AICPA®

Audit and Accounting Guide

Not-for-Profit Entities

March 1, 2018

AICPA

A resource of the

Enhancing Audit Quality Initiative

23574-349

1 2 3 4 5 6 7 8 9 0 AAP 1 9 8

ISBN 978-1-94830-619-5

Printed in Canada

Preface

AICPA

A resource of the
Enhancing Audit
Quality Initiative

(Updated as of March 1, 2018)

This guide was prepared by the Not-For-Profit Organizations Committee.

About AICPA Guides

This AICPA Guide has been developed by the AICPA Not-for-Profit Entities Expert Panel and Guide Task Force to assist practitioners in performing and reporting on their audit engagements and to assist management of not-for-profit entities (NFPs) in the preparation of their financial statements in conformity with U.S. generally accepted accounting principles (GAAP).

An AICPA Guide containing auditing guidance related to generally accepted auditing standards (GAAS) is recognized as an *interpretive publication* as defined in AU-C section 200, *Overall Objectives of the Independent Auditor and the Conduct of an Audit in Accordance With Generally Accepted Auditing Standards*.[1] Interpretive publications are recommendations on the application of GAAS in specific circumstances, including engagements for entities in specialized industries.

Interpretive publications are issued under the authority of the AICPA Auditing Standards Board (ASB) after all ASB members have been provided an opportunity to consider and comment on whether the proposed interpretive publication is consistent with GAAS. The members of the ASB have found the auditing guidance in this guide to be consistent with existing GAAS.

Although interpretive publications are not auditing standards, AU-C section 200 requires the auditor to consider applicable interpretive publications in planning and performing the audit because interpretive publications are relevant to the proper application of GAAS in specific circumstances. If the auditor does not apply the auditing guidance in an applicable interpretive publication, the auditor should document how the requirements of GAAS were complied with in the circumstances addressed by such auditing guidance.

The ASB is the designated senior committee of the AICPA authorized to speak for the AICPA on all matters related to auditing. Conforming changes made to the auditing guidance contained in this guide are approved by the ASB Chair

[1] All AU-C sections can be found in AICPA *Professional Standards*.

(or his or her designee) and the Director of the AICPA Audit and Attest Standards Staff. Any changes to the auditing guidance in this guide exceeding that of conforming changes are issued after all ASB members have been provided an opportunity to consider and comment on whether the guide is consistent with the Statements on Auditing Standards (SASs).

The Financial Reporting Executive Committee (FinREC) is the designated senior committee of the AICPA authorized to speak for the AICPA in the areas of financial accounting and reporting. The financial accounting and reporting guidance contained in this guide was approved by the affirmative vote of at least two-thirds of the members of FinREC in November 2012. Conforming changes made to the financial accounting and reporting guidance after that vote are approved by the FinREC Chair (or his or her designee). Updates made to the financial accounting and reporting guidance in this guide exceeding that of conforming changes are approved by the affirmative vote of at least two-thirds of the members of FinREC.

This guide does the following:

- Identifies certain requirements set forth in FASB *Accounting Standards Codification®* (ASC).
- Describes FinREC's understanding of prevalent or sole industry practice concerning certain issues. In addition, this guide may indicate that FinREC expresses a preference for the prevalent or sole industry practice, or it may indicate that FinREC expresses a preference for another practice that is not the prevalent or sole industry practice; alternatively, FinREC may express no view on the matter.
- Identifies certain other, but not necessarily all, industry practices concerning certain accounting issues without expressing FinREC's views on them.
- Provides guidance that has been supported by FinREC on the accounting, reporting, or disclosure treatment of transactions or events that are not set forth in FASB ASC.

Accounting guidance for nongovernmental entities included in an AICPA Guide is a source of nonauthoritative accounting guidance. As discussed in paragraph 1.13, FASB ASC is the authoritative source of U.S. accounting and reporting standards for nongovernmental NFPs. This guide does not include accounting guidance for governmental entities. AICPA members should be prepared to justify departures from GAAP, as discussed in the "Accounting Principles Rule" (ET sec. 1.320.001 and 2.320.001).[2]

Any auditing guidance in a guide appendix or chapter appendix in a guide, or in an exhibit, while not authoritative, is considered an "other auditing publication." In applying such guidance, the auditor should, exercising professional judgment, assess the relevance and appropriateness of such guidance to the circumstances of the audit. Although the auditor determines the relevance of other auditing guidance, auditing guidance in a guide appendix or exhibit has been reviewed by the AICPA Audit and Attest Standards staff, and the auditor may presume that it is appropriate.

AICPA Guides may include certain content presented as "Supplement", "Appendix", or "Exhibit." A supplement is a reproduction, in whole or in part, of

---

[2] All ET sections can be found in AICPA *Professional Standards*.

authoritative guidance originally issued by a standard setting body (including regulatory bodies) and applicable to entities or engagements within the purview of that standard setter, independent of the authoritative status of the applicable AICPA Guide. Both appendixes and exhibits are included for informational purposes and have no authoritative status.

Purpose and Applicability

This guide applies to the financial statements of nongovernmental NFPs that meet the definition of an NFP included in the FASB ASC glossary. See chapter 1, "Introduction," for further information.

This guide does not discuss the application of all GAAP and all GAAS that are relevant to the preparation and audit of financial statements of NFPs. This guide is directed primarily to those aspects of the preparation and audit of financial statements that are unique to NFPs or are considered particularly significant to them.

Recognition

2018 Guide Edition

AICPA Senior Committees

Auditing Standards Board

Mike Santay, *Chair*
Rick Reisig, *ASB Member*

Financial Reporting Executive Committee

Jim Dolinar, *Chair*
Cathy Clarke, *FinREC Member*

The AICPA gratefully acknowledges those current and former members of the AICPA Not-for-Profit Entities Expert Panel who reviewed or otherwise contributed to the development of this edition of the guide: Jennifer Brenner, Karen Craig, Susan L. Davis, Christina A. Dutch, Lisa Hinkson, Andrew Prather, and James R. Summer III.

The AICPA also thanks Susan E. Budak for her invaluable assistance in updating the 2018 edition of the guide.

AICPA Staff

Christopher Cole
Associate Director
Member Learning and Competency
and
Staff Liaison
to the Not-for-Profit Entities Expert Panel and Guide Task Force

2013 Guide Edition

Not-for-Profit Entities Expert Panel and Guide Task Force (2005-2012)

(members when this edition was completed)

Gregory Capin, *Co-Chair*
Cathy J. Clarke, *Co-Chair*
Frank Jakosz, *Former Co-Chair*

(past members who contributed to this edition)

Stephen Kattell, *Former Co-Chair*
Robert Batarla
Susan E. Budak

Amanda E. Nelson, *Former Co-Chair*
Elaine Allen
Jennifer Brenner
Karen Craig
W. Michael Fritz
Ellen Hobby
Jennifer Hoffman
Laurie Horvath
John A. Mattie
Catherine E. Mickle
Stuart J. Miller
Andrew M. Prather
Susan C. Stewart
Andrea Wright

John M. Cotman
Marianne E. DeVries
Julie L. Floch
Larry Goldstein
Richard C. Holt
J. Mark Jenkins
Bliss Jones
Peter Knutson
Elizabeth E. Krisher
Richard F. Larkin
Tim McCutcheon
Drew M. Paluf
James Remis
John Ring
Nancy E. Shelmon
Kathleen Spencer
Paul C. Sullivan

AICPA Senior Committees

Auditing Standards Board

(members when this edition was completed)

Darrel R. Schubert, *Chair*
Brian Bluhm
Robert E. Chevalier
Sam K. Cotterell
Jim Dalkin
David Duree
Jennifer Haskell
Ed G. Jolicoeur
Barbara Lewis
Carolyn H. McNerney

David Morris
Kenneth R. Odom
Don M. Pallais
Brian R. Richson
Mike Santay
Kay W. Tatum
Kim L. Tredinnick
H. Steven Vogel
Kurtis A. Wolff

Financial Reporting Executive Committee

(members when this edition was completed)

Rich Paul, *Chair*
Aaron Anderson
Linda Bergen
Adam Brown
Terry Cooper
Lawrence Gray
Randolph Green
Mary E. Kane
Jack Markey
Joseph D. McGrath
Rebecca Mihalko
Steve Moehrle
Angela Newell
Mark Scoles
Brad Sparks
Dusty Stallings

(past members who contributed to this edition)

Jay Hanson, *Former Chair*
Benjamin S. Neuhausen, *Former Chair*
David Alexander
Robert Axel
Rick Arpin
Kimber Bascom
Glenn Bradley
Neri Bukspan
Brett Cohen
Pascal Desroches
James A. Dolinar
L. Charles Evans
Faye Feger
Bruce Johnson
Richard Jones
Carl Kampel
Lisa Kelley
David Morris
Jonathon Nus
Richard Petersen
Roy Rendino

Terry Spidell
Randall Sogoloff
Richard K. Stuart
Enrique Tejerina
Robert Uhl
Dan Weaver
Dan Zwarn

The AICPA and the Not-for-Profit Entities Expert Panel and Guide Task Force gratefully acknowledge the invaluable assistance of Joel Tanenbaum to the development and content of this guide.

Guidance Considered in This Edition

This edition of the guide has been modified by the AICPA staff to include certain changes necessary due to the issuance of authoritative guidance since the guide was originally issued (March 1, 2013, edition), and other revisions as deemed appropriate. Relevant guidance issued through March 1, 2018, has been considered in the development of this edition of the guide. However, this guide does not include all audit, accounting, reporting, regulatory, and other requirements applicable to an entity or a particular engagement. This guide is intended to be used in conjunction with all applicable sources of relevant guidance.

Relevant guidance that is issued and effective for fiscal years ending on or before March 1, 2018, is incorporated directly in the text of this guide.

Relevant guidance issued but not yet effective as of March 1, 2018 but becoming effective for fiscal years ending on or before June 30, 2018 is also presented directly in the text of the guide, but it is shaded gray and accompanied by a footnote indicating the effective date of the new guidance. In addition, because of the significance of the changes, relevant guidance for FASB Accounting Standards Update (ASU) No. 2016-14, *Presentation of Financial Statements for Not-for-Profit Entities (Topic 958)*, is also included as shaded text within the guide, even though the amendments in FASB ASU No. 2016-14 are effective for annual financial statements issued for fiscal years beginning after December 15, 2017 (for example, years ending December 31, 2018 and years ending June 30, 2019), and for interim periods within fiscal years beginning after December 15, 2018. Limited guidance from FASB ASU No. 2014-09, *Revenue from Contracts with Customers (Topic 606)*, appears as shaded text, primarily within chapter 12, "Revenues and Receivables From Exchange Transactions," to help readers prepare for the effective date of those amendments, which for most NFPs is annual reporting periods beginning after December 15, 2018, and interim periods within annual periods beginning after December 15, 2019, with a year earlier application required for those that have issued, or are conduit bond obligors for, securities that are traded, listed, or quoted on an exchange or an over-the-counter market, The distinct presentation of this content is intended to aid the reader in differentiating content that may not be effective for the reader's purposes (as part of the guide's "dual guidance" treatment of applicable new guidance).

Relevant guidance issued but not yet effective as of March 1, 2018 and not becoming effective until after June 30, 2018, is referenced in a "guidance update" box; that is, a box that contains summary information on the guidance issued but not yet effective.

In updating this guide, all guidance issued up to and including the following was considered, but not necessarily incorporated, as determined based on applicability:

- FASB ASU No. 2018-03, *Technical Corrections and Improvements to Financial Instruments—Overall (Subtopic 825-10): Recognition and Measurement of Financial Assets and Financial Liabilities*
- SAS No. 133, *Auditor Involvement With Exempt Offering Documents* (AU-C sec. 945)
- Interpretation No. 4, "Performing and Reporting on an Attestation Engagement Under Two Sets of Attestation Standards," (AT-C sec. 9105 par. .31–.35) of AT-C section 105, *Concepts Common to All Attestation Engagements*[3]
- Statement of Position 17-1, *Performing Agreed-Upon Procedures Related to Rated Exchange Act Asset-Backed Securities Third-Party Due Diligence Services as Defined by SEC Release No. 34-72936* (AUD sec. 60)[4]

Users of this guide should consider guidance issued subsequent to those items listed previously to determine their effect on entities and engagements covered by this guide. In determining the applicability of recently issued guidance, its effective date should also be considered.

The changes made to this edition of the guide are identified in appendix G, "Schedule of Changes Made to the Text From the Previous Edition." The changes do not include all those that might be considered necessary if the guide were subjected to a comprehensive review and revision.

Auditors who perform audits under *Government Auditing Standards*; the Single Audit Act Amendments of 1996; and Office of Management and Budget (OMB) Circular A-133, *Audits of States, Local Governments, and Non-Profit Organizations*; or Title 2 U.S. Code of Federal Regulations Part 200, *Uniform Administrative Requirements, Cost Principles, and Audit Requirements for Federal Awards* (Uniform Guidance), should also refer to the AICPA Audit Guide *Government Auditing Standards* and Single Audits.

FASB ASC Pending Content

Presentation of Pending Content in FASB ASC

Amendments to FASB ASC (issued in the form of ASUs) are initially incorporated into FASB ASC in "pending content" boxes following the paragraphs being amended with links to the transition information. The pending content boxes are meant to provide users with information about how the guidance in a paragraph will change as a result of the new guidance.

Pending content applies to different entities at different times due to varying fiscal year-ends, and because certain guidance may be effective on different dates for public and nonpublic entities. As such, FASB maintains amended

[3] All AT-C sections can be found in AICPA *Professional Standards*.

[4] All AUD sections can be found in AICPA *Professional Standards*.

guidance in pending content boxes within FASB ASC until the roll-off date. Generally, the roll-off date is six months following the latest fiscal year end for which the original guidance being amended could still be applied.

Presentation of FASB ASC Pending Content in AICPA Guides

Amended FASB ASC guidance that is included in pending content boxes in FASB ASC on March 1, 2018, is referenced as "Pending Content" in this guide. Readers should be aware that "Pending Content" referenced in this guide will eventually be subjected to FASB's roll-off process and no longer be labeled as "Pending Content" in FASB ASC (as discussed in the previous paragraph).

Terms Used to Define Professional Requirements in This AICPA Guide

Any requirements described in this guide are normally referenced to the applicable standards or regulations from which they are derived. Generally, the terms used in this guide describing the professional requirements of the referenced standard setter (for example, the ASB) are the same as those used in the applicable standards or regulations (for example, *must* or *should*). However, where the accounting requirements are derived from FASB ASC, this guide uses *should*, whereas FASB uses *shall*. In its resource document, "About the Codification," that accompanies FASB ASC, FASB states that it considers the terms *should* and *shall* to be comparable terms and to represent the same concept—the requirement to apply a standard.

Readers should refer to the applicable standards and regulations for more information on the requirements imposed by the use of the various terms used to define professional requirements in the context of the standards and regulations in which they appear.

Certain exceptions apply to these general rules, particularly in those circumstances where the guide describes prevailing and preferred industry practices for the application of a standard or regulation. In these circumstances, the applicable senior committee responsible for reviewing the guide's content believes the guidance contained herein is appropriate for the circumstances.

Applicability of GAAS and PCAOB Standards

Audits of the financial statements of those entities not subject to the oversight authority of the PCAOB (that is, those audit reports not within the PCAOB's jurisdiction as defined by the Sarbanes-Oxley Act of 2002, as amended—hereinafter referred to as *nonissuers*)[5] are to be conducted in accordance with GAAS as issued by the ASB. The ASB develops and issues standards in the form of SASs through a due process that includes deliberation in meetings open to the public, public exposure of proposed SASs, and a formal vote. SASs and their related interpretations are codified in AICPA *Professional Standards*. In citing GAAS and the related interpretations, references generally use section numbers within the codification of currently effective SASs and not the original statement number, as appropriate.

In rare situations, an auditor may be engaged to also follow PCAOB auditing standards in the audit of an NFP. This guide does not provide information

[5] See the definition of the term *nonissuer* in the AU-C Glossary.

about audits conducted in accordance with PCAOB standards. When the audit is not under the jurisdiction of the PCAOB but the entity desires, or is required by an agency, by a regulator, or by contractual agreement, to obtain an audit conducted under PCAOB standards, the AICPA Code of Professional Conduct requires the auditor to also conduct the audit in accordance with GAAS. Paragraph .44 and paragraphs .A43–.A47 of AU-C section 700, *Forming an Opinion and Reporting on Financial Statements*, clarify the format of the auditor's report that should be issued when the auditor conducts an audit in accordance with the standards of the PCAOB, but the audit is not under the jurisdiction of the PCAOB.

Applicability of Quality Control Standards

QC section 10, *A Firm's System of Quality Control*,[6] addresses a CPA firm's responsibilities for its system of quality control for its accounting and auditing practice. A system of quality control consists of policies that a firm establishes and maintains to provide it with reasonable assurance that the firm and its personnel comply with professional standards, as well as applicable legal and regulatory requirements. The policies also provide the firm with reasonable assurance that reports issued by the firm are appropriate in the circumstances.

QC section 10 applies to all CPA firms with respect to engagements in their accounting and auditing practice. In paragraph .06 of QC section 10, an accounting and auditing practice is defined as "a practice that performs engagements covered by this section, which are audit, attestation, compilation, review, and any other services for which standards have been promulgated by the ASB or the AICPA Accounting and Review Services Committee (ARSC) under the "General Standards Rule" (ET sec. 1.300.001) or the "Compliance With Standards Rule" (ET sec. 1.310.001) of the AICPA Code of Professional Conduct. Although standards for other engagements may be promulgated by other AICPA technical committees, engagements performed in accordance with those standards are not encompassed in the definition of an accounting and auditing practice."

In addition to the provisions of QC section 10, readers should be aware of other sections within AICPA *Professional Standards* that address quality control considerations, including the following provisions that address engagement level quality control matters for various types of engagements that an accounting and auditing practice might perform:

- AU-C section 220, *Quality Control for an Engagement Conducted in Accordance With Generally Accepted Auditing Standards*
- AT-C section 105, *Concepts Common to All Attestation Engagements*
- AR-C section 60, *General Principles for Engagements Performed in Accordance With Statements on Standards for Accounting and Review Services*[7]

Because of the importance of engagement quality, this guide includes appendix F, "Overview of Statements on Quality Control Standards." This appendix summarizes key aspects of the quality control standard. This summarization should

---

[6] All QC sections can be found in AICPA *Professional Standards*.

[7] All AR-C sections can be found in AICPA *Professional Standards*.

be read in conjunction with QC section 10, AU-C section 220, AT-C section 105, and AR-C section 60, as applicable.

AICPA Website

The AICPA encourages you to visit its website at aicpa.org and the Financial Reporting Center (FRC) at www.aicpa.org/frc. The FRC supports members in the execution of high-quality financial reporting. Whether you are a financial statement preparer or a member in public practice, this center provides exclusive member-only resources for the entire financial reporting process, and provides timely and relevant news, guidance and examples supporting the financial reporting process. Another important focus of the FRC is keeping those in public practice up to date on issues pertaining to preparation, compilation, review, audit, attestation, or assurance and advisory engagements. Certain content on the AICPA's websites referenced in this guide may be restricted to AICPA members only.

Select Recent Developments Significant to This Guide

Uniform Administrative Requirements, Cost Principles, and Audit Requirements for Federal Awards

In December 2013, the OMB issued the Uniform Guidance, which establishes cost principles and audit requirements for federal awards to nonfederal entities and administrative requirements for all federal grants and cooperative agreements. This guide has been updated for the Uniform Guidance. Appendix E, "Information Sources," of this guide provides website addresses for accessing that guidance.

The Uniform Guidance is effective for nonfederal entities for all federal awards and certain funding increments provided on or after December 26, 2014. This effective date requires an auditor to use the cost principles and administrative requirements found in the pre-Uniform Guidance OMB circulars for awards and funding increments awarded prior to December 26, 2014, and the Uniform Guidance cost principles and administrative requirements for federal awards and certain funding increments awarded on or after December 26, 2014.

Funding Increments Subject to the Uniform Guidance

A federal award may provide for additional funding to an existing award (a funding increment). The "Frequently Asked Questions" document issued by the Council on Financial Assistance Reform (COFAR) clarifies that federal awards made with modified award terms and conditions at the time of the incremental funding action are subject to the Uniform Guidance if that action occurred on or after December 26, 2014. Funding increments with no change to award terms and conditions continue to be subject to pre-Uniform Guidance cost principles and administrative requirements (for example, those found in Circular A-122, *Cost Principles for Non-Profit Organizations*) if the related award was made prior to December 26, 2014. Often, the terms and conditions of the federal award will identify whether the funding increment is subject to the Uniform Guidance requirements or whether it will continue to be subject to the pre-Uniform Guidance requirements.

Depending upon federal award dates, an auditor may be required to use two sources of guidance when testing compliance for major programs because some federal awards (those awarded prior to December 26, 2014) are subject to the pre-Uniform Guidance OMB circulars (for example, Circular A-122, *Cost Principles for Non-Profit Organizations*), while other federal awards (those awarded on or after December 26, 2014) are subject to the cost principles and administrative requirements of the Uniform Guidance. This requirement is not linked to the audit requirements used to perform the compliance audit.

The standards in Subpart F, "Audit Requirements," of the Uniform Guidance are effective for audits of fiscal years beginning on or after December 26, 2014. Therefore, auditees subject to a single audit with December 25, 2015, or later year ends will be required to undergo the audit under the Uniform Guidance audit requirements. The AICPA Audit Guide *Government Auditing Standards* and Single Audits has been fully updated for the Uniform Guidance audit requirements.

FASB's Revenue Recognition

FASB ASU No. 2014-09 was issued by FASB to improve the financial reporting of revenue from contracts with customers and related costs and to align the reporting with International Financial Reporting Standards. ASU No. 2014-09 provides a framework for revenue recognition and supersedes or amends several of the revenue recognition requirements in FASB ASC 605, *Revenue Recognition*, as well as guidance within the industry-specific topics, including FASB ASC 958, *Not-for-Profit Entities*. The standard applies to any entity that either enters into contracts with customers to transfer goods or services or enters into contracts for the transfer of nonfinancial assets unless those contracts are within the scope of other standards (for example, insurance or lease contracts). As discussed later in this preface, FASB has a related project on revenue recognition of grants and contracts, the purpose of which is to provide standards for characterizing grants and similar contracts with resource providers as either exchange transactions or contributions and in distinguishing between conditional contributions and unconditional contributions.

The AICPA has formed 16 industry task forces to assist in developing a new guide on revenue recognition that will provide insights and illustrative examples on how to apply the new standards. Revenue recognition implementation issues identified by the Not-for-Profit Entities Revenue Recognition Task Force will be available at aicpa.org for informal comment, after review by FinREC. Readers are encouraged to submit comments to revreccomments@aicpa.org.

Chapter 12 includes the following changes to help readers prepare for the effective date of the amendments in ASU No. 2014-09:

- Limited guidance appears within Chapter 12 as shaded text. The distinct presentation of this content is intended to aid the reader in identifying the content that will be deleted upon the effective date of the amendments in ASU No. 2014-09 as well as the text that will replace it (the guide's "dual guidance" treatment of applicable new guidance.)
- Appendix A," Implementation Guidance for Accounting Standards Update (ASU) No. 2014-09, *Revenue from Contracts with Customers (Topic 606)*," to chapter 12 of this guide, includes excerpts from chapter 8, "Not-for-Profit Entities," of the AICPA Audit and Accounting Guide *Revenue Recognition*. That guide, developed by

the AICPA Industry Revenue Recognition Task Forces, Revenue Recognition Working Group, and Auditing Revenue Task Force, is intended to help entities and auditors prepare for changes related to revenue recognition.

Throughout the remaining guide, only the effects of ASU No. 2014-09's amendments on FASB ASC 958 are provided in gray-shaded text following the paragraph. The distinct presentation of this content is intended to aid the reader in identifying the content that will be deleted upon the effective date of the amendments in ASU No. 2014-09 as well as the text that will replace it (the guide's "dual guidance" treatment of applicable new guidance). Each gray-shaded paragraph includes a footnote showing the effective date of the ASU. A more comprehensive update for the effects of ASU No. 2014-09's amendments will appear in a future edition.

Appendix B, "The New Revenue Recognition Standard: FASB ASC 606," of this guide provides additional discussion of the new standards. The appendix is prepared for informational and reference purposes only. It has not been reviewed, approved, disapproved, or otherwise acted on by any senior committee of the AICPA and does not represent official positions or pronouncements of the AICPA.

FASB's Recognition and Measurement of Financial Assets and Financial Liabilities

FASB ASU No. 2016-01, *Financial Instruments—Overall (Subtopic 825-10): Recognition and Measurement of Financial Assets and Financial Liabilities*, was issued by FASB in January 2016 to improve the financial reporting of financial assets and liabilities. For NFPs, ASU No. 2016-01 makes the following changes:

- Expands the scope of the standards for equity investments to all equity securities and other ownership interests in an entity, including investments in partnerships, unincorporated joint ventures, and limited liability companies.
- Allows an NFP to choose, on an investment-by-investment basis, to report an equity investment at its cost minus impairment, if any, plus or minus changes resulting from observable price changes in orderly transactions for the identical or a similar investment of the same issue, provided that the equity investment (a) does not have a readily determinable fair value, and (b) does not qualify for the practical expedient to estimate fair value using net asset value per share or its equivalent (in accordance with FASB ASC 820-10-35-59). The ASU requires additional disclosures about those investments.
- Requires the impairment of equity investments without readily determinable fair values to be assessed qualitatively at each reporting period. That impairment assessment will be similar to the qualitative assessment for long-lived assets, goodwill, and indefinite-lived intangible assets. Upon determining that impairment exists, an entity should calculate the fair value of that investment and recognize the impairment in change in net assets. The impairment is measured as the amount by which the carrying value exceeds the fair value of the investment.

- Eliminates the requirement for NFPs to disclose the fair value of financial instruments measured at amortized cost, which is currently required if the NFP is a public entity, if it is a nonpublic entity that has assets of $100 million or more on the date of the financial statements, or if it has derivative instruments.
- Requires disclosure of financial assets and financial liabilities by measurement category and form of financial asset (that is, securities or loans and receivables) either on the face of the statement of financial position or in the accompanying notes.

In February 2018, FASB issued ASU No. 2018-03 for technical corrections and improvements related to ASU No. 2016-01. ASU No. 2018-03 has the same effective date as ASU No. 2016-01. All entities may early adopt the amendments for fiscal years beginning after December 15, 2017, including interim periods within those fiscal years, as long as they have adopted ASU No. 2016-01.

An NFP's equity securities that have readily determinable fair value will continue to be reported at fair value, except for those accounted for under the equity method of accounting or those that result in consolidation of the investee. The standards for those investments, however, will move from FASB ASC 958-320 to FASB ASC 958-321.

Because the amendments in ASU No. 2016-01 and ASU No. 2018–03 are effective for fiscal years beginning after December 15, 2018, and interim periods within fiscal years beginning after December 15, 2019, and they cannot be adopted earlier than for fiscal years beginning after December 15, 2017, this guide will be updated for ASU No. 2016-01 in a future edition. However, because ASU No. 2016-01 allows NFPs to elect not to disclose information about fair value of financial instruments measured at amortized cost (paragraphs 10–19 of FASB ASC 825-10-50) in financial statements that have not yet been made available for issuance, this guide no longer includes those disclosures.

FASB's Leases

FASB ASU No. 2016-02, *Leases (Topic 842)*, issued February 2016, changes the accounting for leases, primarily by the recognition of lease assets and lease liabilities by lessees for leases classified as operating leases under current GAAP. A lessee should recognize in the statement of financial position a liability to make lease payments (the lease liability) and an asset representing its right to use the underlying asset for the lease term (the right-of-use asset). The right-of-use asset and the lease liability are initially measured at the present value of the lease payments.

Leases will continue to be classified as either operating or finance leases (currently referred to as capital leases). However, in contrast to existing lease standards, there are no percentage tests to apply, and there can be more judgment exercised in applying the criteria that determine whether a lease is a finance lease. As a practical matter, most existing capital leases are finance leases, and most existing operating leases remain operating leases. For finance leases, a lessee is required to recognize interest on the lease liability separately from amortization of the right-of-use asset. For operating leases, a lessee is required to recognize a single lease cost, calculated so that the cost of the lease is allocated over the lease term on a generally straight-line basis.

For leases with a term of 12 months or less, a lessee is permitted to make an accounting policy election by class of underlying asset not to recognize lease assets and lease liabilities. If a lessee makes this election, it should recognize lease expense for such leases generally on a straight-line basis over the lease term.

The accounting applied by a lessor is largely unchanged from that applied under existing GAAP. Lessors will account for leases using an approach that is substantially equivalent to existing standards for sales-type leases, direct financing leases and operating leases. Leveraged lease accounting is eliminated, except for grandfathering existing leveraged leases during transition.

ASU No. 2016-02 is effective for fiscal years beginning after December 15, 2018, including interim periods within those fiscal years, for NFPs that have issued, or are conduit bond obligors for, securities that are traded, listed, or quoted on an exchange or an over-the-counter market. For all other NFPs, the amendments in this ASU are effective for fiscal years beginning after December 15, 2019, and interim periods within fiscal years beginning after December 15, 2020. Early adoption is permitted.

FASB's Consolidation

The following ASUs change the analysis that a reporting entity must perform to determine whether it should consolidate certain types of legal entities:

- FASB ASU No. 2015-02, *Consolidation (Topic 810): Amendments to the Consolidation Analysis*, issued in February 2015
- FASB ASU No. 2017-02, *Not-for-Profit Entities—Consolidation (Subtopic 958-810): Clarifying When a Not-for-Profit Entity That Is a General Partner or a Limited Partner Should Consolidate a For-Profit Limited Partnership or Similar Entity*, issued in January 2017

The ASUs are effective for NFPs for fiscal years beginning after December 15, 2016, and for interim periods within fiscal years beginning after December 15, 2017. Early adoption is permitted, provided that both ASUs are adopted at the same time and using the same transition method. Special transition guidance is provided if the NFP already adopted FASB ASU No. 2015-02.

The provisions in FASB ASU No. 2015-02 that modify the evaluation of variable interest entities and FASB ASU No. 2016-17, *Consolidation (Topic 810): Interests Held through Related Parties That Are under Common Control*, do not apply to NFPs.

Together, the two ASUs clarify whether an NFP that is a general partner or a limited partner of a for-profit limited partnership or similar legal entity should consolidate that entity.

Continuing existing standards, NFPs that are general partners are presumed to control a for-profit limited partnership, regardless of the extent of their ownership interest, unless that presumption is overcome. If a limited partnership has multiple general partners, the determination of which, if any, general partner within the group controls and, therefore, should consolidate the limited partnership is based on an analysis of the relevant facts and circumstances.

The guidance in paragraphs 19–29 of FASB ASC 958-810-25 should be considered in evaluating whether rights held by the limited partners overcome the presumption of control by the general partners. The presumption that a general partner controls is overcome if the limited partners have either substantive kick-out rights or substantive participating rights.

If the presumption of control by a general partner is overcome, then one of the limited partners may have a controlling financial interest, and if so, that limited partner should consolidate the limited partnership. A limited partner is deemed to have a controlling financial interest if the limited partner directly or indirectly owns more than 50 percent of the limited partnership's kick-out rights through voting interests. However, if noncontrolling limited partners have substantive participating rights, then the limited partner with a majority of kick-out rights through voting interests does not have a controlling financial interest. Those standards for limited partners, which originally appeared in FASB ASU No. 2015-02, were incorporated in FASB ASC 958-810 for ease of reference and to make conforming revisions to the application guidance.

In addition, FASB ASU No. 2017-02 clarifies that NFPs may elect to report their interests in for-profit limited partnerships at fair value, even if the limited partnership would otherwise be consolidated, provided that all such investments are measured at fair value and the changes in fair value are reported in the statement of activities.

Because of their effective dates, the amendments in FASB ASU No. 2015-02 and FASB ASU No. 2017-02 are incorporated into chapter 3, "Financial Statements, the Reporting Entity, and General Financial Reporting Matters," and chapter 4, "Cash, Cash Equivalents, and Investments," as shaded text. The distinct presentation of this content is intended to aid the reader in identifying the content that will be deleted upon the effective date of the amendments in those ASUs as well as the text that will replace it (the guide's "dual guidance" treatment of applicable new guidance).

FASB's Project on Financial Statements of NFPs

On August 18, 2016, FASB issued ASU No. 2016-14. The new standards are effective for annual financial statements issued for fiscal years beginning after December 15, 2017 (for example, years ending December 31, 2018 and years ending June 30, 2019). Early application of the amendments in the ASU is permitted. The ASU, which is the first phase of a two-phase project, makes significant changes in seven areas:

- Net asset classes
- Liquidity and availability of resources
- Classification and disclosure of underwater endowment funds
- Expense reporting
- Statement of cash flows
- Investment return
- Release of restrictions on capital assets.

Because of the significance of the changes, relevant guidance for ASU No. 2016-14 is included within this guide, even though the amendments are not yet effective. This guide includes the following changes to help readers prepare for the effective date of the amendments in ASU No. 2016-14:

- Appendix A, "Financial Statements Prepared in Accordance with FASB ASU No. 2016-14," was added to chapter 3 to identify replacement and deleted paragraphs for the amendments relating to the statement of financial position, statement of activities, and statement of cash flows, as well as liquidity disclosures because gray-shading of those extensive changes would have been inconvenient for readers' use.

- Appendix A, "Financial Statements Prepared in Accordance with FASB ASU No. 2016-14," was added to chapter 11, "Net Assets and Reclassifications of Net Assets," to identify replacement and deleted paragraphs for the entire chapter because gray-shading of those extensive changes would have been inconvenient for readers' use.
- Throughout the remaining guide, the effect of amendments in ASU No. 2016-14 on guide paragraphs is provided in gray-shaded text following the paragraph. The distinct presentation of this content is intended to aid the reader in identifying the content that will be deleted upon the effective date of the amendments in ASU No. 2016-14 as well as the text that will replace it (the guide's "dual guidance" treatment of applicable new guidance). Each gray-shaded paragraph includes a footnote showing the effective date of the ASU.

In addition, Appendix A, "The New Not-for-Profit Financial Reporting Model Standards: FASB ASU No. 2016-14," of this guide provides discussion of the new standards. The appendix is prepared for informational and reference purposes only. It has not been reviewed, approved, disapproved, or otherwise acted on by any senior committee of the AICPA and does not represent official positions or pronouncements of the AICPA.

The second phase of the project is expected to address the following issues:

- Whether to require a measure of operations.
- Whether and how to define a measure of operations.
- Realignment of certain items in the statement of cash flows to better align operating cash flows with an operating measure on the statement of activities

These three issues will be considered within the scope of a research project about structuring the performance statement (or statement of activities) by both business entities and NFPs. Initially, the second phase was also expected to address segment reporting for NFP health care entities in lieu of an analysis of expenses by both natural and functional classification, but FASB decided in September 2017 not to pursue that alternative further.

FASB's Project on Revenue Recognition of Grants and Contracts by NFPs

On August 3, 2017, FASB issued Proposed Accounting Standards Update, *Not-for-Profit Entities (Topic 958): Clarifying the Scope and the Accounting Guidance for Contributions Received and Contributions Made*. The purpose of the project is to improve standards for characterizing grants and similar contracts with resource providers as either exchange transactions or contributions and for distinguishing between conditional contributions and unconditional contributions. The due date for comment letters was November 1, 2017, and FASB is currently redeliberating the tentative conclusions in that proposed ASU. For more information, see www.fasb.org.

SAS No. 133, *Auditor Involvement With Exempt Offering Documents*

In July 2017, the ASB issued SAS No. 133, which clarifies auditors' responsibilities related to offerings of securities exempt from registration under the

Securities Act of 1933 and franchise offerings (collectively, exempt offerings). SAS No. 133 will be effective for exempt offering documents with which the auditor is involved that are initially distributed, circulated, or submitted on or after June 15, 2018. This SAS is incorporated in Appendix B, "Auditor Involvement With Municipal Securities Filings," of chapter 10, "Debt and Other Liabilities," as gray shaded text, which is used to identify guidance issued but not yet effective as of the date of this guide. Each gray-shaded addition includes a footnote showing the effective date of the SAS.

TABLE OF CONTENTS

Chapter 1

Introduction

Gray shaded text in this chapter reflects guidance issued but not yet effective as of the date of this guide, March 1, 2018, but becoming effective on or prior to June 30, 2018, exclusive of any option to early adopt ahead of the mandatory effective date. Unless otherwise indicated, all unshaded text reflects guidance that was already effective as of the date of this guide.

Scope

Entities

1.01 This Audit and Accounting Guide covers entities that meet the definition of a *not-for-profit entity* (NFP) included in the FASB *Accounting Standards Codification* (ASC) glossary. That definition is

> an entity that possesses the following characteristics, in varying degrees, that distinguish it from a business entity:
>
> *a.* Contributions of significant amounts of resources from resource providers who do not expect commensurate or proportionate pecuniary return
>
> *b.* Operating purposes other than to provide goods or services at a profit
>
> *c.* Absence of ownership interests like those of business entities.
>
> Entities that clearly fall outside this definition include the following:
>
> *a.* All investor-owned entities
>
> *b.* Entities that provide dividends, lower costs, or other economic benefits directly and proportionately to their owners, members, or participants, such as mutual insurance entities, credit unions, farm and rural electric cooperatives, and employee benefit plans.

As noted in the preceding definition, NFPs have characteristics (*a*), (*b*), and (*c*) in varying degrees. An entity could meet the definition of an NFP without possessing characteristic (*a*), (*b*), or (*c*). For example, some NFPs, such as those that receive all their revenue from exchange transactions, receive no contributions.

1.02 This guide applies to the following nongovernmental NFPs:

- Animal protection and humane organizations
- Cemetery organizations
- Civic and community organizations
- Colleges and universities
- Elementary and secondary schools
- Federated fund-raising organizations
- Fraternal organizations
- Labor unions

- Libraries
- Museums
- Other cultural organizations
- Performing arts organizations
- Political action committees
- Political parties
- Private and community foundations
- Professional associations
- Public broadcasting stations
- Religious organizations
- Research and scientific organizations
- Social and country clubs
- Trade associations
- Voluntary health and welfare entities
- Zoological and botanical societies

Additionally, the guidance in this guide applies to all entities that meet the definition of an NFP in paragraph 1.01, regardless of whether they are included in this list.

1.03 Paragraph 1.02 states that this guide applies to certain nongovernmental NFPs. The FASB ASC glossary defines a *nongovernmental entity* as an entity that is not required to issue financial reports in accordance with guidance promulgated by GASB or the Federal Accounting Standards Advisory Board (FASAB). When an NFP meets the definition for a governmental entity in paragraph 1.04, the appropriate generally accepted accounting principles (GAAP) for the financial statements of the NFP is promulgated by GASB. Therefore, other than paragraph 1.04, the accounting and financial reporting guidance in this guide does not constitute category (b) accounting and financial reporting guidance for NFPs that meet the definition for a governmental entity because the AICPA did not make this guide applicable to such governmental NFPs, and GASB did not clear it.

1.04 As noted in AICPA Audit and Accounting Guide *State and Local Governments*, public corporations[1] and bodies corporate and politic are governmental organizations. Other organizations are governmental if they have one or more of the following characteristics:

- Popular election of officers or appointment (or approval) of a controlling majority of the members of the organization's governing body by officials of one or more state or local governments

---

[1] Black's Law Dictionary defines a *public corporation* as:

An artificial person (for example, [a] municipality or a governmental corporation) created for the administration of public affairs. Unlike a private corporation it has no protection against legislative acts altering or even repealing its charter. Instrumentalities created by [the] state, formed and owned by it in [the] public interest, supported in whole or part by public funds, and governed by managers deriving their authority from [the] state. Sharon Realty Co. v. Westlake, Ohio Com. Pl., 188 N.E.2d 318, 323, 25 O.O.2d 322. A public corporation is an instrumentality of the state, founded and owned in the public interest, supported by public funds and governed by those deriving their authority from the state. York County Fair Ass'n v. South Carolina Tax Commission, 249 S.C. 337, 154 S.E.2d 361, 362.

- The potential for unilateral dissolution by a government with the net assets reverting to a government
- The power to enact and enforce a tax levy

Furthermore, organizations are presumed to be governmental if they have the ability to issue directly (rather than through a state or municipal authority) debt that pays interest exempt from federal taxation. However, organizations possessing only that ability (to issue tax-exempt debt) and none of the other governmental characteristics may rebut the presumption that they are governmental if their determination is supported by compelling, relevant evidence.

> The preceding definition of a government is category (b) accounting and financial reporting guidance for governmental entities because GASB has cleared it. Therefore, NFPs meeting the previously listed criteria are subject to the accounting standards promulgated by GASB and, as applicable, should refer to those standards and the related interpretive guidance in AICPA Audit and Accounting Guide *State and Local Governments*.

1.05 Providers of health care services that are described in FASB ASC 954-10-15 are not covered by this guide and should refer to the AICPA Audit and Accounting Guide *Health Care Entities*. That guide applies to entities whose principal operations consist of providing or agreeing to provide health care services and that derive all or almost all of their revenues from the sale of goods or services; it also applies to entities whose primary activities are the planning, organization, and oversight of such entities, such as parent or holding companies of health care entities. The health care guide does not apply to voluntary health and welfare entities (see paragraph 1.06), but it does apply to not-for-profit health care entities that have no ownership interest and are essentially self-sustaining from fees charged for goods and services (as described in paragraph 8 of FASB Concept No. 4, *Objectives of Financial Reporting by Nonbusiness Organizations*).

1.06 If a provider of health care services meets the definition of a *voluntary health and welfare entity* in the FASB ASC glossary, it should follow this guide. That definition is as follows:

> A not-for-profit entity (NFP) that is formed for the purpose of performing voluntary services for various segments of society and that is tax exempt (organized for the benefit of the public), supported by the public, and operated on a not-for-profit basis. Most voluntary health and welfare entities concentrate their efforts and expend their resources in an attempt to solve health and welfare problems of our society and, in many cases, those of specific individuals. As a group, voluntary health and welfare entities include those NFPs that derive their revenue primarily from voluntary contributions from the general public to be used for general or specific purposes connected with health, welfare, or community services. For purposes of this definition, the general public excludes governmental entities when determining whether an NFP is a voluntary health and welfare entity.

Basis of Accounting

1.07 The focus of this guide is financial statements prepared in accordance with GAAP in the United States under the assumption that the NFP will continue to operate as a going concern. Unless liquidation is imminent, an NFP prepares its financial statements under the assumption that it will continue to operate as a going concern. When liquidation is imminent, FASB ASC 205-30 provides guidance on how an entity should prepare its financial statements using the liquidation basis of accounting and describes the related disclosures that should be made. FASB ASC 205-30-25-2 provides the characteristics that determine whether liquidation is imminent.

1.08 Cash-, modified cash-, or tax-basis financial statements can be a viable alternative to GAAP-basis financial statements whenever the NFP is not contractually required—legally or otherwise—to issue GAAP financial statements. Guidance on financial statements prepared with a special purpose framework (formerly referred to as an other comprehensive basis of accounting or OCBOA) is found in the audit, not accounting, literature. AU-C section 800, *Special Considerations—Audits of Financial Statements Prepared in Accordance With Special Purpose Frameworks*,[2] addresses special considerations in the application of auditing standards to an audit of financial statements prepared in accordance with a special purpose framework, which is a cash, tax, regulatory, contractual, or an other basis of accounting.

1.09 In addition, the Practice Aid *Accounting and Financial Reporting Guidelines for Cash- and Tax-Basis Financial Statements* provides nonauthoritative guidance on financial statements prepared in conformity with a special purpose framework.

1.10 This guide is not intended for use in preparing financial statements in accordance with International Financial Reporting Standards (IFRSs). The council of the AICPA has designated the International Accounting Standards Board (IASB) as the body to establish IFRSs for both private and public entities pursuant to the "Compliance With Standards Rule" (ET sec. 1.310.001) and the "Accounting Principles Rule" (ET sec. 1.320.001) of the AICPA Code of Professional Conduct.[3] The IASB does not have a reporting model designed specifically for NFPs; however, the IASB and FASB have indicated that they will jointly consider the applicability of their conceptual framework project to private sector not-for-profit organizations after FASB completes its work for a conceptual framework for private sector business entities Paragraph 1.12 discusses situations when an auditor practicing in the United States is engaged to audit and report on financial statements prepared in conformity with accounting principles generally accepted in another country or to perform an audit in accordance with International Standards on Auditing (ISAs).

Level of Service

1.11 This guide provides auditing considerations and reporting guidance for CPAs that are engaged to audit and report on financial statements in accordance with generally accepted auditing standards (GAAS) for nonissuers.[4]

---

[2] All AU-C sections can be found in AICPA *Professional Standards*.

[3] All ET sections can be found in AICPA *Professional Standards*.

[4] Not-for-profit entities (NFPs) are not issuers subject to oversight by the PCAOB, thus, auditing standards issued by the Auditing Standards Board apply to audits of NFPs.

Many NFPs are required by state regulations, bond covenants, or grantors to have an audit. Other levels of service are offered by CPAs, but those are not the focus of this guide.

1.12 This guide also assumes that the independent auditor will be reporting on financial statements prepared in accordance with U.S. GAAP. If an auditor practicing in the United States is engaged to audit and report on financial statements prepared in conformity with accounting principles generally accepted in another country or to perform an audit in accordance with ISAs, the auditor should be aware of and consider the following additional publications:

- Paragraphs .42–.43 and .A42 of AU-C section 700, *Forming an Opinion and Reporting on Financial Statements*, which discusses auditor's reports for audits conducted in accordance with both GAAS and another set of auditing standards
- Paragraph .A9 of AU-C section 706, *Emphasis-of-Matter Paragraphs and Other-Matter Paragraphs in the Independent Auditor's Report*, which discusses reporting if an entity prepares one set of financial statements in accordance with accounting principles generally accepted in the United States of America and another set of financial statements in accordance with another general purpose framework (for example, IFRSs promulgated by the IASB)
- AU-C section 910, *Financial Statements Prepared in Accordance With a Financial Reporting Framework Generally Accepted in Another Country*

GAAP for NFPs

1.13 FASB ASC is the single authoritative source of U.S. accounting and reporting standards for nongovernmental entities; that is, it is the source of GAAP for nongovernmental entities. The council of the AICPA has resolved that FASB ASC constitutes accounting principles as contemplated in the "Accounting Principles Rule" of the AICPA Code of Professional Conduct.

1.14 NFPs should follow the guidance in all effective provisions of FASB ASC unless the specific provision explicitly exempts NFPs or its subject matter precludes such applicability. FASB ASC 958, *Not-for-Profit Entities*, contains only incremental industry-specific guidance. NFPs should follow that industry-specific guidance and all other relevant guidance contained in other FASB ASC topics that does not conflict with FASB ASC 958.

1.15 Most of the guidance in FASB ASC topics 105–899 applies to NFPs, although the application of certain provisions by NFPs may be unclear because those provisions specify the financial statement display of financial statement elements or items without considering the net asset reporting model included in FASB ASC 958. Nevertheless, NFPs are required to follow those effective provisions. FASB ASC 958-10-45-1 states that NFPs should consider the reporting objectives of the guidance when exercising judgment about how to best display elements, such as in which net asset class. Examples of those provisions include the following:

- FASB ASC 205-20, about discontinued operations
- FASB ASC 220-20, about unusual or infrequently occurring items

- FASB ASC 250, *Accounting Changes and Error Corrections*
- FASB ASC 470-50, about modifications and extinguishments of debt
- FASB ASC 740, *Income Taxes*
- FASB ASC 830, *Foreign Currency Matters*

1.16 The guidance in FASB ASC topics 905–999 applies to entities operating in certain industries. An example of such guidance is FASB ASC 920, *Entertainment—Broadcasters*. Some NFPs conduct activities[5] in those industries and should apply the guidance concerning the recognition and measurement of assets, liabilities, revenues, expenses, and gains and losses to the transactions unique to those industries. However, in applying that guidance, NFPs should follow the financial statement display guidance in FASB ASC 958, even though it may conflict with display that would result from applying the other industry's guidance.

1.17 Per FASB ASC 105-10-05-2, if the guidance for a transaction or event is not specified within a source of authoritative GAAP for that entity, an entity should first consider accounting principles for similar transactions or events within a source of authoritative GAAP for that entity and then consider nonauthoritative guidance from other sources. An entity should not follow the accounting treatment specified in accounting guidance for similar transactions or events if that guidance either (*a*) prohibits the application of the accounting treatment to the particular transaction or event, or (*b*) indicates that the accounting treatment should not be applied to other transactions or events by analogy.

1.18 Accounting and financial reporting practices not included in FASB ASC are nonauthoritative. Sources of nonauthoritative accounting guidance and literature include, for example, practices that are widely recognized and prevalent either generally or in the industry; FASB Concept Statements; AICPA Audit and Accounting Guides; AICPA Issues Papers; IFRSs; pronouncements of professional associations or regulatory agencies; *Technical Questions and Answers*; and accounting textbooks, handbooks, and articles. The appropriateness of other sources of accounting guidance depends on its relevance to particular circumstances, the specificity of the guidance, the general recognition of the issuer or author as an authority, and the extent of its use in practice. For example, FASB Concept Statements would normally be more influential than other sources in this category.

1.19 The guidance in FASB ASC that specifically exempts NFPs from its scope includes guidance on earnings per share, reporting comprehensive income, segment disclosure, and variable interest entities.[6] Other financial reporting guidance, such as that concerning common stock, issuance of convertible debt, stock purchase warrants, share-based payments, payment of dividends, and certain financial instruments with characteristics of both liabilities and equity, typically does not apply to the kinds of entities covered by

---

[5] Such activities may be conducted by (*a*) for-profit entities owned and consolidated by NFPs, (*b*) divisions of NFPs, or (*c*) entire NFPs, such as those operating as not-for-profit broadcasters.

[6] In accordance with FASB *Accounting Standards Codification* 810-10-15-17(a), an NFP is subject to the variable interest entities standards only in the unlikely case of an NFP that is used by business reporting entities in a manner similar to a variable interest entity in an effort to circumvent the provisions of the variable interest entities subsections.

this guide because NFPs do not have ownership interests similar to business entities. However, the guidance included in the effective provisions of those topics applies to all for-profit entities owned by NFPs, whether owned wholly or in part.

Fund Accounting and Net Asset Classes

1.20 Fund accounting is a technique used by some NFPs for purposes of internal recordkeeping and managerial control and to help ensure that the use of resources is in accordance with stipulations imposed by donors and other resource providers and with self-imposed limitations designated by those charged with governance. Under fund accounting, resources are classified into funds associated with specific activities and objectives.

1.21 *Montgomery's Auditing* notes that

> as used in nonprofit accounting, a fund is an accounting entity with a self-balancing set of accounts for recording assets, liabilities, the fund balance, and changes in the fund balance. Separate accounts are maintained for each fund to ensure that the limitations and restrictions on the use of resources are observed. Though the fund concept involves separate accounting records, it does not entail the physical segregation of resources. Fund accounting is basically a mechanism to assist in exercising control over the purpose of particular resources and amounts of those resources available for use."[7]

Fund accounting is discussed further in chapter 16, "Fund Accounting," of this guide.

1.22 FASB ASC 958-205-05-7 states that "[t]he Not-for-Profit Entities Topic does not use the terms *fund balance* or *changes in fund balances* because in current practice those terms are commonly used to refer to individual groups of assets and related liabilities rather than to an entity's net assets or changes in net assets taken as a whole..." As discussed in chapter 3, "Financial Statements, the Reporting Entity, and General Financial Reporting Matters," of this guide, FASB ASC 958-210-45-1 requires that the amounts for each of three classes of net assets (permanently restricted, temporarily restricted, and unrestricted) be displayed in a statement of financial position. FASB ASC 958-220-45-1 also requires that the amounts of change in each of those classes of net assets be displayed in a statement of activities.

FASB ASC 958-205-05-7 states that "[t]he Not-for-Profit Entities Topic does not use the terms fund balance or changes in fund balances because in current practice those terms are commonly used to refer to individual groups of assets and related liabilities rather than to an entity's net assets or changes in net assets taken as a whole..." As discussed in chapter 3, "Financial Statements, the Reporting Entity, and General Financial Reporting Matters," of this guide, the "Pending Content" in FASB ASC 958-210-45-1 requires that the amounts for each of the classes of net assets (net assets with donor restrictions and net assets without donor restrictions) be displayed in a statement of financial

[7] Vincent M. O'Reilly, Murray B. Hirsch, Philip L. Defliese, and Henry R. Jaenicke, Montgomery's Auditing, 11th ed. (New York: John Wiley & Sons, 1990), 791.

position. The "Pending Content" in FASB ASC 958-220-45-1 also requires that the amounts of change in each of those classes of net assets be displayed in a statement of activities.[8]

1.23 Therefore, reporting by individual funds or fund groups is not required. However, FASB ASC 958-205-45-3 does not preclude providing disaggregated information by individual funds or fund groups, as long as the required aggregated amount for each class of net assets is displayed as indicated previously. How an NFP maintains its internal accounting and recordkeeping systems is a matter outside the purview of standard setting.

1.24 Some NFPs may continue to use fund accounting for purposes other than reporting in conformity with GAAP, and some may provide disaggregated information in the financial statements beyond the minimum requirements of GAAP. A particular fund balance may fall completely into one of the net asset classes or may be allocated to more than one net asset class, as discussed in chapter 16.

1.25 The accounting and auditing issues concerning each particular asset, liability, or class of net assets (financial statement elements) are not a function of the element's internal classification or financial statement subclassification. Accordingly, this guide is organized by financial statement elements and not by type of fund or groups of funds. Chapter 16 contains a discussion of the relationship of an NFP's fund balances to its net asset classes.

Other Resources for Financial Reporting by NFPs

1.26 As a complement to this guide, the Financial Reporting Alert *Not-for-Profit Entities* (for management) and the Audit Risk Alert *Not-for-Profit Entities Industry Developments* (for auditors) are issued annually. The Audit Risk Alert provides an overview of economic and industry conditions, regulatory developments, and recently issued accounting and auditing pronouncements that may affect audits of NFPs. It also includes information about how to obtain many of the publications referred to in this guide and a list of useful internet sites.

1.27 Examples of financial statements of NFPs are not included in this guide. The following AICPA publications and websites, some of which have financial statements that can be used as examples, may assist in preparing or auditing financial statements of NFPs:

- The Audit Guide Government Auditing Standards *and Single Audits*
- The Audit Risk Alert Government Auditing Standards *and Single Audit Developments*
- *Not-for-Profit Entities: Checklists and Illustrative Financial Statements*

---

[8] The amendments in FASB Accounting Standards Update No. 2016-14, *Not-for-Profit Entities (Topic 958): Presentation of Financial Statements of Not-for-Profit Entities*, are effective for annual financial statements issued for fiscal years beginning after December 15, 2017 (for example, years ending December 31, 2018 and years ending June 30, 2019), and for interim periods within fiscal years beginning after December 15, 2018. Application to interim financial statements is permitted but not required in the initial year of application. Early application of the amendments is permitted.

- The website of the AICPA's Not-for-Profit Section, which is a centralized resource developed to support NFPs and the professionals who serve NFPs, found at www.aicpa.org/nfp
- *The AICPA Audit Committee Toolkit: Not-for-Profit Organizations*
- *Not-for-Profit Entities—Best Practices in Presentation and Disclosure*
- The website for Electronic Municipal Market Access (EMMA), (http://emma.msrb.org), which is the official source for municipal disclosures and market data maintained by the Municipal Securities Rulemaking Board. EMMA contains official statements and continuing disclosures for NFPs with tax-exempt bonds
- The websites of membership associations that represent the interests of subsectors of the nonprofit sector, such as the National Association of Colleges and University Business Officers and the Council on Foundations
- The websites of NFPs that are considered peers of the reporting entity
- The websites of regulatory agencies, such as the secretary of state
- The websites of organizations that collect and provide information about NFPs, such as guidestar.org

Chapter 2

General Auditing Considerations[1]

Gray shaded text in this chapter reflects guidance issued but not yet effective as of the date of this guide, March 1, 2018, but becoming effective on or prior to June 30, 2018, exclusive of any option to early adopt ahead of the mandatory effective date. Unless otherwise indicated, all unshaded text reflects guidance that was already effective as of the date of this guide.

Overview

2.01 AU-C section 200, *Overall Objectives of the Independent Auditor and the Conduct of an Audit in Accordance With Generally Accepted Auditing Standards*,[2] addresses the independent auditor's overall responsibilities when conducting an audit of financial statements in accordance with generally accepted auditing standards (GAAS). Specifically, it sets out the overall objectives of the independent auditor (the auditor) and explains the nature and scope of an audit designed to enable the auditor to meet those objectives. It also explains the scope, authority, and structure of GAAS and includes requirements establishing the general responsibilities of the auditor applicable in all audits, including the obligation to comply with GAAS.

2.02 Paragraph .12 of AU-C section 200 states that the overall objectives of the auditor, in conducting an audit of financial statements, are to

a. obtain reasonable assurance about whether the financial statements as a whole are free from material misstatement, whether due to fraud or error, thereby enabling the auditor to express an opinion on whether the financial statements are presented fairly, in all material respects, in accordance with an applicable financial reporting framework; and

b. report on the financial statements, and communicate as required by GAAS, in accordance with the auditor's findings.

Purpose of an Audit of Financial Statements

2.03 Consistent with the guidance presented in paragraph .04 of AU-C section 200, the purpose of an audit of a not-for-profit entity's (NFP's) financial statements is to provide financial statement users with an opinion by the auditor about whether the financial statements are presented fairly, in all material respects, in accordance with an applicable financial reporting framework, which enhances the degree of confidence that intended users can place in the financial statements. An audit conducted in accordance with GAAS, including relevant ethical requirements, enables the auditor to form that opinion. As the basis for the auditor's opinion, paragraph .06 of AU-C section 200 states that GAAS require the auditor to obtain reasonable assurance about whether the

---

[1] Not-for-profit entities (NFPs) are not issuers subject to oversight by the PCAOB. Thus, auditing standards issued by the PCAOB do not apply to audits of NFPs. The AICPA Auditing Standards Board sets auditing and assurance standards for nonissuers.

[2] All AU-C sections can be found in AICPA *Professional Standards*.

financial statements as a whole are free from material misstatement, whether due to fraud or error. Reasonable assurance is a high, but not absolute, level of assurance. It is obtained when the auditor has obtained sufficient appropriate audit evidence to reduce *audit risk* (as defined for purposes of GAAS as the risk that the auditor expresses an inappropriate opinion when the financial statements are materially misstated) to an acceptably low level.

2.04 Paragraphs .08 and .10 of AU-C section 200 state that GAAS contain objectives, requirements, and application and other explanatory material that are designed to support the auditor in obtaining reasonable assurance. GAAS require that the auditor exercise professional judgment and maintain professional skepticism throughout the planning and performance of the audit and, among other things,

- identify and assess risks of material misstatement, whether due to fraud or error, based on an understanding of the entity and its environment, including the entity's internal control.
- obtain sufficient appropriate audit evidence about whether material misstatements exist, through designing and implementing appropriate responses to the assessed risks.
- form an opinion on the financial statements, or determine that an opinion cannot be formed, based on an evaluation of the audit evidence obtained.

The auditor also may have certain other communication and reporting responsibilities to management, those charged with governance, users, or other parties outside the entity, regarding matters arising from the audit. These responsibilities may be established by GAAS or by applicable law or regulation.

Audit Risk

2.05 Paragraph .A36 of AU-C section 200 explains that audit risk is a function of the risks of material misstatement and detection risk. The assessment of risks is based on audit procedures to obtain information necessary for that purpose and evidence obtained throughout the audit. The assessment of risks is a matter of professional judgment rather than a matter capable of precise measurement.

2.06 Paragraphs .A38–.A40 of AU-C section 200 provide further explanation on the two levels of the risks of material misstatement. The risks of material misstatement exist at the overall financial statement level and the assertion level for classes of transactions, account balances, and disclosures. Risks of material misstatement at the overall financial statement level refer to risks of material misstatement that relate pervasively to the financial statements as a whole and potentially affect many assertions. Risks of material misstatement at the assertion level are assessed in order to determine the nature, timing, and extent of further audit procedures necessary to obtain sufficient appropriate audit evidence. This evidence enables the auditor to express an opinion on the financial statements at an acceptably low level of audit risk.

2.07 It is not acceptable to simply deem risk to be "at the maximum." Paragraph .A44 of AU-C section 200 explains that the assessment of the risks of material misstatement may be expressed in quantitative terms, such as in percentages or in nonquantitative terms (for example, high, medium, or low).

2.08 Paragraphs .A41–.A44 and .A46–.A47 of AU-C section 200 provide further guidance on the two components of the risk of material misstatement (inherent risk and control risk) and characteristics of detection risk.

Terms of Engagement

2.09 The scope of services rendered by auditors generally depends on the types of reports to be issued as a result of the engagement. Paragraphs .09–.10 of AU-C section 210, *Terms of Engagement*, state that the auditor should agree upon the terms of the audit engagement with management or those charged with governance, as appropriate. The agreed-upon terms of the audit engagement should be documented in an audit engagement letter or other suitable form of written agreement (see paragraph .10 of AU-C section 210 for a listing of agreed-upon terms that should be included). Both management and the auditor have an interest in documenting the agreed-upon terms of the audit engagement before the commencement of the audit to help avoid misunderstandings with respect to the audit as stated in paragraph .A22 of AU-C section 210.

2.10 In accordance with paragraphs .A23–.A24 of AU-C section 210, the form and content of the audit engagement letter may vary for each entity. When relevant, additional services to be provided, such as those relating to regulatory requirements, could be addressed in the audit engagement letter. [If a regulator, or a duly appointed representative, requests access to engagement documentation, refer to Interpretation No. 3, "Providing Access to or Copies of Engagement Documentation to a Regulator" (AT-C sec. 9105 par. .15–.30), of AT-C section 105, *Concepts Common to All Attestation Engagements*.[3]] The audit engagement letter may also address, when applicable, all relevant contractual, legal, and regulatory requirements so that the needs and expectations related to these requirements are not misinterpreted. For example, the auditor may be engaged to perform the audit and issue reports that meet requirements found in *Government Auditing Standards* (often called the Yellow Book) issued by the Comptroller General of the United States.[4] Also, the auditor may be engaged to perform the audit and issue reports as required under the Single Audit Act Amendments of 1996 and Title 2 U.S. *Code of Federal Regulations* Part 200, *Uniform Administrative Requirements, Cost Principles, and Audit Requirements for Federal Awards* (Uniform Guidance). (The preface discusses the effective date of Uniform Guidance for federal awards and funding increments.) The auditor may also be engaged to prepare special reports on various financial data prepared by the NFP, such as those related to bond indentures and other debt instruments and annual state information returns required by state attorneys general.

2.11 An auditor may become aware that the entity is subject to an audit requirement that may not be encompassed in the terms of the engagement. Paragraph .A27 of AU-C section 260, *The Auditor's Communication With Those*

---

[3] All AT-C sections can be found in AICPA *Professional Standards*.

[4] *Government Auditing Standards* contains requirements and guidance for financial audits, attestation engagements, and performance audits. The references to *Government Auditing Standards* (sometimes referred to as the Yellow Book) in this guide pertain only to the standards for financial audits. Auditors who perform audits under *Government Auditing Standards*; the Single Audit Act Amendments of 1996; and the audit requirements of Title 2 U.S. Code of Federal Regulations (CFR) Part 200, *Uniform Administrative Requirements, Cost Principles, and Audit Requirements for Federal Awards*, should also refer to the AICPA Audit Guide Government Auditing Standards *and Single Audits*.

Charged With Governance, states that the communication to those charged with governance that an audit conducted in accordance with GAAS may not satisfy the relevant legal, regulatory, or contractual requirements may be necessary if, for example, an entity engages an auditor to perform an audit of its financial statements in accordance with GAAS and the auditor becomes aware that by law, regulation, or contractual agreement the entity also is required to have an audit performed in accordance with one or more of the following:

a. *Government Auditing Standards*

b. Uniform Guidance

c. Other compliance audit requirements, such as state or local laws or program-specific audits under federal audit guides

Audit Planning Considerations

2.12 AU-C section 300, *Planning an Audit*, addresses the auditor's responsibilities to plan an audit of financial statements. AU-C section 300 is written in the context of recurring audits. Planning activities involve performing preliminary engagement activities; establishing an overall audit strategy and communicating with those charged with governance an overview of the planned scope and timing of the audit; developing a detailed, written audit plan; determining direction and supervision of engagement team members and review of their work; and determining the extent of involvement of professionals with specialized skills. Adequate planning benefits the audit of financial statements in several ways, including the following:

- Helping the auditor identify and devote appropriate attention to important areas of the audit
- Helping the auditor identify and resolve potential problems on a timely basis
- Helping the auditor properly organize and manage the audit engagement so that it is performed in an effective and efficient manner
- Assisting in the selection of engagement team members with appropriate levels of capabilities and competence to respond to anticipated risks and allocating team member responsibilities
- Facilitating the direction and supervision of engagement team members and the review of their work
- Assisting, when applicable, in coordination of work done by auditors of components and specialists

Paragraph .A1 of AU-C section 300 further explains that the nature, timing, and extent of planning activities will vary according to the size and complexity of the entity, the key engagement team members' previous experience with the entity, and changes in circumstances that occur during the audit.

2.13 In accordance with paragraph .09 of AU-C section 300, the auditor should develop an audit plan that includes a description of the nature and extent of planned risk assessment procedures, as determined under AU-C section 315, *Understanding the Entity and Its Environment and Assessing the Risks of Material Misstatement*; the nature, timing, and extent of planned further audit procedures at the relevant assertion level, as determined under AU-C section

330, *Performing Audit Procedures in Response to Assessed Risks and Evaluating the Audit Evidence Obtained*; and other planned audit procedures that are required to be carried out so that the engagement complies with GAAS. Paragraph .A2 of AU-C section 300 explains that planning is not a discrete phase of an audit, but rather a continual and iterative process that often begins shortly after (or in connection with) the completion of the previous audit and continues until the completion of the current audit engagement.

Group Audits

2.14 Under AU-C section 600, *Special Considerations—Audits of Group Financial Statements (Including the Work of Component Auditors)*, the scope of group audits has been expanded beyond those engagements that utilize the concept of "principal auditor" and "other auditors." Group audits involve an audit of financial statements that include the financial information of more than one component (group financial statements). AU-C section 600 introduces a number of new terms, concepts, and requirements related to group audits that will significantly affect current practice.

2.15 The concept of group financial statements is broader than consolidated or combined financial statements because it encompasses business activities in addition to separate entities. Additionally, this standard applies in all audits of group financial statements regardless of whether or not different auditors are involved in the audit. A *component* is defined as an entity or business activity for which group or component management prepares financial information that is required to be included in the group financial statements. A component may include, but is not limited to, subsidiaries, geographical locations, divisions, investments, products or services, functions, processes, or component units of state or local governments.

2.16 AU-C section 600 applies to audits of group financial statements and addresses special considerations that apply to group audits, in particular those that involve component auditors. Accordingly, a critical aspect of this section is the identification of the components that are included in the group financial statements. The requirements in paragraphs .51–.65 of AU-C section 600 are applicable only when the auditor of the group financial statements is assuming responsibility for the work of a component auditor. All other requirements of AU-C section 600 apply to all audits of group financial statements, including components for which the auditor of the group financial statements does not assume responsibility for the work of component auditors (that is, the auditor of the group financial statements makes reference to the audit of the component auditor in the auditor's report on the group financial statements). Accordingly, AU-C section 600 provides guidance when the auditor of the group financial statements assumes responsibility for the work of a component auditor and also when the auditor of the group financial statements makes reference to the work of a component auditor.

2.17 An audit of group financial statements involves identifying the components that are part of the group and considering the effect of the components on the overall group audit strategy and group audit plan (including the extent to which the group engagement team will use the work of component auditors). The decision about whether the auditor's report on the group financial statements will make reference to the audit of a component auditor should be made by the group engagement partner. When the auditor of the group financial statements assumes responsibility for the work of a component auditor, no reference is made to the component auditor in the auditor's report on the group financial statements. Alternatively, the auditor of the group financial statements may decide to make reference to the component auditor in the auditor's report on the group financial statements if two conditions are met. Reference to the audit of a component auditor in the auditor's report on the group financial statements should not be made unless (*a*) the group engagement partner has determined that the component auditor has performed an audit of the financial statements of the component in accordance with the relevant requirements of GAAS, and (*b*) the component auditor has issued an auditor's report that is not restricted regarding use. Reference in the auditor's report on the group financial statements to the fact that part of the audit was conducted by a component auditor is not to be construed as a qualification of the opinion. Rather, such reference is intended to communicate (1) that the auditor of the group financial statements is not assuming responsibility for the work of the component auditor, and (2) the source of the audit evidence with respect to those components for which reference to the audit of component auditors is made.

2.18 The Audit Risk Alert *Understanding the Responsibilities of Auditors for Audits of Group Financial Statements* and Technical Questions and Answers (Q&A) section 8800, *Audits of Group Financial Statements and Work of Others*,[5] have been issued to assist auditors in implementing AU-C section 600.

Using the Work of an Auditor's Specialist

2.19 AU-C section 620, *Using the Work of an Auditor's Specialist*, addresses the auditor's responsibilities relating to the work of an auditor's specialist. For purposes of GAAS, AU-C section 620 defines an *auditor's specialist* as an individual or organization possessing expertise in a field other than accounting or auditing, whose work in that field is used by the auditor to assist the auditor in obtaining sufficient appropriate audit evidence. An auditor's specialist may be either an internal specialist (who is a partner or staff, including temporary staff, of the auditor's firm or a network firm) or an external specialist.

2.20 AU-C section 620 does not address the following:

- Situations in which the engagement team includes a member or consults an individual or organization with expertise in a specialized area of accounting or auditing, which are addressed in AU-C section 220, *Quality Control for an Engagement Conducted in Accordance With Generally Accepted Auditing Standards*, and AU-C section 300
- An auditor's use of the work of an individual or organization possessing expertise in a field other than accounting or auditing, whose work in that field is used by the entity to assist the entity in preparing the financial statements (a management's specialist), which is addressed in AU-C section 500, *Audit Evidence*

2.21 In accordance with AU-C section 620, the objectives of the auditor are (*a*) to determine whether to use the work of an auditor's specialist, and (*b*) if using the work of an auditor's specialist, to determine whether that work is adequate for the auditor's purposes. In reaching these objectives, the auditor should

[5] All Q&A sections can be found in *Technical Questions and Answers*.

- determine the need for an auditor's specialist if expertise in a field other than accounting or auditing is necessary to obtain sufficient appropriate audit evidence;
- evaluate the competence, capabilities, and objectivity of the auditor's specialist; and
- obtain a sufficient understanding of the field of expertise of the auditor's specialist to enable the auditor to
  - — determine the nature, scope, and objectives of the work of the auditor's specialist for the auditor's purposes, and
  - — evaluate the adequacy of that work for the auditor's purposes.

2.22 Paragraph .09 of AU-C section 620 states that the auditor should evaluate whether the auditor's specialist has the necessary competence, capabilities, and objectivity for the auditor's purposes. For example, if the auditor is using an appraisal of commercial real estate values in connection with the audit of financial statements, he or she should evaluate the appraiser's professional qualifications and his or her experience with commercial real estate.

2.23 AU-C section 620 does not preclude the auditor from using an auditor's specialist who has a relationship with the client, including situations when the client has the ability to directly or indirectly control or significantly influence the specialist. However, paragraph .09 of AU-C section 620 states that, in the case of an auditor's external specialist, the evaluation of objectivity should include inquiry regarding interests and relationships that may create a threat to the objectivity of the auditor's specialist. If the auditor believes that a relationship between the entity and the auditor's specialist might impair the objectivity of the auditor's specialist, paragraph .A22 of AU-C section 620 states that the auditor may perform additional procedures with respect to some or all of the assumptions, methods, or findings of the auditor's specialist to determine that the findings are reasonable or may engage another specialist for that purpose.

2.24 Paragraph .10 of AU-C section 620 states that the auditor should obtain a sufficient understanding of the field of expertise of the auditor's specialist to enable the auditor to determine the nature, scope, and objectives of the work of the auditor's specialist for the auditor's purposes, and to evaluate the adequacy of that work for the auditor's purposes.

Materiality

Planning Materiality

2.25 AU-C section 320, *Materiality in Planning and Performing an Audit*, addresses the auditor's responsibility to apply the concept of materiality in planning and performing an audit of financial statements. AU-C section 450, *Evaluation of Misstatements Identified During the Audit*, explains how materiality is applied in evaluating the effect of identified misstatements on the audit and the effect of uncorrected misstatements, if any, on the financial statements.

2.26 Paragraphs .04 and .06 of AU-C section 320 state that the auditor's determination of materiality is a matter of professional judgment and is influenced by the auditor's perception of the financial information needs of users of the financial statements. In planning the audit, the auditor makes judgments about the size of misstatements that will be considered material. Although it is not practicable to design audit procedures to detect misstatements that could be material solely because of their nature (that is, qualitative considerations), the auditor considers not only the size but also the nature of uncorrected misstatements, and the particular circumstances of their occurrence, when evaluating their effect on the financial statements.

2.27 In accordance with paragraphs .10 and .A5 of AU-C section 320, the auditor should determine materiality for the financial statements as a whole when establishing the overall audit strategy. Determining materiality involves the exercise of professional judgment. A percentage is often applied to a chosen benchmark as a starting point in determining materiality for the financial statements as a whole. If, in the specific circumstances of the entity, one or more particular classes of transactions, account balances, or disclosures exist for which misstatements of lesser amounts than materiality for the financial statements as a whole could reasonably be expected to influence the economic decisions of users, then, taken on the basis of the financial statements, the auditor also should determine the materiality level or levels to be applied to those particular classes of transactions, account balances, or disclosures. See paragraphs .A12–.A13 of AU-C section 320 for further application guidance on materiality level or levels for particular classes of transactions, account balances, or disclosures.

2.28 Expenditures of NFPs are often tightly controlled and based on the concept of a balanced budget with relatively small or zero operating margins. Examples of appropriate benchmarks include total net assets, various net asset classes, changes in net assets, changes in each class of net assets, total revenues, revenues of each net asset class, total expenses, total unrestricted contributions, total program expenses, or the effect on important measures, such as the ratio of program expenses to total expenses and the ratio of fund-raising expenses to contributions.

Expenditures of NFPs are often tightly controlled and based on the concept of a balanced budget with relatively small or zero operating margins. Examples of appropriate benchmarks include total net assets, various net asset classes, changes in net assets, changes in each class of net assets, total revenues, revenues of each net asset class, total expenses, total contributions without donor restrictions, total program expenses, or the effect on important measures, such as the ratio of program expenses to total expenses and the ratio of fund-raising expenses to contributions.[6]

2.29 As required by AU-C section 935, *Compliance Audits*, in an audit of compliance, the auditor should establish and apply materiality levels based on the governmental audit requirement. Generally, the auditor's consideration of materiality is in relation to the government program taken as a whole. However, the governmental audit requirement may specify a different level of materiality. For example, for purposes of reporting findings of noncompliance, Subpart F of

---

[6] The amendments in FASB Accounting Standards Update No. 2016-14, *Not-for-Profit Entities (Topic 958): Presentation of Financial Statements of Not-for-Profit Entities*, are effective for annual financial statements issued for fiscal years beginning after December 15, 2017 (for example, years ending December 31, 2018 and years ending June 30, 2019), and for interim periods within fiscal years beginning after December 15, 2018. Application to interim financial statements is permitted but not required in the initial year of application. Early application of the amendments is permitted.

Uniform Guidance requires that noncompliance that is material in relation to 1 of the 12 types of compliance requirements identified in the Appendix XI to Part 200, *Compliance Supplement*, be reported.

Performance Materiality

2.30 Paragraph .A14 of AU-C section 320 explains that planning the audit solely to detect individual material misstatements overlooks the fact that the aggregate of individually immaterial misstatements may cause the financial statements to be materially misstated and leaves no margin for possible undetected misstatements. Therefore, in accordance with paragraph .11 of AU-C section 320, the auditor should determine performance materiality for purposes of assessing the risks of material misstatement and determining the nature, timing, and extent of further audit procedures. *Performance materiality*, for purposes of GAAS, is defined in AU-C section 320 as the amount or amounts set by the auditor at less than materiality for the financial statements as a whole to reduce to an appropriately low level the probability that the aggregate of uncorrected and undetected misstatements exceeds materiality for the financial statements as a whole. If applicable, *performance materiality* also refers to the amount or amounts set by the auditor at less than the materiality level or levels for particular classes of transactions, account balances, or disclosures. Performance materiality is to be distinguished from *tolerable misstatement*, which is the application of performance materiality to a particular sampling procedure. AU-C section 530, *Audit Sampling*, defines tolerable misstatement and provides further application guidance about the concept.

2.31 Paragraph .A14 of AU-C section 320 goes on to explain that the determination of performance materiality is not a simple mechanical calculation and involves the exercise of professional judgment. It is affected by the auditor's understanding of the entity, updated during the performance of the risk assessment procedures, and the nature and extent of misstatements identified in previous audits and, thereby, the auditor's expectations regarding misstatements in the current period.

Qualitative Aspects of Materiality

2.32 As indicated previously, judgments about materiality include both quantitative and qualitative information. As a result of the interaction of quantitative and qualitative considerations in materiality judgments, misstatements of relatively small amounts that come to the auditor's attention could have a material effect on the financial statements. For example, it recently was revealed that an officer of an NFP had been improperly spending the NFP's money to support a lavish personal lifestyle. Although the amount of the improper spending was only a small fraction of 1 percent of the charity's annual budget, the wide publicity surrounding the officer's behavior led to an estimated 10 percent decrease in public contributions for several years and severely affected the charity's ability to fund its programs. Further, as discussed in chapter 3, "Financial Statements, the Reporting Entity, and General Financial Reporting Matters," noncompliance with donor-imposed restrictions (even of an otherwise immaterial amount) could be material if there is a reasonable possibility that the noncompliance could lead to a material loss of revenue or could cause an entity to be unable to continue as a going concern.

2.33 Qualitative considerations also influence the auditor in reaching a conclusion about whether misstatements are material. Paragraph .A23 of

AU-C section 450 provides circumstances that the auditor may consider relevant in determining whether misstatements are material.

Related-Party Transactions

2.34 Obtaining knowledge of the NFP's organization and operations should include performing the procedures in AU-C section 550, *Related Parties*, to determine the existence of related-party relationships and transactions with such parties and to examine those transactions. The definition of *related parties* in FASB *Accounting Standards Codification* (ASC) 850, *Related Party Disclosures*, includes an NFP's management and members of management's immediate family, as well as affiliated entities. Accordingly, transactions with brother-sister entities and certain national and local affiliates as well as entities whose officers or directors are members of the NFP's governing board may have to be disclosed under FASB ASC 850-10-50.

2.35 AU-C section 550 provides guidance on, among other matters, procedures that the auditor should perform to identify related party relationships and transactions and to obtain satisfaction about the related financial statement reporting and disclosure. Obtaining that information will be enhanced if the NFP has a policy that requires an annual written disclosure by governing board members of the details of their transactions and other business involvements with the NFP, as well as disclosure of their other board memberships. Some states require that these kinds of disclosures be made on the annual reporting form filed by the NFP.

2.36 Some states have exhibited a heightened concern about whether the governing board members of NFPs are meeting their stewardship responsibilities, particularly if there are potential conflicts between the governing board members' financial interests and their duties as governing board members. Responses by an NFP to that concern might include increased sensitivity when it enters into business relationships with governing board members and might include developing appropriate controls for addressing potential conflicts of interests that could arise in related-party transactions and for ensuring that such transactions are disclosed to and approved by the governing board.

2.37 Paragraph .A2 of AU-C section 550 states that the substance of a particular transaction may be significantly different from its form. Accordingly, financial statements prepared in accordance with generally accepted accounting principles (GAAP) generally recognize the substance of particular transactions rather than merely their legal form. Paragraph .A45 of AU-C section 550 explains that it will generally not be possible to determine whether a particular transaction would have taken place if the parties had not been related, or assuming it would have taken place, what the terms and manner of settlement would have been. Accordingly, it is difficult to substantiate representations that a transaction was consummated on terms equivalent to those that prevail in arm's-length transactions. Paragraphs .A47 and .A49 of AU-C section 550 further state that the preparation and fair presentation of the financial statements require management to substantiate an assertion included in financial statements that a related party transaction was conducted on terms equivalent to those prevailing in an arm's-length transaction. If the auditor believes that management's assertions is unsubstantiated or the auditor cannot obtain sufficient appropriate audit evidence to support the assertion, the auditor, in accordance with AU-C section 705, *Modifications to the Opinion in the Independent Auditor's Report*, considers the implications for the audit, including the opinion in the auditor's report. AU-C section 705 addresses the auditor's responsibility to issue an appropriate report in circumstances when, in forming an opinion in accordance with AU-C section 700, *Forming an Opinion and Reporting on Financial Statements*, the auditor concludes that a modification to the auditor's opinion on the financial statements is necessary.

Consideration of Errors and Fraud

2.38 As described in AU-C section 240, *Consideration of Fraud in a Financial Statement Audit*, an auditor conducting an audit in accordance with GAAS is responsible for obtaining reasonable assurance that the financial statements as a whole are free from material misstatement, whether caused by fraud or error. Due to the inherent limitations of an audit, an unavoidable risk exists that some material misstatements of the financial statements may not be detected, even though the audit is properly planned and performed in accordance with GAAS.

2.39 Additionally, as discussed in AU-C section 200, the potential effects of inherent limitations are particularly significant in the case of misstatement resulting from fraud. The risk of not detecting a material misstatement resulting from fraud is higher than the risk of not detecting one resulting from error. This is because fraud may involve sophisticated and carefully organized schemes designed to conceal it, such as forgery, deliberate failure to record transactions, or intentional misrepresentations being made to the auditor. Such attempts at concealment may be even more difficult to detect when accompanied by collusion. Collusion may cause the auditor to believe that audit evidence is persuasive when it is, in fact, false. The auditor's ability to detect a fraud depends on factors such as the skillfulness of the perpetrator, the frequency and extent of manipulation, the degree of collusion involved, the relative size of individual amounts manipulated, and the seniority of those individuals involved. Although the auditor may be able to identify potential opportunities for fraud to be perpetrated, it is difficult for the auditor to determine whether misstatements in judgment areas, such as accounting estimates, are caused by fraud or error.

2.40 Furthermore, the risk of the auditor not detecting a material misstatement resulting from management fraud is greater than for employee fraud because management is frequently in a position to directly or indirectly manipulate accounting records, present fraudulent financial information, or override control procedures designed to prevent similar frauds by other employees.

2.41 When obtaining reasonable assurance, the auditor is responsible for maintaining professional skepticism throughout the audit, considering the potential for management override of controls, and recognizing the fact that audit procedures that are effective for detecting error may not be effective in detecting fraud. The requirements in AU-C section 240 are designed to assist the auditor in identifying and assessing the risks of material misstatement due to fraud and in designing procedures to detect such misstatement. Additional information about the implementation of AU-C section 240 is provided in appendix A of this chapter, "Consideration of Fraud in a Financial Statement Audit."

Compliance With Laws and Regulations

2.42 AU-C section 250, *Consideration of Laws and Regulations in an Audit of Financial Statements*, addresses the auditor's responsibility to consider laws and regulations in an audit of financial statements. However, it does not apply to other assurance engagements in which the auditor is specifically engaged to test and report separately on compliance with specific laws and regulations.

Responsibility for Compliance With Laws and Regulations

Responsibility of Management

2.43 In accordance with paragraph .03 of AU-C section 250, it is the responsibility of management, with the oversight of those charged with governance, to ensure that the entity's operations are conducted in accordance with the provisions of laws and regulations, including compliance with the provisions of laws and regulations that determine the reported amounts and disclosures in an entity's financial statements.

Responsibility of the Auditor

2.44 The requirements in AU-C section 250 are designed to assist the auditor in identifying material misstatement of the financial statements due to noncompliance with laws and regulations. However, paragraph .04 of AU-C section 250 recognizes that the auditor is not responsible for preventing noncompliance and cannot be expected to detect noncompliance with all laws and regulations. For purposes of discussion in AU-C section 250, the term *noncompliance* is defined as acts of omission or commission by the entity, either intentional or unintentional, which are contrary to the prevailing laws or regulations.

2.45 The auditor is responsible for obtaining reasonable assurance that the financial statements as a whole are free from material misstatement, whether caused by fraud or error. In conducting an audit of financial statements, the auditor takes into account the applicable legal and regulatory framework. Because of the inherent limitations of an audit, an unavoidable risk exists that some material misstatements in the financial statements may not be detected, even though the audit is properly planned and performed in accordance with GAAS. In the context of laws and regulations, the potential effects of inherent limitations on the auditor's ability to detect material misstatements are greater for the reasons set forth in paragraph .05 of AU-C section 250. Paragraph .05 of AU-C section 250 further states that the further removed noncompliance is from the events and transactions reflected in the financial statements, the less likely the auditor is to become aware of, or recognize, the noncompliance.

2.46 Paragraph .06 of AU-C section 250 distinguishes the auditor's responsibilities regarding compliance with the following two categories of laws and regulations:

a. The provisions of those laws and regulations generally recognized to have a direct effect on the determination of material amounts and disclosures in the financial statements, such as tax and pension laws, and

b. The provisions of other laws and regulations that do not have a direct effect on the determination of the amounts and disclosures in the financial statements but compliance that may be

   i. fundamental to the operating aspects of the business,

   ii. fundamental to an entity's ability to continue its business, or

iii. necessary for the entity to avoid material penalties

(for example, compliance with the terms of an operating license, regulatory solvency requirements, or environmental regulations); therefore, noncompliance with such laws and regulations may have a material effect on the financial statements.

The Auditor's Consideration of Compliance With Laws and Regulations

2.47 Paragraph .A9 of AU-C section 250 states that certain laws and regulations are well established, known to the entity and within the entity's industry or sector, and relevant to the entity's financial statements. These laws and regulations generally are directly relevant to the determination of material amounts and disclosures in the financial statements and readily evident to the auditor. For such laws and regulations, paragraph .13 of AU-C section 250 states that the auditor should obtain sufficient appropriate audit evidence regarding material amounts and disclosures in the financial statements that are determined by the provisions of those laws and regulations.

Procedures to Identify Instances of Noncompliance—Other Laws and Regulations

2.48 As discussed in paragraphs .A12–.A14 of AU-C section 250, certain other laws and regulations may need particular attention by the auditor because they have a fundamental effect on the operations of the entity. Noncompliance with laws and regulations that have a fundamental effect on the operations of the entity may cause the entity to cease operations or call into question the entity's continuance as a going concern (for example, noncompliance with capital or investment requirements).

2.49 In addition, many laws and regulations relating principally to an NFP's operations do not directly affect the financial statements (their financial statement effect is indirect) and are not captured by the entity's information systems relevant to financial reporting. Their indirect effect may result from the need to disclose a contingent liability because of the allegation or determination of identified or suspected noncompliance. Those other laws or regulations may include those related to securities trading, occupational safety and health, food and drug administration, environmental protection, equal employment opportunities, and price-fixing or other antitrust violations.

2.50 For these other such laws and regulations, paragraph .14 of AU-C section 250 states that the auditor should perform the following audit procedures that may identify instances of noncompliance with other laws and regulations that may have a material effect on the financial statements:

a. Inquiring of management and, when appropriate, those charged with governance about whether the entity is in compliance with such laws and regulations

b. Inspecting correspondence, if any, with the relevant licensing or regulatory authorities (additional application and explanatory material can be found at paragraph .A16 of AU-C section 250)

However, even when those procedures are performed, the auditor may not become aware of the existence of noncompliance unless there is evidence of noncompliance in the records, documents, or other information normally inspected in an audit of financial statements.

Noncompliance Brought to the Auditor's Attention by Other Audit Procedures

2.51 During the audit, paragraph .15 of AU-C section 250 states that the auditor should remain alert to the possibility that other audit procedures applied may bring instances of noncompliance or suspected noncompliance with laws and regulations to the auditor's attention. For example, paragraph .A17 of AU-C section 250 states that such audit procedures may include reading minutes; inquiring of NFP's management and in-house or external legal counsel concerning litigation, claims, and assessments; and performing substantive tests of details of classes of transactions, account balances, or disclosures.

2.52 Further discussion regarding audit procedures when noncompliance is identified or suspected, reporting of identified or suspected noncompliance, and documentation requirements can be found in paragraphs .17–.28 of AU-C section 250.

Compliance Auditing Under Government Auditing Standards

2.53 NFPs that receive government financial assistance may be required to have their financial statement audits performed in accordance with *Government Auditing Standards* in addition to GAAS. *Government Auditing Standards* include additional requirements. In performing an audit in accordance with the Yellow Book, the auditor must report on compliance with laws and regulations, violations of which may affect financial statement amounts, and on the NFP's internal control over financial reporting.

Single Audits and Related Considerations

2.54 A *single audit* is an audit of an entity's financial statements and an audit of compliance with federal regulations relating to federal financial assistance in accordance with the Single Audit Act Amendments of 1996. The Uniform Guidance prescribes audit requirements for NFPs receiving federal awards. AU-C section 935 establishes standards and provides guidance when an auditor is engaged, or required by law or regulation, to perform a compliance audit in accordance with all of the following:

- GAAS
- *Government Auditing Standards*
- A governmental audit requirement that requires an auditor to express an opinion on compliance

It requires the auditor to adapt and apply the requirements of AICPA professional standards to a compliance audit and provides guidance on how to do so. It identifies the AU-C sections that are not applicable to a compliance audit, defines terms related to compliance audits, and identifies the elements to be included in an auditor's report on a compliance audit.

2.55 For audits performed in accordance with the Uniform Guidance, the auditor has responsibilities that go beyond GAAS. In such audits, the auditor must perform additional procedures to test and report on compliance with federal statutes, regulations, and the terms and conditions of federal awards that may have a direct and material effect on major federal award programs. Other requirements of the Uniform Guidance relate to the financial statements, including the supplementary schedule of expenditures of federal awards.

2.56 AU-C section 935 and the AICPA Audit Guide Government Auditing Standards *and Single Audits* provide guidance on testing and reporting on compliance with laws and regulations in engagements performed under GAAS, the Yellow Book, and the Uniform Guidance. They provide auditors of NFPs with a basic understanding of the work they should do and the type of reports they should issue under the Yellow Book and the Uniform Guidance.

Processing of Transactions by Service Organizations

2.57 In addition to transactions, such as discretionary investment management services and payroll, for which for-profit entities might use service organizations, NFPs may also use such organizations to process transactions that are unique to the not-for-profit industry, such as student financial aid payments and receipt of contributions. AU-C section 402, *Audit Considerations Relating to an Entity Using a Service Organization*, addresses the user auditor's responsibility for obtaining sufficient appropriate audit evidence in an audit of the financial statements of a user entity that uses one or more service organizations. Specifically, it expands on how the user auditor applies AU-C section 315 and AU-C section 330 when obtaining an understanding of the user entity, including internal control relevant to the audit, sufficient to identify and assess the risks of material misstatement and in designing and performing further audit procedures responsive to those risks.

2.58 Paragraphs .03–.05 of AU-C section 402 state that services provided by a service organization are relevant to the audit of a user entity's financial statements when those services and the controls over them affect the user entity's information system, including related business processes, relevant to financial reporting. Although most controls at the service organization are likely to relate to financial reporting, other controls also may be relevant to the audit, such as controls over the safeguarding of assets. A service organization's services are part of a user entity's information system, including related business processes, relevant to financial reporting if these services affect any of the following:

- *a.* The classes of transactions in the user entity's operations that are significant to the user entity's financial statements;
- *b.* The procedures within both IT and manual systems by which the user entity's transactions are initiated, authorized, recorded, processed, corrected as necessary, transferred to the general ledger, and reported in the financial statements;
- *c.* The related accounting records, supporting information, and specific accounts in the user entity's financial statements that are used to initiate, authorize, record, process, and report the user entity's transactions. This includes the correction of incorrect information and how information is transferred to the general ledger; the records may be in either manual or electronic form;
- *d.* How the user entity's information system captures events and conditions, other than transactions, that are significant to the financial statements;
- *e.* The financial reporting process used to prepare the user entity's financial statements, including significant accounting estimates and disclosures; and

f. Controls surrounding journal entries, including nonstandard journal entries used to record nonrecurring, unusual transactions, or adjustments.

The nature and extent of work to be performed by the user auditor regarding the services provided by a service organization depend on the nature and significance of those services to the user entity and the relevance of those services to the audit.

2.59 AU-C section 402 does not apply to services that are limited to processing an entity's transactions that are specifically authorized by the entity, such as the processing of checking account transactions by a bank or the processing of securities transactions by a broker (that is, when the user entity retains responsibility for authorizing the transactions and maintaining the related accountability). In addition, AU-C section 402 does not apply to the audit of transactions arising from an entity that holds a proprietary financial interest in another entity, such as a partnership, corporation, or joint venture, when the partnership, corporation, or joint venture performs no processing on behalf of the entity.

Use of Assertions in Assessment of Risks of Material Misstatement

2.60 Paragraphs .A113–.A118 of AU-C section 315 discuss the use of assertions in assessment of risks of material misstatement. When representing that the financial statements are in accordance with the applicable financial reporting framework, management implicitly or explicitly makes assertions regarding the recognition, measurement, presentation, and disclosure of the various elements of financial statements and related disclosures. Assertions used by the auditor to consider the different types of potential misstatements that may occur fall into the following categories and may take the following forms.

Categories of Assertions

	Description of Assertions		
	Classes of Transactions and Events During the Period	***Account Balances at the End of the Period***	***Presentation and Disclosure***
Occurrence/ Existence	Transactions and events that have been recorded have occurred and pertain to the entity.	Assets and liabilities exist.	Disclosed events and transactions have occurred.
Rights and Obligations	—	The entity holds or controls the rights to assets, and liabilities are the obligations of the entity.	Disclosed events and transactions pertain to the entity.
Completeness	All transactions and events that should have been recorded are recorded.	All assets, liabilities, and restrictions on net assets that should have been recorded are recorded.	All disclosures that should have been included in the financial statements are included.

Categories of Assertions—*(continued)*

	Description of Assertions		
	Classes of Transactions and Events During the Period	***Account Balances at the End of the Period***	***Presentation and Disclosure***
Accuracy/ Valuation and Allocation	Amounts and other data relating to recorded transactions and events have been recorded appropriately.	Assets, liabilities, and restricted net assets are included in the financial statements at appropriate amounts and any resulting valuation or allocation adjustments are recorded appropriately.	Financial and other information is disclosed fairly and at appropriate amounts.
Cut-off	Transactions and events have been recorded in the correct accounting period.	—	—
Classification and Under-standability	Transactions and events have been recorded in the proper accounts.	—	Financial information is appropriately presented and described and information in disclosures is expressed clearly.

2.61 According to paragraph .A116 of AU-C section 315, the auditor is required to use relevant assertions for classes of transactions, account balances, and disclosures in sufficient detail to form a basis for the assessment of risks of material misstatement and the design and performance of further audit procedures. The auditor is required to use relevant assertions when assessing risks by relating the identified risks to what can go wrong at the relevant assertion, taking into account the relevant controls that the auditor intends to test, and designing further audit procedures that are responsive to the assessed risks.

2.62 The purpose of the use of assertions, specific audit objectives, and control objectives in the tables titled "Auditing Considerations," which are presented in the auditing sections of several of the following chapters, and the examples of audit procedures following those tables, is to assist the auditor in linking the auditor's risk assessments and further audit procedures. The tables include only those matters that are unique to NFPs. Accordingly, they do not represent a complete listing of all of the audit objectives, controls, and auditing procedures that the auditor may need to consider when auditing an NFP. In addition, the absence of examples of selected controls related to a particular assertion is intended to indicate that the assertion does not ordinarily lend itself to specific controls that would provide reasonable assurance that the related audit objective has been achieved.

2.63 There is not necessarily a one-to-one relationship between audit objectives and auditing procedures. Some procedures may relate to more than one objective. On the other hand, a combination of procedures may be necessary to achieve a single objective. The tables and example procedures are not intended to be all-inclusive or to suggest that specific audit objectives, controls, and auditing procedures need to be applied. Some of the audit objectives may not be relevant to a particular NFP because of the nature of its operations or the absence of certain types of transactions. The absence of one or more of the illustrative controls would not necessarily indicate a deficiency in internal control.

2.64 Many of the illustrative controls are premised on the existence of certain essential characteristics of internal control: authorization of transactions, segregation of duties, documentation, supervision and review, and timeliness of controls. To avoid repetition, these characteristics have not been explicitly incorporated in the tables.

Risk Assessment Procedures

2.65 AU-C section 315 addresses the auditor's responsibility to identify and assess the risks of material misstatement in the financial statements through understanding the entity and its environment, including the entity's internal control.

2.66 Obtaining an understanding of the entity and its environment, including the entity's internal control (referred to hereafter as an understanding of the entity), is a continuous, dynamic process of gathering, updating, and analyzing information throughout the audit. As stated in paragraph .A1 of AU-C section 315, the understanding of the entity establishes a frame of reference within which the auditor plans the audit and exercises professional judgment throughout the audit when, for example,

- assessing risks of material misstatement of the financial statements;
- determining materiality in accordance with AU-C section 320;
- considering the appropriateness of the selection and application of accounting policies and the adequacy of financial statement disclosures;
- identifying areas for which special audit consideration may be necessary (for example, related party transactions, the appropriateness of management's use of the going concern assumption, considering the business purpose of transactions, or the existence of complex and unusual transactions);
- developing expectations for use when performing analytical procedures;
- responding to the assessed risks of material misstatement, including designing and performing further audit procedures to obtain sufficient appropriate audit evidence; and
- evaluating the sufficiency and appropriateness of audit evidence obtained, such as the appropriateness of assumptions and management's oral and written representations.

Appendix A of this chapter addresses the unique aspects of NFPs that may be helpful in developing the required understanding of the entity, its environment, and its internal control.

Risk Assessment Procedures and Related Activities

2.67 In accordance with paragraph .05 of AU-C section 315, the auditor should perform risk assessment procedures to provide a basis for the identification and assessment of risks of material misstatement at the financial statement and relevant assertion levels. Risk assessment procedures by themselves, however, do not provide sufficient appropriate audit evidence on which to base the audit opinion. For purposes of GAAS, *risk assessment procedures* are defined in AU-C section 315 as audit procedures performed to obtain an understanding of the entity and its environment, including the entity's internal control, to identify and assess the risks of material misstatement, whether due to fraud or error, at the financial statement and relevant assertion levels.

2.68 As described in paragraph .18 of AU-C section 200, the auditor is required to exercise professional judgment to determine the extent of the required understanding of the entity. Paragraph .A3 of AU-C section 315 states that the auditor's primary consideration is whether the understanding of the entity that has been obtained is sufficient to meet the objectives of AU-C section 315. The depth of the overall understanding that is required by the auditor is less than that possessed by management in managing the entity.

2.69 Paragraph .06 of AU-C section 315 states that the risk assessment procedures should include the following:

- Inquiries of management and others within the entity who, in the auditor's professional judgment, may have information that is likely to assist in identifying risks of material misstatement due to fraud or error
- Analytical procedures
- Observation and inspection

Analytical Procedures

2.70 Paragraphs .A7–.A10 of AU-C section 315 provide additional explanation for analytical procedures performed during the risk assessment process. Analytical procedures performed as risk assessment procedures may identify aspects of the entity of which the auditor was unaware and may assist in assessing the risks of material misstatement in order to provide a basis for designing and implementing responses to the assessed risks. Analytical procedures may enhance the auditor's understanding of the NFP's activities and the significant transactions and events that have occurred since the prior audit and help to identify the existence of unusual transactions or events and amounts, ratios, and trends that might indicate matters that have audit implications.

2.71 In performing analytical procedures as risk assessment procedures, the auditor may identify unusual or unexpected relationships, which may assist the auditor in identifying risks of material misstatement. However, when such analytical procedures use data aggregated at a high level (which is often the situation), the results of those analytical procedures provide only a broad initial indication about whether a material misstatement may exist. Accordingly, consideration of the results of such analytical procedures along with other information gathered in identifying the risks of material misstatement may assist the auditor in understanding and evaluating the results of the analytical procedures.

2.72 Paragraphs .A2–.A3 of AU-C section 520, *Analytical Procedures*, provide examples of sources of information that can be used to develop the necessary expectations for applying analytical procedures. The sources of information that may be unique to NFPs are (1) information regarding the industry in which the client operates, and (2) relationships of financial information with relevant nonfinancial information. The first of these utilizes industry-wide data for comparisons (such as data on endowment return, contributions, or program, fund-raising, and management and general costs that can be obtained from industry trade and professional associations). The second uses the auditor to formulate relevant relationships that are usually unique to a particular type of NFP, such as the relationship that might be expected to exist at a college or university between the number of students registered at standard tuition rates and tuition revenues, the relationship between the number of members in an NFP and its dues revenue, and the relationship between stagehand costs and the number of theatrical, dance, orchestral, or similar performances.

Discussion Among the Audit Team

2.73 In accordance with paragraph .11 of AU-C section 315, the engagement partner and other key engagement team members should discuss the susceptibility of the entity's financial statements to material misstatement and the application of the applicable financial reporting framework to the entity's facts and circumstances. The engagement partner should determine which matters are to be communicated to engagement team members not involved in the discussion. Paragraph .A14 of AU-C section 315 states this discussion may be held concurrently with the discussion among the engagement team that is required by AU-C section 240 to discuss the susceptibility of the entity's financial statements to fraud. Appendix A of this chapter further addresses the discussion among the engagement team about the risks of fraud.

Understanding of the Entity and Its Environment, Including the Entity's Internal Control[7]

2.74 Paragraph .12 of AU-C section 315 states that the auditor should obtain an understanding of the following:

a. Relevant industry, regulatory, and other external factors, including the applicable financial reporting framework.

b. The nature of the entity, including

   i. its operations;

   ii. its ownership and governance structures;

   iii. the types of investments that the entity is making and plans to make, including investments in entities formed to accomplish specific objectives; and

   iv. the way that the entity is structured and how it is financed,

   to enable the auditor to understand the classes of transactions, account balances, and disclosures to be expected in the financial statements.

---

[7] In May 2013, the Committee of Sponsoring Organizations of the Treadway Commission issued its updated *Internal Control—Integrated Framework* and related illustrative documents.

c. The entity's selection and application of accounting policies, including the reasons for changes thereto. The auditor should evaluate whether the entity's accounting policies are appropriate for its business and consistent with the applicable financial reporting framework and accounting policies used in the relevant industry.

d. The entity's objectives and strategies and those related business risks that may result in risks of material misstatement.

e. The measurement and review of the entity's financial performance.

2.75 Appendix A, "Understanding the Entity and Its Environment," of AU-C section 315 contains examples of matters that the auditor may consider in obtaining an understanding of the entity and its environment. Appendix B, "Internal Control Components," of AU-C section 315 contains a detailed explanation of the internal control components.[8]

Industry Characteristics

2.76 The operations of NFPs differ from those of for-profit entities in several significant ways, and those differences affect the auditor's assessment of the risk of material misstatement. NFPs use their resources to accomplish the purpose or mission for which they exist, not to generate net income. These resources often come from contributions, grants, or appropriations, some of which may be subject to limitations on how the resources may be used.[9] These limitations, which may be imposed by donor restrictions, by contractual terms, or by the NFP's governing board, may affect the way in which revenues and net assets are recorded and presented in the financial statements.

2.77 NFPs are also required to comply with numerous other provisions of statutes, contractual agreements, terms of grants and trust agreements, and similar limitations. As discussed earlier in this chapter, these compliance requirements may have an effect on the financial statements. Finally, though NFPs are usually eligible for tax-exempt status under IRC Section 501, income from activities not related to an NFP's exempt purpose may be subject to tax and the NFP may own or control for-profit subsidiaries. Taxes on unrelated business income and other tax matters related to the assessment of the risk of material misstatement for an NFP are addressed in chapter 15, "Tax and Regulatory Considerations."

2.78 NFPs often have revenue and expense transactions that are unique to the industry, and these transactions have attendant implications for assessing the risk of material misstatement. For example, some NFPs solicit contributions from various sources; some receive revenues from grants; and some NFPs collect dues from members. Fund-raising may take place through telemarketing, direct mail solicitations, door-to-door solicitations, telethons, various kinds of special events, and other activities. Some NFPs collect substantial amounts

---

[8] In addition to industry characteristics, the auditor's understanding of the entity and its environment also consists of regulatory and other external factors; the nature of the entity; objectives and strategies and related business risks; and measurement and review of the entity's financial performance. The Audit Risk Alert *Not-for-Profit Entities Industry Developments* is intended to provide auditors of financial statements of NFPs with an overview of recent economic, industry, technical, regulatory, and professional developments that may affect the audits and other engagements they perform.

[9] As used in this guide, *limitation* refers broadly to any constraints imposed on the use of assets or net assets, restriction refers to donor-imposed limitations, and *designation* refers to governing-board-imposed limitations.

of contributions in the form of currency. Each of these sources of cash flows is associated with different kinds of risk. On the expenditure side, some NFPs must also comply with restrictions imposed by resource providers. The revenue and expenditure transaction cycles of NFPs may also include transactions that are similar to those entered into by for-profit entities—for example, buying and selling merchandise, purchasing investments, property and equipment, and other assets; providing services for fees, and earning income from investments. These cycles may include transactions that do not immediately result in revenues and expenses.

2.79 FASB ASC 958-605-25-8 requires NFPs to recognize agreements for future nonreciprocal transfers of cash, other assets, and services that are unconditional (that is, promises to give). Chapter 5, "Contributions Received and Agency Transactions," discusses recognition and measurement principles for the assets and revenues related to such transactions. Applying those principles often involves the use of significant accounting estimates. AU-C section 540, *Auditing Accounting Estimates, Including Fair Value Accounting Estimates, and Related Disclosures*, addresses the auditor's responsibilities relating to accounting estimates, including fair value accounting estimates and related disclosures, in an audit of financial statements. Specifically, it expands on how AU-C section 315 and other relevant AU-C sections are to be applied with regard to accounting estimates. It also includes requirements and guidance related to misstatements of individual accounting estimates and indicators of possible management bias.

2.80 NFPs also have unique reporting requirements under GAAP. For example, they must report their expenses by function, such as major classes of program services and supporting activities, in conformity with FASB ASC 958-720-45-2. They are also subject to specific disclosure requirements under FASB ASC 958-310-50 and FASB ASC 958-605-50, such as disclosures about endowments, promises to give, contributed services, and collections.

2.81 Each of these kinds of transactions and reporting requirements increases the risk of material misstatement. NFPs usually have controls designed to achieve control objectives related to these transactions.

2.82 Many NFPs face financial and operating pressures that are similar to those faced by for-profit entities. NFPs may also face pressures that are unique to entities that seek revenues in the form of contributions and grants, transactions that often depend on the state of the economy. These pressures generate operating, financial, and accounting responses by management, and such responses may increase the risk of material misstatement. The following are examples:

- Certain donors may tie contribution allocation formulas to the NFP's actual or budgeted revenues, leading management to attempt to manage revenues to achieve the largest allocation possible.
- A sluggish economy may reduce contributions and the collection of promises to give that were made in prior years. The reduced receipts may lead the NFP to pursue a more aggressive investment strategy involving complex financial instruments. Accounting for these instruments may represent significant risks. As part of performing his or her risk assessment procedures, the auditor should

obtain an understanding the substance of these instruments and determine that they are reported in conformity with GAAP.

- Adverse demographics may lead an NFP that charges fees for its services to pursue a more aggressive marketing strategy in its quest for constituents; this could decrease the collectability of its receivables.
- Shortfalls in contributions, especially in contributions available for general use, may induce an NFP to use restricted contributions for purposes that violate donor restrictions.
- Acceptance by an NFP of federal research and other grants carries with it an obligation to comply with federal regulations when the NFP administers those grants. Such regulations include those governing overhead and other costs charged to these grants. The terms of the grants may induce NFPs to charge unallowable costs to the grants, possibly resulting in liabilities for fines and repayment of any unallowable costs.
- An attempt to appear as efficient as possible may increase the likelihood of misstatement of the allocation of costs between program services and supporting activities. (Because some financial statement users view program expenses more favorably than supporting services, some NFPs have incentive to report costs as program rather than supporting services.)

Understanding of the Entity's Internal Control

2.83 Paragraphs .13–.14 of AU-C section 315 state that the auditor should obtain an understanding of internal control relevant to the audit. Although most controls relevant to the audit are likely to relate to financial reporting, not all controls that relate to financial reporting are relevant to the audit. It is a matter of the auditor's professional judgment whether a control, individually or in combination with others, is relevant to the audit. When obtaining an understanding of controls that are relevant to the audit, the auditor should evaluate the design of those controls and determine whether they have been implemented by performing procedures in addition to inquiry of the entity's personnel.

2.84 Paragraph .A44 of AU-C section 315 explains that internal control is designed, implemented, and maintained to address identified business risks that threaten the achievement of any of the entity's objectives that concern (*a*) the reliability of the entity's financial reporting, (*b*) the effectiveness and efficiency of its operations, and (*c*) its compliance with applicable laws and regulations.

2.85 For purposes of GAAS, internal control is divided into the following five components:

a. *Control environment* sets the tone of an entity, influencing the control consciousness of its people. It is the foundation for all other components of internal control, providing discipline and structure.

b. *Risk assessment* is the entity's identification, analysis, and management of risks relevant to the preparation and fair presentation of financial statements.

c. *Information system, including the related business processes relevant to financial reporting and communication* consists of the procedures and records designed and established to

i. initiate, authorize, record, process, and report entity transactions (as well as events and conditions) and maintain accountability for the related assets, liabilities, and net assets;

ii. resolve incorrect processing of transactions (for example, automated suspense files and procedures followed to remove suspense items on a timely basis);

iii. process and account for system overrides or bypasses of controls;

iv. transfer information from transaction processing systems to the general ledger;

v. capture information relevant to financial reporting for events and conditions other than transactions, such as the depreciation and amortization of assets and changes in the recoverability of accounts receivables; and

vi. ensure information required to be disclosed by the applicable financial reporting framework is accumulated, recorded, processed, summarized, and appropriately reported in the financial statements.

d. *Control activities* are the policies and procedures that help ensure management directives are carried out.

e. *Monitoring* is a process that assesses the quality of internal control performance over time.

Audit requirements and application guidance related to the preceding components can be found in paragraphs .15–.25 and .A71–.A107, respectively, of AU-C section 315.

2.86 Certain characteristics of internal control, particularly in the control environment, may be unique to NFPs. The following are examples of characteristics of an NFP's control environment that the auditor may consider in obtaining an understanding of that environment:

- The role of management and the governing board
- The frequency of governing board meetings
- The qualifications of management and governing board members
- The governing board members' involvement in the NFP's operations
- The organizational structure

2.87 The other four components of internal control for NFPs may also include characteristics that would not ordinarily exist in for-profit entities. Some areas of NFPs that may include control activities relevant to the audit are how

- restricted contributions are identified, evaluated, and accepted;
- promises to give are valued and recorded;
- contributed goods, services, utilities, facilities, and the use of long-lived assets are valued and recorded;
- compliance with donor restrictions and board designations is monitored;
- reporting requirements imposed by donors, contractors, and regulators are met;

- conformity with accounting presentation and disclosure principles, including those related to functional and natural expense reporting and allocation of joint costs, is achieved; and
- new programs are identified and accounted for.

2.88 Paragraphs .A61–.A62 of AU-C section 315 state that a direct relationship exists between an entity's objectives and the controls it implements to provide reasonable assurance about their achievement. The entity's objectives and, therefore, its controls, relate to financial reporting, operations, and compliance; however, not all of these objectives and controls are relevant to the auditor's risk assessment. Factors relevant to the auditor's professional judgment about whether a control, individually or in combination with others, is relevant to the audit may include such matters as the following:

- Materiality
- The significance of the related risk
- The NFP's size
- The diversity and complexity of the NFP's operations
- Applicable legal and regulatory requirements
- The circumstances and the applicable component of internal control
- The nature and complexity of the systems that are part of the NFP's internal control, including the use of service organizations
- Whether and how a specific control, individually or in combination with other controls, prevents, or detects and corrects, material misstatements

Using Risk Assessment to Design Further Audit Procedures

2.89 As discussed previously, risk assessment procedures allow the auditor to gather the information necessary to obtain an understanding of the entity and its environment, including its internal control. This knowledge provides a basis for assessing the risks of material misstatement of the financial statements. These risk assessments are then used to design further audit procedures, such as tests of controls, substantive tests, or both. This section provides guidance on assessing the risk of material misstatement and how to design further audit procedures that effectively respond to those risks.

Identifying and Assessing the Risks of Material Misstatement

2.90 To provide a basis for designing and performing further audit procedures, paragraphs .26–.27 of AU-C section 315 state that the auditor should identify and assess the risks of material misstatement at the financial statement level and at the relevant assertion level related to classes of transactions, account balances, and disclosures. For this purpose, the auditor should

a. identify risks throughout the process of obtaining an understanding of the entity and its environment, including relevant controls that relate to the risks, by considering the classes of transactions, account balances, and disclosures in the financial statements;

b. assess the identified risks and evaluate whether they relate more pervasively to the financial statements as a whole and potentially affect many assertions;

c. relate the identified risks to what can go wrong at the relevant assertion level, taking into account the relevant controls that the auditor intends to test; and

d. consider the likelihood of misstatement, including the possibility of multiple misstatements, and whether the potential misstatement is of a magnitude that could result in a material misstatement.

2.91 Paragraph .A108 of AU-C section 315 explains that the risks of material misstatement at the financial statement level refer to risks that relate pervasively to the financial statements as a whole and potentially affect many assertions. Risks of this nature are not necessarily risks identifiable with specific assertions at the class of transactions, account balance, or disclosure level. Rather, they represent circumstances that may increase the risks of material misstatement at the assertion level (for example, through management override of internal control). Financial statement level risks may be especially relevant to the auditor's consideration of the risks of material misstatement arising from fraud.

2.92 Paragraph .A120 of AU-C section 315 explains that information gathered by performing risk assessment procedures, including the audit evidence obtained in evaluating the design of controls and determining whether they have been implemented, is used as audit evidence to support the risk assessment. The risk assessment determines the nature, timing, and extent of further audit procedures to be performed.

Risks That Require Special Audit Consideration

2.93 Paragraphs .28–.29 of AU-C section 315 state that as part of the risk assessment described in paragraph .26 of AU-C section 315, the auditor should determine whether any of the risks identified are, in the auditor's professional judgment, a significant risk. In exercising this judgment, the auditor should exclude the effects of identified controls related to the risk. In addition, the auditor should consider at least

a. whether the risk is a risk of fraud;

b. whether the risk is related to recent significant economic, accounting, or other developments and, therefore, requires specific attention;

c. the complexity of transactions;

d. whether the risk involves significant transactions with related parties;

e. the degree of subjectivity in the measurement of financial information related to the risk, especially those measurements involving a wide range of measurement uncertainty; and

f. whether the risk involves significant transactions that are outside the normal course of business for the entity or that otherwise appear to be unusual.

2.94 If the auditor has determined that a significant risk exists, paragraph .30 of AU-C section 315 states that the auditor should obtain an understanding of the entity's controls, including control activities, relevant to that risk and, based on that understanding, evaluate whether such controls have been suitably designed and implemented to mitigate such risks. Examples of risks of material misstatements due to fraud can be found in appendix A of this chapter.

Designing and Performing Further Audit Procedures

2.95 AU-C section 330 addresses the auditor's responsibility to design and implement responses to the risks of material misstatement identified and assessed by the auditor in accordance with AU-C section 315 and to evaluate the audit evidence obtained in an audit of financial statements.

Overall Responses

2.96 Paragraph .05 of AU-C section 330 states that the auditor should design and implement overall responses to address the assessed risks of material misstatement at the financial statement level. Paragraph .A1 of AU-C section 330 states that overall responses to address the assessed risks of material misstatement at the financial statement level may include emphasizing to the audit team the need to maintain professional skepticism, assigning more experienced staff or those with specialized skills or using specialists, providing more supervision, incorporating additional elements of unpredictability in the selection of further audit procedures to be performed, or making general changes to the nature, timing, or extent of further audit procedures (for example, performing substantive procedures at period end instead of at an interim date or modifying the nature of audit procedures to obtain more persuasive audit evidence).

2.97 Paragraphs .A2–.A3 of AU-C section 330 explain that the assessment of the risks of material misstatement at the financial statement level and, thereby, the auditor's overall responses, are affected by the auditor's understanding of the control environment. An effective control environment may allow the auditor to have more confidence in internal control and the reliability of audit evidence generated internally within the entity and, thus, for example, allow the auditor to conduct some audit procedures at an interim date rather than at the period-end. Deficiencies in the control environment, however, have the opposite effect. For example, the auditor may respond to an ineffective control environment by

- conducting more audit procedures as of the period-end rather than at an interim date,
- obtaining more extensive audit evidence from substantive procedures, and
- increasing the number of locations to be included in the audit scope.

Such considerations have a significant bearing on the auditor's general approach (for example, an emphasis on substantive procedures [substantive approach] or an approach that uses tests of controls as well as substantive procedures [combined approach]).

Further Audit Procedures

2.98 Further audit procedures provide important audit evidence to support an audit opinion. These procedures consist of tests of controls and substantive tests. The nature, timing, and extent of the further audit procedures to be performed by the auditor should be based on, and are responsive to, the auditor's assessment of risk of material misstatement at the relevant assertion level.

2.99 In designing the further audit procedures to be performed, paragraph .07 of AU-C section 330 states that the auditor should

a. consider the reasons for the assessed risk of material misstatement at the relevant assertion level for each class of transactions, account balance, and disclosure, including

   i. the likelihood of material misstatement due to the particular characteristics of the relevant class of transactions, account balance, or disclosure (the inherent risk) and

   ii. whether the risk assessment takes into account the relevant controls (the control risk), thereby requiring the auditor to obtain audit evidence to determine whether the controls are operating effectively (that is, the auditor intends to rely on the operating effectiveness of controls in determining the nature, timing, and extent of substantive procedures), and

b. obtain more persuasive audit evidence the higher the auditor's assessment of risk.

2.100 In accordance with paragraph .08 of AU-C section 330, the auditor should design and perform tests of controls to obtain sufficient appropriate audit evidence about the operating effectiveness of relevant controls if (*a*) the auditor's assessment of risks of material misstatement at the relevant assertion level includes an expectation that the controls are operating effectively (that is, the auditor intends to rely on the operating effectiveness of controls in determining the nature, timing, and extent of substantive procedures), or (*b*) when substantive procedures alone cannot provide sufficient appropriate audit evidence at the relevant assertion level. In accordance with paragraph .A21 of AU-C section 330, tests of controls are performed only on those controls that the auditor has determined are suitably designed to prevent, or detect and correct, a material misstatement in a relevant assertion. If substantially different controls were used at different times during the period under audit, each is considered separately. The auditor may adopt a substantive audit strategy that excludes testing controls (as described in Q&A section 8200.07, "Considering a Substantive Audit Strategy," which is nonauthoritative) if the auditor believes that the benefit of testing control operating effectiveness—both in terms of audit efficiency and effectiveness—is less than the cost of testing controls. If testing the operating effectiveness of controls would not be effective or efficient, it will then be necessary to perform substantive procedures that respond to the assessed risks for specific assertions.[10]

2.101 Paragraph .A22 of AU-C section 330 states that testing the operating effectiveness of controls is different from obtaining an understanding of and evaluating the design and implementation of controls. However, the same types of audit procedures are used. The auditor may, therefore, decide it is efficient to test the operating effectiveness of controls at the same time the auditor is evaluating their design and determining that they have been implemented.

---

[10] For nonauthoritative guidance pertaining to internal control and risk assessment, refer to Q&A sections 8200.05–.16.

2.102 Paragraph .A23 of AU-C section 330 states that although some risk assessment procedures may not have been specifically designed as tests of controls, they may nevertheless provide audit evidence about the operating effectiveness of the controls and, consequently, serve as tests of controls. For example,

- inquiries with management and accounting staff about the preparation of interim financial reports, the review of those reports by management, and follow-up that management performs as a result of the review, and
- review of minutes of the meetings of board of directors or committees, or both, to verify that financial reports are provided to and reviewed by those charged with governance.

2.103 One or more significant risks normally arise on most audits.[11] Paragraph .15 of AU-C section 330 states that if the auditor plans to rely on controls over a risk the auditor has determined to be a significant risk, the auditor should test the operating effectiveness of those controls in the current period.

2.104 Irrespective of the audit approach selected, the auditor should design and perform substantive procedures for all relevant assertions related to each material class of transactions, account balances, and disclosures.

2.105 Paragraph .21 of AU-C section 330 states that the auditor's substantive procedures should include audit procedures related to the financial statement closing process, such as

- agreeing or reconciling the financial statements with the underlying accounting records and
- examining material journal entries and other adjustments made during the course of preparing the financial statements.

Paragraph .A57 of AU-C section 330 states that the nature and extent of the auditor's examination of journal entries and other adjustments depend on the nature and complexity of the entity's financial reporting process and the related risks of material misstatement.

2.106 If the auditor has determined that an assessed risk of material misstatement at the relevant assertion level is a significant risk, paragraph .22 of AU-C section 330 states that the auditor should perform substantive procedures that are specifically responsive to that risk. When the approach to a significant risk consists only of substantive procedures, those procedures should include tests of details.

2.107 AU-C section 520 addresses the auditor's use of analytical procedures as substantive procedures (substantive analytical procedures). It also addresses the auditor's responsibility to perform analytical procedures near the end of the audit that assist the auditor when forming an overall conclusion on the financial statements.

---

[11] According to paragraph .27 of AU-C section 240, *Consideration of Fraud in a Financial Statement Audit*, the auditor should treat those assessed risks of material misstatement due to fraud as significant risks. Paragraph .26 of AU-C section 240 states that there is a presumption that risks of fraud exist in revenue recognition. Paragraph .31 of AU-C section 240 states that the risk of management override of controls is present in all entities and is a risk of material misstatement due to fraud and thus is a significant risk.

2.108 As explained in paragraphs .A2–.A3 of AU-C section 520, analytical procedures include the consideration of comparisons of the entity's financial information with, for example, comparable information for prior periods, anticipated results of the entity (such as, budgets or forecasts) or expectations of the auditor, or similar industry information. Analytical procedures also include consideration of relationships; for example, among elements of financial information that would be expected to conform to a predictable pattern based on recent history of the entity and industry or between financial information and relevant nonfinancial information (such as, payroll costs to number of employees). When designing and performing analytical procedures, either alone or in combination with tests of details, as substantive procedures, paragraph .05 of AU-C section 520 states that the auditor should

a. determine the suitability of particular substantive analytical procedures for given assertions, taking into account the assessed risks of material misstatement and tests of details, if any, for these assertions;

b. evaluate the reliability of data from which the auditor's expectation of recorded amounts or ratios is developed, taking into account the source, comparability, and nature and relevance of information available and controls over preparation;

c. develop an expectation of recorded amounts or ratios and evaluate whether the expectation is sufficiently precise (taking into account whether substantive analytical procedures are to be performed alone or in combination with tests of details) to identify a misstatement that, individually or when aggregated with other misstatements, may cause the financial statements to be materially misstated; and

d. determine the amount of any difference of recorded amounts from expected values that is acceptable without further investigation and compare the recorded amounts, or ratios developed from recorded amounts, with the expectations.

2.109 Paragraphs .A13–.A14 of AU-C section 520 explain that different types of analytical procedures provide different levels of assurance. The determination of the suitability of particular substantive analytical procedures is influenced by the nature of the assertion and the auditor's assessment of the risk of material misstatement. Paragraph .A8 of AU-C section 520 states that the effectiveness and efficiency of a substantive analytical procedure in addressing risks of material misstatement depends on, among other things, (*a*) the nature of the assertion, (*b*) the plausibility and predictability of the relationship, (*c*) the availability and reliability of the data used to develop the expectation, and (*d*) the precision of the expectation. For this reason, substantive analytical procedures alone are not well suited to detecting fraud. In addition, paragraph .A19 of AU-C section 520 notes that the auditor may consider testing the operating effectiveness of controls, if any, over the entity's preparation of information used by the auditor in performing the substantive analytical procedures in response to assessed risks. When such controls are effective, the auditor may have greater confidence in the reliability of the information and, therefore, in the results of analytical procedures. The operating effectiveness of controls over nonfinancial information may be tested in conjunction with other tests of controls or other procedures may be performed to support the completeness and accuracy of the underlying information.

2.110 Paragraph .08 of AU-C section 520 states that when substantive analytical procedures have been performed, the auditor should include in the audit documentation the following:

a. The expectation referred to in paragraph 2.108*c* of this guide and the factors considered in its development when that expectation or those factors are not otherwise readily determinable from the audit documentation

b. Results of the comparison referred to in paragraph 2.108*d* of this guide of the recorded amounts, or ratios developed from recorded amounts, with the expectations

c. Any additional auditing procedures performed relating to the investigation of fluctuations or relationships that are inconsistent with other relevant information or that differ from expected values by a significant amount and the results of such additional procedures

Evaluating the Sufficiency and Appropriateness of Audit Evidence

2.111 Paragraph .28 of AU-C section 330 states the auditor should conclude whether sufficient appropriate audit evidence has been obtained. In forming a conclusion, the auditor should consider all relevant audit evidence, regardless of whether it appears to corroborate or to contradict the relevant assertions in the financial statements.

Evaluation of Misstatements Identified During the Audit

2.112 Based on the results of substantive procedures, the auditor may identify misstatements in accounts or notes to the financial statements. AU-C section 450 addresses the auditor's responsibility to evaluate the effect of identified misstatements on the audit and the effect of uncorrected misstatements, if any, on the financial statements. Paragraphs .05–.12 of AU-C section 450 address specific requirements related to the accumulation of identified misstatements, the consideration of identified misstatements as the audit progresses, the communication and correction of misstatements, evaluating the effect of uncorrected misstatements, and documentation.

2.113 The circumstances related to some misstatements may cause the auditor to evaluate them as material, individually or when considered together with other misstatements accumulated during the audit, even if they are lower than materiality for the financial statements as a whole. For example, a loan made to a related party of an otherwise immaterial amount could be material if there is a reasonable possibility that it could lead to a material contingent liability or a material loss of revenue. Paragraph .A23 of AU-C section 450 provides circumstances that the auditor may consider relevant in determining whether misstatements are material.

2.114 AU-C section 700 addresses the auditor's responsibility in forming an opinion on the financial statements based on the evaluation of the audit evidence obtained. The auditor's conclusion, required by AU-C section 700, takes into account the auditor's evaluation of uncorrected misstatements, if any, on the financial statements, in accordance with AU-C section 450.

Communication With Those Charged With Governance

2.115 AU-C section 260 addresses the auditor's responsibility to communicate with those charged with governance in an audit of financial statements. Although this section applies regardless of an entity's governance structure or size, particular considerations apply where all of those charged with governance are involved in managing an entity. This section does not establish requirements regarding the auditor's communication with an entity's management or owners unless they are also charged with a governance role.

2.116 AU-C section 265, *Communicating Internal Control Related Matters Identified in an Audit*, addresses the auditor's responsibility to appropriately communicate to those charged with governance and management deficiencies in internal control that the auditor has identified in an audit of financial statements. In particular, AU-C section 265

- defines the terms *deficiency in internal control, significant deficiency*, and *material weakness*.
- provides guidance on evaluating the severity of deficiencies in internal control identified in an audit of financial statements.
- requires the auditor to communicate significant deficiencies and material weaknesses identified in an audit.

2.117 Paragraphs .11–.13 of AU-C section 265 state that the auditor should communicate in writing to those charged with governance on a timely basis significant deficiencies and material weaknesses identified during the audit, including those that were remediated during the audit. The auditor also should communicate to management at an appropriate level of responsibility, on a timely basis

a. in writing, significant deficiencies and material weaknesses that the auditor has communicated or intends to communicate to those charged with governance, unless it would be inappropriate to communicate directly to management in the circumstances.

b. in writing or orally, other deficiencies in internal control identified during the audit that have not been communicated to management by other parties and that, in the auditor's professional judgment, are of sufficient importance to merit management's attention. If other deficiencies in internal control are communicated orally, the auditor should document the communication.

2.118 The communication referred to should be made no later than 60 days following the report release date. However, paragraph .A15 of AU-C section 265 further explains that the communication is best made by the report release date because receipt of such communication may be an important factor in enabling those charged with governance to discharge their oversight responsibilities.

2.119 As stated in paragraph .03 of AU-C section 265, nothing in AU-C section 265 precludes the auditor from communicating to those charged with governance or management other internal control matters that the auditor has identified during the audit.

2.120 The appendix, "Examples of Circumstances That May Be Deficiencies, Significant Deficiencies, or Material Weaknesses," of AU-C section 265 includes examples of circumstances that may be deficiencies, significant deficiencies, or material weaknesses.

2.121 AU-C section 265 is not applicable if the auditor is engaged to report on the effectiveness of an entity's internal control over financial reporting under AU-C section 940, *An Audit of Internal Control Over Financial Reporting That Is Integrated With an Audit of Financial Statements*.

Completing the Audit

Going-Concern Considerations

2.122 "Pending Content" in FASB ASC 205-40-50 requires that, in connection with preparing financial statements, an entity's management evaluate whether there are conditions and events, considered in the aggregate, that raise substantial doubt about an entity's ability to continue as a going concern within one year after the date that the financial statements are issued (or within one year after the date that the financial statements are available to be issued, when applicable) and to provide related disclosures. Statement on Auditing Standards No. 132, *The Auditor's Consideration of an Entity's Ability to Continue as a Going Concern* (AU-C sec. 570), addresses the auditor's responsibilities in the audit of financial statements relating to the entity's ability to continue as a going concern and the implications for the auditor's report. This section applies to all audits of a complete set of financial statements, regardless of which financial reporting framework, as defined in AU-C section 700 and AU-C section 800, *Special Considerations—Audits of Financial Statements Prepared in Accordance With Special Purpose Frameworks*, was used to prepare the financial statements. The auditor's evaluation of an NFP's ability to continue as a going concern may be one of the most complex and important portions of the audit. This section describes the unique issues that an auditor may encounter in evaluating an NFP's ability to continue as a going concern.

The Auditor's Responsibility

2.123 In accordance with paragraph .10 of AU-C section 570, the auditor's objectives are as follows:

a. To obtain sufficient appropriate audit evidence regarding, and to conclude on, the appropriateness of management's use of the going concern basis of accounting, when relevant, in the preparation of the financial statements

b. To conclude, based on the audit evidence obtained, whether substantial doubt about an entity's ability to continue as a going concern for a reasonable period of time exists

c. To evaluate the possible financial statement effects, including the adequacy of disclosure regarding the entity's ability to continue as a going concern for a reasonable period of time

d. To report in accordance with AU-C section 570.

AU-C section 570 does not define *substantial doubt*. However, the "Pending Content" in the FASB ASC glossary states that *substantial doubt about an entity's ability to continue as a going concern* "exists when conditions and events, considered in the aggregate, indicate that it is probable that the entity will be unable to meet its obligations as they become due." Paragraph .11 of AU-C section 570 defines *reasonable period of time* as "the period of time required by the applicable financial reporting framework or, if no such requirement exists, within one year after the date that the financial statements are issued (or within one year after the date that the financial statements are available to be issued, when applicable)." As explained in paragraph .A6 of AU-C section 570, most financial reporting frameworks requiring an explicit management evaluation of the entity's ability to continue as a going concern specify the period of time to be evaluated. For example, the FASB ASC glossary definition of *substantial doubt* specifies the period as within one year after the date that the financial statements are issued (or within one year after the date that the financial statements are available to be issued, when applicable).

Conditions or Events That Raise Substantial Doubt About an Entity's Ability to Continue as a Going Concern

2.124 Pursuant to paragraph .12 of AU-C section 570, when performing risk assessment procedures as required by AU-C section 315, the auditor should consider whether there are conditions or events, considered in the aggregate, that raise substantial doubt about an entity's ability to continue as a going concern for a reasonable period of time. In doing so, the auditor should determine whether management has performed a preliminary evaluation of whether such conditions or events exist. If management has performed that evaluation, the auditor should discuss the evaluation with management and determine whether management has identified conditions or events that raise substantial doubt about an entity's ability to continue as a going concern for a reasonable period of time and, if so, understand management's plans to address them. If management has not performed that evaluation, the auditor should discuss with management the basis for the intended use of the going concern basis of accounting and inquire of management whether conditions or events exist that raise substantial doubt about an entity's ability to continue as a going concern for a reasonable period of time. Paragraphs .14.15 of AU-C section 570 discuss the auditor's evaluation of management's evaluation, including the period the evaluation should cover. Paragraphs .16.18 and .A28.A40 of AU-C section 570 describe audit procedures to be performed to determine whether conditions and events identified, considered in the aggregate, raise substantial doubt about an entity's ability to continue as a going concern for a reasonable period of time and to gather audit evidence.

2.125 Pursuant to paragraph .13 of AU-C section 570, the auditor should remain alert throughout the audit for audit evidence of conditions or events that raise substantial doubt about an entity's ability to continue as a going concern for a reasonable period of time. The following are examples of such conditions and events in audits of NFPs that, when considered in the aggregate, could indicate that there is substantial doubt:

- Insufficient resources to provide supporting services to activities funded by restricted contributions
- A high ratio of fund-raising expenses to contributions received or a low ratio of program expenses to total expenses
- Insufficient resources to meet donor's restrictions (this may result from the use of restricted resources for purposes that do not satisfy the donor's restrictions, sometimes referred to as interfund borrowing)

- Activities that could jeopardize the NFP's tax-exempt status and thus endanger current contribution levels
- Violation of debt covenants that allow the lender to accelerate payment of debt
- Concerns expressed by governmental authorities regarding alleged violations of state laws governing an NFP's maintenance or preservation of certain assets, such as collection items
- A loss of key governing board members or volunteers
- External events that could affect donors' motivations to continue to contribute
- Decreases in revenues contributed by repeat donors
- A loss of major funding sources

Consideration of Conditions and Events

2.126 Pursuant to paragraph .16 of AU-C section 570, the auditor should obtain sufficient appropriate audit evidence to determine whether conditions and events identified, considered in the aggregate, raise substantial doubt about an entity's ability to continue as a going concern for a reasonable period of time by performing additional audit procedures, including consideration of mitigating factors. These procedures should include the following:

a. Requesting management to make an evaluation when management has not yet performed an evaluation

b. Evaluating management's plans in relation to its going concern evaluation, with regard to whether it is probable that

   i. management's plans can be effectively implemented and

   ii. the plans would mitigate the relevant conditions or events that raise substantial doubt about the entity's ability to continue as a going concern for a reasonable period of time

c. When the entity has prepared a cash flow forecast, and analysis of the forecast is a significant factor in evaluating management's plans,

   i. evaluating the reliability of the underlying data generated to prepare the forecast and

   ii. determining whether there is adequate support for the assumptions underlying the forecast, which includes considering contradictory audit evidence

d. Considering whether any additional facts or information have become available since the date on which management made its evaluation

2.127 Paragraph .17 of AU-C section 570 states that when management's plans include financial support by third parties or the entity's owner-manager (for example, parent) and such support is necessary in supporting management's assertions about the NFP's ability to continue as a going concern for a reasonable period of time, the auditor should obtain sufficient appropriate audit evidence about the intent and ability of such supporting parties to provide the necessary financial support. The failure to obtain written evidence regarding the intent of the supporting parties to provide financial support constitutes a lack of sufficient appropriate audit evidence. Therefore, the auditor should conclude that management's plans are insufficient to alleviate the determination that substantial doubt exists about the entity's ability to continue as a going concern.

Adequacy of Disclosure When Substantial Doubt Has Been Alleviated

2.128 FASB ASC 205-40-50-12 requires certain disclosures when substantial doubt about an entity's ability to continue as a going concern is alleviated as a result of consideration of management's plans. The auditor's assessment of the financial statement effects under AU-C section 570 would be based on those disclosure requirements. When the auditor concludes, primarily because of the auditor's consideration of management's plans, that substantial doubt about the entity's ability to continue as a going concern for a reasonable period of time has been alleviated, paragraph .22 of AU-C section 570 requires the auditor to evaluate the adequacy of the financial statement disclosures required by the applicable financial reporting framework. The auditor's evaluation about whether the financial statements achieve fair presentation includes the consideration of the overall presentation, structure, and content of the financial statements and whether the financial statements, including the related notes, represent the underlying transactions and events in a manner that achieves fair presentation. Depending on the facts and circumstances, the auditor may determine that additional disclosures are necessary to achieve fair presentation.

Adequacy of Disclosure When Substantial Doubt Remains

2.129 The auditor should evaluate whether sufficient appropriate audit evidence has been obtained and conclude on the appropriateness of management's use of the going concern basis of accounting, when relevant, in the preparation of the financial statements. If the auditor concludes that management's use of the going concern basis of accounting is appropriate in the circumstances but substantial doubt exists about an entity's ability to continue as a going concern for a reasonable period of time, the auditor should evaluate the adequacy of the financial statement disclosures as required by the applicable financial reporting framework. If the substantial doubt is not alleviated, a statement in the notes to financial statements is required by FASB ASC 205-40-50-13 indicating that there is substantial doubt about the NFP's ability to continue as a going concern within one year after the date that the financial statements are issued (or within one year after the date that the financial statements are available to be issued when applicable), as well as the additional information in paragraphs 13–14 of FASB ASC 205-40-50. The auditor's assessment of the financial statement effects under AU-C section 570 would be based on those disclosure requirements. The auditor's evaluation about whether the financial statements achieve fair presentation includes the consideration of the overall presentation, structure, and content of the financial statements and whether the financial statements, including the related notes, represent the underlying transactions and events in a manner that achieves fair presentation. Depending on the facts and circumstances, the auditor may determine that additional disclosures are necessary to achieve fair presentation. Paragraph 14.11 describes the implications for the auditor's report when substantial doubt remains.

Communication With Those Charged With Governance

2.130 Unless all those charged with governance are involved in managing the entity, the auditor should communicate with those charged with governance regarding conditions and events, considered in the aggregate, that raise substantial doubt about an entity's ability to continue as a going concern for a reasonable period of time. Paragraph .28 of AU-C section 570 describes the content of the required communication.

Documentation of the Auditor's Considerations

2.131 Paragraph .32 of AU-C section 570 describes the required documentation.

Considerations if Liquidation Is Imminent

2.132 As discussed in paragraph 1.07, when liquidation is imminent, an NFP should prepare its financial statements in accordance with the requirements of FASB ASC 205-30. AU-C section 570 does not apply to an audit of financial statements based on the assumption of liquidation. Interpretation No. 1, "Reporting on Financial Statements Prepared on a Liquidation Basis of Accounting" (AU-C sec. 9700 par. .01–.05), of AU-C section 700 states that if financial statements using the liquidation basis of accounting are presented along with financial statements of a prior period in which the entity was a going concern, the entity has changed the basis of accounting used to determine the amounts at which assets and liabilities are carried from the going concern basis to a liquidation basis, and the auditor should include an emphasis-of-matter paragraph if, in the auditor's professional judgment, that information is fundamental to users' understanding of the financial statements.

Written Representations

2.133 AU-C section 580, *Written Representations*, addresses the auditor's responsibility to obtain written representations from management and, when appropriate, those charged with governance in an audit of financial statements.

Written Representations as Audit Evidence

2.134 According to paragraphs .03–.04 of AU-C section 580, written representations are necessary information that the auditor requires in connection with the audit of the entity's financial statements. Accordingly, similar to responses to inquiries, written representations are audit evidence. Although written representations provide necessary audit evidence, they complement other auditing procedures and do not provide sufficient appropriate audit evidence on their own about any of the matters with which they deal. Furthermore, obtaining reliable written representations does not affect the nature or extent of other audit procedures that the auditor applies to obtain audit evidence about the fulfillment of management's responsibilities or about specific assertions.

Management From Whom Written Representations Are Requested

2.135 As explained in paragraph .A2 of AU-C section 580, written representations are requested from those with overall responsibility for financial and operating matters whom the auditor believes are responsible for, and knowledgeable about, directly or through others in the organization, the matters covered by the representations, including the preparation and fair presentation of the financial statements. As such, in accordance with paragraph .09 of AU-C section 580, the auditor should request written representations from management with appropriate responsibilities for the financial statements and knowledge of the matters concerned.

2.136 Paragraph .A2 of AU-C section 580 further states that those individuals with overall responsibility may vary depending on the governance structure of the entity; however, management (rather than those charged with governance) is often the responsible party. Written representations may therefore be requested from the entity's CEO and CFO or other equivalent persons in entities that do not use such titles. In some circumstances, however, other parties, such as those charged with governance, also are responsible for the preparation and fair presentation of the financial statements.

Written Representations About Management's Responsibilities and Other Written Representations

2.137 Paragraphs .10–.18 of AU-C section 580 discuss matters the auditor is required to request management to provide written representation about, such as preparation and fair presentation of the financial statements, information provided and completeness of transactions, fraud, laws and regulations, uncorrected misstatements, litigation and claims, estimates, related party transactions, and subsequent events. If, in addition to such required representations and those addressed in other AU-C sections, the auditor determines that it is necessary to obtain one or more written representations to support other audit evidence relevant to the financial statements or one or more specific assertions in the financial statements, paragraph .19 of AU-C section 580 states that the auditor should request such other written representations.

2.138 Paragraph .A22 of AU-C section 580 states that management's representations may be limited to matters that are considered either individually or collectively material to the financial statements, provided management and the auditor have reached an understanding on materiality for this purpose. Materiality may be different for different representations. A discussion of materiality may be included explicitly in the representation letter in either qualitative or quantitative terms. Materiality considerations do not apply to those representations that are not directly related to amounts included in the financial statements (for example, management's representations about the premise underlying the audit). In addition, because of the possible effects of fraud on other aspects of the audit, materiality would not apply to management's acknowledgment regarding its responsibility for the design, implementation, and maintenance of internal control to prevent and detect fraud.

Date of, and Period(s) Covered by, Written Representations

2.139 Paragraph .20 of AU-C section 580 states that the date of the written representations should be as of the date of the auditor's report on the financial statements. The written representations should be for all financial statements and period(s) referred to in the auditor's report.

Form of Written Representations

2.140 In accordance with paragraph .21 of AU-C section 580, the written representations should be in the form of a representation letter addressed to the auditor.

Doubt About the Reliability of Written Representations and Requested Written Representations Not Provided

2.141 Paragraph .25 of AU-C section 580 states that the auditor should disclaim an opinion on the financial statements in accordance with AU-C section 705 or withdraw from the engagement if

a. the auditor concludes that sufficient doubt exists about the integrity of management such that the written representations required by paragraphs .10–.11 of AU-C section 580 are not reliable or

b. management does not provide the written representations required by paragraphs .10–.11 of AU-C section 580.

Audit Documentation

2.142 AU-C section 230, *Audit Documentation*, addresses the auditor's responsibility to prepare audit documentation for an audit of financial statements. The exhibit, "Audit Documentation Requirements in Other AU-C Sections," in AU-C section 230 lists other AU-C sections that contain specific documentation requirements and guidance. The specific documentation requirements of other AU-C sections do not limit the application of AU-C section 230. Law, regulation, or other standards may establish additional documentation requirements.

2.143 Paragraph .02 of AU-C section 230 states that audit documentation that meets the requirements of AU-C section 230 and the specific documentation requirements of other relevant AU-C sections provide

a. evidence of the auditor's basis for a conclusion about the achievement of the overall objectives of the auditor; and

b. evidence that the audit was planned and performed in accordance with GAAS and applicable legal and regulatory requirements.

2.144 For purposes of GAAS, *audit documentation*, as defined in paragraph .06 of AU-C section 230, is the record of audit procedures performed, relevant audit evidence obtained, and conclusions the auditor reached (terms such as *working papers* or *workpapers* are also sometimes used).

Timely Preparation of Audit Documentation

2.145 Paragraph .07 of AU-C section 230 states that the auditor should prepare audit documentation on a timely basis. Paragraph .A3 of AU-C section 230 further explains that preparing sufficient and appropriate audit documentation on a timely basis throughout the audit helps to enhance the quality of the audit and facilitates the effective review and evaluation of the audit evidence obtained and conclusions reached before the auditor's report is finalized. Documentation prepared at the time such work is performed or shortly thereafter is likely to be more accurate than documentation prepared at a much later time.[12]

Documentation of the Audit Procedures Performed and Audit Evidence Obtained

2.146 Paragraphs .08–.12 of AU-C section 230 address the auditor's responsibilities regarding documentation of the auditor procedures performed

---

[12] A firm of independent auditors has a responsibility to adopt a system of quality control policies and procedures to provide the firm with reasonable assurance that its personnel comply with applicable professional standards, including generally accepted auditing standards, and the firm's standards of quality in conducting individual audit engagements. Review of audit documentation and discussions with engagement team members are among the procedures a firm performs when monitoring compliance with the quality control policies and procedures that it has established. The elements of quality control are identified in QC section 10, *A Firm's System of Quality Control* (AICPA, *Professional Standards*). See also AU-C section 220, *Quality Control for an Engagement Conducted in Accordance With Generally Accepted Auditing Standards*.

and audit evidence obtained including form, content, and extent of audit documentation. In accordance with paragraph .08 of AU-C section 230, the auditor should prepare audit documentation that is sufficient to enable an experienced auditor, having no previous connection with the audit, to understand

a. the nature, timing, and extent of the audit procedures performed to comply with GAAS and applicable legal and regulatory requirements; (Readers can find additional application and explanatory material in paragraphs .A8–.A9 of AU-C section 230.)

b. the results of the audit procedures performed, and the audit evidence obtained; and

c. significant findings or issues arising during the audit, the conclusions reached thereon, and significant professional judgments made in reaching those conclusions. (Readers can find additional application and explanatory material in paragraphs .A10–.A13 of AU-C section 230.)

As stated in paragraph .A5 of AU-C section 230, examples of audit documentation include audit plans, analyses, issues memorandums, summaries of significant findings or issues, letters of confirmation and representation, checklists, and correspondence (including email) concerning significant findings or issues.

2.147 For audit procedures related to the inspection of significant contracts or agreements, paragraph .10 of AU-C section 230 states that the auditor should include abstracts or copies of those contracts or agreements in the audit documentation.

2.148 In addition to the requirements discussed previously, paragraph .11 of AU-C section 230 addresses further documentation requirements about discussions of significant findings or issues with management, those charged with governance, and others; paragraph .12 of AU-C section 230 addresses documentation requirements for identified information that is inconsistent with the auditor's final conclusion regarding significant issues; and paragraphs .13–.14 of AU-C section 230 address further documentation requirements related to departures from relevant requirements and matters arising after the date of the auditor's report.

Assembly and Retention of the Final Audit File

2.149 Paragraphs .15–.19 of AU-C section 230 address an auditor's responsibilities regarding assembly and retention of the final audit file. Paragraph .16 of AU-C section 230 states that the auditor should assemble the audit documentation in an audit file and complete the administrative process of assembling the final audit file on a timely basis, no later than 60 days following the report release date. After the documentation completion date, paragraph .17 of AU-C section 230 prohibits the auditor from deleting or discarding audit documentation of any nature before the end of the specified retention period. If it is necessary to modify existing audit documentation or add new audit documentation after the documentation date, paragraph .18 of AU-C section 230 requires the auditor to document the specific reasons for making the changes and when and by whom the changes were made and reviewed.

2.150

Appendix A—Consideration of Fraud in a Financial Statement Audit

A-1 AU-C section 240, *Consideration of Fraud in a Financial Statement Audit*,[1] addresses the auditor's responsibilities relating to fraud in an audit of financial statements. Specifically, it expands on how AU-C sections 315, *Understanding the Entity and Its Environment and Assessing the Risks of Material Misstatement*, and 330, *Performing Audit Procedures in Response to Assessed Risks and Evaluating the Audit Evidence Obtained*, are to be applied regarding risks of material misstatement due to fraud.

A-2 Although fraud is a broad legal concept, for the purposes of GAAS, the auditor is primarily concerned with fraud that causes a material misstatement in the financial statements. In accordance with paragraph .03 of AU-C section 240, two types of intentional misstatements are relevant to the auditor:

- Misstatements resulting from fraudulent financial reporting
- Misstatements resulting from misappropriation of assets

Although the auditor may suspect or, in rare cases, identify the occurrence of fraud, the auditor does not make legal determinations of whether fraud has actually occurred.

A-3 Paragraph .A1 of AU-C section 240 states that fraud, whether fraudulent financial reporting or misappropriation of assets, involves incentive or pressure to commit fraud, a perceived opportunity to do so, and some rationalization of the act.

A-4 The auditor of governmental entities and not-for-profit organizations may have additional responsibilities relating to fraud

- as a result of being engaged to conduct an audit in accordance with law or regulation applicable to governmental entities and not-for-profit organizations,
- because of a governmental audit organization's mandate, or
- because of the need to comply with *Government Auditing Standards*.

Consequently, the responsibilities of the auditor of governmental entities and not-for-profit organizations may not be limited to consideration of risks of material misstatement of the financial statements, but may also include a broader responsibility to consider risks of fraud.

The Importance of Exercising Professional Skepticism

A-5 Consistent with paragraph .15 of AU-C section 200, *Overall Objectives of the Independent Auditor and the Conduct of an Audit in Accordance With Generally Accepted Auditing Standards*, paragraph .12 of AU-C section 240 states that the auditor should maintain professional skepticism throughout the audit, recognizing the possibility that a material misstatement due to fraud could exist, notwithstanding the auditor's past experience of the honesty and integrity of the entity's management and those charged with governance.

---

[1] All AU-C sections can be found in AICPA *Professional Standards*.

A-6 Paragraphs .A9–.A10 of AU-C section 240 state that maintaining professional skepticism requires an ongoing questioning of whether the information and audit evidence obtained suggests that a material misstatement due to fraud may exist. It includes considering the reliability of the information to be used as audit evidence and the controls over its preparation and maintenance when relevant. Although the auditor cannot be expected to disregard past experience of the honesty and integrity of the entity's management and those charged with governance, the auditor's professional skepticism is particularly important in considering the risk of material misstatement due to fraud because there may have been changes in circumstances.

A-7 When responses to inquiries of management, those charged with governance, or others are inconsistent or otherwise unsatisfactory (for example, vague or implausible), paragraph .14 of AU-C section 240 states that the auditor should further investigate the inconsistencies or unsatisfactory responses.

Discussion Among Engagement Personnel Regarding the Risks of Material Misstatement Due to Fraud

A-8 AU-C section 315 requires a discussion among the key engagement team members. Paragraph .15 of AU-C section 240 states this discussion should include an exchange of ideas or brainstorming among the engagement team members about how and where the entity's financial statements might be susceptible to material misstatement due to fraud, how management could perpetrate and conceal fraudulent financial reporting, and how assets of the entity could be misappropriated. The discussion should occur setting aside beliefs that the engagement team members may have that management and those charged with governance are honest and have integrity, and should, in particular, also address

a. known external and internal factors affecting the entity that may create an incentive or pressure for management or others to commit fraud, provide the opportunity for fraud to be perpetrated, and indicate a culture or environment that enables management or others to rationalize committing fraud;

b. the risk of management override of controls;

c. consideration of circumstances that might be indicative of earnings management or manipulation of other financial measures and the practices that might be followed by management to manage earnings or other financial measures that could lead to fraudulent financial reporting;

d. the importance of maintaining professional skepticism throughout the audit regarding the potential for material misstatement due to fraud; and

e. how the auditor might respond to the susceptibility of the entity's financial statements to material misstatement due to fraud.

Communication among the engagement team members about the risks of material misstatement due to fraud should continue throughout the audit, particularly upon discovery of new facts during the audit.

A-9 Paragraph .A12 of AU-C section 240 states that discussing the susceptibility of the entity's financial statements to material misstatement due to fraud with the engagement team

- provides an opportunity for more experienced engagement team members to share their insights about how and where the financial statements may be susceptible to material misstatement due to fraud.

- enables the auditor to consider an appropriate response to such susceptibility and to determine which members of the engagement team will conduct certain audit procedures.
- permits the auditor to determine how the results of audit procedures will be shared among the engagement team and how to deal with any allegations of fraud that may come to the auditor's attention during the audit.

A-10 In addition, paragraph .A13 of AU-C section 240 states the discussion may include the following matters:

- A consideration of management's involvement in overseeing employees with access to cash or other assets susceptible to misappropriation
- A consideration of any unusual or unexplained changes in behavior or lifestyle of management or employees that have come to the attention of the engagement team
- A consideration of the types of circumstances that, if encountered, might indicate the possibility of fraud
- A consideration of how an element of unpredictability will be incorporated into the nature, timing, and extent of the audit procedures to be performed
- A consideration of the audit procedures that might be selected to respond to the susceptibility of the entity's financial statements to material misstatement due to fraud and whether certain types of audit procedures are more effective than others
- A consideration of any allegations of fraud that have come to the auditor's attention

A number of factors may influence the extent of the discussion and how it may occur. For example, if the audit involves more than one location, there could be multiple discussions with team members in differing locations. Another factor in planning the discussions is whether to include specialists assigned to the audit team.

A-11 When brainstorming about the incentives and pressures for management and others to commit fraud, the audit team members may want to discuss whether any of the following exist:

- Incentive to minimize reported fund-raising and management and general expenses, and maximize reported program expenses, to make the not-for-profit entity (NFP) appear worthy of contributions, especially if some potential resource providers have stated or implied limits in these areas (for example, the resource provider will not fund NFPs with more than 25 percent overhead), or if the NFP desires to be in compliance with standards of the charitable organization rating agencies
- Incentive to defer fund-raising expenses to future periods if the related contributions will not be received until those future periods
- Incentive to make the NFP look poor (but not too poor) to induce contributors to contribute

- Incentive to mischaracterize the relationship with related parties (for example, affiliated chapters, fund-raising organizations, foundations, guilds, trusts, funds, student clubs, and auxiliaries) to avoid consolidating those entities or reporting the assets held by them for the NFP's benefit if the NFP wants to appear poorer
- Incentive to achieve certain fund-raising goals, especially to meet terms of matching gifts
- Incentive to misstate financial information if contributions are conditioned on achieving certain financial performance goals
- Incentive to report that donor gifts (or restricted income from donor endowments) have been used in accordance with donor restrictions when, in fact, that is not the case (this incentive may be particularly strong if there is a deficit change in unrestricted net assets)

  Incentive to report that donor gifts (or restricted income from donor endowments) have been used in accordance with donor restrictions when, in fact, that is not the case (this incentive may be particularly strong if there is a current year deficit in the change in net assets without donor restrictions or a deficit in net assets without donor restrictions on the statement of financial position.)[2]

- Incentive to "borrow" from restricted funds to cover a current unrestricted deficit

  Incentive to "borrow" from donor-restricted funds to cover a deficit change in net assets without donor restrictions[3]

- Incentive to mischaracterize revenue so as not to fail the IRS public support test
- Incentive to recognize intentions to give as contributions made in order to reduce the private foundation excise tax on the net investment income, avoid the excise tax for failure to distribute income, or both
- Incentive to misallocate expenses to avoid exceeding IRS limits on allowable lobbying
- Incentive to inappropriately minimize unrelated business income taxes, such as by over-allocating costs against taxable unrelated business income
- Incentive to mischaracterize overhead expenses as direct program expenses when grantors limit the amount of their grants that may be used for overhead (sometimes such limits are zero)

---

[2] The amendments in FASB Accounting Standards Update (ASU) No. 2016-14, *Not-for-Profit Entities (Topic 958): Presentation of Financial Statements of Not-for-Profit Entities*, are effective for annual financial statements issued for fiscal years beginning after December 15, 2017 (for example, years ending December 31, 2018 and years ending June 30, 2019), and for interim periods within fiscal years beginning after December 15, 2018. Application to interim financial statements is permitted but not required in the initial year of application. Early application of the amendments is permitted.

[3] The amendments in FASB ASU No. 2016-14 are effective for annual financial statements issued for fiscal years beginning after December 15, 2017 (for example, years ending December 31, 2018 and years ending June 30, 2019), and for interim periods within fiscal years beginning after December 15, 2018. Application to interim financial statements is permitted but not required in the initial year of application. Early application of the amendments is permitted.

- Incentive to avoid surplus funds in grants that require that surplus funds be returned to the grantor

A-12 When brainstorming about the opportunities for fraud to be perpetrated, the audit team members may want to discuss whether the following exist:

- Domination of management by a single person (such as an executive director) or small group without compensating controls, for example, a charismatic executive combined with a reluctance of employees or those charged with governance to disagree with him or her
- Limited number of staff involved in the accounting functions, if the result is inadequate internal control over assets that increases the susceptibility of misappropriation of those assets
- The attitude among management of, "We're a charity, no one would steal from us!" with an attendant lack of appreciation for the importance of strong internal controls
- Unjustified trust in employees or volunteers because "we know they are committed to the cause"
- Key management functions and controls are in the hands of volunteers not subject to normal levels of supervision
- Management lacks the necessary background, experience, or commitment to fulfill their duties
- A hands-off governing board or one with insufficient financial expertise to oversee the financial reporting process and internal controls
- Special events or fund-raising methods result in large amounts of cash on hand or processed, for example, church plate collections, and door-to-door and other off-premises fund-raising
- Revenue (including contributions) received in the form of coins or currency, or both, or in the form of checks personally handed to the NFP's staff and volunteers
- Inadequate investigation of past-due promises to give, especially conditional promises, which are not recognized in the financial statements
- Numerous restricted grants received under the control of a single individual or a small group of individuals, which could lead to allocating expenses to an inappropriate grant account when grant limits are reached on the appropriate one
- Programs are supported by mixed types of grants (fixed price, units of service, cost reimbursement) that could motivate charging inappropriate expenses against certain grants or charging multiple grants for the same expenditure
- Fixed assets not subject to existing general ledger controls because they are not recorded, for example, fixed assets legally owned by a grantor or collection items that the NFP has chosen not to capitalize
- Grant programs for which the recipients are individuals (for example, food, clothing, or other assets are distributed) or scholarships, fellowships, or other financial assistance is paid out

- Research projects in which payments to test subjects are made in cash, especially if lists of payments are not prepared so that the confidentiality of the subjects' identities is preserved
- A complex organizational structure (often including several entities under common control), especially if there are numerous inter-entity transactions

A-13 When brainstorming about a culture or environment that enables management to rationalize committing fraud, the audit team members may want to discuss whether any of the following exist:

- An organizational culture that lets concern for provision of program services completely override sound internal controls
- Misguided attempts to preserve the NFP's program services no matter what the cost or risk, for example, by not remitting payroll withholdings
- An employee's attitude that because his or her compensation is lower than what the employee perceives could be earned in the for-profit sector, special perquisites are justified (such as rights to take donated noncash items for personal use)
- An employee who has access to assets subject to misappropriation is dissatisfied, perhaps because of long work hours or inability to get resources assigned to the employee's projects
- Governing board members have personally guaranteed debt of the NFP and the NFP is experiencing a deteriorating financial condition

A-14 The preceding lists highlight incentives or pressures, or both; opportunities; and cultures or environments that are unique to or more common in the not-for-profit industry than in other industries. Additionally, appendix A, "Examples of Fraud Risk Factors," of AU-C section 240 provides examples of fraud risk factors that the audit team members might consider.

Risk Assessment Procedures and Related Activities

A-15 When performing risk assessment procedures and related activities to obtain an understanding of the entity and its environment, including the entity's internal control, required by AU-C section 315, paragraph .16 of AU-C section 240 states that the auditor should perform the procedures in paragraphs .17–.24 of AU-C section 240 to obtain information for use in identifying the risk of material misstatement due to fraud. As part of this work, the auditor should perform the following procedures:

a. Hold fraud discussions with management, others within the entity, and those charged with governance (unless all those charged with governance are involved in managing the entity). See specific inquiries the auditor should make in paragraphs .17–.19 and .21 of AU-C section 240.

b. Obtain an understanding of how those charged with governance exercise oversight of management's process for identifying and responding to the risks of fraud in the entity and the internal control that management has established to mitigate these risks, unless all those charged with governance are involved in managing the entity. (See paragraphs .20 and .A21–.A23 of AU-C section 240.)

c. Evaluate whether unusual or unexpected relationships that have been identified (based on analytical procedures performed as part of risk assessment procedures) indicate risks of material misstatement due to fraud. (See paragraphs .22, .A24–.A26, and .A46 of AU-C section 240.)

d. Consider whether other information obtained by the auditor indicates risks of material misstatement due to fraud. (See further application guidance in paragraph .A27 of AU-C section 240.)

e. Evaluate whether the information obtained from the risk assessment procedures and related activities performed indicates that one or more fraud risk factors are present. (See paragraphs .24 and .A28–.A32 of AU-C section 240.)

A-16 Performance of analytical procedures relating to revenue with the objective of identifying unusual or unexpected relationships involving revenue accounts may indicate a material misstatement due to fraudulent financial reporting. For example, in the not-for-profit industry, the following unusual or unexpected relationships may indicate a material misstatement due to fraud:

- Changes in contribution revenue as compared to a prior period are not as expected, considering changes in the surrounding circumstances (state of the economy, changed fund-raising efforts, known major gifts or grants, or both)
- Revenue does not change in the direction or magnitude, or both, that is expected based on observed changes in related expenses (for example, revenue and expenses of a clinic)
- Earned revenue is inconsistent with known levels of services provided
- A significant amount of expenditures on cost-reimbursement grants are recognized at the tail end of the grant period
- Investment return overall, or for an individual fund, is not reasonable

Evaluation of Fraud Risk Factors

A-17 As indicated in item (*e*) previously, the auditor may identify events or conditions that indicate incentives or pressures, or both, to perpetrate fraud, opportunities to carry out the fraud, or attitudes or rationalizations, or both, to justify a fraudulent action. Such events or conditions are referred to as fraud risk factors. Although fraud risk factors may not necessarily indicate the existence of fraud, paragraph .24 of AU-C section 240 states that they have often been present in circumstances in which frauds have occurred and therefore may indicate risks of material misstatement due to fraud.

A-18 Paragraph .A31 of AU-C section 240 states that the size, complexity, and ownership characteristics of the entity have a significant influence on the consideration of relevant fraud risk factors. Additional fraud risk factor considerations on large and smaller, less complex entities can be found in paragraphs .A31–.A32 of AU-C section 240.

A-19 Appendix A of AU-C section 240 identifies examples of fraud risk factors that may be faced by auditors in a broad range of situations. The section about brainstorming sessions that are conducted by the audit team members (paragraphs A-8–A-14 of this appendix) contains a list of fraud risk factors specific to the not-for-profit industry. Remember that fraud risk factors are only one of several sources of information an auditor considers when identifying and assessing risk of material misstatement due to fraud.

Identifying Risks That May Result in a Material Misstatement Due to Fraud

A-20 In accordance with AU-C section 315, paragraph .25 of AU-C section 240 states that the auditor should identify and assess the risks of material misstatement due to fraud at the financial statement level, and at the assertion level for classes of transactions, account balances, and disclosures. The auditor's risk assessment should be ongoing throughout the audit, following the initial assessment.

A-21 Recognition of the following items might involve a high degree of management judgment and subjectivity:

Contributions Receivable and Revenue

- Measurement of noncash contributions in the absence of publicly available market quotations
- Whether the allowance for uncollectible pledges is appropriate (This involves a higher degree of subjectivity than normal trade or loans receivable, due to the voluntary nature of the underlying transaction.)
- Whether a donor communication is an expression of an intention to give or a promise to give
- Whether promises to give are conditional or unconditional
- Whether donor stipulations are conditions or restrictions
- Whether a donor-imposed condition on a promise to give has been substantially met
- Whether donated services require specialized skills
- Whether the NFP would typically have had to purchase services if they were not provided by donation
- Whether assets received that must be passed on to another entity meet the criteria for recognition as contribution revenue by the reporting (recipient) entity (that is, is there variance power; are the NFPs financially interrelated; is a transfer revocable; and so forth)

Revenues Other Than Contributions

- Whether revenue transactions (for example, membership dues, grants, contracts) are contributions or exchange transactions (or whether they have a contribution element)
- Whether a revenue source results from an activity that is subject to tax as an unrelated business

Contributions Payable and Expense

- Whether a communication with another NFP is an expression of an intention to give or a promise to give
- Whether promises to give are conditional or unconditional
- Whether stipulations are conditions or restrictions

- Whether a condition on a promise to give to another NFP has been met, especially if the donor NFP's monitoring system is inadequate

Expenses, in General

- Allocation of costs of joint activities, both concerning whether the criteria for allocation are met and whether the allocation bases and methods chosen are appropriate
- Allocation of expenses among functional categories, especially if that allocation is made at year end based on percentages
- Whether an expenditure satisfies a restriction on net assets

Other Items

- Whether an NFP maintains its collection in a manner that qualifies for nonrecognition, especially if they have occasionally sold collection items in the past without purchasing new items for the collection
- Recoverability of assets with possibly limited future use (for example, sets and costumes owned by a theater)
- Whether a related entity meets the criteria for consolidation or for financially interrelated entities accounted for under the equity method, especially if one NFP has significant influence over the other but not a majority voting interest in the governing board of the other

A Presumption That Improper Revenue Recognition Is a Fraud Risk

A-22 Paragraph .26 of AU-C section 240 states that when identifying and assessing the risks of material misstatement due to fraud, the auditor should, based on a presumption that risks of fraud exist in revenue recognition, evaluate which types of revenue, revenue transactions, or assertions give rise to such risks. Paragraph .46 of AU-C section 240 specifies the documentation required when the auditor concludes that the presumption is not applicable in the circumstances of the engagement and, accordingly, has not identified revenue recognition as a risk of material misstatement due to fraud. (See paragraphs .A33–.A35 of AU-C section 240 for application guidance of fraud risks in revenue recognition.)

A-23 Paragraph .27 of AU-C section 240 states that the auditor should treat those assessed risks of material misstatement due to fraud as significant risks and accordingly, to the extent not already done, the auditor should obtain an understanding of the entity's related controls, including control activities, relevant to such risks, including the evaluation of whether such controls have been suitably designed and implemented to mitigate such fraud risks. (See paragraphs .A36–.A37 of AU-C section 240 for application guidance on identifying and assessing the risks of material misstatement due to fraud and understanding the entity's related controls.)

A-24 Revenue may be improperly recognized due to fraudulent financial reporting if

- revenue is improperly classified among the net asset classes, restrictions are released before they are met, or restrictions are not released even though they are met;

- conditional promises to give are recognized as unconditional, or vice versa;
- intentions to give are recognized as promises to give, or promises to give are not recognized because it is asserted that they are intentions to give;
- unconditional grants that are in-substance contributions are recognized as exchange transactions, or vice versa;
- membership dues that are in-substance contributions are recognized as exchange transactions, or vice versa;
- improper periods for amortization of income from membership dues, tuition, and season ticket sales are used;
- agency transactions are recognized as contribution revenue and program expense, particularly if the reported fair value of noncash items changes without cause between receipt and disbursement;
- works of art, historical treasures, and similar items are not recognized but should be because the collection does not meet the criteria for nonrecognition;
- in-kind contributions are selectively recognized to maximize the reported ratio of program expenses to total expenses (that is, the NFP makes every attempt to recognize and maximize the fair value of contributions of items for program purposes, but ignores or minimizes the estimated fair value of items used for management and general or fund-raising purposes);
- discount rates used in measuring promises to give or split-interest gifts are inappropriate;
- revenue is recognized for services that were not delivered; and
- sliding scales used to charge service recipients are not appropriately applied.

Key Estimates

A-25 Fraudulent financial reporting is often accomplished through the intentional misstatement of accounting estimates. Estimates by management are common in the following areas:

- Measurement of noncash contributions other than marketable securities and especially of unusual noncash assets
- Allowance for uncollectible promises to give
- Present value calculations for unconditional promises to give and split-interest agreements
- Methods and factors used in allocating the costs of joint activities
- Allocation of expenses to functional categories
- Future cash flows related to assets that are possibly impaired

A-26 Review and evaluation of the financial results reported by the NFP or its individual operating units also may detect fraudulent financial reporting. Unusual fluctuations in results of a particular reporting unit, or the lack of expected fluctuations, may indicate potential manipulation by management. Examples of key ratios or trends to evaluate include the following:

- Percentage of revenue by major source, particularly if compared over a series of years or between similar individual operating units

- Percentage of expenses in each of the major programs and in management and general and fund-raising categories, particularly if compared over a series of years or between similar individual operating units
- Fund-raising expenses as a percentage of contribution revenue
- Investment income as a percentage of investment assets
- Comparisons of budget to actual for revenues and expenses
- Per capita calculations such as payroll expense per employee, average fee per service recipient, average gift shop sales per person admitted, and average contribution per person solicited, particularly if the denominator (head count) can be determined independent of the accounting function
- Comparison of the amount of gifts received in the accounting records and the development records

Responses to the Assessed Risks of Material Misstatement Due to Fraud

Overall Responses

A-27 In accordance with AU-C section 330, paragraphs .28–.29 of AU-C section 240 state that the auditor should determine overall responses to address the assessed risks of material misstatement due to fraud at the financial statement level. Accordingly, the auditor should

a. assign and supervise personnel, taking into account the knowledge, skill, and ability of the individuals to be given significant engagement responsibilities and the auditor's assessment of the risks of material misstatement due to fraud for the engagement;

b. evaluate whether the selection and application of accounting policies by the entity, particularly those related to subjective measurements and complex transactions, may be indicative of fraudulent financial reporting resulting from management's effort to manage earnings, or a bias that may create a material misstatement; and

c. incorporate an element of unpredictability in the selection of the nature, timing, and extent of audit procedures.

See paragraphs .A38–.A42 of AU-C section 240 for additional application guidance on overall responses to the assessed risks of material misstatement due to fraud.

Audit Procedures Responsive to Assessed Risks of Material Misstatement Due to Fraud at the Assertion Level

A-28 In accordance with AU-C section 330, paragraph .30 of AU-C section 240 states that the auditor should design and perform further audit procedures whose nature, timing, and extent are responsive to the assessed risks of material misstatement due to fraud at the assertion level (see paragraphs .A43–.A46 for further application guidance).

Audit Procedures Responsive to the Risk of Management Override of Controls

A-29 Even if specific risks of material misstatement due to fraud are not identified by the auditor, paragraph .32 of AU-C section 240 states that a possibility exists that management override of controls could occur. Accordingly, the auditor should address the risk of management override of controls apart from any conclusions regarding the existence of more specifically identifiable risks by designing and performing audit procedures, such as

a. testing the appropriateness of journal entries recorded in the general ledger and other adjustments made in preparation of the financial statements, including entries posted directly to financial statement drafts,

b. reviewing accounting estimates for biases and evaluate whether the circumstances producing the bias, if any, represent a risk of material misstatement due to fraud, and

c. evaluating, for significant transactions that are outside the normal course of business for the entity or that otherwise appear to be unusual given the auditor's understanding of the entity and its environment and other information obtained during the audit, whether the business rationale (or lack thereof) of the transactions suggests that they may have been entered into to engage in fraudulent financial reporting or to conceal misappropriation of assets.

Other Audit Procedures

A-30 Paragraph .33 of AU-C section 240 states that the auditor should determine whether, in order to respond to the identified risks of management override of controls, the auditor needs to perform other audit procedures in addition to those specifically referred to previously (that is, when specific additional risks of management override exist that are not covered as part of the procedures performed to address the requirements in paragraph .32 of AU-C section 240.)

Evaluating Audit Evidence

A-31 Paragraphs .34–.37 and .A56–.A62 of AU-C section 240 provide requirements and application guidance for evaluating audit evidence. As stated in paragraph .34 of AU-C section 240, the auditor should evaluate, at or near the end of the audit, whether the accumulated results of auditing procedures, including analytical procedures, that were performed as substantive tests or when forming an overall conclusion, affect the assessment of the risks of material misstatement due to fraud made earlier in the audit or indicate a previously unrecognized risk of material misstatement due to fraud.

A-32 Paragraph .35 of AU-C section 240 states that, if the auditor identifies a misstatement, the auditor should evaluate whether such a misstatement is indicative of fraud. If such an indication exists, the auditor should evaluate the implications of the misstatement with regard to other aspects of the audit, particularly the auditor's evaluation of materiality, management and employee integrity, and the reliability of management representations, recognizing that an instance of fraud is unlikely to be an isolated occurrence. Furthermore, paragraph .36 of AU-C section 240 states that, if the auditor identifies a misstatement, whether material or not, and the auditor has reason to believe that it is, or may be, the result of fraud and that management (in particular, senior management) is involved, the auditor should reevaluate the assessment of the risks of material misstatement due to fraud and its resulting effect on the nature, timing, and extent of audit procedures to respond to the assessed risks. The auditor should also consider whether circumstances or conditions indicate possible collusion involving employees, management, or third parties when reconsidering the reliability of evidence previously obtained.

A-33 Paragraph .A60 of AU-C section 240 states that the implications of identified fraud depend on the circumstances. For example, an otherwise insignificant fraud may be significant if it involves senior management. In such circumstances, the reliability of evidence previously obtained may be called into question because there may be doubts about the completeness and truthfulness of representations made and the genuineness of accounting records and documentation. There may also be a possibility of collusion involving employees, management, or third parties.

A-34 Paragraph .37 of AU-C section 240 states that if the auditor concludes that, or is unable to conclude whether, the financial statements are materially misstated as a result of fraud, the auditor should evaluate the implications for the audit. AU-C section 450, *Evaluation of Misstatements Identified During the Audit*, and AU-C section 700, *Forming an Opinion and Reporting on Financial Statements*, address the evaluation and disposition of misstatements and the effect on the auditor's opinion in the auditor's report.

Auditor Unable to Continue the Engagement

A-35 Paragraph .38 of AU-C section 240 states that if, as a result of identified fraud or suspected fraud, the auditor encounters circumstances that bring into question the auditor's ability to continue performing the audit, the auditor should

a. determine the professional and legal responsibilities applicable in the circumstances, including whether a requirement exists for the auditor to report to the person or persons who engaged the auditor or, in some cases, to regulatory authorities;

b. consider whether it is appropriate to withdraw from the engagement, when withdrawal is possible under applicable law or regulation; and

c. if the auditor withdraws

   i. discuss with the appropriate level of management and those charged with governance the auditor's withdrawal from the engagement and the reasons for the withdrawal, and

   ii. determine whether a professional or legal requirement exists to report to the person or persons who engaged the auditor or, in some cases, to regulatory authorities, the auditor's withdrawal from the engagement and the reasons for the withdrawal.

Given the nature of the circumstances and the need to consider the legal requirements, paragraph .A65 of AU-C section 240 states that the auditor may consider it appropriate to seek legal advice when deciding whether to withdraw from an engagement and in determining an appropriate course of action, including the possibility of reporting to regulators or others. For additional application guidance, including examples of circumstances that may arise and bring into question the auditor's ability to continue performing the audit, see paragraphs .A63–.A65 of AU-C section 240.

A-36 In some circumstances relating to audits of governmental entities and NFPs, the option of withdrawing from the engagement may not be available to the auditor due to the nature of the mandate, public interest considerations, contractual requirements, or law or regulation.

Communications to Management and With Those Charged With Governance

A-37 Paragraph .39 of AU-C section 240 states that if the auditor has identified a fraud or has obtained information that indicates that a fraud may exist, the auditor should communicate these matters on a timely basis to the appropriate level of management in order to inform those with primary responsibility for the prevention and detection of fraud of matters relevant to their responsibilities. As stated in paragraph .A67 of AU-C section 240, this is true even if the matter might be considered inconsequential (for example, a minor defalcation by an employee at a low level in the entity's organization). Unless all of those charged with governance are involved in managing the entity, paragraphs .40–.41 of AU-C section 240 state that, if the auditor has identified or suspects fraud involving (*a*) management, (*b*) employees who have significant roles in internal control, or (*c*) others, when the fraud results in a material misstatement in the financial statements, the auditor should communicate these matters to those charged with governance on a timely basis. If the auditor suspects fraud involving management, the auditor should communicate these suspicions to those charged with governance and discuss with them the nature, timing, and extent of audit procedures necessary to complete the audit. In addition, the auditor should communicate with those charged with governance any other matters related to fraud that are, in the auditor's professional judgment, relevant to their responsibilities. See paragraphs .A68–.A71 of AU-C section 240 for further application guidance concerning communications with those charged with governance.

Communications to Regulatory and Enforcement Authorities

A-38 If the auditor has identified or suspects fraud, paragraph .42 of AU-C section 240 states that the auditor should determine whether the auditor has a responsibility to report the occurrence or suspicion to a party outside the entity. Although the auditor's professional duty to maintain the confidentiality of client information may preclude such reporting, the auditor's legal responsibilities may override the duty of confidentiality in some circumstances.

A-39 In certain circumstances for engagements involving governmental entities and NFPs, requirements for reporting fraud, whether or not discovered through the audit process, may be subject to specific provisions of the audit mandate or related law or regulation.

Documenting the Auditor's Consideration of Fraud

A-40 Paragraphs .43–.46 of AU-C section 240 address requirements on certain items and events to be documented by the auditor in relation to assessed risks of material misstatement due to fraud.

Chapter 3

Financial Statements, the Reporting Entity, and General Financial Reporting Matters

> ***Note:*** *For financial statements prepared in accordance with FASB Accounting Standards Update (ASU) No. 2016-14,* Not-for-Profit Entities (Topic 958): Presentation of Financial Statements of Not-for-Profit Entities, *use appendix A, "Financial Statements Prepared in Accordance With FASB ASU No. 2016-14," of this chapter for the amendments relating to the statement of financial position, statement of activities, and statement of cash flows, as well as liquidity disclosures. Throughout the remainder of this chapter, the effect of amendments in FASB ASU No. 2016-14 on guide paragraphs is provided in gray-shaded text following the paragraph. The distinct presentation of this content is intended to aid the reader in identifying the content that will be deleted upon the effective date of the amendments in FASB ASU No. 2016-14, as well as the text that will replace it (the guide's "dual guidance" treatment of applicable new guidance). Each gray-shaded paragraph includes a footnote showing the effective date of the ASU.*

Introduction

3.01 This chapter discusses the following matters:

- Financial statements (that is, the statement of financial position, statement of activities, statement of cash flows, and statement of functional expenses)
- Reporting related entities, including consolidations
- Mergers and acquisitions
- Collaborative arrangements
- The use of fair value measures
- Financial statement disclosures not discussed elsewhere in this guide, including noncompliance with donor restrictions, risks and uncertainties, subsequent events, and related party transactions

3.02 FASB *Accounting Standards Codification* (ASC) includes the unique standards relating to the general-purpose external financial statements for a not-for-profit entity (NFP) in four subtopics, as follows:

a. FASB ASC 958-205, about presentation of financial statements

b. FASB ASC 958-210, about the statement of financial position

c. FASB ASC 958-220, about the statement of activities

d. FASB ASC 958-230, about the statement of cash flows

In addition to that industry-specific guidance, an NFP should follow all effective provisions of FASB ASC unless the specific provision explicitly exempts NFPs or its subject matter precludes such applicability. For example, FASB ASC contains presentation topics (FASB ASC 205, *Presentation of Financial Statements*, to FASB ASC 280, *Segment Reporting*), many of which provide guidance for general presentation and display items applicable to NFPs. The guidance in this chapter summarizes many of those unique standards but is not intended as a substitute for reading those topics and subtopics.

3.03 FASB ASC 958-205-45-4 specifies that a complete set of financial statements should include a statement of financial position as of the end of the reporting period, a statement of activities and a statement of cash flows for the reporting period, and accompanying notes to financial statements. In addition, a voluntary health and welfare entity[1] should provide a statement of functional expenses.[2]

The "Pending Content" in FASB ASC 958-205-45-4 specifies that a complete set of financial statements of an NFP should include a statement of financial position as of the end of the reporting period, a statement of activities and a statement of cash flows for the reporting period, and accompanying notes to financial statements.[3,4]

3.04 FASB ASC 958-205-45-5 requires that a set of financial statements includes, either in the body of the financial statements or in the accompanying notes, information required by generally accepted accounting principles (GAAP) that do not specifically exempt NFPs and information required by applicable specialized accounting and reporting principles and practices. Per FASB ASC 958-205-45-1, the requirements generally are no more stringent

---

[1] The FASB *Accounting Standards Codification* (ASC) glossary definition of *voluntary health and welfare entity* includes a provision that those not-for-profit entities (NFPs) derive their revenue primarily from voluntary contributions from the general public. It specifies that for purposes of that definition, the *general public* excludes governmental entities when determining whether an NFP is a voluntary health and welfare entity.

[2] FASB ASC and this guide use certain statement titles and the terms *permanently restricted*, *temporarily restricted*, and *unrestricted net assets*. Other titles and other labels may also be used, pursuant to FASB ASC 958-205-55-2 and FASB ASC 958-210-55-3. The terms *statement of financial position* and *statement of activities* indicate the content and purpose of the respective statements and serve as possible titles for those statements. Other appropriately descriptive titles may also be used. Similarly, a statement of functional expenses might have another appropriately descriptive title. For example, a statement reporting financial position could be called a *balance sheet* as well as a *statement of financial position*. Current practice and the statement's purpose suggest, however, that a statement of cash flows only be titled "Statement of Cash Flows." FASB ASC 958-210-55-3 states that other labels exist for net assets and its classes. For example, *equity* may be used for net assets, and *other* or *not donor-restricted* may be used with care to distinguish unrestricted net assets from the temporarily and permanently restricted classes of net assets.

[3] FASB ASC and this guide use certain statement titles and the terms *net assets with donor restrictions* and *net assets without donor restrictions*. Other titles and other labels may also be used, pursuant to FASB ASC 958-205-55-2 and FASB ASC 958-210-55-3. The terms *statement of financial position* and *statement of activities* indicate the content and purpose of the respective statements and serve as possible titles for those statements. Other appropriately descriptive titles may also be used. For example, a statement reporting financial position could be called a *balance sheet* as well as a *statement of financial position*. Current practice and the statement's purpose suggest, however, that a statement of cash flows only be titled "Statement of Cash Flows." FASB ASC 958-210-55-3 states that other labels exist for net assets and its classes. For example, *equity* may be used for net assets, and *other* or *not donor-restricted* may be used with care to distinguish net assets with donor restrictions from net assets without donor restrictions.

[4] The amendments in FASB Accounting Standards Update (ASU) No. 2016-14, *Not-for-Profit Entities (Topic 958): Presentation of Financial Statements of Not-for-Profit Entities*, are effective for annual financial statements issued for fiscal years beginning after December 15, 2017 (for example, years ending December 31, 2018 and years ending June 30, 2019), and for interim periods within fiscal years beginning after December 15, 2018. Application to interim financial statements is permitted but not required in the initial year of application. Early application of the amendments is permitted. Readers preparing financial statements in accordance with the amendments in FASB ASU No. 2016-14 should use appendix A to this chapter (paragraph 3.194) for guidance in preparing the statement of financial position, the statement of activities, and the statement of cash flows.

than the requirements for business entities. The degree of aggregation and order of presentation of items of assets and liabilities in statements of financial position or of items of revenues and expenses in statements of activities of NFPs, although not specified, generally should be similar to those required or permitted for business entities. Particular formats for a statement of financial position, a statement of activities, or a statement of cash flows are neither prescribed nor prohibited in part because similar prescriptions and proscriptions do not exist for business entities.

The "Pending Content" in FASB ASC 958-205-45-5 requires that a set of financial statements include, either in the body of financial statements or in the accompanying notes, information required by generally accepted accounting principles (GAAP) or required by applicable specialized accounting and reporting principles and practices unless NFPs are specifically exempt from providing that information. Per FASB ASC 958-205-45-1, the requirements generally are no more stringent than the requirements for business entities. The degree of aggregation and order of presentation of items of assets and liabilities in statements of financial position or of items of revenues and expenses in statements of activities of NFPs, although not specified, generally should be similar to those required or permitted for business entities. Particular formats for a statement of financial position, a statement of activities, or a statement of cash flows are neither prescribed nor prohibited in part because similar prescriptions and proscriptions do not exist for business entities.[5]

3.05 FASB ASC 958-205-55 includes illustrations of the required financial statements that illustrate some of the ways in which the requirements can be met.

Statement of Financial Position[6]

3.06 FASB ASC 958-210 describes the unique standards relating to a statement of financial position of an NFP. In addition to that industry-specific guidance, an NFP should follow all effective provisions of FASB ASC unless the specific provision explicitly exempts NFPs or its subject matter precludes such applicability. For example, NFPs should apply the guidance contained in FASB ASC 210, *Balance Sheet*, that does not conflict with the industry guidance.

3.07 FASB ASC 958-210-45-1 requires that a statement of financial position focus on the NFP as a whole and report all of the following amounts:

- Total assets
- Total liabilities
- Total net assets

---

[5] The amendments in FASB ASU No. 2016-14 are effective for annual financial statements issued for fiscal years beginning after December 15, 2017 (for example, years ending December 31, 2018 and years ending June 30, 2019), and for interim periods within fiscal years beginning after December 15, 2018. Application to interim financial statements is permitted but not required in the initial year of application. Early application of the amendments is permitted. Readers preparing financial statements in accordance with the amendments in FASB ASU No. 2016-14 should use appendix A to this chapter (paragraph 3.194) for guidance in preparing the statement of financial position, the statement of activities, and the statement of cash flows.

[6] Readers preparing financial statements in accordance with the amendments in FASB ASU No. 2016-14 should use appendix A to this chapter (paragraph 3.194) for guidance in preparing the statement of financial position, the statement of activities, and the statement of cash flows.

- Permanently restricted net assets
- Temporarily restricted net assets
- Unrestricted net assets

3.08 FASB ASC 958-210-45-5 describes how classifying assets and liabilities into reasonably homogeneous groups (paragraph 3.04) increases the usefulness of information. FASB ASC 958-210-45-6 states that assets need not be disaggregated on the basis of the presence of donor-imposed restrictions on their use; for example, cash available for unrestricted current use need not be reported separately from cash received with donor-imposed restrictions that is also available for current use.[7] However, cash or other assets received with a donor-imposed restriction that limits their use to long-term purposes should not be classified with cash or other assets that are unrestricted and available for current use. FASB ASC 958-210-45-6 also states that the kind of asset whose use is limited should be described in the notes to the financial statements if its nature is not clear from the description on the face of the statement of financial position.

Effects of Restrictions, Designations, and Other Limitations on Liquidity

3.09 FASB ASC 958-210-45-8 requires that information about the NFP's liquidity be provided by any of the following:

a. Sequencing assets according to their nearness of conversion to cash and sequencing liabilities according to the nearness of their maturity and resulting use of cash

b. Classifying assets and liabilities as current and noncurrent, as defined by FASB ASC 210-10 (required by FASB ASC 954-210-45-1 for statements of financial position prepared by not-for-profit, business-oriented health care entities)

c. Disclosing in notes to financial statements relevant information about the liquidity or maturity of assets and liabilities, including restrictions on the use of particular assets

3.10 Per FASB ASC 958-210-50-1, information about the liquidity or maturity of assets and liabilities, including restrictions on the use of particular items, should be disclosed in notes to financial statements unless that information is provided on the face of the statement of financial position. FASB ASC 958-205-55-7 explains that when an NFP presents a statement of financial position that sequences assets and liabilities based on their relative liquidity, cash and cash equivalents that are held temporarily in permanent endowment funds until suitable long-term investment opportunities are identified are included in the classification long-term investments. Similarly, cash and contributions receivable restricted by donors to investment in land, buildings, and equipment are not included with the line items cash and cash equivalents or contributions receivable. Rather, those items are reported as assets restricted to investment in land, buildings, and equipment and are sequenced closer to land, buildings, and equipment. Likewise, FASB ASC 958-210-45-12 states that cash held temporarily by a custodian for investment purposes may be included as part of

---

[7] FASB ASC 958-205-45-6 notes that assets may be restricted by donors. For example, land could be restricted to use as a public park. Generally, however, restrictions apply to net assets, not to specific assets.

investments in a statement of financial position rather than as cash. Similarly, FASB ASC 210-10-45-4 states that the concept of the nature of current assets contemplates the exclusion from that classification of such resources as cash that is designated for expenditure in the acquisition or construction of noncurrent assets or is segregated for the liquidation of long-term debts. Even though not actually set aside in special accounts, funds that are clearly to be used in the near future for the liquidation of long-term debts, payments to sinking funds, or for similar purposes should also, under this concept, be excluded from current assets. However, if such funds are considered to pay off maturing debt that has been set up properly as a current liability, they may be included within the current asset classification.

3.11 Application of the guidance discussed in paragraphs 3.09–.10 results in certain (*a*) donor restrictions, (*b*) governing board designations (which are presumed to reflect management intent), and (*c*) legal limitations affecting the classification of or disclosures about assets, or both. In meeting the requirements of FASB ASC 958-210 and FASB ASC 210-10-45 to provide information about liquidity, NFP's should consider not only maturity (nearness to conversion to cash or use of cash), but the effects on liquidity of donor-imposed restrictions, management's intent to meet those restrictions, and management's intent to use assets for long-term purposes (such as liquidation of long-term debts, payments to sinking funds, establishment of quasi endowment funds, and so forth).

3.12 For example, if a split-interest agreement is in trust form, such as a unitrust or annuity trust, or if the assets held for a split-interest agreement are required by state law to be separately invested, the NFP should either separately display the asset on the face of the statement of financial position or should display the asset with similar assets of similar liquidity to meet the requirements of FASB ASC 958-210 and FASB ASC 210-10-45. Cash and investments held in the trust should not be combined with cash and investments that are available for operations. Further, if not apparent from the face of the financial statements, the NFP should disclose the nature and amount of the limitation imposed by a donor restriction, law, or contract in the notes to the financial statements in accordance with paragraphs 6–10 of FASB ASC 958-210-45.

3.13 The Financial Reporting Executive Committee (FinREC) believes if the use of a specific asset is not explicitly limited by a donor restriction, but net assets reflect a donor's restriction to use the contributed assets for a permanent or term endowment, for purchase of a long-lived asset, or for another noncurrent purpose, the liquidity of the NFP is impacted by its responsibility to hold an appropriate composition of assets to comply with those restrictions. (Paragraphs 3.173–.175 discuss requirements if an NFP has not maintained an appropriate composition of assets to comply with donor-imposed restrictions.) In implementing the guidance in FASB ASC 958-210-45-8 pertaining to presenting information about liquidity, FinREC believes assets identified by the NFP as held to meet a donor restriction for noncurrent purposes should be displayed using any of the following methods:

- If the NFP provides information about liquidity by sequencing assets according to their nearness of conversion to cash (that is, a nonclassified statement of financial position), assets held for meeting donor restrictions that limit use to long-term purposes should be

- — separately displayed on the face of the statement of financial position in a position of longer-term relative liquidity as compared to similar assets available for current operating purposes (that is, using a description that identifies the nature of the asset, such as cash or contributions receivable, but displayed lower), or
- — displayed on the face of the statement of financial position using a separate line item, such as "assets whose use has been limited or restricted," in a position of relative liquidity consistent with its noncurrent purpose.

- If information about liquidity is provided by classifying assets as current and noncurrent (that is, a classified statement of financial position), assets held for meeting donor restrictions that limit use to long-term purposes should be classified as noncurrent. For example, assets restricted to the payment of long-term debt would be classified as noncurrent to the extent that they exceed the current portion of long-term debt. A separate line item, such as "assets whose use has been limited or restricted," may be used.

Regardless of which of the preceding methods is used, if the nature of the assets or the related restrictions is not evident from the description on the line item, that information should be disclosed in the notes to the financial statements, as required by paragraphs 6–10 of FASB ASC 958-210-45.

3.14 In some cases, assets held to meet a donor restriction are easily identified. In other cases, the identification process may be subjective. For example, if the NFP conducts a fund-raising campaign to build a new building, unconditional promises to give received in response to that campaign are easily identified as assets held to meet a donor restriction for purchase of a building. If cash gifts to the same campaign are invested until needed to make expenditures for the new building and commingled with the NFP's other investments, a portion of investments may be assigned as assets held to meet a donor restriction for purchase of a building.

3.15 In implementing the guidance in FASB ASC 210-10-45-4 pertaining to the classification of current assets, if the governing board identifies specific assets to be invested or held pursuant to a designation for noncurrent purposes, those assets would be reported in a classified statement of financial position outside the current assets section. FinREC believes that in a nonclassified statement of financial position, those assets would be sequenced with other assets that will be consumed in a similar term. Further, FinREC believes best practice is to report those designated assets separately from donor-restricted assets on the face of the statement of financial position or disclose in the notes to the financial statements the amount of designated assets included in a line item that contains both amounts designated and restricted for noncurrent purposes.

3.16 FinREC believes that when preparing consolidated financial statements, best practice is to apply the guidance in paragraphs 3.09–.23 at the reporting-entity (that is, parent) level in consolidated financial statements, focusing on the entity as a whole, as required by FASB ASC 958-210-45-1. Accordingly, assets that are not separately reported or segregated at the subsidiary level (based on the guidance herein) might be required to be separately reported or segregated at the parent level or vice versa. (A related discussion about the classification of net assets in consolidation is presented in paragraphs 3.102–.105.)

3.17 The following examples illustrate the conclusions in paragraphs 3.09–.16:

- Paragraph 3.18—A specific asset is restricted by the donor, by law, or by contract.
- Paragraph 3.19—Cash, receivables, or other assets are restricted by donor, by law, or by contract to use in an ongoing program of the NFP (that is, current operating purposes).
- Paragraph 3.20—Cash, receivables, or other assets are restricted by donor, by law, or by contract to certain long-term purposes.
- Paragraph 3.21—Cash, receivables, or other assets are designated by the governing board for long-term purposes.
- Paragraph 3.22—Cash, receivables, or other assets are unrestricted in a subsidiary's financial statements but restricted for long-term purposes in the consolidated financial statements.

3.18 Occasionally, specific assets are restricted by donors, by law, or by contract. For example, assume land gifted by a donor is restricted in perpetuity for use as open green space. Such restricted land should be distinguished from land that is not subject to donor-imposed restrictions. Similarly, investments held subject to a split-interest trust agreement should be distinguished from unrestricted investments, as should assets held for a split-interest agreement that is required by state law to be separately invested. Cash required by law or contract to be set aside in compliance with bond sinking fund requirements should be distinguished from cash with no such stipulations. Those restricted assets should be displayed separately on the statement of financial position or disclosed in the notes to financial statements in a way that distinguishes them from similar assets that are not subject to those specific asset stipulations.

3.19 Cash, receivables, or other assets that are restricted by donor, by law, or by contract to current operating purposes are permitted, but not required, to be reported separately from unrestricted current assets. For example, cash that is received in response to a campaign to support Program A, which is an ongoing program of the donee, is permitted, but not required, to be reported separately from unrestricted current assets. FinREC believes that as long as the restrictions on them are quickly met, the assets do not need to be segregated. Because the restrictions on them are quickly met during the normal course of operations, they generally are available to creditors.

3.20 Cash, receivables, or other assets that are restricted by donor, by law, or by contract for certain noncurrent purposes should be reported in a classified statement of financial position outside the current assets section or in a nonclassified statement of financial position sequenced with other assets that will be consumed in a similar term. For example, if an NFP has cash, investments, or contributions receivable resulting from a capital campaign for a permanent endowment fund or for acquisition of a long-lived asset, those assets should not be displayed with similar assets to be used for current operations. They could be reported under a separate caption, such as "cash and other assets restricted to investment in property and equipment," and displayed near the section of the statement where property and equipment is displayed. Although net assets are either temporarily restricted (purpose or time) or permanently restricted when donor-imposed restrictions limit the use of the assets, it is important to reflect in the asset section of the statement of financial position that assets required to be used to satisfy donor restrictions of a long-term nature generally are unavailable to meet current operating obligations.

3.21 The governing boards of some NFPs designate resources to be held for long-term purposes, such as debt-service reserves, quasi endowment, or the future acquisition of property and equipment. Consistent with FASB ASC 210-10-45-4(a), if the governing board identifies specific assets to be invested or held pursuant to the designation of net assets for noncurrent purposes, those assets should be reported in a classified statement of financial position outside the current assets section, or in a nonclassified statement of financial position sequenced with other assets that will be consumed in a similar term. Accordingly, cash, receivables, or other assets designated for long-term purposes generally are not aggregated on a statement of financial position with cash, receivables, or other assets that are available for current use.

3.22 Cash, receivables, or other assets that are unrestricted in a subsidiary's financial statements may need to be reported as restricted in consolidated financial statements. For example, a voluntary health and welfare entity has a broad mission of helping low income families and is the parent of an NFP that has a mission of running a day care and after-school care center for children in the county. The subsidiary NFP received a gift of a small office building subject to the donor's restriction that it be used for providing day care or after-school care or for the administrative support of those programs. In the separate financial statements of the subsidiary, those assets are not separately reported as restricted assets because the use of the assets is no narrower than the nature of the NFP and the purposes specified in its articles of incorporation and bylaws. However, when the subsidiary NFP is consolidated with its voluntary health and welfare entity parent, the office building would be reported separately with related disclosures because the donor-imposed restriction to use the building for day care, after-school care, or the administrative support of those two programs is narrower than the broad mission of helping low income families of the reporting entity. (Related information about the classification of net assets in consolidation is presented in paragraphs 3.103–.105.)

3.23 For each item on the statement of financial position that is segregated because of donor-imposed restrictions, limitations, or board designations, either the face of the financial statements or the notes should disclose the following:

- The nature of the assets comprising the line item (for example, cash, receivables, investments, and so on) (FASB ASC 958-210-45-6)
- The purpose for which the asset is segregated (for example, specific asset is held in perpetuity; held for construction of long-term assets; held for investment in endowment; and so on) (FASB ASC 958-210-45-8)
- The act causing the asset to be segregated (for example, [*a*] a specific asset is donor restricted, [*b*] the NFP is maintaining an appropriate composition of assets to fulfill donor restrictions, or [*c*] the NFP is maintaining an appropriate composition of assets to meet board designations) (FASB ASC 958-210-45-8)

Classification of Net Assets

3.24 Classification of net assets is discussed in paragraphs 9–11 of FASB ASC 958-210-45. The amounts for each of the three net asset classes are based on the existence or absence of donor-imposed restrictions.

3.25 The FASB ASC glossary defines *permanently restricted net assets* as the part of net assets of an NFP resulting from the following: (*a*) contributions and other inflows of assets whose use by the NFP is limited by donor-imposed stipulations that neither expire by passage of time nor can be fulfilled or otherwise removed by the actions of the NFP, (*b*) other asset enhancements and diminishments subject to the same kinds of stipulations, and (*c*) reclassifications from or to other classes of net assets as a consequence of donor-imposed stipulations.

3.26 The FASB ASC glossary defines *temporarily restricted net assets* as the part of the net assets of an NFP that result from the following: (*a*) contributions and other inflows of assets whose use by the NFP is limited by donor-imposed stipulations that either expire by passage of time or can be fulfilled and removed by actions of the NFP pursuant to those stipulations, (*b*) other asset enhancements and diminishments subject to the same kinds of stipulations, and (*c*) reclassifications from or to other classes of net assets as a consequence of donor-imposed stipulations, their expiration by passage of time, or their fulfillment and removal by actions of the NFP pursuant to those stipulations. Paragraphs 9–10 of FASB ASC 958-210-45 describe various purposes for which net assets might be restricted, such as use in future periods or use for specified purposes.

3.27 The FASB ASC glossary defines *unrestricted net assets* as the part of net assets of an NFP that is neither permanently restricted nor temporarily restricted by donor-imposed stipulations. FASB ASC 958-210-45-11 permits information about self-imposed limits, including voluntary resolutions by the governing board to designate a portion of unrestricted net assets (such as board-designated endowments) to be provided in the notes to or on the face of financial statements, provided that the requirement of FASB ASC 958-210-45-1 to display total unrestricted net assets is also met. FASB ASC 958-210-45-7 requires that, if not disclosed in the notes to financial statements, contractual limitations on the use of particular assets (such as cash held on deposit as a compensating balance) should be displayed on the face of the statement of financial position. Paragraphs 1A–1B of FASB ASC 958-205-50 require certain disclosures about board-designated endowment funds.

Statement of Activities[8]

3.28 FASB ASC 958-220 describes the unique standards relating to a statement of activities of an NFP. In addition to that industry-specific guidance, an NFP should follow all effective provisions of FASB ASC unless the specific provision explicitly exempts NFPs or its subject matter precludes such applicability. For example, NFPs should apply the guidance contained in FASB

---

[8] Readers preparing financial statements in accordance with the amendments in FASB ASU No. 2016-14 should use appendix A to this chapter (paragraph 3.194) for guidance in preparing the statement of financial position, the statement of activities, and the statement of cash flows.

ASC 220, *Income Statement—Reporting Comprehensive Income*, that does not conflict with the industry guidance.

3.29 Paragraphs 1–2 of FASB ASC 958-220-45 require that a statement of activities focus on the NFP as a whole and report the following amounts for the period: the change in net assets, using a descriptive term such as *change in net assets* or *change in equity*; the change in permanently restricted net assets; the change in temporarily restricted net assets; and the change in unrestricted net assets.

3.30 In accordance with paragraphs 14–18 of FASB ASC 958-220-45, the statement of activities should report the gross amounts of revenues and expenses for an NFP's ongoing major or central operations and activities; gains and losses may be reported as net amounts if they result from peripheral or incidental transactions or from other events and circumstances that may be largely beyond the control of the NFP and its management. The frequency of the events and the significance of the gross revenues and expenses distinguish major or central events from peripheral or incidental events. Events are ongoing major and central activities if they are normally part of an NFP's strategy and it normally carries on such activities or if the event's gross revenues or expenses are significant in relation to the NFP's annual budget.

3.31 Paragraphs 4–8 of FASB ASC 958-220-45 discuss the classification by net asset class of revenues, expenses, and gains and losses. The determination of the net asset class in which revenues and gains and losses are reported is based on the existence or absence of donor-imposed restrictions and the type of restriction. A statement of activities should report revenues as increases in unrestricted net assets unless the use of the assets received is limited by donor imposed restrictions. All expenses should be reported as decreases in unrestricted net assets. Gains should be reported as increases and losses as decreases in unrestricted net assets unless their use is temporarily or permanently restricted by explicit donor stipulations or by law.

3.32 Pursuant to FASB ASC 958-220-45-3, *reclassifications*, which are defined in the FASB ASC glossary as the simultaneous increase of one net asset class and decrease of another, should be reported as separate items. FASB ASC 958-220-45-13 describes the events that require reclassifications of net assets, including donor-imposed restrictions that are fulfilled by the NFP or that expire with the passage of time or the death of a split-interest agreement's beneficiary.

3.33 Paragraphs 6–7 of FASB ASC 958-220-55 illustrates the requirement for the display of an appropriately labeled subtotal within a statement of activities for the change in a class of net assets before the effects of discontinued operating segments. NFPs should apply the appropriate disclosure and display requirements of, among other things, FASB ASC 250, *Accounting Changes and Error Corrections*; FASB 205-20-45 for discontinued operations; and FASB ASC 220-20-45-1 for unusual or infrequently occurring items. Corrections of prior-period errors are not included in change in net assets. Instead, in accordance with FASB ASC 250-10-45, any error in the financial statements of a prior period discovered after the financial statements are issued or are available to be issued should be reported by restating the prior-period financial statements. The cumulative effect of the error on periods prior to those presented should be made to the opening balance(s) of the appropriate class(es) of net assets of the earliest year presented.

3.34 The cumulative effect of a change in accounting principle also is not included in change in net assets. Instead, it is reported through retrospective application of the new accounting principle to all prior periods, unless it is impracticable to do so (or transition guidance for a newly issued standard requires otherwise). The cumulative effect of the change to the new accounting principle on periods prior to those presented should be made to the opening balance(s) of the appropriate class(es) of net assets of the earliest year presented. FASB ASC 250 provides examples of display and further information about accounting changes and corrections of errors, including discussions of impracticability and materiality. Paragraph 11.60 provides guidance if an NFP corrects net asset classifications previously reported in prior years' financial statements.

3.35 As noted in FASB ASC 958-205-45-1, particular formats for the statement of activities are neither prescribed nor prohibited, in part because similar prescriptions and proscriptions do not exist for business entities. FASB ASC 958-205-55-11 suggests three ways that items could be sequenced: (*a*) revenues and gains first, then expenses, then losses; reclassifications, which must be shown separately, are reported with revenues and gains; (*b*) revenues, expenses, gains and losses, and reclassifications shown last; and (*c*) certain revenues, less directly related expenses, followed by a subtotal, then other revenues, other expenses, gains and losses, and reclassifications. Those items could be arranged in other ways, and other subtotals may be included.

3.36 Pursuant to FASB ASC 958-220-45-9, classifying revenues, expenses, gains, and losses within classes of net assets does not preclude incorporating additional classifications within a statement of activities. For example, within a class or classes of net assets, an NFP may classify items as follows: operating and nonoperating, expendable and nonexpendable, earned and unearned, recurring and nonrecurring, or in other ways.

© Update 3-1 *Accounting and Reporting*: Presentation of Net Periodic Pension Cost and Net Periodic Postretirement Benefit Cost

FASB ASU No. 2017-07, *Compensation—Retirement Benefits (Topic 715): Improving the Presentation of Net Periodic Pension Cost and Net Periodic Postretirement Benefit Cost*, issued in March 2017, is effective for NFPs for annual periods beginning after December 15, 2018, and interim periods within annual periods beginning after December 15, 2019. Early adoption is permitted as of the beginning of an annual period for which financial statements have not been issued or made available for issuance.

FASB ASU No. 2017-07 requires that an employer separate pension and postretirement costs into service and other cost components. The service cost portion would be presented in the same financial statement line item as the related compensation costs arising from services rendered by the pertinent employees during the period. The other components of net benefit cost are required to be presented separately, outside of an intermediate measure of operations, if one is presented.

This edition of the guide has not been updated to reflect changes as a result of this ASU; however, the paragraph that follows will be updated in a future edition.

Readers are encouraged to consult the full text of the ASU on FASB's website at www.fasb.org.

3.37 Paragraphs 9–12 of FASB ASC 958-220-45 discuss reporting a measure of operations. If an intermediate measure of operations, such as an excess or deficit of operating revenues over expenses, is reported in a statement of activities, (*a*) a note to financial statements should describe the nature of the reported measure of operations or the items excluded from operations if the NFP's use of the term *operations* is not apparent from the details provided on the face of the statement, and (*b*) it must be in a financial statement that, at a minimum, reports the change in unrestricted net assets for the period. Some limitations on an NFP's use of an intermediate measure of operations are imposed by other standards. For example, if a subtotal such as income from operations is presented, it should include the following amounts:

a. An impairment loss recognized for a long-lived asset (or asset group) to be held and used pursuant to FASB ASC 360-10-45-4

b. Any gain or loss recognized on the sale of a long-lived asset (or disposal group) if that asset (or group) is not a component of the NFP pursuant to FASB ASC 360-10-45-5

c. Costs associated with an exit or disposal activity that does not involve a discontinued operation pursuant to FASB ASC 420-10-45-3

d. Amortization expenses and impairment losses recognized on intangible assets including goodwill pursuant to FASB ASC 350-30-45-2 and FASB ASC 350-20-45-2

3.38 FinREC believes that in the absence of guidance specific to NFPs, as a best practice, most items that a business entity would report as part of other comprehensive income would be presented by an NFP in the statement of activities outside of an intermediate measure of operations, if one is presented. (Those items are listed in FASB ASC 220-10-45-10A.) However, unrealized gains and losses on available-for-sale and held-to-maturity securities, although reported in other comprehensive income by a business entity, would be the exception to that suggested practice. Unrealized gains and losses are typically presented as described in paragraphs 4.84–.89 because most NFPs do not classify investments into the three categories used in FASB ASC 320-10. For example, an NFP might report the following in its statement of activities:

Change in unrestricted net assets from operations	XX,XXX
Foreign currency translation adjustments	X,XXX
Prior service costs or credits associated with pension benefits[a]	X,XXX
Gains or losses associated with pension benefits that are not recognized immediately as a component of net periodic benefit cost[a]	X,XXX
Investment return in excess of amounts designated for current operations	X,XXX
Change in unrestricted net assets	$XX,XXX

[a] These two lines may be combined if desired.

When doing so, it is important to remember that all changes for the reporting period are reported as part of (that is, above) change in net assets. Paragraphs 3.32–.33 discuss presentation of corrections of errors and changes in accounting principles.

3.39 Classification of revenues, expenses, gains and losses, and reclassifications is discussed in greater detail in subsequent chapters of this guide. Paragraphs 4.86–.89 describe reporting investment return in a statement of activities that includes an intermediate measure of operations. Chapter 13, "Expenses, Gains, and Losses," discusses alternative ways of reporting costs related to sales of goods and services and the direct costs of special events.

Reporting Expenses, Including in a Statement of Functional Expenses

3.40 FASB ASC 958-720-05-4 states that to help donors, creditors, and others assess an NFP's service efforts, including the costs of its services and how it uses resources, a statement of activities or notes to financial statements should provide information about expenses reported by their functional classification, such as major classes of program services and supporting activities. In contrast, FASB ASC 958-205-45-6 states that a natural classification of expenses may include expense categories such as salaries, rent, electricity, interest expense, depreciation, awards and grants to others, and professional fees.

3.41 FASB ASC 958-205-45-6 provides guidance for presenting a statement of functional expenses, which is useful in associating expenses with service efforts and accomplishments. A statement of functional expenses reports information about expenses by their functional classes, as well as information about expenses by their natural classification in a matrix format in a separate financial statement—statement of functional expenses. To the extent that expenses are reported by other than their natural classification (such as salaries included in cost of goods sold or facility rental costs of special events reported as direct benefits to donors), they should be reported by their natural classification if a statement of functional expenses is presented. For example, salaries, wages, and fringe benefits that are included as part of the cost of goods sold on the statement of activities should be included with other salaries, wages, and fringe benefits in the statement of functional expenses. In addition, as discussed in FASB ASC 958-205-45-6, expenses that are netted against investment revenues should be reported by their functional classification on the statement of functional expenses (if the NFP presents that statement).

3.42 FASB ASC 958-720-45-15 requires that voluntary health and welfare entities provide a statement of functional expenses. Pursuant to FASB ASC 958-720-45-16, other NFPs are encouraged, but not required, to provide information about expenses by their natural expense classification. FinREC has observed diversity in practice in the implementation of these standards, in part because of the diversity in applying the definition of a voluntary health and welfare entity. To achieve consistency of reporting as well as the goal of FASB in encouraging disclosure of expenses by their natural classification, FinREC recommends that all NFPs that are supported by the general public present a statement of functional expenses as a basic financial statement or in the notes to the financial statements.

3.43 For example, an NFP could be presumed to be supported by the general public if contributions are 20 percent to 30 percent or more of total revenue and support, including both cash and in-kind contributions recognized in the financial statements but excluding government support. (Conversely, an NFP that receives contributions of less than 20 percent of total revenue and support is presumed not to be supported by the general public.) If the percentage of contributions to total revenue and support guideline is met, an NFP should consider the facts and circumstances surrounding its contributions. For example, a very large contribution from a single donor might overcome the presumption that an NFP is supported by the general public.

3.44 Although a statement of functional expenses potentially can be useful to donors of any NFP, FinREC considered an NFP's cost to prepare the statement and have it audited as an additional primary financial statement. To limit the recommendation to situations for which the benefit of the statement of functional expenses is most likely to exceed those costs, FinREC recommends that a statement of functional expenses be presented by NFPs that receive a significant portion of its total revenues and support in the form of contributions from individuals, federated fund-raisers, corporations, and foundations.

3.45 Paragraphs 13.53.63 include information useful in determining the major programs to include in a statement of activities and in a statement of functional expenses. NFPs frequently report similar levels of major classes of program services and supporting activities in their statements of activities and statements of functional expenses.

Statement of Cash Flows[9]

Update 3-2 *Accounting and Reporting*: Statement of Cash Flows

FASB ASU No. 2016-15, *Statement of Cash Flows (Topic 230): Classification of Certain Cash Receipts and Cash Payments (a consensus of the Emerging Issues Task Force)*, was issued in August 2016 to increase the consistency of reporting the following cash flows: debt prepayment or debt extinguishment costs, settlement of debt instruments with coupon interest rates that are insignificant in relation to the effective interest rate of the borrowing (such as zero-coupon bonds), cash payments made to settle a contingent consideration liability arising from an acquisition, proceeds from the settlement of insurance claims, proceeds from the settlement of corporate-owned life insurance policies, distributions received from equity method investees, and beneficial interests in securitization transactions. In addition, the ASU includes guidance for classification of cash receipts and payments that have aspects of more than one class of cash flows.

FASB ASU No. 2016-15 is effective for NFPs for fiscal years beginning after December 15, 2018, and interim periods within fiscal years beginning after December 15, 2019. Early adoption is permitted.

This edition of the guide has not been updated to reflect changes as a result of this FASB ASU; however, the section that follows will be updated in a future edition. Readers are encouraged to consult the full text of the FASB ASU on FASB's website at www.fasb.org.

[9] Readers preparing financial statements in accordance with the amendments in FASB ASU No. 2016-14 should use appendix A to this chapter (paragraph 3.194) for guidance in preparing the statement of financial position, the statement of activities, and the statement of cash flows.

Update 3-3 *Accounting and Reporting*: Statement of Cash Flows

FASB ASU No. 2016-18, *Statement of Cash Flows (Topic 230): Restricted Cash (a consensus of the FASB Emerging Issues Task Force)*, was issued in October 2016 to increase the consistency of reporting cash flows into and out of restricted cash accounts. It requires that a statement of cash flows explain the change during the period in the total of cash, cash equivalents, and amounts generally described as restricted cash or restricted cash equivalents. It does not define restricted cash.

FASB ASU No. 2016-18 is effective for NFPs for fiscal years beginning after December 15, 2018, and interim periods within fiscal years beginning after December 15, 2019. Early adoption is permitted.

This edition of the guide has not been updated to reflect changes as a result of this FASB ASU; however, the section that follows will be updated in a future edition. Readers are encouraged to consult the full text of the FASB ASU on FASB's website at www.fasb.org.

3.46 FASB ASC 958-230 describes the unique standards relating to a statement of cash flows of an NFP. In addition to that industry-specific guidance, an NFP should follow all effective provisions of FASB ASC unless the specific provision explicitly exempts NFPs or its subject matter precludes such applicability. For example, NFPs should apply the guidance contained in FASB ASC 230, *Statement of Cash Flows*, that does not conflict with the industry guidance.

3.47 FASB ASC 230-10-10-1 explains that the primary purpose of a statement of cash flows is to provide relevant information about the cash receipts and cash payments of an entity during a period. FASB ASC 230-10-45-10 requires that the statement of cash flows classify cash receipts and cash payments as resulting from investing, financing, or operating activities. Exhibit 3-1, "Classification of Cash and Cash Flows," provides examples of cash flows unique to or common to NFPs and their appropriate classification. FASB ASC 958-230-55-5 requires separate disclosure of noncash investing and financing activities (for example, receiving contributions of buildings, securities, or recognized collection items).

Exhibit 3-1

Classification of Cash and Cash Flows

Cash and Cash Equivalents
• Cash held temporarily in the long-term investment portfolio (until suitable investments are identified) is excluded from cash and cash equivalents in accordance with FASB ASC 958-205-55-7 and should be disclosed in the note that defines cash and cash equivalents.
Operating Cash Flows
• Unrestricted cash contributions. • Restricted contributions, provided that the contributed resources are not restricted for fixed assets, endowments, split-interest gifts, and other long-term purposes. • Cash receipts resulting from the sale of donated financial assets (for example, donated debt or equity instruments) that upon receipt were directed without any NFP-imposed limitations for sale and were converted nearly immediately into cash, provided that the donor did not restrict the use of the contributed resources to a long-term purpose. • Agency transactions are generally included as operating activities.
Investing Cash Flows
• Gross purchases of investments should be adjusted for amounts payable for investment purchases at period ends to arrive at cash outflows for purchases. • Gross sales of investments, which should be adjusted for amounts receivable from investment sales at period ends to arrive at cash inflows from sales.
Financing Cash Flows
• Securities lending would generally be classified as a financing activity. • Cash receipts resulting from the sale of donated financial assets (for example, donated debt or equity instruments) that upon receipt were directed without any NFP-imposed limitations for sale and were converted nearly immediately into cash if the donor restricted the use of the contributed resources to a long-term purpose. • Contributions restricted for fixed assets, endowments, split-interest gifts, and other long-term purposes should be reported as a financing activity; the amount would be the actual cash received, not the change in the contributions receivable. • Changes in cash overdrafts generally are considered financing activities and not as operating activities.
Noncash Transactions
• If construction in process and other fixed asset purchases are included in accounts payable at the fiscal year end, they should be disclosed as a noncash transaction and excluded from the change in accounts payable.

Classification of Cash and Cash Flows—*continued*

- Contributions of securities should be disclosed as a noncash transaction and as an adjustment reducing the change in net assets to arrive at operating cash flows if the securities were retained as investments rather than converted nearly immediately into cash.
- Contributions of beneficial interests should be disclosed as a noncash transaction and as an adjustment reducing the change in net assets to arrive at operating cash flows.
- The net change in value for an interest rate swap should be a noncash adjustment to arrive at operating activities. The amount will not equal the amount in the statement of activities if the statement of activities amount includes amounts paid in cash.
- Debt refinancing and refundings are disclosed as a noncash activity if no cash is transferred to the NFP's control and it only enters into new terms (for example, change in interest rate, payment terms, and so forth). Any incremental borrowings are financing inflows.

3.48 The FASB ASC glossary defines *operating activities* as including all transactions and other events that are not defined as investing or financing activities. Operating activities generally involve producing and delivering goods and providing services. Per FASB ASC 958-230-55-4, operating activities also include cash received and paid in agency transactions.

3.49 Some NFPs receive resources in agency transactions, as discussed in chapter 5, "Contributions Received and Agency Transactions." For some of those NFPs, receiving resources as agents may be a primary component of their mission. Because cash flows from operating activities include cash flows from agency transactions, an NFP that acts as an agent as a primary component of its mission might consider presenting the statement of cash flows as the first financial statement in its set of financial statements to emphasize the importance of the information presented in that statement.

3.50 FASB ASC 230-10-45-25 encourages entities to report major classes of gross cash receipts and gross cash payments and their arithmetic sum—the net cash flow from operating activities (the direct method). Paragraphs 28–32 of FASB ASC 230-10-45 describe how to determine and report the amount of net cash flow from operating activities indirectly by adjusting the change in (total) net assets to reconcile it to net cash flow from operating activities (the indirect or reconciliation method). That reconciliation of the change in (total) net assets to the net cash flow from operating activities should be provided in a separate schedule if the direct method of reporting net cash flow from operating activities is used.

3.51 As discussed in FASB ASC 958-210-45-6, cash received with a donor-imposed restriction that limits its use to long-term purposes should not be classified on a statement of financial position with cash that is unrestricted and available for current use.[10] FASB ASC 958-230-55-3 explains that when an NFP reports cash received with a donor-imposed restriction that limits its use to long-term purposes in conformity with FASB ASC 958-210-45-6, an

---

[10] Paragraphs 3.09–.23 and .52–.53 discuss the classification on a statement of financial position of cash received with donor-imposed restrictions limiting its use to long-term purposes.

adjustment is necessary for the statement of cash flows to reconcile beginning and ending cash and cash equivalents. To report in conformity with FASB ASC 230, the receipt of a cash contribution that is restricted for the purchase of equipment should be reported as a cash flow from financing activities (using a caption such as contributions restricted for purchasing equipment), and it should be simultaneously reported as a cash outflow from investing activities (using a caption such as purchase of assets restricted to investment in property and equipment or, if the equipment was purchased in the same period, purchase of equipment). An adjustment to reconcile the change in net assets to net cash used or provided by operating activities would also be needed if the contributed asset is not classified as cash or cash equivalents on the statement of financial position. When the equipment is purchased in a subsequent period, both the proceeds from the sale of assets restricted to investment in the equipment and the purchase of the equipment should be reported as cash flows from investing activities.

3.52 FASB ASC 958-230-55-2 notes that not all assets of NFPs that meet the definition of *cash equivalents* in the FASB ASC glossary are cash equivalents for purposes of preparing statements of financial position and cash flows. Restrictions can prevent them from being included as cash equivalents even if they otherwise qualify. For example, short-term highly liquid investments are not cash equivalents if they are purchased with resources that have donor-imposed restrictions that limit their use to long-term investment. Further, FASB ASC 230-10-45-6 states that an entity should establish a policy concerning which short-term, highly liquid investments that satisfy the definition of cash equivalents are treated as cash equivalents. FASB ASC 230-10-50-1 requires entities to disclose their policy for determining which items are treated as cash equivalents.

3.53 For example, an NFP may hold a portion of its donor-restricted endowment portfolio in cash or instruments with maturities of less than three months. In accordance with FASB ASC 958-210-45-6, those amounts should not be classified with cash or other assets that are unrestricted and available for current use, and thus should be excluded from cash and cash equivalents. Similarly, as discussed in paragraph 3.21, cash and instruments with maturities of less than three months that are identified as a board-designated endowment fund may be excluded from cash and cash equivalents.

3.54 As discussed in chapter 4, "Cash, Cash Equivalents, and Investments," NFPs sometimes apply a spending rate to their investment return. The existence of a spending rate does not affect the classification of cash inflows and outflows on the statement of cash flows. Sales of investments are investing activities even in circumstances in which the NFP uses the sales proceeds to fund current operations. For example, assume NFP has an endowment of $10 million and a spending rate of 5 percent ($500,000). Further, assume interest and dividends are $200,000 and sales of endowment investments in the current year are $800,000. In that circumstance, presumably $300,000 of sales of endowment investments would be used for spending. The NFP should report the full $800,000 of sales of endowment investments as cash inflows from investing activities.

Comparative Financial Information

3.55 FASB ASC 958-205-45-8 provides guidance if NFPs present comparative information for a prior year or years only in total rather than by net asset class.[11] Such summarized information may not include sufficient detail to constitute a presentation in conformity with GAAP. If the prior year's financial information is summarized and does not include the minimum information required by FASB ASC 958, *Not-for-Profit Entities* (for example, if the statement of activities does not present revenues, expenses, gains, and losses by net asset class), the nature of the prior year information should be described by the use of appropriate titles on the face of the financial statements and in a note to the financial statements. The use of appropriate titles includes a phrase such as with summarized financial information for the year ended June 30, 20PY, following the title of the statement or column headings that indicate the summarized nature of the information. Labeling the prior year summarized financial information for comparative purposes only without further disclosure in the notes to financial statements would not constitute the use of an appropriate title.

3.56 An example of a note to the financial statements[12] that describes the nature of the prior period(s) information would be as follows:

> The financial statements include certain prior year summarized comparative information in total but not by net asset class. Such information does not include sufficient detail to constitute a presentation in conformity with GAAP. Accordingly, such information should be read in conjunction with the Organization's financial statements for the year ended June 30, 20PY, from which the summarized information was derived.

3.57 When an NFP presents summarized prior-year financial statements that do not include sufficient detail to constitute a presentation in conformity with GAAP, FinREC recommends including all the disclosures required by GAAP for the prior year.

Reporting of Related Entities, Including Consolidation

> **Update 3-4 *Accounting and Reporting*: Gains and Losses on Sales of Nonfinancial Assets**
>
> FASB ASU No. 2017-05, *Other Income—Gains and Losses from the Derecognition of Nonfinancial Assets (Subtopic 610-20): Clarifying the Scope of Asset Derecognition Guidance and Accounting for Partial Sales of Nonfinancial Assets*, was issued in February 2017 to clarify the scope of FASB ASC 610-20. Among its amendments, it requires that the guidance in FASB ASC 610-20 apply to transfers of nonfinancial assets to a joint venture or other equity method investee.
>
> FASB ASU No. 2017-05 is effective concurrently with the amendments in FASB ASU No. 2014-09, *Revenue from Contracts with Customers (Topic 606)*. As a result, most NFPs will apply the new standards for annual reporting periods beginning after December 15, 2018, and interim periods within annual periods beginning after December 15, 2019. However, NFPs that have issued, or are conduit bond obligors for, securities that are traded, listed, or quoted

[11] Chapter 14, "Reports of Independent Auditors," discusses auditors' reports on comparative financial information.

[12] Because the note discusses information that does not pertain to the current-period financial statements, the note is not considered to be part of the current-period financial statements.

on an exchange or an over-the-counter market are required to apply the standards for annual reporting periods beginning after December 15, 2017, including interim periods within that reporting period.

This edition of the guide has not been updated to reflect changes as a result of this ASU; however, the section that follows will be updated in a future edition. Readers are encouraged to consult the full text of the ASU on FASB's website at www.fasb.org.

3.58 FASB ASC 810-10-10-1 states that the purpose of consolidated financial statements is to present, primarily for the benefit of the shareholders and creditors of the parent entity, the results of operations and the financial position of a parent entity and its subsidiaries essentially as if the group were a single entity with one or more branches or divisions. There is a presumption that consolidated financial statements are more meaningful than separate statements and that they are usually necessary for a fair presentation when one of the entities in the group directly or indirectly has a controlling financial interest in the other entities.

3.59 The guidance for reporting of related entities in this chapter is organized as follows:

- Relationships with another NFP
- Relationships with a for-profit entity
- Consolidation of a special-purpose leasing entity

Pursuant to FASB ASC 810-10-15-17, NFPs do not apply the guidance for variable interest entities in FASB ASC 810, *Consolidation*, to their relationships with other entities.

3.60 The appropriate guidance depends upon an initial assessment of whether the related entity is a for-profit entity or an NFP. Using the definition of an NFP from the FASB ASC glossary (see paragraph 1.01 of this guide), an NFP should determine whether the related entity is also an NFP. FinREC believes that often in cases in which an NFP has an interest in an entity with a nonprofit corporation or a nonprofit membership corporation structure, that entity will meet that definition. FinREC also believes that often in cases in which an NFP has an interest in an entity with a noncorporate structure (such as a partnership, limited liability partnership, or similar entity), that entity is not an NFP, either because of the existence of ownership interests or because it provides lower costs or other economic benefits directly and proportionally to the owners, members, or participants, or both. After making that determination, the flowcharts in supplement A of this chapter, "Flowcharts," and exhibit 3-2, "Relationships of a Not-for-Profit Reporting Entity," can assist in applying the accounting standards.

3.61 Chapter 4 provides guidance about reporting ownership of for-profit entities in circumstances in which the objective is to invest in the entity for investment return (including an objective to realize current income, capital appreciation, or both) and the entities are not required to be consolidated. If the interest is in an entity that provides goods or services that accomplish the purpose or mission for which the NFP exists or that serves the NFP's administrative purposes, the NFP would follow the guidance in this chapter.

Ⓒ Update 3-5 *Accounting and Reporting*: Financial Assets and Financial Liabilities

FASB ASU No. 2016-01, *Financial Instruments—Overall (Subtopic 825-10): Recognition and Measurement of Financial Assets and Financial Liabilities*, issued in January 2016, is effective for NFPs for fiscal years beginning after December 15, 2018, and interim periods within fiscal years beginning after December 15, 2019, and cannot be adopted earlier than for fiscal years beginning after December 15, 2017. However, NFPs may elect not to disclose the information about fair value of financial instruments measured at amortized cost (paragraphs 10–19 of FASB ASC 825-10-50) in any financial statements that have not yet been made available for issuance.

The "Pending Content" resulting from this ASU changes the measurement of equity securities without readily determinable fair value and the disclosures related to those investments, although an NFP is still allowed to elect to report them at fair value. The amendments also change disclosure requirements for financial instruments. This ASU is discussed further in the preface.

FASB ASU No. 2018-03, *Technical Corrections and Improvements to Financial Instruments—Overall (Subtopic 825-10): Recognition and Measurement of Financial Assets and Financial Liabilities*, issued in February 2018, includes technical corrections and improvements related to FASB ASU No. 2016-01. FASB ASU No. 2018-03 has the same effective date as FASB ASU No. 2016-01. Entities may early adopt the amendments for fiscal years beginning after December 15, 2017, including interim periods within those fiscal years, provided they have adopted FASB ASU No. 2016-01.

This edition of the guide has not been updated to reflect changes as a result of these ASUs; however, the text that follows will be updated in a future edition. Readers are encouraged to consult the full text of the ASU at FASB's website at www.fasb.org.

3.62 Exhibit 3-2 describes some common relationships with other entities and identifies where these relationships are discussed in this chapter and in FASB ASC. Exhibit 3-2 and this chapter summarize certain guidance in FASB ASC but are not intended as a substitute for reading the guidance itself.

Exhibit 3-2

Relationships of a Not-for-Profit Reporting Entity[a]

Relationship	FASB ASC Reference	Discussion in This Chapter
Relationships With Not-for-Profit Entities (NFPs)		
The reporting entity is the sole corporate member of an NFP.	Use the guidance in FASB ASC 958-810-25-2 and 954-810-45-3A.	Paragraph 3.65
The reporting entity has a controlling financial interest through direct or indirect ownership of a majority voting interest in the other NFP.	Use the guidance in FASB ASC 958-810-25-2.	Paragraphs 3.65–.66
The reporting entity controls another NFP through a majority voting interest in its board and has an economic interest in that other entity.	Use the guidance in FASB ASC 958-810-25-3.	Paragraphs 3.67–.69
The reporting entity controls an NFP through a form other than majority ownership, sole corporate membership, or majority voting interest in the board of the other entity and has an economic interest in that other entity.	Use the guidance in FASB ASC 958-810-25-4.	Paragraph 3.70
The reporting entity has control over another NFP or an economic interest in the other, but not both.	Use the guidance in FASB ASC 958-810-25-5.	Paragraph 3.71
The reporting entity receives distributions from a related fund-raising entity, but it does not control that entity.	Use the guidance in the "Transfers of Assets to a Not-for-Profit Entity or Charitable Trust that Raises or Holds Contributions for Others" subsections of FASB ASC 958-605.	Paragraphs 5.28–.32

Relationships of a Not-for-Profit Reporting Entity—*continued*

Relationship	FASB ASC Reference	Discussion in This Chapter
Relationships With For-Profit Entities		
The reporting entity owns a majority of a for-profit entity's common voting stock.	Use the guidance in the "General" subsections of FASB ASC 810-10 to determine whether that interest constitutes a controlling financial interest.	Paragraphs 3.73–.74
The reporting entity owns 50 percent or less of the common voting stock of an investee and can exercise significant influence over the investee's operating and financial policies.	Except where the reporting entity elects to report such interests at fair value in accordance with the "Fair Value Option" sections of FASB 825-10, use the equity method of accounting in accordance with FASB ASC 323-10.	Paragraphs 3.76–.79
The reporting entity owns 50 percent or less of the common voting stock of an investee and the reporting entity neither controls nor can exercise significant influence over the investee's operating and financial policies.	Use the guidance in FASB ASC 958-320-35-1 or FASB ASC 958-325-35. The interest may also be reported at fair value in conformity with the "Fair Value Option" sections of FASB 825-10.	Paragraph 3.80
The reporting entity is the general partner of a for-profit limited partnership or similar entity, such as a limited liability company that has governing provisions that are the functional equivalent of a limited partnership.	Use the guidance in paragraphs 1129 of FASB ASC 958-810-25 to determine whether the general partner within the group controls and, therefore, should consolidate the limited partnership or similar entity. If not required to consolidate, use the equity method, unless that partnership interest is reported at fair value in conformity with the "Fair Value Option" sections of FASB 825-10.	Paragraphs 3.81–.83 and paragraphs 3.87–.89

(continued)

Relationships of a Not-for-Profit Reporting Entity—*continued*

Relationship	FASB ASC Reference	Discussion in This Chapter
The reporting entity is a limited partner of a for-profit limited partnership or similar entity.	Use the guidance in paragraphs 11–29 of FASB ASC 958-810-25 to determine if a limited partner has a controlling financial interest and, therefore, should consolidate. If not required to consolidate, the Financial Reporting Executive Committee (FinREC) observes that entities typically use by analogy the guidance in FASB ASC 970-323 for noncontrolling interests in entities engaged in activities other than real estate activities.	Paragraphs 3.84–.89
The reporting entity has an interest in a limited liability company.	Use the guidance in paragraphs 11–29 of FASB ASC 958-810-25 if the functional equivalent of a limited partnership, or paragraphs 114 of FASB ASC 810-10-25 and FASB ASC 323-10 if the functional equivalent of a regular corporation. Unless required to consolidate, the reporting entity may elect to report its interest at fair value in accordance with the "Fair Value Option" sections of FASB 825-10.	Paragraphs 3.90–.91
The reporting entity has a noncontrolling interest that constitutes more than a minor interest in a for-profit partnership, limited liability entity, or similar entity engaged in real estate activities.	Except where the reporting entity elects to report such interests at fair value in accordance with the "Fair Value Option" sections of FASB 825-10, use the equity method in accordance with the guidance in FASB ASC 970-323.	Paragraphs 3.92–.97

Relationships of a Not-for-Profit Reporting Entity—*continued*

Relationship	FASB ASC Reference	Discussion in This Chapter
The reporting entity has a noncontrolling interest that constitutes a minor interest in a for-profit partnership, limited liability entity, or similar entity engaged in real estate activities.	Entities typically apply the guidance in FASB ASC 958-325.	Paragraph 3.96
The reporting entity has an interest in a general partnership that is engaged in activities other than real estate activities, or the reporting entity has the power to control a general partnership engaged in real estate activities.	Except when the reporting entity elects to report such interests at fair value, in accordance with the "Fair Value Option" sections of FASB 825-10, FinREC observes that entities typically use by analogy the guidance in FASB ASC 970-810.	Paragraphs 3.98–.99
The reporting entity has a contractual management relationship with another entity and that contractual management relationship has a term that is either the entire remaining legal life of the other entity or a period of 10 years or more.	Use the guidance in the "Consolidation of Entities Controlled by Contract" subsections of FASB ASC 810-10 to determine whether the arrangement constitutes a controlling financial interest.	Paragraph 3.75
Relationships With Special Entities		
The reporting entity has a relationship with a variable interest entity (VIE) as described in the "Variable Interest Entities" subsections of FASB ASC 810-10.	Pursuant to FASB ASC 810-10-15-17, NFPs are not subject to the "Variable Interest Entities" subsections of FASB ASC 810-10 unless the NFP is used by a business entity in a manner similar to a VIE in an effort to circumvent the provisions of those standards.	

(continued)

Relationships of a Not-for-Profit Reporting Entity—*continued*

Relationship	FASB ASC Reference	Discussion in This Chapter
The reporting entity is engaged in a leasing transaction with a special purpose entity lessor.	Use the guidance in paragraphs 8–10 of FASB ASC 958-810-25 and paragraphs 7–16 of FASB ASC 958-810-55 to determine whether to consolidate the lessor.	Paragraphs 3.100–.101
The reporting entity has entered into a joint operating agreement with another entity. They agree to jointly conduct an activity while sharing the operating results and a residual interest upon dissolution.	If housed in a separate legal entity, use the method of accounting for that entity type; otherwise, use the guidance in FASB ASC 808, *Collaborative Arrangements.*	Paragraphs 3.136–.137
The reporting entity is a sponsor in a research and development arrangement.	Use the guidance in FASB ASC 810-30.	Paragraph 3.75
The reporting entity has another type of relationship with a special purpose entity.	FinREC observes that entities typically analogize to the guidance in paragraphs 8–10 of FASB ASC 958-810-25 and paragraphs 7–16 of FASB ASC 958-810-55.	

[a] As discussed in paragraph 3.61, the guidance in this table applies to relationships with entities that provide goods or services that accomplish the purpose or mission for which the NFP exists or that serve the NFP's administrative purposes.

Relationships With Another NFP

3.63 FASB ASC 958-810-05-3 explains that ownership of NFPs may be evidenced in various ways because NFPs may exist in various legal forms, such as corporations issuing stock, corporations issuing ownership certificates, membership corporations issuing membership certificates, joint ventures, and partnerships, among other forms. FASB ASC 958-810-25-1 states that a relationship with another NFP can take any one of the following forms, which determines the appropriate reporting:

a. A controlling financial interest through direct or indirect ownership of a majority voting interest or sole corporate membership in the other NFP (see FASB ASC 958-810-25-2)

b. Control of a related but separate NFP through a majority voting interest in the board of that NFP by means other than ownership or sole corporate membership and an economic interest in that other NFP (see FASB ASC 958-810-25-3)

c. An economic interest in the other NFP combined with control through means other than those listed in (*a*)–(*b*) (see FASB ASC 958-810-25-4)

d. Either an economic interest in the other NFP or control of the other NFP, but not both (see FASB ASC 958-810-25-5)

3.64 For purposes of applying the guidance for relationships with other NFPs, the FASB ASC glossary defines *control* as the direct or indirect ability to determine the direction of management and policies through ownership, contract, or otherwise. The FASB ASC glossary defines *economic interest* as an NFP's interest in another entity that exists if any of the following criteria are met: (*a*) the other entity holds or utilizes significant resources that must be used for the unrestricted or restricted purposes of the NFP, either directly or indirectly by producing income or providing services, or (*b*) the NFP is responsible for the liabilities of the other entity. FASB ASC 958-810-55-6 provides the following examples of economic interests:

a. Other entities solicit funds in the name of and with the expressed or implied approval of the NFP, and substantially all of the funds solicited are intended by the contributor or are otherwise required to be transferred to the NFP or used at its discretion or direction.

b. An NFP transfers significant resources to another entity whose resources are held for the benefit of the NFP.

c. An NFP assigns certain significant functions to another entity.

d. An NFP provides or is committed to provide funds for another entity or guarantees significant debt of another entity.

e. An NFP has a right to or a responsibility for the operating results of another entity. Or upon dissolution, the reporting entity is entitled to the net assets or is responsible for any deficit of another entity.

For purposes of applying the guidance for relationships with other NFPs, the FASB ASC glossary defines *control* as the direct or indirect ability to determine the direction of management and policies through ownership, contract, or otherwise. The FASB ASC glossary defines *economic interest* as an NFP's interest in another entity that exists if any of the following criteria are met: (*a*) the other entity holds or utilizes significant resources that must be used for the purposes of the NFP, either directly or indirectly by producing income or providing services, or (*b*) the NFP is responsible for the liabilities of the other entity. FASB ASC 958-810-55-6 provides the following examples of economic interests:

a. Other entities solicit funds in the name of and with the expressed or implied approval of the NFP, and substantially all of the funds solicited are intended by the contributor or are otherwise required to be transferred to the NFP or used at its discretion or direction.

b. An NFP transfers significant resources to another entity whose resources are held for the benefit of the NFP.

c. An NFP assigns certain significant functions to another entity.

d. An NFP provides or is committed to provide funds for another entity or guarantees significant debt of another entity.

e. An NFP has a right to or a responsibility for the operating results of another entity. Or upon dissolution, the reporting entity is entitled to the net assets or is responsible for any deficit of another entity.[13]

Controlling Financial Interests

3.65 FASB ASC 958-810-25-2 states that an NFP with a controlling financial interest in another NFP through direct or indirect ownership of a majority voting interest or sole corporate membership in that other NFP should consolidate that other NFP, unless control does not rest with the majority owner or sole corporate member (for instance, if the other NFP is in legal reorganization or in bankruptcy or if other legal or contractual limitations are so severe that control does not rest with the sole corporate member), in which case consolidation is prohibited, as discussed in FASB ASC 810-10-15-10. See FASB ASC 958-810-25-2A for an example in which control may not rest with the holder of the majority voting interest. (This example is included in the next paragraph.) Sole corporate membership in an NFP, like ownership of a majority voting interest in a for-profit entity, should be considered a controlling financial interest, unless control does not rest with the sole corporate member (for instance, if the other [membership] entity is in bankruptcy or if other legal or contractual limitations are so severe that control does not rest with the sole corporate member).

3.66 FASB ASC 958-810-25-2A provides the following example of a situation in which control might not rest with the holder of the majority voting interest. In some situations, certain actions require approval by a supermajority vote of the board. Such voting requirements might overcome the presumption of control by the owner or holder of a majority voting interest. FASB ASC 958-810-55-4A provides the following implementation guidance for that paragraph. An NFP should exercise judgment in evaluating such situations. If supermajority voting requirements exist—for example, a specified supermajority of the board is needed to approve fundamental actions such as amending the articles of incorporation or dissolving the entity—an NFP should consider whether those voting requirements have little or no effect on the ability to control the other entity's operations or assets or, alternatively, whether those voting requirements are so restrictive that they call into question whether control rests with the holder of the majority voting interest. Paragraphs 2–14 of FASB ASC 810-10-25 may be helpful in considering whether the inability of the majority voting interest to unilaterally approve certain actions due to supermajority voting requirements is substantial enough to overcome the presumption of control.

Control Combined With an Economic Interest

3.67 FASB ASC 958-810-25-3 states that in the case of control of a related but separate NFP through a majority voting interest in the board of the other NFP by means other than ownership or sole corporate membership and an economic interest in that other NFP, consolidation is required, unless control does not rest with the holder of the majority voting interest, in which case consolidation is prohibited. An NFP has a majority voting interest in the board of

[13] The amendments in FASB ASU No. 2016-14 are effective for annual financial statements issued for fiscal years beginning after December 15, 2017 (for example, years ending December 31, 2018 and years ending June 30, 2019), and for interim periods within fiscal years beginning after December 15, 2018. Application to interim financial statements is permitted but not required in the initial year of application. Early application of the amendments is permitted.

another NFP if it has the direct or indirect ability to appoint individuals that together constitute a majority of the votes of the fully constituted board (that is, including any vacant board positions).

3.68 FASB ASC 958-810-55-5 provides the following example of a majority voting interest in the board of another entity:

> Entity B has a five-member board, and a simple voting majority is required to approve board actions. Entity A will have a majority voting interest in the board of Entity B if Entity A has the ability to appoint three or more of Entity B's board members. If three of Entity A's board members, employees, or officers serve on the board of Entity B but Entity A does not have the ability to require that those members serve on the Entity B board, Entity A does not have a majority voting interest in the board of Entity B.

3.69 Technical Questions and Answers (Q&A) section 6140.10, "Consolidation of Political Action Committee,"[14] provides the following example:

> An NFP may be related to another NFP that performs political activities that the reporting entity does not wish to perform, perhaps because performing those activities may threaten the reporting entity's tax exempt status, the reporting entity is precluded from conducting such activities, or for other reasons. For example, a membership entity may establish and sponsor a political action committee (PAC) whose mission is to further the interests of the membership entity. The resources held by the PAC are used for the purposes of the membership entity and the governing board of the PAC is appointed by the board of the membership entity. In the circumstances described, both control and economic interest are present and the PAC should be consolidated. Control through a majority voting interest in the board of the PAC exists because the governing board of the PAC is appointed by the board of the membership entity. An economic interest exists because the PAC holds significant resources that must be used for the purposes of the membership entity.

3.70 FASB ASC 958-810-25-4 states that control of a related but separate NFP in which the reporting entity has an economic interest may take forms other than majority ownership interest, sole corporate membership, or majority voting interest in the board of the other NFP; for example, control may be through contract or affiliation agreement. In circumstances such as these, consolidation is permitted but not required, and the reporting entity should disclose the following information required by FASB ASC 958-810-50-2 if it does not present consolidated financial statements:

a. Identification of the other NFP and the nature of its relationship with the reporting entity that results in control

b. Summarized financial data of the other NFP, which should include the following information:

    i. Total assets, liabilities, net assets, revenue, and expenses

    ii. Resources that are held for the benefit of the reporting entity or that are under its control

---

[14] All Q&A sections can be found in *Technical Questions and Answers*.

c. The disclosures required by paragraphs 1–6 of FASB ASC 850-10-50

Control or Economic Interest, But Not Both

3.71 FASB ASC 958-810-25-5 states that the existence of control or an economic interest, but not both, precludes consolidation. Pursuant to FASB ASC 958-810-50-3, the reporting entity should disclose the information about related parties required by paragraphs 1–6 of FASB ASC 850-10-50 for these relationships.

Relationships With a For-Profit Entity

3.72 FASB ASC 958-810-15-4 lists the locations of guidance for reporting relationships between NFPs and for-profit entities. Paragraphs 3.73–.101 provide a brief summary of that guidance but are not intended as a substitute for reading the referenced subtopics.

Controlling Financial Interests in Entities Other Than Limited Partnerships or Similar Legal Entities

3.73 FASB ASC 958-810-15-4(a) states that an NFP with a controlling financial interest through direct or indirect ownership of a majority voting interest in a for-profit entity that is other than a limited partnership or similar legal entity should apply the guidance in the "General" subsections of FASB ASC 810-10. Per FASB ASC 810-10-15-8 and FASB ASC 810-10-25-1, the usual condition for a controlling financial interest is ownership of a majority voting interest, and, therefore, as a general rule ownership by one reporting entity, directly or indirectly, of more than 50 percent of the outstanding voting shares of another entity is a condition pointing toward consolidation. The power to control may also exist with a lesser percentage of ownership, for example, by contract, lease, agreement with other stockholders, or by court decree. However, when applying the guidance in FASB ASC 810-10, NFPs are not subject to the guidance for variable interest entities.

3.74 FASB ASC 810-10-15-10(a)(1) provides an exception if control does not rest with the majority owner. For instance, a majority-owned subsidiary should not be consolidated if any of the following are present: (*a*) the subsidiary is in legal reorganization; (*b*) the subsidiary is in bankruptcy; (*c*) the subsidiary operates under foreign exchange restrictions, controls, or other governmentally-imposed uncertainties that are so severe that they cast significant doubt on the parent's ability to control the subsidiary; and (*d*) the rights of noncontrolling shareholder(s) are so restrictive that it is questioned whether control rests with the majority owner. The guidance in paragraphs 2–14 of FASB ASC 810-10-25 should be applied in assessing the impact of consolidation on noncontrolling shareholder approval or veto rights.

3.75 Additional guidance for determining whether a controlling financial interest exists is located as follows:

a. Per FASB ASC 810-30-15, if the reporting entity has a research and development arrangement in which all of the funds for the research and development activities are provided by the sponsor, the reporting entity should follow the guidance in FASB ASC 810-30 to determine whether and how the sponsor should consolidate that arrangement. Per FASB ASC 810-10-15-17, NFPs do not apply tests to determine whether the research and development entity is determined to be a VIE.

b. Per FASB ASC 810-10-15-3(c), if the reporting entity has a contractual management relationship with another entity, the reporting entity should use the guidance in the "Consolidation of Entities Controlled by Contract" subsections of FASB ASC 810-10 to determine whether the arrangement constitutes a controlling financial interest. Per FASB ASC 810-10-15-17, NFPs do not apply tests to determine whether the other entity is a VIE.

Noncontrolling Interests in Voting Stock

3.76 FASB ASC 958-810-15-4(c) states that an NFP that owns 50 percent or less of the voting stock in a for-profit entity should apply the guidance in FASB ASC 323-10 unless that investment is reported at fair value in conformity with the guidance described in FASB ASC 958-810-15-4(e).

3.77 FASB ASC 323-10 requires that the equity method of accounting be used if investments in common stock or in-substance common stock (or both common stock and in-substance common stock), including investments in common stock of joint ventures, give the investor the ability to exercise significant influence over operating and financial policies of an investee, even though the investor holds 50 percent or less of the common stock or in-substance common stock (or both common stock and in-substance common stock).

3.78 *Significant influence* is defined by paragraphs 6–11 of FASB ASC 323-10-15. Determining the ability of an investor to exercise significant influence is not always clear and applying judgment is necessary to assess the status of each investment. An investment of less than 20 percent of the voting stock of an investee should lead to a presumption that an investor does not have the ability to exercise significant influence unless such ability can be demonstrated. Conversely, an investment (direct or indirect) of 20 percent or more of the voting stock of an investee should lead to a presumption that, in the absence of predominant evidence to the contrary, an investor has the ability to exercise significant influence over an investee. However, this presumption can be overcome in certain instances. FASB ASC 323-10-15-6 provides indications of significant influence that could exist even if the investor owns less than 20 percent of the voting stock. Paragraphs 10–11 of FASB ASC 323-10-15 provide examples of indications that an investor may be unable to exercise significant influence. Additionally, according to FASB ASC 323-10-25-2, the limitations under which a majority-owned subsidiary should not be consolidated, as discussed in paragraph 3.74, should also be applied as limitations to the use of the equity method.

3.79 An NFP that would otherwise be required to use the equity method may be permitted to report at fair value by making an election pursuant to FASB ASC 825-10-25-1 (the fair value option).

3.80 If the NFP's ownership of voting stock in a for-profit business entity is not sufficient to result in a controlling financial interest or significant influence, the NFP may be required to report its interest in the for-profit business entity at fair value in conformity with FASB ASC 958-320-35-1. That guidance applies to equity securities with a readily determinable fair value, other than consolidated subsidiaries and investments reported under the equity method. If the voting stock does not have a readily determinable fair value and the ownership is not sufficient to result in a controlling financial interest or significant influence, the investment is within the scope of FASB ASC 958-325. For more information, see paragraph 4.38. Alternatively, the NFP can report the individual investment at fair value if it makes an election pursuant to FASB ASC 825-10-25-1 (the fair value option).

Limited Partnerships and Similar Entities

3.81 FASB ASC 958-810-15-4(b) states that an NFP that is a general partner or a limited partner of a for-profit limited partnership or a similar legal entity (such as a limited liability company that has governing provisions that are the functional equivalent of a limited partnership) should apply the guidance in paragraphs 1129 of FASB ASC 958-810-25 and paragraphs 16A16I of FASB ASC 958-810-55 unless that partnership interest is an investment within the scope of FASB ASC 958-325 and the NFP has elected to report all other investments at fair value. FASB ASC 958-810-25-11 states that a similar legal entity is an entity (such as a limited liability company) that has governing provisions that are the functional equivalent of a limited partnership. In those entities, a managing member is the functional equivalent of a general partner, and a nonmanaging member is the functional equivalent of a limited partner. Throughout those paragraphs, any reference to a limited partnership includes limited partnerships and similar legal entities. (See paragraph 3.61 for a discussion of which relationships with for-profit entities are discussed in chapter 4 of this guide.)

3.82 Paragraphs 1129 of FASB ASC 958-810-25 discuss the potential consolidation of limited partnerships and similar entities. Paragraphs 1213 of FASB ASC 958-810-25 state that the general partners in a limited partnership are presumed to control a limited partnership regardless of the extent of the general partners' ownership interest in the limited partnership. If a limited partnership has multiple general partners, the determination of which, if any, general partner within the group controls and, therefore, should consolidate the limited partnership is based on an analysis of the relevant facts and circumstances. Paragraphs 1429 of FASB ASC 958-810-25 provide guidance for purposes of assessing whether the limited partners' rights might preclude a general partner from controlling a limited partnership. For example, the general partner might not control a limited partnership in either of the two following circumstances:

- The limited partners have the substantive ability to dissolve the partnership or otherwise remove the general partner without cause (referred to as substantive kick-out rights, which are further defined in paragraphs 1920 of FASB ASC 958-810-25).
- The limited partners have the ability to effectively participate in significant decisions that would be expected to be made in the ordinary course of the limited partnership's business (referred to as substantive participating rights, which are further defined in paragraphs 2127 of FASB ASC 958-810-25).

FASB ASC 958-810-25-15 states that if the presumption of control by the general partner(s) is overcome, each of the general partners should account for its investment in the limited partnership using the equity method of accounting.

3.83 Alternatively, if the presumption of control by the general partner(s) is overcome, an NFP that is a general partner of a for-profit limited partnership or similar entity may report the partnership interest at fair value (instead of the equity method) if it makes an election pursuant to FASB ASC 825-10-25-1 (the fair value option).

3.84 If instead an NFP is a limited partner in a for-profit limited partnership, the accounting depends upon the level of ownership and the type of activities conducted by the limited partnership. If one limited partner has a controlling financial interest (paragraph 3.85), that limited partner consolidates the limited partnership. If the limited partner has a noncontrolling interest and the limited partnership is engaged in real estate activities, refer to the standards discussed in paragraphs 3.92–.97. If the limited partner has a noncontrolling interest and the limited partnership is engaged in activities other than real estate, practice is diverse. Some NFPs apply the guidance in FASB ASC 970-323 even though they are not required to do so. That guidance is summarized in paragraphs 3.86–.89.

3.85 FASB ASC 958-810-25-16 states that if one limited partner directly or indirectly owns more than 50 percent of a limited partnership's kick-out rights through voting interests, then that limited partner is deemed to have a controlling financial interest in the limited partnership and should consolidate the limited partnership. However, if noncontrolling limited partners have substantive participating rights, then the limited partner with a majority of kick-out rights through voting interests does not have a controlling financial interest and would not consolidate. Substantive kick out rights are described in paragraphs 1920 of FASB ASC 958-810-25, and substantive participating rights are described in paragraphs 2127 of FASB ASC 958-810-25.

3.86 If an NFP is a limited partner with a noncontrolling interest and the limited partnership is engaged in activities other than real estate, the NFP might analogize to the guidance in FASB ASC 970-323-25-6, which states that the equity method of accounting is generally appropriate for accounting by limited partners for their noncontrolling investments in limited partnerships. However, the NFP may elect to report that investment at fair value, in accordance with the "Fair Value Option" sections of FASB ASC 825-10. If a limited partner's interest is so minor that the limited partner has virtually no influence over partnership operating and financial policies, accounting for the investment using the guidance in FASB ASC 958-325 may be appropriate.

3.87 For example, NFP A sets up a limited partnership with 2 other NFPs (NFP B and NFP C) to form a shared services entity for computing services. NFP A is the general partner and has an 80 percent interest. NFP B and NFP C each have a 10 percent interest, including a right to or responsibility for the partnership's operating results. NFP A (the general partner) should consolidate the limited partnership unless the presumption of its control is overcome by the rights of the limited partners. If NFP A is in control, FinREC recommends that NFP B and NFP C apply the equity method of accounting by analogy to the guidance in FASB ASC 970-323-25-6. Alternatively, NFP B or NFP C may report at fair value instead of the equity method by making an election pursuant to the "Fair Value Option" subsections of FASB ASC 825-10.

3.88 If NFP B and NFP C have substantive kick-out or participating rights, the presumption of NFP A's control is overcome, and NFP A should report using the equity method. If one of the limited partners has a controlling financial interest, that limited partner consolidates the limited partnership (paragraph 3.85). FinREC recommends that the noncontrolling limited partner(s) use the equity method by analogy to the guidance in FASB ASC 970-323-25-6. Alternatively, any noncontrolling limited partner may report at fair value instead of the equity method by making an election pursuant to the "Fair Value Option" subsections of FASB ASC 825-10.

3.89 Note that the accounting in the preceding example would remain the same even if NFP A (the general partner) had a 5 percent interest and NFP B and NFP C each had a 47.5 percent interest. It is the combination of the facts that (*a*) NFP A controls the decisions that would be expected to be made in the ordinary course of the limited partnership's business and (*b*) neither NFP B nor NFP C has substantive kick-out rights or participating rights, that determines the accounting—not the percentage interest in the limited partnership.

Limited Liability Companies

3.90 Some limited liability companies have governing provisions that are the functional equivalent of a regular corporation. Pursuant to FASB ASC 810-10-25-3, the guidance in paragraphs 114 of FASB ASC 810-10 is used to determine whether an interest in that type of limited liability company should be consolidated. Those standards are described briefly in paragraphs 3.73–.74.

3.91 Other limited liability companies maintain a specific ownership account for each investor—similar to a partnership capital account structure—and are the functional equivalent of a limited partnership (FASB ASC 323-30-35-3). Pursuant to the "Pending Content" in FASB ASC 958-810-25-11, the guidance in paragraphs 1129 of FASB ASC 958-810-25 and paragraphs 16A–16I of FASB ASC 958-810-55 address the potential consolidation of a limited liability company that is similar to a limited partnership. Those standards are described briefly in paragraphs 3.81.89. (See paragraph 3.61 for a discussion of which relationships with for-profit entities are discussed in chapter 4 of this guide.)

Noncontrolling Interests in Real Estate Partnerships and Similar Real Estate Entities

3.92 FASB ASC 958-810-15-4(d) states that an NFP with a more than minor noncontrolling interest in a for-profit real estate partnership, a for-profit real estate limited liability company, or similar for-profit real estate legal entity should report its noncontrolling interest in such an entity using the equity method in accordance with the guidance in FASB ASC 970-323 unless that interest is reported at fair value by making an election pursuant to the "Fair Value Option" subsections of FASB ASC 825-10. Pursuant to FASB ASC 810-10-15-17, when applying the guidance in FASB ASC 970-323, NFPs apply the guidance without considering whether the for-profit real estate entity is possibly a VIE.

3.93 Although not registrants, NFPs might analogize to the guidance in FASB ASC 323-30-S99-1 to determine what is more than a minor interest. FASB ASC 323-30-S99-1 states that the SEC staff understands that practice generally has viewed investments of more than 3 percent to 5 percent to be more than minor.

3.94 To determine whether the interest is noncontrolling, an NFP should apply the following guidance:

- If the for-profit real estate entity is a general partnership, apply the guidance in FASB ASC 970-810-25-1.
- If the for-profit real estate entity is a limited partnership or a similar legal entity, apply the guidance in paragraphs 1129 of FASB

ASC 958-810-25 and paragraphs 16A16I of FASB ASC 958-810-55 (described briefly in paragraphs 3.81.89).

- If the for-profit real estate entity is a limited liability company that maintains a specific ownership account for each investor (similar to a partnership capital account structure), apply the guidance in paragraphs 1129 of FASB ASC 958-810-25 and paragraphs 16A16I of FASB ASC 958-810-55 (described briefly in paragraphs 3.81.89).
- If the for-profit real estate entity is a limited liability company that is similar to a corporation (that is, it does not maintain a specific ownership account for each investor), apply the guidance for corporations in FASB ASC 810-10 and FASB ASC 323-10.

3.95 FASB ASC 970-323-25-2 states that a noncontrolling investor in a real estate general partnership should account for its investment by the equity method and should be guided by the provisions of FASB ASC 323, *Investments—Equity Method and Joint Ventures*. FASB ASC 970-810-25-3 requires that the general partners of a real estate limited partnership apply the equity method of accounting to their interests in either of the following circumstances: (1) if the presumption of control by the general partners is overcome by the rights of the limited partners, or (2) if the presumption of control by the general partners is not overcome by the rights of the limited partners and no single general partner controls the limited partnership. An NFP that would otherwise be required to use the equity method may be permitted to report at fair value by making an election pursuant to FASB ASC 825-10-25-1 (the fair value option).

3.96 FASB ASC 970-323-25-8 states that noncontrolling limited partners in a real estate limited partnership should account for their investments by the equity method and should be guided by the provisions of FASB ASC 323. However, a limited partner's interest may be so minor that the limited partner may have virtually no influence over partnership operating and financial policies. Such a limited partner is, in substance, in the same position with respect to the investment as an investor that owns a minor common stock interest in a corporation, and, accordingly, accounting for the investment using the cost method may be appropriate. An NFP may be permitted to report at fair value by making an election pursuant to FASB ASC 825-10-25-1 (the fair value option).

3.97 NFP D establishes a limited partnership with 2 other NFPs (NFP E and NFP F). The limited partnership buys a building that will house the NFPs' computer labs. NFP D is the general partner and has a 10 percent interest. NFP E and NFP F each have 45 percent interests including a right to and responsibility for the partnership operating results, but the limited partners do not have substantive kick-out or participating rights. As the general partner, NFP D should consolidate the limited partnership as discussed in paragraphs 3.81–.82. NFP E and NFP F should apply the equity method of accounting in accordance with FASB ASC 958-810-15-4(d). Alternatively, NFP E or NFP F may report at fair value in conformity with the fair value option described in FASB ASC 825-10.

General Partnerships

3.98 An NFP that is a partner in a general partnership might apply the guidance in FASB ASC 970-810 even though it is not required to do so. FASB

ASC 970-810 provides consolidation guidance for partners of general partnerships engaged in real estate activities. FASB ASC 970-810-25-1 states that a general partnership that is directly or indirectly controlled by an investor is, in substance, a subsidiary of the investor. Ownership by one entity, directly or indirectly, of over 50 percent of the partnership voting interests is a condition pointing toward consolidation. However, if partnership voting interests are not clearly indicated, a condition that would usually indicate control is ownership of a majority (over 50 percent) of the financial interests in profits or losses. FASB ASC 970-810-25-2 states that a noncontrolling investor in a general partnership should account for its investment by the equity method and be guided by the provisions of FASB ASC 323. Similarly, as noted in paragraph 3.95, FASB ASC 970-323-25-2 states that a noncontrolling investor in a real estate general partnership should account for its investment by the equity method and should be guided by the provisions of FASB ASC 323. Alternatively, the reporting entity may elect to report that noncontrolling interest at fair value, in accordance with the "Fair Value Option" sections of FASB ASC 825-10.

3.99 For example, NFP G and NFP H hold their annual meetings at the same time and in the same city. In order to save costs, they create a general partnership to conduct their meetings, negotiating better rates with the hotel and realizing other synergies. Though they share equally in the decision-making, NFP G has a 70 percent ownership account and NFP B has a 30 percent ownership account. Neither NFP G nor NFP H has control because they share equally in decision-making and therefore neither entity should consolidate the general partnership. If they analogize to the guidance in FASB ASC 970-810-25-2, the NFPs would apply the equity method to their general partnership interests. Alternatively, the NFPs might elect to report their interests at fair value in accordance with the "Fair Value Option" sections of FASB ASC 825-10. (See paragraph 3.137 for a similar example involving an unincorporated joint venture.)

Consolidation of a Special-Purpose Leasing Entity

> **Update 3-6 *Accounting and Reporting*: Leases**
>
> FASB ASU No. 2016-02, *Leases (Topic 842)*, issued February 2016, changes the accounting for leases, primarily by the recognition of lease assets and lease liabilities by lessees for those leases classified as operating leases under current GAAP. FASB ASU No. 2016-02 is effective for fiscal years beginning after December 15, 2018, including interim periods within those fiscal years, for NFPs that have issued, or are conduit bond obligors for, securities that are traded, listed, or quoted on an exchange or an over-the-counter market. For all other NFPs, the amendments in this ASU are effective for fiscal years beginning after December 15, 2019, and interim periods within fiscal years beginning after December 15, 2020. Early adoption is permitted.
>
> This edition of the guide has not been updated to reflect changes as a result of this ASU; however, the section that follows will be updated in a future edition. Readers are encouraged to consult the full text of the ASU on FASB's website at www.fasb.org.

3.100 FASB ASC 958-810-25-8 states that an NFP lessee should consolidate a special-purpose entity lessor (SPE) if all of the following conditions are met:

a. Substantially all of the activities of the SPE involve assets that are to be leased to a single lessee.

b. The expected substantive residual risks and substantially all the residual rewards of the leased asset(s) and the obligation imposed by the underlying debt of the SPE reside directly or indirectly with the lessee through means such as any of the following:

i. The lease agreement.

ii. A residual value guarantee through, for example, the assumption of first-dollar-of-loss provisions.

iii. A guarantee of the SPE's debt.

iv. An option granting the lessee a right to either (*a*) purchase the leased asset at a fixed price or at a defined price other than fair value determined at the date of exercise, or (*b*) receive any of the lessor's sales proceeds in excess of a stipulated amount.

c. The owner (or owners) of record of the SPE has not made an initial substantive residual equity capital investment that is at risk during the entire lease term. This criterion should be considered met if the majority owner (or owners) of the lessor is not an independent third party, regardless of the level of capital investment.

3.101 FinREC believes that 3 percent is the minimum acceptable investment to qualify as an initial, substantive, residual equity capital investment. A greater investment may be necessary depending on the facts and circumstances, including the credit risk associated with the lessee and market risk factors associated with the leased property. For example, the cost of borrowed funds for the transaction might be indicative of the risk associated with the transaction and whether an equity investment greater than 3 percent is needed. Additional information about the application of the preceding criteria and guidance for consolidation of the SPE is located in FASB ASC 958-840.

Consolidated Financial Statements

3.102 FASB ASC 810-10-25-15 states that the industry-specific guidance in FASB ASC that is applicable to a subsidiary should be retained in consolidation of that subsidiary. For example, if a hospital is a subsidiary of a university, the hospital specific guidance for reporting patient revenues and investments is retained in the consolidated statements. Likewise, the specialized guidance for the insurance industry (FASB ASC 944, *Financial Services—Insurance*) is retained when a wholly owned captive insurance company is consolidated with its parent. Further, if an NFP parent has a controlling financial interest in a for-profit subsidiary, and that subsidiary has interests in other for-profit entities, the subsidiary should consider the guidance in FASB ASC 810, including the "Variable Interest Entity" subsections, when evaluating those interests for consolidation. However, as discussed in Q&A section 6140.26, "Not-for-Profit Entity with For-Profit Subsidiary and Adoption of FASB ASU No. 2014-02 on Goodwill," a for-profit subsidiary that is part of a consolidated reporting entity that is an NFP is not permitted to use the amortization accounting alternative in FASB ASU No. 2014-02, *Intangibles—Goodwill and Other (Topic 350): Accounting for Goodwill (a consensus of the Private Company Council)*, in the consolidated financial statements. The for-profit subsidiary could adopt that accounting alternative in its standalone financial statements.

Consolidation of an NFP

3.103 In circumstances in which the net assets of two or more NFPs are combined into a single set of financial statements as parent and subsidiary, the definitions of unrestricted, temporarily restricted, and permanently restricted net assets should be applied from the perspective of the reporting entity as a whole, looking through the existence of separate entities. This may result in classifications for the reporting entity that differ from classifications in the separate financial statements. (Similarly, classification of net assets should be considered from the reporting entity perspective when the net assets of a financially interrelated recipient entity are included in the financial statements of its beneficiary NFP and when the net assets of NFPs under common control are included in combined financial statements.) A related discussion about the presentation of restrictions on assets in consolidation is included in paragraphs 3.16 and 3.22.

In circumstances in which the net assets of two or more NFPs are combined into a single set of financial statements as parent and subsidiary, the definitions of net assets without donor restrictions and net assets with donor restrictions should be applied from the perspective of the reporting entity as a whole, looking through the existence of separate entities. This may result in classifications for the reporting entity that differ from classifications in the separate financial statements. (Similarly, classification of net assets should be considered from the reporting entity perspective when the net assets of a financially interrelated recipient entity are included in the financial statements of its beneficiary NFP and when the net assets of NFPs under common control are included in combined financial statements.) A related discussion about the presentation of restrictions on assets in consolidation is included in paragraphs 3A.16 and 3A.22 in appendix A of this chapter (paragraph 3.194).[15]

3.104 All or a portion of a subsidiary's unrestricted net assets might need to be reported as restricted net assets in the consolidated financial statements. In a subsidiary's separately issued financial statements, net assets are reported as unrestricted if the donor stipulations pertaining to the use of the contributed assets are no more specific than broad limits resulting from the nature of the NFP, the environment in which the NFP operates, and the purposes specified in the NFP's articles of incorporation or bylaws (or comparable documents for an unincorporated association). In the consolidated financial statements, however, the unrestricted net assets of the subsidiary arising from contributions (or investment income on donor-restricted endowment funds) would be reported as temporarily restricted net assets if in fact donor restrictions limit the use of the gift to a purpose narrower than that of the reporting entity. For example, a membership association has a subsidiary foundation that has as its sole mission to provide scholarships. Donors make unrestricted contributions to the subsidiary with the intent that the subsidiary use the contributions to support its mission, including granting scholarships and incurring fund-raising and general and administrative expenses. The gifts to the subsidiary are

[15] The amendments in FASB ASU No. 2016-14 are effective for annual financial statements issued for fiscal years beginning after December 15, 2017 (for example, years ending December 31, 2018 and years ending June 30, 2019), and for interim periods within fiscal years beginning after December 15, 2018. Application to interim financial statements is permitted but not required in the initial year of application. Early application of the amendments is permitted.

therefore classified as increases in unrestricted net assets in the separately issued financial statements of the subsidiary. However, when the subsidiary's financial statements are consolidated with those of the membership association, the classification of the net assets of the subsidiary would be changed to reflect that they are temporarily restricted net assets from the perspective of the consolidated financial statements. Likewise, investment income on donor-restricted endowment funds of the subsidiary would be reported as temporarily restricted net assets in the consolidated financial statements if they were required to be used for scholarships, even if an appropriation had released the time restriction.

All or a portion of a subsidiary's net assets without donor restrictions might need to be reported as net assets with donor restrictions in the consolidated financial statements. In a subsidiary's separately issued financial statements, net assets are reported as without donor restrictions if the donor stipulations pertaining to the use of the contributed assets are no more specific than broad limits resulting from the nature of the NFP, the environment in which the NFP operates, and the purposes specified in the NFP's articles of incorporation or bylaws (or comparable documents for an unincorporated association). In the consolidated financial statements, however, the net assets of the subsidiary arising from contributions (or investment income on donor-restricted endowment funds) would be reported as net assets with donor restrictions if in fact donor restrictions limit the use of the gift to a purpose narrower than that of the reporting entity. For example, a membership association has a subsidiary foundation that has as its sole mission to provide scholarships. Donors make contributions to the subsidiary with the intent that the subsidiary use the contributions to support its mission without restriction, including granting scholarships and incurring fund-raising and general and administrative expenses. The gifts to the subsidiary are therefore classified as increases in net assets without donor restrictions in the separately issued financial statements of the subsidiary. However, when the subsidiary's financial statements are consolidated with those of the membership association, the classification of the net assets of the subsidiary would be changed to reflect that they are net assets with donor restrictions from the perspective of the consolidated financial statements. Likewise, investment income on donor-restricted endowment funds of the subsidiary would be reported as net assets with donor restrictions in the consolidated financial statements if they were required to be used for scholarships, even if an appropriation had released the time restriction.[16]

3.105 Similarly, but less likely, all or a portion of a subsidiary's temporarily restricted net assets might need to be reported as unrestricted net assets in the consolidated financial statements. In the subsidiary's separately issued financial statements, net assets are reported as restricted if donor restrictions limit the use of the contributed assets to a purpose more specific than broad limits resulting from the nature of the NFP, the environment in which the NFP operates, and the purposes specified in the NFP's articles of incorporation or bylaws (or comparable documents for an unincorporated association). In the

---

[16] The amendments in FASB ASU No. 2016-14 are effective for annual financial statements issued for fiscal years beginning after December 15, 2017 (for example, years ending December 31, 2018 and years ending June 30, 2019), and for interim periods within fiscal years beginning after December 15, 2018. Application to interim financial statements is permitted but not required in the initial year of application. Early application of the amendments is permitted.

consolidated financial statements, however, the restricted net assets of the subsidiary arising from contributions (or investment income on donor-restricted endowment funds) would be reported as unrestricted net assets if in fact those donor restrictions are no more specific than broad limits resulting from the nature of the reporting entity, the environment in which it operates, and so on. For example, an NFP adoption agency has a subsidiary whose mission is to raise funds for various children's causes, including adoption, foster care, and parental training. If donors restrict their contributions for adoption services, the subsidiary classifies them as increases in restricted net assets. However, when the subsidiary's financial statements are consolidated with those of the adoption entity, the classification of the net assets of the subsidiary would be changed to reflect that they are unrestricted net assets from the perspective of the reporting entity, which remains primarily an adoption agency.

Similarly, but less likely, all or a portion of a subsidiary's net assets with donor restrictions might need to be reported as net assets without donor restrictions in the consolidated financial statements. In the subsidiary's separately issued financial statements, net assets are reported as having donor restrictions if donor restrictions limit the use of the contributed assets to a purpose more specific than broad limits resulting from the nature of the NFP, the environment in which the NFP operates, and the purposes specified in the NFP's articles of incorporation or bylaws (or comparable documents for an unincorporated association). In the consolidated financial statements, however, the net assets of the subsidiary arising from contributions (or investment return on donor-restricted endowment funds) would be reported as net assets without donor restrictions if in fact those donor restrictions are no more specific than broad limits resulting from the nature of the reporting entity, the environment in which it operates, and so on. For example, an NFP adoption agency has a subsidiary whose mission is to raise funds for various children's causes, including adoption, foster care, and parental training. If donors restrict their contributions for adoption services, the subsidiary classifies them as increases in net assets with donor restrictions. However, when the subsidiary's financial statements are consolidated with those of the adoption entity, the classification of the net assets of the subsidiary would be changed to reflect that they are without donor restrictions from the perspective of the reporting entity, which remains primarily an adoption agency.[17]

3.106 In addition, when the net assets of two or more NFPs are combined into a single set of financial statements as parent and subsidiary, there is no noncontrolling interest in the NFP subsidiary, even if the NFP parent has less than a complete interest. FASB ASC 958-810-25-6 provides the following example:

> An NFP may appoint 80 percent of the board of the other NFP. For NFPs other than health care entities (that is, within the scope of FASB ASC 954, *Health Care Entities*), if the conditions for consolidation in paragraphs 2–4 of FASB ASC 958-810-25 are met, the basis of that

[17] The amendments in FASB ASU No. 2016-14 are effective for annual financial statements issued for fiscal years beginning after December 15, 2017 (for example, years ending December 31, 2018 and years ending June 30, 2019), and for interim periods within fiscal years beginning after December 15, 2018. Application to interim financial statements is permitted but not required in the initial year of application. Early application of the amendments is permitted.

consolidation would not reflect a noncontrolling interest for the portion of the board that the reporting entity does not control because there is no ownership interest other than the interest of the reporting entity.

3.107 FASB ASC 958-810-50-1 requires that if consolidated financial statements are presented, the reporting entity (parent) should disclose any restrictions made by entities outside of the reporting entity on distributions from the controlled NFP (subsidiary) to the parent and any resulting unavailability of the net assets of the subsidiary for use by the parent.

3.108 NFPs that otherwise would be prohibited from presenting consolidated financial statements under paragraph 3.71, but that presented consolidated financial statements prior to December 1994 in conformity with the guidance in AICPA Statement of Position 78-10, *Accounting Principles and Reporting Practices for Certain Nonprofit Organizations*, may continue to do so.

Consolidation of a For-Profit Entity

3.109 NFPs typically provide varying levels of detail in presenting information about for-profit subsidiaries, ranging from (*a*) full consolidated amounts with no discrete information about the for-profit subsidiary to (*b*) consolidating financial statements providing the same level of detail about the for-profit subsidiary as would be presented in the for-profit subsidiary's separately issued financial statements. FinREC believes that in determining the relevance of the for-profit subsidiary, and therefore the most meaningful manner of presenting information about it in consolidated financial statements, best practice is for NFPs to consider the following factors:

- The size of the for-profit subsidiary in relation to the NFP parent. The larger the for-profit subsidiary is in relation to the NFP, the more likely it is that discrete information about the for-profit subsidiary would be meaningful to financial statement users.
- The activities of the for-profit subsidiary in relation to the mission of the NFP parent. The more marginal the activities of the for-profit subsidiary are to the mission of the NFP, the more likely it is that discrete information about the for-profit subsidiary would be meaningful to financial statement users.
- The need for creditors to have separate information about the for-profit subsidiary, including information about guarantees of the for-profit subsidiary's debt or limitations on transferring cash to or from the subsidiary. If the assets of a for-profit subsidiary are encumbered (for example, by mortgages, contracts, or other matters), it may be meaningful to include discrete information about the for-profit subsidiary's total assets, equity, and changes in equity, similar to the disclosures required to be reported by business entities pursuant to FASB ASC 280.

3.110 FinREC believes that NFPs should present such information in a manner that is most meaningful to financial statement users. FinREC recommends that a similar level of detail be included in each of the statement of financial position, the statement of activities, and the statement of cash flows. In circumstances in which the statement of financial position and the statement of activities include discrete information about a for-profit subsidiary, however, FinREC believes it may be meaningful for the statement of cash flows to include a similar level of detail about operating cash flows (that is, discrete information about the for-profit subsidiary), but display fully consolidated cash flows pertaining to investing and financing activities.

3.111 Paragraphs 3.112–.118 provide three examples of the guidance discussed in paragraphs 3.109–.110. These examples present one manner of displaying consolidated information; other presentations may also be appropriate.

Example A

3.112 NFP Trade Association creates a wholly owned for-profit subsidiary (For-Profit Training Facility) to provide continuing professional education to its members. For-Profit Training Facility subsidiary incurs debt in order to build a classroom building. The debt is secured solely by a mortgage on For-Profit Training Facility's assets. NFP Trade Association's mission includes providing training to its members. Although members could obtain training from other service providers, the training is integral to NFP Trade Association's overall mission.

3.113 It may be most meaningful to report For-Profit Training Facility's assets, liabilities, revenues, expenses, and cash flows as part of the overall activities of NFP Trade Association, without discrete information presented on the face of the financial statements about For-Profit Training Facility. However, the notes to the financial statements would include any material disclosures that relate only to the For-Profit Training Facility, such as to disclose any collateral-based debt for which the For-Profit Training Facility is obligated or any assets restricted solely for the use of the Facility.

Example B

3.114 NFP College creates a wholly owned for-profit subsidiary, For-Profit Day Care Center, that operates a day care center for the benefit of its students and faculty. The College does not use the day care center as a teaching resource for its students. For-Profit Day Care Center has no outstanding debt.

3.115 Because the day care center provides services to students, but is peripheral and incidental to the mission of the college, it may be most meaningful to report the assets, liabilities, activities, and cash flows of For-Profit Day Care Center in a manner similar to an auxiliary operation in the college's financial statements. (Auxiliary operations typically are reported on the statement of activities with one line for total revenues and one line for total expenses; the statement of financial position and statement of cash flows do not separate information associated with auxiliary operations.) Alternatively, it may be meaningful to present the operations of the day care center separately on the statement of activities.

Example C

3.116 NFP Community Organization received a contribution of 100 percent of the voting common stock of a For-Profit Plastics Company. The terms of the contribution agreement state that For-Profit Plastics Company's net income may be used for NFP Community Organization's general operations. NFP Community Organization is not involved in the day-to-day management of For-Profit Plastics Company.

3.117 If For-Profit Plastics Company is material to NFP Community Organization's financial statements, it may be meaningful to report the assets, liabilities, activities, and cash flows of For-Profit Plastics Company separately from those of NFP Community Organization. Acceptable methods of doing so include, but are not limited to, presenting (*a*) consolidating financial statements, or (*b*) consolidated financial statements with note disclosure of the assets, liabilities, net assets, activities, and cash flows of For-Profit Plastics Company.

Noncontrolling Interests

3.118 FASB ASC 958-810-45-1 describes how to report noncontrolling interests in the equity (net assets) of consolidated subsidiaries within the appropriate class(es) of net assets. Noncontrolling interests of consolidated subsidiaries should be reported as a separate component of the appropriate class of net assets in the consolidated statement of financial position of an NFP. That amount should be clearly identified and described (for example, as noncontrolling ownership interest in subsidiaries) to distinguish it from the components of net assets of the parent, which includes the parent's controlling financial interest in its subsidiaries. The effects of donor-imposed restrictions, if any, on a partially owned subsidiary's net assets should be reported in accordance with FASB ASC 958-205 and 958-320. Paragraphs 17–25 of FASB ASC 958-810-55 illustrate one way in which the consolidated financial statements of an NFP might satisfy the presentation and disclosure requirements for noncontrolling interests in a consolidated subsidiary and subsequent changes in ownership interests of that subsidiary.

3.119 In accordance with FASB ASC 958-810-50, the consolidated financial statements should provide a schedule of changes in consolidated net assets attributable to the parent and the noncontrolling interest. The schedule is typically included in notes to the consolidated financial statements, although it may appear on the face of financial statements, if practicable. That schedule should reconcile beginning and ending balances of the parent's controlling interest and the noncontrolling interests for each class of net assets for which a noncontrolling interest exists during the reporting period. At a minimum, the schedule includes the following:

- A performance indicator, if the reporting entity is an NFP health care entity (as described in FASB ASC 954-10-15)
- Amounts of discontinued operations
- Changes in ownership interests in a subsidiary, including investments by and distributions to noncontrolling interests acting in their capacity as owners, which should be reported separate from any revenues, expenses, gains, or losses and outside any measure of operations, if reported
- An aggregate amount of all other changes in unrestricted net assets (or other net asset classes, if restricted) for the period

  An aggregate amount of all other changes in net assets without donor restrictions and net assets with donor restrictions for the period[18]

An example of the schedule appears in FASB ASC 958-810-55-25.

---

[18] The amendments in FASB ASU No. 2016-14 are effective for annual financial statements issued for fiscal years beginning after December 15, 2017 (for example, years ending December 31, 2018 and years ending June 30, 2019), and for interim periods within fiscal years beginning after December 15, 2018. Application to interim financial statements is permitted but not required in the initial year of application. Early application of the amendments is permitted.

Parent-Only and Subsidiary-Only Financial Statements

3.120 FASB ASC 810-10-45-11 states that parent-entity financial statements may be needed in addition to consolidated financial statements and that consolidating financial statements, in which one column is used for the parent and other columns for particular subsidiaries or groups of subsidiaries, often are an effective means of presenting the pertinent information. However, consolidated financial statements are the general-purpose financial statements of a parent having one or more subsidiaries; thus, parent-entity financial statements are not a valid substitute for consolidated financial statements. Q&A section 1400.32, "Parent-Only Financial Statements and Relationship to GAAP," states that if consolidation is required under GAAP, no circumstances exist in which an entity may present parent-only financial statements without presenting related consolidated financial statements and claim that the parent-only financial statements are in conformity with GAAP. For example, if, as a condition of a legal or regulatory agreement, an NFP is required to submit parent-only financial statements without related consolidated financial statements as financial statements prepared in accordance with a special-purpose framework (as that term is used in AU-C section 800, *Special Considerations—Audits of Financial Statements Prepared in Accordance With Special Purpose Frameworks*[19]), the parent-only financial statements are not in accordance with GAAP. FinREC observes that GAAP does not preclude the issuance of subsidiary-only financial statements. Care should be taken, however, to include all disclosures required by FASB ASC 850, *Related Party Disclosures*, and other relevant GAAP.

Combined Financial Statements

3.121 FASB ASC 810-10-55-1B provides guidance for circumstances in which combined financial statements of commonly controlled entities would be useful. It states that there are circumstances in which combined financial statements (as distinguished from consolidated financial statements) of commonly controlled entities are likely to be more meaningful than their separate financial statements. For example, combined financial statements would be useful if one individual owns a controlling financial interest in several entities that are related in their operations. Combined financial statements might also be used to present the financial position and the results of operations of entities under common management. FASB ASC 810-10-45-10 states that if combined statements are prepared for a group of related entities, such as a group of commonly controlled entities, intra-entity transactions and profits or losses should be eliminated, and noncontrolling interests, foreign operations, different fiscal periods, or income taxes, should be treated in the same manner as in consolidated statements. (Paragraphs 3.102–.119 discuss presentation of consolidated financial statements.)

Mergers and Acquisitions

3.122 FASB ASC 958-805 provides guidance on a transaction or other event in which an NFP that is the reporting entity combines with one or more other NFPs, businesses, or nonprofit activities. Paragraphs 3.123–.135 summarize the guidance in FASB ASC 958-805, but are not a substitute for reading that subtopic.

---

[19] All AU-C sections can be found in AICPA *Professional Standards*.

3.123 FASB ASC 958-805-25-1 requires that an NFP determine whether that transaction or other event is a merger of NFPs or an acquisition by an NFP by applying the definitions. FASB ASC 958-805-55-1 states that ceding control to a new NFP is the sole definitive criterion for identifying a merger, and one entity obtaining control over the other is the sole definitive criterion for an acquisition. Paragraphs 1–31 of FASB ASC 958-805-55 provide guidance on distinguishing between a merger and an acquisition. FASB ASC 958-805-55-6 discusses some of the more common characteristics that distinguish a merger from an acquisition by an NFP. It states:

> For example, one entity appointing significantly more of the governing board of the newly formed entity, retaining significantly more of its key senior officers, or retaining its bylaws, operating policies, and practices substantially unchanged is more likely to be a feature of an acquisition than of a merger. Similarly, the relative financial strength and relative size of the participants in the combination may help to determine whether one participant is able to dominate the process leading to the combination. For example, if one entity is financially strong and the other is experiencing financial difficulty, the stronger entity may be able to dominate the transaction, which would indicate that the transaction is an acquisition rather than a merger. Similarly, a participant that is substantially larger than each of the others in terms of revenues, assets, and net assets may be able to dominate the transaction. However, relative size, like relative financial strength and the other indicators discussed, is only one characteristic that may help to distinguish between a merger and an acquisition in particular situations—none of the indicators, by itself, is determinative. As discussed in FASB ASC 958-805-55-1, ceding of control is the sole definitive criterion for a merger.

Merger of Not-for-Profit Entities

3.124 The FASB ASC glossary defines *merger of not-for-profit entities* as a transaction or other event in which the governing bodies of two or more NFPs cede control of those entities to create a new NFP. FASB ASC 958-805-25 requires that the NFP resulting from a merger (the new entity) account for the merger by applying the carryover method described in the "Merger of Not-for-Profit Entities" subsections of FASB ASC 958-805.

3.125 Applying the carryover method requires combining the assets and liabilities recognized in the separate financial statements of the merging entities as of the merger date (or that would be recognized if the entities issued financial statements as of that date), with certain adjustments. The new NFP does not recognize additional assets or liabilities, such as internally developed intangible assets, that GAAP did not require or permit the merging entities to recognize. However, if a merging entity's separate financial statements are not prepared in accordance with GAAP, those statements should be adjusted to GAAP before the new entity recognizes the assets and liabilities. The new NFP should carry forward at the merger date the merging entities' classifications and designations of their assets and liabilities unless one of the exceptions in FASB ASC 958-805-25-9 applies. Those exceptions are for certain modifications in contracts as a result of the merger and for conforming accounting policies to reflect a consistent method of accounting.

Acquisition by a Not-for-Profit Entity

3.126 The FASB ASC glossary defines *acquisition by a not-for-profit entity* as a transaction or other event in which an NFP acquirer obtains control of one or more nonprofit activities or businesses and initially recognizes their assets and liabilities in the acquirer's financial statements. An NFP should account for each acquisition of a business or nonprofit activity by applying the acquisition method described in the "Acquisition by a Not-for-Profit Entity" subsections of FASB ASC 958-805. That acquisition method is the same as the acquisition method described in FASB ASC 805, *Business Combinations*; however, FASB ASC 958-805 includes guidance on aspects of the items that are unique or especially significant to an NFP.

3.127 Pursuant to FASB ASC 805-10-05-4 as modified by FASB ASC 958-805-25, the following are steps for applying the acquisition method:

a. Identifying the acquirer

b. Identifying the acquisition date

c. Recognizing the identifiable assets acquired, the liabilities assumed, and any noncontrolling interest in the acquiree

d. Recognizing goodwill acquired or a contribution received, including consideration transferred

3.128 FASB ASC 805-10-25-4 requires that one of the combining entities be identified as the acquirer. The guidance on control and consolidation of NFPs should be used to identify the acquirer: For an NFP acquirer other than a health care entity the guidance to be used is the guidance in FASB ASC 958-810, including the guidance referenced in FASB ASC 958-810-15-4. (Consolidation of NFPs is discussed beginning at paragraph 3.58.) If that guidance does not clearly indicate which of the combining entities is the acquirer, the factors in paragraphs 42–46 of FASB ASC 958-805-55 should be considered in making that determination.

3.129 Paragraphs 6–7 of FASB ASC 805-10-25 require that the acquirer identify the acquisition date, which is the date on which it obtains control of the acquiree. The date on which the acquirer obtains control of the acquiree generally is the date on which the acquirer legally transfers the consideration (if any), acquires the assets, and assumes the liabilities of the acquiree—the closing date. In addition, FASB ASC 958-805-25-17 states that the date on which an NFP acquirer obtains control of an NFP with sole corporate membership generally also is the date on which the acquirer becomes the sole corporate member of that entity.

3.130 FASB ASC 805-20 requires that as of the acquisition date, the acquirer recognize, separately from goodwill, the identifiable assets acquired, the liabilities assumed, and any noncontrolling interest in the acquiree.[20] FASB ASC 805-50-25-4 permits an acquiree to irrevocably elect to apply pushdown accounting in its separate financial statements when the acquirer obtains control of the acquiree (that is, as of the acquisition date). Pushdown accounting refers to establishing a new basis for reporting assets and liabilities in the acquiree's financial statements based on the acquirer's basis. If it elects to change

[20] Reporting noncontrolling interests in financial statements is discussed in chapter 11, "Net Assets and Reclassification of Net Assets."

its basis, the acquiree would report its assets and liabilities at the acquirer's assigned value and record goodwill (if any).

3.131 In conformity with FASB ASC 958-805-30-6(b), an NFP acquirer determines the net of the acquisition-date amounts of the identifiable assets acquired and the liabilities assumed measured in accordance with FASB ASC 805-20 and FASB ASC 958-805. Most assets and liabilities are measured at fair value. However, FASB ASC 805-20-25-16 notes that there are limited exceptions to the recognition and measurement principles applicable to business combinations, including acquisitions by an NFP. The limited exceptions are specified in paragraphs 16–28 of FASB ASC 805-20-25, paragraphs 12–23 of FASB ASC 805-20-30, and paragraphs 11–26 of FASB ASC 958-805-25. Examples of items that are either not recognized or are measured at an amount other than their acquisition-date fair values include income taxes, employee benefits, assets held for sale, collections, conditional promises to give, donor relationships, and certain assets and liabilities arising from contingencies.

3.132 Next, in conformity with FASB ASC 958-805-30-6(a), an NFP acquirer determines the aggregate of the following:

a. The consideration transferred measured at its acquisition-date fair value (see paragraphs 10–13 of FASB ASC 958-805-30)

b. The fair value of any noncontrolling interest in the acquiree

c. In an acquisition by an NFP achieved in stages, the acquisition-date fair value of the acquirer's previously held equity interest in the acquiree

3.133 If the amount determined in accordance with FASB ASC 958-805-30-6(a) is greater than the amount determined in accordance with FASB 958-805-30-6(b), an NFP acquirer should determine whether the operations of the acquiree as part of the combined entity are expected to be predominantly supported by contributions and returns on investments. If not, in conformity with FASB ASC 958-805-25-28, an NFP acquirer should recognize goodwill as of the acquisition date, measured as of the acquisition date as required by FASB ASC 958-805-30-6. (Accounting for goodwill after acquisition is discussed in chapter 7, "Other Assets.") If instead the operations of the acquiree as part of the combined entity are expected to be predominantly supported by contributions and returns on investments, FASB ASC 958-805-25-29 states that an NFP acquirer should recognize a separate charge in its statement of activities as of the acquisition date, measured as the excess of FASB ASC 958-805-30-6(a) over FASB 958-805-30-6(b), rather than goodwill. *Predominantly supported* by means that contributions and returns on investments are expected to be significantly more than the total of all other sources of revenues.

3.134 If the amount determined in accordance with FASB ASC 958-805-30-6(b) is greater than the amount determined in accordance with FASB 958-805-30-6(a), FASB ASC 958-805-25-31 requires an NFP acquirer to recognize the inherent contribution received. The inherent contribution is measured as the excess of the amount in FASB ASC 958-805-30-6(b) over the amount in FASB ASC 958-805-30-6(a). The inherent contribution is reported as a separate credit in the statement of activities as of the acquisition date and, in accordance with FASB ASC 958-805-45-6, is classified on the basis of the type of restrictions imposed on the related net assets. FASB ASC 958-805-45-6 states that those restrictions include restrictions imposed on the net assets of the acquiree by a donor before the acquisition and those imposed by the donor of the business or nonprofit activity acquired, if any. Donor-restricted contributions are reported as restricted support even if the restrictions are met in the same reporting period in which the acquisition occurs. That is, the acquirer should not apply the reporting exception in FASB ASC 958-605-45-4 (see paragraph 5.85) to restricted net assets acquired in an acquisition.

If the amount determined in accordance with FASB ASC 958-805-30-6(b) is greater than the amount determined in accordance with FASB 958-805-30-6(a), FASB ASC 958-805-25-31 requires an NFP acquirer to recognize the inherent contribution received. The inherent contribution is measured as the excess of the amount in FASB ASC 958-805-30-6(b) over the amount in FASB ASC 958-805-30-6(a). The inherent contribution is reported as a separate credit in the statement of activities as of the acquisition date and, in accordance with the "Pending Content" in FASB ASC 958-805-45-6, is classified on the basis of the donor restrictions imposed on the related net assets. The "Pending Content" in FASB ASC 958-805-45-6 states that those restrictions include restrictions imposed on the net assets of the acquiree by a donor before the acquisition and those imposed by the donor of the business or nonprofit activity acquired, if any. Donor-restricted contributions are reported as donor-restricted support even if the restrictions are met in the same reporting period in which the acquisition occurs. That is, the acquirer should not apply the reporting exception in FASB ASC 958-605-45-4 (see paragraph 5.85) to net assets with donor restrictions acquired in an acquisition.[21]

Disclosures

3.135 FASB ASC 958-805-50 requires an NFP to disclose information that enables users of its financial statements to evaluate the nature and financial effect of a merger of NFPs or an acquisition by an NFP. If acquisitions are individually immaterial but are material collectively, the NFP should disclose the required information in the aggregate. Disclosures are also required if an acquisition date is after the reporting date but before the financial statements are issued or available for issue (unless the initial accounting for an acquisition by an NFP is incomplete at the time the financial statements are issued or available for issue, in which case the acquirer describes which disclosures could not be made and the reason why they could not be made). If amounts that relate to acquisitions that occurred in the current or previous reporting periods are adjusted, the NFP should disclose information that enables users of its financial statements to evaluate the financial effects of those adjustments in the current reporting period.

Collaborative Arrangements

3.136 FASB ASC 808 provides display and disclosure guidance for a collaborative arrangement. The FASB ASC glossary defines a *collaborative arrangement* as a contractual arrangement that involves a joint operating activity (see FASB ASC 808-10-15-7) that involves two (or more) parties who are

---

[21] The amendments in FASB ASU No. 2016-14 are effective for annual financial statements issued for fiscal years beginning after December 15, 2017 (for example, years ending December 31, 2018 and years ending June 30, 2019), and for interim periods within fiscal years beginning after December 15, 2018. Application to interim financial statements is permitted but not required in the initial year of application. Early application of the amendments is permitted.

both (*a*) active participants in the activity (see paragraphs 8–9 of FASB ASC 808-10-15), and (*b*) exposed to significant risks and rewards dependent on the commercial success of the activity (see paragraphs 10–13 of FASB ASC 808-10-15). A collaborative arrangement within the scope of FASB ASC 808 is not primarily conducted through a separate legal entity created for that activity. FASB ASC 808-10-45-1 states that an entity should not apply the equity method of accounting to the activities of a collaborative arrangement. Per FASB ASC 808-10-15-3, the guidance in FASB ASC 808 does not apply to arrangements for which the accounting is specifically addressed within the scope of other authoritative accounting literature.

3.137 For example, two unrelated NFPs hold their annual meetings at the same time and in the same city. In order to save costs, they merge their meetings via an unincorporated joint venture, negotiating better rates with the hotel and realizing other synergies. They share equally in the decision-making and net proceeds from the meeting. In accordance with FASB ASC 808-10-45, each NFP should report costs incurred and revenue generated from transactions with third parties (that is, parties that do not participate in the arrangement) in its respective statement of activities on a gross basis if it is deemed to be the principal participant for a given transaction. The guidance in FASB ASC 605-45 should be used to determine which participant in the collaborative arrangement is the principal participant. (See paragraph 3.99 for a similar example involving a general partnership.)

The Use of Fair Value Measures

3.138 The use of fair value measures is pervasive in the preparation of financial statements. Among other uses, fair value is used in the following items:

- Measurement of noncash contributions received (discussed in chapter 5)
- Measurement of financial assets held as an agent (discussed in chapter 5)
- Measurement of the contribution portion of a split-interest agreement (discussed in chapter 6, "Split-Interest Agreements and Beneficial Interests in Trusts")
- Measurement of a beneficial interest in a trust (discussed in chapters 5 and 6)
- Measurement of certain investments (discussed in chapter 4 and chapter 8, "Programmatic Investments")
- Measurement of derivative instruments (discussed in chapter 4)
- Disclosures about the fair value of financial instruments (discussed in chapter 4)
- Measurement of impairment losses for long-lived assets (discussed in chapter 9, "Property and Equipment")
- Measurement of asset retirement obligations (discussed in chapter 9)
- Measurement of a guarantee obligation (discussed in chapter 10, "Debt and Other Liabilities")
- Measurement of exit and disposal costs (discussed in chapter 10)
- Measurement of nonmonetary transactions in conformity with FASB ASC 845, *Nonmonetary Transactions*

- Measurement of transfers of financial assets in conformity with FASB ASC 860, *Transfers and Servicing*
- Measurement of a financial asset or financial liability for which an election is made pursuant to FASB ASC 815-15-25 or the "Fair Value Option" subsections of FASB ASC 825-10 (discussed in paragraphs 3.169–.171)

3.139 FASB ASC 820, *Fair Value Measurement*, defines *fair value*, establishes a framework for measuring fair value, and requires disclosures about fair value measurements. The following paragraphs summarize FASB ASC 820 but are not a substitute for reading FASB ASC 820 itself. FASB ASC 820-10-15 states that, with certain exceptions, the guidance in FASB ASC 820 applies when GAAP requires or permits fair value measurements or disclosures about fair value measurements. It also applies to measurements, such as fair value less costs to sell, based on fair value or disclosures about those measurements.

3.140 To assist practitioners, in October 2011, the AICPA issued the white paper, *Measurement of Fair Value for Certain Transactions of Not-for-Profit Entities*. The white paper discusses fair value measurement for the following types of transactions:

- Unconditional promises to give cash or other financial assets
- Beneficial interests in trusts
- Split-interest agreements

Excerpts from the white paper are incorporated into chapters 5 and 6.

Definition of *Fair Value*

3.141 The FASB ASC glossary defines *fair value* as "the price that would be received to sell an asset or paid to transfer a liability in an orderly transaction between market participants at the measurement date." A fair value measurement assumes that the transaction to sell the asset or transfer the liability occurs in the principal market for the asset or liability or, in the absence of a principal market, the most advantageous market for the asset or liability. FASB ASC 820-10-20 defines the *principal market* as the market with the greatest volume and level of activity for the asset or liability and the *most advantageous market* as the market that maximizes the amount that would be received to sell the asset or minimizes the amount that would be paid to transfer the liability, after taking into account transaction costs and transportation costs. Although an NFP must be able to access the market, it does not need to be able to sell the particular asset or transfer the particular liability on the measurement date to be able to measure fair value on the basis of the price in that market.

3.142 FASB ASC 820-10-35-6C states that even when there is no observable market to provide pricing information about the sale of an asset or the transfer of a liability at the measurement date, a fair value measurement assumes that a transaction takes place at that date, considered from the perspective of a market participant that holds the asset or owes the liability. That assumed transaction establishes a basis for estimating the price to sell the asset or to transfer the liability.

3.143 The definition of fair value focuses on the price that would be received to sell the asset or paid to transfer the liability (an *exit price*), not the price that would be paid to acquire the asset or received to assume the liability (an *entry price*). Conceptually, entry prices and exit prices are different. However, FASB ASC 820-10-30-3 explains that, in many cases, a transaction price (entry price) will equal the exit price and, therefore, will represent the fair value of the asset or liability at initial recognition. FASB ASC 820-10-30-3A provides conditions for which a transaction price might not represent the fair value of an asset or a liability.

3.144 One such condition is if the transaction price includes transaction costs (costs that result directly from and are essential to a transaction and that would not have been incurred by the entity had it not decided to sell the asset or transfer the liability). FASB ASC 820-10-35-9B states that the price in the principal (or most advantageous) market should not be adjusted for transaction costs. Transaction costs are not a characteristic of the asset or liability measured. However, as noted in FASB ASC 820-10-35-9C, if location is a characteristic of the asset (as might be the case, for example, for a commodity), the price in the principal (or most advantageous) market should be adjusted for the costs, if any, that would be incurred to transport the asset from its current location to that market. That is, transaction costs do not include costs that would be incurred to transport an asset from its current location to its principal (or most advantageous) market.

Fair Value of Nonfinancial Assets

3.145 Paragraphs 10A–14 of FASB ASC 820-10-35 provide guidance for the fair value measurement of nonfinancial assets. A fair value measurement of a nonfinancial asset takes into account a market participant's ability to generate economic benefits by using the asset in its highest and best use or by selling it to another market participant that would use the asset in its highest and best use, considering the use of the asset that is physically possible, legally permissible, and financially feasible at the measurement date. An NFP may not intend to use the nonfinancial asset according to its highest and best use; nevertheless, the NFP should measure the fair value of a nonfinancial asset assuming its highest and best use by market participants.

3.146 FASB ASC 820-10-35-10E states that the highest and best use for a nonfinancial asset establishes the valuation premise used to measure its fair value. A nonfinancial asset might provide maximum value to market participants through its use in combination with other assets as a group (as installed or otherwise configured for use) or in combination with other assets and liabilities (for example, a business). If so, a nonfinancial asset's fair value should be based on the price that would be received in a current transaction to sell the asset assuming that the asset would be used with other assets or with other assets and liabilities and that those assets and liabilities (that is, its complementary assets and the associated liabilities) would be available to market participants. Alternatively, a nonfinancial asset might provide maximum value to market participants on a standalone basis. If the highest and best use of the asset is to use it on a standalone basis, the fair value of the asset is the price that would be received in a current transaction to sell the asset to market participants that would use the asset on a standalone basis.

Fair Value of Liabilities

3.147 Paragraphs 16–18C of FASB ASC 820-10-35 provide guidance for the fair value measurement of liabilities. The fair value of a liability reflects the effect of nonperformance risk (the risk that an entity will not fulfill an obligation). Nonperformance risk is assumed to be the same before and after the transfer of the liability. Because nonperformance risk includes (but may not be limited to) a reporting entity's own credit risk, an NFP should take into account the effect of its credit standing and any other factors that might influence the likelihood that the obligation will or will not be fulfilled when measuring the fair value of a liability. If a liability issued with an inseparable third-party credit enhancement (for example, debt that is issued with a contractual third-party guarantee) is measured at fair value, FASB ASC 825-10-25-13 states the unit of accounting for the liability does not include the effects of the third-party credit enhancement when the issuer of the liability measures or discloses the fair value of the liability.

Valuation Approaches and Techniques

3.148 To measure fair value, an NFP should use valuation techniques that are appropriate in the circumstances and for which sufficient data are available, maximizing the use of relevant observable inputs and minimizing the use of unobservable inputs. Three widely used valuation approaches are the market approach, cost approach, and income approach. An NFP should use valuation techniques consistent with one or more of those approaches to measure fair value. Paragraphs 3A–3G of FASB ASC 820-10-55 describe the main aspects of valuation techniques consistent with those approaches as follows:

- The market approach uses prices and other relevant information generated by market transactions involving identical or comparable (that is, similar) assets, liabilities, or a group of assets and liabilities, such as a business. Valuation techniques consistent with the market approach include matrix pricing and often use market multiples derived from a set of comparables.
- The income approach converts future amounts (for example, cash flows or income and expenses) to a single current (that is, discounted) amount. When the income approach is used, the fair value measurement reflects current market expectations about those future amounts. Valuation techniques consistent with the income approach include present value techniques, option-pricing models, and the multiperiod excess earnings method.
- The cost approach reflects the amount that would be required currently to replace the service capacity of an asset (often referred to as current replacement cost). Fair value is determined based on the cost to a market participant (buyer) to acquire or construct a substitute asset of comparable utility, adjusted for obsolescence.

3.149 FASB ASC 820-10-35-24B explains that in some cases, a single valuation technique will be appropriate (for example, when valuing an asset or a liability using quoted prices in an active market for identical assets or liabilities). In other cases, multiple valuation techniques will be appropriate (for example, that might be the case when valuing a reporting unit). If multiple valuation techniques are used to measure fair value, the results (that is, respective indications of fair value) should be evaluated considering the reasonableness of the range of values indicated by those results. A fair value measurement is the point within that range that is most representative of fair value in the circumstances. Example 3 (paragraphs 35–41) of FASB ASC 820-10-55 illustrates the use of multiple valuation approaches.

3.150 Valuation techniques used to measure fair value should be applied consistently. However, a change in a valuation technique or its application is appropriate if the change results in a measurement that is equally or more representative of fair value in the circumstances. Such a change would be accounted for as a change in accounting estimate in accordance with the provisions of FASB ASC 250.

Present Value Techniques

3.151 Paragraphs 4–20 of FASB ASC 820-10-55 provide guidance on present value techniques. Those paragraphs neither prescribe the use of one specific present value technique nor limit the use of present value techniques to the three techniques discussed therein. They say that a fair value measurement of an asset or liability using present value techniques should capture the following elements from the perspective of market participants as of the measurement date: an estimate of future cash flows, expectations about possible variations in the amount and timing of the cash flows, the time value of money, the price for bearing the uncertainty inherent in the cash flows (risk premium), other factors that market participants would take into account in the circumstances, and in the case of a liability, the nonperformance risk relating to that liability, including the reporting entity's (obligor's) own credit risk.

3.152 FASB ASC 820-10-55-6 provides the general principles that govern any present value technique, as follows:

- Cash flows and discount rates should reflect assumptions that market participants would use in pricing the asset or liability.
- Cash flows and discount rates should consider only factors attributed to the asset (or liability) being measured.
- To avoid double counting or omitting the effects of risk factors, discount rates should reflect assumptions that are consistent with those inherent in the cash flows. For example, a discount rate that reflects expectations about future defaults is appropriate if using the contractual cash flows of a loan, but is not appropriate if the cash flows themselves are adjusted to reflect possible defaults.
- Assumptions about cash flows and discount rates should be internally consistent. For example, nominal cash flows (that include the effects of inflation) should be discounted at a rate that includes the effects of inflation.
- Discount rates should be consistent with the underlying economic factors of the currency in which the cash flows are denominated.

3.153 Present value techniques differ in how they adjust for risk and in the type of cash flows they use. For example, the discount rate adjustment technique (also called the traditional present value technique) uses a risk-adjusted discount rate and contractual, promised, or most likely cash flows. In contrast, expected present value techniques use the probability-weighted average of all possible cash flows (referred to as expected cash flows). The traditional present value technique and two methods of expected present value techniques are discussed more fully in paragraphs 4–20 of FASB ASC 820-10-55.

3.154 This guide includes guidance about measuring assets (promises to give and beneficial interests in trusts) and liabilities (split-interest obligations) using traditional present value techniques. That guidance is not intended to suggest that the income approach is the only one of the three approaches that is appropriate in the circumstances, nor is it intended to suggest that the traditional present value technique described in the guide is preferred over other present value techniques. Rather, the inclusion of that guidance in the guide merely reflects that prior to the issuance of the framework for fair value measurement, present value techniques were specifically mentioned in the standards as appropriate for measuring promises to give cash and beneficial interests in trusts, and the guide had been drafted reflecting those standards. In conforming this guide to the framework for fair value measurement, guidance that previously specified the use of the traditional present value technique was modified to indicate that the technique was a possible technique to consider for fair value measurement.

The Fair Value Hierarchy

3.155 FASB ASC 820 emphasizes that fair value is a market-based measurement, not an entity-specific measurement. Therefore, a fair value measurement should be determined based on the assumptions that market participants would use in pricing the asset or liability (referred to as inputs). Paragraphs 37–54A of FASB ASC 820-10-35 establish a fair value hierarchy that distinguishes between (1) inputs that are developed using market data, such as publicly available information about actual events or transactions, and that reflect the assumptions that market participants would use when pricing the asset or liability (observable inputs) and (2) inputs for which market data are not available and that are developed using the best information available about the assumptions that market participants would use when pricing the asset or liability (unobservable inputs). Valuation techniques used to measure fair value should maximize the use of observable inputs and minimize the use of unobservable inputs.

3.156 The fair value hierarchy in FASB ASC 820 categorizes into three levels the inputs to valuation techniques used to measure fair value. The three levels, which are described in paragraphs 40–54A of FASB ASC 820-10-35, are as follows:

- Level 1 inputs are quoted prices (unadjusted) in active markets for identical assets or liabilities that the reporting entity has the ability to access at the measurement date. An active market is a market in which transactions for the asset or liability take place with sufficient frequency and volume to provide pricing information on an ongoing basis. A quoted price in an active market provides the most reliable evidence of fair value and should be used without adjustment to measure fair value whenever available, except as discussed in FASB ASC 820-10-35-41C.
- Level 2 inputs are inputs other than quoted prices included within level 1 that are observable for the asset or liability, either directly or indirectly. If the asset or liability has a specified (contractual) term, a level 2 input must be observable for substantially the full term of the asset or liability. Adjustments to level 2 inputs will vary depending on factors specific to the asset or liability. An adjustment to a level 2 input that is significant to the entire measurement might result in a fair value measurement categorized within level 3 of the fair value hierarchy if the adjustment uses significant unobservable inputs. Level 2 inputs include the following:
    - Quoted prices for similar assets or liabilities in active markets

- Quoted prices for identical or similar assets or liabilities in markets that are not active
- Inputs other than quoted prices that are observable for the asset or liability (for example, interest rates and yield curves observable at commonly quoted intervals, volatilities, and credit spreads)
- Inputs that are derived principally from or corroborated by observable market data by correlation or other means (market-corroborated inputs)

- Level 3 inputs are unobservable inputs for the asset or liability. Unobservable inputs should be used to measure fair value to the extent that relevant observable inputs are not available, thereby allowing for situations in which there is little, if any, market activity for the asset or liability at the measurement date. In developing unobservable inputs, the reporting entity need not undertake exhaustive efforts to obtain information about market participant assumptions. However, a reporting entity should take into account all information about market participant assumptions that is reasonably available. Unobservable inputs are developed using the best information available about the assumptions that market participants would use when pricing the asset or liability.

3.157 In some cases, the inputs used to measure the fair value of an asset or a liability might be categorized within different levels of the fair value hierarchy. In those cases, FASB ASC 820-10-35-37A states that the fair value measurement is categorized in its entirety in the same level of the fair value hierarchy as the lowest level input that is significant to the entire measurement.

3.158 As discussed in FASB ASC 820-10-35-38, the availability of relevant inputs and their relative subjectivity might affect the selection of appropriate valuation techniques. However, the fair value hierarchy prioritizes the inputs to valuation techniques, not the valuation techniques used to measure fair value. For example, a fair value measurement developed using a present value technique might be categorized within level 2 or level 3, depending on the inputs that are significant to the entire measurement and the level of the fair value hierarchy within which those inputs are categorized.

Additional Guidance for Fair Value Measurement in Special Circumstances

3.159 FASB ASC 820-10-35 provides additional guidance for fair value measurements in the following circumstances:

- Measuring fair value of liabilities held by other parties as assets (paragraphs 16B–16D of FASB ASC 820-10-35)
- Measuring fair value when the volume or level of activity for an asset or a liability has significantly decreased (paragraphs 54C–54H of FASB ASC 820-10-35)
- Identifying transactions that are not orderly (paragraphs 54I–54J of FASB ASC 820-10-35)
- Using quoted prices provided by third parties (paragraphs 54K–54M of FASB ASC 820-10-35)

- Measuring the fair value of investments in certain entities that calculate net asset value per share or its equivalent (paragraphs 59–62 of FASB ASC 820-10-35)
- Effects of restrictions on fair value measurements (paragraphs 18B and 38A of FASB ASC 820-10-35 and paragraphs 51–55 of FASB ASC 820-10-55)

Liabilities Held by Other Parties as Assets

3.160 When a quoted price for the transfer of an identical or a similar liability is not available and the identical item is held by another party as an asset, an NFP should measure the fair value of the liability from the perspective of a market participant that holds the identical item as an asset at the measurement date. An NFP should adjust the quoted price of the liability held by another party as an asset only if there are factors specific to the asset that are not applicable to the fair value measurement of the liability. An NFP should ensure that the price of the asset does not reflect the effect of a restriction preventing the sale of that asset. FASB ASC 820-10-35-16D includes some factors, including a third-party credit enhancement, that may indicate that the quoted price of the asset should be adjusted.

Decrease in Market Activity

3.161 If there has been a significant decrease in the volume or level of activity for the asset or liability in relation to normal market activity for the asset or liability (or similar assets or liabilities), further analysis of the transactions or quoted prices is needed. A decrease in the volume or level of activity on its own may not indicate that a transaction price or quoted price does not represent fair value. However, if a reporting entity determines that a transaction or quoted price does not represent fair value (for example, there may be transactions that are not orderly), an adjustment will be necessary if the reporting entity uses those transactions or prices as a basis for measuring fair value. That adjustment may be significant to the fair value measurement in its entirety. Adjustments also may be necessary in other circumstances (for example, when a price for a similar asset requires significant adjustment to make it comparable to the asset being measured or when the price is stale). Further, if there has been a significant decrease in the volume or level of activity for the asset or liability, a change in valuation technique or the use of multiple valuation techniques may be appropriate (for example, the use of a market approach and a present value technique).

Transactions That Are Not Orderly

3.162 When measuring fair value, an NFP should take into account transaction prices for orderly transactions. If evidence indicates that a transaction is not orderly, an NFP should place little, if any, weight (compared with other indications of fair value) on that transaction price. When an NFP does not have sufficient information to conclude whether particular transactions are orderly, it should place less weight on those transactions when compared with other transactions that are known to be orderly.

Quoted Prices Provided by Third Parties

3.163 An NFP may use quoted prices provided by third parties, such as pricing services or brokers, if it has determined that those prices are developed in accordance with FASB ASC 820. More weight should be given to quotes provided by third parties that represent binding offers than to quotes that are indicative prices. Less weight (when compared with other indications of fair value that reflect the results of transactions) should be placed on quotes that do not reflect the result of transactions.

Investments in Entities That Calculate Net Asset Value per Share

3.164 If an investment does not have a readily determinable fair value, an NFP is permitted, as a practical expedient, to estimate the fair value of the investment using its net asset value per share (or its equivalent, such as member units or an ownership interest in partners' capital to which a proportionate share of net assets is attributed), if the criteria in FASB ASC 820-10-15-4 are met. Paragraph 4.43 provides additional information about the circumstances in which this practical expedient is permitted.

If an investment does not have a readily determinable fair value, an NFP is permitted, as a practical expedient, to estimate the fair value of the investment using its net asset value per share (or its equivalent, such as member units or an ownership interest in partners' capital to which a proportionate share of net assets is attributed), if the criteria in FASB ASC 820-10-15-4 are met. The "Pending Content" in FASB ASC 820-10-35-54B states that an investment that meets those criteria and is measured using net asset value per share (or its equivalent) as a practical expedient should not be categorized within the fair value hierarchy. In addition, the disclosure requirements in FASB ASC 820-10-50-2 do not apply to that investment, instead the NFP discloses information required by FASB ASC 820-10-50-6A. Although the investment is not categorized within the fair value hierarchy, the NFP should provide the amount measured using the net asset value per share (or its equivalent) practical expedient to permit reconciliation of the fair value of investments included in the fair value hierarchy to the line items presented in the statement of financial position. Paragraph 4.43 provides additional information about the circumstances in which this practical expedient is permitted.[22]

Effects of Restrictions

3.165 FASB ASC 820-10-55-51 states that the effect of a restriction on the sale or use of an asset by a reporting entity will differ depending on whether the restriction would be taken into account by market participants when pricing the asset. Example 6 (paragraphs 51–55) of FASB ASC 820-10-55 illustrates that restrictions that are a characteristic of the asset and, therefore, would be transferred to market participants, are the only restrictions reflected in fair value. Donor restrictions that are specific to the donee are reflected in the classification of the associated net assets and in disclosure of the nature of the restriction, not in the measurement of fair value or the level in the fair value hierarchy within which that measurement in its entirety falls.

3.166 FASB ASC 820-10-35-38A states that if a market participant would take into account the effect of a restriction on the sale of an asset when

---

[22] The amendments in FASB ASU No. 2016-14 are effective for annual financial statements issued for fiscal years beginning after December 15, 2017 (for example, years ending December 31, 2018 and years ending June 30, 2019), and for interim periods within fiscal years beginning after December 15, 2018. Application to interim financial statements is permitted but not required in the initial year of application. Early application of the amendments is permitted.

estimating the price for the asset, an NFP would adjust the quoted price to reflect the effect of that restriction. If the asset is measured based on a quoted price that is a level 2 input, and the adjustment is an unobservable input that is significant to the entire measurement, the measurement would be categorized within level 3 of the fair value hierarchy.

3.167 Paragraphs 16D and 18B of FASB ASC 820-10-35 state that when measuring the fair value of a liability, an NFP should not include a separate input or an adjustment to other inputs relating to a restriction that prevents the transfer of the item. The effect of a restriction is either implicitly or explicitly included in the other inputs to the fair value measurement.

Disclosures

3.168 Paragraphs 1–8 of FASB ASC 820-10-50 require disclosures about assets and liabilities measured at fair value on a recurring or nonrecurring basis in the statement of financial position after initial recognition. The quantitative disclosures required should be presented in a tabular format. The disclosures do not apply to the initial measurement of an asset or liability at fair value. For assets and liabilities that are measured at fair value in the statement of financial position after initial recognition, an NFP should disclose information to help users of its financial statements assess the valuation techniques and inputs used to develop those measurements. For recurring fair value measurements using significant unobservable inputs (level 3), an NFP should disclose information to help users assess the effects of the measurements on changes in net assets. To meet those two objectives an NFP should consider all of the following, and disclose additional information necessary to meet the objectives:

- The level of detail necessary to satisfy the disclosure requirements
- How much emphasis to place on each of the various requirements
- How much aggregation or disaggregation to undertake
- Whether users of financial statements need additional information to evaluate the quantitative information disclosed

Certain of the disclosures in FASB ASC 820-10-50 apply only to public entities, including NFPs that are conduit bond obligors for conduit debt securities that are traded in a public market (a domestic or foreign stock exchange or an over-the-counter market, including local or regional markets). For example, only public entities are required to disclose information about assets and liabilities that are not measured at fair value in the statement of financial position but for which the fair value is disclosed.

Fair Value Option

3.169 The "Fair Value Option" subsections of FASB ASC 825-10 permit an entity to irrevocably elect fair value as the initial and subsequent measure for many financial instruments and certain other items, with changes in fair value recognized in the statement of activities as those changes occur. Paragraphs 4–6 of FASB ASC 815-15-25 similarly permit an elective fair value re-measurement for any hybrid financial instrument that contains an embedded derivative, if that embedded derivative would otherwise have to be separated from its debt host contract in conformity with FASB ASC 815-15. An election is made on an instrument-by-instrument basis (with certain exceptions), generally when an instrument is initially recognized in the financial statements.

3.170 The "Fair Value Option" subsection of FASB ASC 825-10-15 describes the financial assets and liabilities for which the option is available. Most financial assets and financial liabilities are eligible to be recognized using the fair value option, as are firm commitments for financial instruments and certain nonfinancial contracts. Specifically excluded from eligibility are investments in other entities that are required to be consolidated, employer's and plan's obligations under postemployment, postretirement plans, and deferred compensation arrangements (or assets representing overfunded positions in those plans), financial assets and liabilities recognized under leases, deposit liabilities of depository institutions, and financial instruments that are, in whole or in part, classified by the issuer as a component of shareholder's equity. Additionally, the election cannot be made for most nonfinancial assets and liabilities or for current or deferred income taxes.

3.171 FASB ASC 825-10-45 and FASB ASC 825-10-50 establish presentation and disclosure requirements designed to facilitate comparisons between entities that choose different measurement attributes for similar types of assets and liabilities. Entities should report assets and liabilities that are measured using the fair value option in a manner that separates those reported fair values from the carrying amounts of similar assets and liabilities measured using another measurement attribute. To accomplish that, an entity should either (*a*) report the aggregate carrying amount for both fair value and nonfair value items on a single line, with the fair value amount parenthetically disclosed, or (*b*) present separate lines for the fair value carrying amounts and the nonfair value carrying amounts.

Financial Statement Disclosures Not Considered Elsewhere

3.172 Financial statement disclosures are generally discussed in this guide in connection with the specific financial statement items to which they pertain. This section discusses disclosures that are unique to NFPs and that are not discussed elsewhere in this guide.

Noncompliance With Donor-Imposed Restrictions

3.173 Noncompliance with donor-imposed restrictions may result in net assets being reported other than in accordance with donor-imposed restrictions. If net assets are reported other than in accordance with donor-imposed restrictions, the financial statements are not presented in conformity with GAAP. Consistent with FASB ASC 958-205-45-2 and the conclusions in Q&A section 6140.23, "Changing Net Asset Classifications Reported in a Prior Year," individual net asset classes, rather than net assets in the aggregate (total net assets), are relevant in determining whether an NFP's classifications in financial statements is appropriate. Further, paragraph 106 of FASB Concept No. 6, *Elements of Financial Statements*, states that because donor-imposed restrictions affect the types and levels of service an NFP can provide, whether an NFP has maintained certain classes of net assets may be more significant than whether it has maintained net assets in the aggregate.

3.174 An NFP may not be in compliance with donor-imposed restrictions, including requirements that it maintain an appropriate composition of assets (usually cash and marketable securities in amounts needed to comply with all donor restrictions). Such noncompliance could result in a material contingent liability, a material loss of future revenue, or could cause the NFP to be unable to continue as a going concern. FASB ASC 958-450-50-2 requires noncompliance with donor-imposed restrictions to be disclosed if either of the following is true: (*a*) there is a reasonable possibility that a material contingent liability has been incurred at the date of the financial statements, or (*b*) there is at least a reasonable possibility that the noncompliance could lead to a material loss of revenue or could cause an entity to be unable to continue as a going concern. If the noncompliance results from an NFP's failure to maintain an appropriate composition of assets in amounts needed to comply with all donor restrictions, the amounts and circumstances should be disclosed. FASB ASC 205-40 provides guidance for evaluating whether there is substantial doubt about an entity's ability to continue as a going concern for a reasonable period of time and about related note disclosures. However, if liquidation is imminent, an NFP should prepare its financial statements in accordance with the requirements of FASB ASC 205-30, including its disclosure requirements.

3.175 As discussed in paragraph 10.102 of this guide, noncompliance with donor-imposed restrictions may require accrual of a liability in conformity with FASB ASC 450-20. For example, noncompliance may require the return of resources to the donor, particularly in grant situations, or may result in litigation. FASB ASC 450, *Contingencies*, provides further guidance for accruing and disclosing contingent liabilities.

Risks and Uncertainties

3.176 FASB ASC 275, *Risks and Uncertainties*, requires entities to include in their financial statements information about the following:

- The nature of their operations
- Use of estimates in the preparation of financial statements

In addition, if specified disclosure criteria are met, it requires entities to include in their financial statements disclosures about the following:

- Certain significant estimates
- Current vulnerability due to certain concentrations

FASB ASC 958-605-55-70 includes an example of a vulnerability of concentration of risk because of reliance on major donors. FASB ASC 275-10-55 includes other examples of disclosures that may be pertinent for NFPs.

Subsequent Events

3.177 FASB ASC 855, *Subsequent Events*, establishes standards for accounting for and disclosure of events that occur after the balance sheet date but before financial statements are issued or are available to be issued. In accordance with FASB ASC 855-10-25, an NFP should recognize in the financial statements the effects of all subsequent events that provide additional evidence about conditions that existed at the date of the balance sheet, including the estimates inherent in the process of preparing financial statements. An NFP should not recognize subsequent events that provide evidence about conditions that did not exist at the date of the balance sheet but arose after the balance sheet date but before financial statements are issued or are available to be issued. Instead, nonrecognized subsequent events are disclosed if they are of such a nature that they must be disclosed to keep the financial statements from being misleading.

3.178 FASB ASC 855-10-50-1 requires the disclosure of the date through which an NFP has evaluated subsequent events and whether that date is the date the financial statements were issued or the date the financial statements were available to be issued. The FASB ASC glossary states that "Financial statements are considered issued when they are widely distributed to shareholders and other financial statement users for general use and reliance in a form and format that complies with GAAP." The FASB ASC glossary also states that

> Financial statements are considered available to be issued when they are complete in a form and format that complies with GAAP and all approvals necessary for issuance have been obtained, for example, from management, the board of directors, and/or significant shareholders. The process involved in creating and distributing the financial statements will vary depending on an entity's management and corporate governance structure as well as statutory and regulatory requirements.

3.179 FASB ASC 855-10-25-1A requires that a conduit bond obligor for conduit debt securities that are traded in a public market (a domestic or foreign stock exchange or an over-the-counter market, including local or regional markets) evaluate subsequent events through the date the financial statements are issued. All other NFPs should evaluate subsequent events through the date that the financial statements are available to be issued.

3.180 Because of their use of conduit debt that trades in public markets, some NFPs fall into the class of entities that are required to evaluate subsequent events through the issuance date of their financial statements. If an NFP does not have conduit debt that trades in a public market, it is required to evaluate subsequent events up through the date the financial statements are available to be issued.

Related Party Transactions

3.181 The FASB ASC glossary defines *related parties* as including the following:

a. Affiliates of the entity (An *affiliate* is defined in the FASB ASC glossary as a party that, directly or indirectly through one or more intermediaries, controls, is controlled by, or is under common control with an entity.)

b. Entities for which investments in their equity securities would be required, absent the election of the fair value option under the "Fair Value Option" subsection of FASB ASC 825–10–15, to be accounted for by the equity method by the investing entity

c. Trusts for the benefit of employees, such as pension and profit-sharing trusts that are managed by or under the trusteeship of management

d. Principal owners of the entity and members of their immediate families

e. Management of the entity and members of their immediate families

f. Other parties with which the entity may deal if one party controls or can significantly influence the management or operating policies of the other to an extent that one of the transacting parties might be prevented from fully pursuing its own separate interests *g.* Other parties that can significantly influence the management or operating policies of the transacting parties or that have an ownership interest in one of the transacting parties and can significantly influence the other to an extent that one or more of the transacting parties might be prevented from fully pursuing its own separate interests

3.182 As noted in paragraph 2.36, disclosure of related party transactions is one of an NFP's possible responses to regulators' concerns about whether the governing board members of not-for-profit organizations are meeting their stewardship responsibilities. For purposes of applying the glossary's definition of related parties for purposes of complying with the requirements of FASB ASC 850, related parties of NFPs might include, but are not limited to, the following:

- Officers, board members, founders, substantial contributors, and their immediate family members
- Members of any related party's immediate family
- Parties providing concentrations in revenues and receivables
- Supporting organizations (such as 509[a][3] organizations)
- Financially interrelated entities
- Certain national and local affiliates that don't necessarily meet the definition of affiliate in FASB ASC[23]
- Other entities whose officers, governing board members, owners, or employees are members of the NFP's governing board or senior management, if those individuals have significant influence to an extent that one or more of the transacting parties might be prevented from fully pursuing its own separate interests

3.183 NFPs should disclose the following:

- Material related party transactions, other than compensation arrangements, expense allowances, and other similar items in the ordinary course of business (FASB ASC 850-10-50-1)
- If the reporting entity and one or more other entities are under common ownership or management control and the existence of that control could result in operating results or financial position of the reporting entity that are significantly different from those that would have been obtained if the entities were autonomous, the nature of the control relationship should be disclosed even though there are no transactions between the entities (FASB ASC 850-10-50-6)

3.184 Examples of related party transactions and circumstances that may be required to be disclosed include but are not limited to the following:

- The NFP receives material contributions from related parties (disclosure required by FASB ASC 850-10-50-1). (FinREC believes the NFP need not identify by name the party making the contribution.)

---

[23] FASB ASC 850-10-20 defines an *affiliate* as "a party that, directly or indirectly through one or more intermediaries, controls, is controlled by, or is under common control with an entity."

- The NFP has significant concentrations of revenues and receivables from related parties (disclosure required by FASB ASC 850-10-50-1, in addition to disclosures about current vulnerability due to certain concentrations, as required by FASB ASC 275, which is discussed in paragraph 3.176. And in addition to required disclosures about significant concentrations of credit risk arising from all financial instruments, required by paragraphs 20–22 of FASB ASC 825-10-50, as discussed in paragraph 4.91).
- The NFP accepts obligations associated with contributions from related parties, such as gift annuities payable to related parties or environmental remediation liabilities associated with real estate donated by related parties (disclosures required by FASB ASC 850-10-50-1).
- The NFP is a religious organization that is commonly controlled by an ecclesiastical body (disclosures required by FASB ASC 850-10-50-6).
- The NFP leases office space from a governing board member (disclosures required by FASB ASC 850-10-50-1).
- The NFP uses legal services provided by a firm in which an officer's immediate family member is a person of influence, such as a partner (disclosures required by FASB ASC 850-10-50-1).
- The NFP purchases printing services from a printing shop owned by a governing board member of the NFP (disclosures required by FASB ASC 850-10-50-1).
- The NFP purchases supplies from a company for which one of the NFP's governing board members is a governing board member (disclosures required by FASB ASC 850-10-50-1).
- The NFP loans money to a founder or significant donor (disclosures required by FASB ASC 850-10-50-1).
- The NFP loans money to the spouse or immediate family member of a founder or significant donor (disclosures required by FASB ASC 850-10-50-1).
- A national NFP provides financial consulting to a local affiliate, either for a fee or for no fee (or one brother-sister organization provides consulting to another, either for a fee or for no fee) (disclosures required by FASB ASC 850-10-50-1 and FASB ASC 850-10-50-6).
- The NFP is a foundation established by a for-profit corporation and the foundation's bylaws provide that the for-profit corporation appoints the foundation's board (disclosures required by FASB ASC 850-10-50-1 and FASB ASC 850-10-50-6).
- The reporting NFP makes grants to an independent NFP whose executive director is a governing board member of the reporting NFP (disclosures required by FASB ASC 850-10-50-1).

Auditing

3.185 Auditing objectives and procedures for the financial statements are generally similar to those of other entities. However, there are some specific and unique aspects for financial statement of NFPs.

Financial Statement Close Process

3.186 In obtaining an understanding of the financial statement closing process, including the preparation of significant disclosures, the auditor may find it helpful to focus on the following:

- Procedures used in the financial statement close process to initiate, authorize and record journal entries, including management's controls
- Procedures used to prepare a consolidation, where appropriate
- Procedures used to prepare financial statement disclosures
- Who participates from management (that is, who has responsibility for, and provides significant input to, the process)

3.187 Complex areas that are typically part of the closing process and may require particular attention include the following:

- Significant classes of transactions involving nonroutine and estimation processes such as functional classification of expenses, allocation of costs of informational materials that include a fund-raising appeal, and fair value measurements
- Financial statement disclosures that are derived from specially extracted data such as related party transactions, commitments, and contingencies

The financial statement close process provides greater opportunity for controls to be overridden as it involves upper management, is pervasive across the financial statements and includes preparing final journal entries, many of which may involve judgment. These areas may pose challenges for some NFPs and, therefore, the auditor will need to determine, based on assessed risks of material misstatement, whether to take a controls reliance approach or substantively test the financial statement close process.

Operating and Nonoperating Classifications in the Statement of Activities

3.188 Paragraphs 3.36–.38 provide guidance for reporting a measure of operations. Suggested audit procedures to consider include determining

- that the disclosure in the notes to the financial statements is complete and accurate.
- whether the presentation of revenue and expense transactions is appropriately classified as operating or nonoperating within the NFP's definition of its operating measure.
- whether items that are required to be reported within the operating measure (paragraph 3.37) or outside of the operating measure (paragraphs 3.33–.34) are properly reported.
- that expenses that an NFP chooses to report outside of an operating measure in its statement of activities (that is, nonoperating expenses) are included in the functional expense allocations, either in the notes or in a statement of functional expenses.
- that when an NFP presents prior-year comparative information in total, rather than by net asset class, such that the financial statements will not be in conformity with GAAP, the nature of

the prior year information is described by the use of appropriate titles on the face of the financial statements and in a note to the financial statements.

Consolidation

3.189 Ownership of NFPs may be present in various legal forms including ownership certificates, joint ventures, and partnerships. The form of the relationship will determine the appropriate reporting. With respect to consolidation, suggested audit procedures to consider include considering

- the appropriateness and completeness of consolidation when there is the existence of a relationship with another NFP, with a for-profit entity, or when there are noncontrolling interests.
- whether consolidation is appropriate and includes all entities where consolidation is required. (Exhibit 3-2 describes some common relationships with other entities and identifies where these relationships are discussed in this chapter and in FASB ASC.)
- whether the classification of net assets is appropriate in consolidated financial statements. In particular, consider the situations that are discussed in paragraphs 3.103–.107.
- situations when an NFP is the general partner of a limited partnership or a limited partner that has a controlling financial interest (paragraph 3.85). Appropriate audit procedures could include
    - — reviewing partnership agreements, board minutes, and correspondence to determine if consolidation is required,
    - — considering interviews and site visits,
    - — considering the absence or presence of substantive kick-out rights or participating rights, and
    - — documenting the results of the reviews and discussions.

Liquidity

3.190 Paragraphs 3.09–.23 discuss the requirement to provide information about the liquidity or maturity of assets and liabilities in financial statements, and the effects of restrictions, designations, and other limitations on liquidity. Paragraphs 10.61–.76 discuss the classification of debt. Suggested audit procedures to consider include the review of restrictions, designations, and other limitations to determine if their effects on liquidity are properly presented in the financial statements. In particular,

- consider the classification of cash and cash equivalents of donor-restricted endowment funds held temporarily until suitable long-term investment opportunities are identified.
- cash, contributions receivable, and other assets restricted by donors to investment in land, buildings, and equipment.
- resources that are designated for long-term investment (such as quasi endowments), for expenditure to acquire or construct noncurrent assets, or for the retirement of long term debt.
- if a classified statement of financial position is presented, review of the composition of current assets and current liabilities to determine that the classification is accurate and complete.

Mergers and Acquisitions

3.191 Paragraphs 3.123–.135 provide guidance on transactions or events in which an NFP that is the reporting entity combines with one or more NFPs. Key to the proper accounting is the determination of whether the transaction or event is a merger of an NFP or an acquisition by an NFP. Ceding control is the sole definitive criterion for a merger. One entity obtaining control over the other is the sole definitive criterion for an acquisition. Suggested audit procedures to consider include

- identifying transactions and reviewing the documentation, paying close attention to the change of control.
- understanding and documenting the significant aspects of the merger or acquisition to determine that the reporting on the financial statements is appropriate whether treated as a merger or acquisition.
- for transactions that are mergers, whether the carryover method was properly applied.
- for transactions that are acquisitions, review management's determination of identifiable assets acquired, liabilities assumed, and whether there are noncontrolling interests.
- test the valuation of assets acquired and liabilities assumed and the fair value of the noncontrolling interest (if any).

Noncompliance With Donor-Imposed Restrictions

3.192 Paragraphs 3.173–.175 discuss noncompliance with donor-imposed restrictions. Paragraph .A21 of AU-C section 250, *Consideration of Laws and Regulations in an Audit of Financial Statements*), provides guidance about matters relevant to an auditor's evaluation of the possible effect on the financial statements of noncompliance. If noncompliance could cause an NFP to be unable to continue as a going concern, AU-C section 570 addresses an auditor's responsibilities relating to the entity's ability to continue as a going concern and the implications for the auditor's report when there is substantial doubt about the entity's ability to continue as a going concern for a reasonable period of time.

Supplement A—Flowcharts

3.193

Ownership of a For-Profit Entity

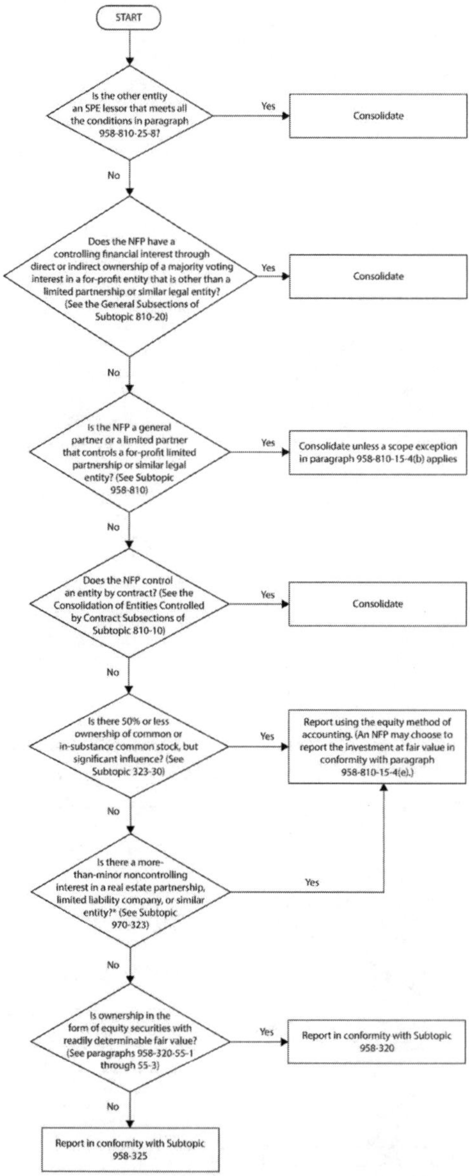

* According to paragraph 323-30-35-3, a limited liability company that maintains a specific ownership account for each investor—similar to a partnership capital account structure—should be viewed as similar to an investment in a limited partnership for purposes of determining whether a noncontrolling investment in a limited liability company should be accounted for using the cost method or the equity method.

Relationship With Another Not-for-Profit Entity

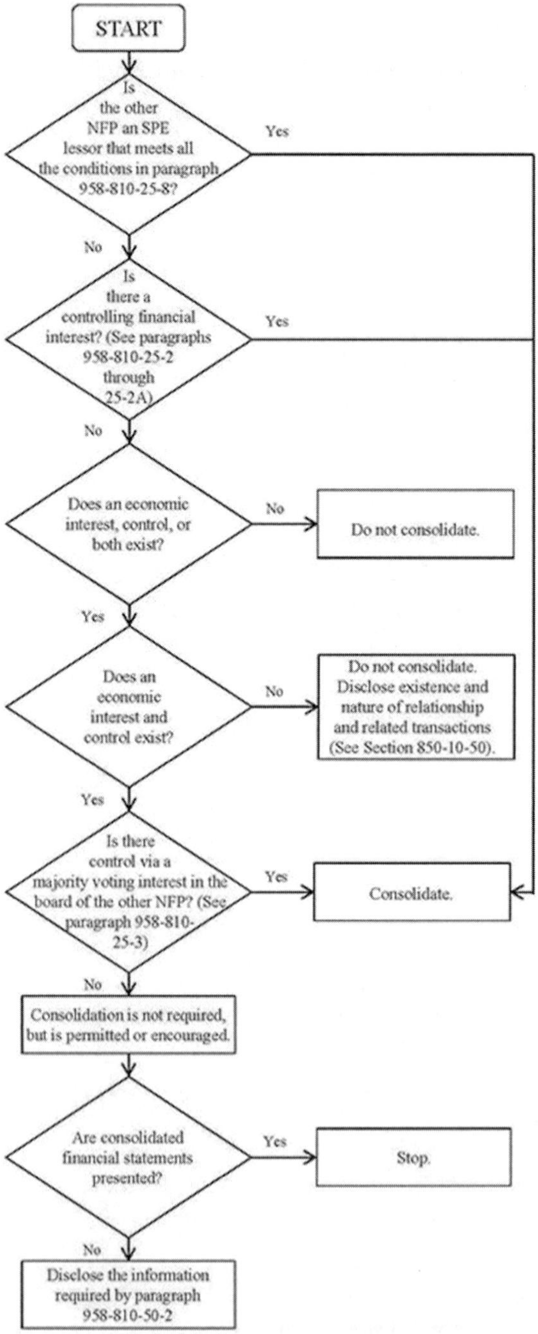

3.194

Appendix A—Financial Statements Prepared in Accordance With FASB ASU No. 2016-14[1]

A-1 This appendix provides guidance for statements of financial position, statements of activities, and statements of cash flows prepared in accordance with the amendments in FASB Accounting Standards Update (ASU) No. 2016-14, *Not-for-Profit Entities (Topic 958): Presentation of Financial Statements of Not-for-Profit Entities*. It also provides guidance for liquidity disclosures and for an analysis that shows the relationship between functional classification and natural classification for all expenses. The amendments in FASB ASU No. 2016-14 are effective for annual financial statements issued for fiscal years beginning after December 15, 2017 (for example, years ending December 31, 2018 and years ending June 30, 2019), and for interim periods within fiscal years beginning after December 15, 2018. Application to interim financial statements is permitted but not required in the initial year of application. Early application of the amendments is permitted. Additional information about the requirements of FASB ASU No. 2016-14 is provided in shaded text throughout this guide, in appendix A, "Financial Statements Prepared in Accordance With FASB ASU No. 2016-14," of chapter 11, and in appendix A, "The New Not-for-Profit Financial Reporting Model: FASB ASU No. 2016-14," of this guide.

A-2 To facilitate the use of this appendix, the paragraph numbers that follow correspond to the paragraphs in chapter 3 that will be replaced upon the effective date of FASB ASU No. 2016-14. For example, paragraph 3A.06 in this appendix corresponds to paragraph 3.06 in the chapter. Paragraphs in this appendix that do not have a corresponding paragraph in the chapter are identified by an A- paragraph number.

Statement of Financial Position

3A.06 The "Pending Content" in FASB ASC 958-210 describes the unique standards relating to a statement of financial position of an NFP. In addition to that industry-specific guidance, an NFP should follow all effective provisions of FASB ASC unless the specific provision explicitly exempts NFPs or its subject matter precludes such applicability. For example, NFPs should apply the guidance contained in FASB ASC 210, *Balance Sheet*, that does not conflict with the industry guidance.

3A.07 The "Pending Content" in FASB ASC 958-210-45-1 requires that a statement of financial position focus on the NFP as a whole and report all of the following amounts:

- Total assets

---

[1] The amendments in FASB Accounting Standards Update (ASU) No. 2016-14, *Not-for-Profit Entities (Topic 958): Presentation of Financial Statements of Not-for-Profit Entities*, are effective for annual financial statements issued for fiscal years beginning after December 15, 2017 (for example, years ending December 31, 2018 and years ending June 30, 2019), and for interim periods within fiscal years beginning after December 15, 2018. Application to interim financial statements is permitted but not required in the initial year of application. Early application of the amendments is permitted.

- Total liabilities
- Total net assets
- Total net assets with donor restrictions
- Total net assets without donor restrictions

3A.08 FASB ASC 958-210-45-5 describes how classifying assets and liabilities into reasonably homogeneous groups (paragraph 3.04) increases the usefulness of information. The "Pending Content" in FASB ASC 958-210-45-6 states that assets need not be disaggregated on the basis of the presence of donor-imposed restrictions on their use; for example, cash available for current use and without donor restrictions need not be reported separately from cash received with donor-imposed restrictions that is also available for current use.[2] However, cash or other assets received with a donor-imposed restriction that limits their use to long-term purposes should not be classified with cash or other assets that are without donor restrictions and available for current use. The "Pending Content" in FASB ASC 958-210-45-6 also states that the kind of asset whose use is limited either by a donor-imposed restriction or by governing board designations should be described in the notes to the financial statements if the nature of the restriction or designation (that is, amount and purpose) is not clear from the description on the face of the statement of financial position.

Effects of Restrictions, Designations, and Other Limitations on Liquidity

3A.09 The "Pending Content" in FASB ASC 958-210-45-7 requires quantitative information, and additional qualitative information in the notes as necessary, about the availability of an NFP's financial assets at the balance sheet date to meet cash needs for general expenditures within one year of the balance sheet date be displayed on the face of the statement of financial position or in notes to the financial statements. The "Pending Content" in FASB ASC 958-210-45-8 requires that additional information about the NFP's liquidity be provided by any of the following:

a. Sequencing assets according to their nearness of conversion to cash and sequencing liabilities according to the nearness of their maturity and resulting use of cash

b. Classifying assets and liabilities as current and noncurrent, as defined by FASB ASC 210-10 (required by FASB ASC 954-210-45-1 for statements of financial position prepared by not-for-profit, business-oriented health care entities)

c. Disclosing in notes to financial statements any additional relevant information about the liquidity or maturity of assets and liabilities, including restrictions on the use of particular assets

3A.10 Per the "Pending Content" in FASB ASC 958-210-50-1, relevant information about the liquidity or maturity of assets and liabilities, including restrictions and self-imposed limits on the use of particular items, should be disclosed in notes to financial statements in addition to information provided

[2] The "Pending Content" in FASB *Accounting Standards Codfication* (ASC) 958-210-45-6 notes that assets may be restricted by donors. For example, land could be restricted to use as a public park. Generally, however, restrictions apply to net assets, not to specific assets.

on the face of the statement of financial position. The "Pending Content" in FASB ASC 958-210-45-5A explains that when an NFP presents a statement of financial position that sequences assets and liabilities based on their relative liquidity, cash and cash equivalents of permanent endowment funds held temporarily until suitable long-term investment opportunities are identified may be included in the classification long-term investments. Likewise, cash held temporarily by a custodian for investment purposes may be included as part of investments in a statement of financial position rather than as cash. The "Pending Content" in FASB ASC 958-205-55-7 states that similarly, cash and contributions receivable restricted by donors to investment in land, buildings, and equipment are not included with the line items cash and cash equivalents or contributions receivable. Rather, those items are reported as assets restricted to investment in land, buildings, and equipment and are sequenced closer to land, buildings, and equipment. Similarly, FASB ASC 210-10-45-4 states that the concept of the nature of current assets contemplates the exclusion from that classification of such resources as cash that is designated for expenditure in the acquisition or construction of noncurrent assets or is segregated for the liquidation of long-term debts. Even though not actually set aside in special accounts, funds that are clearly to be used in the near future for the liquidation of long-term debts, payments to sinking funds, or for similar purposes should also, under this concept, be excluded from current assets. However, if such funds are considered to pay off maturing debt that has been set up properly as a current liability, they may be included within the current asset classification.

3A.11 Application of the guidance discussed in paragraphs 3A.09–.10 results in certain (*a*) donor restrictions, (*b*) governing board designations, and (*c*) legal limitations affecting the classification of or disclosures about assets, or both. In meeting the requirements of FASB ASC 958-210 and FASB ASC 210-10-45 to provide information about liquidity, NFP's should consider not only maturity (nearness to conversion to cash or use of cash), but the effects on liquidity of donor-imposed restrictions, management's intent to meet those restrictions, and management's intent to use assets for long-term purposes (such as liquidation of long-term debts, payments to sinking funds, establishment of quasi endowment funds, and so forth).

3A.12 For example, if a split-interest agreement is in trust form, such as a unitrust or annuity trust, or if the assets held for a split-interest agreement are required by state law to be separately invested, the NFP should either separately display the asset on the face of the statement of financial position or should display the asset with similar assets of similar liquidity to meet the requirements of FASB ASC 958-210 and FASB ASC 210-10-45. Cash and investments held in the trust should not be combined with cash and investments that are available for operations. Further, if not apparent from the face of the financial statements, the NFP should disclose the nature and amount of the limitation imposed by a donor restriction, law, or contract in the notes to the financial statements in accordance with the "Pending Content" in paragraphs 6–7 of FASB ASC 958-210-45.

3A.13 The Financial Reporting Executive Committee (FinREC) believes if the use of a specific asset is not explicitly limited by a donor restriction, but net assets reflect a donor's restriction to use the contributed assets for a perpetual or term endowment, for purchase of a long-lived asset, or for another noncurrent purpose, the liquidity of the NFP is impacted by its responsibility to hold an appropriate composition of assets to comply with those restrictions. (Paragraphs 3.173–.175 discuss requirements if an NFP has not maintained an appropriate composition of assets to comply with donor-imposed restrictions.) In implementing the guidance in the "Pending Content" in FASB ASC 958-210-45-8 pertaining to presenting information about liquidity, FinREC believes assets identified by the NFP as held to meet a donor restriction for noncurrent purposes should be displayed using any of the following methods:

- If the NFP provides information about liquidity by sequencing assets according to their nearness of conversion to cash (that is, a nonclassified statement of financial position), assets held for meeting donor restrictions that limit use to long-term purposes should be
  - — separately displayed on the face of the statement of financial position in a position of longer-term relative liquidity as compared to similar assets available for current operating purposes (that is, using a description that identifies the nature of the asset, such as cash or contributions receivable, but displayed lower), or
  - — displayed on the face of the statement of financial position using a separate line item, such as "assets whose use has been limited or restricted," in a position of relative liquidity consistent with its noncurrent purpose.
- If information about liquidity is provided by classifying assets as current and noncurrent (that is, a classified statement of financial position), assets held for meeting donor restrictions that limit use to long-term purposes should be classified as noncurrent. For example, assets restricted to the payment of long-term debt would be classified as noncurrent to the extent that they exceed the current portion of long-term debt. A separate line item, such as "assets whose use has been limited or restricted," may be used.

Regardless of which of the preceding methods is used, if the nature of the assets or the related restrictions is not evident from the description on the line item, that information should be disclosed in the notes to the financial statements, as required by the "Pending Content" in paragraphs 6–7 of FASB ASC 958-210-45.

3A.14 In some cases, assets held to meet a donor restriction are easily identified. In other cases, the identification process may be subjective. For example, if the NFP conducts a fund-raising campaign to build a new building, unconditional promises to give received in response to that campaign are easily identified as assets held to meet a donor restriction for purchase of a building. If cash gifts to the same campaign are invested until needed to make expenditures for the new building and commingled with the NFP's other investments, a portion of investments may be assigned as assets held to meet a donor restriction for purchase of a building.

3A.15 In implementing the guidance in FASB ASC 210-10-45-4 pertaining to the classification of current assets and the "Pending Content" in FASB ASC 958-210-45-11 pertaining to information about self-imposed limits, if the governing board identifies specific assets to be invested or held pursuant to a designation for noncurrent purposes, those assets would be reported in a classified statement of financial position outside the current assets section. FinREC believes that in a nonclassified statement of financial position, those assets would be sequenced with other assets that will be consumed in a similar term. Further, FinREC believes best practice is to report those designated assets separately from donor-restricted assets on the face of the statement of financial position or disclose in the notes to the financial statements the amount of designated assets included in a line item that contains both amounts designated and restricted for noncurrent purposes.

3A.16 FinREC believes that when preparing consolidated financial statements, best practice is to apply the guidance in paragraphs 3A.09–.23 at the reporting-entity (that is, parent) level in consolidated financial statements, focusing on the entity as a whole, as required by the "Pending Content" in FASB ASC 958-210-45-1. Accordingly, assets that are not separately reported or segregated at the subsidiary level (based on the guidance herein) might be required to be separately reported or segregated at the parent level or vice versa. (A related discussion about the classification of net assets in consolidation is presented in paragraphs 3.102–.105.)

3A.17 The following examples illustrate the conclusions in paragraphs 3A.09–.16:

- Paragraph 3A.18—A specific asset is restricted by the donor, by law, or by contract.
- Paragraph 3A.19—Cash, receivables, or other assets are restricted by donor, by law, or by contract to use in an ongoing program of the NFP (that is, current operating purposes).
- Paragraph 3A.20—Cash, receivables, or other assets are restricted by donor, by law, or by contract to certain long-term purposes.
- Paragraph 3A.21—Cash, receivables, or other assets are designated by the governing board for long-term purposes.
- Paragraph 3A.22—Cash, receivables, or other assets are reported without donor restrictions when presented in a subsidiary's financial statements but are restricted for long-term purposes in the consolidated financial statements.

3A.18 Occasionally, specific assets are restricted by donors, by law, or by contract. For example, assume land gifted by a donor is restricted in perpetuity for use as open green space. Such restricted land should be distinguished from land that is not subject to donor-imposed restrictions. Similarly, investments held subject to a split-interest trust agreement should be distinguished from investments that are not subject to donor-imposed restrictions (for example, investments purchased with excess operating cash), as should assets held for a split-interest agreement that is required by state law to be separately invested. Cash required by law or contract to be set aside in compliance with bond sinking fund requirements should be distinguished from cash with no such stipulations. In accordance with the "Pending Content" in paragraphs 6–7 of FASB ASC 958-210-45, assets restricted by donors, contract, or law should be displayed separately on the statement of financial position or disclosed in the notes to financial statements in a way that distinguishes them from similar assets that are not subject to those specific asset stipulations.

3A.19 Cash, receivables, or other assets that are restricted by donor, by law, or by contract to current operating purposes are permitted, but not required, to be reported separately from similar current assets that are not subject to those types of restrictions. For example, cash that is received in response to a campaign to support Program A, which is an ongoing program of the donee, is permitted, but not required, to be reported separately from operating cash. FinREC believes that as long as the restrictions on them are quickly met, the assets do not need to be segregated. Because the restrictions on them are quickly met during the normal course of operations, they generally are available to creditors.

3A.20 Cash, receivables, or other assets that are restricted by donor, by law, or by contract for certain noncurrent purposes should be reported in a classified statement of financial position outside the current assets section, or if reported in a nonclassified statement of financial position, sequenced with other assets that will be consumed in a similar term. For example, if an NFP has cash, investments, or contributions receivable resulting from a capital campaign for a donor-restricted endowment fund or for acquisition of a long-lived asset, those assets should not be displayed with similar assets to be used for current operations. They could be reported under a separate caption, such as "cash and other assets restricted to investment in property and equipment," and displayed near the section of the statement where property and equipment is displayed. Although net assets are restricted when donor-imposed restrictions limit the use of the assets, it is important to reflect in the asset section of the statement of financial position that assets required to be used to satisfy donor restrictions of a long-term nature generally are unavailable to meet current operating obligations.

3A.21 The governing boards of some NFPs designate resources to be held for long-term purposes, such as debt-service reserves, quasi endowment, or the future acquisition of property and equipment. Consistent with FASB ASC 210-10-45-4(a) and the "Pending Content" in FASB ASC 958-210-45-11, if the governing board identifies specific assets to be invested or held pursuant to the designation of net assets for noncurrent purposes, those assets should be reported in a classified statement of financial position outside the current assets section, or in a nonclassified statement of financial position sequenced with other assets that will be consumed in a similar term. Accordingly, cash, receivables, or other assets designated for long-term purposes generally are not aggregated on a statement of financial position with cash, receivables, or other assets that are available for current use.

3A.22 Cash, receivables, or other assets that are reported without donor restrictions when presented in a subsidiary's financial statements may need to be reported as donor-restricted in consolidated financial statements. For example, a voluntary health and welfare entity has a broad mission of helping low income families and is the parent of an NFP that has a mission of running a day care and after-school care center for children in the county. The subsidiary NFP received a gift of a small office building subject to the donor's restriction that it be used for providing day care or after-school care or for the administrative support of those programs. In the separate financial statements of the subsidiary, those assets are not separately reported as restricted assets because the use of the assets is no narrower than the nature of the NFP and the purposes specified in its articles of incorporation and bylaws. However, when the subsidiary NFP is consolidated with its voluntary health and welfare entity parent, the office building would be reported separately with related disclosures because the donor-imposed restriction to use the building for day care, after-school care, or the administrative support of those two programs is narrower than the broad mission of helping low income families of the reporting entity. (Related information about the classification of net assets in consolidation is presented in paragraphs 3.103–.105.)

3A.23 For each item on the statement of financial position that is segregated because of donor-imposed restrictions, limitations, or board designations, either the face of the financial statements or the notes should disclose the following:

- The kinds of assets comprising the line item (for example, cash, receivables, investments, and so on) (the "Pending Content" in FASB ASC 958-210-45-6)
- The amount of the assets segregated because of a restriction or designation (the "Pending Content" in FASB ASC 958-210-45-6)
- The purpose for which the assets are segregated (for example, specific assets are held in perpetuity; held for construction of long-term assets; held for investment in endowment; and so on) (the "Pending Content" in FASB ASC 958-210-45-6)

In addition, an NFP might disclose the act causing the asset to be segregated (for example, [*a*] a specific asset is donor restricted, [*b*] the NFP is maintaining an appropriate composition of assets to fulfill donor restrictions, or [*c*] the NFP is maintaining an appropriate composition of assets to meet board designations).

Classification of Net Assets

3A.24 Classification of net assets is discussed in the "Pending Content" in paragraphs 9–11 of FASB ASC 958-210-45. The total amounts for each of the two net asset classes—with donor restrictions and without donor restrictions—are based on the existence or absence of donor-imposed restrictions. As explained in the "Pending Content" in FASB ASC 958-205-05-6B, the two required net asset classes are a minimum classification scheme, if they are applicable. An NFP can choose to further disaggregate the two net asset classes. For example, an NFP may wish to disaggregate net assets with donor restrictions between those expected to be maintained in perpetuity and those expected to be spent over time or for a particular purpose. However, the "Pending Content" in FASB ASC 958-210-45-1 does require that the amounts for each of the two classes of net assets and the total of net assets be reported in a statement of financial position.

3A.25 The "Pending Content" in the FASB ASC glossary defines *net assets with donor restrictions* as the part of net assets of an NFP that is subject to donor-imposed restrictions. A *donor-imposed restriction* is defined in the "Pending Content" in the FASB ASC glossary as a donor stipulation that specifies a use for a contributed asset that is more specific than broad limits resulting from the following:

a. The nature of the NFP

b. The environment in which it operates

c. The purposes specified in its articles of incorporation or bylaws or comparable documents for an unincorporated association.

3A.26 The "Pending Content" in the FASB ASC glossary of *donor-imposed restriction* explains that some donors impose restrictions that are temporary in nature, for example, stipulating that resources be used after a specified date, for particular programs or services, or to acquire buildings or equipment. Other donors impose restrictions that are perpetual in nature, for example, stipulating that resources be maintained in perpetuity. Laws may extend those limits to investment returns from those resources and to other enhancements (diminishments) of those resources. Thus, those laws extend donor-imposed restrictions. Both the definition of *donor-imposed restriction* and *net assets with donor restrictions* state that donors include other types of contributors, including makers of certain grants. Paragraphs 9–10 of FASB ASC 958-210-45 describe various purposes for which net assets might be restricted, such as use in future periods or use for specified purposes. The "Pending Content" in FASB ASC 958-210-45-9 requires information about the nature and amount of donor-imposed restrictions to be disclosed in the net asset section of the statement of financial position or in the notes to the financial statements.

3A.27 The "Pending Content" in the FASB ASC glossary defines *net assets without donor restrictions* as the part of net assets of an NFP that is not subject to donor-imposed restrictions (donors include other types of contributors, including makers of certain grants). The "Pending Content" in FASB ASC 958-210-45-11 explains that information about self-imposed limits is useful, including information about voluntary resolutions by the governing board of an entity,[3] such as resolutions to designate a portion of its net assets without donor restrictions to function as an endowment (sometimes called a board-designated endowment fund) or to designate a portion for a specific future expenditure (called board designated net assets). Information about the amounts and purposes of board designations of net assets without donor restrictions should be provided in the notes to or on the face of financial statements. In addition, the "Pending Content" in FASB ASC 958-205-45-13A states that in rare circumstances, a board-designated endowment fund also can include a portion of net assets with donor restrictions. For example, if an NFP is unable to spend donor-restricted contributions in the near term, then the board sometimes considers the long-term investment of these funds. The "Pending Content" in paragraphs 1A–1B of FASB ASC 958-205-50 requires certain additional disclosures about board-designated endowment funds.

The "Pending Content" in the FASB ASC 958-210-45-7 requires that relevant information about the nature and amount of limitations on the use of cash and cash equivalents (such as cash held on deposit as a compensating balance) and contractual limitations on the use of particular assets (such as restricted cash or other assets set aside under debt agreements, assets set aside under self-insurance funding arrangements, assets set aside under collateral arrangements, or assets set aside to satisfy reserve requirements that states may impose under charitable gift annuity agreements) should be displayed either on the face of the statement of financial position or in the notes to financial statements, unless otherwise required on the face of the statement of financial position.

---

[3] The definition of *board-designated net assets* states that some governing boards may delegate designation decisions to internal management, and that such designations are considered to be included in board-designated net assets.

Statement of Activities

3A.28 FASB ASC 958-220 describes the unique standards relating to a statement of activities of an NFP. In addition to that industry-specific guidance, an NFP should follow all effective provisions of FASB ASC unless the specific provision explicitly exempts NFPs or its subject matter precludes such applicability. For example, NFPs should apply the guidance contained in FASB ASC 220, *Income Statement—Reporting Comprehensive Income*, that does not conflict with the industry guidance.

3A.29 The "Pending Content" in paragraphs 1–2 of FASB ASC 958-220-45 requires that a statement of activities focus on the NFP as a whole and report the following amounts for the period: the change in net assets, using a descriptive term such as *change in net assets* or *change in equity*; the change in net assets with donor restrictions and the change in net assets without donor restrictions.

3A.30 In accordance with the "Pending Content" of FASB ASC 958-220-45-14 and the guidance in paragraphs 17–18 of FASB ASC 958-220-45, the statement of activities generally should report the gross amounts of revenues and expenses for an NFP's ongoing major or central operations and activities;[4] gains and losses may be reported as net amounts if they result from peripheral or incidental transactions or from other events and circumstances that may be largely beyond the control of the NFP and its management. The frequency of the events and the significance of the gross revenues and expenses distinguish major or central events from peripheral or incidental events. Events are ongoing major and central activities if they are normally part of an NFP's strategy and it normally carries on such activities or if the event's gross revenues or expenses are significant in relation to the NFP's annual budget.

3A.31 The "Pending Content" in paragraphs 4–8 of FASB ASC 958-220-45 discusses the classification by net asset class of revenues, expenses, and gains and losses. The determination of the net asset class in which revenues and gains and losses are reported is based on the existence or absence of donor-imposed restrictions and the type of restriction. A statement of activities should report revenues as increases in net assets without donor restrictions unless the use of the assets received is limited by donor-imposed restrictions. All expenses should be reported as decreases in net assets without donor restrictions, with the exception of investment expenses, which should be netted against investment return and reported in the net asset class in which the net investment return is reported. Gains should be reported as increases and losses as decreases in net assets without donor restrictions unless their use is restricted by explicit donor stipulations or by law that extends donor restrictions.

3A.32 Pursuant to the "Pending Content" in FASB ASC 958-220-45-3, *reclassifications of net assets*, which are defined in the FASB ASC glossary as the simultaneous increase of one net asset class and decrease of another, should be reported as separate items. The "Pending Content" in FASB ASC 958-220-45-13 describes the events that require reclassifications of net assets, including

---

[4] The "Pending Content" in paragraphs 14–16 of FASB ASC 958-220-45 discusses the requirement that investment return (related to total return investing and not programmatic investing) be reported net of external and direct internal investment expenses. That exception to gross reporting of revenues and expenses is discussed in paragraph 4.47.

donor-imposed restrictions that are fulfilled by the NFP or that expire with the passage of time or the death of a split-interest agreement's beneficiary.

A-3 The FASB ASC glossary defines an *equity transfer* as a nonreciprocal transaction directly between a transferor and a transferee. Equity transfers are similar to ownership transactions between a for-profit parent and its owned subsidiary (for example, additional paid-in capital or dividends). However, equity transfers can occur only between related NFPs if one controls the other or both are under common control. An equity transfer embodies no expectation of repayment, nor does the transferor receive anything of immediate economic value (such as a financial interest or ownership). The "Pending Content" in FASB ASC 958-220-45-20 requires that equity transfers be reported separately as changes in net assets. Equity transfers do not result in any step-up in basis of the underlying assets transferred. However, a service received from personnel of an affiliate that directly benefits the recipient NFP and for which the affiliate does not charge the recipient NFP may be recorded at the fair value of that service in the circumstances indicated in FASB ASC 958-720-30-3 (see paragraphs 13.19–.23).

A-4 As described in the "Pending Content" in FASB ASC 958-20-55-2B, an equity transaction (see paragraph 5.36) differs from an equity transfer in that an equity transaction involves a financially interrelated party either as a third party in a transfer from an entity to one of its affiliates or as a counterparty in a transfer from an entity to itself. In addition, an equity transaction, unlike an equity transfer, is reciprocal; the NFP or its affiliate named as the beneficiary receives an ongoing economic interest in the assets held by the recipient entity.

3A.33 The "Pending Content" in paragraphs 6–7 of FASB ASC 958-220-55 illustrates the requirement for the display of an appropriately labeled subtotal within a statement of activities for the change in a class of net assets before the effects of discontinued operating segments. NFPs should apply the appropriate disclosure and display requirements of, among other things, FASB ASC 250, *Accounting Changes and Error Corrections*; FASB 205-20-45 for discontinued operations; and FASB ASC 220-20-45-1 for unusual or infrequently occurring items. Corrections of prior-period errors are not included in change in net assets. Instead, in accordance with FASB ASC 250-10-45, any error in the financial statements of a prior period discovered after the financial statements are issued or are available to be issued should be reported by restating the prior-period financial statements. The cumulative effect of the error on periods prior to those presented should be made to the opening balance(s) of the appropriate class(es) of net assets of the earliest year presented.

3A.34 The cumulative effect of a change in accounting principle also is not included in change in net assets. Instead, it is reported through retrospective application of the new accounting principle to all prior periods, unless it is impracticable to do so (or transition guidance for a newly issued standard requires otherwise). The cumulative effect of the change to the new accounting principle on periods prior to those presented should be made to the opening balance(s) of the appropriate class(es) of net assets of the earliest year presented. FASB ASC 250 provides examples of display and further information about accounting changes and corrections of errors, including discussions of impracticability and materiality. Paragraph 11.60 provides guidance if an NFP corrects net asset classifications previously reported in prior years' financial statements.

3A.35 As noted in FASB ASC 958-205-45-1, particular formats for the statement of activities are neither prescribed nor prohibited, in part because similar prescriptions and proscriptions do not exist for business entities. The "Pending Content" in FASB ASC 958-205-55-11 suggests four ways that items could be sequenced: (*a*) revenues and gains first, then expenses, then losses; reclassifications of net assets, which must be shown separately, are reported with revenues and gains; (*b*) revenues, expenses, gains and losses, and reclassifications of net assets shown last; (*c*) certain revenues, less directly related expenses, followed by a subtotal, then other revenues, other expenses, gains and losses, and reclassifications of net assets, and (*d*) expenses followed by revenues, gains and losses, and the reclassification of net assets. Those items could be arranged in other ways, and other subtotals may be included.

3A.36 Pursuant to FASB ASC 958-220-45-9, classifying revenues, expenses, gains, and losses within classes of net assets does not preclude incorporating additional classifications within a statement of activities. For example, within a class or classes of net assets, an NFP may classify items as follows: operating and nonoperating, expendable and nonexpendable, earned and unearned, recurring and nonrecurring, or in other ways.

© Update 3A-1 *Accounting and Reporting*: Presentation of Net Periodic Pension Cost and Net Periodic Postretirement Benefit Cost

FASB ASU No. 2017-07, *Compensation—Retirement Benefits (Topic 715): Improving the Presentation of Net Periodic Pension Cost and Net Periodic Postretirement Benefit Cost*, issued in March 2017, is effective for not-for-profit entities for annual periods beginning after December 15, 2018, and interim periods within annual periods beginning after December 15, 2019. Early adoption is permitted as of the beginning of an annual period for which financial statements have not been issued or made available for issuance.

FASB ASU No. 2017-07 requires that an employer separate pension and postretirement costs into service and other cost components. The service cost portion would be presented in the same financial statement line item as the related compensation costs arising from services rendered by the pertinent employees during the period. The other components of net benefit cost are required to be presented separately, outside of an intermediate measure of operations, if one is presented.

This edition of the guide has not been updated to reflect changes as a result of this ASU; however, the paragraph that follows will be updated in a future edition.

Readers are encouraged to consult the full text of the ASU on FASB's website at www.fasb.org.

3A.37 The "Pending Content" in paragraphs 9–12 of FASB ASC 958-220-45 discuss reporting a measure of operations. If an intermediate measure of operations, such as an excess or deficit of operating revenues over expenses, is reported in a statement of activities, (*a*) a note to financial statements should describe the nature of the reported measure of operations or the items excluded from operations if the NFP's use of the term *operations* is not apparent from the details provided on the face of the statement, and (*b*) it must be in a financial statement that, at a minimum, reports the change in net assets without donor restrictions for the period. Example 5 (the "Pending Content" in paragraphs 16–19) of FASB ASC 958-220-55-16 illustrates two alternatives for providing the required information–one in which the information is apparent on the face of the financial statements and one in which the information is disclosed in the notes to the financial statements, and states that there are multiple ways in which the information could be presented. Some limitations on an NFP's use of an intermediate measure of operations are imposed by other standards. For example, if a subtotal such as income from operations is presented, it should include the following amounts:

a. An impairment loss recognized for a long-lived asset (or asset group) to be held and used pursuant to FASB ASC 360-10-45-4

b. Any gain or loss recognized on the sale of a long-lived asset (or disposal group) if that asset (or group) is not a component of an NFP that qualifies for discontinued operations treatment, as defined in FASB ASC 205-20, and pursuant to FASB ASC 360-10-45-5

c. Costs associated with an exit or disposal activity that does not involve a discontinued operation pursuant to FASB ASC 420-10-45-3

d. Amortization expenses and impairment losses recognized on intangible assets including goodwill pursuant to FASB ASC 350-30-45-2 and FASB ASC 350-20-45-2

A-5 Providing a measure of operations in a statement of activities may include internal board designations, appropriations, and similar actions affecting that measure. As required by the "Pending Content" in FASB ASC 958-220-45-12, if an NFP presents internal board designations, appropriations, and similar actions on the face of the financial statements, a note to financial statements should provide an appropriate disaggregation and description by type of these actions if not provided on the face of the financial statements.

3A.38 FinREC believes that in the absence of guidance specific to NFPs, as a best practice, most items that a business entity would report as part of other comprehensive income would be presented by an NFP in the statement of activities outside of an intermediate measure of operations, if one is presented. (Those items are listed in FASB ASC 220-10-45-10A.) However, unrealized gains and losses on available-for-sale and held-to-maturity securities, although reported in other comprehensive income by a business entity, would be the exception to that suggested practice. Unrealized gains and losses are typically presented as described in paragraphs 4.84–.89 because most NFPs do not classify investments into the three categories used in FASB ASC 320-10. For example, an NFP might report the following in its statement of activities:

Change from operations in net assets without donor restrictions	XX,XXX
Foreign currency translation adjustments	X,XXX
Prior service costs or credits associated with pension benefits[a]	X,XXX
Gains or losses associated with pension benefits that are not recognized immediately as a component of net periodic benefit cost[a]	X,XXX

Investment return in excess of amounts designated for current operations	X,XXX
Change in net assets without donor restrictions	$XX,XXX

[a] These two lines may be combined if desired.

When doing so, it is important to remember that all changes for the reporting period are reported as part of (that is, above) change in net assets. Paragraphs 3A.32–.33 discuss presentation of corrections of errors and changes in accounting principles.

3A.39 Classification of revenues, expenses, gains and losses, and reclassifications is discussed in greater detail in subsequent chapters of this guide. Paragraphs 4.86–.89 describe reporting investment return in a statement of activities that includes an intermediate measure of operations. Chapter 13, "Expenses, Gains, and Losses," discusses alternative ways of reporting costs related to sales of goods and services and the direct costs of special events.

Reporting Expenses by Nature and Function

3A.40 The "Pending Content" in FASB ASC 958-205-45-6 states that reporting expenses by nature and function is useful in associating expenses with service efforts and accomplishments of NFPs. The "Pending Content" in the FASB ASC glossary defines *functional expense classification* as a method of grouping expenses according to the purpose for which costs are incurred. The primary functional classifications of an NFP are program services and supporting activities. The "Pending Content" in the FASB ASC glossary defines *natural expense classification* as a method of grouping expenses according to the kinds of economic benefits received in incurring those expenses. Examples of natural expense classifications include salaries and wages, employee benefits, professional services, supplies, interest expense, rent, utilities, and depreciation.

3A.41 The "Pending Content" in FASB ASC 958-720-45-15 requires all NFPs to report information about all expenses in one location on the face of the statement of activities, as a schedule in the notes to financial statements, or in a separate financial statement, presenting the relationship between functional classification and natural classification for all expenses in an analysis that disaggregates functional expense classifications, such as major classes of program services and supporting activities, by their natural expense classifications, such as salaries, rent, electricity, supplies, interest expense, depreciation, awards and grants to others, and professional fees. The analysis is discussed further in paragraph 13.04.

3A.42 This paragraph will be deleted upon the effective date of FASB ASU No. 2016-14.

3A.43 This paragraph will be deleted upon the effective date of FASB ASU No. 2016-14.

3A.44 This paragraph will be deleted upon the effective date of FASB ASU No. 2016-14.

3A.45 This paragraph will be deleted upon the effective date of FASB ASU No. 2016-14.

Statement of Cash Flows

© Update 3A-2 *Accounting and Reporting*: Statement of Cash Flows

FASB ASU No. 2016-15, *Statement of Cash Flows (Topic 230): Classification of Certain Cash Receipts and Cash Payments (a consensus of the Emerging Issues Task Force)*, was issued in August 2016 to increase the consistency of reporting the following cash flows: debt prepayment or debt extinguishment costs, settlement of debt instruments with coupon interest rates that are insignificant in relation to the effective interest rate of the borrowing (such as zero-coupon bonds), cash payments made to settle a contingent consideration liability arising from an acquisition, proceeds from the settlement of insurance claims, proceeds from the settlement of corporate-owned life insurance policies, distributions received from equity method investees, and beneficial interests in securitization transactions. In addition, the ASU includes guidance for classification of cash receipts and payments that have aspects of more than one class of cash flows.

FASB ASU No. 2016-15 is effective for NFPs for fiscal years beginning after December 15, 2018, and interim periods within fiscal years beginning after December 15, 2019. Early adoption is permitted.

This edition of the guide has not been updated to reflect changes as a result of this FASB ASU; however, the section that follows will be updated in a future edition. Readers are encouraged to consult the full text of the FASB ASU on FASB's website at www.fasb.org.

© Update 3A-3 *Accounting and Reporting*: Statement of Cash Flows

FASB ASU No. 2016-18, *Statement of Cash Flows (Topic 230): Restricted Cash (a consensus of the FASB Emerging Issues Task Force)*, was issued in October 2016 to increase the consistency of reporting cash flows into and out of restricted cash accounts. It requires that a statement of cash flows explain the change during the period in the total of cash, cash equivalents, and amounts generally described as restricted cash or restricted cash equivalents. It does not define restricted cash.

FASB ASU No. 2016-18 is effective for NFPs for fiscal years beginning after December 15, 2018, and interim periods within fiscal years beginning after December 15, 2019. Early adoption is permitted.

This edition of the guide has not been updated to reflect changes as a result of this FASB ASU; however, the section that follows will be updated in a future edition. Readers are encouraged to consult the full text of the FASB ASU on FASB's website at www.fasb.org.

3A.46 FASB ASC 958-230 describes the unique standards relating to a statement of cash flows of an NFP. In addition to that industry-specific guidance, an NFP should follow all effective provisions of FASB ASC unless the specific provision explicitly exempts NFPs or its subject matter precludes such applicability. For example, NFPs should apply the guidance contained in FASB ASC 230, *Statement of Cash Flows*, that does not conflict with the industry guidance.

3A.47 FASB ASC 230-10-10-1 explains that the primary purpose of a statement of cash flows is to provide relevant information about the cash receipts and cash payments of an entity during a period. FASB ASC 230-10-45-10 requires that the statement of cash flows classify cash receipts and cash payments as resulting from investing, financing, or operating activities. Exhibit 3A-1, "Classification of Cash and Cash Flows," provides examples of cash flows unique to or common to NFPs and their appropriate classification. FASB ASC 958-230-55-5 requires separate disclosure of noncash investing and financing activities (for example, receiving contributions of buildings, securities, or recognized collection items).

Exhibit 3A-1

Classification of Cash and Cash Flows
Cash and Cash Equivalents
• Cash held temporarily in the long-term investment portfolio (until suitable investments are identified) is excluded from cash and cash equivalents in accordance with FASB ASC 958-205-55-7 and should be disclosed in the note that defines cash and cash equivalents.
Operating Cash Flows
• Cash contributions that are not subject to donor restrictions. • Restricted contributions, provided that the contributed resources are not restricted for fixed assets, endowments, split-interest gifts, and other long-term purposes. • Cash receipts resulting from the sale of donated financial assets (for example, donated debt or equity instruments) that upon receipt were directed without any not-for-profit entity- (NFP-) imposed limitations for sale and were converted nearly immediately into cash, provided that the donor did not restrict the use of the contributed resources to a long-term purpose. • Agency transactions are generally included as operating activities.
Investing Cash Flows
• Gross purchases of investments should be adjusted for amounts payable for investment purchases at period ends to arrive at cash outflows for purchases. • Gross sales of investments, which should be adjusted for amounts receivable from investment sales at period ends to arrive at cash inflows from sales.
Financing Cash Flows
• Securities lending would generally be classified as a financing activity. • Cash receipts resulting from the sale of donated financial assets (for example, donated debt or equity instruments) that upon receipt were directed without any NFP-imposed limitations for sale and were converted nearly immediately into cash if the donor restricted the use of the contributed resources to a long-term purpose. • Contributions restricted for fixed assets, endowments, split-interest gifts, and other long-term purposes should be reported as a financing activity; the amount would be the actual cash received, not the change in the contributions receivable. • Changes in cash overdrafts generally are considered financing activities and not as operating activities.
Noncash Transactions
• If construction in process and other fixed asset purchases are included in accounts payable at the fiscal year end, they should be disclosed as a noncash transaction and excluded from the change in accounts payable.

Classification of Cash and Cash Flows—*continued*

- Contributions of securities should be disclosed as a noncash transaction and as an adjustment reducing the change in net assets to arrive at operating cash flows if the securities were retained as investments rather than converted nearly immediately into cash.
- Contributions of beneficial interests should be disclosed as a noncash transaction and as an adjustment reducing the change in net assets to arrive at operating cash flows.
- The net change in value for an interest rate swap should be a noncash adjustment to arrive at operating activities. The amount will not equal the amount in the statement of activities if the statement of activities amount includes amounts paid in cash.
- Debt refinancing and refundings are disclosed as a noncash activity if no cash is transferred to the NFP's control and it only enters into new terms (for example, change in interest rate, payment terms, and so forth). Any incremental borrowings are financing inflows.

3A.48 The FASB ASC glossary defines *operating activities* as including all transactions and other events that are not defined as investing or financing activities. Operating activities generally involve producing and delivering goods and providing services. Per FASB ASC 958-230-55-4, operating activities also include cash received and paid in agency transactions.

3A.49 Some NFPs receive resources in agency transactions, as discussed in chapter 5, "Contributions Received and Agency Transactions." For some of those NFPs, receiving resources as agents may be a primary component of their mission. Because cash flows from operating activities include cash flows from agency transactions, an NFP that acts as an agent as a primary component of its mission might consider presenting the statement of cash flows as the first financial statement in its set of financial statements to emphasize the importance of the information presented in that statement.

3A.50 FASB ASC 230-10-45-25 encourages entities to report major classes of gross cash receipts and gross cash payments and their arithmetic sum—the net cash flow from operating activities (the direct method) and identifies the minimum classes of operating receipts and disbursements to report. The "Pending Content": in FASB ASC 230-10-45-29 states that NFPs that use the direct method of reporting net cash flows from operations are not required to provide a reconciliation of change in net assets to net cash flow from operating activities. In accordance with FASB ASC 230-10-45-28, NFPs that choose not to provide information by the direct method should determine and report the same amount for net cash flow from operating activities indirectly by adjusting change in net assets to reconcile it to net cash flow from operating activities (the indirect or reconciliation method). Paragraphs 28 and 31–32 of FASB ASC 230-10-45 and the "Pending Content" in paragraphs 29–30 of FASB ASC 230-10-45 describe how to determine and report the amount of net cash flow from operating activities using the indirect method.

3A.51 As discussed in the "Pending Content" in FASB ASC 958-210-45-6, cash received with a donor-imposed restriction that limits its use to long-term purposes should not be classified on a statement of financial position with cash that is available for current use and without donor restrictions.[5] FASB ASC 958-230-55-3 explains that when an NFP reports cash received with a donor-imposed restriction that limits its use to long-term purposes in conformity with the "Pending Content" in FASB ASC 958-210-45-6, an adjustment is necessary for the statement of cash flows to reconcile beginning and ending cash and cash equivalents. To report in conformity with FASB ASC 230, the receipt of a cash contribution that is restricted for the purchase of equipment should be reported as a cash flow from financing activities (using a caption such as contributions restricted for purchasing equipment), and it should be simultaneously reported as a cash outflow from investing activities (using a caption such as purchase of assets restricted to investment in property and equipment or, if the equipment was purchased in the same period, purchase of equipment). An adjustment to reconcile the change in net assets to net cash used or provided by operating activities would also be needed if the contributed asset is not classified as cash or cash equivalents on the statement of financial position. When the equipment is purchased in a subsequent period, both the proceeds from the sale of assets restricted to investment in the equipment and the purchase of the equipment should be reported as cash flows from investing activities.

3.A52 FASB ASC 958-230-55-2 notes that not all assets of NFPs that meet the definition of *cash equivalents* in the FASB ASC glossary are cash equivalents for purposes of preparing statements of financial position and cash flows. Restrictions can prevent them from being included as cash equivalents even if they otherwise qualify. For example, short-term highly liquid investments are not cash equivalents if they are purchased with resources that have donor-imposed restrictions that limit their use to long-term investment. Further, FASB ASC 230-10-45-6 states that an entity should establish a policy concerning which short-term, highly liquid investments that satisfy the definition of cash equivalents are treated as cash equivalents. FASB ASC 230-10-50-1 requires entities to disclose their policy for determining which items are treated as cash equivalents.

3A.53 For example, an NFP may hold a portion of its donor-restricted endowment portfolio in cash or instruments with maturities of less than three months. In accordance with the "Pending Content" in FASB ASC 958-210-45-6, those amounts should not be classified with cash or other assets that are available for current use and without donor restriction, and thus should be excluded from cash and cash equivalents. Similarly, as discussed in paragraph 3.21, cash and instruments with maturities of less than three months that are identified as a board-designated endowment fund may be excluded from cash and cash equivalents.

3A.54 As discussed in chapter 4, "Cash, Cash Equivalents, and Investments," NFPs sometimes apply a spending rate to their investment return. The existence of a spending rate does not affect the classification of cash inflows and outflows on the statement of cash flows. Sales of investments are investing activities even in circumstances in which the NFP uses the sales proceeds to fund current operations. For example, assume NFP has an endowment of $10 million and a spending rate of 5 percent ($500,000). Further, assume interest

[5] Paragraphs 3.09–.23 and .52–.53 discuss the classification on a statement of financial position of cash received with donor-imposed restrictions limiting its use to long term purposes.

and dividends are $200,000 and sales of endowment investments in the current year are $800,000. In that circumstance, presumably $300,000 of sales of endowment investments would be used for spending. The NFP should report the full $800,000 of sales of endowment investments as cash inflows from investing activities.

Liquidity and Availability Disclosure

A-5 The "Pending Content" in FASB ASC 958-210-50-1A requires an NFP to disclose the following:

a. Qualitative information in the notes to financial statements that is useful in assessing an entity's liquidity and that communicates how an NFP manages its liquid resources available to meet cash needs for general expenditures within one year of the date of the statement of financial position

b. Quantitative information either on the face of the statement of financial position or in the notes, and additional qualitative information in the notes as necessary, that communicates the availability of an NFP's financial assets at the date of the statement of financial position to meet cash needs for general expenditures within one year of the date of the statement of financial position. Availability of a financial asset may be affected by any of the following: (1) its nature, (2) external limits imposed by donors, laws, and contracts with others, or (3) internal limits imposed by governing board decisions.

A-6 The term *general expenditures* is undefined. Because the determination of which expenditures are general expenditures affects the determination of whether a financial asset is available to meet cash needs for general expenditures, the additional qualitative information required by the "Pending Content" in FASB ASC 958-210-50-1A(b) may need to include a description of how both general expenditures and availability of financial assets are determined by the NFP.

A-7 There are three examples of notes that meet the requirements of the "Pending Content" in FASB ASC 958-210-50-1A:

- Note G in the "Pending Content" in FASB ASC 958-205-55-21, which provides quantitative information in the form of a reconciliation, as of the financial statement date, of total financial assets to financial assets available to meet cash needs for general expenditures within one year. The reconciling items include amounts for financial assets that are not available for general expenditures. Additional qualitative information about availability of resources and liquidity is also included in the note.
- Case A, Example 2 (the "Pending Content in paragraphs 5–7 in FASB ASC 958-210-55), which provides a narrative discussion of availability of its financial assets and liquidity
- Case B, Example 2 (the "Pending Content in FASB ASC 958-210-55-8), which provides a classified statement of financial position with additional qualitative information about availability of resources and liquidity in a note

A-8 Combined (but not each individually), those examples include qualitative disclosures about:

- The NFP's responsibility to maintain resources to meet donor restrictions, which may make those resources unavailable for general expenditures
- The NFP's goals for maintaining financial assets
- The NFP's policies for investing excess cash
- The NFP's policies for spending from board designated endowment funds
- Contractual agreements that make certain financial assets unavailable to fund general expenditures
- Lines of credit that would be drawn down if the NFP did not have adequate liquid, available financial assets.[6]

---

[6] The amendments in FASB ASU No. 2016-14 are effective for annual financial statements issued for fiscal years beginning after December 15, 2017 (for example, years ending December 31, 2018 and years ending June 30, 2019), and for interim periods within fiscal years beginning after December 15, 2018. Application to interim financial statements is permitted but not required in the initial year of application. Early application of the amendments is permitted.

Chapter 4

Cash, Cash Equivalents, and Investments

Gray shaded text in this chapter reflects guidance issued but not yet effective as of the date of this guide, March 1, 2018, but becoming effective on or prior to June 30, 2018, exclusive of any option to early adopt ahead of the mandatory effective date. Unless otherwise indicated, all unshaded text reflects guidance that was already effective as of the date of this guide.

Cash and Cash Equivalents

4.01 Like for-profit enterprises, not-for-profit entities (NFPs) hold cash balances to meet payments arising in the ordinary course of operations and payments for unanticipated contingencies. These balances may be held as cash or cash equivalents. Cash includes currency on hand and deposits held by financial institutions that can be added to or withdrawn without limitation, such as demand deposits. NFPs may invest excess cash in cash equivalents (such as Treasury bills, commercial paper, and money-market mutual funds) to earn greater returns.

4.02 The FASB *Accounting Standards Codification* (ASC) glossary defines *cash equivalents* as

> short-term, highly liquid investments that have both of the following characteristics: (*a*) readily convertible to known amounts of cash [and] (*b*) so near their maturity that they present insignificant risk of changes in value because of changes in interest rates. Generally, only investments with original maturities of three months or less qualify under that definition. Original maturity means original maturity to the entity holding the investment. For example, both a three-month U.S. Treasury bill and a three-year Treasury note purchased three months from maturity qualify as cash equivalents. However, a Treasury note purchased three years ago does not become a cash equivalent when its remaining maturity is three months. Examples of items commonly considered to be cash equivalents are Treasury bills, commercial paper, money market funds, and federal funds sold (for an entity with banking operations).

4.03 Investments that would otherwise meet the preceding definition may not meet the definition of a cash equivalent if they are subject to donor restrictions, governing board designations, and other limitations on use. For example, NFPs may hold cash and cash equivalents of permanent endowment funds temporarily until suitable long-term investment opportunities are identified. As stated in FASB ASC 958-320-45-10 and illustrated in FASB ASC 958-205-55-7, that cash may be included in the classification *long-term investments* on a statement of financial position rather than as *cash*. The effects of donor restrictions, governing board designations, and other limitations on the classification of cash and cash equivalents are discussed further in paragraphs 3.09–.23 and 3.52–.53. In addition, cash held temporarily by a custodian for investment purposes may be included as part of investments in a statement of financial position rather than as cash.

Investments that would otherwise meet the preceding definition may not meet the definition of a cash equivalent if they are subject to donor restrictions, governing board designations, and other limitations on use. For example, NFPs may hold cash and cash equivalents of donor-restricted endowment funds temporarily until suitable long-term investment opportunities are identified. As stated in the "Pending Content" in 958-210-45-5A and illustrated in the "Pending Content" in FASB ASC 958-205-55-7, that cash may be included in the classification *long-term investments* on a statement of financial position rather than as *cash*. The effects of donor restrictions, governing board designations, and other limitations on the classification of cash and cash equivalents are discussed further in paragraphs 3A.09–.23 and 3A.52–.53. In addition, cash held temporarily by a custodian for investment purposes may be included as part of investments in a statement of financial position rather than as cash.[1]

4.04 Some NFPs deposit funds with a related entity, such as a local organization that deposits funds with its national headquarters or a church that deposits funds with its denominational body. The Financial Reporting Executive Committee (FinREC) believes that funds deposited by an NFP in a related entity's cash account under a centralized cash management arrangement generally would not be classified as cash and cash equivalents in the NFP's financial statements unless the NFP has legal title to the cash on deposit. Generally, legal title in a cash account is evidenced by the cash or cash equivalent being deposited in a demand deposit account at a bank or other financial institution in the NFP's name. An NFP's deposit in a cash pool generally is not a short-term highly-liquid investment, as contemplated in the definition of a *cash equivalent* in paragraph 4.02; rather, the deposit is considered a loan, and the NFP would classify the deposit in the cash pool as a receivable from a related entity.

Investments Discussed in This Chapter

© Update 4-1 *Accounting and Reporting*: Financial Assets and Financial Liabilities

FASB Accounting Standards Update (ASU) No. 2016-01, *Financial Instruments—Overall (Subtopic 825-10): Recognition and Measurement of Financial Assets and Financial Liabilities*, issued in January 2016, is effective for NFPs for fiscal years beginning after December 15, 2018, and interim periods within fiscal years beginning after December 15, 2019, and cannot be adopted earlier than for fiscal years beginning after December 15, 2017. However, NFPs may elect not to disclose the information about fair value of financial instruments measured at amortized cost (paragraphs 10–19 of FASB ASC 825-10-50) in any financial statements that have not yet been made available for issuance.

---

[1] The amendments in FASB Accounting Standards Update (ASU) No. 2016-14, *Not-for-Profit Entities (Topic 958): Presentation of Financial Statements of Not-for-Profit Entities*, are effective for annual financial statements issued for fiscal years beginning after December 15, 2017 (for example, years ending December 31, 2018, and years ending June 30, 2019), and for interim periods within fiscal years beginning after December 15, 2018. Application to interim financial statements is permitted but not required in the initial year of application. Early application of the amendments is permitted.

The "Pending Content" resulting from this ASU changes the measurement of equity securities without readily determinable fair value and the disclosures related to those investments, although a not-for-profit entity is still allowed to elect to report them at fair value. The amendments also change disclosure requirements for financial instruments. This ASU is discussed further in the preface.

FASB ASU No. 2018-03, *Technical Corrections and Improvements to Financial Instruments—Overall (Subtopic 825-10): Recognition and Measurement of Financial Assets and Financial Liabilities*, issued in February 2018, includes technical corrections and improvements related to FASB ASU No. 2016-01. FASB ASU No. 2018-03 has the same effective date as FASB ASU No. 2016-01. Entities may early adopt the amendments for fiscal years beginning after December 15, 2017, including interim periods within those fiscal years, provided they have adopted FASB ASU No. 2016-01.

This edition of the guide has not been updated to reflect changes as a result of these ASUs; however, the text that follows will be updated in a future edition. Readers are encouraged to consult the full text of the ASU at FASB's website at www.fasb.org.

4.05 NFPs acquire various kinds of investments by contribution or purchase. This chapter provides accounting and auditing guidance concerning the initial recognition and measurement, investment income and expenses, the measurement attributes used for subsequent valuation, unrealized and realized gains and losses, and financial statement display and disclosure. Many of the requirements under generally accepted accounting principles in these areas are the same as those for for-profit entities. Accordingly, this chapter focuses on those issues that are unique to NFPs.

4.06 This chapter does not discuss the standards for investments in consolidated subsidiaries. A requirement to consolidate precludes reporting an investment at fair value with two exceptions, which are discussed in paragraph 4.20 (for general partners in a limited partnership or similar entity) and paragraph 4.23 (for limited partners in a limited partnership or similar entity). The standards for consolidation are discussed in chapter 3, "Financial Statements, the Reporting Entity, and General Financial Reporting Matters," because the investee is part of the reporting entity. NFPs can use exhibit 3-2, "Relationships of a Not-for-Profit Reporting Entity," to assist with the determination of which investees are required to be consolidated.

4.07 When considering whether an investee should be consolidated, standards for consolidation of for-profit entities typically would be used to evaluate the relationship. If an interest in another entity is owned with the objective of investment return, FinREC believes that often the investee is a for-profit entity. An investee owned with the objective of investment return typically would not meet the FASB ASC glossary definition of an NFP (see paragraph 1.01) because the investee provides lower costs or other economic benefits directly and proportionally to its owners, members, or participants, or it has ownership interests, or both.

4.08 This chapter provides guidance about reporting investments. If an investment is in the form of an ownership interest in another entity, this chapter provides guidance if the objective is to invest in the entity for investment return (including an objective to realize current income, capital appreciation, or both) and the other entity is not required to be consolidated. If the interest is in an entity that provides goods or services that accomplish the purpose or mission for which the NFP exists or that serves the NFP's administrative purposes, the NFP would follow the guidance in chapter 3.

4.09 Although the valuation (measurement) guidance in this chapter applies to investments held by the NFP as trustee or other fiscal agent under a split-interest agreement, reporting the changes in valuation and reporting investment income earned on those split-interest gifts, including investments held in trust by others, are discussed more fully in chapter 6, "Split-Interest Agreements and Beneficial Interests in Trusts."

4.10 Investments that are made with a primary purpose of furthering the mission-related objectives of the NFP rather than the production of current income or capital appreciation are discussed in chapter 8, "Programmatic Investments."

Initial Recognition and Measurement of Investments

> **© Update 4-2 *Accounting and Reporting*: Gains and Losses on Sales of Nonfinancial Assets**
>
> FASB ASU No. 2017-05, *Other Income—Gains and Losses from the Derecognition of Nonfinancial Assets (Subtopic 610-20): Clarifying the Scope of Asset Derecognition Guidance and Accounting for Partial Sales of Nonfinancial Assets*, was issued in February 2017 to clarify the scope of FASB ASC 610-20. Among its amendments, it requires that the guidance in FASB ASC 610-20 apply to transfers of nonfinancial assets to a joint venture or other equity method investee.
>
> FASB ASU No. 2017-05 is effective concurrently with the amendments in FASB ASU No. 2014-09, *Revenue from Contracts with Customers (Topic 606)*. As a result, most NFPs will apply the new standards for annual reporting periods beginning after December 15, 2018, and interim periods within annual periods beginning after December 15, 2019. However, NFPs that have issued, or are conduit bond obligors for, securities that are traded, listed, or quoted on an exchange or an over-the-counter market are required to apply the standards for annual reporting periods beginning after December 15, 2017, including interim periods within that reporting period.
>
> This edition of the guide has not been updated to reflect changes as a result of this ASU; however, the section that follows will be updated in a future edition. Readers are encouraged to consult the full text of the ASU on FASB's website at www.fasb.org.

4.11 Pursuant to FASB ASC 958-320-30-1 and FASB ASC 958-325-30-1, investments included within the scope of FASB ASC 958-320 and FASB ASC 958-325 are initially measured at their acquisition cost (including brokerage and other transaction fees) if they are purchased and are initially measured at fair value if they are received as a contribution or through an agency transaction. Pursuant to FASB ASC 815-10-30, all derivative instruments are measured initially at fair value. Investments that are accounted for under the equity method generally are measured initially at cost pursuant to FASB ASC 323-10-30, although FASB ASC 970-323-30 provides more specific guidance for real estate ventures, and FASB ASC 323-10-30-2 requires initial measurement at fair value for a retained investment in the common stock of an investee (including a joint venture) in a deconsolidation transaction.

4.12 Paragraphs 3.138–.168 discuss FASB ASC 820, *Fair Value Measurement*, which defines *fair value*, establishes a framework for measuring fair value, and requires disclosures about fair value measurements.

Valuation of Investments Subsequent to Acquisition

4.13 For purposes of the discussion of subsequent measurement, investments are divided into the following four broad categories:

- Investments in equity securities with readily determinable fair values (other than consolidated subsidiaries and equity securities reported under the equity method) and all investments in debt securities, which are investments that are subject to the requirements of FASB ASC 958-320.
- Investments that are accounted for under the equity method, which are investments that are subject to the requirements of FASB ASC 323-10, FASB ASC 323-30, and FASB ASC 970-323, including certain investments in common stock, partnerships, limited liability partnerships, and limited liability corporations.
- Investments in derivative instruments that are subject to the requirements of FASB ASC 815, *Derivatives and Hedging*. If an investment would otherwise be in the scope of FASB ASC 958-320 and it has within it an embedded derivative that is subject to FASB ASC 815, the host contract (as described in FASB ASC 815-15-05-1) remains within the scope of FASB ASC 958-320.
- Other investments, which are those included in the scope of FASB ASC 958-325. Those investments include, among others, certain investments in real estate, mortgage notes that are not debt securities, venture capital funds, certain partnership interests, oil and gas interests, and certain equity securities that do not have a readily determinable fair value. Other investments do not include investments described in the preceding three bullets or investments in consolidated subsidiaries.

4.14 Exhibit 4-1, "Investments of a Not-for-Profit Reporting Entity," describes some common investments and identifies where they are discussed in this chapter and in FASB ASC. Exhibit 4-1 and this chapter summarize certain guidance in FASB ASC but are not a substitute for reading the guidance itself.

4.15 NFPs can choose to report certain investments at fair value under the following elections:

- An NFP may elect to report "other investments" at fair value in accordance with FASB ASC 958-325-35. That election requires that the same measurement attribute be used for all "other investments" excluding those for which the NFP chose, at a specified election date, to measure at fair value pursuant to FASB ASC 815-15-25 or the "Fair Value Option" subsections of FASB ASC 825-10. The election applies to the investments described in FASB ASC 958-325-15.

- An NFP may elect to measure an investee entity at fair value pursuant to the "Fair Value Option" subsections of FASB ASC 825-10. That election can be made only at the specified election dates described in paragraphs 4–5 of FASB ASC 825-10-25 and apply only to the financial instruments described in paragraphs 4–5 of FASB ASC 825-10-15.

4.16 Because there is industry-specific guidance for other investments in FASB ASC 958-325-35, an NFP cannot use by analogy the guidance in FASB ASC 970, *Real Estate—General*, for partnerships that are owned with the objective of total return (that is, as an investment). An NFP uses the guidance in FASB ASC 970 for investments only as required by FASB ASC 958-810-15-4(d); that is, only for a noncontrolling interest in a for-profit real estate partnership, limited liability company, or similar entity that constitutes more than a minor interest, and then only if the NFP has not elected to report that investment at fair value. (However, if the partnership is not held for investment, such as a partnership that provides goods or services that accomplish the purpose or mission for which the NFP exists or that serves the NFP's administrative purposes, the NFP may be permitted to analogize to FASB ASC 970, as discussed in chapter 3.)

Exhibit 4-1

Investments of a Not-for-Profit Reporting Entity[a]

Relationship	*FASB* Accounting Standards Codification (ASC) *Reference*	*Discussion in This Chapter*
Relationships With Entities Held for Investment		
The reporting entity owns 50 percent or less of the common voting stock of an investee and the reporting entity neither controls nor can exercise significant influence over the investee's operating and financial policies. The stock is an equity security that has a readily determinable fair value.	FASB ASC 958-320-35-1	Paragraph 4.17
The reporting entity owns 50 percent or less of the common voting stock of an investee and the reporting entity neither controls nor can exercise significant influence over the investee's operating and financial policies. The stock does not have a readily determinable fair value.	FASB ASC 958-325-35	Paragraph 4.38
The reporting entity owns debt securities that are not derivative instruments.	FASB ASC 958-320-35-1	Paragraph 4.17
The reporting entity owns 50 percent or less of the common voting stock of an investee and can exercise significant influence over the investee's operating and financial policies.	If the reporting entity elects to report such interests at fair value,[b] measure at fair value, If the reporting entity elects to report "other investments" at cost or lower of cost or fair value, use the equity method of accounting in accordance with FASB ASC 323-10.	Paragraphs 4.18–.19

(continued)

Investments of a Not-for-Profit Reporting Entity—*(continued)*

Relationship	*FASB* Accounting Standards Codification (ASC) *Reference*	*Discussion in This Chapter*
Relationships With Entities Held for Investment		
The reporting entity is the general partner of a for-profit limited partnership or similar entity, such as a limited liability company that has governing provisions that are the functional equivalent of a limited partnership.	If the reporting entity has made an election to use fair value for all "other investments," in accordance with FASB ASC 958-325-35, the interest is reported at fair value. Otherwise, use the guidance in paragraphs 11–29 of FASB ASC 958-810-25 to determine whether the general partner within the group controls and, therefore, should consolidate the limited partnership or similar entity. If not required to consolidate, use the equity method unless the partnership interest is reported at fair value in conformity with the "Fair Value Option" sections of FASB 825-10.	Paragraphs 4.20–.22
The reporting entity is a limited partner of a for-profit limited partnership or similar entity.	If the reporting entity has made an election to use fair value for all "other investments," in accordance with FASB ASC 958-325-35, the interest is reported at fair value. Otherwise, use the guidance in paragraphs 1129 of FASB ASC 958-810-25 to determine whether the limited partner has a controlling financial interest, and, therefore, should consolidate the limited partnership or similar entity. If not required to consolidate, use FASB ASC 958-325-35 for noncontrolling interests in entities engaged in activities other than real estate activities.	Paragraphs 4.23–.25 and 4.38

Investments of a Not-for-Profit Reporting Entity—*(continued)*

Relationship	*FASB* Accounting Standards Codification (ASC) *Reference*	*Discussion in This Chapter*
Relationships With Entities Held for Investment		
The reporting entity has an interest in a limited liability company.	If the reporting entity has made an election to use fair value for all "other investments," in accordance with FASB ASC 958-325-35, the interest is reported at fair value. Otherwise, apply the guidance in paragraphs 1129 of FASB ASC 958-810-25 if the functional equivalent of a limited partnership, or paragraphs 114 of FASB ASC 810-10-25 and FASB ASC 323-10 if the functional equivalent of a corporation.	Paragraphs 4.26–.27
The reporting entity has a noncontrolling interest that constitutes *more than* a minor interest in a for-profit partnership (limited or general), limited liability entity, or similar entity engaged in real estate activities.	If the reporting entity elects to report such interests at fair value,[b] measure at fair value. If the reporting entity elects to report "other investments" at cost or lower of cost or fair value, use the equity method in accordance with the guidance in FASB ASC 970-323.	Paragraphs 4.23–.25 and 4.28
The reporting entity has a noncontrolling interest that constitutes a minor interest in a for-profit partnership, limited liability entity, or similar entity engaged in real estate activities.	FASB ASC 958-325-35	Paragraph 4.38
The reporting entity has an interest in a general partnership that is engaged in activities other than real estate activities.	FASB ASC 958-325-35	Paragraph 4.38
The reporting entity holds derivative instruments that are within the scope of FASB ASC 815.	FASB ASC 815	Paragraphs 4.29–.37

(continued)

Investments of a Not-for-Profit Reporting Entity—*(continued)*

Relationship	*FASB* Accounting Standards Codification (ASC) *Reference*	*Discussion in This Chapter*
Relationships With Entities Held for Investment		
The reporting entity has an interest in an investment pool.		Paragraphs 4.58–.64

[a] As discussed in paragraph 4.08, the guidance in this exhibit applies when an ownership interest in another entity is an investment. See exhibit 3-2 for relationships with entities that provide goods or services that accomplish the purpose or mission for which the not-for-profit entity (NFP) exists or that serve the NFP's administrative purposes.

[b] The election to report at fair value refers to the election to report "other investments" at fair value in accordance with FASB ASC 958-325-35 or the election pursuant to the "Fair Value Option" subsections of FASB ASC 825-10. As discussed in paragraph 4.15, the scope sections of those subtopics indicate the types of investments for which the elections are available.

Equity Securities With Readily Determinable Fair Value (Other Than Consolidated Subsidiaries and Equity Securities Reported Under the Equity Method) and All Debt Securities

4.17 FASB ASC 958-320-35-1 requires that investments in equity securities with readily determinable fair value and all investments in debt securities be measured at fair value in the statement of financial position. FASB ASC 958-320 does not apply to the investments described in FASB ASC 958-320-15-4, including investments in consolidated subsidiaries and investments required to be accounted for by the equity method.

Investments That Are Accounted for Under the Equity Method or a Fair Value Election

Investments in Common Stock and In-Substance Common Stock

4.18 Investments in common stock and in-substance common stock of for-profit entities should be reported under the equity method if required by FASB ASC 323-10. FASB ASC 323-10 requires that the equity method of accounting be used if investments in common stock or in-substance common stock (or both common stock and in-substance common stock), including investments in common stock of joint ventures, give the investor the ability to exercise significant influence over operating and financial policies of an investee, even though the investor holds 50 percent or less of the common stock or in-substance common stock (or both common stock and in-substance common stock). (For additional information, see paragraphs 3.76–.78.) However, NFPs that choose to report all "other investments" at fair value in conformity with FASB ASC 958-325-35 (paragraph 4.38) or that make an election to report an investment at fair value pursuant to the "Fair Value Option" subsections of FASB ASC 825-10 may do so instead of applying the equity method of accounting to investments covered by this paragraph.

4.19 The FASB ASC glossary defines *in-substance common stock* as an investment in an entity that has risk and reward characteristics that are substantially similar to that entity's common stock. The characteristics of in-substance common stock are discussed in paragraphs 13–14 of FASB ASC 323-10-15. Paragraphs 1–18 of FASB ASC 323-10-55 provide examples applying the characteristics to various investments.

Limited Partnerships and Similar Entities

4.20 If the NFP is the general partner of a limited partnership or similar entity and the NFP has elected to report all "other investments" at fair value in accordance with FASB ASC 958-325-35, the interest is reported at fair value. In other words, in this situation, the industry-specific guidance in FASB ASC 958-325-35 is applied rather than the general requirement to consolidate. FASB ASC 958-810-25-11 states that a similar legal entity is an entity (such as a limited liability company) that has governing provisions that are the functional equivalent of a limited partnership. In those entities, a managing member is the functional equivalent of a general partner, and a nonmanaging member is the functional equivalent of a limited partner. Throughout these paragraphs, any reference to a limited partnership includes limited partnerships and similar legal entities.

4.21 If, instead, the NFP is the general partner of a limited partnership or similar entity and has not elected to report all "other investments" at fair value in accordance with FASB ASC 958-325-35, paragraphs 12–13 of FASB ASC 958-810-25 require consolidation unless the general partner does not control the limited partnership. The general partners in a limited partnership are presumed to control that limited partnership regardless of the extent of the general partners' ownership interest in the limited partnership. If a limited partnership has multiple general partners, the determination of which, if any, general partner within the group controls and, therefore, should consolidate the limited partnership is based on an analysis of the relevant facts and circumstances. Paragraphs 1429 of FASB ASC 958-810-25 provide guidance for purposes of assessing whether the limited partners' rights might preclude a general partner from controlling a limited partnership. For example, the general partner might not control a limited partnership in either of the two following circumstances:

- The limited partners have the substantive ability to dissolve the partnership or otherwise remove the general partner without cause (referred to as substantive kick-out rights, which are further defined in paragraphs 19–20 of FASB ASC 958-810-25).
- The limited partners have the ability to effectively participate in significant decisions that would be expected to be made in the ordinary course of the limited partnership's business (referred to as participating rights, which are further defined in paragraphs 21–27 of FASB ASC 958-810-25).

If the limited partners have substantive kick-out rights or participating rights, the NFP that is the general partner would account for its investment using the equity method unless the general partnership interest is reported at fair value in conformity with the "Fair Value Option" subsections of FASB ASC 825-10. (For additional information, see paragraphs 3.81–.83 and 3.87–.89.)

4.22 For example, NFP A forms a for-profit limited partnership with NFP B and NFP C to acquire a building that none of the founding NFPs will use in a mission-related activity; rather, the building will be used to generate current income and, eventually, capital appreciation. NFP A is the general partner. It is NFP A's policy to report all "other investments" at fair value in accordance with FASB ASC 958-325-35. Because NFP A has that policy, it reports its general partner interest at fair value. If NFP A did not have that policy, it would consolidate the limited partnership per paragraphs 12–13 of FASB ASC 958-810-25, unless the presumption of control is overcome by the rights of the limited partners. If NFP B or NFP C has substantive kick-out or participating rights, the presumption of control is overcome, and the NFP A would report its interest using the equity method; however, NFP A may report that investment at fair value in conformity with the "Fair Value Option" subsections of FASB ASC 825-10, as an alternative to the equity method.

4.23 If the NFP is a limited partner in a limited partnership or similar entity and has elected to report all "other investments" at fair value in accordance with FASB ASC 958-325-35, the limited partnership interest is reported at fair value. In other words, in this situation, the industry-specific guidance in FASB ASC 958-325-35 is applied rather than the limited partner considering the potential consolidation of the limited partnership.

4.24 If the NFP is a limited partner in a limited partnership or similar entity and has not elected to report all "other investments" at fair value in accordance with FASB ASC 958-325-35, the accounting depends upon the level of ownership and the type of activities conducted by the limited partnership. If one limited partner has a controlling financial interest (paragraph 3.85), that limited partner consolidates the limited partnership. If the limited partner has a noncontrolling interest and the limited partnership is engaged in real estate activities, refer to the standards discussed in paragraphs 3.92.97. If the limited partner has a noncontrolling interest and the limited partnership is engaged in activities other than real estate, the limited partnership interest is an "other investment" to be accounted for at cost or lower or cost or market in accordance with FASB ASC 958-325-35; however, an NFP that is a limited partner may report that investment at fair value in conformity with the "Fair Value Option" subsections of FASB ASC 825-10 without jeopardizing the requirement to use the same measurement attribute for all "other investments." (Reporting "other investments" is discussed more fully in paragraph 4.38.)

4.25 For example, the NFP invests in Private Equity LLP. NFP is a 10 percent limited partner. The limited partnership interest is an "other investment" within the scope of FASB ASC 958-325. Because of that guidance, NFP cannot analogize to the guidance for noncontrolling interests in limited partnerships engaged in real estate activities. NFP uses the guidance in FASB ASC 958-325-35 and reports at either fair value or cost or lower of cost or fair value, depending on its policy for reporting all "other investments." Alternatively, an NFP that is a limited partner may report that investment at fair value in conformity with the "Fair Value Option" subsections of FASB ASC 825-10 without jeopardizing the requirement to use the same measurement attribute for all "other investments." (Reporting "other investments" is discussed more fully in paragraph 4.38.)

4.26 If the investment is in a limited liability company, FASB ASC 958-810-15-4(d) states that an NFP should apply the guidance in FASB ASC 323-30-35-3 to determine whether a limited liability company should be viewed as similar to a limited partnership, as opposed to a corporation, for purposes of determining whether noncontrolling interests should be accounted for in accordance with FASB ASC 970-323 or FASB ASC 323-10. FASB ASC 323-30-35-3 states that if a limited liability company maintains a specific ownership account for each investor—similar to a partnership capital account structure—it should be viewed as similar to an investment in a limited partnership.

4.27 If the investment in the limited liability company is viewed as similar to an investment in a limited partnership and the NFP is the equivalent of a general partner, see paragraphs 4.20–.22. If similar to an investment in a limited partnership and the NFP is the equivalent of a limited partner, see paragraphs 4.23–.25. If, instead, the investment in the limited liability company is viewed as similar to an investment in a corporation, then the NFP would use the standards in paragraphs 1 and 2–14 of FASB ASC 810-10-25 (which are discussed in paragraphs 3.73–.75) to determine if the interest is a controlling interest that should be consolidated. If it is not a controlling interest, then the guidance in FASB ASC 323-10 would be used to determine if the noncontrolling interest should be reported by the equity method (as discussed in paragraphs 4.18–.19). If the entity is not required to be reported by the equity method, then the standards in FASB ASC 958-320-35 apply if the interest is an equity security with a readily determinable fair value; if it is not, the standards in FASB ASC 958-325-35 apply. An NFP that has a noncontrolling interest in a limited liability company may report that investment at fair value in conformity with the "Fair Value Option" subsections of FASB ASC 825-10 without jeopardizing the requirement to use the same measurement attribute for all "other investments." (Reporting "other investments" is discussed more fully in paragraph 4.38.)

General Partnerships

4.28 An NFP that is a partner in a general partnership reports the interest using the equity method in accordance with the guidance in FASB ASC 970-323 and FASB ASC 958-810-15-4(d) if all of the following criteria are met:

- The general partnership is a for-profit entity engaged in real estate activities
- The interest is a noncontrolling interest, as determined by applying the guidance in FASB ASC 970-810-25-1
- The NFP has not elected to report all "other investments" at fair value in accordance with FASB ASC 958-325-35

If any of the three criteria is not met, the interest in the general partnership is an "other investment" to be accounted for in accordance with FASB ASC 958-325-35 (paragraph 4.38); however, an NFP may report its investment in the general partnership at fair value in conformity with the "Fair Value Option" subsections of FASB ASC 825-10 without jeopardizing the requirement to use the same measurement attribute for all "other investments."

Derivative Instruments

© Update 4-3 *Accounting and Reporting*: Derivative Instruments

FASB ASU No. 2017-12, *Derivatives and Hedging (Topic 815): Targeted Improvements to Accounting for Hedging Activities*, issued in August 2017, is effective for NFPs for fiscal years beginning after December 15, 2019, and interim periods within fiscal years beginning after December 15, 2020.

The "Pending Content" resulting from this ASU changes the guidance for (1) fair value hedges of interest rate risk by adding the Securities Industry and Financial Markets Association (SIFMA) Municipal Swap Rate as an eligible benchmark interest rate in the United States, thereby allowing an entity that issues or invests in fixed-rate tax-exempt financial instruments to designate as the hedged risk changes in fair value attributable to interest rate risk related to the SIFMA Municipal Swap Rate rather than overall changes in fair value, (2) designating fair value hedges of interest rate risk and for measuring the change in fair value of the hedged item in fair value hedges of interest rate risk, and (3) recognition and presentation of the effects of the hedging instrument and the hedged item in the financial statements, by requiring the entire change in the fair value of the hedging instrument to be included in the same line item in the statement of activities that is used to present the change in value of the hedged item. The "Pending Content" also makes certain changes to cash flow hedges, which do not affect NFPs because they are not permitted to use cash flow hedge accounting.

This edition of the guide has not been updated to reflect changes as a result of this ASU; however, the section that follows will be updated in a future edition. Readers are encouraged to consult the full text of the ASU at FASB's website at www.fasb.org.

4.29 Options, futures, forwards, and swaps are common examples of derivative instruments. Investments in convertible debt securities are an example of an instrument with an embedded derivative. Unique to NFPs are embedded derivatives related to certain split interest agreements, as discussed in paragraphs 6.34–.39. Accounting and reporting of investments in derivative instruments, including certain derivative instruments embedded in other contracts (collectively referred to as derivatives), is subject to the requirements of FASB ASC 815. A brief summary of FASB ASC 815 is provided in this chapter but is not a substitute for the reading FASB ASC 815.

4.30 Paragraphs 83–139 of FASB ASC 815-10-15 define a *derivative financial instrument*. FASB ASC 815-10-15-83 states that a *derivative instrument* is a financial instrument or other contract with all of the following characteristics:

a. Underlying, notional amount, payment provision. The contract has both of the following terms, which determine the amount of the settlement or settlements, and, in some cases, whether or not a settlement is required:
   i. One or more underlyings and
   ii. One or more notional amounts or payment provisions, or both.

b. Initial net investment. The contract requires no initial net investment or an initial investment that is smaller than would be required for other types of contracts that would be expected to have a similar response to changes in market factors.

c. Net settlement. The contract can be settled net by any of the following means:
   i. Its terms implicitly or explicitly require or permit net settlement,

ii. It can readily be settled net by a means outside the contract, or

iii. It provides for delivery of an asset that puts the recipient in a position not substantially different from net settlement.

4.31 The FASB ASC glossary defines an *underlying* as a variable that, along with either a notional amount or a payment provision, determines the settlement of a derivative instrument. Per paragraphs 88–89 of FASB ASC 815-10-15, an underlying usually is one or a combination of the following:

a. A security price or security price index

b. A commodity price or commodity price index

c. An interest rate or interest rate index

d. A credit rating or credit index

e. An exchange rate or exchange rate index

f. An insurance index or catastrophe loss index

g. A climatic or geological condition (such as temperature, earthquake severity, or rainfall), another physical variable, or a related index

h. The occurrence or nonoccurrence of a specified event (such as a scheduled payment under a contract)

However, an underlying may be any variable whose changes are observable or otherwise objectively verifiable. An underlying may be a price or rate of an asset or liability but is not the asset or liability itself.

4.32 The FASB ASC glossary defines a *notional amount* as a number of currency units, shares, bushels, pounds, or other units specified in a derivative instrument. Sometimes other names are used. For example, the notional amount is called a *face amount* in some contracts. Per FASB ASC 815-10-15-92, the settlement of a derivative instrument with a notional amount is determined by interaction of that notional amount with the underlying. The interaction may be simple multiplication, or it may involve a formula with leverage factors or other constants. The FASB ASC glossary states that a *payment provision* specifies a fixed or determinable settlement to be made if the underlying behaves in a specified manner.

4.33 FASB ASC 815-10-05-4 explains that an entity should recognize derivative instruments, including certain derivative instruments embedded in other contracts, as assets or liabilities in the statement of financial position and measure them at fair value. If certain conditions are met, an entity may elect, under FASB ASC 815, to designate a derivative instrument in any one of the following ways:

a. A hedge of the exposure to changes in the fair value of a recognized asset or liability or of an unrecognized firm commitment that are attributable to a particular risk (referred to as a fair value hedge)

b. A hedge of the exposure to variability in the cash flows of a recognized asset or liability, or of a forecasted transaction, that is attributable to a particular risk (referred to as a cash flow hedge)

c. A hedge of the foreign currency exposure of any one of the following:

i. An unrecognized firm commitment (a foreign currency fair value hedge)

ii. An available-for-sale security (a foreign currency fair value hedge)

iii. A forecasted transaction (a foreign currency cash flow hedge)

iv. A net investment in a foreign operation

FASB ASC 815-30-15-2 states that NFPs and other entities that do not report earnings are not permitted to use cash flow hedge accounting because they do not report earnings separately. Fair value hedge accounting is not discussed in the guide because most NFPs do not take advantage of the specialized accounting for hedging.

4.34 FASB ASC 815-10-25-1 and FASB ASC 815-10-35-1 require that investments in derivative instruments be reported as either assets or liabilities depending on the rights or obligations under the contracts and should be subsequently remeasured at fair value. Similarly, an embedded derivative should be separated from the host contract and accounted for as a derivative instrument pursuant to FASB ASC 815-10 if and only if all of the criteria in FASB ASC 815-15-25-1 are met.

4.35 The accounting for changes in the fair value of a derivative (that is, gains and losses) depends on the intended use of the derivative and the resulting designation. The changes in fair value of derivative instruments or hedged items are classified as unrestricted unless their use is temporarily or permanently restricted by donors or by law.[2]

The accounting for changes in the fair value of a derivative (that is, gains and losses) depends on the intended use of the derivative and the resulting designation. The changes in fair value of derivative instruments or hedged items are classified as increases or decreases in net assets without donor restrictions unless their use is limited by donor-imposed restrictions or by law that extends donor restrictions, in which case those amounts should be reported as increases or decreases in net assets with donor restrictions.[3,4]

4.36 FASB ASC 815-10-35-3 states that an NFP should recognize the gain or loss on a derivative instrument as a change in net assets in the period of change unless the derivative instrument qualifies for the specialized accounting for a fair value hedge or a hedge of the foreign currency exposure of a net investment in a foreign operation. The qualifications for the specialized accounting for hedges are described in FASB ASC 815-20. FASB ASC 815-25 provides the additional standards for fair value hedges and FASB ASC 815-35 provides the additional standards for hedges of net investment in a foreign operation.

4.37 One of the most common uses of derivatives by NFPs is a variable rate debt with a variable-to-fixed interest rate swap, which is a *cash flow hedge*. Cash flow hedge accounting is not available to NFPs in accordance with FASB ASC

---

[2] Paragraph 4.84 discusses an alternative accounting policy for circumstances in which restrictions on investment income and gains are met in the same period in which they are recognized.

[3] Paragraph 4.84 discusses an alternative accounting policy for circumstances in which restrictions on investment income and gains are met in the same period in which they are recognized.

[4] The amendments in FASB ASU No. 2016-14 are effective for annual financial statements issued for fiscal years beginning after December 15, 2017 (for example, years ending December 31, 2018, and years ending June 30, 2019), and for interim periods within fiscal years beginning after December 15, 2018. Application to interim financial statements is permitted but not required in the initial year of application. Early application of the amendments is permitted.

815-30-15-2. Therefore, as required by FASB ASC 815-10-35-1, a variable-to-fixed rate swap should be recorded as either an asset or liability and the changes in its fair value recorded in unrestricted net assets in the period in which the change in value occurs. As noted in FASB ASC 815-10-45-8, FASB ASC 815 does not provide guidance about the classification in the statement of activities of a derivative instrument's gains or losses. As a result, the change in the fair value of the derivative instrument and payments to or receipts from the counterparty to the swap might be classified as interest expense, other income, general and administrative expense, other losses, or an expense that is allocated among the functional expense categories similar to interest expense. The variable rate debt should be reported in subsequent periods using the interest method in FASB ASC 835-30-35, and its carrying value should not be changed by any gains or losses on the derivative instrument, in accordance with FASB ASC 815-10-35-3. Payments at the variable rate on the debt are interest expense and should be allocated among the functional expense categories. Disclosures about this interest rate swap are required by FASB ASC 815-10-50.

One of the most common uses of derivatives by NFPs is a variable rate debt with a variable-to-fixed interest rate swap, which is a *cash flow hedge*. Cash flow hedge accounting is not available to NFPs in accordance with FASB ASC 815-30-15-2. Therefore, as required by FASB ASC 815-10-35-1, a variable-to-fixed rate swap should be recorded as either an asset or liability and the changes in its fair value recorded in net assets without donor restrictions in the period in which the change in value occurs. As noted in FASB ASC 815-10-45-8, FASB ASC 815 does not provide guidance about the classification in the statement of activities of a derivative instrument's gains or losses. As a result, the change in the fair value of the derivative instrument and payments to or receipts from the counterparty to the swap might be classified as interest expense, other income, general and administrative expense, other losses, or an expense that is allocated among the functional expense categories similar to interest expense. The variable rate debt should be reported in subsequent periods using the interest method in FASB ASC 835-30-35, and its carrying value should not be changed by any gains or losses on the derivative instrument, in accordance with FASB ASC 815-10-35-3. Payments at the variable rate on the debt are interest expense and should be allocated among the functional expense categories. Disclosures about this interest rate swap are required by FASB ASC 815-10-50.[5]

Other Investments

4.38 Other investments are described in paragraph 4.13. FASB ASC 958-325-35 provides the standards for subsequent measurement of other investments held by NFPs. Guidance concerning the carrying amounts of other investments subsequent to acquisition differs depending upon the type of NFP, as follows:

- Per paragraphs 1–2 of FASB ASC 958-325-35, institutions of higher education, including colleges, universities, and community or junior colleges, should subsequently report other investments

[5] The amendments in FASB ASU No. 2016-14 are effective for annual financial statements issued for fiscal years beginning after December 15, 2017 (for example, years ending December 31, 2018, and years ending June 30, 2019), and for interim periods within fiscal years beginning after December 15, 2018. Application to interim financial statements is permitted but not required in the initial year of application. Early application of the amendments is permitted.

at either of the following measures: (*a*) fair value or (*b*) carrying value (that is, those that were acquired by purchase are reported at cost and those that were contributed other investments are reported at their fair value at the date of the gift). However, the carrying value should be adjusted if there has been an impairment of value that is not considered to be temporary. The same measurement attribute should be used for all other investments excluding those for which the institution chose, at a specified election date, to measure at fair value pursuant to FASB ASC 815-15-25 or the "Fair Value Option" subsections of FASB ASC 825-10. (For more information about the election to report at fair value, see paragraphs 3.169–.171.) Investments in wasting assets are usually reported net of an allowance for depreciation or depletion if reported at carrying value.

- Per paragraphs 3–4 of FASB ASC 958-325-35, voluntary health and welfare entities should report other investments at either of the following measures: (*a*) carrying value (that is, cost if purchased and fair value at the date of the contribution if contributed) or (*b*) fair value. The same measurement attribute should be used for all other investments excluding those for which the voluntary health and welfare entity chose, at a specified election date, to measure at fair value pursuant to FASB ASC 815-15-25 or the "Fair Value Option" subsections of FASB ASC 825-10. (For more information about the election to report at fair value, see paragraphs 3.169–.171.) If other investments are not equity securities and the fair value of the portfolio of those investments is below the recorded amount, it may be necessary to reduce the carrying amount of the portfolio to fair value or to provide an allowance for decline in fair value. If it can reasonably be expected that the voluntary health and welfare entity will suffer a loss on the disposition of an investment, an impairment loss should be recognized in the period in which the decline in fair value occurs.
- Per paragraphs 6–7 of FASB ASC 958-325-35, NFPs that are not colleges, universities, voluntary health and welfare entities, or health care entities should report other investments using one of the following measures: (*a*) fair value or (*b*) the lower of cost or fair value. The same measurement attribute should be used for all other investments excluding those for which the NFP chose, at a specified election date, to measure at fair value pursuant to FASB ASC 815-15-25 or the "Fair Value Option" subsections of FASB ASC 825-10. (For more information about the election to report at fair value, see paragraphs 3.169–.171.) If other investments are not equity securities and are carried at the lower of cost or fair value, declines in the value of those investments should be recognized if their aggregate fair value is less than their carrying amount, recoveries of aggregate fair value in subsequent periods should be recorded in those periods subject only to the limitation that the carrying amount should not exceed the original cost.
- Notwithstanding the preceding bullet points, if other investments are equity securities that are reported at cost (carrying value), all NFPs, regardless of type, should apply paragraphs 8–13 of FASB ASC 958-325-35 to determine if an impairment loss should be recognized. In conformity with FASB ASC 320-10-35-17, NFPs do not

apply tests for other-than-temporary impairment to debt securities unless the NFP reports a performance indicator as defined in FASB ASC 954-205-45 (health care entities).

Decline in Fair Value After the Date of the Financial Statements

4.39 FASB ASC 855-10-55-2 states that changes in the fair value of assets or liabilities (financial or nonfinancial) after the balance sheet date but before the financial statements are issued or are available to be issued should not be recognized as of the reporting date. Some nonrecognized subsequent events may be of such a nature that they must be disclosed to keep the financial statements from being misleading. For such events, FASB ASC 855-10-50-2 requires that an NFP disclose the nature of the event and an estimate of its financial effect (or a statement that such an estimate cannot be made).

Fair Value Measurements

4.40 FASB ASC 820 defines *fair value*, establishes a framework for measuring fair value, and requires disclosures about fair value measurements. Paragraphs 3.138–.168 summarize FASB ASC 820 but are not a substitute for reading FASB ASC 820 itself.

4.41 For many investments held by NFPs, quoted prices for identical investments are available in active markets at the measurement date (level 1 inputs). For investments without quoted prices in active markets, quoted prices for similar investments in active markets or quoted prices for identical or similar assets in markets that are not active (level 2 inputs) may need to be used, possibly with adjustments. For example, U.S. Treasury securities trade at what is called "on the run" and "off the run." A recently issued U.S. Treasury security will trade "on the run" for a period of time after issuance and can be measured using a quoted price in an active market at the measurement date (level 1). If, after the U.S. Treasury issues new securities of the same duration, investors stop trading the earlier issue and start trading in the newer issue, the market for the earlier issues (referred to as off the run) often becomes inactive. If the market is inactive, a common way to measure those off-the-run U.S. Treasury securities is by using the yield curves on the newer issues (that is, level 2 inputs). Unobservable inputs (level 3) are used to measure fair value to the extent that observable inputs are not available.

4.42 FASB ASC 820-10-35-44 states that if an NFP holds a position in a single investment and the investment is traded in an active market, the fair value of the investment should be measured within level 1 as the product of the quoted price for an individual investment and the quantity held by the NFP. That is the case even if a market's normal daily trading volume is not sufficient to absorb the quantity held and placing orders to sell the position in a single transaction might affect the quoted price. In other words, the quoted price should not be adjusted because of the size of the position relative to trading volume (blockage factor). As noted in FASB ASC 820-10-35-36B, a blockage factor that adjusts because of the size of the investor's position relative to trading volume is not permitted in a fair value measurement.

4.43 Some NFPs invest in alternative investments, such as hedge funds, private equity funds, real estate funds, venture capital funds, offshore fund vehicles, and funds of funds, that provide their investors with a net asset value per share (or its equivalent such as member units or an ownership interest in partners' capital to which a proportionate share of net assets is attributed). If an alternative investment does not have a readily determinable fair value, its fair value may be estimated as of the reporting entity's measurement date using the net asset value per share (or its equivalent) if the investment is in an investment company within the scope of FASB ASC 946, *Financial Services—Investment Companies*, or a real estate fund for which it is industry practice to measure investment assets at fair value on a recurring basis and to issue financial statements that are consistent with the measurement principles in FASB ASC 946. An NFP is not permitted to estimate the fair value of an investment using the net asset value per share of the investment (or its equivalent) as a practical expedient if, as of the measurement date, it is probable that the NFP will sell the investment for an amount different from the net asset value per share (or its equivalent). A sale is considered probable only if all of the criteria in FASB ASC 820-10-35-62 have been met as of the measurement date. FASB ASC 820-10-50-6A requires certain disclosures for these investments, regardless of whether net asset value is used as a practical expedient.

Some NFPs invest in alternative investments, such as hedge funds, private equity funds, real estate funds, venture capital funds, offshore fund vehicles, and funds of funds, that provide their investors with a net asset value per share (or its equivalent such as member units or an ownership interest in partners' capital to which a proportionate share of net assets is attributed). If an alternative investment does not have a readily determinable fair value, as a practical expedient, its fair value may be estimated as of the reporting entity's measurement date using the net asset value per share (or its equivalent) if the investment is in an investment company within the scope of FASB ASC 946, *Financial Services—Investment Companies*, or a real estate fund for which it is industry practice to measure investment assets at fair value on a recurring basis and to issue financial statements that are consistent with the measurement principles in FASB ASC 946. The "Pending Content" in FASB ASC 820-10-35-54B states that an investment that meets those criteria and is measured using net asset value per share (or its equivalent) as a practical expedient should not be categorized within the fair value hierarchy. Although the investment is not categorized within the fair value hierarchy, the NFP should provide the amount measured using the net asset value per share (or its equivalent) practical expedient to permit reconciliation of the fair value of investments included in the fair value hierarchy to the line items presented in the statement of financial position. An NFP is not permitted to estimate the fair value of an investment using the net asset value per share of the investment (or its equivalent) as a practical expedient if, as of the measurement date, it is probable that the NFP will sell the investment for an amount different from the net asset value per share (or its equivalent). A sale is considered probable only if all of the criteria in FASB ASC 820-10-35-62 have been met as of the measurement date. FASB ASC 820-10-50-6A requires certain disclosures for these investments, regardless of whether net asset value is used as a practical expedient.[6]

---

[6] FASB ASU No. 2015-07, *Fair Value Measurement (Topic 820): Disclosures for Investments in Certain Entities That Calculate Net Asset Value per Share (or Its Equivalent) (a consensus of the FASB Emerging Issues Task Force)*, is effective for NFPs for fiscal years beginning after December 15, 2016, and for interim periods within those fiscal years. Early adoption is permitted.

4.44 Technical Questions and Answers (Q&A) sections 2220.18–.26 and 2220.28[7] are intended to assist reporting entities in applying the provisions of FASB ASC 820 discussed in the preceding paragraph. Q&A section 2220.27, "Determining Fair Value of Investments When the Practical Expedient Is Not Used or Is Not Available," assists reporting entities in determining the fair value of investments in circumstances in which the practical expedient (net asset value) is not used or is not available. Q&A sections 2220.18–.28 are reproduced in appendix A of this chapter.

Investment Income and Expenses

4.45 Investment revenue, which is often referred to as investment income, includes dividends, interest, rents, royalties, and similar payments on assets held as investments. Per FASB ASC 958-320-45-2, dividend, interest, and other investment income should be reported in the period earned as increases in unrestricted net assets unless the use of the assets received is limited by donor-imposed restrictions. Donor restricted investment income should be reported as an increase in temporarily restricted net assets or permanently restricted net assets, depending on the type of restriction.[8]

Investment revenue, which is often referred to as investment income, includes dividends, interest, rents, royalties, and similar payments on assets held as investments. Per the "Pending Content" in FASB ASC 958-220-45-22 and FASB ASC 958-220-45-8, gains and losses on investments and dividends, interest, and other investment income should be reported in the statement of activities as increases or decreases in net assets without donor restrictions unless their use is limited by donor-imposed restrictions or by law that extends donor restrictions, in which case those amounts should be reported as increases or decreases in net assets with donor restrictions.[9,10]

4.46 For example, if there are no donor-imposed restrictions on the use of the income, it should be reported as an increase in unrestricted net assets. On the other hand, a donor may stipulate that a gift be invested in perpetuity with the income to be used to support the NFP without restriction or to support a specified program or capital expenditure. The initial gift creates permanently restricted net assets. Unless the NFP elects the alternative accounting policy described in paragraph 4.84 or there is a donor's explicit restriction to the contrary, the investment income of a donor-restricted endowment fund increases temporarily restricted net assets. As discussed further in paragraphs 4.71–.72, the income and gains of a donor-restricted endowment fund are temporarily restricted (time restricted) until appropriated for expenditure, and are also purpose restricted if the donor specified the income be used for support of a donor-specified program or capital expenditure.

---

[7] All Q&A sections can be found in *Technical Questions and Answers*

[8] See footnote 2.

[9] See footnote 2.

[10] The amendments in FASB ASU No. 2016-14 are effective for annual financial statements issued for fiscal years beginning after December 15, 2017 (for example, years ending December 31, 2018, and years ending June 30, 2019), and for interim periods within fiscal years beginning after December 15, 2018. Application to interim financial statements is permitted but not required in the initial year of application. Early application of the amendments is permitted.

For example, if there are no donor-imposed restrictions on the use of the income, it should be reported as an increase in net assets without donor restrictions. On the other hand, a donor may stipulate that a gift be invested in perpetuity with the income to be used to support the NFP without restriction or to support a specified program or capital expenditure. The initial gift creates net assets with donor restrictions. Unless the NFP elects the alternative accounting policy described in paragraph 4.84 or there is a donor's explicit restriction to the contrary, the investment income of a donor-restricted endowment fund increases net assets with donor restrictions. As discussed further in paragraphs 4.71–.72, the income and gains of a donor-restricted endowment fund are time restricted until appropriated for expenditure, and are also purpose restricted if the donor specified the income be used for support of a donor-specified program or capital expenditure.[11]

4.47 FASB ASC 958-220-45-14 specifies that a statement of activities should report the gross amounts of revenues and expenses. It also notes, however, that investment revenues may be reported net of related expenses, such as custodial fees and internal and external investment advisory costs, provided that the amount of the expenses is disclosed either in the statement of activities or in notes to financial statements.

The "Pending Content" in FASB ASC 958-220-45-14 states that to help explain the relationships of an NFP's ongoing major or central operations and activities, a statement of activities generally should report the gross amounts of revenues and expenses. However, investment return (related to total return investing and not programmatic investing) should be reported net of external and direct internal investment expenses. An NFP may present the amounts of net investment return from portfolios that are managed differently or derived from different sources as separate, appropriately labeled line items on the statement of activities. For example, if an NFP has net investment return generated from operating cash, it may present that return separately from net investment return generated from its endowment. In addition, if appropriately labeled, an NFP may present the amounts of net investment return appropriated for spending separate from net investment return in excess of amounts appropriated for spending.[12]

4.48 FinREC observes diversity in the types of costs that have been included as related expenses, which are referred to herein as investment expenses. Investment expenses include, but are not limited to, the costs of the following activities if conducted by the NFP or directly on its behalf:

- Investment advice (includes advice provided by employees as well as third parties)
- Investment acquisition due diligence
- Custodian services

---

[11] The amendments in FASB ASU No. 2016-14 are effective for annual financial statements issued for fiscal years beginning after December 15, 2017 (for example, years ending December 31, 2018, and years ending June 30, 2019), and for interim periods within fiscal years beginning after December 15, 2018. Application to interim financial statements is permitted but not required in the initial year of application. Early application of the amendments is permitted.

[12] The amendments in FASB ASU No. 2016-14 are effective for annual financial statements issued for fiscal years beginning after December 15, 2017 (for example, years ending December 31, 2018, and years ending June 30, 2019), and for interim periods within fiscal years beginning after December 15, 2018. Application to interim financial statements is permitted but not required in the initial year of application. Early application of the amendments is permitted.

- Other administrative activities in connection with investments
- Other professional services in connection with investment activities, such as legal and accounting services
- Interim and year-end monitoring
- Valuation procedures and processes

The preceding paragraph will be deleted upon the effective date of FASB ASU No. 2016-14, *Not-for-Profit Entities (Topic 958): Presentation of Financial Statements of Not-for-Profit Entities.*[13]

4.49 In some circumstances, NFPs have investments that involve several layers of activity. FinREC recommends that an NFP include in investment expenses only the costs of activities conducted by the NFP or directly on its behalf to generate an investment return. Accordingly, if activities in the preceding list are conducted by or on behalf of entities in which the NFP invests, the costs of those activities generally would not be included in investment expense.

The preceding paragraph will be deleted upon the effective date of FASB ASU No. 2016-14.[14]

4.50 For example, assume an NFP provides money to Hedge Fund, a limited partnership, in exchange for a limited partnership interest. The NFP pays a 2 percent advisory fee to Broker for identifying and recommending Hedge Fund. Further, assume Hedge Fund Manager, the General Partner of Hedge Fund, receives as compensation from Hedge Fund 2 percent of average assets managed, plus a performance fee of 20 percent of the total return of Hedge Fund; and that the compensation is deducted from Hedge Fund's returns before remitting amounts to the limited partners. Hedge Fund invests in a mix of investments that includes several other hedge funds, publicly traded equity securities, private equity securities, publicly traded debt, and real estate partnerships. Some of the entities in which Hedge Fund invests conduct investment activities as described in paragraph 4.48. The NFP may or may not be aware of such activities and their costs, which may be (*a*) remitted as discrete amounts from 1 entity to another or (*b*) embedded in total return on investment and therefore deducted (with or without disclosure of amounts) before remitting returns to the investor. The NFP would report as investment expense only the amounts it pays directly—that is, the 2 percent advisory fee paid to Broker. None of the other amounts in this example would be reported by the NFP as investment expense.

The preceding paragraph will be deleted upon the effective date of FASB ASU No. 2016-14.[15]

---

[13] The amendments in FASB ASU No. 2016-14 are effective for annual financial statements issued for fiscal years beginning after December 15, 2017 (for example, years ending December 31, 2018, and years ending June 30, 2019), and for interim periods within fiscal years beginning after December 15, 2018. Application to interim financial statements is permitted but not required in the initial year of application. Early application of the amendments is permitted.

[14] The amendments in FASB ASU No. 2016-14 are effective for annual financial statements issued for fiscal years beginning after December 15, 2017 (for example, years ending December 31, 2018, and years ending June 30, 2019), and for interim periods within fiscal years beginning after December 15, 2018. Application to interim financial statements is permitted but not required in the initial year of application. Early application of the amendments is permitted.

[15] The amendments in FASB ASU No. 2016-14 are effective for annual financial statements issued for fiscal years beginning after December 15, 2017 (for example, years ending December 31, 2018, and years ending June 30, 2019), and for interim periods within fiscal years beginning after December 15, 2018. Application to interim financial statements is permitted but not required in the initial year of application. Early application of the amendments is permitted.

4.51 As another example, assume an NFP hires a Money Manager to manage the NFP's investments. The NFP directly pays Money Manager as compensation 2 percent of average assets managed, plus a performance fee of 20 percent of the total return on investments managed. In addition, Money Manager charges the NFP custodial fees and other administrative charges in connection with the activities that Money Manager conducts to generate an investment return for NFP. Money Manager invests the NFP's money in a mix of investments that includes several hedge funds, publicly traded equity securities, private equity securities, publicly traded debt, and real estate partnerships. Some of the entities in which Money Manager invests conduct investment activities as described in paragraph 4.48. The NFP may or may not be aware of such activities and their costs, which may be (*a*) remitted as discrete amounts from 1 entity to another or (*b*) embedded in total return on investment and therefore deducted (with or without disclosure of amounts) before remitting returns to Money Manager. The NFP would report as investment expense the amounts paid to Money Manager as compensation (that is, 2 percent of average assets managed; the performance fee of 20 percent of the total return on investments managed) and custodial fees and other administrative charges paid to Money Manager in connection with activities Money Manager conducts to generate an investment return for the NFP. None of the other amounts in this example would be reported by the NFP as investment expense.

The preceding paragraph will be deleted upon the effective date of FASB ASU No. 2016-14.[16]

4.52 Further, FinREC recommends that to the extent investment expenses include the costs of activities conducted by employees, the amounts should include employee benefit, occupancy, and other related costs. In some circumstances, it is impracticable to measure and allocate all employee benefit, occupancy, and other related costs pertaining to investment activities conducted by employees. Considerations about which costs should be measured and allocated, such as considerations about materiality and the costs and benefits of developing and providing the information, are the same as considerations about cost allocations in other circumstances.

The Pending Content in paragraphs 1516 of FASB ASC 958-220-45 describes direct internal investment expenses, which are expenses that involve the direct conduct or direct supervision of the strategic and tactical activities involved in generating investment return. These include, but are not limited to, both of the following:

a. Salaries, benefits, travel, and other costs associated with the officer and staff responsible for the development and execution of investment strategy

b. Allocable costs associated with internal investment management and supervising, selecting, and monitoring of external investment management firms

---

[16] The amendments in FASB ASU No. 2016-14 are effective for annual financial statements issued for fiscal years beginning after December 15, 2017 (for example, years ending December 31, 2018, and years ending June 30, 2019), and for interim periods within fiscal years beginning after December 15, 2018. Application to interim financial statements is permitted but not required in the initial year of application. Early application of the amendments is permitted.

Direct internal investment expenses do not include items that are not associated with generating investment return. For example, the costs associated with unitization and other such aspects of endowment management would not be allocated.[17]

4.53 FASB ASC 958-205-45-6 requires that expenses that are netted against investment revenues should be reported by their functional classification on the statement of functional expenses (if the NFP presents that statement). Further, to the extent that expenses are reported by other than their natural classification (such as salaries included in cost of goods sold or facility rental costs of special events reported as direct benefits to donors), FASB ASC 958-205-45-6 requires that they be reported by their natural classification if a statement of functional expenses is presented. Accordingly, if investment expenses are netted against investment revenues and the NFP presents a statement of functional expenses, investment expenses should be reported by their natural classification as part of management and general expenses on the statement of functional expenses.

The "Pending Content" in FASB ASC 958-720-45-15 states that external and direct internal investment expenses that have been netted against investment return should not be included in the analysis of expenses by function and nature (see paragraph 13.04).[18]

Unrealized and Realized Gains and Losses

4.54 Unrealized gains and losses arise from changes in the fair value of investments, exclusive of dividend and interest income recognized but not yet received and exclusive of any write-down of the carrying amount of investments for impairment. Unrealized gains and losses are recognized in some circumstances (for example, when the investments are carried at fair value), but not in others (for example, when the investments are carried at cost). Paragraph 4.38, however, provides guidance pertaining to circumstances in which unrealized losses on investments carried at cost should be recognized.

4.55 Realized gains and losses arise from selling or otherwise disposing of investments. If realized gains and losses arise from selling or otherwise disposing of investments for which unrealized gains and losses have been recognized in the statement of activities of prior reporting periods, the amount reported in the statement of activities as gains or losses upon the sale or other disposition of the investments should exclude the amount that has previously been recognized in the statement of activities. However, the components of that gain or loss may be reported as the realized amount (the difference between amortized cost and the sales proceeds) and the unrealized amount recognized in prior reporting periods. Exhibit 4-2 illustrates this reporting.

---

[17] The amendments in FASB ASU No. 2016-14 are effective for annual financial statements issued for fiscal years beginning after December 15, 2017 (for example, years ending December 31, 2018, and years ending June 30, 2019), and for interim periods within fiscal years beginning after December 15, 2018. Application to interim financial statements is permitted but not required in the initial year of application. Early application of the amendments is permitted.

[18] The amendments in FASB ASU No. 2016-14 are effective for annual financial statements issued for fiscal years beginning after December 15, 2017 (for example, years ending December 31, 2018, and years ending June 30, 2019), and for interim periods within fiscal years beginning after December 15, 2018. Application to interim financial statements is permitted but not required in the initial year of application. Early application of the amendments is permitted.

Exhibit 4-2

Facts	
1.	In 20X1, a not-for-profit entity with a December 31 year end purchases an equity security with a readily determinable fair value for $5,000.
2.	At December 31, 20X1, the fair value of the security is $7,000.
3.	During 20X2, the security is sold for $11,000.
Reporting Gains and Losses	
20X1	Recognize a $2,000 gain and adjust the carrying value to $7,000. (The reported gain equals $7,000 fair value less $5,000 carrying value.)
20X2	Recognize a $4,000 gain and adjust the carrying value to zero. (The gain may be reported as the net of $11,000 selling price less the $7,000 carrying value at the time the security was sold. Alternatively, the gain may be displayed as the realized gain of $6,000 [$11,000 selling price less $5,000 cost] less the $2,000 unrealized gain previously recognized.)

4.56 To the extent that they are recognized, FASB ASC 958-320-45-1 requires that investment gains and losses should be reported in the statement of activities as increases or decreases in unrestricted net assets unless their use is temporarily or permanently restricted by explicit donor stipulations or by law.[19] Presentation of investment gains and losses in the statement of activities is discussed further in paragraphs 4.84–.89.

To the extent they are recognized, the "Pending Content" in FASB ASC 958-320-45-1 requires that gains and losses on investments be reported in the statement of activities as increases or decreases in net assets without donor restrictions unless their use is limited by donor-imposed restrictions or by law that extends donor restrictions, in which case those amounts should be reported as increases or decreases in net assets with donor restrictions.[20] Presentation of investment gains and losses in the statement of activities is discussed further in paragraphs 4.84–.89.[21]

Investments Held as an Agent

4.57 The guidance in paragraphs 4.45–.56 does not apply to investments held by an NFP as an agent. Pursuant to FASB ASC 958-320-25-3, FASB ASC 958-320-35-3, FASB ASC 958-325-25-2, and FASB ASC 958-325-35-16, an NFP is holding an investment as an agent if it has little or no discretion in determining how the investment income, unrealized gains and losses, and realized

---

[19] See footnote 2.

[20] See footnote 2.

[21] The amendments in FASB ASU No. 2016-14 are effective for annual financial statements issued for fiscal years beginning after December 15, 2017 (for example, years ending December 31, 2018, and years ending June 30, 2019), and for interim periods within fiscal years beginning after December 15, 2018. Application to interim financial statements is permitted but not required in the initial year of application. Early application of the amendments is permitted.

gains and losses resulting from those investments will be used. Investment activities of investments held by an NFP as an agent should be reported as agency transactions and, therefore, as changes in assets and liabilities rather than as changes in net assets. Paragraphs 5.07–.22 include guidance concerning distinguishing contributions from agency transactions, including transactions in which a donor grants variance power and those in which the donor transfers the assets to a financially interrelated entity.

Investment Pools

Self-Managed Investment Pools

4.58 An NFP may pool part or all of its investments (including investments arising from contributions with different kinds of restrictions) for portfolio management purposes. The number and the nature of the pools may vary from NFP to NFP. When an NFP establishes a pool, the NFP assigns ownership interests (typically through unitization) to the various funds[22] investing in the pool (sometimes referred to as participants) based on the fair value of the cash and securities placed in the pool by each fund. The NFP uses current fair value to determine the number of units allocated to additional assets placed in the pool by the funds and to amounts withdrawn (redeemed) from the pool by the funds. Investment income and realized gains and losses (and any recognized unrealized gains and losses) are allocated equitably to the funds based on the number of units assigned to each.

Investment Pools Managed by a Financially Interrelated Entity

4.59 If the NFP and the entity that manages the investment pool are financially interrelated entities, as described in the FASB ASC glossary and in FASB ASC 958-20-15-2, the NFP (which is the specified beneficiary) would account for its investment in the pool as part of its interest in the pool manager (which is the recipient entity). FASB ASC 958-20-25-2 requires that if a beneficiary and recipient entity are financially interrelated entities, the beneficiary should recognize its interest in the net assets of the recipient entity. Recognizing an interest in the net assets of the recipient entity and adjusting that interest for a share of the change in net assets of the recipient entity is similar to the equity method, which is described in FASB ASC 323-10. Financially interrelated entities are discussed further in paragraphs 5.28–.32.

Investment Pools Managed by Third Parties

4.60 Instead of the self-managed investment pools discussed in paragraph 4.58 or the pools managed by financially interrelated entities discussed in paragraph 4.59, some NFPs invest in a pool that is managed by another entity. (If that pool is managed by an entity that is consolidated with the reporting entity, it is a self-managed pool, not a third-party pool.) Examples of circumstances in which an NFP transfers some or all of its investments to a pool that is held and invested by a third-party entity include the following:

---

[22] Fund accounting segregates assets, liabilities, and fund balances into separate accounting entities (funds) associated with specific activities, donor-imposed restrictions, or objectives. Each fund has a self-balancing set of accounts consisting of assets, liabilities, fund balance and, when appropriate, revenue and expense or expenditure accounts. Chapter 16, "Fund Accounting," provides additional information.

- Community foundations—Some NFPs transfer their endowment and other assets to investment pools managed by community foundations. Community foundations sometimes refer to these arrangements as agency endowments.
- Colleges and universities—NFPs such as alumni clubs and supporting foundations may participate in a pool of investments handled and managed by a related college or university.
- National organizations and their local organizations—NFPs (commonly referred to as local organizations) that are affiliated with or otherwise related to a national organization with a similar mission may have deposits or investments held by the national organization on its behalf. (If the national and local organizations are consolidated, the pool is considered a self-managed investment pool.)

Most investment pools are managed in a manner similar to a mutual fund or a hedge fund, whereby the investing entity receives units or shares (equity ownership) in the pool and may withdraw or purchase additional shares either monthly or quarterly, at net asset value. In a few investment pools, NFPs own identifiable investments (similar to a brokerage account). The accounting for investment pools depends upon the type of rights the NFP investor has (units, shares, or identifiable investments) and the relationship of the NFP investor to the NFP pool manager.

4.61 This guide discusses three common structures for investment pools:

- The interest in the investment pool is akin to an interest in a mutual fund or a unit in a hedge fund. Some of these interests may be in trust form.
- The interest in the investment pool is like a brokerage account, in that investments are specifically identified in the name of each investor entity.
- The interest in the investment pool is effectively a deposit with a money-market fund.

4.62 If the NFP's interest in a third party's investment pool is akin to an interest in a mutual fund or a unit in a hedge fund, the NFP's investment asset is that particular unit or share interest. By analogy to the guidance in FASB ASC 320-10-55-9, which states that it is not appropriate to look through an investment in a limited partnership interest, venture capital entity, or a mutual fund to the underlying securities it owns, FinREC believes that the NFP would not look through to the investment pool's specific underlying investments in reporting. Q&A section 2220.19, "Unit of Account," states the appropriate unit of account is the interest in the investee fund itself, not the underlying investments within the investee pool, because the reporting entity owns an undivided interest in the whole of the investee fund portfolio and typically lacks the ability to dispose of individual assets and liabilities in the investee pool portfolio. If the NFP is neither consolidated with the pool manager nor financially interrelated with it, the NFP would recognize its rights to the assets held by the pool manager as a beneficial interest in an identifiable pool of assets from a transfer described in FASB ASC 958-605-25-33(d). FASB ASC 958-605-30-14 and 958-605-35-3 state that if a beneficiary has an unconditional right to receive all or a portion of the specified cash flows from a charitable trust or other identifiable pool of assets, the beneficiary should measure and subsequently remeasure that beneficial interest at fair value. If the investment pool meets the criteria specified in paragraphs 4–5 of FASB ASC 820-10-15, the net asset value per unit or share may be used as a practical expedient to measure the fair value of the NFP's interest. (That practical expedient is discussed in paragraph 4.43.)

4.63 If the NFP's interest in the third party's investment pool is like a brokerage account (in that investments are specifically identified in the name of each investor entity), FinREC believes that the NFP would report as though it held the investment directly, including making financial statement disclosures. This reporting is similar to reporting investments held on an NFP's behalf by a broker.

4.64 In circumstances in which the NFP's interest in the third party's investment pool is effectively money on deposit in a money-market fund or bank, whether that deposit is classified as cash, a cash equivalent, or an investment depends on facts and circumstances. As noted in paragraph 4.04, FinREC believes that funds deposited by an NFP in a related entity's cash account under a centralized cash management arrangement generally would not be classified as cash and cash equivalents in the NFP's financial statements unless the NFP has legal title to the cash on deposit (that is, the cash is deposited in a demand deposit account at a bank or other financial institution in the NFP's name). In many cases, an interest in a third-party's investment pool is subject to some withdrawal restrictions. Q&A section 1100.15, "Liquidity Restrictions," states that withdrawal restrictions should be considered in determining whether assets meet the definition of cash equivalents and when determining the sequencing of assets on the statement of financial position (or classification as current assets) or disclosures in the notes to financial statements providing relevant information about the liquidity or maturity of assets.

Endowment Funds

4.65 The FASB ASC glossary defines an *endowment fund* as

> an established fund of cash, securities, or other assets to provide income for the maintenance of a not-for-profit entity (NFP). The use of the assets of the fund may be permanently restricted, temporarily restricted, or unrestricted. Endowment funds generally are established by donor-restricted gifts and bequests to provide either of the following:
>
> *a.* A permanent endowment, which is to provide a permanent source of income
>
> *b.* A term endowment, which is to provide income for a specified period.
>
> Alternatively, an NFP's governing board may earmark a portion of its unrestricted net assets as a board-designated endowment fund.

The "Pending Content" in the FASB ASC glossary defines an endowment fund as

> an established fund of cash, securities, or other assets to provide income for the maintenance of a not-for-profit entity (NFP). The use of the assets of the fund may be with or without donor-imposed restrictions. Endowment funds generally are established by donor-restricted gifts and bequests to provide a source of income in

perpetuity or for a specified period. Alternatively, an NFP's governing board may earmark a portion of its net assets as a board-designated endowment fund.[23]

4.66 The term *endowment* is sometimes used to refer to the aggregate of all gifts received for endowment purposes combined with all board-designated endowment funds that are managed collectively for investment. (Additionally, some NFPs pool excess operating cash with endowment cash for investing, but that does not make that operating cash an endowment or a board-designated endowment.) This discussion does not use the term in that manner. Instead, this discussion focuses on each endowment fund individually—the assets, liabilities, and net assets associated with an NFP's fiduciary responsibilities under a gift agreement with a donor (a donor-restricted endowment fund) or an action by its governing body (a board-designated endowment). Depending on a donor's stipulations, a donor-restricted endowment fund may be created by a single gift agreement with a single donor, or it may be created to combine gifts of many donors that have the same donor-imposed restrictions on investment and use.

4.67 The FASB ASC glossary defines a *donor-restricted endowment fund* as an endowment fund that is created by a donor stipulation requiring investment of the gift in perpetuity or for a specified term. Some donors may require that a portion of income, gains, or both be added to the gift and invested subject to similar restrictions.

The "Pending Content" in the FASB ASC glossary defines a *donor-restricted endowment fund* as an endowment fund that is created by a donor stipulation (donors include other types of contributors, including makers of certain grants) requiring investment of the gift in perpetuity or for a specified term. Some donors or laws may require that a portion of income, gains, or both be added to the gift and invested subject to similar restrictions. The term does not include a *board-designated endowment fund*, which is defined in the "Pending Content" of the FASB ASC glossary as an endowment fund created by an NFP's governing board by designating a portion of its net assets without donor restrictions to be invested to provide income for a long but not necessarily specified period (sometimes called funds functioning as endowment or quasi-endowment funds). In rare circumstances, a board-designated endowment fund also can include a portion of net assets with donor restrictions. For example, if an NFP is unable to spend donor-restricted contributions in the near term, then the board sometimes considers the long-term investment of these funds.[24]

4.68 FASB ASC 958-205-45-14 states that

> when classifying an endowment fund, each source—original gift, gains and losses, and interest and dividends—must be evaluated separately.

---

[23] The amendments in FASB ASU No. 2016-14 are effective for annual financial statements issued for fiscal years beginning after December 15, 2017 (for example, years ending December 31, 2018, and years ending June 30, 2019), and for interim periods within fiscal years beginning after December 15, 2018. Application to interim financial statements is permitted but not required in the initial year of application. Early application of the amendments is permitted.

[24] The amendments in FASB ASU No. 2016-14 are effective for annual financial statements issued for fiscal years beginning after December 15, 2017 (for example, years ending December 31, 2018, and years ending June 30, 2019), and for interim periods within fiscal years beginning after December 15, 2018. Application to interim financial statements is permitted but not required in the initial year of application. Early application of the amendments is permitted.

Each source is unrestricted unless its use is temporarily or permanently restricted by explicit donor stipulations or by law. Thus, an endowment fund that is created by a governing board from unrestricted net assets is classified as unrestricted because all three sources are free of donor restrictions. If an endowment fund is created by a donor, the donor may have placed different restrictions on each of the three sources. Generally, classification of the original gifts and the income earned by endowments is straightforward because usually donors explicitly state any time or purpose restrictions on those two sources. Determining how to classify gains on endowments may not be as easy because agreements with donors often are silent on how gains should be used and whether losses must be restored immediately from future gains, or not at all.

The "Pending Content" in FASB ASC 958-205-45-13A requires an NFP to report the net assets of an endowment fund in a statement of financial position within the two classes of net assets on the basis of the existence or absence of donor-imposed restrictions. The "Pending Content" in FASB ASC 958-205-45-13B states that

> when classifying a donor-restricted endowment fund, consideration should be given to both the donor's explicit stipulations and the applicable laws that extend donor restrictions. Investment return generally is considered free of donor restrictions unless its use is limited by a donor-imposed restriction or by law. In the United States, most donor-restricted endowment funds are subject to an enacted version of the Uniform Prudent Management of Institutional Funds Act of 2006 (UPMIFA) that extends a donor's restriction to use of the funds, including the investment return, until the funds are appropriated for expenditure by the governing board. Thus, if a donor or law imposes a restriction on the investment return, those returns should be reported within net assets with donor restrictions until appropriated for expenditure. Conversely, for an endowment fund that is created by a governing board (board-designated endowment fund), assuming no other purpose-type restrictions exist on the use of those funds, that original fund and all investment returns are free of donor restrictions and should be reported in net assets without donor restrictions.[25]

4.69 FASB ASC 958-205-45-28 and FASB ASC 958-205-45-33 provide guidance for determining the permanently restricted portion of a donor-restricted endowment fund.[26] Those paragraphs state that

> an NFP that is subject to an enacted version of the Uniform Prudent Management of Institutional Funds Act (UPMIFA) shall classify a portion of a donor-restricted endowment fund of perpetual duration as permanently restricted net assets. The amount classified as permanently restricted shall be either (a) the amount of the fund that must be retained permanently in accordance with explicit donor stipulations

---

[25] The amendments in FASB ASU No. 2016-14 are effective for annual financial statements issued for fiscal years beginning after December 15, 2017 (for example, years ending December 31, 2018, and years ending June 30, 2019), and for interim periods within fiscal years beginning after December 15, 2018. Application to interim financial statements is permitted but not required in the initial year of application. Early application of the amendments is permitted.

[26] Paragraphs 5.75–.83 provide additional guidance about classifying the original gift of an endowment fund.

(see paragraphs 958-605-45-3 through 45-4) or (b) the amount of the fund that, in the absence of explicit donor stipulations, the NFP's governing board determines must be retained (preserved) permanently consistent with the relevant law (see paragraph 958-205-45-21).

In states that have enacted a version of the Uniform Management of Institutional Funds Act of 1972 (UMIFA) or states whose relevant law is based on trust law, it is generally understood that at least the amount of the original gift(s) and any required accumulations is not expendable, although the value of the investments purchased may occasionally fall below that amount. Future appreciation of the investments generally restores the value to the required level. In states that have enacted its provisions, UMIFA describes "historic dollar value" as the amount that is not expendable.

The preceding paragraph will be deleted upon the effective date of FASB ASU No. 2016-14.[27]

4.70 As discussed in paragraphs 15.51–.56, a form of UPMIFA is the law for the management of donor-restricted endowment funds in all states but Pennsylvania. UPMIFA replaced the prior legislation, UMIFA. One of the primary differences between UPMIFA and its predecessor is the elimination of the concept of historic dollar value. Under UMIFA, asset growth and income of an endowment could be appropriated for program purposes, subject to the rule that a fund could not be spent below its historic dollar value. *Historic dollar value* was defined as the amount of original contributions to the fund, any additional gifts to the fund, and any additions to historic dollar value made pursuant to the donor's gift instrument. UPMIFA provides more guidance on what is prudent spending, making the need for a spending floor unnecessary. Instead, subject to the intent of the donor expressed in the gift instrument (and in some states, a rebuttable presumption of imprudence), an NFP may appropriate for expenditure or accumulate so much of an endowment fund as it determines is prudent after considering the factors in the law. Thus, FASB ASC 958-205-45-28 requires that the governing board make a determination that the law does not. UPMIFA does not define an amount that must be retained permanently, but for accounting purposes the governing board must determine the amount of the fund that, in the absence of explicit donor stipulations, must be retained permanently. For accounting purposes, most NFPs continue to embrace historic dollar value as the permanently restricted portion of a donor-restricted endowment fund.

The preceding paragraph will be deleted upon the effective date of FASB ASU No. 2016-14.[28]

4.71 FASB ASC 958-205-05-9 notes that because donor stipulations and laws vary, NFPs must assess the relevant facts and circumstances for their

---

[27] The amendments in FASB ASU No. 2016-14 are effective for annual financial statements issued for fiscal years beginning after December 15, 2017 (for example, years ending December 31, 2018, and years ending June 30, 2019), and for interim periods within fiscal years beginning after December 15, 2018. Application to interim financial statements is permitted but not required in the initial year of application. Early application of the amendments is permitted.

[28] The amendments in FASB ASU No. 2016-14 are effective for annual financial statements issued for fiscal years beginning after December 15, 2017 (for example, years ending December 31, 2018, and years ending June 30, 2019), and for interim periods within fiscal years beginning after December 15, 2018. Application to interim financial statements is permitted but not required in the initial year of application. Early application of the amendments is permitted.

endowment gifts and their relevant laws to determine if net appreciation on endowments is available for spending or is permanently restricted. Paragraphs 16–21A of FASB ASC 958-205-45 discuss the classification of net appreciation (net gains) of an endowment fund. In a state with UPMIFA-based legislation, in the absence of a donor's explicit restriction to the contrary, gains on the investments of a donor-restricted endowment fund are temporarily restricted (time restricted) until appropriated for expenditure, and are also purpose restricted if the use of the endowment's income is restricted as to purpose. (As noted in FASB ASC 958-205-05-10, subsection 4(a) of UPMIFA states that, unless stated otherwise in the gift instrument, the assets in an endowment fund are donor-restricted assets until appropriated for expenditure by the institution; in states with legislation that includes similar language, that subsection creates a time restriction.) For example, if a donor stipulates that net gains be added to the principal of its gift until that endowed gift plus accumulated gains increases to a specified dollar level, the gains are permanently restricted. Similarly, if a donor states that a specific investment security must be held in perpetuity, the gains and losses on that security are subject to that same permanent restriction unless the donor specifies otherwise. However, if a donor allows the NFP to choose suitable investments, the gains are not permanently restricted unless the donor or the law requires that an amount be retained permanently.

As discussed in paragraphs 15.51–.56, a form of UPMIFA is the law for the management of donor-restricted endowment funds in all states but Pennsylvania. The "Pending Content" in FASB ASC 958-205-05-9 notes that because donor stipulations and laws vary, NFPs must assess the relevant facts and circumstances for their endowment gifts and their relevant laws to determine if some or all of the investment return on endowments is available for spending. The "Pending Content" in paragraphs 13D13F of FASB ASC 958-205-45 provide guidance for classification of net assets of donor-restricted endowment funds for NFPs that follow an enacted version of UPMIFA.[29]

4.72 In a state that has enacted a version of UPMIFA, legal limitations may state that, "unless stated otherwise in the gift instrument, the assets in an endowment fund are donor-restricted assets until appropriated for expenditure by the institution" (subsection 4(a) of UPMIFA). FASB ASC 958-205-45-30 states that for each donor-restricted endowment fund for which the restriction described in subsection 4(a) of UPMIFA applies, an NFP should classify the portion of the fund that is not classified as permanently restricted net assets as temporarily restricted net assets (time restricted) until appropriated for expenditure by the NFP. Pursuant to FASB ASC 958-205-45-31, in the absence of interpretation of the phrase "appropriated for expenditure" in subsection 4(a) of UPMIFA by legal or regulatory authorities (for example, court decisions or interpretations by state attorneys general), appropriation for expenditure is deemed to occur upon approval for expenditure, unless approval is for a future period, in which case appropriation is deemed to occur when that period is reached. Approval for expenditure may occur through different means within and across NFPs. For example, expenditures could be approved as part of a formal, annual budget. Expenditures also could be approved during the year as unexpected needs arise (such as for emergency relief efforts).

---

[29] The amendments in FASB ASU No. 2016-14 are effective for annual financial statements issued for fiscal years beginning after December 15, 2017 (for example, years ending December 31, 2018, and years ending June 30, 2019), and for interim periods within fiscal years beginning after December 15, 2018. Application to interim financial statements is permitted but not required in the initial year of application. Early application of the amendments is permitted.

The "Pending Content" in FASB ASC 958-205-13D states that donor-restricted endowment funds generally result from a donor's stipulation or by extension of a donor restriction imposed through UPMIFA that limits an NFP's use of an endowment fund, and the original gifted amount, any additional gifts to that fund, and any resulting investment returns should initially be classified as net assets with donor restrictions. Therefore, unless stated otherwise in the gift instrument, the assets in an endowment fund are donor-restricted assets until they are appropriated for expenditure by the NFP's governing board. Donors may provide specific instructions on spending from a donor-restricted endowment fund or from the components of investment return generated from the fund.[30]

4.73 FASB ASC 958-205-45-31 states that upon appropriation for expenditure, the time restriction expires to the extent of the amount appropriated and, in the absence of any purpose restrictions, results in a reclassification of that amount to unrestricted net assets. If the fund is also subject to a purpose restriction, the reclassification of the appropriated amount to unrestricted net assets would not occur until that purpose restriction also has been met, in accordance with the guidance beginning in FASB ASC 958-205-45-9. Pursuant to FASB ASC 958-205-45-11, temporarily restricted net assets with time restrictions are not available to support expenses until the time restrictions have expired. Reclassifications upon the expiration of restrictions are discussed further in paragraphs 11.29–.52.

The "Pending Content" in paragraphs 13E13F of FASB ASC 958-205-45 discusses appropriation from donor-restricted endowment funds. The amount of net assets with donor restrictions in the donor-restricted endowment fund is reduced when the governing board appropriates for expenditure funds from the endowment fund. Upon appropriation for expenditure, the restriction expires to the extent of the amount appropriated as long as all of the time restrictions have lapsed and all of the purpose restrictions have been met. At that time, the appropriated amount is reclassified from net assets with donor restrictions to net assets without donor restrictions in accordance with the "Pending Content" in FASB ASC 958-205-45-9. However, if purpose restrictions from a donor have not yet been met, those funds should remain in net assets with donor restrictions until those purpose restrictions have been satisfied.

In the absence of interpretation of the phrase *appropriated for expenditure* in subsection 4(a) of UPMIFA (see paragraph 958-205-05-10) by legal or regulatory authorities (for example, court decisions or interpretations by state attorneys general), for purposes of the guidance in FASB ASC 958-205, appropriation for expenditure is deemed to occur upon approval for expenditure, unless approval is for a future period, in which case appropriation is deemed to occur when that period is reached. Approval for expenditure may occur through different means within and across NFPs. For example, expenditures could be approved as part of a formal, annual budget. Expenditures also could

---

[30] The amendments in FASB ASU No. 2016-14 are effective for annual financial statements issued for fiscal years beginning after December 15, 2017 (for example, years ending December 31, 2018, and years ending June 30, 2019), and for interim periods within fiscal years beginning after December 15, 2018. Application to interim financial statements is permitted but not required in the initial year of application. Early application of the amendments is permitted.

be approved during the year as unexpected needs arise (such as for emergency relief efforts).[31]

4.74 Pursuant to FASB ASC 958-205-45-29, the amount of permanently restricted net assets is not reduced by an NFP's appropriations from the fund. Thus, if an appropriation is made when a donor-restricted endowment fund has no temporarily restricted net assets, there is no reclassification to make. However, in the accounting records of the donor-restricted endowment fund, the fund would redeem investments and report a transfer to the operating fund (or other fund) in which the appropriated amount is to be spent. The deficit balance of the donor-restricted endowment fund would be reflected in unrestricted net assets. FinREC believes that, similar to the guidance in FASB ASC 958-205-45-24, if appropriations reduce the assets of a donor-restricted endowment fund below the permanently restricted net assets amount, future investment income or gains that restore the fair value of the assets of the endowment fund to the required level should be classified as increases in unrestricted net assets. This accounting for future investment income and gains is similar to accounting for future gains if investment losses reduce the assets of a donor-restricted endowment fund below the level required by the donor stipulations or law, as discussed in the next paragraph.

The preceding paragraph will be deleted upon the effective date of FASB ASU No. 2016-14.[32]

4.75 Paragraphs 22–27 of FASB ASC 958-205-45 discuss the classification of losses of an endowment fund. In the absence of donor stipulations or law to the contrary, losses on the investments of a donor-restricted endowment fund should reduce temporarily restricted net assets to the extent that donor-imposed temporary restrictions on net appreciation of the fund have not been met before a loss occurs. Any remaining loss should reduce unrestricted net assets. Per FASB ASC 958-205-45-29, the amount of permanently restricted net assets is not reduced by losses on the investments of the fund. If losses reduce the assets of a donor-restricted endowment fund below the level required by the donor stipulations or law, gains that restore the fair value of the assets of the endowment fund to the required level should be classified as increases in unrestricted net assets.

In accordance with the "Pending Content" FASB ASC 958-320-45-1 and FASB ASC 958-205-45-13A, losses on the investments of a donor-restricted endowment fund are reported within net assets with donor restrictions. In some cases, the fair value of the fund at the reporting date is less than either the original gift amount or the amount required to be maintained by the donor or by law that extends donor restrictions (an *underwater endowment fund*, as defined in the "Pending Content" of the FASB ASC glossary). The "Pending Content" in FASB ASC 958-205-45-13H states that if a donor-restricted

---

[31] The amendments in FASB ASU No. 2016-14 are effective for annual financial statements issued for fiscal years beginning after December 15, 2017 (for example, years ending December 31, 2018, and years ending June 30, 2019), and for interim periods within fiscal years beginning after December 15, 2018. Application to interim financial statements is permitted but not required in the initial year of application. Early application of the amendments is permitted.

[32] The amendments in FASB ASU No. 2016-14 are effective for annual financial statements issued for fiscal years beginning after December 15, 2017 (for example, years ending December 31, 2018, and years ending June 30, 2019), and for interim periods within fiscal years beginning after December 15, 2018. Application to interim financial statements is permitted but not required in the initial year of application. Early application of the amendments is permitted.

endowment fund is an underwater endowment fund, the accumulated losses should be included together with that fund in net assets with donor restrictions. Information about underwater endowment funds is disclosed in accordance with the "Pending Content" in FASB ASC 958-205-50-2.[33]

4.76 After the fair value of the assets of the endowment fund equals the required level, gains that are restricted by the donor should be classified as increases in temporarily restricted net assets or permanently restricted net assets, depending on the donor's restrictions on the endowment fund.

The preceding paragraph will be deleted upon the effective date of FASB ASU No. 2016-14.[34]

4.77 FinREC believes that, in determining whether a loss or appropriation is reported as a deficit in the net assets of a donor-restricted endowment fund, the calculation should be done on a fund-by-fund basis, rather than in the aggregate for all donor-restricted endowment funds. This approach is consistent with UPMIFA; the commissioners' comments to the definition of an endowment fund in the act state that Section 4 (which is titled "Appropriation for Expenditure or Accumulation of Endowment Fund; Rules of Construction") must be applied to individual funds and cannot be applied to a group of funds that may be managed collectively for investment purposes. This approach also is consistent with the fact set and example disclosure paragraphs 31–52 of FASB ASC 958-205-55, which refer to the fair value of assets associated with individual donor-restricted endowment funds falling below the level that the donor or the state's UPMIFA requires.

FinREC believes that, in determining whether a loss or appropriation is reported as a deficit in the net assets of a donor-restricted endowment fund, the calculation should be done on a fund-by-fund basis, rather than in the aggregate for all donor-restricted endowment funds. This approach is consistent with UPMIFA; the commissioners' comments to the definition of an endowment fund in the act state that Section 4 (which is titled "Appropriation for Expenditure or Accumulation of Endowment Fund; Rules of Construction") must be applied to individual funds and cannot be applied to a group of funds that may be managed collectively for investment purposes. This approach also is consistent with the fact set and example disclosures in the "Pending Content" in paragraphs 31–52 of FASB ASC 958-205-55, especially the "Pending Content" of FASB ASC 958-205-55-49, which refers to the fair value of assets associated with three donor-restricted endowment funds falling below the level that the donor or the state's UPMIFA requires in an NFP with approximately 100 individual funds.[35]

---

[33] The amendments in FASB ASU No. 2016-14 are effective for annual financial statements issued for fiscal years beginning after December 15, 2017 (for example, years ending December 31, 2018, and years ending June 30, 2019), and for interim periods within fiscal years beginning after December 15, 2018. Application to interim financial statements is permitted but not required in the initial year of application. Early application of the amendments is permitted.

[34] The amendments in FASB ASU No. 2016-14 are effective for annual financial statements issued for fiscal years beginning after December 15, 2017 (for example, years ending December 31, 2018, and years ending June 30, 2019), and for interim periods within fiscal years beginning after December 15, 2018. Application to interim financial statements is permitted but not required in the initial year of application. Early application of the amendments is permitted.

[35] The amendments in FASB ASU No. 2016-14 are effective for annual financial statements issued for fiscal years beginning after December 15, 2017 (for example, years ending December 31, 2018, and years ending June 30, 2019), and for interim periods within fiscal years beginning after December 15, 2018. Application to interim financial statements is permitted but not required in the initial year of application. Early application of the amendments is permitted.

4.78 FASB ASC 958-205-55-1 states that how an enacted version of UPMIFA will be interpreted and enforced in a particular state will become clearer with the passage of time. Because the legislation is recently enacted, no case law currently exists for its interpretation. In the meantime, NFPs could look to other sources, such as the discussion that occurred in the legislative committees leading to the law adopted in a particular state, announcements from the state attorney general, a consensus of learned lawyers in the state, or similar information, to help them understand what the law requires. In the absence of new legislation, clarifying court decisions, additional guidance issued by the state attorney general, or similar developments, the governing board's interpretation of the relevant law should be consistent from year to year.

The "Pending Content" in FASB ASC 958-205-55-1 states that enacted versions of UPMIFA vary across jurisdictions, so an NFP would have to assess the specific law applicable to its operations for guidance. Other sources that may be helpful in that assessment could include the discussion that occurred in the legislative committees leading to the law adopted in a particular state, announcements from the state attorney general, a consensus of learned lawyers in the state, or similar information. In the absence of new legislation, clarifying court decisions, additional guidance issued by the state attorney general, or similar developments, the governing board's interpretation of the relevant law should be consistent from year to year.[36]

4.79 Because so few states have UMIFA-based law or have endowment law based on trust law, those standards for classification of donor-restricted endowment funds are not discussed in this guide. They are located in paragraphs 33–35 of FASB ASC 958-205-45.

As discussed in the "Pending Content" in FASB ASC 958-205-45-13G, for donor-restricted endowment funds that are subject to trust law, typically at least, the amount of the original gift(s) and any gains or net appreciation of the fund are not considered to be available for expenditure. Generally, interest, dividends, rents, or other forms of ordinary income are available for spending and are classified as net assets without donor restrictions unless a purpose or other donor restriction exists on use of the investment income.[37]

Financial Statement Presentation

Cash and Cash Equivalents

4.80 A statement of financial position should include a separate line item for "Cash" or "Cash and Cash Equivalents." As noted in paragraphs 3.09–.23, cash and cash equivalents received with donor-imposed stipulations restricting the use of the cash contributed to long-term purposes and cash set aside for

---

[36] The amendments in FASB ASU No. 2016-14 are effective for annual financial statements issued for fiscal years beginning after December 15, 2017 (for example, years ending December 31, 2018, and years ending June 30, 2019), and for interim periods within fiscal years beginning after December 15, 2018. Application to interim financial statements is permitted but not required in the initial year of application. Early application of the amendments is permitted.

[37] The amendments in FASB ASU No. 2016-14 are effective for annual financial statements issued for fiscal years beginning after December 15, 2017 (for example, years ending December 31, 2018, and years ending June 30, 2019), and for interim periods within fiscal years beginning after December 15, 2018. Application to interim financial statements is permitted but not required in the initial year of application. Early application of the amendments is permitted.

long-term purposes should not be classified on a statement of financial position with assets that are available for current use. As noted in paragraph 3.09, NFPs are required to provide information about liquidity or maturity of assets and liabilities, including restriction on the use of particular items.

4.81 Some limitations may exist on an NFP's ability to withdraw or use cash and cash equivalents. These limitations may be imposed by (*a*) creditors and other outside parties (such as limitations on cash held by financial institutions to meet compensating balance requirements, cash and cash equivalents held as collateral on debt obligations, cash received as collateral on loaned securities, and cash held for students, clients, and others under agency agreements); (*b*) donors, who place restrictions on their cash contributions (such as restricting the contributions to investments in buildings or creation of endowments, as described in paragraph 4.03); or (*c*) governing boards, which may designate cash for investment purposes (traditionally known as "funds functioning as endowment" or "quasi endowment"). NFPs are permitted, but not required, to disaggregate assets based on those limitations. Paragraphs 3.09–.23 discuss reporting similar limitations on assets other than cash.

4.82 FASB ASC 958-210-45-7 requires that relevant information about the nature and amount of limitations on the use of cash and cash equivalents (such as cash held on deposit as a compensating balance) be included on the face of the financial statements or in the notes. FASB ASC 958-210-45-9 requires information about the nature and amount of different types of donor-imposed restrictions to be disclosed in the net asset section of the statement of financial position or in the notes to the financial statements. (Chapter 11, "Net Assets and Reclassifications of Net Assets," discusses accounting for net assets.) FASB ASC 958-210-50-2 requires disclosure in the notes to the financial statements if unusual circumstances (such as special borrowing arrangements, requirements imposed by resource providers that cash be held in separate accounts, and known significant liquidity problems) are present, or if the NFP has not maintained appropriate amounts of cash and cash equivalents to comply with donor-imposed restrictions. (Paragraphs 3.173–.175 discuss reporting requirements if an NFP is not in compliance with donor-imposed restrictions.)

The "Pending Content" in FASB ASC 958-210-45-7 requires that relevant information about the nature and amount of limitations on the use of cash and cash equivalents (such as cash held on deposit as a compensating balance) be included on the face of the financial statements or in the notes to the financial statements, as well as contractual limitations on the use of particular assets. These include, for example, restricted cash or other assets set aside under debt agreements, assets set aside under self-insurance funding arrangements, assets set aside under collateral arrangements, or assets set aside to satisfy reserve requirements that states may impose under charitable gift annuity agreements. The "Pending Content" in FASB ASC 958-210-45-9 requires information about the nature and amount of different types of donor-imposed restrictions to be disclosed in the net asset section of the statement of financial position or in the notes to the financial statements. (Chapter 11, "Net Assets and Reclassifications of Net Assets," discusses accounting for net assets.) The "Pending Content" in FASB ASC 958-210-50-2 requires disclosure in the notes to the financial statements if unusual circumstances (such as special borrowing arrangements, requirements imposed by resource providers that cash be held in separate accounts, and known significant liquidity problems) are present, or if the NFP has not maintained appropriate amounts of cash and cash equivalents to comply with donor-imposed restrictions. (Paragraphs 3.173–.175 discuss reporting requirements if an NFP is not in compliance with donor-imposed restrictions.)[38]

4.83 Q&A sections 2130.38–.40 discuss the classification of certificates of deposit on the statement of financial position and whether certificates of deposit are debt securities that must be recognized at fair value. Certificates of deposit with original maturities of 90 days or less are commonly considered "cash and cash equivalents" under FASB ASC 305, *Cash and Cash Equivalents*. A certificate of deposit with an original maturity greater than 90 days would not be included in cash and cash equivalents. Certificates of deposit generally are not debt securities as defined in FASB ASC 958-320. However, some negotiable certificates of deposit may meet the definition of a security. Certificates of deposit that are not debt securities are "other investments," as discussed in paragraph 4.38 of this guide.

Investments

Update 4-4 *Accounting and Reporting*: Derivative Instruments

FASB ASU No. 2017-12, issued in August 2017, is effective for NFPs for fiscal years beginning after December 15, 2019, and interim periods within fiscal years beginning after December 15, 2020.

The "Pending Content" resulting from this ASU changes the guidance for (1) fair value hedges of interest rate risk by adding the Securities Industry and Financial Markets Association (SIFMA) Municipal Swap Rate as an eligible benchmark interest rate in the United States, thereby allowing an entity that issues or invests in fixed-rate tax-exempt financial instruments to designate as the hedged risk changes in fair value attributable to interest rate risk related to the SIFMA Municipal Swap Rate rather than overall changes in fair value, (2) designating fair value hedges of interest rate risk and for measuring the change in fair value of the hedged item in fair value hedges of interest rate risk, and (3) recognition and presentation of the effects of the hedging instrument and the hedged item in the financial statements, by requiring the entire change in the fair value of the hedging instrument to be included in the same line item in the statement of activities that is used to present the change in value of the hedged item. The "Pending Content" also makes certain changes to cash flow hedges, which do not affect NFPs because they are not permitted to use cash flow hedge accounting.

This edition of the guide has not been updated to reflect changes as a result of this ASU; however, the section that follows will be updated in a future edition. Readers are encouraged to consult the full text of the ASU at FASB's website at www.fasb.org.

4.84 FASB ASC 958-320-45-3 states that gains and investment income that are limited to specific uses by donor-imposed restrictions may be reported

[38] The amendments in FASB ASU No. 2016-14 are effective for annual financial statements issued for fiscal years beginning after December 15, 2017 (for example, years ending December 31, 2018, and years ending June 30, 2019), and for interim periods within fiscal years beginning after December 15, 2018. Application to interim financial statements is permitted but not required in the initial year of application. Early application of the amendments is permitted.

as increases in unrestricted net assets if the restrictions are met in the same reporting period as the gains and income are recognized, provided that the NFP has a similar policy for reporting contributions received,[39] reports consistently from period to period, and discloses its accounting policy in the notes to the financial statements.

The "Pending Content" in FASB ASC 958-320-45-3 states that gains and investment income that are limited to specific uses by donor-imposed restrictions may be reported as increases in net assets without donor restrictions if the restrictions are met in the same reporting period as the gains and income are recognized, provided that the NFP has a similar policy for reporting contributions received,[40] reports consistently from period to period, and discloses its accounting policy in the notes to the financial statements.[41]

4.85 Realized and unrealized losses on investments may be netted against realized and unrealized gains on a statement of activities.

4.86 FASB ASC 958-320-45-9 explains that some NFPs, in managing their endowment funds, use a spending-rate or total return policy. Those policies consider total investment return—investment income (interest, dividends, rents, and so forth) plus net realized and unrealized gains (or minus net losses). Typically, spending-rate or total return policies emphasize the use of prudence and a rational and systematic formula to determine the portion of cumulative investment return that can be used to support operations of the current period and the protection of endowment gifts from a loss of purchasing power as a consideration in determining the formula to be used. Example 1 (FASB ASC 958-320-55-4) illustrates a statement of activities and example disclosures of an NFP that uses a spending rate policy to include only a portion of its investment return in its operating measure.

4.87 Even if an NFP uses a spending-rate formula to determine how much of that return will be used for current operations, all investment income and recognized gains and losses should be reported on the statement of activities and classified as unrestricted unless restricted by the donor or applicable law. NFPs are permitted to provide information on the face of the statement of activities and the notes to the financial statements about the total return on investments by segregating the total return between operating and nonoperating components based on a spending-rate formula.

Even if an NFP uses a spending-rate formula to determine how much of that return will be used for current operations, all investment income and recognized gains and losses should be reported on the statement of activities and classified as net assets without donor restrictions unless restricted by the donor or applicable law. NFPs are permitted to provide information on the face of the statement of activities and the notes to the financial statements

---

[39] Chapter 5, "Contributions Received and Agency Transactions," discusses the accounting policy for reporting contributions received if the organization meets donor-imposed restrictions on all or a portion of the amount contributed in the same reporting period as the contribution is received.

[40] Chapter 5, "Contributions Received and Agency Transactions," discusses the accounting policy for reporting contributions received if the organization meets donor-imposed restrictions on all or a portion of the amount contributed in the same reporting period as the contribution is received.

[41] The amendments in FASB ASU No. 2016-14 are effective for annual financial statements issued for fiscal years beginning after December 15, 2017 (for example, years ending December 31, 2018, and years ending June 30, 2019), and for interim periods within fiscal years beginning after December 15, 2018. Application to interim financial statements is permitted but not required in the initial year of application. Early application of the amendments is permitted.

about the total return on investments by segregating the total return between operating and nonoperating components based on a spending-rate formula.[42]

4.88 FASB ASC 958-320-45-6 explains that some NFPs—primarily health care entities—would like to compare their results to business entities in the same industry. An NFP with those comparability concerns may report in a manner similar to business entities by classifying securities as available-for-sale or held-to-maturity as described in paragraphs 1–6 of FASB ASC 320-10-25 and excluding the unrealized gains and losses on those securities (which are recognized in accordance with FASB ASC 958-320) from an operating measure within the statement of activities. Per FASB ASC 958-320-50-1, a reconciliation of investment return to amounts reported in the statement of activities is required to be presented if investment return is separated into operating and nonoperating amounts.

FASB ASC 958-320-45-6 explains that some NFPs—primarily health care entities—would like to compare their results to business entities in the same industry. An NFP with those comparability concerns may report in a manner similar to business entities by classifying securities as available-for-sale or held-to-maturity as described in paragraphs 1–6 of FASB ASC 320-10-25 and excluding the unrealized gains and losses on those securities (which are recognized in accordance with FASB ASC 958-320) from an operating measure within the statement of activities.[43]

4.89 Example 1 (paragraphs 4–10 of FASB ASC 958-320-55) illustrates a statement of activities that reports a portion of investment return within a measure of operations. If investment return is separated into operating and nonoperating amounts, certain information, as discussed in paragraph 4.95, is required to be disclosed. Those disclosures are also illustrated in the example.

The preceding paragraph will be deleted upon the effective date of FASB ASU No. 2016-14.[44]

Disclosures

Update 4-5 *Accounting and Reporting*: Financial Assets and Financial Liabilities

FASB ASU No. 2016-01, issued in January 2016, is effective for NFPs for fiscal years beginning after December 15, 2018, and interim periods within

---

[42] The amendments in FASB ASU No. 2016-14 are effective for annual financial statements issued for fiscal years beginning after December 15, 2017 (for example, years ending December 31, 2018, and years ending June 30, 2019), and for interim periods within fiscal years beginning after December 15, 2018. Application to interim financial statements is permitted but not required in the initial year of application. Early application of the amendments is permitted.

[43] The amendments in FASB ASU No. 2016-14 are effective for annual financial statements issued for fiscal years beginning after December 15, 2017 (for example, years ending December 31, 2018, and years ending June 30, 2019), and for interim periods within fiscal years beginning after December 15, 2018. Application to interim financial statements is permitted but not required in the initial year of application. Early application of the amendments is permitted.

[44] The amendments in FASB ASU No. 2016-14 are effective for annual financial statements issued for fiscal years beginning after December 15, 2017 (for example, years ending December 31, 2018, and years ending June 30, 2019), and for interim periods within fiscal years beginning after December 15, 2018. Application to interim financial statements is permitted but not required in the initial year of application. Early application of the amendments is permitted.

fiscal years beginning after December 15, 2019, and cannot be adopted earlier than for fiscal years beginning after December 15, 2017. However, NFPs may elect not to disclose the information about fair value of financial instruments measured at amortized cost (paragraphs 10–19 of FASB ASC 825-10-50) in any financial statements that have not yet been made available for issuance.

The "Pending Content" resulting from this ASU changes the measurement of equity securities without readily determinable fair value and the disclosures related to those investments, although an NFP is still allowed to elect to report them at fair value. The amendments also change disclosure requirements for financial instruments. This ASU is discussed further in the preface.

FASB ASU No. 2018-03, issued in February 2018, includes technical corrections and improvements related to FASB ASU No. 2016-01. FASB ASU No. 2018-03 has the same effective date as FASB ASU No. 2016-01. Entities may early adopt the amendments for fiscal years beginning after December 15, 2017, including interim periods within those fiscal years, provided they have adopted FASB ASU No. 2016-01.

This edition of the guide has not been updated to reflect changes as a result of these ASUs; however, the text that follows will be updated in a future edition. Readers are encouraged to consult the full text of the ASU at FASB's website at www.fasb.org.

4.90 The majority of the disclosures for investments are located in the "Disclosure" subsections (sections 50) of FASB ASC 958-320, FASB ASC 958-325, and FASB ASC 825-10. The following paragraphs discuss the more common disclosures but are not a substitute for reading the "Disclosure" subsections of FASB ASC. Certain disclosures are illustrated in FASB ASC 958-320-55.

4.91 Paragraphs 20–22 of FASB ASC 825-10-50 require that an NFP disclose all significant concentrations of credit risk arising from all financial instruments, including significant concentrations of credit risk arising from derivative instruments, whether from an individual counterparty or groups of counterparties. Q&A section 2110.06, "Disclosure of Cash Balances in Excess of Federally Insured Amounts," states that the existence of cash on deposit with banks in excess of Federal Deposit Insurance Corporation-insured limits should be disclosed if the uninsured balances represent a significant concentration of credit risk. Further, as explained in FASB ASC 825-10-55-1, the terms of certain loan products may increase a reporting entity's exposure to credit risk and thereby may result in a concentration of credit risk.

4.92 An individual concentration of risk could exist, for example, if an NFP invests a significant amount in the securities of a single corporation or government entity. A group concentration could exist, for example, if an NFP invests a significant amount in debt securities of a single industry or a single geographic region. Programmatic loan investments that permit low payments in early years of the loan and higher payments later in the loan's life also may result in a concentration of credit risk.

4.93 FASB ASC 815-10-50 requires disclosures if an NFP has investments in derivative financial instruments. Additional disclosures are required by FASB ASC 815-15-50 for embedded derivatives, and FASB ASC 815-20-50, 815-25-50, 815-30-50, and 815-30-50 for derivatives designated as hedging exposures to risk.

4.94 FASB 860-30-50-1A(a) requires that NFPs that enter into repurchase agreements or securities lending transactions disclose their policies for requiring collateral or other security. FASB ASC 860-30-50-1A(c) requires that if an NFP accepts collateral that it is permitted by contract or custom to sell or repledge, it should disclose (1) the fair value as of the date of each statement of financial position presented of that collateral, (2) the fair value as of the date of each statement of financial position presented of the portion of that collateral that it has sold or repledged, and (3) information about the sources and uses of that collateral.

4.95 For each period for which a statement of activities is presented, an NFP should disclose

a. pursuant to FASB ASC 958-320-50-1, the composition of investment return including, at a minimum, investment income, net realized gains or losses on investments reported at other than fair value, and net gains or losses on investments reported at fair value.

b. pursuant to FASB ASC 958-320-50-1, a reconciliation of investment return to amounts reported in the statement of activities if investment return is separated into operating and nonoperating amounts, together with a description of the policy used to determine the amount that is included in the measure of operations and a discussion of circumstances leading to a change, if any, in that policy. The reconciliation need not be provided if an NFP includes all investment return in its measure of operations or excludes it from that measure entirely.

c. pursuant to FASB ASC 958-320-50-1, the amount of the expenses, if investment revenues are reported net of related expenses, such as custodial fees and internal and external investment advisory costs (if not provided on the face of the statement of activities.

d. the information required by FASB ASC 825-10-50-30, as modified by FASB ASC 815-10-15-7.

e. the information required by FASB ASC 825-10-50-32 if the NFP made an election pursuant to FASB 825-10-25-4(d) or 9(e) during the period.

For each period for which a statement of activities is presented, an NFP should disclose

a. the information required by FASB ASC 825-10-50-30, as modified by FASB ASC 815-10-15-7.

b. the information required by FASB ASC 825-10-50-32 if the NFP made an election pursuant to FASB 825-10-25-4(d) or 9(e) during the period.

c. the information required by FASB ASC 825-10-50-30, as modified by FASB ASC 815-10-15-7.

d. the information required by FASB ASC 825-10-50-32 if the NFP made an election pursuant to FASB 825-10-25-4(d) or 9(e) during the period.[45]

---

[45] The amendments in FASB ASU No. 2016-14 are effective for annual financial statements issued for fiscal years beginning after December 15, 2017 (for example, years ending December 31, 2018, and years ending June 30, 2019), and for interim periods within fiscal years beginning after December 15, 2018. Application to interim financial statements is permitted but not required in the initial year of application. Early application of the amendments is permitted.

4.96 Per FASB ASC 958-325-45-2, the statement of activities of an institution of higher education should set forth the total performance (that is, investment income and realized and unrealized gains and losses) of the other investment portfolio unless that information is disclosed in the notes.

The preceding paragraph will be deleted upon the effective date of FASB ASU No. 2016-14.[46]

4.97 For each period for which a statement of financial position is presented, an NFP should disclose

a. pursuant to FASB ASC 958-320-50-2, the aggregate carrying amount of investments by major types, for example, equity securities, U.S. Treasury securities, corporate debt securities, mortgage-backed securities, oil and gas properties, and real estate.

b. pursuant to FASB ASC 958-325-50-2(a), the basis for determining the carrying amount for investments within the scope of FASB ASC 958-325.

c. pursuant to FASB ASC 958-325-50-2(b), the method(s) and significant assumptions used to estimate the fair values of investments other than financial instruments if those other investments are reported at fair value.

d. pursuant to FASB ASC 958-205-50-2, the aggregate amount of the deficiencies for all donor-restricted endowment funds for which the fair value of the assets at the reporting date is less than the level required by donor stipulations or law.

pursuant to the "Pending Content" in FASB ASC 958-205-50-2, (*a*) the fair value of the underwater endowment funds, (*b*) the original endowment gift amount or level required to be maintained by donor stipulations or by law that extends donor restrictions and (*c*) the amount of the deficiencies of the underwater endowment funds ((a)less (b)).[47]

e. the information required by FASB ASC 320-10-50-6(a) if the NFP holds cost-method investments in an unrealized loss position for which impairment losses have not been recognized.

f. the information required by FASB ASC 325-20-50-1 if the NFP has cost-method investments.

g. the information required by paragraphs 1–3 of FASB ASC 820-10-50 for investments measured at fair value, if applicable. Only NFPs that are public entities are required to disclose the information required by FASB ASC 820-10-50-2(bb) and (g) and FASB ASC 820-10-50-2E.

---

[46] The amendments in FASB ASU No. 2016-14 are effective for annual financial statements issued for fiscal years beginning after December 15, 2017 (for example, years ending December 31, 2018, and years ending June 30, 2019), and for interim periods within fiscal years beginning after December 15, 2018. Application to interim financial statements is permitted but not required in the initial year of application. Early application of the amendments is permitted.

[47] The amendments in FASB ASU No. 2016-14 are effective for annual financial statements issued for fiscal years beginning after December 15, 2017 (for example, years ending December 31, 2018, and years ending June 30, 2019), and for interim periods within fiscal years beginning after December 15, 2018. Application to interim financial statements is permitted but not required in the initial year of application. Early application of the amendments is permitted.

h. the information required by paragraphs 28–29 of FASB ASC 825-10-50, if the NFP has made an election as described in the "Fair Value Option" subsections of FASB ASC 825-10.

i. the information required by FASB ASC 820-10-50-6A if investments meet the criteria in paragraphs 45 of FASB ASC 820-10-35 to be measured using net asset value as a practical expedient to a fair value measure.

the information required by FASB ASC 820-10-50-6A if investments are measured at net asset value as a practical expedient for a fair value measure. FASB ASC 820-10-35-54B states that the disclosure requirements in FASB ASC 820-10-50-2 do not apply to those investments.[48]

4.98 Paragraphs 1A–1B of FASB ASC 958-205-50 require disclosures about an NFP's endowment fund. At a minimum, those disclosures should include the following information about the NFP's donor-restricted endowment funds and its board-designated endowment funds:

a. A description of the governing board's interpretation of the law(s) that underlies the NFP's net asset classification of donor-restricted endowment funds. (The term *endowment fund* as defined in UPMIFA does not include assets that an institution designates as an endowment fund for its own use.)

b. A description of the NFP's policy(ies) for the appropriation of endowment assets for expenditure (its endowment spending policy[ies]).

c. A description of the NFP's endowment investment policies. The description should include the NFP's return objectives and risk parameters; how those return objectives relate to the NFP's endowment spending policy(ies); and the strategies employed for achieving those return objectives.

d. The composition of the NFP's endowment by net asset class at the end of the period, in total and by type of endowment fund, showing donor-restricted endowment funds separately from board-designated endowment funds.

e. A reconciliation of the beginning and ending balance of the NFP's endowment, in total and by net asset class, including, at a minimum, all of the following line items (as applicable): investment return, separated into investment income (for example, interest, dividends, rents) and net appreciation or depreciation of investments; contributions; amounts appropriated for expenditure; reclassifications; and other changes.

The "Pending Content" in paragraphs 1A–1B of FASB ASC 958-205-50 requires disclosures about an NFP's endowment fund. At a minimum, those disclosures should include the following information about the NFP's donor-restricted endowment funds and its board-designated endowment funds:

a. A description of the governing board's interpretation of the law(s) that underlies the NFP's net asset classification of donor-restricted endowment funds including its interpretation of the

[48] FASB ASU No. 2015-07 is effective for NFPs for fiscal years beginning after December 15, 2016, and for interim periods within those fiscal years. Early adoption is permitted.

ability to spend from underwater endowment funds. (The term *endowment fund* as defined in UPMIFA does not include assets that an institution designates as an endowment fund for its own use.)

b. A description of the NFP's policy(ies) for the appropriation of endowment assets for expenditure (its endowment spending policy[ies]), including its policy, and any actions taken during the period, concerning appropriation from underwater endowment funds.

c. A description of the NFP's endowment investment policies. The description should include the NFP's return objectives and risk parameters; how those return objectives relate to the NFP's endowment spending policy(ies); and the strategies employed for achieving those return objectives.

d. The composition of the NFP's endowment by net asset class at the end of the period, in total and by type of endowment fund, showing donor-restricted endowment funds separately from board-designated endowment funds.

e. A reconciliation of the beginning and ending balance of the NFP's endowment, in total and by net asset class, including, at a minimum, all of the following line items (as applicable): investment return (net), contributions; amounts appropriated for expenditure, and other changes.[49]

4.99 For the most recent period for which a statement of financial position is presented, an NFP should disclose

a. pursuant to FASB ASC 958-320-50-3, the nature of and carrying amount for each individual investment or group of investments that represents a significant concentration of market risk, such as risks that result from the nature of the investments or from a lack of diversity of industry, currency, or geographic location.

b. the information required by FASB ASC 320-10-50-6(b) if the NFP has cost-method investments in an unrealized loss position for which impairment losses have not been recognized.

c. the information required by FASB ASC 825-10-50-30, if the NFP has made an election as described in the "Fair Value Option" subsections of FASB ASC 825-10.

Additionally, paragraphs 1–2 of FASB ASC 825-10-45 require that, if an NFP elects the fair value option, it display on the face of its statement of financial position (either by separate line items or parenthetically) the assets and liabilities reported at fair value separately from the carrying amounts of similar assets and liabilities measured using another measurement attribute.

4.100 In circumstances in which an NFP transfers some or all of its investments to a pool that is managed by a third party, the NFP may be subject to additional financial statement disclosures. FASB ASC 958-605-50-6 requires

---

[49] The amendments in FASB ASU No. 2016-14 are effective for annual financial statements issued for fiscal years beginning after December 15, 2017 (for example, years ending December 31, 2018, and years ending June 30, 2019), and for interim periods within fiscal years beginning after December 15, 2018. Application to interim financial statements is permitted but not required in the initial year of application. Early application of the amendments is permitted.

the following disclosures for each period for which a statement of financial position is presented if an NFP transfers assets to a recipient entity and specifies itself or its affiliate as the beneficiary:

a. The identity of the recipient entity to which the transfer was made

b. Whether variance power was granted to the recipient entity and, if so, a description of the terms of the variance power

c. The terms under which amounts will be distributed to the resource provider or its affiliate

d. The aggregate amount recognized in the statement of financial position for those transfers and whether that amount is recorded as an interest in the net assets of the recipient entity or as another asset (for example, as a beneficial interest in assets held by others or a refundable advance)

4.101 If an interest in an investment pool managed by a third party is reported using net asset value per unit or share as an input for a fair value measurement, as discussed in paragraph 4.43, FASB ASC 820-10-35-54B provides guidance for making disclosures about the level within the fair value hierarchy in which the fair value measurement falls. The level depends upon whether and how soon the NFP can redeem its investment in the pool and whether that redemption would be at net asset value. If an NFP has the ability to redeem its investment in the pool at net asset value per share (or its equivalent) at the reporting date, the fair value measurement of the investment is categorized within level 2 of the fair value hierarchy. If an NFP will never have the ability to redeem its investment in the pool at net asset value per share (or its equivalent), the fair value measurement of the investment should be categorized within level 3 of the fair value hierarchy. If an NFP cannot redeem its investment with the investee at net asset value per share (or its equivalent) at the reporting date but the investment may be redeemable at a future date, the NFP should take into account the length of time until the investment will become redeemable in determining whether the fair value measurement of the interest in the investment pool should be categorized within level 2 or level 3 of the fair value hierarchy. For example, if the NFP does not know when it will have the ability to redeem the investment or it does not have the ability to redeem the investment in the near term at net asset value per share (or its equivalent), the fair value measurement of the investment should be categorized within level 3 of the fair value hierarchy.

If an investment pool is managed by a third party that has substantive activities in addition to investing funds solely for returns from capital appreciation, investment income, or both (for example, a community foundation that makes grants in addition to its investing activities), that investment pool would not meet the fundamental characteristics of an investment company under FASB ASC 946-10-15-6 and an interest in that investment pool is not eligible to being reported at net asset value per unit or share as a practical expedient for fair value, as discussed in paragraph 4.43. Net asset value, however, may be used as an input to measuring fair value. When determining the level within the fair value hierarchy in which the resulting fair value measurement falls. NFPs might consider whether and how soon it can redeem its investment in the pool and whether that redemption would be at net asset value. For example, if the NFP has the ability to redeem its investment in the pool at net asset value per share (or its equivalent) at the reporting date, that fact is evidence that there is less uncertainty of the measurement, and the fair value measurement of the investment might be categorized within level 2 of the fair value hierarchy. If an NFP will never have the ability to redeem its investment in the pool at net asset value per share (or its equivalent), that fact is evidence that there is more uncertainty in the measurement of the investment, and the fair value measurement of the interest in the investment pool might be categorized within level 3 of the fair value hierarchy.[50]

4.102 In circumstances in which NFPs invest in hedge funds or similar investment vehicles that invest in other funds (sometimes referred to as fund-of-funds), FinREC recommends that the notes to the financial statements disclose the nature of amounts included in investment expenses so that it is clear to financial statement users that investment expenses do not reflect the proportionate share of expenses of the underlying investee funds.

The preceding paragraph will be deleted upon the effective date of FASB ASU No. 2016-14.[51]

Auditing

4.103 Many audit objectives and auditing procedures, including the auditor's consideration of controls, related to investments of NFPs are similar to those of other entities. AU-C section 540, *Auditing Accounting Estimates, Including Fair Value Accounting Estimates, and Related Disclosures*,[52] addresses auditing fair value accounting estimates, including requirements and guidance relating to the auditor's understanding of the applicable financial reporting framework relevant to accounting estimates and the method used in making the estimate and the auditor's determination of whether management has appropriately applied the requirements of the applicable financial reporting framework relevant to the accounting estimate. In addition, the auditor may need to consider the specific audit objectives, auditing procedures, and selected controls that are unique to NFPs and that are presented at the end of this chapter.

4.104 NFPs may elect to report securities for which a readily determinable fair value does not exist, such as hedge funds, at fair value as described in paragraph 4.38. In circumstances in which the auditor determines that the nature and extent of auditing procedures would include verifying the existence and testing the measurement of investments in securities, simply receiving a confirmation from a third party, either in aggregate or on a security-by-security basis, would not in and of itself constitute relevant and reliable audit evidence with respect to the valuation assertion.

4.105 As stated in paragraph .07 of AU-C section 501, *Audit Evidence—Specific Considerations for Selected Items*, if estimates of fair value of derivative instruments or securities are obtained from broker-dealers or other third-party

---

[50] FASB ASU No. 2015-07 is effective for NFPs for fiscal years beginning after December 15, 2016, and for interim periods within those fiscal years. Early adoption is permitted.

[51] The amendments in FASB ASU No. 2016-14 are effective for annual financial statements issued for fiscal years beginning after December 15, 2017 (for example, years ending December 31, 2018, and years ending June 30, 2019), and for interim periods within fiscal years beginning after December 15, 2018. Application to interim financial statements is permitted but not required in the initial year of application. Early application of the amendments is permitted.

[52] All AU-C sections can be found in AICPA *Professional Standards*.

sources based on valuation models, the auditor should understand the method used by the broker-dealer or other third-party source in developing the estimate and consider the applicability of AU-C section 500, *Audit Evidence*. Understanding the method used by the broker-dealer or other third-party source in developing the estimate may include, for example, understanding whether a pricing model or cash flow projection was used. The auditor also may determine that it is necessary to obtain estimates from more than one pricing source. For example, this may be appropriate if either of the following occurs:

- The pricing source has a relationship with an entity that might impair its objectivity, such as an affiliate or a counterparty involved in selling or structuring the product.
- The valuation is based on assumptions that are highly subjective or particularly sensitive to changes in the underlying circumstances.

4.106 If derivative instruments or securities are valued by the entity using a valuation model, the auditor should obtain sufficient appropriate audit evidence supporting management's assertions about fair value determined using the model. The auditor may refer to AU-C section 540 for the auditor's procedures to obtain evidence supporting management's assertions about fair value that are determined using a valuation model.

4.107 In circumstances in which the auditor is unable to audit the existence or measurement of interests in investments in securities at the financial statement date, the auditor should consider whether a scope limitation exists that could require the auditor to either qualify his or her opinion or to disclaim an opinion, as discussed in AU-C section 705, *Modifications to the Opinion in the Independent Auditor's Report*. The more complex or illiquid the underlying investments of an alternative investment are, the greater the inherent uncertainty in management's estimated fair value. As the inherent uncertainty in the estimate increases, as well as the significance of the alternative investments to the financial statements, auditors may consider inclusion of an emphasis-of-matter paragraph in the auditors' report.

Endowment Funds

4.108 Auditors may find information available from State Societies of Certified Public Accountants, state Attorneys General, and industry publications useful in obtaining an understanding of laws for management of endowment funds. As required by paragraph .12 of AU-C section 250, *Consideration of Laws and Regulations in an Audit of Financial Statements*, the auditor should obtain a general understanding of the legal and regulatory framework applicable to the entity and the industry or sector in which the entity operates and how the entity is complying with that framework. As noted in paragraph .A18 of AU-C section 580, *Written Representations,* an auditor may request management to provide a written representation about aspects of laws and regulations that may affect the financial statements—an example being the interpretations made by the NFP's governing board concerning whether laws limit the amount of net appreciation of donor-restricted endowment funds that may be spent. However, for NFPs operating in jurisdictions in which there may be questions concerning interpretations of the applicable laws or in which there are conflicting interpretations by various legal counsel, auditors may find it helpful to request that the NFP obtain a specific opinion from legal counsel concerning interpretation of the legal requirements. In such cases, the legal counsel may be considered to be a *management's specialist*, which is defined in AU-C section 500 as an individual or organization possessing expertise in a field other than accounting or auditing, whose work in that field is used by the entity to assist the entity in preparing the financial statements. Paragraph .08 of AU-C section 500 provides requirements concerning circumstances in which information to be used as audit evidence has been prepared using the work of a management's specialist.

Investment Pools

4.109 Paragraphs 4.60–.64 discuss interests in investment pools managed by third parties.

4.110 If an NFP operates an investment pool on behalf of itself and other entities (a self-managed pool), suggested audit procedures to consider include testing the following: (Valuation and Allocation)

- The number of shares or units held in the pool at the beginning of the year, by agreeing to prior-year documentation
- The purchases and sales of units or shares throughout the year and the prices at which the unit or share purchases and sales were made
- The entity's methodology for assessing fair value of the pool and the price per unit or share prior to allowing purchases into or withdrawals from the pool
- The method of distribution of income, gains, and losses to the pool participants and its consistency with the method used in the prior year
- The NFP's compliance with the stated investment allocation and diversification of the pool
- The entity's communication of the pool's investment results to the investors in the pool, including disclosures necessary for the pool investors to satisfy their own fair value reporting and disclosure requirements at year end

4.111 If an NFP is an investor in a pool managed by a third party and the auditor determines that the nature and extent of auditing procedures would include verifying the existence and testing the measurement of investments held in that pool, the auditor typically would satisfy the existence assertion through confirmation, examination of legal documents, or other means. In confirming the existence, the auditor may request that the pool's manager indicate or confirm the pool's fair value, including the fair value of investments held in the pool. In some circumstances, the pool's manager will not provide management or the auditor detailed information about the basis and method for measuring those investments, nor will it provide information about the specific investments held by the pool. For example, in some circumstances the pool's manager may inform management or the auditor that investments are held by the pool as follows:

- In aggregate, such as "$XXX of total investments"
- In aggregate, such as "$XXX of total investments in private equity securities, $YYY of total investments in interests in limited partnerships, and $ZZZ of total investments in debt securities"

- On an investment-by-investment basis, such as "AA shares of common stock of private company A, with a fair value of $AAA; BB shares of preferred stock of private company B, with a fair value of $BBB; CC units of limited partnership interest CCC, with a fair value of $CCC; and real estate property DDD, with a fair value of $DDDD"

4.112 In circumstances in which the auditor determines that the nature and extent of auditing procedures would include verifying the existence and testing the measurement of investments held by an investment pool, simply receiving a confirmation from the pool's manager, either in aggregate or on an investment-by-investment basis, would not in and of itself constitute adequate audit evidence with respect to the requirements for auditing the fair value of the interest in the pool. In addition, receiving confirmation from the pool's manager for investments in aggregate (illustrated by the first two preceding bullets) would not constitute adequate audit evidence with respect to the existence assertion. Receiving confirmation from the pool's manager on an investment-by-investment basis (illustrated by the third preceding bullet), however, typically would constitute adequate audit evidence with respect to the existence assertion.

4.113 Other suggested audit procedures to consider include collecting relevant and reliable audit evidence to verify the number of shares or units the NFP holds in the pool, and recomputing the value of the NFP's interest using the aggregate fair value of the pool, the number of shares or units in the pool held by all investors, and the number of NFP's shares or units.

4.114 In circumstances in which the auditor is unable to audit the existence or measurement of interests in investment pools managed by third parties at the financial statement date, the auditor should consider whether a scope limitation exists that requires the auditor to either qualify his or her opinion or to disclaim an opinion, as discussed in AU-C section 705.

Audit Objectives and Procedures

4.115 The following table illustrates the use of assertions in developing audit objectives and designing substantive tests. The examples are not intended to be all-inclusive nor is it expected that all the procedures would necessarily be applied in an audit. The use of assertions in assessing risks and designing appropriate audit procedures to obtain audit evidence is described in paragraphs .26–.32 of AU-C section 315, *Understanding the Entity and Its Environment and Assessing the Risks of Material Misstatement*. Paragraph .18 of AU-C section 330, *Performing Audit Procedures in Response to Assessed Risks and Evaluating the Audit Evidence Obtained*, requires the auditor to design and perform substantive procedures for all relevant assertions related to each material class of transactions, account balance, and disclosure, irrespective of the assessed risks of material misstatement. This requirement reflects the facts that (1) the auditor's assessment of risk is judgmental and may not identify all risks of material misstatement, and (2) inherent limitations to internal control exist, including management override. Various audit procedures and the purposes for which they may be performed are described in paragraphs .A10–.A26 of AU-C section 500.

Auditing Considerations

Financial Statement Assertions	*Specific Audit Objectives*	*Select Control Objectives*
Rights and obligations; Classification	Restrictions on contributed investments are reflected in the classification of net assets. Restrictions on investment income, net realized gains, and net recognized unrealized gains that are imposed by donors or by law are reflected in the classification of revenue and gains.	Contributions of investments and investment income, gains, and losses are reviewed for restrictions and management monitors compliance with restrictions.
Occurrence/ Existence; Classification	Restricted net assets are reclassified in the statement of activities when restrictions are met on investment income or net appreciation restricted for support of donor-specified programs.	

4.116 Suggested audit procedures to consider include the following:

a. Inquire of management and review documents relating to restrictions on cash arising from donors or legal agreements, or both. (Rights and Obligations, Classifications)

b. Inquire of management regarding their policy for recording of "other investments" per FASB ASC 958-325-35. Determine that the NFP is appropriately and consistently accounting for "other investments" at either a cost-based measure or fair value consistent with the policy. (Valuation)

c. Review donor correspondence to determine the existence of restrictions on and classification of investments and related income, gains, and losses. (Rights and Obligations, Classifications)

d. Review minutes of governing board and governing board committee meetings for evidence of donor or statutory restrictions on and classification of investments and related income, gains, and losses. (Rights and Obligations, Classifications)

e. If specific investments are restricted, review investment transactions for the propriety of dispositions and use of the proceeds of sale consistent with the donor's restrictions. (Rights and Obligations, Classifications)

f. Determine that appropriate reclassifications are made in the statement of activities when restrictions are met on investment income or net appreciation restricted for donor-specified programs. (Occurrence/Existence, Classifications, Completeness)

g. Determine that management has appropriately identified and disclosed the aggregate amount of the deficiencies for all donor-restricted endowments funds for which the fair value of the assets at the reporting date is less than the level required by donor stipulations or law. (Classification, Understandability, Valuation and Allocation)

4.117 If the NFP has donor-restricted endowments, consider testing a sample of funds based on materiality and inherent risk. Suggested procedures to test the allocation of investment returns to the endowment funds and the release of restrictions include the following: (Completeness, Valuation and Allocation)

a. Inquire of management whether they have consulted with legal counsel relating to the nature of the donor endowment restrictions. If legal counsel informs them that the endowment restrictions are not subject to UPMIFA, obtain a legal opinion.

b. If the NFP utilizes a spending rate, obtain an understanding of the spending rate policy.

c. Review the minutes of the annual board meeting where approval of the spending for the fiscal year was obtained and compare amounts (or rates) approved to amounts (or rates) distributed for spending to determine that the institution is in compliance with the approved spending formula.

d. Recalculate the amount distributed for spending to verify that it is in accordance with the approved amount. If the NFP uses a spending rate policy, recalculate the amount to determine that the policy is correctly applied.

e. Recalculate the allocation of the total investment return to the individual endowment funds or to the major groupings of endowment funds by restriction type (for example, scholarship, professorship, prizes, library, and so on).

f. Test the release from restriction of the endowment spending rate and any other appropriated amounts and the endowment total return by performing the following steps:

i. Obtain an understanding of the restrictions for the selected fund from the gift agreement (or other documentation).

ii. Obtain an understanding of how the NFP determines whether restrictions have been met on investment return.

iii. Verify that expenditures were incurred to satisfy those restrictions. Specifically determine if the NFP has sufficient expenses meeting the terms of each restriction (either by general category for broadly restricted endowment funds or by individual expense for specifically restricted endowment funds) to utilize the entire spending rate allocation, and recalculate the release from restriction for all or a selection of endowment funds.

iv. For the portion of the total return not utilized by the NFP through the spending rate or other appropriation, verify that the excess remained classified as temporary restricted net assets.

For the portion of the total return not utilized by the NFP through the spending rate or other appropriation, verify that the excess remained classified as net assets with donor restrictions.[53]

[53] The amendments in FASB ASU No. 2016-14 are effective for annual financial statements issued for fiscal years beginning after December 15, 2017 (for example, years ending December 31, 2018, and years ending June 30, 2019), and for interim periods within fiscal years beginning after December 15, 2018. Application to interim financial statements is permitted but not required in the initial year of application. Early application of the amendments is permitted.

4.118

Appendix A—Determining Fair Value of Alternative Investments

A-1 Technical Questions and Answers (Q&A) sections 2220.18–.28 (*Technical Questions and Answers*) are intended to assist reporting entities in applying the provisions of FASB *Accounting Standards Codification* 820, *Fair Value Measurement*, to alternative investments.

.18 Applicability of Practical Expedient

Inquiry—Which investments are permitted, as a practical expedient, to be measured at fair value on the basis of the net asset value (NAV)?

Reply—FASB ASC 820-10-35-59 permits reporting entities, as a practical expedient, to estimate the fair value of their investments in certain entities that calculate NAV per share (or its equivalent) by using NAV. FASB ASC 820-10-15-4 indicates that the practical expedient in FASB ASC 820-10-35-59

> shall apply only to an investment that meets both of the following criteria as of the reporting entity's measurement date:
>
> *a.* The investment does not have a readily determinable fair value
>
> *b.* The investment is in an investment company within the scope of Topic 946 or is an investment in a real estate fund for which it is industry practice to measure investment assets at fair value on a recurring basis and to issue financial statements that are consistent with the measurement principles in Topic 946.

See section 2220.28 for a definition of *readily determinable fair value* and its interaction with the ability to use the NAV practical expedient.

However, as discussed in FASB ASC 820-10-35-61, if it is probable at the measurement date that a reporting entity will sell an investment (or a portion of the investment) for an amount different from NAV, and the criteria described in FASB ASC 820-10-35-62 are met, the reporting entity is not permitted to estimate the fair value of the investment using the NAV as a practical expedient.

Investments, depending on their characteristics, that may qualify for the practical expedient to be measured at fair value on the basis of NAV (which are often referred to as *alternative investments*) may include interests in hedge funds, private equity funds, real estate funds, venture capital funds, commodity funds, offshore fund vehicles, and funds of funds, as well as some bank common/collective trust funds and other similar funds. Companies in various industries, including investment companies, broker-dealers, banks, insurance companies, employee benefit plans, healthcare organizations, and not-for-profit organizations, often invest in these alternative investments.

[Issue Date: December 2009; Revised November 2017, to include the guidance from FASB ASC 820-10-15-4 and FASB ASC 820-10-35-61.]

.19 Unit of Account

Inquiry—According to the FASB ASC glossary, the *unit of account* is "[t]he level at which an asset or a liability is aggregated or disaggregated in a Topic for recognition purposes." How should the unit of account be identified for an interest in an alternative investment?

Reply—For interests in alternative investments, the appropriate unit of account is the interest in the investee fund itself, not the underlying investments within the investee fund; this is because the reporting entity owns an undivided interest in the whole of the investee fund portfolio and typically lacks the ability to dispose of individual assets and liabilities in the investee fund portfolio. However, as discussed in FASB ASC 820-10-35-61, if it is probable at the measurement date that a reporting entity will sell a portion of an investment at an amount different from NAV, and the criteria described in FASB ASC 820-10-35-62 are met, the portion that the reporting entity intends to sell is valued in accordance with other provisions of FASB ASC 820. The remaining portion of the interest that is not probable of being sold may be valued by using NAV as a practical expedient in accordance with FASB ASC 820-10-35-59.

[Issue Date: December 2009; Revised, May 2016, to reflect conforming changes necessary due to the issuance of FASB ASU No. 2011-04.]

.20 Determining Whether NAV Is Calculated Consistent With FASB ASC 946, *Financial Services—Investment Companies*

Inquiry—FASB ASC 820-10-35-59 states:

> A reporting entity is permitted, as a practical expedient, to estimate the fair value of an investment within the scope of paragraphs 820-10-15-4 through 15-5 using the net asset value per share (or its equivalent, such as member units or an ownership interest in partners' capital to which a proportionate share of net assets is attributed) of the investment, if the net asset value per share of the investment (or its equivalent) is calculated in a manner consistent with the measurement principles of Topic 946 as of the reporting entity's measurement date.

How does a reporting entity conclude that the NAV, as most recently reported by the manager of the alternative investment (reported NAV), has been calculated in a manner consistent with the measurement principles of FASB ASC 946, *Financial Services—Investment Companies*?

Reply—A reporting entity's management is responsible for the valuation assertions in its financial statements. Determining that reported NAV is calculated consistently with FASB ASC 946, including measurement of all or substantially all of the underlying investments of the investee in accordance with FASB ASC 820, requires a reporting entity to independently evaluate the fair value measurement process utilized by the investee fund manager to calculate the NAV. Such an evaluation is a matter of professional judgment and includes determining that the investee fund manager has an effective process and related internal controls in place to estimate the fair value of its investments that are included in the calculation of NAV. The reporting entity's controls used to evaluate the process of the investee fund manager may include the following:

- *Initial due diligence* (procedures performed before the initial investment)
- *Ongoing monitoring* (procedures performed after the initial investment)
- *Financial reporting controls* (procedures related to the accounting for, and reporting of, the investment) (Refer to the AICPA Audit

Guide *Special Considerations in Auditing Financial Instruments* for examples of these controls.[1])

Before concluding that the reported NAV is calculated in a manner consistent with the measurement principles of FASB ASC 946, the reporting entity might evaluate the evidence that is gathered via the initial due diligence and ongoing monitoring of the investee fund. Only after considering all relevant factors can the reporting entity reach a conclusion about whether the reported NAV is calculated in a manner consistent with the measurement principles of FASB ASC 946. For example, the reporting entity might consider the following key factors relating to the valuation received from the investee fund manager:

- The investee fund's fair value estimation processes and control environment, and any changes to those processes or the control environment[2]
- The investee fund's policies and procedures for estimating fair value of underlying investments, and any changes to those policies or procedures[3]
- The use of independent third party valuation experts to augment and validate the investee fund's procedures for estimating fair value
- The portion of the underlying securities held by the investee fund that are traded on active markets
- The professional reputation and standing of the investee fund's auditor (this is not intended to suggest that the auditor is an element of the investee fund's internal control system, but as a general risk factor in evaluating the integrity of the data obtained from the investee fund manager)
- Qualifications, if any, of the auditor's report on the investee fund's financial statements
- Whether there is a history of significant adjustments to the NAV reported by the investee fund manager as a result of the annual financial statement audit or otherwise
- Findings in the investee fund's adviser or administrator's type 1 or type 2 service auditor's report prepared under AT section 801, *Reporting on Controls at a Service Organization* (AICPA, *Professional Standards*), if any.[4] (a type 1 report is a report on management's description of a service organization's system and the

---

[1] The AICPA also has a project to develop guidance which addresses the challenges associated with auditing an entity's investments in alternative investment funds that calculate net asset value per share, or its equivalent (NAV) and the reporting entity uses NAV as a practical expedient. Please be alert to further developments. [Footnote revised, May 2016, to reflect removal of the nonauthoritative practice aid *Alternative Investments—Audit Considerations* from the AICPA's website and the project to address auditing the NAV practical expedient.]

[2] For further guidance, see AU-C section 501, *Audit Evidence—Specific Considerations for Selected Items* (AICPA, *Professional Standards*). Also see footnote 1. [Footnote revised, December 2012, to reflect conforming changes necessary due to the issuance of SAS Nos. 122–126. Footnote revised, May 2016, to reflect removal of the nonauthoritative practice aid *Alternative Investments—Audit Considerations* from the AICPA's website.]

[3] See footnote 2.

[4] AT section 801, *Reporting on Controls at a Service Organization*, establishes the requirements and application guidance for a service auditor reporting on controls at a service organization relevant to user entities' internal control over financial reporting. AU-C section 402, *Audit Considerations Relating to an Entity Using a Service Organization* (AICPA, *Professional Standards*), contains the

(continued)

suitability of the design of controls; a type 2 report is a report on management's description of a service organization's system and the suitability of the design and operating effectiveness of controls)

- Whether NAV has been appropriately adjusted for items such as carried interest and clawbacks (more fully described in section 6910.29, "Allocation of Unrealized Gain (Loss), Recognition of Carried Interest, and Clawback Obligations")
- Comparison of historical realizations to last reported fair value

If the last reported NAV is not as of the reporting entity's measurement date, refer to section 2220.22 for further considerations.

In cases when the reporting entity invests in a fund of funds (the investee fund invests in other funds that do not have readily determinable fair values), the reporting entity might conclude that the NAV reported by the fund of funds manager is calculated in a manner consistent with FASB ASC 946 by assessing whether the fund of funds manager has a process that considers the previously listed items in the calculation of the NAV reported by the fund of funds, and that the fund of funds manager has obtained or estimated NAV from underlying fund managers in a manner consistent with paragraphs 59–62 of FASB ASC 820-10-35 as of the measurement date. The reporting entity is not required to look through the fund of funds interest to underlying fund investments if the reporting entity has concluded that the fund of funds manager reports NAV consistent with FASB ASC 946 for the fund of funds interest.

[Issue Date: December 2009; Revised, June and August 2011, to reflect conforming changes necessary due to the issuance of SSAE No. 16; Revised, December 2012, to reflect conforming changes necessary due to the issuance of SAS Nos. 122–126; Revised, May 2016, to reflect removal of the nonauthoritative practice aid *Alternative Investments—Audit Considerations* from the AICPA's website and the project to address auditing the NAV practical expedient.]

.21 Determining Whether an Adjustment to NAV Is Necessary

Inquiry—FASB ASC 820-10-35-59 allows the reporting entity, as a practical expedient, to estimate the fair value of an investment within the scope of paragraphs 4 and 5 of FASB ASC 820-10-15 using the NAV as reported by the investee when the reporting entity has satisfied itself that (*a*) the investee has calculated NAV consistent with FASB ASC 946 (see section 2220.20), and (*b*) the NAV has been calculated as of the reporting entity's financial reporting (measurement) date.

(footnote continued)

requirements and application guidance for an auditor auditing the financial statements of an entity that uses a service organization.

In April 2016, the AICPA Auditing Standards Board issued Statement on Standards for Attestation Engagements (SSAE) No. 18, *Attestation Standards: Clarification and Recodification*, which, among other things, supersedes AT section 801. As a result of this, AT section 801 will be superseded by AT-C Section 320, *Reporting on an Examination of Controls at a Service Organization Relevant to User Entities' Internal Control Over Financial Reporting* (AICPA, *Professional Standards*), which is effective for service auditors' reports dated on or after May 1, 2017. SSAE No. 18 is available at www.aicpa.org/research/standards/auditattest/downloadabledocuments/ssae_no_18.pdf. [Footnote revised, August 2011, to reflect conforming changes necessary due to the issuance of SSAE No. 16. Footnote revised, December 2012, to reflect conforming changes necessary due to the issuance of SAS Nos. 122–126. Footnote revised, May 2016, to reflect conforming changes necessary due to the issuance of SSAE No. 18.]

FASB ASC 820-10-35-60 further states:

> If the net asset value per share of the investment obtained from the investee is not as of the reporting entity's measurement date or is not calculated in a manner consistent with the measurement principles of Topic 946, the reporting entity shall consider whether an adjustment to the most recent net asset value per share is necessary. The objective of any adjustment is to estimate a net asset value per share for the investment that is calculated in a manner consistent with the measurement principles of Topic 946 as of the reporting entity's measurement date.

How does a reporting entity determine whether an adjustment to the last reported NAV is necessary?

Reply—Examples of when an adjustment to the last reported NAV may be necessary include, but are not limited to the following:

- NAV is not as of the reporting entity's measurement date
- NAV is not calculated in a manner consistent with the measurement principles of FASB ASC 946 (which requires, among other things, measurement of all or substantially all of the underlying investments of the investee in accordance with FASB ASC 820)
- Both

The existence of either of these factors may lead the reporting entity to conclude that an adjustment to the last reported NAV may be necessary. Practically, it is difficult to assess whether an adjustment is necessary unless an estimate of the adjustment is calculated.

[Issue Date: December 2009.]

.22 Adjusting NAV When It Is Not as of the Reporting Entity's Measurement Date

Inquiry—If the reporting entity concludes that the reported NAV is calculated consistently with FASB ASC 946, but an adjustment is necessary because the NAV is not as of the reporting entity's measurement date, how should the reporting entity estimate the adjustment? (Refer to the inquiry in section 2220.21 for applicable FASB literature.)

Reply—FASB ASC 820-10-35-60 states that "The objective of any adjustment is to estimate a net asset value per share for the investment that is calculated in a manner consistent with the measurement principles of Topic 946 as of the reporting entity's measurement date." If the last reported NAV is calculated consistently with FASB ASC 946 but is not as of the reporting entity's measurement date, the reporting entity may either request the investee fund manager to provide a supplemental NAV calculation consistent with the measurement principles of FASB ASC 946 as of the reporting entity's measurement date, or it may be necessary to adjust or roll forward (or roll back)[5] the reported NAV for factors that might cause it to differ from the NAV at the measurement date. For example, the following factors might necessitate an adjustment to the reported NAV when it is not calculated as of the reporting entity's measurement date:

[5] When the reporting entity's measurement date is prior to the NAV calculation date, it may be more appropriate to use that NAV and perform a roll back rather than using a reported NAV calculated prior to the entity's measurement date.

- The reporting entity has made an additional investment(s) (capital contributions) since the calculation date of the reported NAV and prior to the reporting entity's measurement date
- The reporting entity has received a distribution(s) or partial redemption since the calculation date of the reported NAV
- The reporting entity has become aware (through inquiry of the investment manager or communication by the investment manager to the reporting entity) of changes in the value of underlying investments since the calculation date of the reported NAV
- Market changes or other economic conditions have changed to affect (favorably or unfavorably) the value of the investee's portfolio after the calculation date of the reported NAV
- Changes have occurred in the composition of the underlying investment portfolio of the investee fund after the NAV calculation date

The roll forward NAV might be calculated as follows:

i. Last Reported NAV (calculated consistently with FASB ASC 946)	$ X,XXX
ii. Add capital contributions/subscriptions	C,CCC
iii. Subtract distributions/redemptions/withdrawals	(D,DDD)
iv. Adjust for changes in valuations[(a)]	V,VVV
Roll forward NAV (as of the reporting entity's measurement date)	$ R,RRR

(a) Market changes refer to market fluctuations between the date of the reported NAV and the reporting entity's measurement date. Examples of other economic conditions for which it may be necessary to adjust a reported NAV include, but are not limited to, a portfolio company being acquired, going public, or declaring bankruptcy between the date of the reported NAV and the reporting entity's measurement date, or changes in the value of underlying investments caused by company performance or market conditions, or both.

[Issue Date: December 2009.]

.23 Adjusting NAV When It Is Not Calculated Consistent With FASB ASC 946

Inquiry—If the reporting entity concludes that an adjustment is necessary because a reported NAV is not calculated consistently with the measurement principles of FASB ASC 946, how does a reporting entity estimate the adjustment? (Refer to the inquiry in section 2220.21 for applicable FASB literature.)

Reply—Although it is not possible to state all the reasons why a reported NAV may not be consistent with the measurement principles of FASB ASC 946 (that is, it is not fair value based), the reporting entity would need to consider and understand the following:

- The reasons why NAV has not been based upon fair value. In some cases investees may appear to function similarly to investment companies, but do not meet the assessment described in paragraphs 4–9 of FASB ASC 946-10-15 to be an *investment company* and it is not industry practice for the investee to issue financial statements using the measurement principles in FASB ASC 946. (In those cases, the practical expedient is unavailable and the entity should be valued using the general measurement principles of FASB ASC 820.)

- Whether a fair value based NAV can be obtained from the investee manager.
- Whether the specific data needed to adjust the reported NAV can be obtained and properly utilized to estimate a fair value based NAV.

Examples of circumstances in which the reporting entity may be able to obtain data to estimate an adjustment include, but are not be limited to the following:

- Reported NAV is on a cash basis. The reporting entity could estimate the fair value of each underlying investment as of the measurement date by obtaining additional information from the investee manager.
- Reported NAV utilizes blockage discounts taken on securities valued using level 1 inputs, which is not consistent with FASB ASC 820. The reporting entity could estimate the adjustment to reported NAV required to remove the blockage discount based on additional information from the financial statements or from the investee manager.
- Reported NAV has not been adjusted for the impact of unrealized carried interest or incentive fees. The reporting entity could estimate the impact of carried interest or incentive fees and adjust reported NAV.

If the reporting entity finds that it is not practicable to calculate an adjusted NAV (for example, because sufficient information is not available or it is not in a position to reasonably evaluate the information available and estimate values consistent with FASB ASC 946), then the practical expedient is not available. The reporting entity may also elect not to utilize the practical expedient. In those instances, the reporting entity should apply the general measurement principles of FASB ASC 820 instead (see section 2220.27).

[Issue Date: December 2009; Revised, May 2016, to reflect conforming changes necessary due to the issuance of FASB ASU No. 2013-08.]

[.24] Reserved

[Deleted, November 2017, due to the issuance of FASB ASU No. 2015-07, *Fair Value Measurement (Topic 820): Disclosures for Investments in Certain Entities That Calculate Net Asset Value per Share (or Its Equivalent) (a consensus of the FASB Emerging Issues Task Force)*.]

[.25] Reserved

[Deleted, November 2017, due to the issuance of FASB ASU No. 2015-07.]

.26 Classification of Investments for Disclosure Purposes

Inquiry—The sample disclosure provided in FASB ASC 820-10-55-107 appears to apply to an institutional investor with a diversified portfolio of hedge and real estate funds. Certain entities, however, specialize in one particular investment class or have a significant investment in one such class, such as private equity or venture capital. Should these reporting entities use a different classification than that appearing in the sample disclosure?

Reply—Yes. FASB ASC 820-10-55-107 indicates that "[t]he classes presented ... are provided as examples only and are not intended to be treated as a template. The classes disclosed should be tailored to the nature, characteristics, and risks of the reporting entity's investments."

Accordingly, the disclosure should be tailored to address the concentrations of risk that are specifically attributable to the investments. For example, a private equity fund of funds should not simply classify its investments as "private equity" as this classification is not specific enough to address the nature and risks of the investee funds. In this example, more specific classification, perhaps relating to industry, geography, vintage year, or the strategy of the investees (venture, buyout, mezzanine, and so on), may be more appropriate and more useful to the reader. Such classification is a matter of judgment and should only be made after careful consideration of the specific risks and attributes of the portfolio investments has been made.

[Issue Date: December 2009; Revised, October 2013, to reflect conforming changes necessary due to the issuance of FASB ASU No. 2011-04; Revised, May 2016, to reflect conforming changes necessary due to the issuance of FASB ASU Nos. 2010-06 and 2015-07.]

.27 Determining Fair Value of Investments When the Practical Expedient Is Not Used or Is Not Available

Inquiry—For entities that do not elect to use NAV as a practical expedient to estimate fair value or are unable to adjust the most recently reported NAV to estimate a NAV that is calculated in a manner consistent with the measurement principles of FASB ASC 946 as of the reporting entity's measurement date, what inputs or investment features should be considered in estimating fair value?

Reply—Section 2220.27 distinguishes between redeemable and nonredeemable types of alternative investments, which are defined as follows:

- **Investments with redeemable interests.** Typically consist of hedge funds (based both in the United States and offshore) and some bank common/collective trust funds. These investment funds permit holders periodic opportunities to subscribe for or redeem interests at frequencies that can run from daily to annually. Certain funds may impose lock-up periods after an initial investment, under which an investor agrees that it may not redeem its investment for a specified period of time (in some cases, an early redemption may be permitted upon payment of an early redemption fee).
- **Investments with nonredeemable interests.** Typically consist of private equity, venture capital, and real estate funds. Generally, these investments have an initial subscription period, under which each investor makes a commitment to contribute a specified amount of capital as called for by the investment manager, typically as investments are identified and money is needed to acquire them. Due to the inherent illiquidity of the underlying investments, redemptions are not permitted during the fund's life; however, typically, as investments are sold or experience another liquidity event (for example, an initial public offering), the proceeds of the sale, less any incentives due to the fund sponsor,

are often distributed back to the investors in the fund immediately following the sale or liquidity event.

Investment Inputs

A reporting entity might first consider the other market participants to whom it could sell the asset. In accordance with FASB ASC 820-10-35-9, "[a] reporting entity shall measure the fair value of an asset or a liability using the assumptions that market participants would use in pricing the asset or liability, assuming that market participants act in their economic best interest." Based on guidance in FASB ASC 820-10-35-53, in the absence of relevant observable inputs, a reporting entity uses "unobservable inputs [that] shall reflect the assumptions that market participants would use when pricing the asset or liability, including assumptions about risk." FASB ASC 820-10-35-54A states the following:

> A reporting entity shall develop unobservable inputs using the best information available in the circumstances, which might include the reporting entity's own data. In developing unobservable inputs, a reporting entity may begin with its own data, but it shall adjust those data if reasonably available information indicates that other market participants would use different data or there is something particular to the reporting entity that is not available to other market participants (for example, an entity-specific synergy). A reporting entity need not undertake exhaustive efforts to obtain information about market participant assumptions. However, a reporting entity shall take into account all information about market participant assumptions that is reasonably available.

When doing so, the reporting entity is reminded that the FASB ASC glossary defines *market participants* as "knowledgeable, having a reasonable understanding about the asset or liability and the transaction using all available information, including information that might be obtained through due diligence efforts that are usual and customary." Thus, it can be presumed that a market participant would be aware of, and may be willing to accept, limitations on conversion to cash inherent to alternative investments. However, in some cases, those types of limitations may also affect the fair value measurement (see "Investment Features").[6] It also can be presumed that market participants may consider other factors such as the investment manager's track record and potentially limited access to desirable investment opportunities. Finally, it should be acknowledged that market participant assumptions normally result in a range of values. According to FASB ASC 820-10-35-24B, "[a] fair value measurement is the point within that range that is most representative of fair value in the circumstances." See FASB ASC 820-10-35-9 for further guidance. The reporting entity should also consider the guidance in paragraphs 54C–54M of FASB ASC 820-10-35.

Alternative investments may lend themselves to valuation techniques consistent with the income or market approaches. If both of these approaches are used to measure fair value, the results should be evaluated as discussed in FASB ASC 820-10-35-24B. When NAV is not used as a practical expedient,

---

[6] FASB *Accounting Standards Codification* (ASC) 820-10-35-2C states that "[t]he effect on the measurement arising from a particular characteristic will differ depending on how that characteristic would be taken into account by market participants." [Footnote revised, May 2016, to reflect conforming changes necessary due to the issuance of FASB ASU No. 2011-04.]

examples of factors that might be used when estimating fair value (depending on the valuation technique(s) and facts and circumstances) are as follows:

- NAV (as one valuation factor)
- Transactions in principal-to-principal or brokered markets (external markets) and overall market conditions
- Features of the alternative investment
- Expected future cash flows appropriately discounted (detailed description is beyond the scope of section 2220.27; however, for many funds with nonredeemable interests, expected future cash flows from the interests might typically coincide with the expected future cash flows from the underlying investments)
- Factors used to determine whether there has been a significant decrease in the volume and level of activity for the asset when compared with normal market activity for the asset (FASB ASC 820-10-35-54C)

The preceding examples are not listed in any order of importance. Rather, the reporting entity might determine the relative weighting and importance of these inputs based on its view of what market participants might consider in estimating fair value.

Investment Features[7]

A valuation technique used to measure the fair value of an asset or a liability should reflect assumptions a market participant might use to price the asset or liability, including assumptions about liquidity and risk, based on the best information available. The following discussion provides a detailed description of features of alternative investments that normally might be expected to be considered by market participants in the estimation of the fair value of an alternative investment. When considering the potential impact of the features of an alternative investment on its fair value, it is important that all relevant features be considered in the aggregate because that is how a market participant might be likely to evaluate them in determining how much it might be willing to pay for an alternative investment.

Other factors that may be considered include observed subscriptions and redemptions in redeemable interests; external market transactions in nonredeemable interests; and other features of the alternative investment. Additionally, a market participant might normally be expected to compare the performance of the alternative investment to publicly available data (for example, benchmarks, indexes, expected returns, and returns of comparable vehicles), and the cash returns of the investment to NAVs reported by the alternative investment during the year. A conclusion may ultimately be reached that the reported NAV is equivalent to fair value, either because no conditions exist to suggest an adjustment is necessary or because factors indicating a discount to the reported NAV may be offset by other factors that might justify a

---

[7] The "Investment Features" section contains important information related to features of alternative investments that a reporting entity may consider in determining fair value when the option to utilize the practical expedient is unavailable or not elected. The list of features highlighted in this section is intended to provide some examples to better explain the types of scenarios that could impact fair values. Because individual investments may have additional terms and features, the examples included in the "Investment Features" section should not be viewed as an all-inclusive "checklist." Professional judgment should be applied in evaluating the assumptions appropriate to any individual investment. The actual computation of fair value requires management's professional judgment and is beyond the scope of this Technical Questions and Answers section.

premium. In other cases, however, the investment may be valued at a discount or premium to the reported NAV because factors indicate that the fair value of the investment is less than, or more than, the reported NAV. Regardless of whether or not NAV is determined to be equivalent to fair value, the reporting entity needs to evaluate the relevant individual factors and their potential impact on fair value, and consider the level of documentation in its evaluation.

Among the factors that market participants might be expected to consider are the various terms and features of the alternative investment. Such features generally fall into one of two categories: initial due diligence features or ongoing monitoring features. The magnitude of any adjustment resulting from consideration of ongoing monitoring features is a matter of judgment and should be evaluated based on the facts and circumstances specific to each investee fund.

Initial Due Diligence Features. Generally, *initial due diligence features* are inherent characteristics that may have been considered by the reporting entity as part of its due diligence when making its initial investment in the particular investee fund. The following provides examples of initial due diligence features of an alternative investment. Not every feature may be relevant to every alternative investment, nor does this list necessarily include all assumptions that market participants may apply in any specific situation.

> <u>Lock-up periods and redemption fees.</u> (Typically applies only to redeemable interests)
>
> Lock-up period refers to the initial amount of time a reporting entity is contractually required to invest before having the ability to redeem. Typically, when the lock-up period expires, the reporting entity may redeem its interests on any scheduled liquidity date, subject to the other liquidity terms described in the investee fund's governing documents. The length of the lock-up period often depends on the quality and reputation of the fund manager as well as the expected liquidity of the underlying investment portfolio. In some instances, alternative investments may offer reduced fees if an investor agrees to a longer lock-up period. Also, some funds may permit investors to redeem during a lock-up period upon payment of a redemption fee. Such fees are typically imposed on the amount to be redeemed and generally range from 1 percent to 3 percent of the gross redemption amount.
>
> Related to the concept of lock-up periods is the general frequency in which an investor is allowed to redeem or withdraw from a fund. In the absence of a lock-up period, investors with redeemable interests typically may only redeem at prescribed liquidity dates (generally monthly, quarterly, or annually).
>
> <u>Notice periods.</u> (Typically applies only to redeemable interests)
>
> Following the expiration of any applicable lock-up period, a reporting entity may, upon specified prior written notice (generally 45–120 days) to the general partner or manager (redemption notice), elect to redeem all or a portion of its interest as of the last day of a calendar month, quarter, or year (redemption date).
>
> <u>Holdbacks.</u> (Typically applies only to redeemable interests)
>
> When the general partner or investment manager receives a redemption notice, the fund will redeem the interests of an investor as specified in the redemption notice, at the redemption price as of the applicable redemption date. The fund will distribute all or a substantial

portion (for example, 90 percent) of the redemption price with respect to the interests being redeemed within a specified number of business days (for example, 30 days) following the applicable redemption date. Any balance (for example, the remaining 10 percent) is distributed within a specific time frame, often following the release of the fund's audited financial statements for the year in which the redemption date falls. Holdback amounts protect the general partner or investment manager from adjustments reducing the NAV of the fund during an audit of the financial statements.

Suspension of redemptions ("gates"). (Typically applies only to redeemable interests)

Pursuant to the fund's governing documents, the general partner or investment manager can suspend or restrict the right of any investor to redeem his or her interests (whether in whole or in part). The general partner or investment manager can implement this restriction for certain reasons, including the aggregate amount of redemption requests, certain adverse regulatory or tax consequences, reduced liquidity of portfolio holdings, and other reasons that may render the manager unable to promptly and accurately calculate the fund's NAV. The most common example is the use of a "gate," whereby certain redemption requests are deferred, in whole or in part, because the aggregate amount of redemption requests as of a particular redemption date exceeds a specified level, generally ranging from 15 percent to 25 percent of the fund's net assets. The mere presence of a provision allowing the imposition of a gate might not normally be expected to have an effect on fair value, in the absence of any evidence suggesting that the provision actually may be exercised (see "Ongoing Monitoring Features," which follows).

Lack of redemption option. (Nonredeemable interests and instances where all or a portion of otherwise redeemable interests have been declared nonredeemable)

As discussed earlier, funds investing in private equity, venture capital, or real estate investments generally do not permit withdrawals or redemptions, primarily to match the liquidity provisions of the fund with the liquidity of the investment portfolio. When the fund sells any of its portfolio holdings, it often distributes the proceeds received on the sale to the investors in the fund.

Fund sponsor approval to transfer. (Redeemable and nonredeemable interests)

In virtually all cases, transfers of interests in alternative investments are not permitted under the governing documents of the fund without the written consent of the fund sponsor or general partner, for regulatory or tax reasons or both, and thus, are inherent to the category of investments. Past experiences, as well as the current operating environment, are both considerations in assessing the likelihood of such approval being granted.

In some private equity, venture capital and real estate funds that require investors to make commitments to invest over time and periodically call on the commitments as needed, the fund sponsor or general partner may allow an investor to withdraw or redeem from the fund and, thus, be absolved of future commitments, but the investor may forfeit its existing interest if no other investors (including the fund sponsor or general partner) are willing to assume the withdrawn partner's interest, including future commitments. If forfeiture occurs (which, in practice, is rare), the investor's interest is generally reallocated to the remaining investors in the fund. (The balance of the withdrawing partner's commitment may also be reallocated to the other investors, or the total size of the fund may be reduced).

Use of "side pockets." (Typically applies only to redeemable interests)

Certain funds issuing redeemable interests may be allowed to invest a portion of their assets in illiquid securities. In such cases, a common mechanism used is a "side pocket," whereby, at the time of an investment in an illiquid security, a proportionate share of an investor's capital account, relative to the entire interest of the fund, is assigned to a separate memorandum capital account or designated account. Typically, the investor loses its redemption rights to the designated account, and even a full redemption request is fulfilled only with that capital ascribed to his or her basic capital account (that is, the nondesignated capital account), while the investor continues to hold its proportionate interest in the designated account. Only when the security is sold (or otherwise deemed liquid) by the fund is the amount moved back to each applicable investor's basic capital account (and otherwise withdrawn investors can redeem the designated account balance). This designated account generally does not pay a performance fee[8] (although one may be levied) until the illiquid investment is sold or otherwise deemed liquid. Designated accounts are often referred to as "side pocket accounts" or as "special investment accounts." Similar to "gates," the mere existence of contractual provisions permitting the use of side pockets typically does not have a material effect on estimating the fair value unless those provisions are actually exercised and access to a portion of the investment is actually limited.

As previously noted, these examples of initial due diligence features are common characteristics of alternative investment funds and, as such, are generally considered and accepted by investors when making investment decisions in these investments. Accordingly, a market participant may or may not require an adjustment to the reported NAV in a transfer of an investment interest in an alternative investment solely due to the existence of these items. However, it is necessary to consider these features in conjunction with other inputs available to the reporting entity. For example, if the reporting entity is valuing redeemable interests and observes that other investors are subscribing for interests at the reported NAV under the same terms as the reporting entity's agreement, that fact may provide evidence that no adjustment to the reported NAV is necessary. However, if other investors are subscribing to the fund at the reported NAV under terms that, in aggregate, are less favorable than those in the reporting entity's agreement (for example, higher fees, greater restrictions on redemption), that fact may provide evidence that the reporting entity's holdings may trade at a premium to the reported NAV. Similarly, if other investors are receiving more favorable terms in aggregate than those in the reporting

[8] Consistent with the definition in the AICPA Audit and Accounting Guide *Investment Companies*, a *performance fee* (also referred to as an *incentive fee*) is a fee paid to an investment adviser based upon the fund's performance for the period. It may be an absolute share of the fund's performance or a share of the performance in excess of a specified benchmark.

entity's agreement (for example, lower fees, fewer restrictions on redemption), that fact may provide evidence that the reporting entity's holding may trade at a discount to the reported NAV. An investor may also typically consider whether the fund's terms are more or less restrictive than those prevailing in the current market. For example, terms that are more restrictive may suggest a discount. Alternatively, the quality of the investment manager may command a premium.

In short, if market participants would be expected to place a discount or premium on the reported NAV because of features, risk, or other factors relating to the interest, then the fair value measurement of the interest would need to be adjusted for that risk or opportunity.[9] However, if market participants might accept the same features, risk, and other factors relating to the interest and might transact at the reported NAV without a premium or discount, that fact may suggest that no adjustment is needed for the factors discussed previously to estimate fair value.

Ongoing Monitoring Features. *Ongoing monitoring features* are characteristics related to activity in an investee fund subsequent to a reporting entity's initial investment. Because ongoing monitoring features often include specific events relating to the investee fund, the fund sponsor, the industry or the asset class, they are more likely to result in consideration of a discount or premium to the reported NAV than initial due diligence features. The following provides some examples of ongoing monitoring features for an alternative investment.

As with initial due diligence features, not every feature may be relevant to a particular investment, nor does this list necessarily include all assumptions that market participants may apply in any specific situation. Also, changes in market conditions may affect the investor's assumptions relating to the significance of any particular feature.

> Imposition of a gate. (Typically applies only to redeemable interests)
>
> Though an investee fund manager's mere ability to impose a gate on redemption requests is a common initial due diligence feature (as noted previously), the actual imposition of a gate by an investee fund manager may warrant further consideration of whether a discount should be applied to the reported NAV. The act of imposing the gate generally implies that the investee fund manager is experiencing liquidity concerns, either related to specific investments or its portfolio as a whole, which the reporting entity and a market participant normally would be expected to consider in estimating fair value of the interest in the investee fund. Further, the imposition of a gate increases the uncertainty of the ultimate timing of receipt of cash upon redemption, sometimes significantly, and, thus, may impose an additional risk premium on the investment.
>
> Redemptions from an investee fund. (Typically applies only to redeemable interests)
>
> Even in the absence of the actual imposition of a gate, when an investee fund experiences material redemption requests this may suggest comparable liquidity issues that could result in a discount from the reported NAV, particularly in situations when the investee fund is leveraged.

---

[9] This is consistent with FASB ASC 820-10-35-54, which states, "A measurement that does not include an adjustment for risk would not represent a fair value measurement if market participants would include one when pricing the asset or liability." [Footnote revised, May 2016, to reflect conforming changes necessary due to the issuance of FASB ASU No. 2011-04.]

Notification of redemption triggers the assessment of redemption fee. (Typically applies only to redeemable interests)

Though, as noted previously, an investee fund manager may have the ability to charge redeeming investors a redemption fee, the mere existence of this feature is generally considered to be an initial due diligence feature which, in many instances, may not cause the reported NAV to exceed the fair value of the investment interest. However, if a reporting entity irrevocably agrees to redeem some or all of its interest, the redemption fee normally would be expected to cause the reported NAV to exceed the fair value of the investment interest.

Significant changes in key terms of the investee fund. (Redeemable and nonredeemable interests)

The initial due diligence features, as previously noted, represent standard or common characteristics of an alternative investment. They are generally known and accepted by the reporting entity at the time of making an initial investment at the reported NAV. As such, a market participant with full knowledge of these features may also likely transact at the reported NAV, so long as the terms remain within the range prevailing in the market.

If, however, the investee fund makes significant changes to the terms (for example, fees, lock-up periods, notification periods, gates) subsequent to the initial investment, the reporting entity normally would be expected to consider these changes when evaluating whether the reported NAV should be adjusted to arrive at fair value. In some cases, changes may be deemed to have little impact on the investment decisions of a market participant, whereas in other cases, changes to key terms may create a distinct difference between the existing interest and other interests (either in the specific alternative investment or comparable investments), which may result in either a discount or premium to the reported NAV.

Closure of fund to new subscriptions. (Redeemable interests)

Some funds may cease accepting subscriptions from new investors because doing so might cause them to exceed the maximum number of investors they can accept without requiring public filings of financial information under securities laws. In other cases, funds may voluntarily suspend the acceptance of subscriptions from new investors, and even in some cases additional subscriptions from existing investors, because of the adviser's view that opportunities to make further investments under the fund's investment strategy may be limited given the size of the markets involved or that they might not bring acceptable returns, or both. Such an event may suggest that existing interests in the fund could trade at a premium because prospective investors may have no other means of investing in the fund. Further, a large number of investors or the intent not to "dilute" the fund's returns by accepting additional investment funds, or both, may provide evidence that the fund may trade at a premium to the reported NAV.

Ability of fund to identify and make acceptable investments. (Nonredeemable interests)

Venture capital, private equity, and real estate funds typically offer interests on the basis of committed capital, which is only called from investors as investments are identified. Investors agree to commit capital under implicit or explicit understandings that committed capital will be called during an initial investment period, often from one to five years. Depending on the market environment, managers may find that they are unable to identify sufficient investments to utilize committed capital on a timely basis. Such funds often are smaller and less diversified than expected at the time of inception of the fund, which may negatively influence fair value. Further, certain vintages (that is, years when funds were organized) may be identified over time as having represented exceptionally good or poor investment opportunities for the particular investment style, and interests in funds organized in those years may be more likely to incur premiums or discounts, respectively. The fund's potential inability to identify and make acceptable investments will often result in unfunded capital commitments, which may need to be considered when estimating the fair value of an investment interest in the fund.

Allegations of fraud against the investee fund manager. (Redeemable and nonredeemable interests)

If the reporting entity is aware of allegations of fraud, noncompliance with laws and regulations, or other improprieties against the investee fund manager or its affiliates, the reporting entity should consider the potential impact of these allegations on the value of its interest in the investee fund. In many cases, such allegations may result in the unexpected inability to obtain any cash proceeds from the investee fund pending the resolution of the investigation or from a general lack of liquidity resulting from historical misrepresentation of the net assets of the fund. In other cases, the ongoing ability of the investee fund manager to manage the fund may be brought into question.

Change in financial strength or key personnel of investment manager. (Redeemable and nonredeemable interests)

In some cases, a key consideration for investment in certain funds is the reputation, and prior investment record, of the investment manager, or specific individuals expected to manage the investee fund's portfolio. In some situations, the desirability of the investment manager or individuals, or both, may influence the nature of the fee, lock-up, and similar terms investors are willing to accept in making an initial investment. If those key personnel no longer provide services to the alternative investment, investors may not be willing to continue to accept those terms. Further, if the advisory organization experiences financial deterioration, it may be less able to retain key personnel or, for certain private equity, venture capital, or real estate funds, to repay previously-received incentive fees to the fund under contractual clawback provisions (if the fund experiences subsequent losses). Those uncertainties may increase the risk of the investment.

[Issue Date: December 2009; Revised, December 2012, to reflect conforming changes necessary due to the issuance of SAS Nos. 122–126; Revised, May 2016, to reflect conforming changes necessary due to the issuance of FASB ASU No. 2011-04.]

.28 Definition of *Readily Determinable Fair Value* and Its Interaction With the NAV Practical Expedient

Inquiry—What is *readily determinable fair value* and how does it interact with the NAV practical expedient?

Reply—FASB ASC Master Glossary defines *readily determinable fair value* as follows:

> An equity security has a readily determinable fair value if it meets any of the following conditions:
>
> *a.* The fair value of an equity security is readily determinable if sales prices or bid-and-asked quotations are currently available on a securities exchange registered with the U.S. Securities and Exchange Commission (SEC) or in the over-the-counter market, provided that those prices or quotations for the over-the-counter market are publicly reported by the National Association of Securities Dealers Automated Quotations systems or by OTC Markets Group Inc. Restricted stock meets that definition if the restriction terminates within one year.
>
> *b.* The fair value of an equity security traded only in a foreign market is readily determinable if that foreign market is of a breadth and scope comparable to one of the U.S. markets referred to above.
>
> *c.* The fair value of an equity security that is an investment in a mutual fund or in a structure similar to a mutual fund (that is, a limited partnership or a venture capital entity) is readily determinable if the fair value per share (unit) is determined and published and is the basis for current transactions.

This definition reflects the amendments made by FASB Accounting Standards Update (ASU) No. 2015-10, *Technical Corrections and Improvements*, to condition (c). Whether an equity security has a readily determinable fair value (RDFV) in accordance with condition (c) is a facts and circumstances determination and requires judgment. Following these amendments, stakeholders questioned whether certain investments (such as common collective trusts and pooled separate accounts) meet condition (c) and, therefore, would be considered to have RDFV.

The conclusion reached regarding RDFV is important because it determines whether an investment is eligible to estimate fair value using the NAV practical expedient as permitted by FASB ASC 820-10-35-59. FASB ASC 820-10-15-4 indicates that the NAV practical expedient in FASB ASC 820-10-35-59 is available only if both of the following criteria are met:

a. The investment does not have a readily determinable fair value.

b. The investment is in an investment company within the scope of FASB ASC 946 or is an investment in a real estate fund for which it is industry practice to measure investment assets at fair value on a recurring basis and to issue financial statements that are consistent with the measurement principles in FASB ASC 946.

Therefore, if an investment has RDFV, it cannot be measured using the NAV practical expedient and would be subject to the fair value measurement disclosures required by FASB ASC 820-10-50-2, including the requirement to categorize the investment within the fair value hierarchy. In contrast, an investment whose fair value is measured using the NAV practical expedient should not be categorized within the fair value hierarchy and would be subject to the disclosures required by FASB ASC 820-10-50-6A (the disclosure requirements in FASB ASC 820-10-50-2 do not apply to that investment.)

FASB discussed questions raised in connection with condition (c) of the definition of RDFV and indicated the following:[10]

> The Board could not identify a pervasive measurement issue on the basis of outreach conducted with stakeholders. While the Board acknowledged that the interpretation of the Master Glossary definition of readily determinable fair value could have implications on which set of disclosures may be used for certain investments (that is, fair value measurement disclosures or net asset value per share practical expedient disclosures), some Board members concluded that users of the financial statements would not be misled when provided either set of disclosures. Therefore, the Board would encourage entities to provide the disclosures that are consistent with the conclusions previously reached on the measurement of the investment.

[Issue Date: November 2017.]

---

[10] For further information, see the Minutes of March 1, 2017, FASB meeting, which are available on the FASB website.

Chapter 5

Contributions Received and Agency Transactions

Gray shaded text in this chapter reflects guidance issued but not yet effective as of the date of this guide, March 1, 2018, but becoming effective on or prior to June 30, 2018, exclusive of any option to early adopt ahead of the mandatory effective date. Unless otherwise indicated, all unshaded text reflects guidance that was already effective as of the date of this guide.

Introduction

5.01 Some not-for-profit entities (NFPs) receive contributions of cash, other assets, and services from individuals, for-profit entities, other NFPs, and governments. Other assets include securities, land, buildings, use of facilities or utilities, material and supplies, intangible assets, and unconditional promises to give in the future.

5.02 The FASB *Accounting Standards Codification* (ASC) glossary, defines a *contribution* as

> an unconditional transfer of cash or other assets to an entity or a settlement or cancellation of its liabilities in a voluntary nonreciprocal transfer by another entity acting other than as an owner. Those characteristics distinguish contributions from exchange transactions, which are reciprocal transfers in which each party receives and sacrifices approximately equal value; from investments by owners and distributions to owners, which are nonreciprocal transfers between an entity and its owners; and from other nonreciprocal transfers, such as impositions of taxes or legal judgments, fines, and thefts, which are not voluntary transfers. In a contribution transaction, the value, if any, returned to the resource provider is incidental to potential public benefits. In an exchange transaction, the potential public benefits are secondary to the potential proprietary benefits to the resource provider. The term contribution revenue is used to apply to transactions that are part of the entity's ongoing major or central activities (revenues), or are peripheral or incidental to the entity (gains).

5.03 The "Contributions Received" subsections of FASB ASC 958-605 provide guidance for contributions of cash and other assets received, including promises to give. FASB ASC 958-605-15-6 states that the guidance in those subsections do not apply to the following transactions and activities:

- Transfers of assets that are in-substance purchases of goods or services—exchange transactions, in which each party receives and sacrifices commensurate value. However, if an entity voluntarily transfers assets to another or performs services for another in exchange for assets of substantially lower value and no unstated rights or privileges are involved, the contribution received that is inherent in that transaction is within the scope of the "Contributions Received" subsections. (For additional information about transfers that include inherent contributions, see paragraph 5.43.)

- Transfers of assets in which the reporting entity is acting as an agent, trustee, or intermediary rather than as a donor or donee. (Those transactions are within the scope of the "Transfers of Assets to a Not-for Profit Entity or Charitable Trust that Raises or Holds Contributions for Others" subsections of FASB ASC 958-605.)
- Tax exemptions, tax incentives, and tax abatements.

5.04 This chapter provides guidance for distinguishing contributions from other kinds of transactions. It also discusses recognition, measurement, and disclosure principles for contribution revenues[1] and related receivables.[2] Chapter 12, "Revenue and Receivables From Exchange Transactions," discusses accounting principles for revenues, gains, and receivables from providing services and from other exchange transactions. Chapter 13, "Expenses, Gains, and Losses," discusses reporting contributions made by NFPs.

Distinguishing Contributions From Other Transactions[3]

5.05 A contribution by definition must be a voluntary transfer. Some resource providers may be required to transfer assets or provide services to NFPs involuntarily; for example, to settle legal disputes or to pay fines. Those transactions are not contributions. Accounting for contributions is different from accounting for other kinds of voluntary transfers, such as conditional transfers, agency transactions, and exchange transactions. Accounting for transfers with donor-imposed conditions is discussed in paragraphs 5.59–.74.

5.06 Flowchart 5-1 provides guidance for determining whether a transfer of assets includes a contribution. To determine the accounting for transactions in which an entity voluntarily transfers assets to an NFP, it is first necessary to assess the extent of discretion the NFP has over the use of the assets that are received. If it has little or no discretion, the transaction is an agency transaction. If it has discretion over the assets' use, the transaction is a contribution, an exchange, or a combination of the two.

---

[1] For purposes of this chapter, the term *contribution revenue* is used to apply to transactions that are part of the not-for-profit entity's (NFP's) ongoing major or central activities (revenues), or are peripheral or incidental to the NFP (gains). Chapter 12, "Revenues and Receivables From Exchange Transactions," discusses the distinction between ongoing major activities and peripheral or incidental transactions and events.

[2] Unconditional promises to give cash or other financial instruments, such as an ownership interest in an entity, are *financial instruments* as defined in the FASB *Accounting Standards Codification* (ASC) glossary, and thus requirements for recognition and disclosure of financial instruments apply.

[3] Federal rules specify the classification of certain transactions for purposes other than reporting in conformity with generally accepted accounting principles (GAAP), such as contractual reporting requirements. For example, certain transactions should be classified as federal awards received and expended by NFPs. The guidance in this guide pertains to financial reporting in conformity with GAAP. Classifications in conformity with GAAP may differ from classifications in accordance with federal rules.

Flowchart 5-1

Determining Whether a Transfer to a Not-For-Profit Entity Includes a Contribution

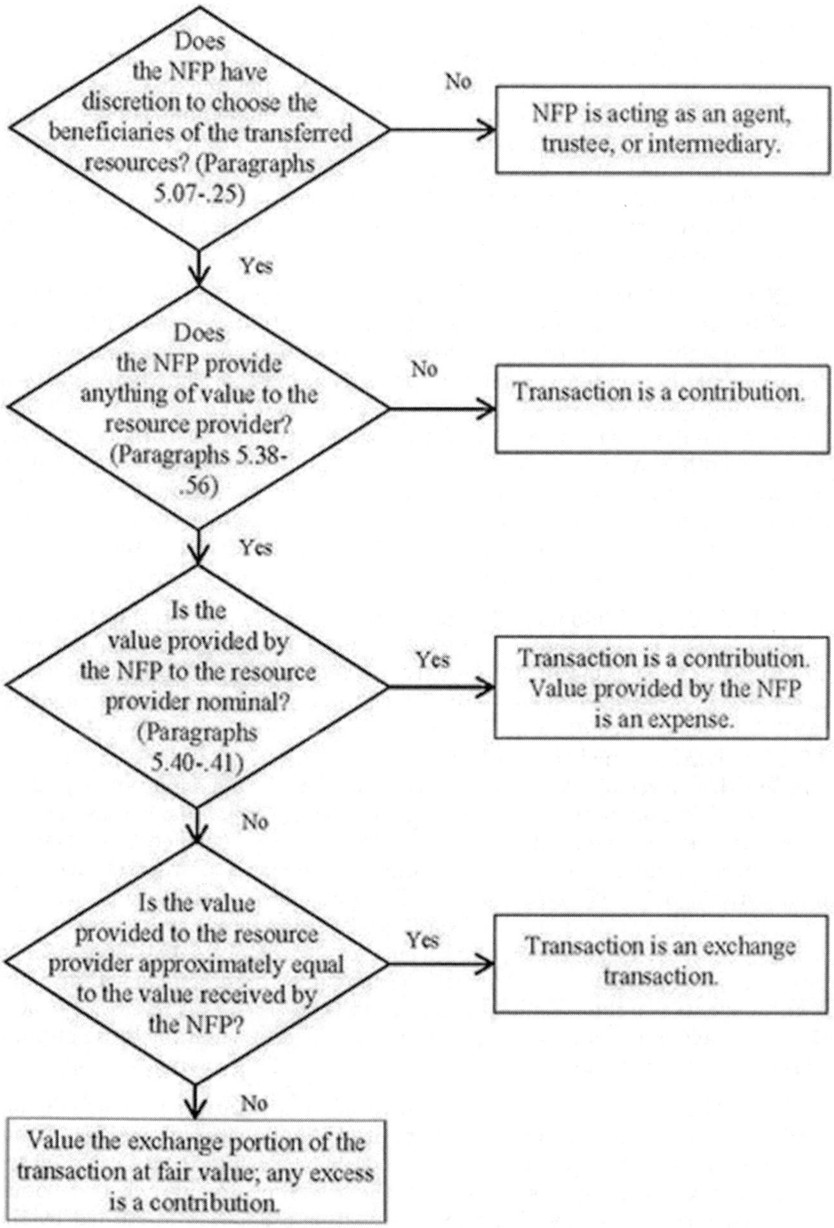

Agency Transactions

5.07 The FASB ASC glossary defines an *agency transaction* as "a type of exchange transaction in which the reporting organization acts as an agent, trustee, or intermediary for another party that may be a donor or donee."

5.08 When NFPs act as agents, trustees, or intermediaries helping donors to make a contribution to another entity or individual, they do not receive a contribution when they receive the assets, nor do they make a contribution when they disburse the assets to the other entity or individual. Instead, they act as go-betweens, passing the assets from the donor through their organization to the specified entity or individual. Federated fund-raising entities, community foundations, and institutionally related entities are examples of NFPs that commonly serve as agents, trustees, or intermediaries, but any NFP can function in those capacities.

5.09 The "Transfers of Assets to a Not-for-Profit Entity or Charitable Trust That Raises or Holds Contributions for Others" subsections of FASB ASC 958-605 establish standards for transactions in which an entity—the donor—makes a contribution by transferring assets to an NFP or charitable trust—a recipient entity—that accepts the assets from the donor and agrees to use those assets on behalf of or transfers those assets, the return on investment of those assets, or both to an unaffiliated entity—the beneficiary—that is specified by the donor. Paragraphs 5.33–.38 discuss the standards for transactions that take place in a similar manner, but are not contributions because the transfers are revocable, repayable, or reciprocal. FASB ASC 958-605 does not set standards for recipient entities that are trustees.[4]

5.10 FASB ASC 958-605-55-76 states that a recipient entity has discretion sufficient to recognize a contribution received if it can choose the beneficiaries of the assets. Paragraphs 76–79 of FASB ASC 958-605 provide guidance to help determine whether a recipient entity has discretion to choose the beneficiary. FASB ASC 958-605-25-24 states that except as described in FASB ASC 958-605-25-25 [variance power] and FASB ASC 958-605-25-27 [financially interrelated entities], a recipient entity that accepts assets from a donor and agrees to use those assets on behalf of [a specified beneficiary] or transfer those assets, the return on investment of those assets, or both to a specified beneficiary is [an agent and] not a donee. (The exceptions for variance power are discussed in paragraphs 5.23–.27 and for financially interrelated entities in paragraphs 5.28–.32.) FASB ASC 958-605-55-78 states that a donor may specify the beneficiary (*a*) by name, (*b*) by stating that all entities that meet a set of donor-defined criteria are beneficiaries, or (*c*) by actions surrounding the transfer that make clear the identity of the beneficiary. (Paragraphs 80–115 of FASB ASC 958-605-55 provide examples of donor stipulations and discuss whether those stipulations specify a beneficiary.)

5.11 The following are three examples of circumstances in which donors specify a beneficiary and the recipient entity should not recognize a contribution (unless the exceptions for variance power or for financially interrelated entities apply). If a donor selects a beneficiary from among a list of potential beneficiaries that have been prequalified or otherwise identified by the

---

[4] Chapter 6, "Split-Interest Agreements and Beneficial Interests in Trusts," discusses split-interest and similar agreements in which NFPs act as trustee for a resource provider and have a beneficial interest in the assets transferred.

recipient entity, the assets received are not contributions to that recipient entity. Similarly, if a grantor specifies eligibility criteria and states that the grant proceeds must be transferred to all who meet those criteria, the recipient entity has not received a contribution even though it may be responsible for determining whether individuals or entities meet those grantor-specified eligibility criteria. Likewise, if a donor responds to a campaign request from an NFP that indicates that the proceeds of the campaign will be distributed to a named beneficiary, then that recipient entity has not received a contribution.

5.12 In contrast, if neither the language used by the donor, the representations of the recipient entity, nor the actions surrounding the transfers cause the donor to believe that he or she is directing the gift to a specified beneficiary, then the NFP is a donee and should recognize a contribution received. For example, an NFP is a donee and should recognize a contribution if it asks the donor to select one or more fields of interest from among a list of community needs prepared by the NFP. Similarly, if a donor uses broad generalizations to describe the beneficiaries, such as homeless individuals, the NFP has received a contribution because the choice of the beneficiary is within its control. Likewise, if an NFP asks its donors to indicate an NFP for consideration by its allocation committee, the NFP is the donee if that request is conveyed in a manner that leads the donor to conclude that its role is merely to propose possible allocations.

5.13 The representations made to the donor during the solicitation of a gift are important in determining whether a transaction is an agency transaction. If an NFP creates a donor's reasonable expectation that a contribution will be transferred to a beneficiary specified by the donor, the NFP is an agent or intermediary. Unless the NFP has variance power or is financially interrelated to the specified beneficiary, it should not recognize a contribution received.

5.14 FASB ASC 958-605-55-75 states that discretion to determine the timing of the distribution to the specified beneficiary, by itself, does not give the recipient entity discretion sufficient to recognize a contribution. That limited discretion is not sufficient. The ability to choose a payment date does not relieve an entity from its obligation to pay.

5.15 Pursuant to FASB ASC 958-605-25-24, an agent should recognize its liability to the specified beneficiary concurrent with its recognition of cash or other financial assets received from the donor. As discussed in FASB ASC 958-605-30-13, both the asset and the liability should be measured at the fair value of the assets received from the donor. FASB ASC 958-605-25-24 states that except as described in [the paragraphs about variance power and financially interrelated entities], a recipient entity that receives nonfinancial assets is permitted, but not required, to recognize its liability and those assets provided that the recipient entity reports consistently from period to period and discloses its accounting policy. An NFP should consider the need for disclosure of its accounting policy in the notes to the financial statements pursuant to FASB ASC 235-10-50-1.

5.16 Distributions of cash or other assets to the specified third-party beneficiaries should be reported as decreases in the assets and liabilities.

5.17 Technical Questions and Answers (Q&A) section 6140.12, "Nondiscretionary Assistance Programs,"[5] provides the following example of a circumstance in which a donor specifies a beneficiary and the recipient entity should

[5] All Q&A sections can be found in *Technical Questions and Answers*.

not recognize a contribution (unless the exceptions for variance power or financially interrelated entities apply). Some NFPs participate in activities wherein the resource provider (donor) determines the eligibility requirements for the ultimate beneficiaries and the NFP (recipient entity) must disburse to any who meet guidelines specified by the resource provider or return the assets. In some of those programs, the NFP receives assets, such as food, food vouchers, public transportation vouchers, and cash, and distributes the assets on behalf of the resource provider (donor) in exchange for a fee for performing that service. Receipts and disbursements of assets under such nondiscretionary programs (other than any fees for performing the service) are agency transactions, and are not contributions to the recipient NFP. A recipient entity that receives financial assets, such as cash or vouchers that can be exchanged for cash, should recognize its liability to the beneficiaries concurrent with its recognition of financial assets received from the donor. A recipient entity that receives nonfinancial assets, such as food vouchers or public transportation vouchers that are denominated in either dollar values or in nonfinancial terms, such as pounds of food or bus rides, but that will not be settled in cash, is permitted, but not required, to recognize its liability and those assets provided that the entity reports consistently from period to period and discloses its accounting policy.

5.18 FASB ASC 958-230-55-4 states that cash received and paid in agency transactions should be reported as cash flows from operating activities in a statement of cash flows. If the statement of cash flows is presented using the indirect method, cash received and paid in such transactions is permitted to be reported either gross or net. FASB ASC 958-605-50-5 states that additional information about transactions in which an NFP acts as an agent, trustee, or intermediary may be required to be disclosed under FASB ASC 850, *Related Party Disclosures*.

5.19 Paragraphs 28–30 of FASB ASC 958-605-25 provide guidance for recognition of an agency transaction by the specified beneficiary. A specified beneficiary should recognize its rights to the assets (financial or nonfinancial) held by a recipient entity as an asset unless the recipient entity is explicitly granted variance power. Those rights are any one of the following: (*a*) an interest in the net assets of the recipient entity (which is discussed in paragraphs 5.28–.32), (*b*) a beneficial interest (which is an unconditional right to receive all or a portion of the specified cash flows from a charitable trust or other identifiable pool of assets), or (*c*) a receivable (which is discussed in the following paragraph). Chapter 6, "Split-Interest Agreements and Beneficial Interests in Trusts," provides additional information about the beneficiaries' rights to trust assets.

5.20 FASB ASC 958-605-25-30 states that if the beneficiary's rights are neither an interest in the net assets of the recipient entity nor a beneficial interest, a beneficiary should recognize its rights to the assets held by a recipient entity as a receivable and contribution revenue in accordance with paragraphs 8–10 of FASB ASC 958-605-25 and FASB ASC 958-605-45-5 for unconditional promises to give. (Paragraphs 5.89–.111 and 5.180–.212 discuss recognition and measurement of promises to give.)

5.21 In some cases, an agent will charge a fee for raising the contributions. In accordance with FASB ASC 958-220-45-14, revenues and expenses should be reported gross. Thus, as discussed in FASB ASC 958-605-55-86, if a federated fund-raising entity charges an administrative fee that will be deducted from all contributions that are to be transferred to a donor's chosen entity, the beneficiaries should report the gross amount of the gifts as contribution revenue and the administrative fees withheld by the federated fund-raising entity as expenses. Q&A section 6140.21, "Should an NPE Report Amounts Charged to the NPE by a Professional Fund-Raiser Gross, as Fund-Raising Expenses, or Net, as a Reduction of Contributions?," and Q&A section 6140.22, "In Circumstances in Which the Reporting NPE Undertakes a Transaction in Which Another NPE (Fund-Raising NPE) Raises Contributions on Behalf of the Reporting NPE, and the Reporting NPE Compensates the Fund-Raising NPE for Raising Those Contributions (Compensation Including, But Not Limited to, an Administrative Fee), Should the Reporting NPE Report the Fund-Raising NPE's Compensation Gross, as Fund-Raising Expenses, or Net, as a Reduction of Contributions?", also discuss situations in which an NFP is charged a fee by a professional fund-raiser, a federated fund-raising entity, or another agent for soliciting contributions on the NFP's behalf. The NFP should report the gross amount of contributions from the donors without reduction. The amount charged or retained as compensation by the professional fund-raiser, federated fund-raising entity, or other entity acting as an agent or intermediary is reported as fund-raising expenses. For example, an NFP enters into a transaction with a professional fund-raiser, whereby the fund-raiser solicits contributions on behalf of the NFP for a fee of 20 percent of the contributions raised. The fund-raiser raises $100,000 from donors and remits $80,000 to the NFP after retaining its fee of $20,000. The NFP should report $100,000 of contribution revenue and $20,000 of fund-raising expense. Q&A sections 6140.21–.22 are discussed further in chapter 13.

5.22 Present value techniques are one valuation technique for measuring the fair value of the contribution and the beneficial interest or receivable; other valuation techniques also are available, as described in FASB ASC 820, *Fair Value Measurement*.[6] If present value techniques are used, the contribution revenue and the beneficial interest or receivable should be measured as the present value of the future cash inflows over the expected term of the agreement. The choice of accounting policies regarding recognition of nonfinancial assets, as discussed in paragraph 5.15, applies only to the agent or intermediary; beneficiaries should recognize their rights to nonfinancial assets held by the recipient entity.

Variance Power

5.23 The FASB ASC glossary defines *variance power* as

> [t]he unilateral power to redirect the use of the transferred assets to another beneficiary. A donor explicitly grants variance power if the recipient entity's unilateral power to redirect the use of the assets is explicitly referred to in the instrument transferring the assets. Unilateral power means that the recipient entity can override the donor's instructions without approval from the donor, specified beneficiary, or any other interested party.

5.24 Paragraphs 25–26 of FASB ASC 958-605-25 discuss the effects of variance power on recognition of the transferred assets by the recipient entity.

---

[6] Paragraphs 3.138–.168 discuss FASB ASC 820, *Fair Value Measurement*, which defines *fair value*, establishes a framework for measuring fair value, and identifies required disclosures about fair value measurements. Paragraphs 4–20 of FASB ASC 820-10-55 provide standards for using present value techniques when the measurement objective is fair value.

A recipient entity that is directed by a donor to distribute the transferred assets, the return on investment of those assets, or both to a specified unaffiliated beneficiary acts as a donee, rather than an agent, trustee, or intermediary, if the donor explicitly grants the recipient entity variance power. A recipient entity that is explicitly granted variance power has the ability to use assets it receives to further its own purpose from the date it accepts the assets. In that situation, the recipient entity should account for receipt of funds by recognizing an asset and corresponding contribution revenue unless the transfer is revocable, repayable, or reciprocal as described in FASB ASC 958-605-25-33 (paragraph 5.34).

5.25 Variance power provides the recipient entity with discretion sufficient to recognize a contribution received despite the specification of a beneficiary by the donor, subject to the exception in the following paragraph. If a donor explicitly grants a recipient entity variance power and names an unaffiliated beneficiary, the recipient entity is a donee and recognizes contribution revenue. Unaffiliated means that the beneficiary is other than the donor or the donor's affiliate as defined in the FASB ASC glossary.

5.26 A recipient entity that receives variance power should not report a contribution if the resource provider specifies itself or its affiliate(s) as the beneficiary of the transferred assets. Because of their reciprocal nature, those transfers are not contributions received by the recipient entity—even if the resource provider granted the recipient entity variance power at the time of the transfer. Paragraphs 5.33–.38 discuss transactions in which a resource provider names itself or its affiliate as beneficiary of a transfer of assets to a recipient entity.

5.27 As discussed in FASB ASC 958-605-25-31, if the donor explicitly grants a recipient entity variance power, the specified unaffiliated beneficiary should not recognize its potential for future distributions from the assets held by the recipient entity. Those future distributions, if they occur, should be recognized as contributions by the specified beneficiary when received or unconditionally promised.

Financially Interrelated Entities

5.28 The FASB ASC glossary defines *financially interrelated entities* stating that a recipient entity and a specified beneficiary are financially interrelated if the relationship between them has both of the following characteristics: (*a*) one of the entities has the ability to influence the operating and financial decisions of the other and (*b*) one of the entities has an ongoing economic interest in the net assets of the other.

5.29 FASB ASC 958-20-15-2 states that the ability to exercise that influence (of the operating and financial decisions of the other) may be demonstrated in several ways, including the following:

a. The entities are affiliates as defined in the FASB ASC glossary.

b. One entity has considerable representation on the governing board of the other entity.

c. The charter or bylaws of one entity limit its activities to those that are beneficial to the other entity.

d. An agreement between the entities allows one entity to actively participate in the policy making processes of the other, such as setting organizational priorities, budgets, and management compensation.

The FASB ASC glossary defines an *ongoing economic interest in the net assets of another* as a residual right to another NFP's net assets that results from an ongoing relationship. The value of those rights increases or decreases as a result of the investment, fund-raising, operating, and other activities of the other entity.

5.30 FASB ASC 958-605-25-27 states that if a recipient entity and a specified beneficiary are financially interrelated entities and the recipient entity is not a trustee, the recipient entity should recognize a contribution received when it receives assets (financial or nonfinancial) from the donor that are specified for the beneficiary. FASB ASC 958-20-25 provides the following example. A foundation that exists to raise, hold, and invest assets for the specified beneficiary or for a group of affiliates of which the specified beneficiary is a member generally is financially interrelated with the NFP or NFPs it supports. The foundation should recognize contribution revenue when it receives assets from the donor. Pursuant to FASB ASC 958-20-25-2, the beneficiary should recognize its interest in the net assets of the recipient entity and adjust that interest for its share of the change in net assets of the recipient entity using a method similar to the equity method of accounting for investments in common stock.[7] Examples 1–3 (paragraphs 3–17) of FASB ASC 958-20-55 illustrate this guidance. (Paragraphs 13.121–.123 of this guide provide guidance pertaining to distributions from financially interrelated fund-raising foundations to specified beneficiaries.) Appendix B, "Technical Questions and Answers About Financially Interrelated Entities," of this chapter includes a series of nonauthoritative technical questions and answers, Q&A sections 6140.13–.18, that discuss the classification of a beneficiary's interest in the net assets of a financially interrelated fund-raising foundation in the beneficiary's financial statements.

5.31 FASB ASC 958-20-55-2A states that although most of the relationships described in the definition of *economic interest* used in FASB ASC 958-810 (see FASB ASC 958-810-55-6) are potentially ongoing economic interests in the net assets of the other, some do not meet the criterion in paragraph 958-20-15-2(b). (The examples of economic interest in FASB ASC 958-810-55-6 are included in paragraph 3.64 of this guide.) Only economic interests that are both ongoing and residual interests in the net assets are ongoing economic interests in the net assets of another.

5.32 Most of the relationships described in FASB ASC 958-810-55-6 are potentially ongoing economic interests in the net assets of a financially interrelated entity. However, some will not meet the definition because they are not ongoing interests; or they are not residual interests; or are neither ongoing nor residual. By specifying that an interest in the net assets of a financially interrelated entity be ongoing, the definition of *financially interrelated entities* includes economic interests in entities that provide ongoing support to the NFP and excludes economic interests that arise only upon the dissolution of the NFP. By specifying that the interest in the net assets be residual, the definition excludes economic interests that are a fixed dollar amount. For example, some NFPs receive equity infusions from another entity, and they are required to return the fixed amount of that equity infusion upon the occurrence of a triggering event, such as the cancelation of an affiliation agreement. Economic interests of that type are not residual rights whose value increases or decreases as a

---

[7] FASB ASC 958-20-55-11 states that an interest in the net assets of an affiliate would be eliminated if that affiliate was included in consolidated financial statements of the interest holder.

result of the investment, fund-raising, operating, and other activities of the other entity.

Similar Transactions That Are Revocable, Repayable, or Reciprocal

5.33 In addition to establishing standards for contributions transferred to beneficiaries via agents, trustees, and intermediaries, the "Transfers of Assets to a Not-for-Profit Entity or Charitable Trust that Raises or Holds Contributions for Others" subsections of FASB ASC 958-605 also set standards for transactions that take place in a similar manner (that is, there is a resource provider, a recipient entity, and a specified beneficiary), but that are not contributions because the terms of the transfer or the relationships between the parties make the transfer revocable, repayable, or reciprocal.

5.34 FASB ASC 958-605-25-33 describes four types of transfers that are not contributions to either the recipient entity or the specified beneficiary. The first three types are the following:

a. The transfer is subject to the resource provider's unilateral right to redirect the use of the transferred assets to another beneficiary.

b. The transfer is accompanied by the resource provider's conditional promise to give or is otherwise revocable or repayable.

c. The resource provider controls the recipient entity and specifies an unaffiliated beneficiary. See the definition of *control* in FASB ASC 958–810.[8]

Those transfers should be reported as an asset of the resource provider and as a liability of the recipient entity.

5.35 Sometimes a resource provider specifies itself or its affiliate as beneficiary of a transfer of assets to a recipient entity. Those transfers are reciprocal and thus are not contributions. Examples of those types of transfers are (*a*) an NFP transfers assets to a community foundation to establish an endowment for the benefit of the NFP and (*b*) an NFP transfers assets to a foundation it creates to hold those assets.

5.36 Paragraphs 4–7 of FASB ASC 958-20-25 describe two types of reciprocal transactions, which are as follows:

a. An equity transaction—A transfer of assets to a recipient entity that meets all of the following conditions:

i. The resource provider specifies itself or its affiliate as the beneficiary,

ii. The resource provider and the recipient entity are financially interrelated entities (paragraphs 5.28–.32 discuss financially interrelated entities), and

iii. Neither the resource provider nor its affiliate expects payment of the transferred assets, although payment of investment return on the transferred assets may be expected.

---

[8] FASB ASC 958-810 defines *control* as "the direct or indirect ability to determine the direction of management and policies through ownership, contract, or otherwise."

b. The resource provider specifies itself or its affiliate as the beneficiary and any of the conditions (ii.) and (iii.) in paragraph (*a*) are not met (that is, the transfer is not an equity transaction).

5.37 Per FASB ASC 958-605-25-33, if the transfer in which the resource provider specifies itself or its affiliate as the beneficiary is not an equity transaction, the resource provider should report an asset and the recipient entity should report a liability. If the transaction is an equity transaction, the reporting depends upon whether the resource provider or its affiliate is the specified beneficiary. Per FASB ASC 958-20-25-5 and FASB ASC 958-20-45-1, if the resource provider specifies itself as the beneficiary, the resource provider should report an equity transaction as an interest in the net assets of the recipient entity (or an increase in a previously recognized interest), and the recipient entity should report an equity transaction as a separate line in its statement of activities. Per FASB ASC 958-605-25-6 and FASB ASC 958-20-45-1, if the resource provider specifies an affiliate as the beneficiary, the resource provider and the recipient entity should report an equity transaction as separate lines in their statements of activities, and the affiliate named as beneficiary should report an interest in the net assets of the recipient entity. Because no donor is involved when an NFP transfers its assets to a recipient entity and names itself as beneficiary (that is, as discussed in paragraph 5.35, the transaction is not a contribution), the transfer does not affect the classification of net assets. Thus, if an NFP transfers assets to the recipient entity that were received from sources other than donor-restricted contributions or donor-restricted investment return, the classification of net assets associated with the assets held by the recipient entity also is without donor restrictions. Likewise, if an NFP transfers assets to the recipient entity that were donor restricted and the restriction was not met prior to or by the transfer, the classification of net assets associated with the assets held by the recipient entity is similarly restricted. If the recipient entity places limitations on the withdrawal of the transferred assets, the NFP should disclose those limitations as part of its disclosure of the terms under which amounts will be distributed to it or its affiliate, as described in paragraph 5.220.

5.38 In accordance with FASB ASC 958-20-45-3, if the beneficiary (resource provider or its affiliate) and the recipient entity are included in consolidated financial statements, the beneficiary's interest in the net assets of the recipient entity (as recognized in the previous paragraph) should be eliminated.

Exchange Transactions[9]

5.39 The FASB ASC glossary defines *exchange transaction* as a reciprocal transfer between two entities that results in one of the entities acquiring assets or services or satisfying liabilities by surrendering other assets or services or incurring other obligations. The FASB ASC glossary definition of *contribution* states that contributions differ from exchange transactions, which are reciprocal transfers in which each party receives and sacrifices something of approximately equal value.

5.40 In some situations, exchange transactions can be easily distinguished from contributions. For example, sales in a museum bookstore or payments of employees' salaries clearly are exchange transactions: each party gives up and

[9] Certain reciprocal transactions that involve transfers to recipient entities are discussed in paragraphs 5.25 and .31–.36.

receives equivalent economic value. In contrast, an example of a contribution is a donation to an NFP's mass fund-raising appeal: donors are providing resources in support of the NFP's mission and expect to receive nothing of direct value in exchange.

5.41 In some cases, NFPs provide premiums to donors or to potential donors. Paragraphs 18–19 of FASB ASC 958-720-45 discuss the cost of premiums and whether premiums are given in exchange for resources provided. The guidance is included in this paragraph and the following paragraph. The cost of premiums (such as postcards, address labels, or calendars) given to potential donors as part of mass fund-raising appeals is a fund-raising expense, and the classification of the donations received from the appeal as contributions is unaffected by the fact that premiums were given to potential donors. The premiums are not provided to potential donors in exchange for the assets contributed; they can be kept by all those from whom funds are solicited, regardless of whether a contribution is made.

5.42 The cost of premiums (such as coffee mugs) that are given to resource providers to acknowledge receipt of a contribution also should be reported as fund-raising expenses if those costs are nominal in value compared with the value of the goods or services donated by the resource provider. For example, an NFP may provide a coffee mug to people making a contribution of $50 or more; the mug costs the NFP $1. The NFP should recognize contributions for the total amount contributed and fund-raising expense of $1 for each coffee mug provided to donors. The cost of premiums that are greater than nominal in value should be reported as cost of sales. If premiums are greater than nominal in value, transactions should be reported as part exchange transaction and part contribution.

5.43 Transactions that are in part a contribution and in part an exchange transaction (also referred to as bargain purchases) include an inherent contribution. The FASB ASC glossary defines an *inherent contribution* as a contribution that results if an entity voluntarily transfers assets (or net assets) or performs services for another entity in exchange for either no assets, or for assets of substantially lower value, and unstated rights or privileges of a commensurate value are not involved. For example, an individual has a home currently valued at $150,000, which is subject to a mortgage of $30,000. If the individual pays off the mortgage and sells the home to an NFP for $50,000, a contribution of $100,000 is inherent in the transaction. The Financial Reporting Executive Committee (FinREC) believes that in circumstances in which the transaction is in part a contribution and in part an exchange, NFPs should first determine the fair value of the exchange portion of the transaction, with the residual (excess of the resources received over the fair value of the exchange portion of the transaction) reported as contributions.

5.44 In other circumstances, however, classifying asset transfers as exchange transactions or as contributions may require the exercise of judgment concerning whether a reciprocal transaction has occurred, that is, whether a recipient NFP has given up assets, rights, or privileges approximately equal to the value of the assets, rights, or privileges received. Value should be assessed from both the recipient NFP's and the resource provider's points of view and can be affected by a wide variety of factors; for example, resource providers can retain the right to share in the use of or income from an asset provided to the NFP or obtain benefit in the marketplace, such as stimulating a positive entity image.

5.45 Table 5-1 contains the list of indicators from FASB ASC 958-605-55-8 that may be helpful in determining whether individual asset transfers are contributions, exchange transactions, or a combination of both. Depending on the facts and circumstances, some indicators may be more significant than others; however, no single indicator is determinative of the classification of a particular transaction. Indicators of a contribution tend to describe transactions in which the value, if any, returned to the resource provider is incidental to potential public benefits. Indicators of an exchange tend to describe transactions in which the potential public benefits are secondary to the potential proprietary benefits to the resource provider.

Table 5-1

Indicators Useful in Distinguishing Contributions From Exchange Transactions

Indicator	*Contribution*	*Exchange Transaction*
Recipient not-for-profit entity's (NFP's) intent in soliciting the asset*	Recipient NFP asserts that it is soliciting the asset as a contribution.	Recipient NFP asserts that it is seeking resources in exchange for specified benefits.
Resource provider's expressed intent about the purpose of the asset to be provided to recipient NFP	Resource provider asserts that it is making a donation to support the NFP's programs.	Resource provider asserts that it is transferring resources in exchange for specified benefits.
Method of delivery	The time or place of delivery of the asset to be provided by the recipient NFP to third-party recipients is at the discretion of the NFP.	The method of delivery of the asset to be provided by the recipient NFP to third-party recipients is specified by the resource provider.
Method of determining amount of payment	The resource provider determines the amount of the payment.	Payment by the resource provider equals the value of the assets to be provided by the recipient NFP, or the assets' cost plus markup; the total payment is based on the quantity of assets to be provided.
Penalties assessed if NFP fails to make timely delivery of assets	Penalties are limited to the delivery of assets already produced and the return of the unspent amount. (The NFP is not penalized for nonperformance.)	Provisions for economic penalties exist beyond the amount of payment. (The NFP is penalized for nonperformance.)
Delivery of assets to be provided by the recipient NFP	Assets are to be delivered to individuals or organizations other than the resource provider.	Assets are to be delivered to the resource provider or to individuals or organizations closely connected to the resource provider.

* This table refers to assets. Assets may include services. The terms *assets* and *services* are used interchangeably in this table.

5.46 The following voluntary asset transfers are discussed in more detail because they may be difficult to classify:

- Membership dues (paragraphs 5.47–.50)
- Grants, awards, and sponsorships (paragraphs 5.51–.52)
- Naming opportunities (paragraphs 5.53–.56)
- Donor status (paragraph 5.57)
- Gifts in kind (paragraphs 5.123–.129)

Membership Dues

5.47 Paragraphs 9–12 of FASB ASC 958-605-55 discuss NFPs that receive dues from their members. This paragraph and the following paragraph and table reproduce that guidance. The term "members" is used broadly by some NFPs to refer to their donors and by other NFPs to refer to individuals or other entities that pay dues in exchange for a defined set of benefits. These transfers often have elements of both a contribution and an exchange transaction because members receive tangible or intangible benefits from their membership in the NFP. Usually, the determination of whether membership dues are contributions rests on whether the value received by the member is commensurate with the dues paid. For example, if an NFP has annual dues of $100 and the only benefit members receive is a monthly newsletter with a fair value of $25, $25 of the dues are received in an exchange transaction and should be recognized as revenue as the earnings process is completed and $75 of the dues are a contribution.

5.48 Member benefits generally have value regardless of how often (or whether) the benefits are used. For example, most would agree that a health club membership is an exchange transaction, even if the member stops using the facilities before the completion of the membership period. It may be difficult, however, to measure the benefits members receive and to determine whether the value of those benefits is approximately equal to the dues paid by the members. Table 5-2 contains the list of indicators from FASB ASC 958-605-55-12 that may be helpful in determining whether membership dues are contributions, exchange transactions, or a combination of both. Depending on the facts and circumstances, some indicators may be more significant than others; however, no single indicator is determinative of the classification of a particular transaction.

5.49 FASB ASC 958-605-25-1 states that revenue derived from membership dues in exchange transactions should be recognized over the period to which the dues relate. Nonrefundable initiation and life membership fees received in exchange transactions should be recognized as revenues in the period in which the fees become receivable if future fees are expected to cover the costs of future services to be provided to members. If nonrefundable initiation and life membership fees, rather than future fees, are expected to cover those costs, nonrefundable initiation and life member fees received in exchange transactions should be recognized as revenue over the average duration of membership, the life expectancy of members, or other appropriate time periods.

The preceding paragraph will be deleted upon the effective date of FASB ASU No. 2014-09, *Revenue from Contracts with Customers (Topic 606).*[10]

Table 5-2

Indicators Useful for Determining the Contribution and Exchange Portions of Membership Dues

Indicator	*Contribution*	*Exchange Transaction*
Recipient not-for-profit entity's (NFP's) expressed intent concerning purpose of dues payment	The request describes the dues as being used to provide benefits to the general public or to the NFP's service beneficiaries.	The request describes the dues as providing economic benefits to members or to other entities or individuals designated by or related to the members.
Extent of benefits to members	The benefits to members are negligible.	The substantive benefits to members (for example, publications, admissions, educational programs, and special events) may be available to nonmembers for a fee.
NFP's service efforts	The NFP provides service to members and nonmembers.	The NFP benefits are provided only to members.
Duration of benefits	The duration is not specified.	The benefits are provided for a defined period; additional payment of dues is required to extend benefits.
Expressed agreement concerning refundability of the payment	The payment is not refundable to the resource provider.	The payment is fully or partially refundable if the resource provider withdraws from membership.
Qualifications for membership	Membership is available to the general public.	Membership is available only to individuals who meet certain criteria (for example, requirements to pursue a specific career or to live in a certain area).

[10] FASB Accounting Standards Update (ASU) No. 2014-09, *Revenue from Contracts with Customers (Topic 606)*, is effective for NFPs for annual reporting periods beginning after December 15, 2018, and interim periods within annual periods beginning after December 15, 2019. However, NFPs that have issued, or are conduit bond obligors for, securities that are traded, listed, or quoted on an exchange or an over-the-counter market are required to apply the standards for annual reporting periods beginning after December 15, 2017, including interim periods within that reporting period.

5.50 Q&A section 6140.02, "Income Recognition of Membership Dues by Not-for-Profit Entity," provides the following example:

> A local NFP collects membership dues and does not provide any services to its members in return for the dues. For an additional cost, the NFP provides services, such as seminars, group insurance, and so on, to its members. It records the dues as contributions and recognizes them as revenue in the period they are received. FASB ASC 958-605-25-2 requires that the dues be recognized as contributions revenue when received because the members receive no benefits from the dues. In accordance with FASB ASC 958-605-25-1, if the member did receive benefits from those dues, dues revenue would be recognized over the period of membership.

The preceding paragraph will be deleted upon the effective date of FASB ASU No. 2014-09, *Revenue from Contracts with Customers (Topic 606).*[11]

Grants, Awards, and Sponsorships

5.51 Paragraphs 2–5 of FASB ASC 958-605-55 discuss transactions in which foundations, business entities, and other types of entities provide resources to NFPs under programs referred to as grants, awards, or sponsorships. A grant, award, or sponsorship may be entirely a contribution, entirely an exchange transaction, or a combination of the two. In addition, those transactions may also have characteristics of agency transactions.[12] Those asset transfers are contributions if the resource providers receive no value in exchange for the assets transferred or if the value received by the resource providers is incidental to the potential public benefit from using the assets transferred. A grant made by a resource provider to an NFP would likely be a contribution if the activity specified by the grant is to be planned and carried out by the NFP and the NFP has the right to the benefits of carrying out the activity. If, however, the grant is made by a resource provider that provides materials to be tested in the activity and that retains the right to any patents or other results of the activity, the grant would likely be an exchange transaction.

5.52 Some transfers of assets between NFPs and governments (such as the sale of goods and services) are clearly exchange transactions. Other transfers of assets between NFPs and governments (such as support given by state and local governments with no stipulation as to its use) are clearly contributions. Other kinds of government transfers (sometimes referred to as grants, awards, or appropriations) have characteristics that require judgment to determine whether they are contributions or exchange transactions. The indicators described in table 5-1 provide guidance on how to classify such transfers. Depending on the facts and circumstances, some indicators may be more significant than others; however, no single indicator is determinative of the classification of a particular transaction.

---

[11] FASB ASU No. 2014-09 is effective for NFPs for annual reporting periods beginning after December 15, 2018, and interim periods within annual periods beginning after December 15, 2019. However, NFPs that have issued, or are conduit bond obligors for, securities that are traded, listed, or quoted on an exchange or an over-the-counter market are required to apply the standards for annual reporting periods beginning after December 15, 2017, including interim periods within that reporting period.

[12] Paragraphs 5.07–.36 discuss agency transactions.

Naming Opportunities

5.53 NFPs may publicly recognize resource providers (individuals, foundations, corporate entities, and others) through what are commonly referred to as naming opportunities. *Naming opportunities*, which may be accompanied by additional rights and privileges, may be either an acknowledgement of a gift or what is effectively advertising (or other benefits) provided by the NFP in exchange for the resources provided, or a combination of both. For example, naming opportunities might include the following:

- An NFP gives resource providers the opportunity to name or sponsor a building or a portion thereof, based on receiving certain dollar amounts. Such naming opportunities may result in the sponsorship being publicized through name and logo placement at the building, in addition to other benefits that may be provided.
- A college or university gives resource providers the opportunity to name a faculty position or to provide scholarships bearing the resource provider's name, based on receiving certain dollar amounts. As part of the transaction, the resource provider may receive certain recruiting privileges.
- An NFP gives resource providers the opportunity to sponsor a particular event, with that sponsorship being publicized through logo placement at the event and in any publications or advertisements connected with the event.
- An NFP conducts a multiyear capital campaign (or similar fundraiser), with different levels of commitment resulting in an escalating variety of sponsorship or advertising benefits to the resource provider. The benefits include future naming options (either for a specified time or in perpetuity), as well as other items of significant value being delivered to the resource provider.

5.54 NFPs should consider whether naming opportunities are contributions, exchange transactions, or some combination of both. FinREC believes that if public recognition and accompanying rights and privileges result in only nominal value to the resource provider, the NFP has received a contribution. However, an NFP should consider the specific facts and circumstances of the naming opportunity and accompanying rights and privileges, such as the type of resource provider (individual or corporation), the length of time that the naming benefit is provided, control over name and logo use, and other contract stipulations. For example, the right to name an endowed research fund "The Jane Doe Cancer Research Fund," is by itself considered of nominal value to Jane Doe. In contrast, the right to name the sports arena of a local college may have value to a local corporation if that corporation includes terms similar to the following in its agreement with the college: the number of years the arena will carry its name, the location of the sign in relation to the nearby highway, the font used for the sign, and the right to rename the arena if the corporation's name changes during the agreement's term.

5.55 Table 5-3 contains a list of indicators that may be helpful in determining whether naming opportunities are contributions, exchange transactions, or a combination of both. Depending on the facts and circumstances, some indicators may be more significant than others; however, no single indicator is determinative of the classification of a particular transaction.

5.56 In determining the value of a naming opportunity and accompanying rights and privileges, if any, FinREC believes that the exchange portion of the transaction, if any, should be valued first at fair value, and any residual would be recognized as a contribution. FinREC believes that the NFP should consider stipulations placed on the use of the resources provided, if any, in determining the net asset classification of the contribution portion received. If multiple deliverables spanning a period of years are part of the exchange transaction, it is possible that the contribution element would be reflected in current year's revenues but some or all portions of the exchange transaction components could be deferred. Chapter 12 provides guidance on the recognition of exchange transactions.

Table 5-3

Naming Opportunities Indicators Useful in Distinguishing Contributions From Exchange Transactions

Indicator	*Contribution*	*Exchange Transaction*
Value of public recognition	Resource provider receives nominal value related to the public recognition and there are no direct benefits provided to the resource provider.	Resource provider receives significant value related to the public recognition or there are direct benefits provided to the resource provider.
Length of time that the naming benefit is provided	Naming benefit is provided for a relatively short time, or the not-for-profit entity (NFP) has the right to change the name at its discretion.	Naming benefit is provided for relatively long time, and the name cannot be changed solely at the NFP's discretion.
Control over name and logo use	Party receiving the naming opportunity cannot change the name.	Party receiving the naming opportunity can change the name, such as if a corporate donor changes its name and requires a corresponding name change at the NFP.
Other rights and privileges	The named party receives no other rights or privileges in connection with the naming opportunity transaction.	The named party receives other rights and privileges in connection with the naming opportunity transaction, such as an exclusive right to sell, exclusive recruitment opportunities, and so forth.

Donor Status

5.57 In some circumstances, NFPs use status or recognition levels such as platinum, gold, silver, and bronze to acknowledge the generosity of their donors. Often those levels include benefits provided by the NFP beyond the mere listing of names under the appropriate heading in a roll of donors. Analogous to the naming opportunity transactions and guidance discussed in paragraphs

5.53–.56, NFPs should consider whether such transactions are contributions, exchange transactions, or a combination of both. Typically, the benefits have some fair value, and the NFP should consider whether amounts received are in excess of the fair value returned to the donor.[13] Some NFPs offer increasing levels of benefits for increasing levels of recognition. For example, an aquarium may offer multiple levels of membership with each level providing different benefits for the members. The basic membership level provides only year-round entry to the aquarium whereas the more advanced levels provide exclusive access to special events and discounts at the gift shop. When benefits provided by the NFP correspond to differing levels of support the NFP receives, the comparison of fair value returned to fair value received needs to be assessed at each level. If the NFP receives assets at a given status or recognition level in exchange for benefits of substantially lower value and no unstated rights or privileges of a commensurate value are involved, the excess should be reported as a contribution.

Core Recognition and Measurement Principles for Contributions

5.58 The core principles for recognition and measurement of contributions are discussed in paragraphs 5.59–.88. That discussion is followed by special accounting considerations related to the following types of contributions:

- Promises to give (paragraphs 5.89–.111)
- Contributed services (paragraphs 5.112–.117)
- Special events (paragraphs 5.118–.122)
- Gifts in kind (paragraphs 5.123–.149)
- Contributed items to be sold at fund-raising events (paragraphs 5.150–.151)
- Contributed fund-raising material, informational material, or advertising, including media time or space (paragraphs 5.152–.163)
- Contributed utilities and use of long-lived assets (paragraphs 5.164–.166)
- Guarantees (paragraphs 5.167–.171)
- Below-market interest rate loans (paragraphs 5.172–.174)
- Contributed collection items (paragraph 5.175)
- Split-interest agreements (paragraph 5.176 and chapter 6)
- Administrative costs of restricted contributions (paragraphs 5.177–.179)

Recognition Principles

5.59 The recognition principles for contributions are discussed in the "Contributions Received" subsections of FASB ASC 958-605. Accounting for contributions depends on whether the transfer of assets, including promises

---

[13] The FASB ASC glossary defines an *inherent contribution* as a contribution that results if an entity voluntarily transfers assets (or net assets) or performs services for another entity in exchange for either no assets or for assets of substantially lower value and unstated rights or privileges of a commensurate value are not involved. For example, as illustrated in case C of example 4 (FASB ASC 958-220-55-15), special events revenue reported as part exchange (for the fair value the participant received) and part contribution (for the excess of the payment over that fair value).

to give, is received by the NFP with donor-imposed conditions, donor-imposed restrictions, or both. Donor-imposed conditions create a barrier that must be overcome before a contribution can be recognized; by definition, a contribution is unconditional (paragraph 5.02). Donor-imposed restrictions do not affect the timing of recognition; instead, they affect the classification of the contribution revenue.

5.60 The FASB ASC glossary defines a *donor-imposed condition* as a donor-imposed stipulation that specifies a future and uncertain event whose occurrence or failure to occur gives the donor the right of return of the assets or releases the donor from the obligation to transfer assets in the future.

5.61 Some promises to give are in part conditional and in part unconditional. For example, an NFP may guarantee the debt of an unaffiliated entity without receiving commensurate consideration in return. That guarantee is in part conditional—the promise to make payments in future periods upon default—and in part unconditional—the gift of the guarantor's credit support, which enables the entity to obtain a lower interest rate on its borrowing. In circumstances in which an NFP provides a guarantee to another without receiving commensurate consideration, the NFP has made a contribution. Likewise, in circumstances in which an NFP receives a guarantee without providing commensurate consideration, the NFP has received a contribution. (Paragraphs 5.167–.171 provide additional information about a recipient's accounting for a guarantee. Paragraphs 10.96–.97 provide additional information about a guarantor's accounting for guarantees.)

5.62 The FASB ASC glossary defines a *donor-imposed restriction* as

> [a] stipulation that specifies a use for a contributed asset that is more specific than the broad limits resulting from the following: (*a*) the nature of the NFP, (*b*) the environment in which it operates, and (*c*) the purposes specified in its articles of incorporation or bylaws or comparable documents for an unincorporated association. A donor-imposed restriction on an NFP's use of the asset contributed may be temporary or permanent. Some donor-imposed restrictions impose limits that are permanent, for example, stipulating that resources be invested in perpetuity (not used up). Others are temporary, for example, stipulating that resources may be used only after a specified date, for particular programs or services, or to acquire buildings and equipment.

The "Pending Content" in FASB ASC glossary defines a *donor-imposed restriction* as

> [a] donor stipulation (donors include other types of contributors, including makers of certain grants) that specifies a use for a contributed asset that is more specific than the broad limits resulting from the following: (a) the nature of the NFP, (b) the environment in which it operates, and (c) the purposes specified in its articles of incorporation or bylaws or comparable documents for an unincorporated association. Some donors impose restrictions that are temporary in nature, for example, stipulating that resources be used after a specified date, for particular programs or services, or to acquire buildings or and equipment. Other donors impose restrictions that are perpetual in nature, for example, stipulating that resources be maintained in perpetuity. Laws may extend those limits to investment returns from those resources and to other enhancements

(diminishments) of those resources. Thus, those laws extend donor-imposed restrictions.[14]

5.63 Paragraphs 15–17 of FASB ASC 958-605-55 provide guidance for distinguishing between a condition stipulated by a donor and a restriction on the use of a contribution imposed by a donor. Those paragraphs are summarized in this paragraph and the next. Making that distinction may require the exercise of judgment. Conditional transfers are not contributions yet; they may become contributions upon the occurrence of one or more future and uncertain events. Because of the uncertainty about whether they will be met, conditions imposed by resource providers may cast doubt on whether the resource provider's intent was to make a contribution, to make a conditional contribution, or to make no contribution. As a result of this uncertainty, donor-imposed conditions should be substantially met by the entity before the receipt of assets is recognized as a contribution or a contribution receivable. In contrast to donor-imposed conditions, donor-imposed restrictions limit the use of the contribution, but they do not change the transaction's fundamental nature from that of a contribution.

5.64 If donor stipulations do not state clearly whether the right to receive payment or take delivery depends on meeting those stipulations, or if those stipulations are ambiguous, distinguishing a conditional promise to give from an unconditional promise to give may be difficult. First, review the facts and circumstances surrounding the gift and communicate with the donor. If the ambiguity cannot be resolved as a result of those efforts, presume a promise containing stipulations that are not clearly unconditional is a conditional promise to give. However, if the possibility that the condition will not be met is remote,[15] a conditional promise to give is considered unconditional. For example, a stipulation that an annual report must be provided by the donee to receive subsequent annual payments on a multiyear promise is not a condition if the possibility of not meeting that administrative requirement is remote. A challenge (or matching) grant is a common form of conditional promise to give.

5.65 FASB ASC 958-605-25-2 states that except as provided (for contributed services and collections), contributions received should be recognized as revenues or gains in the period received and as assets, decreases of liabilities, or expenses depending on the form of the benefits received.[16] The classification of contributions received as revenues or gains depends on whether the transactions are part of the NFP's ongoing major or central activities (revenues), or are peripheral or incidental to the NFP (gains).

5.66 Depending on the kind of benefit received, in addition to recognizing contribution revenue, the NFP should also recognize (*a*) an increase in assets (for example, cash, securities, contributions receivable, collections [if capitalized, see chapter 7, "Other Assets"], and property and equipment); (*b*) a decrease

---

[14] The amendments in FASB ASU No. 2016-14, *Not-for-Profit Entities (Topic 958): Presentation of Financial Statements of Not-for-Profit Entities*, are effective for annual financial statements issued for fiscal years beginning after December 15, 2017 (for example, years ending December 31, 2018 and years ending June 30, 2019), and for interim periods within fiscal years beginning after December 15, 2018. Application to interim financial statements is permitted but not required in the initial year of application. Early application of the amendments is permitted.

[15] The FASB ASC glossary defines *remote* as "the chance of the future event or events occurring is slight."

[16] Unconditional contributions of services and collection items are subject to different recognition criteria. Paragraphs 5.91–.94 and chapter 7, "Other Assets," discuss those transactions.

in liabilities (for example, accounts payable or notes payable); or (*c*) an expense (for example, donated legal services).

Measurement Principles

5.67 The "Contributions Received" subsections of FASB ASC 958-605-30 discuss the initial measurement of contributions received. Specifically, FASB ASC 958-605-30-2 states that a contribution received should be measured at its fair value, although FASB ASC 958-605-30-6 states that unconditional promises to give that are expected to be collected in less than one year may be measured at net realizable value because that amount results in a reasonable estimate of fair value. FASB ASC 820 establishes a framework for measuring fair value. FASB ASC 820-10-35-9 states that a reporting entity should measure the fair value of an asset using the assumptions that market participants would use in pricing the asset, assuming that market participants act in their economic best interest. FASB ASC 820-10-35-2B states that when measuring fair value, a reporting entity should take into account the characteristics of the asset, including restrictions on the sale or use of the asset, if market participants would take those characteristics into account when pricing the asset. Example 6 (paragraphs 51–55 of FASB ASC 820-10-55) illustrates that restrictions that are a characteristic of an asset, and therefore would transfer to a market participant, are the only restrictions reflected in fair value. Donor restrictions that are specific to the donee are reflected in the classification of net assets, not in the measurement of fair value.

5.68 Contribution revenue should be measured at the fair value of the assets or services received or promised or the fair value of the liabilities satisfied. However, FASB ASC 958-605-25-4 states that a major uncertainty about the existence of value may indicate that an item received or given should not be recognized. For example, a gift of clothing or furniture has no value unless it can be utilized in either of the following ways: (*a*) used internally by the NFP or for program purposes, or (*b*) sold by the NFP. Chapter 7 provides additional information about gifts of clothing or furniture.

5.69 FASB ASC 958-605-25-4 also states that if an item is accepted solely to be saved for its potential future use in scientific or educational research, it may have uncertain value, or perhaps no value, and should not be recognized. For example, contributions of flora, fauna, photographs, and objects identified with historic persons, places, or events often have no value or have highly restricted alternative uses.

5.70 Some items that NFPs receive as contributions are more difficult to measure than others, but difficulty in measuring fair value is not, in and of itself, a reason for not recognizing a contribution. As noted in FASB ASC 958-605-25-5, certain forms of contributed resources may be more difficult to measure reliably than others, but the form of the contributed resources alone should not change conclusions about whether to recognize the underlying event.

Recognition If a Donor Imposes a Condition

5.71 Per FASB ASC 958-605-25-13, a transfer of assets with a conditional promise to contribute them should be accounted for as a refundable advance until the conditions have been substantially met or explicitly waived by the donor. A change in the original conditions of the agreement between the promisor and the promisee should not be implied without an explicit waiver.

5.72 Transfers of assets, including promises to give, on which resource providers have imposed conditions should be recognized as contributions if the likelihood of not meeting the conditions is remote (because the transfer is considered unconditional as discussed in paragraphs 5.63–.64). Consistent with paragraph 62 of the basis for conclusions of superseded FASB Statement No. 116, *Accounting for Contributions Received and Contributions Made,* FinREC believes that conditions as described in FASB ASC 958-605 are similar to those described in federal income tax laws and regulations. Those regulations provide, in part, that "if a transfer for charitable purposes is dependent upon the performance of some act or the happening of a precedent event in order that it might become effective, no deduction is allowable unless the possibility that the charitable transfer will not become effective is so remote as to be negligible." Paragraph 5.64 provides an example from FASB ASC 958-605-55-16 of a condition for which the likelihood of not meeting that condition is remote.

5.73 FASB ASC 958-605-55-21 discusses promises that become unconditional in stages because they are dependent on several or a series of conditions—milestones—rather than on a single future and uncertain event. Those promises are recognized in increments as each of the conditions is met. Similarly, other promises are conditioned on promisees incurring certain qualifying expenses (or costs). Those promises become unconditional and are recognized to the extent that the expenses are incurred. A portion of those contributions should be recognized as revenue as each of those stages is met.

5.74 FASB ASC 958-605-55-17 provides the following example. A resource provider promises to contribute $1 for each $1 of contributions received by an NFP, up to $100,000, over the next 6 months. As contributions are received from other resource providers, the conditions would be met and the promise would become unconditional. For example, if $10,000 is received in the first month from donors, $10,000 of the conditional promise would become unconditional and should be recognized as contribution revenue.

Recognition If a Donor Imposes a Restriction

5.75 Contributions may be received with donor-imposed restrictions. Donor's restrictions impose special responsibilities on management of an NFP to ensure that it uses donated assets as stipulated. They also place limits on the use of resources. Some restrictions limit the NFP's use of contributed assets in perpetuity. Other restrictions are temporary in nature, limiting the NFP's use of contributed assets to (*a*) later periods or after specific dates (time restrictions), (*b*) specific purposes (purpose restrictions), or (*c*) both. The responsibilities of management to use restricted resources in accordance with the donors' stipulations are discussed more fully in paragraphs 11.03–.08.

5.76 FASB ASC 958-605-45-4 notes that a restriction on an NFP's use of the assets contributed results either from a donor's explicit stipulation or from circumstances surrounding the receipt of the contribution that make clear the donor's implicit restriction on use.

5.77 For example, restrictions may (*a*) be stipulated explicitly by the donor in a written or oral communication accompanying the contribution—an explicit restriction or (*b*) result implicitly from the circumstances surrounding receipt of the contributed asset—an implicit restriction. For example, restrictions can result from the following:

- Contributions accompanied by a letter (or oral statement) from the donor, stating that the contribution should be used for Program Z (explicit)
- Contributions to a capital campaign whose stated objective is to raise funds for a new building (implicit)
- Contributions to a fund-raising appeal in which the stated objective is to raise funds for Program A (implicit)

5.78 FASB ASC 958-220-45-13(d) notes that a donor can impose restrictions on otherwise unrestricted net assets. For example, a donor may make a restricted contribution that is conditioned on the NFP restricting a stated amount of its unrestricted net assets. Such restrictions that are not reversible without donors' consent result in a reclassification of unrestricted net assets to restricted net assets.

The "Pending Content" in FASB ASC 958-220-45-13(d) notes that a donor can impose restrictions on net assets without donor restrictions. For example, a donor may make a restricted contribution that is conditioned on the NFP restricting a stated amount of its net assets without donor restrictions. Such restrictions that are not reversible without donors' consent result in a reclassification of net assets without donor restrictions to net assets with donor restrictions.[17]

5.79 Paragraphs 3–7 of FASB ASC 958-605-45 provide guidance on classification of contributions received. Contributions without donor-imposed restrictions should be reported as unrestricted support that increases unrestricted net assets. Contributions with donor-imposed restrictions should be reported as restricted support, which increases permanently restricted or temporarily restricted net assets, depending on the nature of the restriction.

The "Pending Content" in paragraphs 3–7 of FASB ASC 958-605-45 provides guidance on classification of contributions received. An NFP should distinguish between contributions received with donor-imposed restrictions and those received without donor-imposed restrictions. The former should be reported as donor-restricted support that increases net assets with donor restrictions. The latter should be reported as support that increases net assets without donor restrictions.[18]

5.80 The FASB ASC glossary defines *permanent restriction* as "a donor-imposed restriction that stipulates that resources be maintained permanently but permits the NFP to use up or expend part or all of the income or other economic benefits derived from the donated assets." For example, the permanently restricted classification should be used for contributions of cash or securities that must be invested in perpetuity to provide a permanent source of income for the NFP, for contributions of permanently restricted collection items (if capitalized), for contributions of cash that must be used to purchase permanently

---

[17] The amendments in FASB ASU No. 2016-14 are effective for annual financial statements issued for fiscal years beginning after December 15, 2017 (for example, years ending December 31, 2018 and years ending June 30, 2019), and for interim periods within fiscal years beginning after December 15, 2018. Application to interim financial statements is permitted but not required in the initial year of application. Early application of the amendments is permitted.

[18] The amendments in FASB ASU No. 2016-14 are effective for annual financial statements issued for fiscal years beginning after December 15, 2017 (for example, years ending December 31, 2018 and years ending June 30, 2019), and for interim periods within fiscal years beginning after December 15, 2018. Application to interim financial statements is permitted but not required in the initial year of application. Early application of the amendments is permitted.

restricted collection items, and for revolving loan funds.[19] The FASB ASC glossary defines *temporary restriction* as "a donor-imposed restriction that permits the donee to use up or expend the donated assets as specified and that is satisfied either by the passage of time or by actions of the donee." The temporarily restricted classification should be used for contributions with restrictions that the contributed assets be used only after some future date, or for some specific program, or to acquire a specific asset.

The preceding paragraph will be deleted upon the effective date of FASB ASU No. 2016-14, *Not-for-Profit Entities (Topic 958): Presentation of Financial Statements of Not-for-Profit Entities.*[20]

5.81 In most cases, whether a restriction is permanent or temporary is clear. Paragraphs 120 and 124 of FASB Concept No. 6, *Elements of Financial Statements—a replacement of FASB Concepts Statement No. 3 (incorporating an amendment of FASB Concepts Statement No. 2)*, may be helpful in resolving cases that might be unclear. Those paragraphs state, in part, that:

> Receipt of a contribution increases permanently restricted net assets if the donor stipulates that the resources received must be maintained permanently and those resources are capable of providing future economic benefit indefinitely. Only assets that are not by their nature used up in carrying out the organization's activities are capable of providing economic benefits indefinitely. Gifts of cash, securities, or nonexhaustible property, such as land and art objects,[21] to be added to an organization's endowment or collections are common examples of those types of assets.
>
> In contrast to permanent restrictions, . . .temporary restrictions pertain to assets that by their nature are spent or used up in carrying out the receiving organization's activities or, if capable of providing economic benefits indefinitely, need not be retained after a stipulated time.

The preceding paragraph will be deleted upon the effective date of FASB ASU No. 2016-14.[22]

5.82 For example, a donor may stipulate that an NFP is a beneficiary of a charitable trust held by a third-party trustee. The trust document states the following:

- The trustee should invest the trust assets as a prudent investor would, using a portfolio approach in making investments and considering the risk and return objectives of the trust.

---

[19] Revolving loan funds are discussed further in paragraphs 8.65 and 16.17.

[20] The amendments in FASB ASU No. 2016-14 are effective for annual financial statements issued for fiscal years beginning after December 15, 2017 (for example, years ending December 31, 2018 and years ending June 30, 2019), and for interim periods within fiscal years beginning after December 15, 2018. Application to interim financial statements is permitted but not required in the initial year of application. Early application of the amendments is permitted.

[21] The recognition of contributions of collection items depends on the collections-capitalization policy adopted by the NFP. Accounting for collections is discussed in chapter 7.

[22] The amendments in FASB ASU No. 2016-14 are effective for annual financial statements issued for fiscal years beginning after December 15, 2017 (for example, years ending December 31, 2018 and years ending June 30, 2019), and for interim periods within fiscal years beginning after December 15, 2018. Application to interim financial statements is permitted but not required in the initial year of application. Early application of the amendments is permitted.

- The trustee may distribute some or all of the net income and principal of the trust at any time or times in equal shares to the beneficiary.
- In each calendar year the trustee shall distribute such amounts of income and principal in equal shares to the beneficiary as shall be necessary to avoid the tax on failure to distribute income imposed by Section 4942 of the IRS code (that is, tax on nonexempt charitable trusts and private foundations).
- The trust document states that the "trust created under this agreement shall be perpetual in duration..."

The trustee has indicated that it will maintain the trust in perpetuity and only distribute the minimum annual amount required by IRS regulations.

The preceding paragraph will be deleted upon the effective date of FASB ASU No. 2016-14.[23]

5.83 FinREC believes that in implementing the guidance in FASB ASC 958-605-45, donor intent is the overriding factor in determining net asset classifications. All other facts and circumstances are information to help determine donor intent. In the fact pattern described in the previous paragraph, FinREC believes that the net asset classification should be permanently restricted. Although losses on trust investments and distributions from the trust that are in excess of the trust income could reduce the trust assets for a time, the trust assets (investments) are capable of providing economic benefits indefinitely and the donor has instructed that the trust should be perpetual in duration.

The preceding paragraph will be deleted upon the effective date of FASB ASU No. 2016-14.[24]

Accounting Policies That Affect the Classification of Contributions

5.84 FASB ASC 958-605-45 allows an NFP's policy decisions to affect classification of net assets in only two situations, which are described in paragraphs 5.85–.88.

The preceding paragraph and the heading that precedes it will be deleted upon the effective date of FASB ASU No. 2016-14.[25]

5.85 In some situations, an NFP may meet donor-imposed restrictions on all or a portion of the amount contributed in the same reporting period in which

---

[23] The amendments in FASB ASU No. 2016-14 are effective for annual financial statements issued for fiscal years beginning after December 15, 2017 (for example, years ending December 31, 2018 and years ending June 30, 2019), and for interim periods within fiscal years beginning after December 15, 2018. Application to interim financial statements is permitted but not required in the initial year of application. Early application of the amendments is permitted.

[24] The amendments in FASB ASU No. 2016-14 are effective for annual financial statements issued for fiscal years beginning after December 15, 2017 (for example, years ending December 31, 2018 and years ending June 30, 2019), and for interim periods within fiscal years beginning after December 15, 2018. Application to interim financial statements is permitted but not required in the initial year of application. Early application of the amendments is permitted.

[25] The amendments in FASB ASU No. 2016-14 are effective for annual financial statements issued for fiscal years beginning after December 15, 2017 (for example, years ending December 31, 2018 and years ending June 30, 2019), and for interim periods within fiscal years beginning after December 15, 2018. Application to interim financial statements is permitted but not required in the initial year of application. Early application of the amendments is permitted.

the contribution is received. In those cases, pursuant to FASB ASC 958-605-45-4, the contribution (to the extent that the restrictions have been met) may be reported as unrestricted support provided that the NFP has a similar policy for reporting investment gains and income (see FASB ASC 958-320-45-3),[26] reports consistently from period to period, and discloses its accounting policy in notes to financial statements.

In some situations, an NFP may meet donor-imposed restrictions on all or a portion of the amount contributed in the same reporting period in which the contribution is received. In those cases, pursuant to the "Pending Content" in FASB ASC 958-605-45-4, the contribution (to the extent that the restrictions have been met) may be reported as support in net assets without donor restrictions, provided that an NFP has a similar policy for reporting investment gains and income,[27] reports consistently from period to period, and discloses its accounting policy.[28]

5.86 NFPs may receive contributions of long-lived assets (such as property and equipment) or of cash and other assets restricted to the purchase of long-lived assets, for which donors have not expressly stipulated how or how long the long-lived asset must be used by the NFP or how to use any proceeds resulting from the asset's disposal. FASB ASC 958-605-45-6 states that gifts of long-lived assets received without stipulations about how long the donated asset must be used should be reported as restricted support if it is an NFP's policy to imply a time restriction that expires over the useful life of the donated assets. NFPs that adopt a policy of implying time restrictions also should imply a time restriction on long-lived assets acquired with gifts of cash or other assets restricted for those acquisitions.

In some cases, NFPs may receive contributions of long-lived assets (such as property and equipment) or cash or other assets to acquire long-lived assets for which donors have expressly stipulated how or how long the long-lived asset must be used or how to use any proceeds resulting from the asset's disposal; those contributions should be reported as donor-restricted support that increases net assets with donor restrictions. In other cases, NFPs may receive contributions of long-lived assets or of cash and other assets restricted to the acquisition or construction of long-lived assets, for which donors have not expressly stipulated how or how long the donated long-lived asset or long-lived asset acquired or purchased must be used by the NFP or how to use any proceeds resulting from the asset's disposal. The "Pending Content" in FASB ASC 958-605-45-6 states that gifts of long-lived assets received without stipulations about how long the donated asset must be used should be reported as revenue without donor restrictions. Gifts of cash or other assets restricted to

---

[26] FASB ASC 958-320-45-3 (see paragraph 4.84) discusses the accounting policy for reporting investment gains and income if the NFP meets donor-imposed restrictions on all or a portion of such gains and income in the same reporting period as the gains and income are recognized.

[27] The "Pending Content" in FASB ASC 958-320-45-3 (see paragraph 4.84) discusses the accounting policy for reporting gains and investment income if the NFP meets donor-imposed restrictions on all or a portion of the gains and income in the same reporting period as the gains and income are recognized.

[28] The amendments in FASB ASU No. 2016-14 are effective for annual financial statements issued for fiscal years beginning after December 15, 2017 (for example, years ending December 31, 2018 and years ending June 30, 2019), and for interim periods within fiscal years beginning after December 15, 2018. Application to interim financial statements is permitted but not required in the initial year of application. Early application of the amendments is permitted.

acquire long-lived assets should initially be reported as donor-restricted support. Expiration of the restrictions is discussed in paragraphs 11.46–.49.[29]

5.87 If an NFP adopts such a policy, the contributions of long-lived assets or of cash and other assets restricted to the purchase of long-lived assets it receives should be reported as restricted support that increases temporarily restricted net assets. Expiration of the restrictions is discussed in paragraphs 11.46–.49.

The preceding paragraph will be deleted upon the effective date of FASB ASU No. 2016-14.[30]

5.88 Alternatively, an NFP may adopt a policy of not implying time restrictions on contributions of long-lived assets (or of other assets restricted to the purchase of long-lived assets) received without donor stipulations about how long the contributed assets must be used. If an NFP adopts such a policy, contributions of long-lived assets with no donor-imposed time restrictions should be reported as unrestricted support, and contributions of long-lived assets with donor-imposed time restrictions should be reported as temporarily restricted support.[31] Contributions of cash and other assets restricted to the acquisition of long-lived assets should be reported as restricted support that increases temporarily restricted net assets.

The preceding paragraph will be deleted upon the effective date of FASB ASU No. 2016-14.[32]

Additional Accounting Considerations for Certain Contributions

Promises to Give

5.89 The FASB ASC glossary defines *promise to give*, *unconditional promise to give*, and *conditional promise to give* as follows:

> A promise to give is a written or oral agreement to contribute cash or other assets to another entity. A promise carries rights and obligations—the recipient of a promise to give has a right to expect that the promised assets will be transferred in the future, and the

[29] The amendments in FASB ASU No. 2016-14 are effective for annual financial statements issued for fiscal years beginning after December 15, 2017 (for example, years ending December 31, 2018 and years ending June 30, 2019), and for interim periods within fiscal years beginning after December 15, 2018. Application to interim financial statements is permitted but not required in the initial year of application. Early application of the amendments is permitted.

[30] The amendments in FASB ASU No. 2016-14 are effective for annual financial statements issued for fiscal years beginning after December 15, 2017 (for example, years ending December 31, 2018 and years ending June 30, 2019), and for interim periods within fiscal years beginning after December 15, 2018. Application to interim financial statements is permitted but not required in the initial year of application. Early application of the amendments is permitted.

[31] In most cases, long-lived assets are not capable of providing future economic benefit indefinitely, as discussed in paragraph 5.81. However, if a donor requires that the proceeds of a sale of the contributed long-lived asset be used to create a permanent endowment fund, the contribution of the long-lived asset would be reported as an increase in permanently restricted net assets.

[32] The amendments in FASB ASU No. 2016-14 are effective for annual financial statements issued for fiscal years beginning after December 15, 2017 (for example, years ending December 31, 2018 and years ending June 30, 2019), and for interim periods within fiscal years beginning after December 15, 2018. Application to interim financial statements is permitted but not required in the initial year of application. Early application of the amendments is permitted.

maker has a social and moral obligation, and generally a legal obligation, to make the promised transfer. A promise to give may be either conditional or unconditional.

An unconditional promise to give is a promise to give that depends only on passage of time or demand by the promisee for performance.

A conditional promise to give is a promise to give that depends on the occurrence of a specified future and uncertain event to bind the promisor.

5.90 NFPs may enter into written or oral agreements with donors involving future nonreciprocal transfers of cash, other assets, and services.[33] These items are sometimes referred to as pledges, a term that FASB ASC 958, *Not-for-Profit Entities*, and this guide avoid because it may be misinterpreted because that term is used by some to include intentions to give as well as promises. Such agreements between NFPs and potential donors should be reported as contribution revenue and receivables if such agreements are, in substance, unconditional promises to give, even if the promises are not legally enforceable.

Recognition of Unconditional Promises to Give

5.91 Paragraphs 8–10 of FASB ASC 958-605-25 provide recognition guidance for unconditional promises to give. An unconditional promise to give should be recognized when it is received. However, to be recognized there must be sufficient evidence in the form of verifiable documentation that a promise was made and received. A communication that does not indicate clearly whether it is a promise is considered an unconditional promise to give if it indicates an unconditional intention to give that is legally enforceable. Legal enforceability refers to the availability of legal remedies, not the intent to use them.

5.92 FASB ASC 958-605-25-15 states that promises to give that are silent about payment terms but otherwise are clearly unconditional should be accounted for as unconditional promises to give. If the parties fail to express the time or place of performance and performance is unconditional, performance within a reasonable time after making a promise is an appropriate expectation; similarly, if a promise is conditional, performance within a reasonable time after fulfilling the condition is an appropriate expectation.

5.93 Per FASB ASC 958-605-55-19, the requirement (that there be sufficient evidence that a promise was received and made) does not preclude recognition of verifiable oral promises, such as those documented by tape recordings, written registers, or other means that permit subsequent verification.

5.94 Other forms of sufficient verifiable evidence documenting that a promise was made by the donor and received by the NFP include (*a*) written agreements, (*b*) pledge cards, (*c*) oral promises documented by contemporaneous written logs, and (*d*) oral promises documented by follow-up written confirmations.

---

[33] FASB ASC 958-605-55-20 notes that "promises to give services generally involve personal services that, if not explicitly conditional, are often implicitly conditioned upon the future and uncertain availability of specific individuals whose services have been promised." It is assumed in the remainder of this chapter that promises to give services are conditional and, hence, not recognized until the services are performed.

5.95 Per FASB 958-605-45-5, contributions of unconditional promises to give with payments due in future periods should be reported as restricted support unless explicit donor stipulations or circumstances surrounding the receipt of a promise make clear that the donor intended it to be used to support activities of the current period. It is reasonable to assume that by specifying future payment dates donors indicate that their gift is to support activities in each period in which a payment is scheduled. For example, receipts of unconditional promises to give cash in future years generally increase temporarily restricted net assets.

Per the "Pending Content" in FASB 958-605-45-5, contributions of unconditional promises to give with payments due in future periods should be reported as donor-restricted support unless explicit donor stipulations or circumstances surrounding the receipt of a promise make clear that the donor intended it to be used to support activities of the current period. It is reasonable to assume that by specifying future payment dates donors indicate that their gift is to support activities in each period in which a payment is scheduled. For example, receipts of unconditional promises to give cash in future years generally increase net assets with donor restrictions.[34]

5.96 Use of the *permanently restricted* classification is appropriate if donor-imposed restrictions stipulate that the resources must be maintained permanently (for example, donors' promises to give cash or securities that must be invested in perpetuity). Use of the unrestricted classification is appropriate if the donor explicitly stipulates that the promise to give is to support current-period activities or if other circumstances surrounding the promise make it clear that the donor's intention is to support current-period activities. The classification of contribution revenue is discussed further in paragraphs 5.75–.88.

The preceding paragraph will be deleted upon the effective date of FASB ASU No. 2016-14.[35]

5.97 FinREC believes that in implementing the guidance in FASB ASC 958-605-45-5, an NFP implies time restrictions that expire in the periods that the payments of the unconditional promise to give are due. For example, absent explicit donor stipulations to the contrary, if a donor promises to give $5,000 a year for 5 years to be used to fund scholarships for students that are accounting majors, it is reasonable to assume that the donor wanted a $5,000 scholarship to be granted in each of the 5 years. The promise to give would be reported as donor-restricted support because there is both a purpose restriction (for scholarships) and 5 time restrictions—one for $5,000 expiring when the first payment is due, another for $5,000 expiring when the second payment is due, and so forth.

5.98 However, FinREC believes that an NFP would not imply time restrictions that expire in the periods that the payments of the unconditional promise

---

[34] The amendments in FASB ASU No. 2016-14 are effective for annual financial statements issued for fiscal years beginning after December 15, 2017 (for example, years ending December 31, 2018 and years ending June 30, 2019), and for interim periods within fiscal years beginning after December 15, 2018. Application to interim financial statements is permitted but not required in the initial year of application. Early application of the amendments is permitted.

[35] The amendments in FASB ASU No. 2016-14 are effective for annual financial statements issued for fiscal years beginning after December 15, 2017 (for example, years ending December 31, 2018 and years ending June 30, 2019), and for interim periods within fiscal years beginning after December 15, 2018. Application to interim financial statements is permitted but not required in the initial year of application. Early application of the amendments is permitted.

to give are due if another time period is inherent in the donor's purpose restriction. For example, a donor may give to be the official sponsor of the Tenth Annual Fund-raising Walk,[36] which takes place in the current fiscal year, but specifies a payment date for the unconditional promise in the next fiscal year. Because the donor's explicit stipulation specified an event of the current year, no time restriction is implied by the donee, and because the purpose restriction is met by holding the fund-raising walk in the current year, the net assets are unrestricted at the end of the year. The contribution revenue relating to the promise would be reported as an increase in unrestricted net assets if the NFP adopted the policy discussed in FASB ASC 958-605-45-4 (see paragraph 5.85); otherwise, it would be reported as an increase in temporarily restricted net assets (to reflect the purpose restriction) along with a release of that restriction in the current year. Similarly, a donor may give to support a traveling exhibit the museum will host in year 2, but specify that the payments on that unconditional promise are due in installments in each of years 1, 2, and 3. The contribution revenue relating to the promise would be reported in year 1 as an increase in temporarily restricted net assets to reflect the purpose restriction, but a time restriction would not be implied because a time period is inherent in the donor's restriction for an event that will occur only in year 2.

However, FinREC believes that an NFP would not imply time restrictions that expire in the periods that the payments of the unconditional promise to give are due if another time period is inherent in the donor's purpose restriction. For example, a donor may give to be the official sponsor of the Tenth Annual Fund-raising Walk,[37] which takes place in the current fiscal year, but specifies a payment date for the unconditional promise in the next fiscal year. Because the donor's explicit stipulation specified an event of the current year, no time restriction is implied by the donee, and because the purpose restriction is met by holding the fund-raising walk in the current year, the net assets are no longer donor-restricted at the end of the year. The contribution revenue relating to the promise would be reported as an increase in net assets without donor restrictions if the NFP adopted the policy discussed in the "Pending Content" in FASB ASC 958-605-45-4 (see paragraph 5.85); otherwise, it would be reported as an increase in net assets with donor restrictions (to reflect the purpose restriction) along with a release of that restriction in the current year. Similarly, a donor may give to support a traveling exhibit the museum will host in year 2, but specify that the payments on that unconditional promise are due in installments in each of years 1, 2, and 3. The contribution revenue relating to the promise would be reported in year 1 as an increase in net assets with donor restrictions to reflect the purpose restriction, but a time restriction would not be implied because a time period is inherent in the donor's restriction for an event that will occur only in year 2.[38]

---

[36] Paragraphs 5.51–.57 discuss whether a sponsorship is entirely a contribution, entirely an exchange transaction, or a combination of the two.

[37] Paragraphs 5.51–.57 discuss whether a sponsorship is entirely a contribution, entirely an exchange transaction, or a combination of the two.

[38] The amendments in FASB ASU No. 2016-14 are effective for annual financial statements issued for fiscal years beginning after December 15, 2017 (for example, years ending December 31, 2018 and years ending June 30, 2019), and for interim periods within fiscal years beginning after December 15, 2018. Application to interim financial statements is permitted but not required in the initial year of application. Early application of the amendments is permitted.

Measurement of Unconditional Promises to Give

5.99 Initial and subsequent measurement of unconditional promises to give is discussed in paragraphs 5.180–.212.

Recognition of Conditional Promises to Give

5.100 Paragraphs 11–13 of FASB ASC 958-605-25 provide recognition guidance for conditional promises to give. Conditional promises to give cash or other assets (such as securities or property and equipment) should be recognized as contribution revenue and receivables when the conditions on which they depend are substantially met or explicitly waived by the donor, that is, when the conditional promise becomes unconditional.

5.101 Pursuant to FASB ASC 958-605-30-7, if a promise to give has not previously been recognized as contribution revenue because it was conditional, fair value should be measured when the conditions are met.

5.102 Recognition and measurement of conditional promises to give should be based on facts and circumstances existing at the reporting date. When information about whether the conditions placed by the donor have been substantially met comes to light after the reporting date (but before financial statements are issued or are available to be issued), the nature of the information determines whether the promise to give is recognized at the reporting date in the statement of financial position. In accordance with FASB ASC 855-10-25-3, if information comes to light that provides evidence that the donor-imposed conditions were substantially met after the reporting date, the conditional promise to give would not be recognized (because the promise became unconditional after the reporting date). In contrast, if the information provides evidence that the donor-imposed conditions had been met prior to the reporting date, then, pursuant to FASB ASC 855-10-25-1, the conditional promise to give is recognized at the reporting date (because the promise became unconditional before the reporting date).

5.103 For example, assume that in March 20X1, an individual makes a conditional promise to give an NFP $1 million if NFP raises $1 million or more in matching contributions by December 31, 20X1. At the end of the fiscal year on June 30, the NFP has raised $800,000. The NFP raises an additional $200,000 by July 15, prior to issuance of the NFP's June 30, 20X1, financial statements. This type of subsequent event provides evidence about facts and circumstances that did not exist at the date of the financial statements. At June 30, 20X1, the condition was not met and the fact that it was met subsequent to June 30, 20X1, should not result in an adjustment to the June 30, 20X1, financial statements. The $1,000,000 contribution from the individual would be recognized on July 15, 20X1, in the fiscal year ended June 30, 20X2.

5.104 As a separate example, assume a company promises to donate $100,000 to an NFP if the NFP raises at least $100,000 at a special fund-raising event to be held on December 31, 20X2. The NFP fiscal year-end is December 31, and when the promise is made, the possibility that the NFP will raise $100,000 at the event is uncertain, therefore the promise is conditional. The NFP holds the special event on December 31, 20X2, but does not complete its recordkeeping and determine the amount raised at the event until January 15, 20X3. On January 15, 20X3, prior to the issuance of its financial statements, the NFP determines that it raised $115,000 at the event. This type of subsequent event provides additional evidence about facts and circumstances that existed at the date of the financial statements (that is, the special event raised $115,000 as of December 31, 20X2). At December 31, 20X2, the condition was met, and the $100,000 contribution would be recognized in the December 31, 20X2, financial statements.

Intentions to Give

5.105 NFPs may receive communications that are intentions to give, rather than promises to give. For example, communications from individuals indicating that the NFP has been included in the individual's will as a beneficiary are intentions to give. Such communications are not unconditional promises to give, because individuals retain the ability to modify their wills during their lifetimes. (When the probate court declares the will valid, the NFP should recognize contribution revenue and a receivable at the fair value of its interest in the estate, unless the promise is conditioned upon future or uncertain events, in which case a contribution should not be recognized until the conditions are substantially met.) Paragraphs 49–51 of FASB ASC 958-605-55 provide an example of an individual naming an NFP as a beneficiary in her will. NFPs should disclose information about conditional promises in valid wills in conformity with FASB ASC 958-310-50-4. In cases in which the testator has not placed a purpose restriction on the gift, the net asset classification of the contribution revenue from a bequest differs in practice among NFPs. Some have concluded that because the contribution is in receivable form and will be paid at a future date, it is inherently time-restricted and therefore should be recognized as donor-restricted support. Others have concluded that because restrictions can only be placed by donors and the receivable is due and payable on the date the will cleared probate, the contribution revenue is not donor restricted. The latter say that although there may be time delays between clearing probate and payment because of administrative dealings of the courts and attorneys, those delays are not the actions of donors, and the timeline is not a function of a time restriction placed by a donor. NFPs should consider the facts and circumstances in determining the classification of the contribution revenue.

5.106 Per FASB ASC 958-605-25-10, solicitations for donations that clearly include wording such as "information to be used for budget purposes only" or that clearly and explicitly allow resource providers to rescind their indications that they will give are intentions to give rather than promises to give and should not be reported as contributions.

5.107 In some cases, it may be unclear whether a donor communication is an intention to give or a promise to give. FASB ASC 958-605-25-9 states that a communication that does not indicate clearly whether it is a promise is considered an unconditional promise to give if it indicates an unconditional intention to give that is legally enforceable. Legal enforceability refers to the availability of legal remedies, not the intent to use them.

5.108 For example, a donor may tell an NFP that he or she promises to give an amount that will be paid upon the donor's death. The donor may also inform the NFP of the manner in which the promise will be funded such as by (*a*) the donor's estate, (*b*) an irrevocable trust, or (*c*) a revocable trust that becomes irrevocable upon the donor's death. Depending on the communication from the donor, it may be unclear whether the communication is a promise to give, as discussed in paragraphs 5.89–.104, or an indication that the NFP has been included in the individual's will, as discussed in paragraph 5.105.

5.109 If the communication is a donor's notification that the NFP has been included in the donor's will, FinREC believes that the donor has communicated an intention to give. If the communication is a donor's notification that the NFP is named as a beneficiary of a trust, the guidance in chapter 6 is used to determine if the beneficial interest in the trust is recognized and, if so, how it is measured. If the communication is a donor's promise to contribute a defined amount of cash or specific assets and the date of death is used as a payment date for the promise, FinREC believes that the donor has communicated a promise to give.

5.110 Using the date of death to define the due date of the payment is not a donor-imposed condition because although the date itself may be unpredictable, its eventuality is not. Thus, the promise is not conditioned on the death of the donor. Unless the communication from the donor specifies a future and uncertain event on which the contribution depends, as discussed in paragraphs 5.59–.66, a donor that makes an irrevocable promise to give that is payable upon his or her death has made an unconditional promise to give. Although the possibility that a donor will deplete the assets of an estate or a trust affects the measurement of the contribution, that ability does not constitute a donor-imposed condition, as defined in the FASB ASC glossary (paragraph 5.60). FinREC believes information about the assets promised (that is, a defined amount of cash or specific assets) and the manner in which the promise will be funded, such as by (*a*) the donor's estate, (*b*) an irrevocable trust, or (*c*) a revocable trust that becomes irrevocable upon the donor's death, would be considered when measuring the fair value of the contribution.

5.111 In measuring the fair value of an unconditional promise to give that is payable upon the donor's death, NFPs should apply the guidance in FASB ASC 820. As noted in the AICPA White Paper *Measurement of Fair Value for Certain Transactions of Not-for-Profit Entities* (fair value white paper), FinREC believes that the income approach (that is, present value techniques) would be the most prevalent valuation approach. FinREC believes that if present value techniques are used to measure the fair value of the contribution in accordance with FASB ASC 820, the NFP should consider the terms of the contribution and other inputs, such as

- whether sufficient assets will exist to fulfill the promise,
- anticipated date of distribution of assets to the NFP, including donor mortality, and
- whether the NFP has been designated as the beneficiary of a trust and whether that designation could change, in the case in which the promise is funded by a trust.

FinREC believes that consideration and assessment of the inputs requires judgment and may lead to a low estimate of fair value (including zero), depending in particular on the funding for the promise and expected date of death. In general, the greater the uncertainty associated with the promise to give, the lower the fair value because market participants generally seek compensation (that is, a risk premium) for bearing uncertainty. For example, a promise of $100,000 received from a healthy 29-year-old individual of modest means would have a lower fair value than a promise of the same amount from a wealthy 89-year-old individual who is not in good health.

Contributed Services

5.112 FASB ASC 958-605-25-16 requires that contributions of services be recognized if the services received meet any of the following criteria:

a. They create or enhance a nonfinancial asset. The FASB ASC glossary defines a *nonfinancial asset* as an asset that is not a financial asset. Nonfinancial assets include land, buildings, use of facilities or utilities, materials and supplies, intangible assets, or services.

b. They require specialized skills, are provided by individuals possessing those skills and would typically need to be purchased if not provided by donation. Services requiring specialized skills are provided by accountants, architects, carpenters, doctors, electricians, lawyers, nurses, plumbers, teachers, and other professionals and craftsmen.

5.113 Recognized contributed services should be reported as contribution revenue and as assets or expenses. Whether such contributions should be recognized is unaffected by whether the NFP could afford to purchase the services at their fair value.

5.114 FASB ASC 958-605-25-16 states that contributed services and promises to give services that do not meet the criteria (in paragraph 5.112) should not be recognized. Examples 7–10 (paragraphs 52–68 of FASB ASC 958-605-55) illustrate the recognition of contributed services. Per FASB ASC 958-605-30-2, if such contributions are recognized, they should be measured at fair value.

5.115 Per FASB ASC 958-605-30-10, the fair value of contributed services that create or enhance nonfinancial assets may be measured by referring to either the fair value of the services received or the fair value of the asset or of the asset enhancement resulting from the services. Fair value should be used for the measure regardless of whether the NFP could afford to purchase the services at their fair value.

5.116 When measuring the fair value of contributed services that create or enhance nonfinancial assets, the prevalent practice is to measure the contributed services at fair value, with an upper limit on the amount recognized (a cap) at the fair value of the asset enhancement or resulting nonfinancial assets. In determining the fair value of the resulting nonfinancial assets, an NFP could take a before and after approach to isolate the portion of the change in the fair value of the nonfinancial asset attributed to the contributed services from the portion attributed to other factors, such as market conditions. Generally, an NFP would use the fair value measure that is more readily determinable to measure contributed services.

5.117 Per FASB ASC 958-605-25-17, the guidance in FASB ASC 958-720 should be followed for services received from personnel of an affiliate that directly benefit the recipient NFP and for which the affiliate does not charge the recipient NFP. An affiliate is a party that, directly or indirectly through one or more intermediaries, controls, is controlled by, or is under common control with an entity. Charging the recipient NFP means requiring payment from the recipient NFP at least for the approximate amount of the direct personnel costs (for example, compensation and any payroll-related fringe benefits) incurred by the affiliate in providing a service to the recipient NFP or the approximate fair value of that service. For additional information, see paragraphs 13.19–.23.

Special Events

5.118 Some NFPs have special events that are in part fund-raising activities and in part exchange transactions, such as fund-raising dinners. In such circumstances, the ticket revenue from such events is divided between contributions and revenue from exchange transactions for financial reporting purposes. The exchange transaction is measured at fair value of the direct donor benefits, and the excess of the ticket price over the fair value of the direct donor benefits is the contribution portion.[39]

5.119 In some circumstances, the event is scheduled to take place after the financial statement date and the revenue from the exchange transaction portion is deferred until the event takes place and the goods or services are transferred to the ticketholder. FinREC's guidance for reporting the revenue of a special event that will be held after year-end, for which amounts are received before year-end, is summarized in flowchart 5-2. FinREC believes that if a special event is scheduled to take place after the financial statement date, the contribution portion of the amount received for ticket sales prior to the end of the reporting period is presumed to be conditioned on the event taking place. Accordingly, the contribution portion that is received before the financial statement date should be accounted for in conformity with paragraphs 12–13 of FASB ASC 958-605-25. The contribution portion would be accounted for as a refundable advance until the event has taken place or the donor explicitly waives the condition of the event taking place. If a donor promises to purchase tickets, that promise is also presumed to be conditioned on the event taking place.

5.120 Assessing the likelihood that the event will take place requires judgment. As discussed in paragraph 5.72, FinREC believes that conditions described in FASB ASC 958-605 are similar to those described in federal income tax laws and regulations; that is, a condition will be disregarded if it is so remote that it is negligible. FinREC believes, in a manner similar to that guidance, concluding that a future special event will take place and that the contribution portion should be recognized at the time of the ticket sale requires overcoming a high hurdle. Unless the ticket purchase is determined to be unconditional, the contribution portion should be recognized as a refundable advance until the condition is substantially met (that is, the event takes place). The exchange transaction portion also should be recognized when the event takes place, in conformity with the same principles that govern recognition of revenue from other kinds of exchange transactions. A receivable for a promise to purchase tickets would not be recognized until the event takes place because, prior to that time, the condition on which the contribution depends has not been substantially met and the revenue from the exchange portion has not yet been earned. (Accounting for exchange transaction is discussed in chapter 12.)

5.121 For example, assume that in November 20X0, an NFP with a December 31 year-end begins selling tickets at $100 each to a February 14, 20X1, fund-raising event. The event includes dinner (the exchange portion) that has a fair value of $30. The NFP will hold the event only if it sells 100 tickets by January 31, 20X1. FinREC believes the $70 contribution revenue is conditioned on the event taking place, and the $30 for the dinner is not earned until the event takes place. For tickets sold before the event takes place, FinREC believes $70

---

[39] See footnote 13.

should be reported as a refundable advance unless the possibility that the event will not take place is so remote that it is negligible or the donor explicitly waives the condition that the event takes place. If at December 31 the possibility that the event will not take place is so remote that it is negligible (for example, the dinner has been held every year for many years, well over 100 tickets have been sold, and all other available evidence indicates the possibility that the event will not take place is remote) would the contribution be considered unconditional, and the $70 contribution revenue recognized when the ticket is sold. The $30 portion of the ticket price allocated for the value of the dinner (that is, the fair value of the exchange transaction) should be accounted for as deferred revenue when received and should be recognized as revenue when the event takes place.

5.122 Presentation of special events in the statement of activities is discussed in paragraphs 13.45–.49.

Flowchart 5-2

FinREC's Guidance for Reporting the Revenue of a Special Event That Will Be Held After Year-End for Which Amounts Are Received Before Year-End

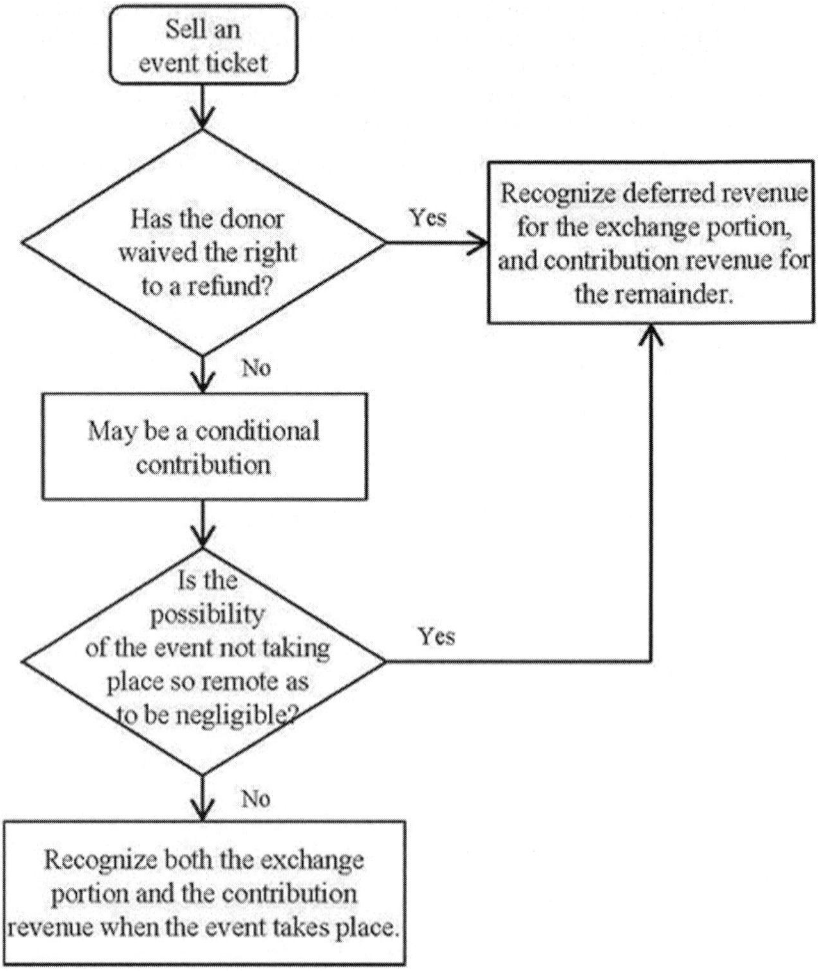

Gifts in Kind

5.123 The term *gifts in kind* is used broadly to refer to all noncash gifts. Paragraphs 5.124–.149 discuss gifts of tangible personal property, such as furniture, equipment, clothing, pharmaceuticals, and supplies. Other types of gifts in kind are discussed in the following paragraphs:

- Contributed items to be sold at fund-raising events (paragraphs 5.150–.151)
- Contributed fund-raising material, informational material, or advertising, including media time or space (paragraphs 5.152–.163)

- Contributed utilities and use of long-lived assets (paragraphs 5.164–.166)
- Contributed collection items (paragraph 5.175)

5.124 Certain types of NFPs, such as thrift stores and international relief organizations, typically receive significant amounts of gifts in kind—such as furniture, equipment, clothing, pharmaceuticals, and supplies—from resource providers. In many cases, the donor contributes the gifts in kind directly to an NFP that sells them as inventory or consumes them as the end user, without involving any other parties in the transaction. In those cases, the NFP has received a contribution.

5.125 In other cases, the donor transfers the gifts in kind to an NFP recipient, and that recipient then transfers the gifts in kind to another NFP that sells them or consumes them as the end user (referred to as the NFP beneficiary). Whether these transfers are reported as agency transactions or as contributions depends on the extent of discretion that the NFP recipient has over the use or subsequent disposition of the assets. Determining whether an NFP recipient receives assets as an agent is discussed in the "Transfers of Assets to a Not-for-Profit Entity or Charitable Trust That Raises or Holds Contributions for Others" subsections of FASB ASC 958-605 and in paragraphs 5.07–.14. Paragraphs 5.15–.17 describe the accounting and disclosure requirements of an agent that receives nonfinancial assets.

5.126 FinREC believes that in implementing that guidance in FASB ASC 958-605, an NFP recipient should recognize gifts in kind as contributions if both of the following conditions are met:

- The NFP recipient has discretion in using or distributing the gifts in kind. FASB ASC 958-605-55-76 states that a recipient entity has discretion sufficient to recognize a contribution received if it can choose the beneficiaries of the assets transferred. The "Transfers of Assets to a Not-for-Profit Entity or Charitable Trust That Raises or Holds Contributions for Others" subsections of FASB ASC 958-605-55 provide examples of donor stipulations and discuss whether an NFP has discretion to choose the beneficiary. If a resource provider specifies a beneficiary to whom the gifts in kind should be transferred, the NFP would meet this condition in circumstances in which it has variance power or is a financially interrelated entity. Variance power is discussed in paragraphs 5.23–.27. Financially interrelated entities are discussed in paragraphs 5.28–32.
- The NFP has risks and rewards of ownership over the gifts in kind, such as the risk of loss if they are lost, damaged, or destroyed and the ability to obtain the benefits of and control others' access to the gifts in kind. This typically, though not necessarily, occurs in circumstances in which the NFP takes physical possession of the gifts in kind. It also occurs in circumstances in which the NFP takes constructive possession; that is, the NFP owns the gifts in kind and can direct their use, but it does not have physical possession of the gifts in kind because they are stored in a third-party facility.

5.127 In circumstances in which the NFP receives gifts in kind, but does not meet both of the conditions in the previous paragraph for recognizing contribution revenue, the NFP is acting as an agent or intermediary pursuant to the "Transfers of Assets to a Not-for Profit Entity or Charitable Trust that Raises or Holds Contributions for Others" subsections of FASB ASC 958-605. An NFP that is acting as an agent or intermediary should not recognize contribution revenue in connection with that gift in kind. Likewise, an NFP that partners or cooperates with other entities in facilitating a gift in kind transaction should not report contribution revenue in connection with that transaction unless it meets both of the conditions in the previous paragraph. An NFP recipient that is an agent or intermediary should follow the accounting policy it adopted for nonfinancial gifts received as an agent or intermediary. In accordance with FASB ASC 958-605-25-24, the agent or intermediary is permitted, but not required, to recognize the nonfinancial assets it receives, along with the liability to distribute the assets to the beneficiary (paragraph 5.15), provided that it reports consistently from period to period and discloses its accounting policy.

5.128 If solicitation materials, contracts, pledge forms, governing board minutes, or other documentation indicates that the NFP recipient is acting as an agent or intermediary rather than a donee, gifts in kind are recognized if it is the NFP recipient's policy to recognize nonfinancial assets that it holds as an agent. In other situations, if the NFP recipient's role is not clear, the following factors may indicate that the NFP is acting as an agent or intermediary. None of these factors is determinative by itself; all applicable facts and circumstances should be considered in the particular situation:

- The NFP recipient does not take physical possession of the gifts in kind.
- The NFP recipient takes possession of gifts in kind for storage or transportation, but
  - does not receive them from the original donor, or
  - does not sell them as inventory or consume them as the end user.
- The NFP recipient receives the gifts in kind from an entity that is its affiliate, that has overlapping board members or management, or both, or that shares physical facilities; and then the NFP recipient distributes the gifts in kind to another entity that is its affiliate, that has overlapping board members or management, or both, or that shares physical facilities.
- The donor would be readily able to make a contribution to the beneficiary, without involving the NFP recipient.
- Several NFP recipients participate in transferring the gifts in kind from the donor to the beneficiary.
- The NFP recipient was created shortly before receiving the gifts in kind from the donor, and appears to have been created specifically to serve as a pass-through between the donor and the beneficiary.
- The nature of the gifts in kind is not consistent (or is only marginally consistent) with the NFP recipient's mission.
- The NFP recipient did not solicit the gifts in kind.
- The NFP recipient receives all or most of its gifts in kind from the same donor or relatively small group of donors. (This is an indicator because the NFP recipient may be an entity created only to

help those donors get the best tax advantages from their gifts, and the NFP recipient is merely carrying out the donors' directives.)

- A pattern exists whereby gifts in kind consistently pass from the same donor, to the same NFP recipient, to the same beneficiary.
- The NFP recipient and either or both the donor and the beneficiary have relatively minimal program activities beyond receipt or distribution of gifts in kind.

5.129 An NFP that is the specified by the donor as the beneficiary of an agency transaction should recognize its rights to gifts in kind held by the NFP recipient unless the NFP recipient is granted variance power. If the donor explicitly grants the NFP recipient variance power, a specified unaffiliated beneficiary should not recognize its potential for future distributions from the gifts in kind held by the NFP recipient. Those future distributions, if they occur, should be recognized as contributions by the specified beneficiary when received or unconditionally promised. (Paragraphs 5.19–.20 describe more fully the specified beneficiary's accounting.) However, FASB ASC 958-605-25-4 states that a major uncertainty about the existence of value may indicate that an item received or given should not be recognized. For example, a gift of clothing or furniture has no value unless it can be utilized in either of the following ways: (*a*) used internally by the NFP or for program purposes, or (*b*) sold by the NFP.

Fair Value Measurement of Gifts in Kind

5.130 Per FASB ASC 958-605-30-11, gifts in kind that can be used or sold should be measured at fair value. FASB ASC 820, which is discussed in paragraphs 3.138–.168, defines *fair value* and establishes a framework for measuring fair value. NFPs may encounter unique measurement challenges for gifts in kind because items contributed to an NFP (*a*) often do not have active markets and some contributed items, such as preservation easements, generally are not bought or sold; (*b*) sometimes are items that the NFP would not otherwise purchase or sell and therefore the NFP is not familiar with markets for the items; and (*c*) sometimes are not used at their highest and best use by the NFP. However, as explained in FASB ASC 958-605-25-5, contributed tangible property worth accepting generally possesses the common characteristic of all assets—future economic benefit or service potential. The future economic benefit or service potential of a tangible item usually can be obtained by exchanging it for cash or by using it to produce goods or services. Certain forms of contributed resources may be more difficult to measure reliably than others, but the form of the contributed resources alone should not change conclusions about whether to recognize the underlying event.

5.131 The highest level (level 1 input) of the fair value hierarchy is a quoted price (unadjusted) in an active market for an identical asset or liability that the reporting entity can access at the measurement date; that price provides the most reliable evidence of fair value. However, an *active market* (that is, a market in which transactions for the asset or liability take place with sufficient frequency and volume to provide pricing information on an ongoing basis) does not exist for many of the nonfinancial assets an NFP receives. In some cases, there may be publicly available information about transactions for the identical items or similar items in inactive markets (such as auction websites), which provide level 2 inputs. In other cases, the only transactions for the contributed item occur in principal-to-principal markets for which little information is made publicly available. When there is little, if any, market activity for the asset or liability at the measurement date and relevant observable inputs are not available, unobservable inputs are used to measure fair value. In those cases, the NFP must determine fair value by making its own assumptions about the assumptions that a market participant would use in pricing the asset in a hypothetical transaction occurring at the measurement date (a level 3 input). In developing those assumptions, an NFP would consider factors specific to the nonfinancial asset, the principal market for the asset or liability (or in the absence of a principal market, the most advantageous market), and market participants with whom the NFP would enter into a transaction in that market, assuming that market participants generally act in their economic best interest. An NFP need not undertake exhaustive efforts to obtain information about market participant assumptions. However, it should take into account all information about market participant assumptions that is reasonably available.

5.132 FASB ASC 820-10-35-5 states that a fair value measurement assumes that the transaction to sell the asset or transfer the liability takes place either in the principal market for the asset or liability or, in the absence of a principal market, the most advantageous market for the asset or liability. If an NFP does not regularly purchase or sell the donated nonfinancial asset, it may not know which market is the principal market. The FASB ASC glossary defines the *principal market* as the market with the greatest volume and level of activity for the asset or liability. An NFP need not undertake an exhaustive search of all possible markets to identify the principal market or, in the absence of a principal market, the most advantageous market, but it should take into account all information that is reasonably available. As noted in FASB ASC 820-10-35-6A, the NFP must have access to the principal (or most advantageous) market at the measurement date. The principal (or most advantageous) market (and thus, market participants) should be considered from the perspective of the reporting entity, thereby allowing for differences between and among entities with different activities. For example, an NFP that receives pharmaceuticals would not look to retail pharmacy sales prices for valuing those gifts in kind unless it was able to sell in that market; most NFPs do not have the proper licenses, controlled substances registrations, and facilities needed to access that market, and it would not be financially feasible to obtain them. In the absence of evidence to the contrary, the market in which the NFP normally would enter into a transaction to sell the asset or to transfer the liability is presumed to be the principal market or, in the absence of a principal market, the most advantageous market.

5.133 FinREC believes that the market in which an NFP would normally sell or distribute the asset may not be the principal, or even the most advantageous, market for the donated nonfinancial item because of evidence to the contrary. As an example, in selling or distributing donated nonfinancial assets, the NFP may be more interested in fulfillment of its mission than it is in maximizing the sales price. Thus, beneficiaries receiving gifts in kind from NFPs are not necessarily the group to whom the NFP should look when identifying the assumptions that market participants would use. For example, beneficiaries receiving gifts in kind from NFPs may be economically disadvantaged and, if the gifts in kind are sold to them, the prices accepted by the NFPs may be significantly less than they could get in another market. Further, certain nonfinancial assets, such as certain medicines, may be unavailable in markets in certain geographic areas, other than through free distribution by NFPs. Although the supply of such gifts in kind distributions may affect the demand, and therefore pricing, in geographically nearby markets, the fact that the NFP will be distributing the gifts in kind to economically disadvantaged beneficiaries has no effect on the principal market in which the goods would normally be sold, which is the market that should be used for valuing the goods.

5.134 For example, pharmaceutical companies have agreed to provide AIDS medicines to NFPs at a price substantially lower than the fair value that such drugs are sold to market participants in the United States and in other countries. Although the NFP may be charged a purchase price or handling charge for the medicines, if that charge is substantially below fair value for the medicines, there is a contribution inherent in the transaction (paragraph 5.43). If a specific AIDS drug has a fair value of $100 per dose in the United States, but is provided to an NFP for use in its programs in the United States at a cost of only $20, the fact that the NFP sells the medicines to its patient beneficiaries for a nominal charge (or provides them for free) does not affect the determination of fair value of the medicine and the amount of the contribution. In this example, the NFP would recognize contribution revenue of $80 and a disbursement of $20 to obtain inventory with a value of $100 to be utilized in its programs.

5.135 FinREC believes transactions at prices substantially less than those observed in the principal market should not be used as inputs in determining the fair value of gifts in kind unless they are adjusted. Additionally, FinREC observes that in some circumstances a market may not exist sufficient to provide observable (level 1 or level 2) inputs, and therefore the NFP should determine fair value using unobservable (level 3) inputs, as discussed in FASB ASC 820-10-35 (see paragraphs 3.155–.158).

5.136 As noted in paragraph 5.133, an NFP may not always use gifts in kind for their highest and best use from the perspective of market participants. A fair value measurement of a nonfinancial asset takes into account a market participant's ability to generate economic benefits by using the asset in its highest and best use or by selling it to another market participant that would use the asset in its highest and best use, which would maximize the value of the gifts in kind. In addition to programmatic reasons for not pursuing highest and best use, in some cases tax law or donor-imposed restrictions limit the use of the nonfinancial asset to a use other than its highest and best use. As explained in FASB ASC 820-10-35-10B, the highest and best use of a nonfinancial asset takes into account the use of the asset that is physically possible, legally permissible, and financially feasible.

5.137 For example, in some circumstances, NFPs obtain gifts in kind that the donor requires be used subject to limitations imposed by IRC Section 170(e)(3). In order to get an enhanced deduction under that section, the donee cannot transfer the gifts in kind in exchange for money, property, or services. In other cases, donors may restrict gifts in kind distributions to certain geographic locations, sometimes due to regulatory or market protection concerns. In still other cases, a donor may restrict the NFP's ability to sell an asset for its highest and best use, such as when a donor places a conservation easement on a piece of land. FASB ASC 820-10-35-6B states that although a reporting entity must be able to access the market, the reporting entity does not need to be able to sell the particular asset or transfer the particular liability on the measurement date to be able to measure fair value on the basis of the price in that market. The fact that the NFP cannot sell the asset because of a donor-imposed restriction does not affect its need to measure fair value on the basis of the price in the principal (or most advantageous) market considering the asset's highest and best use.

5.138 As discussed in paragraph 3.165, FASB ASC 820-10-35-2B and FASB ASC 820-10-55-51 state that when measuring fair value, an NFP should take into account the characteristics of an asset (such as certain legal restrictions on sale or use) if market participants would take those characteristics into account when pricing the asset or liability at the measurement date. The effect on the measurement arising from a particular characteristic will differ depending on whether that restriction will transfer to market participants. Thus, a conservation easement, which is recorded like a deed and is binding upon future owners of the property, would be considered in pricing the asset if a donor places that restriction on use of the property.

5.139 In comparison, restrictions that are specific to the donee should be reflected in the classification of net assets, not in the measurement of fair value. FinREC believes that in implementing that guidance, limitations imposed by IRC Section 170(e)(3), prohibiting NFPs from selling the gifts in kind, as well as donor restrictions limiting the geographic locations area in which the gifts in kind may be distributed, are restrictions specific to the entity. Because those restrictions are not a characteristic of the asset, they would not transfer to market participants, and therefore should not be considered in pricing the asset.

5.140 Some NFPs receive commodities with restrictions requiring that the commodities be sold (monetized) upon receipt. Commodities transferred for monetization usually have specific restrictions on their sale, limiting the sale to a specific country and only after performing a study to ensure that such a sale will not disrupt the marketplace in that country. Those contracts are discussed in chapter 7.

5.141 FASB ASC 958-605-30-11 states that in determining fair value of gifts in kind, entities should consider the quality and quantity of the gifts, as well as any applicable discounts that would have been received by the entity, including discounts based on that quantity if the assets had been acquired in exchange transactions.

5.142 For example, if the gift in kind is received in wholesale quantity but only retail values are readily available to use as inputs to fair value, a wholesale discount generally would be applied. Similarly, if the gifts in kind that are received have a product expiration date that is sooner than products typically sold in the marketplace or if technological advances have made the gifts in kind less desirable than similar items in the marketplace, a discount should be applied. Whenever a gift in kind differs from the item observed in the marketplace transaction, the NFP should consider whether an adjustment is needed to determine fair value.

5.143 FASB ASC 820-10-35-38A states that if an observable input requires an adjustment using an unobservable input and that adjustment results in a significantly higher or lower fair value measurement, the resulting measurement would be categorized within level 3 of the fair value hierarchy.

5.144 An NFP has a responsibility to determine the fair value of gifts in kind in accordance with the standards in FASB ASC 820. Therefore, if a donor provides a valuation or an appraisal, the NFP should independently and without bias ascertain whether that value is determined in accordance with FASB ASC 820. Likewise, published sources exist that purport to provide the value of various assets that may be received as gifts in kind, such as pharmaceuticals or motor vehicles. FinREC believes that in measuring fair value in conformity with FASB ASC 820, NFPs should consider whether those published sources are appropriate inputs for measuring fair value. The value that a donor recognizes for tax purposes or that a published source indicates is not necessarily fair value and may differ significantly from fair value.

5.145 FASB ASC 958-605-30-11 states that fair value would generally not increase when a gift in kind is passed from one entity to another. However, fair value could increase if an entity adds value to the gift, such as by cleaning and packaging the gift. Any increases should be evaluated to determine whether the entity did, in fact, add to the fair value of the assets.

5.146 Additional examples of activities that might increase the fair value of gifts in kind before they are passed to another entity include repairing and refurbishing used goods or repackaging items that were contributed in bulk quantities so that they can be sold individually.

Gross or Net Presentation of Gifts in Kind

5.147 According to FASB ASC 958-220-45-14, sales of contributed inventory or other gifts in kind should be reported gross if the sales are part of an entity's ongoing major or central operations and activities; that is, the sales are reported separately from (and therefore in addition to) the initial recording of the contribution of that inventory or other gifts in kind, with a corresponding cost of sales (subject to the exception in paragraphs 5.150–.151 that pertains to certain fund-raising events). For sales of contributed inventory or other gifts in kind that result from incidental or peripheral transactions, either gross reporting, as discussed in FASB ASC 958-220-45-14, or net reporting, as discussed in FASB ASC 958-220-45-17, is permitted, subject to the exception in paragraphs 5.150–.151. FinREC recommends that sales that result from incidental or peripheral transactions, such as sales of contributed inventory or other gifts in kind, be reported net, similar to gains and losses. As discussed in paragraph 13.39, FASB ASC 958-220-45-18 includes guidance to help distinguish events that are ongoing major or central, from peripheral or incidental.

5.148 Examples of transactions that typically result in reporting the sale of contributed assets as sales and costs of sales (gross reporting) include the following:

- Items contributed to an NFP that are used to produce inventory or that are further processed in vocational training workshops that are part of the NFP's mission
- Items contributed to an NFP and subsequently sold in its thrift shops that are part of the NFP's mission
- Sports equipment contributed to an NFP that is an athletic organization and subsequently sold to participants in the NFP's programs that provide opportunities to participate in the sport in which that equipment is used

5.149 Examples of transactions that typically result in reporting the sale of contributed assets net include the following:

- Charity auctions or other fund-raising events in which contributed gifts in kind can be linked to asset transfers from the original resource providers to the ultimate resource providers (recipients) because they are, in substance, part of the same transaction, as discussed in FASB ASC 958-605-25-20 (paragraph 5.150)

- Excess food, medicine, clothing, and other items received by the NFP as a contribution but that are beyond its current needs, assuming the sales transaction is peripheral or incidental
- Fixed assets, such as office equipment or real estate, received by the NFP as a contribution but that are beyond its current needs, assuming the sales transaction is peripheral or incidental

Contributed Items to Be Sold at Fund-raising Events

5.150 As discussed in FASB ASC 958-605-25-20, NFPs may also receive items, such as tickets, gift certificates, works of art, and merchandise, that are to be used for fund-raising purposes by transferring them to other resource providers (the ultimate resource provider or recipient) during fund-raising events. Those gifts in kind can be linked to asset transfers from the original resource providers to the ultimate resource providers (recipients) because they are, in substance, part of the same transaction; those gifts in kind should be reported as contributions and measured at fair value when originally received by an NFP. The difference between the amount received for those items from the ultimate resource providers (recipients) and the fair value of the gifts in kind when originally contributed to the NFP should be recognized as adjustments to the original contributions when the items are transferred to the ultimate resource providers (recipients).

5.151 For example, a public radio station receives a ticket with a fair value of $75 from the local community theater (the original resource provider), which is to be auctioned to the highest bidder; a listener (the ultimate resource provider or recipient) subsequently acquires the ticket at auction for $100. The initial transfer of the ticket to the NFP should be reported as a $75 contribution and the ticket should be reported as an asset; an additional $25 contribution should be reported when the ticket is transferred to the listener at auction, and no cost for the ticket should be reported on the statement of activities. In that example, the ultimate resource provider or recipient acquires the ticket in a transaction that is in part an exchange transaction and in part a contribution.[40] If instead a listener acquires the ticket for $45, rather than $100, a reduction of $30 in contributions should be reported when the ticket is transferred to the listener at auction, because the transfer at auction is part of the transaction that was initiated when the NFP received the ticket. Holding the ticket from the time of initial receipt to the time of ultimate transfer at auction does not create a transaction separate from the initial contribution.

Contributed Fund-raising Material, Informational Material, or Advertising, Including Media Time or Space

5.152 In some cases, entities other than an NFP use for an NFP's benefit (or provide at no charge to an NFP) certain nonfinancial assets that encourage the public to contribute to the NFP or help the NFP communicate its message or mission. Examples of these include fund-raising material, informational material, or advertising, including media time or space for public service announcements or other purposes. As noted in FASB ASC 958-605-55-23,

[40] Paragraphs 13.26–.31 discuss reporting special events associated with an NFP's fund-raising efforts.

the use of property, utilities, or advertising time are considered to be forms of contributed assets rather than contributed services. Therefore, the criteria for recognition of contributed services in FASB ASC 958-605-25-16, as discussed in paragraph 5.112, are not applicable.

5.153 Q&A section 6140.24, "Contributions of Certain Nonfinancial Assets, Such as Fundraising Material, Informational Material, or Advertising, Including Media Time or Space for Public Service Announcements or Other Purposes," states that when such nonfinancial assets are used for the NFP's benefit (or provided to the NFP at no charge) and they encourage the public to contribute to an NFP or help the NFP communicate its message or mission, NFPs should consider whether they have received a contribution. If they have received a contribution, the nonfinancial asset received should be measured at fair value, pursuant to FASB ASC 958-605-30-2; and the related expense, at the time the expense is recognized, should be reported by function, based on the nature of the contributed item.

5.154 Examples of such activities include the following:

- An advertising agency, television station, or newspaper provides design services or professional talent services.
- A radio or television station gives an NFP (or uses for the NFP's benefit) commercial air time at no charge.
- A radio or television station airs a public service announcement provided to it by the NFP. (Some stations air the announcement and report information about the airings to the NFP.)
- A magazine, newspaper, or other print media gives an NFP (or uses for the NFP's benefit) advertising space at no charge.
- An internet site gives an NFP (or uses for the NFP's benefit) advertising space at no charge.

5.155 FinREC believes that in the case of fund-raising material, informational material, advertising, and media time or space, the NFP has received an asset (future economic benefit) and can control others' access to the benefit, and therefore has received a contribution, if the NFP has an active involvement in determining and managing the message and the use of the materials. The future economic benefit received may be either (*a*) cash inflows, such as contributions arising from fund-raising activities or revenues arising from exchange transactions, or (*b*) service potential in conducting program or management and general activities.

5.156 FinREC believes that the NFP's involvement in determining and managing the content need not be absolute in order to conclude that a transfer of assets has occurred and therefore a contribution has been received. For example, the NFP may receive assistance from a television station, publication, or website in the production of a public service announcement. FinREC believes that receiving such assistance would not lead to the conclusion that the NFP does not determine the content. As another example, if a radio or television station gives an NFP commercial air time at no charge, the NFP need not determine the timeslot in which the message will air in order to conclude that a transfer of assets occurred and therefore a contribution has been received.

5.157 Determining whether a transfer occurred based on the extent of the NFP's involvement may be a subjective determination. FinREC believes that in making such a determination, NFPs should consider all relevant facts and circumstances. The greater the NFP's involvement in determining and managing the message and the use of the materials, the greater the evidence that the NFP has received a contribution.

5.158 The following facts and circumstances are indicators that the NFP has received a contribution:

- The NFP approves the advertisement before it is placed in the newspaper (or other media).
- The NFP provides or actively grants its permission to include its logo (or other materials or information) in an advertisement before the advertisement is placed in the newspaper (or other media). For purposes of applying this indicator, the NFP's silence or failure to defend the use of its logo (or other materials or information) is not considered implicit approval of such usage.
- The NFP provides input to the person or entity producing and placing the advertisement (or materials produced and disseminated), and has significant influence, but not absolute approval power, in determining the content of the advertisement (or materials produced and disseminated). For example, an NFP that reviews an advertisement demonstrates significant influence but not absolute approval power.
- The NFP provides artwork or other materials to the person or entity producing and placing the advertisement (or materials produced and disseminated).
- Representatives of the NFP appear in an audio or video advertisement (or materials produced and disseminated).

5.159 The following facts and circumstances are evidence that the NFP has not received a contribution:

- Another entity designs a newspaper advertisement encouraging the public to contribute to an NFP and places that advertisement in the newspaper without seeking or receiving input from the NFP.
- The NFP is aware that the advertisement will be placed (or materials produced and disseminated), but is unable to provide significant input or objection.
- The NFP provides minimal input to the person or entity producing and placing the advertisement (or materials produced and disseminated), and does not have significant influence in determining the content of the advertisement (or materials produced and disseminated).

5.160 In circumstances in which fund-raising material, informational material, advertising, and media time or space are used for the NFP's benefit (or provided to the NFP at no charge) and encourage the public to contribute to an NFP, NFPs should consider whether the fund-raising activity is combined with program, management and general, membership development or other activities (that is, the activity is a joint activity). For example, an NFP receives as a contribution the production of a public service announcement, as well as media time to show that public service announcement. Further, assume the public service announcement is a joint activity because the message is part fund-raising and part program. FinREC believes that in such circumstances, expenses associated with reporting that activity should be reported pursuant to the "Accounting for Costs of Activities that Include Fundraising" subsections of FASB ASC 958-720. Those subsections are discussed in paragraphs 13.79–.118.

5.161 FinREC believes that whether fund-raising materials, informational materials, or advertising, including media time or space for public service announcements or other purposes, are recognized as contributions received is unaffected by (*a*) whether the NFP could afford to purchase them or (*b*) whether they would typically need to be purchased by the NFP if they had not been provided by contribution. In reaching that conclusion, FinREC analogized to FASB ASC 958-605-55-23, which states that whether contributions of utilities and use of long-lived assets should be reported is unaffected by whether the NFP could afford to purchase the utilities or facilities at their fair value.

5.162 However, those criteria do apply to graphic design services, professional talent services, and similar contributed services associated with the contribution of the nonfinancial assets. FinREC believes that those services create or enhance a nonfinancial asset and they should be recognized as a contribution in accordance with FASB ASC 958-605-25-16, as discussed in paragraph 5.112. For example, assume an NFP receives a solicitation from an advertising agency to create a multimedia advertising campaign promoting the NFP's new program and soliciting contributions to help fund the program. The NFP is involved in the design and content of the advertising campaign at the outset and has approval rights before the advertisements are produced in final form. All services associated with the production of the advertising and the professional talent used to produce the television and radio advertisements are donated. The advertisements are placed on television, radio, and in print. In this example, the NFP would recognize a contribution for the contributed services because the NFP has the ability to approve design and content and the contributed services enhance a nonfinancial asset (the multimedia advertising campaign).

5.163 In determining fair value of contributions of fund-raising materials, informational materials, advertising, and media time or space, FinREC believes the following facts and circumstances may be relevant:

- The donor's own historical experience of receiving payment in the form of cash, marketable securities, or other consideration that is readily convertible to a known amount of cash for similar advertising from buyers unrelated to the NFP.
- Placement of the ad, such as the time of day or position within a website or publication.
- Number of viewers or readers.
- Demographics of the viewers or readers, such as income, age, gender, and other relevant factors, and whether those demographics correlate with the targeted audience for the NFP's message.
- Standard discounts given for similarly placed commercial messages or programs, such as discounts on unsold commercial time or space.
- Type of space, such as color or black and white. For internet ads, consider whether the advertisement is a banner ad, the length of time displayed, the type of display (for example, flashing versus still), and the number of clicks required to get to the ad.

- Whether the NFP shares the message, advertising, or materials with others or is the only entity receiving the benefit of the message, advertising, or materials.

Contributed Utilities and Use of Long-Lived Assets

> **Update 5-1 *Accounting and Reporting*: Leases**
>
> FASB Accounting Standards Update (ASU) No. 2016-02, *Leases (Topic 842)*, issued February 2016, changes the accounting for leases, primarily by the recognition of lease assets and lease liabilities by lessees for those leases classified as operating leases under current generally accepted accounting principles (GAAP). FASB ASU No. 2016-02 is effective for fiscal years beginning after December 15, 2018, including interim periods within those fiscal years, for NFPs that have issued, or are conduit bond obligors for, securities that are traded, listed, or quoted on an exchange or an over-the-counter market. For all other NFPs, the amendments in this FASB ASU are effective for fiscal years beginning after December 15, 2019, and interim periods within fiscal years beginning after December 15, 2020. Early adoption is permitted.
>
> This edition of the guide has not been updated to reflect changes as a result of this FASB ASU; however, the section that follows will be updated in a future edition. Readers are encouraged to consult the full text of the FASB ASU on FASB's website at www.fasb.org.

5.164 NFPs may receive unconditional contributions of the use of electric, telephone, and other utilities and of long-lived assets (such as a building or the use of facilities) in which the donor retains legal title to the long-lived asset. Pursuant to FASB ASC 958-605-55-23 and FASB ASC 958-605-25-2, an NFP should recognize the fair value of the use of property or utilities as contribution revenue in the period in which the contribution[41] is received and expenses in the period the utilities or long-lived assets are used.[42] If the transaction is an unconditional promise to give (as described in paragraphs 5.89–.111) for a specified number of periods, the promise should be reported as contributions receivable and as restricted support that increases temporarily restricted net assets.[43]

NFPs may receive unconditional contributions of the use of electric, telephone, and other utilities and of long-lived assets (such as a building or the use of facilities) in which the donor retains legal title to the long-lived asset. Pursuant to FASB ASC 958-605-25-2 and the "Pending Content" in FASB ASC 958-605-55-23, an NFP should recognize the fair value of the use of property or utilities as contribution revenue in the period in which the contribution[44] is received

[41] As discussed in FASB ASC 958-605-55-26, contributions are received in several different forms, which include both the use of facilities and utilities, as well as unconditional promises to give those items in the future.

[42] FASB ASC 958-605-55-23 states that whether those contributions should be reported is unaffected by whether the NFP could afford to purchase the utilities or facilities at their fair value.

[43] Paragraph 5.58 discusses measurement principles for initial recognition of contributions received.

[44] As discussed in FASB ASC 958-605-55-26, contributions are received in several different forms, which include both the use of facilities and utilities, as well as unconditional promises to give those items in the future.

and expenses in the period the utilities or long-lived assets are used.[45] If the transaction is an unconditional promise to give (as described in paragraphs 5.89–.111) for a specified number of periods, the promise should be reported as a contribution receivable and as donor-restricted support that increases net assets with donor restrictions.[46,47]

5.165 FASB ASC 958-605-55-24 discusses unconditional promises to give the use of long-lived assets (such as a building or other facilities) for a specified number of periods in which the donor retains legal title to the long-lived asset. Those promises may be received in connection with leases or may be similar to leases but have no lease payments. For example, an NFP may use facilities under lease agreements that call for lease payments at amounts below the fair rental value of the property. In circumstances in which an NFP receives an unconditional promise to give for a specified number of periods, the promise should be reported as revenue and as a contribution receivable for the difference between the fair rental value of the property and the stated amount of the lease payments.[48] In other words, if a donor promises that the NFP can use a facility for 10 years, the NFP has received a multiyear promise to give and should report the fair value of that promise as a contribution with a donor-imposed restriction in Year 1. Amounts reported as contributions should not exceed the fair value of the long-lived asset at the time the NFP receives the unconditional promise to give. The contribution receivable may be described in the financial statements based on the item whose use is being contributed, such as a building, rather than as contributions receivable. The contribution of the use of the property could be subject to donor-imposed restrictions or conditions.

5.166 FinREC believes that in implementing the guidance in the previous paragraph, NFPs should consider whether a promise to give the use of property or equipment is similar to a capital lease, even though the lease payments are contributed and there is no lease obligation. FinREC also believes that when considering the limitation on the amount recognized as contribution revenue, the comparison is between the amount recognized *at the date the unconditional promise to give is received* and the fair value of the underlying long-lived asset at that same date. That is, the limitation on the amount recognized does not include additional contributions that the NFP may receive in the form of (*a*) promises to pay executory costs (that is, maintenance, insurance, and taxes), make renovations, or address environmental remediation obligations on the NFP's behalf, or (*b*) forgiveness of payments that would have been due under the gift agreement, such as to reimburse the donor (lessor) for expenses or to pay the donor (lessor) an amount computed based on the NFP's (lessee's) sales at the leased property or another metric. For example, a donor may promise the free use of equipment for 5 years, which is more than 75 percent of the equipment's useful life. The donor also agrees to pay the costs of the installation

---

[45] FASB ASC 958-605-55-23 states that whether those contributions should be reported is unaffected by whether the NFP could afford to purchase the utilities or facilities at their fair value.

[46] Paragraph 5.58 discusses measurement principles for initial recognition of contributions received.

[47] The amendments in FASB ASU No. 2016-14 are effective for annual financial statements issued for fiscal years beginning after December 15, 2017 (for example, years ending December 31, 2018 and years ending June 30, 2019), and for interim periods within fiscal years beginning after December 15, 2018. Application to interim financial statements is permitted but not required in the initial year of application. Early application of the amendments is permitted.

[48] See footnote 13.

of the equipment and the costs of shipping the equipment to the NFP. If the equipment has a fair value of $10,000, and installation and shipping costs are $2,000, the limitation on the amount recognized for the equipment is $10,000, but the NFP would also recognize a contribution of $2,000 for the installation and shipping. The $2,000 would also be capitalized as part of the cost of the equipment.

Guarantees

5.167 As discussed in paragraph 5.61, an NFP may receive a guarantee of its debt from an unaffiliated entity without providing commensurate consideration in return. FinREC believes that in circumstances in which an NFP receives a guarantee without providing commensurate consideration, the NFP has received a contribution that should be initially measured at fair value. That guarantee is in part a conditional contribution—the promise to make payments in future periods upon default—and in part an unconditional contribution—the gift of the guarantor's credit support, which enables the NFP to obtain a lower interest rate on its borrowing. (Paragraphs 10.100–.101 provide additional information about a guarantor's accounting for guarantees.)

5.168 FASB ASC 460, *Guarantees,* provides guidance pertaining to guarantees.[49] Among other transactions, FASB ASC 460 applies to contracts that contingently require a guarantor to make payments to a guaranteed party based on another entity's failure to perform under an obligating agreement (performance guarantees).

5.169 FASB ASC 460-10-30-2 states that if a guarantee is issued in a standalone arm's-length transaction with an unrelated party, the liability recognized at the inception of the guarantee should be the premium received or receivable by the guarantor as a practical expedient. In implementing the guidance discussed in paragraphs 5.167–.168, the prevalent practice for determining the fair value of a guarantee of indebtedness is to use an estimate of the premium that would be required by the guarantor to issue the same guarantee in a stand-alone arm's-length transaction with an unrelated party. In the absence of observable market inputs for a premium amount, FinREC believes that the fair value of the guarantee might be estimated by using present value techniques, such as the present value of the interest savings (that is, the difference between the debt payments using the stated interest rate and the debt payments using a market interest rate, which is determined as the rate that the NFP would otherwise pay had the guarantor not provided the guarantee).

5.170 In subsequent periods, FinREC believes that the recipient of a guarantee should amortize the amount of the guarantee over the life of the debt using the effective interest method, or if immaterially different, the straight-line method. That accounting is computationally similar to a below-market interest rate loan, as discussed in paragraphs 5.172–.174. If the NFP defaults on

---

[49] FASB ASC 460-10-25-1 states that the guidance in the "General" subsections of FASB ASC 460-10-25 and FASB ASC 460-10-30 does not apply to the following circumstances, among others:

- A guarantee issued either between parents and their subsidiaries or between corporations under common control.
- A parent's guarantee of its subsidiary's debt to a third party (whether the parent is a corporation or an individual).
- A subsidiary's guarantee of the debt owed to a third party by either its parent or another subsidiary of that parent.

its debt (or another event triggers the payment of funds to the lender by the guarantor), the NFP should recognize contribution revenue if the amount that the guarantor pays on its behalf is not repayable to the guarantor, or the NFP should recognize its liability to the guarantor if the guarantee agreement requires the NFP to repay the guarantor.

5.171 As an alternative to the accounting in the previous paragraph, the NFP might irrevocably elect to use fair value as the initial and subsequent measurement of the guarantee, in accordance with the Fair Value Option subsections of FASB ASC 825-10.

Below-Market Interest Rate Loans

5.172 Some NFPs receive loans of cash that are interest free or that have below-market interest rates. Interest expense and contribution revenue should be reported in connection with loans of cash to NFPs that are interest free or that have below-market interest rates (regardless of whether the loan is between related parties). Those contributions should be measured at fair value. FinREC believes that the difference between the fair value of the loan at a market interest rate and the fair value of the loan at its stated rate is one method of determining the fair value of the contribution. Donor accounting for below-market interest rate loans is further discussed in chapter 8, "Programmatic Investments."

5.173 For example, on January 1, 20X8, an NFP with a December year-end receives an interest-free loan of $200,000, payable on December 31, 20Y0. The purpose of the loan is to pay operating expenses and the appropriate imputed market rate of interest is 6 percent. The journal entries over the life of the loan would be as follows.

1/1/X8		
Cash	200,000	
Loan payable		167,924
Contribution revenue—temporarily restricted		32,076
(Receipt of cash; liability reported at the fair value of the loan using the present value of $200,000 due in 3 years, discounted at 6 percent.)		
12/31/X8		
Interest expense	10,075	
Loan payable		10,075
(Accretion of loan using the effective interest method.)		
Reclass: Temporarily restricted net assets	10,075	
Reclass: Unrestricted net assets		10,075
(Reclassification due to lapse of restriction.)		
12/31/X9		
Interest expense	10,680	
Loan payable		10,680
(Accretion of loan using the effective interest method.)		

Reclass: Temporarily restricted net assets	10,680	
Reclass: Unrestricted net assets		10,680
(Reclassification due to lapse of restriction.)		
12/31/Y0		
Interest expense	11,321	
Loan payable		11,321
(Accretion of loan using the effective interest method.)		
Reclass: Temporarily restricted net assets	11,321	
Reclass: Unrestricted net assets		11,321
(Reclassification due to lapse of restriction.)		
Loan payable	200,000	
Cash		200,000
(Payment of the loan.)		

1/1/X8		
Cash	200,000	
Loan payable		167,924
Contribution revenue—net assets with donor restrictions		32,076
(Receipt of cash; liability reported at the fair value of the loan using the present value of $200,000 due in 3 years, discounted at 6 percent.)		
12/31/X8		
Interest expense	10,075	
Loan payable		10,075
(Accretion of loan using the effective interest method.)		
Reclass: Net assets with donor restrictions	10,075	
Reclass: Net assets without donor restrictions		10,075
(Reclassification due to lapse of restriction.)		
12/31/X9		
Interest expense	10,680	
Loan payable		10,680
(Accretion of loan using the effective interest method.)		
Reclass: Net assets with donor restrictions	10,680	
Reclass: Net assets without donor restrictions		10,680
(Reclassification due to lapse of restriction.)		
12/31/Y0		

Interest expense	11,321	
Loan payable		11,321
(Accretion of loan using the effective interest method.)		
Reclass: Net assets with donor restrictions	11,321	
Reclass: Net assets without donor restrictions		11,321
(Reclassification due to lapse of restriction.)		
Loan payable	200,000	
Cash		200,000
(Payment of the loan.)[50]		

5.174 As another example, on January 1, 19X8, an NFP with a December year-end receives an interest-free loan of $200,000. The purpose of the loan is to pay operating expenses and the appropriate imputed rate of interest is 6 percent. Unlike the example in paragraph 5.173, the loan is payable on demand. The loan is repaid on December 31, 20Y0.

1/1/X8		
Cash	200,000	
Loan payable		200,000
(Receipt of cash.)		
12/31/X8		
Interest expense	12,000	
Contribution revenue—Unrestricted		12,000
(Contribution revenue for below-market rate of interest on loan [loan balance × interest rate: $200,000 × .06].)		
12/31/X9		
Interest expense	12,000	
Contribution revenue—Unrestricted		12,000
(Contribution revenue for below-market rate of interest on loan.)		
12/31/Y0		
Interest expense	12,000	
Contribution revenue—Unrestricted		12,000
(Contribution revenue for below-market rate of interest on loan.)		
Loan payable	200,000	
Cash		200,000
(Payment of the loan.)		

[50] The amendments in FASB ASU No. 2016-14 are effective for annual financial statements issued for fiscal years beginning after December 15, 2017 (for example, years ending December 31, 2018 and years ending June 30, 2019), and for interim periods within fiscal years beginning after December 15, 2018. Application to interim financial statements is permitted but not required in the initial year of application. Early application of the amendments is permitted.

1/1/X8		
Cash	200,000	
Loan payable		200,000
(Receipt of cash.)		
12/31/X8		
Interest expense	12,000	
Contribution revenue—net assets without donor restrictions		12,000
(Contribution revenue for below-market rate of interest on loan [loan balance × interest rate: $200,000 × .06].)		
12/31/X9		
Interest expense	12,000	
Contribution revenue—net assets without donor restrictions		12,000
(Contribution revenue for below-market rate of interest on loan.)		
12/31/Y0		
Interest expense	12,000	
Contribution revenue—net assets without donor restrictions		12,000
(Contribution revenue for below-market rate of interest on loan.)		
Loan payable	200,000	
Cash		200,000
(Payment of the loan.)[51]		

Contributed Collection Items

5.175 NFPs may receive contributions of works of art, historical treasures, and similar items that meet the definition of collections in the FASB ASC glossary. The recognition and measurement principles for contributions of collection items depend on the collections-capitalization policy adopted by the NFP. Accounting for collections is discussed in chapter 7.

Split-Interest Agreements

5.176 A *split-interest agreement* is a form of contribution in which an NFP receives benefits that are shared with other beneficiaries designated by the donor. Common kinds of such agreements include charitable lead and remainder trusts, charitable gift annuities, and pooled (life) income funds. Because of the specialized nature of these arrangements, they are discussed separately in chapter 6.

---

[51] The amendments in FASB ASU No. 2016-14 are effective for annual financial statements issued for fiscal years beginning after December 15, 2017 (for example, years ending December 31, 2018 and years ending June 30, 2019), and for interim periods within fiscal years beginning after December 15, 2018. Application to interim financial statements is permitted but not required in the initial year of application. Early application of the amendments is permitted.

Administrative Costs of Restricted Contributions

5.177 Some NFPs have a policy of designating a certain percentage of restricted gifts to offset the costs of raising and administering those gifts. In applying the guidance in paragraphs 5.75–.83, NFPs may be required to determine whether an implicit restriction exists if an NFP has a policy that allocates a percentage of certain contributions to supporting services. In order to conclude that the policy to allocate a portion of the contribution to supporting services is an implicit donor restriction, FinREC believes that policy needs to be effectively communicated to or from the donor prior to receipt of the contribution.

5.178 For example, assume a donor contributes $100 restricted for Program A to an NFP that has a policy of allocating 5 percent of all purpose-restricted contributions to supporting services. In determining whether that policy has been effectively communicated to or from the donor prior to receipt of the contribution, FinREC believes that

- in circumstances in which the NFP discloses the policy to donors when soliciting the contribution, an implicit restriction exists, and 95 percent of the gift is donor-restricted for Program A and 5 percent of the gift is restricted for supporting services,
- in circumstances in which the donor is unaware of that policy, no implicit restriction exists and 100 percent of the gift is donor restricted for Program A, and
- in circumstances in which the NFP discloses that policy in the notes to its financial statements, but does not otherwise disclose that policy directly to the donor, no implicit restriction exists and 100 percent of the gift is donor restricted for Program A. Disclosure of that policy in the financial statements, in and of itself, would not be considered sufficient evidence that the donor intends a portion of the contribution to be restricted for supporting services because (1) the donor may not read the financial statements and (2) that type of communication might come after the contribution was already received.

5.179 If the NFP has not communicated to the donor its policy for cost allocations, charges, assessments, or assignments as it pertains to meeting donor restrictions, the NFP may be in noncompliance with donor restrictions. Paragraphs 3.173–.175 discuss noncompliance with donor-imposed restrictions, including illegal acts. Paragraphs 11.03–.08 discuss an NFP's fiduciary responsibilities to meet donor's restrictions.

Measurement Principles for Contributions Receivable

5.180 In accordance with FASB ASC 958-605-30-1, contributions receivable (unconditional promises to give) are initially measured at fair value. NFPs also have the option of electing to subsequently measure a contribution receivable at fair value in conformity with the "Fair Value Option" subsections of FASB ASC 825-10. *Fair value* is the price that would be received to sell an unconditional promise to give (an asset) in an orderly transaction between market participants at the measurement date.

5.181 FASB ASC 958-605-55-22 states that the present value of the future cash flows is one valuation technique for measuring the fair value of contributions arising from unconditional promises to give cash; other valuation techniques also are available, as described in FASB ASC 820.[52] The fair value white paper states that FinREC believes that a present value technique (an application of the income approach) will be the most prevalent valuation technique used to measure fair value of an unconditional promise to give that is expected to be collected in one year or more. In reaching that conclusion, FinREC observes that the market approach typically would not be operational for measuring the fair value of unconditional promises to give cash because no market exists, and the cost approach is not used for valuing financial assets such as promises to give. Because no market exists for unconditional promises to give, assumptions regarding what a hypothetical acquirer would pay for these assets (the right to receive from the donor the cash flow inherent in the promise), determined under current market conditions, are necessary in determining fair value. (The portions of the fair value white paper that discuss unconditional promises to give cash and other financial assets are included in appendix A of this chapter.)

5.182 Most NFPs do not elect to subsequently measure contributions receivable at fair value. Instead, they report contributions receivable using updated present value assumptions of cash flows, discounted at the rate used when the receivable was initially recognized. Those NFPs compute and disclose an allowance for uncollectible receivables and an allowance for the unamortized discount.

Present Value Techniques

5.183 FASB ASC 820-10-55 and the fair value white paper discuss two present value techniques, the (*a*) traditional or discount rate adjustment technique and (*b*) expected present value technique, which may be applied using one of two methods. Conceptually, the three present value methods should give the same results. FinREC observes that in practice, however, certain techniques may be easier, more practical, or more appropriate to apply to certain facts and circumstances.

5.184 Key pricing inputs used in a fair value measurement should reflect the factors that market participants would consider in setting a price for the promise to give. The fair value hierarchy in FASB ASC 820-10-35 prioritizes market observable inputs, but also allows for the use of unobservable (internally derived) inputs when relevant market observable inputs are unavailable. When using a present value technique, two key pricing inputs are the cash flows and the discount rate. The factors considered in determining the cash flows and the discount rate used should be documented.

5.185 Paragraphs 19–32 of the fair value white paper (appendix A) provide information about determining the discount rate for promises to give cash. FASB ASC 958-605-30-5 states that if present value techniques are used to measure fair value, the present value of unconditional promises to give should be measured using a discount rate that is consistent with the general principles for present value measurement discussed in paragraphs 5–9 of FASB ASC 820-10-55. FASB ASC 820-10-55-6 discusses general principles for determining the discount rate when applying present value techniques. As noted in FASB ASC 820-10-55-6(c), to avoid double counting or omitting the effects of risk factors, discount rates should reflect assumptions that are consistent with those

---

[52] See footnote 6.

inherent in the cash flows. For example, a discount rate that reflects the uncertainty in expectations about future defaults is appropriate if using promised cash flows of an unconditional promise to give. That same rate should not be used if using most likely cash flows or expected (that is, probability-weighted) cash flows because those cash flows already reflect assumptions about the uncertainty of future defaults.

5.186 The use of the word *expected* in the phrase *expected to be received* or the phrase *expected to be collected*, when used to describe the receipt of cash or other assets from an unconditional promise to give, is not intended to limit the NFP's choice of present value techniques to an expected present value technique as described in paragraphs 13–20 of FASB ASC 820-10-55.

Organization of the Measurement Guidance

5.187 The guidance for measurement of contributions receivable is organized as follows:

	Initial Measurement		*Subsequent Measurement*	
Contribution Receivable	*FASB ASC*	*This Guide*	*FASB ASC*	*This Guide*
Due in less than one year	958-605-30-6	Paragraphs 5.188–.189		Paragraph 5.198
Due in more than one year				
Promise to give cash	Paragraphs 4-5 of 958-605-30	Paragraphs 5.190–.192	Paragraphs 6–10 of 958-310-35	Paragraphs 5.199–.205
Promise to give equity securities with readily determinable fair value or debt securities	958-605-30-8	Paragraphs 5.193–.196	958-310-35-11	Paragraphs 5.199–.207
Promise to give other assets	958-605-30-8	Paragraphs 5.193–.196	Paragraphs 12–13 of 958-310-35	Paragraphs 5.204–.205; paragraphs 5.208–.211

Initial Measurement

Contributions Receivable in Less Than One Year

5.188 FASB ASC 958-605-30-6 states that unconditional promises to give that are expected to be collected in less than one year may be measured at net realizable value because that amount results in a reasonable estimate of fair value. FASB Concept No. 5, *Recognition and Measurement in Financial Statements of Business Enterprises*, states that net realizable value is "the nondiscounted amount of cash, or its equivalent, into which an asset is expected to be converted in due course of business, less direct costs, if any, necessary to make that conversion." That means, for contributions receivable, an NFP assesses whether the contribution is reasonably assured of collection, and only recognizes the amount that it estimates will be collected, less direct costs of collection, if any.

5.189 For contributions receivable that result from mass fund-raising appeals, an NFP may estimate the collectible portion by using the experience it gained from similar appeals. Paragraph 114 of the basis for conclusions of FASB Statement No. 116 explains:

> Annual campaigns, mail solicitations, telethons, or phonathons generally result in many promises of small donor amounts that are due in less than one year and are unconditional. To measure individually the present value of estimated cash flows for promises to give resulting from those campaigns generally is impracticable. Measurement difficulties are compounded because the solicitation process may result in some spurious promises.

Contributions Receivable in One Year or More

5.190 FASB ASC 958-605-30-4 discusses initial measurement of unconditional promises to give using present value techniques to measure the fair value of unconditional promises to give. An NFP should determine the amount and timing of the future cash flows of unconditional promises to give cash (or, for promises to give noncash assets, the quantity and nature of assets expected to be received). In making that determination, the NFP should consider all the elements in FASB ASC 820-10-55-5, including the following: when the receivable is expected to be collected, the creditworthiness of the other parties, the NFP's past collection experience, the NFP's policies concerning the enforcement of promises to give, expectations about possible variations in the amount or timing of the cash flows (that is, the uncertainty inherent in the cash flows), and other factors concerning the receivable's collectibility.

Unconditional Promises to Give Cash

5.191 Table 5-4 reproduces the table in FASB ASC 958-605-55-22, which illustrates the use of present value techniques for initial recognition and measurement of unconditional promises to give cash that are expected to be collected one year or more after the financial statement date.

Table 5-4

Initial Recognition of Unconditional Promises to Give Cash

Facts

Assume that a not-for-profit entity receives a promise (or promises from a group of homogeneous donors) to give $100 in 5 years, that the anticipated future cash flows from the promise(s) are $70, and that the present value of the future cash flows is $50.

Solution

dr.		Contributions Receivable	$70	
	cr.	Contribution Revenue—Temporarily Restricted		$50
	cr.	Discount on Contributions Receivable		$20

(To report contributions receivable and revenue using a present value technique to measure fair value.)

[*Note:* Many entities may use a subsidiary ledger to retain information concerning the $100 face amount of contributions promised in order to monitor collections of contributions promised.]

Initial Recognition of Unconditional Promises to Give Cash—*continued*

Facts

Assume that a not-for-profit entity receives a promise (or promises from a group of homogeneous donors) to give $100 in 5 years, that the anticipated future cash flows from the promise(s) are $70, and that the present value of the future cash flows is $50.

Solution

dr.		Contributions Receivable	$70	
	cr.	Contribution Revenue—Donor-restricted Support		$50
	cr.	Discount on Contributions Receivable		$20

(To report contributions receivable and revenue using a present value technique to measure fair value.)

[***Note:*** Many entities may use a subsidiary ledger to retain information concerning the $100 face amount of contributions promised in order to monitor collections of contributions promised.][53]

5.192 In conformity with FASB ASC 835-30-25-11, the discount rate should be determined at the time the unconditional promise to give is initially recognized and should not be revised subsequently unless the NFP has elected to measure the promise to give at fair value in conformity with the "Fair Value Option" subsections of FASB ASC 825-10, as discussed further in paragraphs 5.199–.200.

Unconditional Promises to Give Noncash Assets

5.193 FASB ASC 958-605-30-8 discusses initial measurement of unconditional promises to give noncash assets. It states that a present value technique is one valuation technique for measuring the fair value of an unconditional promise to give noncash assets; other valuation techniques also are available, as described in FASB ASC 820.[54] If present value techniques are used, the fair value of contributions arising from unconditional promises to give noncash assets might be determined based on the present value of the projected fair value of the underlying noncash assets at the date that those assets are expected to be received (that projected fair value is referred to in this section as the future fair value) and in the quantities that those assets are expected to be received, if the date is one year or more after the financial statement date.

5.194 In determining the future amount to be discounted, FASB ASC 958-605-30-8 requires that the NFP consider both the likelihood of the promise

---

[53] The amendments in FASB ASU No. 2016-14 are effective for annual financial statements issued for fiscal years beginning after December 15, 2017 (for example, years ending December 31, 2018 and years ending June 30, 2019), and for interim periods within fiscal years beginning after December 15, 2018. Application to interim financial statements is permitted but not required in the initial year of application. Early application of the amendments is permitted.

[54] See footnote 6.

being fulfilled and the future fair value of those underlying assets, such as the future fair value per share of a promised equity security. The quantity, nature, and timing of assets expected to be received, such as the number of shares of a promised equity security, the entity in which those shares represent an equity interest, and when those shares will be received should be considered in determining the likelihood of the promise being fulfilled.

5.195 Similar to paragraphs 49 and 91 in the fair value white paper (appendix A), FinREC believes that if the NFP determines the fair value of unconditional promises to give noncash assets based on the present value of the future fair value of the underlying noncash assets in the quantities that those assets are expected to be received, the appropriate discount rate would equal or exceed the expected growth rate (rate of return) on the noncash assets. If, for example, the NFP expects, a promised equity security's value to grow at a rate of 5 percent, then as the recipient of a promise of those securities, the NFP also bears at least that same risk. Thus, FinREC believes that best practice is for the discount rate to also reflect that risk, and the discount rate in this example would be, at a minimum, 5 percent.

5.196 FASB ASC 958-605-30-8 also states that, in cases in which the future fair value of the underlying asset is difficult to determine, the fair value of an unconditional promise to give noncash assets may be based on the fair value of the underlying asset at the date of initial recognition. No discount for the time value of money should be reported if an asset's fair value at the date of initial recognition is used to measure the fair value of the contribution. FinREC believes that the future fair value of the underlying asset typically is difficult or impossible to determine, and that best practice typically is to use the fair value of the underlying asset as the measure at the date of initial recognition for a promise to give a noncash asset. For example, it might be difficult or impossible to determine future fair value if there is a lack of open and available market for the underlying asset.

Subsequent Measurement

5.197 FASB ASC 958-310-35 discusses the subsequent measurement of receivables. It states that after recognition, the value of a contribution arising from an unconditional promise to give cash or noncash assets (contribution receivable) may change because of any of the following reasons: (*a*) accrual of the interest element for a promise to give measured using present value techniques, (*b*) changes in the quantity or nature of assets expected to be received (such as changes in the amounts of future cash flows), (*c*) changes in the future fair value of the underlying noncash assets at the date that those assets are expected to be received (referred to as the future fair value of underlying noncash assets), (*d*) changes in the timing of assets expected to be received, and (*e*) changes in the time value of money.

Contributions Receivable in Less Than One Year

5.198 Often, contributions receivable that are due in less than one year are outstanding at the end of the fiscal year. If they are outstanding, net realizable value is updated at the date of the statement of financial position. Net realizable value is the nondiscounted amount of cash, or its equivalent, into which the receivables are expected to be converted in due course of operations, less direct costs, if any, necessary to make that conversion.

Contributions Receivable in One Year or More

Election to Subsequently Measure Contributions Receivable at Fair Value

5.199 The "Fair Value Option" subsections of FASB ASC 825-10 create a fair value option under which an NFP may irrevocably elect fair value as the initial and subsequent measure for most contributions receivable. Unconditional promises to give cash and unconditional promises to give financial instruments (such as equity and debt securities) are financial assets, and an NFP may choose, when it first recognizes the receivable, to measure it at fair value (the fair value option) on an ongoing basis. The decision about whether to elect the fair value option should be (*a*) applied instrument by instrument, except as discussed in FASB ASC 825-10-25-7, (*b*) irrevocable (unless a new election date occurs, as discussed in FASB ASC 825-10-25-4), and (*c*) applied only to an entire instrument and not to only specified risks, specific cash flows, or portions of that instrument. An NFP may decide whether to elect the fair value option for each eligible item on its election date; alternatively, it may elect the fair value option according to a preexisting policy for contributions receivable. Most NFPs do not elect the fair value option for their contributions receivable.

5.200 FASB ASC 958-310-35-1 states that if an NFP elects to measure a receivable at fair value and uses a present value technique to measure fair value, the discount rate assumptions, and all other elements discussed in FASB ASC 820-10-55-5, should be revised at each measurement date to reflect current market conditions.

If the Election to Subsequently Measure Contributions Receivable at Fair Value Is Not Made

> **© Update 5-2 *Accounting and Reporting*: Credit Losses**
>
> FASB ASU No. 2016-13, *Financial Instruments—Credit Losses (Topic 326): Measurement of Credit Losses on Financial Instruments*, was issued in June 2016 to provide financial statement users with more decision-useful information about the expected credit losses on financial instruments and other commitments to extend credit held by a reporting entity at each reporting date. To achieve this objective, the amendments in this ASU replace the incurred loss impairment methodology in current GAAP with a methodology that reflects expected credit losses and requires consideration of a broader range of reasonable and supportable information to inform credit loss estimates.
>
> FASB ASU No. 2016-13 is effective for NFPs for fiscal years beginning after December 15, 2020, and interim periods within fiscal years beginning after December 15, 2021. Early adoption is permitted for fiscal years beginning after December 15, 2018, including interim periods within those fiscal years.
>
> This edition of the guide has not been updated to reflect changes as a result of this ASU; however, the section that follows will be updated in a future edition. Readers are encouraged to consult the full text of the ASU on FASB's website at www.fasb.org.

5.201 If an NFP does not elect to subsequently measure its contributions receivable at fair value, accounting for contributions receivable in one year or more is similar to trade receivables due in one year or more. Paragraphs 5–11 of FASB ASC 310-10-35 provide general principles for measurement impairment of receivables. An allowance for uncollectible amounts is established when both (*a*) it is probable that the NFP will be unable to collect all amounts promised according to the terms of the contribution receivable and (*b*) the amount of the loss can be reasonably estimated. Q&A section 6140.09, "Reporting Bad Debt Losses," states that bad debt losses on unconditional promises to give cash or noncash assets are prohibited from being netted against contribution revenue under FASB ASC 958-220-45-17.

5.202 As noted in Q&A section 6140.25, "Multiyear Unconditional Promises to Give—Measurement Objective and the Effect of Changes in Interest Rates," if an NFP has not elected the fair value option (as discussed in paragraphs 5.199–.200), and market interest rates change in periods subsequent to initial recognition of the contribution receivable, in conformity with FASB ASC 835-30-25-11, the discount rate used in a present value technique should not be revised to reflect those changes in market rates.

5.203 Discounts on contributions receivable should be amortized between the date the promise to give is initially recognized and the date the cash or other contributed assets are received. In conformity with FASB ASC 835-30-35, the interest method should be used to amortize the discount. Other methods of amortization may be used if the results are not materially different. FASB ASC 958-310-35-6 and FASB ASC 958-310-45-2 require that the subsequent accruals of the interest element be accounted for by donees as contribution revenue that increases either temporarily or permanently restricted net assets if the underlying promise to give is donor restricted.

Discounts on contributions receivable should be amortized between the date the promise to give is initially recognized and the date the cash or other contributed assets are received. In conformity with FASB ASC 835-30-35, the interest method should be used to amortize the discount. Other methods of amortization may be used if the results are not materially different. FASB ASC 958-310-35-6 and FASB ASC 958-310-45-2 require that the subsequent accruals of the interest element be accounted for by donees as contribution revenue that increases net assets with donor restrictions if the underlying promise to give is donor restricted.[55]

Changes in the Quantity or Nature of Assets Expected to Be Received

5.204 This paragraph and the next discuss the guidance in paragraphs 7–10 of FASB ASC 958-310-35 for subsequent measurement of unconditional promises to give if there are changes in the quantity or nature of the promised assets. If the value of a contribution receivable decreases because of changes in the quantity or nature of assets expected to be received, the decrease should be recognized in the period(s) in which the expectation changes. As discussed in FASB ASC 958-310-45-3, that decrease should be reported as an expense or loss (bad debt) in the net asset class in which the net assets are represented. Because all expenses are reported as decreases in the unrestricted net asset

---

[55] The amendments in FASB ASU No. 2016-14 are effective for annual financial statements issued for fiscal years beginning after December 15, 2017 (for example, years ending December 31, 2018 and years ending June 30, 2019), and for interim periods within fiscal years beginning after December 15, 2018. Application to interim financial statements is permitted but not required in the initial year of application. Early application of the amendments is permitted.

class, those decreases should be reported as losses if they are decreases in temporarily restricted net assets or permanently restricted net assets.

This paragraph and the next discuss the guidance in paragraphs 7–10 of FASB ASC 958-310-35 for subsequent measurement of unconditional promises to give if there are changes in the quantity or nature of the promised assets. If the value of a contribution receivable decreases because of changes in the quantity or nature of assets expected to be received, the decrease should be recognized in the period(s) in which the expectation changes. As discussed in the "Pending Content" in FASB ASC 958-310-45-3, that decrease should be reported as an expense or loss (bad debt) in the net asset class in which the net assets are represented. Because all expenses are reported as decreases in the net assets without donor restrictions class, those decreases should be reported as losses if they are decreases in net assets with donor restrictions.[56]

5.205 No increase in net assets should be recognized if the value of a contribution receivable increases because of a change in the quantity or nature of assets expected to be received between the date the unconditional promise to give is recognized and the date it is collected, unless the promise was previously written down because of expenses or losses from bad debts. If the value of a contribution receivable increases because of changes in the quantity or nature of assets expected to be received, and previous decreases in the value of that unconditional promise to give resulted in expenses or losses from bad debts, the increase should be reported as a recovery of those expenses or losses to the extent that those expenses or losses were previously recognized. The recovery should be reported in the net asset classes in which the net assets are represented. Amounts collected, other than a recovery of bad debt expenses or losses, in excess of the carrying amount of contributions receivable should be reported as contribution revenue in the appropriate net asset class.

Changes in the Fair Value of Underlying Noncash Assets—Gifts of Certain Securities

5.206 As discussed in FASB ASC 958-310-35-11, the value of a contribution receivable arising from an unconditional promise to give equity securities with readily determinable fair values or debt securities may change between the date the unconditional promise to give is recognized and the date the asset promised is received because of changes in the future fair value of the underlying securities. For purposes of subsequent measurement, the method of determining the future fair value of the underlying securities should be the same as the method used for determining that amount for purposes of initial measurement. Thus, if a promise to give securities is measured based on the fair value of the underlying securities at the date of gift, as described in FASB ASC 958-605-30-8 (paragraph 5.196), an observed change in the current fair value of the underlying securities should be recognized. The change should be reported as an increase or decrease in contribution revenue in the period(s) in which the change occurs. The change should be recognized in the net asset class in which the contribution was originally reported or in the net asset class in which the net assets are represented.

---

[56] The amendments in FASB ASU No. 2016-14 are effective for annual financial statements issued for fiscal years beginning after December 15, 2017 (for example, years ending December 31, 2018 and years ending June 30, 2019), and for interim periods within fiscal years beginning after December 15, 2018. Application to interim financial statements is permitted but not required in the initial year of application. Early application of the amendments is permitted.

5.207 Assumed relationships, such as the relationship between the market price of the security at the time the initial measurement is made and its projected market price at the date the asset is expected to be received, should be presumed to continue in determining whether the future fair value of the underlying noncash asset has changed.

Changes in the Fair Value of Underlying Noncash Assets—Gifts of Other Assets

5.208 As discussed in paragraph 5.197 and FASB ASC 958-310-35-12, the value of a contribution receivable arising from an unconditional promise to give noncash assets other than equity securities with readily determinable fair values or debt securities may change between the date the unconditional promise to give is recognized and the date the asset promised is received because of changes in the future fair value of the underlying noncash assets. If, in a period subsequent to initial measurement, an observed change in the current fair value of the asset to be contributed occurs, that change in fair value may or may not result in changes in the future fair value of the underlying noncash asset, depending on the method and assumptions used for determining the future fair value of the underlying noncash asset.

5.209 As discussed in FASB ASC 958-310-35-12, for purposes of subsequent measurement, the method for determining the future fair value of the underlying noncash asset should be the same as the method used for determining that amount for purposes of initial measurement. (Paragraphs 5.193–.196 discuss the measurement principles for initial recognition of unconditional promises to give noncash assets, including consideration of the future fair value of the underlying asset.) Accordingly, assumed relationships, such as the relationship between the market price of the noncash asset at the time the initial measurement is made and its projected market price at the date the asset is expected to be received, should be presumed to continue in determining whether the future fair value of the underlying noncash asset has changed.

5.210 As discussed in paragraph 5.196, the fair value of an unconditional promise to give noncash assets may be based on the fair value of the underlying noncash asset at the date of initial recognition. If that method is used at initial measurement, for subsequent measurement, observed changes in the current fair value of the asset to be contributed should be treated as if they were changes in the fair value of contributions arising from unconditional promises to give noncash assets because of changes in the future fair value of the underlying asset. If that method is not used at initial measurement, for subsequent measurement, observed changes in the current fair value of the asset to be contributed may or may not result in changes in the future fair value of the underlying asset, and, therefore, may or may not result in changes in the fair value of contributions arising from unconditional promises to give noncash assets because of changes in the future fair value of the underlying asset.

5.211 As discussed in FASB ASC 958-310-35-13, if the future fair value of the underlying noncash asset (that is, other than equity securities with readily determinable fair values or debt securities) decreases, that decrease should be reported as a decrease in contribution revenue in the period(s) in which the decrease occurs. The decrease should be reported in the net asset class in which the contribution was originally reported or in the net asset class in which the net assets are represented. Thus, if a promise to give noncash assets is measured based on the fair value of those underlying noncash assets at the date of gift, as described in FASB ASC 958-605-30-8 (paragraph 5.196), an observed decrease in the current fair value of the underlying noncash asset should be recognized. If the future fair value of the underlying noncash asset increases between the date the unconditional promise to give is recognized and the date the asset promised is received, no additional revenue should be recognized.

Illustration

5.212 Table 5-5 reproduces the table in FASB ASC 958-310-55-1, which illustrates the accounting for changes in the value of unconditional promises to give subsequent to initial recognition, but before collection if those promises to give are not measured subsequently at fair value.

Table 5-5

Accounting for Unconditional Promises to Give That Are Not Measured Subsequently at Fair Value (Subsequent to Initial Recognition But Before Collection)

	Reason for the Change in Value			
Underlying Asset	*Change in Collectibility of the Receivable*		*Change in the Fair Value of the Underlying Asset*	
	Increase in Value	*Decrease in Value*	*Increase in Future Fair Value*	*Decrease in Future Fair Value*
Cash	No adjustment[a]	Recognize expense or loss (bad debt)	Not applicable	Not applicable
Securities[b]	No adjustment[a]	Recognize expense or loss (bad debt)	Recognize additional contribution revenue	Recognize a decrease in contribution revenue
Other assets	No adjustment[a]	Recognize expense or loss (bad debt)	No adjustment	Recognize a decrease in contribution revenue

[a] Recoveries of previously recognized decreases in value resulting from changes in estimates of collectibility (up to the amount of decreases previously recognized), however, should be recognized as reductions of bad debt expense or loss.

[b] For purposes of this table, *securities* are defined as equity securities with readily determinable fair values and all debt securities, consistent with the use of the terms in FASB *Accounting Standards Codification* 958-320.

Financial Statement Presentation

5.213 FASB ASC 958-605-45-1 states that resources received in exchange transactions should be classified as unrestricted revenues and net assets, even in circumstances in which resource providers place limitations on the use of the resources. For example, resources received from governments in exchange transactions in which those governments have placed limitations on the use of the resources should be reported as unrestricted revenues and net assets, because those limitations are not donor-imposed restrictions on contributions. (Classification of net assets is discussed further in paragraphs 5.75–.88; in chapter 3, "Financial Statements, the Reporting Entity, and General Financial Reporting Matters;" and in chapter 11, "Net Assets and Reclassifications of Net Assets.") Similar guidance applies to resources received from entities other than governments. For example, resources received from a manufacturer in an exchange transaction to test a potential product should be reported as unrestricted revenues and net assets, even if the manufacturer placed limitations on the use of the resources. Those limitations are not donor-imposed restrictions on contributions.

The "Pending Content" in FASB ASC 958-605-45-1 states that resources received in exchange transactions should be classified as revenues in the net assets without donor restrictions class, even in circumstances in which resource providers place limitations on the use of the resources. For example, resources received from governments in exchange transactions in which those governments have placed limitations on the use of the resources should be reported as revenues in the net assets without donor restrictions class, because those limitations are not donor-imposed restrictions on contributions. (Classification of net assets is discussed further in paragraphs 5.75–.88; in chapter 3, "Financial Statements, the Reporting Entity, and General Financial Reporting Matters;" and in chapter 11, "Net Assets and Reclassifications of Net Assets.") Similar guidance applies to resources received from entities other than governments. For example, resources received from a manufacturer in an exchange transaction to test a potential product should be reported as revenues in the net assets without donor restrictions class, even if the manufacturer placed limitations on the use of the resources. Those limitations are not donor-imposed restrictions on contributions.[57]

5.214 Contribution revenue may be reported as a separate line item on a statement of activities. However, this does not preclude reporting separate line items for government contracts, membership dues,[58] special events, or similar revenue sources in other revenue categories or in the notes to the financial statements.

5.215 As discussed in FASB ASC 958-310-45-1, contributions receivable should be reported net of the discount that arises if measuring a promise to give at present value. The discount should be separately disclosed by reporting it as a deduction from contributions receivable either on the face of a statement of financial position or in the notes to the financial statements. In accordance with FASB ASC 210-10-45-13, the valuation allowances for uncollectible contributions receivable should be deducted from the receivables account to which it relates. FASB ASC 958-310-50-2 states that the allowance for uncollectible promises to give does not include amounts determined to be uncollectible when the contributions receivable were initially measured. Thus, for the example

---

[57] The amendments in FASB ASU No. 2016-14 are effective for annual financial statements issued for fiscal years beginning after December 15, 2017 (for example, years ending December 31, 2018 and years ending June 30, 2019), and for interim periods within fiscal years beginning after December 15, 2018. Application to interim financial statements is permitted but not required in the initial year of application. Early application of the amendments is permitted.

[58] Accounting for the portion of membership dues that is an exchange transaction is different than accounting for the portion that is a contribution. Paragraphs 5.45–.47 discuss revenue recognition principles for membership dues.

in table 5-4, the notes to financial statements should disclose unconditional promises to give of $70 and unamortized discount of $20.

Disclosures

5.216 The majority of the disclosure requirements for contributions received and agency transactions are located in the "Disclosure" sections (sections 50) of FASB ASC 958-310 and FASB ASC 958-605. The following paragraphs discuss the more common of those disclosures, but are not a substitute for the "Disclosure" sections of FASB ASC.

5.217 The notes to financial statements should include information about the accounting policies adopted by the NFP, including the following:

- Whether the NFP implies time restrictions on the use of contributed long-lived assets (and contributions of cash and other assets restricted to purchasing them) received without donor stipulations about how long the contributed assets must be used. (Paragraphs 5.86–.88 provide guidance concerning the application of this policy.)
- Whether the NFP classifies donor-restricted contributions as unrestricted or restricted support if restrictions are satisfied in the same reporting period in which the contributions are received. (Paragraph 5.85 provides guidance concerning the application of this policy.)
- Whether the NFP recognizes contributions of collection items. (Chapter 7 provides guidance concerning the application of this policy.)
- Disclosure of how the NFP computes its fund-raising ratio if it includes that ratio in its financial statements, as described in FASB ASC 958-205-50-3.

The notes to financial statements should include information about the accounting policies adopted by the NFP, including the following:

- Whether the NFP classifies donor-restricted contributions as increases in net assets without donor restrictions or net assets with donor restrictions if restrictions are satisfied in the same reporting period in which the contributions are received (Paragraph 5.85 provides guidance concerning the application of this policy.)
- Whether the NFP recognizes contributions of collection items (Chapter 7 provides guidance concerning the application of this policy.)
- Disclosure of how the NFP computes its fund-raising ratio if it includes that ratio in its financial statements, as described in FASB ASC 958-205-50-3[59]

---

[59] The amendments in FASB ASU No. 2016-14 are effective for annual financial statements issued for fiscal years beginning after December 15, 2017 (for example, years ending December 31, 2018 and years ending June 30, 2019), and for interim periods within fiscal years beginning after December 15, 2018. Application to interim financial statements is permitted but not required in the initial year of application. Early application of the amendments is permitted.

5.218 The notes to financial statements should include the following information about contributions receivable:

- Contributions receivable pledged as collateral or otherwise limited with regard to use.
- A schedule of contributions receivable (showing the total amount separated into amounts receivable in less than one year, in one to five years, and in more than five years) and the related allowance for uncollectible contributions receivable arising from subsequent decreases due to changes in the quantity or nature of assets expected to be received (see paragraphs 5.204–.205), and the unamortized discount.
- The amount of conditional promises to give—in total and, with descriptions, the amount of each group of similar promises (for example, those conditioned upon the development of new programs, upon the purchase or construction of new property and equipment, and upon the raising of matching funds within a specified time period).
- Disclosures required by paragraphs 20–21 of FASB ASC 825-10-50 if an individual donor or groups of donors constitutes a significant concentration of credit risk arising from contributions receivable, unless those disclosures are optional because the three criteria of FASB ASC 825-10-50-3 are met.
- Disclosures required by paragraphs 1–3 of FASB ASC 820-10-50 in the format described in FASB ASC 820-10-50-8, if contributions receivable are subsequently measured at fair value.
- Disclosures required by FASB ASC 820-10-50-2E if unconditional promises to give are not measured at fair value in the statement of financial position but their fair value is disclosed (public entities only).
- Disclosures required by paragraphs 28–31 of FASB ASC 825-10-50, if contributions receivable are subsequently measured at fair value.
- Disclosures required by FASB ASC 825-10-50-32, if an election to report contributions receivable at fair value is made after initial recognition pursuant to FASB ASC 825-10-25-4(e).
- Disclosures required by FASB ASC 835-30-45 for imputation of interest.

5.219 The notes to financial statements should include the following disclosures concerning contributions of services received during the period:

- The nature and extent of contributed services received by the NFP
- A description of the programs or activities for which the services were used
- The amount of contributed services recognized during the period

NFPs are encouraged to report in the notes to the financial statements, if practical, the fair value of contributed services received but not recognized.

5.220 If an NFP transfers assets to a recipient entity and specifies itself or its affiliate as beneficiary, the NFP should disclose the following information for each period for which a statement of financial position is presented:

a. The identity of the recipient entity to which the transfer was made

b. Whether variance power was granted to the recipient entity and, if so, a description of the terms of the variance power

c. The terms under which amounts will be distributed to the resource provider or its affiliate

d. The aggregate amount recognized in the statement of financial position for those transfers and whether that amount is recorded as an interest in the net assets of the recipient entity or as another asset (for example, as a beneficial interest in assets held by others or a refundable advance)

5.221 Information about gifts-in-kind transactions may be required to be disclosed under FASB ASC 850. FinREC recommends that, in addition, NFPs with significant gift-in-kind activities disclose in the notes to the financial statements their accounting policies for gifts in kind; general sources of gifts in kind (such as governments, other NFPs, and private donors); as well as the gift-in-kind activity during the year, including the amount utilized by the NFP in its own programs and the amount donated to other NFPs. FinREC recommends that those disclosures include information about gifts in kind received from agency transactions, as well as gifts in kind received from contributions.

Illustrative Disclosures

5.222 The following section provides examples of notes to financial statements that illustrate some of the disclosures discussed in this chapter.

Example 1—Donor-Imposed Restrictions

Note X: Summary of Significant Accounting Policies

All contributions are considered to be available for unrestricted use unless specifically restricted by the donor. Amounts received that are designated for future periods or restricted by the donor for specific purposes are reported as temporarily restricted or permanently restricted support that increases those net asset classes. However, if a restriction is fulfilled in the same time period in which the contribution is received, the NFP reports the support as unrestricted.

All contributions are considered to be available for use at the discretion of the NFP unless specifically restricted by the donor. Amounts received that are designated for future periods or restricted by the donor for specific purposes are reported as donor-restricted support that increases the net assets with donor restrictions class. However, if a restriction is fulfilled in the same time period in which the contribution is received, the NFP reports the support as an increase in net assets without donor restrictions.[60]

Example 2—Promises to Give

Note X: Summary of Significant Accounting Policies

Unconditional promises to give that are expected to be collected within one year are recorded at net realizable value. Unconditional promises to give that are expected to be collected in future years are recorded

---

[60] The amendments in FASB ASU No. 2016-14 are effective for annual financial statements issued for fiscal years beginning after December 15, 2017 (for example, years ending December 31, 2018 and years ending June 30, 2019), and for interim periods within fiscal years beginning after December 15, 2018. Application to interim financial statements is permitted but not required in the initial year of application. Early application of the amendments is permitted.

at fair value, which is measured as the present value of their future cash flows. The discounts on those amounts are computed using risk-adjusted interest rates applicable to the years in which the promises are received. Amortization of the discounts is included in contribution revenue. Conditional promises to give are not included as support until the conditions are substantially met.

Note Y: Promises to Give

Included in "Contributions Receivable" are the following unconditional promises to give:

	20X1	*20X0*
Capital campaign	$1,220	
Restricted to future periods	795	$530
Unconditional promises to give before unamortized discount and allowance for uncollectibles	2,015	530
Less: Unamortized discount	(180)	(24)
Subtotal	1,835	506
Less: Allowance for uncollectibles	(150)	(30)
Net unconditional promises to give	$1,685	$476
Amounts due in:		
Less than one year	$1,220	
One to five years	725	
More than five years	70	
Total	$2,015	

Discount rates ranged from 4 percent to 4.5 percent and from 3.5 percent to 4 percent for 20X1 and 20X0, respectively.

In 20X0, the NFP received $650 for a capital campaign which must be returned if the NFP does not receive $1,300 in donations to the capital campaign. The $650 received was recorded on the 20X0 statement of financial position as a refundable advance. In 20X1, the NFP received $500 in cash donations and $865 in unconditional promises to give to this campaign. As a result, the $650 was recognized as a donor-restricted contribution in 20X1.

In addition, the NFP received the following conditional promises to give that are not recognized as assets in the statements of financial position:

	20X1	*20X0*
Conditional promise to give upon the establishment of a library program	$100	$100
Conditional promise to give upon obtaining $2,500 in unconditional promises to give to the capital campaign	5,000	

[*The following disclosure is encouraged but not required.*]

The NFP received an indication of an intention to give from an individual long-time donor. The anticipated gift is an extensive collection of pre-Columbian textiles with great historical and artistic significance. The value of this intended gift has not been established, nor has the gift been recognized as an asset or contribution revenue.

Example 3—Accounting Policy for Contributed Property and Equipment

Note X: Summary of Significant Accounting Policies

Contributed property and equipment is recorded at fair value at the date of donation. In the absence of donor stipulations regarding how long the contributed assets must be used, the NFP has adopted a policy of implying a time restriction on contributions of such assets that expires over the assets' useful lives. As a result, all contributions of property and equipment, and of assets contributed to acquire property and equipment, are recorded as restricted support.

OR

Contributed property and equipment is recorded at fair value at the date of donation. If donors stipulate how long the assets must be used, the contributions are recorded as restricted support. In the absence of such stipulations, contributions of property and equipment are recorded as unrestricted support.

Example 3 will be deleted upon the effective date of FASB ASU No. 2016-14.[61]

Example 4—Contributed Services

The NFP recognizes contribution revenue for certain services received at the fair value of those services. Those services include the following items:

	20X1	*20X0*
Home outreach program:		
Salaries:		
Social work interns—261 and 315 hours at $12.00 per hour	$3,132	$3,780
Registered nurse—200 and 220 hours at $15.00 per hour	3,000	3,300
Total salaries	6,132	7,080
Management and general:		
Accounting services	10,000	19,000
Total contributed services	$16,132	$26,080

[61] The amendments in FASB ASU No. 2016-14 are effective for annual financial statements issued for fiscal years beginning after December 15, 2017 (for example, years ending December 31, 2018 and years ending June 30, 2019), and for interim periods within fiscal years beginning after December 15, 2018. Application to interim financial statements is permitted but not required in the initial year of application. Early application of the amendments is permitted.

In addition, approximately 80,000 hours, for which no value has been assigned, were volunteered by tutors in the home outreach program.

Example 5—Beneficial Interest in Assets Held by Others

In 19XX, the NFP transferred $1,000,000 from its investment portfolio to the Any Town Community Foundation to establish an endowment fund. Under the terms of the agreement, in the first quarter of each year, the NFP receives a distribution equal to the investment return generated by the transferred assets during the prior year. The NFP can withdraw all or a portion of the original amount transferred, any appreciation on those transferred assets, or both, provided that a majority of the governing boards of the NFP and the Foundation approve of the withdrawal. At the time of the transfer, the NFP granted variance power to the Foundation. That power gives the Foundation the right to distribute the investment income to another not-for-profit entity of its choice if the NFP ceases to exist or if the governing board of Any Town Community Foundation votes that support of the NFP (*a*) is no longer necessary or (*b*) is inconsistent with the needs of the Any Town community. At June 30, 20X1, the endowment fund has a value of $1,234,567, which is reported in the statement of financial position as beneficial interest in assets held by others.

Example 6—Gifts in Kind Accounting Policy Note

Gifts in kind: The NFP receives gifts in kind, such as medical equipment, prescription drugs, and other medical supplies for use in treating disaster victims. Gifts in kind revenue is recognized in circumstances in which the NFP has sufficient discretion over the use and disposition of the items to recognize a contribution in conformity with FASB ASC 958-605-25. Accordingly, the recognition of gifts in kind revenue is limited to circumstances in which the NFP takes constructive possession of the gifts in kind and the NFP is the recipient of the gift, rather than an agent or intermediary (as defined by accounting standards). Gifts in kind received through donations are valued and recorded as revenue at their fair value at the time the contribution is received.

In circumstances in which the NFP is functioning as an agent or intermediary with respect to the gifts in kind, the NFP reports an asset and corresponding liability measured at the fair value at the earlier of the time the goods are promised or received from the resource provider, and until the NFP remits the gifts in kind to the ultimate beneficiary.

In circumstances in which the NFP distributes gifts in kind as part of its own programs, it reports an expense, which is reported in the functional classification for the program in which the gifts in kind were used. Although it is the NFP's policy to distribute gifts in kind as promptly as possible, the NFP may hold some gifts in kind at year-end. Undistributed gifts in kind at year-end are reported as inventory. Inventory is valued at the lower of cost or net realizable value (cost is determined as fair value at the date of gift plus any costs incurred).

Example 7—Gifts in Kind Inventory

	Medical Equipment	*Prescription Drugs*	*Other Medical Supplies*	*Total*
Undistributed gifts in kind inventory,				
Beginning of year	$10,000	$5,000	$15,000	$30,000
Gifts in kind:				
Donations	150,000	175,000	125,000	450,000
Agency transactions	50,000			50,000
Labor costs added			45,000	45,000
Obsolete inventory written off	(5,000)		(1,000)	(6,000)
Gifts in kind distributed:				
Used in NFP's programs	(40,000)	(80,000)	(115,000)	(235,000)
Distributed to other NFPs:				
Contributions	(75,000)	(90,000)	(40,000)	(205,000)
Agency transactions	(50,000)			(50,000)
Undistributed gifts in kind inventory,				
End of year	$ 40,000	$10,000	$29,000	$79,000

The donations were received from the following sources:

Source	*Total*	*Contribution*	*Agency Transactions*
U.S. Agency for International Development	$150,000	$100,000	$50,000
U.S. Department of Agriculture	25,000	25,000	
Total government	175,000	125,000	50,000
Private corporations	300,000	300,000	
Other NFPs	25,000	25,000	
Total donations	$500,000	$450,000	$50,000

Auditing

5.223 Because business entities do not usually receive contributions or enter into agency transactions, the specific audit objectives and auditing procedures, including consideration of controls, related to contributions, contributions receivable, and agency transactions are unique to NFPs and are presented in the following paragraphs.

5.224 An NFP that receives a significant amount of contributions may have an increased risk of material misstatement if it does not have proper internal controls. Paragraph .14 of AU-C section 315, *Understanding the Entity and Its Environment and Assessing the Risks of Material Misstatement*,[62] states

[62] All AU-C sections can be found in AICPA *Professional Standards*.

that when obtaining an understanding of controls that are relevant to the audit, the auditor should evaluate the design of those controls and determine whether they have been implemented by performing procedures in addition to inquiry of the entity's personnel. Evaluating the design of a control involves considering whether the control, individually or in combination with other controls, is capable of effectively preventing or detecting and correcting material misstatements. Implementation of a control means that the control exists and that the entity is using it. An improperly designed control may, individually or in combination with other design deficiencies, represent a significant deficiency or a material weakness in the entity's internal control. AU-C section 265, *Communicating Internal Control Related Matters Identified in an Audit*, describes the auditor's responsibility to appropriately communicate to those charged with governance and management certain deficiencies in internal control that the auditor has identified in an audit of financial statements.

5.225 An effective system of internal control for an NFP that receives significant amounts of contributions includes controls that ensure that all contributions received and contributions receivable are properly recorded, that revenues arising from conditional promises to give are recognized when the conditions have been substantially met, and that restrictions on contributions are recognized in the appropriate net asset class.

5.226 Contributions received are measured at fair value. AU-C section 540, *Auditing Accounting Estimates, Including Fair Value Accounting Estimates, and Related Disclosures*, addresses audit considerations relating to the measurement and disclosure of assets, liabilities and specific components of equity presented or disclosed at fair value in financial statements.

5.227 The following tables illustrate the use of assertions in developing audit objectives and designing substantive tests. The examples are not intended to be all-inclusive nor is it expected that all the procedures would necessarily be applied in an audit. The use of assertions in assessing risks and designing appropriate audit procedures to obtain audit evidence is described in paragraphs .26–.32 of AU-C section 315. Paragraph .18 of AU-C section 330, *Performing Audit Procedures in Response to Assessed Risks and Evaluating the Audit Evidence Obtained*, requires the auditor to design and perform substantive procedures for all relevant assertions related to each material class of transactions, account balance, and disclosure, irrespective of the assessed risks of material misstatement. This requirement reflects the facts that (1) the auditor's assessment of risk is judgmental and may not identify all risks of material misstatement, and (2) inherent limitations to internal control exist, including management override. Various audit procedures and the purposes for which they may be performed are described in paragraphs .A10–.A26 of AU-C section 500, *Audit Evidence*.

Auditing Considerations

Financial Statement Assertions	*Specific Audit Objectives*	*Select Control Objectives*
Contribution Transactions, in General		
Occurrence/ Existence	Amounts recognized as contribution revenues represent valid unconditional contributions.	Controls ensure that only unconditional contributions are recognized in the financial statements.

Auditing Considerations—*continued*

Financial Statement Assertions	*Specific Audit Objectives*	*Select Control Objectives*
Completeness	All unconditional contributions are recognized.	Controls ensure that all unconditional contributions are recognized in the financial statements. Controls ensure that revenue is recognized when the conditions on conditional promises to give have been substantially met.
Valuation and Allocation	Contribution revenues are appropriately valued.	Controls ensure the appropriate valuation of contribution revenue at the time of initial recognition.
Cut-off	Contributions are reported in the period in which they were given.	Controls ensure that contributions occurring near fiscal period end are recorded in the proper period.
Classification and understandability	Contributions are reported in the proper net asset class. Disclosures related to contributions are clear and understandable.	Contributions are reviewed for restrictions and other limitations. Controls ensure that contributions are appropriately presented and disclosed.
Noncash Contributions		
Occurrence; Completeness; Valuation and allocation	Assets, expenses, and revenues from contributed services, utilities, facilities, and use of long-lived assets meet the appropriate recognition criteria; all such contributions that meet the recognition criteria are recognized and appropriately measured.	Controls ensure that only contributed services, utilities, facilities, and use of long-lived assets that meet the appropriate recognition criteria are recognized; controls ensure that all such contributions that meet the recognition criteria are recognized and appropriately measured.

5.228 Suggested audit procedures to consider for cash and noncash contributions include the following:

- Examine documentation supporting recognition of contribution revenues noting information such as whether the donor imposed any conditions or restrictions or whether the NFP might be acting as an agent. (Rights and Obligations; Occurrence/Existence; Classification)
- Select from data accumulated and maintained by the fund-raising function, and determine whether a contribution should have been recognized and, if so, vouch it to a recognized contribution, investigating reconciling items. (Completeness)
- Review and test the methods and assumptions used to measure contribution revenue at the time of initial recognition. (Valuation)

- Examine contributions reported before and after fiscal period end to determine if they are reported in the appropriate period. (Cut-off)
- Review the documentation underlying contributions and promises to give (including donor correspondence and governing board minutes) for propriety of classification. (Classification and Understandability)
- Determine the appropriateness of disclosures for conditional and unconditional promises to give. (Completeness, Classification and Understandability)
- Inquire of management, read the governing board minutes or other minutes, searching for contributions or contributions receivable. Particular focus should be on related party contributions, including those from board members and management. (Completeness, Classification, Existence, Valuation)
- Consider the tests for expiration of restrictions in the auditing section of chapter 11. Determine whether classification of contributions is consistent with the NFP's policy if restrictions are met in the same period as contributions are received (as described in paragraph 5.85). (Classification)

5.229 Given the wide range and types of contributed services, utilities, facilities, use of long-lived assets and gifts in kind transactions, thoughtful assessment of the risk of material misstatement and evaluation of the sources of possible audit evidence to support the existence and valuation assertions are necessary in order to design appropriate and effective audit procedures.

Contributed Services, Facilities, or Utilities

5.230 In addition to those possible procedures identified in paragraph 5.228, suggested audit procedures to consider include the following:

- Through inquiry, determine if the NFP receives contributed services (for example, discounted or free legal services), facilities, utilities, or use of long-lived assets. (Occurrence/Existence)
- If the NFP receives contributed services, examine supporting documentation for the recognition of contributed services and determine that the services meet the recognition criteria in FASB ASC 958-605-25-16 (paragraph 5.112). (Rights and Obligations, Completeness)
- Review and test the assumptions used to measure and value contributed services. (Valuation)
- Determine that the costs incurred to induce donors to contribute services (regardless of whether those services meet the recognition criteria) are classified as fund-raising expenses by the NFP. (Allocation)
- Consider if any specific disclosure is required. For example, if an NFP has land and buildings leased at a below market rate, it may want to disclose how the transaction is recorded. (Completeness)

5.231 Some NFPs rely heavily on substantial amounts of contributed services, such as docents at a museum or volunteers at a call-in center. Although these services may not meet the criteria allowing recognition in the financial statements, the NFP may want to disclose the level of effort and value of the contributed services in the notes to the financial statements. If the NFP maintains sufficiently detailed time records of the volunteer effort that the auditor could test, the hours contributed could be disclosed. Otherwise those disclosures would be marked as unaudited. A value would be assigned based on the work performed, rather than based on the individual performing the work. For example, if an attorney provides administrative services, the value would be based on the administrative services value not the attorney's standard billing rate.

Contributed Property and Equipment

> © **Update 5-3 *Accounting and Reporting*: Leases**
>
> FASB ASU No. 2016-02, issued February 2016, changes the accounting for leases, primarily by the recognition of lease assets and lease liabilities by lessees for those leases classified as operating leases under current GAAP. FASB ASU No. 2016-02 is effective for fiscal years beginning after December 15, 2018, including interim periods within those fiscal years, for NFPs that have issued, or are conduit bond obligors for, securities that are traded, listed, or quoted on an exchange or an over-the-counter market. For all other NFPs, the amendments in this FASB ASU are effective for fiscal years beginning after December 15, 2019, and interim periods within fiscal years beginning after December 15, 2020. Early adoption is permitted.
>
> This edition of the guide has not been updated to reflect changes as a result of this FASB ASU; however, the section that follows will be updated in a future edition. Readers are encouraged to consult the full text of the FASB ASU on FASB's website at www.fasb.org.

5.232 In addition to those possible procedures identified in paragraph 5.228, suggested audit procedures to consider include the following:

- Review management's process for identifying contributed property and equipment. (Completeness)
- Be alert to the identification of contributed property and equipment while performing other audit procedures, such as the review of minutes and lease agreements and test of controls over contributions. (Completeness)
- Verify that contributions of property and equipment are properly recognized at fair value at the date of contribution. (Valuation)
- Verify that assets are properly classified based upon any restrictions on contributed property and equipment. Review donor correspondence and the NFP's accounting policies for contributions of long-lived assets. For further information about those policies, see paragraphs 5.86–.88. (Allocation)
- If the donor retains legal title to contributed facilities, verify that the NFP is recording contribution revenue and expense in the period received and used. The receipt of multiyear commitments to provide contributed facilities is recorded similar to a multiyear contribution receivable or a capital lease. Verify that the amount recognized as contributions revenue at the date the contributed

facilities are recognized does not exceed the fair value of the underlying long-lived asset at that date. For further information, see paragraphs 5.164–.166. (Completeness, Valuation)

Gifts in Kind Transactions

5.233 Some NFPs receive substantial amounts of donated gifts in kind such as pharmaceuticals, agricultural equipment, medical equipment, and so forth. The auditor's risk assessment depends on the particular facts and circumstances, including the following:

- The significance of the gifts in kind to the financial statements
- The nature and complexity of the valuation of the gifts in kind (for example, pharmaceuticals that are not approved by the U.S. Food and Drug Administration [FDA] may be more difficult to value than FDA-approved pharmaceuticals)
- The nature and extent of management's processes and related internal controls associated with valuation of gifts in kind, including their experience with such transactions
- The nature and extent of information available to management to support its valuation process and valuation conclusions

5.234 Auditors could review the historical patterns of the distribution of gifts in kind and determine the extent of the NFP's discretion over those distributions. As explained in paragraphs 5.07–.32, the extent of discretion that the NFP has over the assets received determines whether the incoming gifts in kind are classified as contributions or as agency transactions.

5.235 These transactions typically result in the NFP recording substantial amounts of revenue and a corresponding program service expense; therefore, it is important for the auditor to obtain an understanding of how the NFP has assessed the fair value of the donated goods. If the NFP utilizes a pricing service or pricing guide, the auditor may need to obtain evidence that the values provided by the service or guide are supportable and verifiable values determined in accordance with the guidance in FASB ASC 820. If the NFP has any undistributed or in-transit gifts in kind in inventory at the end of the fiscal year, it is typically necessary to perform tests of the inventory unless the risks of material misstatement are at an acceptably low level.

5.236 For the purpose of assessing risk, when an NFP receives a significant number of individual gifts-in-kind transactions, the auditor may need to group the gifts in kind based on similar characteristics, valuation processes, or both. The auditor often obtains sufficient appropriate audit evidence for the valuation assertions associated with gifts in kind from observable market prices (for example, from recent sales or purchase transactions).

Contributions Receivable

5.237 Paragraph .20 of AU-C section 330 states that the auditor should use external confirmation procedures for accounts receivable except under certain specified circumstances. Paragraph .A55 of AU-C section 330 defines *accounts receivable* as (*a*) the entity's claims against customers that have arisen from the sale of goods or services in the normal course of business, and (*b*) a financial institution's loans. Though under that definition contributions receivable are not accounts receivable to which that presumption would apply, the auditor may nevertheless determine that it is appropriate to request external confirmation of contributions receivable.

5.238 Receivables are usually confirmed principally to provide evidence about the existence assertion. FASB ASC 958-605-25-8 specifies that for a promise to give to be recognized in financial statements, there must be sufficient evidence in the form of verifiable documentation that a promise was made and received. If the documentation is not present, an asset should not be recognized. The verifiable documentation for recognition of promises to give may not be sufficient evidence concerning the existence assertion. Confirming contributions receivable may provide additional evidence about the existence of promises to give, the existence or absence of restrictions, the existence or absence of conditions, and the periods over which the promises to give become due. If the auditor confirms contributions receivable, AU-C section 505, *External Confirmations*, provides requirements and guidance concerning the external confirmation process.

Auditing Considerations

Financial Statement Assertions	*Specific Audit Objectives*	*Select Control Objectives*
Account Balances		
Occurrence/ Existence	Amounts recognized as contributions receivable represent valid unconditional promises to give.	Controls ensure that only unconditional promises to give are recognized in the financial statements.
Completeness	All unconditional promises to give are recognized.	Controls ensure that all unconditional promises to give are recognized in the financial statements. Controls ensure that conditional promises to give are recognized when the conditions have been substantially met.
Valuation and Allocation	Contributions receivable are appropriately valued.	Controls ensure the appropriate valuation of promises to give at the time of initial recognition. The valuation of promises to give is periodically reviewed by management. Write-offs of uncollectible promises to give are identified and approved in accordance with the entity's established policy.

5.239 Suggested audit procedures to consider include the following:

- Inquire of management (including development office) and members of governance regarding the existence of oral promises to give. (Existence/Occurrence)

- Review the reconciliation of the development office's listing of receivables to that recorded in the general ledger. (Completeness)
- Examine documentation supporting recognition of promises to give, noting information such as absence of conditions or restrictions and the periods over which the promises to give become due. (Existence/Occurrence, Rights and Obligations)
- Consider confirmation, as discussed in paragraphs 5.237–.238. (Existence)
- If confirmation is not performed, test contributions receivable by vouching subsequent receipts or other alternative procedures. (Existence)
- Compare detail of contributions receivable with data accumulated and maintained by the fund-raising function and investigate reconciling items. (Completeness)
- Review and test the methods and assumptions used to measure promises to give at fair value at the time of initial recognition. (Valuation)
- Review promises to give for collectibility, and, if appropriate, changes in fair value of the underlying asset. (Valuation)

Agency Transactions

Auditing Considerations

Financial Statement Assertions	***Specific Audit Objectives***	***Select Control Objectives***
Account Balances		
Occurrence/Existence and Completeness	Assets and liabilities from agency transactions meet the criteria for classification and recognition as agency transactions. All agency transactions are recognized.	Controls ensure that (1) only resources received and paid in agency transactions are recognized as agency transactions and (2) all such transactions are recognized.
Presentation and Disclosures		
Rights and obligations	Agency transactions are not included in reported amounts of contributions.	Controls ensure that agency transactions are identified and are not included in contribution totals.

5.240 Suggested audit procedures to consider include the following:

- Obtain solicitation materials. Review for donor expectations based on representations within those materials of whether gifts will be transferred to a beneficiary specified by the donor, as described in paragraphs 5.10–.13. (Rights and Obligations)

- Review the documentation underlying the receipt of assets from resource providers for propriety of classification and recognition as resources that are to be transferred to others. (Occurrence/Existence; Completeness; Rights and Obligations)
- Review the documentation underlying the distribution of assets to others for propriety of classification and recognition. (Occurrence, Rights and Obligations)
- Review the historical patterns of the distribution of gifts in kind and determine the extent of the NFP's discretion over those distributions, and whether the incoming gifts in kind should be classified as contributions or agency transactions. As explained in paragraphs 5.07–.32, the extent of discretion that the NFP has over the assets received determines whether the incoming gifts are classified as contributions or as agency transactions. (Rights and Obligations)
- Determine whether agency transactions are excluded from the statement of activities. If they are not, determine that agency transactions are reported as described in the "Transfers of Assets to a Not-for-Profit Entity or Charitable Trust that Raises or Holds Contributions for Others" subsections of FASB ASC 958-605. (Classification and Understandability)

5.241

Appendix A—Excerpt From AICPA Financial Reporting White Paper *Measurement of Fair Value for Certain Transactions of Not-for-Profit Entities*[1]

A-1 Not-for-profit entities face various challenges in applying the provisions of Financial Accounting Standards Board *Accounting Standards Codification* 820, *Fair Value Measurement*, in part because markets do not exist for certain assets and liabilities. To assist practitioners, on October 14, 2011, the AICPA issued the white paper Measurement of Fair Value for Certain Transactions of Not-for-Profit Entities. The following excerpt provides assistance for measuring unconditional promises to give cash or other financial assets due in one year or more.

Unconditional Promises to Give Cash

1. Financial Accounting Standards Board (FASB) *Accounting Standards Codification* (ASC) 958-605,[2] in discussing measurement principles for contributions, generally requires not-for-profit entities (NFPs) to measure at fair value recognized contributions of cash or other assets (for example, marketable securities, land, buildings, use of facilities or utilities, materials and supplies, other goods or services) and unconditional promises to give those items in the future.

2. The discussion of fair value measurements in FASB ASC 820-10-35 includes an exit price approach (that is, the price that would be received for a promise to give [asset] in an exchange involving hypothetical market participants, determined under current market conditions). Because no market exists for unconditional promises to give, assumptions about what a hypothetical acquirer would pay for these assets (the right to receive from the donor the cash flow inherent in the promise) are necessary in determining fair value. FASB ASC 820-10-35 and its interpretive guidance in FASB ASC 820-10-55 emphasize that because fair value is a market-based (not an entity-specific) measurement, the exit price is determined without regard to whether an entity intends to sell or hold an asset or a liability that is measured at fair value.

3. Paragraphs 4–32 address the application of FASB ASC 820-10-35 in determining the fair value of a promise to give cash at a date one year or more in the future. This white paper does not discuss the fair value of a promise to give nonfinancial assets. It also does not discuss how to determine the fair value of unconditional promises to give that are due in less than one year. As explained in FASB ASC 958-605-30-6, unconditional promises to give that are expected to be collected in less than one year may be measured at net realizable value because that amount results in a reasonable estimate of fair value.

---

[1] As a benefit of AICPA membership, all AICPA members can access the AICPA White Paper *Measurement of Fair Value for Certain Transactions of Not-for-Profit Entities* at www.aicpa.org/interestareas/frc/industryinsights/pages/fv_and_disclosures_nfp.aspx.

[2] Pursuant to Financial Accounting Standards Board (FASB) Statement No. 168, *The* FASB Accounting Standards Codification *and the Hierarchy of Generally Accepted Accounting Principles—a replacement of FASB Statement No. 162*, FASB *Accounting Standards Codification* (ASC) is the sole source of authoritative generally accepted accounting principles. To aid readers in using this white paper, as a drafting convention in referencing FASB ASC, this white paper sometimes references pronouncements that were issued prior to the effective date of FASB ASC and from which the FASB ASC paragraphs are derived.

What Is the Unit of Account for an Unconditional Promise to Give That Is Expected to Be Collected in One Year or More?

4. For an unconditional promise to give that is expected to be collected in one year or more, the unit of account implied in FASB ASC 958-605 is the individual (stand-alone) promise to give.[3] That means that the focus of the fair value measurement is on the individual (stand-alone) promise to give in which the exit price represents the amount that a hypothetical market participant would pay to acquire the right to receive from the donor the cash flows inherent in the promise to pay the NFP. The Financial Reporting Executive Committee (FinREC) believes that, consistent with the guidance in FASB ASC 820-10-35-17 on the measurement of the fair value of liabilities, it is appropriate to assume when measuring the fair value of a promise to give that the cash flows received by the hypothetical acquirer would be the same as the cash flows that would be received by the NFP and that no additional credit risk needs to be considered as a result of a hypothetical change in ownership.

What Valuation Technique(s) Should an NFP Use to Measure the Fair Value of an Unconditional Promise to Give That Is Expected to Be Collected in One Year or More?

5. FASB ASC 820-10-35-24A provides that valuation techniques consistent with the market approach, income approach, cost approach, or all three should be used to measure fair value. Paragraphs 3A–3G of FASB ASC 820-10-55 explain those valuation techniques.

6. FASB ASC 820-10-35-24 clarifies that "[a] reporting entity shall use valuation techniques that are appropriate in the circumstances and for which sufficient data are available to measure fair value, maximizing the use of relevant observable inputs and minimizing the use of unobservable inputs." For an unconditional promise to give that is expected to be collected in one year or more, FinREC believes that a present value (PV) technique (an application of the income approach) will be the most prevalent valuation technique used to measure fair value. In reaching that conclusion, FinREC observes that the market approach typically would not be operational for measuring the fair value of unconditional promises to give cash because no market exists, and the cost approach is not used for valuing financial assets, such as promises to give.

PV Techniques

7. Paragraphs 4–20 of FASB ASC 820-10-55 discuss PV techniques. FASB ASC 820-10-55-5 states that

> [p]resent value (that is, an application of the income approach) is a tool used to link future amounts (for example, cash flows or values) to a present amount using a discount rate. A fair value measurement of an asset or a liability using a present value technique captures all of the following elements from the perspective of market participants at the measurement date:
>
> a. An estimate of future cash flows for the asset or liability being measured.

[3] In practice, some not-for-profit entities (NFPs) have pooled unconditional promises to give with certain similar characteristics. The Financial Reporting Executive Committee (FinREC) believes that such pooling is permissible in circumstances in which the measurement of fair value would not be materially different from a measurement that considers each unconditional promise to give as the unit of account.

b. Expectations about possible variations in the amount and timing of the cash flows representing the uncertainty inherent in the cash flows.

c. The time value of money, represented by the rate on risk-free monetary assets that have maturity dates or durations that coincide with the period covered by the cash flows and pose neither uncertainty in timing nor risk of default to the holder (that is, a risk-free interest rate). For present value computations denominated in nominal U.S. dollars, the yield curve for U.S. Treasury securities determines the appropriate risk-free interest rate.

d. The price for bearing the uncertainty inherent in the cash flows (that is, a risk premium).

e. Other factors that market participants would take into account in the circumstances.

f. For a liability, the nonperformance risk relating to that liability, including the reporting entity's (that is, the obligor's) own credit risk.

8. Risk and uncertainty associated with the amount, timing, or both, of cash flows of an asset (or a liability) are key considerations when measuring fair value because risk-averse market participants would demand compensation for bearing the uncertainty inherent in the cash flows (the risk premium).[4] Paragraphs 7–8 of FASB ASC 820-10-55 explain that

> [a] fair value measurement using present value techniques is made under conditions of uncertainty because the cash flows used are estimates rather than known amounts. In many cases, both the amount and timing of the cash flows are uncertain. Even contractually fixed amounts, such as the payments on a loan, are uncertain if there is risk of default.
>
> Market participants generally seek compensation (that is, a risk premium) for bearing the uncertainty inherent in the cash flows of an asset or a liability. A fair value measurement should include a risk premium reflecting the amount that market participants would demand as compensation for the uncertainty inherent in the cash flows. Otherwise, the measurement would not faithfully represent fair value. In some cases, determining the appropriate risk premium might be difficult. However, the degree of difficulty alone is not a sufficient reason to exclude a risk premium.

9. FinREC observes that the requisite risk assessment requires judgments and that those judgments are significant in some cases. In making that assessment, consistent with FASB ASC 820-10-35-54A, FinREC believes that an NFP need not undertake exhaustive efforts to obtain information from or about the donor.

---

[4] The FASB ASC glossary term *promise to give* notes that "the recipient of a promise to give has a right to expect that the promised assets will be transferred in the future, and the maker has a social and moral obligation, and generally a legal obligation, to make the promised transfer." As noted in paragraph 108 of FASB Statement No. 116, *Accounting for Contributions Received and Contributions Made*, in developing FASB Statement No. 116, FASB found that although legal remedies are available, they are seldom necessary because promises generally are kept. FinREC believes, however, that in many (if not most) cases, uncertainty will exist; therefore, it will be necessary to consider risk in a fair value measurement.

Rather, the NFP would assess the risk associated with the promise to give using information that is reasonably available in the circumstances, considering factors specific to the donor and promise to give. FinREC believes that those factors may include, but are not limited to, the following:

- The ability of the donor to pay (credit risk), which may be indicated by published credit ratings (for example, a credit rating might be available for an enterprise that is a donor or comparable to the donor); financial analysis (for example, cash flow and ratio analysis); or credit reports for an individual donor
- Factors specific to the donor that might be relevant in assessing the donor's commitment to honor its promise, such as the extent to which the donor is committed to, or otherwise involved in, the activities of the NFP (for example, whether the donor is a member of the governing board); the donor's history of charitable giving and involvement with charitable organizations, including, but not limited to, the NFP; and the donor's financial circumstances and history (past bankruptcies or defaults); financial condition (including other debt); current employment (including its stability); earnings potential over the term of the promise; and personal circumstances (including family situation, age, and health)
- Risk factors that affect certain groups of donors (for example, economic conditions in certain geographical areas or industry sectors)
- The NFP's prior experience in collecting similar types of promises to give, including the extent to which the NFP has enforced the promises
- Whether the underlying asset is held in an irrevocable trust or escrow, which may reduce default risk

10. FASB ASC 820-10-55 discusses two PV techniques: (*a*) the traditional or discount rate adjustment (DRA) technique and (*b*) the expected PV (EPV) technique, which may be applied using one of two methods. Those PV techniques differ in how they adjust for risk. Key differences are summarized in the following table:

	DRA	*EPV Method 1*	*EPV Method 2*
Cash Flows	Single set of cash flows (contractual or promised, most likely).[5]	Expected (probability-weighted) cash flows (or expected value), adjusted for general market (systematic) risk by subtracting the cash risk premium. The risk-adjusted expected cash flows represent a certainty-equivalent cash flow.	Expected (probability-weighted) cash flows (or expected value).
	The single set of cash flows are conditional cash flows (in other words, contractual or promised cash flows are conditional on the event of no default by the debtor).	The risk-adjusted expected cash flows are not conditional upon the occurrence of specific events because they are probability weighted.	The expected cash flows are not conditional upon the occurrence of specific events because they are probability weighted.
Discount Rate	Risk-adjusted discount rate derived from observed rates of return for comparable assets or liabilities that are traded in the market (that is, a market rate of return that corresponds to an observed market rate associated with such conditional cash flows and that, therefore, represents the amount that market participants would demand for bearing the uncertainty inherent in such cash flows).	Risk-free interest rate (for example, yield to maturity on U.S. Treasuries).	Risk-free interest rate (for example, yield to maturity on U.S. Treasuries), adjusted for general market (systematic) risk by adding risk premium. The risk-adjusted discount rate represents the expected rate of return that corresponds to an expected rate associated with such probability-weighted cash flows.

What Are Some of the Key Issues That an NFP Should Consider in Determining Which PV Technique to Use to Measure the Fair Value of an Unconditional Promise to Give That Is Expected to Be Collected in One Year or More?

11. Conceptually, the three PV methods discussed in the chart in the previous paragraph should give the same results. FinREC observes that in practice,

[5] Such nonprobability-weighted cash flows are referred to in this white paper as projected cash flows to distinguish them from expected cash flows, which are probability weighted.

however, certain techniques may be easier, more practical, or more appropriate to apply to certain facts and circumstances. FASB ASC 820-10-55-4 states that the "present value technique used to measure fair value will depend on facts and circumstances specific to the asset or liability being measured (for example, whether prices for comparable assets or liabilities can be observed in the market) and the availability of sufficient data."

12. A DRA technique using promised cash flows and observable market rates that reflect expectations about future defaults may be easier to apply at initial recognition than the EPV techniques, which require an NFP to probability weight the cash flows or estimate the systematic risk premium. However, to account for the unconditional promises to give in subsequent periods, the NFP must be able to identify when the level of defaults on its promises surpasses the level incorporated in the discount rate that it used for initial recognition, so that it can recognize an allowance for uncollectible promises on a timely basis if the actual uncollectible amounts exceed the amounts originally projected. This can be particularly challenging if the discount rate used is a market rate for which the level of default incorporated in the rate is not publicly available. The use of most likely cash flows, rather than promised cash flows, and a discount rate that is consistent with those cash flows will mitigate some of the challenges for subsequent measurement. That DRA technique is discussed in the next paragraph.

13. Although it might appear that the DRA technique may be easy to apply because it does not require an NFP to probability weight the cash flows or estimate the systematic risk premium, as required by the EPV technique, FinREC observes that the DRA technique using promised cash flows may be impractical to apply. FinREC observes that if an NFP uses the DRA technique with promised cash flows, it must use a discount rate that reflects expectations about future defaults, and the NFP must be able to identify when the level of defaults on its unconditional promises to give surpasses the level incorporated in the discount rate it used. This is particularly challenging if the discount rate used is a market rate, such as for unsecured borrowings in which the level of default incorporated in the rate is typically not available. If the NFP does not identify the level of defaults incorporated in the discount rate, it would be unable to timely report a credit impairment loss when the actual uncollectible amounts exceed the amounts originally projected. Thus, the benefit of avoiding the calculation of probability-weighted cash flows on initial measurement (if using the DRA technique with promised cash flows) would be substantially negated by the fact that the NFP would nevertheless have to estimate the cash flows initially expected when determining the allowance for doubtful accounts in subsequent measurements.[6]

14. A DRA technique that uses most likely cash flows (rather than promised cash flows) might be practical to apply because the cash flows initially projected are known, but that technique requires the NFP to use a discount rate that reflects market participant assumptions that are consistent with risks inherent in most likely cash flows to avoid double counting or omitting the effects of risk factors. As explained in paragraph 19, the discount rate would be higher

---

[6] The discussion in paragraphs 12–14 assumes that the NFP does not elect to report contributions receivable pursuant to an election under FASB ASC 825, *Financial Instruments*. Instead, the discussion assumes that an NFP initially measures contributions receivable at fair value using present value techniques, which then is used as cost. In subsequent periods, that cost is amortized, with the interest element reported as additional contribution revenue, and a valuation allowance is reported to reflect credit impairment occurring after initial measurement.

than the risk-free rate used in EPV method 1 or the discount rate used in EPV method 2 because most likely cash flows are uncertain, but the discount rate would be lower than the discount rate used with promised cash flows because some of the uncertainty of promised cash flows is removed in the determination of most likely cash flows. Because the three PV techniques trade off the ease of determining a discount rate against the ease of determining the cash flows, FinREC observes that no one PV technique is inherently better than another for measuring unconditional promises to give.

15. FinREC observes that in estimating fair value, an entity is not precluded from using fair value estimates provided by third parties, such as valuation specialists, in circumstances in which a reporting entity has determined that the estimates provided by those parties are determined in accordance with FASB ASC 820-10-35. For example, in using a PV technique, valuation specialists may be helpful in determining a discount rate that is consistent with the cash flows used.

What Are the Key Pricing Inputs When Using a PV Technique?

16. Key pricing inputs should reflect the factors that market participants would consider in setting a price for the promise to give. The FASB ASC 820-10-35 fair value hierarchy prioritizes market observable inputs but also allows for the use of unobservable (internally derived) inputs when relevant market observable inputs are unavailable. When using a PV technique, two key pricing inputs are the cash flows and discount rate. The factors considered in determining the cash flows and discount rate used should be documented.

17. As noted in FASB ASC 820-10-55-6(c), to avoid double counting or omitting the effects of risk factors, discount rates should reflect assumptions that are consistent with those inherent in the cash flows. For example, a discount rate that reflects the uncertainty in expectations about future defaults is appropriate if using contractual cash flows of a loan. That same rate should not be used if using expected (that is, probability-weighted) cash flows because the expected cash flows already reflect assumptions about the uncertainty of future defaults.

18. The cash flows used in a PV technique differ depending on the method used. Following is an illustration of cash flow estimates under the three methods (DRA, EPV method 1, and EPV method 2). Assume that an NFP holds a promise to give $100 in one year. The NFP believes that there is a 70 percent chance that it will collect the full amount, a 20 percent chance that it will collect $80, and a 10 percent chance that it will collect nothing. Under EPV method 2, expected cash flow would be calculated as follows:

$100 × 70% =	$70
$80 × 20% =	$16
$0 × 10% =	$0
	$86

Under EPV method 1, the expected cash flow would be less than $86 because it would be adjusted (reduced) for systematic risk. Because of the challenges in determining an adjustment for systematic risk, utilization of EPV method 1 may not be practical. Under the DRA technique, both the promised cash flow and most likely cash flow are $100.

19. FASB ASC 820-10-55-6 discusses general principles for determining the discount rate when applying PV techniques. FinREC believes that the discount rate used would fall on a continuum between the risk-free rate (minimum) and unsecured borrowing rate (maximum).

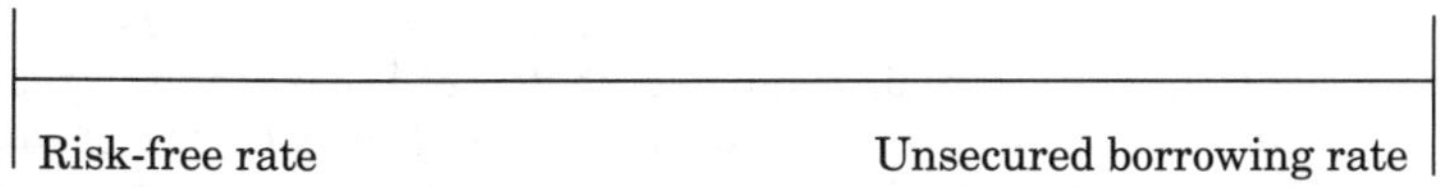

Where the rate falls on the continuum would depend on the extent to which risk factors such as those discussed in paragraph 9 have been incorporated into the projected cash flows. (The lowest discount rate would be used for EPV method 1, and the highest discount rate would be used for the DRA technique using contractual cash flows,[7] as discussed in paragraphs 21–32.) The relationship between cash flows and discount rates is depicted as follows:

This diagram depicts the inverse relationship between risks being incorporated in projected cash flows and risks being incorporated in discount rates (that is, the discount rate increases as projected cash flows incorporate fewer risk factors and vice versa).

EPV Method 1

20. When using EPV method 1, the risk-adjusted expected cash flows are discounted by the risk-free interest rate, which may be indicated by the yield to maturity on U.S. Treasuries. The risk-free interest rate is appropriate in this case because all risk is built into the expected cash flows, which therefore represent a certainty-equivalent cash flow. As discussed in FASB ASC 820-10-55-15, EPV method 1 adjusts the expected cash flows for the systematic (market) risk by subtracting a cash risk premium in arriving at risk-adjusted expected cash flows. However, as previously discussed, determining a certainty-equivalent cash flow typically would be impracticable for unconditional promises to give.

EPV Method 2

21. When using EPV method 2, the expected cash flows are discounted by a risk-adjusted rate, which is determined based on the risk-free interest rate, adjusted for general market (systematic) risk by adding a risk premium.

22. In EPV method 2, some but not all risk is built into the expected cash flows. The expected cash flows are probability weighted and, therefore, adjusted for the likelihood of possible outcomes affecting the timing and amount of the

[7] For an unconditional promise to give, the contractual cash flows are the amounts promised by the donor, which are referred to as promised cash flows in this white paper.

cash flows. Probability weighting is not enough, however. It is also necessary to adjust for the risk premium that market participants would seek for accepting uncertainty. The following example illustrates this point:

> Asset B is a *certain* undiscounted cash flow of $10,000 due 10 years hence (a U.S. Treasury instrument is an example of asset B). Asset E has an *expected* undiscounted cash flow of $10,000 due 10 years hence; however, the actual cash flow from asset E may be as high as $12,000 or as low as $8,000 or some other amount within that range. A risk-averse individual would pay something less for asset E than asset B because of the uncertainty involved. Although the expected cash flow of $10,000 incorporates the uncertainty in cash flows from asset E, that amount does not incorporate the premium that market participants demand for bearing that uncertainty.

23. In EPV method 2, the compensation that market participants would seek for accepting uncertainty (the risk premium) is built into the discount rate. The risk-adjusted discount rate represents an expected rate of return that corresponds to an expected rate associated with such probability-weighted cash flows.

DRA

24. When using the DRA technique, the projected cash flows are discounted by a risk-adjusted rate. As discussed in FASB ASC 820-10-55-10

> the [DRA] technique uses a single set of cash flows from the range of possible estimated amounts, whether contractual or promised (as is the case for a bond) or most likely cash flows. In all cases, those cash flows are conditional upon the occurrence of specified events (for example, contractual or promised cash flows for a bond are conditional on the event of no default by the debtor).

25. The risk-adjusted discount rate used in the DRA technique is derived from observed rates of return for comparable assets or liabilities that are traded in the market. Accordingly, the contractual, promised, or most likely cash flows are discounted at an observed or estimated market rate for such conditional cash flows (that is, a market rate of return). Therefore, it represents the amount that market participants would demand for bearing the uncertainty inherent in such cash flows. In circumstances in which the projected cash flows already reflect assumptions about future defaults, NFPs should apply a discount rate that is commensurate with the reduced risk inherent in the cash flows that anticipate defaults, in order to avoid double counting that credit risk, as discussed in FASB ASC 820-10-55-6.

26. Determining the observed rate of return for comparable assets that are traded in the market requires an analysis of market data for comparable assets. FASB ASC 820-10-55-11 explains that "[c]omparability is established by considering the nature of the cash flows (for example, whether the cash flows are contractual or noncontractual and are likely to respond similarly to changes in economic conditions), as well as other factors (for example, credit standing, collateral, duration, restrictive covenants, and liquidity)." As a basis for assessing comparability, FinREC believes that best practice is for the NFP to assess the likelihood that the donor will not honor its promise to give (default risk), as well as the risk premium reflecting the amount that market participants would demand because of the risk (uncertainty) in the cash flows.[8]

27. Market comparable data that might be relevant in determining the risk-adjusted discount rate used in the DRA technique will differ depending on the donor (for example, whether the donor is an individual, a corporation, or a foundation). Some examples follow.

28. If the donor is an individual, FinREC believes that the risk-adjusted discount rate might be determined using unsecured consumer lending rates that are generally available from published sources (major financial institutions). FinREC believes that best practice is to use those unsecured consumer lending rates in circumstances in which the credit characteristics of the donor are similar to the credit characteristics of those with unsecured debt.

29. FinREC believes that in applying the DRA technique using promised cash flows for promises from individuals, an unsecured consumer lending rate might be a starting point for determining an observable market interest rate. The NFP, however, may need to make adjustments to that rate, as discussed in paragraph 32, including, but not limited to, adjustments based on differences in the credit characteristics of the donor compared with the credit characteristics of borrowers of unsecured debt. (FinREC believes that such adjustments might be made based on the average credit characteristics of a homogeneous group of donors in circumstances in which the results would not be materially different from making such adjustments based on the specific credit characteristics of an individual donor.)

30. If the donor is a corporation, and the DRA technique using promised cash flows is used, FinREC believes that the risk-adjusted discount rate might be determined using the yield on publicly traded debt, whether issued by the corporation itself or a comparable corporation. FinREC believes that best practice is to use that yield on publicly traded debt in circumstances in which the promise to give is similar to the publicly traded debt. If the donor is a private foundation, FinREC believes that the risk-adjusted discount rate might be similarly determined using the yield on publicly traded debt, whether issued by the foundation itself, a comparable foundation, or a comparable corporation.[9]

31. In either case (whether the donor is a corporation or foundation), the NFP would consider factors specific to the promise, including its terms and risk, in assessing the extent to which the promise to give is similar to publicly traded debt. For example, FinREC believes that a promise to give a single fixed contribution at a future date likely would be more analogous to publicly traded

---

[8] FinREC believes that a promise to give is different from a trade receivable. A promise to give arises from a donative intent. It is not an exchange transaction in which each of the parties to the exchange receives equivalent value and, generally, will be expected to exercise rights created by the exchange to enforce the terms of the transaction. FinREC believes that information derived from a trade receivable might be relevant in determining the discount rate used in the discount rate adjustment technique. However, adjustments to that information might be needed to incorporate the risk inherent in the cash flows in situations in which the NFP does not have a practice of enforcing its rights to receive promises to pay.

[9] In considering the yield on debt issued by a foundation or other NFP, FinREC believes that the relevant input is the taxable yield, not the tax-exempt yield.

zero coupon debt that pays a single amount at a future date than to a debt instrument that periodically pays interest or principal, or both.[10]

32. In all cases, the NFP would evaluate comparability and adjust available market data for differences, so that the risk-adjusted discount rate used to measure fair value (such as unsecured lending rates or yield on publicly traded debt) is reasonable when considered in the context of the donor and cash flows used. For example, as discussed in paragraphs 12–14, if the NFP uses most likely cash flows, rather than promised cash flows, to mitigate some of the challenges for subsequent measurement, an observed market rate based on promised cash flows (such as an unsecured lending rate or a yield on publicly traded debt) would be adjusted downward to reflect the fact that most likely cash flows incorporate an assessment of default.

[10] For publicly traded zero coupon debt, comparability should be established based on its remaining term to maturity. For a debt instrument that periodically pays interest, principal, or both, FinREC believes that comparability should be established based on its duration, not its remaining term to maturity. Duration refers to the weighted average term over which the debt cash flows will be received.

5.242

Appendix B—Technical Questions and Answers About Financially Interrelated Entities

> ***Note:*** *Technical Questions and Answers* has not been updated for the amendments in FASB Accounting Standards Update (ASU) No. 2016-14, *Not-for-Profit Entities (Topic 958): Presentation of Financial Statements of Not-for-Profit Entities*. Therefore, this appendix does not reflect changes that might be necessary because of the amendments in that ASU.

Technical Questions and Answers sections 6140.13–.18 (*Technical Questions and Answers*) provide guidance for the classification of a beneficiary's interest in the net assets of a financially interrelated fund-raising foundation.

.13 Note to Sections 6140.14–.18—Implementation of FASB ASC 958—Classification of a Beneficiary's Interest in the Net Assets of a Financially Interrelated Fund-Raising Foundation (in the Beneficiary's Financial Statements)

Some not-for-profit entities have separate fund-raising foundations (commonly referred to as *institutionally related foundations*) that solicit contributions on their behalf. FASB ASC 958 provides guidance on (among other things) the accounting that should be followed by such institutionally related foundations and their related beneficiary entity(ies) with respect to contributions received by the foundation.

Some institutionally related foundations and their beneficiary entities meet the characteristics of financially interrelated entities provided in FASB ASC 958-20-15-2. If entities are financially interrelated, FASB ASC 958 provides that the balance sheet of the beneficiary entity(ies) should reflect that entity's interest in the net assets of the foundation, and that interest should be periodically adjusted to reflect the beneficiary's share of the changes in the net assets of the foundation. This accounting is similar to the equity method of accounting, which is described in FASB ASC 323, *Investments—Equity Method and Joint Ventures*.

FASB ASC 323-10-35-5 requires that the periodic adjustment of the investment be included in the determination of the investor's net income. The purpose of sections 6140.14–.18 (applicable to NPEs other than health care [HC] entities) and sections 6400.36–.42 (applicable to not-for-profit HC entities) is to clarify that in circumstances in which the recipient and the beneficiary are financially interrelated:

- Beneficiary entities should segregate the adjustment into changes in restricted and unrestricted net assets. (NPE TPA [sections 6140.14–.16]; HC TPA [section 6400.36–37 and .39])
- In circumstances in which the beneficiary can influence the financial decisions of the recipient entity to such an extent that the beneficiary can determine the timing and amount of distributions

from the recipient to the beneficiary, the existence of the recipient entity should be transparent in determining the net asset classifications in the beneficiary's financial statements. In other words, the recipient cannot impose time or purpose restrictions beyond those imposed by the donor. (NPE TPA [sections 6140.14 and .16]; HC TPA [sections 6400.36 and .39])

- In circumstances in which the beneficiary cannot influence the financial decisions of the recipient entity to such an extent that the beneficiary can determine the timing and amount of distributions from the recipient to the beneficiary, the existence of the recipient entity creates an implied time restriction on the beneficiary's net assets attributable to the beneficiary's interest in the net assets of the recipient (in addition to any other restrictions that may exist). Accordingly, in recognizing its interest in the net assets of the recipient entity and the changes in that interest, the beneficiary should classify the resulting net assets and changes in those net assets as temporarily restricted (unless donors placed permanent restrictions on their contributions). (NPE TPA [section 6140.15]; HC TPA [section 6400.37])
- In circumstances in which the beneficiary can influence the financial decisions of the recipient entity to such an extent that the beneficiary can determine the timing and amount of distributions from the recipient to the beneficiary and some net assets held by the recipient for the benefit of the beneficiary are subject to purpose restrictions (for example, net assets of the recipient restricted to the beneficiary's purchase of property, plant, and equipment [PPE]), expenditures by the beneficiary that meet those purpose restrictions result in the beneficiary (and recipient) reporting reclassifications from temporarily restricted to unrestricted net assets (assuming that the beneficiary has no other net assets subject to similar purpose restrictions), unless those net assets are subject to time restrictions that have not expired, including time restrictions that are implied on contributed long-lived assets as a result of the beneficiary's accounting policy pursuant to FASB ASC 958-605-45-6. (If those net assets are subject to time restrictions that have not expired and the beneficiary has other net assets with similar purpose restrictions, the restrictions on those other net assets would expire in accordance with FASB ASC 958. These sections do not, however, establish a hierarchy pertaining to which restrictions are released first—restrictions on net assets held by the recipient or purpose restrictions on net assets held by the beneficiary.) (NPE TPA [section 6140.17]; HC TPA [section 6400.40])
- In circumstances in which the beneficiary cannot influence the financial decisions of the recipient entity to such an extent that the beneficiary can determine the timing and amount of distributions from the recipient to the beneficiary and some net assets held by the recipient for the benefit of the beneficiary are subject to purpose restrictions, though not subject to time restrictions other than the implied time restrictions that exist because the beneficiary cannot determine the timing and amount of distributions from the recipient to the beneficiary, expenditures by the beneficiary that are consistent with those purpose restrictions should

not result in the beneficiary reporting a reclassification from temporarily restricted to unrestricted net assets, subject to the exceptions in the following sentence. Expenditures by the beneficiary that are consistent with those purpose restrictions should result in the beneficiary reporting a reclassification from temporarily restricted to unrestricted net assets if (*a*) the recipient has no discretion in deciding whether the purpose restriction is met[1] or (*b*) the recipient distributes or obligates itself to distribute to the beneficiary amounts attributable to net assets restricted for the particular purpose, or otherwise indicates that the recipient intends for those net assets to be used to support the particular purpose as an activity of the current period. In all other circumstances, (*a*) purpose restrictions and (*b*) implied time restrictions on the net assets attributable to the interest in the recipient entity exist and have not yet expired. (However, if the beneficiary has other net assets with similar purpose restrictions, those restrictions would expire in accordance with FASB ASC 958. These TPAs do not establish a hierarchy pertaining to which restrictions are released first—restrictions on net assets held by the recipient or restrictions on net assets held by the beneficiary.) (NPE TPA [section 6140.18]; HC TPA [section 6400.41])

- *For HC NPEs Only.* In circumstances in which the beneficiary can influence the financial decisions of the recipient to such an extent that the beneficiary can determine the timing and amount of distributions from the recipient to the beneficiary, changes in the beneficiary's interest in the net assets of a recipient entity attributable to unrealized gains and losses on investments should be included or excluded from the performance indicator in accordance with FASB ASC 954-10, FASB ASC 954-205-45, FASB ASC 954-320-45, FASB ASC 954-320-55, and FASB ASC 954-605 in the same manner that they would have been had the beneficiary had the transactions itself. Similarly, in applying this guidance, the determination of whether amounts are included or excluded from the performance measure should comprehend that if the beneficiary cannot influence the financial decisions of the recipient entity to such an extent that the beneficiary can determine the timing and amount of distributions from the recipient to the beneficiary, an implied time restriction exists on the beneficiary's net assets attributable to the beneficiary's interest in the net assets of the recipient (in addition to any other restrictions that may exist). Accordingly, in circumstances in which the beneficiary cannot influence the financial decisions of the recipient entity to such an extent that the beneficiary can determine the timing and amount

[1] In some circumstances, the purpose restrictions may be so broad that the recipient entity has discretion in deciding whether expenditures by the beneficiary that are consistent with those purpose restrictions actually meet those purpose restrictions. For example, the recipient's net assets may have arisen from a contribution that was restricted for the beneficiary's purchase of research equipment, with no particular research equipment specified. Purchasing an XYZ microscope, which is consistent with that purpose restriction, may or may not meet that purpose restriction, depending on the decision of the recipient. In contrast, the net assets may have arisen from a contribution that was restricted for an XYZ microscope. Purchasing an XYZ microscope, which also is consistent with that purpose restriction, would result in the recipient having no discretion in determining whether that purpose restriction is met.

of distributions from the recipient to the beneficiary, the beneficiary should classify the resulting net assets and changes in those net assets as temporarily restricted (unless donors placed permanent restrictions on their contributions) and therefore exclude those changes from the performance indicator. (HC TPA [section 6400.42])

- *For HC NPEs Only.* In circumstances in which the recipient entity and the beneficiary are both controlled by the same entity, entities should consider the specific facts and circumstances to determine whether the beneficiary can influence the financial decisions of the recipient entity to such an extent that the beneficiary can determine the timing and amount of distributions from the recipient to the beneficiary. (HC TPA [section 6400.38])

Technical Practice Aids for Not-for-Profit Entities Implementation of FASB ASC 958—Classification of a Beneficiary's Interest in the Net Assets of a Financially Interrelated Fund-Raising Foundation (in the Beneficiary's Financial Statements)

<table>
<tr><th colspan="4">HC NPEs</th></tr>
<tr><th colspan="3">NPEs that are not HC NPEs</th><th></th></tr>
<tr><th>Can the beneficiary determine the timing and amount of distributions from the recipient to the beneficiary? [Not-for-profit health care entities (HC NPEs) under common control consider HC Technical Practice Aid (TPA) section 6400.38]</th><th>How does the existence of the recipient affect the beneficiary's reporting of its interest?</th><th>Are any net assets held by the recipient for the benefit of the beneficiary subject to donor-imposed purpose restrictions and has the beneficiary made expenditures that meet those purpose restrictions (in circumstances in which the beneficiary can determine the timing and amount of distributions from the recipient to the beneficiary) or that are consistent with those purpose restrictions (in circumstances in which the beneficiary cannot determine the timing and amount of distributions from the recipient to the beneficiary)?</th><th>Are any changes in the beneficiary's interest in the net assets of the recipient attributable to unrealized gains and losses on investments?</th></tr>
</table>

(continued)

HC NPEs			
NPEs that are not HC NPEs			
Yes	Existence of recipient is transparent in determining net asset classifications. (NPE TPA [sections 6140.14 and .16]; HC TPA [sections 6400.36 and .39])	Reclass the applicable net assets from temporarily restricted (TR) to unrestricted (UR) unless those net assets are subject to time restrictions that have not expired. (NPE TPA [section 6140.17]; HC TPA [section 6400.40])	Changes in the beneficiary's interest in the net assets of a recipient entity attributable to unrealized gains and losses on investments should be included or excluded from the performance indicator in accordance with FASB ASC 954-10, FASB ASC 954-205-45, FASB ASC 954-320-45, FASB ASC 954-320-55, and FASB ASC 954-605 in the same manner that they would have been had the beneficiary had the transactions itself. (HC TPA [section 6400.42])
No	Existence of the recipient creates an implied time restriction on the beneficiary's net assets attributable to the beneficiary's interest in the net assets of the recipient. (NPE TPA [section 6140.15]; HC TPA [section 6400.37])	Reclass the applicable net assets from TR to UR only if the purpose restriction and the implied time restriction are met. Whether the purpose restriction is met depends in part on (1) whether the recipient has discretion in determining whether the purpose restriction is met and (2) the recipient's decision in exercising that discretion, if any. (NPE TPA [section 6140.18]; HC TPA [section 6400.41])	An implied time restriction exists on the beneficiary's net assets attributable to the beneficiary's interest in the net assets of the recipient. The beneficiary should classify the resulting net assets and changes in those net assets as temporarily restricted (unless donors placed permanent restrictions on their contributions) and therefore exclude those changes from the performance indicator. (HC TPA [section 6400.42])

[Revised, June 2009, to reflect conforming changes necessary due to the issuance of FASB ASC.]

.14 Application of FASB ASC 958—Classification of a Beneficiary's Interest in the Net Assets of a Financially Interrelated Fund-Raising Foundation (The beneficiary can influence the operating and financial decisions of the foundation to such an extent that the beneficiary can determine the timing and amount of distributions from the foundation.)

Inquiry—ABC Research Institute, a not-for-profit entity subject to FASB ASC 958[2] and ABC Foundation are financially interrelated entities as described in FASB ASC 958-20-15-2. ABC Foundation's bylaws state that it is organized for the purpose of stimulating voluntary financial support from donors for the sole benefit of ABC Research Institute. Assume that ABC Research Institute can influence the operating and financial decisions of ABC Foundation to such an extent that ABC Research Institute can determine the timing and amount of distributions from ABC Foundation to ABC Research Institute.

During its most recent fiscal year, ABC Foundation's activities resulted in an increase in net assets (before distributions) of $3,200, comprised of $2,000 in unrestricted contributions, $1,000 in temporarily restricted contributions (purpose restrictions), $500 in unrestricted dividend and interest income, and $300 in expenses. In addition, ABC Foundation distributed $2,500 in cash representing unrestricted net assets to ABC Research Institute. How should this activity be reported in ABC Research Institute's financial statements?

Reply—Because ABC Foundation (the recipient entity) and ABC Research Institute (the beneficiary) are financially interrelated, FASB ASC 958-20-25-2 requires ABC Research Institute to recognize its interest in the net assets of ABC Foundation and periodically adjust that interest for its share of the change in net assets of ABC Foundation. This is similar to the equity method of accounting described in FASB ASC 323.

In recognizing its interest in the net assets of ABC Foundation and the changes in that interest, ABC Research Institute should classify the resulting net assets as if contributions were received by ABC Research Institute directly from the donor, because ABC Research Institute can influence the operating and financial decisions of ABC Foundation to such an extent that ABC Research Institute can determine the timing and amount of distributions from ABC Foundation to ABC Research Institute. In other words, the existence of ABC Foundation should be transparent in determining the net asset classifications in ABC Research Institute's financial statements because ABC Foundation cannot impose time or purpose restrictions beyond those imposed by the donor. (Any instructions given by ABC Foundation are designations, rather than restrictions.)

In the circumstances described in the preceding, ABC Research Institute would initially increase its asset, "Interest in Net Assets of ABC Foundation" for the change in ABC Foundation's net assets ($3,200). ABC Research Institute's Statement of Activity would include "Change in Unrestricted Interest in ABC Foundation" of $2,200, which would be reported as an increase in unrestricted net assets, and "Change in Temporarily Restricted Interest in ABC Foundation" of $1,000 as an increase in temporarily restricted net assets.

---

[2] This section addresses not-for-profit entities subject to FASB ASC 958. Section 6400.36, "Application of FASB ASC 958—Classification of a Beneficiary's Interest in the Net Assets of a Financially Interrelated Fund-Raising Foundation (The beneficiary can influence the operating and financial decisions of the foundation to such an extent that the beneficiary can determine the timing and amount of distributions from the foundation.)," addresses a similar issue for not-for-profit health care entities subject to FASB ASC 954, *Health Care Entities*.

The $2,500 distribution from ABC Foundation to ABC Research Institute would not be reported as an increase in net assets on ABC Research Institute's Statement of Activity. By analogy to equity method accounting, the $2,500 would be reported in a manner similar to a distribution from a subsidiary to its parent (for example, a dividend). ABC Research Institute should report the distribution by increasing cash and decreasing its interest in the net assets of ABC Foundation.

If the distribution represented restricted net assets, ABC Research Institute would not reclassify the net assets from temporarily restricted to unrestricted at the time of the distribution. Instead, ABC Research Institute would reclassify the net assets from temporarily restricted to unrestricted when those restrictions were met.

[Revised, June 2009, to reflect conforming changes necessary due to the issuance of FASB ASC.]

.15 Application of FASB ASC 958—Classification of a Beneficiary's Interest in the Net Assets of a Financially Interrelated Fund-Raising Foundation (The beneficiary cannot influence the operating and financial decisions of the foundation to such an extent that the beneficiary can determine the timing and amount of distributions from the foundation.)

Inquiry—ABC Research Institute, a not-for-profit entity subject to FASB ASC 958[3] and ABC Foundation are financially interrelated entities as described in FASB ASC 958-20-15-2. ABC Foundation's bylaws state that it is organized for the purpose of stimulating voluntary financial support from donors for the sole benefit of ABC Research Institute. Assume that ABC Research Institute cannot, however, influence the operating and financial decisions of ABC Foundation to such an extent that ABC Research Institute can determine the timing and amount of distributions from ABC Foundation to ABC Research Institute.

During its most recent fiscal year, ABC Foundation's activities resulted in an increase in net assets (before distributions) of $3,200, comprised of $2,000 in unrestricted contributions, $1,000 in temporarily restricted contributions (purpose restrictions), $500 in unrestricted dividend and interest income, and $300 in expenses. In addition, ABC Foundation elected to distribute $2,500 in cash representing unrestricted net assets to ABC Research Institute. How should this activity be reported in ABC Research Institute's financial statements?

Reply—Because ABC Foundation (the recipient entity) and ABC Research Institute (the beneficiary) are financially interrelated, FASB ASC 958-20-25-2 requires ABC Research Institute to recognize its interest in the net assets of ABC Foundation and periodically adjust that interest for its share of the change in net assets of ABC Foundation. This is similar to the equity method of accounting described in FASB ASC 323.

ABC Research Institute cannot influence the operating and financial decisions of ABC Foundation to such an extent that ABC Research Institute can determine the timing and amount of distributions from ABC Foundation to ABC

---

[3] This section addresses not-for-profit entities subject to FASB ASC 958. Section 6400.37, "Application of FASB ASC 958—Classification of a Beneficiary's Interest in the Net Assets of a Financially Interrelated Fund-Raising Foundation (The beneficiary cannot influence the operating and financial decisions of the foundation to such an extent that the beneficiary can determine the timing and amount of distributions from the foundation.)," addresses a similar issue for not-for-profit health care entities subject to FASB ASC 954.

Research Institute. Therefore, an implied time restriction exists on ABC Research Institute's interest in the net assets of ABC Foundation (in addition to any other restrictions that may exist). Accordingly, in recognizing its interest in the net assets of ABC Foundation and the changes in that interest, ABC Research Institute should classify the resulting net assets as changes in temporarily restricted net assets (unless donors placed permanent restrictions on their contributions).

In the circumstances described in the preceding, ABC Research Institute would initially increase its asset, "Interest in Net Assets of ABC Foundation" for the change in ABC Foundation's net assets ($3,200). ABC Research Institute's Statement of Activity would include "Change in Temporarily Restricted Interest in ABC Foundation" of $3,200 as an increase in temporarily restricted net assets.

The $2,500 distribution from ABC Foundation to ABC Research Institute would not be reported as an increase in net assets on ABC Research Institute's Statement of Activity. By analogy to equity method accounting, the $2,500 would be treated similar to a distribution from a subsidiary to its parent (for example, a dividend). ABC Research Institute should report the distribution by increasing cash and decreasing its interest in the net assets of ABC Foundation.

ABC Research Institute would reclassify the net assets from temporarily restricted to unrestricted at the time of the distribution, because the time restriction would expire at the time of the distribution. (If those net assets were subject to purpose or time restrictions that remained even after the net assets had been distributed to ABC Research Institute, ABC Research Institute would not reclassify the net assets from temporarily restricted to unrestricted at the time of the distribution. Instead, ABC Research Institute would reclassify the net assets from temporarily restricted to unrestricted when those restrictions were met.)

[Revised, June 2009, to reflect conforming changes necessary due to the issuance of FASB ASC.]

.16 Application of FASB ASC 958—Classification of a Beneficiary's Interest in the Net Assets of a Financially Interrelated Fund-Raising Foundation (More Than One Beneficiary—Some Contributions Are Designated)

Inquiry—DEF Arts Entity is the parent of three brother-sister not-for-profit entities: Ballet, Orchestra, a not-for-profit entity subject to FASB ASC 958[4] and Foundation. Foundation is organized for the purpose of raising contributions for the benefit of both Ballet and Orchestra. The four entities are legally separate not-for-profit entities that are financially interrelated pursuant to the guidance in FASB ASC 958-20-15-2. Assume that Orchestra can influence the financial decisions of Foundation to such an extent that Orchestra can determine the timing and amount of distributions from Foundation to Orchestra.

A donor contributes $5,000 cash to Foundation and stipulates that the contribution is for the benefit of Orchestra. Foundation would record the contribution as temporarily restricted revenue (because Foundation must use the contribution for the benefit of Orchestra). In its separately issued financial statements,

---

[4] This section addresses not-for-profit entities subject to FASB ASC 958. Section 6400.39, "Application of FASB ASC 958—Classification of a Beneficiary's Interest in the Net Assets of a Financially Interrelated Fund-Raising Foundation (More Than One Beneficiary—Some Contributions Are Designated)," addresses a similar issue for not-for-profit health care entities subject to FASB ASC 954.

Orchestra would recognize its interest in the net assets attributable to that contribution by debiting "Interest in Net Assets of Foundation" for $5,000. Would the offsetting credit be reported as temporarily restricted revenue (because the net assets attributable to the contribution are restricted on Foundation's Balance Sheet) or unrestricted revenue (because there are no donor-imposed time restrictions or purpose restrictions on how Orchestra must use the contribution)?

Reply—Orchestra should report the offsetting credit as unrestricted revenue. Because Orchestra can influence the financial decisions of Foundation to such an extent that Orchestra can determine the timing and amount of distributions from Foundation to Orchestra, no implied time restriction exists on Orchestra's net assets attributable to its interest in the net assets of Foundation. Accordingly, in recognizing its interest in the net assets of Foundation and the changes in that interest, Orchestra should classify the resulting net assets as if contributions were received by Orchestra directly from the donor. In other words, the existence of Foundation should be transparent in determining the net asset classifications in Orchestra's separately issued financial statements because Foundation cannot impose time or purpose restrictions beyond those imposed by the donor. (Any instructions given by Foundation are designations, rather than restrictions.)

Because there are no donor-imposed restrictions on how Orchestra must use the contribution, Orchestra should report the change in its interest in the net assets attributable to the contribution as an increase in unrestricted net assets in its separately issued Statement of Activity. When Foundation actually distributes the funds, Orchestra should increase cash and decrease its interest in net assets of Foundation; the distributions would have no effect on Orchestra's Statement of Activity.

[Revised, June 2009, to reflect conforming changes necessary due to the issuance of FASB ASC.]

.17 Application of FASB ASC 958—Classification of a Beneficiary's Interest in the Net Assets of a Financially Interrelated Fund-Raising Foundation (The beneficiary makes an expenditure that meets a purpose restriction on net assets held for its benefit by the recipient entity—The beneficiary can influence the operating and financial decisions of the recipient to such an extent that the beneficiary can determine the timing and amount of distributions from the recipient.)

Inquiry—ABC Research Institute, a not-for-profit entity subject to FASB ASC 958[5] and ABC Foundation are financially interrelated entities as described in FASB ASC 958-20-15-2. ABC Foundation's bylaws state that it is organized for the purpose of stimulating voluntary financial support from donors for the sole benefit of ABC Research Institute. Assume that ABC Research Institute can influence the operating and financial decisions of ABC Foundation to such an extent that ABC Research Institute can determine the timing and amount of distributions from ABC Foundation to ABC Research Institute.

---

[5] This section addresses not-for-profit entities subject to FASB ASC 958. Section 6400.40,"Application of FASB ASC 958—Classification of a Beneficiary's Interest in the Net Assets of a Financially Interrelated Fund-Raising Foundation (The beneficiary makes an expenditure that meets a purpose restriction on net assets held for its benefit by the recipient organization—The beneficiary can influence the operating and financial decisions of the recipient to such an extent that the beneficiary can determine the timing and amount of distributions from the recipient.)," addresses a similar issue for not-for-profit health care entities subject to FASB ASC 954.

ABC Foundation's net assets consist of $3,000,000 resulting from cash contributions restricted for the purchase of property, plant, and equipment (PPE) by ABC Research Institute. ABC Research Institute has recorded its interest in those net assets by debiting "Interest in net assets of ABC Foundation" and crediting "Change in interest in ABC Foundation," which is reported as an increase in temporarily restricted net assets. ABC Research Institute's accounting policy is to not imply a time restriction that expires over the useful life of the donated long-lived assets pursuant to FASB ASC 958-605-45-6 and it has no other net assets restricted for the purchase of PPE.[6] ABC Research Institute subsequently purchased and placed into service $3,000,000 of PPE that meets those donor restrictions prior to receiving a distribution from ABC Foundation. Should ABC Research Institute reclassify $3,000,000 from temporarily-restricted net assets to unrestricted net assets as a result of building and placing into service the $3,000,000 of PPE?

Reply—Because ABC Foundation (the recipient entity) and ABC Research Institute (the beneficiary) are financially interrelated, FASB ASC 958-20-25-2 requires ABC Research Institute to recognize its interest in the net assets of ABC Foundation and periodically adjust that interest for its share of the change in net assets of ABC Foundation. This is similar to the equity method of accounting described in FASB ASC 323.

In recognizing its interest in the net assets of ABC Foundation and the changes in that interest, ABC Research Institute should classify the resulting net assets as if contributions were received by ABC Research directly from the donor, because ABC Research Institute can influence the operating and financial decisions of ABC Foundation to such an extent that ABC Research Institute can determine the timing and amount of distributions from ABC Foundation to ABC Research Institute. Accordingly, the net assets representing contributions restricted for the purchase of PPE should be reported as temporarily restricted net assets (purpose restricted) in ABC Research Institute's financial statements. Upon purchasing and placing into service the PPE, ABC Research Institute (and ABC Foundation) should reclassify $3,000,000 from temporarily restricted to unrestricted net assets.[7] In other words, the existence of ABC Foundation should be transparent in determining the net asset classifications in ABC Research Institute's financial statements because ABC Foundation cannot impose time or purpose restrictions beyond those imposed by the donor. (Any instructions given by ABC Foundation are designations, rather than restrictions.)

[Revised, June 2009, to reflect conforming changes necessary due to the issuance of FASB ASC.]

---

[6] The assumption that ABC Research Institute has no other net assets restricted for the purchase of PPE is intended to avoid establishing a hierarchy pertaining to which restrictions are released first—restrictions on net assets held by the recipient or restrictions on net assets held by the beneficiary. That issue is not addressed in this TPA.

[7] In this fact pattern, ABC Research Institute's interest in the net assets of ABC Foundation is subject to only purpose restrictions because the net assets arose from cash contributions with no time restrictions. If instead the net assets arose from promises to give rather than from cash contributions, the net assets might be subject to time restrictions in addition to the purpose restrictions. In determining whether net assets that arose from promises to give are subject to time restrictions, NPEs should consider the guidance in section 6140.04, "Lapsing of Restrictions on Receivables if Purpose Restrictions Pertaining to Long-Lived Assets Are Met Before the Receivables Are Due," which discusses whether restrictions on net assets arising from promises to give that are restricted by donors for investments in long-lived assets are met when the assets are placed in service or when the receivables are due.

.18 Application of FASB ASC 958—Classification of a Beneficiary's Interest in the Net Assets of a Financially Interrelated Fund-Raising Foundation (The beneficiary makes an expenditure that is consistent with a purpose restriction on net assets held for its benefit by the recipient entity—The beneficiary cannot influence the operating and financial decisions of the recipient to such an extent that the beneficiary can determine the timing and amount of distributions from the recipient.)

Inquiry—ABC Research Institute, a not-for-profit entity subject to FASB ASC 958[8] and ABC Foundation are financially interrelated entities as described in FASB ASC 958-20-15-2. ABC Foundation's bylaws state that it is organized for the purpose of stimulating voluntary financial support from donors for the sole benefit of ABC Research Institute. Assume that ABC Research Institute cannot, however, influence the operating and financial decisions of ABC Foundation to such an extent that ABC Research Institute can determine the timing and amount of distributions from ABC Foundation to ABC Research Institute.

ABC Foundation's net assets consist of $3,000,000 resulting from cash contributions restricted for the purchase of property, plant, and equipment (PPE) by ABC Research Institute. ABC Research Institute has recorded its interest in those net assets by debiting "Interest in net assets of ABC Foundation" and crediting "Change in interest in ABC Foundation," which is reported as an increase in temporarily restricted net assets. ABC Research Institute has no other net assets restricted for the purchase of PPE.[9]

ABC Research Institute subsequently built and placed into service the New Modern Wing of the Research Building prior to receiving a distribution from ABC Foundation or any indication that it intends to support building and placing into service the New Modern Wing of the Research Building. Should ABC Research Institute reclassify $3,000,000 from temporarily-restricted net assets to unrestricted net assets as a result of building and placing into service the $3,000,000 of PPE?

Reply—From ABC Research Institute's perspective, its interest in the net assets of ABC Foundation has two restrictions—a purpose restriction (the purchase of the PPE) and an implied time restriction. (ABC Research Institute cannot influence the operating and financial decisions of ABC Foundation to such an extent that ABC Research Institute can determine the timing and amount of distributions from ABC Foundation to ABC Research Institute, including distributions pertaining to expenditures by ABC Research Institute that meet the donor-imposed purpose restrictions. Therefore, an implied time restriction exists on ABC Research Institute's interest in the net assets of ABC Foundation.) FASB ASC 958-205-45-9 provides, in part, as follows:

---

[8] This section addresses not-for-profit entities subject to FASB ASC 958. Section 6400.41, "Application of FASB Statement No. 136—Classification of a Beneficiary's Interest in the Net Assets of a Financially Interrelated Fund-Raising Foundation (The beneficiary makes an expenditure that is consistent with a purpose restriction on net assets held for its benefit by the recipient organization—The beneficiary cannot influence the operating and financial decisions of the recipient to such an extent that the beneficiary can determine the timing and amount of distributions from the recipient.)," addresses a similar issue for not-for-profit health care entities subject to FASB ASC 954.

[9] The assumption that ABC Research Institute has no other net assets restricted for the purchase of PPE is intended to avoid establishing a hierarchy pertaining to which restrictions are released first—restrictions on net assets held by the recipient or restrictions on net assets held by the beneficiary. That issue is not addressed in this section.

> If two or more temporary restrictions are imposed on a contribution, the effect of the expiration of those restrictions shall be recognized in the period in which the last remaining restriction has expired.

FASB ASC 958-205-45-11 further provides, in part, as follows:

> Temporarily restricted net assets with time restrictions are not available to support expenses until the time restrictions have expired.

In considering whether the purpose restriction on ABC Research Institute's interest in the net assets of ABC Foundation is met, ABC Research Institute should determine whether ABC Foundation has discretion in deciding whether an expenditure by ABC Research Institute that is consistent with the purpose restriction satisfies that purpose restriction. For example, if the restricted net assets arose from a contribution that was restricted for "building projects of ABC Research Institute," with no particular building project specified, purchasing and placing into service the New Modern Wing of the Research Building is consistent with the purpose restriction but may or may not meet it, because ABC Foundation has some discretion in deciding which building project releases the purpose restriction. In other words, ABC Foundation may, at its discretion, either release restricted net assets in support of building the New Modern Wing of the Research Building or not, because the purpose restriction imposed by the donor was broad enough to give ABC Foundation discretion in deciding which building projects meet the purpose restriction. If ABC Foundation has such discretion, a purpose restriction and an implied time restriction on ABC Research Institute's interest in the net assets of ABC Foundation exist. Therefore, ABC Research Institute should not reclassify $3,000,000 from temporarily-restricted net assets to unrestricted net assets as a result of building and placing into service the New Modern Wing of the Research Building unless ABC Foundation distributes or obligates itself to distribute to ABC Research Institute amounts attributable to net assets restricted for the purchase of PPE by ABC Research Institute, or ABC Foundation otherwise indicates that it intends for those net assets to be used to support the building and placing into service the New Modern Wing of the Research Building as an activity of the current period (assuming that ABC Research Institute had no other net assets that were restricted for the purchase of PPE).[10,11]

---

[10] In this fact pattern, the expenditure is made prior to meeting the purpose restriction and the implied time restriction that exists because ABC Research Institute cannot determine the timing and amount of distributions from ABC Foundation to ABC Research Institute. FASB ASC 958-205-45-11 provides that in circumstances in which both purpose and time restrictions exist, expenditures meeting the purpose restriction must be made simultaneous with or after the time restriction has expired in order to satisfy both the purpose and time restriction and result in a reclassification of net assets from temporarily restricted to unrestricted. In other words, time restrictions, if any, must be met before expenditures can result in purpose restrictions being met. In this fact pattern, however, the time restriction is an implied time restriction that exists because the beneficiary cannot determine the timing and amount of distributions from the recipient to the beneficiary, rather than an implied time restriction that exists because a promise to give is due in a future period or because of an explicit donor stipulation. Accordingly, in this fact pattern, temporarily restricted net assets with implied time restrictions are available to support expenditures made before the expiration of the time restrictions and the net assets should be reclassified from temporarily restricted to unrestricted in the period in which the last remaining restriction has expired. In other words, in this fact pattern, if the expenditure that meets the purpose restriction is made before meeting the implied time restriction that exists because the beneficiary cannot determine the timing and amount of distributions from the recipient to the beneficiary, all the restrictions should be considered met once the implied time restriction is met.

[11] In this fact pattern, ABC Research Institute's interest in the net assets of ABC Foundation is subject to an implied time restriction that exists because ABC Research Institute cannot determine

(continued)

In contrast to the example in the previous paragraph, if the restricted net assets arose from a contribution that was restricted for "building and placing into service the New Modern Wing of the Research Building," ABC Foundation has no discretion in deciding whether that purpose restriction is met by building and placing into service the New Modern Wing of the Research Building. Therefore, if ABC Research Institute builds and places into service the New Modern Wing of the Research Building, the purpose restriction is met (assuming that ABC Research Institute had no other net assets that were restricted for building and placing into service the New Modern Wing). In addition, the implied time restriction is met because ABC Foundation is required to distribute the funds to ABC in order to meet the donor's stipulations. Therefore, ABC Research Institute (and ABC Foundation) should reclassify $3,000,000 from temporarily-restricted net assets to unrestricted net assets as a result of building and placing into service the New Modern Wing of the Research Building.

In summary, ABC Research Institute should not reclassify $3,000,000 from temporarily-restricted net assets to unrestricted net assets as a result of building and placing into service the New Modern Wing of the Research Building until both the purpose restriction and the implied time restriction are met. If both the purpose restriction and the implied time restriction are met, ABC Research Institute should decrease its interest in the net assets of ABC Foundation and increase cash (or a receivable, if the Foundation has merely obligated itself to make the distribution) by the amount of the distribution, and simultaneously reclassify the same amount from temporarily restricted net assets to unrestricted net assets.

[Revised, June 2009, to reflect conforming changes necessary due to the issuance of FASB ASC.]

(footnote continued)

the timing and amount of distributions from ABC Foundation to ABC Research Institute and a purpose restriction. Because the net assets arose from cash contributions with no other donor-imposed time restrictions, no time restrictions other than those imposed by ABC Foundation exist. If instead the net assets arose from promises to give rather than from cash contributions, the net assets might be subject to donor-imposed time restrictions in addition to the time restriction imposed by ABC Foundation and the purpose restriction. In determining whether net assets that arose from promises to give are subject to donor-imposed time restrictions in addition to the time restrictions imposed by ABC Foundation, NPEs should consider the guidance in section 6140.04, which discusses whether restrictions on net assets arising from promises to give that are restricted by donors for investments in long-lived assets are met when the assets are placed in service or when the receivables are due. In circumstances in which the net assets are subject to (*a*) donor-imposed time restrictions in addition to the (*b*) implied time restrictions that exist because ABC Research Institute cannot determine the timing and amount of distributions from ABC Foundation to ABC Research Institute and (*c*) purpose restrictions, the last remaining time restriction should be considered in applying the guidance in FASB ASC 958-205-45-11 that provides that temporarily restricted net assets with time restrictions are not available to support expenses until the time restrictions have expired.

Chapter 6

Split-Interest Agreements and Beneficial Interests in Trusts

Gray shaded text in this chapter reflects guidance issued but not yet effective as of the date of this guide, March 1, 2018, but becoming effective on or prior to June 30, 2018, exclusive of any option to early adopt ahead of the mandatory effective date. Unless otherwise indicated, all unshaded text reflects guidance that was already effective as of the date of this guide.

Introduction

6.01 Some donors enter into trust or other arrangements under which not-for-profit entities (NFPs) receive benefits that are shared with other beneficiaries. Recognition and measurement principles for these arrangements, commonly known as *split-interest agreements*, are discussed in FASB *Accounting Standards Codification* (ASC) 958-30 and this chapter. The application of these principles to six widely used types of such agreements—charitable lead trusts, perpetual trusts held by third parties,[1] charitable remainder trusts, charitable gift annuities, pooled (life) income funds, and a gift of real estate with a retained life interest—is also illustrated.

Types of Split-Interest Agreements

6.02 Under a split-interest agreement, a donor makes an initial transfer of assets to a trust, a fiscal agent, or directly to the NFP in which the NFP has a beneficial interest but is not the sole beneficiary. The terms of some agreements do not allow donors to revoke their gifts; other agreements may be revocable by donors in certain situations; still others may be irrevocable by the donor, but the NFP's rights to distributions are revocable because the agreement allows the donor to change the beneficiaries. The time period covered by the agreement is expressed either as a specific number of years (or in perpetuity) or as the remaining life of an individual or individuals designated by the donor. The assets are invested and administered by the NFP, a trustee, or a fiscal agent, and distributions are made to a beneficiary or beneficiaries during the term of the agreement (or in the case of gifts of real estate, the beneficiary may have a use interest). At the end of the agreement's term, the remaining assets covered by the agreement are distributed to or retained by either the NFP or another beneficiary or beneficiaries.

6.03 Under some kinds of agreements, referred to in this guide as lead interests, the NFP receives the distributions during the agreement's term. In other kinds of agreements, referred to as remainder interests, the donor (or other individuals or entities designated by the donor) receives distributions during the agreement's term and the NFP receives all or a portion of the assets

---

[1] Though perpetual trusts held by third parties may not meet the definition of a *split-interest agreement* because the not-for-profit entity (NFP) may be the sole beneficiary, they are included in this chapter because they present some of the same recognition and measurement issues as do split-interest agreements.

remaining at the end of the agreement's term. Under either kind of agreement, donors may impose restrictions on the NFP's use of all or a portion of any assets received.

Recognition and Measurement Principles

6.04 In accordance with FASB ASC 958-30-45-7, the contribution portion of a split-interest agreement (that is, the part that represents the unconditional transfer of assets in a voluntary nonreciprocal transaction) should be recognized as revenue or gain. (As discussed in the FASB ASC glossary definition of *contribution*, the term *contribution revenue* in FASB ASC is used to apply to transactions that are part of the entity's ongoing major or central activities [revenues], or are peripheral or incidental to the entity [gains]. This guide also uses that convention.) In accordance with FASB ASC 958-605-30-2, a contribution should be measured at its fair value.

Use of Fair Value Measures

6.05 Recognition of split-interest agreements also requires assets and liabilities to be initially measured at fair value and, in certain cases, requires them to be remeasured at fair value subsequently. FASB ASC 820, *Fair Value Measurement*, establishes a framework for measuring fair value.[2] This guide uses present value techniques as one possible technique to measure the contribution revenue and obligation to other beneficiaries of a split-interest agreement. See paragraphs 4–20 of FASB ASC 820-10-55 for implementation guidance for using present value techniques if the measurement objective is fair value. Other valuation techniques are also available, as described in FASB ASC 820-10-35. For example, paragraphs 71–80 of the AICPA white paper *Measurement of Fair Value for Certain Transactions of Not-for-Profit Entities* (fair value white paper), describes using a market approach and level 2 inputs for valuing certain liabilities under split-interest remainder agreements with fixed payments. Excerpts from the fair value white paper, which are included in appendix A of this chapter, discuss fair value measurement of perpetual and nonperpetual beneficial interests in trusts and the liabilities of split-interest agreements.

6.06 Reference to IRS guidelines and actuarial tables or commercially available software that is used in calculating the donor's charitable deduction for income tax purposes may be helpful in assessing the reasonableness of the method used for measuring fair value. However, the objective of those tools (guidelines, tables, and software) is to measure the tax deductibility of the gift, which may not necessarily result in a fair value measurement. To use those tools for measuring in accordance with generally accepted accounting principles (GAAP), NFPs would need to consider the assumptions that are inherent in the calculations (primarily interest rates and mortality) and determine whether those assumptions are market participant assumptions appropriate for the measurement of fair value.

Recognition of Revocable Agreements

6.07 FASB ASC 958-30-25-2, FASB ASC 958-30-30-3, and paragraphs 11–12 of FASB ASC 958-30-35 discuss recognition and measurement of revocable

---

[2] Paragraphs 3.138–.168 discuss FASB *Accounting Standards Codification* (ASC) 820, *Fair Value Measurement*, which defines *fair value*, establishes a framework for measuring fair value, and requires disclosures about fair value measurements.

split-interest agreements. Revocable split-interest agreements should be accounted for as intentions to give. Assets received by an NFP acting as a trustee under a revocable split-interest agreement should be recognized at fair value when received as assets and as a refundable advance. If those assets are investments, they should be recognized in conformity with FASB ASC 958-320 or 958-325 as appropriate. Contribution revenue for the assets received should be recognized when the agreements become irrevocable or when the assets are distributed to the NFP for its unconditional use, whichever occurs first. Income earned on assets held under revocable agreements that is not available for the NFP's unconditional use, and any subsequent adjustments to the carrying value of those assets, should be recognized as adjustments to the assets and as refundable advances.

Recognition of Irrevocable Agreements

6.08 Recognition and measurement of an irrevocable split-interest agreement varies depending on three factors: whether the NFP's rights to distributions in accordance with the agreement are revocable or irrevocable (paragraph 6.09), whether the assets are held by the NFP or a third party (paragraphs 6.09–.10), and the type of agreement (paragraph 6.12).

6.09 An NFP's interest in the assets of a split-interest agreement is revocable if the donor, a trustee, or a third party can cancel the agreement and redirect the assets. An NFP's interest in the assets of a split-interest agreement can be revocable even if the agreement itself is irrevocable. For example, in a charitable remainder unitrust agreement, a donor can retain, or give to a third party, the power to substitute another charitable beneficiary without jeopardizing the donor's charitable deduction. Unless the use of that power is limited by the agreement to situations that are remote of occurrence (such as the failure of the named charitable beneficiary to qualify as a charitable organization under IRC Section 170) or unless the parties that can change the beneficiary are no longer living, the interest of the named NFP is revocable and the guidance in paragraph 6.07 applies.

6.10 If an NFP serves as the trustee for a split-interest trust agreement or if the assets transferred by the donor are otherwise under the NFP's control, the NFP records the assets received from the donor, a liability for the future payments to be made to the donor or third parties designated by the donor, and contribution revenue for the difference (assuming the right to those assets is irrevocable). If a third party appointed by the donor serves as the trustee for a split-interest trust agreement or as a fiscal agent, the NFP records its beneficial interest and contribution revenue.

6.11 Serving as the trustee or fiscal agent for a split-interest agreement carries the duties of annual tax filings and, in some states, compliance with state insurance regulations. Some NFPs that are appointed as trustee or fiscal agent under split-interest agreements choose a bank or other third party to hold the assets and administer those duties. If an NFP has appointed the trustee or fiscal agent and has the ability to replace that party, the NFP follows the guidance for an NFP that is a trustee or fiscal agent because the assets remain under the NFP's control.

6.12 This guide and FASB ASC 958-30 organize and present guidance by type of split-interest agreement. The following classifications are used:

- Pooled income funds or net income unitrusts

- Irrevocable agreements other than pooled income funds or net income unitrusts, which includes guidance for charitable lead trusts, charitable remainder trusts, and charitable gift annuities

Initial Recognition and Measurement of Unconditional Irrevocable Agreements Other Than Pooled Income Funds or Net Income Unitrusts

NFP Is the Trustee or Fiscal Agent

6.13 Paragraphs 4–14 of FASB ASC 958-30-25 discuss recognition of unconditional irrevocable agreements for which the NFP serves as trustee or if the assets contributed by the donor are otherwise under the control of the NFP. Per FASB ASC 958-30-25-4, in the absence of donor-imposed conditions, an NFP should recognize contribution revenue and related assets and liabilities when an irrevocable split-interest agreement naming it trustee or fiscal agent is executed. Assets received under those agreements should be recorded when received. If those assets are investments, they should be recognized in conformity with the guidance in FASB ASC 958-320 or FASB ASC 958-325, as appropriate. The contribution portion of an agreement (that is, the part that represents the unconditional transfer of assets in a voluntary nonreciprocal transaction) should be recognized as revenue or gain.

6.14 Per paragraphs 4–6 of FASB ASC 958-30-30, at the date of initial recognition of a split-interest agreement, contributions should be measured at fair value. The cash and other assets received under split-interest agreements should be recognized at fair value at the date of initial recognition. If the transferred assets, or a portion of those assets, are being held for the benefit of others, such as the donor or third parties designated by the donor, a liability, measured at fair value, should also be recognized at the date of initial recognition. If present value techniques are used to measure fair value, the liability generally is measured at the present value of the future payments to be made to the other beneficiaries. Any present value technique for measuring the fair value of the contribution or payments to be made to other beneficiaries must consider the elements described in FASB ASC 820-10-55-5, including the following:

a. The estimated return on the invested assets during the expected term of the agreement

b. The contractual payment obligations under the agreement

c. A discount rate commensurate with the risks involved

6.15 Per FASB ASC 958-30-30-7, under a lead interest agreement, the fair value of the contribution can be estimated directly based on the present value of the future distributions to be received by the NFP as a beneficiary. Under lead interest agreements, the future payments to be made to other beneficiaries will be made by the NFP only after the NFP receives its benefits. In those situations, the present value of the future payments to be made to other beneficiaries may be estimated by the fair value of the assets contributed by the donor under the agreement less the fair value of the benefits to be received by the NFP. If present value techniques are used, the fair value of the benefits to be received by the NFP should be measured at the present value of the benefits to be received over the expected term of the agreement.

6.16 Per FASB ASC 958-30-30-8, under remainder interest agreements, the present value of the future payments to be made to other beneficiaries can be estimated directly based on the terms of the agreement. Future distributions will be received by the NFP only after obligations to other beneficiaries are satisfied. In those cases, the fair value of the contribution may be estimated based on the fair value of the assets contributed by the donor less the fair value of the payments to be made to other beneficiaries.

6.17 As noted in paragraph 90 of the fair value white paper, when determining the appropriate discount rate to be used if present value techniques are used for the valuations described in paragraphs 6.15–.16, it is important to remember that because the payments to the beneficiary depend upon the risk and return level of the assets in the trust (or other identifiable pool of assets), the cash flows from the trust (or pool) to the beneficiary are at least as risky as the cash flows of the trust (or pool) investments. That is, if the rate of return on the trust investments is 6 percent (due to the risk of investing the trust assets), then the beneficiary of the cash flows from the trust (or pool) also bears at least that same risk. Because the beneficiary also bears that risk, best practice is for the discount rate to also reflect that risk, and therefore the discount rate in this example would be at a minimum 6 percent.

6.18 Per FASB ASC 958-30-45-1, contribution revenues recognized under split-interest agreements should be classified as increases in temporarily restricted net assets unless either of the following conditions exists:

a. The donor has permanently restricted the NFP's use of its interest (lead or remainder) in the assets. If the donor has permanently restricted the NFP's use of its interest, the contribution should be classified as an increase in permanently restricted net assets.

b. The donor gives the NFP the immediate right to use without restrictions the assets it receives. If the NFP has the immediate right to use its interest without restrictions, the contribution should be classified as increases in unrestricted net assets.

Per the "Pending Content" in FASB ASC 958-30-45-1, contribution revenues recognized under split-interest agreements should be classified as increases in net assets with donor restrictions unless the donor gives the NFP the immediate right to use, without restrictions, the assets it receives, in which case the contribution should be classified as an increase in net assets without donor restrictions.[3]

6.19 As discussed in FASB ASC 958-30-45-2, under many charitable gift annuity agreements, the assets received from the donor are held by the NFP as part of its general assets and are available for its unrestricted use. The contribution portion of a charitable gift annuity agreement should be recognized as unrestricted support if both (*a*) the donor does not restrict the use of the assets contributed to the NFP and (*b*) neither the charitable gift annuity agreement nor state law requires the assets received by the NFP to be invested until the income beneficiary's death. If either of those criteria is not met, the contribution should be classified as restricted in accordance with FASB ASC 958-30-45-1.

---

[3] The amendments in FASB Accounting Standards Update (ASU) No. 2016-14, *Not-for-Profit Entities (Topic 958): Presentation of Financial Statements of Note-for-Profit Entities*, are effective for annual financial statements issued for fiscal years beginning after December 15, 2017 (for example, years ending December 31, 2018, and years ending June 30, 2019), and for interim periods within fiscal years beginning after December 15, 2018. Application to interim financial statements is permitted but not required in the initial year of application. Early application of the amendments is permitted.

As discussed in the "Pending Content" in FASB ASC 958-30-45-2, under many charitable gift annuity agreements, the assets received from the donor are held by the NFP as part of its general assets and are available for its general use. The contribution portion of a charitable gift annuity agreement should be recognized as revenue without donor restrictions if both (*a*) the donor does not restrict the use of the assets contributed to the NFP and (*b*) neither the charitable gift annuity agreement nor laws and regulations require the assets received by the NFP to be invested until the income beneficiary's death. If either of those criteria is not met, the contribution should be classified as donor-restricted support that increases net assets with donor restrictions and should be reclassified as net assets without donor restrictions when donor-imposed restrictions or legal requirements are satisfied. Additional annuity reserves required by state laws, as described in FASB ASC 958-30-50-2, do not create donor restrictions.[4]

Unrelated Third Party Is the Trustee or Fiscal Agent

6.20 Paragraphs 16–19 of FASB ASC 958-30-25 and FASB ASC 958-30-30-11 discuss recognition and initial measurement of irrevocable split-interest agreements for which a third party maintains control of the donor's contributed assets. In a split-interest agreement in which cash or other assets contributed by a donor are held by an independent trustee (such as a charitable trust for which a bank, trust company, foundation, or private individual is the trustee) or by another fiscal agent of the donor or the cash or other assets are otherwise not controlled by the NFP, the NFP should recognize its beneficial interest in those assets. The contribution should be recognized when the NFP is notified of the agreement's existence. Contribution revenues recognized should be classified in accordance with FASB ASC 958-30-45-1, which is reproduced in paragraph 6.18. If, however, the trustee or fiscal agent has variance power to redirect the benefits to another entity or if the NFP's rights to the benefits are conditional, the NFP should not recognize its potential for future distributions from the split-interest agreement until the NFP has an unconditional right to receive benefits under the agreement. (See FASB ASC 958-605-25-31.)

6.21 Occasionally, an NFP is named a beneficiary of a charitable trust without being informed. Also, an NFP may have discussions with donors and potential donors about establishing charitable trusts but may not know if a trust was established. An NFP should make reasonable efforts to obtain the information necessary to evaluate its beneficial interest if it does not receive a finalized executed copy of the trust agreement, regular trustee investment statements, or both. In some of these situations, donors or their representatives resist disclosing their personal information or their trust arrangements to the NFP.

6.22 As discussed in paragraph 6.20, NFPs should report irrevocable beneficial interests in trusts. In some circumstances, however, the NFP may have reliable and verifiable evidence that the beneficial interest exists, but may be unable to obtain the necessary information to measure the interest. The Financial Reporting Executive Committee (FinREC) believes that, for practical

[4] The amendments in FASB ASU No. 2016-14 are effective for annual financial statements issued for fiscal years beginning after December 15, 2017 (for example, years ending December 31, 2018, and years ending June 30, 2019), and for interim periods within fiscal years beginning after December 15, 2018. Application to interim financial statements is permitted but not required in the initial year of application. Early application of the amendments is permitted.

purposes, an NFP generally would need the following information in order to record its beneficial interests in a trust:

- A copy of the executed trust document, a statement from the trustee, or other information, to verify the trust's existence.
- Sufficient information about the trust in order to value the beneficial interest. In circumstances in which fair value is determined using the income approach, such information would include the assets held by the trust, payout rate or amount, and the age(s) of all life beneficiaries.

FinREC recommends that if the NFP has reliable and verifiable evidence that the beneficial interest exists but, after making and continuing to make reasonable efforts, the NFP is unable to obtain the necessary information to measure such interests, best practice is for the NFP to disclose the known facts and circumstances pertaining to the interest without reporting it as an asset.

6.23 FinREC believes that if sufficient information was unavailable in the year that the NFP initially became aware of the existence of the trust, the NFP should recognize the beneficial interest in the trust and contribution revenue in the first year in which the necessary information becomes available. The NFP should not report a prior period adjustment to correct an error (pursuant to FASB ASC 250, *Accounting Changes and Error Corrections*) if the NFP made, and continued to make, reasonable efforts to obtain the necessary information to measure the beneficial interest.

6.24 Pursuant to FASB ASC 958-605-30-14, if an NFP is the beneficiary of a split-interest agreement held by a trustee or fiscal agent and has an unconditional right to receive all or a portion of the specified cash flows from the assets held pursuant to that agreement, the NFP should measure its beneficial interest at fair value.

6.25 Present value techniques are one valuation technique for measuring the fair value of the contribution and the beneficial interest. If present value techniques are used, the contribution revenue and the beneficial interest in the trust should be measured at the present value of the future distributions expected to be received over the term of the agreement. However, if the trust held by a third party is a perpetual trust, FASB ASC 958-605-30-14 states that the fair value generally can be measured using the fair value of the assets contributed to the trust, unless facts and circumstances indicate that the fair value of the beneficial interest differs from the fair value of the assets contributed to the trust.

6.26 As noted in paragraph 49 of the fair value white paper, if present value techniques are used to value a beneficial interest in a charitable trust (or other identifiable pool of assets), it is important to remember when determining the appropriate discount rate that the cash flows from the trust (or pool) to the NFP are at least as risky as the cash flows within the trust (or pool) itself. That is, if the trustee or fiscal agent is receiving a yield to maturity of 4 percent to cover the risk of investing the trust assets, then the risk as a beneficiary of the cash flows from the investments of the trust (or pool) is at least 4 percent. (The risk can be higher because there is a possibility that the trustee or fiscal agent will not perform its duties as assigned.) In other words, the discount rate should always be greater than or equal to the assumed rate of the return on the trust (or pool) itself. As a result, an estimate of the fair value of the beneficial interest will never exceed the fair value of the trust (or pool) assets (or the proportionate share thereof if there is more than one charitable beneficiary.)

6.27 As noted in paragraph 5.09, FASB ASC 958-605-25 establishes standards for a beneficiary's reporting of assets held in trust, but does not establish standards for a trustee's reporting of those assets. Paragraphs 5.33–.38 discuss the requirements for transactions in which a perpetual trust held by a third party (trustee or other recipient entity) is established by an NFP for its own benefit or for the benefit of its affiliate. Paragraphs 6.62–.66 provide an example of a perpetual trust held by a third party.

Initial Recognition and Measurement of Pooled Income Funds and Net Income Unitrusts

6.28 Per FASB ASC 958-30-25-15 and FASB ASC 958-30-30-10, the assets received from the donor under a pooled income fund agreement or a net income unitrust should be recognized when received and measured at fair value. An NFP should recognize its remainder interest in the assets received as contribution revenue in the period in which the assets are received from the donor. The contribution should be measured at fair value. Present value techniques are one valuation technique for measuring the fair value of the contribution; other valuation techniques are also available, as described in FASB ASC 820-10-35. If present value techniques are used, the contribution may be measured at the fair value of the assets to be received, discounted for the estimated time period until the donor's death. The contributed assets should be recognized at fair value. The difference between the fair value of the assets when received and the revenue recognized should be recorded as deferred revenue, representing the amount of the discount for future interest. Contribution revenues recognized under a pooled income fund agreement or a net income unitrust should be classified in accordance with FASB ASC 958-30-45-1, which is reproduced in paragraph 6.18.

Recognition and Measurement During the Agreement's Term for Unconditional Irrevocable Agreements Other Than Pooled Income Funds or Net Income Unitrusts

6.29 Per FASB ASC 958-30-35-6 and 958-30-45-3, during the term of the agreement, certain transactions and events should be recognized as changes in the value of split-interest agreements in a statement of activities and should be classified as temporarily restricted, permanently restricted, or unrestricted net assets, depending on the classification used when the contribution revenue was recognized initially.

Per FASB ASC 958-30-35-6 and the "Pending Content" in FASB ASC 958-30-45-3, during the term of the agreement, certain transactions and events should be recognized as changes in the value of split-interest agreements in a statement of activities and should be classified as net assets with donor restrictions or net assets without donor restrictions, depending on the classification used when the contribution revenue was recognized initially.[5]

[5] The amendments in FASB ASU No. 2016-14 are effective for annual financial statements issued for fiscal years beginning after December 15, 2017 (for example, years ending December 31, 2018, and years ending June 30, 2019), and for interim periods within fiscal years beginning after December 15, 2018. Application to interim financial statements is permitted but not required in the initial year of application. Early application of the amendments is permitted.

6.30 Pursuant to FASB ASC 958-30-45-4, amounts should be reclassified from temporarily restricted net assets to unrestricted net assets as distributions are received by NFPs under the terms of split-interest agreements, unless those assets are otherwise temporarily restricted by the donor. In that case, they should be reclassified to unrestricted net assets when the restrictions expire.

Pursuant to the "Pending Content" in FASB ASC 958-30-45-4, amounts should be reclassified from net assets with donor restrictions to net assets without donor restrictions as distributions are received by NFPs under the terms of split-interest agreements, unless those assets are otherwise further restricted by the donor. In that case, they should be reclassified to net assets without donor restrictions when the restrictions expire.[6]

Unrelated Third Party Is the Trustee or Fiscal Agent

6.31 Pursuant to FASB ASC 958-30-35-2, in circumstances in which cash or other assets contributed by donors under split-interest agreements are held by independent trustees, such as a charitable trust for which a bank is a trustee, or by other fiscal agents of the donors or otherwise not controlled by the NFP, the measurement objective for the beneficial interest for periods subsequent to the period of initial recognition is fair value. Per FASB ASC 958-30-35-10, the change in the value of split-interest agreements should be the change in the fair value of the NFP's beneficial interest, which should be determined using the same valuation technique that was used to measure the asset initially. In accordance with FASB ASC 958-30-35-3, in circumstances in which the fair value is measured at the present value of the future cash flows, all elements discussed in FASB ASC 820-10-55-5, including discount rate assumptions, should be revised at each measurement date to reflect current market conditions. Distributions from the trust should be reflected as a reduction in the beneficial interest. As discussed in FASB ASC 958-30-45-4, as distributions are received by the NFP under the terms of the split-interest agreement, amounts should be reclassified from temporarily restricted net assets to unrestricted net assets unless those assets are otherwise temporarily restricted by the donor. In that case, they should be reclassified to unrestricted net assets when the restrictions expire.

Pursuant to FASB ASC 958-30-35-2, in circumstances in which cash or other assets contributed by donors under split-interest agreements are held by independent trustees, such as a charitable trust for which a bank is a trustee, or by other fiscal agents of the donors or otherwise not controlled by the NFP, the measurement objective for the beneficial interest for periods subsequent to the period of initial recognition is fair value. Per FASB ASC 958-30-35-10, the change in the value of split-interest agreements should be the change in the fair value of the NFP's beneficial interest, which should be determined using the same valuation technique that was used to measure the asset initially. In accordance with FASB ASC 958-30-35-3, in circumstances in which

---

[6] The amendments in FASB ASU No. 2016-14 are effective for annual financial statements issued for fiscal years beginning after December 15, 2017 (for example, years ending December 31, 2018, and years ending June 30, 2019), and for interim periods within fiscal years beginning after December 15, 2018. Application to interim financial statements is permitted but not required in the initial year of application. Early application of the amendments is permitted.

the fair value is measured at the present value of the future cash flows, all elements discussed in FASB ASC 820-10-55-5, including discount rate assumptions, should be revised at each measurement date to reflect current market conditions. Distributions from the trust should be reflected as a reduction in the beneficial interest. As discussed in the "Pending Content" in FASB ASC 958-30-45-4, as distributions are received by the NFP under the terms of the split-interest agreement, amounts should be reclassified from net assets with donor restrictions to net assets without donor restrictions as distributions are received by NFPs under the terms of split-interest agreements, unless those assets are otherwise further restricted by the donor. In that case, they should be reclassified to net assets without donor restrictions when the restrictions expire.[7]

NFP Is the Trustee or Fiscal Agent

6.32 FASB ASC 958-30-35-4 states that assets held by the NFP under irrevocable split-interest agreements as investments should be subsequently measured in conformity with FASB ASC 958-320-35 or FASB ASC 958-325-35.

6.33 Paragraphs 5–8 of FASB ASC 958-30-35 discuss the recognition of transactions and events during the term of a split-interest agreement in circumstances in which assets and related liabilities are recognized under lead and remainder interest agreements for which an NFP serves as a trustee or fiscal agent. Pursuant to FASB ASC 958-30-35-6, if the NFP does not elect to measure the liability at the fair value as described in the next paragraph, the following adjustments to the liability should be recognized as changes in the value of split-interest agreements in a statement of activities: (*a*) amortization of the discount associated with the contribution and (*b*) revaluations of future payments to beneficiaries, based on changes in life expectancy, and other actuarial assumptions. In conformity with FASB ASC 310-10-30-6 and FASB ASC 958-30-35-6, the discount rate should not be revised after initial recognition, unless the measurement objective for periods subsequent to the period of initial recognition is fair value.

6.34 As discussed in FASB ASC 958-30-35-2, the measurement objective is fair value for the following split-interest obligations:

a. Embedded derivatives subject to the measurement provisions of FASB ASC 815-15, as discussed in paragraph 6.37

b. Obligations for which the NFP elects the fair value option pursuant to the "Fair Value Option" subsections of FASB ASC 825-10, as discussed in paragraphs 6.38–.39

c. Obligations containing embedded derivatives that the NFP has irrevocably elected to measure in their entirety at fair value in conformity with FASB ASC 815-15-25 as discussed in paragraphs 6.37–.39.

6.35 FinREC recommends the use of fair value for measuring the assets and liabilities of split-interest agreements held by an NFP as trustee. Most assets held by NFPs under split-interest agreements are required to be measured

[7] The amendments in FASB ASU No. 2016-14 are effective for annual financial statements issued for fiscal years beginning after December 15, 2017 (for example, years ending December 31, 2018, and years ending June 30, 2019), and for interim periods within fiscal years beginning after December 15, 2018. Application to interim financial statements is permitted but not required in the initial year of application. Early application of the amendments is permitted.

at fair value by FASB ASC 958-320-35 or NFPs make an election to report the investments at fair value as permitted by FASB ASC 958-325-35. FinREC believes that reporting unrealized gains and losses on the investments held under a split-interest agreement without reporting the corresponding liability at fair value results in an effect on change in net assets that is not representative of how the NFP is affected by economic events, such as changes in interest rates. (Measuring split-interest obligations at fair value in subsequent periods is discussed in paragraphs 6.38–.39.) FinREC believes that holding an investment that is within the scope of FASB ASC 958-325-15 under a split-interest agreement and reporting it at fair value does not limit the available elections (fair value or cost) described in paragraphs 2, 4, and 6 of FASB ASC 958-325-35 (paragraph 4.38). For example, a house held as an investment of the NFP can be reported at cost even if a house held under a split-interest agreement is reported at fair value (or vice versa).

6.36 As discussed in paragraphs 7–14 of FASB ASC 958-30-25, the obligation for certain split-interest agreements contains embedded derivatives. Example 2 (paragraphs 6–29) of FASB ASC 958-30-55 provides illustrations for determining whether a split-interest agreement has an embedded derivative that requires bifurcation. The following paragraph summarizes the subsequent measurement guidance for embedded derivatives, but is not a substitute for the reading of paragraphs 7–8 of FASB ASC 958-30-35 or FASB ASC 815-15.

6.37 If an NFP does not elect to report a split-interest obligation at fair value, a split-interest obligation with an embedded derivative (for example, the liability for remainder unitrusts with either period-certain payments or period-certain-plus-life-contingent payments and certain lead interest trusts) is bifurcated into a debt host contract and an embedded derivative that is measured at fair value. (Paragraph 6.34 discusses alternative treatments for reporting split-interest agreements that contain embedded derivatives.) The debt host contract is the liability for the payment to the beneficiary that would be required if the fair value of the trust assets does not change over the specified period. The embedded derivative represents the liability (or contra-liability) for the increase (or decrease) in the payments to the beneficiary due to changes in the fair value of the trust assets over the specified period. Thus, in circumstances in which the liability is measured using present value techniques, the discount rate assumptions on the debt host contract should not be revised subsequent to initial recognition, consistent with paragraphs 5.192 and 6.33. In accordance with FASB ASC 815-10-35-1, the embedded derivative is subsequently measured at fair value. If the fair value of the embedded derivative is measured using present value techniques, all elements discussed in FASB ASC 820-10-55-5, including the discount rate assumptions on the embedded derivative should be revised at each measurement date to reflect current market conditions. In conformity with FASB ASC 815-15-25-53, if an NFP cannot reliably identify and measure the embedded derivative, the entire split-interest liability should be measured at fair value (that is, all elements discussed in FASB ASC 820-10-55-5, including discount rate assumptions, should be revised to reflect current market conditions).

6.38 If the NFP elects the fair value option pursuant to FASB ASC 958-30-35-6 in circumstances in which assets and related liabilities are recognized under lead and remainder interest agreements for which an NFP serves as a trustee or fiscal agent, the liability for future payments to be made to other beneficiaries is measured at fair value. The following paragraph summarizes the guidance for making the election and subsequently measuring at fair value, but is not a substitute for the reading of FASB ASC 815-15 or the "Fair Value Option" subsections of FASB ASC 825-10.

6.39 The election may be made on an instrument-by-instrument basis, and should be supported by concurrent documentation or a preexisting documented policy for automatic election. If an NFP elects to measure the obligation for future payments to be made to other beneficiaries at fair value, the entire liability should be remeasured at fair value (that is, if the fair value is measured using a present value technique, all the elements discussed in FASB ASC 820-10-55-5, including the discount rate assumptions for the entire obligation should be revised at each measurement date to reflect current market conditions).[8]

6.40 Per FASB ASC 958-30-35-5, when assets and related liabilities are recognized under charitable gift annuity, charitable lead trust, or charitable remainder trust agreements for which an NFP serves as a trustee or fiscal agent, income earned on those assets, gains and losses, and distributions made to other beneficiaries under the agreements should be reported in the NFP's statements of financial position, activities, and cash flows.

Recognition and Measurement During the Agreement's Term for Pooled Income Funds and Net Income Unitrusts

6.41 FASB ASC 958-30-35-4 states that assets held by the NFP under irrevocable split-interest agreements as investments should be subsequently measured in conformity with FASB ASC 958-320-35 or FASB ASC 958-325-35. Per FASB ASC 958-30-35-9, periodic income on a pooled income fund or net income unitrust and payments to the donor should be reflected as increases and decreases in a liability to the donor. Amortization of the discount should be recognized as a reduction in the deferred revenue account and as a change in the value of split-interest agreements. In accordance with FASB ASC 958-30-45-7, changes in the value of split-interest agreements recognized should be reported as separate line items in a statement of activities if not disclosed in the related notes. Pursuant to FASB ASC 958-30-45-3, changes in the value of split-interest agreements should be classified as temporarily restricted, permanently restricted, or unrestricted net assets, depending on the classification used when the contribution revenue was recognized initially.

FASB ASC 958-30-35-4 states that assets held by the NFP under irrevocable split-interest agreements as investments should be subsequently measured in conformity with FASB ASC 958-320-35 or FASB ASC 958-325-35. Per FASB ASC 958-30-35-9, periodic income on a pooled income fund or net income unitrust and payments to the donor should be reflected as increases and decreases in a liability to the donor. Amortization of the discount should be recognized as a reduction in the deferred revenue account and as a change in the value of split-interest agreements. In accordance with FASB ASC 958-30-45-7, changes in the value of split-interest agreements recognized should be reported as separate line items in a statement of activities if not disclosed in the related notes. Pursuant to the "Pending Content" in FASB ASC 958-30-45-3, changes in the value of split-interest agreements should be classified

[8] Paragraphs 3.169–.171 provide additional information about FASB ASC 815-15 or the "Fair Value Option" subsections of FASB ASC 825-10.

as net assets with donor restrictions or net assets without donor restrictions, depending on the classification used when the contribution revenue was recognized initially.[9]

Recognition Upon Termination of Agreement

6.42 Pursuant to FASB ASC 958-30-40-1, upon termination of a split-interest agreement, asset and liability accounts related to the agreement should be closed. Any remaining amounts in the asset or liability accounts should be recognized as changes in the value of split-interest agreements. The changes should be classified as changes in permanently restricted, temporarily restricted, or unrestricted net assets, pursuant to FASB ASC 958-30-45-3, as appropriate. Per FASB ASC 958-30-45-5, if assets previously distributed to the NFP become available for its unrestricted use upon termination of the agreement, appropriate amounts should be reclassified from temporarily restricted to unrestricted net assets.

Pursuant to FASB ASC 958-30-40-1, upon termination of a split-interest agreement, asset and liability accounts related to the agreement should be closed. Any remaining amounts in the asset or liability accounts should be recognized as changes in the value of split-interest agreements. The changes should be classified as changes in net assets with donor restrictions or net assets without donor restrictions, as appropriate. Per the "Pending Content" in FASB ASC 958-30-45-5, if assets previously distributed to the NFP become available for its general use upon termination of the split-interest agreement, a reclassification of net assets should be made from net assets with donor restrictions to net assets without donor restrictions.[10]

Purchase of Annuity Contracts to Make Distributions to the Beneficiaries

6.43 Some NFPs that serve as trustee or fiscal agents for split-interest agreements enter into annuity contracts with insurance companies or financial institutions to make the required distributions to the beneficiary specified by the donor. The purchase of those contracts is similar to reinsurance. In accordance with FASB ASC 405-20-40 and FASB ASC 944-20-40, an obligation is extinguished only if the debtor or ceding entity is legally relieved of its obligation for the liability. Whether the NFP has been legally relieved of its entire obligation to the beneficiary is a factual question that depends on the settlement's terms.

6.44 If the beneficiary legally releases the NFP as trustee from being the primary obligor under the split-interest agreement, the obligation to make

---

[9] The amendments in FASB ASU No. 2016-14 are effective for annual financial statements issued for fiscal years beginning after December 15, 2017 (for example, years ending December 31, 2018, and years ending June 30, 2019), and for interim periods within fiscal years beginning after December 15, 2018. Application to interim financial statements is permitted but not required in the initial year of application. Early application of the amendments is permitted.

[10] The amendments in FASB ASU No. 2016-14 are effective for annual financial statements issued for fiscal years beginning after December 15, 2017 (for example, years ending December 31, 2018, and years ending June 30, 2019), and for interim periods within fiscal years beginning after December 15, 2018. Application to interim financial statements is permitted but not required in the initial year of application. Early application of the amendments is permitted.

payments to the beneficiary is extinguished and a gain or loss on the extinguishment of the obligation can be recognized. However, FASB ASC 405-20-40-2 applies if the NFP remains secondarily liable to the beneficiary. FASB ASC 405-20-40-2 states that whether or not explicit consideration was paid for the guarantee, the original debtor (the NFP) becomes a guarantor. As a guarantor, it should recognize a guarantee obligation in the same manner as would a guarantor that had never been primarily liable to that creditor (beneficiary), with due regard for the likelihood that the third party [the insurance company or financial institution] will carry out its obligations. The guarantee obligation should be initially measured at fair value, and that amount reduces the gain or increases the loss recognized on extinguishment.

6.45 If the NFP as trustee is not relieved from being the primary obligor, the annuity contract is reported as an asset held under a split-interest agreement and the obligation to make payments continues to be reported as a liability. FASB ASC 210-20-45 permits an asset and a liability to be offset only if a right of setoff exists. That right would not exist in the situation described in paragraphs 6.43–.44 because the NFP as trustee owes the beneficiary, but the annuity contract that is making the payments is between the NFP and an insurance company or financial institution.

Financial Statement Presentation

Statement of Financial Position

6.46 As discussed in paragraph 3.12, if a split-interest agreement is in trust form, such as a unitrust or annuity trust, or if the assets held for a split-interest agreement are required by state law to be separately invested, the NFP should either separately display the asset on the face of the statement of financial position or should display the asset with similar assets of similar liquidity to meet the requirements of FASB ASC 958-210 and FASB ASC 210-10-45. Cash and investments held in the trust should not be combined with cash and investments that are available for operations.

Statement of Activities

6.47 As discussed in footnote 1 to chapter 5, "Contributions Received and Agency Transactions," contributions may be reported as revenues or gains, depending on whether they are part of the NFP's ongoing major activities or are peripheral or incidental transactions. For purposes of this chapter, the term contribution revenue is used to apply to either situation.

Disclosures

6.48 The majority of the unique disclosures for split-interest agreements are located in FASB ASC 958-30-50. The following three paragraphs discuss the more common of those disclosures, but are not intended as a substitute for the "Disclosure" sections of FASB ASC.

6.49 The notes to the financial statements should include all of the following disclosures related to split-interest agreements:

- A description of the general terms of existing split-interest agreements

- Assets and liabilities recognized under split-interest agreements, if not reported separately from other assets and liabilities in a statement of financial position
- The limitation(s) imposed on assets by the split-interest agreement, if not apparent from the face of the financial statements, as discussed in paragraphs 3.12 and 3.23
- If the nature of the assets held under the split-interest agreements and the related donor and legal restrictions, if not evident from the description(s) on the line item(s) on the statement of financial position, as discussed in paragraph 3.23
- The basis used (for example, cost, lower of cost or fair value, fair value) for recognized assets
- The discount rates and actuarial assumptions used, if present value techniques are used in reporting the assets and liabilities related to split-interest agreements
- Contribution revenue recognized under such agreements, if not reported as a separate line item in a statement of activities
- Changes in the value of split-interest agreements recognized, if not reported as a separate line item in a statement of activities
- The disclosures required by the "Fair Value Option" subsections of FASB ASC 825-10, if an NFP elects the fair value option pursuant to FASB ASC 958-30-35-2(b) or 958-30-35-2(c)
- The disclosures required by paragraphs 1–2, 2B, and 2E of FASB ASC 820-10-50 in the format described in FASB ASC 820-10-50-8, if the assets and liabilities of split-interest agreements are measured at fair value on a recurring basis in periods subsequent to initial recognition or if the fair value of split-interest assets and liabilities are disclosed

6.50 Annuity reserves may be required by the laws of the state where the NFP is located or by the state where the donor resides. An NFP that issues split-interest agreement contracts should disclose any legally mandated reserves in the notes to financial statements. If state law imposes other limitations on the NFP, such as limitations on the manner in which some net assets are invested, those limitations also should be disclosed in the notes to financial statements.

6.51 In addition, some NFPs voluntarily set aside additional reserves as a cushion against unexpected actuarial losses. Voluntary reserves should be included as part of unrestricted net assets, but may be disclosed as a separate component, such as board-designated unrestricted net assets (see FASB ASC 958-210-55-3).

In addition, some NFPs voluntarily set aside additional reserves for unexpected actuarial losses. The "Pending Content" in FASB ASC 958-30-50-3 requires that voluntary reserves be included as part of net assets without donor restrictions, but they may be presented as a separate component of board-designated net assets on the face of the statement of financial position (see the "Pending Content" in FASB ASC 958-210-55-3). If not provided on the face of that statement, the reserves set aside by the NFP's governing board should be disclosed in the notes in accordance with the "Pending Content" in FASB

ASC 958-210-50-3 to disclose information about the amounts and purposes of board designations of net assets without donor restrictions.[11]

6.52 As noted in paragraph 53 of the fair value white paper, when making disclosures about the inputs to fair value measurement, as required by FASB ASC 820-10-50-1, FinREC believes that if the fair value of the beneficial interest in a perpetual trust is measured using the fair value of the trust assets, best practice is for an NFP to disclose (*a*) the terms of the trust and practice of the trustee pertaining to distributions, and (*b*) that the NFP has used the fair value of the trust assets to determine the fair value of the beneficial interest.

6.53 If an NFP is unable to obtain sufficient information to make a reasonable estimate of the fair value of a beneficial interest (see paragraphs 6.21–.23), FinREC recommends as a best practice that the NFP disclose the following information about each potentially material beneficial interest or in the aggregate for individually immaterial beneficial interests that are material collectively:

- The characteristics of the agreement, to the extent known
- What factor(s) are limiting the ability to measure the beneficial interest(s)
- How much the NFP received from the beneficial interest(s) in each of the periods for which a statement of activities is presented.

Examples of Split-Interest Agreements

6.54 Many kinds of split-interest agreements have been developed. The examples in this section demonstrate how the recognition and measurement principles discussed in this chapter apply to some common kinds of agreements. Appendix B, "Journal Entries," of this chapter provides journal entries related to these examples.

Charitable Lead Trust

6.55 A charitable lead trust is an arrangement in which a donor establishes and funds a trust with specific distributions to be made to a designated NFP over a specified period. The NFP's use of the assets distributed may be restricted by the donor. The distributions may be for a fixed dollar amount, an arrangement called a *charitable lead annuity trust*, or for a fixed percentage of the trust's fair value as determined annually, a *charitable lead unitrust*. Upon termination of the trust, the remainder of the trust assets is paid to the donor or to the beneficiaries designated by the donor.

6.56 For example, NFP A receives cash from a donor under an irrevocable charitable lead annuity trust agreement designating NFP A as trustee and lead beneficiary. Under the terms of the trust, NFP A will invest the assets and receive a specified dollar amount each year for its general use until the death of the donor. At that time, the remaining assets in the trust revert to the donor's estate.

---

[11] The amendments in FASB ASU No. 2016-14 are effective for annual financial statements issued for fiscal years beginning after December 15, 2017 (for example, years ending December 31, 2018, and years ending June 30, 2019), and for interim periods within fiscal years beginning after December 15, 2018. Application to interim financial statements is permitted but not required in the initial year of application. Early application of the amendments is permitted.

6.57 Contribution revenue, assets held in trust, and a liability for amounts held for others should be recognized by NFP A in the period in which the trust is established. Revenue should be reported as temporarily restricted support and measured at fair value. The present value of the specified dollar amount to be received annually over the expected life of the donor is one possible technique to measure the fair value of the contribution. The assets held in trust by NFP A should be recorded at fair value at the date of initial recognition. The difference between the fair value of the assets received and the contribution revenue represents the present value of the liability to pay the donor's estate upon the termination of the trust.

Contribution revenue, assets held in trust, and a liability for amounts held for others should be recognized by NFP A in the period in which the trust is established. Revenue should be reported as an increase in net assets with donor restrictions and measured at fair value. The present value of the specified dollar amount to be received annually over the expected life of the donor is one possible technique to measure the fair value of the contribution. The assets held in trust by NFP A should be recorded at fair value at the date of initial recognition. The difference between the fair value of the assets received and the contribution revenue represents the present value of the liability to pay the donor's estate upon the termination of the trust.[12]

6.58 In subsequent periods, both the income earned on the trust assets and recognized gains and losses should be reflected in the trust asset and liability accounts. Adjustments of the liability to reflect amortization of the discount and revaluations of the future cash flows based on revisions in the donor's life expectancy should be recognized as changes in the value of split-interest agreements and classified as changes in temporarily restricted net assets in a statement of activities. Amounts should be reclassified from temporarily restricted to unrestricted net assets as the annual distributions to NFP A are made and recognized during the term of the trust. Upon the death of the donor, the assets are distributed to the donor's estate, the asset and liability accounts are closed, and any difference between the balances in those accounts should be recognized as a change in the value of split-interest agreements in the temporarily restricted net asset class. (In this example, the timing of the distribution of the remainder interest to the beneficiary was dependent on the donor's death. If instead the distribution were required to be paid at the end of a specified period, the liability to the beneficiary would have contained an embedded derivative as described in paragraph 6.36. Paragraphs 6.34–.39 discuss measuring an obligation that contains an embedded derivative.)

In subsequent periods, both the income earned on the trust assets and recognized gains and losses should be reflected in the trust asset and liability accounts. Adjustments of the liability to reflect amortization of the discount and revaluations of the future cash flows based on revisions in the donor's life expectancy should be recognized as changes in the value of split-interest agreements and classified as changes in net assets with donor restrictions in

---

[12] The amendments in FASB ASU No. 2016-14 are effective for annual financial statements issued for fiscal years beginning after December 15, 2017 (for example, years ending December 31, 2018, and years ending June 30, 2019), and for interim periods within fiscal years beginning after December 15, 2018. Application to interim financial statements is permitted but not required in the initial year of application. Early application of the amendments is permitted.

a statement of activities. Amounts should be reclassified from net assets with donor restrictions to net assets without donor restrictions as the annual distributions to NFP A are made and recognized during the term of the trust. Upon the death of the donor, the assets are distributed to the donor's estate, the asset and liability accounts are closed, and any difference between the balances in those accounts should be recognized as a change in the value of split-interest agreements in the net assets with donor restrictions class. (In this example, the timing of the distribution of the remainder interest to the beneficiary was dependent on the donor's death. If instead the distribution were required to be paid at the end of a specified period, the liability to the beneficiary would have contained an embedded derivative as described in paragraph 6.36. Paragraphs 6.34–.39 discuss measuring an obligation that contains an embedded derivative.)[13]

6.59 Paragraph B-2 of appendix B provides the journal entries related to the previous example.

6.60 If NFP A is not the trustee and does not exercise control over the trust's assets, it should recognize its beneficial interest in those assets as temporarily restricted contribution revenue and as a beneficial interest, measured at fair value as discussed in paragraphs 6.20–.27. Distributions from the trust should be reflected as a reduction in the beneficial interest and as reclassifications from temporarily restricted net assets to unrestricted net assets. Changes in the fair value of the beneficial interest should be recognized as adjustments to the beneficial interest in the statement of financial position and as changes in the value of split-interest agreements in the statement of activities in the temporarily restricted net asset class. If present value techniques are used to estimate fair value, those changes would reflect the revision of all elements discussed in FASB ASC 820-10-55-5, including the passage of time, revaluations of expected future cash flows based on revisions in the donor's life expectancy, and discount rate assumptions to reflect current market conditions. Any balance in the beneficial interest account remaining upon termination of the trust should be recognized as a change in the value of split-interest agreements in the statement of activities in the temporarily restricted net asset class. Paragraph B-3 of appendix B provides the journal entries related to this example.

If NFP A is not the trustee and does not exercise control over the trust's assets, it should recognize its beneficial interest in those assets as donor-restricted contribution revenue and as a beneficial interest, measured at fair value as discussed in paragraphs 6.20–.27. Distributions from the trust should be reflected as a reduction in the beneficial interest and as reclassifications from net assets with donor restrictions to net assets without donor restrictions. Changes in the fair value of the beneficial interest should be recognized as adjustments to the beneficial interest in the statement of financial position and as changes in the value of split-interest agreements in the statement of activities in the net assets with donor restrictions class. If present value techniques are used to estimate fair value, those changes would reflect the

[13] The amendments in FASB ASU No. 2016-14 are effective for annual financial statements issued for fiscal years beginning after December 15, 2017 (for example, years ending December 31, 2018, and years ending June 30, 2019), and for interim periods within fiscal years beginning after December 15, 2018. Application to interim financial statements is permitted but not required in the initial year of application. Early application of the amendments is permitted.

revision of all elements discussed in FASB ASC 820-10-55-5, including the passage of time, revaluations of expected future cash flows based on revisions in the donor's life expectancy, and discount rate assumptions to reflect current market conditions. Any balance in the beneficial interest account remaining upon termination of the trust should be recognized as a change in the value of split-interest agreements in the statement of activities in the net assets with donor restrictions class. Paragraph B-3 of appendix B provides the journal entries related to this example.[14]

6.61 Paragraphs 6.56–.60 are examples in which the donor specified that the distributions of the charitable lead annuity trust are to be distributed to NFP A for its unrestricted use. Accordingly, the initial contribution and subsequent changes to net assets as a result of this charitable lead annuity trust are reported as changes in temporarily restricted net assets, and amounts were reclassified from temporarily restricted to unrestricted net assets as the annual distributions to NFP A were made during the term of the trust. Had the donor instead specified that the remaining assets of the trust were to be distributed to NFP A to create a permanent endowment, the initial contribution, as well as subsequent changes to net assets as a result of this charitable lead annuity trust, would be reported as changes in permanently restricted net assets. Upon the death of the donor, when the assets are distributed to the donor's estate and the asset and liability accounts are closed, any difference between the balances in those accounts also would be recognized as a change in the value of split-interest agreements in the permanently restricted net asset class.

The preceding paragraph will be deleted upon the effective date of FASB ASU No. 2016-14.[15]

Perpetual Trust Held by a Third Party

6.62 According to the FASB ASC glossary, a *perpetual trust held by a third party* is an arrangement in which a donor establishes and funds a perpetual trust administered by an individual or entity other than the NFP that is the beneficiary.[16] Under the terms of the trust, the NFP has the irrevocable right to receive the income earned on the trust assets in perpetuity, but never receives the assets held in trust. Distributions received by the NFP may be restricted by the donor.

6.63 For example, a donor establishes a trust with the donor's bank serving as trustee. Funds contributed to the trust are to be invested in perpetuity. Under the terms of the trust, NFP B is to be the sole beneficiary and is to

---

[14] The amendments in FASB ASU No. 2016-14 are effective for annual financial statements issued for fiscal years beginning after December 15, 2017 (for example, years ending December 31, 2018, and years ending June 30, 2019), and for interim periods within fiscal years beginning after December 15, 2018. Application to interim financial statements is permitted but not required in the initial year of application. Early application of the amendments is permitted.

[15] The amendments in FASB ASU No. 2016-14 are effective for annual financial statements issued for fiscal years beginning after December 15, 2017 (for example, years ending December 31, 2018, and years ending June 30, 2019), and for interim periods within fiscal years beginning after December 15, 2018. Application to interim financial statements is permitted but not required in the initial year of application. Early application of the amendments is permitted.

[16] Paragraphs 5.33–.38 provide guidance for transactions in which a perpetual trust held by a third party (trustee or other recipient organization) is established by an NFP for its own benefit or for the benefit of its affiliate.

receive annually the income on the trust's assets as earned in perpetuity. NFP B can use the distributions from the trust in any way that is consistent with its mission.

6.64 The arrangement should be recognized by NFP B as contribution revenue and as an asset, measured at fair value, when NFP B is notified of the trust's existence, as discussed in paragraphs 6.20–.27. FASB ASC 958-605-30-14 states that the fair value of a perpetual trust held by a third party generally can be measured using the fair value of the assets contributed to the trust, unless facts and circumstances indicate that the fair value of the beneficial interest differs from the fair value of the assets contributed to the trust. The contribution should be classified as permanently restricted support, because the trust is similar to a donor-restricted permanent endowment that NFP B does not control, rather than a multiyear promise to give. Pursuant to FASB ASC 958-605-35-3, annual distributions from the trust are reported as investment income. In this example, the investment income increases unrestricted net assets.

The arrangement should be recognized by NFP B as contribution revenue and as an asset, measured at fair value, when NFP B is notified of the trust's existence, as discussed in paragraphs 6.20–.27. FASB ASC 958-605-30-14 states that the fair value of a perpetual trust held by a third party generally can be measured using the fair value of the assets contributed to the trust, unless facts and circumstances indicate that the fair value of the beneficial interest differs from the fair value of the assets contributed to the trust. The contribution should be classified as donor-restricted support, because the trust is similar to a donor-restricted perpetual endowment that NFP B does not control, rather than a multiyear promise to give. Pursuant to FASB ASC 958-605-35-3, annual distributions from the trust are reported as investment income. In this example, the investment income increases net assets without donor restrictions.[17]

6.65 Periodically in conjunction with preparing its financial statements, NFP B should remeasure its beneficial interest at fair value, using the same valuation technique that was used to measure the asset initially, as described in paragraph 6.31. If the fair value of the perpetual trust was initially measured using the fair value of the assets contributed to the trust, the fair value in subsequent periods generally can be measured using the fair value of the assets of the trust at the date of remeasurement, as explained in FASB ASC 958-605-35-3, unless facts and circumstances indicate that the fair value of the beneficial interest differs from the fair value of the assets contributed to the trust. In this example, the adjustment should be recognized as permanently restricted gains or losses.

Periodically in conjunction with preparing its financial statements, NFP B should remeasure its beneficial interest at fair value, using the same valuation technique that was used to measure the asset initially, as described in paragraph 6.31. If the fair value of the perpetual trust was initially measured

---

[17] The amendments in FASB ASU No. 2016-14 are effective for annual financial statements issued for fiscal years beginning after December 15, 2017 (for example, years ending December 31, 2018, and years ending June 30, 2019), and for interim periods within fiscal years beginning after December 15, 2018. Application to interim financial statements is permitted but not required in the initial year of application. Early application of the amendments is permitted.

using the fair value of the assets contributed to the trust, the fair value in subsequent periods generally can be measured using the fair value of the assets of the trust at the date of remeasurement, as explained in FASB ASC 958-605-35-3, unless facts and circumstances indicate that the fair value of the beneficial interest differs from the fair value of the assets contributed to the trust. In this example, the adjustment should be recognized as gains or losses in the net assets with donor restrictions class.[18]

6.66 Paragraph B-4 of appendix B provides the journal entries related to the previous example.

Charitable Remainder Trust

6.67 A charitable remainder trust is an arrangement in which a donor establishes and funds a trust with specified distributions to be made to a designated beneficiary or beneficiaries over the trust's term. Upon termination of the trust, an NFP receives the assets remaining in the trust. The NFP may ultimately have general use of those assets, or the donor may place restrictions on their use. The distributions to the beneficiaries may be for a specified dollar amount, an arrangement called a *charitable remainder annuity trust*, or for a specified percentage of the trust's fair value as determined annually, a *charitable remainder unitrust*. Some charitable remainder unitrusts limit the annual payout to the lesser of the stated percentage or the actual income earned. Obligations to the beneficiaries are limited to the trust's assets.

6.68 For example, a donor establishes a charitable remainder unitrust, with NFP C serving as trustee. Under the trust's terms, the donor's spouse is to receive an annual distribution equal in value to a specified percentage of the fair value of the trust's assets each year until the spouse dies. The income earned on the trust's assets must remain in the trust until the spouse dies. At that time, the remaining assets of the trust are to be distributed to NFP C for use as a perpetual endowment.

6.69 NFP C should recognize the contribution in the period in which the trust is established. The assets held in trust by NFP C and the liability to the donor's spouse should be recorded at fair value when received, as discussed in paragraphs 6.13–.19. If the liability is measured using present value techniques, the liability to the donor's spouse should be recorded at the present value of the future payments to be distributed over the spouse's expected life. The amount of the contribution is the difference between these amounts and should be classified as permanently restricted support because the donor has specified that NFP C must use the assets to create a perpetual endowment.

NFP C should recognize the contribution in the period in which the trust is established. The assets held in trust by NFP C and the liability to the donor's spouse should be recorded at fair value when received, as discussed in paragraphs 6.13–.19. If the liability is measured using present value techniques, the liability to the donor's spouse should be recorded at the present value of the future payments to be distributed over the spouse's expected life.

---

[18] The amendments in FASB ASU No. 2016-14 are effective for annual financial statements issued for fiscal years beginning after December 15, 2017 (for example, years ending December 31, 2018, and years ending June 30, 2019), and for interim periods within fiscal years beginning after December 15, 2018. Application to interim financial statements is permitted but not required in the initial year of application. Early application of the amendments is permitted.

The amount of the contribution is the difference between these amounts and should be classified as donor-restricted support because the donor has specified that NFP C must use the assets to create a perpetual endowment.[19]

6.70 In subsequent periods, income earned on trust assets, recognized gains and losses, and distributions paid to the spouse should be reflected in the NFP C's statement of financial position. Adjustments to the liability to reflect amortization of the discount, revaluations of the present value of the estimated future payments to the spouse, and changes in actuarial assumptions should be recognized in a statement of activities as a change in the value of split-interest agreements in the permanently restricted net asset class. Upon the death of the spouse, the liability should be closed and any balance should be recognized as a change in the value of split-interest agreements in the statement of activities in the permanently restricted net asset class. (In this example, the period for which distributions were made to the beneficiary was dependent solely on the spouse's death and the payment amounts varied based on the fair value of the unitrust assets. If instead the variable-amount distributions were required to be paid for a specified number of years—or for the greater of the spouse's life or a specified number of years, the liability to the beneficiary would have contained an embedded derivative, as discussed in paragraph 6.36. Paragraphs 6.34–.39 discuss measuring an obligation that contains an embedded derivative.

In subsequent periods, income earned on trust assets, recognized gains and losses, and distributions paid to the spouse should be reflected in the NFP C's statement of financial position. Adjustments to the liability to reflect amortization of the discount, revaluations of the present value of the estimated future payments to the spouse, and changes in actuarial assumptions should be recognized in a statement of activities as a change in the value of split-interest agreements in the net assets with donor restrictions class. Upon the death of the spouse, the liability should be closed and any balance should be recognized as a change in the value of split-interest agreements in the statement of activities in the net assets with donor restrictions class. (In this example, the period for which distributions were made to the beneficiary was dependent solely on the spouse's death and the payment amounts varied based on the fair value of the unitrust assets. If instead the variable-amount distributions were required to be paid for a specified number of years—or for the greater of the spouse's life or a specified number of years, the liability to the beneficiary would have contained an embedded derivative, as discussed in paragraph 6.36. Paragraphs 6.34–.39 discuss measuring an obligation that contains an embedded derivative.[20]

---

[19] The amendments in FASB ASU No. 2016-14 are effective for annual financial statements issued for fiscal years beginning after December 15, 2017 (for example, years ending December 31, 2018, and years ending June 30, 2019), and for interim periods within fiscal years beginning after December 15, 2018. Application to interim financial statements is permitted but not required in the initial year of application. Early application of the amendments is permitted.

[20] The amendments in FASB ASU No. 2016-14 are effective for annual financial statements issued for fiscal years beginning after December 15, 2017 (for example, years ending December 31, 2018, and years ending June 30, 2019), and for interim periods within fiscal years beginning after December 15, 2018. Application to interim financial statements is permitted but not required in the initial year of application. Early application of the amendments is permitted.

6.71 Paragraph B-5 of appendix B provides the journal entries related to the previous example.

6.72 If NFP C is not the trustee and does not exercise control over the assets contributed to the trust, the agreement should be recognized as a beneficial interest in a trust. NFP C should recognize, as permanently restricted contribution revenue and as a beneficial interest, the fair value of the beneficial interest, as discussed in paragraphs 6.20–.27. Adjustments to the beneficial interest to reflect changes in the fair value should be measured using the same valuation technique as was used to measure the asset initially and recognized as changes in the value of split-interest agreements. For example, if present value techniques were used to estimate fair value, the adjustment would reflect the revision of all elements discussed in FASB ASC 820-10-55-5, including the passage of time, revaluation of the present value of the future payments to the spouse, changes in actuarial assumptions during the term of the trust, and discount rates based on current market conditions. Upon the death of the spouse, the beneficial interest is closed, the assets received from the trust are recognized at fair value, and any difference is reported as a change in the value of split-interest agreements in permanently restricted net assets. Paragraph B-6 of appendix B provides the journal entries related to this example.

If NFP C is not the trustee and does not exercise control over the assets contributed to the trust, the agreement should be recognized as a beneficial interest in a trust. NFP C should recognize, as donor-restricted contribution revenue and as a beneficial interest, the fair value of the beneficial interest, as discussed in paragraphs 6.20–.27. Adjustments to the beneficial interest to reflect changes in the fair value should be measured using the same valuation technique as was used to measure the asset initially and recognized as changes in the value of split-interest agreements. For example, if present value techniques were used to estimate fair value, the adjustment would reflect the revision of all elements discussed in FASB ASC 820-10-55-5, including the passage of time, revaluation of the present value of the future payments to the spouse, changes in actuarial assumptions during the term of the trust, and discount rates based on current market conditions. Upon the death of the spouse, the beneficial interest is closed, the assets received from the trust are recognized at fair value, and any difference is reported as a change in the value of split-interest agreements in the net assets with donor restrictions class. Paragraph B-6 of appendix B provides the journal entries related to this example.[21]

6.73 Paragraphs 6.68–.72 are an example in which the donor specified that the remaining assets of the charitable remainder unitrust are to be distributed to NFP C for use as a perpetual endowment. Accordingly, the initial contribution and subsequent changes to net assets as a result of this charitable remainder unitrust are reported as changes in permanently restricted net assets. Had the donor instead specified that the remaining assets of the trust were to be distributed to NFP C for its unrestricted use, the initial contribution, as well as subsequent changes to net assets as a result of this charitable

[21] The amendments in FASB ASU No. 2016-14 are effective for annual financial statements issued for fiscal years beginning after December 15, 2017 (for example, years ending December 31, 2018, and years ending June 30, 2019), and for interim periods within fiscal years beginning after December 15, 2018. Application to interim financial statements is permitted but not required in the initial year of application. Early application of the amendments is permitted.

remainder unitrust, would be reported as changes in temporarily restricted net assets because their use is time restricted (they must be held in the split-interest trust until the donor's spouse dies). Upon the death of the spouse, the liability would be closed and any balance would be recognized as a change in the value of split-interest agreements in the statement of activities in the temporarily restricted net asset class, with a reclassification from temporarily restricted net assets to unrestricted net assets to recognize the expiration of the time restriction upon the donor's death.

Paragraphs 6.68–.72 are an example in which the donor specified that the remaining assets of the charitable remainder unitrust are to be distributed to NFP C for use as a perpetual endowment. Accordingly, the initial contribution and subsequent changes to net assets as a result of this charitable remainder unitrust are reported as changes in net assets with donor restrictions due to the perpetual nature of the restriction. Had the donor instead specified that the remaining assets of the trust were to be distributed to NFP C for its general use, the initial contribution, as well as subsequent changes to net assets as a result of this charitable remainder unitrust, still would be reported as changes in net assets with donor restrictions, but in this case, the classification reflects that their use is time restricted (they must be held in the split-interest trust until the donor's spouse dies). Upon the death of the spouse, the liability would be closed and any balance would be recognized as a change in the value of split-interest agreements in the statement of activities in the net asset with donor restrictions class, with a reclassification from net assets with donor restrictions to net assets without donor restrictions to recognize the expiration of the time restriction upon the donor's death.[22]

Charitable Gift Annuity

6.74 A charitable gift annuity is an arrangement between a donor and an NFP in which the donor contributes assets to the NFP in exchange for a promise by the NFP to pay a fixed amount for a specified period of time to the donor or to individuals or entities designated by the donor. The agreements are similar to charitable remainder annuity trusts except that no trust exists, the assets received are held as general assets of the NFP, and the annuity liability is a general obligation of the NFP.

6.75 For example, NFP D and a donor enter into an arrangement whereby assets are transferred from the donor to NFP D. NFP D agrees to pay a stated dollar amount annually to the donor's spouse until the spouse dies.

6.76 NFP D should recognize the agreement in the period in which the contract is executed. The assets received should be recognized at fair value when received, and an annuity payment liability should be recognized at fair value as discussed in paragraphs 6.13–.19. As noted in paragraphs 71–76 of the fair value white paper, using a market approach and level 2 inputs may be the best valuation approach for measuring the fair value of certain liabilities under split-interest remainder agreements with fixed payments; for others, the

[22] The amendments in FASB ASU No. 2016-14 are effective for annual financial statements issued for fiscal years beginning after December 15, 2017 (for example, years ending December 31, 2018, and years ending June 30, 2019), and for interim periods within fiscal years beginning after December 15, 2018. Application to interim financial statements is permitted but not required in the initial year of application. Early application of the amendments is permitted.

income approach in the form of present value techniques will be the best valuation technique. In this example, unrestricted[23] contribution revenue should be recognized as the difference between these two amounts.

NFP D should recognize the agreement in the period in which the contract is executed. The assets received should be recognized at fair value when received, and an annuity payment liability should be recognized at fair value as discussed in paragraphs 6.18–.19. As noted in paragraphs 71–76 of the fair value white paper, using a market approach and level 2 inputs may be the best valuation approach for measuring the fair value of certain liabilities under split-interest remainder agreements with fixed payments; for others, the income approach in the form of present value techniques will be the best valuation technique. In this example, contribution revenue increasing the net assets without donor restrictions class should be recognized as the difference between these two amounts.[24]

6.77 In subsequent periods, payments to the donor's spouse reduce the annuity liability. Adjustments to the annuity liability to reflect amortization of the discount and changes in the life expectancy of the donor's spouse should be recognized in a statement of activities as changes in the value of split-interest agreements in unrestricted net assets. Upon the death of the donor's spouse, the annuity liability should be closed and a change in the value of split-interest agreements should be recognized in the statement of activities.

In subsequent periods, payments to the donor's spouse reduce the annuity liability. Adjustments to the annuity liability to reflect amortization of the discount and changes in the life expectancy of the donor's spouse should be recognized in a statement of activities as changes in the value of split-interest agreements in net assets without donor restrictions. Upon the death of the donor's spouse, the annuity liability should be closed and a change in the value of split-interest agreements should be recognized in the statement of activities.[25]

6.78 Paragraph B-7 of appendix B provides the journal entries related to the previous example.

Pooled (Life) Income Fund

6.79 Some NFPs form, invest, and manage pooled (or life) income funds.[26] These funds are divided into units, and contributions of many donors'

---

[23] Paragraphs 6.18–.19 discuss the classification of the contribution portion of a charitable gift annuity agreement. Paragraphs 6.50–.51 discuss classification and disclosure of reserve requirements or other limitations imposed by state law on NFPs that hold charitable gift annuities.

[24] The amendments in FASB ASU No. 2016-14 are effective for annual financial statements issued for fiscal years beginning after December 15, 2017 (for example, years ending December 31, 2018, and years ending June 30, 2019), and for interim periods within fiscal years beginning after December 15, 2018. Application to interim financial statements is permitted but not required in the initial year of application. Early application of the amendments is permitted.

[25] The amendments in FASB ASU No. 2016-14 are effective for annual financial statements issued for fiscal years beginning after December 15, 2017 (for example, years ending December 31, 2018, and years ending June 30, 2019), and for interim periods within fiscal years beginning after December 15, 2018. Application to interim financial statements is permitted but not required in the initial year of application. Early application of the amendments is permitted.

[26] Net income unitrusts are similar to pooled life-income funds because the corpus is maintained. Accordingly, financial reporting for net income unitrusts is similar to reporting for pooled life-income funds.

life-income gifts are pooled and invested as a group. The FASB ASC glossary defines a *pooled income fund* as a trust in which donors are assigned a specific number of units based on the proportion of the fair value of their contributions to the total fair value of the pooled income fund on the date of the donor's entry to the pooled fund. Until a donor's death, the donor (or the donor's designated beneficiary or beneficiaries) is paid the actual income (as defined under the arrangement) earned on the donor's assigned units. Upon the donor's death, the value of these assigned units reverts to the NFP.

6.80 For example, a donor contributes assets to NFP E's pooled (life) income fund and is assigned a specific number of units in the pool. The donor is to receive a life interest in any income earned on those units. Upon the donor's death, the value of the units is available to NFP E for its general use.

6.81 NFP E should recognize its remainder interest in the assets received as temporarily restricted contribution revenue in the period in which the assets are received from the donor. The contribution should be measured at fair value. Present value techniques are one valuation technique for measuring the fair value of the contribution. If present value techniques are used, the contribution may be measured at the fair value of the assets to be received, discounted for the estimated time period until the donor's death. The contributed assets should be recognized at fair value when received. The difference between the fair value of the assets when received and the revenue recognized should be recorded as deferred revenue, representing the amount of the discount for future interest.

NFP E should recognize its remainder interest in the assets received as donor-restricted contribution revenue in the period in which the assets are received from the donor. The contribution should be measured at fair value. Present value techniques are one valuation technique for measuring the fair value of the contribution. If present value techniques are used, the contribution may be measured at the fair value of the assets to be received, discounted for the estimated time period until the donor's death. The contributed assets should be recognized at fair value when received. The difference between the fair value of the assets when received and the revenue recognized should be recorded as deferred revenue, representing the amount of the discount for future interest.[27]

6.82 Periodic income on the fund and payments to the donor should be reflected as increases and decreases in a liability to the donor. Amortization of the discount should be recognized as a reduction in the deferred revenue account and as a change in the value of split-interest agreements and reported as a change in temporarily restricted net assets. Upon the donor's death, any remaining balance in the deferred revenue account should be closed and a change in the value of split-interest agreements should be recognized. A reclassification to unrestricted net assets is also necessary to record the satisfaction of the time restriction on temporarily restricted net assets.

---

[27] The amendments in FASB ASU No. 2016-14 are effective for annual financial statements issued for fiscal years beginning after December 15, 2017 (for example, years ending December 31, 2018, and years ending June 30, 2019), and for interim periods within fiscal years beginning after December 15, 2018. Application to interim financial statements is permitted but not required in the initial year of application. Early application of the amendments is permitted.

Periodic income on the fund and payments to the donor should be reflected as increases and decreases in a liability to the donor. Amortization of the discount should be recognized as a reduction in the deferred revenue account and as a change in the value of split-interest agreements in the net assets with donor restrictions class. Upon the donor's death, any remaining balance in the deferred revenue account should be closed and a change in the value of split-interest agreements should be recognized. A reclassification to net assets without donor restrictions is also necessary to record the satisfaction of the time restriction on the restricted net assets.[28]

6.83 Paragraph B-8 of appendix B provides the journal entries related to the previous example.

Life Interest in Real Estate

6.84 Occasionally an NFP receives a contribution of real estate (such as a personal residence or farm) and the donor retains the right to use the real estate until his or her death (referred to as an irrevocable life interest). Paragraphs 6.85–.88 provide an example showing how that contribution would be reported.

6.85 A donor irrevocably transfers title to her personal residence to NFP G, retaining the right for the donor and the donor's spouse to use the residence until their deaths. The contract between the donor and NFP G specifies that the donor continues to pay the executory costs for the property, including maintenance costs, property taxes, insurance, utilities, and similar costs. NFP G should recognize the agreement in the period in which the contract and deed are executed. The residence received should be recognized at its fair value, and an obligation for the life interest should be recognized at fair value. The fair value of the use obligation for the donor's life interest should consider the fair value rent for similar properties, actuarial life expectancy of the donor and the donor's spouse, as well as whether the donor or the NFP is responsible for any executory costs, and other factors pursuant to FASB ASC 840, *Leases*. Because the use interest is reported as a separate obligation, NFP G should measure the fair value of the residence received without regard to the use interest. The use obligation should be considered deferred revenue. The difference between the fair value of the residence and the fair value of the use obligation for the donor's life interest is recognized as contribution revenue that is temporarily restricted (time restriction that exists until the expiration of the donor's life interest) unless the donor has specified that the proceeds from the sale of the residence must be used by NFP G to create a permanent endowment fund (or other permanent restriction on use), in which case the contribution revenue is permanently restricted.

A donor irrevocably transfers title to her personal residence to NFP G, retaining the right for the donor and the donor's spouse to use the residence until their deaths. The contract between the donor and NFP G specifies that the donor continues to pay the executory costs for the property, including maintenance costs, property taxes, insurance, utilities, and similar costs. NFP G

---

[28] The amendments in FASB ASU No. 2016-14 are effective for annual financial statements issued for fiscal years beginning after December 15, 2017 (for example, years ending December 31, 2018, and years ending June 30, 2019), and for interim periods within fiscal years beginning after December 15, 2018. Application to interim financial statements is permitted but not required in the initial year of application. Early application of the amendments is permitted.

should recognize the agreement in the period in which the contract and deed are executed. The residence received should be recognized at its fair value, and an obligation for the life interest should be recognized at fair value. The fair value of the use obligation for the donor's life interest should consider the fair value rent for similar properties, actuarial life expectancy of the donor and the donor's spouse, as well as whether the donor or the NFP is responsible for any executory costs, and other factors pursuant to FASB ASC 840, *Leases*. Because the use interest is reported as a separate obligation, NFP G should measure the fair value of the residence received without regard to the use interest. The use obligation should be considered deferred revenue. The difference between the fair value of the residence and the fair value of the use obligation for the donor's life interest is recognized as donor-restricted contribution revenue (recognizing the time restriction that exists until the expiration of the donor's life interest and a purpose restriction if the donor restricted the use of the proceeds from the sale of the residence).[29]

6.86 In subsequent periods, NFP G should amortize the use obligation based on the actuarial life expectancy of the donor and the donor's spouse. (Because the use interest is a lease, it is not eligible for the fair value option pursuant to the Fair Value Option subsections of FASB ASC 825-10, as discussed in 825-10-15-5, and should not otherwise be adjusted to reflect changes in the rental market.) Adjustments to the use obligation to reflect amortization of the discount, the amortization of the use obligation, and changes in the life expectancy of the donor are recognized in a statement of activities as changes in the value of split-interest agreements in the same class of net assets as the contribution. Because the residence is held as an investment, the guidance in FASB ASC 958-325-35, which is discussed in paragraph 4.38, should be used for subsequent measurement of the residence. Upon the death of both the donor and the donor's spouse, the use obligation should be closed and a change in the value of split-interest agreements should be recognized in the statement of activities in the same net asset class as the contribution. If the residence is then available for the NFP's general use (that is, the donor has not further restricted the use of the residence or the proceeds of its sale), the carrying amount of the residence should be reclassified from temporarily restricted to unrestricted net assets. In this example, the donor was responsible for executory costs of the residence. If instead NFP G were responsible, it would report cash flows for maintaining the real estate, such as property taxes, utilities, and repairs and maintenance as period costs (as opposed to initially recognizing a liability for future period expenses).

In subsequent periods, NFP G should amortize the use obligation based on the actuarial life expectancy of the donor and the donor's spouse. (Because the use interest is a lease, it is not eligible for the fair value option pursuant to the Fair Value Option subsections of FASB ASC 825-10, as discussed in 825-10-15-5, and should not otherwise be adjusted to reflect changes in the rental market.) Adjustments to the use obligation to reflect amortization of the discount, the amortization of the use obligation, and changes in the life

[29] The amendments in FASB ASU No. 2016-14 are effective for annual financial statements issued for fiscal years beginning after December 15, 2017 (for example, years ending December 31, 2018, and years ending June 30, 2019), and for interim periods within fiscal years beginning after December 15, 2018. Application to interim financial statements is permitted but not required in the initial year of application. Early application of the amendments is permitted.

expectancy of the donor are recognized in a statement of activities as changes in the value of split-interest agreements in the same class of net assets as the contribution. Because the residence is held as an investment, the guidance in FASB ASC 958-325-35, which is discussed in paragraph 4.38, should be used for subsequent measurement of the residence. Upon the death of both the donor and the donor's spouse, the use obligation should be closed and a change in the value of split-interest agreements should be recognized in the statement of activities in the same net asset class as the contribution. If the residence is then available for the NFP's general use (that is, the donor has not further restricted the use of the residence or the proceeds of its sale), the carrying amount of the residence should be reclassified from net assets with donor restrictions to net assets without donor restrictions. In this example, the donor was responsible for executory costs of the residence. If instead NFP G were responsible, it would report cash flows for maintaining the real estate, such as property taxes, utilities, and repairs and maintenance as period costs (as opposed to initially recognizing a liability for future period expenses).[30]

6.87 The disclosures required by FASB ASC 958-325-50 for other investments should include the residence. FinREC believes that NFP G should also disclose the following information pertaining to a life interest in real estate. The disclosures may be aggregated if the NFP holds more than one life interest in real estate.

- The carrying amount of property (fair value at date of gift plus any capitalized additions or fair value, dependent upon the type of NFP and its election for subsequent measurement, as described in paragraph 4.38) as of the date of the latest statement of financial position presented. Further, as required by FASB ASC 958-325-35-2 and 360-10-50-1, if NFP G is a college or university, it should disclose the amount of accumulated depreciation if it subsequently measures the contributed property at fair value at date of gift plus any capitalized additions.
- The property should not be included in the statement of financial position with property and equipment used in operations, but it may be included with investments.
- The amount of the use obligation at the date of the latest statement of financial position presented, if not separately displayed on the face of the statement of financial position.
- That the donor and the donor's spouse are responsible for executory costs.
- In accordance with FASB ASC 958-210-45-6, the donor-imposed restrictions on the use of the residence and that it cannot be sold until the death of both the donor and the donor's spouse.

6.88 Paragraph B-9 of appendix B provides the journal entries related to the previous example.

---

[30] The amendments in FASB ASU No. 2016-14 are effective for annual financial statements issued for fiscal years beginning after December 15, 2017 (for example, years ending December 31, 2018, and years ending June 30, 2019), and for interim periods within fiscal years beginning after December 15, 2018. Application to interim financial statements is permitted but not required in the initial year of application. Early application of the amendments is permitted.

Auditing

6.89 Because for-profit entities do not usually enter into split-interest agreements, the specific audit objectives and auditing procedures, including consideration of controls, related to such agreements are unique to NFPs and are presented in the following paragraphs. (See also the discussion concerning confirming receivables in paragraphs 5.237–.238.)

6.90 Reporting split-interest agreements requires the NFP to measure fair value of assets and liabilities. AU-C section 540, *Auditing Accounting Estimates, Including Fair Value Accounting Estimates, and Related Disclosures*,[31] addresses audit considerations relating to the measurement and disclosure of assets, liabilities, and specific components of equity presented or disclosed at fair value in financial statements.

6.91 The following table illustrates the use of assertions in developing audit objectives and designing substantive tests. The examples are not intended to be all-inclusive nor is it expected that all the procedures would necessarily be applied in an audit. The use of assertions in assessing risks and designing appropriate audit procedures to obtain audit evidence is described in paragraphs .26–.32 of AU-C section 315, *Understanding the Entity and Its Environment and Assessing the Risks of Material Misstatement*. Paragraph .18 of AU-C section 330, *Performing Audit Procedures in Response to Assessed Risks and Evaluating the Audit Evidence Obtained*, requires the auditor to design and perform substantive procedures for all relevant assertions related to each material class of transactions, account balance, and disclosure, irrespective of the assessed risks of material misstatement. This requirement reflects the facts that (1) the auditor's assessment of risk is judgmental and may not identify all risks of material misstatement, and (2) inherent limitations to internal control exist, including management override. Various audit procedures and the purposes for which they may be performed are described in paragraphs .A10–.A26 of AU-C section 500, *Audit Evidence*.

Auditing Considerations

Financial Statement Assertions	*Specific Audit Objectives*	*Select Control Objectives*
Transactions		
Occurrence/ Existence	Amounts recognized as contribution revenues or change in value resulting from split-interest agreements represent valid revenues.	Management has established procedures to track and support the existence of split-interest agreements. If NFP is the trustee, management authorizes split-interest agreements.

[31] All AU-C sections can be found in AICPA *Professional Standards*.

Auditing Considerations—*continued*

Financial Statement Assertions	***Specific Audit Objectives***	***Select Control Objectives***
Completeness	All unconditional split-interest agreements are recognized. All income received under split-interest agreements is recorded.	Controls ensure that split-interest agreements are known and recorded. Management reviews income distribution terms of split-interest agreements and determines that periodic reports and remittances from trustees conform to those terms. Donor relations and fund-raising staff notify appropriate management upon death of beneficiaries.
Valuation and Allocation	Assets, liabilities, and revenues recognized at the inception of split-interest agreements are measured at fair value when received. Fair value is measured using appropriate measurement methods.	Documentation supports the determination of assets, liabilities, revenues, and changes in the value of split-interest agreements at the inception of the agreements. If the not-for-profit entity (NFP) elects fair value measurements as described in FASB *Accounting Standards Codification* (ASC) 815-15-25 or the "Fair Value Option" subsections of FASB ASC 825-10, documentation supports the election.
Rights and Obligations	Restrictions on contributions arising from split-interest agreements have been met and recorded.	Split-interest agreements are reviewed for restrictions.
Account Balances		
Occurrence	Amounts recognized as (1) cash, investments, contributions receivable, and other assets held under split-interest agreements, (2) beneficial interests in trusts held by others, and (3) liabilities for amounts held for others resulting from split-interest agreements represent valid revenues, assets, and liabilities.	If NFP is the trustee, management authorizes split-interest agreements. Donor relations and fund-raising staff notify appropriate management upon death of beneficiaries.

(continued)

Auditing Considerations—*continued*

Financial Statement Assertions	*Specific Audit Objectives*	*Select Control Objectives*
Completeness	All irrevocable split-interest agreements are recognized. All income received under split-interest agreements is recorded.	Controls ensure that donor relations and fund-raising staff notify management upon receipt of a split-interest arrangement. Controls ensure that split-interest agreements are known and recorded. Management reviews income distribution terms of split-interest agreements and determines that periodic reports and remittances from trustees conform to those terms.
Valuation and Allocation	Assets and liabilities are measured using appropriate measurement methods. If present value techniques are used to initially measure the liability to other beneficiaries and a fair value election is not made for subsequent measurements, amortization of the discount associated with the contribution and revaluations (based on changes in actuarial assumptions) of the liabilities to beneficiaries are recognized during the term of split-interest agreements. (*a*) Beneficial interests in trusts held by others, (*b*) embedded derivatives subject to the measurement provisions of FASB ASC 815-15, and (*c*) assets and liabilities for which an election pursuant to FASB ASC 815-15-25 or the "Fair Value Option" subsections of FASB ASC 825-10 was made are remeasured at fair value and changes recognized during the term of split-interest agreements. Restrictions on contributions arising from split-interest agreements have been met.	Documentation supports the determination of assets, liabilities, revenues, and changes in the value of split-interest agreements over the term of the agreements. If the NFP elects fair value measurements as described in FASB ASC 815-15-25 or the "Fair Value Option" subsections of FASB ASC 825-10, documentation supports the election. Split-interest agreements are reviewed for restrictions.

Auditing Considerations—*continued*

Financial Statement Assertions	***Specific Audit Objectives***	***Select Control Objectives***
Presentation and Disclosure		
Rights and Obligations	Net assets arising from split-interest agreements have been reported in the appropriate net asset class. Contribution revenues and changes in the value of split-interest agreements that are recognized during the term of split-interest agreements are reported in the proper net asset class. Net assets are reclassified as restrictions expire.	Split-interest agreements are reviewed for restrictions.

6.92 Additionally, for irrevocable rights under split-interest agreements, suggested audit procedures to consider include the following:

1. Obtain a detailed, comparative summary of irrevocable split-interest agreements by type of agreement (for example, charitable remainder trust, perpetual trust, charitable gift annuity). The summary should include all aspects of the split-interest agreement, such as investments, receivables, refundable advances, and deferred revenue depending on the type of agreement. Consider performing the following procedures, as appropriate (Accuracy):
   a. Reconcile the comparative summary to the general ledger.
   b. Test the mathematical accuracy of the comparative summary.
2. Test completeness of the detailed listing (Completeness):
   a. Document how the NFP ensures completeness of the detailed listing.
   b. Discuss with management their procedures for identifying new irrevocable split-interest agreements.
   c. Review donor and trustee correspondence.
   d. Compare current year detailed listing to prior year and inquire about changes in the detail. For example, determine why an account on the prior-year summary is not included on the current year's summary.
   e. Reconcile any new gifts to reports, if any, from the development office (or equivalent) and to written acknowledgements for large donors.
   f. Compare significant gifts mentioned in minutes of governing board meetings to detailed listing.

   g. Be alert during other test work. For example, during contribution testing and review of journal entries be alert that a gift may actually reflect a split-interest agreement that the NFP has not properly recorded. In tests of cash receipts, be alert that a distribution from a trust held by a third party might improperly be recognized as contribution revenue or other revenue.

3. For split-interest agreements initially recognized in the current year, obtain copies of the split-interest agreement to understand the terms of the contribution and to determine that the agreement is accounted for correctly. Review agreements to determine whether (*a*) the agreement is irrevocable and (*b*) the NFP has been named irrevocably as a beneficiary of the trust or (*c*) any persons granted the power to change beneficiaries are no longer living. If terms are ambiguous, consider asking the NFP to provide documentation of the assessment of an attorney. (Rights and Obligations, Completeness, Valuation and Allocation)

4. Agree key information used in the valuation to supporting documentation, such as the split-interest agreement. (Rights and Obligations, Completeness, Valuation and Allocation) Key information might include the following:
   a. Type of agreement
   b. Conditions that may affect or prohibit current recognition
   c. Whether the agreement is irrevocable or revocable
   d. Whether there are any restrictions on the use of the proceeds
   e. Who serves as the trustee or fiscal agent
   f. Fair value of the transferred assets at date of gift
   g. Number, age(s), and sex of beneficiaries
   h. Beneficiary payment type, frequency, duration, and amount
   i. NFP's beneficial interest percentage
   j. Specific bequests or other distributions of the agreement
   k. Other relevant information

5. For trust agreements initially recognized in prior years and related trust distributions in the current year determine that trust distributions that were expected based on the terms of the trust were received, identified, and recorded. (Completeness)

6. If the NFP is the trustee or fiscal agent, consider the following procedures to test the valuation of the obligation: (Valuation and Allocation)
   a. If the NFP engaged an actuarial firm to assist in the valuation of the obligation, obtain a report from the actuary that documents the valuation and assumptions used and review it for reasonableness. Refer to paragraph .08 of AU-C section 500, which provides requirements concerning circumstances in which information to be used as audit evidence has been prepared using the work of a management's specialist. A *management's specialist* is defined in

AU-C section 500 as an individual or organization possessing expertise in a field other than accounting or auditing, whose work in that field is used by the entity to assist the entity in preparing the financial statements.

b. For obligation amounts calculated using a purchased or internally-developed application, test the controls in place surrounding the application. Determine whether the application is appropriate for determining amounts computed in accordance with GAAP. (For example, paragraph 6.06 discusses the use of software that is used to determine the donor's tax deduction.)

c. Test the valuation methodology utilized. Valuation approaches and techniques are discussed in paragraphs 3.148–.154 of this guide and in appendix A of this chapter. Refer to AU-C section 540 for further guidance in auditing fair value measurements and paragraphs 5–8 of FASB ASC 958-30-35.

d. Obtain mortality tables used for establishing the expected life of the beneficiaries and thereby, the term of the existence of any agreements that are life-dependent (that is, the discount period, if present value techniques are used for valuation). Recompute the agreement's projected term used in the valuation. Consider the need for updated tables. Technical Questions and Answers section 3700.01, "Effect of New Mortality Tables on Nongovernmental Employee Benefit Plans (EBPs) and Nongovernmental Entities That Sponsor EBPs" (*Technical Questions and Answers*), can be helpful when determining the effect of newly issued mortality tables on estimates and how to evaluate the new mortality tables as a subsequent event.

e. On a test basis, recalculate the liability to beneficiaries.

7. Test assets held under the split-interest agreement. (Existence, Completeness, Valuation)

   a. If the institution acts as trustee or fiscal agent, perform customary tests of investments.

   b. For assets held by third-party trustees or fiscal agents, request a listing of the assets held and their fair values from the third-party trustees as of the end of the fiscal year. (Note: The trustee may confirm the full value of the trust assets but the NFP may only be entitled to a percentage of those assets. Determine that only the percentage to be received by the NFP is considered in determining the carrying amount for the beneficial interest in the trust [which is the NFP's unit of account].) Test the fair value of the investments in the trust as described in paragraph 6.93. Apply the NFP's ownership percentage to the fair value of the investments in the trust to recalculate the fair value of the beneficial interest (as discussed in paragraphs 6.25–.26).

8. For life interests in real estate, verify who is responsible for paying the property taxes and other executory costs and determine whether they are being paid. (Rights and obligations)

9. Review the presentation in the statement of activities. (Classification and Understandability)
    - *a.* For split-interest agreements initially recognized in the current year, assess the classification of contribution revenue by referring to any donor restrictions within the split-interest agreement.
    - *b.* Assess classification of change in value of split-interest agreements by recomputing the year-end value change and verifying that the change increased or decreased the same class of net assets as the original contribution.
    - *c.* Determine if the NFP properly accounted for any expiration of restrictions through its release from restrictions line item.
10. Review the presentation on the statement of financial position. (Classification and Understandability)
    - *a.* Verify that the financial statement presentation of assets is correct. If the NFP is the trustee or fiscal agent, both the carrying amount of the assets and the liabilities should be reflected. If a third party is the trustee or fiscal agent, the fair value of the beneficial interest should be presented.
    - *b.* Determine whether beneficiaries are still living if term of agreement is based on a beneficiary's life. Some NFPs with large numbers of split-interest agreements may subscribe to death lists from the federal or state governments to ensure the death of any donors or beneficiaries is known in a timely manner.
    - *c.* Determine if there are state laws requiring legally mandated annuity reserves as described in paragraph 6.50. If so, verify that the NFP's reserves meet legal requirements.
    - *d.* If the NFP has legally required or voluntary reserves, verify that the disclosures described in paragraphs 6.50–.51 are presented on the face of the statement of financial position or in the notes to the financial statements.
11. Review the presentation on the statement of cash flows. Verify that the financial statement presentation of changes in cash flows is correct. If the NFP is the trustee, cash transferred to the NFP under new split-interest agreements and payments to beneficiaries are reported as financing cash flows. (Classification and Understandability)
12. Some states restrict the types of investments that can be held under split-interest agreements. Inquire of the client regarding any such restrictions and consider whether disclosure in the notes to the financial statements would be useful. (Rights and Obligations)

6.93 In circumstances in which a third party is the fiscal agent or trustee and the auditor determines that the nature and extent of auditing procedures would include verifying the existence and testing the measurement of investments held by a trust, simply receiving a confirmation from the trustee, either in aggregate or on an investment-by-investment basis, would not in and of itself constitute relevant and reliable audit evidence with respect to the requirements for auditing the fair value of the interest in the trust under AU-C section 540. In addition, receiving confirmation from the trustee for investments in aggregate (such as "$XXX of total investments" or "$XXX of total investments in private equity securities, $YYY of total investments in interests in limited partnerships, and $ZZZ of total investments in debt securities") would not constitute relevant and reliable audit evidence with respect to the existence assertion. Receiving confirmation from the trustee on an investment-by-investment basis, however, typically would constitute adequate audit evidence with respect to the existence assertion. In circumstances in which the auditor is unable to audit the existence or measurement of interests in trusts at the financial statement date, the auditor should consider whether a scope limitation exists that requires the auditor to either qualify his or her opinion or to disclaim an opinion, as discussed in paragraphs .A8–.A12 of AU-C section 705, *Modifications to the Opinion in the Independent Auditor's Report*.

6.94 For revocable rights under split-interest agreements, suggested audit procedures to consider include the following:

1. Obtain a detailed, comparative listing of revocable split-interest agreements for which the NFP acts as trustee or fiscal agent and perform the following tests: (Completeness)
    a. Agree the comparative summary to the general ledger and compare to the prior-year working papers.
    b. Check the mathematical accuracy of the comparative summary.
2. For new revocable agreements: (Rights and Obligations)
    a. Obtain and examine the supporting documentation, such as the split-interest agreement, donor correspondence, and governing board minutes.
    b. Read the agreement and verify that the NFP's interest is revocable.
3. For revocable agreements for which a third party acts as trustee or fiscal agent, examine correspondence from the third party to determine whether conditions are substantially met and the agreement should be recognized. (Completeness)
4. Verify the financial statement presentation of revocable agreements for which the NFP acts as trustee or fiscal agent. Assets held under the agreement should be reflected at fair value with a refundable advance of the same amount. Perform customary tests of investments on any investments held under the agreement. Revenue should not be recognized until the agreement becomes irrevocable or until the assets are distributed to the NFP for its unconditional use, whichever comes first. (Completeness, Valuation)
5. Verify the financial statement presentation of revocable agreements for which a third party acts as trustee. Those agreements should not be reflected on the NFP's statement of financial position. However, disclosure in accordance with FASB ASC 958-310-50-4 should be considered by management. (Completeness)

6.95

Appendix A—Excerpt From AICPA White Paper *Measurement of Fair Value for Certain Transactions of Not-for-Profit Entities*[1]

A-1 Not-for-profit entities (NFPs) face various challenges in applying the provisions of FASB *Accounting Standards Codification* (ASC) 820, *Fair Value Measurement*, in part because markets do not exist for certain assets and liabilities. To assist practitioners, on October 14, 2011, the AICPA issued a white paper, *Measurement of Fair Value for Certain Transactions of Not-for-Profit Entities*. The following excerpt provides assistance for measuring beneficial interests in trusts and the liabilities of split-interest agreements.

Beneficial Interests in Trusts

33. An NFP may have a beneficial interest in a trust that is reported at fair value, pursuant to FASB ASC 958-605-30-14. A beneficial interest is recognized by an NFP if a donor transfers cash or other assets to an independent trustee (such as a bank, trust company, foundation, or private individual) or other fiscal agent of the donor,[2] and the donor specifies that the NFP will receive a distribution from the trust assets. In such circumstances, the NFP's asset is the irrevocable right to the stream of cash flows (an interest in the cash flows). The trustee typically controls the investment decisions and timing of distributions to the NFP, and the NFP cannot transfer its interest. Although the cash or other assets in the trust are not controlled by the NFP, the NFP recognizes as its asset the beneficial interest in the trust assets. (If, however, the trustee has variance power to redirect the benefits to another entity, or if the NFP's rights to the benefits are conditional, the NFP would not recognize its potential for distributions from the trust until the NFP has received a distribution or otherwise receives an unconditional right to distributions under the trust agreement.)

34. For purposes of the discussion in this white paper, charitable trusts fall into one of two types: nonperpetual trusts or perpetual trusts. In a nonperpetual trust held by a third party, the NFP will receive its distributions during the term of the trust agreement, and at some point, no later than the end of the term specified in the trust agreement (for example, the end of a specified number of years or upon the death of the donor), the distributions to the NFP will cease. Interests in charitable lead trusts and charitable remainder trusts are examples of these types of beneficial interests in trusts. In contrast, the distributions from a perpetual trust never end. Beneficial interests in perpetual trusts exist because the NFP has the irrevocable right to receive the income earned on trust assets in perpetuity, but the NFP will never receive the assets held in trust.

35. Paragraphs 36–54 address questions related to the application of FASB ASC 820-10-35 in determining the fair value of a beneficial interest in a trust held by a third party.

---

[1] As a benefit of AICPA membership, all AICPA members can access the AICPA Financial Reporting white paper *Measurement of Fair Value for Certain Transactions of Not-for-Profit Entities* at www.aicpa.org/interestareas/frc/industryinsights/pages/fv_and_disclosures_nfp.aspx.

[2] To ease readability, this white paper uses the term *trustee* to encompass both a trustee and fiscal agent of the donor that is not a trustee.

What Is the Unit of Account for a Beneficial Interest in a Trust?

36. The subject of the fair value measurement (unit of account) for a beneficial interest in a trust is each individual beneficial interest. An NFP that receives distributions from three trusts has three beneficial interests and three units of account for which it must determine fair value.

37. There currently is no market in which beneficial interests in charitable trusts trade; therefore, no observable exit price will exist for a beneficial interest. The fair value of a beneficial interest in trust must be determined by assuming a hypothetical transaction at the measurement date, considered from the perspective of a hypothetical market participant that would purchase the beneficial interest. The objective of a fair value measurement is to determine the price that would be received to sell the beneficial interest at the measurement date, even though it is not possible to sell the beneficial interest because of donor-imposed or legal restrictions.

38. The NFP's asset is the right to receive cash flows from the trust, not the assets of the trust itself. Although the trust assets may be investments for which quoted prices in an active market are available, the NFP does not control those investments; they are not the NFP's assets, and they are not the unit of account for the fair value measurement.

How Should NFPs Estimate the Fair Value of Interests in Perpetual Trusts?

39. FASB ASC 958-605-30-14 (footnote 7 to paragraph 6.45 of the AICPA Audit and Accounting Guide *Not-for-Profit Entities*[3]) discusses circumstances in which an NFP has the irrevocable right to receive the income earned on trust assets in perpetuity but never receives the assets held in trust. It provides as follows:

> The fair value of a perpetual trust held by a third party generally can be measured using the fair value of the assets contributed to the trust, unless facts and circumstances indicate that the fair value of the beneficial interest differs from the fair value of the assets contributed to the trust.

40. FinREC believes that this guidance continues to be relevant in measuring an NFP's interest in a perpetual trust, in accordance with FASB ASC 820, *Fair Value Measurement*. FinREC believes that in practice, the fair value of the assets in the trust can be used as an input when measuring a beneficial interest in a perpetual trust, generally without further adjustment (see paragraphs 50–51 for adjustments that FinREC considered and rejected). Circumstances may exist, however, in which the fair value of the beneficial interest differs from the fair value of the assets held by the trust.

41. For example, if the trustee has been instructed not to distribute assets from the trust for a period of years or to distribute only a minor portion of the income that is available for distribution from the trust, the fair value of the beneficial interest may differ from the fair value of the assets contributed to the trust. Similarly, in circumstances in which the trustee has the ability to determine the amount of the distributions and chooses not to distribute assets from the trust or to distribute only a minor portion of the income available for distribution from the trust, the fair value of the beneficial interest may differ from the fair

[3] References are to the 2011 edition of the AICPA Audit and Accounting Guide *Not-for-Profit Entities*, unless otherwise noted.

value of the assets in the trust. The fair value of the beneficial interest will also differ from the fair value of the assets of the trust if the trust distributions are shared among two or more NFPs; in that case, the proportionate share of the trust assets may be used to measure the beneficial interest.

42. If facts and circumstances indicate that the fair value of the beneficial interest differs from the fair value of the assets contributed to the trust, the income approach (PV technique) may also be utilized to measure the fair value of the beneficial interest in the trust. If the PV technique is used, a beneficial interest in a trust would be measured as the PV of the future distributions projected to be received, discounted at an appropriate rate. For a perpetual trust, the formula for an annuity in perpetuity would be used.[4] Assuming that payments begin at the end of the current period, the formula for an annuity in perpetuity is simply the distribution amount divided by the appropriate discount rate or yield (paragraphs 48–49 discuss determining an appropriate discount rate).

43. If an NFP is uncertain whether facts and circumstances indicate that the fair value of the beneficial interest differs from the fair value of the assets contributed to the trust, the NFP might compute the fair value of the trust under both methods. Then, as instructed in FASB ASC 820-10-35-24B, the results of the valuation techniques (respective indications of fair value) would be evaluated, considering the reasonableness of the range of values indicated by those results. A fair value measurement is the point within that range that is most representative of fair value in the circumstances.

How Should NFPs Estimate the Fair Value of Interests in Nonperpetual Trusts?

44. If a charitable trust exists for a term, the income approach for measuring the fair value (PV techniques) is likely the most practical method for measuring the beneficial interest in the trust. The beneficial interest in the trust would be measured as the PV of the future distributions projected to be received over the expected term of the agreement, discounted at an appropriate rate (paragraphs 48–49 discuss determining an appropriate discount rate). The fair value of the assets of a trust would not be used to measure a beneficial interest unless that interest was in a perpetual trust. The following example uses a discount rate adjustment technique (paragraphs 24–32 and the appendix "Present Value Techniques in Paragraphs 4–20 of Financial Accounting Standards Board *Accounting Standards Codification* 820-10-55" provide additional information about the discount rate adjustment technique).

45. For example, assume that a donor establishes a charitable lead unitrust with assets valued at $100,000, naming Main Bank as trustee, the donor as the noncharitable beneficiary, and Charity as the charitable beneficiary. Main Bank is to invest and manage the trust assets, paying out 5 percent of the fair value of the trust assets as of the valuation date each year to Charity until the donor's death and then paying the remaining trust assets to the donor's estate. The donor's life expectancy is 10 years. For information about determining life expectancy, see paragraph 92.

46. To use PV techniques, Charity would begin by estimating the cash flows that it will receive. Main Bank has invested the trust assets in its collective trust, and it estimates that the trust will have an average return of 4 percent,

[4] The value of the distributions in perpetuity is measurable because the distributions that are anticipated far in the future have extremely low present value. Because the corpus of the trust is never paid, there is no present value for the corpus.

net of trustee fees, over the next 5 years. For simplicity's sake, assume that the valuation date is as of the beginning of the year.

Date	*Projected Trust Income*	*Projected Payout*	*Projected Fair Value of the Trust*
Beginning			$100,000
Year 1	$4,000	$5,000	99,000
Year 2	3,960	4,950	98,010
Year 3	3,920	4,900	97,030
Year 4	3,881	4,851	96,060
Year 5	3,842	4,803	95,099
Year 6	3,804	4,756	94,147
Year 7	3,766	4,707	93,206
Year 8	3,728	4,660	92,274
Year 9	3,691	4,614	91,351
Year 10	3,654	4,568	90,437

Charity would then apply a discount rate to the projected payouts. The discount rate should reflect the risks associated with the cash flows; it cannot be less than 4 percent because that is the rate of return of the trust assets (see paragraphs 48–49). The PV of the projected payments is computed as follows, using PV factors for a single amount due in the future at 4 percent:

Date	*Projected Payout*	*PV Factor*	*PV of Payout*
Year 1	$5,000	0.96154	$4,808
Year 2	4,950	0.92456	4,577
Year 3	4,900	0.88900	4,356
Year 4	4,851	0.85480	4,147
Year 5	4,803	0.82193	3,948
Year 6	4,756	0.79031	3,759
Year 7	4,707	0.75992	3,577
Year 8	4,660	0.73069	3,405
Year 9	4,614	0.70259	3,242
Year 10	4,568	0.67556	3,086
Estimate of fair value			$38,905

Charity would recognize $38,905 as the fair value of the beneficial interest and its contribution when notified of the irrevocable gift at the beginning of year 1.

47. The preceding method can also be used to estimate the fair value of remainder interests in charitable trusts that are held by third-party trustees. Assume the same trust as in paragraph 46 but that Charity holds the remainder interest. Using the first table in paragraph 46, Charity computes the amount that it expects to receive upon the death of the donor as $90,437. To estimate the fair value of that payment, Charity uses the factor for a single payment of $90,437 due in 10 years at 4 percent (0.67556) and computes a fair value of the remainder interest of $61,095. Note that the values of the lead interest ($38,905) and remainder interest ($61,095) equal the value of the trust assets ($100,000).

If PV Techniques Are Used to Measure a Beneficial Interest in a Trust, How Is the Appropriate Discount Rate Determined?

48. Much of the discussion about PV techniques in paragraphs 7–15 is equally applicable when using PV techniques to measure beneficial interests in trusts. When estimating future distributions from the trust and discount rates, assumptions that market participants would use in their estimates should be used, and the discount rates should reflect assumptions that are consistent with those inherent in the cash flows. This prevents double counting or omitting the effects of risk factors.

49. When determining the appropriate discount rate to be used to value a beneficial interest in a charitable trust, it is important to remember that the cash flows from the trust to the NFP beneficiary are at least as risky as the cash flows within the trust itself. That is, if the trustee is receiving a yield to maturity of 4 percent to cover the risk of investing the trust assets, then the risk as a beneficiary of the cash flows from the investments of the trust is at least 4 percent. Risks that change the pattern of the cash flows can cause the discount rate to be higher. In other words, the discount rate should always be greater than or equal to the assumed rate of the return on the trust itself. As a result, an estimate of the fair value of the beneficial interest in the trust assets should never exceed the fair value of the trust assets (or the proportionate share thereof if there is more than one charitable beneficiary).

What Other Factors Did FinREC Consider Regarding the Measurement of the Fair Value of a Beneficial Interest in a Trust?

50. FinREC considered whether the fact that the trustee controls the investment decisions should affect the fair value of the NFP's beneficial interest in the trust. FinREC believes the fact that the trustee controls the investment decisions typically has no effect on the fair value of the asset (the beneficial interest in the trust). Assuming that the trustee exercises its fiduciary responsibilities, FinREC believes that the trustee's control over such investment decisions generally is neither an enhancement nor a diminishment of the NFP's interest in the trust.

51. FinREC also considered whether the risk premium related to the individual investments held in the trust should be considered in estimating the fair value of the beneficial interest in the trust. FinREC believes that the risk premium related to the individual investments held in the trust should not be separately considered in estimating the fair value of the asset (interest in the trust) because that risk premium is already built into the price of each individual investment held in the trust. However, as noted in paragraphs 48–49, the rate of return on the assets of the trust is a consideration when determining the appropriate discount rate if the income approach and PV techniques are used to measure fair value.

How Are Subsequent Measurements of Fair Value Made?

52. FASB ASC 958-30-35-2 and 958-605-35-3 require that an NFP remeasure at fair value at each reporting date its beneficial interest in a trust held by a third-party trustee. The NFP should remeasure its beneficial interest by applying the same technique that it used upon initial measurement, but it should update all the assumptions, including the discount rate, to reflect current market conditions. However, a change in a valuation technique or its application (for example, a change in its weighting when multiple valuation techniques are used or a change in an adjustment applied to a valuation technique) is appropriate if the change results in a measurement that is equally or more representative of fair value in the circumstances. For further information, see paragraph 103.

What Considerations, if Any, Are There for Making Required Disclosures of Fair Value When the Asset Measured Is a Beneficial Interest in a Perpetual Trust Held by a Third Party?

53. An NFP should make the disclosures about fair value measures required by FASB ASC 820-10-50. In making disclosures about the inputs to fair value measurement, as required by FASB ASC 820-10-50-1, FinREC believes that if the fair value of the beneficial interest in a perpetual trust is measured using the fair value of the trust assets, best practice is for an NFP to disclose (*a*) the terms of the trust and practice of the trustee pertaining to distributions and (*b*) that the NFP has used the fair value of the trust assets to determine the fair value of the beneficial interest.

54. As noted in paragraphs 36–38, the unit of account is the beneficial interest in the trust itself. In making the disclosures about the level of the fair value hierarchy within which the fair value measurements are categorized in their entirety, as required by FASB ASC 820-10-50-2, FinREC believes that it is reasonable to analogize to the guidance in FASB ASC 820-10-35-54B,[5] which addresses how a fair value measurement should be categorized if net asset value per share is used as a practical expedient to measure an investment in an entity that measures all of its investments at fair value. That guidance says that if a reporting entity will never have the ability to redeem its investment at net asset value per share (or its equivalent), the fair value measurement of the investment should be categorized as a level 3 fair value measurement. Accordingly, by analogy, the measurement for a beneficial interest in a perpetual trust should also be categorized as a level 3 fair value measurement because the NFP will never receive the trust's assets.

55. Because a beneficial interest in a perpetual trust is categorized as a level 3 measure, an NFP is required to disclose the information required for recurring fair value measurements using significant unobservable inputs. NFPs that are public entities are required to disclose the sensitivity of the fair value measurement to changes in unobservable inputs; other NFPs are not so required.

Split-Interest Agreements

56. *Split-interest agreements* (sometimes referred to as deferred giving) are agreements in which a donor makes an initial gift to a trust or directly to an

---

[5] FASB Accounting Standards Update (ASU) No. 2015-07, *Fair Value Measurement (Topic 820): Disclosures for Investments in Certain Entities That Calculate Net Asset Value per Share (or Its Equivalent) (a consensus of the Emerging Issues Task Force)*, issued May 2015, deleted the referenced paragraph. The AICPA white paper *Measurement of Fair Value for Certain Transactions of Not-for-Profit Entities* has not been updated to reflect that change. ASU No. 2015-07 was effective for not-for-profit entities for fiscal years beginning after December 15, 2016, and for interim periods within those fiscal years. See also paragraph 4.101.

NFP in which the NFP has a beneficial interest but is not the sole beneficiary. The period covered by the agreement is expressed either as a specific number of years or the remaining life of an individual or individuals designated by the donor. The assets are invested and administered by the NFP, a trustee, or a fiscal agent. Under agreements referred to as lead interests, the NFP receives any distributions or income during the agreement's term, and the donor (or other individuals or entities designated by the donor) receives all or a portion of the assets remaining at the end of the agreement's term. In agreements referred to as remainder interests, the donor (or other individuals or entities designated by the donor) receives the distributions during the term, and the NFP receives all or a portion of the assets remaining at the end of the agreement's term. Split-interest agreements, therefore, are a combination of a contribution and an exchange transaction.

Remainder Interests

57. Three primary types of remainder agreements exist: charitable remainder trusts, charitable gift annuities, and pooled income funds.

Charitable Remainder Trusts

58. Under charitable remainder trusts, as described in the glossary of FASB ASC and paragraph 6.47 of the Audit and Accounting Guide *Not-for-Profit Entities* [2012 Edition], the donor establishes and funds a trust, the terms of which provide that specified distributions are to be made to a designated beneficiary or beneficiaries over the trust's term. The distributions to the beneficiaries may be for a specified dollar amount (an arrangement called a charitable remainder annuity trust) or specified percentage of the trust's fair market value, as determined annually (an arrangement called a charitable remainder unitrust). Some charitable remainder unitrusts limit the annual payout to the lesser of the stated percentage or actual income earned. Obligations to the beneficiaries are limited to the trust's assets.

Charitable Gift Annuities

59. Charitable gift annuities are similar to charitable remainder trusts except that, as described in FASB ASC 958-30-05-11 (paragraph 6.52 of the Audit and Accounting Guide *Not-for-Profit Entities* [2012 Edition]), no trust exists. The assets received are held as general assets of the NFP, and the annuity liability is a general obligation of the NFP. Under charitable gift annuities, the NFP agrees to pay a fixed amount for a specified period of time to the donor or to individuals or entities designated by the donor.

Pooled Income Funds

60. The third type of remainder agreement, described in the FASB ASC glossary and paragraph 6.56 of the Audit and Accounting Guide *Not-for-Profit Entities* [2012 Edition], is a pooled income fund. A *pooled income fund* is a trust for which the NFP is trustee. These trusts pool the contributions of many donors and invest those gifts as a group. Donors are assigned a specific number of units in the pooled income fund based on the proportion of the fair value of their contributions to the total fair value of the pooled income fund on the date of the donor's entry to the pooled fund. Until his or her death, the donor (or the donor's designated beneficiary or beneficiaries) is paid the actual income (as defined under the arrangement) earned on the donor's assigned units. Upon the donor's death, the value of the assigned units reverts to the NFP.

Lead Interests

61. The most common type of lead interest arrangement is one in which a donor establishes and funds a trust with specific distributions to be made to a designated NFP over a specified period. The distributions may be a fixed dollar amount (an arrangement called a charitable lead annuity trust) or fixed percentage of the trust's fair market value, as determined annually (a charitable lead unitrust). Upon termination of the trust, the remainder of the trust assets is paid to the donor or beneficiaries designated by the donor.

Recognition of Split-Interest Agreements

62. As noted in FASB ASC 958-30-30 (chapter 6, "Split-Interest Agreements," of the Audit and Accounting Guide *Not-for-Profit Entities*), recognition of split-interest agreements generally requires the assets, liabilities, and contribution to be initially measured at fair value. FASB ASC 958-30 provides guidance for determining the fair value of the contribution of either a lead or remainder interest.

63. Prior to FASB Statement No. 157, which is reflected in FASB ASC 820, the fair value of the contribution inherent in a split-interest agreement was estimated using the income approach (PV technique). Beginning with the 2007 edition, the Audit and Accounting Guide *Not-for-Profit Organizations* was conformed to FASB Statement No. 157, and it (and FASB ASC) indicates that PV techniques are one valuation technique for measuring the fair value of the contribution and liability; other valuation techniques are also available, as described in FASB Statement No. 157.

64. Paragraphs 6.10–.11 of the 2011 edition of the Audit and Accounting Guide *Not-for-Profit Entities*, which has been conformed to FASB ASC, in discussing initial measurement of lead and remainder agreements (other than pooled income funds or net income unit trusts), provide as follows:

> **6.10** Per FASB ASC 958-30-30-7, under a lead interest agreement, the fair value of the contribution can be estimated directly based on the present value of the future distributions to be received by the NFP as a beneficiary. Under lead interest agreements, the future payments to be made to other beneficiaries will be made by the NFP only after the NFP receives its benefits. In those situations, the present value of the future payments to be made to other beneficiaries may be estimated by the fair value of the assets contributed by the donor under the agreement less the fair value of the benefits to be received by the NFP. If present value techniques are used, the fair value of the benefits to be received by the NFP should be measured at the present value of the benefits to be received over the expected term of the agreement.
>
> **6.11** Per FASB ASC 958-30-30-8, under remainder interest agreements, the present value of the future payments to be made to other beneficiaries can be estimated directly based on the terms of the agreement. Future distributions will be received by the NFP only after obligations to other beneficiaries are satisfied. In those cases, the fair value of the contribution may be estimated based on the fair value of the assets contributed by the donor less the fair value of the payments to be made to other beneficiaries.

65. Prevalent practice is to measure the fair value of the contribution and liability using commercially available software aimed at determining the amount of the donor's tax deduction. The objective of that software is to measure the tax deductibility of the gift, which may not necessarily result in a fair value measurement. To use that software for measuring in accordance with generally accepted accounting principles (GAAP), NFPs would need to consider the assumptions that are inherent in the software's calculations (such as interest rate and mortality) and determine whether those assumptions are market participant assumptions that are appropriate for the measurement of fair value. If the assumptions are inappropriate, the NFP must determine whether the output from the software can be adjusted to reflect a fair value measurement that complies with GAAP. The NFP must consider whether the differences in the resulting values are significant enough that the software should not be used to determine the fair value of the contribution for financial statement purposes. One method to test whether the software can be used would be to use sampling to select split-interest agreements for testing and then compare the measurements arrived at using the methods described in this white paper with the measurements from the software.

66. Paragraphs 67–102 of this white paper address questions related to the application of FASB ASC 820-10-35 in determining the fair value of split-interest agreements.

Can the Market Approach Be Used to Value the Liability?

67. In some respects, assets and liabilities related to split-interest agreements are similar to assets and liabilities related to fixed- and variable-rate annuity contracts that are sold by insurance companies. However, certain differences exist between annuities offered by insurance companies and annuities offered by NFPs. The following are the most significant differences:

- For most types of agreements, a donor who enters into a split-interest agreement is able to take a charitable contribution deduction on his or her tax return in the year that the agreement is signed and funded. Split-interest agreements that do not result in an initial charitable contribution deduction have other tax benefits. Insurance company contracts are investment vehicles, some of which offer tax-deferral opportunities.
- Annuities offered by insurance companies generally pay out at a higher rate of return than annuities offered by NFPs. Because of the individual's intention to make a tax-deductible contribution, an individual generally is willing to accept a lower payout rate from an NFP than he or she would accept from an insurance company.
- The insurance industry is highly regulated, and states have insurance guarantee associations that provide the purchasers of insurance company products with varying degrees of limited protection against the inability of the insurance company to pay its obligations under the agreements. (As of May 2011, 22 of the 50 states provided protection for the PV of an annuity contract to a maximum of $100,000, and another 18 provided protection of $250,000. The other 10 states provided higher degrees of protection. Most states, however, restrict insurance agents and companies from advertising the existence of that protection.) Some states do not regulate split-interest agreements; other states regulate them but not to the extent that insurance companies are regulated. For example, a state may require the NFP to do one, two, or all of the following: maintain minimum reserves, create a segregated trust, or

limit its investment options to those perceived to be conservative. Those NFP requirements, however, are not as pervasive or extensive as requirements for insurance companies, and reserves, when required, typically are held by the NFP rather than a third party.

- An insurance company typically includes fees, a profit margin, or both in its contracts, whereas an NFP that enters into an annuity or unitrust agreement typically does not build any fees (or only very low fees to cover costs) into the agreement because the NFP will receive its benefits via the contribution portion of the agreement.
- It may be difficult to find a marketplace for annuities offered by insurance companies that is similar to the marketplace for variable annuities offered by NFPs (unitrusts). Variable annuities offered by insurance companies include a plethora of investment returns, tax deferral strategies, and payout terms. In addition, variable annuities offered by insurance companies are structured differently than variable annuities offered by NFPs. Variable annuities offered by NFPs hold the assets funding the annuity in trust. Further, variable annuities offered by NFPs pay an agreed-upon rate that is applied to the fair value of the trust assets on the annual measurement date. In comparison, variable annuities offered by insurance companies generally have a guaranteed lifetime income component that results in a liquidation of the assets. The variable component of such annuities offered by insurance companies generally increases in circumstances in which the total return on the assets exceeds a defined value.

68. FASB ASC 820-10-35-50 requires an entity using a market approach to adjust the observed market prices for the differences between the item being measured and the item for which the price was observed. It is unclear whether and how the NFP should adjust for the tax deductibility, adjust for the protection provided by the guarantee association, and remove the profit and fee components from the observed market prices for the insurance company contracts. FinREC observes that for these reasons, it may not be practical to utilize the market approach for all split-interest agreements.

69. FinREC believes that the market approach is generally not feasible for split-interest agreements with variable payments. Variable annuities offered by insurance companies include a plethora of investment returns, tax deferral strategies, and payout terms. In addition, variable annuities offered by insurance companies are structured differently than variable annuities offered by NFPs. Variable annuities offered by NFPs pay an agreed-upon rate that is applied to the fair value of the trust assets on the annual measurement date. In comparison, variable annuities offered by insurance companies generally have a guaranteed lifetime income component that results in a liquidation of the assets. The variable component of annuities offered by insurance companies generally increases in circumstances in which the total return on the assets exceeds a defined value. The market approach, therefore, is not feasible for split-interest agreements with variable payments because prices in an active market for obligations similar to split-interest agreements with variable payments cannot be observed with a reasonable cost and effort.

70. In contrast to split-interest agreements with variable payments, FinREC observes that there are many similarities between annuities offered by insurance companies and split-interest agreements with fixed payments. Given these similarities, FinREC believes that NFPs may use market information about annuities offered by insurance companies as inputs into a fair value measurement when determining the fair value of the liabilities under split-interest remainder agreements with fixed payments. FinREC believes that the fair value of a liability for a series of fixed payments would be similar, assuming the risk of nonperformance (credit standing) was the same. (Paragraphs 73–77 discuss credit standing.) Thus, the market approach is feasible for certain split-interest agreements with fixed payments.

How Should NFPs Estimate the Fair Value of Liabilities Under Split-Interest Remainder Agreements With Fixed Payments?

71. For liabilities under split-interest remainder agreements with fixed payments, FinREC believes that one of two approaches will be the best valuation approach for measuring fair value. In the circumstances described in paragraph 76, FinREC believes that a market approach using level 2 inputs, as described in paragraphs 3A–3C of FASB ASC 820-10-55, will provide the best measure. In other circumstances, as described in paragraph 78, FinREC believes that the income approach, in the form of PV techniques using level 2 inputs for interest rates, yield curves, and life expectancy tables, will provide the best measure. NFPs could, of course, use other valuation techniques to measure the fair value of liabilities under split-interest remainder agreements with fixed payments.

72. FinREC notes that observable prices are readily available from the websites of insurance companies and brokers for annuities with fixed payments and terms that are similar to split-interest liabilities with fixed payments. FinREC believes that for split-interest agreements with fixed payments, those quoted prices may be considered level 2 inputs, pursuant to the FASB ASC glossary definition of *level 2 inputs* and FASB ASC 820-10-35-48, because they are an observable quoted price for a similar liability and in an active market.

73. NFPs should consider the need to make adjustments to market prices of annuities offered by insurance companies (level 2 inputs) in estimating the fair value of liabilities under split-interest remainder agreements with fixed payments to reflect the difference in credit risk.

74. Market participants may have reasons for placing little or no emphasis on the credit standing of the payer, such as the following:

- Historically and in the current market, few defaults are observed on annuities from either NFPs or insurance companies.
- If an NFP is the payer, their affinity for the NFP and their donative intent.
- If an insurance company is the payer, the high degree of regulation of the insurance industry, including the protection provided by state guarantee associations that assume some or all of the liability to the annuitant if the insurance company defaults.

75. Even though market participants may place little or no emphasis on the credit standing of the payer, the following characteristics may cause annuity obligations of an NFP to have a different risk profile than annuities offered by insurance companies:

- Differences in credit standing
- The existence and extent of insurance company regulation, including protection provided by state guarantee associations

- Whether the NFP annuity obligation is adequately funded through a trust
- The existence and extent of minimum reserve requirements related to NFP annuity obligations

Therefore, it may be difficult to find a marketplace for annuities offered by insurance companies that is similar to the marketplace for annuities offered by NFPs, and market quotes for fixed payment annuities offered by insurance companies may need to be adjusted for credit quality or credit enhancement features.

76. FASB ASC 820-10-35-50 requires that observed market prices be adjusted if they are for liabilities that are similar to, rather than the same as, the liability being measured (level 2 measures). FinREC observes that the insurance industry is highly regulated, which results in (*a*) annuities being offered by insurance companies that have a strong, superior, or excellent capacity to meet their financial commitments (creditworthiness), or (*b*) market participants viewing insurance companies as equally creditworthy because of protection provided by a state guarantee association. Thus, FinREC believes that the use of market quotes for fixed payment annuities offered by insurance companies should be limited to situations for which the credit risk associated with an NFP's obligation to make fixed payments is similarly low. Specifically, FinREC believes that the market quotes for fixed payment annuities offered by insurance companies will be most representative for measuring split-interest obligations in any of the following situations:

- The annuity obligation is adequately funded from assets held in an irrevocable trust, and the NFP is observing its fiduciary responsibilities as trustee.
- The NFP has a credit standing similar to that of the insurance companies whose quotes are observed in the marketplace. That is, the NFP has an "investment grade" credit standing reflecting strong, superior, or excellent capacity to meet financial commitments. Note that the NFP's credit standing may be based on the NFP's own assessment, rather than a rating by a third-party rating agency.
- The NFP holds a commercially available annuity that provides cash flows to the beneficiary in the amount of and for the entire term of the agreement.

77. In situations similar to those in the preceding paragraph, facts and circumstances may lead to a conclusion that an NFP would make no adjustment for credit risk to the market prices of annuities offered by insurance companies when it estimates the fair value of liabilities under split-interest remainder agreements with fixed payments.

78. In situations dissimilar to those described in paragraph 76, FinREC believes that the income approach, in the form of PV techniques that maximize the use of observable inputs for interest rates, yield curves, and life expectancy tables, will be the best valuation approach for split-interest agreements with fixed payments. The income approach, including considerations for determining the discount rate, is discussed further in paragraphs 93–102.

79. FinREC believes that when using PV techniques to determine the fair value of a split-interest agreement's obligation to make fixed payments, NFPs should consider the risk premium that hypothetical market participants would demand for bearing the uncertainty inherent in the cash flows of the obligation. For example, a market participant would likely demand a premium to be compensated for uncertainties associated with the life span of an annuitant. Market quotes for annuities of insurance companies already include this risk premium.

80. Some NFPs have used tables provided by the IRS or similar tables in planned giving software to estimate the fair value of liabilities under split-interest remainder agreements with fixed payments. FinREC believes that such tables may be inappropriate for estimating the fair value of liabilities under split-interest remainder agreements with fixed payments because they are not regularly updated and are based on the population at large, rather than the population likely to buy an annuity or enter into a split-interest agreement. FinREC believes that quoted market prices for fixed-payment annuities in active markets appropriately consider the expected life of the relevant pool of annuitants. As a result, entities may want to use the life expectancy date from other sources, such as those discussed in paragraph 92.

How Should Discount Rates Be Determined if the Income Approach Is Used, Including Should Any Risk Premium That Hypothetical Market Participants Would Demand for Bearing the Inherent Uncertainties Be Incorporated in the Cash Flows?

81. In discussing discount rates used in PV measurements, FASB ASC 958-30-30-6 (paragraph 6.09 of the Audit and Accounting Guide *Not-for-Profit Entities* [2012 Edition]) specifies that a discount rate commensurate with the risks involved should be used if PV techniques are used to measure the fair value of split-interest obligations. In practice, some NFPs have used surrogates for a discount rate commensurate with the risks involved, such as average rate of return on the investment portfolio or average interest rate on outstanding borrowings, asserting that those surrogates generally did not result in measures that resulted in material misstatements in the financial statements.

82. FASB ASC 820-10-55-5 lists the elements that a fair value measurement of an asset or a liability should capture when using PV techniques (see paragraph 7).

83. In determining fair value, entities should consider the risk that actual cash flows (in both timing and amount) may differ from the cash flows used in the PV calculation. All other factors being equal, therefore, the higher the risk that actual cash flows may differ from the cash flows used in the PV calculation, the higher the discount rate or rate of return.

How Should NFPs Account for the Changes in the Liabilities Under Split-Interest Agreements With Fixed Payments in Subsequent Periods?

84. FASB ASC 958-30-35 (chapter 6 of the Audit and Accounting Guide *Not-for-Profit Entities*) discusses recognition and measurement during the term of a split-interest agreement. The NFP has two options available for reporting the liabilities under split-interest agreements with fixed payments: it can elect the fair value option, pursuant to FASB ASC 825-10-25, or amortize the discount associated with the obligation (remainder trust) or contribution (lead interest) and adjust for changes in life expectancies (if payments are life dependent).

85. FASB ASC 820-10-35-25 requires that valuation techniques be applied consistently, unless a change in valuation techniques results in a measurement that is equally or more representative of fair value in the circumstances (also see "Changes in Valuation Techniques" in exhibit 3). If the NFP elects to report the annuity payment liability at fair value in subsequent periods, it should use the same method to determine fair value as it used at initial recognition, unless a change in valuation techniques results in a measurement that is equally or more representative of fair value in the circumstances. That is, if, at initial recognition, the NFP used market quotations gathered from the Internet for commercially available annuity products with similar terms, it should repeat that process, unless a change in valuation techniques results in a measurement that is equally or more representative of fair value in the circumstances, and the liability would be adjusted upward or downward to reflect the new market quote. If, at initial recognition, the NFP used PV techniques to estimate the fair value, it should update all the elements described in paragraph 81, including the discount rate assumptions, in arriving at the current fair value estimate.

86. If the NFP does not elect to report the annuity liability at fair value, it should not adjust the discount rate assumptions. It should update only the actuarial assumptions, including life expectancy. FinREC observes that if the NFP initially measured the liability using market quotes, it would determine the imputed discount rate to be used in amortizing the liability.[6] To do so, the NFP might solve for the discount rate using the fixed payment amount; the life expectancies at the inception of the contract (obtained from a reliable published source, such as the National Center for Health Statistics [NCHS]); and the market quote (the PV at initial measurement). That imputed discount rate would be used in the subsequent periods' remeasurements over the life of the agreement.

How Should NFPs Estimate the Fair Value of Split-Interest Liabilities With Variable Payments?

87. For liabilities under split-interest agreements with variable payments (sometimes referred to as charitable unitrusts), FinREC believes that an income approach, using PV techniques and level 2 inputs for interest rates, as described in the FASB ASC glossary and paragraphs 3F–3G of FASB ASC 820-10-55, often will be the best valuation approach for measuring fair value. This white paper, therefore, discusses various techniques under an income approach for measuring the fair value of liabilities under split-interest remainder agreements with variable payments.

88. All variable payment split-interest agreements hold the assets in trust; therefore, the trust is the obligor, not the NFP that serves as trustee. Holding the assets in trust provides significant protection (similar to collateral) against the risk of default because

- the variable payments are computed as a percentage of the trust assets; thus, the payments decrease if investment losses cause a decrease in the trust assets.
- split-interest remainder agreements that result in tax deductions must have a remainder interest equal to or greater than 10 percent of the fair value of the assets initially transferred to the trust, which provides additional protection against default.

89. To use the income approach to measure the fair value of the contribution and obligation of a split-interest agreement with variable payments, an NFP must make assumptions about the following inputs to the PV techniques:

---

[6] Accounting for split-interest agreements with embedded derivatives is outside the scope of this white paper.

- Projected rate of return on the investments in the trust
- Discount rate for the obligation
- The expected mortality of the individual on which termination of the agreement depends, if the agreement is life dependent

90. In circumstances in which cash is invested, the investor is subject to various types of risk, including market risk, credit risk, inflation risk, and so forth. FinREC observes that because the payments to the beneficiary depend upon the assets in the trust, the cash flows from the trust are at least as risky as the cash flows of the trust investments. That is, if the trustee expects, for example, a rate of return on the trust investments of 6 percent (due to the risk of investing the trust assets), then the beneficiary of the cash flows from the trust also bears at least that same risk. FinREC believes that because the beneficiary also bears that risk, best practice is for the discount rate to also reflect that risk; therefore, the discount rate in this example would be at a minimum 6 percent.

91. FinREC observes that defaults rarely occur on split-interest agreements with variable payments because they are collateralized obligations, and NFPs generally perform their trust duties as assigned. Therefore, FinREC believes that if the NFP is complying with all of its fiduciary duties as trustee, best practice is to use the same rate for the projected rate of return on the investments and discount rate. The NFP can use either the risk-neutral rate or projected earnings rate on the trust assets.

92. Life expectancy information can be obtained from various sources, such as recent annuity tables published by the Society of Actuaries, including the Annuity 2000 Mortality Table (adopted by the National Association of Insurance Commissioners in 1996), or the NCHS ("United States Life Tables" in the *National Vital Statistics Reports*). The Annuity 2000 Mortality Tables reflect the fact that individuals who purchase annuities tend to be wealthier and, thus, healthier than the general public.[7] The tables published by the NCHS are based on the general public. Some sources suggest that a minimum of two years and a maximum of six years would be added to the life expectancies in mortality tables based upon the general public to reflect annuitants' expected longer lives.

93. An example of an income approach calculation for a charitable remainder unitrust appears in exhibit 1; the example uses a discount rate adjustment technique. Paragraphs 24–32 and appendix A provide additional information about the discount rate adjustment technique.

---

[7] This mortality table can be adjusted to reflect the fact that mortality rates improve over time. For example, projection scale G is used to adjust annual rates of mortality in individual annuity tables.

EXHIBIT 1

FACT SET

94. James Joyce establishes a charitable remainder unitrust with assets valued at $100,000, naming ABC Charity as the remainder beneficiary and trustee. The unitrust agreement specifies that Mr. Joyce will receive 6 percent of the value of the trust assets annually, based on the fair value of the trust assets on the measurement date. Mr. Joyce is 75 years old when the agreement is signed. Payments are made at the end of the year.

95. The following table provides information for determining a risk-neutral rate, which is measured as the risk-free rate adjusted for the credit swap spread rate.[8] The credit swap spread measures a more liquid market in which AA banks lend to each other. The credit swap spread rate is measured as the difference between the London Interbank Offered Rate (LIBOR) and the Treasury bill (T bill) rate. The boxes indicate observable market returns.

Portfolio return and discount rate:			
	LIBOR	0.83%	
	T-bill	0.16%	
Assume constant by duration	Swap spread	0.67%	
	1-year Treasury	0.47%	
	2-year Treasury	0.86%	
	3-year Treasury	1.29%	
Linear interpolation between years 3 and 5	4-year Treasury	1.64%	
	5-year Treasury	1.98%	
	6-year Treasury	2.21%	
Linear interpolation between years 5 and 10	7-year Treasury	2.44%	
	8-year Treasury	2.67%	
	9-year Treasury	2.90%	
	10-year Treasury	3.12%	
Linear interpolation between years 10 and 30	30-year Treasury	4.07%	0.048% per year

The preceding observable market rates are used to compute the return on the investments in the portfolio for purposes of estimating the trust assets at the beginning of the year. They are also used to develop the discount factors. For

[8] The Treasury yield curve rates published by the U.S. Treasury are an alternative set of risk-free rates.

example, the trust assets at the beginning of year 2 are computed as $100,000 × (1 + 0.0047 [the 1-year Treasury rate] + 0.0067 [the swap spread]) – ($100,000 × 6% payment). The discount factor for year 2 is computed as the year 1 discount factor × (1 / (1 + 0.0086 [the 2-year Treasury rate] + 0.0067 [the swap spread])).

Estimate of Fair Valueof Obligation to the Beneficiary and ABC Charity's Contribution

Yr.	*Mortality*	*Probability of Payment*	*Trust Assets at Beginning of the Year*	*Trust Return/ Discount Rate*	*Payout*	*Projected Payment*	*Discount Factor*	*Present Value of Payout*
	A	$B = B^{prev} \times (1 - A)$	$C = C^{prev} \times (1 + D^{prev}/100) - E^{prev}$	D	$E = 6\% \times C$	$F = B \times E$	G	$H = F \times G$
1	0.028304	0.971696	$100,000	1.140	$6,000	$5,830	0.98873	$5,764
2	0.030830	0.941739	95,140	1.530	5,708	5,376	0.97383	5,235
3	0.033570	0.910125	90,887	1.960	5,453	4,963	0.95511	4,740
4	0.036543	0.876867	87,215	2.305	5,233	4,589	0.93359	4,284
5	0.039760	0.842002	83,993	2.650	5,040	4,243	0.90949	3,859
6	0.043231	0.805602	81,179	2.878	4,871	3,924	0.88405	3,469
7	0.046962	0.767769	78,645	3.108	4,719	3,623	0.85740	3,106
8	0.050960	0.728644	76,370	3.338	4,582	3,339	0.82970	2,770
9	0.055233	0.688399	74,337	3.568	4,460	3,070	0.80112	2,460
10	0.059782	0.647245	72,529	3.790	4,352	2,817	0.77186	2,174
11	0.064614	0.605424	70,926	3.838	4,256	2,576	0.76637	1,974
12	0.069729	0.563208	69,393	3.885	4,164	2,345	0.76055	1,783
13	0.075129	0.520895	67,925	3.933	4,076	2,123	0.75442	1,602
14	0.081346	0.478522	66,521	3.980	3,991	1,910	0.74799	1,429
15	0.087988	0.436418	65,177	4.028	3,911	1,707	0.74126	1,265
16	0.095054	0.394935	63,891	4.075	3,833	1,514	0.73425	1,112
17	0.102537	0.354440	62,661	4.123	3,760	1,333	0.72696	969
18	0.110440	0.315295	61,485	4.170	3,689	1,163	0.71940	837
19	0.117691	0.278188	60,360	4.218	3,622	1,007	0.71159	717
20	0.125100	0.243386	59,284	4.265	3,557	866	0.70354	609

(continued)

Estimate of Fair Valueof Obligation to the Beneficiary and ABC Charity's Contribution—*continued*

Yr.	*Mortality*	*Probability of Payment*	*Trust Assets at Beginning of the Year*	*Trust Return/ Discount Rate*	*Payout*	*Projected Payment*	*Discount Factor*	*Present Value of Payout*
	A	$B = B^{prev} \times (1 - A)$	$C = C^{prev} \times (1 + D^{prev}/100) - E^{prev}$	D	E = 6% × C	F = B × E	G	H = F × G
21	0.132647	0.211102	58,255	4.313	3,495	738	0.69525	513
22	0.140309	0.181482	57,272	4.360	3,436	624	0.68673	428
23	0.148066	0.154611	56,333	4.408	3,380	523	0.67800	354
24	0.163725	0.129297	55,436	4.455	3,326	430	0.66907	288
25	0.182176	0.105742	54,579	4.503	3,275	346	0.65995	229
26	0.204277	0.084142	53,762	4.550	3,226	271	0.65064	177
27	0.231053	0.064701	52,983	4.598	3,179	206	0.64117	132
28	0.263745	0.047636	52,239	4.645	3,134	149	0.63154	94
29	0.287334	0.033949	51,532	4.693	3,092	105	0.62176	65
30	0.314649	0.023267	50,858	4.740	3,051	71	0.61185	43
31	0.346177	0.015212	50,217	4.788	3,013	46	0.60181	28
32	0.382403	0.009395	49,608	4.835	2,976	28	0.59167	17
33	0.423813	0.005413	49,030	4.883	2,942	16	0.58142	9
34	0.470893	0.002864	48,482	4.930	2,909	8	0.57108	5
35	0.524128	0.001363	47,964	4.978	2,878	4	0.56067	2
36	0.584004	0.000567	47,473	5.025	2,848	2	0.55019	1
37	0.651007	0.000198	47,010	5.073	2,821	1	0.53965	0
38	0.725622	0.000054	46,574	5.120	2,794	0	0.52907	0
					Total Fair Value of Donor's Interest			**$52,543**
Life expectancy		13.442			**Total Fair Value of ABC Charity's Interest**			**$47,457**

96. The calculation in exhibit 1 incorporates a yield curve and mortality probabilities. The Financial Reporting Executive Committee believes that a shortcut method would provide an adequate estimate of fair value in circumstances in which the results would not be materially different than the more precise method illustrated in exhibit 1. Exhibit 2 presents a shortcut calculation for the same fact set as exhibit 1.

EXHIBIT 2

97. Rather than using annual mortality statistics, the beneficiary's life expectancy is used, and 13.44 years (exhibit 1) is rounded to 14 years. Instead of using the yield curve used in exhibit 1, the average return over the life of the beneficiary is projected. The boxes indicate observable market returns. As in exhibit 1, the return on Treasuries after year 10 is imputed using a linear interpolation of the 10-year and 30-year rates. Thus, the average return is computed as follows:

1-year Treasury	0.47%
2-year Treasury	0.86%
3-year Treasury	1.29%
4-year Treasury	1.64%
5-year Treasury	1.98%
6-year Treasury	2.21%
7-year Treasury	2.44%
8-year Treasury	2.67%
9-year Treasury	2.90%
10-year Treasury	3.12%
11-year Treasury	3.17%
12-year Treasury	3.22%
13-year Treasury	3.26%
14-year Treasury	3.31%
	32.55%
Average Treasury	2.32%
Swap spread	0.67%
Average return	2.99%

The average return is used to compute the return on the investments in the portfolio for purposes of estimating the trust assets at the beginning of the year. It is also used as the discount rate, which is computed using the formula $1 / (1 + \text{interest rate})^n$ in which n is the number of years. The estimate of the obligation to the beneficiary and ABC Charity's contribution is as follows, using the shortcut method:

Estimate of Fair Value of Obligation to the Beneficiary and ABC Charity's Contribution

	Projected Trust Balance: Beginning of Year	*Projected Trust Income*	*Projected Trust Payout*	*Present Value Factor*	*Present Value of Payout*
	$A = A^{prev} + B^{prev} - C^{prev}$	$B = A \times 2.993\%$	$C = A \times 6\%$	D	$E = C \times D$
Year 1	$100,000	$2,993	$6,000	0.9709	$5,826
Year 2	96,993	2,903	5,820	0.9427	5,486
Year 3	94,077	2,816	5,645	0.9153	5,167
Year 4	91,249	2,731	5,475	0.8887	4,866
Year 5	88,505	2,649	5,310	0.8629	4,582
Year 6	85,844	2,570	5,151	0.8378	4,315
Year 7	83,263	2,492	4,996	0.8135	4,064
Year 8	80,760	2,417	4,846	0.7898	3,827
Year 9	78,331	2,345	4,700	0.7669	3,604
Year 10	75,976	2,274	4,559	0.7446	3,394
Year 11	73,692	2,206	4,422	0.7229	3,196
Year 12	71,476	2,140	4,289	0.7019	3,010
Year 13	69,327	2,075	4,160	0.6815	2,835
Year 14	67,243	2,013	4,035	0.6617	2,670
			Total Fair Value of Donor's Interest		**$56,842**
			Total Fair Value of ABC Charity's Interest		**$43,158**

98. The shortcut method in exhibit 2 results in an obligation to the beneficiary of $56,842 as compared with $52,543 in the more exact method in exhibit 1, which is a difference of $4,299 or 8 percent. The primary reason for the difference is the use of the average return over the life expectancy of the beneficiary instead of the yield curve. In circumstances in which the average return is used, and the yield curve is upward sloping (as is typical), the trust assets are not depleted as rapidly, and the projected payments to the beneficiary are larger.

99. Exhibits 1 and 2 used a risk-neutral rate adjusted by the swap spread as the projected return on the trust assets and discount rate. As discussed in paragraph 90, if a not-for-profit entity (NFP) uses the projected earnings rate on the trust assets in the PV calculation, and the NFP is complying with all its fiduciary duties as trustee, best practice is to use that projected earnings rate as the discount rate. Exhibit 3 presents a shortcut calculation for the same fact set as exhibits 1 and 2 but uses the projected earning rate on the trust assets as the discount rate, rather than the risk-neutral rate.

EXHIBIT 3

100. The beneficiary's life expectancy from exhibit 1 (13.44 years) is rounded to 14 years. Instead of using the yield curve used in exhibit 1 or the average return over the life of the beneficiary used in exhibit 2, the projected return on the portfolio of 4 percent is used as the discount rate and rate of return on the trust assets.

101. The shortcut method in exhibit 3 results in an obligation to the beneficiary of $56,479 as compared with $52,543 in the more exact method in exhibit 1, a difference from exhibit 1 of $3,936 or 7.5 percent. The primary reason for the difference is the use of the average return on trust investments over the life expectancy of the beneficiary instead of the yield curve. In circumstances in which the average return is used, and the yield curve is upward sloping (as is typical), the trust assets are not depleted as rapidly, and the projected payments to the beneficiary are larger. The difference from the shortcut method using the risk-neutral rate is negligible ($56,842 compared with $56,479).

Estimate of Fair Value of Obligation to the Beneficiary and ABC Charity's Contribution

	Projected Trust Balance: Beginning of Year	***Projected Trust Income***	***Projected Trust Payout***	***Present Value Factor***	***Present Value of Payout***
	A = A^{prev} + B^{prev} – C^{prev}	**B = A × 4%**	**C = A × 6%**	**D**	**E = C × D**
Year 1	$100,000	$4,000	$6,000	0.9615	$5,769
Year 2	98,000	3,920	5,880	0.9246	5,436
Year 3	96,040	3,842	5,762	0.8890	5,123
Year 4	94,119	3,765	5,647	0.8548	4,827
Year 5	92,237	3,689	5,534	0.8219	4,549
Year 6	90,392	3,616	5,424	0.7903	4,286
Year 7	88,584	3,543	5,315	0.7599	4,039
Year 8	86,813	3,473	5,209	0.7307	3,806
Year 9	85,076	3,403	5,105	0.7026	3,586
Year 10	83,375	3,335	5,002	0.6756	3,380
Year 11	81,707	3,268	4,902	0.6496	3,185
Year 12	80,073	3,203	4,804	0.6246	3,001
Year 13	78,472	3,139	4,708	0.6006	2,828
Year 14	76,902	3,076	4,614	0.5775	2,665
			Total Fair Value of Donor's Interest		**$56,479**
			Total Fair Value of ABC Charity's Interest		**$43,521**

102. To determine the sensitivity of the fair value measurements to changes in the rate used for the investment return, a not-for-profit entity (NFP) or its auditors can perform a sensitivity analysis by substituting different rates of return and discount rates into the spreadsheet used to compute the fair value estimates. Doing so results in the following values of the obligation, using the shortcut method, and the following rates. Readers are reminded that the discount rate would equal the projected rate of return on the investments if the NFP is complying with all of its fiduciary duties as trustee.

Portfolio Return	*Discount Rate*	*Obligation*
2.99%	2.99%	$56,842
1.00	1.00	57,574
2.00	2.00	57,205
4.00	4.00	56,479
5.00	5.00	56,122

Changes in Valuation Techniques

103. In accordance with paragraphs 25–26 of Financial Accounting Standards Board (FASB) *Accounting Standards Codification* (ASC) 820-10-35, a change in a valuation technique or its application (for example, a change in its weighting when multiple valuation techniques are used or a change in an adjustment applied to a valuation technique) is appropriate if the change results in a measurement that is equally or more representative of fair value in the circumstances. That might be the case if, for example, any of the following events occur:

a. New markets develop.

b. New information becomes available.

c. Information previously used is no longer available.

d. Valuation techniques improve.

e. Market conditions change.

Revisions resulting from a change in the valuation technique or its application are accounted for as a change in accounting estimate. The disclosure provisions of FASB ASC 250, *Accounting Changes and Error Corrections*, for a change in accounting estimate are not required for revisions resulting from a change in a valuation technique or its application.

6.96

Appendix B—Journal Entries

B-1 This appendix provides journal entries related to the examples in paragraphs 6.54–.88.

B-2 ***Charitable Lead Trust (not-for-profit entity [NFP] is trustee)*** (paragraphs 6.55–.58). NFP A enters into an irrevocable charitable lead annuity trust arrangement with a donor whereby

- the donor establishes a trust with NFP A serving as trustee.
- the terms of the trust are that NFP A is to receive an annuity of $X per year until the donor's death.
- distributions received from the trust by NFP A are unrestricted.
- upon the death of the donor, the remaining balance in the trust passes to the donor's estate.

Solution:

Creation of the trust:

dr.	Assets Held in Charitable Lead Trust	
cr.		Liability for Amounts Held for Others
cr.		Contribution Revenue—Temporarily Restricted

(Assets and revenue measured at fair value when received, as discussed in paragraphs 6.13–.15)

Over the term of the trust:

dr.	Assets Held in Charitable Lead Trust	
cr.		Liability for Amounts Held for Others

(Trust income and changes in fair value of assets held in trust, to the extent recognized)

dr.	Cash	
cr.		Assets Held in Charitable Lead Trust

(Distribution of income to NFP)

dr.	Temporarily Restricted Net Assets—Reclassifications Out	
cr.		Unrestricted Net Assets—Reclassifications In

(Reclassification of amounts received by NFP)

dr.	Liability for Amounts Held for Others	
cr.		Change in Value of Split-Interest Agreements—Temporarily Restricted

(Amortization of discount and revaluation based on changes in actuarial assumptions—debit and credit could be reversed)

Termination of the trust:

dr.	Liability for Amounts Held for Others
dr.	Change in Value of Split-Interest Agreements—Temporarily Restricted (or cr.)
cr.	Assets Held in Charitable Lead Trust

(Return of assets to donor's estate)

B-3 ***Charitable Lead Trust (NFP is not trustee)*** (paragraph 6.60). The fact situation is the same as in the previous example except that the NFP is not the trustee.

Solution:

Creation of the trust:

dr.	Beneficial Interest in Lead Trust
cr.	Contribution Revenue—Temporarily Restricted

(Beneficial interest in trust assets measured at fair value, as discussed in paragraphs 6.20–.27.)

Over the term of the trust:

dr.	Cash
cr.	Beneficial Interest in Lead Trust

(Distribution of income to NFP)

dr.	Temporarily Restricted Net Assets—Reclassifications Out
cr.	Unrestricted Net Assets—Reclassifications In

(Reclassification of amount received by NFP)

dr.	Beneficial Interest in Lead Trust
cr.	Change in Value of Split-Interest Agreements—Temporarily Restricted

(Change in fair value—debit and credit could be reversed)

Termination of the trust:

dr.	Change in Value of Split-Interest Agreements—Temporarily Restricted
cr.	Beneficial Interest in Lead Trust

(Closeout interest)

B-4 ***Perpetual Trust Held by a Third Party*** (paragraphs 6.62–.65). Donor enters into an irrevocable perpetual trust agreement with a third-party trustee with NFP B as the income beneficiary whereby

- the donor establishes a trust with its bank serving as trustee, with a payment to the trust to be invested in perpetuity by the trustee.

- the terms of the trust are that NFP B is to be the sole beneficiary and receive the income on the trust assets as earned in perpetuity with no restrictions on its use.

Solution:

Creation of the trust:

dr. Beneficial Interest in Perpetual Trust

cr. Contribution Revenue—Permanently Restricted

(Assets and revenue measured at fair value, as discussed in paragraphs 6.24–.27 and in paragraph 6.64.)

Each period:

dr. Cash

cr. Investment Income (Unrestricted)

(Income received from trust [net asset class based on stipulations of the trust])

dr. Beneficial Interest in Perpetual Trust

cr. Gain or Loss—Permanently Restricted

(To adjust asset for changes in fair value—debit and credit could be reversed)

B-5 ***Charitable Remainder Trust (NFP is trustee)*** (paragraphs 6.67–.70). NFP C enters into a charitable remainder unitrust agreement with a donor whereby

- a trust is established by the donor to be administered by NFP C.
- the donor's spouse is to receive an annual distribution of X percent of the fair value of the trust's assets each year until the spouse dies.
- at the time of death of the donor's spouse, the remaining assets of the trust are to be distributed to NFP C as permanent endowment.

Solution:

Creation of the trust:

dr. Assets Held in Charitable Remainder Trust

cr. Liability Under Unitrust Agreement

cr. Contribution Revenue—Permanently Restricted

(Assets and liability, as discussed in paragraphs 6.13–.18.)

Over the term of the trust:

dr. Assets Held in Charitable Remainder Trust

cr. Liability Under Unitrust Agreement

(Trust income and change in fair value of assets held in trust, to the extent recognized) dr. Liability Under Unitrust Agreement

cr. Assets Held in Charitable Remainder Trust

(Payment to beneficiary)

dr. Liability Under Unitrust Agreement

cr. Change in Value of Split-Interest Agreements—Permanently Restricted

(Amortization of discount and adjustment of liability to reflect change in actuarial assumptions—debit and credit could be reversed)

Termination of the trust:

dr. Liability Under Unitrust Agreement

cr. Change in Value of Split-Interest Agreements—Permanently Restricted

(To close liability)

dr. Endowment Assets

cr. Assets Held in Charitable Remainder Trust

(To close trust and recognize assets as endowment)

B-6 ***Charitable Remainder Trust (NFP is not trustee)*** (paragraph 6.72). The fact situation is the same as in the previous example, except that the NFP does not serve as trustee.

Solution:

Creation of the trust:

dr. Beneficial Interest in Remainder Trust

cr. Contribution Revenue—Permanently Restricted

(Beneficial interest measured at fair value, as discussed in paragraphs 6.20–.27.)

Over the term of the trust:

dr. Beneficial Interest in Remainder Trust

cr. Change in Value of Split-Interest Agreements—Permanently Restricted

(Change in fair value—debit and credit could be reversed)

Termination of the trust:

dr. Endowment Assets

cr. Beneficial Interest in Remainder Trust

cr. Change in Value of Split-Interest Agreements—Permanently Restricted

(NFP receives distribution of trust assets from trustee, measured at fair value; the receivable account is closed and the change in value of split-interest agreements reflects the difference)

B-7 ***Charitable Gift Annuity*** (paragraphs 6.74–.77). NFP D enters into a charitable gift annuity contract with a donor whereby

- assets are transferred to NFP D and are available for unrestricted use by NFP D.
- NFP D agrees to pay a stated dollar amount annually to the donor's spouse until the spouse dies, at which time the remaining assets are available for the unrestricted use of NFP D.

Solution:

Creation of the annuity:

dr.	Assets	
cr.		Annuity Payment Liability
cr.		Contribution Revenue—Unrestricted

(Assets and liabilities are measured at fair value when received, as discussed in paragraphs 6.13–.19.)

Over the term of the annuity:

dr.	Annuity Payment Liability	
cr.		Cash

(Payment to annuity beneficiary)

dr.	Change in Value of Split-Interest Agreements—Unrestricted	
cr.		Annuity Payment Liability

(Amortization of discount on liability and recording of any change in the life expectancy of the beneficiary—debit and credit could be reversed)

Termination of the annuity:

dr.	Annuity Payment Liability	
cr.		Change in Value of Split-Interest Agreements—Unrestricted

(To close the annuity payment liability)

B-8 ***Pooled (Life) Income Fund*** (paragraphs 6.79–.82). NFP E forms, invests, and manages a pooled income (or life-income) fund. The fund is divided into units, and contributions from many donors are pooled. Donors are assigned a specific number of units based on the proportion of the fair value of the contribution to the total fair value of the fund. A donor makes a contribution to the fund, is assigned a specific number of units, and will receive the actual income earned on those units until his or her death. The assets contributed must be invested in the fund until the donor's death. At that time, the value of the units assigned to the donor will revert to NFP E, and those assets will be available to NFP E without restriction.

Solution:

Contribution of assets:

dr.	Assets of Pooled Income Fund	
cr.		Contribution Revenue—Temporarily Restricted
cr.		Discount for Future Interest (Deferred Revenue)

(Assets and contribution revenue recorded at fair value on date of receipt, as discussed in paragraph 6.28.)

Over the term of the agreement:

dr.	Assets of Pooled Income Fund	
cr.		Liability to Life Beneficiary

(Income earned on units assigned to donor)

dr.	Liability to Life Beneficiary	
cr.		Assets of Pooled Income Fund

(Payment to life beneficiary)

dr.	Discount for Future Interest (Deferred Revenue)	
cr.		Change in Value of Split-Interest Agreements—Temporarily Restricted

(Amortization of discount and changes in the life expectancy of the beneficiary)

Termination of the agreement:

dr.	Discount for Future Interest (Deferred Revenue)	
cr.		Change in Value of Split-Interest Agreement—Unrestricted

(To close discount upon the death of the life beneficiary)

dr.	Cash or Investment Assets	
cr.		Assets of Pooled Income Fund

(To recognize assets available for use upon the death of the life beneficiary)

dr.	Temporarily Restricted Net Assets—Reclassification Out	
cr.		Unrestricted Net Assets—Reclassification In

(Reclassification based on the expiration of the time restriction)

B-9 ***Life Interest in Real Estate*** (paragraphs 6.84–.87).

A donor irrevocably transfers title to her personal residence to NFP G, retaining the right for the donor and the donor's spouse to use the residence until their deaths. The contract between the donor and NFP G specifies that the donor continues to pay the executory costs for the property, including maintenance costs, property taxes, insurance, utilities, and similar costs.

Solution:

Contribution of assets:

dr.	Residence Held Subject to a Life Interest
cr.	Contribution Revenue—Temporarily Restricted
cr.	Use Interest of Beneficiary (Deferred Revenue)

(Assets and contribution revenue recorded at fair value on date of receipt, as discussed in paragraph 6.85)

Over the term of the agreement:

dr.	Use Interest of Beneficiary (Deferred Revenue)
cr.	Change in Value of Split-Interest Agreements—Temporarily Restricted

(Amortize use obligation for donor's use of residence for a year)

dr.	Use Interest of Beneficiary (Deferred Revenue)
cr.	Change in Value of Split-Interest Agreements—Temporarily Restricted

(Amortization of discount and changes in the life expectancy of the beneficiary)

Termination of the agreement:

dr.	Use Interest of Beneficiary (Deferred Revenue)
cr.	Change in Value of Split-Interest Agreement—Temporarily Restricted

(To close use interest upon the death of both the donor and the donor's spouse)

dr.	Temporarily Restricted Net Assets—Reclassification Out
cr.	Unrestricted Net Assets—Reclassification In

(Reclassification based on the expiration of the time restriction)

dr.	Investment or Assets Held for Sale
cr.	Residence Held Subject to Life Interest

(To recognize assets available for use upon the death of donor and the donor's spouse)

B-1 This appendix provides journal entries related to the examples in paragraphs 6.54–.88 for NFPs that prepare financial statements in accordance with the amendments in FASB Accounting Standards Update (ASU) 2016-14, *Not-for-Profit Entities (Topic 958): Presentation of Financial Statements of Not-for-Profit Entities*. The amendments in ASU No. 2016-14 are effective for annual financial statements issued for fiscal years beginning after December 15, 2017 (for example, years ending December 31, 2018, and years ending June 30, 2019), and for interim periods within fiscal years beginning after December 15, 2018. Application to interim financial statements is permitted but not required in the initial year of application. Early application of the amendments is permitted. Additional information about the requirements of ASU No. 2016-14 is provided in shaded text throughout this guide, in appendix A, "Financial Statements Prepared in Accordance with FASB ASU No. 2016-14," of chapter 3, and in appendix A, "The New Not-for-Profit Financial Reporting Model: FASB ASU No. 2016-14," of this guide.

B-2 ***Charitable Lead Trust (not-for-profit entity [NFP] is trustee)*** (paragraphs 6.55–.58). NFP A enters into an irrevocable charitable lead annuity trust arrangement with a donor whereby

- the donor establishes a trust with NFP A serving as trustee.
- the terms of the trust are that NFP A is to receive an annuity of $X per year until the donor's death.
- distributions received from the trust by NFP A do not contain donor restrictions.
- upon the death of the donor, the remaining balance in the trust passes to the donor's estate.

Solution:

Creation of the trust:

dr. Assets Held in Charitable Lead Trust

cr. Liability for Amounts Held for Others

cr. Contribution Revenue—Donor Restricted

(Assets and revenue measured at fair value when received, as discussed in paragraphs 6.13–.15)

Over the term of the trust:

dr. Assets Held in Charitable Lead Trust

cr. Liability for Amounts Held for Others

(Trust income and changes in fair value of assets held in trust, to the extent recognized)

dr. Cash

cr. Assets Held in Charitable Lead Trust

(Distribution of income to NFP)

dr. Net Assets with Donor Restrictions—Reclassifications Out

cr. Net Asset without Donor Restrictions—Reclassifications In

(Reclassification of amounts received by NFP)

dr. Liability for Amounts Held for Others

cr. Change in Value of Split-Interest Agreements—Donor Restricted

(Amortization of discount and revaluation based on changes in actuarial assumptions—debit and credit could be reversed)

Termination of the trust:

dr. Liability for Amounts Held for Others

dr. Change in Value of Split-Interest Agreements—Donor Restricted (or cr.)

cr. Assets Held in Charitable Lead Trust

(Return of assets to donor's estate)

B-3 ***Charitable Lead Trust (NFP is not trustee)*** (paragraph 6.60). The fact situation is the same as in the previous example except that the NFP is not the trustee.

Solution:

Creation of the trust:

dr. Beneficial Interest in Lead Trust

cr. Contribution Revenue—Donor Restricted

(Beneficial interest in trust assets measured at fair value, as discussed in paragraphs 6.20–.27.)

Over the term of the trust:

dr. Cash

cr. Beneficial Interest in Lead Trust

(Distribution of income to NFP)

dr. Net Assets with Donor Restrictions—Reclassifications Out

cr. Net Assets without Donor Restrictions—Reclassifications In

(Reclassification of amount received by NFP)

dr. Beneficial Interest in Lead Trust

cr. Change in Value of Split-Interest Agreements—Donor Restricted

(Change in fair value—debit and credit could be reversed)

Termination of the trust:

dr. Change in Value of Split-Interest Agreements—Donor Restricted

cr. Beneficial Interest in Lead Trust

(Closeout interest)

B-4 ***Perpetual Trust Held by a Third Party*** (paragraphs 6.62–.65). Donor enters into an irrevocable perpetual trust agreement with a third-party trustee with NFP B as the income beneficiary whereby

- the donor establishes a trust with its bank serving as trustee, with a payment to the trust to be invested in perpetuity by the trustee.
- the terms of the trust are that NFP B is to be the sole beneficiary and receive the income on the trust assets as earned in perpetuity with no restrictions on its use.

Solution:

Creation of the trust:

dr.	Beneficial Interest in Perpetual Trust
cr.	Contribution Revenue—Donor Restricted

(Assets and revenue measured at fair value, as discussed in paragraphs 6.24–.27 and in paragraph 6.64.)

Each period:

dr.	Cash
cr.	Investment Income (Without Donor Restrictions)

(Income received from trust [net asset class based on stipulations of the trust])

dr.	Beneficial Interest in Perpetual Trust
cr.	Gain or Loss—Donor Restricted

(To adjust asset for changes in fair value—debit and credit could be reversed)

B-5 ***Charitable Remainder Trust (NFP is trustee)*** (paragraphs 6.67–.70). NFP C enters into a charitable remainder unitrust agreement with a donor whereby

- a trust is established by the donor to be administered by NFP C.
- the donor's spouse is to receive an annual distribution of X percent of the fair value of the trust's assets each year until the spouse dies.
- at the time of death of the donor's spouse, the remaining assets of the trust are to be distributed to NFP C as perpetual endowment.

Solution:

Creation of the trust:

dr.	Assets Held in Charitable Remainder Trust
cr.	Liability Under Unitrust Agreement

cr. Contribution Revenue—Donor Restricted

(Assets and liability, as discussed in paragraphs 6.13–.18.)

Over the term of the trust:

dr. Assets Held in Charitable Remainder Trust

cr. Liability Under Unitrust Agreement

(Trust income and change in fair value of assets held in trust, to the extent recognized)

dr. Liability Under Unitrust Agreement

cr. Assets Held in Charitable Remainder Trust

(Payment to beneficiary)

dr. Liability Under Unitrust Agreement

cr. Change in Value of Split-Interest Agreements—Donor Restricted

(Amortization of discount and adjustment of liability to reflect change in actuarial assumptions—debit and credit could be reversed)

Termination of the trust:

dr. Liability Under Unitrust Agreement

cr. Change in Value of Split-Interest Agreements—Donor Restricted

(To close liability)

dr. Endowment Assets

cr. Assets Held in Charitable Remainder Trust

(To close trust and recognize assets as endowment)

B-6 ***Charitable Remainder Trust (NFP is not trustee)*** (paragraph 6.72). The fact situation is the same as in the previous example, except that the NFP does not serve as trustee.

Solution:

Creation of the trust:

dr. Beneficial Interest in Remainder Trust

cr. Contribution Revenue—Donor Restricted

(Beneficial interest measured at fair value, as discussed in paragraphs 6.20–.27.)

Over the term of the trust:

dr. Beneficial Interest in Remainder Trust

cr. Change in Value of Split-Interest Agreements—Donor Restricted

(Change in fair value—debit and credit could be reversed)

Termination of the trust:

dr.	Endowment Assets	
cr.		Beneficial Interest in Remainder Trust
cr.		Change in Value of Split-Interest Agreements—Donor Restricted

(NFP receives distribution of trust assets from trustee, measured at fair value; the receivable account is closed and the change in value of split-interest agreements reflects the difference)

B-7 ***Charitable Gift Annuity*** (paragraphs 6.74–.77). NFP D enters into a charitable gift annuity contract with a donor whereby

- assets are transferred to NFP D and are available for general purposes by NFP D.
- NFP D agrees to pay a stated dollar amount annually to the donor's spouse until the spouse dies, at which time the remaining assets are available for general purposes of NFP D.

Solution:

Creation of the annuity:

dr.	Assets	
cr.		Annuity Payment Liability
cr.		Contribution Revenue—Without Donor Restriction

(Assets and liabilities are measured at fair value when received, as discussed in paragraphs 6.13–.19.)

Over the term of the annuity:

dr.	Annuity Payment Liability	
cr.		Cash

(Payment to annuity beneficiary)

dr.	Change in Value of Split-Interest Agreements—Without Donor Restrictions	
cr.		Annuity Payment Liability

(Amortization of discount on liability and recording of any change in the life expectancy of the beneficiary—debit and credit could be reversed)

Termination of the annuity:

dr.	Annuity Payment Liability	
cr.		Change in Value of Split-Interest Agreements—Without Donor Restrictions

(To close the annuity payment liability)

B-8 ***Pooled (Life) Income Fund*** (paragraphs 6.79–.82). NFP E forms, invests, and manages a pooled income (or life-income) fund. The fund is divided into units, and contributions from many donors are pooled. Donors are assigned a specific number of units based on the proportion of the fair value of the contribution to the total fair value of the fund. A donor makes a contribution to the fund, is assigned a specific number of units, and will receive the actual income earned on those units until his or her death. The assets contributed must be invested in the fund until the donor's death. At that time, the value of the units assigned to the donor will revert to NFP E, and those assets will be available to NFP E without restriction.

Solution:

Contribution of assets:

dr.		Assets of Pooled Income Fund	
	cr.		Contribution Revenue—Donor Restricted
	cr.		Discount for Future Interest (Deferred Revenue)

(Assets and contribution revenue recorded at fair value on date of receipt, as discussed in paragraph 6.28.)

Over the term of the agreement:

dr.		Assets of Pooled Income Fund	
	cr.		Liability to Life Beneficiary

(Income earned on units assigned to donor)

dr.		Liability to Life Beneficiary	
	cr.		Assets of Pooled Income Fund

(Payment to life beneficiary)

dr.		Discount for Future Interest (Deferred Revenue)	
	cr.		Change in Value of Split-Interest Agreements—Donor Restricted

(Amortization of discount and changes in the life expectancy of the beneficiary)

Termination of the agreement:

dr.		Discount for Future Interest (Deferred Revenue)	
	cr.		Change in Value of Split-Interest Agreement—Without Donor Restrictions

(To close discount upon the death of the life beneficiary)

dr.		Cash or Investment Assets	
	cr.		Assets of Pooled Income Fund

(To recognize assets available for use upon the death of the life beneficiary) dr. Net Assets with Donor Restrictions—Reclassification Out

cr. Net Assets without Donor Restrictions—Reclassification In

(Reclassification based on the expiration of the time restriction)

B-9 *Life Interest in Real Estate* (paragraphs 6.84–.87).

A donor irrevocably transfers title to her personal residence to NFP G, retaining the right for the donor and the donor's spouse to use the residence until their deaths. The contract between the donor and NFP G specifies that the donor continues to pay the executory costs for the property, including maintenance costs, property taxes, insurance, utilities, and similar costs.

Solution:

Contribution of assets:

dr. Residence Held Subject to a Life Interest

cr. Contribution Revenue—Donor Restricted

cr. Use Interest of Beneficiary (Deferred Revenue)

(Assets and contribution revenue recorded at fair value on date of receipt, as discussed in paragraph 6.85)

Over the term of the agreement:

dr. Use Interest of Beneficiary (Deferred Revenue)

cr. Change in Value of Split-Interest Agreements—Donor Restricted

(Amortize use obligation for donor's use of residence for a year)

dr. Use Interest of Beneficiary (Deferred Revenue)

cr. Change in Value of Split-Interest Agreements—Donor Restricted

(Amortization of discount and changes in the life expectancy of the beneficiary)

Termination of the agreement:

dr. Use Interest of Beneficiary (Deferred Revenue)

cr. Change in Value of Split-Interest Agreement—Donor Restricted

(To close use interest upon the death of both the donor and the donor's spouse)

dr. Net Assets with Donor Restrictions—Reclassification Out

cr. Net Assets without Donor Restrictions—Reclassification In

(Reclassification based on the expiration of the time restriction)

dr.	Investment or Assets Held for Sale	
	cr.	Residence Held Subject to Life Interest

(To recognize assets available for use upon the death of donor and the donor's spouse)[1]

---

[1] The amendments in FASB ASU No. 2016-14, *Not-for-Profit Entities (Topic 958): Presentation of Financial Statements of Not-for-Profit Entities*, are effective for annual financial statements issued for fiscal years beginning after December 15, 2017 (for example, years ending December 31, 2018, and years ending June 30, 2019), and for interim periods within fiscal years beginning after December 15, 2018. Application to interim financial statements is permitted but not required in the initial year of application. Early application of the amendments is permitted.

Chapter 7

Other Assets

Gray shaded text in this chapter reflects guidance issued but not yet effective as of the date of this guide, March 1, 2018, but becoming effective on or prior to June 30, 2018, exclusive of any option to early adopt ahead of the mandatory effective date. Unless otherwise indicated, all unshaded text reflects guidance that was already effective as of the date of this guide.

Introduction

7.01 Some assets held by not-for-profit entities (NFPs) are similar to those held by for-profit entities. This chapter considers assets that are not discussed elsewhere in this guide and that present accounting issues unique to NFPs.

Inventory

7.02 NFPs may acquire merchandise inventory for resale; for example, items held for sale by a bookstore, dining service, kitchen, or thrift shop. Merchandise inventory may be acquired by NFPs in exchange transactions or from contributions. FASB *Accounting Standards Codification* (ASC) 330, *Inventory*, discusses the general principles applicable to inventory.

7.03 Pursuant to the recognition and measurement standards for contributions in FASB ASC 958-605-25-2 and FASB ASC 958-605-30-2, contributions of inventory should be reported in the period received and should be measured at fair value. The FASB ASC glossary defines *fair value* as "the price that would be received to sell an asset or paid to transfer a liability in an orderly transaction between market participants at the measurement date." Consistent with the FASB ASC glossary definition of fair value, the fair value of contributed inventory is its estimated selling price. (Paragraphs 3.138–.168 discuss FASB ASC 820, *Fair Value Measurement*, which defines fair value, establishes a framework for measuring fair value, and identifies required disclosures about fair value measurements.)

7.04 Pursuant to FASB ASC 958-605-25-4, a major uncertainty about the existence of value may indicate that an item received or given should not be recognized. For example, a gift of clothing or furniture has no value unless it can be utilized in either of the following ways: (*a*) used internally by the NFP or for program purposes or (*b*) sold by the NFP. (Paragraphs 5.123–.149 discuss gifts in kind.)

7.05 Pursuant to FASB ASC 958-605-30-9, inputs for measuring fair value may be obtained from published catalogs, vendors, independent appraisals, and other sources. If methods such as estimates, averages, or computational approximations, such as average value per pound or subsequent sales, can reduce the cost of measuring the fair value of inventory, use of those methods is appropriate, provided the methods are applied consistently, and the results of applying those methods are reasonably expected not to be materially different from the results of a detailed measurement of the fair value of contributed inventory.

7.06 Reporting inventory at cost (or fair value at date of donation) is satisfactory only if the utility of the goods has not diminished since their acquisition. FASB ASC 330-10-35-1 states that when there is evidence that the utility of goods, in their disposal in the ordinary course of business, will be less than cost, whether due to physical deterioration, obsolescence, changes in price levels, or other causes, the difference should be recognized as a loss of the current period. This is generally accomplished by stating such goods at a lower level commonly designated as market. The term *market* means current replacement cost (by purchase or by reproduction, as the case may be) provided that it meets both of the following conditions: (*a*) market should not exceed the net realizable value, and (*b*) market should not be less than net realizable value reduced by an allowance for an approximately normal profit margin. Technical Questions and Answers (Q&A) section 6140.01, "Inventory Valuation for a Not-for-Profit Scientific Entity,"[1] provides an example of an NFP that produces products that are sold at a price less than cost. The difference between cost and sale proceeds is covered by contributions. Q&A section 6140.01 states that the fact that the difference between the sales proceeds and the costs is covered by contributions does not change the application of the requirements of FASB ASC 330-10, and that inventories should be valued at lower of cost or market. As noted in FASB ASC 330-10-35-3, the rule of lower of cost or market is intended to provide a means of measuring the residual usefulness of an inventory expenditure. The term *market* is therefore to be interpreted as indicating utility on the inventory date and may be thought of in terms of the equivalent expenditure which would have to be made in the ordinary course at that date to procure corresponding utility.

The "Pending Content" in FASB ASC 330-10-35-1B states that inventory measured using any method other than LIFO or the retail inventory method (for example, inventory measured using first-in, first-out (FIFO) or average cost) should be measured at the lower of cost and net realizable value. When evidence exists that the net realizable value of inventory is lower than its cost, the difference should be recognized as a loss in earnings in the period in which it occurs. That loss may be required, for example, due to damage, physical deterioration, obsolescence, changes in price levels, or other causes. The FASB ASC glossary defines *net realizable value* as "estimated selling prices in the ordinary course of business, less reasonably predictable costs of completion, disposal, and transportation."

Net realizable value is not a relevant measure for inventories of NFPs if the inventory items will be provided to program beneficiaries without charge or for a minimal fee. Thus, reporting those inventories at cost (or fair value at date of donation) is satisfactory if the utility of the inventory items has not diminished since their acquisition.[2]

7.07 Consistent with FASB ASC 958-220-45-4, sales of inventory or other assets that are part of an NFP's ongoing major or central operations and activities should be reported separately from (and therefore in addition to) the

[1] All Q&A sections can be found in *Technical Questions and Answers*.

[2] FASB Accounting Standards Update (ASU) No. 2015-11, *Inventory (Topic 330): Simplifying the Measurement of Inventory*, is effective for not-for-profit entities for fiscal years beginning after December 15, 2016, and interim periods within fiscal years beginning after December 15, 2017.

reporting of the contribution of the inventory items, with a corresponding cost of sales. As noted in paragraphs 5.150–.151, sales of tickets, gift certificates, works of art, and other merchandise that were contributed for the purpose of being transferred to others during fund-raising events should be recognized as adjustments to the original contributions when the items are sold to the ultimate resource providers (recipients) during the fund-raising event. For other sales of inventory, either gross or net reporting is permitted if the sales are incidental or peripheral transactions. The Financial Reporting Executive Committee (FinREC) recommends that sales that result from incidental or peripheral transactions be reported net, similar to gains and losses.

7.08 Examples of transactions that typically result in reporting the sale of contributed assets as sales and costs of sales (gross reporting) include the following:

- Items produced or processed in vocational training workshops that are part of the NFP's mission
- Items contributed to the NFP and subsequently sold in its thrift shops that are operated as part of the NFP's mission
- Used cars contributed and sold by an NFP that has a vehicle donation program

7.09 Examples of transactions that typically result in reporting the sale of contributed assets as a gain or loss (net reporting) include the following:

- Excess food, medicine, clothing, and so on that was received by the NFP as a contribution but that is beyond the NFP's current needs, assuming the transaction is peripheral or incidental
- Sales of long-lived assets, such as office equipment or real estate, that was received by the NFP as a contribution but that is beyond the NFP's current needs, assuming the transaction is peripheral or incidental
- A used car sold by an NFP that only occasionally receives donated vehicles

Acting as an Agent in a Sale of Commodities

7.10 Some NFPs receive commodities subject to agreements that require that the commodities be sold (monetized) upon receipt and the proceeds be used to perform under a grant agreement. Commodities received for monetization usually have specific limitations on their sale, such as limiting the sale to purchasers in a specific country, specifying a minimum price that must be obtained upon sale, and requiring that the NFP perform a study to ensure that the sale will not disrupt the marketplace in that country. The NFP typically is acting as an agent in the transaction to monetize the commodities, and does not recognize revenue or cost of goods sold for the sale of the commodities. Instead the cash proceeds of the sale are recognized as if the grant were a cash grant. If the NFP holds title to the commodities at the reporting date, FinREC recommends that the NFP include the value of the commodities on the statement of financial position as an asset and an offsetting liability. The amount to be reported would be the value of the commodities as contractually agreed upon with the principal in the transaction.

Prepaid Expenses, Deferred Costs, and Similar Items

7.11 NFPs may incur costs that will result in benefits to future periods rather than solely to current-period activities. Except as discussed elsewhere in this guide, the recognition and measurement principles for those costs are similar to those used by business entities. Accordingly, amounts expended for prepaid expenses and deposits should be reported as assets. As noted in FASB ASC 340-10-05-4, prepaid expenses are typically used up or expire within the normal operating cycle of an entity. The term *prepaid expense* derives from the fact that they are paid in advance of their use or consumption.

7.12 For example, a performing arts organization might report as assets production costs relating to performances that will occur in the next fiscal period; or a museum might report exhibit costs for hosting an upcoming traveling exhibit. (Certain of these costs might be characterized as property or equipment, or as start-up costs.) Whether the costs of such activities should be reported as assets, rather than expensed, depends on whether a future economic benefit exists, either in the form of future cash inflows or service potential.

7.13 Future benefits of prepaid assets may be realized through service potential by providing desired or needed goods or services to beneficiaries or other constituents, particularly if the NFP does not intend to charge a fee for the future activity to which the costs relate. Accordingly, deferral of costs may be appropriate even in circumstances in which the activity is expected to generate no net cash inflows.

7.14 NFPs should consider the following guidance when determining whether they have transactions and activities that result in prepaid expenses and deferred costs as of the date of the statement of financial position:

- Chapter 13, "Expenses, Gains and Losses," which provides specific guidance pertaining to fund-raising costs, advertising costs, start-up activities, organization costs, and internal-use computer software costs.
- FASB ASC 835-30, which requires that debt issuance costs related to a recognized debt liability be presented in the statement of financial position as a direct deduction from the carrying amount of that debt liability, consistent with debt discounts.
- FASB ASC 985-20, which applies to computer software to be sold, leased, or otherwise marketed as a separate product or as part of a product or process.
- FASB ASC 985-705-S99, which applies to film and software costs associated with developing entertainment and educational software products. Although that guidance applies only to public registrants, FinREC believes it provides appropriate guidance for NFPs undertaking similar projects.
- FASB ASC 926-20, which applies to costs incurred by producers or distributors of feature films, television specials, television series, or similar products (including animated films and television programming) that are sold, licensed, or exhibited, regardless of whether the content is produced on film, videotape, digital or other video recording format.
- FASB ASC 350-50, which applies to website development costs.

7.15 If an NFP has prepaid expenses or deferred costs, it should determine the period over which the asset is consumed (and therefore amortized) based on how the economic benefit underlying the asset is used up or lost. Long-term prepaid assets are subject to impairment tests under FASB ASC 360-10.

Collections and Works of Art, Historical Treasures, or Similar Assets

7.16 The FASB ASC glossary defines *collections* as follows:

> Works of art, historical treasures, or similar assets that meet all of the following criteria: (*a*) They are held for public exhibition, education, or research in furtherance of public service rather than financial gain, (*b*) They are protected, kept unencumbered, cared for, and preserved, and (*c*) They are subject to an organizational policy that requires the proceeds of items that are sold to be used to acquire other items for collections.

7.17 FASB ASC 958-360-25-3 states that an NFP that holds works of art, historical treasures, and similar items that meet the definition of a collection has the following three alternative policies for reporting that collection: (*a*) capitalization of all collection items, (*b*) capitalization of all collection items on a prospective basis (that is, all items acquired after a stated date), or (*c*) no capitalization. Capitalization of selected collections or items is precluded.

7.18 Accounting for collections depends on whether an NFP adopts a policy of recognizing collections as assets. If an NFP adopts a policy of capitalizing collections, items acquired in exchange transactions should be recognized as assets in the period in which they are acquired and should be measured at cost. Per FASB ASC 958-605-25-19 and FASB ASC 958-605-30-2, contributed collection items should be recognized as assets and as revenues or gains if collections are capitalized[3] and should be measured at fair value. Items acquired in a nonmonetary exchange should be measured in accordance with FASB ASC 845-10-30. As discussed in FASB ASC 958-605-25-4, if an item is accepted solely to be saved for its potential future use in scientific or educational research and has no alternative use, it may have uncertain value, or perhaps no value, and should not be recognized.

7.19 As discussed in FASB ASC 820-10-35-9, an NFP should measure the fair value of an asset using the assumptions that market participants would use in pricing the asset, assuming that market participants act in their economic best interest. When developing those assumptions, an NFP need not identify specific market participants; rather, the reporting entity should identify characteristics that distinguish market participants. When doing so, the NFP would generally consider factors specific to all of the following: the asset, the principal (or most advantageous) market for the asset, and market participants with whom the NFP would enter into a transaction in that market. Market participant assumptions should include assumptions about the effect of a restriction on the sale or use of an asset if market participants would consider the effect of the restriction in pricing the asset. Example 6 (paragraphs 51–55) of FASB

---

[3] As discussed in paragraphs 3–6 of FASB *Accounting Standards Codification* (ASC) 958-605-45, contributions should be classified as increases in unrestricted, temporarily restricted, or permanently restricted net assets, depending on the existence and type of restrictions imposed by donors. Chapter 5, "Contributions Received and Agency Transactions," provides guidance concerning accounting for contributions with donor-imposed restrictions.

ASC 820-10-55 explains that restrictions that are a characteristic of an asset—and therefore would transfer to a market participant—are the only restrictions reflected in fair value. Donor restrictions that are specific to the donee are reflected in the classification of net assets, not in the measurement of fair value. For example, a donor contributes a painting to a museum and specifies that the painting be added to the museum's permanent collection and, if it is sold, the proceeds of the sale be used to purchase another collection item. That restriction is not a characteristic of the painting itself and would not transfer to a purchaser of the painting; therefore, the donor-imposed restriction has no effect on the fair value of the painting (or the amount of the donor-restricted contribution if the museum capitalizes its collections).

7.20 FASB ASC 958-605-25-19 states that contributed collection items should not be recognized as revenues or gains if collections are not capitalized.

7.21 FASB ASC 958-230-55-5A states that cash flows from purchases, sales, and insurance recoveries of unrecognized, noncapitalized collection items should be reported as investing activities in a statement of cash flows. Additional disclosures described in paragraphs 7.26–.27 should be made if an NFP elects not to capitalize collections.

7.22 If collection items are capitalized, FASB ASC 958-360-35-5 requires depreciation to be recognized. The future economic benefits or service potentials of individual items comprising collections, works of art, historical treasures, and similar items—including those designated as landmarks, monuments, cathedrals, or historical treasures—are used up not only by wear and tear in intended uses but also by the continuous destructive effects of pollutants, vibrations, and so forth. The cultural, aesthetic, or historical values of those assets can be preserved, if at all, only by periodic major efforts to protect, clean, and restore them, usually at significant cost. Depreciation need not be recognized on collection items that meet the criteria in FASB ASC 958-360-35-3. Additionally, if collection items are capitalized, a collection item should be tested for impairment in accordance with FASB ASC 360-10-35 whenever events or changes in circumstances indicate that its carrying amount may not be recoverable.

7.23 Per paragraphs 2–3 of FASB ASC 958-360-40, a contribution made by an NFP of a previously recognized collection item should be reported as an expense and a decrease in assets in the period in which the contribution is made, and should be measured at fair value. A gain or loss should be recognized on that contribution made if the collection item's fair value differs from its carrying amount. A contribution made by an NFP of a previously unrecognized collection item should not be recognized on the face of the financial statements. FASB ASC 958-360-50-6 requires disclosure of those contributions in notes to the financial statements.

7.24 FASB ASC 958-605-25-18 requires that contributions of works of art, historical treasures, and similar assets that are not part of a collection should be recognized as assets and as revenue or gains.[4] Per FASB ASC 958-605-30-2, those contributions should be measured at fair value. Items acquired in exchange transactions should be measured at cost. Works of art, historical treasures, and similar items that are not added to collections should be accounted for as either held for sale or held and used in accordance with FASB ASC 360-10-35, as discussed in chapter 9, "Property and Equipment."

---

[4] See footnote 3.

Financial Statement Presentation of Collections

7.25 In accordance with FASB ASC 958-360-45-3, if an NFP adopts a policy of capitalizing collections (as defined in the FASB ASC glossary) a statement of financial position should include the total amount capitalized on a separate line item, "Collections" or "Collection Items." Per FASB ASC 958-360-45-4, the amount capitalized for works of art, historical treasures, and similar assets that do not meet the definition of a collection should be disclosed separately on the face of the statement of financial position or in the notes.

7.26 FASB ASC 958-360-45-5 states that an NFP that does not recognize and capitalize its collections should report the following on the face of its statement of activities, separately from revenues, expenses, gains, and losses:

- Costs of collection items purchased as a decrease in the appropriate class of net assets
- Proceeds from sale of collection items as an increase in the appropriate class of net assets
- Proceeds from insurance recoveries of lost or destroyed collection items as an increase in the appropriate class of net assets

Similarly, an entity that capitalizes its collections prospectively should report proceeds from sales and insurance recoveries of items not previously capitalized separately from revenues, expenses, gains, and losses. Example 1 (paragraph 2) of FASB ASC 958-360-55 illustrates a statement of activities that satisfies these requirements. In that example, the statement of activities reports purchases of collection items as a decrease in permanently restricted net assets if the collection items were purchased with contributions restricted for that purpose and the entity does not capitalize collections. It reports the proceeds of sales of collection items that had not been capitalized as increases in permanently restricted net assets if those collection items were contributed (or purchased with contributions restricted for that purpose). Purchases of collection items and proceeds of their sale are changes in unrestricted net assets if the collection items were neither donated nor purchased with contributions restricted for that purpose.

FASB ASC 958-360-45-5 states that an NFP that does not recognize and capitalize its collections should report the following on the face of its statement of activities, separately from revenues, expenses, gains, and losses:

- Costs of collection items purchased as a decrease in the appropriate class of net assets
- Proceeds from sale of collection items as an increase in the appropriate class of net assets
- Proceeds from insurance recoveries of lost or destroyed collection items as an increase in the appropriate class of net assets

Similarly, an entity that capitalizes its collections prospectively should report proceeds from sales and insurance recoveries of items not previously capitalized separately from revenues, expenses, gains, and losses. The "Pending Content" in Example 1 (paragraph 2) of FASB ASC 958-360-55 illustrates a statement of activities that satisfies these requirements. In that example, the statement of activities reports purchases of collection items as a decrease in net assets with donor restrictions if the collection items were purchased with contributions restricted for that purpose and the entity does not capitalize collections. It reports the proceeds of sales of collection items that had not been capitalized as increases in net assets with donor restrictions if those collection items were contributed (or purchased with contributions restricted for that purpose). Purchases of collection items and proceeds of their sale are changes in net assets without donor restrictions if the collection items were neither donated nor purchased with contributions restricted for that purpose.[5]

7.27 FASB ASC 958-360-50-6 states that an NFP that does not recognize and capitalize its collections or that capitalizes collections prospectively should describe its collections, including their relative significance, and its stewardship policies for collections. If collection items not capitalized are deaccessed during that period, it also should describe the items given away, damaged, destroyed, lost, or otherwise deaccessed during the period or disclose their fair value. In addition, FASB ASC 958-360-45-3 requires that a line item should be shown on the face of the statement of financial position that refers to the disclosures required by this paragraph. That line item should be dated if collections are capitalized prospectively, for example, "Collections acquired since January 1, 19X1 (Note X)." FASB ASC 958-360-50-1 requires that an NFP disclose (its chosen) capitalization policy for collections (capitalization, prospective capitalization, or no capitalization).

Illustrative Disclosures About Collections

7.28 This section provides examples of notes to the financial statements that illustrate some of the financial statement disclosures concerning collection items.

Example 1—NFPs That Capitalize Collections

Note X: Summary of Significant Accounting Policies

The organization has capitalized its collections since its inception. If purchased, items accessioned into the collection are capitalized at cost, and if donated, they are capitalized at their fair value on the accession date (the date on which the item is accepted by the Acquisitions Committee of the Board of Trustees). Gains or losses on the deaccession of collection items are classified on the statement of activities as unrestricted or temporarily restricted support depending on donor restrictions, if any, placed on the item at the time of accession. Collection items are depreciated over their estimated useful lives unless they have cultural, aesthetic, or historical value that is worth preserving perpetually, and the organization is protecting and preserving essentially undiminished the service potential of the collection item.

The organization has capitalized its collections since its inception. If purchased, items accessioned into the collection are capitalized at cost, and if donated, they are capitalized at their fair value on the

[5] The amendments in FASB ASU No. 2016-14, *Not-for-Profit Entities (Topic 958): Presentation of Financial Statements of Not-for-Profit Entities*, are effective for annual financial statements issued for fiscal years beginning after December 15, 2017 (for example, years ending December 31, 2018, and years ending June 30, 2019), and for interim periods within fiscal years beginning after December 15, 2018. Application to interim financial statements is permitted but not required in the initial year of application. Early application of the amendments is permitted.

accession date (the date on which the item is accepted by the Acquisitions Committee of the Board of Trustees). Gains or losses on the deaccession of collection items are classified on the statement of activities as support without donor restrictions or donor-restricted support depending on donor restrictions, if any, placed on the item at the time of accession. Collection items are depreciated over their estimated useful lives unless they have cultural, aesthetic, or historical value that is worth preserving perpetually, and the organization is protecting and preserving essentially undiminished the service potential of the collection item.[6]

Example 2—NFPs That Capitalize Their Collections Prospectively

Note X: Summary of Significant Accounting Policies

Collection items acquired on or after July 1, 19X0: Accessions of these collection items are capitalized at cost, if the items were purchased, or at their fair value on the accession date (the date on which the item is accepted by the Acquisitions Committee of the Board of Trustees), if the items were contributed. Gains or losses from deaccessions of these items are reflected on the statement of activities as changes in the appropriate net asset classes, depending on the existence and type of donor-imposed restrictions. Collection items are depreciated over their estimated useful lives unless they have cultural, aesthetic, or historical value that is worth preserving perpetually, and the organization is protecting and preserving essentially undiminished the service potential of the collection item.

Collection items acquired prior to July 1, 19X0: Collection items purchased prior to July 1, 19X0, were recorded as decreases in unrestricted net assets. No financial statement recognition was made for contributed collection items. Proceeds from insurance recoveries or deaccessions of these items are reflected on the statements of activities as changes in the appropriate net asset classes, depending on the existence and type of donor-imposed restrictions.

Collection items acquired prior to July 1, 19X0: Collection items purchased prior to July 1, 19X0, were recorded as decreases in net assets without donor restrictions. No financial statement recognition was made for contributed collection items. Proceeds from insurance recoveries or deaccessions of these items are reflected on the statements of activities as changes in the appropriate net asset classes, depending on the existence and type of donor-imposed restrictions.[7]

---

[6] The amendments in FASB ASU No. 2016-14 are effective for annual financial statements issued for fiscal years beginning after December 15, 2017 (for example, years ending December 31, 2018, and years ending June 30, 2019), and for interim periods within fiscal years beginning after December 15, 2018. Application to interim financial statements is permitted but not required in the initial year of application. Early application of the amendments is permitted.

[7] The amendments in FASB ASU No. 2016-14 are effective for annual financial statements issued for fiscal years beginning after December 15, 2017 (for example, years ending December 31, 2018, and years ending June 30, 2019), and for interim periods within fiscal years beginning after December 15, 2018. Application to interim financial statements is permitted but not required in the initial year of application. Early application of the amendments is permitted.

Note Z: Collections

The organization's collections are made up of artifacts of historical significance, scientific specimens, and art objects. Each of the items is cataloged for educational, research, scientific, and curatorial purposes, and activities verifying their existence and assessing their condition are performed continuously.

During 20X1, a significant number of American pioneer artifacts from the 1800s were destroyed while in transit to an exhibition in which they were to be displayed. Because those items were purchased prior to July 1, 19X0, the insurance proceeds of $22,000, which reimbursed the organization in full for the artifacts' fair value, are reflected as an increase in unrestricted net assets on the statement of activities. No other collection items were deaccessioned in 20X1 or 20X0.

During 20X1, a significant number of American pioneer artifacts from the 1800s were destroyed while in transit to an exhibition in which they were to be displayed. Because those items were purchased prior to July 1, 19X0, the insurance proceeds of $22,000, which reimbursed the organization in full for the artifacts' fair value, are reflected as an increase in net assets without donor restrictions on the statement of activities. No other collection items were deaccessioned in 20X1 or 20X0.[8]

Example 3—NFPs That Do Not Capitalize Collections

Note X: Summary of Significant Accounting Policies

The collections, which were acquired through purchases and contributions since the organization's inception, are not recognized as assets on the statement of financial position. Purchases of collection items are recorded as decreases in unrestricted net assets in the year in which the items are acquired, or as temporarily or permanently restricted net assets if the assets used to purchase the items are restricted by donors. Contributed collection items are not reflected on the financial statements. Proceeds from deaccessions or insurance recoveries are reflected as increases in the appropriate net asset classes.

The collections, which were acquired through purchases and contributions since the organization's inception, are not recognized as assets on the statement of financial position. Purchases of collection items are recorded as decreases in net assets without donor restrictions in the year in which the items are acquired, or as decreases in net assets with donor restrictions if the assets used to purchase the items were restricted by donors. Contributed collection items are not reflected on the financial statements. Proceeds from deaccessions or

[8] The amendments in FASB ASU No. 2016-14 are effective for annual financial statements issued for fiscal years beginning after December 15, 2017 (for example, years ending December 31, 2018, and years ending June 30, 2019), and for interim periods within fiscal years beginning after December 15, 2018. Application to interim financial statements is permitted but not required in the initial year of application. Early application of the amendments is permitted.

insurance recoveries are reflected as increases in the appropriate net asset classes.[9]

Note Z: Collections

The organization's collections are made up of artifacts of historical significance, scientific specimens, and art objects that are held for educational, research, scientific, and curatorial purposes. Each of the items is cataloged, preserved, and cared for, and activities verifying their existence and assessing their condition are performed continuously. Collection items are subject to a policy that requires proceeds from their sales to be used to acquire other items for collections.

During 20X1, a significant number of American pioneer artifacts from the 1800s were destroyed while in transit to an exhibition in which they were to be displayed. These artifacts were contributed in 20XX, with a restriction that limited any future proceeds from deaccessions to acquisitions of artifacts from a similar period. As a result, the insurance proceeds of $22,000, which reimbursed the organization in full for the artifacts' fair value, are reflected as an increase in temporarily restricted net assets on the statement of activities. No other collection items were deaccessioned in 20X1 or 20X0.

During 20X1, a significant number of American pioneer artifacts from the 1800s were destroyed while in transit to an exhibition in which they were to be displayed. These artifacts were contributed in 20XX, with a restriction that limited any future proceeds from deaccessions to acquisitions of artifacts from a similar period. As a result, the insurance proceeds of $22,000, which reimbursed the organization in full for the artifacts' fair value, are reflected as an increase in net assets with donor restrictions on the statement of activities. No other collection items were deaccessioned in 20X1 or 20X0.[10]

Goodwill

Update 7-1 *Accounting and Reporting*: Goodwill Impairment Test

FASB Accounting Standards Update (ASU) No. 2017-04, *Intangibles—Goodwill and Other (Topic 350): Simplifying the Test for Goodwill Impairment*, was issued in January 2017 to simplify how an entity is required to test goodwill for impairment. It eliminates step 2 from the goodwill

[9] The amendments in FASB ASU No. 2016-14 are effective for annual financial statements issued for fiscal years beginning after December 15, 2017 (for example, years ending December 31, 2018, and years ending June 30, 2019), and for interim periods within fiscal years beginning after December 15, 2018. Application to interim financial statements is permitted but not required in the initial year of application. Early application of the amendments is permitted.

[10] The amendments in FASB ASU No. 2016-14 are effective for annual financial statements issued for fiscal years beginning after December 15, 2017 (for example, years ending December 31, 2018, and years ending June 30, 2019), and for interim periods within fiscal years beginning after December 15, 2018. Application to interim financial statements is permitted but not required in the initial year of application. Early application of the amendments is permitted.

impairment test. Step 2 measures a goodwill impairment loss by comparing the implied fair value of a reporting unit's goodwill with the carrying amount of that goodwill. This ASU modified the concept of impairment from the condition that exists when the carrying amount of goodwill exceeds its implied fair value to the condition that exists when the carrying amount of a reporting unit exceeds its fair value.

FASB ASU No. 2017-04 is effective for NFPs for their annual or any interim goodwill impairment tests in fiscal years beginning after December 15, 2021. Early adoption is permitted for interim or annual goodwill impairment tests performed on testing dates after January 1, 2017.

This edition of the guide has not been updated to reflect changes as a result of this ASU; however, the section that follows will be updated in a future edition. Readers are encouraged to consult the full text of the ASU on FASB's website at www.fasb.org.

7.29 An NFP recognizes goodwill in an acquisition by an NFP only if the operations of the acquiree are not expected to be predominantly supported by contributions and returns on investments. (As discussed in paragraph 3.133, goodwill is immediately charged to the statement of activities as of the acquisition date if the operations of the acquiree as part of the combined entity are expected to be predominantly supported by contributions and returns on investments.) FASB ASC 350-20 provides guidance for measuring goodwill subsequent to its acquisition. The following paragraphs summarize the guidance in FASB ASC 350-20, but are not a substitute for reading that guidance.

7.30 Goodwill that is recognized as an asset on the acquisition date should not be amortized. Instead, it should be tested annually for impairment at a level of reporting referred to as a reporting unit. (Paragraphs 33–46 of FASB ASC 350-20-35 provide guidance on determining reporting units.) Impairment is the condition that exists when the carrying amount of goodwill exceeds its implied fair value. The fair value of goodwill can be measured only as a residual and cannot be measured directly. Therefore, FASB ASC 350-20 includes a methodology to determine an amount that achieves a reasonable estimate of the value of goodwill for purposes of measuring an impairment loss. That estimate is referred to as the implied fair value of goodwill. Paragraphs 4–19 of FASB ASC 350-20-35 describe a two-step impairment test used to identify potential goodwill impairment and measure the amount of an impairment loss to be recognized (if any). An NFP has an unconditional option to assess qualitative factors before performing the two-step impairment test. If the NFP chooses to assess qualitative factors, it would assess relevant events and circumstances that could affect the fair value of the reporting unit, such as those in FASB ASC 350-20-35-3C. If, after assessing the qualitative factors, an entity determines that it is not more likely than not that the fair value of a reporting unit is less than its carrying amount, then the two-step goodwill impairment test is unnecessary. If an entity determines that it is more likely than not that the fair value of a reporting unit is less than its carrying amount, the two-step impairment test should be used to identify potential goodwill impairment and measure the amount of a goodwill impairment loss to be recognized (if any). If desired, an NFP may bypass the qualitative assessment described for any reporting unit in any period and proceed directly to performing the two-step goodwill impairment test.

7.31 AICPA Accounting and Valuation Guide *Testing Goodwill for Impairment* provides accounting and valuation guidance for impairment testing of goodwill. It focuses on practice issues related to the qualitative assessment and the first step of the two-step test. It also provides an illustration of the second step of the two-step goodwill impairment test. This guide addresses the following issues:

- Identifying reporting units
- Assigning assets and liabilities to a reporting unit
- Performing the optional qualitative assessment, including an illustration of one approach of performing it
- Measuring the fair value of a reporting unit in accordance with the guidance in FASB ASC 820, including an illustration of the valuation techniques often utilized for this purpose

Intangible Assets Other Than Goodwill

> **© Update 7-2 *Accounting and Reporting*: Gains and Losses on Sales of Nonfinancial Assets**
>
> FASB ASU No. 2017-05, *Other Income—Gains and Losses from the Derecognition of Nonfinancial Assets (Subtopic 610-20): Clarifying the Scope of Asset Derecognition Guidance and Accounting for Partial Sales of Nonfinancial Assets*, was issued in February 2017 to clarify the scope of FASB ASC 610-20. Among its amendments, it requires an entity to account for the derecognition of a nonfinancial asset, including an intangible asset, in accordance with FASB ASC 610-20, unless a scope exception from FASBASC 610-20 applies. For example, the derecognition of a nonfinancial asset in a contract with a customer would be accounted for in accordance with FASB ASC 606, *Revenue from Contracts with Customers*, instead of FASB ASC 610-20.
>
> FASB ASU No. 2017-05 is effective concurrently with the amendments in FASB ASU No. 2014-09, *Revenue from Contracts with Customers (Topic 606)*. As a result, most NFPs will apply the new standards for annual reporting periods beginning after December 15, 2018, and interim periods within annual periods beginning after December 15, 2019. However, NFPs that have issued, or are conduit bond obligors for, securities that are traded, listed, or quoted on an exchange or an over-the-counter market are required to apply the standards for annual reporting periods beginning after December 15, 2017, including interim periods within that reporting period.
>
> This edition of the guide has not been updated to reflect changes as a result of this ASU; however, the section that follows will be updated in a future edition. Readers are encouraged to consult the full text of the ASU on FASB's website at www.fasb.org.

7.32 Some common examples of intangible assets of NFPs are brand identification (such as trademarks, service marks, collective marks, internet domain names, and other marketing-related intangibles), donor lists, copyrights, and similar artistic-related intangibles, noncommercial broadcasting licenses, and patents.[11] FASB ASC 350-30-55 provides additional examples of intangible assets other than goodwill. The cost of an intangible asset acquired other than in an acquisition by an NFP is capitalized in accordance with FASB ASC 350-30-25 and should be initially measured using the guidance in FASB ASC 805-50-15-3 and paragraphs 1–4 of FASB ASC 805-50-30. Capitalization of an intangible asset acquired in an acquisition by an NFP is discussed in paragraphs 3.126–.134.) After initial recognition and measurement, FASB ASC 350-30 provides the accounting and reporting of intangible assets other than goodwill. The following paragraphs summarize the guidance in FASB ASC 350-30, but are not a substitute for reading that guidance.

7.33 Under the requirements of FASB ASC 350-30, accounting for a recognized intangible asset is based on its useful life to the reporting entity. An intangible asset with a finite useful life should be amortized; an intangible asset with an indefinite useful life should not be amortized. FASB ASC 350-30-55 provides examples of intangible assets other than goodwill.

7.34 If an intangible asset has a finite useful life, but the precise length of that life is not known, that intangible asset should be amortized over the best estimate of its useful life. The method of amortization should reflect the pattern in which the economic benefits of the intangible asset are consumed or otherwise used up. If that pattern cannot be reliably determined, a straight-line amortization method should be used.

7.35 If an intangible asset is determined to have an indefinite useful life, it should not be amortized until its useful life is determined to be no longer indefinite. Instead, an intangible asset that is not subject to amortization should be tested for impairment annually and more frequently if events or changes in circumstances indicate that it is more likely than not that the asset is impaired. An intangible asset with an indefinite useful life should be tested for impairment in accordance with paragraphs 18–19 of FASB ASC 350-30-35. An NFP may first assess qualitative factors to determine whether it is more likely than not (that is, a likelihood of more than 50 percent) that an indefinite-lived intangible asset is impaired. Paragraphs 18B–18C of FASB ASC 350-30-35 include examples of relevant events and circumstances that could affect the significant inputs used to determine the fair value of an indefinite-lived intangible asset. If, after assessing the totality of events and circumstances and their potential effect on significant inputs to the fair value determination, the NFP determines that it is more likely than not that the indefinite-lived intangible asset is impaired, the NFP performs the quantitative impairment test in FASB ASC 350-30-35-19 to measure the impairment. The quantitative impairment test is a comparison of the fair value of the intangible asset with its carrying amount. If the carrying amount of the intangible asset exceeds its fair value, an impairment loss should be recognized in an amount equal to that excess.

Auditing

7.36 Many audit objectives and auditing procedures, including the consideration of controls, related to other assets of NFPs are similar to those of other

---

[11] In accordance with FASB ASC 350-30-25-3, costs of internally developing, maintaining, or restoring intangible assets that are not specifically identifiable, that have indeterminate lives, or that are inherent in a continuing business or nonprofit activity and related to an entity as a whole, should be recognized as an expense when incurred. Thus, many internally developed intangible assets are never recognized as assets.

entities. In addition, the auditor may need to consider the specific audit objectives, auditing procedures, and selected controls that are unique to NFPs and that are presented at the end of this chapter.

Inventory

7.37 As discussed in paragraph 7.05, in certain circumstances, the fair value of contributed inventory may be measured using methods such as estimates, averages, or computational approximations. Such methods may be used in connection with the financial statement assertion of valuation. However, such methods are unrelated to the assertions of existence and occurrence. AU-C section 540, *Auditing Accounting Estimates, Including Fair Value Accounting Estimates, and Related Disclosures*,[12] sets forth requirements and guidance when auditing the measurement and disclosure of assets, liabilities, and specific components of equity presented or disclosed at fair value in financial statements. Paragraphs .A16–.A17 of AU-C section 500, *Audit Evidence*, and paragraphs .11–.15 and .A20–.A38 of AU-C section 501, *Audit Evidence—Specific Considerations for Selected Items*, provide requirements and guidance concerning inventory observation.

Goodwill

7.38 Examples of auditing procedures that might be applied for goodwill recognized from an acquisition include the following:

- Review the supporting documents and agreements related to the acquisition to determine if goodwill should be recognized and whether the operations of the acquiree as part of the combined entity are not expected to be predominantly supported by contributions and returns on investment. (Classification, Understandability)
- Review relevant valuation documents at the acquisition date supporting the value of goodwill recognized, based on the consideration transferred, fair value of noncontrolling interest, and the amounts of the identifiable assets acquired and liabilities assumed. (Completeness, Valuation)
- Determine that acquisition related costs are recorded as expenses in the periods in which the costs are incurred and services are received (except for costs to issue debt securities). (Classification)
- Annually, understand and test the process used by management to perform its goodwill impairment assessment, including its qualitative assessment. (Valuation)

7.39 Examples of auditing procedures that might be applied in the year of acquisition when the operations of the acquiree as part of the combined entity are predominantly supported by contributions and returns on investments, or when an inherent contribution is received (that is, when the fair value of the consideration transferred is less than the fair value of net assets acquired), include the following:

- Review the supporting documents and agreements to determine whether the expected operations of the acquiree, when included

[12] All AU-C sections can be found in AICPA *Professional Standards*.

as part of the combined entity, would be predominantly supported by contributions and returns on investments. (Classification, Understandability)

- When the operations of the acquiree as part of the combined entity is predominantly supported by contributions and returns on investments, determine that a separate charge is recognized in the statements of activities for the excess of consideration transferred over the fair value of net assets acquired (rather than goodwill). (Accuracy, Classification)
- When an inherent contribution is received, determine that the excess of the net assets acquired over consideration paid is presented as a separate line in the statement of activities. (Accuracy, Classification)
- When an inherent contribution is received, determine that proper net assets classification of the excess of the net assets acquired over consideration paid, based on restrictions imposed by the donor before the acquisition. (Accuracy, Classification)

Collection Items

7.40 Whether collections are capitalized or not, the auditor may determine that it is necessary to perform procedures to understand the NFP's controls over recording accessions (including contributions) and deaccessions of collection items, controlling the collections, and periodically physically inspecting them. Procedures such as walk-throughs of relevant custodial controls might be adequate for the auditor to gain the requisite level of knowledge about the design and implementation of controls over the collection items.

7.41 The auditor's understanding assists the auditor in assessing risks and, in part, provides evidence supporting the disclosures required by FASB ASC 958-360-50-6. Examples of auditing procedures that might be applied for collection items are presented in the table at the end of this chapter.

7.42 The following table illustrates the use of assertions in developing audit objectives and designing substantive tests. The examples are not intended to be all-inclusive nor is it expected that all the procedures would necessarily be applied in an audit. The use of assertions in assessing risks and designing appropriate audit procedures to obtain audit evidence is described in paragraphs .26–.32 of AU-C section 315, *Understanding the Entity and Its Environment and Assessing the Risks of Material Misstatement*. Paragraph .18 of AU-C section 330, *Performing Audit Procedures in Response to Assessed Risks and Evaluating the Audit Evidence Obtained*, requires the auditor to design and perform substantive procedures for all relevant assertions related to each material class of transactions, account balance, and disclosure, irrespective of the assessed risks of material misstatement. This requirement reflects the facts that (1) the auditor's assessment of risk is judgmental and may not identify all risks of material misstatement, and (2) inherent limitations to internal control exist, including management override. Various audit procedures and the purposes for which they may be performed are described in paragraphs .A10–.A26 of AU-C section 500.

Auditing Considerations

Financial Statement Assertions	***Specific Audit Objectives***	***Select Control Objectives***
Transactions		
All Collection Items		
Occurrence	Collection items acquired in the current period by purchase and contribution were authorized. Deaccessions from collections occurred and were authorized.	Controls ensure that purchased collection items are authorized and supported, contributed collection items are appropriately accessioned, and deaccessions are authorized and supported.
Capitalized Collection Items		
Completeness; Valuation and allocation	All collection items acquired in exchange transactions are recognized as assets at cost. All contributed collection items are recognized as assets and as contributions at fair value.	Controls exist to ensure that all purchases and contributions of collection items are recognized as assets (at cost and fair value, respectively) and that contribution revenues are recognized for contributed collection items based on adequate support.
Account Balances		
All Collection Items		
Occurrence/ Existence	Collection items exist.	Collections items are safeguarded and are physically inspected periodically.
Rights and obligations	Restrictions on contributed collection items have been met.	Contributions of collection items are reviewed for restrictions and management monitors compliance with restrictions.
Presentation and Disclosure		
Noncapitalized Collection Items		
Valuation	Noncapitalized works of art, historical treasures, and similar assets meet the definition of *collections* in the FASB *Accounting Standards Codification* glossary.	Policies and procedures for determining that noncapitalized assets are *collections*.

(*continued*)

Auditing Considerations—*continued*

Financial Statement Assertions	*Specific Audit Objectives*	*Select Control Objectives*
Completeness	Appropriate disclosures referenced in a line item on the face of the statement of financial position.	
Classification	Purchases, sales, involuntary conversions, and other deaccessions of noncapitalized collection items are appropriately displayed in the statement of activities and the statement of cash flows.	
Capitalized Collection Items		
Classification	Contributed and deaccessioned collection items are reported in the appropriate net asset class.	

All Collections

7.43 Suggested audit procedures to consider include the following:

- Obtain an understanding of the NFP's policies over collection items and determine whether the requirements for a collection (paragraph 7.16) are included in the policy. (Completeness, Classification)
- Review documentation supporting accessions and deaccessions of collection items. (Completeness, Occurrence)
- Review minutes of governing board and governing board committee meetings for the following:
  - — Authorization of major accessions and deaccessions. (Completeness)
  - — Evidence of current period purchases and contributions. (Completeness, Cut-off)
  - — Evidence of restrictions on collection items. (Allocation, Classification)
- Review donor correspondence to determine the presence or absence of restrictions. (Allocation, Classification)
- If specific collection items are restricted, review collection item transactions for propriety of use and disposition. (Rights and Obligations)
- Make inquiries of curatorial personnel about deaccessioned collection items. (Completeness)
- Review the NFP's procedures for controlling collections and physically inspecting them. (Existence)
- For tests of the collection inventory

- — consider whether to observe the physical inspection. (Existence)
- — test the inventory of collection items by going from items to the inventory list as well as from the list to inventory items. (Existence, Completeness)
- — review actions taken by management to investigate discrepancies disclosed by the physical inspection and to adjust the records. (Completeness, Accuracy)

- Determine that works of art, historical treasures, and similar assets that are not added to the collection are capitalized and disclosed separately on the face of the statement of financial position or in the notes. (Completeness, Understandability)
- Compare the list of collections to lists provided to third parties (such as insurance companies), including the values. (Completeness)
- For collection items acquired in an exchange transaction, consider if the cost includes the costs necessarily incurred to bring the item to the condition and location necessary for its intended use. (Completeness, Accuracy)

Capitalized Collection Items

7.44 Suggested audit procedures to consider include the following:

- Review documentation and procedures supporting the determination of cost or fair value. (Valuation)
- Review donor correspondence to determine the presence or absence of restrictions and the propriety of classification. (Allocation, Classification)
- Review minutes of governing board and governing board committee meetings for evidence of restrictions. (Allocation, Classification, Completeness)
- Determine that the statement of financial position includes the total amount capitalized on a separate line item, titled "collections" or "collection items." (Completeness, Understandability)
- If prospective capitalization is used for collection items, determine that
    - — a line item is shown on the face of the statement of financial position as required by FASB ASC 958-360-45-4.
    - — that line item refers to the disclosures about collections required by FASB ASC 958-360-50-6.
    - — that line item is dated as of the date capitalization of the collection began; for example, "collections acquired since January 1, 1995 (Note X)." (Completeness, Understandability)
- Consider the need to apply provisions of AU-C section 620, *Using the Work of an Auditor's Specialist*, in conjunction with determining the reliability of carrying values. (Valuation)

Noncapitalized Collections

7.45 Suggested audit procedures to consider include the following:

- Review policies and procedures determining the appropriateness of classifying assets as noncapitalized collections. (Completeness, Classification, Understandability)
- Determine whether proceeds of sales of collection items are used to acquire other items for the collection. (Completeness, Classification, Understandability)
- Determine that the line item required by FASB ASC 958-360-45-3 is present and that it refers to the note disclosures about collections. (Completeness, Understandability)
- Determine the appropriateness of disclosures related to noncapitalized collections. (Completeness, Understandability)

Chapter 8

Programmatic Investments

Gray shaded text in this chapter reflects guidance issued but not yet effective as of the date of this guide, March 1, 2018, but becoming effective on or prior to June 30, 2018, exclusive of any option to early adopt ahead of the mandatory effective date. Unless otherwise indicated, all unshaded text reflects guidance that was already effective as of the date of this guide.

Introduction

8.01 Instead of making cash grants to other entities, some not-for-profit entities (NFPs) provide benefits to their constituencies in the form of financial instruments. Like grants, these financial instruments have as their primary purpose the achievement of the NFP's programmatic mission. For example, an NFP might make a seed money grant to support a new performing arts organization or it might instead make a seed money loan. A foundation might make a grant to capitalize a community development loan fund or it might make long-term low interest loan to serve a similar purpose. However, as financial instruments, these other forms of financial support have the possibility of producing financial returns, and thus they share characteristics with an NFP's traditional investments. These financial instruments, referred to as programmatic investments, offer both financial and programmatic returns.

8.02 This chapter discusses the three most common types of programmatic investments—those in the form of loans, equity interests, or guarantees—and the accounting and disclosures by the NFP investor. This chapter does not provide guidance for the investees.

8.03 Examples of those types of programmatic investments include the following:

- Low-interest or interest-free loans to students with demonstrated financial need
- Student loans that will be forgiven upon the completion of a defined amount of community service after graduation
- Investments in nonprofit, low income housing projects
- Loans to small for-profit businesses owned by members of economically disadvantaged groups or individuals who are members of those groups, for whom commercial loans are not available or are not available at affordable interest rates
- Loans, typically of small dollar amounts, made to small businesses or individuals who lack access to banking and related services as a way to help the borrower out of poverty (referred to as microfinance)
- Investments in businesses in deteriorated urban areas under a plan to improve the economy of the area by providing employment or job training for residents
- Investments in NFPs that have a mission of combating community deterioration

- Guarantees of an NFP's debt, which increases the amount of credit available to that NFP because the guarantor assumes part or all of the third-party lender's risk

8.04 *Programmatic investments* are defined for the purpose of this chapter as any investment by an NFP that meets the following two criteria:

- Its primary purpose is to further the tax exempt objectives of the NFP.
- The production of income or the appreciation of the asset is not a significant purpose (that is, an investor seeking a market return would not enter into the investment).

The preceding definition is similar to that of the term *program-related investment*, which is defined in IRS Section 4944(c).

Programmatic investments are defined for the purpose of this chapter as any investment by an NFP that meets the following two criteria:

- Its primary purpose is to further the tax exempt objectives of the NFP.
- The production of income or the appreciation of the asset is not a significant purpose (that is, an investor seeking a market return would not enter into the investment).

The preceding definition is similar to that of the term *programmatic investing*, which is defined in the FASB ASC glossary, and *program-related investment*, which is defined in IRS Section 4944(c).[1]

8.05 For the recipient, the primary benefit of a programmatic investment is access to capital, typically at more affordable terms than might otherwise be available. For the NFP investor, the principal benefits are the achievement and sustainability of the mission-related program—the repayment of the loan or the return of equity can be used again for a future charitable purpose. Thus, programmatic investments are a means of leveraging philanthropic dollars.

8.06 Some NFPs maintain formal programs that make programmatic investments on an annual basis. Others make programmatic investments when the opportunity presents itself.

8.07 As with any transfer of assets, a programmatic investment may not be used to generate significant private inurement or private benefit for any entity. (Private inurement and private benefit are discussed in paragraphs 15.09–.12.) When considering whether a programmatic investment results in private benefit or private inurement, the overall objectives of the investment should be documented. In Revenue Ruling 74-587, the IRS found that although some of the individuals receiving financial assistance may not themselves qualify for charitable assistance, that fact did not detract from the charitable character of

---

[1] The amendments in FASB Accounting Standards Update (ASU) No. 2016-14, *Not-for-Profit Entities (Topic 958): Presentation of Financial Statements of Not-for-Profit Entities*, are effective for annual financial statements issued for fiscal years beginning after December 15, 2017 (for example, years ending December 31, 2018, and years ending June 30, 2019), and for interim periods within fiscal years beginning after December 15, 2018. Application to interim financial statements is permitted but not required in the initial year of application. Early application of the amendments is permitted.

the organization's program because the assistance to area businesses helped to relieve poverty, provide employment opportunities, and combat community deterioration, as well as helped to lessen prejudice and discrimination against minority groups.

Core Considerations for Accounting and Reporting

8.08 The following are core considerations for determining the proper accounting for programmatic investments, regardless of their form:

- An assessment of whether an investment is programmatic or not is made when the initial investment transaction occurs.
- Because one of the goals of making programmatic investments is furthering the mission of the NFP and because, by definition, the production of income or the appreciation of the asset is not a significant consideration in the determination of whether to invest, programmatic investments often have a contribution element. If they do, the contribution made should be accounted for in accordance with the standards in FASB *Accounting Standards Codification* (ASC) 720-25 and FASB ASC 958-720.
- Programmatic investments are subject to the same accounting standards as similar financial instruments, except for the contribution element, if any. Thus, loans are within the scope of the standards in FASB ASC 310, *Receivables*; ownership interests are subject to the standards for reporting relationships with related entities, including consolidation, equity method, and so forth (discussed in paragraphs 3.58–.121); and guarantees are subject to the standards in FASB ASC 460, *Guarantees*.
- The relative significance of the investments to an NFP's operations and financial position and the quantitative and qualitative risks arising from them is considered when determining the type of financial statement presentation and the extent of the disclosures. Thus, even though the amount of programmatic investments might quantitatively be considered immaterial, user needs for qualitative information are a consideration in determining the appropriate financial reporting.

Loans

© Update 8-1 *Accounting and Reporting*: Credit Losses

FASB Accounting Standards Update (ASU) No. 2016-13, *Financial Instruments—Credit Losses (Topic 326): Measurement of Credit Losses on Financial Instruments*, was issued in June 2016 to provide financial statement users with more decision-useful information about the expected credit losses on financial instruments and other commitments to extend credit held by a reporting entity at each reporting date. To achieve this objective, the amendments in the ASU replace the incurred loss impairment methodology in current generally accepted accounting principles (GAAP) with a methodology that reflects expected credit losses and requires consideration of a broader range of reasonable and supportable information to inform credit loss estimates.

FASB ASU No. 2016-13 is effective for NFPs for fiscal years beginning after December 15, 2020, and interim periods within fiscal years beginning after December 15, 2021. Early adoption is permitted for fiscal years beginning after December 15, 2018, including interim periods within those fiscal years.

This edition of the guide has not been updated to reflect changes as a result of this ASU; however, the section that follows will be updated in a future edition. Readers are encouraged to consult the full text of the ASU on FASB's website at www.fasb.org.

8.09 Loans are the most common programmatic investment. Stated interest rates on programmatic investments may be below market when compared to loans to entities of similar credit risk, and often are set at very low interest rates. Loan terms vary considerably, based both on the needs of the borrower, the type of project and the needs and expectations of the NFP investor. Terms can range from periods of a few months to more than a decade. Longer term loans are typically associated with community development and real estate development projects.

8.10 When accounting for programmatic loans, NFPs look to one of two areas of FASB ASC, which may result in diversity of practice. Some NFPs look to the standards for loan accounting in FASB ASC 310 and to FASB ASC 835-30 on imputation of interest, and they impute a market interest rate on the loan that incorporates the risk that the NFP may be unable to collect from the borrower all contractually required payments of principal and interest, as discussed in paragraphs 8.11–.17. Other NFPs look to the FASB ASC definition of an inherent contribution, and they recognize the transaction as entirely a loan receivable, entirely a contribution, or in part a contribution and in part a loan receivable, as discussed in paragraphs 8.18–.33. The NFP should determine which method is most appropriate and apply those standards to all programmatic loan transactions, reporting consistently from period to period, and disclosing its accounting policy.

Effective Interest Rate Approach

Loan Origination (Initial Recognition and Measurement)

8.11 In some cases, a programmatic loan (*a*) bears a market interest rate, and (*b*) the NFP expects at origination to collect all contractually required payments when due. In that case, at origination, the loan should be recognized at the amount of cash (or other assets) transferred to the borrower. In other cases, programmatic loans are interest free or have below-market interest rates, because a loan at an interest rate commensurate with the risk inherent in the expected cash flows would be unaffordable by the borrowers. FASB ASC 835-30-05-3 states that the use of an interest rate that varies from prevailing interest rates warrants evaluation of whether the face amount and the stated interest rate of a note or obligation provide reliable evidence for properly recording the exchange and subsequent related interest.

8.12 FASB ASC 835-30 provides guidance on the imputation of interest for receivables that are contractual rights to receive money on fixed or determinable dates, whether or not there is any stated provision for interest. As noted in paragraphs 2–3 of FASB ASC 835-30-25, when notes are traded in an open market, the market rate of interest and quoted prices of the notes provide the evidence of the present value. When notes have no ready market, the problem of determining present value is more difficult. To estimate the present value of a note under such circumstances, an applicable interest rate is approximated that may differ from the stated rate. This process of approximation is called *imputation*, and the resulting rate is called an *imputed interest rate*.

8.13 Although, as noted in FASB ASC 835-30-25-6, a note issued solely for cash equal to its face amount is presumed to earn the stated rate of interest, in some cases the parties may also exchange unstated (or stated) rights or privileges, which are given accounting recognition by establishing a note discount or premium account. In the case of a programmatic loan, the difference between the cash transferred to the borrower and the present value of the contractual payments for the loan at the effective interest rate is typically recognized as a contribution expense.

8.14 Guidance for determining the appropriate rate to use in a present value calculation can be found in the following sources:

- Paragraphs 4–20 of FASB ASC 820-10-55
- Paragraphs 12–13 of FASB ASC 835-30-25
- Paragraphs 16–32 of the nonauthoritative AICPA White Paper *Measurement of Fair Value for Certain Transactions of Not-for-Profit Entities*, which are reproduced in appendix A of chapter 5, "Contributions Received and Agency Transactions"

When determining an appropriate interest rate, to the extent possible, an NFP would consider market inputs of the jurisdiction in which the loan is made. These might include the time value of money, credit standing of the borrower, collateral, duration of the loan, restrictive covenants, and liquidity. In the absence of market inputs, the NFP would use its own assumptions about the assumptions that market participants would use in the jurisdiction in which the loan is made.

8.15 For example, a community foundation lends $100,000 to an arts organization. The note is noninterest bearing, is unsecured, and a balloon payment is due at the end of the 5-year term. The community foundation determines that a market rate for a loan with the same terms and a borrower of equal credit worthiness as the arts organization is 15 percent. The present value of the contractual payments due under the loan is $49,720. Using the interest method, the community foundation would make the following entry:

Loan receivable	$100,000	
Contribution expense	50,280	
Cash		$100,000
Discount on loan receivable		50,280

Use of the Interest Method While the Loan Is Outstanding

8.16 The discount on the loan is amortized as interest income over the life of the note in such a way as to result in a constant rate of interest when applied to the amount outstanding at the beginning of any given period, as described in FASB ASC 835-30-35-2. The difference between the periodic interest cost calculated using the interest method and the nominal interest on the outstanding amount of the debt is the amount of periodic amortization.

8.17 Continuing the example in paragraph 8.15, at the end of year 1, the community foundation would make the following entry to record the imputed interest income at 15 percent and the periodic amortization of the discount:

Discount on loan receivable	$7,458	
Interest income		$7,458

The carrying value of the loan after the previous entry is $57,178 ($100,000 - $50,280 + $7,458). This is the amount used when the community foundation tests for impairment, which is discussed in paragraphs 8.38–.47.

Inherent Contribution Approach

Loan Origination (Initial Recognition and Measurement)

8.18 At origination, programmatic loans fit into one of following three categories—entirely a loan receivable, entirely a contribution, or in part a contribution and in part a loan receivable. Which of those is appropriate is determined by management's best judgment after evaluation of the facts and circumstances available at the time of first accounting for the loan. Flowchart 8-1, which should be used in conjunction with the discussion in paragraphs 8.19–.33, may be helpful in making that determination.

Flowchart 8-1

Origination of a Programmatic Loan, Inherent Contribution Method

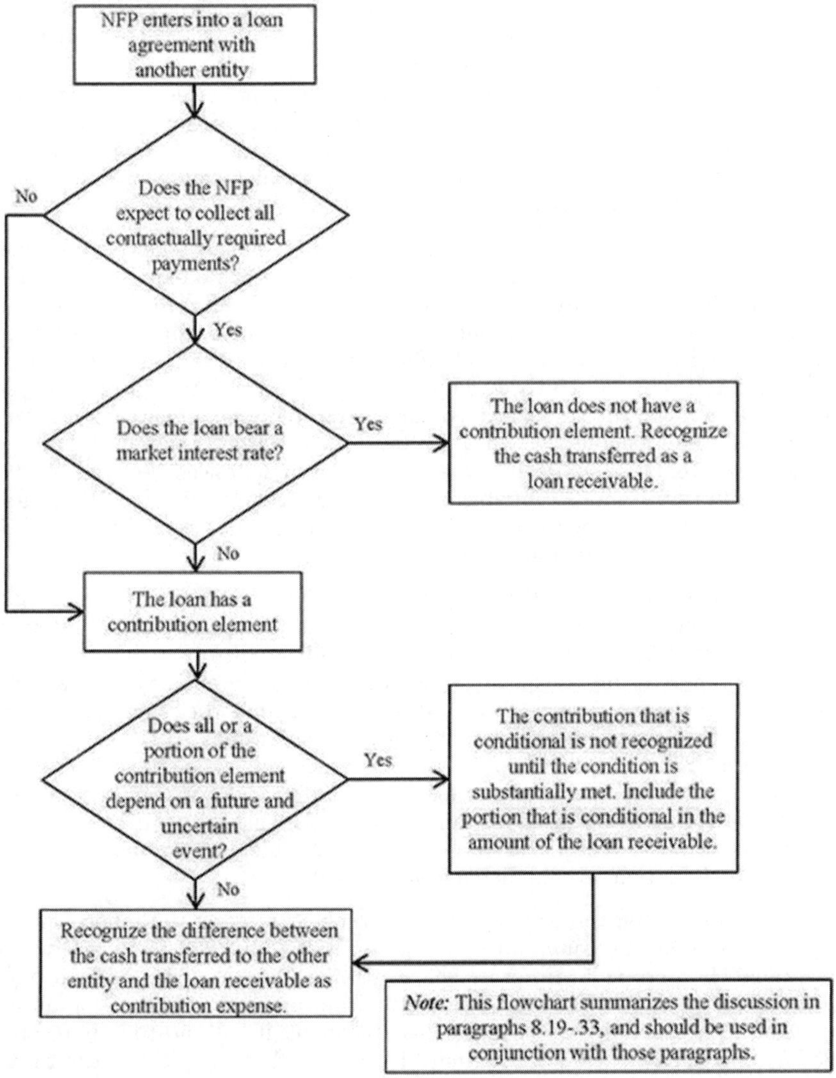

8.19 In some cases, a programmatic loan (*a*) bears a market interest rate, and (*b*) the NFP expects at origination to collect all contractually required payments when due. Those loans do not contain a contribution element, and the NFP recognizes a loan receivable for the amount of the cash (or other assets) transferred to the borrower. For many programmatic loans, however, one or both of those criteria are not met at origination, and the amount of the loan receivable recognized will differ from the amount of cash (or other assets) transferred to the borrower.

Loans for Which the NFP Does Not Expect to Collect All Required Payments

8.20 In some cases, upon origination of a programmatic loan, it is probable that the NFP investor will be unable to collect from the borrower[2] all contractually required payments of principal and interest. Those loans typically have a contribution element. The timing of recognition of the contribution element depends upon whether the contribution is unconditional or depends upon the occurrence of a specified future and uncertain event (conditional). Some loans contain both unconditional and conditional contribution elements. Paragraphs 8.21–.22 and 8.26–.27 provide examples that help to determine when to recognize the contribution element(s).

8.21 Some NFPs make contributions to individuals or other entities and use a loan format even though the NFPs have little or no expectation of repayment. Those NFPs prefer to provide financial assistance in a loan format because loans are thought to be more effective instruments than grant agreements if the goal is helping the individual or entity achieve economic productivity and self-reliance. The body empowered to approve loan applications typically does not consider the so-called borrower's creditworthiness when determining whether to make the loan, and often does not intend to pursue collection if the loan becomes past due. In those facts and circumstances, the loan may be considered in substance a contribution to the borrower. At the origination date, those NFPs typically report the value of the cash (or other assets) transferred to the borrower as a contribution made.

8.22 In other cases, NFPs make loans to individuals or other entities with an expectation that some, but generally not all, of the principal and interest will be collected. The borrowers may be marginally creditworthy, but there is a lot of risk inherent in the expected cash flows, and it is probable or reasonably possible that the borrower will default. In those facts and circumstances, the loan contains a contribution element that is unconditional. At the origination date, those NFPs typically recognize the loan receivable at the present value of the cash flows most likely to be collected. The difference between the present value and the cash advanced (or fair value of other assets transferred to the borrower) would be recognized as a contribution made. It would not be appropriate, at origination, to establish a loss allowance.

8.23 Repeating the example in paragraph 8.15 using the inherent contribution approach, a community foundation lends $100,000 to an arts organization. The note is noninterest bearing, is unsecured, and a balloon payment is due at the end of the 5-year term. The community foundation anticipates that at the due date of the balloon payment, it will most likely receive $57,640. The present value of that most likely cash flow using the interest rate commensurate with the risks (3 percent) is also $49,720.[3] Using the inherent

[2] This chapter uses the term *borrower* for the individual or entity to whom a loan is made, even though at origination there may be no expectation that the loan will be repaid.

[3] Conceptually, the effective interest method and the inherent contribution method should yield the same loan value at origination because the objective of both measurements is to estimate the fair value (market value) of the loan at the origination date. The effective interest method uses contractual cash flows, which have a high uncertainty of collection. Therefore, the interest rate associated with contractual cash flows reflects that uncertainty, and is 15 percent in this example. In contrast, the

(continued)

contribution approach, the community foundation would make the following entry:

Loan receivable	$57,640	
Contribution expense	50,280	
Cash		$100,000
Discount on loans receivable		7,920

Use of the Interest Method While the Loan Is Outstanding

8.24 The discount on the loan is amortized as interest income over the life of the note in such a way as to result in a constant rate of interest when applied to the amount outstanding at the beginning of any given period, as described in FASB ASC 835-30-35-2. The difference between the periodic interest cost so calculated using the interest method and the nominal interest on the outstanding amount of the debt is the amount of periodic amortization.

8.25 Continuing the example in paragraph 8.23, at the end of year 1, the community foundation would make the following entry to record the imputed interest income at 3 percent and the periodic amortization of the discount:

Discount on loan receivable	$1,492	
Interest income		$1,492

The carrying value of the loan after the previous entry is $51,212 ($57,640 - $7,920 + $1,492). This is the amount used when the community foundation tests for impairment, which is discussed in paragraphs 8.38–.47.

8.26 Still, in other cases, NFPs make loans to creditworthy borrowers, but to encourage the borrower to take a specific action that achieves programmatic objectives, the loan document includes conditions upon which all or a portion of the loan principal will be forgiven. Those loan documents contain conditional promises to give. Pursuant to FASB ASC 720-25-25 and FASB ASC 958-605-25-11, conditional promises to give, which depend on the occurrence of a specified future and uncertain event to bind the promisor, should be recognized when the conditions on which they depend are substantially met. Imposing a condition creates a barrier that must be overcome before the recipient of the transferred assets (in this case, the borrower) has an unconditional right to retain the promised assets (the loan proceeds). Thus, at origination, the loan typically would be recognized at the amount of cash (or other assets) transferred to the borrower. In other words, if there is a possibility that the loan will not be forgiven, the NFP would account for the loan at origination as described in this paragraph. The forgiveness of the principal amount would be recognized as a

(footnote continued)

inherent contribution method uses most likely cash flows, which incorporate some of the uncertainty of collection into the amount recognized as the inherent contribution. The interest rate associated with most likely cash flows is correspondingly lower, and is 3 percent in this example. Paragraphs 11–32 of the nonauthoritative AICPA White Paper *Measurement of Fair Value for Certain Transactions of Not-for-Profit Entities* provide additional information about the relationship between cash flows and interest rates when using present value techniques. Although those paragraphs discuss the present value concepts in terms of promises to give, the concepts themselves are the same. Those paragraphs are reproduced in appendix A of chapter 5, "Contributions Received and Agency Transactions."

contribution made by reducing the loan's carrying amount and recognizing contribution expense when the condition(s) for forgiveness are substantially met; that is, when the conditional promise becomes unconditional.

8.27 For example, a loan would be recognized at the amount of cash (or other assets) transferred to a law school student even though the loan agreement contains a clause that a portion of the loan principal will be forgiven if the student graduates, passes the bar, and performs pro bono services for one year. Because it is at least possible, and perhaps even probable, that the student will not complete all the necessary conditions for forgiveness (that is, the possibility that the condition[s] for forgiveness will not be met is other than remote), the forgiveness of the loan is not recognized at the origination of the loan.

8.28 However, FASB ASC 958-605-25-12 provides that a conditional promise to give is considered unconditional if the possibility that the condition will not be met is remote. Therefore, if the contribution portion of a loan is unconditional because the chance that it will not be forgiven is remote, the loan would be initially recognized at the present value of the cash flows expected to be collected. Contribution expense is recognized at origination in the amount of the difference between the present value of the cash flows expected to be collected and the cash (or other assets) transferred to the borrower.

Loans That Do Not Bear a Market Interest Rate but the NFP Expects to Collect All Required Payments

8.29 Programmatic investments may be in the form of loans that are interest free or have below-market interest rates. The NFP expects to collect all the payments required under the terms of the loan agreement, but because a loan at an interest rate commensurate with the risk inherent in the expected cash flows would be unaffordable by the borrowers, the NFP reduces the interest rate. To estimate the present value of a note under such circumstances, an applicable market interest rate is approximated that may differ from the stated or coupon rate. This process of approximation, which is discussed in FASB ASC 835-30, is called *imputation*, and the resulting rate is called an *imputed interest rate*.

8.30 In the circumstances described in the previous paragraph, an interest-free or below-market interest rate loan issued by an NFP in exchange for cash has an unstated (or stated) right or privilege, which is its contribution element. The NFP lender gives accounting recognition to the contribution element by recognizing a contribution made and establishing a valuation discount. The valuation discount and contribution expense should be reported regardless of whether the loan is between related parties. The valuation discount should be amortized as interest income by the NFP lender over the life of the note, as required by FASB ASC 835-30-35. The difference between the periodic interest cost calculated using the market rate and the interest method and the interest at the stated or coupon interest rate on the outstanding amount of the loan is the amount of periodic amortization. Paragraph 8.14 provides sources for guidance for determining the appropriate rate to use.

8.31 In accordance with FASB ASC 720-25-25-1, contributions made should be recognized as expenses in the period made and as decreases of assets or increases of liabilities depending on the form of the benefits given. In practice, the difference between the fair value of the loan at a market interest rate and the present value of the loan at its stated rate is often used to determine the fair value of the contribution. (Donee accounting for below-market interest rate loans is discussed in paragraphs 5.172–.174.)

8.32 The following example of the NFP lender's accounting uses the same fact set as that in paragraph 5.173. On January 1, 20X8, an NFP lender with a December year-end makes an interest-free programmatic loan of $200,000, payable on December 31, 20Y0. The purpose of the loan is to support the borrower's operating expenses and the appropriate imputed market rate of interest is 6 percent. The journal entries over the life of the loan would be as follows.

1/1/X8			
	Loan receivable	167,924	
	Contribution expense	32,076	
	Cash		200,000
(Transfer of cash; receivable reported at the fair value of the loan using the present value of $200,000 due in 3 years, discounted at 6 percent. Alternatively, as discussed in FASB ASC 835-30-55-8, the loan receivable could be recognized at $200,000, with an offsetting discount for imputed interest of $32,076. In that case, accretion in future periods would be recognized by reducing the discount account and reporting interest income.)			
12/31/X8			
	Loan receivable	10,075	
	Interest income		10,075
(Accretion of loan using the interest method.)			
12/31/X9			
	Loan receivable	10,680	
	Interest income		10,680
(Accretion of loan using the interest method.)			
12/31/Y0			
	Loan receivable	11,321	
	Interest income		11,321
(Accretion of loan using the interest method.)			
	Cash	200,000	
	Loan receivable		200,000
(Payment of the loan.)			

8.33 The following example of the NFP lender's accounting uses the same fact set as that in paragraph 5.174. On January 1, 19X8, an NFP lender with a December year-end makes an interest-free loan of $200,000. The purpose of the loan is to support the borrower's operating expenses, and the appropriate imputed rate of interest is 6 percent. Unlike the example in paragraph 8.32, the loan is payable on demand. Because the NFP can demand the full $200,000 at any time, the loan amount is not discounted at inception and interest is therefore calculated on the full original balance. The loan is repaid on December 31, 20Y0.

1/1/X8			
	Loan receivable	200,000	
	Cash		200,000
(Transfer of cash.)			
12/31/X8			
	Contribution expense	12,000	
	Interest income		12,000
(Contribution expense for below-market rate of interest on loan [loan balance × interest rate: $200,000 × .06].)			
12/31/X9			
	Contribution expense	12,000	
	Interest income		12,000
(Contribution expense for below-market rate of interest on loan.)			
12/31/Y0			
	Contribution expense	12,000	
	Interest income		12,000
(Contribution expense for below-market rate of interest on loan.)			
	Cash	200,000	
	Loan receivable		200,000
(Payment of the loan.)			

Loans That Contain a Right to Profit From the Sale or Refinancing of Property

8.34 If the loan contains a right to participate in expected residual profit from the sale or refinancing of property, the "Acquisition, Development, and Construction Arrangements" subsections of FASB ASC 310-10 provide guidance for determining whether an NFP lender should account for an acquisition, development, and construction arrangement as a loan or as an investment in real estate or a joint venture.

Forgiveness of Programmatic Loans

8.35 In some cases, the terms of a programmatic loan include forgiveness, in whole or in part, upon the occurrence of a specified future and uncertain event. As discussed in paragraphs 8.26–.28, those promises to forgive future payments are conditional promises to give.

8.36 In other cases, the terms of a programmatic loan do not include forgiveness, but the NFP investor decides to forgive all or a portion of the loan amount. Determining whether a loan is forgiven, or is impaired (as discussed in paragraphs 8.38–.47) is a matter of judgment, and sometimes challenging as both a loan impairment and a decision to forgive may occur within a short period of time. The loan is impaired if, at the time a decision is made to forgive a programmatic loan (or a portion of a loan), it is probable that the NFP investor will be unable to collect all amounts due according to the contractual terms of the loan agreement (paragraphs 8.38–.47). Further, if a borrower's financial difficulties cause the NFP to grant a concession to the borrower that it would not otherwise consider, the restructuring of the debt may be a troubled debt restructuring (paragraphs 8.48–.50). FASB ASC 310-40-15-20 includes indicators that the NFP investor should consider when determining if a borrower is experiencing financial difficulties.

8.37 However, if a loan that is not impaired is forgiven and the body empowered to forgive the loan communicates to the borrower that the amount is forgiven, the NFP investor would recognize a contribution made that would be classified as a program expense. Communication of the forgiveness to the borrower is key to the classification, because in accordance with FASB ASC 405-20-40-1, the debt is not extinguished until the debtor is legally released from being the primary obligor under the liability. In the absence of that communication, the NFP continues to act as a lender rather than a donor.

Impairment of Programmatic Loans

> **Update 8-2 *Accounting and Reporting*: Credit Losses**
>
> FASB ASU No. 2016-13 was issued in June 2016 to provide financial statement users with more decision-useful information about the expected credit losses on financial instruments and other commitments to extend credit held by a reporting entity at each reporting date. To achieve this objective, the amendments in the ASU replace the incurred loss impairment methodology in current GAAP with a methodology that reflects expected credit losses and requires consideration of a broader range of reasonable and supportable information to inform credit loss estimates.
>
> FASB ASU No. 2016-13 is effective for NFPs for fiscal years beginning after December 15, 2020, and interim periods within fiscal years beginning after December 15, 2021. Early adoption is permitted for fiscal years beginning after December 15, 2018, including interim periods within those fiscal years.
>
> This edition of the guide has not been updated to reflect changes as a result of this ASU; however, the section that follows will be updated in a future edition. Readers are encouraged to consult the full text of the ASU on FASB's website at www.fasb.org.

8.38 Typically, programmatic loans would not meet the definition of a security, as defined in FASB ASC 958-320-20, and therefore are not subject to the standards in FASB ASC 958-320 for debt securities. As a result, unless the NFP has elected to report programmatic investments at fair value by making an election pursuant to the "Fair Value Option" subsections of FASB ASC 825-10 (the fair value option), programmatic loans are reported at amortized cost.

8.39 FASB ASC 310-10-35 provides standards for impairment of loans. The guidance is divided into parts, as follows:

- Paragraphs 7–11 of FASB ASC 310-10-35 apply to groups of smaller-balance homogeneous loans, as well as loans that are not identified for evaluation or that are evaluated but are not individually considered impaired.

- Paragraphs 12–40 of FASB ASC 310-10-35 apply to loans that are identified for evaluation or that are individually deemed to be impaired. An NFP might evaluate programmatic investments using these standards if the loan amount crosses a size criterion or delinquency criterion (or both) identified by the NFP.

Smaller-Balance Loans

8.40 FASB ASC 310-10-35-9 requires that losses from uncollectible receivables be accrued when both of the following conditions are met:

- Information available before the financial statements are issued or are available to be issued indicates that it is probable that an asset has been impaired at the date of the financial statements.
- The amount of the loss can be reasonably estimated.

Those conditions may be considered in relation to individual receivables or in relation to groups of similar types of receivables. If the conditions are met, accrual should be made even though the particular receivables that are uncollectible may not be identifiable.

8.41 FASB ASC 310-10-35-10 provides further guidance. If, based on current information and events, it is probable that the NFP will be unable to collect all amounts due according to the contractual terms of the receivable, the probability condition is met. All amounts due according to the contractual terms means that both the contractual interest payments and the contractual principal payments will be collected as scheduled according to the receivable's contractual terms. However, a creditor need not consider an insignificant delay or insignificant shortfall in amount of payments as meeting the probability condition. Whether the amount of loss can be reasonably estimated will normally depend on, among other things, the experience of the entity, information about the ability of individual debtors to pay, and appraisal of the receivables in light of the current economic environment. In the case of an entity that has no experience of its own, reference to the experience of other entities in the same business may be appropriate.

Loans That Are Identified for Evaluation and That Are Individually Deemed to Be Impaired

8.42 FASB ASC 310-10-35-14 provides a list of characteristics that an entity might use to identify loans for evaluation of impairment. Those characteristics include, among others, a specific materiality criterion; loans to borrowers in industries or countries experiencing economic instability; borrowers experiencing problems such as operating losses, marginal working capital, inadequate cash flow, or business interruptions; and internally generated listings such as watch lists, past due reports, and overdraft listings.

8.43 FASB ASC 310-10-35-16 states that upon evaluation, a loan is impaired when, based on current information and events, it is probable that a creditor will be unable to collect all amounts due according to the contractual terms of the loan agreement. (See paragraph 8.41 for further guidance about the meaning of all amounts due according to the contractual terms.)

8.44 When a loan is impaired, FASB ASC 310-10-35-22 requires that impairment be measured based on the present value of expected future cash flows discounted at the loan's effective interest rate. Paragraphs 20–32 of FASB ASC 310-10-35 provide further guidance on how to measure the impairment.

8.45 Continuing the example in paragraph 8.17, which uses the effective interest approach, the community foundation identifies this loan for evaluation of impairment at the end of year 1. Because the community foundation believes that it will collect only $57,640 at the due date 4 years from now, it determines that the loan is impaired. The community foundation is required to measure the impairment based on the $57,640 payment at the loan's effective interest rate of 15 percent, which is $32,956. The carrying value of the loan is $57,178, so the community foundation recognizes a valuation allowance of $24,222.

8.46 In contrast, if the inherent contribution approach has been used, as in paragraph 8.25, and the community foundation identifies this loan for evaluation of impairment at the end of year 1, there is no impairment to recognize at this time. The community foundation expects to receive a $57,640 payment 4 years from now. The present value of $57,640 at 3 percent is $51,212, which is the loan's carrying value. The loan will not be impaired until the amount expected to be collected at the due date is less than $57,640.

8.47 Paragraphs 37–40 of FASB ASC 310-10-35 describe accounting for a loan after the initial measurement of impairment. If there is a significant change (increase or decrease) in the amount or timing of an impaired loan's expected future cash flows, or if actual cash flows are significantly different from the cash flows previously projected, a creditor should recalculate the impairment by re-applying the procedures specified in paragraphs 21–22 and paragraphs 24–26 of FASB ASC 310-10-35 and adjusting the valuation allowance. Similarly, if a creditor measured the impairment based on the observable market price of an impaired loan or the fair value of the collateral, the valuation allowance should be adjusted if there is a significant change (increase or decrease) in either of those bases. However, the net carrying amount of the loan should at no time exceed the recorded investment in the loan, which is the amount of the loan disregarding the valuation allowance.

Troubled Debt Restructuring

8.48 In some cases, a concession is granted by an NFP investor in an attempt to protect as much of its investment in a programmatic loan as possible. The concession can take the form of (*a*) modification in the terms of the loan, (*b*) a receipt of assets (including an equity interest in the borrower) in partial satisfaction of the programmatic loan and a modification of terms of the remaining loan, or (*c*) a receipt of assets (including an equity interest in the borrower) in satisfaction of the programmatic loan even though the value received is less than the amount of the loan. The NFP investor expects to obtain more cash or other value from the borrower, or to increase the probability of receipt, by granting the concession than by not granting it. If an NFP investor, for economic or legal reasons related to the borrower's financial difficulties, grants a concession to the borrower that it would not otherwise consider, the granting of that concession (that is, restructuring the loan) may be a troubled debt restructuring.

8.49 In general, if a borrower can obtain funds from sources other than the NFP investor at market interest rates at or near those for nontroubled debt, the restructuring of the loan is not a troubled debt restructuring. A borrower in a troubled debt restructuring can obtain funds from sources other than the NFP investor, if at all, only at effective interest rates (based on market prices) so high that the borrower cannot afford to pay them. Even if the borrower is experiencing some financial difficulties, a restructuring is not necessarily a troubled debt restructuring. The guidance in FASB ASC 310-40-15 is used to determine if a restructuring is a troubled debt restructuring. FASB ASC 310-40-15-12 provides examples of debt restructurings that are not troubled debt restructurings.

8.50 If an NFP investor, by applying the guidance in FASB ASC 310-40-15, determines that a restructuring is a troubled debt restructuring, the NFP investor applies the guidance from the following:

- FASB ASC 310-40-35 if the loan terms are modified, regardless of whether assets are received when the concession is granted.
- FASB ASC 310-40-40 if the loan is settled by the assets received and the concessions granted in the restructurings (including foreclosure, a deed in lieu of foreclosure, or similar legal agreement).
- FASB ASC 310-40-40 if a new borrower is substituted for the existing borrower as part of the restructuring.

Disclosures About Programmatic Loans

> **Update 8-3 *Accounting and Reporting*: Credit Losses**
>
> FASB ASU No. 2016-13 was issued in June 2016 to provide financial statement users with more decision-useful information about the expected credit losses on financial instruments and other commitments to extend credit held by a reporting entity at each reporting date. To achieve this objective, the amendments in the ASU replace the incurred loss impairment methodology in current GAAP with a methodology that reflects expected credit losses and requires consideration of a broader range of reasonable and supportable information to inform credit loss estimates.
>
> FASB ASU No. 2016-13 is effective for NFPs for fiscal years beginning after December 15, 2020, and interim periods within fiscal years beginning after December 15, 2021. Early adoption is permitted for fiscal years beginning after December 15, 2018, including interim periods within those fiscal years.
>
> This edition of the guide has not been updated to reflect changes as a result of this ASU; however, the section that follows will be updated in a future edition. Readers are encouraged to consult the full text of the ASU on FASB's website at www.fasb.org.

8.51 Programmatic loans are subject to the standards in FASB ASC 310-10-50, including its requirements for financing receivables and loan products that have contractual terms that expose entities to risks and uncertainties. Further, if loans are made to related parties, the NFP should also consider the requirements of FASB ASC 850, *Related Party Disclosures.* In implementing those requirements, an NFP investor would consider the relative significance of programmatic loans to its mission-related operations and to its financial position, and the quantitative and qualitative risks arising from the transactions. For example, disclosures about the allowance for credit losses related to financing receivables (paragraphs 11A–14 of FASB ASC 310-10-50), disclosures about impaired loans (paragraphs 14A–20 of FASB ASC 310-10-50), and disclosures about credit quality indicators (paragraphs 27–30 of FASB ASC 310-10-50) are required unless the amount of programmatic loans is immaterial to the financial statements.

8.52 If making programmatic loans is one of the NFP's major class of programs,[4] FinREC recommends that, in addition to the disclosures in FASB ASC 310-10-50, an NFP disclose the following:

- The number of loans outstanding
- The average face amount and average carrying amount of the loans at origination and the reason for the difference
- The program purpose that is being accomplished by the loan activity
- The amount of impairment losses in total and by program expense line item(s)

Equity Instruments

8.53 By definition, programmatic investments that are equity instruments are interests in entities that provide goods or services that accomplish the purpose or mission for which the NFP exists or that serve the NFP's administrative purposes. Thus, when determining the proper accounting and reporting, an NFP investor follows the guidance in chapter 3, "Financial Statements, the Reporting Entity, and General Financial Reporting Matters." Exhibit 3-2, "Relationships of a Not-for-Profit Reporting Entity," describes some common relationships with other entities and identifies where these relationships are discussed in chapter 3 and in FASB ASC. Exhibit 3-2 and chapter 3 summarize certain guidance in FASB ASC but are not a substitute for reading the guidance itself.

8.54 Programmatic equity interests typically are in for-profit entities and, therefore, generally would not have a contribution element at origination. In some cases, the agreement for the equity interest will contain additional rights or privileges, such as the investor's right to obtain future services from the investee at reduced rates. In those cases, those additional rights and privileges should be accounted for in accordance with relevant generally accepted accounting principles and the consideration specified in the agreement is allocated between the equity interest and those additional rights and privileges.

Programmatic Equity Investments That Are Consolidated

8.55 Although unusual, a programmatic equity investment in another entity might provide the NFP investor with sufficient control that consolidation is required. The standards for consolidation are discussed in chapter 3. NFPs can use exhibit 3-2 to assist with the determination of which investees are required to be consolidated.

Programmatic Equity Investments Reported Using the Equity Method

8.56 NFPs can use exhibit 3-2 to assist with the determination of which investees are required to be reported using the equity method. FASB

[4] Guidance for determination of a not-for-profit entity's major classes of programs is included in paragraphs 13.48–.58.

ASC 323-10-35 provides guidance for the application of the equity method. Because programmatic equity investments are often made to newly created entities or entities in economic distress, the investee may experience losses rather than net income. Paragraphs 19–30 of FASB ASC 323-10-35 provide standards if an NFP investor's share of losses of an investee equals or exceeds the carrying amount of a programmatic investment; that is, the losses have reduced the carrying amount of the equity-method investment to zero. An NFP investor ordinarily should discontinue applying the equity method if the investment (and net advances) is reduced to zero. It should not provide for additional losses unless it has guaranteed obligations of the investee or is otherwise committed to provide further financial support for the investee. However, if the imminent return to profitable operations by an investee appears to be assured, the NFP investor should provide for additional losses. (For example, a material, nonrecurring loss of an isolated nature may reduce an investment below zero even though the underlying profitable operating pattern of an investee is unimpaired.) If the investee subsequently reports net income (or an increase in net assets), the NFP investor should resume applying the equity method only after its share of that net income (or increase in net assets) equals the share of net losses not recognized during the period the equity method was suspended.

8.57 Timely identification of impairment is a consideration for any interest that is reported using the equity method. Impairment of equity method investments is discussed in paragraphs 31–32A of FASB ASC 323-10-35. A decrease in value of an equity method investment should be recognized if that decrease is other than temporary, even though the decrease in value is in excess of what would otherwise be recognized by application of the equity method.

8.58 A series of operating losses of an investee or other factors may indicate that a decrease in value of a programmatic equity investment has occurred. Evidence of a loss in value might include, but would not necessarily be limited to, absence of an ability to recover the carrying amount of the investment or inability of the investee to sustain an earnings capacity that would justify the carrying amount of the investment. Although programmatic equity investments seldom have readily determinable fair values, a current fair value that is less than the carrying amount also may indicate a loss in value of the investment. All are factors that should be evaluated.

Programmatic Equity Investments Reported Using Fair Value

8.59 Typically, programmatic equity investments do not meet the definition of an equity security with readily determinable fair value, as defined in FASB ASC 958-320-20, and therefore are not subject to the fair value measurement requirements in FASB ASC 958-320. An NFP that would otherwise be required to use the equity method or the cost method for an equity instrument may be permitted to report at fair value by making an election pursuant to FASB ASC 825-10-25-1 (the fair value option).

Programmatic Equity Investments Reported Using a Cost Method

8.60 Timely identification of impairment is a consideration for any equity interest that is reported using the cost method. Impairment of cost-method investments is discussed in paragraphs 8–13 of FASB ASC 958-325-35. Because the fair value of cost-method investments is not readily determinable, the evaluation of whether an investment is impaired should be determined in accordance with FASB ASC 320-10-35-25. If the value is impaired, the NFP investor should determine whether the impairment is other than temporary using the guidance in paragraphs 30–33 of FASB ASC 320-10-35. If the impairment is other than temporary, a loss is recognized in accordance with FASB ASC 320-10-35-34. The fair value of the investment would then become the new amortized cost basis of the investment and should not be adjusted for subsequent recoveries in fair value.

Disclosures About Programmatic Equity Instruments

8.61 The disclosures for programmatic equity instruments are the same as those required for other equity instruments (that is, disclosures for consolidated subsidiaries, equity-method investments, related parties, and so forth, as applicable). In addition to the disclosures required by those other topics in FASB ASC, the Financial Reporting Executive Committee (FinREC) recommends that an NFP that makes programmatic equity investments disclose the following:

- The number of programmatic equity investees
- The carrying amount recognized in the statement of financial position for the programmatic equity instruments
- The program purpose that is being accomplished by the programmatic equity relationship(s)
- The amount of impairment losses in total and by program expense line item(s)

Guarantees

8.62 Some programmatic investments take the form of guarantees. FASB ASC 460 establishes the accounting and disclosure requirements to be met by a guarantor for certain guarantees issued and outstanding. Those standards are briefly discussed in paragraphs 10.100–.101.

Concentrations of Risk

8.63 As explained in FASB ASC 825-10-55-1, the terms of certain loan products increase a reporting entity's exposure to credit risk, and thereby may result in a concentration of credit risk. FASB ASC 825-10-50-20 requires entities to disclose all significant concentrations of credit risk arising from all financial instruments, whether from an individual counterparty or groups of counterparties. Group concentrations of credit risk exist if a number of counterparties are engaged in similar activities and have similar economic characteristics that would cause their ability to meet contractual obligations to be similarly affected by changes in economic or other conditions. Judgment is required to determine whether loan products have terms that give rise to a concentration of credit risk.

Presentation of Programmatic Investments

Contributed Resources for Making Programmatic Investments

8.64 If the resources to make a programmatic investment are restricted by donors, the net assets related to the contributed resources should be reported as restricted until the restrictions are met, in accordance with FASB ASC 958-210-45-1.

8.65 Therefore, FinREC believes that if a donor provides resources with a restriction that the resources be used to make a programmatic investment, the net assets would be reported as temporarily restricted until that investment is made. However, if the donor specifies that the contributed resources should create a revolving fund, such that repayments of loans or proceeds from sales of programmatic investments must be reinvested to make additional programmatic investments, the net assets related to the revolving fund are subject to a permanent restriction. Although the net assets may be reduced from time to time by losses, and may eventually be exhausted, the resources are capable of providing economic benefits indefinitely and the donor has instructed that the fund should be revolving in duration. (Paragraphs 5.80–.83 provide additional information about the classification of net assets as permanently restricted.)

Therefore, FinREC believes that if a donor provides resources with a restriction that the resources be used to make a programmatic investment, the net assets would be reported as net assets with donor restrictions until that investment is made, and then be reclassified to net assets without donor restrictions. However, if the donor specifies that the contributed resources should create a revolving fund, such that repayments of loans or proceeds from sales of programmatic investments must be reinvested to make additional programmatic investments, the net assets related to the revolving fund are subject to a perpetual restriction, and would not be reclassified when the programmatic investment was made. (The restriction is perpetual because, although the net assets may be reduced from time to time by losses, and may eventually be exhausted, the resources are capable of providing economic benefits indefinitely and the donor has instructed that the fund should be revolving in duration.)[5]

8.66 In some cases, a donor that provides resources restricted to making a programmatic investment will also restrict the use of the income earned by the programmatic investment or the proceeds of its sale or maturity. If so, those restrictions on income, gains, and losses should be recognized in accordance with FASB ASC 958-320-45 when the income, sale, or maturity is recognized.

Agency Resources for Making Programmatic Investments

8.67 In some cases, the NFP investor is acting as an agent for a principal (often a governmental entity) when it makes programmatic investments. If so, any cash received by the NFP prior to making the investment is reported as an agency liability, as described in paragraphs 10.86 and 10.93. The Federal Perkins Loan Program, the Health Professions Loan Program, and the Nursing Student Loan Program are examples of revolving funds that are recorded as agency transactions.

---

[5] The amendments in FASB ASU No. 2016-14 are effective for annual financial statements issued for fiscal years beginning after December 15, 2017 (for example, years ending December 31, 2018, and years ending June 30, 2019), and for interim periods within fiscal years beginning after December 15, 2018. Application to interim financial statements is permitted but not required in the initial year of application. Early application of the amendments is permitted.

8.68 In accordance with FASB ASC 958-325-25-2, when a programmatic investment is made using resources supplied by the principal, cash is reduced and the investment recognized. If the programmatic investment has a contribution element, the contribution made is not the agent's contribution expense; the contribution has been made by the principal. If an agreement for an equity interest provides the principal with additional rights and privileges that require separate accounting, those rights and privileges are not the agent's assets. To the extent that a programmatic investment reduces the assets held on behalf of the principal, the offsetting liability to the principal is also reduced. The liability to the principal is typically satisfied by transferring the programmatic investment(s) or the cash received at maturity or sale of the programmatic investment to the principal. In some cases in which the principal is a government agency, the government agency might forgive the liability.

8.69 In accordance with FASB ASC 958-325-35-16, if an NFP is holding an investment as an agent and has little or no discretion in determining how the investment income, unrealized gains and losses, and realized gains and losses resulting from that investment will be used, those investment activities should be reported as agency transactions and, therefore, as changes in assets and liabilities, rather than as changes in net assets. If the programmatic investment is funded in part by the NFP and in part by the principal, the investment income, unrealized gains and losses, and realized gains and losses would be shared between the two entities in accordance with their agreement.

Program-Related Investments of Private Foundations

8.70 In the year that a program-related investment is made, the IRS allows private foundations to count the investment as part of the required 5 percent charitable distribution. Principal repayments on program-related loans count as "recaptured distributions," increasing the payout requirement in the years that the principal repayments are made by the amount of the repayment. (That is, the amount of any principal repayment will be effectively added to that year's minimum distribution requirement.) Interest and dividend payments are considered regular income. The IRS exempts program-related investments from the "prudent man" rule on investments.

Auditing

8.71 Auditing objectives and procedures for programmatic investments can be similar to investments held by other entities. However, there are some specific and unique aspects for NFPs that hold such investments. Suggested audit procedures to consider include the following:

- Review the NFP's policies for programmatic investments, which might include
  - — the criteria for determining what constitutes a programmatic investment,
  - — a description of the approval process,
  - — the type of program purposes for which the NFP is allowed to invest,
  - — potential limits, if any, on the total number of programmatic investments,

- the extent to which the NFP intends to pursue collection, and
- the process the NFP will use to evaluate impairment of the programmatic investment.

- Understand the guidance in paragraph 8.04 and review the initial investment transaction to determine if it has the characteristics of a programmatic investment. (Completeness, Valuation and Allocation)
- Review the NFP's disclosures to determine whether proper qualitative and quantitative information has been included. Due to the nature of an NFP's activities, often times programmatic investments involve mission critical decisions that may be of importance to the users of the financial statements. Paragraphs 8.51–.52, 8.61, and 8.63 discuss disclosures for programmatic investments. (Valuation)
- For programmatic investments in the form of loans,
  - review the loan documents to determine if the stated or implied interest rate represents a market rate commensurate with the risks inherent in the expected cash flows. If the rate is considered below a market rate, review the calculation prepared by the NFP to determine that the contribution portion is properly reflected in the financial statements and notes thereto (paragraphs 8.11–.17 and 8.29–.33). (Valuation and Allocation)
  - review the loan documents and promissory notes to assess the intended collectibility upon origination. As discussed in paragraphs 8.11–.17 and 8.18–.25, at times the NFP investor does not expect to collect all contractually required payments when due. In that case, determine whether the amounts recognized as contribution expense and loan receivable are reasonable considering the expectations. (Valuation and Allocation, Rights and Obligations)
  - consider the guidance in paragraphs 8.26–.28 and 8.35–.36, determine whether the NFP has forgiven a portion of or the entire outstanding loan. (Valuation and Allocation, Rights and Obligations)
  - review the loan documents to determine if the terms describe a contribution element that is conditioned on a future and uncertain event. If so, determine whether the NFP has procedures to identify whether the conditions have been substantially met and to recognize the contribution. (Valuation and Allocation, Rights and Obligations)
- For programmatic investments in the form of equity interests,
  - review the investment agreement to determine whether any additional rights and privileges that should be recognized separately have been identified and recorded (paragraph 8.54). (Valuation and Allocation, Rights and Obligations)

  - determine whether consolidation is required. Consider the guidance in paragraph 8.55 and in chapter 3. (Classification)
  - for programmatic equity investments that do not require consolidation, determine whether the equity method, cost method, or fair value is required. Consider the guidance in paragraphs 8.56–.60. (Valuation)
- Review the programmatic investments to determine if an impairment loss should be recognized. For loans, refer to the guidance in paragraphs 8.37–.46. For equity investments, refer to the guidance in paragraphs 8.56–.60. (Valuation and Allocation, Rights and Obligations)
- Inquire whether the NFP has guaranteed the debt of other entities. If so, determine whether the recorded amount is appropriate and whether the NFP has procedures for monitoring the entities it guarantees and adjusting the amount of the guarantee liability in subsequent periods. (Valuation and Allocation, Rights and Obligations)

Chapter 9

Property and Equipment

Gray shaded text in this chapter reflects guidance issued but not yet effective as of the date of this guide, March 1, 2018, but becoming effective on or prior to June 30, 2018, exclusive of any option to early adopt ahead of the mandatory effective date. Unless otherwise indicated, all unshaded text reflects guidance that was already effective as of the date of this guide.

Introduction

9.01 Not-for-profit entities (NFPs) use various kinds of property and equipment to provide goods and services to beneficiaries, customers, and members. Property and equipment includes all long-lived tangible assets held by NFPs, except collection items[1] and assets held for investment purposes.

9.02 Property and equipment commonly held by NFPs includes the following:

- Land and land improvements
- Buildings and building improvements, equipment, furniture and office equipment, library books, motor vehicles, and similar depreciable assets
- Leased property and equipment (capitalized in conformity with FASB *Accounting Standards Codification* [ASC] 840-30)
- Improvements to leased property
- Construction in process
- Contributed use of facilities and equipment (recognized in conformity with the "Contributions Received and Agency Transactions" subsections of FASB ASC 958-605, as illustrated in paragraphs 23–25 of FASB ASC 958-605-55)

Recognition and Measurement Principles

9.03 NFPs acquire the use of property and equipment through purchases, trade-ins, self-construction, leases, and contributions. NFPs should apply the guidance in FASB ASC 360, *Property, Plant, and Equipment*, except when it conflicts with the specialized guidance for NFPs in FASB ASC 958-360.

Contributed Property and Equipment

9.04 Pursuant to FASB ASC 958-605-25-2; 958-605-30-2; and 958-605-45-3, contributions of property and equipment (including unconditional promises to give property and equipment) should be recognized at fair value[2] at the date

---

[1] Because of their unique nature, collection items are reported differently than how other long-lived tangible assets are reported. Chapter 7, "Other Assets," discusses accounting for collection items.

[2] FASB *Accounting Standards Codification* (ASC) 820, *Fair Value Measurement*, defines *fair value* and establishes a framework for measuring fair value. Paragraphs 3.138–.168 discuss those standards. In addition, chapter 5, "Contributions Received and Agency Transactions," discusses measuring the fair value of contributed assets.

of contribution and, depending on donor restrictions and the NFP's accounting policy, should be included in permanently restricted, temporarily restricted, or unrestricted net assets.[3] If the donors stipulate how or how long contributed property and equipment must be used by the NFP, the contribution should be reported as restricted support. If the donors do not specify such restrictions, the contribution should be reported as restricted support if the NFP has adopted an accounting policy of implying a time restriction on the use of such assets that expires over the assets' useful lives. (The policy is discussed further in paragraphs 5.86–.88.) In the absence of donor restrictions or an NFP's policy of implying time restrictions, contributions of long-lived assets should be reported as unrestricted support.

Pursuant to FASB ASC 958-605-25-2; 958-605-30-2; and the "Pending Content" in FASB ASC 958-605-45-3, contributions of property and equipment (including unconditional promises to give property and equipment) should be recognized at fair value[4] at the date of contribution and, depending on donor restrictions, should be included in net assets with donor restrictions or net assets without donor restrictions.[5] If the donors stipulate how or how long contributed property and equipment must be used by the NFP, the contribution should be reported as donor-restricted support. Pursuant to the "Pending Content" in FASB ASC 958-605-45-6, if the donors do not specify such restrictions, the contribution should be reported as support increasing net assets without donor restrictions. Gifts of cash or other assets restricted to acquire long-lived assets should initially be reported as donor-restricted support. Paragraphs 11.41–.49 discuss when restrictions on gifts of property and equipment or on gifts for their purchase expire.[6]

9.05 In practice, contributions of depreciable assets generally do not increase permanently restricted net assets. As noted in paragraph 5.81, only contributions of assets that are not by their nature used up in carrying out the NFP's activities and thus are capable of providing economic benefits indefinitely should be classified as increases in permanently restricted net assets. For example, if a donor contributes a depreciable long-lived asset and specifies that it is to be sold and the proceeds used to create a permanent endowment, that contribution would be capable of providing economic benefits indefinitely and would increase permanently restricted net assets.

---

[3] As discussed in paragraphs 7.16–.28, separate standards apply to contributions of works of art, historical treasures, or similar assets that are added to collections, as defined.

[4] FASB *Accounting Standards Codification* (ASC) 820, *Fair Value Measurement*, defines *fair value* and establishes a framework for measuring fair value. Paragraphs 3.138–.168 discuss those standards. In addition, chapter 5, "Contributions Received and Agency Transactions," discusses measuring the fair value of contributed assets.

[5] As discussed in paragraphs 7.16–.28, separate standards apply to contributions of works of art, historical treasures, or similar assets that are added to collections, as defined.

[6] The amendments in FASB Accounting Standards Update (ASU) No. 2016-14, *Not-for-Profit Entities (Topic 958): Presentation of Financial Statements of Note-for-Profit Entities*, are effective for annual financial statements issued for fiscal years beginning after December 15, 2017 (for example, years ending December 31, 2018, and years ending June 30, 2019), and for interim periods within fiscal years beginning after December 15, 2018. Application to interim financial statements is permitted but not required in the initial year of application. Early application of the amendments is permitted.

The preceding paragraph will be deleted upon the effective date of FASB ASU No. 2016-14, *Not-for-Profit Entities (Topic 958): Presentation of Financial Statements of Not-for-Profit Entities*.[7]

9.06 Unconditional promises to give property and equipment to an NFP should be recognized by the NFP as receivables in conformity with paragraphs 8–10 of FASB ASC 958-605-25. Contributions of the use of property and equipment in which the donor retains legal title to the assets are discussed in paragraphs 5.164–.166.

9.07 Per FASB ASC 958-360-30-1, similar to items acquired in exchange transactions, the amount initially recognized for contributed property and equipment should include all the costs incurred by the entity to place those assets in use. Examples of such costs include the freight and installation costs of contributed equipment and cataloging costs for contributed library books.

Use of Property and Equipment Owned by Others

Update 9-1 *Accounting and Reporting*: Leases

FASB Accounting Standards Update (ASU) No. 2016-02, *Leases (Topic 842)*, issued February 2016, changes the accounting for leases, primarily by the recognition of lease assets and lease liabilities by lessees for those leases classified as operating leases under current generally accepted accounting principles (GAAP). FASB ASU No. 2016-02 is effective for fiscal years beginning after December 15, 2018, including interim periods within those fiscal years, for NFPs that have issued, or are conduit bond obligors for, securities that are traded, listed, or quoted on an exchange or an over-the-counter market. For all other NFPs, the amendments in this ASU are effective for fiscal years beginning after December 15, 2019, and interim periods within fiscal years beginning after December 15, 2020. Early adoption is permitted.

This edition of the guide has not been updated to reflect changes as a result of this ASU; however, the section that follows will be updated in a future edition. Readers are encouraged to consult the full text of the ASU on FASB's website at www.fasb.org.

9.08 An NFP may have access to use property or equipment that it does not own. If the property or equipment is used under the terms of a lease agreement that at its inception requires lease payments at fair value, the NFP should apply the guidance in FASB ASC 840, *Leases*. In many cases, an NFP has the right to use property without making lease payments or makes lease payments that are significantly below market rates. For example, property or equipment may be provided by a donor, by a related NFP, by an unrelated entity under an affiliation program, by a sponsor of research, or by a governmental agency or unit.

[7] The amendments in FASB ASU No. 2016-14 are effective for annual financial statements issued for fiscal years beginning after December 15, 2017 (for example, years ending December 31, 2018, and years ending June 30, 2019), and for interim periods within fiscal years beginning after December 15, 2018. Application to interim financial statements is permitted but not required in the initial year of application. Early application of the amendments is permitted.

9.09 Contributed use of property is discussed in paragraphs 5.164–.166. If the NFP is not required to make lease payments or if lease payments are significantly below fair value, a contribution is inherent in the use of the property, unless the agreement includes other rights or privileges of a commensurate value. For example, an NFP may receive use of a vehicle for a year from a local car dealer, and no lease payments are required. In determining whether lease payments are below fair value, the payments would be compared to payments for similar property that is rented under similar terms.

9.10 In other cases, an NFP uses property owned by another entity to fulfill its obligations under an agreement with that entity. For example, some NFPs provide research or testing services using property owned by the entity that sponsors the research or testing. FASB ASC 958-605-55-25 applies if the agreement between the owner of the property (sponsor) and the NFP is an exchange transaction and it is probable that the NFP will be permitted to keep the asset when the arrangement terminates. The paragraph states that property and equipment used in exchange transactions (other than lease transactions), such as federal contracts, in which the resource provider retains legal title during the term of the arrangement, should be reported as a contribution at fair value at the date received by the NFPs only if it is probable that the NFP will be permitted to keep the assets when the arrangement terminates. Per FASB ASC 958-360-50-4, the terms of such arrangements should be disclosed in notes to the financial statements.

9.11 In many cases, the sponsoring entity transfers cash to the NFP rather than the property or equipment itself, with the directive that the cash be used to buy the property and equipment to be used in the exchange transaction. The sponsoring entity will retain legal title to the property and equipment during the term of the arrangement. Analogizing to the guidance in FASB ASC 958-605-55-25 (which is discussed in the preceding paragraph), if it is probable that the NFP will be permitted to keep the asset when the arrangement terminates, the cash received would be reported as revenue (for example, a contribution or grants and contracts revenue) and the property, when purchased, would be capitalized in accordance with the NFP's capitalization policy and depreciated in subsequent periods. At the completion of the arrangement, the NFP should test the equipment for recoverability if, as expected, the NFP is permitted to keep the asset. If the sponsoring entity requires return of the equipment, the equipment would be derecognized when it ceases to be used and is returned to the sponsoring entity.

9.12 When making a determination of whether it will be permitted to keep the asset when the arrangement terminates, the NFP would consider facts and circumstances that include the following:

- The NFP's prior experience with the sponsoring entity and whether the sponsoring entity typically transfers title to the property at the end of the agreement's term
- The experience of other NFPs who have contracted with the same sponsoring entity
- The term of the agreement as compared to the useful life of the property, and the expected salvage value of the property at the end of the term
- Whether the property will be technologically obsolete at the end of the term of the agreement

9.13 If, after considering the facts and circumstances, the NFP concludes that it is not probable that it will be permitted to keep the asset when the arrangement terminates, the NFP should report the transaction as an agent. It would report an asset (first cash, and then property held as an agent upon the property's purchase) and an offsetting liability (amount owed pursuant to an agency transaction). During the term, the NFP would decrease the asset to reflect its use, charging an expense such as rent expense. A decrease in the liability of a similar amount would also be recognizing, crediting the same revenue source that is used for the contract revenue. At the end of the term, the NFP would derecognize any amount remaining for the property held as an agent and the offsetting liability. If the sponsoring entity transfers title at the end of the term, the NFP would report revenue, measuring the property at its fair value at that time.

Capitalized Interest

9.14 Many NFPs finance acquisitions, additions, and renovations of facilities by issuing tax-exempt debt, as discussed in chapter 10, "Debt and Other Liabilities." If the proceeds of tax-exempt borrowings are externally restricted to finance the acquisition of specified qualifying assets or to service the related debt, the amount of interest cost to be capitalized is determined in accordance with paragraphs 8–12 of FASB ASC 835-20-30. If the NFP uses taxable debt or otherwise does not qualify for interest capitalization under those paragraphs, then the amount of interest cost to be capitalized is determined pursuant to paragraphs 2–7 of FASB ASC 835-20-30. Frequently, an NFP is required to capitalize interest under paragraphs 2–7 of FASB ASC 835-20-30 for some projects and paragraphs 8–12 of FASB ASC 835-20-30 for others.

9.15 Among the differences between the two sets of guidance are the interest cost to be capitalized and the capitalization period. For interest costs on qualifying assets acquired with proceeds of tax-exempt borrowings that are externally restricted, FASB ASC 835-20-30-11 requires that the amount of capitalized interest be all interest cost of the borrowing less any interest earned on related interest-bearing investments acquired with proceeds of the related tax-exempt borrowings from the date of the borrowing until the assets are ready for their intended use. For other borrowings, paragraphs 2–7 of FASB ASC 835-20-30 use a weighted average construction expenditures concept that is applied during the period for which the three criteria in FASB ASC 835-20-25-3 are present. Those criteria are (*a*) expenditures for the asset have been made, (*b*) activities that are necessary to get the asset ready for its intended use are in progress, and (*c*) interest cost is being incurred.

9.16 In accordance with FASB ASC 835-20-30-12, the interest cost of a tax-exempt borrowing should be eligible for capitalization on other qualifying assets of the entity when the specified qualifying assets are no longer eligible for interest capitalization. The entire interest cost on that portion of the proceeds that is available for other uses, such as refunding an existing debt issue other than a construction loan related to those assets, also is eligible for capitalization on other qualifying assets. Example 1 in FASB ASC 835-20-55-4 illustrates this guidance.

9.17 In certain circumstances in which an NFP has an investment (equity, loans, and advances) accounted for by the equity method and the investee has not begun its planned principal operations, FASB ASC 835-20-35-2 requires capitalization of interest cost. As explained in FASB ASC 835-20-15-5(c), the investor's investment in the investee, not the individual assets or projects of the investee, is the qualifying asset for purposes of interest capitalization. Interest is capitalized while the investee has activities in progress necessary to commence its planned principal operations, provided that the investee's activities include the use of funds to acquire qualifying assets for operations.

9.18 FASB ASC 835-20-15 specifies the types of assets for which interest is not capitalized. Among the listed items are assets acquired with gifts and grants that are restricted by the donor or grantor to acquisition of those assets, to the extent that funds are available from such gifts and grants; interest earned from the temporary investment of those funds that is similarly restricted should be considered an addition to the gift or grant for this purpose. Other items include assets not included in the consolidated balance sheet of the parent company and consolidated subsidiaries and assets that are not being used in the earning activities of the entity and not undergoing the activities necessary to get them ready for use.

9.19 Some NFPs finance construction projects with municipal securities that have both taxable and tax-exempt components. The aggregate proceeds are to finance a specific construction project and are restricted by a common indenture or trust agreement to use only for construction of the project, repayment of the debt, or both. In such situations, the interest to be capitalized on the taxable portion of the issue is accounted for separate from the interest on the tax-exempt portion, based on paragraphs 2–7 of FASB ASC 835-20-30.

Depreciation and Amortization

9.20 FASB ASC 360-10-35-4 states that *depreciation* is a system of accounting that aims to distribute the cost or other basic value of tangible capital assets, less salvage (if any), over the estimated useful life of the unit (which may be a group of assets) in a systematic and rational manner. Depreciation should be recognized for contributed property and equipment, as well as for purchased property and equipment.

9.21 Paragraphs 1–6 of FASB ASC 958-360-35 require all NFPs to recognize depreciation for all property and equipment except land used as a building site, certain works of art or historical treasures with extraordinarily long lives, and similar assets.

9.22 Per FASB ASC 958-360-35-7, the terms of certain grants and reimbursements from other entities may specify whether depreciation or the entire cost of the asset in the year of acquisition should be included as a cost of activities associated with those grants or reimbursements for contractual purposes (sometimes referred to as allowable costs). Those terms should not affect the recognition and measurement of depreciation for financial reporting purposes.

Update 9-2 *Accounting and Reporting*: Leases

FASB ASU No. 2016-02, issued February 2016, changes the accounting for leases, primarily by the recognition of lease assets and lease liabilities by lessees for those leases classified as operating leases under current GAAP. FASB ASU No. 2016-02 is effective for fiscal years beginning after December 15, 2018, including interim periods within those fiscal years, for NFPs that have issued, or are conduit bond obligors for, securities that are traded, listed, or quoted on an exchange or an over-the-counter market. For all other NFPs, the amendments in this ASU are effective for fiscal years beginning after

December 15, 2019, and interim periods within fiscal years beginning after December 15, 2020. Early adoption is permitted.

This edition of the guide has not been updated to reflect changes as a result of this ASU; however, the section that follows will be updated in a future edition. Readers are encouraged to consult the full text of the ASU on FASB's website at www.fasb.org.

9.23 FASB ASC 840-10-35-6 states that leasehold improvements that are placed in service significantly after and not contemplated at or near the beginning of the lease term should be amortized over the shorter of the following terms:

a. The useful life of the assets, or

b. A term that includes required lease periods and renewals that are deemed to be reasonably assured (as used in the context of the definition of *lease term*) at the date the leasehold improvements are purchased

Expiration of Restrictions on Property and Equipment

9.24 The expiration of restrictions on gifts of property and equipment or on gifts for their purchase is discussed in paragraphs 11.46–.49. The expiration of restrictions on a promise to give that is restricted to the purchase or construction of long-lived assets is discussed in paragraphs 11.37–.45.

Impairment or Disposal of Long-Lived Assets

Update 9-3 *Accounting and Reporting*: Gains and Losses on Sales of Nonfinancial Assets

FASB ASU No. 2017-05, *Other Income—Gains and Losses from the Derecognition of Nonfinancial Assets (Subtopic 610-20): Clarifying the Scope of Asset Derecognition Guidance and Accounting for Partial Sales of Nonfinancial Assets*, was issued in February 2017 to clarify the scope of FASB ASC 610-20. Among its amendments, it requires an entity to account for the derecognition of a nonfinancial asset, including the transfer or sale of property, plant, and equipment, in accordance with FASB ASC 610-20, unless a scope exception from FASB ASC 610-20 applies. For example, the derecognition of a nonfinancial asset in a contract with a customer would be accounted for in accordance with FASB ASC 606, *Revenue from Contracts with Customers*, instead of FASB ASC 610-20.

FASB ASU No. 2017-05 is effective concurrently with the amendments in FASB ASU No. 2014-09, *Revenue from Contracts with Customers (Topic 606)*. As a result, most not-for-profit entities (NFPs) will apply the new standards for annual reporting periods beginning after December 15, 2018, and interim periods within annual periods beginning after December 15, 2019. However, NFPs that have issued, or are conduit bond obligors for, securities that are traded, listed, or quoted on an exchange or an over-the-counter market are required to apply the standards for annual reporting periods beginning after December 15, 2017, including interim periods within that reporting period.

This edition of the guide has not been updated to reflect changes as a result of this ASU; however, the section that follows will be updated in a future edition. Readers are encouraged to consult the full text of the ASU on FASB's website at www.fasb.org.

9.25 The "Impairment or Disposal of Long-Lived Assets" subsections of FASB ASC 360-10 provide guidance whenever events or changes in circumstances indicate that the carrying amount of a long-lived asset (asset group)[8] may not be recoverable. This paragraph and the next three summarize that guidance but are not a substitute for reading those subsections. FASB ASC 360-10-35-17 states that an impairment loss should be recognized only if the carrying amount of the long-lived asset (or asset group) is not recoverable and exceeds its fair value. The carrying amount of a long-lived asset (asset group) is not recoverable if it exceeds the sum of the undiscounted cash flows expected to result from use and eventual disposition of the asset (asset group). That assessment should be based on the carrying amount of the asset (asset group) at the date it is tested for recoverability, whether in use (see FASB ASC 360-10-35-33) or under development (see FASB ASC 360-10-35-34). An impairment loss should be measured as the amount by which the carrying amount of a long-lived asset (asset group) exceeds its fair value.

9.26 FASB ASC 958-360-35-8 states that when grouping assets for impairment testing, an NFP that relies in part on contributions to maintain its assets may need to consider those contributions in determining the appropriate cash flows to compare with the carrying amount of an asset. If future unrestricted contributions to the entity as a whole are not considered, the sum of the expected future cash flows may be negative, or positive but less than the carrying amount of the asset. For example, the costs of administering a museum may exceed the admission fees charged, but the museum may fund the cash flow deficit with unrestricted contributions.

The "Pending Content" in FASB ASC 958-360-35-8 states that when grouping assets for impairment testing, an NFP that relies in part on contributions to maintain its assets may need to consider those contributions in determining the appropriate cash flows to compare with the carrying amount of an asset. If future contributions without donor restrictions to the entity as a whole are not considered, the sum of the expected future cash flows may be negative, or positive but less than the carrying amount of the asset. For example, the costs of administering a museum may exceed the admission fees charged, but

[8] The FASB ASC glossary defines an *asset group* as the unit of accounting for a long-lived asset or assets to be held and used, which represents the lowest level for which identifiable cash flows are largely independent of the cash flows of other groups of assets and liabilities. The FASB ASC glossary states that a *disposal group* for a long-lived asset or assets to be disposed of by sale or otherwise represents assets to be disposed of together as a group in a single transaction and liabilities directly associated with those assets that will be transferred in the transaction. Per FASB ASC 360-10-15-4, examples of liabilities included in a disposal group are legal obligations that transfer with a long-lived asset, such as certain environmental obligations, and obligations that, for business reasons, a potential buyer would prefer to settle when assumed as part of a group, such as warranty obligations that relate to an acquired customer base. Per FASB ASC 360-10-35-24, in limited circumstances, a long-lived asset (for example, a corporate headquarters facility) may not have identifiable cash flows that are largely independent of the cash flows of other assets and liabilities and of other asset groups. In those circumstances, the asset group for that long-lived asset should include all assets and liabilities of the entity.

the museum may fund the cash flow deficit with contributions without donor restrictions.[9]

9.27 A long-lived asset is classified as held and used until it is disposed of or it meets the criteria to be classified as held for sale. A long-lived asset that is disposed of by gift should be recognized in accordance with FASB ASC 720-25. The contribution of the long-lived asset should be measured at the fair value of the asset given, and if the fair value of the asset transferred differs from its carrying amount, a gain or loss should be recognized on the disposition of the asset. An asset (disposal group) should be classified as held for sale in the period in which all of the criteria in FASB ASC 360-10-45-9 are met. If at any time afterwards the criteria are no longer met (except in certain limited circumstances beyond the entity's control, as discussed in FASB ASC 360-10-45-11), a long-lived asset (disposal group) classified as held for sale should be reclassified as held and used in accordance with FASB ASC 360-10-35-44. Further, if the criteria in FASB ASC 360-10-45-9 for classifying a long-lived asset (disposal group) as held for sale are met after the balance sheet date, but before the issuance of the financial statements, a long-lived asset (disposal group) should be classified as held and used in those financial statements when issued and certain disclosures are required.

9.28 A long-lived asset (disposal group) that is held for sale should be measured at the lower of its carrying amount or fair value less cost to sell. A long-lived asset should not be depreciated (amortized) while it is classified as held for sale. (Interest and other expenses attributable to the liabilities of a disposal group held for sale should continue to be accrued.) FASB ASC 205-20 provides guidance on when the results of operations of a component of an entity that either has been disposed of or is classified as held for sale would be reported as a discontinued operation in the financial statements. Paragraphs 1B–1D of FASB ASC 205-20-45 state that only the following are reported as discontinued operations:

- Disposals of components of an entity that represent a strategic shift that has (or will have) a major effect on the NFP's operations and financial results
- A business or nonprofit activity that, on acquisition, meets the criteria in FASB ASC 205-20-45-1E to be classified as held for sale. If the one-year requirement in FASB ASC 205-20-45-1E(d) is met (except as permitted by FASB ASC 205-20-45-1G), a business or nonprofit activity should be classified as held for sale as a discontinued operation at the acquisition date if the other criteria in FASB ASC 205-20-45-1E are probable of being met within a short period following the acquisition (usually within three months).

If a long-lived asset (asset group) that is disposed of is a subsidiary, a business, or a nonprofit activity, the NFP should also consider the guidance in FASB ASC 810-10-40.

---

[9] The amendments in FASB ASU No. 2016-14 are effective for annual financial statements issued for fiscal years beginning after December 15, 2017 (for example, years ending December 31, 2018, and years ending June 30, 2019), and for interim periods within fiscal years beginning after December 15, 2018. Application to interim financial statements is permitted but not required in the initial year of application. Early application of the amendments is permitted.

9.29 FASB ASC 958-360-40-1 applies if contributed long-lived assets are disposed of before the end of their useful lives and those assets are subject to an accounting policy implying time restrictions on the use of contributed long-lived assets. In those situations, the gain or loss on the disposal of that asset should be reported as a change in unrestricted net assets and a reclassification should be reported for any remaining temporarily restricted net assets.

The preceding paragraph will be deleted upon the effective date of FASB ASU No. 2016-14.[10]

Asset Retirement Obligations

9.30 FASB ASC 410-20 establishes accounting standards for recognition and measurement of a liability for an asset retirement obligation and the associated asset retirement cost. It applies to legal obligations associated with the retirement of a tangible long-lived asset if those obligations result from the acquisition, construction, development, or normal operation of a long-lived asset. FASB ASC 410-20 also applies to any legal obligations that require disposal of a replaced part that is a component of a tangible long-lived asset, with exceptions for certain obligations. An NFP is required to recognize a liability if the obligation to perform the asset retirement activity is unconditional, even though the timing or method of settlement may be uncertain.

9.31 An NFP should recognize the fair value of a liability for an asset retirement obligation in the period in which it is incurred if a reasonable estimate of fair value can be made. (Per FASB ASC 410-20-30-1, an expected present value technique will usually be the only appropriate technique with which to estimate the fair value of a liability for an asset retirement obligation.) The asset retirement cost should be capitalized by increasing the carrying amount of the related long-lived asset by the same amount as the liability.

9.32 For example, an NFP would have an asset retirement obligation if it accepted a gift of a building with the stipulation that in 10 years the building would be destroyed and the land converted to a garden that would be open to the public. Paragraphs 57–58 of FASB ASC 410-20-55 discuss an example of regulations that create a duty or responsibility for an entity to remove and dispose of asbestos in a special manner.

Gains and Losses

9.33 In accordance with FASB ASC 958-220-45-8, gains and losses recognized on property and equipment, including impairment losses, should be classified in a statement of activities as changes in unrestricted net assets unless explicit donor stipulations or law require their use to be restricted. In those situations, gains or losses should be classified as increases or decreases in temporarily restricted or permanently restricted net assets, as appropriate. For example, if a donor requires the proceeds from a sale of property to be used to establish a donor-restricted endowment to be maintained in perpetuity, the

[10] The amendments in FASB ASU No. 2016-14 are effective for annual financial statements issued for fiscal years beginning after December 15, 2017 (for example, years ending December 31, 2018, and years ending June 30, 2019), and for interim periods within fiscal years beginning after December 15, 2018. Application to interim financial statements is permitted but not required in the initial year of application. Early application of the amendments is permitted.

gain (or loss) on the sale of the property would increase (or decrease) permanently restricted net assets.

In accordance with the "Pending Content" in FASB ASC 958-220-45-8, gains and losses recognized on property and equipment, including impairment losses, should be classified in a statement of activities as changes in net assets without donor restrictions unless their use is restricted by explicit donor stipulations or by law that extends donor restrictions. In those situations, gains or losses should be classified as increases or decreases in net assets with donor restrictions.[11]

Financial Statement Presentation

9.34 FASB ASC 958-220-45-11 describes limitations on an NFP's use of an intermediate measure of operations. It states that if that subtotal, such as income from operations, is presented, it should include the amount of an impairment loss recognized for a long-lived asset (asset group) to be held and used, pursuant to FASB ASC 360-10-45-4. It also should include the amount of a gain or loss recognized on the sale of a long-lived asset (disposal group) if that long-lived asset (disposal group) is not a component of the NFP, that qualifies for discontinued operations treatment, as defined in FASB ASC 205-20, and pursuant to FASB ASC 360-10-45-5.

9.35 FASB ASC 958-360-50 and FASB ASC 360-10-50 list most of the disclosures required for property and equipment. The following paragraphs list some of the more common of those disclosures, as well as references to other locations in FASB ASC that include required disclosures about property and equipment.

9.36 An NFP should disclose significant accounting policies concerning property and equipment, such as the following:

- The capitalization policy adopted
- Whether time restrictions are implied on the use of contributed long-lived assets (and contributions of assets restricted to purchase them) received without donor stipulations regarding how long the contributed assets must be used
- Whether donor-restricted contributions of long-lived assets are reported as unrestricted when restrictions are satisfied in the same reporting period in which the contributions are received, pursuant to FASB ASC 958-605-45-4

An NFP should disclose significant accounting policies concerning property and equipment, such as the following:

- The capitalization policy adopted

---

[11] The amendments in FASB ASU No. 2016-14 are effective for annual financial statements issued for fiscal years beginning after December 15, 2017 (for example, years ending December 31, 2018, and years ending June 30, 2019), and for interim periods within fiscal years beginning after December 15, 2018. Application to interim financial statements is permitted but not required in the initial year of application. Early application of the amendments is permitted.

- Whether donor-restricted contributions of long-lived assets are reported as support within net assets without donor restrictions when restrictions are satisfied in the same reporting period in which the contributions are received, pursuant to the "Pending Content" in FASB ASC 958-605-45-4.[12]

Update 9-4 *Accounting and Reporting*: Leases

FASB ASU No. 2016-02, issued February 2016, changes the accounting for leases, primarily by the recognition of lease assets and lease liabilities by lessees for those leases classified as operating leases under current GAAP. FASB ASU No. 2016-02 is effective for fiscal years beginning after December 15, 2018, including interim periods within those fiscal years, for NFPs that have issued, or are conduit bond obligors for, securities that are traded, listed, or quoted on an exchange or an over-the-counter market. For all other NFPs, the amendments in this ASU are effective for fiscal years beginning after December 15, 2019, and interim periods within fiscal years beginning after December 15, 2020. Early adoption is permitted.

This edition of the guide has not been updated to reflect changes as a result of this ASU; however, the section that follows will be updated in a future edition. Readers are encouraged to consult the full text of the ASU on FASB's website at www.fasb.org.

9.37 A statement of financial position or related notes should include the balances of each major class of property and equipment. The basis of valuation—for example, cost for purchased items and fair value for contributed items—should also be disclosed. Separate disclosure should also be made of the following items:

- Nondepreciable assets.
- Property and equipment not held for use in operations, for example, items held for sale or for investment purposes or construction in process.
- FASB ASC 958-210-50-3 requires disclosure of the nature and amount of limitations on the use of cash and cash equivalents and assets whose use is limited, including assets restricted by donors for the acquisition of property and equipment.
- Improvements to leased facilities and equipment.
- FASB ASC 840-30-50 requires disclosures about assets (and related obligations) recognized under capital leases.
- FASB ASC 835-20-50 requires disclosures about capitalized interest.
- FASB ASC 205-20-50 requires disclosures about assets sold or held for sale.

[12] The amendments in FASB ASU No. 2016-14 are effective for annual financial statements issued for fiscal years beginning after December 15, 2017 (for example, years ending December 31, 2018, and years ending June 30, 2019), and for interim periods within fiscal years beginning after December 15, 2018. Application to interim financial statements is permitted but not required in the initial year of application. Early application of the amendments is permitted.

- FASB ASC 360-10-50 requires disclosure about impairment losses recognized on long-lived assets.

9.38 Accumulated depreciation, either for each major class of property and equipment or in total, should be disclosed (*a*) as a deduction or parenthetically in a statement of financial position, or (*b*) in the notes to the financial statements. The amount of depreciation expense for the period and the method or methods used to compute depreciation for the major classes of property and equipment should also be disclosed.

9.39 The notes to the financial statements should include disclosures concerning the liquidity of the NFP's property and equipment, including information about limitations on their use. For example, information should be provided about

- property and equipment pledged as collateral or otherwise subject to lien.
- property and equipment acquired with restricted assets where title may revert to another party, such as a resource provider.
- donor or legal limitations on the use of or proceeds from the disposal of property and equipment.
- impaired long-lived assets reported at fair value, as required by FASB ASC 820-10-50-2.

9.40 Example 3 in paragraph 5.222 illustrates how an NFP might disclose alternative policies for implying time restrictions on the use of contributed long-lived assets (and contributions of assets restricted to purchase them) received without donor stipulations concerning how long the contributed assets must be used in notes to the financial statements. Paragraph 9.04 discusses those alternative accounting policies.

The preceding paragraph will be deleted upon the effective date of FASB ASU No. 2016-14.[13]

Auditing

9.41 Many audit objectives and auditing procedures, including the consideration of controls, related to property and equipment of NFPs are similar to those of other entities. In addition, the auditor may need to consider specific audit objectives, auditing procedures, and selected controls in the table in paragraph 9.42, which are unique to NFPs.

9.42 The following table illustrates the use of assertions in developing audit objectives and designing substantive tests. The examples are not intended to be all-inclusive nor is it expected that all the procedures would necessarily be applied in an audit. The use of assertions in assessing risks and designing appropriate audit procedures to obtain audit evidence is described in paragraphs

---

[13] The amendments in FASB ASU No. 2016-14 are effective for annual financial statements issued for fiscal years beginning after December 15, 2017 (for example, years ending December 31, 2018, and years ending June 30, 2019), and for interim periods within fiscal years beginning after December 15, 2018. Application to interim financial statements is permitted but not required in the initial year of application. Early application of the amendments is permitted.

.26–.32 of AU-C section 315, *Understanding the Entity and Its Environment and Assessing the Risks of Material Misstatement.*[14] Paragraph .18 of AU-C section 330, *Performing Audit Procedures in Response to Assessed Risks and Evaluating the Audit Evidence Obtained*, requires the auditor to design and perform substantive procedures for all relevant assertions related to each material class of transactions, account balance, and disclosure, irrespective of the assessed risks of material misstatement. This requirement reflects the facts that (1) the auditor's assessment of risk is judgmental and may not identify all risks of material misstatement, and (2) inherent limitations to internal control exist, including management override. Various audit procedures and the purposes for which they may be performed are described in paragraphs .A10–.A26 of AU-C section 500, *Audit Evidence*.

Auditing Considerations

Financial Statement Assertions	*Specific Audit Objectives*	*Select Control Objectives*
Transactions		
Contributed Property and Equipment		
Valuation and allocation	Contributed property and equipment is reported at fair value at the date of contribution.	Controls ensure that contributions of property and equipment are known and recorded and that documentation supports the determination of their fair value.
Presentation and Disclosures		
Rights and obligations; Classification	Restrictions on contributed property and equipment are reflected in the classification of net assets.	Contributions of property and equipment are reviewed for restrictions and management monitors compliance with restrictions.
Reclassification of Temporarily Restricted Net Assets		
Occurrence/ Existence; Classification	Temporarily restricted net assets are reclassified as unrestricted net assets in the statement of activities over the term of the donor-imposed restrictions or when placed in service if the donor did not specify a term and one is not implied.	

[14] All AU-C sections can be found in AICPA *Professional Standards*.

Auditing Considerations—*continued*

Financial Statement Assertions	*Specific Audit Objectives*	*Select Control Objectives*
Reclassification of Net Assets with Donor Restrictions[15]		
Occurrence/ Existence; Classification	Net assets with donor restrictions are reclassified as net assets without donor restrictions in the statement of activities over the term of the donor-imposed restrictions or when placed in service if the donor did not specify a term.	

Property and Equipment Additions

9.43 Audit procedures for purchased property and equipment are similar to those for business entities, with the exception of testing related to contributions and their donor-imposed restrictions.

9.44 For property and equipment contributed in the current year, also refer to the tests in paragraph 5.232. If restricted resources were used for the purchase of property and equipment, the auditor may find it necessary to consider whether reclassifications are made on the statement of activities when the asset is placed in service, provided that the donor did not specify a term of use and the NFP does not have a policy that implies a time restriction that expires over the useful life of the asset (as discussed in paragraphs 5.86–.88). (Classification)

For property and equipment contributed in the current year, also refer to the tests in paragraph 5.232. If restricted resources were used for the purchase of property and equipment, the auditor may find it necessary to consider whether reclassifications are made on the statement of activities when the asset is placed in service. (Classification)[16]

9.45 Contributions of property or its use received by the NFP are measured at fair value. AU-C section 540, *Auditing Accounting Estimates, Including Fair Value Accounting Measurements, and Related Disclosures*, addresses audit considerations relating to the measurement and disclosure of assets,

---

[15] The amendments in FASB ASU No. 2016-14 are effective for annual financial statements issued for fiscal years beginning after December 15, 2017 (for example, years ending December 31, 2018, and years ending June 30, 2019), and for interim periods within fiscal years beginning after December 15, 2018. Application to interim financial statements is permitted but not required in the initial year of application. Early application of the amendments is permitted.

[16] The amendments in FASB ASU No. 2016-14 are effective for annual financial statements issued for fiscal years beginning after December 15, 2017 (for example, years ending December 31, 2018, and years ending June 30, 2019), and for interim periods within fiscal years beginning after December 15, 2018. Application to interim financial statements is permitted but not required in the initial year of application. Early application of the amendments is permitted.

liabilities, and specific components of equity presented or disclosed at fair value in financial statements. (Valuation)

9.46 In evaluating capitalization policies, the auditor may find it necessary to consider whether interest has been appropriately capitalized in accordance with FASB ASC 835-20 (paragraphs 9.14–.19). (Classification and Disclosure)

Account Balances

9.47 Audit procedures for property and equipment balances are the same as for business entities, except for tests of contributed long-lived assets and the use of long-lived assets owned by others. For those items, suggested audit procedures to consider include the following:

- If specific property or equipment is restricted, review the use of the asset for compliance with donor restrictions. (Rights and Obligations, Classification)
- If specific property or equipment is subject to a donor restriction that requires that it be sold and the proceeds of its sale used for a restricted purpose, determine if the NFP has internal controls to identify that equipment and to ensure that upon sale, the proceeds are restricted for the required purpose. (Rights and Obligations, Classification)
- If the NFP has a policy that implies a time restriction that expires over the useful life of contributed property and equipment (as discussed in paragraphs 5.86–88), determine whether reclassifications are made on the statement of activities over the asset's useful life unless the donor specified a different term of use. (Classification)

The preceding bullet will be deleted upon the effective date of FASB ASU No. 2016-14.[17]

- If the NFP plans to sell or abandon property or the property is impaired, in addition to the tests typically performed to test the financial statement assertions, consider whether a reclassification should be reported for any remaining temporarily restricted net assets, as discussed in paragraph 9.29. (Classification)

The preceding bullet will be deleted upon the effective date of FASB ASU No. 2016-14.[18]

---

[17] The amendments in FASB ASU No. 2016-14 are effective for annual financial statements issued for fiscal years beginning after December 15, 2017 (for example, years ending December 31, 2018, and years ending June 30, 2019), and for interim periods within fiscal years beginning after December 15, 2018. Application to interim financial statements is permitted but not required in the initial year of application. Early application of the amendments is permitted.

[18] The amendments in FASB ASU No. 2016-14 are effective for annual financial statements issued for fiscal years beginning after December 15, 2017 (for example, years ending December 31, 2018, and years ending June 30, 2019), and for interim periods within fiscal years beginning after December 15, 2018. Application to interim financial statements is permitted but not required in the initial year of application. Early application of the amendments is permitted.

- If the NFP uses property and equipment owned by others,
  - — inquire into the nature of any relationship between the NFP and the owners of the property or equipment.
  - — review disclosure of the nature of any relationship between the NFP and the owners of the property or equipment.
  - — determine compliance with donor, grantor, or other resource provider's requirements. (Rights and Obligations)
  - — if asset has been recorded because the NFP asserts that it is probable that it will be permitted to keep the asset when the arrangement terminates, test that assertion against the NFP's historical experience, correspondence related to the agreement, and other relevant evidence. (Rights and Obligations)

9.48 When evaluating the disclosures in the financial statements, the auditor should consider whether the required disclosures (paragraphs 9.35–.39) have been made.

9.49 When considering an NFP's application of the impairment or disposal of long-lived assets subsections of FASB ASC 360-10, auditors may inquire about the policies and procedures used by management to determine whether all impaired assets have been properly identified. In addition to evaluating the NFP's procedures for identifying indicators of impairment, the auditor may consider information obtained during the audit in determining whether the NFP has identified appropriate indicators of impairment. As noted in paragraph 9.26, an NFP that relies in part on contributions to maintain its assets may need to consider those contributions in performing the impairment tests.

Chapter 10

Debt and Other Liabilities

Gray shaded text in this chapter reflects guidance issued but not yet effective as of the date of this guide, March 1, 2018, but becoming effective on or prior to June 30, 2018, exclusive of any option to early adopt ahead of the mandatory effective date. Unless otherwise indicated, all unshaded text reflects guidance that was already effective as of the date of this guide.

Introduction

10.01 Many obligations of not-for-profit entities (NFPs) are similar to those of for-profit entities. This chapter considers debt and other liabilities that are not discussed elsewhere in this guide and that present accounting and auditing issues unique to NFPs.

Fair Value Measurement

10.02 The "Fair Value Option" subsections of FASB *Accounting Standards Codification* (ASC) 825-10 permit an NFP to irrevocably elect fair value as the initial and subsequent measure for certain financial liabilities, with changes in fair value recognized in the statement of activities as those changes occur. The following liabilities that might exist for NFPs are outside the scope of the "Fair Value Option" subsections and thus cannot be reported at fair value: employers' and plans' obligations for pension benefits, other postretirement benefits (including health care and life insurance benefits), postemployment benefits, deferred compensation arrangements, financial liabilities recognized under lease contracts, current and deferred tax assets and liabilities, and liabilities that require the NFP to provide services, rather than cash or another financial asset, to the obligee.

10.03 Liabilities are rarely transferred in the marketplace because of contractual or other legal restrictions preventing their transfer. Paragraphs 16–18C of FASB ASC 820-10-35, which are briefly summarized in paragraphs 10.04–.08, provide guidance for determining the fair value of a liability. Even when there is no observable market to provide pricing information about the transfer of a liability, there might be an observable market for the liability if it is held by other parties as an asset. When a quoted price for the transfer of an identical or a similar liability is not available and the identical item is held by another party as an asset, an NFP should measure the fair value of the liability from the perspective of a market participant that holds the identical item as an asset at the measurement date, adjusting if necessary (paragraph 10.05).

10.04 In such cases, an NFP should measure the fair value of the liability as follows:

- Using the quoted price in an active market for the identical liability held by another party as an asset, if that price is available
- If that price is not available, using other observable inputs, such as the quoted price in a market that is not active for the identical liability held by another party as an asset

- If observable prices are not available for an identical liability held as an asset, using another valuation approach, such as the following:
  - — An income approach (for example, a present value technique that takes into account the future cash flows that a market participant would expect to receive from holding the liability as an asset)
  - — A market approach (for example, using quoted prices for similar liabilities held by other parties as assets)

10.05 An NFP should adjust the quoted price of the liability held by another party as an asset only if there are factors specific to the asset that are not applicable to the fair value measurement of the liability. An NFP should ensure that the price of the asset does not reflect the effect of a restriction preventing the sale of that asset. FASB ASC 820-10-35-16D includes some factors, including a third-party credit enhancement, that may indicate that the quoted price of the asset should be adjusted.

10.06 When a quoted price for the transfer of an identical or a similar liability is not available and the identical item is not held by another party as an asset, an NFP should measure the fair value of the liability using a valuation technique from the perspective of a market participant that owes the liability. Paragraphs 16I–16L of FASB ASC 820-10-35 provide guidance for using present value techniques to measure the fair value of a liability.

10.07 The fair value of a liability reflects the effect of *nonperformance risk* (the risk that the entity will not fulfill the obligation). Nonperformance risk includes, but may not be limited to, a reporting entity's own credit risk. Nonperformance risk is assumed to be the same before and after the transfer of the liability. When measuring the fair value of a liability, an NFP should take into account the effect of its credit risk (credit standing) and any other factors that might influence the likelihood that the obligation will or will not be fulfilled. FASB ASC 820-10-35-18A states that an issuer of a liability issued with an inseparable third-party credit enhancement that is accounted for separately from the liability should not include the effect of the credit enhancement (for example, a third-party guarantee of debt) in the fair value measurement of the liability. If the credit enhancement is accounted for separately from the liability, the issuer would take into account its own credit standing and not that of the third-party guarantor when measuring the fair value of the liability. Thus, if fair value is determined based on the prices at which the liabilities are trading in markets, an adjustment needs to be made for the difference between the credit standing of the guarantor (on which the market trades are based) and the credit standing of the NFP. In other words, the observed price for the debt traded as an asset is adjusted to exclude the effect of the third-party credit enhancement. (Paragraphs 10.21–.23 provide additional information about credit enhancements.)

10.08 When measuring the fair value of a liability, an NFP should not include a separate input or an adjustment to other inputs relating to the existence of a restriction that prevents the transfer of the liability. The effect of a restriction that prevents the transfer of a liability is either implicitly or explicitly included in the other inputs to the fair value measurement.

Municipal Bond Financing and Other Long-Term Debt

10.09 An NFP may finance part of its activities from the proceeds of tax-exempt bonds or other obligations issued through state and local financing authorities. FASB ASC 958-470-25-1 states that because the NFP is responsible for the repayment of those obligations, that financing should be recognized as a liability in its statement of financial position. The FASB ASC glossary defines *conduit debt securities* as

> Certain limited-obligation revenue bonds, certificates of participation, or similar debt instruments issued by a state or local governmental entity for the express purpose of providing financing for a specific third party (the conduit bond obligor) that is not a part of the state or local government's financial reporting entity. Although conduit debt securities bear the name of the governmental entity that issues them, the governmental entity often has no obligation for such debt beyond the resources provided by a lease or loan agreement with the third party on whose behalf the securities are issued. Further, the conduit bond obligor is responsible for any future financial reporting requirements.

10.10 Typically, a qualified governmental agency such as a financing authority (the issuer) issues the securities and then lends the proceeds to the NFP (the obligor). In these "conduit financings," although the securities bear the name of the issuing government, the issuer has no obligation for repayment of the debt; the bondholders' principal and interest will be paid solely from resources of the obligor. This is a simplistic explanation of the obligations under the bond; the nature of municipal debt financing can vary in complexity and terms. A careful reading of the agreements between the obligor and the issuing agency, the trustee of master trust, and any credit-enhancing entities is useful to fully understanding the structure of the transactions.[1]

10.11 Various types of collateral are offered for municipal bonds issued on behalf of NFPs. For revenue bond issues, the NFP pledges a specific revenue stream; typically revenue derived from the project or enterprise being funded. There may also be a mortgage on the property financed and other restrictive covenants. To obtain project financing, a financing authority may require an NFP to enter into a lease arrangement, a sublease arrangement, or both. The Audit and Accounting Guide *Health Care Entities* provides guidance if an NFP is part of an obligated group of affiliated entities, the assets and revenues of which serve as collateral for the bonds.

10.12 Municipal bonds are issued with either a variable or a fixed interest rate. A *fixed-rate bond* bears interest at a specified, constant rate. *Variable-rate* (or floating-rate) *bonds* bear interest at a rate that is reset from time to time. Some documents provide the ability to change the interest mode (for example, from auction-rate[2] to variable-rate). In addition, a common financing structure involves initially issuing lower cost variable-rate debt and a floating-to-fixed interest rate swap, which results in economics similar to fixed-rate debt. Paragraph 4.37 discusses accounting for variable-rate debt with a variable-to-fixed interest rate swap.

---

[1] "Report on the Municipal Securities Market," issued by the SEC on July 31, 2012, provides an overview of the municipal securities marketplace, including conduit debt securities.

[2] In a Dutch auction, investors bid for the bonds, which are sold at the lowest yield necessary to sell the bonds that are offered for sale.

10.13 The type of project or projects that are funded with municipal bond proceeds affects the taxability of income received by the bondholders and, thus, whether the bonds are characterized as "tax-exempt" or "taxable." Generally, tax-exempt bonds are issued to finance services or facilities that are for the public good. Interest paid to holders of tax-exempt bonds is often exempt from federal income taxes and sometimes from state or local taxes as well. Taxable bonds may be issued for uses not qualifying for tax-exempt financing (for example, rental real estate). Tax considerations are discussed in paragraphs 10.54–.58.

Joint and Several Liability Arrangements

10.14 Under joint and several liability, the total amount of an obligation is enforceable against any and all of the parties to the arrangement. Each party is considered primarily responsible for the entire obligation and cannot refuse to pay on the basis that individually it borrowed only a portion of the total or on the basis that the other parties also are obligated to pay. For example, in a lending arrangement, the lender can demand payment for the total amount of the obligation from any party to the arrangement or any combination of the parties. However, if a party pays the obligation, it may be able to pursue the other parties for repayment. The difference between a joint and several liability arrangement and a guarantee is that guarantors are required to make payment only contingently, upon nonperformance by the primary obligor (that is, a guarantor is secondarily liable). Guarantees are discussed in paragraphs 10.100–.101.

10.15 Often the parties in a joint and several liability arrangement are entities that are under common control. For example, entities that are under common control may be jointly and severally liable for obligations of the parent or for brother/sister entities. By borrowing under a joint and several liability arrangement, the members of the consolidated entity that borrow under the arrangement (sometimes referred to as an obligated group) can finance programs and capital expansions by borrowing on the basis of the group's revenues and assets. Thus, financially weaker entities benefit from the credit strength of the stronger entities in the group. Joint and several liability arrangements can also exist between unrelated parties. For instance, several unrelated entities may be jointly and severally liable as a result of a legal settlement.

10.16 FASB ASC 405-40 applies to joint and several liability arrangements for which the total amount of an obligation is fixed at the reporting date. For the total amount of an obligation under an arrangement to be considered fixed at the reporting date there can be no measurement uncertainty at the reporting date relating to the total amount of the obligation, although the amount that an NFP expects to pay on behalf of other parties to the arrangement (its co-obligors) may be uncertain at the reporting date. Examples of obligations within the scope of FASB ASC 405-40 include certain debt arrangements, other contractual obligations, and settled litigation and judicial rulings. Examples of obligations outside of the scope of FASB ASC 405-40 are asset retirement and environmental obligations, retirement benefits, contingencies within the scope of FASB ASC 450, *Contingencies*, and guarantees within the scope of FASB ASC 460, *Guarantees*.

10.17 For arrangements within the scope of FASB ASC 405-40, an NFP measures its obligation as the sum of the following:

a. The amount the NFP agreed to pay on the basis of its arrangement among its co-obligors

b. Any additional amount the reporting entity expects to pay on behalf of its co-obligors. If there is a range of additional amounts that the NFP expects to pay, and some amount within that range is a better estimate than any other amount within the range, that amount should be the additional amount included in the measurement of the obligation. If no amount within the range is a better estimate than any other amount, then the minimum amount in the range should be the additional amount included in the measurement of the obligation.

Disclosures about joint and several arrangements are required by FASB ASC 405-40-50.

Conduit Bonds That Trade in Public Markets

10.18 Certain accounting standards require entities that have securities that trade in public markets to provide more extensive disclosures and adopt standards earlier than is required for entities that do not have securities trading in public markets. Generally, the rationale behind these requirements is that the entity's financial statements are being utilized in public markets for making decisions about whether to buy, sell, or hold that entity's securities.

10.19 The FASB ASC glossary has multiple definitions for the term *public entity*. Generally, these are entities that have debt or equity securities that trade in public markets. When applying accounting standards that refer to public entities, careful attention should be paid to the requirements to determine which definition applies and whether the definition includes conduit bond obligors within its scope. If within its scope, it is also necessary to determine whether the obligor's securities trade in public markets (for example, over-the-counter markets). Technical Questions and Answers (Q&A) section 7100, *Definition of a Public Business Entity*,[3] although not intended to serve as guidance to NFPs, may assist NFPs in understanding the key terms used in the various definitions of public entity, including the definitions of security, over-the-counter market, and conduit debt obligor. As discussed in paragraph 10.24, if conduit bonds have been issued on behalf of an NFP in a competitive or negotiated offering, they are deemed to trade in public markets; bonds issued in a private placement would not be deemed to trade in public markets for as long as the bonds are privately held.

10.20 The fact that an NFP with conduit bonds that trade in public markets is considered a public entity does not change that entity's status for purposes of applying accounting standards with requirements that are specific to NFPs, or that explicitly exclude NFPs. If the scope of an accounting standard that contains expanded disclosure requirements (or additional accounting requirements) for public entities explicitly excludes NFPs, NFPs would not apply that standard. Additionally, classification as a public entity under generally accepted accounting principles (GAAP) does not impose SEC or other regulatory filing requirements (such as Regulation S-X or S-K) on NFPs that are conduit debt obligors, nor does it result in an NFP being required to comply with the portions of the Sarbanes-Oxley Act that apply only to issuers, as defined by the Securities and Exchange Act of 1934.

---

[3] All Q&A sections can be found in *Technical Questions and Answers*.

Credit Enhancement[4]

10.21 NFPs may utilize credit enhancements to make their debt more attractive to lenders and investors or to allow them to access the market at more favorable rates. *Credit enhancement* involves the use of the credit standing of an entity other than the issuer or obligor to provide additional security in a bond or note financing. The term typically refers to bond insurance, bank letters of credit, and similar facilities, but also may refer more broadly to the use of any form of guaranty, secondary source of payment, or similar additional credit-improving instruments. For example, foundations may provide guarantees on bank borrowings of other NFPs or a governing board member may guarantee the debt of the NFP.

10.22 When credit enhancement is provided through a bank letter of credit, the debt bears the rating of the issuing bank that commits to pay the principal of and interest on the securities in the event the obligor is unable to do so. Letters of credit cover a specified time period. Bond insurance is an unconditional and irrevocable commitment from a municipal bond insurance company to make scheduled bond debt service payments in the event of nonpayment by the obligor. Bonds secured by a municipal bond insurance policy carry the rating of the municipal bond insurer. Once acquired, a bond insurance policy generally is in place for the life of the bonds.

10.23 Because credit-enhanced debt is rated based on the credit standing of another entity, downgrades of the other entity's ratings can have implications for the obligor's own credit ratings, as well as potentially triggering defaults under debt agreements and derivative contracts.

Issuance of Municipal Bonds

10.24 Municipal bonds are issued through negotiated sales, competitive bids, or private placements. In a *negotiated sale*, the issuer or obligor negotiates a price with one or more underwriters. In a *competitive bid sale*, the securities are sold to one or more underwriters who submitted the best acceptable bid(s). The underwriters then resell the securities to the general investing public. Municipal bonds issued in negotiated sales or competitive bids are deemed to be traded in public markets; thus, conduit borrowers under those arrangements are considered public entities for purposes of providing certain disclosures or adopting certain accounting standards earlier than nonpublic entities (see the discussion in paragraphs 10.18–.20). In addition, when underwriters sell municipal securities to the general investing public, the SEC imposes certain requirements on the underwriters, who in turn require the obligors to file certain disclosure documents. An overview of SEC considerations related to municipal bonds is provided in appendix A, "Municipal Securities Regulation," of this chapter and in paragraphs 15.57–.60. In a *private placement*, the securities generally are sold only to qualified investors (for example, an institutional investor), rather than through an offering to the general investing public. As noted in Q&A section 7100.03, "Use of the Term 'Over-the-Counter Market' in the Definition of a Public Business Entity," markets accessible by only certain investors (for example, qualified institutional or accredited investors) are not

---

[4] Paragraph 10.07 discusses the fair value of bonds with third-party credit enhancements, whether measured for purposes of disclosure or reporting under the "Fair Value Option" subsections of FASB ASC 825-10.

considered accessible by the public. Municipal bonds issued in private placements are not deemed to trade in public markets because the investors typically are subject to restrictions on resale.

10.25 An NFP that is issuing municipal bonds through a financing authority prepares an official statement that offers the securities for sale and provides appropriate financial and other information about the offering, the NFP, and any guarantors or credit enhancement providers. Financial advisers, bond counsel, and, frequently, engineers and appraisers assist the NFP in preparing information for the official statement. The following are important stages in a municipal securities offering; the time periods between these stages may vary.

- The preliminary official statement is issued to all prospective buyers of the securities.
- The financing authority, NFP, and the underwriters execute the bond purchase agreement.
- The official statement is issued at the time of sale (sometimes referred to as the effective date) and identifies the actual debt service requirements of the securities.
- The closing date is the date the transaction is finalized and the proceeds are transferred from the buyers to the NFP.

Extinguishment and Modification Transactions

10.26 NFPs generally follow the same accounting and financial reporting standards for extinguishment and modification of debt as investor-owned entities. Those standards are found in FASB ASC 405-20, FASB ASC 470-50, and FASB ASC 470-60.

10.27 FASB ASC 405-20-40 states that a liability is extinguished either when the debtor pays the creditor and is relieved of its obligation for the liability or when the debtor is legally released from being the primary obligor under the liability, either judicially or by the creditor. FASB ASC 405-20-40-1(a)(4) states that paying the creditor includes reacquisition by the debtor of its outstanding debt securities whether the securities are cancelled or held as so-called treasury bonds.

10.28 Thus, a debt obligation is derecognized if an NFP reacquires its bonds in a secondary market purchase, regardless of whether the reacquired securities are then held by the debtor as treasury bonds or retired. Treasury bonds held should never be reported as an asset of the NFP, even if the entity intends to remarket the bonds at a future date or hold and manage them as part of its investment portfolio. (Bonds that are repurchased in a failed-debt remarketing are discussed further in paragraph 10.51.)

10.29 Another way that an NFP may extinguish its debt is by issuing new debt whose proceeds are used to repay the previously-issued debt (a refunding transaction). If the new debt is held by the same creditor as the old debt, the refunding may be a modification of debt terms rather than an extinguishment, as discussed in paragraphs 6–12 of FASB ASC 470-50-40 (see paragraphs 10.39–.43). Current refunding, advance refunding, and crossover refunding are 3 types of refunding transactions. In a *current refunding*, the new debt proceeds may be used to repay the old debt within 90 days of the first call date or maturity of the debt to be refunded. In an *advance refunding*, the new debt proceeds are placed with an escrow agent and invested until they are used to pay principal and interest of the old debt at a future time. In an advance refunding, outstanding securities are refinanced more than 90 days prior to their call or maturity date.[5] In a *crossover refunding*, debt (referred to as crossover bonds) is issued for the purpose of paying off an existing debt issue (referred to as the refunded bonds). The crossover bonds are collateralized initially by an escrow of investments purchased with the crossover bond proceeds, and the refunded bonds continue to be secured by their original collateral or revenue stream. On a specified date, the investments held in escrow are sold and the refunded bonds are redeemed. Then, the crossover bonds become collateralized by the original collateral or payable from the original revenue stream. In refunding transactions, the entity must either call the bonds (if allowed) to redeem them early, or must irrevocably set aside the funds to pay them off (in a defeasance). These situations are discussed in the following paragraphs.

Calls and Mode Conversions

10.30 Some bond contracts allow an NFP to repay the bonds prior to their scheduled maturity date, which is referred to as a call option. Typically, new bonds are issued to pay off the outstanding bonds (a refunding).

10.31 Some bonds are structured as multimodal, which permits the NFP to exercise an interest mode conversion. A multimodal feature provides the NFP with a contractual right to change the interest feature of the bond from one form to another (for example, an auction-based interest rate to a fixed-rate or index-based variable interest rate). In most cases, a mode conversion involves a call (referred to as a mandatory tender) of the old bonds and marketing of new bonds to new investors as well as existing bondholders. Thus, the mode conversion is similar to a traditional refunding, and the same accounting considerations apply to mode conversions regarding refunding.

Defeasance

10.32 If the NFP would like to retire the debt early but does not have a call option, *defeasance* is a financing tool that allows it to obtain some or all of the benefits of repaying bondholders prior to actually retiring the debt. In a defeasance, the NFP purchases government securities for deposit into an escrow account, and irrevocably pledges the securities to the payment of the outstanding debt. The securities and their related earnings are sufficient to pay the principal and interest on the debt when it comes due. (In essence, the NFP is substituting collateral on the debt.) Often, some or all of the funds deposited into the escrow arise from an advance refunding. Generally, the revenues originally pledged as security on the outstanding securities switch over to become security for payment of the refunding debt (the new issue) on the date the advance refunding debt is issued.

10.33 Defeasances are categorized as legal or in-substance (sometimes referred to as an economic defeasance). When a defeasance occurs, the debtor has not paid the creditor, therefore, in accordance with FASB ASC 405-20-40-1(b), the liability is considered extinguished only if the debtor is legally released from being the primary obligor under the liability, either judicially or by the creditor. As described in FASB ASC 405-20-55-9, in a legal defeasance, generally the creditor legally releases the debtor from being the primary obligor under the

---

[5] Per the Tax Reform Act of 1986, new money bonds issued prior to January 1, 1986, can be advance refunded twice, whereas bonds issued on or after that date can only be advance refunded once.

liability; however, whether the debtor has in fact been released and the condition in FASB ASC 405-20-40-1(b) is satisfied is a matter of law. Conversely, in an in-substance defeasance, the debtor is not released from the debt by putting assets in the trust. For the reasons identified in FASB ASC 405-20-55-4, an in-substance defeasance is different from a legal defeasance and the liability is not extinguished.

10.34 The terms of some debt contracts allow for legal defeasance, which is the termination of the rights and interests of the debtholders and of their lien on the pledged revenues or other security. When the conditions specified in the debt contract for legal defeasance are met, the NFP's obligation for repayment of the debt is satisfied in full and the debt is extinguished, provided that the debtor is legally released from being the primary obligor under the liability, as discussed in FASB ASC 405-20-40-1(b). A legal opinion may be required.

10.35 In other situations, referred to as an in-substance defeasance, establishing a defeasance escrow makes the revenues pledged as collateral available for other purposes without actually affecting a legal defeasance. This might be used if, for example, the debt contract does not provide a procedure for termination of the debtholders' rights and interests other than through redemption of the debt. In an in-substance defeasance, if for some reason the escrowed funds prove insufficient to make future payments on the old debt, the NFP must make up the difference (that is, the NFP is still legally obligated to make payment on such debt).

10.36 FASB ASC 405-20-55 provides implementation guidance on extinguishment of liabilities, including in-substance and legal defeasances.

10.37 Paragraphs 4–6 of FASB ASC 860-10-40 provide standards for determining whether financial assets should be derecognized.

10.38 Derecognition of the assets in the defeasance trust may need to be separately evaluated even if the defeased debt has met the criteria for derecognition. Because the obligor must surrender control over the assets transferred to the trust, and the transferred assets must be legally isolated from the obligor (for example, presumptively put beyond the reach of the obligor and its creditors even in bankruptcy or other receivership), if the obligor has any type of continuing involvement with the transferred assets (for example, if the obligor has the ability to direct the investment of trust assets or is entitled to residual assets upon termination of the trust), a separate legal isolation opinion may be required in order to conclude that the conditions for derecognition have been met.

Bond Modifications and Exchanges

10.39 When one debt instrument is replaced with another (such as occurs in refundings or interest mode conversions), and the new debt instrument is held by the same creditor(s) as the old, questions may arise regarding whether the transaction is considered a debt modification or a debt extinguishment.

10.40 For a conduit bond offering involving a governmental financing agency, an NFP should determine whether the financing agency is acting as a principal or as an agent of the obligor in order to determine whether the transaction is an extinguishment or a modification. Paragraphs 19–20 of FASB ASC 470-50-40 discuss these considerations.

10.41 Paragraphs 6–12 of FASB ASC 470-50-40 provide guidance for determining whether a replacement of one debt instrument with another is a modification of the original debt terms or the extinguishment of one obligation and the issuance of another. FASB ASC 470-50-40-6 states that an exchange of debt instruments with substantially different terms is a debt extinguishment and should be accounted for in accordance with FASB ASC 405-20-40-1 (by derecognizing the liability). FASB ASC 470-50-40-10 states that from the debtor's perspective, an exchange of debt instruments between a debtor and a creditor in a nontroubled debt situation is deemed to have been accomplished with debt instruments that are substantially different if the present value of the cash flows under the terms of the new debt instrument is at least 10 percent different from the present value of the remaining cash flows under the terms of the original instrument. However, if the debt modification is considered a troubled debt restructuring, the guidance in FASB ASC 470-60 would apply.

10.42 When applying the guidance in paragraphs 9–12 of FASB ASC 470-50-40 and evaluating whether a modification or an exchange has occurred between the same debtor and creditor with a municipal bond issuance, the debt instrument is the individual bond held by an investor, and the creditor is the bondholder. Thus, the unit of account is not for the bond issue in total, but on a bondholder-by-bondholder basis. In certain cases, if the bonds are widely held, it may be appropriate to conclude that the issuance of new bonds to pay off old bonds is not a refinancing of debt with the same creditors and thus is an extinguishment, rather than a modification. If the bonds are not widely held and the transaction is in essence a refinancing of debt with the same creditor(s), it is necessary to determine whether the difference between the present value of the remaining cash flows associated with the original obligation and the present value of the cash flows associated with the new obligation is less than 10 percent. If the difference is less than 10 percent, the transaction is a modification.

10.43 Paragraphs 19–20 of FASB ASC 470-50-40 and paragraphs 4–7 of FASB ASC 470-50-55 provide guidance and indicators to consider in making such a determination.

Gain or Loss on Debt Extinguishment

10.44 FASB ASC 470-50 addresses how a gain or loss on a debt extinguishment should be measured. It applies to all extinguishments of debt, whether early or not, except debt that is extinguished through a troubled debt restructuring (or convertible debt). Per FASB ASC 470-50-40-2, the difference between the reacquisition price and the net carrying amount of the extinguished debt should be recognized currently in income of the period of extinguishment as losses or gains and identified as a separate item. Gains and losses should not be amortized to future periods. Classification of the gain or loss is discussed in FASB ASC 470-50-45 (see paragraph 10.81).

10.45 The *reacquisition price* of debt is the amount paid on extinguishment, including a call premium and miscellaneous costs of reacquisition. If extinguishment is achieved by a direct exchange of new securities, the reacquisition price is the fair value of the new securities. The net carrying amount of the extinguished debt is the amount due at maturity, adjusted for unamortized premium, discount, and cost of issuance.

Debt Issuance Costs

10.46 Paragraphs 17–18 of FASB ASC 470-50-40 provide guidance for reporting costs incurred by the debtor in connection with an exchange or modification of debt instruments. The accounting treatment depends on whether the fees are paid to the creditor or to other third-parties. The following paragraph summarizes that guidance but is not a substitute for reading the referenced paragraphs.

10.47 If the exchange or modification is to be accounted for in the same manner as a debt extinguishment and the new debt instrument is initially recorded at fair value, then (*a*) the fees between the debtor and creditor should be associated with the extinguishment of the old debt instrument and are included in determining the debt extinguishment gain or loss to be recognized, and (*b*) the third-party costs directly related to the exchange or modification are amortized over the term of the new debt instrument using the interest method in a manner similar to debt issue costs. If the exchange or modification is not accounted for in the same manner as a debt extinguishment, then (*a*) the fees between the debtor and the creditor should be associated with the replacement or modified debt instrument and, along with any existing unamortized premium or discount, are amortized as an adjustment of interest expense over the remaining term of the replacement or modified debt instrument using the interest method, and (*b*) the third-party costs directly related to the exchange or modification are expensed as incurred.

10.48 As discussed in paragraphs 17–18 and 21 of FASB ASC 470-50-40, in the event of a mode conversion, modification, or extinguishment of debt, there may be effects on any related prepaid issuance costs or deferred issuance costs, such as impairment adjustments or revised amortization periods.

Puts/Tender Options

10.49 Some bond contracts allow the bonds to be repaid prior to their stated maturity at the option of the bondholder. The bondholder's right to request earlier payment is referred to as a tender option (or sometimes as a put option). An NFP applies paragraphs 26–27 and 40–43 of FASB ASC 815-15-25 to determine if the put options are embedded derivatives that must be accounted for separately from the debt host contract. Some NFPs utilize bank agreements such as letters of credit or standby bond purchase agreements (a liquidity facility) to provide liquidity for the put or tender feature so that the put bonds can be remarketed to another investor. Paragraphs 26–53 of FASB ASC 815-15-55 provide illustrations of several remarketable put bond structures.

10.50 If a bondholder exercises its put option, the NFP (through its remarketing agent) generally will seek to sell the put bonds to another investor. If another investor is found who accepts the same terms as the original bondholder, the transaction occurs between the bondholders and does not affect the accounting by the NFP.

10.51 If another investor cannot be found (that is, a failed remarketing), the NFP is required to pay the bondholder. If the NFP has a liquidity facility, then the liquidity provider generally advances the funds needed to pay the bondholder. At that point, ownership of the bonds transfers to the liquidity provider, and they become bank bonds. The interest rate payable on bank bonds converts to the rate stipulated in the liquidity facility agreement. Efforts continue to remarket the bank bonds for the period of time stipulated in the liquidity facility agreement. If another bondholder is found within that period, the proceeds generally are used to pay off the liquidity facility, the interest rate returns to the terms in the original bond agreement, and the bonds revert to their normal status, unless the NFP acquires its own bonds, as discussed in paragraph 10.27.

10.52 If another buyer cannot be found after a certain period, the liquidity facility generally ceases to be interest-only and converts to a term loan. The NFP repays the debt over a relatively short period of time, rather than over the original stated maturity of the bonds. In effect, the bank (the liquidity facility) exchanges the term loan for the bond, and the bond is derecognized because its terms are substantially different, as discussed in paragraphs 9–12 of FASB ASC 470-50-40, from those of the term loan.

10.53 In some cases, an NFP may forego using an external liquidity facility. If a failed remarketing occurs, the NFP pays the holder of the put bonds using its own cash and liquid investments ("self-liquidity"). In these situations, the bonds are considered extinguished when the failed remarketing occurs, regardless of whether the put bonds are retained by the NFP as treasury bonds or retired (paragraph 10.27).

IRS Considerations

10.54 As discussed in paragraph 10.13, interest paid to holders of tax-exempt bonds is often exempt from federal income taxes and sometimes from state or local taxes as well. In order to maintain the bonds' tax-exempt status, an NFP must comply with all applicable federal tax laws and Treasury regulations including (but not limited to) the use of bond-financed property and arbitrage requirements. The IRS encourages Section 501(c)(3) organizations to implement procedures that will enable them to adequately safeguard against postissuance violations that could result in loss of the tax-exempt status of the bonds. IRS Publication 4078, *Tax-Exempt Private Activity Bonds* (available for download at www.irs.gov), is a helpful source of information regarding the requirements. Other IRS information for the tax-exempt bond community is available at www.irs.gov/tax-exempt-bonds. Requirements related to arbitrage and the qualified use of proceeds are briefly summarized in the following paragraphs.

10.55 Tax-exempt bonds bear interest at lower rates than taxable bonds due to the inherent federal tax subsidy. Safeguards exist so that entities do not attempt to benefit inappropriately from this subsidy by issuing tax-exempt bonds and then investing the proceeds to earn *arbitrage* (the difference between the interest earned on the invested funds and the interest rate the NFP must pay to the bondholders). Specific IRS requirements control arbitrage, dictating which bond issues are subject to rebate (that is, remitting excess earnings to the federal government) and when the yield on investments must be restricted. Certain exceptions apply to these provisions based on the nature and timing of the expenditures paid by the bond proceeds.

10.56 FASB ASC 954-470-25-2, which applies to health care entities but is equally relevant to NFPs, states that IRS regulations concerning tax-exempt bonds prohibit the yield realized from the investment of the proceeds of tax-exempt bonds from exceeding the interest rate to be paid on such bonds. Whenever an NFP invests tax-exempt bond proceeds and the ultimate yield is higher than the interest rate on the bonds, the entity may be subject to an arbitrage rebate liability. The arbitrage determination is made as of the date of the issue;

however, intentional acts undertaken after the date of the issue can disqualify the issue retroactively. The earnings in excess of interest expense represent a liability that must be paid to the U.S. Treasury in order for the bonds to maintain their tax-exempt status. The arbitrage rebate liability may be a substantial amount if the bond proceeds are not spent as quickly as planned. For example, this may occur if a provider encounters a delay in a major construction project.

10.57 The type of project or projects that are funded by the bond proceeds affects the taxability of income received by the bondholders. Conduit bonds issued for projects that only benefit private parties (private activity bonds) normally are taxable. Conduit bonds issued to finance facilities owned and utilized by IRC Section 501(c)(3) nonprofit organizations are exempt from federal income tax if they are qualified Section 501(c)(3) bonds. To qualify for tax-exemption, at least 95 percent of the net bond proceeds must be used for exempt activities. Thus, no more than 5 percent of the net proceeds may be used in any private business use or by the NFP in an unrelated trade or business activity. Bond issuance costs are considered part of the 5 percent private use and reduce the net proceeds available for other types of private use. IRC Section 501(c)(3) borrowers must ensure that the IRS rules on private use are met both at the time that the bonds are issued and throughout the life of the bonds.

10.58 Treasury Regulations provide for certain remedial actions to cure uses of proceeds that would otherwise cause the qualified Section 501(c)(3) bonds to lose their exempt status. Those remedial actions can include redemption or defeasance of bonds, alternative qualified use of disposition proceeds, or alternative use of the bond-financed facilities. NFPs may also be eligible to enter into a closing agreement under the Tax Exempt Bonds Voluntary Closing Agreement Program (IRS Notice 2008-31).

Financial Statement Presentation and Disclosure

Statement of Financial Position

10.59 According to FASB ASC 958-470-25-1, if an NFP finances part of its activities using the proceeds of tax-exempt bonds or other obligations issued through state and local financing authorities and the NFP is responsible for the repayment of those obligations, that financing should be recognized as a liability in the NFP's statement of financial position.

10.60 FASB ASC 835-30-45-1A requires that a discount or premium be reported in the statement of financial position as a direct deduction from or addition to the face amount of the note. Similarly, debt issuance costs related to a note should be reported in the balance sheet as a direct deduction from the face amount of that note. The discount, premium, or debt issuance costs should not be classified as a deferred charge or deferred credit.

10.61 Although debt typically has a stated maturity of many years, careful consideration should be given to classification of the liability as current or noncurrent based on the features of the debt. Debt that appears to be long-term based on its legal maturity might not be considered long-term for financial reporting purposes because of subjective acceleration clauses or due on demand (put) provisions. Careful consideration of the debt agreements and related documents (for example, the indenture, loan and trust agreement, liquidity facility, and so on) may be required in order to make a determination whether debt is properly classified.

10.62 The principal guidance for evaluating the appropriate classification of debt obligations in the statement of financial position is found in FASB ASC 210-10-45, FASB ASC 470-10-45, and FASB ASC 470-10-55.

Classification of Debt With Due on Demand or Put Provisions, Including Remarketing Agreements and Auction-Rate Securities

10.63 FASB ASC 470-10-45-10 states that the current liability classification should include obligations that, by their terms, are due on demand or will be due on demand within one year (or operating cycle, if longer) from the balance sheet date, even though liquidation may not be expected within that period.

10.64 FASB ASC 470-10-55-8 states that debt agreements that allow a debt holder to redeem (or put) a debt instrument on demand (or within one year) should be classified as short-term liabilities despite the existence of a best-efforts remarketing agreement. That is, unless the issuer (the NFP) of the redeemable debt instrument has the ability and intent to refinance the debt on a long-term basis as provided for in FASB ASC 470-10-45-14, the debt should be classified as a current liability in a classified statement of financial position and in order of relative liquidity in an unclassified statement of financial position.

10.65 For example, some variable-rate bonds have a demand feature (a put or tender option) whereby the bondholder may require the NFP or its remarketing agent to repurchase the bonds, often on short notice. Demand obligations normally are classified as current liabilities despite the fact that the bond's stated maturities cover many years. However, such obligations often are supported by a liquidity facility (such as a standby bond purchase agreement or letter of credit from a financial institution) that provides the NFP with the ability to refinance, on a long-term basis, any obligation that may arise if tendered bonds cannot immediately be remarketed to another investor (see paragraphs 10.51–.53).

10.66 FASB ASC 470-10-45-14 requires that the intent to refinance a short-term obligation on a long-term basis be supported by an ability to consummate the refinancing that is demonstrated in either of the following ways: (*a*) post-balance-sheet-date issuance of a long-term obligation or equity securities, or (*b*) a financing agreement. If a financing agreement is used to justify noncurrent classification of the debt, FASB ASC 470-10-45-14(b) requires that before the statement of financial position is issued or is available to be issued, the entity must have entered into a financing agreement that clearly permits the entity to refinance the short-term obligation on a long-term basis on terms that are readily determinable, and all of the three conditions in FASB ASC 470-10-45-14(b) must be met.

10.67 In summary, those three conditions are the following:

1. The agreement does not expire within one year from the date of the entity's statement of financial position, and during that period the agreement is not cancelable by the lender except for violation of a provision with which compliance is objectively determinable or measurable. Further, any obligations incurred under the agreement are not callable during that period.
2. No violation of any provision in the financing agreement exists at the date of the entity's statement of financial position and no available information indicates that a violation has occurred

thereafter or, if a violation has occurred thereafter, a waiver has been obtained.

3. The lender is expected to be financially capable of honoring the agreement.

However, the conditions are very complex, and the preceding summary is not intended as a substitute for reading paragraphs 14–20 of FASB ASC 470-10-45.

10.68 If the liquidity facility (which is the financing agreement) contains a subjective acceleration clause, the liquidity facility does not meet the first condition in the previous paragraph because compliance with that clause is not objectively determinable or measureable. The NFP is not deemed to have the ability and intent to finance on a long-term basis and thus, cannot classify the debt as noncurrent, even if the repayment terms of the liquidity facility would otherwise support such classification. (See paragraph 10.70 for the definition of a *subjective acceleration clause*). The probability of the subjective acceleration clause being exercised is irrelevant when attempting to demonstrate the ability to refinance a short-term obligation on a long-term basis. See the related discussion in paragraph 10.71.

10.69 Rather than utilizing a liquidity facility issued by an external third party, some NFPs choose to utilize their own funds for satisfying puts or tenders. NFPs that do so have no basis for excluding those put and tender obligations from current liabilities, because there is no third party providing liquidity that would effectively allow the entity to refinance the debt on a long-term basis.

Classification of Long-Term Debt With a Subjective Acceleration Clause

10.70 The FASB ASC glossary defines a *subjective acceleration clause* as a provision in a debt agreement that states that the creditor may accelerate the scheduled maturities of the obligation under conditions that are not objectively determinable (for example, if the debtor fails to maintain satisfactory operations or if a material adverse change occurs). For long-term obligations, the effect of a subjective acceleration clause on classification in the statement of financial position is determined by FASB ASC 470-10-45-2. That paragraph states that in some situations, the circumstances (for example, recurring losses or liquidity problems) would indicate that long-term debt subject to a subjective acceleration clause should be classified as a current liability. Other situations would indicate only disclosure of the existence of such clauses. Neither reclassification nor disclosure would be required if the likelihood of the acceleration of the due date were remote, such as if the lender historically has not accelerated due dates of loans containing similar clauses and the financial condition of the borrower is strong and its prospects are bright.

10.71 In other words, a long-term obligation with a subjective acceleration clause could continue to be classified as noncurrent unless it was probable it would be called. For an obligation that by its terms is short term, FASB ASC 470-10-55-1 states that a higher standard is required for a financing agreement that permits an entity to refinance a short-term obligation on a long-term basis than is required for an existing long-term loan for which early repayment might be requested. As discussed in paragraph 10.68, if a financing agreement that permits an entity to refinance a short-term obligation on a long-term basis contains a subjective acceleration clause, the mere presence of that clause is enough to preclude long-term classification.

Classification of Long-Term Debt With a Covenant Violation

10.72 Violations of covenants could cause termination of the financing agreement or demand for immediate repayment. Thus, debt covenant violations can affect classification in the statement of financial position.

10.73 Paragraphs 11–12 of FASB ASC 470-10-45 discuss the classification of long-term obligations that (*a*) are callable by the creditor either because the debtor's violation of a provision of the debt agreement at the balance sheet date makes the obligation callable, or (*b*) may become callable because the violation, if not cured within a specified grace period, will make the obligation callable. Those paragraphs require that such callable obligations be classified as current liabilities unless either of the two conditions in FASB ASC 470-10-45-11 is met.

10.74 In summary, those two conditions are the following:

1. The creditor has waived or subsequently lost the right to demand repayment for more than one year from the date of the statement of financial position, or
2. The long-term obligation contains a grace period within which the debtor may cure the violation, and it is probable that the violation will be cured within that period.

However, the conditions are complex and the preceding summary is not a substitute for reading paragraphs 11–12 of FASB ASC 470-10-45.

10.75 If neither of those two conditions is met, the debt is classified as short term, regardless of the fact that the creditor has not demanded repayment and there is no indication that the creditor intends to do so within the next year. Further, no distinction between significant and insignificant violations should be drawn. That is the right of the creditor, and if the violation is considered insignificant by the creditor, the debtor should be able to obtain a waiver.

10.76 Paragraphs 2–6 of FASB ASC 470-10-55 provide examples of classification of long-term debt when a debt covenant violation at the balance sheet date is waived by a lender for a period greater than a year (sometimes referred to as an in-substance grace period), but the entity must meet the covenant on a quarterly or semiannual basis.

Cash and Cash Equivalents Restricted by Debt Agreements

10.77 Debt-financing instruments may require cash, investments, or both to be set aside in special accounts that can only be used for debt-related purposes, such as unexpended proceeds of debt issues and funds deposited with a trustee and limited to use in accordance with the requirements of a bond indenture or similar document (for example, sinking funds, debt reserve funds, or defeasance-related escrows). Such assets are usually reported in the statement of financial position as "cash and cash equivalents restricted by debt agreements" or "bond funds held by trustee" with a corresponding note disclosing the contractual restrictions. The portion of those assets that is required for liquidation of current liabilities is reported as current assets, with the remainder reported as noncurrent.

10.78 FASB ASC 860-30-50-1A requires disclosures if an entity pledges any of its assets as collateral. NFPs should disclose the carrying amount and classifications of both assets pledged as collateral (if those assets are not reclassified and separately reported in the statement of financial position) and associated liabilities. NFPs also should disclose qualitative information about the relationship(s) between collateral assets and associated liabilities. For example, if assets are restricted solely to satisfy a specific obligation, the nature of restrictions placed on the assets should be disclosed.

Subsequent Events

10.79 Events occurring subsequent to the date of the statement of financial position but before the financial statements are issued or available to be issued may need to be reflected in the financial statements, either by changing the classification of the debt or by disclosure. For example, debt restructuring transactions occurring after the date of the statement of financial position may have an effect on the debtor's current or noncurrent classifications as of that date, and extinguishing or modifying the terms of a debt issue may require disclosure. Chapter 3, "Financial Statements, Reporting Entity, and General Financial Reporting Matters," includes additional information about subsequent events, including a discussion of whether an NFP evaluates subsequent events through the issuance date of the financial statements or the available to be issued date.

Statement of Activities

10.80 If the proceeds of tax-exempt borrowings are externally restricted to the acquisition of specified qualifying assets or to service the related debt, the amount of interest cost capitalized should be determined in accordance with paragraphs 10–12 of FASB ASC 835-20-30. Those considerations are discussed in chapter 9, "Property and Equipment."

10.81 FASB ASC 835-30-45-3 requires that amortization of debt issuance costs be reported as interest expense. Pursuant to FASB ASC 470-50-40-2, gains or losses on extinguishment of debt should be recognized currently in income of the period of extinguishment and identified as a separate item.

Disclosures

10.82 General disclosure requirements for debt (such as description of the debt, collateral, interest rate, covenants, and guarantees) are set forth in FASB ASC 470-10-50. If debt was considered to be extinguished by in-substance defeasance under the provisions of FASB Statement No. 76, *Extinguishment of Debt*, before the effective date of FASB Statement No. 125, *Accounting for Transfers and Servicing of Financial Assets and Extinguishments of Liabilities* (that is, before December 31, 1996), FASB ASC 470-50-50-1 requires disclosure of the amount of the debt and a description of the transaction as long as the debt remains outstanding. FASB ASC 860-30-50-2 provides disclosure requirements for assets that are set aside solely for the purpose of satisfying scheduled payments of a specific obligation.

10.83 If short-term obligations are classified in the statement of financial position as a long-term liability because the NFP has the ability and intent to refinance the debt on a long-term basis (see paragraph 10.66), those obligations need to be included in the disclosure of the combined aggregate amount of maturities and sinking fund requirements for all long-term borrowings that is required by FASB ASC 470-10-50-1. In those situations, the NFP must ensure that disclosure is made of both the debt repayment schedule of the liquidity facility and the stated maturity of the debt. This can be done by either (*a*) by providing two tabular schedules (one for the liquidity facility payment schedule and the other based on the stated maturity of the debt), or (*b*) including one repayment schedule in the table and providing narrative disclosure related to the other.

10.84 As discussed in paragraphs 10.18–.20, additional disclosures are required for entities defined as public entities. Generally, *public entities* are those that have debt or equity securities that trade in public markets. Because FASB ASC has multiple definitions for the term *public entity,* careful attention should be paid to such disclosure requirements to determine if their scope includes conduit bond obligors whose bonds trade in public markets.

10.85 FASB ASC 855-10-55-2 cites the sale of a bond after the balance sheet date but before financial statements are issued or are available to be issued as an example of an event that requires disclosure in the notes to the financial statements.

10.86 Other events occurring after the balance sheet date, such as failed auctions, potential or actual cancellation of a liquidity facility, defaults, or a mandatory tender of bonds, may also need to be disclosed in the financial statements as subsequent events.

Annual Filing Requirements

10.87 Some debt agreements require audited financial statements to be provided to the creditor, underwriters, and bond repositories on an annual ongoing basis. Some NFPs are required to annually submit audited financial statements to the Municipal Securities Rulemaking Board's (MSRB's) Electronic Municipal Market Access (EMMA) system, which is a system for disseminating the information to investors in municipal securities and other interested parties (see appendix A and appendix B, "Auditor Involvement With Municipal Securities Filings," of this chapter).

Tax Liabilities

10.88 Chapter 15, "Tax and Regulatory Considerations," discusses tax issues concerning NFPs, including recognition and measurement guidance for deferred tax assets and liabilities and tax positions taken or expected to be taken in a tax return.

Deferred Revenue

10.89 Resources received in exchange transactions from customers, patients, and other service beneficiaries for specific projects, programs, or activities that have not yet taken place should be recognized as liabilities to the extent that the earnings process has not been completed. For example, resources received from the advance sale of season theater tickets should be recognized as deferred revenue, representing the obligation to hold the performances. That revenue is earned as the theater performances are held. Paragraphs 5.119–.122 discuss ticket sales of special events that are scheduled to take place after the financial statement date.

Refunds Due to and Advances From Third Parties

10.90 Some NFPs receive (*a*) advances from third parties, such as government agencies, based on the estimated cost of providing services to constituents, (*b*) advances from donors with a conditional promise to contribute the transferred assets, and (*c*) resources from third parties to be used to make loans to the NFP's constituents. Advances from third parties for services not yet performed, as well as refunds due to third parties for amounts previously received under such agreements, should be included as liabilities on a statement of financial position.

Promises to Give

10.91 The FASB ASC glossary defines a *promise to give* as "a written or oral agreement to contribute cash or other assets to another entity. A promise carries rights and obligations—the recipient of a promise to give has a right to expect that the promised assets will be transferred in the future, and the maker has a social and moral obligation, and generally a legal obligation, to make the promised transfer. A promise to give may be either conditional or unconditional." Per FASB ASC 958-605-25-11, conditional promises to give should not be recognized until the conditions are substantially met.[6] FASB ASC 720-25-25 requires contributions made to be recognized as expenses in the period made and as decreases of assets or increases of liabilities depending on the form of the benefits given. In accordance with FASB ASC 958-720-25-2, unconditional promises to give should be recognized at the time the donor has an obligation to transfer the promised assets in the future, which generally occurs when the donor approves a specific grant or when the recipient of the promise is notified. If a donor explicitly reserves the right to rescind an intention to contribute, or if a solicitation explicitly allows a donor to rescind the intention, a promise to give should not be recognized by the donor. If payments of the unconditional promise to give are to be made to a recipient over several fiscal periods and the recipient is subject only to routine performance requirements, a liability and an expense for the entire amount payable should be recognized. FASB ASC 958-720-30-1 requires that the liability and expense be measured initially at fair value. Paragraphs 10.02–.08 discuss fair value measurement of liabilities, and paragraphs 3.151–.154 of this guide discuss present value techniques for measuring fair value. Appendix A to chapter 5, "Contributions Received and Agency Transactions," of this guide includes excerpts from the AICPA Financial Reporting white paper *Measurement of Fair Value for Certain Transactions of Not-for-Profit Entities*, which discusses fair value measurement of unconditional promises to give cash. Although that white paper is for measurement by an NFP receiving a promise to give, much of its discussion is useful to measurement by an NFP making a promise to give. Unconditional promises to give that are expected to be paid in less than one year may be measured at net settlement value.

10.92 Per FASB ASC 958-720-25-3, if an NFP makes contributions or awards grants to other NFPs upon specific requests of others, the NFP may be acting as an agent, trustee, or intermediary in a transfer between the donor and the beneficiary specified by the donor (agency transaction). The terms *agent*, *trustee*, and *intermediary* are defined in the FASB ASC glossary. Paragraph 10.97 describes liabilities for amounts held for others in agency transactions. Paragraphs 5.07–.32 provide further guidance about agency transactions.

---

[6] Chapter 5, "Contributions Received and Agency Transactions," provides additional guidance for recognizing conditional promises to give.

10.93 Per FASB ASC 958-405-35-1, if the present value of the amounts to be paid is used to measure fair value[7] of an unconditional promise to give, the discount rate should be determined at the time the unconditional promise to give is initially recognized and should not be revised, unless the promise to give is subsequently remeasured at fair value pursuant to the "Fair Value Option" subsections of FASB ASC 825-10. The interest method, described in FASB ASC 835-30-35-2, should be used to amortize discounts. Per FASB ASC 958-405-45-1, the amortization of any discount related to unconditional promises to give should be reported as a component of contribution expense, in the same functional expense classification in which the promise to give was reported.

10.94 If contributions payable are measured using present value techniques and the NFP has not elected to measure the payable at fair value as described in paragraph 10.02, methods of amortization other than the interest method may be used if the results are not materially different. The discount should be amortized between the date the promise to give is initially recognized and the date the cash or other contributed assets are paid.

10.95 In addition to disclosures required by FASB ASC 450-20-50, FASB ASC 958-405-50 requires that the notes to financial statements include a schedule of unconditional promises to give that shows the total amount separated into amounts payable in each of the next five years, the aggregate amount due in more than five years, and for unconditional promises to give that are reported using present value techniques, the unamortized discount.

Split-Interest Obligations

10.96 Some contributions received by NFPs, such as interests in charitable gift annuity contracts and charitable remainder and lead trusts, impose obligations on the NFP to make future payments to others. Guidance for reporting such contributions, often referred to as split-interest agreements, is included in chapter 6, "Split-Interest Agreements and Beneficial Interests in Trusts." Obligations arising from split-interest gifts should be recognized as liabilities. Paragraphs 6.32–.40 discuss periodic revaluations of the obligations under split-interest agreements, including whether the discount rate assumptions should be revised at each measurement date to reflect current market conditions. Periodic revaluations of these obligations result in changes in the value of split-interest agreements, which should be included as changes in the appropriate net asset classes in a statement of activities.

Amounts Held for Others Under Agency Transactions

10.97 Some NFPs receive assets in agency transactions. Paragraphs 23–24 of FASB ASC 958-605-25 discuss recognition of resources received by intermediaries and agents in agency transactions. If cash and other financial assets are held under agency transactions, the NFP should report a liability to the specified beneficiary concurrently with its recognition of those assets received from the donor. If the assets received from the donor are donated materials, supplies, or other nonfinancial assets, the intermediary or recipient entity may

---

[7] Paragraphs 3.138–.168 discuss FASB ASC 820, *Fair Value Measurement*, which defines *fair value* and establishes a framework for measuring fair value. Paragraphs 4–20 of FASB ASC 820-10-55 provide standards for using present value techniques when the measurement objective is fair value.

choose either to (*a*) report the receipt of the asset as a liability to the beneficiary concurrent with recognition of the assets received or (*b*) not to report the transaction at all. The choice is an accounting policy that should be applied consistently from period to period. FASB ASC 958-605-50-4 states that an intermediary or other recipient entity should disclose its accounting policy for recognizing nonfinancial assets that it accepts from a donor on behalf of a specified beneficiary. Paragraphs 5.07–.32 discuss agency transactions in more detail.

Revenue Sharing and Other Agreements

10.98 FASB ASC 958-810-25-7 notes that some NFPs enter into agreements with other entities, such as sharing revenue, resulting in liabilities to those other entities. In such circumstances, those liabilities should be reported. If NFPs agree to share revenue from fund-raising campaigns, the appropriate accounting depends on the relationship between the NFPs. FASB ASC 958-20 discusses agreements for which an NFP agrees to raise or hold contributions for a financially interrelated entity (see paragraph 5.28). FASB ASC 958-605-25-24 discusses agreements in which an NFP agrees to raise or hold contributions for another NFP as its agent (see paragraph 10.97).

Exit or Disposal Activities

10.99 FASB ASC 420, *Exit or Disposal Cost Obligations*, provides financial accounting and reporting standards for costs associated with exit or disposal activities, including restructurings. Per FASB ASC 420-10-15-4, an exit activity includes, but is not limited to, a restructuring, such as the sale or termination of a line of business, the closure of business activities in a particular location, the relocation of business activities from one location to another, changes in management structure, or a fundamental reorganization that affects the nature and focus of operations. FASB ASC 420 discusses recognition of liabilities for the costs of exit activities, including one-time termination benefits provided to current employees that are involuntarily terminated, costs to terminate a contract that is not a capital lease, costs to consolidate facilities or relocate employees, costs associated with a disposal activity covered by FASB ASC 205-20, and costs associated with an exit activity, including exit activities associated with an entity newly acquired in a merger or acquisition. FASB ASC 360-10 and FASB ASC 410-20 and paragraphs 9.25–.29 discusses exit and disposal obligations associated with the retirement (sale, abandonment, recycling, disposal, or other other-than-temporary idling) of tangible long-lived assets and the associated asset retirement costs.

Guarantees

10.100 An NFP that issues certain guarantees, including guarantees of the debt of others, should recognize a liability for those guarantees, even in circumstances in which it is not probable that payments will be required under the guarantee. Guarantees are not conditional promises to give because the guarantor has given something of value. For example, a community foundation may guarantee the debt of a local arts organization without charging a premium. The fact that the arts organization is able to obtain financing not otherwise available, or to be charged a lower interest rate on its borrowing as a result of the guarantee, is evidence that something of value has been given to the arts organization at the inception of the guarantee. When the community foundation enters into the guarantee agreement, it assumes a noncontingent obligation to stand ready to make payments in the event that the arts organization fails to pay.

10.101 FASB ASC 460, *Guarantees*, establishes the accounting and disclosure requirements to be met by a guarantor for certain guarantees issued and outstanding. FASB ASC 460-10-25-4 requires that at the inception of a guarantee, a guarantor should recognize in its statement of financial position a liability for that guarantee. Per paragraphs 2–3 of FASB ASC 460-10-30, if a guarantee is issued as a contribution to an unrelated party, the liability recognized at the inception of the guarantee should be measured at its fair value unless at the inception of the guarantee, the contingent liability amount required to be recognized at inception of the guarantee by FASB ASC 450-20-30 is greater. If a guarantee is issued in a standalone arm's-length transaction with an unrelated party, the liability recognized at the inception of the guarantee may be the premium received or receivable by the guarantor as a practical expedient. Per FASB ASC 460-10-35-1, the liability that the guarantor initially recognized would typically be reduced as the guarantor is released from risk under the guarantee. Disclosures about guarantees are required by FASB ASC 460-10-50.

Contingencies

10.102 In conformity with FASB ASC 450-20, notes to the financial statements may have to include information about, or a liability may have to be accrued for, loss contingencies. FASB ASC 958-450-25-1 provides the following examples of circumstances that may result in such contingencies:

- Noncompliance with donor-imposed restrictions on contributed assets
- A problem with the NFP's tax-exempt status, or that a determination letter regarding that status has not been received (Paragraphs 15.06–.07 further discuss considerations related to loss of tax-exempt status. Paragraphs 15.39–.43 discuss tax positions, including the position that an entity is tax-exempt.)

Pension and Other Defined Benefit Postretirement Plan Obligations

Single-Employer Plans

10.103 An NFP that sponsors a single-employer defined benefit pension or postretirement plan should recognize the overfunded or underfunded status of that plan in its statement of financial position. The NFP should also recognize changes in that funded status in the year in which the changes occur as changes in unrestricted net assets. The underfunded status of a plan is a liability, and the overfunded status of a plan is an asset.

An NFP that sponsors a single-employer defined benefit pension or postretirement plan should recognize the overfunded or underfunded status of that plan in its statement of financial position. The NFP should also recognize changes in that funded status in the year in which the changes occur as changes in net assets without donor restrictions. The underfunded status of a plan is a liability, and the overfunded status of a plan is an asset.[8]

10.104 For a single-employer defined benefit pension plan, FASB ASC 715-30-25-1 states that if the projected benefit obligation exceeds the fair value of plan assets, the employer should recognize in its statement of financial position a liability that equals the unfunded projected benefit obligation. If the fair value of plan assets exceeds the projected benefit obligation, the employer should recognize in its statement of financial position an asset that equals the overfunded projected benefit obligation. Per FASB ASC 715-30-35-62, the measurements of plan assets and benefit obligations required should be as of the date of the employer's fiscal year-end statement of financial position, with limited exceptions.

10.105 For single-employer defined benefit postretirement plans other than pensions, FASB ASC 715-60-25-1 and FASB ASC 715-60-35-6 state that an employer that sponsors 1 or more plans should recognize in its statement of financial position the funded statuses of those plans, and should measure the funded status for each plan as the difference between the fair value of plan assets and the accumulated postretirement benefit obligation. Per FASB ASC 715-60-35-121, the measurements of plan assets and benefit obligations should be as of the date of the employer's fiscal year-end statement of financial position, with limited exceptions.

Multiemployer Plans[9]

10.106 Some NFPs participate in multiemployer pension plans. The following are characteristics of a multiemployer plan:

- The assets contributed by one employer may be used to provide benefits to employees of other participating employers because they are not specifically earmarked only for its employees.
- If a participating employer fails to make its required contributions, the unfunded obligations of the plan may be borne by the remaining participating employers.
- If an employer chooses to stop participating in a multiemployer plan, the withdrawing company may be required to pay to the plan a final payment (the withdrawal liability).

10.107 Paragraphs 62–64 of FASB ASC 715-30-55 describe a multiemployer defined benefit pension plan sponsored by a national NFP, which covers employees at the national level and all local chapters. In that example, each

---

[8] The amendments in FASB Accounting Standards Update No. 2016-14, *Not-for-Profit Entities (Topic 958): Presentation of Financial Statements of Not-for-Profit Entities*, are effective for annual financial statements issued for fiscal years beginning after December 15, 2017 (for example, years ending December 31, 2018, and years ending June 30, 2019), and for interim periods within fiscal years beginning after December 15, 2018. Application to interim financial statements is permitted but not required in the initial year of application. Early application of the amendments is permitted.

[9] Some defined benefit plans to which two or more unrelated employers contribute are not multiemployer plans. Rather, they are in-substance aggregations of single-employer plans designed to allow participating employers to pool their assets for investment purposes and to reduce the costs of plan administration. Those multiple-employer plans ordinarily do not involve collective-bargaining agreements. They may also have features that allow participating employers to have different benefit formulas, with the employer's contributions to the plan based on the benefit formula selected by the employer. FASB ASC 715, *Compensation—Retirement Benefits*, requires such plans to be considered single-employer plans rather than multiemployer plans, and each employer's accounting should be based on its respective interest in the plan.

chapter is required to contribute to the pension plan based on a predetermined formula, plan assets are not segregated or restricted on a chapter-by-chapter basis, and if a chapter withdraws from the pension plan, the pension obligations for its employees are retained by the pension plan as opposed to being allocated to the withdrawing chapter. The national NFP should account for the plan as a single-employer pension plan in its financial statements. In each chapter's separate financial statements (if issued) the arrangement should be accounted for as a multiemployer pension plan. A chapter's contribution for the period is its net periodic pension cost. A chapter would recognize a liability for any contributions due and unpaid. Instead of the disclosures required by FASB ASC 715-80-50, each chapter should disclose the name of the plan in which it participates and the amount of contributions it made in each annual period for which statement of activities is presented, as well as any related-party disclosures required by FASB ASC 850-10.

10.108 FASB ASC 715-80-35 states that the provisions of FASB ASC 450 apply if withdrawal from a multiemployer plan may result in an employer having an obligation to the plan for a portion of the unfunded benefit obligation of the pension or other postretirement benefit plans and that obligation is either probable or reasonably possible.

10.109 FASB ASC 715-80-50 requires disclosures to help users of financial statements assess the potential future cash flow implications relating to an employer's participation in multiemployer pension plans. The disclosures also indicate the financial health of all of the significant plans in which the employer participates and assist a financial statement user in locating additional information that is available outside the financial statements. The disclosures of the employer's contributions made to the plan include all items recognized as net pension costs (see FASB ASC 715-80-35-1). The disclosures based on the most recently available information should include information available through the date at which the employer has evaluated subsequent events.

10.110 If an NFP participates in a multiemployer plan that provides postretirement benefits other than pensions, disclosures are required for each annual period for which a statement of activities is presented. The disclosures should include a description of the nature of the benefits and the types of employees covered by these benefits, as well as a description of the nature and effect of any changes that affect comparability of total employer contributions from period to period. Examples of events that affect comparability are provided in FASB ASC 715-80-50-11.

Auditing

General

10.111 Many audit objectives and auditing procedures, including consideration of controls, related to debt and other liabilities of NFPs are similar to those of other entities. In addition, the auditor may need to consider the specific audit objectives, auditing procedures, and selected controls listed in the following table, which are unique to NFPs.

10.112 The following table illustrates the use of assertions in developing audit objectives and designing substantive tests. The examples are not intended to be all-inclusive nor is it expected that all the procedures would necessarily be applied in an audit. The use of assertions in assessing risks and designing appropriate audit procedures to obtain audit evidence is described in paragraphs .26–.32 of AU-C section 315, *Understanding the Entity and Its Environment and Assessing the Risks of Material Misstatement*.[10] Paragraph .18 of AU-C section 330, *Performing Audit Procedures in Response to Assessed Risks and Evaluating the Audit Evidence Obtained*, requires the auditor to design and perform substantive procedures for all relevant assertions related to each material class of transactions, account balance, and disclosure, irrespective of the assessed risks of material misstatement. This requirement reflects the facts that (1) the auditor's assessment of risk is judgmental and may not identify all risks of material misstatement, and (2) inherent limitations to internal control exist, including management override. Various audit procedures and the purposes for which they may be performed are described in paragraphs .A10–.A26 of AU-C section 500, *Audit Evidence*.

Auditing Considerations

Financial Statement Assertions	*Specific Audit Objectives*	*Select Control Objectives*
Transactions		
Contributions Made		
Occurrence	Amounts recognized as contributions made are properly authorized and are reported in the period in which they become unconditional.	Controls ensure that only unconditional contributions made and promises to give are recognized in the financial statements.
Completeness	All unconditional contributions made are recognized.	Controls ensure that all unconditional contributions made are recognized in the financial statements.
Accuracy/ Valuation and allocation	Contributions made are measured at fair value at initial recognition.	Controls ensure the appropriate valuation of contributions made, including promises to give, at the time of initial recognition.
Account Balances		
Debt		
Completeness/ Accuracy	Amounts related to arbitrage on unexpended tax-exempt debt offerings are recognized in the financial statements. Amounts related to conduit debt obligations are recognized in the financial statements.	Controls ensure that the earnings yield on unexpended tax-exempt debt offerings is compared to the interest rate paid on the debt and any excess amount is recorded as a potential liability. Controls ensure that all conduit debt obligations have been recognized.

(continued)

[10] All AU-C sections can be found in AICPA *Professional Standards*.

Financial Statement Assertions	*Specific Audit Objectives*	*Select Control Objectives*
Contributions Payable (Promises to Give)		
Occurrence	Amounts recognized as contributions payable represent valid unconditional promises to give.	Controls ensure that only unconditional promises to give are recognized in the financial statements.
Completeness	All unconditional promises to give are recognized.	Controls ensure that all unconditional promises to give are recognized in the financial statements. Controls ensure that the conditions on which conditional promises to give depend are monitored to determine whether they have been substantially met.
Cut-off	All unconditional promises to give are recognized in the proper period.	Controls ensure that contributions made near fiscal period end are recorded in the appropriate period.
Accuracy/ Valuation and allocation	Contributions payable beyond one year are measured using the method elected by the not-for-profit entity (NFP).	Controls ensure the appropriate valuation of contributions payable at the end of the fiscal period.
Presentation and Disclosure		
Debt		
Completeness	All disclosures related to debt, including conduit debt obligations, and letters of credit have been included.	Management monitors compliance with debt covenants and is aware of possible events of default. Controls ensure that all conduit debt obligations and lines of credit have been disclosed.

10.113 Suggested audit procedures to consider for these assertions include the following:

- Contributions made
  - Examine documentation supporting recognition of contributions made including notification of donee and whether the contribution is conditional or unconditional. (Occurrence)
  - Review minutes of governing board and governing board committee meetings for information about contributions. (Completeness)
  - Review and test the method used for valuing contributions made, including promises to give. (Accuracy/ Valuation and Allocation)

- Debt, including letters of credit
  - — Review the entity's calculation of the arbitrage liability related to excess yield earned on tax-exempt borrowings. (Completeness/Accuracy)
  - — Inquire about the existence of any conduit debt obligations that may need to be recognized in the statement of financial position and disclosed in the notes to the financial statements. (Completeness/Accuracy)
- Unconditional promises to give made (contributions payable)
  - — Examine documentation supporting recognition of contributions payable, including information such as the absence of conditions and the periods over which the promises to give become due. (Occurrence)
  - — Review minutes of governing board and governing board committee meetings for information about promises to give. (Chapter 5 provides guidance on distinguishing between contributions and exchange transactions.) (Completeness)
  - — Review cash disbursements subsequent to year-end to ascertain that contributions made were recorded in the proper period. (Cut-off)
  - — Review and test the method and assumptions used for valuing promises to give payable more than one year from the date of the financial statements. (Accuracy/Valuation and Allocation)

Debt

Subsequent Events

10.114 Q&A section 8700.03, "Auditor's Responsibilities for Subsequent Events Relative to a Conduit Debt Obligor," provides guidance when an NFP is a conduit debt obligor with conduit debt securities that trade in a public market. Management is required to evaluate subsequent events through the date the financial statements are first widely distributed (that is, issued). The auditor, using his or her professional judgment, needs to evaluate management's assertion about the financial statement issuance date and decide whether the manner in which the NFP has made its financial statements available does or does not constitute issuance for purposes of complying with GAAP and completing the auditor's subsequent event procedures. The auditor is required, in accordance with AU-C section 560, *Subsequent Events and Subsequently Discovered Facts*, to perform subsequent event procedures so that they cover the period from the date of the financial statements to the date of the auditor's report or as near as practicable thereto. As discussed more fully in Q&A section 8700.02, "Auditor Responsibilities for Subsequent Events," (in most cases, this will be the same date that management discloses as the date through which they have evaluated subsequent events. In accordance with AU-C section 560, the auditor is not required to perform any audit procedures regarding the financial statements after the date of the auditor's report, unless facts become known to the auditor after the date of the auditor's report that, had they been known to the auditor at that date, may have caused the auditor to revise the auditor's report (that is, a subsequently discovered fact).

Offering Statements and Continuing Disclosures

10.115 Appendix B to this chapter discusses auditor involvement with municipal securities filings. Although an NFP should be concerned with all compliance requirements for filings, for an audit of financial statements, generally accepted auditing standards focus the auditor's concern on those compliance requirements that could have a direct and material effect on the determination of financial statement amounts.

10.116

Appendix A—Municipal Securities Regulation

A-1 Currently, municipal securities are exempt from all of the provisions of the Securities Act of 1933 (1933 Act) and the Securities Exchange Act of 1934 (1934 Act) except the antifraud provisions of Section 17(a) of the 1933 Act and Section 10(b) of the 1934 Act (and the associated Rule 10b-5). Those antifraud provisions prohibit any person from misrepresenting or omitting material facts in the offering or sale of securities. Instances of application of the antifraud provisions in SEC enforcement actions offer guidance within the context of actual transactions.

A-2 The SEC published its views with respect to the disclosure obligations of participants in the municipal securities markets under the antifraud provisions of the federal securities laws in its 1994 Interpretive Release, "Statement of the Commission Regarding Disclosure Obligations of Municipal Securities Issuers and Others."[1] In it, the SEC reviews numerous municipal disclosure practices needing improvement in light of the antifraud provisions.

A-3 SEC Rule 15c2-12 and associated SEC releases impose certain requirements on the underwriters of municipal securities.[2] Because of Rule 15c2-12, obligors of most municipal securities offerings over set dollar amounts must provide certain disclosure documents when issuing securities (primary market disclosures) as well as at certain times thereafter (referred to as continuing disclosures or secondary market disclosures). Primary market disclosures are made by issuing an official statement. Secondary market disclosures consist of (*a*) annual continuing disclosures as contractually established and (*b*) material events notices. Both primary and secondary market disclosure documents are available through the nationally-recognized municipal securities information repository (the Electronic Municipal Market Access system, or EMMA) and to state information depositories, if one exists in the obligor's state.

SEC's Office of Municipal Securities

A-4 The Office of Municipal Securities (OMS), which is located in the Division of Trading and Markets, coordinates the SEC's municipal securities activities, advises the SEC on policy matters relating to the municipal bond market, and provides technical assistance in the development and implementation of major SEC initiatives in the municipal securities area. In addition, OMS assists the Division of Enforcement and other SEC offices and divisions on a wide array municipal securities matters. OMS works closely with the municipal securities industry to educate state and local officials and conduit borrowers about risk management issues and foster a thorough understanding of the SEC's policies. OMS maintains a website of helpful information specifically directed to municipal securities issues and conduit obligors (www.sec.gov/info/municipal.shtml).

Secondary Market Disclosure Requirements

A-5 In 1994, the SEC issued rules requiring, as a condition of issuance of debt securities, that the obligor agree to implement a system of continuing disclosure that remains in effect as long as the bonds are outstanding. The core of this system is the continuing disclosure agreement (sometimes referred to as

---

[1] Securities Act Release No. 33-7049, 59 FR 12748.

[2] For the adopting release, see www.sec.gov/rules/final/adpt6.txt.

a "15c2-12 contract" or "15c2-12 agreement"). This is a covenant entered into by the obligor in which the obligor agrees to provide certain specified information to bondholders and beneficial owners throughout the life of the bond issue. The terms of the obligor's continuing disclosure agreement are spelled out in the indenture or bond resolution, and also are summarized in the official statement.

A-6 The system is much less prescriptive than the system of periodic reporting required of publicly traded companies. The primary elements are (1) annual reporting of financial and operating information, and (2) material events reporting. Quarterly reporting is encouraged but not required (unless agreed to in the continuing disclosure covenant for a particular issue).

A-7 There is no prescribed reporting format (similar to the 10-K) for submission of the annual financial and operating information. The specific list of items to be included in the annual report will be agreed upon by the parties to the financing transaction and enumerated in the continuing disclosure agreement and in an appendix to the official statement. Usually, it consists largely of audited financial statements and updates of specified categories of financial information and operating data or specific sections and charts in the final official statements, or both.

A-8 There is no statutory due date for the filing of annual financial information, as there is with 10-K filings. Instead, the filing deadline is contractually agreed to in the continuing disclosure agreement. If an obligor fails to file information by the agreed-upon deadline and subsequently issues an official statement for new bonds, it must disclose its failure to file in that official statement. Failure to disclose this information constitutes a material omission in the official statement.

A-9 The annual report does not have to be submitted all at once, in a single document; it may be submitted as a single document or as separate documents comprising a package.

A-10 The continuing disclosure agreement also requires the obligor to file disclosures related to significant events within 10 days of their occurrence. Events for which notice is to be provided (that is, that are not subject to a materiality determination) are as follows:

- Principal and interest payment delinquencies
- Unscheduled draws on debt-service reserves reflecting financial difficulties
- Unscheduled draws on credit enhancements reflecting financial difficulties
- Substitution of credit or liquidity providers, or their failure to perform
- Adverse tax opinions or events affecting the tax-exempt status of the security
- Defeasances
- Rating changes
- Tender offers
- Bankruptcy, insolvency, receivership, or a similar event
- Notices of failure to provide annual financial information on or before the date specified on the continuing disclosure agreement

Events that are subject to a materiality determination before triggering a requirement to provide notice are as follows:

- Appointment of successor additional trustees or the change of name of a trustee
- Nonpayment related defaults
- Modifications of rights to security holders
- Bond calls
- Matters affecting collateral (for example, release, substitution, or sale of property securing repayment of the securities)
- Consummation of a merger, consolidation, or acquisition involving an obligated person, or the sale of substantially all of the assets of an obligated person, other than in the ordinary course of business, the entry into definitive agreements to undertake such an action, or the termination of an agreement as it relates to any such sale, other than pursuant to its terms

Electronic Municipal Market Access System

A-11 Effective July 1, 2009, the Electronic Municipal Market Access System (EMMA) became the nationally recognized municipal securities information repository for filing annual reports, material event notices, and voluntarily-submitted information. EMMA is an internet-based centralized database that provides free public access to disclosure and transaction information about municipal bonds to the municipal market. EMMA also provides access to official statements, advance refunding documents, real-time trade and historical trade information, daily market information, and other educational materials about municipal bonds. Technical Questions and Answers section 7100.05, "FINRA TRACE and MSRB EMMA Data and a Public Business Entity" (*Technical Questions and Answers*), states that although EMMA provides historical trade prices, credit ratings and other information related to those securities, it does not allow execution of trades, and therefore it is not an over-the-counter market. Essentially, EMMA makes municipal disclosure information available to the market in a manner similar to the SEC's Electronic Data-Gathering, Analysis, and Retrieval System, or EDGAR, for the disclosures of publicly traded companies. Rule 15c2-12 requires all continuing disclosure information to be filed using EMMA. EMMA's web address is http://emma.msrb.org. The SEC release concerning this amendment to SEC Rule 15c2-12 is available at www.sec.gov/rules/sro/msrb/2008/34-59061.pdf.

10.117

Appendix B—Auditor Involvement With Municipal Securities Filings

Continuing Disclosure Documents

B-1 As discussed in paragraph A-3 of appendix A, "Municipal Securities Regulation," of this chapter, obligors of many municipal security offerings make continuing disclosures by providing to the Municipal Securities Rulemaking Board (MSRB) (*a*) annual continuing disclosures as contractually established and (*b*) events notices. Annual continuing disclosures are financial information, including audited financial statements, which are updated annually. Events notices, which are required for specific events with respect to municipal securities, such as principal and interest payment delinquencies and nonpayment related defaults, are provided on an as-needed basis and do not involve financial statements. If the primary offering of municipal securities subject to Rule 15c2-12 occurred on or before November 30, 2010, obligors under continuing disclosure agreements are required to notify the MSRB of any of 11 specific events, if determined material, in a timely manner. If the primary offering of municipal securities subject to Rule 15c2-12 occurred after December 1, 2010, obligors under continuing disclosure agreements are required to notify the MSRB of any of 15 events "in a timely manner not in excess of ten business days after the occurrence of the event." For these obligors, certain events are required to be reported without regard to materiality, whereas certain other events are reported based on materiality. (The list of events is included in paragraph A-10 of appendix A in this chapter.)

B-2 Rule 15c2-12, as amended, requires the underwriter of a municipal securities offering to reasonably determine that the issuer or obligated person (hereafter referred to as the obligor) has undertaken in its continuing disclosure agreement to provide continuing disclosure documents (*a*) solely to the MSRB and (*b*) in an electronic format and accompanied by identifying information as prescribed by the MSRB. An obligor provides continuing disclosure information using the MSRB's Electronic Municipal Market Access (EMMA) system.[1] However, such filings with the MSRB (using the EMMA system) do not affect the legal obligations or contractual disclosure agreements of issuers and obligated persons to provide continuing disclosure documents, along with any other submissions, to the appropriate state information depositories, as required under the appropriate state law. This does not affect the obligation of issuers and obligated persons under outstanding continuing disclosure agreements entered into prior to July 1, 2009, to submit continuing disclosure documents to the appropriate State Information Depository, if any, as stated in their continuing disclosure agreements, nor on their obligation to make any other submissions that may be required under appropriate state law.

B-3 A not-for-profit entity's (NFP's) continuing disclosures uploaded to the MSRB's EMMA system are not considered other information as discussed in AU-C section 720, *Other Information in Documents Containing Audited*

---

[1] Electronic Municipal Market Access (EMMA) receives electronic submissions of, and makes publicly available, continuing disclosure documents and related information on the EMMA website at http://emma.msrb.org.

Financial Statements.[2] Therefore, an auditor is not required to apply the requirements of AU-C section 720 to such continuing disclosures.

B-4 In its Release No. 33-7049 and 34-33741,[3] *Statement of the Commission Regarding Disclosure Obligations of Municipal Securities Issuers and Others*, the SEC encourages market participants to continue to refer to voluntary guidelines (such as the guidelines prepared by the Government Finance Officers Association) and the SEC's Interpretive Release in preparing official statements and continuing disclosure documents.

Auditor Involvement With Exempt Offering Documents

Statement on Auditing Standards No. 133, *Auditor Involvement with Exempt Offering Documents* (AU-C sec. 945), issued in July 2017, provides guidance as to when an auditor is considered involved with an exempt offering document and, when involved as defined by the standard, the auditor's responsibilities with regard to the offering. Municipal securities are exempt from the registration requirements of Section 5 of the Securities Act of 1933, thus are within the scope of AU-C section 945. An *exempt offering document* is the disclosure document that provides financial and nonfinancial information related to the entity issuing the exempt offering and the offering itself. As discussed in paragraph 10.25, the exempt offering document related to a municipal security offering is an official statement.[4]

Conditions Establishing Auditor Involvement

B-5 Because there is no SEC requirement for auditor involvement with official statements of nonissuers, an auditor generally is not required to participate in, or undertake any procedures with respect to, an NFP's official statement.[5] The following are activities the auditor may become involved in with respect to the official statement:

- Assisting in preparing the financial information[6] included in the official statement
- Reviewing a draft of the official statement at the NFP's request
- Signing (either manually or electronically) the independent auditor's report for inclusion in a specific official statement[7]
- Providing written agreement (for example, through a consent letter or signed authorization form) for the use of the independent auditor's report in a specific official statement (See paragraphs B-16–B-20.)

---

[2] All AU-C sections can be found in AICPA *Professional Standards*.

[3] Note that the SEC release is one release that has two numbers: one for the Securities Exchange Act of 1933 and one for the Securities Exchange Act of 1934.

[4] AU-C section 945, *Auditor Involvement With Exempt Offering Documents*, is effective for municipal securities offering documents with which the auditor is involved that are initially distributed, circulated, or submitted on or after June 15, 2018.

[5] As discussed in paragraph B-7, some auditors require that they become involved with a not-for-profit entity's (NFP's) official statements even though the conditions described in this paragraph establishing involvement would not otherwise exist.

[6] For the purpose of this requirement, *financial information* does not include the financial statements covered by the auditor's opinion.

[7] This situation involves an original manual or electronic signature on the auditor's report, not a reproduction of an auditor's report that was manually or electronically signed. For example, the underwriter or bond counsel may require a copy of the auditor's report with an original manual or electronic signature to file with the official closing documents for the offering.

- Providing a revised independent auditor's report[8] for inclusion in a specific official statement
- Issuing a comfort letter, the letter described in paragraph .12 of AU-C section 920, *Letters for Underwriters and Certain Other Requesting Parties*, or an attestation engagement report in lieu of a comfort or similar letter on information included in the official statement (See paragraphs B-11–B-15.)
- Issuing a practitioner's report on an attestation engagement relating to the debt offering (See paragraph B-21.)

Paragraph .08 of AU-C section 945 provides two conditions that both have to exist to establish involvement with an official statement:

a. The auditor's report is included or incorporated by reference in the official statement.

b. The auditor performs one or more of the following activities with respect to the official statement:

   i. Assisting the entity in preparing information included in the official statement

   ii. Reading a draft of the official statement at the entity's request

   iii. Issuing a comfort or similar letter in accordance with AU-C section 920, *Letters for Underwriters and Certain Other Requesting Parties*, or an agreed-upon procedures report in accordance with AT-C section 215, *Agreed-Upon Procedures Engagements*,[9] in lieu of a comfort or similar letter on information included in the official statement

   iv. Participating in due diligence discussions with underwriters, placement agents, broker-dealers, or other financial intermediaries in connection with the exempt offering

   v. Issuing a practitioner's attestation report on information relating to the exempt offering

   vi. Providing written agreement for the use of the auditor's report in the official statement

   vii. Updating an auditor's report for inclusion in the official statement

Each of the triggering activities is discussed in more depth in this section.

Auditors may become aware of an offering through a communication from an entity or through the receipt of a draft official statement from an underwriter, placement agent, broker-dealer, or the entity. Awareness of an exempt offering by the auditor does not, by itself, constitute involvement. Conversely, there is nothing that precludes the auditor from following the procedures in AU-C section 945 if the conditions are not met. See related discussion in paragraph B-7.

---

[8] A revised report would, for example, eliminate the references made by the auditor in the original report to (*a*) supplementary information that the auditor reported on in relation to the financial statements or (*b*) the audit and reports required by *Government Auditing Standards* (also referred to as the Yellow Book), issued by the Comptroller General of the United States.

[9] All AT-C sections can be found in AICPA *Professional Standards*.

Assisting in Preparing Information

Assistance in preparing information as described in paragraph B-5*b*(i) is predicated upon the auditor being reasonably aware that the information will be included in a specific official statement. For example, an auditor assisting the entity with the preparation of a schedule for the entity's internal purposes that the entity later includes in its official statement would not be considered assisting the entity in preparing information as described in paragraph B-5*b*(i).

Information does not include the audited financial statements or interim financial information covered by the auditor's report. Further, information does not include required supplementary information, or other information that accompanied those financial statements that the auditor already considered during the audit of the financial statements or review of interim financial information.

AU-C section 945 highlights that self-review, management participation, and advocacy threats to a covered member's compliance with the AICPA Code of Professional Conduct may exist when a member provides corporate finance consulting services to an entity.[10] A member may assist the entity in drafting its official statement or memorandum without impairing independence[11] if the member complies with the AICPA Code of Professional Conduct.[12,13]

It is important to note that providing written or oral comments to the entity on the official statement is considered assisting the entity in preparing information included in the official statement, regardless of whether the entity requested the auditor to read the document or the auditor did so voluntarily.

Reading a Draft of the Official Statement

Reading a draft of the official statement encompasses situations in which the auditor reads the official statement at the request of the entity even if the auditor does not ultimately provide written or oral comments.

Issuing a Comfort or Similar Letter or an Agreed-Upon Procedures Report in Accordance With AT-C Section 215

Underwriting agreements between an entity and its underwriters may include a request for the entity's auditor to prepare and issue a comfort letter that will assist the underwriters with their due diligence in connection with the exempt offering. Comfort letters may also be requested by parties other than the underwriters. AU-C section 920 addresses the auditor's responsibilities related to the issuance of comfort letters and is further discussed in paragraphs B-10–B-15.

Participating in Due Diligence Discussions

As part of their due diligence process, underwriters and their counsel may ask to meet with the entity's auditors and discuss the specific official statement,

---

[10] The "Independence Rule" (ET sec. 1.200.001) of the AICPA Code of Professional Conduct. All ET sections can be found in AICPA *Professional Standards*.

[11] The "Corporate Finance Consulting" interpretation (ET sec. 1.295.130.02*f*) of the "Nonattest Services" subtopic under the "Independence Rule" of the AICPA Code of Professional Conduct.

[12] The "General Requirements for Performing Nonattest Services" interpretation (ET sec. 1.295.040) of the "Nonattest Services" subtopic under the "Independence Rule."

[13] The "Corporate Finance Consulting" interpretation (ET sec. 1.295.130.03) of the "Nonattest Services" subtopic under the "Independence Rule" also lists examples of types of corporate finance consulting services that would impair a member's independence in connection with an offering.

either formally or informally.[14] Such meetings are often referred to as oral due diligence meetings; however, other communication methods may be used. The discussion typically focuses on the audit engagement, the entity's financial statements, and the entity's system of internal control over financial reporting. Auditors use professional judgment in determining whether to participate in due diligence discussions if the underwriter has not provided the written opinion from external legal counsel or representation letter as described in AU-C section 920.[15] If the auditor agrees to participate, auditors use professional judgment in determining which questions in an oral due diligence meeting can be addressed.

Issuing a Practitioner's Attestation Report on Information Relating to the Official Statement

During the offering process, management or other parties to the offering may engage a practitioner to perform an attestation engagement on information related to the offering. For example, management or its legal advisers may engage a practitioner to perform agreed-upon procedures on the entity's compliance with the revenue coverage requirements on outstanding debt securities or to recompute the calculation of escrow account requirements for an advance refunding of debt securities. If the practitioner engaged to perform the attestation engagement is the auditor whose report accompanies the financial statements included in the exempt offering document, the auditor is deemed to be involved with the official statement. A practitioner's attestation report relating to an exempt offering need not be referred to or included in the exempt offering document to involve the auditor of the financial statements with the offering.

If the practitioner engaged to perform the attestation engagement is not the financial statement auditor, the practitioner engaged to perform the attestation engagement is not deemed to be involved with the official statement in the manner described in AU-C section 945.

Providing Written Agreement for the Use of the Auditor's Report in the Official Statement

For municipal securities offerings, generally there is no regulatory requirement for the auditor to provide any type of written agreement to use the auditor's report in the offering. If the auditor is asked to provide written agreement, the auditor may provide an inclusion letter indicating that the auditor agrees to the inclusion of the auditor's report in the official statement. An inclusion letter is a letter requested by and addressed to the entity that is signed and dated by the auditor indicating that the auditor agrees to the inclusion or incorporation by reference of the auditor's report in the official statement. The following example language may be used to indicate that the auditor agrees to inclusion of the auditor's report on financial statements in an official statement:

Independent Auditor's Inclusion Letter

> We agree to the inclusion [*or incorporation by reference*] in the [*name of offering document*] dated [*insert issuance date of offering document*] of our report, dated [*insert date of auditor's report on the*

---

[14] The "Confidential Client Information Rule" (ET sec 1.700.001) of the AICPA Code of Professional Conduct states that the auditor should not disclose any confidential client information without the specific consent of the client.

[15] Paragraphs .07, .11, and .A92 of AU-C section 920 .

financial statements], on our audit of the financial statements of [*name of entity*] as of December 31, 20X2 [*and 20X1*], and for the year[*s*] then ended.

When the auditor is asked to issue a letter agreeing to the inclusion of the auditor's report in the offering document, the effective date of the letter can be the preliminary official statement date or the official statement date.

Updating an Auditor's Report for Inclusion in the Official Statement

Updating an auditor's report involves, for example, signing an updated auditor's report when the previously issued financial statements are corrected for an accounting error or reflect a retrospective application of a change in accounting principle.

The following examples would not constitute updating an auditor's report for purposes of paragraph B-5*b*(vii):

- Providing a copy of or re-signing a previously issued auditor's report
- Revising an originally issued auditor's report to eliminate references made by the auditor in the original report required by *Government Auditing Standards*
- Revising an originally issued report to eliminate references made by the auditor in the original report to supplementary information that the auditor reported on in relation to the basic financial statements

Auditor Responsibilities When Involved in an Official Statement

The objectives of the auditor when involved with an official statement are to perform procedures specified in AU-C section 945 and respond appropriately as follows:

a. When the auditor determines that information included or incorporated by reference in the official statement could undermine the credibility of the financial statements and the auditor's report thereon

b. To facts that become known to the auditor after the date of the auditor's report that, had they been known to the auditor at that date, may have caused the auditor to revise the auditor's report.

As discussed in paragraph 10.25, municipal securities offerings have multiple stages. Thus, a single offering could involve multiple applications of the required procedures. Requesting management to keep the auditor advised of the progress of the preparation of the offering document proceedings through the final distribution, circulation, or submission of the final offering statement is important so that the auditor's consideration of events occurring after the date of the auditor's report up to the distribution, circulation, or submission of the final offering statement can be completed.[16]

B-6 Although AU-C section 720, *Other Information in Documents Containing Audited Financial Statements*, addresses auditor responsibilities with respect to other information contained in annual reports (or similar documents) of organizations for charitable or philanthropic purposes if they are available to

---

[16] AU-C section 945 is effective for municipal securities offering documents with which the auditor is involved that are initially distributed, circulated, or submitted on or after June 15, 2018.

the public and they contain audited financial statements and the auditor's report thereon, paragraph .02 of AU-C section 720 states that it may be applied, adapted as necessary in the circumstances, to other documents to which the auditor devotes attention. Therefore, if the auditor is involved with an official statement, the guidance in AU-C section 720 may be applied. If the guidance in AU-C section 720 is applied, the auditor should communicate with those charged with governance the auditor's responsibility for other information in a document containing audited financial statements, any procedures performed, and the results.

In accordance with paragraph .09 of AU-C section 945, the auditor should perform the procedures described in paragraphs .06–.18 of AU-C section 720, *Other Information in Documents Containing Audited Financial Statements*, on the official statement. When revision of the other information in the official statement is necessary due to a material inconsistency or a material misstatement of fact that management refuses to correct, AU-C section 720 requires the auditor to notify those charged with governance of the auditor's concerns regarding the other information and take any further appropriate action. With regard to exempt offerings, actions may also include determining whether to withhold the auditor's agreement to include the auditor's report. In such cases, the auditor may consider it appropriate to obtain legal advice.

In addition to the procedures related to other information, paragraph .10 of AU-C section 945 requires the following when the auditor is involved with an official statement of a municipal security offering:

a. Perform procedures designed to identify events occurring between the date of the auditor's report and the date of the distribution, circulation, or submission of the official statement that, had they been known to the auditor as of the date of the auditor's report, may have caused the auditor to revise the auditor's report (hereafter referred to as "subsequent events" for purposes of this appendix). Such procedures should include the following:

   i. Obtaining an understanding of any procedures that management may have performed to identify such events

   ii. Inquiring of management and, when appropriate, those charged with governance about whether any such events have occurred that might affect the financial statements

   iii. Reading minutes, if any, of the meetings of the entity's management and those charged with governance that have been held since the date of the auditor's report and inquiring about matters discussed at any such meetings for which minutes are not yet available

   iv. Reading the entity's most recent subsequent interim financial statements, if any

b. Obtain updated written representations from management about the following:

   i. Whether any information has come to management's attention that would cause management to believe that any of the previous representations should be modified

   ii. Whether any events have occurred subsequent to the date of the auditor's report that would require adjustment to, or disclosure in, the financial statements

iii. That management provided complete minutes of the meetings of the entity's management and those charged with governance, or summaries of actions of recent meetings for which minutes have not yet been prepared since previous representations were provided

iv. That management provided communications received from regulatory agencies concerning noncompliance with, or deficiencies in, financial reporting practices since previous representations were provided.

Paragraphs .11–.12 of AU-C section 945 provide requirements and guidance when a predecessor auditor's report on a prior period is included in the official statement and when a predecessor auditor of an acquired entity is involved with an official statement.

Paragraph .13 of AU-C section 945 states that if the auditor identifies subsequent events that may require adjustment of, or disclosure in, the audited financial statements or reviewed interim financial information, the auditor should not agree to the inclusion of the auditor's report in the official statement until the auditor's consideration of the subsequent events, including the effect on the auditor's report, has been satisfactorily evaluated in accordance with AU-C section 560, *Subsequent Events and Subsequently Discovered Facts*.[17]

As noted in paragraph .14 of AU-C section 945, if the auditor becomes aware of subsequently discovered facts, the auditor should not agree to the inclusion of the auditor's report in the official statement until the auditor's consideration of the subsequently discovered facts, including the effect on the auditor's report, has been satisfactorily evaluated in accordance with AU-C section 560.[18]

If management does not revise the financial statements in circumstances in which the auditor believes they need to be revised, in addition to following the requirements in AU-C section 560, paragraph .15 of AU-C section 945 states the auditor should not agree to the inclusion of the auditor's report in the official statement.[19,20]

Engagement Terms Regarding Auditor Involvement

B-7 Although an auditor is not required to become involved with an NFP's official statements, some auditors include a provision in the terms of the engagement requiring the NFP to obtain permission from the auditor before using the independent auditor's report in the official statement. Such a provision may be used by the auditor to establish a requirement that the auditor become involved with the NFP's official statements, as discussed in paragraphs B-5–B-6, when the NFP requests the required permission from the auditor.

Auditors may include a provision in the terms of the engagement requiring the entity to obtain permission from the auditor before using the auditor's report in connection with an exempt offering document. The existence of such a provision in an engagement letter does not establish involvement unless the

---

[17] Paragraph .11 of AU-C section 560, *Subsequent Events and Subsequently Discovered Facts*.

[18] Paragraphs .15–.18 of AU-C section 560.

[19] Paragraphs .17–.18 of AU-C section 560.

[20] AU-C section 945 is effective for municipal securities offering documents with which the auditor is involved that are initially distributed, circulated, or submitted on or after June 15, 2018.

auditor performs one or more of the activities in paragraph .B-5*b* with respect to the exempt offering document. An example provision for an engagement letter may read as follows:

> The Entity may wish to include our report on these financial statements in an exempt offering document. The Entity agrees that the aforementioned auditor's report, or reference to our Firm, will not be included in any such offering document without our prior permission or consent. Any agreement to perform work in connection with an exempt offering document, including an agreement to provide permission or consent, will be a separate engagement.[21]

Clarification in the Official Statement When There Is No Auditor Involvement

B-8 When the auditor and client agree not to include a provision in the terms of the engagement that would require auditor involvement (see paragraph B-7), the auditor may include in the terms of the engagement a requirement that any official statements issued by the NFP with which the auditor is not involved clearly indicate that the auditor is not involved with the contents of such official statements. An example disclosure may read as follows:

> [*Name of firm*], our independent auditor, has not been engaged to perform and has not performed, since the date of its report included herein, any procedures on the financial statements addressed in that report. [*Name of firm*] also has not performed any procedures relating to this official statement.

Paragraph .A3 of AU-C section 945 states that the auditor may include in the terms of the engagement a provision that any exempt offering document issued by the entity with which the auditor is not involved, other than as determined by paragraph B-5, will clearly indicate the auditor is not involved with the contents of such offering document. An example disclosure related to an exempt offering document may read as follows:

> [*Name of firm*], our independent auditor, has not been engaged to perform and has not performed, since the date of its report included herein, any procedures on the financial statements addressed in that report. [*Name of firm*] also has not performed any procedures relating to this offering document.[22]

Using *Government Auditing Standards* Reports and References in the Official Statement

B-9 NFPs sometimes request that auditors revise an originally issued auditor's report to eliminate references made by the auditor to *Government Auditing Standards* for use in a municipal security offering. Issuing a separate GAAS only report is permitted for this purpose because *Government Auditing Standards* acknowledge that an auditee may need a financial statement audit for purposes other than to comply with a requirement calling for an audit in accordance with *Government Auditing Standards*.

---

[21] AU-C section 945 is effective for municipal securities offering documents with which the auditor is involved that are initially distributed, circulated, or submitted on or after June 15, 2018.

[22] AU-C section 945 is effective for municipal securities offering documents with which the auditor is involved that are initially distributed, circulated, or submitted on or after June 15, 2018.

NFPs sometimes request that auditors revise an originally issued auditor's report to eliminate references made by the auditor to *Government Auditing Standards* for use in a municipal security offering. Issuing a separate GAAS only report is permitted for this purpose because *Government Auditing Standards* acknowledge that an auditee may need a financial statement audit for purposes other than to comply with a requirement calling for an audit in accordance with *Government Auditing Standards*. As noted in paragraph B-5, when such requests are made of the auditor it would not be considered a triggering activity to establish involvement.[23]

Letters for Underwriters and Other Requesting Parties

B-10 Underwriting agreements between an NFP and its underwriters may require the auditor to prepare a comfort letter addressed to the underwriters. An auditor is neither required to accept an engagement to issue a comfort letter nor required to provide comfort on every matter requested when accepting an engagement to issue a comfort letter. AU-C section 920 defines the term underwriters and gives guidance to auditors[24] when engaged to issue letters to underwriters and to certain other requesting parties in connection with a nonissuer entity's financial statements included in registration statements filed with the SEC under the 1933 Act. An auditor may provide a comfort letter to a broker-dealer or other financial intermediary acting as principal or agent in offerings of securities issued or backed by NFPs exempt from registration under the 1933 Act only if the broker-dealer or other financial intermediary provides the required representation letter described in paragraph .11 of AU-C section 920. The required elements of the representation letter from the broker-dealer or other financial intermediary are as follows:

- The letter should be addressed to the auditor.
- The letter should contain the following:

  > The review process applied to the information relating to the issuer of the securities, is (will be) substantially consistent with the due diligence process that we would perform if this securities offering were being registered pursuant to the Securities Act of 1933. We are knowledgeable with respect to that due diligence process.

- The letter should be signed by the requesting broker-dealer or other financial intermediary.

B-11 When a party requesting a comfort letter has provided the auditor with the required representation letter, the auditor should refer to the requesting party's representations in the comfort letter. See example A-2 of exhibit B, "Examples of Comfort Letters," in paragraph .A93 of AU-C section 920, which is a typical comfort letter in a non-1933 Act offering, including the required underwriter representations. If the required representation letter is not provided by the broker-dealer or other financial intermediary, paragraph .12 of AU-C section 920 provides requirements and guidance for auditors. See example Q, "Letter to a Requesting Party That Has Not Provided the Legal Opinion or the

---

[23] AU-C section 945 is effective for municipal securities offering documents with which the auditor is involved that are initially distributed, circulated, or submitted on or after June 15, 2018.

[24] Because of its use in SEC literature, certain auditing literature uses the term *accountant* to refer to the auditor. However, this chapter replaces the term *accountant* with the term *auditor*.

Representation Letter Required by Paragraph .11," of exhibit B in paragraph .A93 of AU-C section 920 for the relevant illustration.

B-12 As discussed in paragraph .13 of AU-C section 920, when a comfort letter is requested by a party other than the underwriter, broker-dealer, or other financial intermediary, the auditor should not provide that party with a comfort letter or the letter described in paragraph .12 of AU-C section 920. Instead, the auditor may provide the party with a practitioner's report on agreed-upon procedures and should refer to AT-C section 215, *Agreed-Upon Procedures Engagements*. (See paragraph .A7 of AU-C section 920).

B-13 If the auditor is engaged to provide negative assurance in a comfort letter on interim financial information, paragraph .45 of AU-C section 920 requires the auditor to perform a review, as discussed in AU-C section 930, *Interim Financial Information*. A review of interim financial information may be conducted under AU-C section 930 if:

- the entity's latest annual financial statements have been audited by the auditor or a predecessor auditor;
- the auditor has been engaged to audit the entity's current year financial statements, or the auditor audited the entity's latest annual financial statements and in situations in which the engagement of another auditor to audit the current year financial statements is not effective prior to the beginning of the period covered by the review;
- the interim financial information is prepared in accordance with the same financial reporting framework as that used to prepare the annual financial statements; and
- any condensed financial statement (*a*) purports to be prepared in accordance with an appropriate financial reporting framework which includes appropriate form and content of the interim financial statements; (*b*) includes a note that the financial information does not represent complete financial statements and is to be read in conjunction with the latest annual audited financial statements; and (*c*) the condensed interim financial information accompanies the entity's latest audited annual financial statements or such audited annual statements are made readily available[25] by the entity.

If AU-C section 930 is not applicable, the review engagement may be performed under Statements on Standards for Attestation Engagements or Statements on Standards for Accounting and Review Services.

B-14 If the auditor has not performed such a review, paragraphs .45 and .60 of AU-C section 920 prohibit the auditor from giving negative assurance with respect to whether any material modifications should be made to the interim financial information for it to be in conformity with generally accepted accounting principles and from providing negative assurance as to subsequent changes in financial statements items from the date of the interim financial information. Instead, the auditor is limited to reporting procedures performed and findings

---

[25] According to paragraph .A3 of AU-C section 930, *Interim Financial Information*, audited financial statements are deemed readily available if a third party user can obtain the statements without any further action by the entity (financial statements on an entity's website would be considered readily available whereas statements that are available on request would not).

obtained. The letter should specifically state that the auditor has not audited the interim financial information in accordance with generally accepted auditing standards and does not express an opinion concerning such information. An example of that language is in the third statement of the example A-1 comfort letter in AU-C section 920.

B-15 When the auditor is asked to prepare a letter for the underwriter, the letter can be as of the preliminary official statement date or the official statement date with updating letters issued as of the official statement date (if applicable) and the closing date. Paragraphs .A24–.A25 of AU-C section 920 state that the letter ordinarily is dated on, or shortly after, the underwriting agreement is signed, and the underwriting agreement ordinarily specifies the date, often referred to as the cutoff date, to which certain procedures described in the letter are to relate (for example, a date five days before the date of the letter). A factor in considering whether to accept the engagement is whether the period between the cut-off date and the date of the letter provides sufficient time to allow the auditor to perform the procedures and prepare the letter. The five-day cut-off period in AU-C section 920 is illustrative only and does not set a requirement, but practice generally does not exceed a five-day cut-off period.

Auditing Interpretations Regarding Official Statements

B-16 Exhibit A, "Background," of AU-C section 925, *Filings With the U.S. Securities and Exchange Commission Under the Securities Act of 1933*, addresses the auditor's agreement[26] to (*a*) being named in and (*b*) the use of an auditor's report in an offering document other than one registered under the of 1933 Act.[27]

The preceding paragraph and the heading that precedes it will be deleted upon the effective date of AU-C section 945, which is effective for municipal securities offering documents with which the auditor is involved that are initially distributed, circulated, or submitted on or after June 15, 2018.

B-17 Paragraph 16 of exhibit A of AU-C section 925 states that when a client wishes to make reference to the auditor's role in an offering document in connection with a securities offering that is not registered under the 1933 Act, the caption "Independent Auditors" (or something similar) would generally be used to title that section of the document rather than "Experts," with no reference to the auditor as an "expert" anywhere in the document. Exhibit B, "Illustrative Disclosures and Reports," of AU-C section 925 provides the following example of a typical description of the auditor's role.[28]

Independent Auditors

> The financial statements of [*name of entity*] as of December 31, 20XX, and for the year then ended, included in this offering circular, have been audited by ABC & Co., independent auditors, as stated in their report(s) appearing herein.

---

[26] The term *consent* is an SEC term that relates to registered securities, and municipal securities are not registered securities. Therefore, this guide uses the term *agreement*, even though the AICPA interpretations discussed refer to *consent*.

[27] NFPs typically refer to the offering document or offering memorandum as an official statement.

[28] As discussed in paragraph B-9, if the auditor is not involved with the offering document and the terms of the engagement require disclosure of this fact, additional disclosure similar to that illustrated in paragraph B-9 should be included here.

If the client refuses to delete from the offering document the reference to the auditor as an expert, the auditor should not permit inclusion of the auditor's report in the offering document.

Reference to the Auditor as an "Expert"

When performing procedures in accordance with AU-C section 945, the auditor should determine that the auditor's role is not described in the official statement in a way that indicates that the auditor's responsibility is greater than the auditor intends. The term *expert* has a specific statutory meaning under the Securities Act of 1933. Outside the Securities Act of 1933 context, the term expert is typically undefined. Accordingly, when an entity wishes to make reference to the auditor's role in connection with an exempt offering, the caption to that section of the document would generally be titled "Independent Auditors" (or something similar) rather than "Experts," with no reference to the auditor as an expert anywhere in the official statement. The following is an example of a typical description of the auditor's role when an entity wishes to make reference to the auditor in an official statement:

Independent Auditors

> The financial statements of [*name of entity*] as of December 31, 20X2 [*and 20X1*], and for the year[*s*] then ended, included in this official statement, have been audited by [*name of firm*], independent auditors, as stated in their report appearing herein.

If the entity refuses to delete references to the auditor as an "expert," the auditor may consider whether to withhold permission to include the auditor's report in the official statement, based on the auditor's professional judgment. In such circumstances, the auditor may consider it appropriate to obtain legal advice.[29]

B-18 Paragraphs 19–20 of exhibit A of AU-C section 925 state that when an auditor's report is used in connection with an offering transaction that is not registered under the 1933 Act, it is usually not necessary for the auditor to provide any type of written consent. If the auditor is asked to provide a written consent for use in connection with a document other than a 1933 Act registration statement, then the auditor may provide a letter indicating that the auditor agrees to the inclusion of the auditor's report on the audited financial statements in the offering materials. This letter would not typically be included in the offering materials. The following example language may be used:

> We agree to the inclusion in the offering circular of our report, dated February 5, 20XX, on our audit of the financial statements of [*name of entity*].

The preceding paragraph will be deleted upon the effective date of AU-C section 945, which is effective for municipal securities offering documents with which the auditor is involved that are initially distributed, circulated, or submitted on or after June 15, 2018. Providing written agreement for the use of the auditor's report in the official statement is a triggering activity for auditor involvement, as discussed in paragraph B-5.

B-19 As stated in paragraph .08 of AU-C section 925, the auditor should determine that the auditor's name is not being used in a way that indicates that

---

[29] AU-C section 945 is effective for municipal securities offering documents with which the auditor is involved that are initially distributed, circulated, or submitted on or after June 15, 2018.

the auditor's responsibility is greater than the auditor intends. Therefore, if the client refuses to delete from the offering document the reference to the auditor as an expert, then the auditor should not permit inclusion of the auditor's report in the offering document.

The preceding paragraph will be deleted upon the effective date of AU-C section 945, which is effective for municipal securities offering documents with which the auditor is involved that are initially distributed, circulated, or submitted on or after June 15, 2018. See paragraph B-17.

B-20 When the auditor is asked to issue a letter agreeing to the use of the auditor's report in the offering document, the effective date of the letter can be the preliminary official statement date or the official statement date.

The preceding paragraph will be deleted upon the effective date of AU-C section 945, which is effective for municipal securities offering documents with which the auditor is involved that are initially distributed, circulated, or submitted on or after June 15, 2018. Content will be included under the heading "Providing Written Agreement for the Use of the Auditor's Report in the Official Statement" (paragraph B-5).

Attestation Engagements Related to Municipal Securities Issuances

B-21 During the process of issuing municipal securities, NFPs or other involved parties often engage practitioners to provide certain needed information. These engagements should be conducted in accordance with the appropriate professional attestation standards as agreed to by the engaging NFP and the practitioner.[30] For example, an NFP or its bond counsel may engage a practitioner to review the NFP's compliance with the revenue coverage requirements on outstanding bonds or to verify the calculation of escrow account requirements for an advance refunding of bonds. If the auditor of the financial statements included in the official statement also provides a practitioner's report on an attestation engagement relating to a debt offering, that establishes an involvement with the official statement, as indicated in paragraph B-5. A practitioner's report on an attestation engagement relating to a debt offering need not be referred to or included in the official statement to involve the auditor of the financial statements with the official statement. Sometimes, the practitioner's report on the attestation engagement may only be included in the official closing documents for the offering. Also, if the practitioner providing the report on the attestation engagement is not the auditor of the financial statements included in the official statements, the issuance of the practitioner's report does not, by itself, involve either the auditor of the financial statements or the practitioner who issued the report on the attestation engagement with the official statement.

B-22 A practitioner should not provide any form of assurance, through an examination, review, or agreed-upon procedures engagement, that an entity

[30] Generally, these attestation engagements are performed only in accordance with AICPA Statements on Standards for Attestation Engagements. However, if the auditor is performing the engagement in accordance with *Government Auditing Standards*, the auditor should apply the guidance of *Government Auditing Standards*, including chapter 5, "Standards for Attestation Engagements." The auditor also should consider the guidance in Interpretation No. 1, "Reporting on Attestation Engagements Performed in Accordance With *Government Auditing Standards*" (AT-C sec. 9205 par. .01–.03), of AT section 205, *Examination Engagements*, which explains how an attestation report should be modified when the engagement is performed in accordance with *Government Auditing Standards* and provides an illustrative attestation report.

(a) is not insolvent at the time the debt is incurred or would not be rendered insolvent thereby, (b) does not have unreasonably small capital, or (c) has the ability to pay its debts as they mature, as discussed in Interpretation No. 1, "Responding to Requests for Reports on Matters Relating to Solvency" (AT-C sec. 9105 par. .01–.11), of AT-C section 105, *Concepts Common to All Attestation Engagements*.

Chapter 11

Net Assets and Reclassifications of Net Assets

> ***Note:*** *For financial statements prepared in accordance with FASB Accounting Standards Update No. 2016-14,* Not-for-Profit Entities (Topic 958): Presentation of Financial Statements of Not-for-Profit Entities, *use appendix A, "Financial Statements Prepared in Accordance with FASB ASU No. 2016-14" of this chapter. The amendments in FASB ASU No. 2016-14 are effective for annual financial statements issued for fiscal years beginning after December 15, 2017 (for example, years ending December 31, 2018 and years ending June 30, 2019), and for interim periods within fiscal years beginning after December 15, 2018. Application to interim financial statements is permitted but not required in the initial year of application. Early application of the amendments is permitted.*

Introduction

11.01 The FASB *Accounting Standards Codification* (ASC) glossary defines *net assets* as "the excess or deficiency of assets over liabilities of a not-for-profit entity (NFP), which is classified into three mutually exclusive classes according to the existence or absence of donor-imposed restrictions."[1] As a residual interest, net assets cannot be measured independently of an NFP's assets and liabilities. Changes in net assets result from transactions and other events and circumstances in which total assets and total liabilities change by different amounts. In many NFPs, such changes include nonreciprocal transfers of assets received from donors who do not expect to receive either repayment or proportionate economic benefit in return. Display of and disclosures about net assets and changes in them are intended to assist donors and other users in assessing an NFP's efforts to provide goods and services to its constituencies, its efficiency and effectiveness in providing such services, and its continuing ability to do so.

11.02 Changes in net assets result from revenues, expenses, gains, and losses; those changes are discussed in chapters 5–10 and 12–13 of this guide. This chapter describes principles for reporting total net assets in statements of financial position and changes in total net assets in statements of activities as well as related disclosures.

Fiduciary Responsibilities to Meet Donor Restrictions

11.03 As noted in paragraph 5.75, the receipt of contributed assets imposes a fiduciary responsibility on an NFP's management to use the resources effectively and efficiently in pursuit of the NFP's mission; a donor's restriction on contributed resources focuses that fiduciary responsibility on a particular use for the contributed resources. As noted in FASB ASC 958-605-25-2, donors' restrictions place limits on the use of contributed resources and may affect an NFP's performance and its ability to provide services. The existence or absence of donors' restrictions forms the basis for the classification of net assets.

[1] Though not-for-profit entities (NFPs) may use other terms, such as *equity*, this guide uses the term *net assets* to describe the residual interest.

11.04 The FASB ASC glossary defines a *donor-imposed restriction* as

> a donor stipulation that specifies a use for a contributed asset that is more specific than the broad limits resulting from the following: (*a*) the nature of the NFP, (*b*) the environment in which it operates, and (*c*) the purposes specified in its articles of incorporation or bylaws or comparable documents for an unincorporated association. A donor-imposed restriction on an NFP's use of the asset contributed may be temporary or permanent. Some donor-imposed restrictions impose limits that are permanent, for example, stipulating that resources be invested in perpetuity (not used up). Others are temporary, for example, stipulating that resources may be used only after a specified date, for particular programs or services, or to acquire buildings and equipment.

11.05 When an NFP accepts a restricted contribution, it accepts a fiduciary responsibility to use the gift for the purposes for which it is given. An NFP needs a method of tracking restrictions on net assets and when those restrictions are satisfied. One way of tracking restricted net assets and their use is fund accounting, which facilitates tracking by segregating resources into funds that are consistent with the restricted use of the contribution. Chapter 16, "Fund Accounting," discusses fund accounting and the fund types typically used by NFPs. Other ways of tracking restricted net assets and their uses are via a subsidiary ledger or a project accounting system.

11.06 No matter which system is used, an NFP needs to maintain documentation about the activities and other purposes for which the net assets in the fund, subsidiary ledger account, or project can be used. Documentation about any restrictions on periods in which the gift can be spent, restrictions on specific assets, limitations on investing, or other donor restrictions that limit the use of the resources also need to be included. For gifts that have complex restrictions, it is advisable to retain a copy of the gift agreement as part of the documentation. Some NFPs include donor names, donor contact information, and the amount(s) and date(s) of the contribution(s) in the documentation. For restrictions that are perpetual, such as donor-restricted endowment funds and perpetual interests in trusts, that documentation should be maintained in perpetuity.

11.07 The end result should be that the NFP is able to produce a listing of the amounts and purposes for which its net assets are restricted. That information supports the disclosure in the financial statement in accordance with FASB ASC 958-210-50-3, which requires that information about the nature and amounts of different types of permanent or temporary restrictions be provided either by reporting their amounts on the face of the statement of financial position or by including the relevant details in notes to financial statements.

Failure to Meet a Donor's Restriction

11.08 As noted in FASB ASC 958-450-25-1, noncompliance with donor-imposed restrictions on contributed assets, although rare, does occur, sometimes as a result of events occurring subsequent to receiving a contribution. Paragraphs 3.173–.175 provide guidance for noncompliance with donor restrictions. FASB ASC 855, *Subsequent Events*, provides guidance if the noncompliance occurs after the date of the statement of financial position but before the financial statements are issued. Paragraphs 3.177–.180 provide additional information about subsequent events.

Net Asset Classes

11.09 Paragraphs 9–11 of FASB ASC 958-210-45 provide guidance for the classification of net assets. The amounts for each of the three classes of net assets—permanently restricted, temporarily restricted, and unrestricted—are based on the existence or absence of donor-imposed restrictions.

11.10 In addition to the three classes of net assets, further disaggregation of total net assets may also be reported. For example, unrestricted net assets may be subdivided into board-designated net assets and undesignated net assets. Donor-imposed restrictions limit an NFP's ability to use or dispose of specific contributed assets or the economic benefits embodied in those assets. Donor stipulations should not be considered restrictions unless they include limitations on the use of contributed assets that are more specific than the broad limits imposed by the NFP's purpose and nature.

11.11 FASB ASC 958-210-45-6 states that, generally, donor-imposed restrictions apply to net assets, not to specific assets. Donors may also restrict specific assets regarding their use (for example, land contributed for a park) or over time (for example, contributed securities that must be held in perpetuity). Paragraphs 3.09–.23 and 11.55 discuss reporting requirements for specific assets that have been received with donor-imposed restrictions.

Permanently Restricted Net Assets

11.12 The FASB ASC glossary defines *permanently restricted net assets* as the part of net assets of an NFP resulting from any of the following:

a. Contributions and other inflows of assets whose use by the NFP is limited by donor-imposed stipulations that neither expire by passage of time nor can be fulfilled or otherwise removed by the actions of the NFP

b. Other asset enhancements and diminishments subject to the same kinds of stipulations

c. Reclassifications from or to other classes of net assets as a consequence of donor-imposed stipulations

11.13 Permanently restricted net assets must be maintained by the NFP in perpetuity. For example, contributions of cash or securities restricted by the donor with the stipulation that they be invested in perpetuity (donor-restricted endowment funds) and contributions of collection items (if they are capitalized)[2] required by the donor to be maintained permanently in the NFP's collections should be recognized as increases in permanently restricted net assets.

11.14 Permanently restricted net assets may also change as a result of increases and decreases in existing assets that are subject to permanent restrictions. For example, FASB ASC 958-205-45-18 states that if a donor stipulates that net gains be added to the principal of its gift until that endowed gift plus accumulated gains increases to a specified dollar level, the gains are permanently restricted. Similarly, if a donor states that a specific investment security must be held in perpetuity, the gains and losses on that security are subject to that same permanent restriction unless the donor specifies otherwise. Increases

---

[2] Chapter 7, "Other Assets," discusses accounting policies concerning the capitalization of collection items.

in the carrying amounts of assets that are invested in perpetuity because of donor-imposed restrictions should be recognized as increases in permanently restricted net assets to the extent that donor stipulations or applicable law requires those increases to be retained permanently. Paragraphs 4.65–.79 further discuss the permanently restricted net assets of donor-restricted endowment funds.

Temporarily Restricted Net Assets

11.15 The FASB ASC glossary defines *temporarily restricted net assets* as the part of the net assets of an NFP that result from any of the following:

a. Contributions and other inflows of assets whose use by the NFP is limited by donor-imposed stipulations that either expire by passage of time or can be fulfilled and removed by actions of the NFP pursuant to those stipulations

b. Other asset enhancements and diminishments subject to the same kinds of stipulations

c. Reclassifications from or to other classes of net assets as a consequence of donor-imposed stipulations, their expiration by passage of time, or their fulfillment and removal by actions of the NFP pursuant to those stipulations

11.16 Temporarily restricted net assets are those net assets whose use by the NFP has been limited by donors (*a*) to later periods of time or after specified dates, or (*b*) to specified purposes.[3] For example, contributions restricted by the donor to use by the NFP over the next five years or to support a specific future program should be recognized as increases in temporarily restricted net assets. Contributions of assets (such as equipment or buildings) that by their nature are used up over time and that the donor stipulates must be used by the NFP should also be recognized as increases in temporarily restricted net assets.[4] Paragraphs 4.65–.79 discuss the temporarily restricted net assets of donor-restricted endowment funds.

11.17 Temporarily restricted net assets may also change as a result of increases and decreases in existing assets or the economic benefits embodied in those assets that are subject to donor-imposed temporary restrictions. For example, if the donor has stipulated that income earned on temporarily restricted net assets must be added to principal until the principal is spent for a restricted purpose, the income should be reported as increases in temporarily restricted net assets.

Unrestricted Net Assets

11.18 The FASB ASC glossary defines *unrestricted net assets* as the part of net assets of an NFP that is neither permanently restricted nor temporarily restricted by donor-imposed stipulations.

---

[3] FASB *Accounting Standards Codification* (ASC) 958-605-45-4 states that donor-restricted contributions whose restrictions are met in the same reporting period may be reported as unrestricted support provided that an NFP has a similar policy for reporting investment gains and income (see FASB ASC 958-320-45-3), reports consistently from period to period and discloses its accounting policy. Paragraph 5.85 provides further guidance concerning that policy.

[4] Some NFPs may adopt an accounting policy of implying time restrictions on contributed long-lived assets in the absence of explicit donor-imposed restrictions. Paragraphs 5.86–.88 provide additional guidance on alternative policies.

11.19 Unrestricted net assets include those net assets whose use is not restricted by donors, even though their use may be limited in other respects, such as by contract or by board designation. Changes in net assets arising from exchange transactions (except income and gains on assets that are restricted by donors or by law) should be included in the unrestricted class. Paragraphs 4.65–.79 discuss the unrestricted net assets of endowment funds.

11.20 NFPs such as social and country clubs may issue membership interests, such as capital shares. If those interests are wholly or partially refundable when the member dies, moves away, resigns his or her membership, or at a fixed date, FASB ASC 480-10 provides guidance.

11.21 FASB ASC 480-10 states that an interest that is mandatorily redeemable at a fixed date for a fixed or indexed amount—that embodies an unconditional obligation requiring the issuer to redeem it by transferring its assets at a fixed date (or dates)—should be classified as a liability and initially measured at fair value. An interest that embodies a conditional obligation to redeem the instrument by transferring assets upon an event not certain to occur becomes mandatorily redeemable if that event occurs, the condition is resolved, or the event becomes certain to occur.

11.22 Thus, a membership interest that embodies a conditional obligation to redeem it upon an event not certain to occur (such as *only* upon moving from the community) is initially classified as unrestricted net assets. If the uncertain event occurs, the condition is resolved, or the event becomes certain to occur, and payment of a fixed or indexed amount is to be made at a fixed date (such as three months from the event's occurrence), the interest is reclassified as a liability.

11.23 Per FASB ASC 480-10-55-10, upon reclassification, the issuing NFP would measure the obligation at fair value and reduce net assets by the amount of that initial measure, recognizing no gain or loss. Subsequently, pursuant to FASB ASC 480-10-35-3, those mandatorily redeemable interests are measured at the present value of the amount to be paid at settlement using the rate implicit at inception if both the amount to be paid and the settlement date are fixed. If the amount to be paid varies by reference to an interest rate index, currency index, or another external index, those instruments are subsequently measured at the amount of cash that would be paid under the conditions specified in the contract if settlement occurred at the reporting date. The change in the liability amount from the prior period is reported as interest cost (reported as described in paragraph 13.77).

11.24 The Financial Reporting Executive Committee believes that for other mandatorily redeemable membership interests, a membership interest would also be classified as a liability if the obligation requiring the club to redeem it is unconditional, unless the redemption is required to occur only upon the liquidation or termination of the social or country club. An obligation to redeem a membership interest that is conditioned upon an event not certain to occur would be initially classified as unrestricted net assets. When the obligation becomes unconditional (that is, if the uncertain event occurs, the condition is resolved, or the event becomes certain to occur), the membership interest would be reclassified as a liability.

Noncontrolling Interests

11.25 FASB ASC 958-810-45-1 states that noncontrolling interests in the equity (net assets) of consolidated subsidiaries should be reported as a separate component of the appropriate class of net assets in the consolidated statement of financial position of an NFP. That amount should be clearly identified and described (for example, as noncontrolling ownership interest in subsidiaries) to distinguish it from the components of net assets of the parent, which includes the parent's controlling financial interest in its subsidiaries. Paragraphs 17–25 of FASB ASC 958-810-55 illustrate the presentation of a noncontrolling interest in a for-profit subsidiary in a consolidated statement of financial position and a consolidated statement of changes in unrestricted net assets.

11.26 The effects of donor-imposed restrictions, if any, on a partially owned subsidiary's net assets should be reported in accordance with FASB ASC 958-205 and 958-320. In other words, the noncontrolling interest would be displayed in unrestricted net assets, temporarily restricted net assets, and permanently restricted net assets in accordance with the nature and existence of donor-imposed restrictions. For example, if Charity A owned a controlling interest in NFP B, its partially owned subsidiary, and NFP B had donor-restricted endowment funds, the net asset section of the statement of financial position of the consolidated entity might appear as follows:

Unrestricted net assets:	
Charity A	$ XX,XXX
Noncontrolling interest in NFP B	XX,XXX
Total unrestricted net assets	XX,XXX
Temporarily restricted net assets:	
Charity A	XX,XXX
Noncontrolling interest in NFP B	XX,XXX
Total temporarily restricted net assets	XX,XXX
Permanently restricted net assets:	
Charity A	XX,XXX
Noncontrolling interest in NFP B	XX,XXX
Total permanently restricted net assets	XX,XXX
Total net assets	$XXX,XXX

11.27 FASB ASC 958-810-25-6 discusses an interest by an NFP in another NFP that is less than a complete interest. For example, an NFP may appoint 80 percent of the board of the other NFP. For NFPs other than health care entities (that is, within the scope of FASB ASC 954, *Health Care Entities*), if the conditions for consolidation in paragraphs 2–4 of FASB ASC 958-810-25 are met, the basis of that consolidation would not reflect a noncontrolling interest for the portion of the board that the reporting entity does not control because there is no ownership interest other than the interest of the reporting entity. Additional information about reporting of related entities, including consolidation, is provided by chapter 3, "Financial Statements, the Reporting Entity, and General Financial Reporting Matters."

Reclassifications

11.28 Per FASB ASC 958-220-45-13, reclassifications of net assets—that is, simultaneous increases in one net asset class and decreases in another—should be made if any of the following events occur:

a. The NFP fulfills the purposes for which the net assets were restricted.

b. Donor-imposed restrictions expire with the passage of time or with the death of a split-interest agreement beneficiary (if the net assets are not otherwise restricted).

c. A donor withdraws, or court action removes, previously imposed restrictions.

d. A donor imposes restrictions on otherwise unrestricted net assets.[5]

Expiration of Donor-imposed Restrictions

11.29 Paragraphs 9–12 of FASB ASC 958-205-45 and FASB ASC 958-220-45-13 provide guidance for reporting reclassifications for the expiration of donor-imposed restrictions. An NFP should recognize the expiration of a donor-imposed restriction on a contribution in the period in which the restriction expires. A restriction expires when the stipulated time has elapsed, when the stipulated purpose for which the resource was restricted has been fulfilled, or both.

11.30 If two or more temporary restrictions are imposed on a contribution, the effect of the expiration of those restrictions should be recognized in the period in which the last remaining restriction has expired. FASB ASC 958-205-45-10A states that when determining when the last of two or more temporary restrictions has expired, explicit donor stipulations generally carry more weight than implied restrictions. (For additional information, see the example in paragraph 11.41.) Expirations of donor-imposed restrictions should be reported in a statement of activities as reclassifications, decreasing temporarily restricted net assets and increasing unrestricted net assets. Paragraphs 11.33–.52 provide information about the expiration of donor restrictions in specific situations.

11.31 For example, the amount of a donor's contribution that must be used by the NFP for a specified program would be reclassified from temporarily restricted to unrestricted net assets in the period in which the NFP conducts the program. The restriction on a contribution to acquire supplies for a particular program activity expires when those supplies are acquired by the NFP. The restriction on a term endowment in which contributed cash is to be invested for 10 years expires at the end of the tenth year.

11.32 The reclassification from temporarily restricted net assets into unrestricted net assets reflects that relationship between a restricted contribution and an expense that it supports because the restriction generally expires (increasing unrestricted net assets) in the same period as the expense occurs (decreasing unrestricted net assets).

---

[5] Paragraph 5.78 discusses donors imposing restrictions on otherwise unrestricted net assets.

Using Restricted Contributions First

11.33 A purpose restriction is typically fulfilled when the NFP incurs an expense or recognizes a liability to a vendor to acquire goods or services that satisfies the restriction. When an expense is incurred or liability recognized, both unrestricted net assets and temporarily restricted net assets may be available for that purpose.

11.34 FASB ASC 958-205-45-11 states that if an expense is incurred for a purpose for which both unrestricted and temporarily restricted net assets are available, a donor-imposed restriction is fulfilled to the extent of the expense incurred unless the expense is for a purpose that is directly attributable to another specific external source of revenue. For example, an expense does not fulfill an existing donor restriction if that expense is incurred for a purpose that is directly attributable to and reimbursed by a sponsored exchange agreement or a conditional award from a government agency, private foundation, or others.

11.35 For example, an employee's salary may meet donor-imposed restrictions to support the program on which the employee is working. In that situation, the restriction is met to the extent of the salary expense incurred unless incurring the salary will lead to inflows of revenues from a specific external source, such as revenues from a cost reimbursement contract or a conditional promise to give that becomes unconditional when the NFP incurs the salary expense.

11.36 In accordance with FASB ASC 958-205-45-11, temporarily restricted net assets with time restrictions are not available to support expenses until the time restrictions have expired. For example, a donor might specify that a gift be invested for a period of five years, with the investment return being added to the original gift during that time. At the end of the five years, the donor specifies that the accumulated amount be spent for a lecture series on a particular environmental topic. Although the NFP may hold lectures on that topic prior to the end of the fifth year, the expenses of those lectures do not release the restriction. Only expenses for lectures on that topic held after the end of the fifth year will release the restriction because the temporarily restricted net assets were not available until the time restriction had expired. Further, as explained in paragraphs 30–31 of FASB ASC 958-205-45, the temporarily restricted net assets of a donor-restricted endowment fund are time restricted until appropriated for expenditure by the NFP. Thus, the temporarily restricted net assets of a donor-restricted endowment fund are not available to support expenses until they are appropriated for expenditure (which is when the time restriction expires). (Paragraphs 11.37–.45 provide additional information about the implied time restrictions on promises to give with payments due in future periods. Paragraphs 4.71–.73 provide additional information about the implied time restrictions on the net assets of donor-restricted endowment funds.)

Expiration of Restrictions on Promises to Give

11.37 Paragraphs 5.95–.98 explain that a time restriction is implied on unconditional promises to give that are due in future periods unless explicit donor stipulations or circumstances surrounding the receipt of the promise make clear that the donor intended it to be used to support activities of the current period. FASB ASC 958-605-45-5 states that it is reasonable to assume that by specifying future payment dates donors indicate that their gift is to support activities in each period in which a payment is scheduled.

11.38 Thus, in the absence of clarifying donor stipulations, it would be inappropriate to look backward at the date the time restriction is met to determine if the purpose restriction was met in a prior year. For example, if a donor promises to give $5,000 a year for 5 years to be used to fund scholarships for students that are accounting majors, it is reasonable to assume that the donor wanted a $5,000 scholarship to be granted in each of the 5 years. In the absence of clarifying donor stipulations, it would be inappropriate to look backwards each year when the promised $5,000 was paid and to conclude that the purpose restriction had been met by scholarships of $25,000 granted in the year of the promise.

11.39 Technical Questions and Answers (Q&A) section 6140.03, "Lapsing of Time Restrictions on Receivables That Are Uncollected at Their Due Date,"[6] explains that time restrictions on contributions receivable lapse when the receivable is due. In some cases, the due date may be explicitly stated. In other cases, circumstances surrounding receipt of the contribution may make clear the implicit due date. In yet other cases, the due date may be unclear. NFPs should consider the facts and circumstances surrounding the promise to give to determine the due date, if any. At the due date, the time restriction expires and the net assets become available for the purpose specified by the donor. If the donor did not specify a purpose or otherwise restrict the contribution, the temporarily restricted net assets are reclassified to unrestricted net assets at the due date.

11.40 An NFP implies time restrictions that expire in the periods that the payments are due unless another time period is inherent in the donor's purpose restriction (that is, explicit donor stipulations or circumstances surrounding the receipt of a promise to give make clear that the donor intended the gift to be used to support activities of a period other than the one in which the payment is due). For example, a museum may receive an unconditional promise to give in year 1 that is restricted to supporting a traveling exhibit the museum will host in year 2. Although payments on that promise are due in installments in each of years 1, 2, and 3, a time restriction would not be implied because the donor restricted the gift to an event that will occur only in year 2.

11.41 FASB ASC 958-205-45-10A provides the following example. Assume in Year 1 that an NFP receives an unconditional promise to give that is payable in two equal installments in Years 2 and 3 with an explicit donor stipulation that its gift is to cover purchases of new equipment for the new School of Chemistry, which is expected to be completed in Year 3. That gift would have a purpose restriction (to be used to acquire new equipment to be housed in the new building), and because the unconditional promise is payable in Years 2 and 3, an entity generally would imply a time restriction (see FASB ASC 958-605-45-5). If, however, the building was completed early and opened in Year 2 and all of the needed equipment was purchased in Year 2 and exceeded the promised amount, absent an explicit stipulation to the contrary, it would be reasonable to conclude that those purchases fulfilled the donor restriction on the promised gift. Because the NFP did not adopt a policy of implying time restrictions on long-lived assets in accordance with FASB ASC 958-205-45-12 (as described in paragraph 11.47), the restriction for the purchase of the equipment expires when the equipment is placed in service. In addition, a reclassification would

---

[6] All Q&A sections can be found in *Technical Questions and Answers*.

be reported to reflect the decrease in temporarily restricted net assets and the increase in unrestricted net assets in Year 2.

11.42 Q&A section 6140.04, "Lapsing of Restrictions on Receivables if Purpose Restrictions Pertaining to Long-Lived Assets Are Met Before the Receivables Are Due," provides guidance for situations in which a donor restricts a contribution to the purchase of particular long-lived assets, and those assets are acquired, placed in service, and the purpose restrictions met, prior to the due date of the contribution. For example, an NFP may have a capital campaign asking for commitments to contribute over the next 5 years so the NFP can build a new building. A donor may promise to give $100,000 in 5 years in response to that request, but the building will be completed in 4 years. Because FASB ASC 958-205-45-11 states that temporarily restricted net assets with time restrictions are not available to support expenses until the time restrictions have expired, it can be unclear when the restrictions on the promise to give expire.

11.43 Q&A section 6140.04 states that NFPs should consider the facts and circumstances surrounding the promise to give and whether those facts and circumstances indicate that the donor intended the contribution to be used to support activities of the current period (that is, the period in which the long-lived asset is constructed or placed in service). If circumstances indicate that the donor intended to support activities of the current period, there is no time restriction and the guidance in paragraphs 9 and 11–12 of FASB ASC 958-205-45 would not be applicable, unless a restriction was placed on the contribution other than constructing the building (such as an additional donor restriction or a policy of implying time restrictions that expire over the useful life of the asset, as discussed in paragraph 11.47).

11.44 It is reasonable to assume that when a donor restricts a contribution to the construction or purchase of a specific long-lived asset, the donor intends to support activities of the period in which that long-lived asset is constructed or placed in service, even though the donor may specify payment dates that extend beyond that period. If circumstances indicate that the donor intended to support activities of the period in which the building is constructed or placed in service, a time restriction that expires when the payments are due should not be implied on the promise to give. If the only restriction on the unconditional promise to give is the construction or purchase of the specified long-lived asset (that is, the donor did not place additional restrictions on the contribution and the NFP does not imply a time restriction that expires over the useful life of the asset, as discussed in paragraph 11.47), the restriction is met as the asset is constructed or, if purchased, when it is placed in service.

11.45 If the donor does not stipulate a specific long-lived asset to be constructed or purchased, but merely states that the gift is to be used for capital acquisitions, it is reasonable to assume that by specifying future payment dates the donor indicates that the gift is to support capital acquisitions in each period in which a payment is scheduled (in accordance with FASB ASC 958-605-45-5). Both a purpose restriction and an implied time restriction exist, and in accordance with FASB ASC 958-205-45-11, the time restriction must expire first, and then the net assets are available for the purchase of capital assets. In accordance with Q&A section 6140.03, the implied time restriction on the promise to give expires when the receivable is due, and the expiration of restrictions is recognized in the future period in which the last remaining purpose restriction expires.

Expiration of Restrictions on Gifts of Long-Lived Assets or Gifts for Their Purchase

11.46 Paragraphs 1–2 of FASB ASC 958-360-45 provide guidance for reclassification of net assets upon the expiration of donor restrictions related to property and equipment. If a donor specifies a time period over which a donated long-lived asset must be used, temporarily restricted net assets should, over time, be reclassified as unrestricted net assets in a statement of activities as those restrictions expire. The amount reclassified may or may not be equal to the amount of the related depreciation. The amount to be reclassified is based on the length of time indicated by the donor-imposed restrictions, and the amount of depreciation is based on the useful economic life of the asset. For example, a vehicle with an estimated useful economic life of five years may be contributed by a donor and restricted for a specific use by the NFP for three years. Although the vehicle is depreciated over five years, the restriction expires over three years.

11.47 If a donor does not specify a time period over which a donated long-lived asset must be used, FASB ASC 958-605-45-6 (which is discussed in paragraphs 5.86–.88) states that an NFP may elect a policy to imply a time restriction that expires over the useful life of the donated long-lived assets. An NFP that adopts a policy of implying time restrictions also should imply a time restriction on long-lived assets acquired with gifts of cash or other assets restricted for those acquisitions. FASB ASC 958-205-45-12 states that if time restrictions are implied on gifts of long-lived assets, those implied time restrictions expire as the economic benefits of the acquired assets are used up; that is, over their estimated useful lives. As discussed in paragraphs 9.20–.23, depreciation should be recorded over the asset's useful life, and net assets should be reclassified periodically from temporarily restricted to unrestricted as depreciation is recognized.

11.48 In the absence of donor stipulations specifying how long donated assets must be used or an NFP's policy of implying time restrictions, FASB ASC 958-205-45-12 states that restrictions on long-lived assets, if any, or cash to acquire long-lived assets expire when the assets are placed in service.

11.49 Paragraphs 11.41–.45 discuss the expiration of restrictions on a promise to give that is restricted to the purchase or construction of long-lived assets.

Expiration of Restrictions on Donor Restricted Endowment Funds

11.50 FASB ASC 958-205-45-10 provides the following example. A gift of a term endowment that is to be invested for five years has two temporary restrictions—a purpose restriction (to be invested) and a time restriction (for a period of five years). After five years of investing, the purpose restriction will be met and the time restriction will lapse. In year five, when that term endowment becomes unrestricted, a reclassification should be reported to reflect the decrease in temporarily restricted net assets and the increase in unrestricted net assets. Thus, the related effects of that time-restricted gift should be reported in the period of receipt as well as the period in which the nature of the restriction changes.

11.51 The expiration of restrictions on donor-restricted endowment funds of permanent duration is discussed in paragraph 4.73.

Restrictions That Are Met in the Same Year as the Contribution Was Received

11.52 As noted in paragraph 5.85, an NFP may meet donor-imposed restrictions on all or a portion of an amount contributed in the same reporting period in which the contribution is received. In those cases, pursuant to FASB ASC 958-605-45-4, the contribution (to the extent that the restrictions have been met) may be reported as unrestricted support provided that the NFP has a similar policy for reporting investment gains and income (pursuant to FASB ASC 958-320-45-3, which is discussed in paragraph 4.84), reports consistently from period to period, and discloses its accounting policy in notes to financial statements. No reclassification is reported because the contribution was never included in temporarily restricted net assets.

Disclosures

11.53 FASB ASC 958-210-45-1 requires that a statement of financial position should report all of the following amounts: total assets, total liabilities, permanently restricted net assets, temporarily restricted net assets, unrestricted net assets, and total net assets. FASB ASC 958-220-45-1 requires that a statement of activities should report the following amounts for the period: the change in net assets, the change in permanently restricted net assets, the change in temporarily restricted net assets, and the change in unrestricted net assets. Per FASB ASC 958-220-45-2, the change in net assets should articulate to the net asset or equity reported in the statement of financial position.

11.54 FASB ASC 958-220-45-3 requires that reclassifications of amounts between net asset classes should be reported separately from other transactions in the statement of activities. If an event described in FASB ASC 958-220-45-13(c) or 13(d) occurs (paragraph 11.29), disclosure may be required by FASB ASC 220-20-50-1 as an unusual or infrequently occurring item. FASB ASC 958-220-45-4 states that information about reclassifications generally is provided by aggregating items that possess similar characteristics into reasonably homogeneous groups. Consistent with illustrative note D of FASB ASC 958-205-55-21, NFPs are encouraged to disclose detailed information about the restrictions that have been met and that therefore resulted in reclassifications from temporarily restricted net assets to unrestricted net assets. The encouraged information illustrated in note D is more detailed than the requirement to aggregate items that possess similar characteristics into reasonably homogeneous groups. Examples of encouraged disclosures include the following:

- Different kinds of restrictions that expired during the reporting period, such as reclassifications pertaining to expiration of time restrictions, satisfaction of purpose restrictions, or other donor-directed releases of restrictions.

- Information about the nature and extent of expenditures that satisfied purpose restrictions during the period (for example, capital expenditures, program service expenses, or supporting activity expenses)

11.55 FASB ASC 958-210-45-9 requires that information about the nature and amounts of different types of permanent restrictions or temporary restrictions be provided either by reporting their amounts on the face of the statement or by including relevant details in notes to financial statements.

11.56 For example, information about the following should be shown on the face of the financial statements or in the notes:

- Different kinds of permanent restrictions, such as those related to collection items and other specific assets to be held in perpetuity and to assets that have been contributed by donors with stipulations that they be invested in perpetuity
- Different kinds of temporary restrictions, such as those concerning the support of specific operating activities, use in specific future periods, or the acquisition of long-term assets

11.57 Paragraphs 1A–1B of FASB ASC 958-205-50 require disclosures about an NFP's donor-restricted endowment funds and its board-designated endowment funds. Those requirements are discussed in paragraph 4.98.

11.58 Separate disclosures of significant limitations other than those imposed by donors are permitted to be made on the face of the financial statements or in the notes to the financial statements. For example, paragraphs 6.50–.51 discuss disclosure of annuity reserves that are required by the laws of the state where the NFP is located or by the state where the donor resides and voluntary reserves set aside as a cushion against unexpected actuarial losses.

11.59 Paragraphs 4–5 of FASB ASC 958-810-50 describe the schedule of changes in consolidated net assets attributable to the parent and the noncontrolling interest that an NFP (parent) should provide if it has one or more consolidated subsidiaries with a noncontrolling interest. The schedule should be in notes to the consolidated financial statements or on the face of financial statements, if practicable. That schedule should reconcile beginning and ending balances of the parent's controlling interest and the noncontrolling interests for each class of net assets for which a noncontrolling interest exists during the reporting period and should include, at a minimum, the items in FASB ASC 958-810-50-5. FASB ASC 958-810-55-25 illustrates the required disclosures.

Changing Net Asset Classifications Reported in a Prior Year

11.60 Q&A section 6140.23, "Changing Net Asset Classifications Reported in a Prior Year," discusses circumstances in which NFPs correct net asset classifications previously reported in prior years' financial statements. It states that individual net asset classes, rather than net assets in the aggregate (total net assets), are relevant in determining whether an NFP's correction of net asset classifications previously reported in prior years' financial statements is an error in previously issued financial statements. As support for that conclusion, Q&A section 6140.23 quotes from paragraph 106 of FASB Concept No. 6, *Elements of Financial Statements—a replacement of FASB Concepts Statement No. 3 (incorporating an amendment of FASB Concepts Statement No. 2)*, which states the following:

> Since donor-imposed restrictions affect the types and levels of service a not-for-profit organization can provide, whether an organization has

> maintained certain classes of net assets may be more significant than whether it has maintained net assets in the aggregate.

As further support, Q&A section 6140.23 quotes FASB ASC 958-205-45-2:

> All NFPs shall ... classify and report net assets in three groups—permanently restricted, temporarily restricted, and unrestricted—based on the existence or absence of donor-imposed restrictions and the nature of those restrictions. Information about the nature and amount of restrictions imposed by donors on the use of contributed assets, including their potential effects on specific assets and on liabilities or classes of net assets, is helpful in assessing the financial flexibility of an NFP.

Auditing

11.61 Because net assets cannot be measured independently of an NFP's assets and liabilities, the auditor's consideration of net asset balances generally focuses on the assertions about rights and obligations and classification and understandability. In addition, the auditor may need to consider the specific audit objectives, auditing procedures, and selected controls listed in the following table, which are unique to NFPs.

11.62 The following table illustrates the use of assertions in developing audit objectives and designing substantive tests. The examples are not intended to be all-inclusive nor is it expected that all the procedures would necessarily be applied in an audit. The use of assertions in assessing risks and designing appropriate audit procedures to obtain audit evidence is described in paragraphs .26–.32 of AU-C section 315, *Understanding the Entity and Its Environment and Assessing the Risks of Material Misstatement*.[7] Paragraph .18 of AU-C section 330, *Performing Audit Procedures in Response to Assessed Risks and Evaluating the Audit Evidence Obtained*, requires the auditor to design and perform substantive procedures for all relevant assertions related to each material class of transactions, account balance, and disclosure, irrespective of the assessed risks of material misstatement. This requirement reflects the facts that (1) the auditor's assessment of risk is judgmental and may not identify all risks of material misstatement and (2) inherent limitations to internal control exist, including management override. Various audit procedures and the purposes for which they may be performed are described in paragraphs .A10–.A26 of AU-C section 500, *Audit Evidence*.

[7] All AU-C sections can be found in AICPA *Professional Standards*.

Auditing Considerations

Financial Statement Assertions	*Specific Audit Objectives*	*Select Control Objectives*
Presentation and Disclosure		
Rights and obligations; Classification and understandability	Net assets are used and accounted for in accordance with the presence or absence of donor restrictions. Temporarily restricted net assets are reclassified as unrestricted net assets in the statement of activities when donor-imposed restrictions have been fulfilled.	Management monitors compliance with donor restrictions. Controls ensure that reclassification of temporarily restricted net assets occurs when donor-imposed restrictions have been fulfilled. Management reviews the temporarily restricted net asset balances to ensure that the net assets are restricted (including unconditional promises to give due in future periods).

11.63 Suggested audit procedures to consider include the following:

1. Review minutes of governing board and governing board committee meetings for evidence of donor restrictions. (Rights and Obligations, Classification and Understandability, Completeness)
2. Obtain or document an understanding of the NFP's processes and controls over classifying net assets into permanently restricted, temporarily restricted, and unrestricted categories. Consider performing tests of controls over changes to each of the net asset classifications. (Classification and Understandability)
3. Obtain an understanding of any changes in legislation related to the net assets classification (for example, an enacted version of the Uniform Prudent Management of Institutional Funds Act) and review management's policies for consistency and interpretation with the provisions of the law. (Classification and Understandability)
4. Document the understanding of processes and controls over releases from restriction at the NFP. Consider testing the controls surrounding this activity. Determine that testing addresses releases of restrictions that have been recorded by the NFP as well as assessing whether any additional releases should have been recorded. (Completeness, Valuation and Allocation)
5. Obtain a detailed roll-forward of net assets, segregated into the appropriate net asset classes, reflecting the following columnar headings: net asset balances at the beginning of the period; net asset additions during the period; net asset reclassifications during the period; net asset reductions during the period; and net asset balances at the end of the period; or a comparative summary of

year-end net asset balances by net asset class. Consider the following tests: (Completeness, Classification and Understandability)

a. Agree beginning balances by net asset class to prior-year audited financial statements; investigate differences, if any (for example, unposted audit adjustments).

b. Trace and agree ending balances to the general ledger.

c. Test the mathematical accuracy of the analysis.

d. Review the composition of each net asset category.

e. Review change from prior year to determine that activity within net asset classification is reasonable and consistent with the requirements of each net asset category. Select a sample of net asset additions and deductions and trace to supporting donor or grantor receipts, correspondence, expenditures fulfilling restrictions, and so forth to test the propriety of the net asset classification. This includes comparing the information to the audit procedures performed on other areas, such as contributions and split-interest agreements.

f. Investigate any significant or unusual changes.

g. Review management's disclosure of the composition of net assets, verifying that information regarding the types of permanent restrictions and temporary restrictions is accurate and in adequate detail to provide the disclosures required by FASB ASC 958-210-45-9 (as discussed in paragraphs 11.03–.07 and 11.55–.56).

h. Consider disclosure of any significant limitations on the use of net assets that are not donor-imposed (for example, board-designated reserves).

6. Verify that the NFP releases temporarily restricted net assets before spending unrestricted net assets unless the expenditure is for a purpose that is directly attributable to another specific external source of revenue (as discussed in paragraphs 11.33–.36). For example, for expenditures selected for testing, determine whether temporarily restricted net assets were available to be spent either from gifts or from endowment return that had been appropriated for expenditure and, if amounts were available, whether the restriction was released. (Paragraphs 4.71–.73 discuss the effects of appropriation on the availability of temporarily restricted endowment return.) (Completeness, Classification and Understandability)

7. For releases from restriction, obtain a detailed schedule of net assets released during the year (or the reclassifications column of the roll-forward in step 4): (Completeness, Classification and Understandability)

a. Verify that the schedule ties to the statement of activities.

b. Test the mathematical accuracy of the schedule.

c. Based on inherent risk and materiality, determine the most efficient testing strategy (target testing, sampling, analytical review) and select items for testing.

d. Trace release from restrictions to the underlying support (for example, an invoice and expense). Determine that the release is appropriate, based on donor restrictions (purpose, time, or both). (Note that this testing will vary based on the NFP as well as the type of restriction.)

e. For releases of restriction on net assets of endowment funds, perform the audit procedures described in chapter 4, "Cash, Cash Equivalents, and Investments."

8. Determine that appropriate reclassifications are reported in the statement of activities when donor-imposed restrictions have been fulfilled and that the releases of restriction from temporarily restricted net assets to unrestricted net assets net to zero. (Rights and Obligations, Classification and Understandability)
9. Consider performing the suggested procedures in paragraphs 4.116–.117 for donor-restricted endowments funds. (Completeness, Accuracy, Classification)
10. Obtain and test the accuracy and adequacy of the disclosures related to net assets (paragraphs 11.53–.59). (Accuracy, Classification)

11.64

Appendix A—Financial Statements Prepared in Accordance with FASB ASU No. 2016-14

A-1 This appendix provides guidance for classification and reclassification of net assets in financial statements prepared in accordance with the amendments in FASB Accounting Standards Update (ASU) 2016-14, *Not-for-Profit Entities (Topic 958): Presentation of Financial Statements of Not-for-Profit Entities*. The amendments in ASU No. 2016-14 are effective for annual financial statements issued for fiscal years beginning after December 15, 2017 (for example, years ending December 31, 2018 and years ending June 30, 2019), and for interim periods within fiscal years beginning after December 15, 2018. Application to interim financial statements is permitted but not required in the initial year of application. Early application of the amendments is permitted. Additional information about the requirements of ASU No. 2016-14 is provided in shaded text throughout this guide, in appendix A, "Financial Statements Prepared in Accordance with FASB ASU No. 2016-14," of chapter 3, and in appendix A, "The New Not-for-Profit Financial Reporting Model: FASB ASU No. 2016-14," of this guide.

A-2 To facilitate the use of this appendix, the paragraph numbers in subsequent paragraphs correspond to the paragraphs in chapter 11 that will be replaced upon the effective date of FASB ASU No. 2016-14. For example, paragraph 11A.01 in this appendix corresponds to paragraph 11.01 in the chapter. Paragraphs in this appendix that do not have a corresponding paragraph in the chapter are identified by an A-paragraph number.

Introduction

11A.01 The "Pending Content" in the FASB *Accounting Standards Codification* (ASC) glossary defines *net assets* as "the excess or deficiency of assets over liabilities of a not-for-profit entity (NFP), which is divided into two mutually exclusive classes according to the existence or absence of donor-imposed restrictions."[1] As a residual interest, net assets cannot be measured independently of an NFP's assets and liabilities. Changes in net assets result from transactions and other events and circumstances in which total assets and total liabilities change by different amounts. In many NFPs, such changes include nonreciprocal transfers of assets received from donors who do not expect to receive either repayment or proportionate economic benefit in return. Display of and disclosures about net assets and changes in them are intended to assist donors and other users in assessing an NFP's efforts to provide goods and services to its constituencies, its efficiency and effectiveness in providing such services, and its continuing ability to do so.

11A.02 Changes in net assets result from revenues, expenses, gains, and losses; those changes are discussed in chapters 5–10 and 12–13 of this guide. This chapter describes principles for reporting total net assets in statements of financial position and changes in total net assets in statements of activities as well as related disclosures.

---

[1] Though not-for-profit entities (NFPs) may use other terms, such as *equity*, this guide uses the term *net assets* to describe the residual interest.

Fiduciary Responsibilities to Meet Donor Restrictions

11A.03 As noted in paragraph 5.75, the receipt of contributed assets imposes a fiduciary responsibility on an NFP's management to use the resources effectively and efficiently in pursuit of the NFP's mission; a donor's restriction on contributed resources focuses that fiduciary responsibility on a particular use for the contributed resources. As noted in FASB ASC 958-605-25-2, donors' restrictions place limits on the use of contributed resources and may affect an NFP's performance and its ability to provide services. The existence or absence of donors' restrictions forms the basis for the classification of net assets.

11A.04 The "Pending Content" in the FASB ASC glossary defines a *donor-imposed restriction* as

> [a] donor stipulation (donors include other types of contributors, including makers of certain grants) that specifies a use for a contributed asset that is more specific than the broad limits resulting from the following: (*a*) the nature of the NFP, (*b*) the environment in which it operates, and (*c*) the purposes specified in its articles of incorporation or bylaws or comparable documents for an unincorporated association. Some donors impose restrictions that are temporary in nature, for example, stipulating that resources be used after a specified date, for particular programs or services, or to acquire buildings or equipment. Other donors impose restrictions that are perpetual in nature, for example, stipulating that resources be maintained in perpetuity. Laws may extend those limits to investment returns from those resources and to other enhancements (diminishments) of those resources. Thus, those laws extend donor-imposed restrictions.

11A.05 When an NFP accepts a restricted contribution, it accepts a fiduciary responsibility to use the gift for the purposes for which it is given. An NFP needs a method of tracking restrictions on net assets and when those restrictions are satisfied. One way of tracking restricted net assets and their use is fund accounting, which facilitates tracking by segregating resources into funds that are consistent with the restricted use of the contribution. Chapter 16, "Fund Accounting," discusses fund accounting and the fund types typically used by NFPs. Other ways of tracking restricted net assets and their uses are via a subsidiary ledger or a project accounting system.

11A.06 No matter which system is used, an NFP needs to maintain documentation about the activities and other purposes for which the net assets in the fund, subsidiary ledger account, or project can be used. Documentation about any restrictions on periods in which the gift can be spent, restrictions on specific assets, limitations on investing, or other donor restrictions that limit the use of the resources also need to be included. For gifts that have complex restrictions, it is advisable to retain a copy of the gift agreement as part of the documentation. Some NFPs include donor names, donor contact information, and the amount(s) and date(s) of the contribution(s) in the documentation. For restrictions that are perpetual, such as donor-restricted endowment funds and perpetual interests in trusts, that documentation should be maintained in perpetuity.

11A.07 The end result should be that the NFP is able to produce a listing of the amounts and purposes for which its net assets are restricted. That information supports the disclosure in the financial statement in accordance with the "Pending Content" in FASB ASC 958-210-50-3, which requires that information about the nature and amounts of different types of donor-imposed restrictions, which affect how and when, if ever, the resources (net assets) can be used, be provided either by reporting their amounts on the face of the statement of financial position or by including the relevant details in notes to financial statements.

Failure to Meet a Donor's Restriction

11A.08 As noted in FASB ASC 958-450-25-1, noncompliance with donor-imposed restrictions on contributed assets, although rare, does occur, sometimes as a result of events occurring subsequent to receiving a contribution. Paragraphs 3.173–.175 provide guidance for noncompliance with donor restrictions. FASB ASC 855, *Subsequent Events*, provides guidance if the noncompliance occurs after the date of the statement of financial position but before the financial statements are issued. Paragraphs 3.177–.180 provide additional information about subsequent events.

Net Asset Classes

11A.09 The "Pending Content" in paragraphs 9–11 of FASB ASC 958-210-45 provides guidance for the classification of net assets. The amounts for each of the two classes of net assets—with donor restrictions and without donor restrictions—are based on the existence or absence of donor-imposed restrictions.

11A.10 As explained in the "Pending Content" in FASB ASC 958-205-05-6B, the two required net asset classes are a minimum classification scheme, if they are applicable. An NFP can choose to further disaggregate the two net asset classes. For example, an NFP may wish to disaggregate net assets with donor restrictions between those expected to be maintained in perpetuity and those expected to be spent over time or for a particular purpose. Additionally, net assets without donor restrictions may be subdivided into board-designated net assets and undesignated net assets to meet the requirements of the "Pending Content" in FASB ASC 958-210-50-3. Donor-imposed restrictions limit an NFP's ability to use or dispose of specific contributed assets or the economic benefits embodied in those assets. Donor stipulations should not be considered restrictions unless they include limitations on the use of contributed assets that are more specific than the broad limits imposed by the NFP's purpose and nature.

11A.11 The "Pending Content" in FASB ASC 958-210-45-6 states that, generally, donor-imposed restrictions apply to net assets, not to specific assets. Donors may also restrict specific assets regarding their use (for example, land contributed for a park) or over time (for example, contributed securities that must be held in perpetuity). Paragraphs 3A.09–.23 and 11A.55 discuss reporting requirements for specific assets that have been received with donor-imposed restrictions.

Net Assets With Donor Restrictions

11A.12 The "Pending Content" in FASB ASC glossary defines *net assets with donor restrictions* as "the part of net assets of an NFP that is subject to donor-imposed restrictions (donors include other types of contributors, including makers of certain grants)."

11A.13 Some contributions have donor-imposed restrictions that require the NFP to maintain their resources in perpetuity. For example, contributions of cash or securities restricted by the donor with the stipulation that they be invested in perpetuity (donor-restricted endowment funds) and contributions of collection items (if collections are capitalized)[2] required by the donor to be maintained permanently in the NFP's collections should be included in net assets with donor restrictions.

11A.14 This paragraph will be deleted upon the effective date of FASB ASU No. 2016-14.

11A.15 This paragraph will be deleted upon the effective date of FASB ASU No. 2016-14.

11A.16 Other contributions have donor-imposed restrictions that limit their use (*a*) to later periods of time or after specified dates, or (*b*) to specified purposes.[3] For example, contributions restricted by the donor to use by the NFP over the next five years or to support a specific future program should be recognized as increases in net assets with donor restrictions.

11A.17 Net assets with donor restrictions may also change as a result of increases and decreases in existing assets or the economic benefits embodied in those assets that are subject to donor-imposed restrictions. For example, if the donor has stipulated that investment return earned on a term endowment must be added to the principal of the endowment fund until the term is expired and the principal can be spent for a restricted purpose, the investment return should be reported as increases in net assets with donor restrictions. Similarly, if the donor has stipulated that investment return on a perpetual endowment be spent for a restricted purpose, the investment return increases net assets with donor restrictions. Investment return on donor-restricted endowments (both term and perpetual) is also subject to a time restriction that results from the Uniform Prudent Management of Institutional Funds Act (UPMIFA) as enacted by a state. UPMIFA, as enacted, is a law that extends a donor's restriction to use of the funds, including the investment return, until the funds are appropriated for expenditure by the governing board. Paragraphs 4.65.79 provide additional information about the classification of donor-restricted endowment funds.

Net Assets Without Donor Restrictions

11A.18 The "Pending Content" in the FASB ASC glossary defines *net assets without donor restrictions* as the part of net assets of an NFP that is not subject to donor-imposed restrictions (donors include other types of contributors, including makers of certain grants).

11A.19 The use of net assets without donor restrictions may be limited in other respects, such as by contract or by board designation. Changes in net assets arising from exchange transactions (except income and gains on

---

[2] Chapter 7, "Other Assets," discusses accounting policies concerning the capitalization of collection items.

[3] The "Pending Content" in FASB *Accounting Standards Codification* (ASC) 958-605-45-4 states that donor-restricted contributions whose restrictions are met in the same reporting period may be reported as support within net assets without donor restrictions provided that an NFP has a similar policy for reporting investment gains and income (see the "Pending Content" in FASB ASC 958-320-45-3), reports consistently from period to period and discloses its accounting policy. Paragraph 5.85 provides further guidance concerning that policy.

assets that are restricted by donors or by law) should be included in net assets without donor restrictions.

11A.20 NFPs such as social and country clubs may issue membership interests, such as capital shares. If those interests are wholly or partially refundable when the member dies, moves away, resigns his or her membership, or at a fixed date, FASB ASC 480-10 provides guidance.

11A.21 FASB ASC 480-10 states that an interest that is mandatorily redeemable at a fixed date for a fixed or indexed amount—that embodies an unconditional obligation requiring the issuer to redeem it by transferring its assets at a fixed date (or dates)—should be classified as a liability and initially measured at fair value. An interest that embodies a conditional obligation to redeem the instrument by transferring assets upon an event not certain to occur becomes mandatorily redeemable if that event occurs, the condition is resolved, or the event becomes certain to occur.

11A.22 Thus, a membership interest that embodies a conditional obligation to redeem it upon an event not certain to occur (such as *only* upon moving from the community) is initially classified as net assets without donor restrictions. If the uncertain event occurs, the condition is resolved, or the event becomes certain to occur, and payment of a fixed or indexed amount is to be made at a fixed date (such as three months from the event's occurrence), the interest is reclassified as a liability.

11A.23 Per FASB ASC 480-10-55-10, upon reclassification, the issuing NFP would measure the obligation at fair value and reduce net assets by the amount of that initial measure, recognizing no gain or loss. Subsequently, pursuant to FASB ASC 480-10-35-3, those mandatorily redeemable interests are measured at the present value of the amount to be paid at settlement using the rate implicit at inception if both the amount to be paid and the settlement date are fixed. If the amount to be paid varies by reference to an interest rate index, currency index, or another external index, those instruments are subsequently measured at the amount of cash that would be paid under the conditions specified in the contract if settlement occurred at the reporting date. The change in the liability amount from the prior period is reported as interest cost (reported as described in paragraph 13.77).

11A.24 The Financial Reporting Executive Committee believes that for other mandatorily redeemable membership interests, a membership interest would also be classified as a liability if the obligation requiring the club to redeem it is unconditional, unless the redemption is required to occur only upon the liquidation or termination of the social or country club. An obligation to redeem a membership interest that is conditioned upon an event not certain to occur would be initially classified as net assets without donor restrictions. When the obligation becomes unconditional (that is, if the uncertain event occurs, the condition is resolved, or the event becomes certain to occur), the membership interest would be reclassified as a liability.

Noncontrolling Interests

11A.25 FASB ASC 958-810-45-1 states that noncontrolling interests in the equity (net assets) of consolidated subsidiaries should be reported as a separate component of the appropriate class of net assets in the consolidated statement of financial position of an NFP. That amount should be clearly identified and described (for example, as noncontrolling ownership interest in subsidiaries) to distinguish it from the components of net assets of the parent, which includes the parent's controlling financial interest in its subsidiaries. The "Pending Content" in paragraphs 17–25 of FASB ASC 958-810-55 illustrates the presentation of a noncontrolling interest in a for-profit subsidiary in a consolidated statement of financial position and a consolidated statement of changes in net assets without donor restrictions.

11A.26 The effects of donor-imposed restrictions, if any, on a partially owned subsidiary's net assets should be reported in accordance with FASB ASC 958-205 and 958-320. In other words, the noncontrolling interest would be displayed in the net asset classes in accordance with the existence (or absence) of donor-imposed restrictions. For example, if Charity A owned a controlling interest in NFP B, its partially owned subsidiary, and NFP B had donor-restricted endowment funds, the net asset section of the statement of financial position of the consolidated entity might appear as follows:

Net assets without donor restrictions:	
Charity A	$ XX,XXX
Noncontrolling interest in NFP B	XX,XXX
Total net assets without donor restrictions	XX,XXX
Net assets with donor restrictions:	
Charity A	XX,XXX
Noncontrolling interest in NFP B	XX,XXX
Total net assets with donor restrictions	XX,XXX
Total net assets	$XXX,XXX

11A.27 FASB ASC 958-810-25-6 discusses an interest by an NFP in another NFP that is less than a complete interest. For example, an NFP may appoint 80 percent of the board of the other NFP. For NFPs other than health care entities (that is, within the scope of FASB ASC 954, *Health Care Entities*), if the conditions for consolidation in paragraphs 2–4 of FASB ASC 958-810-25 are met, the basis of that consolidation would not reflect a noncontrolling interest for the portion of the board that the reporting entity does not control because there is no ownership interest other than the interest of the reporting entity. Additional information about reporting of related entities, including consolidation, is provided by chapter 3, "Financial Statements, the Reporting Entity, and General Financial Reporting Matters."

Reclassifications of Net Assets

11A.28 Per the "Pending Content" in FASB ASC 958-220-45-13, reclassifications of net assets—that is, simultaneous increases in one net asset class and decreases in another—should be made if any of the following events occur:

a. The NFP fulfills the purposes for which the net assets were restricted.

b. Donor-imposed restrictions expire with the passage of time or with the death of a split-interest agreement beneficiary (if the net assets are not otherwise restricted).

c. A donor withdraws, or court action removes, previously imposed restrictions.

d. A donor imposes restrictions on net assets without donor restrictions.[4]

Expiration of Donor-imposed Restrictions

11A.29 The "Pending Content" in paragraphs 9–12 of FASB ASC 958-205-45 and the "Pending Content" in FASB ASC 958-220-45-13 provides guidance for reporting reclassifications for the expiration of donor-imposed restrictions. An NFP should recognize the expiration of a donor-imposed restriction on a contribution in the period in which the restriction expires. A restriction expires when the stipulated time has elapsed, when the stipulated purpose for which the resource was restricted has been fulfilled, or both.

11A.30 If two or more restrictions that are temporary in nature are imposed on a contribution, the effect of the expiration of those restrictions should be recognized in the period in which the last remaining restriction has expired. The "Pending Content" in FASB ASC 958-205-45-10A states that when determining when the last of two or more donor-imposed restrictions that are temporary in nature has expired, explicit donor stipulations generally carry more weight than implied restrictions. (For additional information, see the example in paragraph 11A.41.) Expirations of donor-imposed restrictions should be reported in a statement of activities as reclassifications of net assets, decreasing net assets with donor restrictions and increasing net assets without donor restrictions. Paragraphs 11A.33–.52 provide information about the expiration of donor restrictions in specific situations.

11A.31 For example, the amount of a donor's contribution that must be used by the NFP for a specified program would be reclassified from net assets with donor restrictions to net assets without donor restrictions in the period in which the NFP conducts the program. The restriction on a contribution to acquire supplies for a particular program activity expires when those supplies are acquired by the NFP. The restriction on a term endowment in which contributed cash is to be invested for 10 years expires at the end of the tenth year.

11A.32 The reclassification of net assets from net assets with donor restrictions into net assets without donor restrictions reflects that relationship between a donor-restricted contribution and an expense that it supports because the restriction generally expires (increasing net assets without donor restrictions) in the same period as the expense occurs (decreasing net assets without donor restrictions).

Using Donor-Restricted Contributions First

11A.33 A purpose restriction is typically fulfilled when the NFP incurs an expense or recognizes a liability to a vendor to acquire goods or services that satisfies the restriction. When an expense is incurred or liability recognized, both net assets without donor restrictions and net assets with donor restrictions may be available for that purpose.

---

[4] Paragraph 5.78 discusses donors imposing restrictions on net assets without donor restrictions.

11A.34 The "Pending Content" in FASB ASC 958-205-45-11 states that if an expense is incurred for a purpose for which both net assets without donor restrictions and net assets with donor restrictions are available, a donor-imposed restriction is fulfilled to the extent of the expense incurred unless the expense is for a purpose that is directly attributable to another specific external source of revenue. For example, an expense does not fulfill an existing donor restriction if that expense is incurred for a purpose that is directly attributable to and reimbursed by a sponsored exchange agreement or a conditional award from a government agency, private foundation, or others.

11A.35 For example, an employee's salary may meet donor-imposed restrictions to support the program on which the employee is working. In that situation, the restriction is met to the extent of the salary expense incurred unless incurring the salary will lead to inflows of revenues from a specific external source, such as revenues from a cost reimbursement contract or a conditional promise to give that becomes unconditional when the NFP incurs the salary expense.

11A.36 In accordance with the "Pending Content" in FASB ASC 958-205-45-11, explicit time restrictions, such as those discussed in the "Pending Content" in FASB ASC 958-205-45-10, and implied time restrictions, such as those discussed in the "Pending Content" in FASB ASC 958-605-45-5, make net assets unavailable to support expenses until the time restrictions have expired. For example, a donor might specify that a gift be invested for a period of five years, with the investment return being added to the original gift during that time. At the end of the five years, the donor specifies that the accumulated amount be spent for a lecture series on a particular environmental topic. Although the NFP may hold lectures on that topic prior to the end of the fifth year, the expenses of those lectures do not release the restriction. Only expenses for lectures on that topic held after the end of the fifth year will release the restriction because the net assets with donor restrictions were not available until the time restriction had expired. Further, as explained in the "Pending Content" in FASB ASC 958-205-45-13D, unless stated otherwise in the gift instrument, the assets in an endowment fund are donor-restricted assets until they are appropriated for expenditure by the NFP's governing board. Thus, the net assets of a donor-restricted endowment fund are not available to support expenses until they are appropriated for expenditure (which is when the time restriction expires). (Paragraphs 11A.37–.45 provide additional information about the implied time restrictions on promises to give with payments due in future periods. Paragraphs 4.71–.73 provide additional information about the time restrictions on the net assets of donor-restricted endowment funds.)

Expiration of Donor Restrictions on Promises to Give

11A.37 Paragraphs 5.95–.98 explain that a time restriction is implied on unconditional promises to give that are due in future periods unless explicit donor stipulations or circumstances surrounding the receipt of the promise make clear that the donor intended it to be used to support activities of the current period. The "Pending Content" in FASB ASC 958-605-45-5 states that it is reasonable to assume that by specifying future payment dates donors indicate that their gift is to support activities in each period in which a payment is scheduled.

11A.38 Thus, in the absence of clarifying donor stipulations, it would be inappropriate to look backward at the date the time restriction is met to determine if the purpose restriction was met in a prior year. For example, if a donor promises to give $5,000 a year for 5 years to be used to fund scholarships for students that are accounting majors, it is reasonable to assume that the donor wanted a $5,000 scholarship to be granted in each of the 5 years. In the absence of clarifying donor stipulations, it would be inappropriate to look backwards each year when the promised $5,000 was paid and to conclude that the purpose restriction had been met by scholarships of $25,000 granted in the year of the promise.

11A.39 Technical Questions and Answers (Q&A) section 6140.03, "Lapsing of Time Restrictions on Receivables That Are Uncollected at Their Due Date,"[5] explains that time restrictions on contributions receivable lapse when the receivable is due. In some cases, the due date may be explicitly stated. In other cases, circumstances surrounding receipt of the contribution may make clear the implicit due date. In yet other cases, the due date may be unclear. NFPs should consider the facts and circumstances surrounding the promise to give to determine the due date, if any. At the due date, the time restriction expires and the net assets become available for the purpose specified by the donor. If the donor did not specify a purpose or otherwise restrict the contribution, the net assets with donor restrictions are reclassified to net assets without donor restrictions at the due date.

11A.40 An NFP implies time restrictions that expire in the periods that the payments are due unless another time period is inherent in the donor's purpose restriction (that is, explicit donor stipulations or circumstances surrounding the receipt of a promise to give make clear that the donor intended the gift to be used to support activities of a period other than the one in which the payment is due). For example, a museum may receive an unconditional promise to give in year 1 that is restricted by the donor to supporting a traveling exhibit the museum will host in year 2. Although payments on that promise are due in installments in each of years 1, 2, and 3, a time restriction would not be implied because the donor restricted the gift to an event that will occur only in year 2.

11A.41 The "Pending Content" in FASB ASC 958-205-45-10A provides the following example. Assume in Year 1 that an NFP receives an unconditional promise to give that is payable in two equal installments in Years 2 and 3 with an explicit donor stipulation that its gift is to cover purchases of new equipment for the new School of Chemistry, which is expected to be completed in Year 3. That gift would have a purpose restriction (to be used to acquire new equipment to be housed in the new building), and because the unconditional promise is payable in Years 2 and 3, an entity generally would imply a time restriction (see the "Pending Content" in FASB ASC 958-605-45-5). If, however, the building was completed early and opened in Year 2 and all of the needed equipment was purchased in Year 2 and exceeded the promised amount, absent an explicit stipulation to the contrary, it would be reasonable to conclude that those purchases fulfilled the donor restriction on the promised gift. The restriction for the purchase of the equipment expires when the equipment is placed in service in accordance with the "Pending Content" in FASB ASC 958-205-45-12. A reclassification of net assets would be reported to reflect the decrease in net assets with donor restrictions and the increase in net assets without donor restrictions in Year 2.

---

[5] All Q&A sections can be found in *Technical Questions and Answers*.

11A.42 This paragraph will be deleted upon the effective date of FASB ASU No. 2016-14.

11A.43 This paragraph will be deleted upon the effective date of FASB ASU No. 2016-14.

11A.44 This paragraph will be deleted upon the effective date of FASB ASU No. 2016-14.

11A.45 This paragraph will be deleted upon the effective date of FASB ASU No. 2016-14.

Expiration of Restrictions on Gifts of Long-Lived Assets or Gifts for Their Purchase

11A.46 The "Pending Content" in paragraphs 1–1A of FASB ASC 958-360-45 provides guidance for reclassification of net assets upon the expiration of donor restrictions related to property and equipment. If the property, plant, and equipment item being depreciated was contributed to the NFP with an explicit donor-imposed restriction on the length of time of the item's use, net assets with donor restrictions should be reclassified as net assets without donor restrictions in a statement of activities as those restrictions expire. The amount reclassified may or may not be equal to the amount of the related depreciation. The amount to be reclassified should be based on the length of time indicated by the donor-imposed restrictions, if restrictions exist, while the amount of depreciation should be based on the useful economic life of the asset. For example, a computer with an estimated useful economic life of five years may be contributed by a donor and restricted for a specific use by the NFP for three years.

A-3 Depreciation should be recorded over the asset's useful life, and net assets should be reclassified periodically from net assets with donor restrictions to net assets without donor restrictions as the asset is used for its restricted purpose. In the example in the "Pending Content" in FASB ASC 958-360-45-1 (paragraph 11A.46), the computer would be depreciated over five years, and the restriction would expire over three years.

11A.47 This paragraph will be deleted upon the effective date of FASB ASU No. 2016-14.

11A.48 The "Pending Content" in FASB ASC 958-360-45-1A states that the following contributions should be reclassified from net assets with donor restrictions to net assets without donor restrictions when the acquired or constructed property, plant, or equipment is placed in service:

a. Purpose-restricted contributions of property, plant, or equipment that are without donor-imposed stipulations specifying how long the donated asset must be used

b. Contributions of cash restricted for the acquisition or construction of property, plant, or equipment.

The entire amount of the contribution of property, plant, or equipment or cash should be reclassified at the time the asset is placed in service. There may be circumstances in which a donor restriction might extend beyond the point at which the property, plant, or equipment is placed in service. For example, a donor might specify that a donation restricted for the acquisition of property, plant, or equipment must continue to be used for a specified period of time. In such circumstances, the restriction would expire over the period of time that the asset is to be used.

11A.49 Paragraph 11A.41 discusses the expiration of restrictions on a promise to give that is restricted to the purchase of long-lived assets.

Expiration of Restrictions on Donor-Restricted Endowment Funds

11A.50 The "Pending Content" in FASB ASC 958-205-45-10 provides the following example. A gift of a term endowment that is to be invested for five years has two donor-imposed restrictions that are temporary in nature—a purpose restriction (to be invested) and a time restriction (for a period of five years). After five years of investing, the purpose restriction will be met and the time restriction will lapse. In year five, when that term endowment is no longer donor-restricted, a reclassification of net assets should be reported to reflect the decrease in net assets with donor restrictions and the increase in net assets without donor restrictions.

11A.51 The expiration of restrictions on donor-restricted endowment funds of perpetual duration is discussed in paragraph 4.73.

Restrictions That Are Met in the Same Year as the Contribution Was Received

11A.52 As noted in paragraph 5.85, an NFP may meet donor-imposed restrictions on all or a portion of an amount contributed in the same reporting period in which the contribution is received. In those cases, pursuant to the "Pending Content" in FASB ASC 958-605-45-4, the donor-restricted contribution (to the extent that the restrictions have been met) may be reported as support within net assets without donor restrictions provided that the NFP has a similar policy for reporting investment gains and income (pursuant to the "Pending Content" in FASB ASC 958-320-45-3, which is discussed in paragraph 4.84), reports consistently from period to period, and discloses its accounting policy in notes to financial statements. No reclassification is reported because the contribution was never included in net assets with donor restrictions.

Disclosures

11A.53 The "Pending Content" in FASB ASC 958-210-45-1 requires that a statement of financial position report all of the following amounts: total assets, total liabilities, total net assets with donor restrictions, total net assets without donor restrictions, and total net assets. The "Pending Content" in FASB ASC 958-220-45-1 requires that a statement of activities report the following amounts for the period: the change in net assets, the change in net assets with donor restrictions, and the change in net assets without donor restrictions. Per FASB ASC 958-220-45-2, the change in net assets should articulate to the net asset or equity reported in the statement of financial position.

11A.54 The "Pending Content" in FASB ASC 958-220-45-3 requires that reclassifications of net assets, such as expirations of donor-imposed restrictions, should be reported separately from other transactions in the statement of activities. If an event described in the "Pending Content" in FASB ASC 958-220-45-13(c) or 13(d) occurs (paragraph 11A.29), disclosure may be required by FASB ASC 220-20-50-1 as an unusual or infrequently occurring item. The "Pending Content" in FASB ASC 958-220-45-4 states that information about reclassifications of net assets generally is provided by aggregating items that possess similar characteristics into reasonably homogeneous groups. Consistent with illustrative note D of the "Pending Content" in FASB ASC 958-205-55-21, NFPs are encouraged to disclose detailed information about the restrictions that have been met and that therefore resulted in reclassifications from net assets with donor restrictions to net assets without donor restrictions. The encouraged information illustrated in note D is more detailed than the requirement to aggregate items that possess similar characteristics into reasonably homogeneous groups. Examples of encouraged disclosures include the following:

- Different kinds of restrictions that expired during the reporting period, such as reclassifications of net assets pertaining to expiration of time restrictions, satisfaction of purpose restrictions, or other donor-directed releases of restrictions.
- Information about the nature and extent of expenditures that satisfied purpose restrictions during the period (for example, capital expenditures, program service expenses, or supporting activity expenses)

11A.55 The "Pending Content" in FASB ASC 958-210-45-9 and FASB ASC 958-210-50-3 requires that information about the nature and amounts of different types of restrictions, including donor-imposed restrictions, that affect how and when, if ever, the resources (net assets) can be used be provided either by reporting their amounts on the face of the statement or by including relevant details in notes to financial statements.

11A.56 For example, information about the following donor-imposed restrictions may be shown on the face of the financial statements or in the notes:

a. Assets, such as land or works of art, donated with stipulations that they be used for a specified purpose, be preserved, and not be sold.

b. Assets donated with stipulations that they be invested to provide a permanent source of income. These result from gifts and bequests that create a donor-restricted endowment that is perpetual in nature.

c. Support of particular operating activities.

d. Investment for a specified term.

e. Use in a specified future period.

f. Acquisition of long-lived assets.

11A.57 The "Pending Content" in paragraphs 1A–1B of FASB ASC 958-205-50 and FASB ASC 958-205-50-2 requires disclosures about an NFP's donor-restricted endowment funds and its board-designated endowment funds. Those requirements are discussed in paragraphs 4.97.98.

11A.58 The Pending Content" in FASB ASC 958-210-50-3 requires disclosure, on the face of the financial statements or in the notes to financial statements, of information about additional limitations placed on net assets, such as information about the amounts and purposes of board designations of net assets without donor restrictions. For example, paragraphs 6.51 discusses disclosure of voluntary reserves set aside as a cushion against unexpected actuarial losses on split-interest agreements. In addition, the "Pending Content" in FASB ASC 958-30-50-2 requires that legally mandated reserves, such as annuity reserves required by laws of the state in which the NFP is located or the donor resides, should be disclosed in the notes to financial statements.

11A.59 The "Pending Content" in paragraphs 4–5 of FASB ASC 958-810-50 describes the schedule of changes in consolidated net assets attributable to the parent and the noncontrolling interest that an NFP (parent) should provide if it has one or more consolidated subsidiaries with a noncontrolling interest. The schedule should be in notes to the consolidated financial statements or on the face of financial statements, if practicable. That schedule should reconcile beginning and ending balances of the parent's controlling interest and the noncontrolling interests for each class of net assets for which a noncontrolling interest exists during the reporting period and should include, at a minimum, the items in the "Pending Content" of FASB ASC 958-810-50-5. The "Pending Content" in FASB ASC 958-810-55-25 illustrates the required disclosures.

Changing Net Asset Classifications Reported in a Prior Year

11A.60 Q&A section 6140.23, "Changing Net Asset Classifications Reported in a Prior Year," discusses circumstances in which NFPs correct net asset classifications previously reported in prior years' financial statements. It states that individual net asset classes, rather than net assets in the aggregate (total net assets), are relevant in determining whether an NFP's correction of net asset classifications previously reported in prior years' financial statements is an error in previously issued financial statements. As support for that conclusion, Q&A section 6140.23 quotes from paragraph 106 of FASB Concept No. 6, *Elements of Financial Statements—a replacement of FASB Concepts Statement No. 3 (incorporating an amendment of FASB Concepts Statement No. 2)*, which states the following:

> Since donor-imposed restrictions affect the types and levels of service a not-for-profit organization can provide, whether an organization has maintained certain classes of net assets may be more significant than whether it has maintained net assets in the aggregate.

As further support, the "Pending Content" in FASB ASC 958-205-45-2 states that information about restrictions imposed by donors on the use of contributed assets, including their potential effects on specific assets and on liabilities or classes of net assets, should be disclosed in accordance with FASB ASC 958-210-50-3, because it is helpful in assessing the financial flexibility of an NFP.

Auditing

11A.61 Because net assets cannot be measured independently of an NFP's assets and liabilities, the auditor's consideration of net asset balances generally focuses on the assertions about rights and obligations and classification and understandability. In addition, the auditor may need to consider the specific audit objectives, auditing procedures, and selected controls listed in the following table, which are unique to NFPs.

11A.62 The following table illustrates the use of assertions in developing audit objectives and designing substantive tests. The examples are not intended to be all-inclusive nor is it expected that all the procedures would necessarily be applied in an audit. The use of assertions in assessing risks and designing appropriate audit procedures to obtain audit evidence is described in paragraphs .26–.32 of AU-C section 315, *Understanding the Entity and Its Environment and Assessing the Risks of Material Misstatement*.[6] Paragraph .18 of AU-C section 330, *Performing Audit Procedures in Response to Assessed Risks and Evaluating the Audit Evidence Obtained*, requires the auditor to design and perform substantive procedures for all relevant assertions related to each material class of transactions, account balance, and disclosure, irrespective of the assessed risks of material misstatement. This requirement reflects the facts that (1) the auditor's assessment of risk is judgmental and may not identify all risks of material misstatement and (2) inherent limitations to internal control exist, including management override. Various audit procedures and the purposes for which they may be performed are described in paragraphs .A10–.A26 of AU-C section 500, *Audit Evidence*.

Auditing Considerations

Financial Statement Assertions	*Specific Audit Objectives*	*Select Control Objectives*
Presentation and Disclosure		
Rights and obligations; Classification and understandability	Net assets are used and accounted for in accordance with the presence or absence of donor restrictions. Net assets with donor restrictions are reclassified as net assets without donor restriction in the statement of activities when donor-imposed restrictions have been fulfilled.	Management monitors compliance with donor restrictions. Controls ensure that reclassification of net assets with donor restrictions occurs when donor-imposed restrictions have been fulfilled. Management reviews the balances of net assets with donor restrictions to ensure that the net assets are restricted (including unconditional promises to give due in future periods).

11A.63 Suggested audit procedures to consider include the following:

1. Review minutes of governing board and governing board committee meetings for evidence of donor restrictions. (Rights and Obligations, Classification and Understandability, Completeness)
2. Obtain or document an understanding of the NFP's processes and controls over classifying net assets into net assets with donor restrictions and net assets without donor restrictions. Consider performing tests of controls over changes to all of the net asset classifications. (Classification and Understandability)
3. Obtain an understanding of any changes in legislation related to the net assets classification (for example, an enacted version of the

---

[6] All AU-C sections can be found in AICPA *Professional Standards*.

Uniform Prudent Management of Institutional Funds Act) and review management's policies for consistency and interpretation with the provisions of the law. (Classification and Understandability)

4. Document the understanding of processes and controls over releases from restriction at the NFP. Consider testing the controls surrounding this activity. Determine that testing addresses releases of restrictions that have been recorded by the NFP as well as assessing whether any additional releases should have been recorded. (Completeness, Valuation and Allocation)

5. Obtain a detailed roll-forward of net assets, segregated into the appropriate net asset classes, reflecting the following columnar headings: net asset balances at the beginning of the period; net asset additions during the period; net asset reclassifications during the period; net asset reductions during the period; and net asset balances at the end of the period; or a comparative summary of year-end net asset balances by net asset class. Consider the following tests: (Completeness, Classification and Understandability)

   a. Agree beginning balances by net asset class to prior-year audited financial statements; investigate differences, if any (for example, unposted audit adjustments).

   b. Trace and agree ending balances to the general ledger.

   c. Test the mathematical accuracy of the analysis.

   d. Review the composition of each net asset category.

   e. Review change from prior year to determine that activity within net asset classification is reasonable and consistent with the requirements of each net asset category. Select a sample of net asset additions and deductions and trace to supporting donor or grantor receipts, correspondence, expenditures fulfilling restrictions, and so forth to test the propriety of the net asset classification. This includes comparing the information to the audit procedures performed on other areas, such as contributions and split-interest agreements.

   f. Investigate any significant or unusual changes.

   g. Review management's disclosure of the composition of net assets, verifying that information regarding the types of donor-imposed restrictions and board designations is accurate and in adequate detail to provide the disclosures required by the "Pending Content" in FASB ASC 958-210-45-9 and the "Pending Content" in FASB ASC FASB ASC 958-210-50-3 (as discussed in paragraphs 11A.03–.07 and 11A.55–.58).

   h. Consider disclosure of any significant limitations on the use of net assets that are neither donor-imposed nor board-designated (for example, reserves of net assets required by state insurance regulations on split-interest gifts).

6. Verify that the NFP releases restricted resources (net assets with donor restrictions) before spending general resources (net assets

without donor restrictions) unless the expenditure is for a purpose that is directly attributable to another specific external source of revenue (as discussed in paragraphs 11A.33–.36). For example, for expenditures selected for testing, determine whether donor-restricted resources were available to be spent either from gifts or from endowment return that had been appropriated for expenditure and, if amounts were available, whether the restriction was released. (Paragraphs 4.71–.73 discuss the effects of appropriation on the availability of endowment return.) (Completeness, Classification and Understandability)

7. For releases from restriction, obtain a detailed schedule of net assets released during the year (or the reclassifications column of the roll-forward in step 4): (Completeness, Classification and Understandability)
   a. Verify that the schedule ties to the statement of activities.
   b. Test the mathematical accuracy of the schedule.
   c. Based on inherent risk and materiality, determine the most efficient testing strategy (target testing, sampling, analytical review) and select items for testing.
   d. Trace release from restrictions to the underlying support (for example, an invoice and expense). Determine that the release is appropriate, based on donor restrictions (purpose, time, or both). (Note that this testing will vary based on the NFP as well as the type of restriction.)
   e. For releases of restriction on net assets of endowment funds, perform the audit procedures described in chapter 4, "Cash, Cash Equivalents, and Investments."
8. Determine that appropriate reclassifications are reported in the statement of activities when donor-imposed restrictions have been fulfilled and that the releases of restriction from net assets with donor restrictions to net assets without donor restrictions net to zero. (Rights and Obligations, Classification and Understandability)
9. Consider performing the suggested procedures in paragraphs 4.116–.117 for donor-restricted endowments funds. (Completeness, Accuracy, Classification)
10. Obtain and test the accuracy and adequacy of the disclosures related to net assets (paragraphs 11.53–.59). (Accuracy, Classification)[7]

---

[7] The amendments in FASB Accounting Standards Update (ASU) No. 2016-14, *Not-for-Profit Entities (Topic 958): Presentation of Financial Statements of Note-for-Profit Entities*, are effective for annual financial statements issued for fiscal years beginning after December 15, 2017 (for example, years ending December 31, 2018, and years ending June 30, 2019), and for interim periods within fiscal years beginning after December 15, 2018. Application to interim financial statements is permitted but not required in the initial year of application. Early application of the amendments is permitted.

Chapter 12

Revenues and Receivables From Exchange Transactions

Gray shaded text in this chapter reflects guidance issued but not yet effective as of the date of this guide, March 1, 2018, but becoming effective on or prior to June 30, 2018, exclusive of any option to early adopt ahead of the mandatory effective date. Unless otherwise indicated, all unshaded text reflects guidance that was already effective as of the date of this guide.

Update 12-1 *Accounting and Reporting:* Revenue Recognition

In May 2014, FASB issued Accounting Standards Update (ASU) No. 2014-09, *Revenue from Contracts with Customers (Topic 606)*, to improve the financial reporting of revenue from contracts with customers and related costs and to align that reporting with International Financial Reporting Standards. In August 2015, FASB issued ASU No. 2015-14, *Revenue from Contracts with Customers (Topic 606): Deferral of the Effective Date*, which deferred the effective date of the amendments in FASB ASU No. 2014-09 for one year. As a result, most not-for-profit entities (NFPs) apply the new standards for annual reporting periods beginning after December 15, 2018, and interim periods within annual periods beginning after December 15, 2019, but they may elect to apply the new standards earlier on one of two dates:

- An annual reporting period beginning after December 15, 2016, including interim periods within that reporting period, or
- An annual reporting period beginning after December 15, 2016, and interim periods within annual periods beginning one year after the annual reporting period in which an entity first applies the standards.

However, NFPs that have issued, or are conduit bond obligors for, securities that are traded, listed, or quoted on an exchange or an over-the-counter market are required to apply the standards for annual reporting periods beginning after December 15, 2017, including interim periods within that reporting period. Earlier application by those NFPs is permitted only as of annual reporting periods beginning after December 15, 2016, including interim reporting periods within that reporting period.

FASB ASU No. 2014-09 provides a framework for revenue recognition and supersedes or amends several of the revenue recognition requirements in FASB ASC 605, *Revenue Recognition*, as well as guidance within the industry-specific topics, including FASB ASC 958, *Not-for-Profit Entities*. The standards apply to any entity that either enters into contracts with customers to transfer goods or services or enters into contracts for the transfer of nonfinancial assets unless those contracts are within the scope of other standards (for example, insurance or lease contracts).

FASB has also issued several ASUs that amend FASB ASU No. 2014-09 to clarify or correct certain aspects of the new revenue recognition standards, as follows:

- FASB ASU No. 2016-08, *Revenue from Contracts with Customers (Topic 606): Principal versus Agent Considerations (Reporting Revenue Gross versus Net)*
- FASB ASU No. 2016-10, *Revenue from Contracts with Customers (Topic 606): Identifying Performance Obligations and Licensing*
- FASB ASU No. 2016-12, *Revenue from Contracts with Customers (Topic 606): Narrow-Scope Improvements and Practical Expedients*
- FASB ASU No. 2016-20, *Technical Corrections and Improvements to Topic 606, Revenue from Contracts with Customers*

The AICPA has formed 16 industry task forces to assist in developing a new accounting guide on revenue recognition that will provide helpful hints and illustrative examples for how to apply the new standards. Revenue recognition implementation issues identified by the Not-for-Profit Entities Revenue Recognition Task Force will be available at aicpa.org for informal comment after review by the AICPA Financial Reporting Executive Committee (FinREC). Readers are encouraged to submit comments to revreccomments@aicpa.org. Appendix A, "Implementation Guidance for FASB Accounting Standards Update No. 2014-09, *Revenue from Contracts with Customers (Topic 606)*," of this chapter includes implementation guidance relevant to NFPs in the form of excerpts from the AICPA Accounting and Auditing Guide *Revenue Recognition*.

Refer to appendix B, "The New Revenue Recognition Standard: FASB ASU No. 2014-09," of this guide for more information on this ASU. Readers are also encouraged to consult the full text of the ASU on FASB's website at www.fasb.org.

Introduction

12.01 The FASB *Accounting Standards Codification* (ASC) glossary defines an *exchange transaction* as a reciprocal transfer between two entities that results in one of the entities acquiring assets or services or satisfying liabilities by surrendering other assets or services or incurring other obligations. The FASB ASC glossary's definition of *contribution* states that contributions differ from exchange transactions, which are reciprocal transfers in which each party receives and sacrifices something of approximately equal value. Chapter 5, "Contributions Received and Agency Transactions," includes guidance on distinguishing exchange transactions from contributions and agency transactions.

12.02 This chapter discusses recognition, measurement, and display issues for revenues and related receivables arising from exchange transactions. Because of their specialized nature, exchange transactions from investment activities are discussed in chapter 4, "Cash, Cash Equivalents, and Investments." The following transactions, which are generally in part contributions and in part exchange transactions, are discussed elsewhere in the guide, as follows:

- Naming opportunities (paragraphs 5.53–.56)
- Donor status (paragraph 5.57)
- Split-interest gifts (chapter 6, "Split-Interest Agreements and Beneficial Interests in Trusts")
- Special events (paragraphs 5.118–.122)

Difference Between Revenues and Gains

12.03 Paragraph 78 of FASB Concept No. 6, *Elements of Financial Statements—a replacement of FASB Concepts Statement No. 3 (incorporating an amendment of FASB Concepts Statement No. 2)*, defines *revenues* as "inflows or other enhancements of assets of an entity or settlements of its liabilities (or a combination of both) from delivering or producing goods, rendering services, or other activities that constitute the entity's ongoing major or central operations." Exchange transactions that give rise to revenues for NFPs typically involve their efforts to provide goods or services to members, clients, students, customers, and other beneficiaries for a fee.

The "Pending Content" in the FASB ASC glossary defines revenues as inflows or other enhancements of assets of an entity or settlements of its liabilities (or a combination of both) from delivering or producing goods, rendering services, or other activities that constitute the entity's ongoing major or central operations. Exchange transactions that give rise to revenues for NFPs typically involve their efforts to provide goods or services to members, clients, students, customers, and other beneficiaries for a fee.[1]

12.04 FASB ASC 605-10-25-1 states that an entity's revenue-earning activities involve delivering or producing goods, rendering services, or other activities that constitute its ongoing major or central operations, and revenues are considered to have been earned when the entity has substantially accomplished what it must do to be entitled to the benefits represented by the revenues. Gains commonly result from transactions and other events that involve no earning process, and for recognizing gains, being earned is generally less significant than being realized or realizable.

The preceding paragraph will be deleted upon the effective date of FASB ASU No. 2014-09.[2]

12.05 In some situations, judgment is required to determine whether an increase in net assets should be reported as revenue or as gain. Consistent with paragraphs 14–19 of FASB ASC 958-220-45, that determination should be based on the relationship of the transaction to the NFP's activities. Transactions and other events that would properly be considered part of one NFP's ongoing major or central activities (and hence give rise to revenues) may be considered peripheral for other NFP's (and hence give rise to gains). For example,

---

[1] Most not-for-profit entities (NFPs) will apply the standards in FASB *Accounting Standards Codification* (ASC) 606, *Revenue from Contracts with Customers*, for annual reporting periods beginning after December 15, 2018, and interim periods within annual periods beginning after December 15, 2019, although they may elect to apply those standards earlier. However, NFPs that have issued, or are conduit bond obligors for, securities that are traded, listed, or quoted on an exchange or an over-the-counter market are required to apply the standards for annual reporting periods beginning after December 15, 2017, including interim periods within that reporting period.

[2] Most NFPs will apply the standards in FASB ASC 606 for annual reporting periods beginning after December 15, 2018, and interim periods within annual periods beginning after December 15, 2019, although they may elect to apply those standards earlier. However, NFPs that have issued, or are conduit bond obligors for, securities that are traded, listed, or quoted on an exchange or an over-the-counter market are required to apply the standards for annual reporting periods beginning after December 15, 2017, including interim periods within that reporting period.

sales of computer equipment by a college store should be reported as revenues if such sales are considered part of the college's ongoing major or central activities. Sales of old computer equipment used in a museum's administrative offices would, however, be reported as gains if such sales are peripheral and if the equipment were sold above book value. Chapter 13, "Expenses, Gains, and Losses," discusses reporting gains from exchange transactions.

Recognition, Measurement, and Display of Revenue

12.06 The recognition, measurement, and display of revenues arising from exchange transactions are similar for both NFPs and for-profit entities. Revenues from exchange transactions should be recognized when earned based on accrual accounting principles and should be measured by the increase in cash, receivables, or other assets or by the decrease in liabilities resulting from the transaction. The following subtopics within FASB ASC provide relevant standards for revenues commonly earned by NFPs via exchange transactions:

- FASB ASC 605-25, which discusses revenue recognition if an entity will perform multiple revenue-generating activities under a single arrangement, such as provide multiple products, services, rights to use assets, or any combination thereof
- FASB ASC 605-28, which discusses revenue recognition for research or development contracts if a portion or all of the consideration is contingent upon achievement of a milestone
- FASB ASC 605-45, which discusses the following:
    - Whether an entity that sells products or services that will be delivered by a third party should report revenue gross or net of certain amounts paid to others
    - Presentation for shipping and handling fees
    - Presentation for out-of-pocket expenses billed to customers (expense reimbursements)
    - Presentation of taxes collected from customers and remitted to governmental authorities
- FASB ASC 835-30, which discusses imputation of interest on notes issued in exchange transactions if the stated interest rate varies from prevailing interest rates
- FASB ASC 912-605, which discusses revenue recognition by government contractors

In addition, as discussed in paragraph 1.16, some NFPs conduct activities similar to industries within the scope of FASB ASC 905–999 and should apply the guidance concerning the recognition and measurement of revenues to the transactions unique to those industries. An example of such guidance is FASB ASC 920, *Entertainment—Broadcasters.*

The recognition, measurement, and display of revenues arising from exchange transactions are similar for both NFPs and for-profit entities. The following subtopics within FASB ASC provide relevant standards for revenues commonly earned by NFPs via exchange transactions:

- FASB ASC 606, *Revenue from Contracts with Customers*, which discusses a five-step principles-based approach for revenue recognition from with customers
- FASB ASC 835-30, which discusses imputation of interest on notes issued in exchange transactions if the stated interest rate varies from prevailing interest rates
- FASB ASC 840, *Leases*, which discusses recognition of rental income by lessors
- FASB ASC 845, *Nonmonetary Transactions*, which discusses recognition of rental income by lessors[3]

12.07 Paragraphs 83–84 of FASB Concept No. 5, *Recognition and Measurement in Financial Statements of Business Enterprises,* provides nonauthoritative guidance for recognition of revenues and gains. In addition, FASB ASC 605-10-S99-1 also provides useful guidance, although it applies only to public registrants. In general, based upon the guidance in those two sources, revenue is not recognized until it is both realized or realizable and earned, which generally occurs when the following four criteria have been met:

- Persuasive evidence of an arrangement exists
- Delivery has occurred or services have been rendered
- The seller's price to the buyer is fixed or determinable
- Collectibility is reasonably assured

When an NFP enters into a contract with a customer to sell goods or services or enters into a contract for the transfer of nonfinancial assets, it applies the standards in FASB ASC 606. The "Pending Content in the FASB ASC glossary defines a customer as "a party that has contracted with an entity to obtain goods or services that are an output of the entity's ordinary activities in exchange for consideration." The "Pending Content" in FASB ASC 606-10-15-2 explains that FASB ASC 606 should be applied by entities to all contracts with customers except for a list of exceptions, which include contracts that are within the scope of other standards (for example, insurance contracts or lease contracts), financial instruments, guarantees (other than product or service warranties), and nonmonetary exchanges between entities in the same line of business to facilitate sales to customers or potential customers.[4]

12.08 If payment is received from a buyer before revenue is able to be recognized, the obligation to the buyer to either perform under the agreement

---

[3] Most NFPs will apply the standards in FASB ASC 606 for annual reporting periods beginning after December 15, 2018, and interim periods within annual periods beginning after December 15, 2019, although they may elect to apply those standards earlier. However, NFPs that have issued, or are conduit bond obligors for, securities that are traded, listed, or quoted on an exchange or an over-the-counter market are required to apply the standards for annual reporting periods beginning after December 15, 2017, including interim periods within that reporting period.

[4] Most NFPs will apply the standards in FASB ASC 606 for annual reporting periods beginning after December 15, 2018, and interim periods within annual periods beginning after December 15, 2019, although they may elect to apply those standards earlier. However, NFPs that have issued, or are conduit bond obligors for, securities that are traded, listed, or quoted on an exchange or an over-the-counter market are required to apply the standards for annual reporting periods beginning after December 15, 2017, including interim periods within that reporting period.

or to return the payment is recognized (generally referred to as deferred revenue). Recognition of that revenue is deferred until the obligation underlying the liability is satisfied and all other revenue recognition criteria have been met.

The "Pending Content" in paragraphs 34 of FASB ASC 606-10-05 states that the core principle is that an entity recognizes revenue to depict the transfer of promised goods or services to customers in an amount that reflects the consideration to which the entity expects to be entitled in exchange for those goods or services. An entity recognizes revenue in accordance with that core principle by applying the five steps, which are summarized as follows:

- Step 1: Identify the contract(s) with a customer
- Step 2: Identify the performance obligations in the contract
- Step 3: Determine the transaction price
- Step 4: Allocate the transaction price to the performance obligations in the contract
- Step 5: Recognize revenue when (or as) the entity satisfies a performance obligation

The five steps are discussed in appendix B of this guide, which summarizes the guidance in FASB ASC 606, but is not a substitute for reading that topic. In addition, appendix A of this chapter provides implementation guidance for NFPs in the form of excerpts from the AICPA Accounting and Auditing Guide *Revenue Recognition*.[5]

12.09 As described in FASB ASC 845-10-05-2, most business transactions involve exchanges of cash or other monetary assets or liabilities for goods or services. The amount of monetary assets or liabilities exchanged generally provides an objective basis for measuring the cost of nonmonetary assets or services received by an entity, as well as for measuring gain or loss on nonmonetary assets transferred from an entity. However, some exchanges involve primarily nonmonetary assets or liabilities. FASB ASC 845-10-30-1 states that, in general, the accounting for nonmonetary transactions should be based on the fair values of the assets (or services) involved, which is the same basis as that used in monetary transactions. Thus, the cost of a nonmonetary asset acquired in exchange for another nonmonetary asset is the fair value of the asset surrendered to obtain it, and a gain or loss should be recognized on the exchange. The fair value of the asset received should be used to measure the cost if it is more clearly evident than the fair value of the asset surrendered.

12.10 In accordance with FASB ASC 958-220-45-5, revenues from exchange transactions should be reported as increases in unrestricted net assets in a statement of activities even when there are legal limitations on the uses of the revenue arising from contracts or other agreements. For example, dormitory fees paid by students to a college that must, under terms of a bond indenture,

---

[5] Most NFPs will apply the standards in FASB ASC 606 for annual reporting periods beginning after December 15, 2018, and interim periods within annual periods beginning after December 15, 2019, although they may elect to apply those standards earlier. However, NFPs that have issued, or are conduit bond obligors for, securities that are traded, listed, or quoted on an exchange or an over-the-counter market are required to apply the standards for annual reporting periods beginning after December 15, 2017, including interim periods within that reporting period.

be immediately deposited in a sinking fund to retire the bonds issued to build the dormitory are unrestricted revenues, as are assessments or fees to cover the cost of a new swimming pool that are received by a country club from its members. Those revenues are not contributions, and restricted revenues arise only from donor's restrictions on contributions or investment return earned on contributed resources. As discussed in chapter 3, "Financial Statements, the Reporting Entity, and General Financial Reporting Matters," further classifications (for example, between operating and nonoperating) may be incorporated within a statement of activities beyond the required net asset classes.

In accordance with the "Pending Content: in FASB ASC 958-220-45-5, a statement of activities should report revenues as increases in net assets without donor restrictions unless the use of the assets received is limited by donor-imposed restrictions. For example, fees from rendering services and income from investments generally are without donor restrictions; however, income from donor-restricted perpetual or term endowments generally would increase net assets with donor restrictions.

There can be legal limitations on the uses of the revenue arising from contracts or other agreements, but if the revenues are not donor restricted, those revenues do not increase net assets with donor restrictions. Donor-restricted revenues arise only from donor's restrictions on contributions or investment return earned on contributed resources. For example, dormitory fees paid by students to a college that must, under terms of a bond indenture, be immediately deposited in a sinking fund to retire the bonds issued to build the dormitory are revenues that increase net assets without donor restrictions, as are assessments or fees to cover the cost of a new swimming pool that are received by a country club from its members.[6]

12.11 Revenues from exchange transactions should generally be reported gross of any related expenses (paragraph 3.30). Expenses that are directly related to specific gross revenues may, however, be displayed sequentially with those revenues. For example, gross revenues from special events less the direct costs related to those events, followed by a subtotal, may be reported in a statement of activities. Chapter 13 discusses reporting of special events.

Discounts

12.12 Per FASB ASC 958-605-45-2, if the NFP regularly provides discounts (such as financial aid for students that is not reported as an expense, reduced fees for services, or free services) to certain recipients of its goods or services, revenues should be reported net of those discounts. Net revenue may be reported as a single line item in a statement of activities, or the gross revenue is permitted to be reported less the related discount, provided that the discount is displayed immediately beneath the revenue. Paragraphs 7–8 of FASB ASC

---

[6] The amendments in FASB Accounting Standards Update (ASU) No. 2016-14, *Not-for-Profit Entities (Topic 958): Presentation of Financial Statements for Not-for-Profit Entities*, are effective for annual financial statements issued for fiscal years beginning after December 15, 2017 (for example, years ending December 31, 2018, and years ending June 30, 2019), and for interim periods within fiscal years beginning after December 15, 2018. Application to interim financial statements is permitted but not required in the initial year of application. Early application of the amendments is permitted.

958-720-25 (paragraph 13.15) provide guidance concerning whether reductions in amounts charged for goods or services should be reported as discounts or expenses.

The preceding paragraph will be deleted upon the effective date of FASB ASU No. 2014-09. See appendix A of this chapter for recognition of tuition and fees.[7]

Membership Dues

12.13 As discussed in Technical Questions and Answers (Q&A) section 6140.02, "Income Recognition of Membership Dues by Not-for-Profit Entity,"[8] if a member receives benefits from those dues, dues revenue would be recognized over the period of membership in accordance with FASB ASC 958-605-25-1.

The preceding paragraph will be deleted upon the effective date of FASB ASU No. 2014-09.[9]

12.14 Nonrefundable initiation and life membership fees received in exchange transactions should be recognized as revenues in the period in which the fees become receivable if future fees are expected to cover the costs of future services to be provided to members. If nonrefundable initiation and life membership fees, rather than future fees, are expected to cover those costs, nonrefundable initiation and life member fees received in exchange transactions should be recognized as revenue over the average duration of membership, the life expectancy of members, or other appropriate time periods. Dues would be recognized as contributions revenue when received if members receive no benefits from the dues, as discussed further in paragraphs 5.47–.50.

The preceding paragraph will be deleted upon the effective date of FASB ASU No. 2014-09.[10]

---

[7] FASB ASU No. 2014-09, *Revenue from Contracts with Customers (Topic 606)*, is effective for NFPs for annual reporting periods beginning after December 15, 2018, and interim periods within annual periods beginning after December 15, 2019. However, NFPs that have issued, or are conduit bond obligors for, securities that are traded, listed, or quoted on an exchange or an over-the-counter market are required to apply the standards for annual reporting periods beginning after December 15, 2017, including interim periods within that reporting period.

[8] All Q&A sections can be found in *Technical Questions and Answers*.

[9] FASB ASU No. 2014-09 is effective for NFPs for annual reporting periods beginning after December 15, 2018, and interim periods within annual periods beginning after December 15, 2019. However, NFPs that have issued, or are conduit bond obligors for, securities that are traded, listed, or quoted on an exchange or an over-the-counter market are required to apply the standards for annual reporting periods beginning after December 15, 2017, including interim periods within that reporting period.

[10] FASB ASU No. 2014-09 is effective for NFPs for annual reporting periods beginning after December 15, 2018, and interim periods within annual periods beginning after December 15, 2019. However, NFPs that have issued, or are conduit bond obligors for, securities that are traded, listed, or quoted on an exchange or an over-the-counter market are required to apply the standards for annual reporting periods beginning after December 15, 2017, including interim periods within that reporting period.

Receivables From Exchange Transactions

Update 12-2 *Accounting and Reporting:* Credit Losses

FASB ASU No. 2016-13, *Financial Instruments—Credit Losses (Topic 326): Measurement of Credit Losses on Financial Instruments*, was issued in June 2016 to provide financial statement users with more decision-useful information about the expected credit losses on financial instruments and other commitments to extend credit held by a reporting entity at each reporting date. To achieve this objective, the amendments in the ASU replace the incurred loss impairment methodology in current generally accepted accounting principles with a methodology that reflects expected credit losses and requires consideration of a broader range of reasonable and supportable information to inform credit loss estimates.

FASB ASU No. 2016-13 is effective for NFPs for fiscal years beginning after December 15, 2020, and interim periods within fiscal years beginning after December 15, 2021. Early adoption is permitted for fiscal years beginning after December 15, 2018, including interim periods within those fiscal years.

This edition of the guide has not been updated to reflect changes as a result of this FASB ASU; however, the section that follows will be updated in a future edition. Readers are encouraged to consult the full text of the FASB ASU on FASB's website at www.fasb.org.

12.15 Unless measured at fair value in conformity with the "Fair Value Option" subsections of FASB ASC 825-10,[11] FASB ASC 958-310-35-3 requires that receivables arising from exchange transactions should be reported at net realizable value if the amounts are due within one year. Longer-term receivables should be reported in conformity with FASB ASC 310-10-35. Pursuant to FASB ASC 210-10-45-13, a valuation allowance for credit losses (also referred to as an allowance for uncollectible receivables or an allowance for doubtful accounts) should be deducted from the receivables to which the allowance relates and should be disclosed. Q&A section 6140.09, "Reporting Bad Debt Losses," states that under FASB ASC 958-220-45-17, bad debt losses are not permitted to be netted against revenues.

12.16 FASB ASC 310-10-50 requires an NFP to provide information about its significant accounting policies for receivables, the credit quality of its financing receivables, and the allowance for credit losses. Examples of financing receivables of NFPs include church mortgages held by church development funds, student loans issued by college and universities, loans receivable in housing associations, microfinance loans, certain program-related investments issued by foundations, and officer and employee notes receivable.[12] The relative significance of the financing receivables to an NFP's operations and financial position and the quantitative and qualitative risks arising from the credit quality of the receivables is considered when determining the extent of the disclosures.

---

[11] Paragraphs 3.169–.171 discuss the option for entities to report certain assets and liabilities at fair value in conformity with FASB ASC 815-15 or the "Fair Value Option" subsections of FASB ASC 825-10.

[12] Chapter 8, "Programmatic Investments," provides additional information on loans if their primary purpose is to further the mission-related objectives of the not-for-profit entity, and the production of income is not a significant purpose.

12.17 FASB ASC 310-10-55 provides examples of disclosures about financing receivables that are useful to NFPs that hold financing receivables as a major program activity. The following examples of disclosures are useful to NFPs that hold financing receivables, but not as a major program activity. Each example indicates the loan portfolio's size as compared to total assets. That disclosure is not required, but provides users with an understanding of the relative significance of the loan portfolio.

Example 1—Student Loans

The University makes uncollateralized loans to students based on financial need under the Perkins federal loan program (federal funding) and the University student loan program (institutional funding). At August 31, 20X1, and 20X0, student loans were $3,654,126 and $3,238,878, respectively, which is about 3 percent of total assets. Of these amounts, as of August 31, 20X1, and 20X0, $2,257,200 and $1,973,900, respectively, were not in repayment status (that is, the borrowers were not yet required to make payments). Most loans that are in repayment status are collected over a period of 10 years.

Allowances for doubtful accounts are established based on prior collection experience and current economic factors that, in management's judgment, could influence the ability of loan recipients to repay the amounts per the loan terms. Amounts due under the federal loan programs are guaranteed by the government and, therefore, no allowances are placed on any past due balances under the program. The allowance for doubtful accounts for the University student loan program was approximately $173,000 for each of the years ended August 31, 20X1, and 20X0. Institutional loan balances are written off only when they are deemed to be permanently uncollectible.

At August 31, 20X1, and 20X0, the following amounts were past due under the student loan programs.

	In Default				
August 31,	*Less than 240 days (8 monthly installments)*	*More than 240 days and less than 2 years*	*More than 2 years, up to 5 years*	*More than 5 years*	*Total past due*
20X1	$224,325	$112,659	$121,925	$70,325	$529,234
20X0	246,436	173,308	129,168	70,575	619,487

The availability of funds for loans under the Perkins federal loan program is dependent on reimbursement to the pool from repayments on outstanding loans. Funds advanced by the federal government of $2,811,563 and $2,663,531 at August 31, 20X1, and 2010, respectively, are ultimately refundable to the government and are classified as liabilities in the statement of financial position. Outstanding loans cancelled under the program result in a reduction of the funds available for loan and a decrease in the liability to the government.

Example 2—Notes Receivable from Staff

As part of a program to attract and retain excellent staff, the Organization provides home purchase down payment assistance. Notes receivable amounting to $208,100 and $222,500 were outstanding at June 30, 20X1, and 20X0, respectively, and are less than 1/2 percent of total assets. The notes are collateralized by second trust deeds on single family residences located in the towns surrounding the Organization. The second trust deeds are subordinated to the first trust deeds on the residences. Interest rates on the notes are determined by market rates for second trust deeds at the origination of the note, and range from X percent to Y percent. The loans have a term of 10 years with due-on-sale and due-on-separation-of-service clauses. Note payments are withheld from staff members' salaries; thus, there are no amounts past due. No allowance for doubtful accounts has been recorded against these notes based on their collateralization and prior collection history.

Example 3—Loan Receivable from Officer

As part of the compensation package, the Charity made a $10,000 loan to an officer, which is less than percent of the Charity's total assets. The loan is due on demand and bears simple interest at the rate of X percent.

Collection is not intended to be pursued in the next year; accordingly, the loan is presented as long term. The loan is unsecured. Collection is fully expected and accordingly, no allowance has been provided.

Auditing

12.18 Many audit objectives and auditing procedures, including consideration of controls, for NFPs are similar to those of other entities. In addition, the auditor may need to consider the specific audit objectives, auditing procedures, and selected controls that are unique to NFPs and that are considered subsequently.

12.19 As discussed in chapter 2, "General Auditing Considerations," of this guide and in paragraph .26 of AU-C section 240, *Consideration of Fraud in a Financial Statement Audit*,[13] when identifying and assessing the risks of material misstatement due to fraud, the auditor should, based on a presumption that risks of fraud exist in revenue recognition, evaluate which types of revenue, revenue transactions, or assertions give rise to such risks. Audit procedures for revenue and receivables from exchange transactions are similar to those for business entities, with the exception of testing related to proper classification of transactions as either contribution or exchange transactions. The auditor may find it necessary to document the method the NFP uses to determine if a transaction is a contribution or an exchange transaction. The auditor could select transactions throughout the year and review the supporting documentation to assess whether such transactions have been properly classified. (Classification)

12.20 Some federal grants are structured as exchange transactions. Federal grants are subject to single audit requirements and related audit procedures, which are discussed in AICPA Audit Guide Government Auditing Standards *and Single Audits*.

12.21 The following table illustrates the use of assertions in developing audit objectives and designing substantive tests related to revenues and

[13] All AU-C sections can be found in AICPA *Professional Standards*.

receivables from exchange transactions. The examples are not intended to be all-inclusive nor is it expected that an auditor would use all these procedures in an audit. The use of assertions in assessing risks and designing appropriate audit procedures to obtain audit evidence is described in paragraphs .26–.32 of AU-C section 315, *Understanding the Entity and Its Environment and Assessing the Risks of Material Misstatement*. Paragraph .18 of AU-C section 330, *Performing Audit Procedures in Response to Assessed Risks and Evaluating the Audit Evidence Obtained*, requires the auditor to design and perform substantive procedures for all relevant assertions related to each material class of transactions, account balance, and disclosure, irrespective of the assessed risks of material misstatement. This requirement reflects the facts that (1) the auditor's assessment of risk is judgmental and may not identify all risks of material misstatement, and (2) inherent limitations to internal control exist, including management override. Various audit procedures and the purposes for which they may be performed are described in paragraphs .A10–.A26 of AU-C section 500, *Audit Evidence*.

Auditing Considerations

Financial Statement Assertions	***Specific Auditing Objectives***	***Select Control Objectives***
Revenues from Exchange Transactions		
Existence and occurrence, Completeness	Revenue and gains are reported in the proper period using the accrual basis of accounting.	Controls ensure that revenue is accrued as services are performed or as contractual obligations are satisfied. Management establishes and monitors controls over the recognition of revenue.
Classification	Consideration given to determine if the transaction is properly classified as a contribution or as an exchange transaction.	Controls ensure that revenue is classified by type of service rendered. Controls ensure that increases in net assets are properly classified between revenues and gains/losses.
Presentation and disclosure	In the statement of activities, revenue from exchange transactions is reported in the unrestricted net asset class.	Controls ensure that revenue is properly classified. Discounts and other adjustments are authorized, controlled, and recorded properly. Controls ensure that expenses that are directly related to specific gross revenues from special events are displayed sequentially with those revenues, as described in paragraph 12.11.

Auditing Considerations—*continued*

Financial Statement Assertions	***Specific Auditing Objectives***	***Select Control Objectives***
Presentation and disclosure	In the statement of activities, revenue from exchange transactions is reported in the net assets without donor restrictions class.[14]	Controls ensure that revenue is properly classified. Discounts and other adjustments are authorized, controlled, and recorded properly. Controls ensure that expenses that are directly related to specific gross revenues from special events are displayed sequentially with those revenues, as described in paragraph 12.11.[15]
Valuation	Revenue amounts have been recorded appropriately.	Discounts and other adjustments are authorized, controlled, and recorded properly.
Cut-off	In the statement of activities, revenue is reported in the proper period.	Controls ensure that revenue is recorded in the proper period.

12.22 Suggested audit procedures to consider for testing revenue include the following:

- Test discounts and other adjustments to determine that they are accounted for in accordance with the NFP's policies. (Valuation)
- Obtain agreements for major sources of revenue and determine if management has properly classified each source an exchange transaction or contribution. (Occurrence/Existence, Classification)
- Determine that management has properly classified transactions that have elements of both exchange transactions and contributions (for example, grants and special events). (Classification)
- Evaluate special event revenue for special considerations relative to timing and revenue recognition. (Cut-off, Classification)

---

[14] The amendments in FASB ASU No. 2016-14 are effective for annual financial statements issued for fiscal years beginning after December 15, 2017 (for example, years ending December 31, 2018, and years ending June 30, 2019), and for interim periods within fiscal years beginning after December 15, 2018. Application to interim financial statements is permitted but not required in the initial year of application. Early application of the amendments is permitted.

[15] The amendments in FASB ASU No. 2016-14 are effective for annual financial statements issued for fiscal years beginning after December 15, 2017 (for example, years ending December 31, 2018, and years ending June 30, 2019), and for interim periods within fiscal years beginning after December 15, 2018. Application to interim financial statements is permitted but not required in the initial year of application. Early application of the amendments is permitted.

- For exchange transactions with contracts that cross the fiscal year end, determine that management has recorded the transactions in the appropriate reporting period. (Cut-off)
- Evaluate managements policies and procedures surrounding classification of revenue versus gain (Classification)

12.23 AU-C section 505, *External Confirmations*, discusses the process that the auditor should follow when using external confirmations. Paragraph .20 of AU-C section 330 states that an auditor should use external confirmation procedures for accounts receivable, except when one or more of the following is applicable:

- The overall account balance is immaterial.
- External confirmation procedures for accounts receivable would be ineffective.
- The auditor's assessed level of risk of material misstatement at the relevant assertion level is low, and the other planned substantive procedures address the assessed risk. In many situations, the use of external confirmation procedures for accounts receivable and the performance of other substantive procedures are necessary to reduce the assessed risk of material misstatement to an acceptably low level.

12.24 It may be ineffective to attempt confirmation of certain receivables. For example, confirmation of grants receivable from government agencies is often ineffective. Paragraphs .A54 and .A56 of AU-C section 330 describe circumstances in which external confirmation procedures for accounts receivable may be ineffective. These circumstances include the following:

- When based on prior years' audit experience or experience with similar entities, response rates to properly designed confirmation requests will be inadequate.
- When based on prior years' audit experience or experience with similar entities, responses are known or expected to be unreliable. For example,
  - — responses to confirmation requests may be less reliable if the confirming party is a related party of the NFP.
  - — responses may be more reliable if provided by a person at the confirming party who has the requisite knowledge about the information being confirmed.
- The intended confirming party is known or expected to be unable or unwilling to respond. For example, the confirming party
  - — may not accept responsibility for responding to a confirmation request;
  - — may consider responding too costly or time consuming;
  - — may have concerns about the potential legal liability resulting from responding;
  - — may account for transactions in different currencies; or
  - — may operate in an environment in which responding to confirmation requests is not a significant aspect of day-to-day operations.

12.25

Appendix A—Implementation Guidance for FASB Accounting Standards Update No. 2014-09, *Revenue from Contracts with Customers (Topic 606)*[1]

A-1 This appendix includes excerpts from chapter 8, "Not-for-Profit Entities," of the AICPA Audit and Accounting Guide *Revenue Recognition* (Revenue Recognition guide). That guide has been developed by the AICPA Industry Revenue Recognition Task Forces, Revenue Recognition Working Group, and Auditing Revenue Task Force to assist management in the preparation of their financial statements in accordance with U.S. generally accepted accounting principles (GAAP) and to assist practitioners in performing and reporting on their audit engagements. Specifically, that guide is intended to help entities and auditors prepare for changes related to revenue recognition as a result of FASB Accounting Standards Update (ASU) No. 2014-09, *Revenue from Contracts with Customers (Topic 606)*, and subsequent ASUs amending FASB *Accounting Standards Codification* (ASC) 606, *Revenue from Contracts with Customers*.

A-2 Four topics are discussed in chapter 8 of the Revenue Recognition guide, as follows:

- Scope, which is discussed in paragraph A-3 (paragraph 8.7.01)
- Bifurcation of transactions between contribution and exchange components, which is discussed in paragraphs A-4–A-5 (paragraphs 8.7.02–8.7.06)
- Tuition and housing revenues, which are discussed in paragraphs A-7–A-75 (paragraphs 8.6.01–8.6.69)
- Dues and subscriptions, which are discussed in paragraphs A-76–A-108.

Scope

A-3 Paragraph 8.7.01 explains that contributions are not in the scope of FASB ASC 606 and states the following:

> At the March 30, 2015 FASB/IASB TRG meeting, the question of whether contributions are included or excluded from the scope of FASB ASC 606 was discussed.[2] As noted in Topic 7, paragraph 40 of TRG Agenda Ref. 34, March 2015 Meeting—Summary of Issues Discussed and Next Steps, TRG members agreed with the staff view that contributions are not in the scope of FASB ASC 606.

---

[1] FASB Accounting Standards Update (ASU) No. 2014-09, *Revenue from Contracts with Customers (Topic 606)*, is effective for NFPs for annual reporting periods beginning after December 15, 2018, and interim periods within annual periods beginning after December 15, 2019. However, NFPs that have issued, or are conduit bond obligors for, securities that are traded, listed, or quoted on an exchange or an over-the-counter market are required to apply the standards for annual reporting periods beginning after December 15, 2017, including interim periods within that reporting period.

[2] See March 2015 FASB/IASB Joint Transition Resource Group for Revenue Recognition Agenda Ref. 26: Whether Contributions are Included or Excluded from the Scope.

Bifurcation of Transactions Between Contribution and Exchange Components

A-4 FASB ASC 606-10-15-4 states the following:

> A contract with a customer may be partially within the scope of this Topic and partially within the scope of other Topics listed in paragraph 606-10-15-2.
>
> *a.* If the other Topics specify how to separate and/or initially measure one or more parts of the contract, then an entity shall first apply the separation and/or measurement guidance in those Topics. An entity shall exclude from the transaction price the amount of the part (or parts) of the contract that are initially measured in accordance with other Topics and shall apply paragraphs 606-10-32-28 through 32-41 to allocate the amount of the transaction price that remains (if any) to each performance obligation within the scope of this Topic and to any other parts of the contract identified by paragraph 606-10-15-4(b).
>
> *b.* If the other Topics do not specify how to separate and/or initially measure one or more parts of the contract, then the entity shall apply the guidance in this Topic to separate and/or initially measure the part (or parts) of the contract.

A-5 Paragraphs 8.7.05–8.7.06 state the following:

> Based on the guidance in FASB ASC 606-10-15-4, to bifurcate a transaction between the portion that is a contribution and portion that is an exchange, a not-for-profit organization (NFP) should apply the guidance in paragraphs 9–12 of FASB ASC 958-605-55 for separating and initially measuring the transaction. That guidance provides an example when a membership dues transaction is bifurcated into contribution and exchange transaction components and, by analogy, other types of transactions, such as [grants, awards, and sponsorships; naming opportunities; donor status; and gifts in kind] would be accounted for in the same manner.
>
> As stated in paragraph 5.43 of this guide, FinREC believes that in circumstances in which the transaction is in part a contribution and in part an exchange, NFPs should first determine the fair value of the exchange portion of the transaction, with the residual (excess of the resources received over the fair value of the exchange portion of the transaction) reported as contributions.

Tuition and Housing Revenues

A-6 FASB ASC 606-10-25-1 includes the following five criteria, which must all be met to determine whether a contract exists within the scope of FASB ASC 606.

a. The parties to the contract have approved the contract (in writing, orally, or in accordance with other customary business practices) and are committed to perform their respective obligations.

b. The entity can identify each party's rights regarding the goods or services to be transferred.

c. The entity can identify the payment terms for the goods or services to be transferred.

d. The contract has commercial substance (that is, the risk, timing, or amount of the entity's future cash flows is expected to change as a result of the contract).

e. It is probable that the entity will collect the consideration to which it will be entitled in exchange for the goods or services that will be transferred to the customer.

Step 1: Identify the Contract

Contract Existence

A-7 The FASB ASC glossary defines a contract as "an agreement between two or more parties that creates enforceable rights and obligations. Contracts may be written, oral, or implied by an entity's customary business practices. The practices and processes for establishing contracts with customers vary across legal jurisdictions, industries, and entities. In accordance with FASB ASC 606-10-25-2, higher education institutions (institutions) will need to consider such practices and processes (including those related to the admission and registration of students) in determining whether and when an agreement with a student creates enforceable rights and obligations between the institution and the student. In certain circumstances, it may be appropriate for an institution to consult with its legal counsel in making this determination. (paragraph 8.6.02)

A-8 Institutions will also need to consider the guidance in FASB ASC 606-10-25-4, which states that a contract does not exist if each party to the contract has the unilateral enforceable right to terminate a wholly unperformed contract without compensating the other party (or parties). FASB ASC 606-10-25-4 also states that a contract is considered *wholly unperformed* if both of the following criteria are met:

a. The entity has not yet transferred any promised goods or services to the customer.

b. The entity has not yet received, and is not yet entitled to receive, any consideration in exchange for the promised goods or services. (paragraph 8.6.03)

A-9 In evaluating whether a contract is wholly unperformed, institutions will need to consider whether consideration has been received from or on behalf of the student (for example, a nonrefundable enrollment or housing deposit); the institution is entitled to receive consideration in exchange for promised services; or the institution has started to perform services. If any of these have occurred, the contract would not be considered wholly unperformed. (paragraph 8.6.04)

A-10 An institution may receive a nonrefundable deposit from a potential student to secure a spot for enrollment or housing. FASB ASC 606-10-55-46 states that upon receipt of a prepayment from a customer, an entity shall recognize a contract liability in the amount of the prepayment for its performance obligation to transfer, or to stand ready to transfer, goods or services in the future. FASB ASC 606-10-55-47 also states that a customer's nonrefundable prepayment to an entity gives the customer a right to receive a good or service in the future. FinREC believes that in cases in which a student pays the institution a nonrefundable deposit to secure a spot for enrollment or housing, this generally gives the student the right to receive the instruction or housing, as applicable, and obliges the institution to stand ready to provide such instruction or housing, as applicable. Students may not, in fact, enroll in the institution or move in to campus housing, and, as a consequence, the associated nonrefundable deposit will be forfeited. FASB ASC 606-10-55-48 provides that if an entity expects to be entitled to a breakage amount in a contract liability, the entity should recognize the expected breakage amount as revenue in proportion to the pattern of rights exercised by the customer. Because whether a student actually enrolls or moves into housing are binary events (that is, the student either exercises his or her right or not), and if there are no other rights being exercised by the student, FinREC believes the institution would not record breakage until the student's right to enroll or be provided housing expires. (paragraph 8.6.05)

Collectibility

A-11 One of the criteria included in FASB ASC 606-10-25-1 that must be met in order to conclude that a contract exists is an explicit collectibility threshold. In accordance with FASB ASC 606-10-25-1(e), an institution will need to determine that it is probable it will collect the tuition and housing charges it will be entitled to in exchange for providing the instruction and housing to students for a contract to exist. FASB ASC 606-10-25-1e also states that in evaluating whether collectibility of the amount of consideration is probable, an entity shall consider only the customer's ability and intention to pay that amount of consideration when it is due. FinREC believes that assessing the customer's ability to pay would incorporate expected payments from parties in addition to the student and his or her parents, where applicable (for example, financial aid packages that combine aid from a variety of sources—federal, state, local, and so on) for a total combined collectibility assessment made by the institution. (paragraph 8.6.06)

A-12 FASB ASC 606-10-25-1(e) further states that the amount of consideration to which the entity will be entitled may be less than the price stated in the contract if the consideration is variable because the entity may offer the customer a price concession.

A-13 Expected price concessions (see paragraph A-45 for more discussion) would result in a lower transaction price. Collectibility would then be evaluated based on the lower amount. (paragraph 8.6.08)

A-14 If an institution concludes that collectibility from a student or others paying on the student's behalf is not probable based on historical experience with that student or based on other factors, in accordance with FASB ASC 606-10-25-1(e), the institution would conclude that there is not yet a contract and would not recognize revenue until the facts and circumstances change such that there is a contract or the conditions for recognizing revenue when there is no contract (as discussed in FASB ASC 606-10-25-7) are satisfied. In accordance with FASB ASC 606-10-25-6, an entity would need to continually reassess the collectibility threshold. If facts and circumstances subsequently change such that the criteria of FASB ASC 606-10-25-1(e) are subsequently met (for example, sufficient consideration is received from such student or other party paying on the student's behalf, or additional information about the credit-worthiness of the student is obtained such that it becomes probable that the institution will collect the amount it expects to be entitled to), the institution would begin applying the revenue model. (paragraph 8.6.09)

A-15 FASB ASC 606-10-25-5 states that if a contract with a customer meets the criteria in FASB ASC 606-10-25-1e at contract inception, an entity should not reassess those criteria unless there is an indication of a significant change in facts or circumstances. For example, if a student's intention or ability to pay the consideration deteriorates significantly, in accordance with FASB ASC 606, an institution would reassess whether it is probable that the institution will collect the consideration to which it will be entitled in exchange for the remaining services that will be transferred to the student. If collection is no longer probable, the institution would no longer apply the revenue recognition model and would cease to recognize further revenue, including any relating to partial consideration received, until the facts and circumstances change such that collectibility again becomes probable or either of the events in FASB ASC 606-10-25-7 is met. (paragraph 8.6.10) FASB ASC 606-10-25-7 states the following:

> When a contract with a customer does not meet the criteria in paragraph 606-10-25-1 and an entity receives consideration from the customer, the entity shall recognize the consideration received as revenue only when either of the following events has occurred:
>
> a. The entity has no remaining obligations to transfer goods or services to the customer, and all, or substantially all, of the consideration promised by the customer has been received by the entity and is nonrefundable.
>
> b. The contract has been terminated, and the consideration received from the customer is nonrefundable.
>
> c. The entity has transferred control of the goods or services to which the consideration that has been received relates, the entity has stopped transferring goods or services to the customer (if applicable) and has no obligation under the contract to transfer additional goods or services, and the consideration received from the customer is nonrefundable.

A-16 As clarified in BC 34 of ASU No. 2014-09, because the reassessment would relate only to the remaining services, institutions would not include in the reassessment (and, therefore, would not reverse) any receivables, revenue, or contract assets already recognized. Institutions would, however, assess the contract assets and receivables for potential impairment in accordance with FASB ASC 310, *Receivables*. (paragraph 8.6.11)

Combination of Contracts

A-17 Institutions will need to determine if tuition and housing (or any other contracts entered into with the student) are contracted for together in a single contract or if in separate contracts, whether such contracts need to be combined for purposes of applying FASB ASC 606. FASB ASC 606-10-25-9 states that an entity shall combine two or more contracts entered into at or near the same time with the same customer and account for the contracts as a single contract if one or more of the stated criteria are met. Specifically, if the contracts are negotiated as a package with a single commercial objective, the amount of consideration to be paid in one contract depends on the price or performance of the other contract, or if the services promised in the contracts are a single performance obligation, then the institution would combine the contracts. When making the determination of whether to combine contracts for tuition and housing, an entity would need to consider whether a discount (for example, financial aid) has been provided in a bundled arrangement (see paragraph A-29 for further discussion on discounts). If none of the stated criteria are met, an institution would treat the contracts as separate contracts and follow the guidance in FASB ASC 606 for each separate contract. (paragraph 8.6.12)

Portfolio Approach

A-18 FASB ASC 606 is generally applied to an individual contract with a customer. FASB ASC 606-10-10-4 states the following:

> However, as a practical expedient, an entity may apply this guidance to a portfolio of contracts (or performance obligations) with similar characteristics if the entity reasonably expects that the effects on the financial statements of applying this guidance to the portfolio would not differ materially from applying the guidance in Topic 606 to the individual contracts (or performance obligations) within that portfolio. When accounting for a portfolio, an entity shall use estimates and assumptions that reflect the size and composition of the portfolio.

A-19 Institutions will need to consider the cost versus benefits of the portfolio approach as they apply the revenue recognition model. For example, institutions may consider whether the benefit to applying the portfolio approach to assess collectibility in step 1 or to estimate refunds in step 3 is more practical than applying the guidance in FASB ASC 606 on an individual contract basis. Although the portfolio approach may be more cost effective than applying FASB ASC 606 on an individual contract basis, FASB ASC 606 provides no specific guidance on how an entity should assess whether the results of a portfolio approach would differ materially from application on a contract-by-contract basis. FASB does indicate in BC 69 of ASU No. 2014-09 that it did not intend for an entity to quantitatively evaluate each outcome and, instead, the entity should be able to take a reasonable approach to determine the portfolios that would be appropriate for its types of contracts. (paragraph 8.6.14)

Step 2: Identify the Performance Obligations

Performance Obligations

A-20 Institutions will need to determine if tuition and housing are distinct services promised by the institution or whether they need to be combined. (paragraph 8.6.15)

A-21 FASB ASC 606-10-05-4b states the following:

> A contract includes promises to transfer goods or services to a customer. If those goods or services are distinct, the promises are performance obligations and are accounted for separately. A good or service is distinct if the customer can benefit from the service on its own or together with other resources that are readily available to the customer and the entity's promise to transfer the good or service to the customer is separately identifiable from other promises in the contract.

A-22 When assessing whether promised goods or services are separately identifiable under FASB ASC 606, the objective is to determine whether the nature of the entity's overall promise in the contract is to transfer (*a*) each of those separate goods or services or (*b*) a combined item (or items) to which the promised goods or services are inputs. FASB ASC 606-10-25-21 provides factors to consider when assessing whether two or more promises to transfer goods or services to a customer are or are not separately identifiable. (paragraph 8.6.17)

A-23 If tuition and housing are included in a single contract or separate contracts, which are combined in accordance with FASB ASC 606-10-25-9, institutions will need to consider the promises included in the contract (or combined contracts) entered into with students and whether the promises are performance obligations, which need to be accounted for separately. FinREC believes that, in most cases, tuition and housing are distinct services and, therefore, separate performance obligations. (paragraphs 8.6.18–.19)

Step 3: Determine the Transaction Price

Transaction Price

A-24 Institutions will need to consider the guidance in paragraphs 2–32 of FASB ASC 606-10-32 to determine the amount that will need to be included in the measurement of tuition and housing revenues.

FASB ASC 606-10-32-2 states the following:

> An entity shall consider the terms of the contract and the customary business practices to determine the transaction price. The transaction price is the amount of consideration to which an entity expects to be entitled in exchange for transferring promised goods or services to a customer, excluding amounts collected on behalf of third parties. The consideration promised in a contract with a customer may include fixed amounts, variable amounts, or both.

A-25 In determining the transaction price(s) in accordance with FASB ASC 606-10-32-2, institutions should include all the consideration it expects to be entitled to for the student's tuition and housing. Certain institutions may offer students different tuition and housing rates based on the category of student (for example, seniors, veterans, first responders, in-state vs. out of state, and so on). As such, the contract price may differ by student and would be based on the individual contract entered into by each student. BC 187 of ASU No. 2014-09 also indicates that amounts to which the entity has rights under the present contract can be paid by any party (that is, not only by the customer). Therefore, the consideration may be paid by the student or by other parties paying on behalf of the student (for example, parent, employer, federal or state governments or other external organizations through student aid awarded specifically to the student by such organizations, and so on). (paragraph 8.6.22)

A-26 Institutions will need to determine a transaction price based on each contract identified. If separate contracts are identified by the institution for housing and tuition, separate transaction prices would be determined for each contract. Conversely, if a combined or single contract exists, one transaction price would be determined (and allocated to the identified separate performance obligations in step 4). (paragraph 8.6.23)

Consideration Payable to the Customer

A-27 FASB ASC 606-10-32-3 states that the nature, timing, and amount of consideration promised by a customer affect the estimate of the transaction price. When determining the transaction price, FASB ASC 606-10-32-3e explains that one item to consider is the effect of consideration payable to the customer. (paragraph 8.6.24)

A-28 FASB ASC 606-10-32-25 states the following:

> Consideration payable to a customer includes cash amounts that an entity pays, or expects to pay, to the customer (or to the other parties that purchase the entity's goods or services from the customer). Consideration payable to a customer also includes credits or other items (for example, a coupon or voucher) that can be applied against amounts owed to the entity (or to other parties that purchased the entity's goods or services from the customer). An entity shall account for consideration payable to a customer as a reduction of the transaction price and, therefore, of revenue, unless the payment to the customer is in exchange for a distinct good or service that the customer transfers to the entity.

A-29 Institutions often provide reductions in amounts charged for tuition and housing (for example, financial aid awarded to the student by the institution may be applied to tuition or housing charges). Institutions will need to evaluate whether such reductions are provided partially or fully in exchange for a distinct good or service. In some cases, such reductions are given in exchange for distinct goods or services provided to the institution, for example, as part of a compensation package (such as tuition remission provided to employees or work-study aid provided to students). Per FASB ASC 958-720-25-7, such reductions are reported as expenses, and per FASB ASC 958-720-45-23, such expenses would be reported in the same functional classification in which the cost of the goods or services provided to the institution is reported. (paragraph 8.6.26)

A-30 Alternatively, reductions in amounts charged for housing or tuition provided by an institution may be provided other than in exchange for a distinct good or service provided directly to the institution. For example, a college may award a scholarship to a student enrolled at the college. In these instances, in accordance with FASB ASC 606-10-32-25, such reductions would be accounted for as a reduction of the transaction price and, therefore, of revenue. (paragraph 8.6.27)

A-31 FASB ASC 606-10-32-27 states that

> if consideration payable to a customer is accounted for as a reduction of the transaction price, an entity shall recognize the reduction in revenue when (or as) the later of either of the following events occurs:
>
> *a.* The entity recognizes the revenue for the transfer of the related goods or services to the customer.
>
> *b.* The entity pays or promises to pay the consideration (even if the payment is conditional on a future event). That promise might be implied by the entity's customary business practice.

A-32 Generally, reductions in amounts charged for housing or tuition are known and agreed to by the institution and the student prior to the recognition of revenue. Therefore, FinREC believes that such reductions would generally be recognized as the institution recognizes the revenue. (paragraph 8.6.29)

A-33 FASB ASC 606-10-32-26 states the following:

> ...If the amount of consideration payable to a customer exceeds the fair value of the distinct good or service, then the entity shall account for such an excess as a reduction of the transaction price. If the entity cannot reasonably estimate the fair value of the good or service received from the customer, it shall account for all of the consideration payable to the customer as a reduction of the transaction price.

A-34 If the reduction in amounts charged for housing or tuition is provided partially in exchange for a distinct good or service, the excess would be accounted for in accordance with FASB ASC 606-10-32-26. (paragraph 8.6.31)

Right to Withdraw

A-35 FASB ASC 606-10-32-5 states that "if the consideration promised in a contract includes a variable amount, an entity shall estimate the amount of consideration to which the entity will be entitled in exchange for transferring the promised goods or services to a customer." FASB ASC 606-10-32-6 further states that "an amount of consideration can vary because of discounts, rebates, refunds, credits, price concessions, incentives, performance bonuses, penalties, or other similar items."

A-36 Institutions may provide a stated period of time during which students may withdraw from classes without further (or reduced) financial obligation (beyond any nonrefundable deposits), which may result in a full or partial refund in those cases in which consideration has been received in advance. (paragraph 8.6.33)

A-37 In accordance with FASB ASC 606-10-32-10, if the institution receives consideration from a student and expects to refund some or all of that consideration to the student, this type of consideration is a form of variable consideration. As a result, the institution would need to recognize a refund liability. The refund liability is measured at the amount of consideration received (or receivable) for which the institution does not expect to be entitled (that is, amounts not included in the transaction price). (paragraph 8.6.34)

A-38 In accordance with FASB ASC 606-10-32-8, an entity shall estimate the amount of variable consideration using one of two methods: the "expected value" or the "most likely amount" method. As discussed in FASB ASC 606-10-32-8a, the "expected value" method, which is the sum of probability-weighted amounts in a range of possible consideration amounts, may provide an appropriate estimate of the amount of variable consideration if the entity has a large number of contracts with similar characteristics.

A-39 Institutions may find it impractical to estimate the refund liability at an individual contract level when it is not known whether a specific student will withdraw. However, the entity may have evidence of withdrawals on a portfolio level. In accordance with the discussion at the July 2015 FASB/IASB TRG meeting on the portfolio practical expedient, institutions are required to consider all information that is reasonably available to the entity to estimate the refund liability, whether the guidance in FASB ASC 606 is applied on a portfolio or contract by contract basis. (paragraph 8.6.36)

A-40 In accordance with FASB ASC 606-10-32-11, "an entity shall include in the transaction price some or all of the amount of variable consideration estimated in accordance with FASB ASC 606-10-32-8 only to the extent that it is probable that a significant reversal in the amount of cumulative revenue recognized will not occur when the uncertainty associated with the variable consideration is subsequently resolved." The institution should consider the factors provided in FASB ASC 606-10-32-12 to assess the likelihood and magnitude of a revenue reversal. For example, although the withdrawals are outside the institution's influence, if the institution has significant predictive experience in estimating withdrawals and the uncertainty regarding a student's withdrawal will be resolved in a short time frame, FinREC believes that these circumstances indicate that a significant reversal in the cumulative amount of revenue recognized may not be expected. As such, FinREC believes it would be appropriate in this instance to include the institution's estimate of withdrawals in the transaction price. (paragraph 8.6.37)

A-41 In accordance with FASB ASC 606-10-55-26, institutions would need to update the measurement of the refund liability at the end of each reporting period for changes in expectations about the amount of refunds and recognize corresponding adjustments as revenue (or reductions of revenue). (paragraph 8.6.38)

Impact of Collectibility to the Measurement of Revenue

A-42 Although collectibility is considered in step 1 of the revenue recognition model, it is not considered when determining the transaction price in step 3. As explained in BC 261 of ASU No. 2014-09, revenue should be recognized at the amount to which the entity expects to be entitled, which would not reflect any adjustments for amounts that the entity might not be able to collect from the customer. (paragraph 8.6.39)

A-43 As such, under step 3 of the revenue recognition model, the transaction price is not adjusted to reflect the effects of a customer's credit risk, except for contracts with a significant financing component, as discussed in FASB ASC 606-10-32-19, that would use a rate that reflects the credit characteristics of the party receiving financing. Institutions would, however, need to separately assess contract assets and receivables for impairment (bad debt) and present and disclose such assets in accordance with FASB ASC 310. (paragraph 8.6.40)

A-44 Judgment will be required in evaluating whether the likelihood that an institution will not receive the full amount of stated consideration gives rise to a collectibility issue or a price concession. In many cases, the institution may have chosen to accept the risk of default by the student of the contractually agreed-upon consideration (customer credit risk). However, there may be instances in which an institution has a history of providing price concessions to students. In accordance with paragraphs 6–7 of FASB ASC 606-10-32, if an entity provides a price concession, the consideration would be considered variable consideration. Consequently, institutions will need to determine the transaction price in step 3 of the model, including any price concessions, before concluding on the collectibility criterion in step 1 of the model. (paragraph 8.6.41)

Step 4: Allocate the Transaction Price to the Performance Obligations in the Contract

Allocating Transaction Price to Performance Obligations

A-45 If tuition and housing are included in a single contract or combined contracts (as discussed in paragraph A-17), institutions will need to consider the guidance in FASB ASC 606 with respect to allocating the transaction price to the performance obligations in the contract. The following analysis in subsequent paragraphs assumes tuition and housing are separate performance obligations. (paragraph 8.6.42)

A-46 As discussed in FASB ASC 606-10-32-28, the transaction price is allocated to each performance obligation (or distinct good or service) in an amount that depicts the amount of consideration to which the entity expects to be entitled in exchange for transferring the promised goods or services to the customer. FASB ASC 606-10-32-29 indicates that the transaction price should be allocated to each performance obligation identified in the contract on a relative standalone selling price basis. (paragraph 8.6.43)

A-47 FASB ASC 606-10-32-32 further states the following:

> The standalone selling price is the price at which an entity would sell a promised good or service separately to a customer. The best evidence of a standalone selling price is the observable price of a good or service when the entity sells that good or service separately in similar circumstances and to similar customers. A contractually stated price or a list price for a good or service may be (but is not presumed to be) the standalone selling price of that good or service.

A-48 Regarding tuition and housing, institutions may sell tuition separately (for example, to commuter students), but rarely would they sell housing separately to a student not also enrolled in classes. As such, although the standalone selling price for tuition may be observable, this may not be the case for housing. Institutions may consider other similar housing prices to estimate the selling price. Paragraphs 33–35 of FASB ASC 606-10-32 provide guidance on estimating the standalone selling price when it is not observable. (paragraph 8.6.45)

A-49 When determining the transaction price, institutions will also need to consider whether any reductions in amounts charged for tuition and housing (for example, financial aid awarded to the student) applies to tuition, housing, or both. (paragraph 8.6.46)

Step 5: Recognize Revenue When (or as) the Entity Satisfies a Performance Obligation

Recognizing Revenue

A-50 Under FASB ASC 606-10-25-23, an entity should recognize revenue when (or as) the entity satisfies a performance obligation by transferring a promised good or service to a customer. (paragraph 8.6.47)

A-51 As explained in FASB ASC 606-10-25-24, for each performance obligation identified, an entity needs to determine whether it satisfies the performance obligation over time or at a point in time. FASB ASC 606-10-25-27 provides criteria, one of which would need to be met, in order for revenue to be recognized over time. For example, FASB ASC 606-10-25-27*(a)* explains that if a customer simultaneously receives and consumes the benefits provided by the entity's performance as the entity performs, the entity transfers control of the good or service over time and, therefore, satisfies a performance obligation and recognizes revenue over time. Paragraphs 4–5 of FASB ASC 606-10-55 provide further guidance on this consideration.

A-52 FinREC believes that generally, students simultaneously receive and consume all of the benefits provided by the institution's performance because the institution provides instruction or housing to the students throughout the academic period, and it would be appropriate for institutions to recognize tuition and housing revenues over time in these circumstances. (paragraph 8.6.49)

A-53 FASB ASC 606-10-55-46 states that "an entity should derecognize the contract liability related to a nonrefundable prepayment from a customer (and recognize revenue) when it transfers those goods or services and, therefore, satisfies its performance obligation."

A-54 Students may not, in fact, enroll in the institution or move in to campus housing and, as a consequence, the associated nonrefundable deposit will be forfeited. FASB ASC 606-10-55-48 provides that if an entity expects to be entitled to a breakage amount in a contract liability, the entity should recognize the expected breakage amount as revenue in proportion to the pattern of rights exercised by the customer. Because actually enrolling or moving into housing are binary events (that is, the student either exercises his or her right or not) and the student is not exercising any other rights, FinREC believes the institution would not record breakage until the student's right to enroll or be provided housing expires. (paragraph 8.6.51)

Measuring Progress Over Time

A-55 An institution should consider the guidance in paragraphs 31–37 of FASB ASC 606-10-25 to determine how to measure progress towards completion of the performance obligation. (paragraph 8.6.52) FASB ASC 606-10-25-31 states the following:

> For each performance obligation satisfied over time, an entity should recognize revenue over time by measuring the progress toward complete satisfaction of that performance obligation. The objective when measuring progress is to depict an entity's performance in transferring control of goods or services promised to a customer (that is, the satisfaction of any entity's performance obligation).

A-56 FASB ASC 606-10-25-33 explains that appropriate methods of measuring progress include output methods and input methods and further states that in determining the appropriate method for measuring progress, an entity shall consider the nature of the good or service that the entity promised to transfer to the customer. (paragraph 8.6.53)

A-57 As further explained in FASB ASC 606-10-55-17, output methods recognize revenue on the basis of direct measurements of the value to the customer of the goods or services transferred to date relative to the remaining goods or services promised under the contract. FASB ASC 606-10-55-19 also states that the outputs used to measure progress may not be directly observable and the information required to apply them may not be available to the entity without undue cost and, therefore, an input method may be necessary. (paragraph 8.6.54)

A-58 As explained in FASB ASC 606-10-55-20, input methods recognize revenue on the basis of the entity's efforts or inputs to the satisfaction of a performance obligation relative to the total expected inputs to the satisfaction of the performance obligation. Inputs may include resources consumed, labor hours expended, costs incurred, or time elapsed. FASB ASC 606-10-55-20 states that if the entity's efforts or inputs are expended evenly throughout the performance period, it may be appropriate for the entity to recognize revenue on a straight-line basis. (paragraph 8.6.55)

A-59 Institutions will need to consider which method would be most appropriate for measuring progress if tuition and housing revenues are recognized over time. Instruction and housing services are generally provided ratably over the academic period. Therefore, FinREC believes it would be appropriate for institutions to recognize revenue ratably over the academic period based on time elapsed. (paragraph 8.6.56)

Presentation of Contracts in the Financial Statements

Statement of Financial Position

A-60 FASB ASC 606-10-45-1 states that when either party to a contract has performed, an entity should present the contract in the statement of financial position as a contract asset or a contract liability, depending on the relationship between the entity's performance and the customer's payment. (paragraph 8.6.57)

A-61 As stated in FASB ASC 606-10-45-3, "a contract asset is an entity's right to consideration in exchange for goods or services that the entity has transferred to a customer." FASB ASC 606-10-45-2 defines a *contract liability* is "an entity's obligation to transfer goods or services to a customer for which the entity has received consideration (or an amount of consideration is due) from the customer." (paragraph 8.6.58)

A-62 FASB ASC 606-10-45-1 also states that "an entity shall present any unconditional rights to consideration separately as a receivable." FASB ASC 606-10-45-4 further states that "a right to consideration is unconditional if only the passage of time is required before payment of that consideration is due."

A-63 FASB ASC 606-10-45-5 states the following:

> This guidance uses the terms *contract asset* and *contract liability*, but does not prohibit an entity from using alternative terms in the statement of financial position for those items. If an entity uses an alternative description for a contract asset, the entity shall provide sufficient information for a user of the financial statements to distinguish between receivables and contract assets.

A-64 *Presentation of advanced cash payments and receivables.* In accordance with FASB ASC 606-10-45-2, if a student pays consideration (or payments are received on their behalf) or an entity has the right to an amount of consideration that is unconditional (that is, a receivable) under a contract before the institution has provided the service to the student, the institution would present the consideration received (or receivable) as a contract liability when the payment is made or the entity has an unconditional right to the consideration. (paragraph 8.6.61)

A-65 *Presentation of amounts due prior to provision of service.* Example 38, Case B in paragraphs 285–286 of FASB ASC 606-10-55 illustrates the guidance in FASB ASC 606 on the presentation of contract balances for a non-cancellable contract. This example suggests that an entity should recognize a receivable (and a corresponding contract liability) when the contract becomes non-cancellable because the entity has an unconditional right to the consideration. (paragraph 8.6.62)

A-66 Institutions will need to consider the rights and obligations included in enrollment contracts to determine whether, and at what point, the contract is non-cancellable. For example, many institutions provide a period during which students may withdraw from classes without further (or reduced) financial obligation. (paragraph 8.6.63)

A-67 *Presentation of entity's rights to consideration based on provision of goods or services.* In accordance with FASB ASC 606-10-45-3, if the institution provides the tuition or housing services before the customer pays or before the entity has an unconditional right to the consideration, FinREC believes it is appropriate to recognize a contract asset for the services provided, excluding any amounts presented as a receivable (see preceding text). (paragraph 8.6.64)

A-68 *Consideration of impairment of contract assets and receivables.* In accordance with paragraphs 3–4 of FASB ASC 606-10-45, impairment of a contract asset or receivable should be measured, presented, and disclosed in accordance with FASB ASC 310. As stated in FASB ASC 606-10-45-4, upon initial recognition of a receivable from a contract with a customer, any difference between the measurement of the receivable in accordance with FASB ASC 310 and the corresponding amount of revenue recognized under FASB ASC 606 should be presented as an expense (for example, as an impairment loss). (paragraph 8.6.65).

A-69 *Presentation of Refund Liability.* As discussed in paragraph A-37, an institution might also be required to present a refund liability to reflect the amount of consideration received for which the institution does not expect to be entitled. (paragraph 8.6.66)

Statement of Activities

A-70 Because FASB ASC 606 prescribes that revenue is recognized based on the transaction price (net of any reductions or consideration payable to customer), presenting the gross amount as revenue is not allowed under FASB ASC 606. However, FASB ASC 606 neither prescribes nor prohibits presentation of the reductions (for example, financial aid or scholarships) in the financial statements. FinREC believes it is acceptable for institutions to disclose the amount of reductions incorporated in the revenue line either parenthetically on the face of the statement of activities or in the notes to the financial statements. (paragraph 8.6.67)

Disclosures

A-71 Institutions should consider the specific disclosure requirements included in FASB ASC 606-10-50 as they prepare the notes to the financial statements as they relate to tuition and housing revenues. (paragraph 8.6.68)

Examples

A-72 The following examples are meant to be illustrative, and the determination of how to account for tuition revenue should be based on the facts and circumstances of an entity's specific situation. In this example, the student is a commuter student (that is, contracts with the institution to provide instruction only). (paragraph 8.6.69)

Example 8-6-1—Student Pays Tuition Bill After Entity Performs

A-73 In this example, a higher education institution has a fiscal year end that occurs during the semester. The student receives an offer to enroll at the institution. A nonrefundable deposit of $1,000 is required upon acceptance of the institution's offer to enroll. The student accepts the enrollment offer and pays the nonrefundable deposit. At this time, the institution determines that a contract is in place in accordance with FASB ASC 606. A bill for $9,000 (remaining tuition balance) is generated by the institution and sent to the student upon enrollment. Payment of the bill is due two weeks prior to the start of classes. The student pays the bill after classes have already begun. The semester spans 100 days. Students are eligible to receive a refund ranging from full to partial tuition paid (based on the number of classes they drop) within the first two weeks after classes have begun, excluding the nonrefundable portion. The student in this example withdraws from one class (with a tuition charge of $900) within the two-week grace period. The institution has decided that it will apply a portfolio approach for calculating refund liabilities. In this case, it has been determined that using this approach would not produce a result that materially differs from determining refunds on a contract-by-contract basis. The institution calculates a refund estimate of 10 percent of tuition (excluding the nonrefundable deposit).

A-74 The following presents the journal entries made by the institution to reflect the preceding:

a. Student pays nonrefundable enrollment deposit of $1,000 prior to enrollment.

DR.	Cash	$1,000	
CR.	Contract Liability (Deferred Revenue)		$1,000

[As the student ultimately enrolls, the deposit will be included in the transaction price and revenue recognized as the institution performs (for example, ratably over the 100-day semester.]

b. Student enrolls. Bill is sent to student for $9,000 balance of tuition.

No entry because revenue recognition has not yet commenced and the institution does not yet have an unconditional right to consideration given the 2-week cancellation (withdrawal) period.

c. Bill is due 2 weeks prior to first day of class.

No entry because the student has the right to cancel the contract (withdraw) through the first 2 weeks of classes.

d. Institution provides the first day of class (the student has made no payment other than the enrollment deposit).

DR.	Contract Liability (Deferred Revenue)	$91	
CR.	Revenue		$91

[The institution adjusts the transaction price based on its estimate of refunds (using the expected value method, determined using a portfolio approach).]

[Revenue is recognized ratably over the 100-day semester ($91.00 = $10,000 revenue/100 days less refund estimate [$9,000/100 × 10% refund estimate])]

[This entry is repeated each day for the nine days remaining in the withdrawal period.]

e. At the end of day 1, student partially withdraws by dropping a class, and tuition is reduced by $900. Balance of tuition bill is reduced to $8,100.

Because no consideration was received (other than the nonrefundable deposit), no funds are returned.

f. End of institution's reporting period:

DR./CR.	Contract Liability (Deferred Revenue)	– 0 –	
	DR./CR. Revenue		– 0 –

[The institution would update its estimate of the transaction price using the portfolio approach at each reporting period until the withdrawal period ends. In this example, the reporting period ends after week 1 of classes. In this example, the actual reduction in tuition for the period ($900) equals the allocated portion of the refund estimate under the portfolio approach ($9,000 × 10%); therefore, no entry at the end of the reporting period is needed in this example.]

g. After end of week 2, withdrawal period has ended.

DR.	Receivable	$8,100	
	CR. Contract Liability (Deferred Revenue)		$8,100

[The receivable for the student is recorded for the unpaid tuition balance (net of withdrawal), with an offsetting contract liability, because the contract is now non-cancellable.]

h. Throughout remainder of semester (90 days):

DR.	Contract Liability (Deferred Revenue)	$8,190	
	CR. Revenue		$8,190

[Continue to recognize revenue ratably over the semester and reduce contract liability.]

[Revenue is recognized ratably over the 100-day semester ($91 per day × 90 days remaining)]

i. Student pays.

DR.	Cash	$8,100	
	CR. Receivable		$8,100

Example 8-6-2—Student Pays Tuition Bill Before Entity Performs

A-75 In this example, assume the same facts as in example 8-6-1, except that the student pays the tuition bill prior to the start of classes.

a. Student pays nonrefundable enrollment deposit of $1,000 prior to enrollment.

DR.	Cash	$1,000	
	CR. Contract Liability (Deferred Revenue)		$1,000

[As the student ultimately enrolls, the deposit will be included in the transaction price and revenue recognized as the institution performs (for example, ratably over the 100-day semester).]

b. Student enrolls. Bill is sent to student for $9,000 balance of tuition.

No entry because revenue recognition has not yet commenced and the institution does not yet have an unconditional right to consideration given the 2-week cancellation (withdrawal) period.

c. Student pays tuition bill.

DR.	Cash	$9,000	
	CR. Contract Liability (Deferred Revenue)		$9,000

d. Institution recognizes refund liability.

DR.	Contract Liability	$900	
	CR. Refund Liability (Deferred Revenue)		$900

[Refund liability is estimated using the expected value method, determined using a portfolio approach. $900 represents the applicable refund estimate per student ($9,000 potentially refundable × 10% refund estimate)]

e. Institution provides the first day of class.

DR.	Contract Liability (Deferred Revenue)	$91	
	CR. Revenue		$91

[Revenue is recognized ratably over the 100-day semester ($91.00 = $10,000 revenue/100 days less refund estimate [$9,000/100 × 10% refund estimate])]

[This entry is repeated each day for the 9 days remaining in the withdrawal period.]

f. At the end of day 1, student partially withdraws by dropping a class, and tuition is reduced by $900.

DR.	Refund Liability	$900	
	CR. Cash		$900

[In this example, the actual refund for this particular student equals the allocated portion of the refund liability calculated under the portfolio approach. If this were not the case, the institution would update its refund estimate.]

g. Throughout remainder of semester (90 days):

DR.	Contract Liability (Deferred Revenue)	$8,190	
	CR. Revenue		$8,190

[Continue to recognize revenue ratably over the semester and reduce contract liability.]

[Revenue is recognized ratably over the 100-day semester ($91 per day × 90 days remaining)]

Dues and Subscriptions

Distinguishing Contributions From Other Transactions: Exchange Transactions

A-76 The FASB ASC glossary defines an *exchange transaction* and *contribution* as follows:

- An exchange transaction is "a reciprocal transfer between two entities that results in one of the entities acquiring assets or services or satisfying liabilities by surrendering other assets or services or incurring other obligations."
- A contribution is as "an unconditional transfer of cash or other assets to an entity or a settlement or cancellation of its liabilities in a voluntary nonreciprocal transfer by another entity acting other than as an owner. Those characteristics distinguish contributions from exchange transactions, which are reciprocal transfers in which each party receives and sacrifices approximately equal value; from investments by owners and distributions to owners, which are nonreciprocal transfers between an entity and its owners; and from other nonreciprocal transfers, such as impositions of taxes or legal judgments, fines, and thefts, which are not voluntary transfers. In a contribution transaction, the value, if any, returned to the resource provider is incidental to potential public benefits. In an exchange transaction, the potential public benefits are secondary to the potential proprietary benefits to the resource provider. The term contribution revenue is used to apply to transactions that are part of the entity's ongoing major or central activities (revenues), or are peripheral or incidental to the entity (gains)."

A-77 Therefore a contribution differs from an exchange transaction because an exchange transaction is a reciprocal transfer in which each party receives and sacrifices something of approximately equal value.

Membership Dues

A-78 Paragraphs 9–12 of FASB ASC 958-605-55 discuss NFPs that receive dues from their members. This paragraph and the following paragraph and Table 5-2 (paragraph 5.49) reproduce that guidance. The term "members" is used broadly by some NFPs to refer to their donors and by other NFPs to refer to individuals or other entities that pay dues in exchange for a defined set of benefits. These transfers often have elements of both a contribution and an exchange transaction because members receive tangible or intangible benefits from their membership in the NFP. For example, the exchange portion of member benefits may include a journal subscription, discounted or free continuing professional education (CPE) classes, conferences and seminars, discounted or free tickets to seats at performing arts events, discounted services, access to locked website contents or a library, networking opportunities, and/or career qualifications. When membership dues carry traits of both contributions and exchange components, they should be bifurcated as required in FASB ASC 606-10-15-4. (See paragraphs A-4–A-5 for additional discussion on bifurcation.) Usually, the determination of whether membership dues are contributions rests on whether the value received by the member is commensurate with the dues paid. For example, if an NFP has annual dues of $100 and the only benefit members receive is a monthly newsletter with a fair value of $25, $25 of the dues are received in an exchange transaction and $75 of the dues are a contribution.

A-79 Member benefits generally have value regardless of how often (or whether) the benefits are used. For example, most would agree that a health club membership is an exchange transaction, even if the member stops using the facilities before the completion of the membership period. It may be difficult, however, to measure the benefits members receive and to determine whether the value of those benefits is approximately equal to the dues paid by the members.

A-80 Table 5-2 (paragraph 5.49) contains the list of indicators from FASB ASC 958-605-55-12 that may be helpful in determining whether memberships are contributions, exchange transactions, or a combination of both. Depending on the facts and circumstances, some indicators may be more significant than others; however, no single indicator is determinative of the classification of a particular transaction. Indicators of a contribution tend to describe transactions in which the value, if any, returned to the resource provider is incidental to potential public benefits. Indicators of an exchange tend to describe transactions in which the potential public benefits are secondary to the potential proprietary benefits to the resource provider.

A-81 FinREC believes that membership dues, excluding any amount determined to be a contribution, generally should be considered an exchange or reciprocal transaction in which the member receives something of value and in return pays the NFP for the benefits of membership. The exchange transaction should be accounted for in accordance with FASB ASC 606 as revenue from contracts with customers.

A-82 For example, a trade association charges its members annual membership dues that include a contribution to its educational foundation that funds a college scholarship for students that major in the same discipline that the trade association represents. Typically, the membership amount and the contribution amount are separately identified, and payment of the contribution is optional. In that case, the amounts specified on the invoice are the amounts to be recognized as membership dues and contribution. However, in the less likely case that the contribution portion is not specified but a contribution is included as part of the membership dues, as discussed in paragraph A-5 and paragraph 5.43, the trade association should bifurcate the exchange from the contribution by determining the fair value of the exchange portion of the transaction (membership dues), with the residual (excess of the resources received over the fair value of the exchange portion of the transaction) reported as contributions. The NFP should apply the guidance in FASB ASC 606 to the exchange portion of the membership dues and apply FASB ASC 958-605 to the contribution.

Discussion of the Five-Step Revenue Recognition Model Related to the Exchange Aspects of Membership Dues and Subscriptions

Step 1: Identify the Contract with a Customer

A-83 In order for the exchange portion of membership dues, a subscription, a life-time subscription, or a life-time membership to be a contract with a customer, it would need to meet the following criteria as required by FASB ASC 606-10-25-1:

a. The contract is approved and the parties are committed to their obligations.

b. The NFP can identify each parties' rights to the goods or services being provided.

c. The NFP can identify the payment terms for the goods or services to be transferred.

d. The contract has commercial substance.

e. It is probable that the NFP will collect substantially all of the consideration to which it will be entitled in exchange for the goods or services that will be transferred to the customer.

A-84 In most cases, NFPs require and receive the payments in advance for memberships and subscriptions, life-time memberships and life-time subscriptions, which are based on pricing and terms established by the NFP. Therefore, FinREC believes that the criteria for contract existence in FASB ASC 606-10-25-1 generally would be met for the exchange aspects of memberships and subscriptions, when the order is placed.

A-85 In the circumstances in which an NFP bills a member or subscriber for a renewal in advance, prior to the beginning of the service period, it is unlikely that the requirements in FASB ASC 606-10-25-1 have been met for the renewal. Even in cases where the requirements in FASB ASC 606-10-25-1 have been met and it is determined that a contract with a customer exists, the NFP would need to consider whether either party to the contract has performed and whether the requirements in FASB ASC 606-10-45-1 through 45-5 have been met to determine the presentation of the contract. FASB ASC 606-10-45-4 states that an entity would only recognize a receivable if it has a present right to payment even though that amount may be subject to refund in the future. Furthermore, as illustrated by Example 38 of FASB ASC 606-10-55 (paragraphs 284–286), an entity should not recognize a receivable and contract liability in the statement of financial position if the entity does not yet have a right to consideration that is unconditional (that is, the contract is cancellable at the invoice date). Therefore, a receivable would not be recorded until the earliest of meeting the performance obligation or, under a noncancellable contract when the entity has an unconditional right to consideration.

Step 2: Identify the Performance Obligations in the Contract

A-86 A *performance obligation* is defined in FASB ASC 606-10-25-14 as a promise in a contract with a customer to transfer to the customer either:

a. A good or service (or a bundle of goods or services) that is distinct.

b. A series of distinct good or services that are substantially the same and that have the same pattern of transfer to the customer.

A-87 If the NFP promises in a contract to transfer more than one good or service to the customer, in accordance with FASB ASC 606-10-25-14, the NFP should account for each promised good or service as a performance obligation only if it is (1) distinct or (2) a series of distinct goods or services that are substantially the same and have the same pattern of transfer.

A-88 Membership dues often entitle the member to a group of benefits, such as the right to identify himself/herself/itself as a member and use the membership organization's logo, the right to access to members' only areas of websites, the ability to serve voluntarily on committees, the ability to participate in online forums, or the right to access job postings. In accordance with FASB ASC 606-10-25-22, if the member benefit is not distinct, then the benefit should be combined with other promised goods or services until the NFP identifies a bundle of promised goods or services that is distinct (that is, general membership benefits).

A-89 A member benefit would be considered distinct, as compared to other promised services included in the contract, if both of the following criteria in FASB ASC 606-10-25-19 are met:

a. *Capable of being distinct*—Can the customer benefit from the promised good or service either on its own or together with other resources that are readily available to the customer?

b. *Distinct within the context of the contract*—Is the promise to transfer the good or service separately identifiable from other promises in the contract?

A-90 Helpful in determining whether a member benefit is capable of being distinct is whether the NFP regularly sells the benefit on a standalone basis, which indicates that a customer can benefit from the good or service on its own or together with other resources that are readily available. (Example 11, Case E in FASB ASC 606-10-55-150G through 55-150J and Example 12, Case A 606-10-55-151 through 55-153A provide examples of this evaluation that may be helpful for NFPs to consider.) For example, if an NFP provided free access to its website to members and separately sold that benefit to nonmembers, that benefit is capable of being distinct.

A-91 NFPs are required under FASB ASC 606-10-25-14 to assess contracts with customers to determine if there are multiple performance obligations. If so, the NFP is required by FASB ASC 606-10-32-28 to allocate the transaction price to each of the identified performance obligations in an amount that depicts the amount of consideration to which the entity expects to be entitled in exchange for transferring the promised good or service to the customer.

A-92 For example, a trade association charges its members annual membership dues, and the membership includes access to an online database, a subscription to its monthly publication (one per month) and discounts on future educational opportunities. The trade association should assess whether access to an online database, each of the monthly publications and each discount related to separate educational programs are separate performance obligations or could be considered to be general membership benefits, and whether the discounts provide material rights. In accordance with paragraphs 16A–16B of FASB ASC 606-10-25, an entity is not required to assess whether promised goods or services are performance obligations if they are immaterial in the context of the contract with the customer, although discounts that provide material rights cannot be deemed immaterial. Consistent with paragraphs 41–45 of FASB ASC 606-10-55, the right to obtain a discount on future purchases does not create a performance obligation to which a portion of the transaction price would need to be allocated unless the discount is considered to be a material right. (If an option provides a material right to the customer, the customer in effect pays the entity in advance for future goods or services, and the entity recognizes revenue when those future goods or services are transferred or when the option expires.) Example 49—Option that Provides the Customer with a Material Right (Discount Voucher) in FASB ASC 606-10-55-336 through 55-339 provides further guidance.

Step 3: Determine the Transaction Price

A-93 As explained in FASB ASC 606-10-32-2, the *transaction price* is the amount of consideration (for example, cash payment) to which an NFP expects to be entitled in exchange for transferring promised goods or services to a member or subscriber (customer), excluding amounts collected on behalf of third parties. To determine the transaction price, an entity should consider the effects of:

a. Variable consideration

b. Constraining estimates of variable consideration

c. The existence of a significant financing component

d. Noncash consideration

e. Consideration payable to the customer

A-94 In general, subscriptions, memberships, life-time memberships, and life-time subscriptions are paid for in advance by the customer to the NFP or they are bundled with other goods or services (e.g. conference and seminars, etc.) and amounts paid are generally not refundable. FASB ASC 606-10-32-15 states, "In determining the transaction price, an entity shall adjust the promised amount of consideration for the effects of the time value of money if the timing of payments agreed to by the parties to the contract (either explicitly or implicitly) provides the customer or the entity with a significant benefit of financing the transfer of goods or services to the customer". However, FASB ASC 606-10-32-17 provides factors that, if present, indicate that a financing component does not exist. That paragraph addresses the circumstances in which a customer paid for the goods or services in advance, and the timing of the transfer of those goods or services is at the discretion of the customer. An example would be online CPE—The customer pays for the course at the time of purchase and can choose when to complete the course within a one- or two-year period.

A-95 The assessment of what constitutes a significant benefit of financing requires judgment. BC234 of FASB ASU No. 2014-09 states, "that for many contracts an entity will not need to adjust the promised amount of customer consideration because the effects of the financing component will not materially change the amount of revenue that should be recognized in relation to a contract with a customer". The assessment of what constitutes a significant benefit of financing will be based upon individual facts and circumstances for each entity. If an entity concludes the financing component is not significant, the entity does not need to adjust the consideration promised in determining the transaction price. Under FASB ASC 606-10-32-18, as a practical expedient, an NFP need not adjust the transaction price for a significant financing component if the NFP expects, at contract inception, that the period between transfer of the goods or services to the customer and payment by the customer will be one year or less.

Step 4: Allocate the Transaction Price to the Performance Obligations in the Contract

A-96 As explained in FASB ASC 606-10-32-28, for a contract with a customer that has more than one performance obligation, an NFP should allocate the transaction price to each performance obligation in an amount that depicts the amount of consideration to which the NFP expects to be entitled in exchange for transferring the promised goods or services to the customer.

A-97 In the case where there are multiple performance obligations, as required by FASB ASC 606-10-32-29, the NFP should allocate the transaction price to each performance obligation identified in a contract on a relative standalone selling price basis. As required by FASB ASC 606-10-32-33, if a standalone selling price is not observable, the NFP should estimate it. FASB ASC 606-10-32-34 provides examples of suitable methods for estimating the standalone selling price of a good or service. If the transaction price includes a discount or variable consideration that relates entirely to one or more, but not all, performance obligations in a contract, then the requirements in paragraphs 36–41 of FASB ASC 606-10-32 specify when an entity should allocate the discount or variable consideration to one (or some) performance obligation(s) rather than to all performance obligations in the contract.

A-98 Continuing the example in paragraph A-92, after determining the transaction price, the association should allocate the transaction price to each separately identifiable performance obligation in an amount that depicts the amount of consideration to which the entity expects to be entitled in exchange for transferring the promised goods or services to the customer, as required by FASB ASC 606-10-32-28. Thus, if the right to obtain a discount on the future educational opportunities is a material right, the membership dues should be allocated among the performance obligations including the discount right.

Step 5: Recognize Revenue When (or As) the Entity Satisfies a Performance Obligation

A-99 As explained in FASB ASC 606-10-25-23, an NFP should recognize revenue when (or as) it satisfies the performance obligation by transferring a promised good or service to the customer. For the membership service and/or subscriptions, whether they are annual or life-time, the recognition point will depend on the specific facts and circumstances. A good or service is transferred when (or as) the customer obtains control of that good or service.

A-100 FASB ASC 606-10-25-27 notes that an entity transfers control of a good or service over time, and, therefore, satisfies a performance obligation over time if one of the following criteria is met:

a. The customer simultaneously receives and consumes the benefits provided by the entity's performance as the entity performs.

b. The entity's performance creates or enhances an asset that the customer controls as the asset is created or enhanced.

c. The entity's performance does not create an asset with an alternative use to the entity, and the entity has an enforceable right to payment for performance completed to date.

A-101 For each performance obligation, an NFP should determine whether the performance obligation will be satisfied over time by transferring control of a good over time or if the NFP satisfies a performance obligation at a point in time. For performance obligations associated with nonrefundable life-time memberships and life-time subscriptions, if the obligation is satisfied over time, exchange transactions would be recognized as revenue over an appropriate time period (such as the life expectancy of the member or subscriber) using an appropriate measure of progress (such as a time-based measure). If the performance obligation is not satisfied over time, an NFP should consider at what point in time control transfers, based on the following indicators as explained in FASB ASC 606-10-25-30:

a. Present right to payment

b. Legal title

c. Physical possession

d. Risks and rewards of ownership

e. Customer acceptance

A-102 Continuing the example in paragraphs A-92 and A-98, the revenue related to the publications would be recognized monthly (as performance obligations are satisfied in separate monthly deliverables, which is a point in time per FASB ASC 606-10-25-30). The revenue allocated to the option is recognized when the educational opportunity is provided (if exercised) or the option expires. The revenue related to access to an online database is recognized ratably over the membership period as the customer simultaneously receives and consumes those benefits.

A-103 If the member exercises the option to participate in the educational opportunity, the exercise might be accounted for by the association either as a contract modification or a continuation of the existing contract (that is, a change in the transaction price for the contract). (Refer to FASB/IASB TRG Agenda Ref. 32: *Accounting for a Customer's Exercise of a Material Right*, and paragraphs 9–12 of Agenda Ref. 34: *March 2015 Meeting—Summary of Issues Discussed and Next Steps*). If the association accounts for the exercise of the option as a contract modification, then it should apply the guidance in paragraphs 10–13 of FASB ASC 606-10-25. If the association accounts for the exercise of the option as a continuation of the existing contract, it should follow the example in paragraphs 14–15 of TRG Agenda Ref. 32 and allocate the additional consideration to the educational opportunity along with the amount previously allocated to the option to participate in the educational opportunity.

A-104 The following examples are meant to be illustrative, and the application of FASB ASC 606 should be based on the facts and circumstances of an entity's specific situation.

Example #1: Subscriptions Received as Part of a Membership

A-105 An NFP trade association produces a quarterly journal that discusses and highlights research, issues and trends of interest to its members and others in the respective discipline related to the NFP's mission. Members receive the NFP's quarterly journal as part of their annual membership dues, which are $300 per year. In addition to the quarterly journal, members receive other membership benefits, such as access to the members-only section of the association's website and legislative advocacy services. The NFP sells individual journals to others that are not members of the NFP for $25 per journal. The NFP has determined there is no contribution included in the payment from the customer.

A-106 The NFP applies the guidance in FASB ASC 606 and determines the following:

Step 1—Identify the Contract: There is a contract between the NFP and the member related to both membership and the journal subscription.

Step 2—Identify Performance Obligations: There are six promised goods or services that are to be evaluated whether they are performance obligations that meet the criteria in FASB ASC 606-10-25-19:

- The promise to the member to provide access to the website during the one-year term.
- The promise to the member to provide legislative advocacy services during the one-year term.
- The promise to the member of a subscription to provide four quarterly journals.

For the purposes of this example, the promises to deliver all of these goods and services are distinct. However, the promise to deliver access to the website and the promise to provide advocacy services are delivered concurrently and have the same measure of progress; therefore, they may be accounted for as if they were a single performance obligation (referred to as "membership benefits").

Step 3—Determine the Transaction Price: The transaction price is the contract price of $300 for a one year membership, which includes the subscription.

Step 4—Allocate the Transaction Price to Performance Obligations: The transaction price should be allocated between the five performance obligations based on the relative standalone selling prices of each performance obligation.

- The standalone selling price for each journal would be the observable price of $25, because that is the price at which the NFP separately sells the journals to customers.
- The NFP does not sell membership separately without including the quarterly journals. Because there is no directly observable selling price, the NFP should estimate the standalone selling price. The NFP determines that the adjusted market assessment approach is a suitable method to use to estimate the standalone selling price for the membership, as the estimate will refer to prices charged by other NFPs for similar services. In this case, the standalone selling price was determined to be $250.
- The NFP would then allocate the transaction price to the performance obligations based on the relative standalone selling price as follows:

Performance Obligation	Standalone selling price	Percentage
1 Quarterly Journal	$ 25	7%
2 Quarterly Journal	25	7%
3 Quarterly Journal	25	7%
4 Quarterly Journal	25	7%
5 Membership	250	72%
Total	$350	100%

Performance Obligation	Allocated Transaction Price
1 Quarterly Journal	$ 21
2 Quarterly Journal	21
3 Quarterly Journal	21
4 Quarterly Journal	21
5 Membership	216
Total	$300

Step 5—Recognize Revenue When Each Performance Obligation is Satisfied: The NFP concludes that:

- The member simultaneously receives and consumes the benefits of membership, and the membership performance obligation is satisfied over time. The NFP also concludes that the best measure of progress toward complete satisfaction of the membership performance obligation over time is a time-based measure. Thus, $216 is recognized ratably over the one-year membership period.
- The performance obligation for each quarterly journal is satisfied at a point in time, and revenue should be recognized when control of the journal has been transferred to the customer. Assuming the NFP concludes that control of the journal transfers to the customer upon shipment, $21 is recognized when each quarterly journal is shipped.

Example #2: One-Year Subscription to an Academic Journal

A-107 An NFP produces an academic journal quarterly that discusses and highlights research, issues and trends of interest to a particular special interest group that the NFP serves. The NFP produces this journal four times a year. The NFP offers the journal for an annual subscription for $120 a year, which represents the standalone selling price. For the purpose of this discussion there is no discount offered to members, members do not receive the subscription as part of their annual dues, and the NFP has determined there is no contribution included in the payment from the customer. The NFP sells the journals to non-subscribers for $35 per issue and distributes the journal for sale in college bookstores and specialty newsstands for the same $35 price per issue.

A-108 The NFP applies the guidance in FASB ASC 606 and determines the following:

Step 1: Identify the Contract: There is a contract between the NFP and subscriber to provide a subscription of the quarterly journal for a one-year period.

Step 2: Identify Performance Obligations: There are four performance obligations that meet the criteria in FASB ASC 606-10-25-19:

- The promise to the subscriber to provide four quarterly journals.

The subscriber obtains the journals within the contract period at a discount to the $35 per issue price, but any additional journals purchased after the contract period would be at the non-subscriber price of $35 per issue. Therefore, the NFP concludes that the discount on the journals provided during the contract term does not provide the customer with a material right.

Step 3: Determine the Transaction Price: After considering whether there is a financing component to the contract (including whether to apply the practical expedient permitted by FASB ASC 606-10-32-18 for contracts of less than one year if a significant financing component does exist), the NFP concludes that there is no significant financing component and the transaction price is the contract price of $120.

Step 4: Allocate the Transaction Price to Performance Obligations: The transaction price should be allocated between the four performance obligations based on the relative standalone selling prices of each performance obligation. Each journal has the same standalone selling price of $35, so 25% of the transaction price is allocated to each journal.

Performance Obligation	Allocated Transaction Price
1 Quarterly Journal	$ 30
2 Quarterly Journal	30
3 Quarterly Journal	30
4 Quarterly Journal	30
Total	$120

Step 5: Recognize Revenue When Each Performance Obligation is Satisfied: The NFP concludes that:

- The performance obligation for each quarterly journal is satisfied at a point in time, and revenue should be recognized when control of the journal has been transferred to the customer. Assuming the NFP concludes that control of the journal transfers to the customer upon shipment, $30 is recognized when each quarterly journal is shipped.

Chapter 13

Expenses, Gains, and Losses

Gray shaded text in this chapter reflects guidance issued but not yet effective as of the date of this guide, March 1, 2018, but becoming effective on or prior to June 30, 2018, exclusive of any option to early adopt ahead of the mandatory effective date. Unless otherwise indicated, all unshaded text reflects guidance that was already effective as of the date of this guide.

Introduction

13.01 Generally, expenses, gains, and losses of not-for-profit entities (NFPs) are similar to those of for-profit entities and are recognized, measured, and displayed similarly. This chapter discusses certain expense, gain, and loss recognition, measurement, and display issues that are unique to NFPs and that are not covered elsewhere in this guide.

Expenses

13.02 Paragraph 80 of FASB Concept No. 6, *Elements of Financial Statements—a replacement of FASB Concepts Statement No. 3 (incorporating an amendment of FASB Concepts Statement No. 2)*, defines *expenses* as "outflows or other using up of assets or incurrences of liabilities (or a combination of both) from delivering or producing goods, rendering services, or carrying out other activities that constitute the entity's ongoing major or central operations." Expenses are distinguished from losses, which are decreases in an NFP's net assets from peripheral or incidental transactions and from all other transactions and other events and circumstances affecting the NFP except those that result from expenses.

13.03 Per FASB *Accounting Standards Codification* (ASC) 958-220-45-7, a statement of activities should report expenses as decreases in unrestricted net assets. As discussed in paragraphs 3.36–.38, further classifications (such as between operating and nonoperating) may be incorporated within a statement of activities beyond the required net asset classes. As explained in chapter 11, "Net Assets and Reclassifications of Net Assets," the relationship between a restricted contribution and an expense that it supports is reported via a reclassification from temporarily restricted net assets into unrestricted net assets; the restriction generally expires (increasing unrestricted net assets) in the same period as the expense occurs (decreasing unrestricted net assets).

Per the "Pending Content" in FASB *Accounting Standards Codification* (ASC) 958-220-45-7, a statement of activities should report expenses as decreases in net assets without donor restrictions, with the exception of investment expenses, which should be netted against investment return and reported in the net asset category in which the net investment return is reported (paragraph 4.47). As discussed in paragraphs 3A.36–.38, further classifications (such as between operating and nonoperating) may be incorporated within a statement of activities beyond the required net asset classes. As explained in chapter 11, "Net Assets and Reclassifications of Net Assets," the relationship between a donor-restricted contribution and an expense that it supports is reported via a reclassification from net assets with donor restrictions into net assets without donor restrictions; the restriction generally expires (increasing net assets without donor restrictions) in the same period as the expense occurs (decreasing net assets with donor restrictions).[1]

13.04 FASB ASC 958-720-45-2 specifies that to help donors, creditors, and others in assessing an NFP's service efforts, including the costs of services and how it uses resources, a statement of activities or notes to financial statements should provide information about expenses reported by their functional classification, such as major classes of program services and supporting activities. FASB ASC 958-205-45-6 requires voluntary health and welfare entities[2] to report information about expenses by their functional classes, such as major classes of program services and supporting activities, as well as information about expenses by their natural classifications (such as salaries, rent, electricity, interest expense, depreciation, awards and grants to others, and professional fees), in a matrix format in a separate financial statement called a *statement of functional expenses*.[3] FASB ASC 958-720-45-16 states that other NFPs are encouraged, but not required, to provide information about expenses by their natural classification.

The "Pending Content" in FASB ASC 958-720-45-2 specifies that to help donors, creditors, and others in assessing an NFP's service efforts, including the costs of services and how it uses resources, a statement of activities or notes to financial statements should provide information about expenses reported by their functional expense classification, such as major classes of program services and supporting activities. The "Pending Content" in FASB ASC 958-720-45-15 requires NFPs to report information about all expenses in one location—on the face of the statement of activities, as a schedule in the notes to financial statements, or in a separate financial statement—presenting the relationship between functional classification and natural classification for all expenses in an analysis that disaggregates functional expense classifications, such as major classes of program services and supporting activities, by their natural expense classifications, such as salaries, rent, electricity, supplies, interest expense, depreciation, awards and grants to others, and professional fees.[4] To the extent that expenses are reported by other than their natural

---

[1] The amendments in FASB Accounting Standards Update (ASU) No. 2016-14, *Not-for-Profit Entities (Topic 958): The Presentation of Financial Statements of Not-for-Profit Entities*, are effective for annual financial statements issued for fiscal years beginning after December 15, 2017 (for example, years ending December 31, 2018, and years ending June 30, 2019), and for interim periods within fiscal years beginning after December 15, 2018. Application to interim financial statements is permitted but not required in the initial year of application. Early application of the amendments is permitted.

[2] *Voluntary health and welfare entities* are defined in the FASB *Accounting Standards Codification* (ASC) glossary and in the glossary of this guide.

[3] Not-for-profit entities may have various kinds of functions. The discussion in this guide focuses on program, management and general, and fund-raising for illustrative purposes, because those functional classifications are the predominant practice. Other functional classifications are possible. Accordingly, the classifications used may include program, management and general, and fund-raising or other classifications, such as cost of sales or investing.

[4] *Voluntary health and welfare entities* are defined in the FASB *Accounting Standards Codification* (ASC) glossary and in the glossary of this guide.

classification (such as salaries included in cost of goods sold or facility rental costs of special events reported as direct benefits to donors), they should be reported by their natural classification in the analysis of expenses by nature and function. For example, salaries, wages, and fringe benefits that are included as part of the cost of goods sold on the statement of activities should be included with other salaries, wages, and fringe benefits in the analysis of expenses by nature and function. External and direct internal investment expenses that have been netted against investment return should not be included in the analysis of expenses by nature and function. Certain items that are typically excluded from net income of for-profit entities, such as those items listed in FASB ASC 220-10-45-10A, are considered gains or losses and, like other gains and losses, should not be included in the analysis of expenses by nature and function. Note F in the "Pending Content" in FASB ASC 958-205-55-21 provides an example of how to report expenses by nature and function. Paragraphs 13.53.63 include information useful in determining the major programs to include in the analysis of expenses by nature and function. NFPs frequently report corresponding levels of major classes of program services and supporting activities in their statements of activities and an analysis of expenses by nature and function.[5]

13.05 Reporting information about the functional classification of expenses may require the allocation of costs that benefit two or more functions. All references in this guide to the allocation of costs of informational materials and activities that include a fund-raising appeal among functions are subject to the provisions of the "Accounting for Costs of Activities that Include Fundraising" subsections of FASB ASC 958-720, which are discussed in paragraphs 13.79–.118.

13.06 There is no requirement to report losses by functional category.[6]

Expense Recognition Issues

13.07 Expenses are recognized when an NFP's economic benefits are used up in delivering or producing goods, rendering services, or other activities or when previously recognized assets are expected to provide reduced or no future benefits. Some expenses, such as cost of goods sold, are recognized simultaneously with revenues that result directly and jointly from the same transactions or other events as the expenses. Some expenses, such as salaries, are recognized when cash is spent or liabilities are incurred for goods and services that are used up either simultaneously with acquisition or soon after. Some expenses, such as depreciation, are allocated by systematic and rational procedures to the periods during which the related assets are expected to provide services. An expense or loss is also recognized if it becomes evident that the previously recognized future economic benefits of an asset have been reduced or eliminated, or that a liability has been incurred or increased, without associated economic benefits.

---

[5] The amendments in FASB ASU No. 2016-14 are effective for annual financial statements issued for fiscal years beginning after December 15, 2017 (for example, years ending December 31, 2018, and years ending June 30, 2019), and for interim periods within fiscal years beginning after December 15, 2018. Application to interim financial statements is permitted but not required in the initial year of application. Early application of the amendments is permitted.

[6] Paragraphs 13.02 and 13.30–.36 discuss the differences between expenses and losses.

Fund-raising Costs

13.08 Fund-raising costs are the costs of *fund-raising activities*, which are defined in the FASB ASC glossary as activities undertaken to induce potential donors to contribute money, securities, services, materials, facilities, other assets, or time. (Paragraphs 13.67–.69 provide additional discussion of fund-raising activities.) As discussed in paragraphs 5.39–.57, in some circumstances, classifying asset transfers as exchange transactions or as contributions may require the exercise of judgment concerning whether a nonreciprocal transfer has occurred. To the extent such transactions are contributions, the costs of soliciting them are fund-raising costs.

13.09 Per FASB ASC 958-720-25-4, costs of fund-raising, including the cost of special fund-raising events, should be expensed as incurred. Costs are incurred when the item or service has been received. Fund-raising costs incurred in one period, such as those made to obtain bequests, compile a mailing list of prospective contributors, or solicit contributions in a direct-response activity, may result in contributions that will be received in future periods. These costs also should be expensed as incurred. Accounting for the costs of premiums, such as address labels, calendars, greeting cards, coffee mugs, and other items of nominal value that are provided to donors and potential donors, is discussed in paragraphs 5.41–.42.

13.10 The Financial Reporting Executive Committee (FinREC) believes that the costs of tangible fund-raising assets, such as brochures and promotional items, may be recorded as an asset upon purchase and expensed when used because the cost is incurred upon use, rather than upon purchase. This is similar to the guidance for advertising materials in FASB ASC 720-35-25-3, which states, "Sales materials, such as brochures and catalogues, may be accounted for as prepaid supplies until they no longer are owned or expected to be used, in which case their cost would be a cost of advertising." Thus, until tangible fund-raising assets are no longer owned or expected to be used, they may be accounted for as an asset. As discussed in paragraph 7.06, the NFP should assess whether the value of that inventory is impaired.

13.11 In some circumstances, fund-raising activities are conducted by professional fund-raisers or federated fund-raising entities (or other such fund-raising NFPs) on behalf of a reporting entity. Often, the professional fund-raiser, federated fund-raising entity, or other such fund-raising NFP charges a fee for its services, and sometimes that fee is deducted from the contributions raised before they are remitted to the reporting entity.

13.12 If the fund-raising activities are conducted by a professional fund-raiser, guidance is provided by Technical Questions and Answers (Q&A) section 6140.21, "Should an NPE Report Amounts Charged to the NPE by a Professional Fund-Raiser Gross, as Fund-Raising Expenses, or Net, as a Reduction of Contributions?"[7] In circumstances in which a professional fund-raiser charges an NFP for soliciting contributions on the NFP's behalf, the NFP should report the amounts charged by the professional fund-raiser gross, as fund-raising expense, rather than net, as a reduction of the contributions received. As discussed in paragraphs 14–17 of FASB ASC 958-220-45, revenues and expenses should be reported gross (except for investment revenues and related expenses, which are permitted to be reported net of related expenses), whereas gains and

---

[7] All Q&A sections can be found in *Technical Questions and Answers*.

losses may be reported net. Q&A section 6140.21 provides the following example:

> NFP A enters into an agreement with Professional Fund-raiser B, whereby Professional Fund-raiser B solicits contributions on behalf of NFP A, for a fee of 20 percent of contributions raised. Professional Fund-raiser B raises $100,000 and remits $80,000 to NFP A after retaining its fee of $20,000. NFP A should report $100,000 contribution revenue and $20,000 fund-raising expense.

If the fund-raising activities are conducted by a professional fund-raiser, guidance is provided by Technical Questions and Answers (Q&A) section 6140.21, "Should an NPE Report Amounts Charged to the NPE by a Professional Fund-Raiser Gross, as Fund-Raising Expenses, or Net, as a Reduction of Contributions?"[8] In circumstances in which a professional fund-raiser charges an NFP for soliciting contributions on the NFP's behalf, the NFP should report the amounts charged by the professional fund-raiser gross, as fund-raising expense, rather than net, as a reduction of the contributions received. As discussed in the "Pending Content" in paragraphs 14–17 of FASB ASC 958-220-45, whereas gains and losses may be reported net, revenues and expenses should be reported gross, except for investment return (related to total return investing and not programmatic investing), which should be reported net of external and direct internal investment expenses. Q&A section 6140.21 provides the following example:

> NFP A enters into an agreement with Professional Fund-raiser B, whereby Professional Fund-raiser B solicits contributions on behalf of NFP A, for a fee of 20 percent of contributions raised. Professional Fund-raiser B raises $100,000 and remits $80,000 to NFP A after retaining its fee of $20,000. NFP A should report $100,000 contribution revenue and $20,000 fund-raising expense.[9]

13.13 If the fund-raiser is a federated fund-raising entity or other such fund-raising NFP, guidance is provided by FASB ASC 958-605-55-86 and Q&A section 6140.22, "In Circumstances in Which the Reporting NPE Undertakes a Transaction in Which Another NPE (Fund-Raising NPE) Raises Contributions on Behalf of the Reporting NPE, and the Reporting NPE Compensates the Fund-Raising NPE for Raising Those Contributions (Compensation Including, But Not Limited to, an Administrative Fee), Should the Reporting NPE Report the Fund-Raising NPE's Compensation Gross, as Fund-Raising Expenses, or Net, as a Reduction of Contributions?" Example 4 of FASB ASC 958-605-55 is an example of a federated fund-raising entity that allows donors to specify that their gifts be transferred to an NFP beneficiary of the donor's choice. FASB ASC 958-605-55-86 states that the beneficiaries specified by the donors would report the gross amounts of the gifts as contribution revenue and the administrative fees withheld by the federated fund-raising entity as

---

[8] All Q&A sections can be found in *Technical Questions and Answers*.

[9] The amendments in FASB ASU No. 2016-14 are effective for annual financial statements issued for fiscal years beginning after December 15, 2017 (for example, years ending December 31, 2018, and years ending June 30, 2019), and for interim periods within fiscal years beginning after December 15, 2018. Application to interim financial statements is permitted but not required in the initial year of application. Early application of the amendments is permitted.

expenses; the net amount would be recognized as a receivable from the federated fund-raising entity. Q&A section 6140.22 contains a similar conclusion and states that if a fund-raising NFP acts as an agent or intermediary for a reporting entity, and the reporting entity compensates the fund-raising NFP for acting as an agent or intermediary, the reporting entity should report fund-raising expenses for that compensation. The reporting entity should report the amount retained as compensation by the fund-raising NFP (that is, the administrative fees) as fund-raising expenses and report contributions for the gross amount contributed from the donor. In functionalizing the administrative fees reported as fund-raising expenses, the reporting entity would classify those expenses as fund-raising activities. (Paragraphs 5.07–.32 of this guide provide further guidance about identifying transactions in which an NFP acts as an agent or intermediary.)

13.14 In other circumstances, an NFP might be the beneficiary of fund-raising activities conducted by another entity, such as a corporation or an individual. The NFP beneficiary has not contracted with the entity conducting the fund-raising and may not have a role in planning or running the campaign or event. In those cases, the NFP should determine whether they have incurred fund-raising expenses by considering the guidance in paragraphs 5.152–.163. In addition to the proceeds forwarded by the entity conducting the fund-raising, the NFP may have also received a contribution of fund-raising material, informational material, advertising, and media time or space. As described in paragraphs 5.152–.163, if the NFP has an active involvement in determining and managing the message and the use of the materials prepared by the entity, a contribution of fund-raising material, informational material, advertising, or media time or space would be recognized as contribution revenue and fund-raising expense.

Financial Aid and Other Reductions in Amounts Charged for Goods and Services

13.15 Some NFPs provide reductions in amounts charged for goods or services, such as financial aid provided by colleges and universities. Per FASB ASC 958-720-25-7, reductions in amounts charged for goods or services provided by an NFP should be reported as expenses if such reductions are given in exchange for goods or services provided to the NFP, such as part of a compensation package. Per FASB ASC 958-720-45-23, amounts reported as expenses for such reductions should be reported in the same functional classification in which the cost of the goods or services provided to the NFP are reported. Per FASB ASC 958-720-25-8, if reductions in amounts charged for goods or services provided by an NFP are given other than in exchange for services provided to the NFP, those amounts should be reported as follows:

- As expenses to the extent that the NFP incurs incremental expense in providing such goods or services
- As discounts[10] if the NFP incurs no incremental expense in providing such goods or services

[10] Chapter 12, "Revenues and Receivables From Exchange Transactions," of this guide provides guidance concerning display of discounts.

Some NFPs provide reductions in amounts charged for goods or services, such as financial aid provided by colleges and universities. Per FASB ASC 958-720-25-7, reductions in amounts charged for goods or services provided by an NFP should be reported as expenses if such reductions are given in exchange for goods or services provided to the NFP, such as part of a compensation package. Per FASB ASC 958-720-45-23, amounts reported as expenses for such reductions should be reported in the same functional classification in which the cost of the goods or services provided to the NFP are reported. Appendix A, "Implementation Guidance for Accounting Standards Update (ASU) No. 2014-09, *Revenue from Contracts with Customers (Topic 606)*" to chapter 12, "Revenues and Receivables From Exchange Transactions," discusses reductions in amounts charged for goods or services provided by an NFP are given other than in exchange for services provided to the NFP.[11]

Advertising Costs

13.16 FASB ASC 720-35 provides recognition, measurement, and disclosure guidance for the advertising activities of all entities, including NFPs. (FASB ASC 720-35-15-3 specifically notes, however, that fund-raising by NFPs is not within the scope of the subtopic.) FASB ASC 720-35-50 requires certain disclosures about advertising activities, including disclosure of total amount charged to advertising expense for each statement of activities presented.

13.17 FASB ASC 720-35-05-4 defines *advertising* as "the promotion of an industry, an entity, a brand, a product name, or specific products or services so as to create or stimulate a positive entity image or to create or stimulate a desire to buy the entity's products or services." Per FASB ASC 958-720-25-6, advertising by an NFP includes activities to create or stimulate a desire to use the NFP's products or services that are provided without charge.

FASB ASC 720-35-05-4 defines *advertising* as "the promotion of an industry, an entity, a brand, a product name, or specific products or services so as to create or stimulate a positive entity image or to create or stimulate a desire to buy the entity's products or services."[12]

13.18 Per FASB ASC 720-35-25-1 and FASB ASC 340-20-25-4, the costs of advertising should be expensed either as incurred or the first time the advertising takes place, subject to the following exception. The costs of

---

[11] Most NFPs will apply the standards in FASB ASC 606, *Revenue from Contracts with Customers*, for annual reporting periods beginning after December 15, 2018, and interim periods within annual periods beginning after December 15, 2019, although they may elect to apply those standards earlier. However, NFPs that have issued, or are conduit bond obligors for, securities that are traded, listed, or quoted on an exchange or an over-the-counter market are required to apply the standards for annual reporting periods beginning after December 15, 2017, including interim periods within that reporting period.

[12] Most NFPs will apply the standards in FASB ASC 606 for annual reporting periods beginning after December 15, 2018, and interim periods within annual periods beginning after December 15, 2019, although they may elect to apply those standards earlier. However, NFPs that have issued, or are conduit bond obligors for, securities that are traded, listed, or quoted on an exchange or an over-the-counter market are required to apply the standards for annual reporting periods beginning after December 15, 2017, including interim periods within that reporting period.

direct-response advertising should be capitalized if both of the following conditions are met: (*a*) the primary purpose of the advertising is to elicit sales to customers who could be shown to have responded specifically to the advertising and (*b*) the direct-response advertising is expected to result in probable future benefits. Per FASB ASC 340-20-25-8, the probable future benefits of direct-response advertising activities are probable future revenues arising from that advertising in excess of future costs to be incurred in realizing those revenues. Per FASB ASC 958-720-25-6, if no future revenues are anticipated because the products or services advertised are being provided by the NFP without charge, there is no basis for capitalizing the costs of direct-response advertising after the first time the advertising takes place.

Per FASB ASC 720-35-25-1, the costs of advertising should be expensed either as incurred or the first time the advertising takes place.[13]

Services Received From an Affiliate

13.19 The "Services Received from Personnel of an Affiliate" subsections of FASB ASC 958-720 provide guidance for reporting services received by an NFP from personnel of an affiliate if those services directly benefit the recipient NFP and the affiliate does not charge the recipient NFP. Charging the recipient NFP means requiring payment from the recipient NFP at least for the approximate amount of the direct personnel costs (for example, compensation and any payroll-related fringe benefits) incurred by the affiliate in providing a service to the recipient NFP or the approximate fair value of that service. The guidance does not address transactions between affiliates for which the affiliate charges the recipient NFP at least for the approximate amount of direct personnel costs or the approximate fair value of the services provided.

13.20 FASB ASC 958-720-25-9 requires that an NFP recognize all services received from personnel of an affiliate that directly benefit the recipient NFP (that is, are similar to personnel directly engaged by the recipient NFP). For example, that would include services performed by personnel of an affiliate for and under the direction of the recipient NFP and shared services. *Shared services* generally refers to services provided by a centralized function (one or more individuals) within the affiliate group that the recipient NFP would otherwise typically need to purchase or have donated, if not provided by those personnel.

13.21 Paragraphs 2–3 of FASB ASC 958-720-30 require that those services be measured by the recipient NFP at the cost recognized by the affiliate in providing those services. Although the components of cost would depend on the nature and type of services provided and could vary from entity to entity, cost should include the direct personnel costs (for example, compensation and any payroll-related fringe benefits) incurred by the affiliate in providing the services to the recipient NFP. However, if recording a service received from personnel of an affiliate at the cost recognized by the affiliate for the personnel providing that service will significantly overstate or understate the value of

---

[13] Most NFPs will apply the standards in FASB ASC 606 for annual reporting periods beginning after December 15, 2018, and interim periods within annual periods beginning after December 15, 2019, although they may elect to apply those standards earlier. However, NFPs that have issued, or are conduit bond obligors for, securities that are traded, listed, or quoted on an exchange or an over-the-counter market are required to apply the standards for annual reporting periods beginning after December 15, 2017, including interim periods within that reporting period.

the service received, the recipient NFP may elect to recognize that service at either of the following:

a. The cost recognized by the affiliate for the personnel providing that service

b. The fair value of that service.

13.22 In accordance with FASB ASC 958-720-45-56, the increase in net assets associated with services received from personnel of an affiliate that directly benefit the recipient NFP and for which the affiliate does not charge the recipient NFP should not be presented as a contra-expense or a contra-asset. The corresponding decrease in net assets or the creation or enhancement of an asset resulting from the use of services received from personnel of an affiliate that directly benefit the recipient NFP and for which the affiliate does not charge the recipient NFP should be presented similar to how other such expenses or assets are presented.

In accordance with FASB ASC 958-720-45-56, the decrease in net assets or the creation or enhancement of an asset resulting from the use of services received from personnel of an affiliate that directly benefit the recipient NFP and for which the affiliate does not charge the recipient NFP should be presented similar to how other such expenses or assets are presented. Per the "Pending Content" in FASB ASC 958-220-45-21, the increase in net assets associated with services received from personnel of an affiliate that directly benefit the recipient NFP and for which the affiliate does not charge the recipient NFP should be reported as an equity transfer, regardless of whether those services are received from personnel of an NFP affiliate or any other affiliate. As discussed in paragraph A-3 of appendix A, "Financial Statements Prepared in Accordance with FASB ASU No. 2016-14," to chapter 3, "Financial Statements, the Reporting Entity, and General Financial Reporting Matters," the "Pending Content" in FASB ASC 958-220-45-20 requires that equity transfers be reported separately as changes in net assets.[14]

13.23 FASB ASC 958-720-50-3 requires that the disclosures in FASB ASC 850-10 be provided for services received by an NFP from personnel of an affiliate.

Start-Up Costs

13.24 FASB ASC 720-15 provides guidance on the financial reporting of start-up costs and organization costs. It requires costs of start-up activities, including organization costs to be expensed as incurred.

13.25 The FASB ASC glossary broadly defines *start-up activities* as those one-time activities related to any of the following: (*a*) opening a new facility, (*b*) introducing a new product or service, (*c*) conducting business in a new territory, (*d*) conducting business with an entirely new class of customer or beneficiary, (*e*) initiating a new process in an existing facility, or (*f*) commencing some new operations. Start-up activities include activities related to organizing a new entity (commonly referred to as organization costs).

---

[14] The amendments in FASB ASU No. 2016-14 are effective for annual financial statements issued for fiscal years beginning after December 15, 2017 (for example, years ending December 31, 2018, and years ending June 30, 2019), and for interim periods within fiscal years beginning after December 15, 2018. Application to interim financial statements is permitted but not required in the initial year of application. Early application of the amendments is permitted.

13.26 FASB ASC 720-15-15 describes certain costs that may be incurred in conjunction with start-up activities that are outside the scope of FASB ASC 720-15. FASB ASC 720-15-55 provides examples to help entities determine what costs are and are not within its scope. Example 3 (paragraphs 8–10) of FASB ASC 720-15-55 describes an NFP that provides meals to the homeless and is opening a shelter to house the homeless. The example shows the costs that might be incurred in conjunction with start-up activities and clarifies which costs are and are not within the scope of the subtopic.

Internal Use Computer Software Costs

13.27 FASB ASC 350-40 provides guidance on accounting for the costs of computer software developed or obtained for internal use. It identifies the characteristics of internal-use software and provides examples to assist in determining when computer software is for internal use. The determination of which costs are capitalized as intangible assets and which costs are expensed depends on the nature of the cost and the stage of the software development project.[15] The guidance in FASB ASC 350-40 does not apply to hosting arrangements (also known as cloud computing arrangements) unless those arrangements meet the criteria in FASB ASC 350-40-15-4A. Instead, FASB ASC 350-40-15-4C states that hosting arrangements that do not meet both criteria in FASB ASC 350-40-15-4A are service contracts and do not constitute a purchase of, or convey a license to, software.

Contributions Made

13.28 As part of their program services, some NFPs make contributions to other NFPs. FASB ASC 720-25 provides standards for contributions made. Contributions made should be recognized as expenses in the period made and as decreases of assets or increases of liabilities depending on the form of the benefits given.

13.29 Unconditional promises to give cash are recognized as payables and contribution expenses. The recognition rules for contributions made in the form of unconditional promises to give are discussed in paragraphs 10.91–.95. As discussed in paragraphs 11–15 of FASB ASC 958-605-25, conditional promises to give should be recognized when the conditions on which they depend are substantially met; that is, when the conditional promise becomes unconditional. However, a conditional promise to give is considered unconditional if the possibility that the condition will not be met is remote. FASB ASC 958-605-55-16 provides an example and states that a stipulation that an annual report must be provided by the donee to receive subsequent annual payments on a multiyear promise is not a condition if the possibility of not meeting that administrative requirement is remote. FASB ASC 450-20-50 should be considered when determining whether disclosures about conditional promises to give are required.

13.30 Contributions made should be measured at the fair values of the assets given or, if made in the form of a settlement or cancellation of a donee's liabilities, at the fair value of the liabilities cancelled. If the fair value of an asset transferred differs from its carrying amount, a gain or loss should be recognized on the disposition of the asset.

13.31 FASB ASC 958-720-25-3 states that if an NFP makes contributions or awards grants to other NFPs upon specific requests of others, the NFP may

---

[15] Related literature includes FASB ASC 720-45, which provides guidance on costs associated with business process reengineering and IT transformation projects.

be acting as an agent, trustee, or intermediary in a transfer between the donor and the beneficiary specified by the donor (an agency transaction). Paragraph 10.97 describes liabilities for amounts held for others in agency transactions. Paragraphs 5.07–.32 provide further guidance about identifying agency transactions.

13.32 Some transfers may appear to be contributions made but are actually reciprocal in nature. Paragraphs 5.33–.38 provide further guidance about a transfer made by an NFP for its own benefit or for the benefit of its affiliate.

13.33 If NFPs make contributions to other NFPs, FinREC believes best practice is to separately identify such contributions to other NFPs (both those to related parties and those to NFPs that are not related), either in the statement of activities or notes to the financial statements. (Though separately identified from other types of expenses, such contributions are nevertheless reported as expenses within the functional classifications.) FinREC believes contributions to other NFPs, including grants that are contributions, are different in concept from expenses incurred in running an organization's own activities, and that distinction may be meaningful to financial statement users.

If NFPs make contributions to other NFPs, FinREC believes best practice is to separately identify such contributions to other NFPs (both those to related parties and those to NFPs that are not related), either in the statement of activities or notes to the financial statements. Unless the transfer is (*a*) between an NFP and another NFP it controls or (*b*) between NFPs under common control (which are equity transfers, as discussed in paragraph A-3 of appendix A to chapter 3), contributions made are reported as expenses within the functional classifications. FinREC believes contributions to other NFPs, including grants that are contributions, are different in concept from expenses incurred in running an organization's own activities, and that distinction may be meaningful to financial statement users.[16]

Contributed Use of Facilities

13.34 Some NFPs provide the free use of facilities to other NFPs. Example 5 (paragraphs 45–48 of FASB ASC 958-605-55) provides an example of an entity providing free use of facilities to an NFP. It states that if the entity explicitly and unconditionally promises the use of the facility for a specified period of time (for example, five years), the donor would recognize that unconditional promise when made as a payable and an expense at its fair value. Although the example does not discuss the accounting in subsequent periods as the space is occupied, the use of real estate for a five-year period without a transfer of ownership is an operating lease, and the donor should report a reduction of the payable and rent income. Paragraphs 5.164–.166 discuss the donee's reporting of the receipt of an unconditional contribution of the use of long-lived assets (such as a building or the use of facilities) in which the donor retains legal title to the long-lived asset.

---

[16] The amendments in FASB ASU No. 2016-14 are effective for annual financial statements issued for fiscal years beginning after December 15, 2017 (for example, years ending December 31, 2018, and years ending June 30, 2019), and for interim periods within fiscal years beginning after December 15, 2018. Application to interim financial statements is permitted but not required in the initial year of application. Early application of the amendments is permitted.

Gains and Losses

13.35 *Revenues* are inflows of assets that result from an NFP's ongoing major or central operations and activities. *Gains* are increases in net assets resulting from an NFP's peripheral or incidental transactions and other events and circumstances affecting the NFP other than those that result from revenues. *Expenses* are outflows of assets or incurrences of liabilities that result from an NFP's ongoing major or central operations and activities. *Losses* are decreases in net assets from an NFP's peripheral or incidental transactions and other events and circumstances affecting the NFP other than those that result from expenses.

13.36 Gains and losses result both from an NFP's peripheral or incidental activities and from events and circumstances that stem from the environment and that are largely beyond the control of a particular organization and its management. Some gains and losses result from holding assets or liabilities while their values change, such as from changes in the fair value of securities or changes in foreign exchange rates. Other gains and losses result from natural catastrophes, such as fires, floods, and earthquakes. Still others result from transactions (such as an NFP's sale of buildings and equipment that are no longer needed for its ongoing operations or from its winning or losing a lawsuit) that are only peripheral or incidental to the NFP.

13.37 Transactions resulting in revenues for one NFP may result in gains for another, which, in turn, determines how the related costs should be classified and displayed.

13.38 Per FASB ASC 958-220-45-14, a statement of activities should report the gross amounts of revenues and expenses (except for investment revenues and related expenses, which are permitted to be reported net of related expenses, as discussed in paragraphs 4.45–.53). FASB ASC 958-220-45-17 states that a statement of activities may report gains and losses as net amounts if they result from peripheral or incidental transactions or from other events and circumstances that may be largely beyond the control of the NFP and its management.

Per the "Pending Content" in FASB ASC 958-220-45-14, a statement of activities should report the gross amounts of revenues and expenses except for investment return (related to total return investing and not programmatic investing), which should be reported net of external and direct internal investment expenses, as discussed in paragraphs 4.45–.55. FASB ASC 958-220-45-17 states that a statement of activities may report gains and losses as net amounts if they result from peripheral or incidental transactions or from other events and circumstances that may be largely beyond the control of the NFP and its management.[17]

13.39 Per FASB ASC 958-220-45-18, the frequency of the events and the significance of the gross revenues and expenses distinguish major or central

---

[17] The amendments in FASB ASU No. 2016-14 are effective for annual financial statements issued for fiscal years beginning after December 15, 2017 (for example, years ending December 31, 2018, and years ending June 30, 2019), and for interim periods within fiscal years beginning after December 15, 2018. Application to interim financial statements is permitted but not required in the initial year of application. Early application of the amendments is permitted.

events from peripheral or incidental events. Events are ongoing major and central activities if (*a*) they are normally part of an NFP's strategy and it normally carries on such activities or if (*b*) the event's gross revenues or expenses are significant in relation to the NFP's annual budget. Events are peripheral or incidental if they are not an integral part of an NFP's usual activities or if their gross revenues or expenses are not significant in relation to the NFP's annual budget. Accordingly, similar events may be reported differently by different NFPs based on the NFP's overall activities.

13.40 Per FASB ASC 958-220-45-8, gains and losses should be recognized as increases or decreases in unrestricted net assets unless their use is temporarily or permanently restricted by explicit donor stipulations or by law. As discussed in paragraph 3.37, certain gains and losses are required to be presented as part of income from operations if that subtotal is presented in the statement of activities.

Per the "Pending Content" in FASB ASC 958-220-45-8, gains and losses recognized on investments and other assets (or liabilities) should be recognized as increases or decreases in net assets without donor restrictions unless their use is restricted by explicit donor stipulations or by law that extends donor restrictions. As discussed in paragraph 3A.37, certain gains and losses are required to be presented as part of income from operations if that subtotal is presented in the statement of activities.[18]

13.41 Losses need not be reported by their functional classification or in the matrix that presents information about expenses according to both their functional and natural classifications.

Losses need not be reported by their functional classification or in the analysis that presents information about expenses according to both their functional and natural classifications (paragraph 13.04).[19]

Reporting Costs Related to Sales of Goods and Services

13.42 Per FASB ASC 958-720-45-20, the way that costs related to sales of goods and services are displayed depends on whether the sales constitute a major or central activity of the NFP or a peripheral or incidental activity. For example, a not-for-profit museum that has a store that is a major or central activity should report and display separately the revenues from the store's sales and the related cost of sales. Cost of sales is permitted to be reported immediately after revenues from sale of merchandise, and may be followed by a descriptive subtotal, or cost of sales may be reported with other expenses. If

---

[18] The amendments in FASB ASU No. 2016-14 are effective for annual financial statements issued for fiscal years beginning after December 15, 2017 (for example, years ending December 31, 2018, and years ending June 30, 2019), and for interim periods within fiscal years beginning after December 15, 2018. Application to interim financial statements is permitted but not required in the initial year of application. Early application of the amendments is permitted.

[19] The amendments in FASB ASU No. 2016-14 are effective for annual financial statements issued for fiscal years beginning after December 15, 2017 (for example, years ending December 31, 2018, and years ending June 30, 2019), and for interim periods within fiscal years beginning after December 15, 2018. Application to interim financial statements is permitted but not required in the initial year of application. Early application of the amendments is permitted.

the store sells merchandise that is related to the museum's program, the store would be a program service and the cost of the store's sales would be reported as a program expense. In other circumstances, cost of sales could be reported as a separate supporting service. For example, if operating a cafeteria is a major or central activity but is not related to the NFP's programs, the cafeteria's cost of sales would be reported as supporting services. Similarly, Q&A section 6140.06, "Functional Category of Cost of Sales of Contributed Inventory," states that cost of sales of contributed inventory would be reported as the cost of a separate supporting service, unless the item sold is related to a program activity, in which case, cost of sales is reported as a cost of a program activity. Cost of sales of contributed inventory would not be reported as fund-raising expenses.

13.43 FASB ASC 958-720-45-22 states that, in contrast, a not-for-profit church that occasionally produces and sells a cookbook (considered to be a peripheral or incidental activity) has gains (or losses) from those sales, and the receipts and related costs are permitted to be offset and only the net gains (or losses) are reported.

13.44 Losses from the church cookbook (a peripheral or incidental activity) described in the previous paragraph are not classified as an expense, so they should not be reported by their functional classification.

Reporting the Cost of Special Events and Other Fund-raising Activities

13.45 Some NFPs conduct fund-raising or joint activities, including special social and educational events (such as symposia, dinners, dances, and theater parties) in which the attendee receives a direct benefit (for example, a meal or theater ticket). As discussed in Q&A section 6140.07, "Functional Category of Costs of Special Events," some, but not necessarily all, costs of special fund-raising events should be reported as fund-raising. Certain costs of special fund-raising events, such as costs of direct donor benefits that are provided in exchange transactions, should be reported in categories other than fund-raising. As discussed in Q&A section 6140.08, "Functional Category of the Costs of Direct Donor Benefits," the costs of donor benefits that are not program related should be reported as a separate supporting category, such as cost of sales, if the benefits are provided in exchange transactions; they should not be reported as fund-raising. If the donor benefits are provided in transactions that are not exchange transactions, such as a fund-raising dinner for which there is no charge to attend, the costs of donor benefits should be reported as fund-raising unless they are program related. Some special events are joint activities; if so, the guidance in the "Accounting for Costs of Activities that Include Fundraising" subsections of FASB ASC 958-720 should be considered in classifying the expenses of the special event. Those standards are discussed in paragraphs 13.79–.118.

13.46 FASB ASC 958-220-45-19 states that an NFP may report net amounts in its statement of activities for its special events if they result from peripheral or incidental transactions. However, so-called "special events" can be ongoing and major activities; if so, an NFP should report the gross revenues and expenses of those activities. Costs netted against receipts from peripheral or incidental special events should be limited to direct costs.

13.47 NFPs may report the gross revenues of special events and other fund-raising activities with the cost of direct benefits to donors (for example, meals and facilities rental) displayed either (1) as a line item deducted from the special event revenues or (2) in the same section of the statement of activities as are other programs or supporting services and allocated, if necessary, among those various functions. Alternatively, the NFP could consider revenue from special events and other fund-raising activities as part exchange (for the fair value the participant received) and part contribution (for the excess of the payment over that fair value) and report the two parts separately.

13.48 Paragraphs 11–15 of FASB ASC 958-220-55 (example 4) illustrate the guidance in FASB ASC 958-220-45-19. NFP B has a special event that is an ongoing and major activity with a ticket price of $100. The activity does not meet the audience criterion in paragraphs 13.100–.106 and, therefore, all costs of the activity, other than the direct donor benefits, should be reported as fund-raising. The event includes a dinner that costs NFP B $25 and that has a fair value of $30. (Chapter 5, "Contributions Received and Agency Transactions," discusses the appropriate reporting if the meal or other items of value are donated to the NFP for resale.) In addition, NFP B incurs other direct costs of the event of $15 in connection with promoting and conducting the event, including incremental direct costs incurred in transactions with independent third parties and the payroll and payroll-related costs for the activities of employees who are directly associated with, and devote time to, the event. The other direct costs are unrelated to the direct benefits to donors and, accordingly, should not be included as costs of benefits to donors. The other direct costs include (*a*) $5 that otherwise might be considered management and general costs if they had been incurred in a different activity, and (*b*) fund-raising costs of $10. In addition, NFP B has the following transactions, which are unrelated to the special event: contributions for the general use of NFP B of $200, program expenses of $60, management and general expenses of $20, and fund-raising expenses of $20.

13.49 Paragraphs 13–15 of FASB ASC 958-220-55 illustrate three ways in which the NFP could display the results of the special event as part of its statement of activities, as follows:

Case A

Changes in unrestricted net assets:		
Contributions		$200
Special event revenue	100	
Less: Costs of direct benefits to donors	(25)	
Net revenues from special events		75
Contributions and net revenues from special events		275
Other expenses:		
Program		60
Management and general		20
Fund-raising		35
Total other expenses		115
Increase in unrestricted net assets		$160

(continued)

Case B		
Changes in unrestricted net assets:		
Revenues:		
Contributions		$200
Special event revenue		100
Total revenues		300
Expenses:		
Program		60
Costs of direct benefits to donors		25
Management and general		20
Fund-raising		35
Total other expenses		140
Increase in unrestricted net assets		$160
Case C		
Changes in unrestricted net assets:		
Contributions		$270
Dinner sales	30	
Less: Costs of direct benefits to donors	(25)	
Gross profit on special events		5
Contributions and net revenues from special events		275
Other expenses:		
Program		60
Management and general		20
Fund-raising		35
Total other expenses		115
Increase in unrestricted net assets		$160

Case A		
Changes in net assets without donor restrictions:		
Contributions		$200
Special event revenue	100	
Less: Costs of direct benefits to donors	(25)	
Net revenues from special events		75
Contributions and net revenues from special events		275

Other expenses:		
Program		60
Management and general		20
Fund-raising		35
Total other expenses		115
Increase in net assets without donor restrictions		$160
Case B		
Changes in net assets without donor restrictions:		
Revenues:		
Contributions		$200
Special event revenue		100
Total revenues		300
Expenses:		
Program		60
Costs of direct benefits to donors		25
Management and general		20
Fund-raising		35
Total other expenses		140
Increase in net assets without donor restrictions		$160
Case C		
Changes in net assets without donor restrictions:		
Contributions		$270
Dinner sales	30	
Less: Costs of direct benefits to donors	(25)	
Gross profit on special events		5
Contributions and net revenues from special events		275
Other expenses:		
Program		60
Management and general		20
Fund-raising		35
Total other expenses		115
Increase in net assets without donor restrictions		$160[20]

[20] The amendments in FASB ASU No. 2016-14 are effective for annual financial statements issued for fiscal years beginning after December 15, 2017 (for example, years ending December 31, 2018, and years ending June 30, 2019), and for interim periods within fiscal years beginning after December 15, 2018. Application to interim financial statements is permitted but not required in the initial year of application. Early application of the amendments is permitted.

Investment Revenues, Expenses, Gains, and Losses

13.50 If the objective is to invest in the entity for total return (including an objective to realize investment income, gains upon sale, or both), investment revenues, expenses, gains, and losses are discussed in chapter 4, "Cash, Cash Equivalents, and Investments." If the primary purpose of the investment is to further the mission-related objectives of the NFP, and the production of income is not a significant purpose, revenues, expenses, gains, and losses are discussed in chapter 8, "Programmatic Investments."

Functional Reporting of Expenses

13.51 FASB ASC 958-720-45-2 requires the presentation, in either a statement of activities or the notes to the financial statements, of information about expenses reported by their functional expense classification, such as major classes of program services and supporting activities. *Program services* are defined in the FASB ASC glossary as "the activities that result in goods and services being distributed to beneficiaries, customers, or members that fulfill the purposes or mission for which the NFP exists. Those services are the major purpose for and the major output of the NFP and often relate to several major programs." *Supporting activities* are defined in the FASB ASC glossary as "all activities of a not-for-profit entity (NFP) other than program services. Generally, they include management and general activities, fundraising activities, and membership-development activities." FASB ASC 958-720-45 provides examples of the kinds of activities that fall into each of those categories.

13.52 Program services may include cost of sales and costs of other revenue-generating activities that are program related. Supporting services may include, as one or more separate categories, cost of sales and costs of other revenue-generating activities that are not program related. Further elaboration of the kinds of activities that fall into each of the functional categories is provided in the following sections.

Program Services

13.53 FASB ASC 958-720-45-2 requires that a statement of activities or notes to financial statements provide information about expenses reported by their functional expense classification, including major classes of program services. The number of functional reporting classifications for program services varies according to the nature of the NFP and the services it renders. Most NFPs incur costs and provide services for several separate and identifiable programs, and the expenses for those programs should be disaggregated and reported either on the face of the statement of activities or in the notes to financial statements by the kind of program or group of related programs. The goal is to report meaningful information about the cost of the NFP's service efforts. For example, assume an NFP has as its mission helping the homeless. It has two programs: one whose function is to operate a soup kitchen to feed the homeless, and another whose function is to help the homeless get into appropriate housing. The NFP typically would disaggregate and report separately information about the two programs. As another example, assume that a large religious organization has, as part of its ministries, similar programs to help the homeless. In addition, it also has programs for worship services, youth instruction, adult instruction, family counseling, and fellowship. That religious organization typically would aggregate the expenses of the two programs for the homeless, and report them as a single line item, such as "support services for the homeless."

13.54 FASB ASC 958-720-45-3 provides the following additional examples. A large university may have programs for student instruction, research, and patient care, among others. A federated fund-raising entity's programs may include making contributions to NFPs supported by the federated fund-raising organization. A health and welfare entity may have programs for health or family services, research, disaster relief, and public education, among others.

13.55 Further, FASB ASC 958-720-45-3 notes that paragraphs 1–19 of FASB ASC 280-10-50 (which address how to determine reportable operating segments) may be helpful in determining what constitutes major classes of programs and supporting activities, even though segment reporting is not required of NFPs. The guidance pertaining to segment reporting considers, among other factors, quantitative thresholds to determine discrete segment data, such as size of revenues, expenses, profits, geographic areas, internal measurements, and availability of discrete financial information.

13.56 Though uncommon, a single functional reporting classification may be adequate to report the program service that an NFP provides. For example, for Housing and Urban Development organizations, private foundations, and Section 509(a)(3) supporting organizations, a single functional reporting classification may be adequate. Additionally, smaller NFPs or younger NFPs may focus their efforts on a single program.

13.57 NFPs have latitude in defining their major programs so that the information provided is meaningful in understanding the expenses of the NFP's service efforts. Factors to consider in determining the programs to present include the following (some factors may be more or less significant than others, depending on the facts and circumstances, and therefore, more or less heavily weighted in identifying major programs):

- Program objectives
- Nature of services
- Constituents served, including as disaggregated by geographic or other demographics
- Magnitude of the program to the NFP's overall activities
- Budgetary categories
- Oversight, regulatory, grant, or other compliance requirements that separate the program from others
- Other factors that may be relevant to financial statement users

13.58 In addition, FinREC believes that program information in the financial statements is most meaningful when it correlates with descriptions of the NFP's mission and the NFP's programs that are used by the NFP in its fund-raising materials, its programmatic promotional materials, website descriptions, tax filings, annual reports, and other public information.

13.59 Paragraphs 13.60–.63 provide four examples that may be helpful in applying the guidance in paragraphs 13.53–.58.

Example A

13.60 NFP A provides training for homeless individuals in order to enable them to enter the workforce. As part of its mission, it conducts outreach (providing food and shelter) to locate homeless individuals who would be best served by the training. It is also an advocate for the rights of the homeless, and runs a small job placement service for the graduates of its program. NFP A budgets and fund-raises separately for these four functions. The major classes of programs it uses in its financial statements are training, outreach services, advocacy, and job placement services.

Example B

13.61 NFP B is similar in all aspects to the NFP in example A, except that its advocacy efforts are minimal, and the job placement services happen more by word of mouth than by formal procedures. The major classes of programs that NFP B uses in its financial statements are training services and outreach services; for financial reporting purposes, the other activities typically would be incorporated into one of these two programs or into an "other programs" line item. If in the future, these other activities become a significant part of NFP B's mission and budget, NFP B would then consider them major classes of programs, similar to NFP A in example A.

Example C

13.62 NFP C provides the same services as the NFP in example A, except that NFP C serves distinct geographic areas, which each have their own funding sources (both governmental and private). It is important to NFP C and its funding sources to identify both of these geographic areas and major funding sources separately, and accordingly the major classes of programs that NFP C uses in its financial statements are segregated by geographic region and funding source.

Example D

13.63 NFP D is a Section 509(a)(3) entity created to provide support to NFP E. NFP D conducts fund-raising activities and grants funds to its supported organization. NFP D only engages in grant-making to its supported organization, and accordingly NFP D uses in its financial statements only one program activity classification, which it titles "grants made to NFP E."

Required Disclosures About Program Services

13.64 Per FASB ASC 958-205-50-1, the financial statements should provide a description of the nature of the NFP's activities, including a description of each of its major classes of programs. If not provided in the notes to financial statements, the description can be presented on the statement of activities (for example, using column headings). Per FASB ASC 958-720-45-5, the components of total program expenses should be evident from the details provided on the face of the statement of activities, unless the notes to the financial statements disclose total program expenses and provide information about why total program expenses disclosed in the notes do not articulate with the statement of activities (FASB ASC 958-720-50-1(b)). As an example, FASB ASC 958-720-50-1 notes that total program expenses are not evident from the details provided on the face of the statement of activities if cost of sales is not identified as either program or supporting services.

Supporting Services

13.65 NFPs may have various kinds of supporting activities, such as management and general, fund-raising, and membership development. Some industries have functional categories of supporting activities that are prevalent in that industry. For example, colleges and universities typically have institutional support and institutional development activities. A single functional reporting classification is ordinarily adequate to portray each kind of supporting service. NFPs may, however, present more detailed disaggregated information for each kind of supporting service. For example, fund-raising expenses and the corresponding resources that are obtained may be reported separately for each kind of fund-raising activity undertaken, either on the face of a statement of activities or in the notes to the financial statements.

Management and General Activities

13.66 Per the FASB ASC glossary, *management and general activities* are activities that are not identifiable with a single program, fund-raising activity, or membership-development activity but that are indispensable to the conduct of those activities and to an entity's existence. Paragraphs 7–8 of FASB ASC 958-720-45 provide additional description of management and general activities. They include oversight; business management; general record keeping; budgeting; financing; soliciting funds other than contributions and membership dues (for example, the costs associated with promoting the sale of goods or services to customers, including advertising costs; responding to government, foundation, and other requests for proposals for customer-sponsored contracts for goods and services; and administering government, foundation, and similar customer-sponsored contracts, including billing and collecting fees); disseminating information to inform the public of the NFP's stewardship of contributed funds; making announcements concerning appointments; producing and disseminating the annual report; and all other management and administration except for direct conduct of program services, fund-raising activities, or membership-development activities. The costs of oversight and management usually include the salaries and expenses of the governing board, the CEO of the NFP, and the supporting staff. However, if such staff spends a portion of their time directly supervising program services or categories of other supporting services, their salaries and expenses should be allocated among those functions.

Per the "Pending Content" in the FASB ASC glossary, *management and general activities* are supporting activities that are not directly identifiable with one or more program, fund-raising, or membership-development activities. The "Pending Content" in paragraphs 7–8 of FASB ASC 958-720-45 provides additional descriptions of management and general activities. They include oversight; business management; general record keeping and payroll; budgeting; financing; soliciting funds other than contributions and membership dues (for example, the costs associated with promoting the sale of goods or services to customers, including advertising costs, and responding to government, foundation, and other requests for proposals for customer-sponsored contracts for goods and services); administering government, foundation, and similar customer-sponsored contracts, including billing and collecting fees and grant and contract financial reporting; disseminating information to inform the public of the NFP's stewardship of contributed funds; making announcements concerning appointments; producing and disseminating the annual report; employee benefits management and oversight (human resources); and all other management and administration except for direct conduct of program services, fund-raising activities, or membership-development activities.

The costs of oversight and management usually include the salaries and expenses of the governing board, the CEO of the NFP, and the supporting staff. However, if such staff spends a portion of their time directly supervising program services or categories of other supporting services, their salaries and expenses should be allocated among those functions. Example 21 (the "Pending Content" in paragraphs 171176) of FASB ASC 958-720-55 provides examples of which activities would constitute direct conduct or supervision of program or support functions.

Case A in Example 21 involves a chief executive officer who spends a portion of time directly overseeing the research program. Additionally, a portion of time is spent with current and potential donors on fundraising cultivation activities. A portion of the chief executive officer's compensation and benefits and other expenses would be allocated to the research program and to the fundraising function representing the portion of time spent on those activities because they reflect direct conduct or direct supervision. If the remainder of the chief executive officer's time is spent indirectly supervising the other areas of NFP A, including the administrative areas, those activities would not constitute direct conduct or direct supervision, and the ratable portion of compensation and benefit amounts would remain in management and general activities.

Case B in Example 21 involves a chief financial officer who has primary responsibility for (*a*) accounting and reporting, (*b*) short-term budgeting and long-term financial planning, (*c*) cash management, and (*d*) direct oversight of the NFP's endowment. A portion of the chief financial officer's compensation and benefits and other expenses would be allocated to management and general activities for the accounting and reporting, the short-term budgeting and long-term financial planning, and cash management functions because they benefit the overall organization. A portion also would be allocated to investment expenses for management of the investment strategy of the endowment and would be netted against investment return. However, any portion of time spent supervising the accounting for investments or other fiduciary oversight would not be allocated to investment expenses because that time is related to an accounting and general management activity that benefits the overall organization and should be allocated to management and general activities.

Case C in Example 21 involves a human resources department that is involved in the benefits administration for all personnel. The human resources department's related costs would not be allocated to any specific program. Rather, those costs would remain a component of management and general activities because benefits administration is a supporting activity for the entire entity.

Case D in Example 21 involves an accountant who is responsible for grant accounting and reporting and a principal investigator. In some cases, under the terms of a grant agreement, a fiscal report is required to be filed that details expenses incurred and charged against the grant. The fiscal report is not part of the direct conduct or direct supervision of the grant but rather is an accounting function. Therefore, the grant accountant's compensation and benefits would not be allocated to the programmatic area. However, a scientific report prepared by a principal investigator who is responsible for the research activity would be indicative of direct conduct or direct supervision of the grant activity (or both), and the principal investigator's compensation and benefits would be allocated to the grant.[21]

Fund-raising Activities

13.67 Per the FASB ASC glossary, *fundraising activities* are activities undertaken to induce potential donors to contribute money, securities, services, materials, facilities, other assets, or time. Paragraphs 9–10 of FASB ASC 958-720-45 provide additional description of fund-raising activities. They include publicizing and conducting fund-raising campaigns; maintaining donor mailing lists; conducting special fund-raising events; preparing and distributing fund-raising manuals, instructions, and other materials; and conducting other activities involved with soliciting contributions from individuals, foundations, government agencies, and others. Fund-raising activities include soliciting contributions of services from individuals, regardless of whether those services meet the recognition criteria for contributions in the "Contributions Received" subsection of FASB ASC 958-605-25. Q&A section 6140.11, "Costs of Soliciting Contributed Services and Time That Do Not Meet the Recognition Criteria in FASB ASC 958," states that certain contributed services are prohibited from being recognized for practical, rather than conceptual, reasons. Those services are nevertheless contributions, regardless of whether or not they are recognized. Therefore, soliciting those contributions meets the definition of fund-raising in the FASB ASC glossary. For example, costs of soliciting contributed services to be used in program functions should be accounted for as fund-raising expenses, even if the contributed services do not meet the recognition criteria. Similarly, costs of soliciting management and general services should be reported as fund-raising, even if the management and general services do not meet the recognition criteria. (Paragraph 13.124 discusses how fund-raising activities of federated fund-raising organizations should be reported.) Per FASB ASC 958-720-50-1, the financial statements should disclose total fund-raising expenses.

13.68 As discussed in Q&A section 6140.20, "NPEs Reporting No Fund-Raising Expenses," it would be unusual for an NFP to have contributions but have minimal or no fund-raising expense. Examples of circumstances in which an NFP could have contributions but minimal or no fund-raising expense typically include those in which (*a*) because of name recognition or custom, donors contribute to the NFP without the NFP undertaking fund-raising activities, (*b*) fund-raising activities are conducted entirely or almost entirely by volunteers whose contributed services do not meet the recognition criteria for contributed services in FASB ASC 958-605-25-16, or (*c*) other entities that the NFP does not control contribute to the NFP with the NFP undertaking minimal or no fund-raising activity or other participation in relation to those contributions. The NFP should consider whether it is required to make financial statement

[21] The amendments in FASB ASU No. 2016-14 are effective for annual financial statements issued for fiscal years beginning after December 15, 2017 (for example, years ending December 31, 2018, and years ending June 30, 2019), and for interim periods within fiscal years beginning after December 15, 2018. Application to interim financial statements is permitted but not required in the initial year of application. Early application of the amendments is permitted.

disclosures required by FASB ASC 850, *Related Party Disclosures*, and FASB ASC 275, *Risks and Uncertainties.*

13.69 Q&A section 6140.20 provides the following examples of circumstances in which an NFP with contributions may have no fund-raising expense or minimal fund-raising expense in relation to contributions:

- A religious entity obtains most or all of its contributions from member tithing.
- An entity has no paid staff and most or all contributions arise from uncompensated board members soliciting contributions (and this board member activity does not meet the recognition criteria for contributed services in FASB ASC 958-605-25-16).
- The reporting entity is a private foundation or is supported by a private foundation, and the reporting entity expends no or minimal resources in soliciting those contributions.
- The reporting entity obtains most or all of its contributions from one or more entities that it does not control (fund-raising NFP), expends minimal resources, and has minimal participation in soliciting those contributions.

Q&A section 6140.20 provides the following examples:

- NPE Relief and Development Entity is one of many entities devoted to cause ABC. NPE Relief and Development Entity receives most or all of its contributions from Relief and Development Entities in the USA, Canada, and the United Kingdom that raise support for cause ABC throughout the world.
- NPE Religious Entity Denomination International Mission Board receives a substantial portion of its support from the NPE Religious Entity Denomination, which supports various entities and causes, including but not limited to NPE Religious Entity Denomination International Mission Board. NPE Religious Entity Denomination allocates, at its discretion, X percent of its contributions from supporting churches and individuals to NPE Religious Entity Denomination International Mission Board.

Membership-Development Activities

13.70 Per the FASB ASC glossary, *membership-development activities* include soliciting for prospective members and membership dues, membership relations, and similar activities. FASB ASC 958-720-45-12 states that if no significant benefits or duties are connected with membership, the substance of membership-development activities may, in fact, be fund-raising. Paragraphs 11–14 of FASB ASC 958-720-45 provide additional description of membership-development activities. The related costs should be reported as fund-raising costs when the substance of membership development is, in fact, fund-raising. (See paragraphs 9–12 of FASB ASC 958-605-55 for indicators useful in determining the contribution and exchange portions of membership dues.)[22] Membership development activities may be conducted in conjunction with other activities. In circumstances in which membership development is conducted in conjunction with other activities but does not include soliciting contributions,

---

[22] Chapter 5, "Contributions Received and Agency Transactions," and table 5-2, "Indicators Useful for Determining the Contribution and Exchange Portions of Membership Dues," of this guide provide the guidance in paragraphs 9–12 of FASB ASC 958-605-55.

the activity is not a joint activity, and the costs should be allocated to membership development and one or more other functions. For example, if an activity involves costs to solicit new members (membership development) and direct costs of providing goods or services to existing members, in accordance with FASB ASC 958-720-45-3, an appropriate part of the costs of soliciting members should be allocated to the membership-development function and a part to program services. In circumstances in which membership development is in part soliciting membership dues and in part soliciting contributions, the activity is a joint activity as discussed in the "Accounting for Costs of Activities that Include Fundraising" subsections of FASB ASC 958-720. Those subsections are discussed in paragraphs 13.79–.118 but are not intended as a substitute for reading them.

Classification of Expenses Related to More Than One Function

13.71 Some expenses are directly related to, and can be assigned to, a single major program or service or a single supporting activity. Other expenses relate to more than one program or supporting activity, or to a combination of programs and supporting services. These expenses should be allocated among the appropriate functions. Examples include a direct mail solicitation that combines fund-raising with program activities (subject to the provisions of paragraphs 13.79–.118), salaries of persons who perform more than one kind of service, and the rental of a building used for various programs and supporting activities.

Some expenses are directly related to, and can be assigned to, a single major program or service or a single supporting activity. Other expenses relate to more than one program or supporting activity, or to a combination of programs and supporting services. Examples include a direct mail solicitation that combines fund-raising with program activities (subject to the provisions of paragraphs 13.79–.118), salaries of persons who perform more than one kind of service, and the rental of a building used for various programs and supporting activities.

The "Pending Content" in FASB ASC 958-720-45-2A states that costs that benefit more than one function should be allocated. Activities that represent direct conduct or direct supervision of program or other supporting activities require allocation from management and general activities. Additionally, information technology generally can be identified as benefiting various functions, such as management and general (for example, accounting and financial reporting and human resources), fund-raising, and program delivery. Therefore, information technology costs generally would be allocated among the functions receiving direct benefit.

The "Pending Content" in paragraph FASB ASC 958-720-50-1(d) requires an NFP to describe the methods used to allocate costs among program and support functions. The "Pending Content" in FASB ASC 958-720-55-176 and Note F in the "Pending Content" in FASB ASC 958-205-55-21 provide examples of note disclosures on the cost allocation methods used.[23]

---

[23] The amendments in FASB ASU No. 2016-14 are effective for annual financial statements issued for fiscal years beginning after December 15, 2017 (for example, years ending December 31, 2018, and years ending June 30, 2019), and for interim periods within fiscal years beginning after December 15, 2018. Application to interim financial statements is permitted but not required in the initial year of application. Early application of the amendments is permitted.

Direct Identification Versus Allocation Methods[24]

13.72 Direct identification of specific expense (also referred to as assigning expenses) is the preferable method of charging expenses to various functions. If an expense can be specifically identified with a program or supporting service, it should be assigned to that function. For example, travel costs incurred in connection with a program activity should be assigned to that program.

13.73 If direct identification (that is, assignment) is impossible or impracticable, an allocation is appropriate. The techniques used to allocate are common to all entities, for-profit and NFP alike. A reasonable allocation of expenses among an NFP's functions may be made on a variety of bases. Objective methods of allocating expenses are preferable to subjective methods. The allocation may be based on related financial or nonfinancial data. The paragraphs that follow provide guidance (in addition to that presented throughout this chapter) on allocating or presenting certain costs that may be incurred by NFPs. The guidance found in Subpart E of Title 2 U.S. Code of Federal Regulations Part 200, *Uniform Administrative Requirements, Cost Principles, and Audit Requirements for Federal Awards* (Uniform Guidance), may also be helpful in allocating costs.

13.74 Per FASB ASC 958-720-45-25, occupying and maintaining a building is not a separate supporting service.

13.75 The expenses associated with occupying and maintaining a building, such as depreciation, utilities, maintenance, and insurance, may be allocated among the NFP's functions based on the square footage of space occupied by each program and supporting service. If floor plans are not available and the measurement of the occupied space is impractical, an estimate of the relative portion of the building occupied by each function may be made.

13.76 Q&A section 6960.12, "Allocation of Overhead," states that allocation of overhead is an interprogram transaction that should not be reported as revenue of the program providing the services, but rather as a reduction of expense of such program.

13.77 Per FASB ASC 958-720-45-24, interest costs, including interest on a building's mortgage, should be allocated to specific programs or supporting services to the extent possible. Interest costs that cannot be allocated should be reported as part of the management and general function. (FASB ASC 835-20-50-1 requires disclosure of total interest costs incurred and the amount thereof that has been capitalized, if any.)

13.78 An NFP should evaluate its expense allocation methods periodically. The evaluation may include, for example, a review of the time records or activity reports of key personnel, the use of space, and the consumption of supplies and postage. The expense allocation methods should be reviewed by management and revised when necessary to reflect significant changes in the nature or level of the NFP's current activities, so that the financial statements appropriately reflect the amounts for program services and supporting activities.

---

[24] This section provides general information about assigning and allocating costs among functional classifications. For costs incurred in joint activities, the guidance in this section is subject to the provisions of paragraphs 13.79–.118.

Expenses of Materials and Activities That Combine Fund-raising Activities With Activities That Have Elements of Another Function (Joint Activities)

13.79 FASB ASC 958-720-05-5 states that some NFPs solicit support through a variety of fund-raising activities, including the following: direct mail, telephone solicitation, door-to-door canvassing, telethons, special events, and others. Sometimes fund-raising activities are conducted with activities related to other functions, such as program activities or supporting services and management and general activities. Sometimes fund-raising activities include components that would otherwise be associated with program or supporting services, but in fact support fund-raising. The "Accounting for Costs of Activities that Include Fundraising" subsections of FASB ASC 958-720 establish financial accounting standards for accounting for costs of those joint activities and require financial statement disclosures about the nature of the activities for which joint costs have been allocated and the amounts of joint costs. The following paragraphs summarize those subsections but are not intended as a substitute for reading them.

13.80 The functional classifications of fund-raising, program, and management and general are discussed throughout the "Accounting for Costs of Activities that Include Fundraising" subsections of FASB ASC 958-720 for purposes of illustrating how the guidance in these paragraphs would be applied by entities that use those functional classifications. Some entities have a functional structure that does not include fund-raising, program, or management and general, or that includes other functional classifications, such as membership development. Use of those functional classifications is not intended to require reporting the functional classifications of fund-raising, program, and management and general.

13.81 For example, some NFPs may conduct membership development activities. As discussed in paragraph 13.70, the substance of membership development activities may, in fact, be fund-raising. To the extent that member benefits are received, however, membership is an exchange transaction. In circumstances in which membership development is in part soliciting revenues from exchange transactions and in part soliciting contributions and the purpose, audience, and content of the activity are appropriate for achieving membership development, joint costs should be allocated between fund-raising and the exchange transaction. Accounting for the costs of a joint activity is discussed in paragraphs 13.79–.118.

Accounting for Joint Activities

13.82 Per FASB ASC 958-720-45-29, if the criteria of purpose, audience, and content are met, the costs of a joint activity should be classified as follows: (*a*) the costs that are identifiable with a particular function should be charged to that function and (*b*) joint costs should be allocated between fund-raising and the appropriate program or management and general function. If any of the criteria are not met, all costs of the joint activity should be reported as fund-raising costs, including costs that might be considered program or management and general costs if they had been incurred in a different activity, subject to the exception in the following sentence. Costs of goods or services provided in exchange transactions that are part of joint activities, such as costs of direct donor benefits of a special event (for example, a meal), should not be reported as fund-raising. Paragraphs 5.118–.123 and paragraphs 13.45–.49 provide additional guidance for the recognition and presentation in financial statements of special events.

13.83 FASB ASC 958-720-55-34 provides guidance for classifying costs of a joint activity that are identifiable with a particular functional classification. That paragraph provides the following example. The purpose for which costs other than joint costs are incurred may be fund-raising, program, or management and general, depending on the context in which they are used in the activity undertaken. For example, a program-related pamphlet may be sent to an audience in need of the program. In that context, the pamphlet is used for program purposes. However, in order to demonstrate to potential donors that the NFP's programs are worthwhile, that same pamphlet may be sent to an audience that is likely to contribute but that has no need or reasonable potential for use of the program. In that context, the pamphlet is used for fund-raising. The classification of the cost of the pamphlets depends upon the use of the pamphlets and the application of the criteria in FASB ASC 958-720-45-29. Thus, if some program-related pamphlets are used in program activities that include no fund-raising, the cost of the pamphlets used in those separate program activities that include no fund-raising should be charged to program. If some pamphlets are used in a joint activity and the criteria in FASB ASC 958-720-45-29 (paragraph 13.82) are met, the costs of materials that accomplish program goals and that are unrelated to fund-raising, such as the costs of a program-related pamphlet included in a joint activity, should be charged to program, whereas joint costs, such as postage, should be allocated between fund-raising and program. However, if the program-related pamphlet is used in fund-raising packets and the criteria are not met, the costs of the pamphlets used in the fund-raising packets, as well as the joint costs, should be charged to fund-raising.

13.84 In circumstances in which entities that have a functional structure that includes other functional classifications conduct joint activities, all costs of those joint activities should be charged to fund-raising (or the category in which fund-raising is reported), unless the purpose, audience, and content of those joint activities are appropriate for achieving those other functions.

Purpose

13.85 The purpose criterion is met if the purpose of the joint activity includes accomplishing program or management and general functions. Paragraphs 33–47 of FASB ASC 958-720-45 (reproduced in part in paragraphs 13.86–.99) provide guidance that should be considered in determining whether the purpose criterion is met. Paragraphs 35–39 of FASB ASC 958-720-45 (paragraphs 13.86–.90) provide guidance pertaining to program functions only. FASB ASC 958-720-45-38 (paragraph 13.91) provides guidance pertaining to both program and management and general functions.

13.86 *Program functions*. To accomplish program functions, the activity should call for specific action by the audience that will help accomplish the NFP's mission. Actions that help accomplish the NFP's mission are actions that do either of the following: (*a*) benefit the recipient (such as by improving the recipient's physical, mental, emotional, or spiritual health and well-being) or (*b*) benefit society (such as by addressing societal problems). If the activity calls for specific action by the audience that will help accomplish the NFP's mission, the guidance in FASB ASC 958-720-45-38 (paragraphs 13.91–.99) should also be considered in determining whether the purpose criterion is met.

13.87 FASB ASC 958-720-55-4 provides the following examples of activities that call for specific action by the audience that will help accomplish the NFP's mission:

- An NFP's mission includes improving individuals' physical health. For that NFP, motivating the audience to take specific action that will improve their physical health is a call for specific action by the audience that will help accomplish the NFP's mission. An example of an activity that motivates the audience to take specific action that will improve their physical health is sending the audience a brochure that urges them to stop smoking and suggests specific methods, instructions, references, and resources that may be used to stop smoking.
- An NFP's mission includes educating individuals in areas other than the causes, conditions, needs, or concerns that the NFP's programs are designed to address (referred to as causes). For that NFP, educating the audience in areas other than causes or motivating the audience to otherwise engage in specific activities that will educate them in areas other than causes is a call for specific action by the audience that will help accomplish the NFP's mission. Examples of NFPs whose mission includes educating individuals in areas other than causes are universities and possibly other NFPs. An example of an activity motivating individuals to engage in education in areas other than causes is a university inviting individuals to attend a lecture or class in which the individuals will learn about the solar system. (Paragraphs 13.89–.90 provide further discussion of NFPs with educational missions.)
- Some educational activities that might otherwise be considered as educating the audience about causes may implicitly call for specific action by the audience that will help accomplish the NFP's mission. For example, activities that educate the audience about environmental problems caused by not recycling implicitly call for that audience to increase recycling. If the need for and benefits of the specific action are clearly evident from the educational message, the message is considered to include an implicit call for specific action by the audience that will help accomplish the NFP's mission.

13.88 FASB ASC 958-720-55-5 provides the following examples of activities that fail to call for a specific action by the audience that will help accomplish the NFP's mission:

- Educating the audience about causes or motivating the audience to otherwise engage in specific activities that will educate them about causes is not a call for specific action by the audience that will help accomplish the NFP's mission. Such activities are considered in support of fund-raising.
- Asking the audience to make contributions is not a call for specific action by the audience that will help accomplish the NFP's mission.

13.89 Paragraphs 22–24 of FASB ASC 958-720-55 provide additional guidance for NFPs with educational missions, which is reproduced in this paragraph and the next. Most transactions in which a student attends a lecture or class are exchange transactions and are not joint activities. Such transactions are joint activities only if the activity includes fund-raising. Some organizations have missions that include educating the public (students) in areas other than causes. FASB ASC 958-720-55-4 states that, for those entities, educating the audience in areas other than causes or motivating the audience to engage in specific activities, such as attending a lecture or class, that will educate them in areas other than causes is considered a call for specific action by the recipients that will help accomplish the NFP's mission. Educating the audience about causes or motivating the audience to engage in specific activities that will educate them about causes without educating them in other subjects is not considered a call for specific action by the audience that will help accomplish the NFP's mission.

13.90 An example of a lecture or class that will educate students in an area other than causes is a lecture on the nesting habits of the bald eagle, given by the Save the Bald Eagle Society, an NFP whose mission is to save the bald eagle from extinction and educate the public about the bald eagle. An example of a lecture or class that will address particular causes is a lecture by the Bald Eagle Society on the potential extinction of bald eagles and the need to raise contributions to prevent their extinction. For purposes of applying this guidance, motivating the audience to attend a lecture on the nesting habits of the bald eagle is a call for specific action that will help accomplish the NFP's mission. If the lecture merely addresses the potential extinction of bald eagles and the need to raise contributions to prevent their extinction without addressing the nesting habits of the bald eagle, motivating the audience to attend the lecture is not considered a call for specific action by the recipient that will help accomplish the NFP's mission.

13.91 *Program and management and general functions*. Per FASB ASC 958-720-45-38, the following factors should be considered, in the order in which they are listed, to determine whether the purpose criterion is met:

a. The compensation or fees test (paragraphs 13.92–.95)

b. The separate and similar activities test (paragraphs 13.96–.97)

c. The other evidence test (paragraphs 13.98–.99)

13.92 *The compensations or fees test.* Paragraphs 40–44 of FASB ASC 958-720-45 provide guidance for the compensation or fees test. The purpose criterion is not met if a majority of compensation or fees for any party's performance of any component of the discrete joint activity varies based on contributions raised for that discrete joint activity.

13.93 Some compensation contracts provide that compensation for performing the activity is based on a factor other than contributions raised, but not to exceed a specified portion of contributions raised. For example, a contract may provide that compensation for performing the activity is $10 per contact hour, but not to exceed 60 percent of contributions raised. In such circumstances, compensation is not considered based on amounts raised unless the stated maximum percentage is met. In circumstances in which it is not yet known whether the stated maximum percentage is met, compensation is not considered based on amounts raised unless it is probable that the stated maximum percentage will be met.

13.94 The compensation or fees test is a negative test in that it either (*a*) results in failing the purpose criterion or (*b*) is not determinative of whether the purpose criterion is met.

13.95 In considering the guidance in FASB ASC 958-720-45-38 (paragraph 13.91), the compensation or fees test is the preeminent guidance. Therefore, if the activity fails the compensation or fees test, the activity fails the purpose criterion and the separate and similar activities test should not be considered. If the purpose criterion is not failed based on the compensation or fees test, this factor (the compensation or fees test) is not determinative of whether the purpose criterion is met, and the factor in paragraphs 45–46 of FASB ASC 958-720-45 (paragraphs 13.96–.97) (separate and similar activities test) should be considered.

13.96 *The separate and similar activities test.* The purpose criterion is met if a similar program or management and general activity is conducted separately and on a similar or greater scale. That is, the purpose criterion is met if either of the following two conditions is met:

a. The first condition is met if both of the following are true:

   i. The program component of the joint activity calls for specific action by the recipient that will help accomplish the NFP's mission (see paragraphs 35–37 of FASB ASC 958-720-45, which are reproduced in part in paragraphs 13.86–.90).

   ii. A similar program component is conducted without the fund-raising component using the same medium and on a scale that is similar to or greater than the scale on which it is conducted with the fund-raising. Determining the scale on which an activity is conducted may be subjective. Factors to consider in determining the scale on which an activity is conducted may include dollars spent, the size of the audience reached, and the degree to which the characteristics of the audience are similar to the characteristics of the audience of the activity being evaluated.

b. The second condition is met if a management and general activity that is similar to the management and general component of the joint activity being accounted for is conducted without the fund-raising component using the same medium and on a scale that is similar to or greater than the scale on which it is conducted with the fund-raising.

13.97 If the purpose criterion is met based on the separate and similar activities test, the other evidence test (paragraphs 13.98–.99) should not be considered. If the separate and similar activities test is not determinative, the other evidence test should be considered.

13.98 *The other evidence test.* The compensation or fees test and the separate and similar activities test may not always be determinative because the attributes they consider may not be present. If the factors in paragraphs 40–44 of FASB ASC 958-720-45 (the compensation or fees test in paragraphs 13.92–.95) or paragraphs 44–45 of FASB ASC 958-720-45 (the separate and similar activities test in paragraphs 13.96–.97) do not determine whether the purpose criterion is met, other evidence may determine whether the criterion is met. All available evidence, both positive and negative, should be considered to determine whether, based on the weight of that evidence, the purpose criterion is met.

13.99 The following are examples of indicators that provide evidence for determining whether the purpose criterion is met:

a. FASB ASC 958-720-55-7 provides the following examples of indicators that provide evidence that the purpose criterion may be met:

   i. *Measuring program results and accomplishments of the activity*. The facts may indicate that the purpose criterion is met if the NFP measures program results and accomplishments of the activity (other than measuring the extent to which the public was educated about causes).

   ii. *Medium*. The facts may indicate that the purpose criterion is met if the program component of the joint activity calls for specific action by the recipient that will help accomplish the NFP's mission and if the NFP conducts the program component without a significant fund-raising component in a different medium. Also, the facts may indicate that the purpose criterion is met if the NFP conducts the management and general component of the joint activity without a significant fund-raising component in a different medium.

b. FASB ASC 958-720-55-8 provides the following examples of indicators that provide evidence that the purpose criterion may not be met:

   i. *Evaluation*. The facts may indicate that the purpose criterion is not met if the evaluation of any party's performance of any component of the discrete joint activity varies based on contributions raised for that discrete joint activity.

   ii. *Compensation*. The facts may indicate that the purpose criterion is not met if some, but less than a majority, of compensation or fees for any party's performance of any component of the discrete joint activity varies based on contributions raised for that discrete joint activity.

c. FASB ASC 958-720-55-9 provides the following examples of indicators that provide evidence that the purpose criterion may be either met or not met:

   i. *Evaluation of measured results of the activity*. The NFP may have a process to evaluate measured program results and accomplishments of the activity (other than measuring the extent to which the public was educated about causes). If the NFP has such a process, in evaluating the effectiveness of the joint activity, the NFP may place significantly greater weight on the activity's effectiveness in accomplishing program goals or may place significantly greater weight on the activity's effectiveness in raising contributions. The former may indicate that the purpose criterion is met. The latter may indicate that the purpose criterion is not met.

   ii. *Qualifications*. The qualifications and duties of those performing the joint activity should be considered. If a third party, such as a consultant or contractor, performs part or all of the joint activity, such as producing brochures or making telephone calls, the third party's experience and the range of services provided to the NFP should be considered in determining whether the third party is performing fund-raising, program (other than educating the public about causes), or management and general activities on behalf of the NFP. If the NFP's employees perform part or all of the joint activity, the full range of their job duties should be considered in determining whether those employees are performing fund-raising, program (other than educating the public about causes), or management and general activities on behalf of the NFP. For example, employees who are not members of the fund-raising department and employees who are members of the fund-raising department but who perform nonfund-raising activities are more likely to perform activities that include program or management and general functions than are employees who otherwise devote significant time to fund-raising.

iii. *Tangible evidence of intent*. Tangible evidence indicating the intended purpose of the joint activity should be considered. Examples of such tangible evidence include the following:

(1) The NFP's written mission statement, as stated in its fund-raising activities, bylaws, or annual report;

(2) Minutes of board of directors', committees', or other meetings;

(3) Restrictions imposed by donors (who are not related parties) on gifts intended to fund the joint activity;

(4) Long-range plans or operating policies;

(5) Written instructions to other entities, such as script writers, consultants, or list brokers, concerning the purpose of the joint activity, audience to be targeted, or method of conducting the joint activity; and

(6) Internal management memoranda.

Audience

13.100 A rebuttable presumption exists that the audience criterion is not met if the audience includes prior donors or is otherwise selected based on its ability or likelihood to contribute to the NFP; that presumption can be overcome if the audience is also selected for one or more of the reasons in FASB ASC 958-720-45-49 (paragraph 13.101*a–c*). In determining whether that presumption is overcome, NFPs should consider the extent to which the audience is selected based on its ability or likelihood to contribute to the NFP and contrast that with the extent to which it is selected for one or more of the reasons in FASB ASC 958-720-45-49 (paragraph 13.101*a–c*). For example, if the audience's ability or likelihood to contribute is a significant factor in its selection and it has a need for the action related to the program component of the joint activity, but having that need is an insignificant factor in its selection, the presumption would not be overcome.

13.101 FASB ASC 958-720-45-49 states that in circumstances in which the audience includes no prior donors and is not otherwise selected based on its ability or likelihood to contribute to the NFP, the audience criterion is met if the audience is selected for any of the following reasons:

a. The audience's need to use or reasonable potential for use of the specific action called for by the program component of the joint activity.

b. The audience's ability to take specific action to assist the NFP in meeting the goals of the program component of the joint activity.

c. The NFP is required to direct the management and general component of the joint activity to the particular audience or the audience has reasonable potential for use of the management and general component.

13.102 Paragraphs 11–15 of FASB ASC 958-720-55 provide additional guidance for the audience criterion, which is reproduced in this paragraph and the following 4 paragraphs. Some NFPs conduct joint activities that are special events, such as symposia, dinners, dances, and theater parties, in which the attendee receives a direct benefit (for example, a meal or theater ticket) and for which the admission price includes a contribution. For example, it may cost $500 to attend a dinner with a fair value of $50. In that case, the audience is required to make a $450 contribution in order to attend.

13.103 In circumstances in which the audience is required to make a contribution to participate in a joint activity, such as attending a special event, the audience's ability or likelihood to contribute is a significant factor in its selection. Therefore, in circumstances in which the audience is required to make a contribution to participate in a joint activity, the extent to which the audience is selected for the program or management and general reasons in FASB ASC 958-720-45-49 (paragraph 13.101) must be overwhelmingly significant in order to rebut the presumption that the audience criterion is not met.

13.104 The source of the names and the characteristics of the audience should be considered in determining the reason for selecting the audience. Some NFPs use lists compiled by others to reach new audiences. The source of such lists may indicate the purpose or purposes for which they were selected. For example, lists acquired from entities with similar or related programs are more likely to meet the audience criterion than are lists acquired from entities with dissimilar or unrelated programs. Also, the characteristics of those on the lists may indicate the purpose or purposes for which they were selected. For example, a list based on a consumer profile of those who buy environmentally friendly products may be useful to an NFP whose mission addresses environmental concerns and could therefore indicate that the audience was selected for its ability to take action to assist the NFP in meeting program goals. However, a list based on net worth would indicate that the audience was selected based on its ability or likelihood to contribute, unless there was a correlation between net worth and the program or management and general components of the activity.

13.105 Some audiences may be selected because they have an interest in or affinity to the program. For example, homeowners may have an interest in the homeless because they are sympathetic to the plight of the homeless. Nevertheless, including homeowners in the audience of a program activity to provide services to the homeless would not meet the audience criterion because they do not have a need or reasonable potential for use of services to the homeless.

13.106 An example of a joint activity in which the audience is selected because the NFP is required to direct the management and general component of the joint activity to the particular audience is an activity in which the NFP sends a written acknowledgment or other information to comply with requirements of the IRS to prior donors and includes a request for contributions. An example of a joint activity in which the audience is selected because the audience has reasonable potential for use of the management and general component is an activity in which the NFP sends its annual report to prior donors and includes a request for contributions.

Content

13.107 FASB ASC 958-720-45-50 states that the content criterion is met if the joint activity supports program or management and general functions, as follows:

a. *Program*. The joint activity calls for specific action by the recipient that will help accomplish the NFP's mission (see paragraphs 35–37 of FASB ASC 958-720-45, which are reproduced in part in paragraphs 13.86–.90). If the need for and benefits of the action are not clearly evident, information describing the action and explaining the need for and benefits of the action is provided.

b. *Management and general*. The joint activity fulfills one or more of the NFP's management and general responsibilities through a component of the joint activity.

13.108 Per FASB ASC 958-720-45-35, actions that help accomplish the NFP's mission are actions that either benefit the recipient or benefit society. FASB ASC 958-720-55-17 provides the following examples of actions that benefit the recipient (such as by improving the recipient's physical, mental, emotional, or spiritual health and well-being) or society (such as by addressing societal problems):

a. Actions that benefit the recipient include the following:

  i. *Stop smoking.* Specific methods, instructions, references, and resources should be suggested.

  ii. *Do not use alcohol or drugs.* Specific methods, instructions, references, and resources should be suggested.

b. Actions that benefit society include the following:

  i. *Write or call.* The party to communicate with and the subject matter to be communicated should be specified.

  ii. *Complete and return the enclosed questionnaire.* The results of the questionnaire should help the NFP achieve its mission. For example, if the NFP discards the questionnaire, it does not help the NFP achieve its mission.

  iii. *Boycott.* The particular product or company to be boycotted should be specified.

13.109 Information identifying and describing the NFP, its causes, or how the contributions provided will be used is considered in support of fund-raising.

13.110 Per FASB ASC 958-720-45-53, activities that are undertaken in order to solicit contributions are fund-raising activities. For example, activities conducted to comply with requirements of regulatory bodies concerning soliciting contributions, such as the requirement by some states or other regulatory bodies that certain disclosures be included when soliciting contributions, are fund-raising activities. For purposes of applying this guidance, communications that include such required disclosures are considered fund-raising activities and are not considered management and general activities.

13.111 FASB ASC 958-720-55-18 provides the following examples of required disclosures that are considered fund-raising activities:

- Information filed with the attorney general concerning this charitable solicitation may be obtained from the attorney general of [*the state*] by calling 123-4567. Registration with the attorney general does not imply endorsement.
- A copy of the registration and financial information may be obtained from the Division of Consumer Services by calling toll-free, within [*the state*], 1 (800) 123-4567. Registration does not imply endorsement, approval, or recommendation by [*the state*].
- Information about the cost of postage and copying, and other information required to be filed under [*the state*] law, can be obtained by calling 123-4567.
- The entity's latest annual report can be obtained by calling 123-4567.

Allocation Methods

13.112 The cost allocation methodology used for joint costs should be rational and systematic, it should result in an allocation of joint costs that is reasonable, and it should be applied consistently given similar facts and circumstances. Paragraphs 25–31 of FASB ASC 958-720-55 (reproduced in supplement C, "Allocation Methods," of this chapter) provide explanations and examples of some acceptable allocation methods for joint costs. The allocation of joint costs should be based on the degree to which costs were incurred for the functions to which the costs are allocated (that is, program, management and general, or fund-raising). For purposes of determining whether the allocation methodology for a particular joint activity should be consistent with methodologies used for other particular joint activities, facts and circumstances that may be considered include factors related to the content and relative costs of the components of the activity. The audience should not be considered in determining whether the facts and circumstances are similar for purposes of determining whether the allocation methodology for a particular joint activity should be consistent with methodologies used for other particular joint activities. A change in cost allocation methodology should be evaluated in accordance with FASB ASC 250, *Accounting Changes and Error Corrections*, to determine if it is a change in accounting principle.

13.113 Paragraphs 32–33 of FASB ASC 958-720-55 provide the following information about which joint costs should be measured and allocated. Some costs, such as utilities, rent, and insurance (commonly referred to as indirect costs), may be joint costs. For example, the telephone bill for a department that, among other things, prepares materials that include both fund-raising and program components may commonly be referred to as an indirect cost. Such telephone bills may also be joint costs. However, for some NFPs, it is impracticable to measure and allocate the portion of the costs that are joint costs. Considerations about which joint costs should be measured and allocated, such as considerations about materiality and the costs and benefits of developing and providing the information, are the same as considerations about cost allocations in other circumstances.

Incidental Activities

13.114 Some fund-raising activities conducted in conjunction with program or management and general activities are incidental to such program or management and general activities. In circumstances in which a fund-raising, program, or management and general activity is conducted in conjunction with another activity and is incidental to that other activity, and the criteria in FASB ASC 958-720-45-29 (paragraph 13.77) for allocation are met, joint costs are permitted but not required to be allocated and may therefore be charged to the functional classification related to the activity that is not the incidental activity. However, in circumstances in which the program or management and general activities are incidental to the fund-raising activities, it is unlikely that the criteria in that paragraph to permit allocation of joint costs would be met.

13.115 Paragraphs 160–165 of FASB ASC 958-720-55 provide the following three examples of incidental activities. NFP Q conducts a fund-raising activity by including a generic message, "Contributions to NFP Q may be sent to [*address*]" on a small area of a message that would otherwise be considered a program or management and general activity based on its purpose, audience, and content. That fund-raising activity likely would be considered incidental to the program or management and general activity being conducted. NFP R conducts a program activity by including a generic program message such as "Continue to pray for [*a particular cause*]" on a small area of a message that would otherwise be considered fund-raising based on its purpose, audience, and content. That program activity would likely be considered incidental to the fund-raising activity being conducted. NFP S conducts a management and general activity by including the brief management and general message—"We recently changed our phone number. Our new number is 123-4567"—on a small area of a message that would otherwise be considered a program or fund-raising activity based on its purpose, audience, and content. That management and general activity would likely be considered incidental to the program or fund-raising activity being conducted.

Disclosures

13.116 FASB ASC 958-720-50-2 requires that an NFP that allocates joint costs should disclose all of the following in the notes to its financial statements:

a. The types of activities for which joint costs have been incurred

b. A statement that such costs have been allocated

c. The total amount allocated during the period and the portion allocated to each functional expense category

13.117 An NFP is also encouraged, but not required, to disclose the amount of joint costs for each kind of joint activity, if practical.

Additional Guidance

13.118 FASB ASC 958-720-55-2 (reproduced in supplement A, "Accounting for Joint Activities," of this chapter) includes a flowchart useful in accounting for joint activities. Paragraphs 35–159 of FASB ASC 958-720-55 (reproduced in supplement B, "Examples of Applying the Criteria of Purpose, Audience, and Content to Determine Whether a Program or Management and

General Activity Has Been Conducted," of this chapter) illustrate the application of the purpose, audience, and content criteria to determine whether a program or management and general activity has been conducted along with the fund-raising activity. Paragraph 25–31 of FASB ASC 958-720-55 (reproduced in supplement C of this chapter) illustrate allocation methods for joint costs. Paragraphs 166–170 of FASB ASC 958-720-55 (reproduced in supplement D, "Examples of Disclosures," of this chapter) illustrate disclosures required when joint activities are conducted.

Support to Related Local and National NFPs

13.119 Some NFPs make payments or provide other support to local or national entities. The specific purposes and benefits of those payments may be for use of the national entity's name; for permission to raise funds in a specified geographical area; for the ability to participate in joint purchasing arrangements; for technical and fund-raising assistance; or for similar functions. Alternatively, the purposes and benefits of those payments may be indeterminable. Payments in the form of grants and dues may also be made to related local and national entities.

13.120 Per FASB ASC 958-720-45-26, payments to related local and national NFPs should be reported by their functional classification to the extent that it is practicable and reasonable to do so and the necessary information is available, even if it is impossible to allocate the entire amount of such payments to functions. Payments to those entities that cannot be allocated to functions should be treated as a separate supporting service, reported on a statement of activities as a separate line item, and labeled "unallocated payments to local (or national) organizations."

Distributions From Financially Interrelated Fund-raising Foundations to Specified Beneficiaries

13.121 FASB ASC 958-20-25-1 states that a foundation that exists to raise, hold, and invest assets for a specified beneficiary or for a group of affiliates of which the specified beneficiary is a member generally is financially interrelated with the NFP or NFPs it supports. (Paragraphs 5.28–.32 describe the standards for determining when NFPs are financially interrelated.) The foundation recognizes contribution revenue when it receives assets from the donor. When it later distributes the contributed assets to the beneficiary (and assuming that the distributions are neither [*a*] loans or repayments of loans, or [*b*] reciprocal transactions, including those discussed in paragraphs 4–7 of FASB ASC 958-20-25), a financially interrelated foundation reduces assets and recognizes an expense when it distributes assets to its financially interrelated beneficiary, as illustrated in examples 1 and 3 in FASB ASC 958-20-55.

13.122 Because they are expenses, distributions to financially interrelated NFPs should be reported by their functional expense classifications, as required by FASB ASC 958-720-45-2. If the foundation has only a single major program, as discussed at paragraph 13.56, the distributions might be reported on the statement of activities as "distributions to {name of beneficiary}." If the foundation has several programs, analogous to the guidance in FASB ASC 958-720-45-26, the payments to the beneficiary would be functionally classified to the extent that it is practicable and reasonable to do so and the necessary information is available, even if it is impossible to allocate the entire amount of such payments. Payments to financially interrelated beneficiaries that cannot be allocated to functions would be treated as a separate supporting service, reported on a statement of activities as a separate line item,[25] and labeled "unallocated payments to financially interrelated entities." The foundation should consider whether the disclosures for related party transactions, as discussed in FASB ASC 850, are necessary.

13.123 Some fund-raising foundations (recipients) raise, hold, and invest assets for health care entities (beneficiaries). As discussed in Q&A section 6140.19, "Application of FASB ASC 958—Classification of Distributions From a Financially Interrelated Fund-Raising Foundation (Recipient Entity) to a Health Care Beneficiary," those foundations are not health care entities as described in FASB ASC 954-10-15, and therefore would not follow the guidance in FASB ASC 954, *Health Care Entities*. Instead, those foundations should report in conformity with the guidance in FASB ASC 958, including consideration of its guidance for financially interrelated entities in FASB ASC 958-20. That guidance applies regardless of whether the recipient entity and the beneficiary are under common control or whether one controls the other in a parent-subsidiary relationship. (Paragraphs 1.05–.06 of this guide discuss further the scope of this guide as it pertains to health care entities.)

Expenses of Federated Fund-raising Entities

13.124 Per FASB ASB 958-720-45-27, federated fund-raising entities solicit and receive designated and undesignated contributions and make grants and awards to other NFPs. The fund-raising activities of federated fund-raising entities, including activities related to fund-raising on behalf of others, should be reported as fund-raising expenses.

Income Taxes

13.125 Per FASB ASC 958-720-50-1, if an NFP incurs income tax expense, the financial statements of the NFP should disclose the amount of income tax expense and describe the nature of the activities that generated the taxes.

Auditing

13.126 Many audit objectives and auditing procedures, including consideration of controls, related to expenses, gains, and losses of NFPs are similar to those of other entities. In addition, the auditor may need to consider the specific audit objectives, auditing procedures, and selected controls listed in the table in paragraph 13.127, which are unique to NFPs.

13.127 The following table illustrates the use of assertions in developing audit objectives and designing substantive tests. The examples are not intended to be all-inclusive nor is it expected that all the procedures would necessarily be applied in an audit. The use of assertions in assessing risks and designing appropriate audit procedures to obtain audit evidence is described in paragraphs .26–.32 of AU-C section 315, *Understanding the Entity and Its Environment and Assessing the Risks of Material Misstatement*.[26] Paragraph .18 of AU-C

---

[25] If the NFP chooses to report expenses by natural classification on the face of the statement of activities, the separate line item would appear in the notes to the financial statements with the functional expense classification.

[26] All AU-C sections can be found in AICPA *Professional Standards*.

section 330, *Performing Audit Procedures in Response to Assessed Risks and Evaluating the Audit Evidence Obtained,* requires the auditor to design and perform substantive procedures for all relevant assertions related to each material class of transactions, account balance, and disclosure, irrespective of the assessed risks of material misstatement. This requirement reflects the facts that (1) the auditor's assessment of risk is judgmental and may not identify all risks of material misstatement, and (2) inherent limitations to internal control exist, including management override. Various audit procedures and the purposes for which they may be performed are described in paragraphs .A10–.A26 of AU-C section 500, *Audit Evidence*.

Auditing Considerations

Financial Statement Assertions	*Specific Audit Objectives*	*Select Control Objectives*
Transactions		
Occurrence	Transactions and events recognized as expenses have occurred and pertain to the entity.	Controls ensure that only transactions that are valid expenses are recognized in the financial statements
Completeness	All expenses incurred are recognized.	Controls ensure that all expenses incurred are recognized in the financial statements.
Presentation and Disclosure		
Classification	Expenses are properly classified and displayed by functional category in the notes or the face of the statement of activities. Expenses are properly classified as gross or netted with revenues.	Controls ensure that expenses are properly classified and displayed.

Expense Recognition Issues

13.128 Suggested audit procedures to consider include the following:

- Determine that fund-raising costs have been expensed as incurred and that there are no fund-raising costs inappropriately reported as an asset, such as prepaid expenses, on the statement of financial position except as described in paragraphs 13.08–.14. (Completeness)
- Review the financial statements to determine that revenue is reported net of discounts and other adjustments as described in paragraph 13.15. (Classification)
- Determine that any reductions in amounts charged for goods or services have been properly reported based on the guidance in paragraph 13.15. (Occurrence, Completeness)

- Obtain and read fund-raising agreements with professional fund-raisers or federated fund-raising entities, or both, to determine if fund-raising expenses associated with contributions received from those entities have been properly reported in accordance with paragraphs 13.08–.14. (Completeness, Classification)
- Examine documentation supporting recognition of contributions made including notification of donee and whether the contribution is conditional or unconditional. (Occurrence)
- Review minutes of governing board and governing board committee meetings for information about contributions made and compare to expense recognized for contributions made. (Completeness)
- Review and test the method used for valuing contributions made, including promises to give. (Accuracy/Valuation)
- Review contributions of use of facilities to verify the contributions made are accounted for in accordance with the guidance in paragraph 13.34. (Completeness)

Gains and Losses

13.129 Suggested audit procedures to consider include the following:

- Review any gains or losses that are reported net on the statement of activities to determine the use of net reporting is appropriate (paragraphs 13.37–.39). (Classification)
- Verify that gains and losses have been properly reported in the net asset classes based on the existence or absence of donor restrictions. (Classification)
- Review any costs of sales that are reported net on the statement of activities with the related sales revenue to determine the use of net reporting is appropriate due to the peripheral or incidental nature of the sales activity as further described in paragraphs 13.42–.44. (Classification)
- Review any costs of special events that are reported net on the statement of activities with the related special event revenue to determine the use of net reporting is appropriate due to the peripheral or incidental nature of the sales activity as further described in paragraphs 13.45–.49. Additionally, review the costs to determine the costs are limited to only direct costs, as further described in paragraph 13.46. (Classification)

Functional Reporting of Expenses

13.130 Suggested audit procedures to consider include the following:

- Review the NFP's functional expense allocation by performing the following procedures:
    - — Obtain or update an understanding of the allocation methodology of expenses by functional classification. (Classification)
    - — If payroll and related costs are a significant part of total expenses, then specifically review the NFPs methodology for allocating payroll and related costs to the functional classifications. (Classification)

- Verify the consistent application of the allocation methodology. Verify the NFP has updated its allocation methodology in a timely manner for any changes in its cost structure (for example, when new construction is completed, new debt is entered into, or a significant new program is started or discontinued). (Classification)
- Review and test management's policies and procedures for allocating costs to the various functional categories that they support. Select a sample for testing to determine if the expenses have been properly allocated. (Classification)
- Perform an analytical review of functional classifications by comparing current period expenses in total and by functional classification with expectations (which could be based on prior-period expenses, budget, or other factors), and investigate significant variances from expectations. (Classification, Occurrence, Completeness)

- Verify that the NFP's presentation of program services in the statement of activities or notes to the financial statements is appropriate, consistent, and includes the appropriate costs. (Classification)
- Verify that the number of programs reported for program expenses is adequate based on the complexity of the NFP and its activities. (Classification)
- Verify that the NFP's presentation of supporting services in the statement of activities or notes to the financial statements is appropriate, consistent, and includes the appropriate categories, such as fund-raising and management and general. (Classification)
- Review the NFP's allocation of any joint costs by performing the following procedures:
  - The allocation of joint costs may involve a high degree of management judgment and subjectivity. Therefore, a risk may exist that management will manipulate the joint activity to meet the purpose, audience, or content criteria to increase the amount of expense allocated to the program classification and reduce the amount of expense allocated to the fund-raising classification to make the NFP look more efficient in the eyes of donors, regulators, or charity watchdog agencies. (Classification)
  - Select a sample of solicitations for testing. (Classification)
  - Inquire with management regarding the procedures management performs to verify the purpose, audience, and content criteria are met for each joint cost activity. (Classification)
  - Obtain evidence to support management's assertion that the purpose, audience, and content criteria are met. (Classification)

- Determine whether costs are appropriately allocated between fund-raising and the appropriate program or management and general function. Determine that the allocation has been performed consistently and in a rational and systematic manner. (Classification)
- Review the notes to financial statements to determine that the required disclosures for joint costs are included. (Completeness)

- Verify that any payments to related local or national NFPs are reported in the appropriate functional classification. (Classification)
- If the auditee is a federated fund-raising entity, verify that the costs of fund-raising activities, including fund-raising on behalf of others, are properly reported as fund-raising expenses. (Classification)

13.131

Supplement A—Accounting for Joint Activities

A-1 The following flowchart from FASB *Accounting Standards Codification* (ASC) 958-720-55-2 summarizes the guidance in paragraphs 29–53 of FASB ASC 958-720-45 (see paragraphs 13.79–.118) and is not intended as a substitute for the guidance therein.

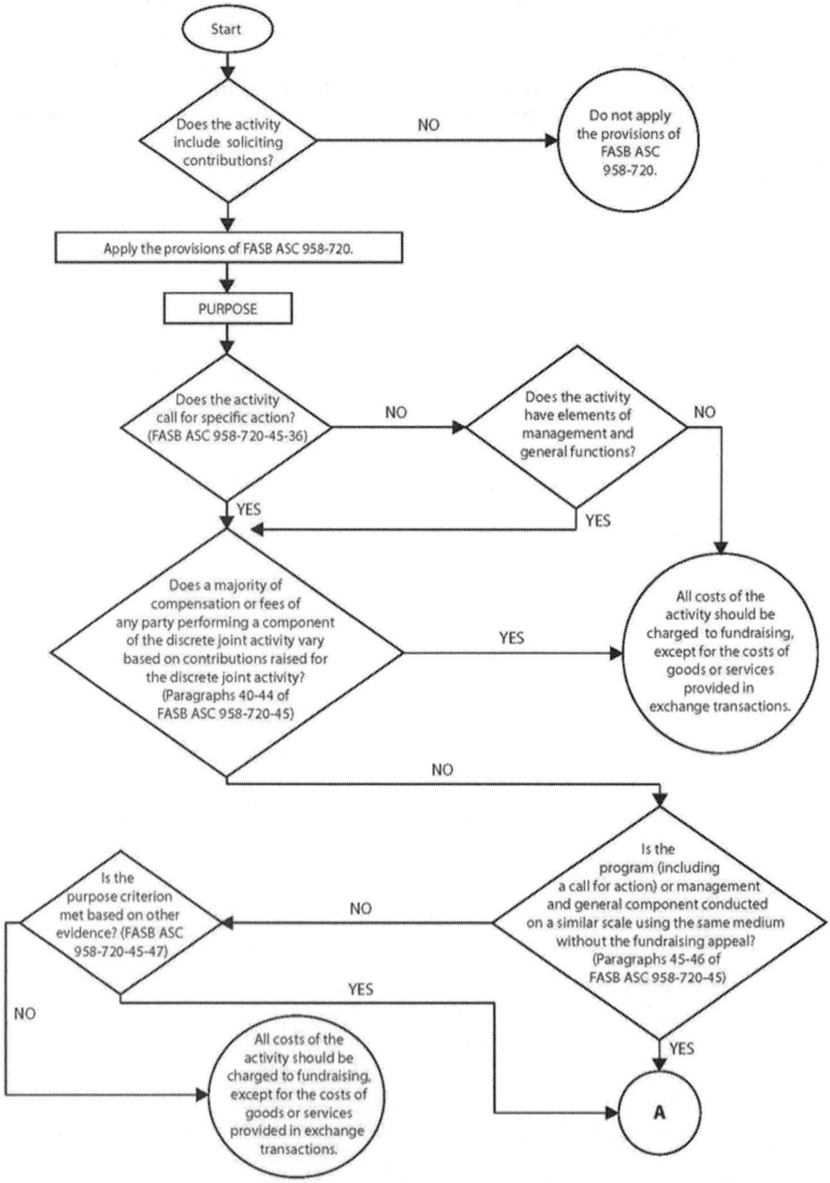

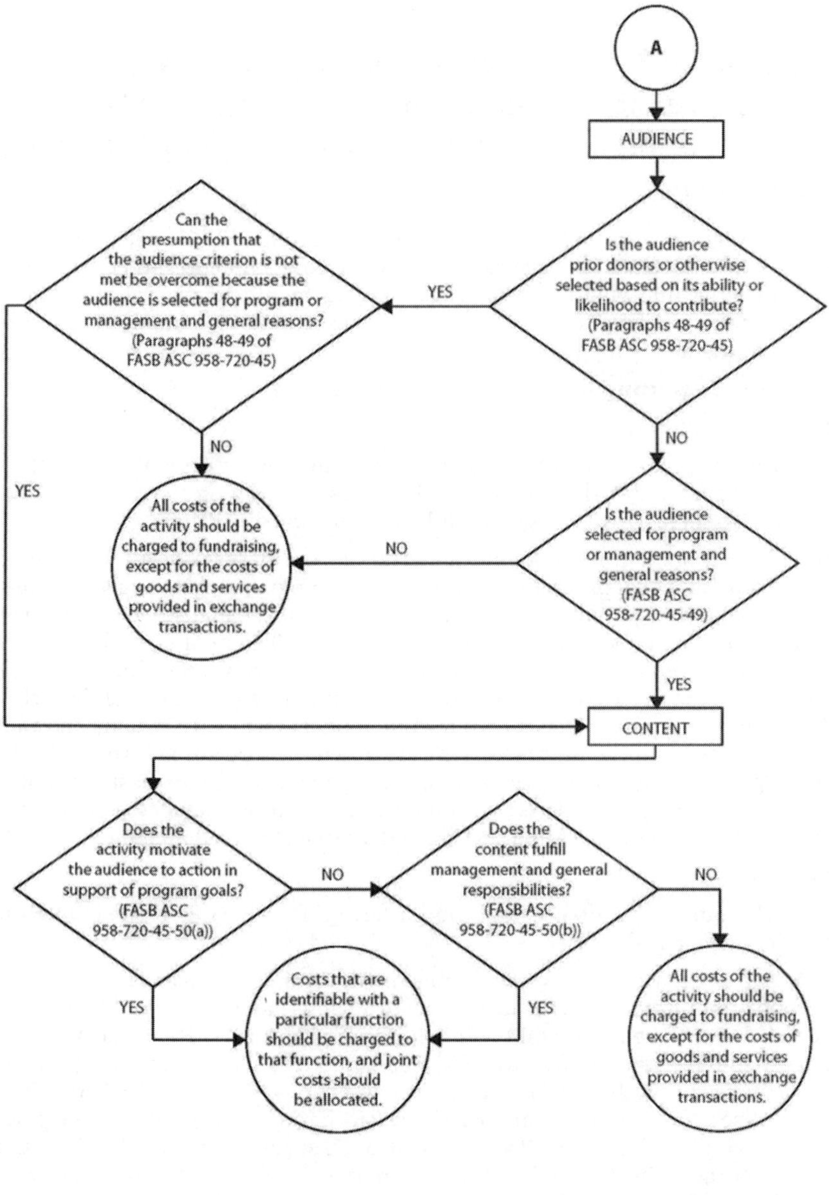
A
AUDIENCE
Is the audience prior donors or otherwise selected based on its ability or likelihood to contribute? (Paragraphs 48-49 of FASB ASC 958-720-45)
YES
Can the presumption that the audience criterion is not met be overcome because the audience is selected for program or management and general reasons? (Paragraphs 48-49 of FASB ASC 958-720-45)
NO
YES
All costs of the activity should be charged to fundraising, except for the costs of goods and services provided in exchange transactions.
NO
Is the audience selected for program or management and general reasons? (FASB ASC 958-720-45-49)
NO
YES
CONTENT
Does the activity motivate the audience to action in support of program goals? (FASB ASC 958-720-45-50(a))
NO
Does the content fulfill management and general responsibilities? (FASB ASC 958-720-45-50(b))
NO
YES
Costs that are identifiable with a particular function should be charged to that function, and joint costs should be allocated.
YES
All costs of the activity should be charged to fundraising, except for the costs of goods and services provided in exchange transactions.

13.132

Supplement B—Examples of Applying the Criteria of Purpose, Audience, and Content to Determine Whether a Program or Management and General Activity Has Been Conducted

B-1 Paragraphs 35–159 of FASB *Accounting Standards Codification* (ASC) 958-720-55 illustrate the application of the purpose, audience, and content criteria to determine whether a program or management and general activity has been conducted along with a fund-raising activity. Those examples are reproduced in the following paragraphs.

Example 1: Mailing of Informational Materials

Facts

B-2 Not-for-profit entity (NFP) A's mission is to prevent drug abuse. NFP A's annual report states that one of its objectives in fulfilling that mission is to assist parents in preventing their children from abusing drugs.

B-3 NFP A mails informational materials to the parents of all junior high school students explaining the prevalence and dangers of drug abuse. The materials encourage parents to counsel children about the dangers of drug abuse and inform them about how to detect drug abuse. The mailing includes a request for contributions. NFP A conducts other activities informing the public about the dangers of drug abuse and encouraging parents to counsel their children about drug abuse that do not include requests for contributions and that are conducted in different media. NFP A's executive director is involved in the development of the informational materials as well as the request for contributions. The executive director's annual compensation includes a significant bonus if total annual contributions exceed a predetermined amount.

Conclusion

B-4 The purpose, audience, and content criteria are met, and the joint costs should be allocated.

B-5 The activity calls for specific action by the recipient (encouraging parents to counsel children about the dangers of drug abuse and informing them about how to detect drug abuse) that will help accomplish the NFP's mission. Therefore, the guidance in FASB ASC 958-720-45-38 (see paragraph 13.91) should be considered. Neither of the factors in paragraphs 40–44 of FASB ASC 958-720-45 (see the compensation or fees test in paragraphs 13.92–.95) or paragraphs 45–46 of FASB ASC 958-720-45 (see the separate and similar activities test in paragraphs 13.96–.97) is determinative of whether the purpose criterion is met. (Although NFP A's executive director's annual compensation varies based on annual contributions, the executive director's compensation does not vary based on contributions raised for this discrete joint activity.) Therefore, other evidence, such as the indicators in paragraphs 6–9 of FASB ASC 958-720-55 (see paragraph 13.99), should be considered. The purpose criterion is met based on the other evidence because (*a*) the program component of this activity calls for specific action by the recipient (encouraging parents to counsel children about the dangers of drug abuse) that will help accomplish the NFP's mission, and it otherwise conducts the program activity in this example without a request for contributions, and (*b*) performing such programs helps accomplish

NFP A's mission. Note that had NFP A conducted the activity using the same medium on a scale that is similar to or greater than the scale on which it is conducted with the request for contributions, the purpose criterion would have been met under paragraphs 45–46 of FASB ASC 958-720-45 (see paragraphs 13.96–.97).

B-6 The audience criterion is met because the audience (parents of junior high school students) is selected based on its need to use or reasonable potential for use of the action called for by the program component.

B-7 The content criterion is met because the activity calls for specific action by the recipient (encouraging parents to counsel children about the dangers of drug abuse and informing them about how to detect drug abuse) that will help accomplish the NFP's mission (assisting parents in preventing their children from abusing drugs), and it explains the need for and benefits of the action (the prevalence and dangers of drug abuse).

Example 2: Mailing to Prior Donors

Facts

B-8 NFP B's mission is to reduce the incidence of illness from ABC disease, which afflicts a broad segment of the population. One of NFP B's objectives in fulfilling that mission is to inform the public about the effects and early warning signs of the disease and specific action that should be taken to prevent the disease.

B-9 NFP B maintains a list of its prior donors and sends them donor renewal mailings. The mailings include messages about the effects and early warning signs of the disease and specific action that should be taken to prevent it. That information is also sent to a similar-sized audience but without the request for contributions. Also, NFP B believes that recent donors are more likely to contribute than nondonors or donors who have not contributed recently. Prior donors are deleted from the mailing list if they have not contributed to NFP B recently, and new donors are added to the list. There is no evidence of a correlation between recent contributions and participation in the program component of the activity. Also, the prior donors' need to use or reasonable potential for use of the messages about the effects and early warning signs of the disease and specific action that should be taken to prevent it is an insignificant factor in their selection.

Conclusion

B-10 The purpose and content criteria are met. The audience criterion is not met. All costs, including those that might otherwise be considered program or management and general costs if they had been incurred in a different activity, should be charged to fund-raising.

B-11 The activity calls for specific action by the recipient (action that should be taken to prevent ABC disease) that will help accomplish the entity's mission. Therefore, the guidance in FASB ASC 958-720-45-38 (see paragraph 13.91) should be considered. The purpose criterion is met because (*a*) the program component of the activity calls for specific action by the recipient that will help accomplish the NFP's mission (to reduce the incidence of illness from the disease), and (*b*) the program is also conducted using the same medium on a scale that is similar to or greater than the scale on which it is conducted with the request for contributions (a similar mailing is done without the request for contributions, to a similar-sized audience).

B-12 The audience criterion is not met. The rebuttable presumption that the audience criterion is not met because the audience includes prior donors is not overcome in this example. Although the audience has a need to use or reasonable potential for use of the program component, that was an insignificant factor in its selection.

B-13 The content criterion is met because the activity calls for specific action by the recipient (actions to prevent ABC disease) that will help accomplish the entity's mission (to reduce the incidence of ABC disease), and it explains the need for and benefits of the action (to prevent ABC disease).

Example 3: Telephone Solicitation of Prior Donors

Facts

B-14 NFP C's mission is to reduce the incidence of illness from ABC disease, which afflicts a broad segment of the population. One of NFP C's objectives in fulfilling that mission is to increase governmental funding for research about ABC disease.

B-15 NFP C maintains a list of its prior donors and its employees call them on the telephone reminding them of the effects of ABC disease, asking for contributions, and encouraging them to contact their elected officials to urge increased governmental funding for research about ABC disease. The callers are educated about ABC, do not otherwise perform fund-raising functions, and are not compensated or evaluated based on contributions raised. NFP C's research indicates that recent donors are likely to contact their elected officials about such funding whereas nonrecent donors are not. Prior donors are deleted from the calling list if they have not contributed to NFP C recently, and new donors are added to the list.

Conclusion

B-16 The purpose, audience, and content criteria are met, and the joint costs should be allocated.

B-17 The activity calls for specific action by the recipient (contacting elected officials concerning funding for research about ABC disease) that will help accomplish the NFP's mission. Therefore, the guidance in FASB ASC 958-720-45-38 (see paragraph 13.91) should be considered. Neither of the factors in paragraphs 40–44 of FASB ASC 958-720-45 (see the compensation or fees test in paragraphs 13.92–.95) or paragraphs 45–46 of FASB ASC 958-720-45 (see the separate and similar activities test in paragraphs 13.96–.97) is determinative of whether the purpose criterion is met. Therefore, other evidence, such as the indicators in paragraphs 6–9 of FASB ASC 958-720-55 (see paragraph 13.99), should be considered. The purpose criterion is met based on the other evidence, because (*a*) the qualifications and duties of the personnel performing the activity indicate that it is a program activity (the callers are educated about ABC and do not otherwise perform fund-raising functions), (*b*) the method of compensation for performing the activity does not indicate that it is a fund-raising activity (the employees are not compensated or evaluated based on contributions raised), and (*c*) performing such programs helps accomplish NFP C's mission.

B-18 The audience criterion is met because the audience (recent donors) is selected based on its ability to assist NFP C in meeting the goals of the program component of the activity (recent donors are likely to contact their elected officials about such funding whereas nonrecent donors are not).

B-19 The content criterion is met because the activity calls for specific action by the recipient (contacting elected officials concerning funding for research about ABC disease) that will help accomplish the NFP's mission (to reduce the incidence of ABC disease), and it explains the need for and benefits of the action (to prevent ABC disease).

Example 4: Mailing Targeted Based on Program-Related Criteria

Facts: Case A

B-20 NFP D's mission is to improve the quality of life for senior citizens. One of NFP D's objectives included in that mission is to increase the physical activity of senior citizens. One of NFP D's programs to attain that objective is to send representatives to speak to groups about the importance of exercise and to conduct exercise classes.

B-21 NFP D mails a brochure on the importance of exercise that encourages exercise in later years to residents over the age of 65 in 3 zip code areas. The last 2 pages of the 4-page brochure include a perforated contribution remittance form on which NFP D explains its program and makes an appeal for contributions. The content of the first 2 pages of the brochure is primarily educational; it explains how seniors can undertake a self-supervised exercise program and encourages them to undertake such a program. In addition, NFP D includes a second brochure on various exercise techniques that can be used by those undertaking an exercise program.

B-22 The brochures are distributed to educate people in this age group about the importance of exercising, to help them exercise properly, and to raise contributions for NFP D. These objectives are documented in a letter to the public relations firm that developed the brochures. The audience is selected based on age, without regard to ability to contribute. NFP D believes that most of the recipients would benefit from the information about exercise.

Conclusion: Case A

B-23 The purpose, audience, and content criteria are met, and the joint costs should be allocated. (Note that the costs of the second brochure should be charged to program because all the costs of the brochure are identifiable with the program function.)

B-24 The activity calls for specific action by the recipient (exercising) that will help accomplish the NFP's mission. Therefore, the guidance in FASB ASC 958-720-45-38 (see paragraph 13.91) should be considered. Neither of the factors in paragraphs 40–44 of FASB ASC 958-720-45 (see the compensation or fees test in paragraphs 13.92–.95) or paragraphs 45–46 of FASB ASC 958-720-45 (see the separate and similar activities test in paragraphs 13.96–.97) is determinative of whether the purpose criterion is met. Therefore, other evidence, such as the indicators in paragraphs 6–9 of FASB ASC 958-720-55 (see paragraph 13.99), should be considered. The purpose criterion is met based on the other evidence, because (*a*) performing such programs helps accomplish NFP D's mission, and (*b*) the objectives of the program are documented in a letter to the public relations firm that developed the brochure.

B-25 The audience criterion is met because the audience (residents over 65 in certain zip codes) is selected based on its need to use or reasonable potential for use of the action called for by the program component.

B-26 The content criterion is met because the activity calls for specific action by the recipient (exercising) that will help accomplish the NFP's mission (increasing the physical activity of senior citizens), and the need for and benefits of the action are clearly evident (explains the importance of exercising).

Facts: Case B

B-27 In this case, NFP D employs a fund-raising consultant to develop the first brochure and pays that consultant 30 percent of contributions raised.

Conclusion: Case B

B-28 The content and audience criteria are met. The purpose criterion is not met, however, because a majority of compensation or fees for the fund-raising consultant varies based on contributions raised for this discrete joint activity (the fund-raising consultant is paid 30 percent of contributions raised). All costs should be charged to fund-raising, including the costs of the second brochure and any other costs that otherwise might be considered program or management and general costs if they had been incurred in a different activity.

Example 5: Door-to-Door Canvass

Facts

B-29 NFP E's mission is to protect the environment. One of NFP E's objectives included in that mission is to take action that will increase the portion of waste recycled by the public.

B-30 NFP E conducts a door-to-door canvass of a community that recycles a low portion of its waste. The purpose of the activity is to help increase recycling by educating the community about environmental problems created by not recycling, and to raise contributions. Based on the information communicated by the canvassers, the need for and benefits of the action are clearly evident. The ability or likelihood of the residents to contribute is not a basis for communities selected, and all neighborhoods in the geographic area are covered if their recycling falls below a predetermined rate. The canvassers are selected from individuals who are well-informed about NFP E's environmental concerns and programs and who previously participated as volunteers in program activities such as answering environmental questions directed to NFP E and developing program activities designed to influence legislators to take actions addressing those concerns. The canvassers have not previously participated in fund-raising activities.

Conclusion

B-31 The purpose, audience, and content criteria are met, and the joint costs should be allocated.

B-32 The activity calls for specific action by the recipient (implicitly—to help increase recycling) that will help accomplish the entity's mission. Therefore, the guidance in FASB ASC 958-720-45-38 (see paragraph 13.91) should be considered. Neither of the factors in paragraphs 40–44 of FASB ASC 958-720-45 (see the compensation or fees test in paragraphs 13.92–.95) or paragraphs 45–46 of FASB ASC 958-720-45 (see the separate and similar activities test in paragraphs 13.96–.97) is determinative of whether the purpose criterion is met. Therefore, other evidence, such as the indicators in paragraphs 6–9 of FASB ASC 958-720-55 (see paragraph 13.99), should be considered. The purpose criterion is met based on the other evidence, because (*a*) the qualifications and duties of the personnel performing the activity indicate that it is a program activity (the canvassers are selected from individuals who are well-informed about NFP E's environmental concerns and programs and who previously participated as volunteers in program activities such as answering environmental questions directed to NFP E and developing program activities designed to influence legislators to take actions addressing those concerns), and (*b*) performing such programs helps accomplish NFP E's mission (to protect the environment).

B-33 The audience criterion is met because the audience (neighborhoods whose recycling falls below a predetermined rate) is selected based on its need to use or reasonable potential for use of the action called for by the program component.

B-34 The content criterion is met because the activity calls for specific action by the recipient (implicitly—to help increase recycling) that will help accomplish NFP E's mission (to protect the environment), and the need for and benefits of the action are clearly evident (increased recycling will help alleviate environmental problems).

Example 6: Door-to-Door Solicitation Campaign

Facts

B-35 NFP F's mission is to provide summer camps for economically disadvantaged youths. Educating the families of ineligible youths about the camps is not one of the program objectives included in that mission.

B-36 NFP F conducts a door-to-door solicitation campaign for its camp programs. In the campaign, volunteers with canisters visit homes in middle class neighborhoods to collect contributions. NFP F believes that people in those neighborhoods would not need the camp's programs but may contribute. The volunteers explain the camp's programs, including why the disadvantaged children benefit from the program, and distribute leaflets to the residents regardless of whether they contribute to the camp. The leaflets describe the camp, its activities, who can attend, and the benefits to attendees. Requests for contributions are not included in the leaflets.

Conclusion

B-37 The purpose, audience, and content criteria are not met. All costs should be charged to fund-raising.

B-38 The activity does not include a call for specific action because it only educates the audience about causes (describing the camp, its activities, who can attend, and the benefits to attendees). Therefore, the purpose criterion is not met.

B-39 The audience criterion is not met, because the audience is selected based on its ability or likelihood to contribute, rather than based on its need to use or reasonable potential for use of the action called for by the program component or its ability to take action to assist the NFP in meeting the goals of the program component of the activity. (NFP F believes that people in those neighborhoods would not need the camp's programs but may contribute.)

B-40 The content criterion is not met because the activity does not call for specific action by the recipient. (The content educates the audience about causes that the program is designed to address without calling for specific action.)

Example 7: Annual National Telethon

Facts

B-41 NFP G's mission is to educate the public about lifesaving techniques in order to increase the number of lives saved. One of NFP G's objectives in fulfilling that mission, as stated in the minutes of the board's meetings, is to produce and show television broadcasts including information about lifesaving techniques.

B-42 NFP G conducts an annual national telethon to raise contributions and to reach the American public with lifesaving educational messages, such as summary instructions concerning dealing with certain life-threatening situations. Based on the information communicated by the messages, the need for and benefits of the action are clearly evident. The broadcast includes segments describing NFP G's services. NFP G broadcasts the telethon to the entire country, not merely to areas selected on the basis of giving potential or prior fund-raising results. Also, NFP G uses national television broadcasts devoted entirely to lifesaving educational messages to conduct program activities without fund-raising.

Conclusion

B-43 The purpose, audience, and content criteria are met, and the joint costs should be allocated.

B-44 The activity calls for specific action by the recipient (implicitly, to save lives) that will help accomplish the NFP's mission. Therefore, the guidance in FASB ASC 958-720-45-38 (see paragraph 13.91) should be considered. The purpose criterion is met because (*a*) the program component of the activity calls for specific action by the recipient that will help accomplish NFP G's mission (to save lives by educating the public), and (*b*) a similar program activity is conducted without the fund-raising using the same medium and on a scale that is similar to or greater than the scale on which it is conducted with the appeal (NFP G uses national television broadcasts devoted entirely to lifesaving educational messages to conduct program activities without fund-raising).

B-45 The audience criterion is met because the audience (a broad segment of the population) is selected based on its need to use or reasonable potential for use of the action called for by the program activity.

B-46 The content criterion is met because the activity calls for specific action by the recipient (implicitly—to save lives) that will help accomplish the NFP's mission (to save lives by educating the public), and the need for and benefits of the action are clearly evident (saving lives is desirable).

Example 8: Television Broadcast Educating the Public

Facts

B-47 NFP H's mission is to provide food, clothing, and medical care to children in developing countries.

B-48 NFP H conducts television broadcasts in the United States that describe its programs, show the needy children, and end with appeals for contributions. NFP H's operating policies and internal management memoranda state that these programs are designed to educate the public about the needs of children in developing countries and to raise contributions. The employees producing the programs are trained in audiovisual production and are familiar with NFP H's programs. Also, the executive producer is paid $25,000 for this activity, with a $5,000 bonus if the activity raises more than $1,000,000.

Conclusion

B-49 The purpose, audience, and content criteria are not met. All costs should be charged to fund-raising.

B-50 The activity does not include a call for specific action because it only educates the audience about causes (describing its programs and showing the needy children). Therefore, the purpose criterion is not met. Also, note that if the factor in paragraphs 40–44 of FASB ASC 958-720-45 (the compensation or fees test; see paragraphs 13.92–.95) were considered, it would not be determinative of whether the purpose criterion is met. Although the executive producer will be paid $5,000 if the activity raises more than $1,000,000, that amount would not be a majority of the executive producer's total compensation for this activity, because $5,000 would not be a majority of the executive producer's total compensation of $30,000 for this activity. Also, note that if other evidence, such as the indicators in paragraphs 6–9 of FASB ASC 958-720-55 (see paragraph 13.99), were considered, the purpose criterion would not be met based on the other evidence. Although the qualifications and duties of the personnel performing the activity indicate that the employees producing the program are familiar with NFP H's programs, the facts that some, but less than a majority, of the executive producer's compensation varies based on contributions raised, and that the operating policies and internal management memoranda state that these programs are designed to educate the public about the needs of children in developing countries with no call for specific action by recipients and to raise contributions, indicate that the purpose is fund-raising.)

B-51 The audience criterion is not met because the audience is selected based on its ability or likelihood to contribute, rather than based on its need to use or reasonable potential for use of the action called for by the program component or its ability to take action to assist the NFP in meeting the goals of the program component of the activity. (The audience is a broad segment of the population of a country that is not in need of or has no reasonable potential for use of the program activity.)

B-52 The content criterion is not met because the activity does not call for specific action by the recipient that will help accomplish the NFP's mission. (The content educates the audience about the causes without calling for specific action.)

Example 9: Distribution of the Annual Report

Facts

B-53 NFP I is a university that distributes its annual report, which includes reports on mission accomplishments, to those who have made significant contributions over the previous year, its board of trustees, and its employees. The annual report is primarily prepared by management and general personnel, such as the accounting department and executive staff. The activity is coordinated by the public relations department. Internal management memoranda indicate that the purpose of the annual report is to report on how management discharged its stewardship responsibilities, including the university's overall performance, goals, financial position, cash flows, and results of operations. Included in the package containing the annual report are requests for contributions and donor reply cards.

Conclusion

B-54 The purpose, audience, and content criteria are met, and the joint costs should be allocated.

B-55 The activity has elements of management and general functions. Therefore, no call for specific action is required. Neither of the factors in paragraphs 40–44 of FASB ASC 958-720-45 (see the compensation or fees test in paragraphs 13.92–.95) or paragraphs 45–46 of FASB ASC 958-720-45 (see the separate and similar activities test in paragraphs 13.96–.97) is determinative of whether the purpose criterion is met. Therefore, other evidence, such as the indicators in paragraphs 6–9 of FASB ASC 958-720-55 (see paragraph 13.99), should be considered. The purpose criterion is met based on the other evidence because (*a*) the employees performing the activity are not members of the fund-raising department and perform other non-fund-raising activities and (*b*) internal management memoranda indicate that the purpose of the annual report is to fulfill one of the university's management and general responsibilities.

B-56 The audience criterion is met because the audience is selected based on its reasonable potential for use of the management and general component. Although the activity is directed primarily at those who have previously made significant contributions, the audience was selected based on its presumed interest in NFP I's annual report (prior donors who have made significant contributions are likely to have an interest in matters discussed in the annual report).

B-57 The content criterion is met because the activity (distributing annual reports) fulfills one of the entity's management and general responsibilities (reporting concerning management's fulfillment of its stewardship function).

Example 10: Compliance With IRS Regulations

Facts

B-58 In accordance with internal management memoranda documenting its policies requiring it to comply with IRS regulations, NFP J mails prior donors the contribution substantiation documentation required by the IRS. The documentation is included on a perforated piece of paper. The information above the perforation line pertains to the documentation required by the IRS. The information below the perforation line includes a request for contributions and may be used as a donor reply card.

Conclusion

B-59 The purpose, audience, and content criteria are met, and the joint costs should be allocated. (Note that the costs of the information below the perforation line are identifiable with fund-raising and therefore should be charged to fund-raising.)

B-60 The activity has elements of management and general functions. Therefore, no call for specific action is required. Neither of the factors in paragraphs 40–44 of FASB ASC 958-720-45 (see the compensation or fees test in paragraphs 13.92–.95) or paragraphs 45–46 of FASB ASC 958-720-45 (see the separate and similar activities test in paragraphs 13.96–.97) is determinative of whether the purpose criterion is met. Therefore, other evidence, such as the indicators in paragraphs 6–9 of FASB ASC 958-720-55 (see paragraph 13.99), should be considered. The purpose criterion is met based on the other evidence because internal management memoranda indicate that the purpose of the activity is to fulfill one of NFP J's management and general responsibilities.

B-61 The audience criterion is met because the NFP is required to direct the management and general component of the activity to the particular audience. Although the activity is directed at those who have previously contributed, the audience was selected based on its need for the documentation.

B-62 The content criterion is met because the activity (sending documentation required by the IRS) fulfills one of the entity's management and general responsibilities (complying with IRS regulations).

Example 11: Mailing to Individuals Targeted Using a Rented List

Facts

B-63 NFP K is an animal rights organization. It mails a package of material to individuals included in lists rented from various environmental and other NFPs that support causes that NFP K believes are congruent with its own. In addition to donor response cards and return envelopes, the package includes (*a*) materials urging recipients to contact their legislators and urge the legislators to support legislation to protect those rights, and (*b*) postcards addressed to legislators urging support for legislation restricting the use of animal testing for cosmetic products. The mail campaign is part of an overall strategy that includes magazine advertisements and the distribution of similar materials at various community events, some of which are undertaken without fund-raising appeals. The advertising and community events reach audiences similar in size and demographics to the audience reached by the mailing.

Conclusion

B-64 The purpose, audience, and content criteria are met, and the joint costs should be allocated.

B-65 The activity calls for specific action by the recipient (mailing postcards to legislators urging support for legislation restricting the use of animal testing for cosmetic products) that will help accomplish the entity's mission. Therefore, the guidance in FASB ASC 958-720-45-38 (see paragraph 13.91) should be considered. Neither of the factors in paragraphs 40–44 of FASB ASC 958-720-45 (see the compensation or fees test in paragraphs 13.92–.95) or paragraphs 45–46 of FASB ASC 958-720-45 (see the separate and similar activities test in paragraphs 13.96–.97) is determinative of whether the purpose criterion is met. Therefore, other evidence, such as the indicators in paragraphs 6–9 of FASB ASC 958-720-55 (see paragraph 13.99), should be considered. The purpose criterion is met based on the other evidence, because (*a*) the program component of this activity calls for specific action by the recipient that will help accomplish the NFP's mission, and it otherwise conducts the program activity in this example without a request for contributions, and (*b*) performing such programs helps accomplish NFP K's mission.

B-66 The audience criterion is met because the audience (individuals included in lists rented from various environmental and other NFPs that support causes that NFP K believes are congruent with its own) is selected based on its ability to take action to assist the NFP in meeting the goals of the program component of the activity.

B-67 The content criterion is met because the activity calls for specific action by the recipient (mailing postcards to legislators urging support for legislation restricting the use of animal testing for cosmetic products) that will help accomplish the NFP's mission (to protect animal rights), and the need for and benefits of the action are clearly evident (to protect animal rights).

Example 12: Advertising of Ticket Subscription With a Request for Contributions

Facts

B-68 NFP L is a performing arts entity whose mission is to make the arts available to residents in its area. NFP L charges a fee for attending performances and sends advertisements, including subscription forms, for the performances to residents in its area. These advertisements include a return envelope with a request for contributions. NFP L evaluates the effectiveness of the advertising based on the number of subscriptions sold as well as contributions received. In performing that evaluation, NFP L places more weight on the number of subscriptions sold than on the contributions received. Also, NFP L advertises the performances on local television and radio without a request for contributions but on a smaller scale than the mail advertising.

Conclusion

B-69 The purpose, audience, and content criteria are met, and the joint costs should be allocated.

B-70 The activity calls for specific action by the recipient (attending the performances) that will help accomplish the NFP's mission. Therefore, the guidance in FASB ASC 958-720-45-38 (see paragraph 13.91) should be considered. Neither of the factors in paragraphs 40–44 of FASB ASC 958-720-45 (see the compensation or fees test in paragraphs 13.92–.95) or paragraphs 45–46 of FASB ASC 958-720-45 (see the separate and similar activities test in paragraphs 13.96–.97) is determinative of whether the purpose criterion is met. Therefore, other evidence, such as the indicators in paragraphs 6–9 of FASB ASC 958-720-55 (see paragraph 13.99), should be considered. The purpose criterion is met based on the other evidence because (*a*) the NFP measures program results and accomplishments of the joint activity and in evaluating the effectiveness of the activity, the NFP places significantly greater weight on the activity's effectiveness in accomplishing program goals than on the activity's effectiveness in raising contributions (NFP L evaluates the effectiveness of the advertising based on the number of subscriptions sold as well as contributions received and places more weight on the number of subscriptions sold than on the contributions received), (*b*) it otherwise conducts the program activity without a request for contributions, and (*c*) performing such programs helps accomplish NFP L's mission (to make the arts available to residents in its area).

B-71 The audience criterion is met because the audience (a broad segment of the population in NFP L's area) is selected based on its need to use or reasonable potential for use of the action called for by the program component.

B-72 The content criterion is met because the activity calls for specific action by the recipient (attending the performances) that will help accomplish the NFP's mission (making the arts available to area residents), and the need for and benefits of the action are clearly evident (attending the performance is a positive cultural experience). (Note that the purchase of subscriptions is an exchange transaction and, therefore, is not a contribution.)

Example 13: University Lecture Series With Fair Value Admission

Facts

B-73 NFP M is a university whose mission is to educate the public (students) in various academic pursuits. NFP M's political science department holds a special lecture series in which prominent world leaders speak about current events. The speakers command relatively high fees and, in order to cover costs and make a modest profit, the university sets a relatively expensive fee to attend. However, the tickets are priced at the fair value of the lecture and no portion of the ticket purchase price is a contribution. NFP M advertises the lectures by sending invitations to prior attendees and to prior donors who have contributed significant amounts, and by placing advertisements in local newspapers read by the general public. At some of the lectures, including the lecture being considered in this example, deans and other faculty members of NFP M solicit significant contributions from attendees. Other lectures in the series are conducted on a scale similar to the scale of the lecture in this example without requesting contributions. NFP M's records indicate that historically 75 percent of the attendees have attended prior lectures. Of the 75 percent who have attended prior lectures, 15 percent have made prior contributions to NFP M. Of the 15 percent who have made prior contributions to NFP M, 5 percent have made contributions in response to solicitations made at the events. (Therefore, one-half of 1 percent of attendees makes contributions in response to solicitations made at the events. However, those contributions are significant.) Overall, the audience's ability or likelihood to contribute is an insignificant factor in its selection. NFP M evaluates the effectiveness of the activity based on the number of tickets sold, as well as contributions received. In performing that evaluation, NFP M places more weight on the number of tickets sold than on the contributions received.

Conclusion

B-74 The purpose, audience, and content criteria are met, and the joint costs should be allocated. The purchase of the tickets is an exchange transaction and, therefore, is not a contribution. As discussed in FASB ASC 958-720-45-29 (see paragraph 13.82), costs of goods or services provided in exchange transactions that are part of joint activities, such as costs of direct donor benefits of a special event, should not be reported as fund-raising. FASB ASC 958-220-45-19 (see paragraph 13.46) provides guidance concerning reporting special events.

B-75 The activity calls for specific action by the recipient (attending the lecture) that will help accomplish the NFP's mission. Therefore, the guidance in FASB ASC 958-720-45-38 (see paragraph 13.91) should be considered. The purpose criterion is met because (*a*) the program component of the activity calls for specific action by the recipient that will help accomplish the NFP's mission (educating the public [students] in various academic pursuits), and (*b*) the program is also conducted using the same medium on a scale that is similar to or greater than the scale on which it is conducted with the request for contributions (other lectures in the series are conducted on a scale similar to the scale of the lecture in this example without requesting contributions).

B-76 The audience criterion is met. The rebuttable presumption that the audience criterion is not met because the audience includes prior donors is overcome in this example because the audience (those who have shown prior interest in the lecture series, prior donors, a broad segment of the population in NFP M's area, and those attending the lecture) is also selected for its reasonable potential for use of the program component (attending the lecture). Although the audience may make significant contributions, that was an insignificant factor in its selection.

B-77 The content criterion is met because the activity calls for specific action by the recipient (attending the lecture) that will help accomplish the NFP's mission (educating the public [students] in various academic pursuits), and the need for and benefits of the action are clearly evident (attending the lecture is a positive educational experience).

Example 14: University Lecture Series With Contribution Inherent in the Admission

Facts

B-78 NFP N is a university whose mission is to educate the public (students) in various academic pursuits. NFP N's political science department holds a special lecture series in which prominent world leaders speak about current events.

Admission is priced at $250, which is above the $50 fair value of the lecture and, therefore, $200 of the admission price is a contribution. Therefore, the audience's likelihood to contribute to the NFP is a significant factor in its selection. NFP N advertises the lectures by sending invitations to prior attendees and to prior donors who have contributed significant amounts, and by placing advertisements in local newspapers read by the general public. NFP N presents similar lectures that are priced at the fair value of those lectures.

Conclusion

B-79 The purpose and criterion are met. The audience criterion is not met. All costs, including those that might otherwise be considered program or management and general costs if they had been incurred in a different activity, except for the costs of the direct donor benefit (the lecture), should be charged to fund-raising. Note that the purchase of the tickets is an exchange transaction and, therefore, is not a contribution. As discussed in FASB ASC 958-720-45-29 (see paragraph 13.82), costs of goods or services provided in exchange transactions that are part of joint activities, such as costs of direct donor benefits of a special event, should not be reported as fund-raising.) FASB ASC 958-220-45-19 (see paragraph 13.46) provides guidance concerning reporting special events.

B-80 The activity calls for specific action by the recipient (attending the lecture) that will help accomplish the NFP's mission. Therefore, the guidance in FASB ASC 958-720-45-38 (see paragraph 13.91) should be considered. The purpose criterion is met because (*a*) the program component of the activity calls for specific action by the recipient that will help accomplish the NFP's mission (educating the public [students] in various academic pursuits), and (*b*) the program is also conducted using the same medium on a scale that is similar to or greater than the scale on which it is conducted with the request for contributions (other lectures in the series are conducted on a scale similar to the scale of the lecture in this example without including a contribution in the admission price).

B-81 The audience criterion is not met. The rebuttable presumption that the audience criterion is not met because the audience is selected based on its likelihood to contribute to the NFP is not overcome in this example. The fact that the $250 admission price includes a $200 contribution leads to the conclusion that the audience's ability or likelihood to contribute is an overwhelmingly significant factor in its selection, whereas there is no evidence that the extent to which the audience is selected for its need to use or reasonable potential for use of the action called for by the program component (attending the lecture) is overwhelmingly significant.

B-82 The content criterion is met because the activity calls for specific action by the recipient (attending the lecture) that will help accomplish the NFP's mission (educating the public [students] in various academic pursuits), and the need for and benefits of the action are clearly evident (attending the lecture is a positive educational experience).

Example 15: Free Health Screenings

Facts

B-83 NFP O's mission is to reduce the incidence of illness from ABC disease, which primarily afflicts people over 65 years of age. One of NFP O's objectives in fulfilling that mission is to have all persons over 65 screened for ABC disease.

B-84 NFP O rents space at events attended primarily by people over 65 years of age and conducts free screening for ABC disease. NFP O's employees, who are educated about ABC disease and screening procedures and do not otherwise perform fund-raising functions, educate interested parties about the effects of ABC disease and the ease and benefits of screening for it. NFP O also solicits contributions at the events. The effectiveness of the activity is evaluated primarily based on how many screening tests are performed, and only minimally based on contributions raised. The employees are not compensated or evaluated based on contributions raised.

Conclusion

B-85 The purpose, audience, and content criteria are met, and the joint costs should be allocated.

B-86 The activity calls for specific action by the recipient (being screened for ABC disease) that will help accomplish the NFP's mission; therefore, the guidance in FASB ASC 958-720-45-38 (see paragraph 13.91) should be considered. Neither of the factors in paragraphs 40–44 of FASB ASC 958-720-45 (see the compensation or fees test in paragraphs 13.92–.95) or paragraphs 45–46 of FASB ASC 958-720-45 (see the separate and similar activities test in paragraphs 13.96–.97) is determinative of whether the purpose criterion is met. Therefore, other evidence, such as the indicators in paragraphs 6–9 of FASB ASC 958-720-55 (see paragraph 13.99), should be considered. The purpose criterion is met based on the other evidence, because (*a*) a process exists to evaluate measured program results and accomplishments and in evaluating the effectiveness of the joint activity, the NFP places significantly greater weight on the activity's effectiveness in accomplishing program goals than on the activity's effectiveness in raising contributions (NFP O evaluates the effectiveness of the activity based on the number of screening tests conducted as well as contributions received and places more weight on the number of tests conducted than on the contributions received); (*b*) the qualifications and duties of the personnel performing the activity indicate that it is a program activity (the employees are educated about ABC disease and the testing procedures and do not otherwise perform fund-raising functions); (*c*) the method of compensation for performing the activity does not indicate that it is a fund-raising activity (the employees are not compensated or evaluated based on contributions raised); and (*d*) performing such programs helps accomplish NFP O's mission (to prevent ABC disease).

B-87 The audience criterion is met because the audience (people over 65 years of age) is selected based on its need to use or reasonable potential for use of the action called for by the program component.

B-88 The content criterion is met because the activity calls for specific action by the recipient (being screened for ABC disease) that will help accomplish the NFP's mission (to reduce the incidence of ABC disease), and it explains the need for and benefits of the action (to prevent ABC disease).

Example 16: Public Television Membership Drive

Facts

B-89 NFP P's mission is to provide cultural and educational television programming to residents in its area. NFP P owns a public television station and holds a membership drive in which it solicits new members. The drive is conducted by station employees and consists of solicitations that are shown during long breaks between the station's regularly scheduled programs. NFP P's internal management memoranda state that these drives are designed to raise contributions. NFP P evaluates the effectiveness of the activity based on the amount of contributions received. NFP P shows the programs on a similar scale, without the request for contributions. The audience is members of the general public who watch the programs shown during the drive. Station member benefits are given to those who contribute and consist of tokens of appreciation with a nominal value.

Conclusion

B-90 The purpose, audience, and content criteria are met, and the joint costs should be allocated. (Note that there would be few, if any, joint costs. Costs associated with the fund-raising activities, such as costs of airtime, would be separately identifiable from costs of the program activities, such as licensing costs for a particular television program. Also, note that because no significant benefits or duties are associated with membership, member dues are contributions. Therefore, the substance of the membership-development activities is, in fact, fund-raising.)

B-91 The activity calls for specific action by the recipient (watching the television program) that will help accomplish the NFP's mission. Therefore, the guidance in FASB ASC 958-720-45-38 (see paragraph 13.91) should be considered. The purpose criterion is met because (*a*) the program component of the activity calls for specific action by the recipient that will help accomplish the NFP's mission, and (*b*) the program is also conducted using the same medium on a scale that is similar to or greater than the scale on which it is conducted with the request for contributions (NFP P shows the television programs on a similar scale, without the request for contributions).

B-92 The audience criterion is met. The rebuttable presumption that the audience criterion is not met because the audience is selected based on its likelihood to contribute is overcome in this example because the audience (members of the general public who watch the television programs shown during the drive) is also selected for its reasonable potential for use of the program component (watching the television programs). Although the audience may make contributions, that was an insignificant factor in its selection.

B-93 The content criterion is met because the activity calls for specific action by the recipient (watching the television programs) that will help accomplish the NFP's mission (providing cultural and educational television programming to residents in its area), and the need for and benefits of the action are clearly evident (watching the programs is a positive cultural and educational experience).

13.133

Supplement C—Allocation Methods for Joint Costs

C-1 Paragraphs 26–31 of FASB *Accounting Standards Codification* (ASC) 958-720-55 provide the following information about commonly used cost allocation methods for joint costs.

Physical Units Method

C-2 Joint costs are allocated to materials and activities in proportion to the number of units of output that can be attributed to each of the materials and activities. Examples of units of output are lines, square inches, and physical content measures. This method assumes that the benefits received by the fund-raising, program, or management and general component of the materials or activity from the joint costs incurred are directly proportional to the lines, square inches, or other physical output measures attributed to each component of the activity. This method may result in an unreasonable allocation of joint costs if the units of output, for example, line counts, do not reflect the degree to which costs are incurred for the joint activity. Use of the physical units method may also result in an unreasonable allocation if the physical units cannot be clearly ascribed to fund-raising, program, or management and general. For example, direct mail and telephone solicitations sometimes include content that is not identifiable with fund-raising, program, or management and general; or the physical units of such content are inseparable.

Illustration

C-3 For example, assume a direct mail campaign is used to conduct programs of the not-for-profit entity (NFP) and to solicit contributions to support the organization and its programs. Further, assume that the appeal meets the criteria for allocation of joint costs to more than one function.

C-4 The letter and reply card include a total of 100 lines; 45 lines pertain to program because they include a call for action by the recipient that will help accomplish the NFP's mission, and 55 lines pertain to the fund-raising appeal. Accordingly, 45 percent of the costs are allocated to program and 55 percent to fund-raising.

Relative Direct Cost Method

C-5 Joint costs are allocated to each of the components on the basis of their respective direct costs. Direct costs are those costs that are incurred in connection with the multipurpose materials or activity and that are specifically identifiable with a function (program, fund-raising, or management and general). This method may result in an unreasonable allocation of joint costs if the joint costs of the materials and activity are not incurred in approximately the same proportion and for the same reasons as the direct costs of the materials and activity. For example, if a relatively costly booklet informing the reader about the NFP's mission (including a call for action by the recipient that will help accomplish the NFP's mission) is included with a relatively inexpensive fund-raising letter, the allocation of joint costs based on the cost of these pieces may be unreasonable, particularly if the booklet and letter weigh approximately the same and therefore contribute equally to the postage costs.

Illustration

C-6 For example, the costs of a direct mail campaign that can be specifically identified with program services are the costs of separate program materials and a postcard which calls for specific action by the recipient that will help accomplish the NFP's mission. They total $20,000. The direct costs of the fund-raising component of the direct mail campaign consist of the costs to develop and produce the fund-raising letter. They total $80,000. Joint costs associated with the direct mail campaign total $40,000 and would be allocated as follows under the relative direct cost method.

Program	$20,000/$100,000 × $40,000 = $8,000
Fund-raising	$80,000/$100,000 × $40,000 = $32,000

Stand-Alone Joint-Cost-Allocation Method

C-7 Joint costs are allocated to each component of the activity based on a ratio that uses estimates of costs of items included in joint costs that would have been incurred had the components been conducted independently. The numerator of the ratio is the cost (of items included in joint costs) of conducting a single component independently; the denominator is the cost (of items included in joint costs) of conducting all components independently. This method assumes that efforts for each component in the stand-alone situation are proportionate to the efforts actually undertaken in the joint cost situation. This method may result in an unreasonable allocation because it ignores the effect of each function, which is performed jointly with other functions, on other such functions. For example, the programmatic impact of a direct mail campaign or a telemarketing phone message may be significantly lessened when performed in conjunction with a fund-raising appeal.

Illustration

C-8 For example, assume that the joint costs associated with a direct mail campaign including both program and fund-raising components are the costs of stationery, postage, and envelopes at a total of $100,000. The costs of stationery, postage, and envelopes to produce and distribute each component separately would have been $90,000 for the program component and $70,000 for the fund-raising component. Under the stand-alone joint cost allocation method, the $100,000 in joint costs would be allocated as follows.

Program	$90,000/$160,000 × $100,000 = $56,250
Fund-raising	$70,000/$160,000 × $100,000 = $43,750

13.134

Supplement D—Examples of Disclosures

D-1 Example 20 (paragraphs 167–170) of FASB *Accounting Standards Codification* (ASC) 958-720-55 illustrates the disclosures discussed in FASB ASC 958-720-50-2 (see paragraphs 13.116–.117). Case A shows the required and encouraged information in narrative format. Case B reports that information in tabular format, as well as information concerning joint costs incurred for each kind of activity by functional expense classification, which is neither required nor encouraged, but which is not prohibited.

Case A: Narrative Format

Note X. Allocation of Joint Costs

In 20XX, Not-for-profit Entity B conducted activities that included requests for contributions as well as program and management and general components. Those activities included direct mail campaigns, special events, and a telethon. The costs of conducting those activities included a total of $310,000 of joint costs, which are not specifically attributable to particular components of the activities (joint costs). [Joint costs for each kind of activity were $50,000, $150,000, and $110,000 respectively.] These joint costs were allocated as follows.

Fund-raising	$180,000
Program A	80,000
Program B	40,000
Management and general	10,000
Total	$310,000

Note that the bracketed sentence is a disclosure that is encouraged but not required.

Case B: Tabular Format

Note X. Allocation of Joint Costs

In 20XX, Not-for-profit Entity B conducted activities that included appeals for contributions and incurred joint costs of $310,000. These activities included direct mail campaigns, special events, and a telethon. Joint costs were allocated as follows.

	Direct Mail	*Special Events*	*Telethon*	*Total*
Fund-raising	$40,000	$50,000	$90,000	$180,000
Program A	10,000	65,000	5,000	80,000
Program B		25,000	15,000	40,000
Management and general		10,000		10,000
Total	$50,000	$150,000	$110,000	$310,000

Note that shading is used to highlight information that is not required, encouraged, or prohibited. However, not-for-profit entities may prefer to disclose it. Disclosing the total joint costs for each kind of activity ($50,000, $150,000, and $110,000) is encouraged but not required.

Chapter 14

Reports of Independent Auditors

Gray shaded text in this chapter reflects guidance issued but not yet effective as of the date of this guide, March 1, 2018, but becoming effective on or prior to June 30, 2018, exclusive of any option to early adopt ahead of the mandatory effective date. Unless otherwise indicated, all unshaded text reflects guidance that was already effective as of the date of this guide.

Reports on Financial Statements

14.01 This chapter discusses the application of generally accepted auditing standards (GAAS) when reporting on the financial statements of not-for-profit entities (NFPs) in specific circumstances. The facts and circumstances of each particular audit will govern the appropriate form of report.

14.02 The auditor's standard report described in paragraphs .22–.41 of AU-C section 700, *Forming an Opinion and Reporting on Financial Statements*,[1] refers to *results of operations*, which is usually understood to refer to an enterprise's net income for a period together with other changes in net worth. As described in chapter 3, "Financial Statements, the Reporting Entity, and General Financial Reporting Matters," an NFP's statement of activities reports the changes in net assets[2] for the period but does not purport to present the results of operations, as would an income statement of a for-profit entity.[3] Accordingly, for NFPs, the opinion paragraph of the auditor's report would refer to changes in net assets because that is more descriptive of the information in the statement of activities than results of operations.

Reports on Comparative Financial Statements and Presentation of Comparative Information

14.03 As noted in chapter 3 of this guide, NFPs sometimes present comparative information for a prior year or years only in total rather than by net

[1] All AU-C sections can be found in AICPA *Professional Standards*.

[2] As discussed in paragraph 3.08, descriptive terms such as *change in equity* may be used.

[3] As discussed in chapter 3, "Financial Statements, the Reporting Entity, and General Financial Reporting Matters," a not-for-profit entity may present an intermediate measure of operations within the statement of activities. As noted in chapter 3, however, if an intermediate measure of operations is reported, it must be in a financial statement that, at a minimum, reports the change in unrestricted net assets for the period. Such a statement would, therefore, ordinarily present more than merely the results of operations.

As discussed in chapter 3, "Financial Statements, the Reporting Entity, and General Financial Reporting Matters," a not-for-profit entity may present an intermediate measure of operations within the statement of activities. As noted in chapter 3, however, if an intermediate measure of operations is reported, it must be in a financial statement that, at a minimum, reports the change in net assets without donor restrictions for the period. Such a statement would, therefore, ordinarily present more than merely the results of operations. This note reflects an amendment in FASB Accounting Standards Update (ASU) No. 2016-14, *Not-for-Profit Entities (Topic 958): Presentation of Financial Statements of Not-for-Profit Entities*. FASB ASU No. 2016-14 is effective for annual financial statements issued for fiscal years beginning after December 15, 2017 (for example, years ending December 31, 2018, and years ending June 30, 2019), and for interim periods within fiscal years beginning after December 15, 2018. Application to interim financial statements is permitted but not required in the initial year of application. Early application of the amendments is permitted.

asset class. Paragraphs .45–.46 of AU-C section 700 provide requirements and guidance for reporting on comparative financial statements and state the following:

> Comparative financial statements may be required by the applicable financial reporting framework, or management may elect to provide such information. When comparative financial statements are presented, the auditor's report should refer to each period for which financial statements are presented and on which an audit opinion is expressed.
>
> When expressing an opinion on all periods presented, a continuing auditor should update the report on the financial statements of one or more prior periods presented on a comparative basis with those of the current period. The auditor's report on comparative financial statements should not be dated earlier than the date on which the auditor has obtained sufficient appropriate audit evidence on which to support the opinion for the most recent audit.

14.04 Paragraphs .47–.48 of AU-C section 700 differentiate between comparative financial statements, discussed previously, and comparative information upon which the auditor has no responsibility to opine, unless requested to do so. Paragraph .A52 of AU-C section 700 states the following:

> Comparative information, which may be condensed financial statements or prior period summarized financial information, is not considered comparative financial statements because it is not a complete set of financial statements. For example, entities such as state and local governmental units frequently present total-all-funds information for the prior periods rather than information by individual funds because of space limitations or to avoid cumbersome or confusing formats. Also, not-for-profit organizations frequently present certain summarized financial information for the prior period(s) in total rather than by net asset class. Accordingly, the auditor need not opine on comparative information in accordance with this section.

14.05 Though the financial reporting model for NFPs does not require fund reporting, FASB *Accounting Standards Codification* (ASC) 958, *Not-for-Profit Entities*, requires, however, that certain basic information, such as reporting total net assets and changes in net assets by net asset class, be provided. If the prior year(s) financial statements include the minimum information required by those standards for a complete set of financial statements (statement of financial position, statement of activities, statements of cash flows, and accompanying notes), the financial statements are not summarized information. Accordingly, the requirements related to comparative financial statements would apply. Alternatively, if the prior year(s) financial statements are summarized and therefore do not include the minimum information required for a complete set of financial statements, the guidance related to comparative information applies, whereby the auditor's report should not mention the summarized information in the introductory paragraph or in the opinion paragraph. However, paragraph .47 of AU-C section 700 requires the auditor to clearly indicate in the auditor's report the character of the auditor's work, if any, and the degree of responsibility the auditor is taking in relation to the prior year(s) summarized information.

14.06 As noted in paragraph 3.55, if the comparative financial information is summarized and does not include the minimum information required by FASB ASC 958—for example, if the statement of activities does not present revenues, expenses, gains, and losses by net asset class—certain disclosures about the nature of the information presented are required. If the disclosures required by paragraph 3.55 are omitted or are incomplete, the auditor should add a paragraph to his or her report calling the omitted or incomplete disclosure to the readers' attention.

14.07 An example of an other-matter paragraph in the auditor's report, following the opinion paragraph, for the circumstances when the comparative summarized financial information presented was derived from prior year financial statements that were audited, is as follows:

> ***Report on Summarized Comparative Information***
>
> We have previously audited the XYZ Not-for-Profit Organization's 20X0 financial statements, and we expressed an unmodified audit opinion on those audited financial statements in our report dated December 15, 20X0. In our opinion, the summarized comparative information presented herein as of and for the year ended September 30, 20X0 is consistent, in all material respects, with the audited financial statements from which it has been derived.

14.08 For circumstances when the comparative summarized financial information presented was derived from prior year financial statements that were not audited, an example of an other-matter paragraph in the auditor's report, following the opinion paragraph, is as follows:

> ***Report on Summarized Comparative Information***
>
> The summarized comparative information presented herein as of and for the year ended September 30, 20X0, derived from those unaudited financial statements, has not been audited, reviewed, or compiled and, accordingly, we express no opinion and provide no assurance on it.

Unmodified Opinions

14.09 The auditor's standard report contains an opinion that the financial statements are presented fairly, in all material respects, in conformity with generally accepted accounting principles (GAAP). That conclusion may be expressed only when the auditor has formed such an opinion on the basis of an audit performed in accordance with GAAS. An example of the auditor's standard report on financial statements covering a single year is as follows:

> **Independent Auditor's Report**
>
> **Report on the Financial Statements**[4]
>
> We have audited the accompanying consolidated financial statements of XYZ Not-for-Profit Entity, which comprise the consolidated statement of financial position as of June 30, 20X1, and the related

[4] The subtitle "Report on the Financial Statements" is unnecessary in circumstances when the second subtitle, "Report on Other Legal and Regulatory Requirements," is not applicable.

consolidated statements of activities and cash flows[5] for the years then ended, and the related notes to the consolidated financial statements.

Management's Responsibility for the Financial Statements

Management is responsible for the preparation and fair presentation of these consolidated financial statements in accordance with accounting principles generally accepted in the United States of America; this includes the design, implementation, and maintenance of internal control relevant to the preparation and fair presentation of consolidated financial statements that are free from material misstatement, whether due to fraud or error.

Auditor's Responsibility

Our responsibility is to express an opinion on these consolidated financial statements based on our audit. We conducted our audit in accordance with auditing standards generally accepted in the United States of America. Those standards require that we plan and perform the audit to obtain reasonable assurance about whether the consolidated financial statements are free from material misstatement.

An audit involves performing procedures to obtain audit evidence about the amounts and disclosures in the consolidated financial statements. The procedures selected depend on the auditor's judgment, including the assessment of the risks of material misstatement of the consolidated financial statements, whether due to fraud or error. In making those risk assessments, the auditor considers internal control relevant to the entity's preparation and fair presentation of the consolidated financial statements in order to design audit procedures that are appropriate in the circumstances, but not for the purpose of expressing an opinion on the effectiveness of the entity's internal control.[6] Accordingly, we express no such opinion. An audit also includes evaluating the appropriateness of accounting policies used and the reasonableness of significant accounting estimates made by management, as well as evaluating the overall presentation of the consolidated financial statements.

We believe that the audit evidence we have obtained is sufficient and appropriate to provide a basis for our audit opinion.

Opinion

In our opinion, the consolidated financial statements referred to above present fairly, in all material respects, the consolidated financial position of XYZ Not-for-Profit Entity as of June 30, 20X1, and the changes in its net assets and its cash flows for the years then ended in accordance with accounting principles generally accepted in the United States of America.

---

[5] Each of the statements presented, which may include a statement of functional expenses, should be identified in the introductory paragraph.

[6] In circumstances when the auditor also has responsibility to express an opinion on the effectiveness of internal control in conjunction with the audit of the consolidated financial statements, this sentence would be worded as follows: "In making those risk assessments, the auditor considers internal control relevant to the entity's preparation and fair presentation of the consolidated financial statements in order to design audit procedures that are appropriate in the circumstances." In addition, the next sentence, "Accordingly, we express no such opinion." would not be included.

Report on Other Legal and Regulatory Requirements

[*Form and content of this section of the auditor's report will vary depending on the nature of the auditor's other reporting responsibilities.*]

[*Auditor's signature*]

[*Auditor's city and state*]

[*Date of the auditor's report*]

Modified Reports and Departures From Unmodified Opinions

14.10 AU-C section 706, *Emphasis-of-Matter Paragraphs and Other-Matter Paragraphs in the Independent Auditor's Report*, indicates the circumstances in which an emphasis-of-matter or other-matter paragraph is required to be added following the standard opinion paragraph. AU-C section 705, *Modifications to the Opinion in the Independent Auditor's Report*, indicates circumstances in which departures from GAAP and limitations on the scope of the audit would require a modified opinion, an adverse opinion, or a disclaimer of opinion, and provides examples of auditors' reports in those circumstances. Examples of possible departures from GAAP that an auditor of an NFP's financial statements might encounter include the NFP's failure to (*a*) recognize or appropriately measure promises to give, contributed services, or depreciation on plant and equipment in conformity with GAAP, and (*b*) provide information about expenses reported by their functional classification. The auditor's inability to obtain sufficient appropriate audit evidence with regard to (*a*) contributed services that the NFP has recorded or (*b*) receivables and revenues from fund-raising activities is an example of possible restrictions on the scope of the audit that an auditor of an NFP's financial statements might encounter.

Going Concern

14.11 Statement on Auditing Standards No. 132, *The Auditor's Consideration of an Entity's Ability to Continue as a Going Concern* (AU-C sec. 570), provides guidance to the auditor in evaluating whether there is substantial doubt about the entity's ability to continue as a going concern for a reasonable period of time. Paragraphs 2.122–.132 of this guide discuss that guidance and the guidance in FASB ASC 205-40, which provides standards for evaluation and disclosure when there is substantial doubt about an entity's ability to continue as a going concern. Paragraph .23 of AU-C section 570 states that if the financial statements have been prepared using the going concern basis of accounting but, in the auditor's judgment, management's use of the going concern basis of accounting in the preparation of the financial statements is inappropriate, the auditor should express an adverse opinion. If the auditor concludes that the going concern basis is appropriate but conditions and events have been identified that raise substantial doubt about the entity's ability to continue as a going concern for a reasonable period of time, and if, after considering the identified conditions or events and management's plans, the auditor concludes that substantial doubt remains, the auditor should include an emphasis-of-matter paragraph in the auditor's report. The emphasis-of-matter paragraph should use the phrase "substantial doubt about its (the entity's) ability to continue as a going concern" if the financial statements are prepared in accordance with GAAP. The auditor should not use conditional language concerning the existence of substantial doubt about the entity's ability to continue as a going concern for a reasonable period of time. If instead, based on the audit evidence obtained, the auditor concludes that substantial doubt has been alleviated by management's plans, the auditor may (but is not required to) include an emphasis-of-matter paragraph, making reference to management's disclosures related to the conditions and events and management's plans related to those conditions and events. Paragraphs .A51.A57 of AU-C section 570 discuss additional considerations and provide example emphasis-of-matter paragraphs. AU-C section 570 does not apply to an audit of financial statements based on the assumption of liquidation, as discussed further in paragraph 2.132. Interpretation No. 1, "Reporting on Financial Statements Prepared on a Liquidation Basis of Accounting" (AU-C sec. 9700 par. .01–.05), of AU-C section 700 provides an example auditor's report for financial statements prepared in the year of adoption of the liquidation basis of accounting.

Reporting on Supplementary Information

14.12 FASB ASC 958-720-45-4 states that information about an NFP's major programs (or segments) can be enhanced by reporting the interrelationships of program expenses and program revenues. Related nonmonetary information about program inputs, outputs, and results also is helpful. Generally, reporting that kind of information is feasible only in supplementary (other) information or management explanations or by other methods of financial reporting.

14.13 Although nonmonetary information about an NFP's activities and programs may be informative and helpful to users of the financial statements, this information is not necessary for fair presentation of financial position, changes in net assets, or cash flows on which the auditor is reporting. In addition, this information may not be auditable if it is obtained from records outside the accounting system that are not subject to controls, rather than being obtained (or derived by analysis or computation) from records subject to controls. AU-C section 720, *Other Information in Documents Containing Audited Financial Statements*, provides guidance to the auditor with regard to other information that may be included in audited financial statements. Paragraph .A2 of AU-C section 720 states that the auditor is not required to reference the other information in the auditor's report on the financial statements. However, the auditor may include an other-matter paragraph disclaiming an opinion on the other information. For example, an auditor may choose to include a disclaimer on the other information when the auditor believes that the auditor could be associated with the information and the user may infer a level of assurance that is not intended. An example follows:

> **Other Matter**
>
> Our audit was conducted for the purpose of forming an opinion on the [basic] financial statements as a whole. The [*identify the other information*] is presented for purposes of additional analysis and is not a required part of the basic financial statements. Such information has not been subjected to the auditing procedures applied in the audit of the basic financial statements, and, accordingly, we do not express an opinion or provide any assurance on it.

14.14 AU-C section 725, *Supplementary Information in Relation to the Financial Statements as a Whole*, applies if an auditor is engaged to report on whether supplementary information is fairly stated, in all material respects, in relation to the financial statements as a whole. If the auditor completes the procedures required by paragraph .07 of AU-C section 725 subsequent to the date of the auditor's report, Interpretation No. 1, "Dating the Auditor's Report on Supplementary Information" (AU-C sec. 9725 par. .01–.04), of AU-C section 725 provides an example report on the supplementary information that makes it clear that the auditor performed no additional procedures on the audited financial statements subsequent to the date of the auditor's report on those financial statements.

Special Considerations[7]

14.15 Some NFPs may find that financial statements prepared on the cash basis or the modified cash basis of accounting are adequate for their governing boards and other users. AU-C section 800, *Special Considerations—Audits of Financial Statements Prepared in Accordance With Special Purpose Frameworks*, describes the auditor's reporting requirements when the financial statements are prepared in accordance with a special purpose framework, which is a cash, tax, regulatory, contractual, or an other basis of accounting.[8]

14.16 AU-C section 806, *Reporting on Compliance With Aspects of Contractual Agreements or Regulatory Requirements in Connection With Audited Financial Statements*, addresses the auditor's responsibility and the form and content of the report when the auditor is requested to report on the entity's compliance with aspects of contractual agreements or regulatory requirements in connection with the audit of financial statements. In that instance, the auditor's report should include an appropriate alert in accordance with AU-C section 905, *Alert That Restricts the Use of the Auditor's Written Communication*. Technical Questions and Answers (Q&A) section 9110.22, "Use of Restricted Alert Language When Financial Statements Are Audited in Accordance With GAAS and *Government Auditing Standards*,"[9] clarifies that the auditor is not prohibited from using the restricted alert language required by paragraph .07 of AU-C section 905 if an auditor's report is not required to be issued in accordance with *Government Auditing Standards* and the report does not refer to *Government Auditing Standards*. For example, an NFP is required to have a financial statement audit conducted in accordance with GAAS and *Government Auditing Standards* because the NFP receives federal funds. In addition to the reports required by *Government Auditing Standards*, the auditor is requested to provide a compliance report to the organization's financial institution about whether the auditor identified any instances of noncompliance with the covenants of a loan agreement. Because that compliance report is not required to be issued in

---

[7] Paragraph .A34 of AU-C section 800, *Special Considerations—Audits of Financial Statements Prepared in Accordance With Special Purpose Frameworks*, provides guidance on evaluating the adequacy of disclosure and presentation in financial statements presented using a special purpose framework. Technical Questions and Answers (Q&A) section 1500, *Financial Statements Prepared in Accordance With a Special Purpose Framework* (*Technical Questions and Answers*), provides nonauthoritative guidance.

[8] The accrual basis of accounting is required by generally accepted accounting principles (GAAP) for a fair presentation of financial position, changes in net assets, and cash flows. Financial statements presented on the cash receipts and disbursements basis of accounting or using modifications of the cash basis having substantial support may only be considered to present financial position, changes in net assets, and cash flows in conformity with GAAP if they do not differ materially from financial statements prepared on an accrual basis and in accordance with GAAP.

[9] All Q&A sections can be found in *Technical Questions and Answers*.

accordance with *Government Auditing Standards* and the report to be issued would refer only to GAAS and not to *Government Auditing Standards*, the auditor may use the restricted alert language required by paragraph .07 of AU-C section 905. Q&A section 9110.23, "Modification of Compliance Report When Financial Statements Are Audited in Accordance With GAAS," states that the auditor would not need to modify the report language to indicate that the financial statement audit was also conducted in accordance with *Government Auditing Standards*; the report would refer only to the audit being conducted in accordance with auditing standards generally accepted in the United States of America.

Reporting Under Other Technical Standards

14.17 As noted in footnote 1 to chapter 2, "General Auditing Considerations," NFPs are not issuers subject to oversight by the PCAOB, and auditors are not required to follow auditing standards issued by the PCAOB in an audit of an NFP.

14.18 However, an auditor may be engaged to follow another set of auditing standards (for example, International Standards on Auditing, the standards of the PCAOB, or *Government Auditing Standards*). As discussed in paragraphs .42–.43 of AU-C section 700, an auditor may indicate that the audit was also conducted in accordance with another set of auditing standards. The auditor should not refer to having conducted an audit in accordance with another set of auditing standards in addition to GAAS, unless the audit was conducted in accordance with both sets of standards in their entirety. When the auditor's report refers to both GAAS and another set of auditing standards, the auditor's report should identify the other set of auditing standards as well as their origin. Interpretation No. 3, "Reporting on Audits Conducted in Accordance With Auditing Standards Generally Accepted in the United States of America and International Standards on Auditing" (AU-C sec. 9700 par. .08–.13), of AU-C section 700 provides further guidance and example auditor's reports. When conducting an audit of financial statements in accordance with the standards of the PCAOB and the audit is not within the jurisdiction of the PCAOB, the auditor is required to also conduct the audit in accordance with GAAS. In such circumstances, when the auditor refers to the standards of the PCAOB in addition to GAAS in the auditor's report, the auditor should use the form of report required by the standards of the PCAOB, amended to state that the audit was also conducted in accordance with GAAS, as discussed in paragraph .44 of AU-C section 700.[10]

14.19 In all audits, the auditor's opinion on the financial statements addresses whether the financial statements are presented fairly, in all material respects, in accordance with the applicable financial reporting framework. A *financial reporting framework* is defined in AU-C section 200, *Overall Objectives of the Independent Auditor and the Conduct of an Audit in Accordance With Generally Accepted Auditing Standards*, as:

---

[10] AU-C section 940, *An Audit of Internal Control Over Financial Reporting That Is Integrated With an Audit of Financial Statements*, establishes requirements and provides guidance that applies when an auditor is engaged to perform an audit of internal control over financial reporting that is integrated with an audit of financial statements in accordance with generally accepted auditing standards (integrated audit).

A set of criteria used to determine measurement, recognition, presentation, and disclosure of all material items appearing in the financial statements; for example, U.S. generally accepted accounting principles, International Financial Reporting Standards (IFRSs) promulgated by the International Accounting Standards Board (IASB), or a special purpose framework.

14.20 AU-C section 700 applies to audits of financial statements prepared under a financial reporting framework that has been promulgated by those entities designated by the council of the AICPA to establish GAAP. A list of those entities is found in ET appendix A, "Council Resolution Designating Bodies to Promulgate Technical Standards," of the AICPA Code of Professional Conduct (AICPA, *Professional Standards*).

14.21 Alternatively, AU-C section 910, *Financial Statements Prepared in Accordance With a Financial Reporting Framework Generally Accepted in Another Country*, applies when an auditor practicing in the United States is engaged to report on financial statements that have been prepared in accordance with a financial reporting framework generally accepted in another country not adopted by a body designated by council to establish generally accepted accounting principles that are intended for use outside the United States.

Reporting on Prescribed Forms

14.22 Some NFPs prepare financial reports using forms prescribed by an affiliated entity. If the financial statements prepared using the prescribed form do not conform with GAAP, either NFP may attach a separate set of financial statements and the auditor's report thereon. Alternatively, the auditor can be engaged to report on the prescribed form. The auditor may be requested to issue a preprinted auditor's report. The auditor's report should refer to GAAS only if the auditor's report includes, at a minimum, each of the elements outlined in paragraph .22 of AU-C section 800. If the prescribed specific layout, form, or wording of the auditor's report is not acceptable or would cause an auditor to make a statement that the auditor has no basis to make, in accordance with paragraph .23 of AU-C section 800, the auditor should reword the prescribed form of report or attach an appropriately worded separate report. When a separate report is issued, the auditor could consider inserting language such as "See attached independent auditor's report" in the space provided for the auditor's signature on the preprinted form.

14.23 IRS Form 990, "Return of Organizations Exempt from Income Tax," may be used in some states as an annual report by NFPs for reporting to both state and federal governments. Some states require an auditor's opinion on the financial statements included in an IRS Form 990 filed in the state. In most states, the report is used primarily to satisfy statutory requirements, but regulatory authorities may make the financial statements and the accompanying auditor's report a matter of public record. In other situations, there may be public distribution of the report.

14.24 As noted in paragraph .A5 of AU-C section 800, certain regulators, including state and local government legislators, regulatory agencies, or departments, require financial statements to be prepared in accordance with a financial reporting framework that is based on U.S. GAAP but does not comply with all of the requirements of U.S. GAAP. Such frameworks are regulatory bases of accounting, as defined in paragraph .07 of AU-C section 800. In some circumstances, however, the cash or tax basis of accounting may be permitted by a regulator. For purposes of AU-C section 800, the cash and tax bases of accounting are not regulatory bases of accounting. If the financial statements are not in conformity with GAAP, the auditor could consider whether the financial statements included in the prescribed form are prepared in accordance with a special purpose framework, such as the tax basis or the financial reporting provisions of a government regulatory agency (a regulatory basis of accounting). In an audit of financial statements prepared in accordance with a special purpose framework, paragraph .11 of AU-C section 800 requires that the auditor obtain the agreement of management that it acknowledges and understands its responsibility to include all informative disclosures that are appropriate for the special purpose framework used to prepare the entity's financial statements. If the prescribed form contains only a single financial statement or specific elements of a financial statement, the auditor should consider whether the application of the financial reporting framework will result in a presentation that provides adequate disclosures to enable the intended users to understand the information conveyed in the financial statement or the specific element and the effect of material transactions and events on the information conveyed in the financial statement or the specific element, as noted in paragraphs .11 and .A9 of AU-C section 805, *Special Considerations—Audits of Single Financial Statements and Specific Elements, Accounts, or Items of a Financial Statement*. The following example illustrates a report expressing an opinion on certain financial statements that are prepared in accordance with the instructions for Form 990 or 990 EZ and that are not accompanied by notes to financial statements:

Independent Auditor's Report

Report on the Financial Statements

We have audited the accompanying balance sheet (Part [*insert part number of Form 990 or 990EZ*]) of XYZ Charity as of December 31, 20XX, and the related statement of revenue, expenses, and changes in net assets (Part [*insert part number of Form 990 or 990EZ*]) and statement of functional expenses (Part [*insert part number of Form 990 or 990EZ*]) for the year then ended included in the accompanying Internal Revenue Service Form [*insert 990 or 990EZ*].

Management's Responsibility for the Financial Statements

Management is responsible for the preparation and fair presentation of these financial statements in accordance with the accounting practices prescribed by the Internal Revenue Service and the Office of the State of ....; this includes the design, implementation, and maintenance of internal control relevant to the preparation and fair presentation of financial statements that are free from material misstatement, whether due to fraud or error.

Auditor's Responsibility

Our responsibility is to express an opinion on these financial statements based on our audit. We conducted our audit in accordance with auditing standards generally accepted in the United States of America. Those standards require that we plan and perform the audit to obtain reasonable assurance about whether the financial statements are free from material misstatement.

An audit involves performing procedures to obtain audit evidence about the amounts and disclosures in the financial statements. The procedures selected depend on the auditor's judgment, including the assessment of the risks of material misstatement of the financial statements, whether due to fraud or error.

In making those risk assessments, the auditor considers internal control relevant to the entity's preparation and fair presentation of the financial statements in order to design audit procedures that are appropriate in the circumstances, but not for the purpose of expressing an opinion on the effectiveness of the entity's internal control. Accordingly, we express no such opinion. An audit also includes evaluating the appropriateness of accounting policies used and the reasonableness of significant accounting estimates made by management, as well as evaluating the overall presentation of the financial statements.

We believe that the audit evidence we have obtained is sufficient and appropriate to provide a basis for our audit opinion.

Opinion

In our opinion, the financial statements referred to above present fairly, in all material respects, the assets, liabilities, and net assets of XYZ Charity as of December 31, 20XX, and its revenue and expenses and changes in net assets for the year then ended on the basis of accounting described in the following paragraph.

Basis of Accounting

The financial statements are prepared in accordance with the accounting practices prescribed by the Internal Revenue Service and the Office of the State of ......, which is a basis of accounting other than accounting principles generally accepted in the United States of America. Our opinion is not modified with respect to this matter.

Restriction on Use

Our report is intended solely for the information and use of the board of directors and management of XYZ Charity, the Internal Revenue Service, and the Office of the State of ......, and is not intended to be and should not be used by anyone other than these specified parties.

Report on Other Legal and Regulatory Requirements

[*Form and content of this section of the auditor's report will vary depending on the nature of the auditor's other reporting responsibilities.*]

[*Signature*]

[*Auditor's city and state*]

[*Date*]

14.25 If special purpose financial statements are prepared in accordance with a regulatory basis of accounting and the special purpose financial statements together with the auditor's report are intended for general use (that is, the financial statements together with the auditor's report are intended for use by parties other than those within the NFP and the regulatory agencies to whose jurisdiction the NFP is subject or the financial statements together with the auditor's report are distributed by the NFP to parties other than the regulatory agencies to whose jurisdiction the NFP is subject, either voluntarily or upon specific request), the auditor should not include the emphasis-of-matter or other-matter paragraphs required by paragraphs .19–.20 of AU-C section 800. Instead, as required by paragraph .21 of AU-C section 800, the auditor should express an opinion about whether the special purpose financial statements are presented fairly, in all material respects, in accordance with GAAP. The auditor should also, in a separate paragraph, express an opinion about whether the financial statements are prepared in accordance with the special purpose framework.

Reports Required by *Government Auditing Standards*, the Single Audit Act Amendments of 1996, and the Uniform Guidance

14.26 *Government Auditing Standards*, the Single Audit Act Amendments of 1996, and Title 2 U.S. Code of Federal Regulations (CFR) Part 200, *Uniform Administrative Requirements, Cost Principles, and Audit Requirements for Federal Awards* (Uniform Guidance), broaden the auditor's responsibility to include reporting on not only an NFP's financial statements but also its internal control and its compliance with federal statutes, regulations, and the terms and conditions of federal awards. AICPA Audit Guide Government Auditing Standards *and Single Audits* describes and illustrates the required reports.

14.27 In addition, as stated in paragraph .11 of AU-C section 905, the report on internal control over financial reporting and on compliance and other matters and the report on compliance with requirements applicable to each major program and on the internal control over compliance, required by *Government Auditing Standards*, each require an alert in a separate paragraph to describe the purpose of the auditor's written communication and state that the auditor's written communication is not suitable for any other purpose. Interpretation No. 2, "Reporting on the Design of Internal Control" (AT-C sec. 9205 par. .04–.14), of AT-C section 205, *Examination Engagements*,[11] is relevant if an NFP applying for a government grant or contract is required to submit a written pre-award survey by management about the suitability of the design of the entity's internal control or a portion of the entity's internal control, together with a practitioner's report thereon.

14.28 The Uniform Guidance requires an auditor to determine and provide an opinion on whether the NFP's Schedule of Expenditures of Federal Awards (SEFA) is presented fairly in all material respects in relation to the financial statements as a whole (often referred to as providing an in-relation-to opinion). The Uniform Guidance, as applicable, does not specifically prescribe the basis of accounting to be used by the NFP to prepare the SEFA. Therefore, an NFP may present its SEFA on a basis of accounting that differs from that used to prepare its financial statements. The NFP is required to disclose the basis of accounting and the significant accounting policies used in preparing the SEFA.

14.29 Q&A section 9160.27, "Providing Opinion on a Schedule of Expenditures of Federal Awards in Relation to an Entity's Financial Statements as a Whole When the Schedule of Expenditures of Federal Awards Is on a Different Basis of Accounting Than the Financial Statements," provides guidance if the SEFA is prepared on a different basis of accounting than that of the financial statements. Paragraph .07*d* of AU-C section 725 requires that the auditor compare and reconcile the SEFA to the underlying accounting and other records

---

[11] All AT-C sections can be found in AICPA *Professional Standards*.

used in preparing the financial statements or to the financial statements themselves. If the SEFA can be reconciled to the underlying accounting and other records used in preparing the financial statements or to the financial statements themselves, the auditor may provide an opinion on whether the SEFA is presented fairly, in all material respects, in relation to the entity's financial statements as a whole.

14.30 Interpretation No. 1, "Reporting on Attestation Engagements Performed in Accordance With *Government Auditing Standards*" (AT-C sec. 9205 par. .01–.03), of AT-C section 205 indicates how a practitioner should modify the scope paragraph of an attestation report to indicate that an examination or review was "conducted in accordance with attestation standards established by the American Institute of Certified Public Accountants and the standards applicable to attestation engagements contained in *Government Auditing Standards* issued by the Comptroller General of the United States."

Chapter 15

Tax and Regulatory Considerations

Introduction

15.01 Some laws and regulations have a direct and significant effect on the determination of financial statement amounts. Other laws and regulations, when violated, have an effect on financial amounts because of resulting financial penalties. Management generally should identify federal, state, local, and foreign laws and regulations that may have a direct and material effect on the determination of financial statement amounts. The auditor should make inquiries of management concerning the client's compliance with laws and regulations. A not-for-profit entity's (NFP's) failure to maintain its tax-exempt status could have serious tax and financial consequences and affect both its financial statements and related disclosures, and it could possibly require modification of the auditor's report. Failure to comply with tax laws and regulations could be an illegal act that may, as discussed in chapter 2, "General Auditing Considerations," have either a direct and material effect on the determination of financial statement amounts (for example, the result of an incorrect accrual for taxes on unrelated business income) or a material indirect effect on the financial statements that would require appropriate disclosures (for example, the result of a potential loss of tax-exempt status).

15.02 The regulatory environment for NFPs is always changing and NFPs and their auditors run the risk of not remaining informed. The AICPA issues two helpful publications annually as a complement to this guide. For members of an NFP's financial management, governing board, and audit committee, the AICPA issues the Financial Reporting Alert *Not-for-Profit Entities: Accounting Issues and Risks*. For auditors, it issues the Audit Risk Alert *Not-for-Profit Entities Industry Developments*. These alerts provide an overview of economic and industry conditions, regulatory developments (including IRS developments), and recently issued accounting and auditing pronouncements that may affect NFPs.

15.03 This chapter discusses certain tax and regulatory considerations relevant to NFPs. It does not include a detailed discussion of the IRC or other laws and regulatory guidance, nor is it intended as a substitute for the appropriate research.

Internal Revenue Service

Basis of Exemption

15.04 The IRS determines whether an NFP qualifies for exemption from federal income tax. There are more than 25 different types of tax exemption. The following are some of the more common types of tax-exempt NFPs:

- Section 501(c)(3)—Corporations, united funds, other funds, and foundations organized and operated (*a*) exclusively for religious, charitable, scientific, testing-for-public-safety, literary, or educational purposes; (*b*) to foster national or international amateur sports competition; or (*c*) for the prevention of cruelty to children or animals

- Section 501(c)(4)—Civic leagues, NFPs operated exclusively for the promotion of social welfare (including certain war veterans' organizations), and certain local associations of employees
- Section 501(c)(5)—Labor, agricultural, and horticultural organizations
- Section 501(c)(6)—Business leagues, chambers of commerce, real estate boards, boards of trade, and professional football leagues that are not organized for profit
- Section 501(c)(7)—Social clubs organized for pleasure, recreation, and other not-for-profit purposes
- Section 501(c)(8)—Fraternal beneficiary societies, orders, associations, and so on that provide life, sick, accident, or other benefits to members
- Section 501(c)(10)—Domestic fraternal societies, orders, associations, and so on that do not provide life, sick, accident, or other benefits
- Section 501(c)(13)—Cemeteries, crematoria, and like corporations
- Section 501(c)(19)—A post, organization, auxiliary unit, and so on, of past or present members of the Armed Forces of the United States

15.05 The IRS considers all charitable organizations (that is, those that are tax-exempt under Section 501[c][3]) to be private foundations unless they qualify as public charities. The distinction is important because private foundations are subject to more restrictions under the tax laws, as discussed in paragraph 15.37. Per Section 509(a), a Section 501(c)(3) entity is classified as a public charity if it meets one of the following descriptions:

- Churches, hospitals, qualified medical research organizations affiliated with hospitals, schools, colleges, and universities.
- Entities formed exclusively for religious, charitable, scientific, testing for public safety, literary, or educational purposes, or to foster national or international amateur sports that normally receive a substantial portion of their support from direct or indirect contributions from many sources, including the general public, governmental agencies, corporations, private foundations, or other public charities.
- Entities that meet both of the following mechanical tests, based on actual support during the previous five years:
  - — The entity receives not more than one-third of its support from gross investment income.
  - — The entity receives more than one-third of its support from a combination of the following:
    - Contributions, gifts, grants, and membership fees, except when such support is received from disqualified persons.

  - Gross receipts from admissions, sale of merchandise, performance of services, or furnishing facilities, all of which must be derived from an activity related to the organization's exempt purpose. Excluded from the gross receipts are any amounts from any one person, governmental unit, or company in excess of $5,000 or 1 percent of total support (whichever is greater) and amounts received from disqualified persons.

- Entities that are organized, and at all times thereafter are operated, exclusively for the benefit of, to perform the functions of, or to carry out the purposes of one or more organizations described previously.

15.06 At the federal level, the IRS has the authority to revoke exemptions for any one of several reasons. Examples of potential threats to an NFP's federal tax-exempt status include, but are not limited to, the following:

- Material changes in the NFP's character, purpose, or method of operation
- Private inurement
- Private benefit
- Commerciality
- Lobbying
- Political campaign activities
- Unrelated business income
- Failure of the NFP to meet the commensurate test
- Violation of public policy by the NFP
- Failure to comply with annual reporting obligations

15.07 Noncompliance with federal and state tax laws and regulations may have direct and material effects on an NFP's financial statements. Noncompliance may also, possibly through the loss of the NFP's tax-exempt status, have indirect effects on the statements, such as causing violations of covenants of tax-exempt debt, affecting exemptions for property taxes and sales and use taxes, affecting the qualification of employee benefit plans, and so forth. Further, because many NFPs depend on their tax-exempt status for funding purposes and could lose their funding if that status was revoked, such indirect effects may also indicate that there is substantial doubt about the NFP's ability to continue as a going concern.

Material Changes in the NFP's Character, Purpose, or Method of Operation

15.08 The IRS requires that an NFP disclose on its annual information return (Form 990, "Return of Organization Exempt From Income Tax;" Form 990-EZ, "Short Form Return of Organization Exempt From Income Tax;" or Form 990-PF, "Return of Private Foundation or Section 4947[a][1] Nonexempt Charitable Trust Treated as a Private Foundation) any changes in the kinds of exempt activities the NFP conducts, any changes in its governing documents, and whether there has been a liquidation, dissolution, or substantial contraction. If an NFP is unsure about whether a proposed change in its purposes or activities is consistent with its status as a tax-exempt organization or as a public charity, it may request IRS guidance in a private letter ruling. An NFP may also request a determination letter to reclassify the NFP as a public charity or a private foundation.

Private Inurement and Private Benefit

15.09 NFPs are generally prohibited from making distributions to individuals who control or substantially support them financially. Private inurement rules regulate transactions between an NFP and insiders. *Insiders* are individuals with a personal or private interest in the NFP, such as governing board members, officers, certain employees, and substantial contributors. Transactions between insiders and NFPs are permitted, but the NFP has the burden of proving to the IRS that the transactions do not result in private inurement. The NFP must be able to prove that the transaction was reasonable, was adequately documented, had independent approval, and did not violate any law or regulation. Employee compensation can create an inurement problem if it is judged to be "unreasonably high." (Paragraphs 15.64–.67 discuss executive compensation.) IRC provisions are stricter for private foundations than for other NFPs. Paragraph 15.37 briefly discusses those more restrictive provisions.

15.10 The concept of private benefit prohibits an NFP from providing excessive benefits for the private interests of any specific individual or group—both insiders and outsiders. Incidental levels of private benefits are permitted, but the NFP is required to demonstrate that such benefits are a necessary concomitant of a public related benefit. The NFP generally should have sound policies for transactions with both insiders and outsiders, and these policies ordinarily should document that the transactions were appropriate and were approved by disinterested parties.

15.11 Intermediate sanctions legislation (IRC Section 4958), enacted in 1996, provides for monetary penalties of 25 percent or 200 percent of the excess benefit against certain individuals who are unjustly benefited at the expense of the NFP. The legislation applies to 501(c)(3) organizations (not including private foundations) and 501(c)(4) organizations. Before this statute was enacted, the only sanction available to the IRS for private inurement was revocation of exempt status, which the IRS was reluctant to impose except in cases of very serious violations. Consequently, lesser violations often went unpunished for lack of an appropriate remedy.

15.12 Under intermediate sanctions, certain individuals who, in general, are in a position of substantial influence with respect to the NFP are *disqualified persons*. Penalties of 10 percent of the excess benefit may be assessed against managers who participated in transactions resulting in excess benefit received by disqualified persons. Examples of excess benefit transactions include excessive compensation, purchases of goods and services at prices in excess of fair value, and sales of goods and services at prices less than fair value.

Commerciality

15.13 An NFP cannot qualify for tax exemption or can have its tax-exempt status revoked if it is, in reality, a commercial enterprise. Engaging in commercial activity, however, does not *per se* disqualify the NFP from tax-exempt status unless the commercial activity becomes the NFP's primary purpose. A gray area exists between commercial and noncommercial activities. To avoid problems with commerciality, many NFPs have found it advantageous to create separate for-profit subsidiaries. These for-profit subsidiaries must file commercial federal and state tax returns. They are also disclosed on Schedule R to the Form 990 of the related NFP.[1]

Lobbying

15.14 The IRC allows public charities (but not private foundations) to lobby to influence federal, state, and local legislation (including initiatives and referenda), but it places limits on how much lobbying they can do. The IRS uses two tests to determine whether lobbying is substantial: the substantial-part test or the expenditure test.

15.15 The *substantial-part test* is a subjective test that looks at all the pertinent facts and circumstances. It considers a variety of factors, including the time that both compensated and volunteer workers devote to lobbying and the expenditures the organization devotes to lobbying. Under this test, an NFP that conducts excessive lobbying in any taxable year may lose its tax-exempt status and may be subject to an excise tax on its lobbying expenditures for the year that it lost its tax-exempt status.

15.16 Alternatively, if an NFP is not a church or a private foundation, it can elect to have its lobbying activities measured using the expenditure test by making a Section 501(h) election. Under the expenditure test, a 501(c)(3)'s lobbying activity will not jeopardize its tax-exempt status so long as its expenditures related to that activity normally do not exceed an amount specified in IRC Section 4911. When electing to use this test, an NFP that engages in excessive lobbying over a four-year period may lose its tax-exempt status, making all its income for that period taxable. If the NFP exceeds its lobbying expenditure dollar limit in a particular year, it must pay an excise tax on the excess.

15.17 Membership organizations that are granted tax-exempt status under IRC Section 501(c)(4), (5), or (6) and lobby are required to make disclosures to their members regarding the portion of membership dues allocable to nondeductible lobbying expenses, as required by IRC Section 6033(e) or pay a proxy tax.

Political Campaign Activities

15.18 Public charities are prohibited from engaging in partisan political campaign activities—that is, directly or indirectly participating or intervening in any political campaign on behalf of, or in opposition to, any candidate for public office. IRS Publication 4221-PC, *Compliance Guide for 501(c)(3) Public Charities*, can be helpful in determining permitted and prohibited activities. Prohibited political activities include contributing to candidates or political organizations, including, for example, in-kind contributions of services, publicity, advertising, paid staff time, facilities, and office space. Also prohibited are (*a*) evaluating candidates and their positions if the NFP concentrates on a narrow range of issues of particular importance to the organization, and (*b*) encouraging voter registration for a specific political group. Certain voter education activities, including holding public forums and publishing voter education guides, are permissible if conducted in a nonpartisan way. In addition, activities intended to encourage people to participate in the electoral process, such as

[1] A for-profit subsidiary's transactions with its not-for-profit (NFP) parent can have unrelated business income tax consequences for the parent, as discussed in paragraph 15.30.

voter registration and "get-out-the-vote" drives, are also allowed if conducted in a nonpartisan way. Violation of the law can result in imposition of an excise tax, or in extreme cases, a loss of tax exempt status.

15.19 NFPs that are not Section 501(c)(3) public charities may be permitted to engage in a limited amount of political activities as long as that is not a primary activity. However, any expenditures the NFP makes for political activities may be subject to tax. A membership entity may establish and sponsor a political action committee (PAC) whose mission is to further the interests of the membership entity by engaging in political campaign activities. Consolidation of a PAC is discussed in paragraph 3.69 of this guide.

Unrelated Business Income

15.20 NFPs can lose their tax-exempt status if the IRS determines that the percentage of their income that is from business activities unrelated to their specific exempt purposes is excessive. There is, however, no specific percentage of unrelated business income defined by the IRS as too large a percentage. The facts and circumstances of each unrelated business income situation would be considered. Unrelated business income and the unrelated business income tax are discussed in more detail in paragraphs 15.28–.31.

Failure to Meet the Commensurate Test

15.21 An NFP can lose its tax-exempt status if it fails the commensurate test, which provides that the scope of the NFP's programs must be commensurate with its financial resources. The test requires that an NFP have a charitable program that is both real and, taking the NFP's circumstances and financial resources into account, substantial. This means that fund-raising expenses and administrative expenses should not be an excessive percentage of total expenses. Although no specific payout percentage has been established and individual facts and circumstances must be considered, low levels of program spending invite IRS scrutiny.

Violation of Public Policy

15.22 An NFP can also lose its tax exemption because it violates public policy. For example, a social club (that is, a section 501[c][7] organization) is not exempt from income tax if any written policy statement, including the governing instrument and bylaws, allows discrimination on the basis of race, color, or religion. A private school must annually file Form 5578, "Annual Certification of Racial Nondiscrimination for a Private School Exempt From Federal Income Tax," to provide the IRS with its certification that it does not discriminate against applicants and students on the basis of race, color, and national or ethnic origin.

Failure to Comply With Reporting Obligations

15.23 Almost all NFPs—even very small ones—have federal annual return or notice filing obligations. As described in Part B of the Form 990 instructions, certain religious organizations, certain government organizations, certain political organizations, and certain organizations that file different types of annual information returns are exempt from filing a Form 990, 990-EZ, 990-PF, or 990-N, "Electronic Notification (e-Postcard) For Tax-Exempt Organizations Not Required to File Form 990 or 990-EZ." Unless specifically exempted, each NFP is required to file Form 990, 990-EZ, 990-PF, or 990-N. For information on which form the NFP must file, see paragraph 15.24. There are consequences for failure to file. If an NFP does not file for three consecutive years, its tax exempt status will be revoked as of the filing due date for the third return. If tax-exempt status is revoked on this basis, the NFP must again apply for tax-exempt status.

IRS Filing Requirements

15.24 As noted in paragraph 15.23, most NFPs must file annual returns with the IRS. There are 3 returns for public charities—the one the charity files depends upon its gross receipts and total assets. Form 990 is filed by NFPs with gross receipts greater than or equal to $200,000 or total assets greater than or equal to $500,000 at the end of the tax year. Form 990-EZ is filed by NFPs with gross receipts less than $200,000 and total assets at the end of the tax year less than $500,000. NFPs that normally have $50,000 or less in gross receipts submit Form 990-N, unless they choose to file a complete Form 990 or Form 990-EZ. All private foundations file Form 990-PF.

15.25 The stated goals of the IRS for Form 990 are to enhance transparency, promote tax compliance, and minimize the burden on filing by NFPs. The form and its instructions are modified by the IRS annually. The basic structure of the form consists of a 12-page core form, which is to be completed by all filers, and 16 schedules designed by topic (lobbying, related parties, compensation, and so on). The form has a checklist that allows a preparer to determine which schedules are required for the NFP. In addition, the Form 990 includes the following:

- A summary page designed to provide a financial "snapshot" of the NFP
- Questions regarding organizational governance practices
- Disclosure of information from the NFP's audited financial statements
- Compensation information
- Disclosures regarding programs and activities of the NFP

15.26 E-filing of Form 990 and 990-PF is required for certain large NFPs. The electronic filing requirement applies to NFPs with $10 million or more in total assets if the NFP files at least 250 returns in a calendar year, including income, excise, employment tax, and information returns (such as Forms W-2 and 1099). Private foundations and nonexempt charitable trusts are required to file Form 990-PF electronically regardless of their asset size, if they file at least 250 returns annually. If an NFP is required to file a return electronically but does not, the NFP is considered not to have filed its return. All Forms 990-N are required to be electronically filed.

15.27 NFPs must provide a copy of their Form 990, Form 990-EZ, or Form 990-PF, and Form 1023, "Application for Recognition of Exemption under Section 501(c)(3) of the Internal Revenue Code," or Form 1024, "Application for Recognition of Exemption under Section 501(a)," to persons requesting it either in person or in writing. A reasonable charge may be made for copying. There are penalties for failure to make the forms available. Donor information on Schedule B, "Schedule of Contributors," is confidential except for private foundations and political organizations. Certain NFPs that file Form 990-T, "Unrelated Business Income Tax Return," must also provide a copy of that return, as discussed in paragraph 15.31.

Unrelated Business Income

15.28 Unrelated business income is gross income from an unrelated trade or business less expenses directly connected with the unrelated trade or business, certain net operating losses, and qualified charitable contributions. An unrelated trade or business of an exempt organization is any trade or business that is regularly carried on and whose conduct is not substantially related to the exercise or performance of its exempt purpose. The IRS is interested in how the unrelated business income was earned, not in how it is used. Thus, unrelated business income is taxable even if it is used to further the NFP's tax-exempt purpose. Unrelated business income is subject to tax at federal corporate rates, including the alternative minimum tax (or in some cases, trust tax rates). The first $1,000 of net unrelated business income is excluded from taxation, and corporate net operating losses carryforwards and various tax credits are allowed. Because the tax is an income tax, the requirements of FASB *Accounting Standards Codification* (ASC) 740, *Income Taxes*, should be applied by the NFP.

15.29 The unrelated-business-income tax requirements apply to all NFPs except (*a*) corporations that have been organized under Acts of Congress and that are instrumentalities of the United States and (*b*) certain charitable trusts not subject to the tax on private foundations.

15.30 Income from certain specified activities that might otherwise be considered unrelated business income is excluded from taxation. For example, unrelated business income does not include dividends, interest, royalties, certain rents from real property, and gains on the sale of property (except for inventory or dealer property). These exclusions generally do not apply to the extent the income is debt-financed. Unrelated business income also excludes income from activities in which substantially all of the work is done by volunteers, income from the sale of donated merchandise, and certain income from activities carried on for the convenience of members, students, patients, officers, or employees. Examples of activities that may produce unrelated business taxable income include the following:

- Advertising income
- Corporate sponsorship activities (in some cases)
- Income from investments in partnerships, subchapter S corporations, and certain other alternative investments that are pass-through entities for tax purposes
- Rents from debt-financed property
- Rents based on a percentage of net income rather than gross income
- Rents on personal property
- Unrelated debt-financed income
- Sales of items unrelated to the NFP's mission in gift shops, pro shops, online storefronts, and similar retail establishments
- The sale of products or services that are available because of excess capacity, such as banquet space and meals sold to the nonmembers by a country club or the sale of unused computer time

- Provision of goods and services that do not relate to the organization's exempt purposes (for example, management, administrative, and consulting services) to unrelated parties
- Interest, annuities, royalties, and rents from a controlled taxable corporation, if those items reduced the tax of the controlled corporation

15.31 Form 990-T and its related schedules are filed to report unrelated income taxes and to compute and remit the tax. 501(c)(3) organizations must make the return available to the public upon request for a period of three years from the date required to be filed (including extensions). All information must be made available unless specifically excluded by statute.

Alternative Investments

15.32 Some NFPs invest in hedge funds, private equity funds, real estate funds, venture capital funds, commodity funds, offshore fund vehicles, and funds of funds, which are commonly referred to as alternative investments. NFPs should be aware of supplementary tax filing responsibilities in connection with investments in these arrangements, which can include returns for unrelated business income tax (Form 990-T), transfers of tangible and nontangible property to a foreign corporation (Form 926), investment activity with foreign partnerships (Form 8865), investment activity with foreign corporations (Form 5471), reportable transactions (Form 8886), and reports of foreign bank accounts (Form TD F90-22.1). Penalties for noncompliance can be severe, so NFPs should be careful to comply with these requirements.

Tax Shelters

15.33 IRC Section 4965 imposes excise taxes and disclosure requirements on any tax-exempt entity (including a public charity, a private foundation, or other tax-exempt organization) that is a party to prohibited tax shelter transactions. In certain cases, penalties are also imposed on the tax-exempt entity's managers. Under the final regulations, issued in July 2010, a tax-exempt entity is a party to a prohibited tax shelter transaction if the entity (*a*) facilitates a prohibited tax shelter transaction by reason of its tax-exempt, tax indifferent, or tax-favored status, or (*b*) is identified in published guidance, by type, class, or role, as a party to a prohibited tax shelter transaction. The regulations provide (1) rules regarding the form, manner, and timing of disclosure obligations, and (2) return requirements accompanying payment of excise taxes.

Employment Taxes

15.34 Personnel costs easily constitute the single largest type of expense for many NFPs. In most ways, including the necessary tax filings, accounting for personnel costs is similar to for-profit entities. Employers do not have broad discretion over whether workers are classified as employees or independent contractors. The burden of proof generally falls to the NFP, and incorrect classifications can result in significant financial consequences. It is important to remember that neither the number of hours worked nor the amount paid affects the classification of a worker. The IRS methodology for distinguishing employees from independent contractors uses the three categories of behavioral control, financial control, and the type of relationship. Those categories provide evidence about the degree of control exercised by the NFP over the worker. IRS

Publication 15-A, *Employer's Supplemental Tax Guide*, provides guidance to help make the proper determination.

15.35 If an NFP has employees, it is responsible for federal income tax withholding and Social Security and Medicare taxes and state and local employment taxes. Section 501(c)(3) organizations are exempt from federal unemployment taxes; other NFPs must pay federal unemployment taxes. In some states, an NFP can elect not to pay into the state unemployment insurance fund. However, this leaves the NFP self-insured, and if an unemployment claim is successfully filed, the NFP will receive a large bill from the state.

15.36 To acknowledge beliefs against socialized insurance that are held by certain religious organizations, Congress provided an elective exemption from social security taxes for churches, including church-controlled organizations and associations and conventions of churches. An objection based on religious beliefs is the only valid reason for making the election. The election must be made by the due date of the church's initial quarterly payroll tax return (Form 941) after hiring a nonminister employee. Thus, unless the church is newly created or made the election in the past, the election is not available. The election by the church does not relieve church employees from paying Social Security taxes; they pay self-employment taxes on their income, although they are employees for all other purposes.

Private Foundations

15.37 Private foundations are subject to more restrictions under the tax law than are public charities. These restrictions include statutory prohibitions against self-dealing, excess business holdings, jeopardy investments, failing to distribute income, and taxable expenditures. In addition, private foundations are subject to an excise tax on their net investment income and are required to make annual distributions of 5 percent of the average market value of their noncharitable-use assets for charitable, educational, scientific, and similar purposes. (Noncharitable-use assets are assets that are not used or held for use directly in carrying on the NFP's exempt purpose; they include assets held for investment and the production of investment income.) The effects of program-related investments on the excise tax calculation are discussed briefly in paragraph 8.70.

15.38 Excise tax is paid on net investment income and is determined in accordance with IRC Section 4940. Although practice is mixed concerning whether the excise tax is an income tax, the Financial Reporting Executive Committee (FinREC) believes that best practice is to follow the requirements of FASB ASC 740. Thus, temporary differences for capital gains and losses may result in deferred tax assets and liabilities. Deferred tax assets and liabilities are discussed further in paragraphs 15.44–.45.

Income Tax Positions

15.39 NFPs adopt many tax positions relative to tax laws, including those adopted in determining whether tax is due, a refund is owed, or a tax return needs to be filed. Tax considerations may result in an NFP (or its for-profit or not-for-profit subsidiaries) taking a tax position pertaining to whether a transaction or event must be reported in a tax return. The FASB ASC glossary defines *tax position* as a position in a previously filed tax return or a position expected to be taken in a future tax return that is reflected in measuring current or deferred income tax assets and liabilities for interim or annual periods. A tax position can result in a permanent reduction of income taxes payable, a deferral of income taxes otherwise currently payable to future years, or a change in the expected realizability of deferred tax assets. A tax position also can result in or affect the measurement of a current or deferred tax asset or liability in the statement of financial position. The term *tax position* encompasses, but is not limited to, the following:

- A decision to classify a transaction, entity, or other position in a tax return as tax exempt or subject to a lower rate of tax
- A decision not to file a tax return, such as a decision that a Form 990T need not be filed
- The characterization of income, such as a characterization of income as passive, or a decision to exclude reporting taxable income in a tax return
- The characterization of an expense as deductible
- An allocation or a shift of income between jurisdictions (federal, state, local, or foreign)
- An entity's status, including its status as a tax-exempt NFP

15.40 The following are among possible tax positions of NFPs:

- That the organization is exempt from federal income taxes.
- Aspects of the definition of *unrelated business income* are subject to judgment concerning whether an activity is considered a "trade or business," is "unrelated" to the NFP's exempt purpose, and is "regularly carried on."
- Whether activities are exceptions from unrelated business income tax—because they are carried on largely by volunteers, involve selling of donated merchandise, or are carried on for the convenience of members, students, patients— is subject to interpretation.
- A change in an NFP's activities over time may cause an NFP to claim that certain activities are related to their exempt purposes but the activity bears little relation to the exempt activities for which it was granted exempt status.
- Once a source of unrelated business income is identified, there may be uncertainty in computing the amount of gross income from the activity or in allocating expenses for personnel costs, occupancy, administrative expenses, and so forth.
- NFPs that have multistate operations or employees may have state nexus and may be required to file state returns. Similarly, NFPs that have operations via partnership investments in other states may be required to file state returns for unrelated business income tax.
- NFPs with foreign operations may not have researched whether tax filings and payments are required by foreign jurisdictions.

15.41 The validity of a tax position is a matter of tax law. In some cases, the law is subject to varied interpretation and whether a tax position will ultimately be sustained may be uncertain. FASB ASC 740-10-25-6, which applies to income taxes, limits the recognition of tax positions to only the financial statement effects of a tax position when it is more likely than not, based on the technical merits, that the position will be sustained upon examination.

15.42 FASB ASC 740-10-55-225 provides examples of tax positions to be considered if an NFP enters into transactions that may be subject to income tax on unrelated business income. If an NFP has unrecognized tax benefits (that is, if a liability is created because the amount of benefit recognized in the statement of financial position differs from the amount taken or expected to be taken in the Form 990-T or any other income tax return for the current year), FASB ASC 740-10-50-15 requires that entities disclose the amounts of income tax-related interest and penalties recognized in the statement of activities, the total amounts of interest and penalties recognized in the statement of financial position, information about positions for which it is reasonably possible that the total amounts of unrecognized tax benefits will significantly increase or decrease within 12 months of the reporting date, and a description of tax years that remain subject to examination by major tax jurisdictions. FASB ASC 740-10-50-15A requires additional disclosures of NFPs that are public entities. Although information returns, including the Form 990, are not within the scope of FASB ASC 740 because they are not income tax returns, FinREC encourages disclosure of relevant information required by FASB ASC 740-10-50-15.

15.43 If an NFP's financial statements for a tax year include a note addressing the NFP's liability for unrecognized tax benefits under FASB ASC 740-10-50, the NFP must provide the text of that note, verbatim, in Schedule D of Form 990. This requirement includes, for example, the description of a liability for unrelated business income tax, or tax that may be assessed as a result of the revocation of exempt status. The instructions to Schedule D of Form 990 state that the full text of the note is required, even if the NFP did not report any liability for uncertain tax positions.

Deferred Tax Assets and Liabilities

Ⓤ Update 15-1 *Accounting and Reporting*: Classification of Deferred Taxes

FASB Accounting Standards Update (ASU) No. 2015-17, *Income Taxes (Topic 740): Balance Sheet Classification of Deferred Taxes*, issued November 2015, is effective for NFPs for fiscal years are effective for financial statements issued for annual periods beginning after December 15, 2017, and interim periods within annual periods beginning after December 15, 2018. Early adoption is permitted.

The "Pending Content" in FASB ASC 740-10-45-4 states that in a classified statement of financial position, an entity should classify deferred tax liabilities and assets as noncurrent amounts.

This edition of the guide has not been updated to reflect changes as a result of this ASU; however, the section that follows will be updated in a future edition. Readers are encouraged to consult the full text of the ASU on FASB's website at www.fasb.org.

15.44 Although NFPs are generally tax-exempt under various IRC sections,[2] some may be subject to taxes on various portions of their income, such as federal excise taxes on investment income or federal and state income taxes on unrelated business income. FASB ASC 740 provides guidance on recognizing (*a*) the amount of taxes payable (or refundable) for the current year and (*b*) deferred-tax liabilities (and assets) for the estimated future tax consequences of temporary differences and carryforwards.

15.45 An NFP may be required by FASB ASC 740-10 to report a deferred tax asset or liability for the estimated future tax effects attributable to temporary differences or net operating loss carryforwards for unrelated business income. If an NFP incurs unrelated business income tax, they may have deferred tax liabilities related to items such as those described in paragraphs 18–29 of FASB ASC 740-10-25. Although practice is mixed regarding whether the excise tax is an income tax, FinREC believes that the excise taxes on unrealized gains and losses for investments of private foundations should also be considered temporary differences for which deferred tax assets and liabilities should be recognized in accordance with FASB ASC 740-10.

State and Local Regulations

State Charitable Solicitation Laws

15.46 NFPs are generally subject to the laws of the state of incorporation as well as the laws of states in which they conduct significant activities. Each state has its own laws that govern exemption from its taxes, and those laws provide the applicable definitions and requirements. Exemptions may be available for state and local sales, real estate, and other taxes and vary from state to state.

15.47 Most states have regulatory bodies that oversee NFPs and can revoke an NFP's state tax-exempt status (without regard to its federal tax-exempt status) and prevent the NFP from operating in that state. Most states require NFPs to register and submit annual filings. These requirements are based on one of the following criteria:

- Registration requirements for NFPs (and their paid solicitors) soliciting funds within the state
- Registration of NFPs (including trusts) holding property in the state
- Registration of entities doing business in the state

15.48 An internet site maintained by the National Association of State Charity Officials (NASCO) and the National Association of Attorneys General (www.multistatefiling.org) provides information with regard to individual state registration and reporting requirements. The information appears with the Unified Registration Statement, a form that is used in most states for filings. Some states require information in addition to the Unified Registration

---

[2] Some NFPs may meet the definition of an NFP as discussed in paragraphs 1.01–.02 but may nevertheless not be tax-exempt under the IRC. For example, an NFP that may otherwise qualify for tax-exempt status under the IRC may lose its tax exemption because it has violated the private inurement rules applicable to tax-exempt entities. Examples of potential threats to an NFP's federal tax-exempt status are discussed in paragraphs 15.06–.23.

Statement, such as submission of annual financial statements. Some states accept a copy of the NFP's information return (discussed in paragraph 15.23) as a filing document, although some states require audited financial statements.

15.49 The application of those individual state registration requirements to NFPs that fund-raise over the internet is addressed by The Charleston Principles. Those principles, developed by NASCO, are a guide to state regulators regarding when NFPs and their fund-raisers may be required to register, in what jurisdictions they may be required to register, and when they may be subject to enforcement action when fund-raising is conducted via the internet. States are encouraged to use the principles to implement their specific state laws, but they are not binding on state regulators. The Charleston Principles can be found at www.nasconet.org.

State and Local Gaming Regulations

15.50 Most states and local jurisdictions have laws about the conduct of raffles, bingo, casino nights, pull-tabs, and other games of chance conducted for fund-raising purposes. In many areas, there may be more than one governmental body that has jurisdiction over gaming. It is advisable to check with both the state and local governments far in advance of hosting a gaming event because the process of obtaining any necessary licenses and permits can be complex or time-consuming or both.

Uniform Prudent Management of Institutional Funds Act

15.51 The Uniform Prudent Management of Institutional Funds Act (UPMIFA) is the law in all states except Pennsylvania for the management of donor-restricted endowment funds. This law affects the classification of the net assets of endowment funds and their investment income, gains, and losses. UPMIFA is a uniform act developed by the Uniform Law Commission (the National Conference of Commissioners on Uniform State Laws) to do three things: provide guidance on the management and investment of charitable funds; provide rules on spending from endowment funds; and provide rules on when and how a charity can release or modify a restriction imposed by a donor. UPMIFA supports two general principles: (*a*) assets should be invested prudently in diversified investments that seek growth as well as income, and (*b*) investments may prudently be spent for the purposes of the endowment fund held by a charitable institution. The discussion in this chapter is based upon UPMIFA, but each state enacts its own version of the law and may make changes to UPMIFA's language. Therefore, an NFP should consult its own state law to determine if there were changes, and it may wish to consult legal counsel.

15.52 When a donor directs a charity to "spend only the income" from a gift or to "hold this gift as an endowment," the donor has created a donor-restricted endowment. But the donor's instructions for the administration of the endowment are usually incomplete (and this is done purposely to allow for flexibility in a fund of perpetual duration). When a donor and a charity have not reached a specific agreement for management of an endowment, then the state law will apply.

15.53 UPMIFA provides a standard of conduct for managing and investing institutional funds. It requires investment "in good faith and with the care an ordinarily prudent person in a like position would exercise under similar circumstances." It requires prudence in incurring investment costs, authorizing "only costs that are appropriate and reasonable in relation to the assets, the purposes of the institution, and the skills available to the institution." UPMIFA emphasizes that in making decisions about whether to acquire or retain an asset, the institution should consider the institution's mission, its current programs, and the desire to cultivate additional donations from a donor, in addition to factors related more directly to the asset's potential as an investment, such as the expected tax consequences, if any, of investment decisions or strategies. No investment decision may be made in isolation, but must be made in light of the institution's entire portfolio, and "as a part of an overall investment strategy having risk and return objectives reasonably suited to the fund and to the institution."

15.54 UPMIFA provides guidance for prudent spending of a donor-restricted endowment fund. It states that the institution "may appropriate for expenditure or accumulate so much of an endowment fund as the institution determines to be prudent for the uses, benefits, purposes and duration for which the endowment fund is established." Seven criteria guide the institution in its annual expenditure decisions:

- Duration and preservation of the endowment fund
- The purposes of the institution and the endowment fund
- General economic conditions
- Possible effect of inflation or deflation
- The expected total return from income and the appreciation of investments
- Other resources of the institution
- The investment policy of the institution

15.55 UPMIFA also provides the following four methods for removal or modification of donor-imposed restrictions on the management, investment or purpose of an endowment fund.

- An institution can remove or modify a restriction provided that the donor consents in writing (or other record) and that any new purpose for the fund is a charitable purpose of the institution.
- An institution can ask the court to modify a donor's restriction if the restriction has become impracticable or wasteful, if it impairs the management or investment of the fund, or if, because of circumstances not anticipated by the donor, a modification of a restriction will further the purposes of the fund.
- An institution can ask the court to modify a donor's restriction for the purpose of a fund if the purpose becomes unlawful, impracticable, impossible to achieve, or wasteful.
- An institution may release or modify a donor's restriction on its own for small funds that have existed for a substantial period of time. The size of the fund and the period of time are specified in the state's law.

In each case except for the first (direct contact with the donor), the institution must notify an official named in the law (generally the state's Attorney General) of the desire to remove or modify the restriction, and the official must be given an opportunity to respond. (In effect, the official represents the donor's interests.) To the extent practicable, any modification is to be consistent with the donor's probable intention.

15.56 Chapter 4, "Cash, Cash Equivalents, and Investments," discusses how state law affects the classification of the net assets of an endowment fund and its investment income, gains, and losses.

Securities Regulation

15.57 NFPs engage in a wide variety of activities that may involve the issuance of securities. They might issue notes, bonds, and other debt instruments to raise funds for general operations or for the construction or purchase of churches, schools, hospitals, retirement homes, or other facilities. Some NFPs, most commonly church extension funds and other religious organizations, might issue taxable bonds for the purpose of raising capital for the construction of churches and the support of other entities affiliated with the denomination. Others may accept contributions in the form of split-interest agreements. In some cases, a group of NFPs may pool their funds for common investment. All of these activities may require NFPs to comply with securities laws.

15.58 Federal and state governmental agencies generally attempt to avoid regulation of nonprofit entities by granting the entities privileges and exemptions not available to others. The Philanthropy Protection Act of 1995 exempts NFPs from regulation by the SEC in most cases, although anti-fraud provisions always apply. However, some states have securities or insurance regulations that apply to the transactions in the previous paragraph. NFPs must look to the laws and rules of each state in which they have activity to determine the applicable requirements. Some states require a registration of nonprofit offerings; a few require the NFP to register as a broker-dealer or issuer-dealer.

15.59 In some states, the acceptance of split-interest agreements, especially charitable gift annuities, may be regulated and overseen by the state's department of insurance or a similar department. States may require registration to offer such products to donors, may require annual reports to be filed, and may limit the types of investments such agreements can hold. The American Council on Gift Annuities maintains a website (www.acga-web.org) that has links to the states' laws.

15.60 The SEC oversees the municipal bond market, in which colleges, universities, and other NFPs actively participate. Some NFPs—either on their own or through conduit debt issued by state government authorities—issue public debt. Appendix A, "Municipal Securities Regulation," of chapter 10, "Debt and Other Liabilities," discusses municipal securities regulation, and paragraphs 10.54–.58 discuss IRS considerations for tax-exempt bonds.

Sarbanes Oxley and Governance Policies

15.61 The Public Company Accounting Reform and Investor Protection Act (commonly referred to as the Sarbanes-Oxley Act or SOX) requires that publicly traded companies adhere to significant governance standards, which are intended to raise the bar for integrity and competence for publicly traded companies. Its effect has also promoted greater accountability within the nonprofit and private sectors. Although nearly all of the provisions of SOX apply only to publicly traded companies, many NFPs have adopted policies and altered governance practices in response to the Act. Two provisions of SOX specifically apply to all entities, including NFPs:

- SOX expanded protection for whistle-blowers and created criminal penalties for entities retaliating against individuals who expose actual or potential conduct of a federal offense.
- SOX criminalized the alteration, destruction, concealment, or falsification of documents when the intent is to interfere with an official investigation, contemplated or active, or a judicial proceeding.

15.62 Partially in reaction to SOX and partially in reaction to reform efforts of the U.S. Senate Finance Committee, the Panel on the Nonprofit Sector, convened by the Independent Sector, developed a publication, *Principles for Good Governance and Ethical Practice: A Guide for Charities and Foundations*. The publication, which is available at https://independentsector.org/programs/principles-for-good-governance-and-ethical-practice/, outlines 33 practices designed to support board members and staff leaders as they work to improve their operations and strengthen governance, transparency, and ethical standards. The publication is not authoritative, but it does provide best practices for governance as developed via a rigorous due process.

15.63 The IRS has also issued a publication on governance policies and practices, which is available on its website (www.irs.gov) as part of its Life Cycle of a Public Charity. The publication discusses the following six topics: mission, organizational documents, governing body, governance and management policies, financial statements and Form 990 reporting, and transparency and accountability.

Executive Compensation

15.64 Executive compensation is an area of significant focus and concern for NFPs, partly due to a public perception that large executive salaries are incompatible with charitable activity, which can make even reasonable compensation front-page news, harming the reputation of the NFP and its ability to attract support. If compensation is excessive, an NFP's tax exempt status may be in jeopardy due to private inurement, and the IRS views unreasonable compensation as an excess benefit transaction, which can result in excise tax penalties (paragraphs 15.09–.12). Compensation of governing board members, officers, and certain employees is included in the Form 990, Form 990-EZ, or Form 990-PF information return filed by the NFP, as is the number of individuals who were paid more than $100,000 in compensation. Because the return is a public document (refer to paragraph 15.27), compensation can't be considered a private matter.

15.65 Compensation included in the information returns includes all compensation that was reported (or should have been reported) on Form W-2 or Form 1099, including salaries, bonuses, and taxable fringe benefits, as well as other forms of compensation described in the instructions to Form 990. The IRS Publication 15-B, *Employer's Tax Guide to Fringe Benefits*, is useful for determining whether fringe benefits should be included as compensation. In the instructions to the Form 990 and Form 990-EZ, the IRS describes three specific procedures that an NFP must follow if it wants to establish a rebuttable presumption that compensation is reasonable. Payments under a compensation arrangement are presumed to be reasonable if the following three conditions are met:

- The transaction is approved by an authorized body of the NFP that is composed of individuals who do not have a conflict of interest concerning the transaction.
- Before making its determination, the authorized body obtained and relied upon appropriate data as to comparability.
- The authorized body adequately documents the basis for its determination concurrently with making the determination. The documentation must contain the information required by the Treasury regulations.

15.66 Compensation and benefits that do not comply with these procedures are referred to as automatic excess benefit transactions. To be protected by the rebuttable presumption, a governing board (or other authorized body) must document the various types of salary, bonuses, and benefits paid to the individual, its intent to include them in compensation, and that it considered them when determining that compensation was reasonable. Care must be taken to include all types of compensation required to be reported, because if an individual receives a taxable benefit that should have been reported as compensation but was not, the amount will be treated automatically as an excess benefit transaction, even if the total compensation including the unreported item would have been reasonable.

15.67 NFPs commonly use a combination of qualified and nonqualified retirement plans as a part of compensation, including defined benefit plans, 403(b) plans, 401(k) plans, 457 plans, and nonqualified deferred compensation plans (such as rabbi trust arrangements). Those plans, like those used by for-profit entities, are subject to complex rules and reporting requirements under the Department of Labor, the IRS, or both.

Other Regulatory Activities

U.S. Department of the Treasury Anti-Terrorist Financing Guidelines: Voluntary Best Practices for U.S.-Based Charities

15.68 An executive order signed on November 13, 2001, and the Uniting and Strengthening America by Providing Appropriate Tools Required to Intercept and Obstruct Terrorism Act of 2001 (USA Patriot Act) prohibit transactions with individuals and organizations deemed to be associated with terrorism. The executive order allows the federal government to freeze all assets controlled by or in the possession of the terrorist entities and those who support them, including during the investigation of the alleged association. The Patriot Act imposes fines, imprisonment, or both to any individual or entity that provides or helps conceal material support or resources knowing or intending that they are to be used in preparation for, or in carrying out, terrorist acts. In addition, the Patriot Act gives private parties a civil cause of action against those who provide material or financial support for terrorism. The United States relies on this executive order and a wide variety of federal criminal statutes in fighting terrorism.

15.69 From the government's perspective, the onus is on grantmakers to understand the counter-terrorism measures in effect and to ensure that grants they make do not end up unintentionally in the hands of terrorists. Two publications are especially helpful to NFPs that attempt to comply with the federal requirements related to anti-terrorist financing:

- U.S. Department of the Treasury *Anti-Terrorist Financing Guidelines: Voluntary Best Practices for U.S.-Based Charities*, a report issued in 2006 that is designed to assist charities that attempt in good faith to protect themselves from terrorist abuse.
- *Principles of International Charity*, a report issued by a working group of more than 40 charities and the Council on Foundations, in response to concerns about the practicality of the Treasury's guidelines and their effectiveness and potential to discourage international charitable activities by U.S. organizations.

15.70 Adherence to the guidelines in either of these reports is voluntary, and following the Treasury guidelines does not constitute a legal defense against any civil or criminal liability for violating any local, state, or federal laws or regulations. Instead, the measures are intended to build upon preexisting controls and protective measures already in place to assist in compliance with the laws.

Auditing

15.71 As stated in paragraph .12 of AU-C section 250, *Consideration of Laws and Regulations in an Audit of Financial Statements*,[3] the auditor should obtain a general understanding of the legal and regulatory framework applicable to the entity and the industry or sector in which the entity operates and how the entity is complying with that framework. An example of this would include the consideration of applicable tax laws that could affect a nonprofit's filing status or tax accruals.

15.72 Many audit objectives and auditing procedures, including consideration of controls, related to the tax provisions and liabilities of NFPs are similar to those of other entities. In addition, the auditor may need to consider the specific audit objectives, auditing procedures, and selected controls listed in the table in paragraph 15.73 that are unique to NFPs.

15.73 The following table illustrates the use of assertions in developing audit objectives and designing substantive tests. The examples are not intended to be all-inclusive, nor is it expected that all the procedures would necessarily be applied in an audit. The use of assertions in assessing risks and designing appropriate audit procedures to obtain audit evidence is described in paragraphs .26–.32 of AU-C section 315, *Understanding the Entity and Its Environment and Assessing the Risks of Material Misstatement*. Paragraph .18 of AU-C section 330, *Performing Audit Procedures in Response to Assessed Risks and Evaluating the Audit Evidence Obtained*, requires the auditor to design and perform substantive procedures for all relevant assertions related to each material class of transactions, account balance, and disclosure, irrespective of the assessed risks of material misstatement. This requirement reflects the facts that (1) the auditor's assessment of risk is judgmental and may not identify all risks of material misstatement, and (2) inherent limitations to internal control exist, including management override. Various audit procedures and the purposes for which they may be performed are described in paragraphs .A10–.A26 of AU-C section 500, *Audit Evidence*.

---

[3] All AU-C sections can be found in AICPA *Professional Standards*.

Auditing Considerations

Financial Statement Assertions	*Specific Audit Objectives*	*Select Control Objectives*
Account Balances		
Completeness; Valuation	All liabilities and contingencies for taxes due and uncertainty in income taxes for the current and prior years are accrued using applicable tax rates, or disclosed, respectively.	Computations of current and deferred tax assets and/or liabilities, and preparation of tax returns are performed and reviewed by knowledgeable personnel.
Presentation and Disclosure		
Rights and Obligations; Classification and Understandability	The not-for-profit entity (NFP) has obtained qualifying tax exemptions from the appropriate government authorities.	Management monitors compliance with applicable tax regulations.
Completeness	The NFP's tax-exempt status, taxes, interest, penalties, any tax contingencies, and positions for which it is reasonably possible that the total amounts of unrecognized tax benefits will significantly increase or decrease within 12 months of the reporting date, are disclosed in the notes to the financial statements.	

15.74 Suggested audit procedures to consider include the following:

- Ascertain whether the NFP has been granted tax-exempt status from the IRS and applicable states by reviewing the determination letter. (Rights and Obligations, Classification and Understandability)
- Review minutes of governing board meetings for changes in the NFP's governing instruments that could affect its tax-exempt status. (Rights and Obligations, Classifications and Understandability)

- Consider the effect of new, expanded, or unusual activities on the NFP's tax-exempt status. (Rights and Obligations, Classifications and Understandability)
- Consider the possibility that the IRS could successfully challenge the NFP's tax-exempt status because of issues such as those discussed in paragraphs 15.06–.23. (Rights and Obligations, Classifications and Understandability)
- Inquire if federal, state, and local tax returns (such as information returns [paragraph 15.23], income tax returns, excise tax returns, and employment tax returns) have been filed on a timely basis. (Completeness)
- Review tax returns or filings and related correspondence for all open years. (Completeness)
- Review revenue agent's reports, if any, for evidence of additional liabilities or contingencies. (Completeness)
- Review minutes of governing board and governing board committee meetings and the accounting records for evidence of significant unrelated business income. (Completeness)
- Review any Schedule K-1s received by the NFP to determine if activities reported thereon generate unrelated business income. (Completeness)
- Review the reasonableness of the computation of any unrelated business income tax liability. (Accuracy/Valuation)
- Inquire about how the NFP identifies whether it conducts activities in jurisdictions requiring registration. Registration may be necessary if the NFP provides services within another state, incurs payroll within another state, conducts solicitations within another state, and so forth. (Completeness)
- Determine whether the NFP's tax-exempt status, taxes, interest, penalties, any tax contingencies, and positions for which it is reasonably possible that the total amounts of unrecognized tax benefits will significantly increase or decrease within 12 months of the reporting date are appropriately disclosed in the notes to the financial statements as required by FASB ASC 740-10-50. (Completeness, Understandability)
- Review private foundation excise tax returns to determine the reasonableness of the computation of any excise tax, and determine that the disclosures required by FASB ASC 740-10-50 are provided, if appropriate. (Completeness, Understandability)

Chapter 16

Fund Accounting

Gray shaded text in this chapter reflects guidance issued but not yet effective as of the date of this guide, March 1, 2018, but becoming effective on or prior to June 30, 2018, exclusive of any option to early adopt ahead of the mandatory effective date. Unless otherwise indicated, all unshaded text reflects guidance that was already effective as of the date of this guide.

Introduction

16.01 Many not-for-profit entities (NFPs) use fund accounting for internal recordkeeping, even though fund accounting is not required by generally accepted accounting principles (GAAP). Fund accounting segregates assets, liabilities, and fund balances into separate accounting entities associated with specific activities, donor-imposed restrictions, or objectives; thus it can be used to track an NFP's fiduciary responsibilities to use assets in accordance with donor-imposed restrictions, legal and contractual limitations, and internal designations. The financial reporting model for NFPs also focuses on an NFP's fiduciary responsibilities, but it differs from fund accounting because it is based on net assets, reflects only donor-imposed restrictions in its classification of net assets, and requires an NFPs' external financial reporting to focus on aggregate information about the entity as a whole, rather than on individual funds.[1] FASB *Accounting Standards Codification* (ASC) 958-205-45-3 permits the continued disclosure, for external financial reporting purposes, of disaggregated data classified by fund groups, provided that the information required by GAAP is presented. This chapter provides an overview of fund accounting and discusses the reporting of information derived from an internal fund accounting system in conformity with the reporting requirements of the financial reporting model for NFPs.[2]

Fund Accounting and External Financial Reporting

16.02 *Fund accounting* is a system of recording resources whose use may be limited by donors, granting agencies, governing boards, other individuals or entities, or by law. To keep records of these limitations for internal purposes, NFPs that use fund accounting maintain separate funds for specific purposes. Each fund consists of a self-balancing set of asset, liability, and fund balance accounts. Prior to 1996, most NFPs prepared fund accounting-based external financial statements by combining funds with similar characteristics into fund groups.

[1] Both fund balances and net assets represent residual interests in assets less liabilities. Fund balances, however, are not the same as net asset balances.

[2] The timing of recognition of changes in net assets under fund accounting and the net asset model may differ. For example, restrictions may expire under the net asset model in different periods than when expenses are reported in a fund. Accordingly, not-for-profit entities that continue to use fund accounting for internal recordkeeping purposes should generally keep records of all transactions and events that have been recognized under one model but not the other and should adjust opening fund accounting balances to amounts representing opening net assets.

16.03 For external financial reporting purposes, the total of all assets and liabilities included in all funds and changes in net assets should be measured and reported on an NFP's financial statements in conformity with FASB ASC 958, *Not-for-Profit Entities*. Fund balances should be classified on a statement of financial position based on the existence and type of donor-imposed restrictions.[3] Because of differences in the types of limitations a fund accounting system tracks, for external financial reporting purposes, a fund balance may have to be divided among more than one net asset class.

16.04 FASB ASC 958-210-45-2 states that the requirement to display total assets and liabilities results in certain practical limits on how interfund items are displayed in a financial statement. For example, because receivables and payables between fund groups are not assets or liabilities of the reporting entity, a statement of financial position should clearly label and arrange those interfund items to eliminate their amounts when displaying total assets or liabilities.

16.05 The remainder of this chapter describes seven commonly used groups of funds and discusses how their fund balances would be reported based on the requirements of FASB ASC 958.

Unrestricted Current (or Unrestricted Operating or General) Funds

16.06 Unrestricted current funds (also called unrestricted operating or general funds) are used to record an NFP's activities that are supported by resources over which governing boards have discretionary control. Amounts designated by governing boards for specific purposes may be included in unrestricted current funds, or those amounts may be accounted for in other funds, such as plant funds, endowment funds, and loan funds. The principal sources of unrestricted current funds are exchange transactions with members, clients, students, customers, and others; and contributions and investment income that are not subject to donor-imposed restrictions or laws that extend donor restrictions. The resources of unrestricted current funds are used to help meet the costs of providing the NFP's programs and supporting services.

16.07 Fund balances of unrestricted current funds should be classified on a statement of financial position as "unrestricted net assets." If the fund balances include some donor-restricted resources, they should be separated into unrestricted net assets and temporarily restricted net assets. For example, if the unrestricted current funds include unconditional promises to give that are for the general support of the NFP, the net assets associated with those promises should be included in temporarily restricted net assets if the promises are subject to time restrictions. In accordance with FASB ASC 958-210-50-2, significant limits on the use of unrestricted current funds that result from contractual agreements with suppliers, creditors, and others should be disclosed on the face of the financial statements or in the notes to the financial statements. Unrestricted current fund balances that have been designated by governing bodies for specific purposes [such as quasi endowment (funds functioning as endowment), funds for long-term investment, self-insurance reserve funds, or future development funds] should be classified as unrestricted net

---

[3] Accounting for contributions received with donor-imposed restrictions is discussed in chapter 5, "Contributions Received and Agency Transactions," of this guide.

assets. The net assets of board-designated endowment funds are required to be disclosed per FASB ASC 958-205-50-1B; other board designations are permitted to be disclosed, as discussed in chapters 3, "Financial Statements, the Reporting Entity, and General Financial Reporting Matters," and 11, "Net Assets and Reclassifications of Net Assets."

Fund balances of unrestricted current funds should be classified on a statement of financial position as net assets without donor restrictions. However, if the fund balances include some donor-restricted resources, they should be separated into net assets without donor restrictions and net assets with donor restrictions. For example, if the unrestricted current funds include unconditional promises to give that are for the general support of the NFP, the net assets associated with those promises should be included in net assets with donor restrictions if the promises are subject to time restrictions. In accordance with FASB ASC 958-210-50-2, significant limits on the use of unrestricted current funds that result from contractual agreements with suppliers, creditors, and others should be disclosed on the face of the financial statements or in the notes to the financial statements. (That information may be included in qualitative disclosures on the availability of an NFP's financial assets in accordance with the "Pending Content" in FASB ASC 958-210-50-1A(b)). Unrestricted current fund balances that have been designated by governing bodies for specific purposes [such as quasi endowment (funds functioning as endowment), funds for long-term investment, self-insurance reserve funds, or future development funds] should be classified as net assets without donor restrictions. The "Pending Content" in FASB ASC 958-210-45-11 requires information about the amounts and purposes of board designations of net assets without donor restrictions to be provided in notes to or on the face of the financial statements. In addition, the net assets of board-designated endowment funds are required to be disclosed per FASB ASC 958-205-50-1B.[4]

Restricted Current (or Restricted Operating or Specific-Purpose) Funds

16.08 Restricted current funds (also called restricted operating or specific-purpose funds) are used to record NFPs' activities that are supported by resources whose use is limited by external parties to specific operating purposes. The principal sources of restricted current funds are contributions from donors; contracts, grants, and appropriations; and income on donor-restricted endowment funds.

16.09 Fund balances of restricted current funds are resources held for specified operating activities that have not yet been used. As stated in FASB ASC 958-210-45-9, the amounts for each of three classes of net assets are based

[4] The amendments in FASB Accounting Standards Update (ASU) No. 2016-14, *Not-for-Profit Entities (Topic 958): The Presentation of Financial Statements of Not-for-Profit Entities*, are effective for annual financial statements issued for fiscal years beginning after December 15, 2017 (for example, years ending December 31, 2018, and years ending June 30, 2019), and for interim periods within fiscal years beginning after December 15, 2018. Application to interim financial statements is permitted but not required in the initial year of application. Early application of the amendments is permitted.

on the existence or absence of donor-imposed restrictions. Thus, the portion of the fund balances that represents amounts contributed subject to donor-imposed restrictions should be classified as temporarily restricted net assets. However, if restricted current fund balances are subject only to legal restrictions imposed by an entity other than a donor, they should be included in unrestricted net assets. For example, fund balances representing amounts received only with contractual limitations should be classified as unrestricted net assets. Any portion of the fund balances that represents unearned revenue resulting from exchange transactions should be classified as a liability.

Fund balances of restricted current funds are resources held for specified operating activities that have not yet been used. As stated in the "Pending Content" in FASB ASC 958-210-45-9, the amounts for each of the two classes of net assets are based on the existence or absence of donor-imposed restrictions. Thus, the portion of the fund balances that represents amounts contributed subject to donor-imposed restrictions should be classified as net assets with donor restrictions. However, if restricted current fund balances are subject only to legal restrictions imposed by an entity other than a donor, they should be included in net assets without donor restrictions. For example, fund balances representing amounts received only with contractual limitations should be classified as net assets without donor restrictions. Any portion of the fund balances that represents unearned revenue resulting from exchange transactions should be classified as a liability.[5]

Plant (or Land, Building, and Equipment) Funds

16.10 Some NFPs record plant and equipment (and resources held to acquire them) in a plant (or land, building, and equipment) fund or funds. A plant fund may be a single group of accounts or may be subdivided into some or all of the following subfund account groups:

- Unexpended plant funds
- Funds for renewal and replacement
- Funds for retirement of indebtedness
- Investment (or net investment) in plant

16.11 Unexpended plant fund balances and renewals and replacement fund balances are resources that have not yet been used to acquire, renew, and replace plant and equipment. Retirement-of-indebtedness fund balances are resources held to service debt related to the acquisition or construction of plant and equipment. The portion of those fund balances that represents amounts received with donor-imposed restrictions that have not yet been met should be classified in a statement of financial position as temporarily restricted or permanently restricted net assets, depending on the nature of the restrictions. Other fund balances, including those arising under agreements with trustees under bond indentures and those designated by the NFP's governing board

---

[5] The amendments in FASB ASU No. 2016-14 are effective for annual financial statements issued for fiscal years beginning after December 15, 2017 (for example, years ending December 31, 2018, and years ending June 30, 2019), and for interim periods within fiscal years beginning after December 15, 2018. Application to interim financial statements is permitted but not required in the initial year of application. Early application of the amendments is permitted.

from unrestricted resources for the purchase, construction, renewal, or replacement of property and equipment should be classified as unrestricted net assets. Board designations and limitations imposed by bond agreements on the use of those unrestricted net assets may be described on the face of the financial statements or in the notes, as discussed in chapters 3 and 11.

Unexpended plant fund balances and renewals and replacement fund balances are resources that have not yet been used to acquire, renew, and replace plant and equipment. Retirement-of-indebtedness fund balances are resources held to service debt related to the acquisition or construction of plant and equipment. The portion of those fund balances that represents amounts received with donor-imposed restrictions that have not yet been met should be classified in a statement of financial position as net assets with donor restrictions. Other fund balances, including those arising under agreements with trustees under bond indentures and those designated for the purchase, construction, renewal, or replacement of property and equipment by the NFP's governing board from net assets without donor restrictions should be classified as net assets without donor restrictions. The "Pending Content" in FASB ASC 958-210-45-11 requires information about the amounts and purposes of board designations of net assets without donor restrictions to be provided in notes to or on the face of financial statements.[6]

16.12 Investment-in-plant fund balances represent assets invested in property and equipment less any liabilities related to those assets. These fund balances should be classified as permanently restricted net assets to the extent that (1) donors have imposed restrictions on the assets' use that neither expire by passage of time nor can be fulfilled or removed by actions of the NFP—for example, land that must be held in perpetuity—or (2) the proceeds from the ultimate sale or disposal of contributed long-lived assets must be reinvested in perpetuity. Amounts representing property and equipment acquired with unrestricted resources or with resources whose use is limited by parties other than donors should be classified as unrestricted net assets. Significant limitations on the use of property and equipment should be described in notes to the financial statements.[7]

Investment-in-plant fund balances represent assets invested in property and equipment less any liabilities related to those assets. These fund balances should be classified as net assets with donor restrictions to the extent that (1) donors have imposed restrictions on how or how long the asset must be used—for example, land that must be held in perpetuity—or if the donor required the proceeds from the ultimate sale or disposal of contributed long-lived assets to be used for a restricted purpose. Amounts representing property and equipment acquired with resources received without donor-imposed restrictions or with resources whose use is limited by parties other than donors

---

[6] The amendments in FASB ASU No. 2016-14 are effective for annual financial statements issued for fiscal years beginning after December 15, 2017 (for example, years ending December 31, 2018, and years ending June 30, 2019), and for interim periods within fiscal years beginning after December 15, 2018. Application to interim financial statements is permitted but not required in the initial year of application. Early application of the amendments is permitted.

[7] Examples of significant limitations on the use of property and equipment that should be described in the notes to the financial statements are provided in chapter 9, "Property and Equipment," of this guide.

should be classified as net assets without donor restrictions. Significant limitations on the use of property and equipment should be described in notes to the financial statements.[8,9]

16.13 If property and equipment were acquired by gift or were acquired with resources contributed by a donor for the purpose of purchasing property and equipment, the classification of the fund balances related to those assets depends upon donors' restrictions and the NFP's policy of implying a time restriction on the use of gifts of long-lived assets or gifts for the purchase of long-lived assets, as discussed in paragraph 9.04.

The preceding paragraph will be deleted upon the effective date of FASB Accounting Standards Update (ASU) No. 2016-14, *Not-for-Profit Entities (Topic 958): The Presentation of Financial Statements of Not-for-Profit Entities.*[10]

16.14 If a donor contributed property or equipment and also specified a time period over which the donated asset must be used, some portion of the fund balance related to that property or equipment would be classified as temporarily restricted net assets, unless the donor-specified time period has expired. The portion classified as temporarily restricted net assets depends upon how much of the donor-specified period has passed. The remainder of the fund balance would be classified as unrestricted net assets because using the equipment over time, as required by the donor, releases the restrictions, as explained in paragraphs 11.46–.49. If the donor contributed cash (or other assets) and restricted the use of the donated cash (or other assets) to the purchase of property or equipment that must be used for a specified time period, the related fund balance would be similarly classified as partly temporarily restricted net assets and partly unrestricted net assets.

If property and equipment were acquired by gift or were acquired with resources contributed by a donor for the purpose of purchasing property and equipment, the classification of the fund balances related to those assets depends upon donors' restrictions. If a donor contributed property or equipment and specified a time period over which the donated asset must be used, some portion of the fund balance related to that property or equipment would be classified as net assets with donor restrictions, unless the donor-specified time period has expired. The portion classified as net assets with donor restrictions depends upon how much of the donor-specified period has passed. The remainder of the fund balance would be classified as net assets without

---

[8] Examples of significant limitations on the use of property and equipment that should be described in the notes to the financial statements are provided in chapter 9, "Property and Equipment," of this guide.

[9] The amendments in FASB ASU No. 2016-14 are effective for annual financial statements issued for fiscal years beginning after December 15, 2017 (for example, years ending December 31, 2018, and years ending June 30, 2019), and for interim periods within fiscal years beginning after December 15, 2018. Application to interim financial statements is permitted but not required in the initial year of application. Early application of the amendments is permitted.

[10] The amendments in FASB ASU No. 2016-14 are effective for annual financial statements issued for fiscal years beginning after December 15, 2017 (for example, years ending December 31, 2018, and years ending June 30, 2019), and for interim periods within fiscal years beginning after December 15, 2018. Application to interim financial statements is permitted but not required in the initial year of application. Early application of the amendments is permitted.

donor restrictions because using the equipment over time, as required by the donor, releases the restrictions, as explained in paragraphs 11.46–.49. If the donor contributed cash (or other assets) and restricted the use of the donated cash (or other assets) to the purchase of property or equipment that must be used for a specified time period, the related fund balance would be similarly classified partly as net assets with donor restrictions and partly as net assets without donor restrictions.[11]

16.15 If a donor contributed property or equipment and did not specify a time period over which the asset must be used, FASB ASC 958-605-45-6 (which is discussed in paragraph 5.86) states that an NFP may elect a policy to imply a time restriction that expires over the useful life of the donated long-lived assets. An NFP that adopts that policy (of implying time restrictions) also should imply a time restriction on long-lived assets acquired with gifts of cash or other assets restricted for those acquisitions. When an NFP's policy is to imply a restriction that expires over the useful life of the asset, some portion of the fund balance for that property or equipment is classified as temporarily restricted net assets unless the useful life of the asset has expired. The portion classified as temporarily restricted net assets depends upon how much of the useful life has passed. The remainder of the fund balance would be classified as unrestricted net assets. Likewise, if the NFP has a policy of implying a time restriction on the use of long-lived assets and it has purchased property or equipment with gifts restricted for that purchase, some portion of the fund balance for the purchased asset will be classified as temporarily restricted net assets until the end of the useful life of the property or equipment that was purchased. If the NFP does not have such a policy, and the donor has not imposed restrictions on the use of the gift, the investment-in-plant funds balance will be classified as unrestricted net assets.

If a donor contributed property or equipment and did not specify a time period over which the asset must be used, the investment-in-plant funds balance will be classified as net assets without donor restrictions unless the donor specified a purpose for which the property and equipment must be used and the asset has not yet been placed in service.[12]

Loan Funds

16.16 Some NFPs use loan funds to account for loans made to students, employees, and other constituents and resources available for those purposes. The assets initially made available for the loans may be provided by donors or various governmental and other granting agencies or designated by governing boards. These entities or individuals may also stipulate qualifications

---

[11] The amendments in FASB ASU No. 2016-14 are effective for annual financial statements issued for fiscal years beginning after December 15, 2017 (for example, years ending December 31, 2018, and years ending June 30, 2019), and for interim periods within fiscal years beginning after December 15, 2018. Application to interim financial statements is permitted but not required in the initial year of application. Early application of the amendments is permitted.

[12] The amendments in FASB ASU No. 2016-14 are effective for annual financial statements issued for fiscal years beginning after December 15, 2017 (for example, years ending December 31, 2018, and years ending June 30, 2019), and for interim periods within fiscal years beginning after December 15, 2018. Application to interim financial statements is permitted but not required in the initial year of application. Early application of the amendments is permitted.

for individual borrowers. Some loan funds are self-perpetuating—that is, the principal and interest repayments on outstanding loans are used to make additional loans. Other loan funds are created on a temporary basis, and the original resource providers must be repaid. In some situations, repayments may be forgiven by resource providers if certain conditions are met.

16.17 Fund balances of loan funds are resources available for lending. The portion of the fund balances representing resources restricted by donors in perpetuity for use in making loans (for example, a revolving fund) should be classified as permanently restricted. If a portion of the loan funds is subject only to donor-imposed restrictions that expire (for example, loan funds that make loans on a one-time, rather than revolving, basis), that portion should be classified as temporarily restricted until the loans are made. If a portion of the loan funds may be used for the unrestricted purposes of the NFP (such as loan program administration), that portion is classified as unrestricted net assets. Amounts that have been designated by governing boards to be used as loan funds, such as amounts designated as matching funds for government loan programs (for example, government loans to students that require colleges and universities to match a portion of those loans) and other amounts used for loans that have not been restricted by donors, should be classified as unrestricted net assets. Any portion of loan fund balances that represents refundable advances, such as under a government loan program, should be reported as a liability.

Fund balances of loan funds are resources available for lending. The portion of the fund balances representing resources restricted by donors in perpetuity for use in making loans (for example, a revolving fund) should be classified as net assets with donor restrictions. If a portion of the loan funds is subject only to donor-imposed restrictions that expire (for example, loan funds that make loans on a one-time, rather than revolving, basis), that portion should be classified as net assets with donor restrictions until the loans are made. If a portion of the loan funds may be used for the general purposes of the NFP (such as loan program administration), that portion is classified as net assets without donor restrictions. Amounts that have been designated by governing boards to be used as loan funds, such as amounts designated as matching funds for government loan programs (for example, government loans to students that require colleges and universities to match a portion of those loans) and other amounts used for loans that have not been restricted by donors, should be classified as net assets without donor restrictions. Any portion of loan fund balances that represents refundable advances, such as under a government loan program, should be reported as a liability.[13]

Endowment Funds

16.18 Some NFPs record cash, securities, or other assets held to provide income for the maintenance of the NFP in an endowment fund or funds. Three kinds of endowment may be identified: perpetual endowment, term endowment, and quasi endowment (also called funds functioning as endowment). *Perpetual*

---

[13] The amendments in FASB ASU No. 2016-14 are effective for annual financial statements issued for fiscal years beginning after December 15, 2017 (for example, years ending December 31, 2018, and years ending June 30, 2019), and for interim periods within fiscal years beginning after December 15, 2018. Application to interim financial statements is permitted but not required in the initial year of application. Early application of the amendments is permitted.

endowment refers to amounts that have been contributed with donor-specified restrictions that the gift be invested to provide a perpetual source of support (often stated as "principal to be invested in perpetuity"); income from those investments may also be restricted by donors. *Term endowment* is similar to perpetual endowment, except that at some future time or upon the occurrence of a specified future event, the resources originally contributed become available for general or purpose-restricted use by the entity. *Quasi endowment* refers to resources designated by an entity's governing board to be retained and invested for specified purposes for a long but unspecified period.

16.19 Fund balances of endowment funds are resources for which various limitations exist on the use of the resources invested and, in some cases, on the income generated by those resources. Amounts that are resources restricted by donors in perpetuity should be classified as permanently restricted. If donor-imposed restrictions exist that preclude the use of gains and losses (net appreciation) on perpetual endowment, either as a result of explicit or implicit donor stipulation or by the NFP's interpretation of the relevant law, those gains and losses should also be classified as permanently restricted. In the absence of such restrictions, those gains and losses should be classified as temporarily restricted until they are appropriated by the governing board for expenditure. If the fair value of the assets of a donor-restricted endowment fund is less than the amount required to be maintained permanently, the deficit is classified as unrestricted net assets. Chapter 4, "Cash, Cash Equivalents, and Investments," provides additional information about the classification of the net assets of endowment funds.

Fund balances of endowment funds are resources for which various limitations exist on the use of the resources invested and, in some cases, on the income generated by those resources. Amounts that are resources restricted by donors in perpetuity should be classified as net assets with donor restrictions. Fund balances that represent term endowments for which the gift must be invested for a specific period and then used at the end of the term for a specified purpose should be classified as net assets with donor restrictions. Investment return on the donor-restricted endowment (both perpetual and term) should be classified as net assets with donor restrictions until they are appropriated by the governing board for expenditure. Although NFPs are no longer required to report in the financial statements the portion of an endowment that must be retained in perpetuity (typically, the original gift amount and any additions to the fund or other amounts that are required by the donor to be held in perpetuity), it is necessary to maintain that information in financial records in order to comply with the requirement in the "Pending Content" in FASB ASC 958-205-50-2 to disclose, in aggregate for all underwater endowment funds, the original endowment gift amount or level required to be maintained by donor stipulations or by law that extends donor restrictions and the amount of the deficiencies of the underwater endowment funds. Chapter 4, "Cash, Cash Equivalents, and Investments," provides additional information about the classification of the net assets of endowment funds.[14]

---

[14] The amendments in FASB ASU No. 2016-14 are effective for annual financial statements issued for fiscal years beginning after December 15, 2017 (for example, years ending December 31, 2018, and years ending June 30, 2019), and for interim periods within fiscal years beginning after December 15, 2018. Application to interim financial statements is permitted but not required in the initial year of application. Early application of the amendments is permitted.

16.20 Fund balances that represent term endowments for which the gift must be invested for a specific period and then used at the end of the term for a specified purpose should be classified as temporarily restricted net assets. Amounts representing resources that will be permanently restricted at the end of the specified term should be classified as permanently restricted net assets.

The preceding paragraph will be deleted upon the effective date of FASB ASU No. 2016-14.[15]

16.21 Fund balances that are quasi endowments should be classified as unrestricted net assets if they were created by a designation of the NFP's governing board from unrestricted net assets. Fund balances that are quasi endowments should be classified as temporarily restricted net assets if they were created by a designation of the NFP's governing board from temporarily restricted resources and the restrictions are not yet met. For example, if an NFP receives a large gift restricted for a specific purpose and the gift is far in excess of the NFP's current needs, the governing board may decide to invest the gift and use a spending rate to determine the amount it will annually spend for the restricted purpose. Over time, temporarily restricted resources of the quasi endowments become unrestricted net assets because of the requirement to use restricted resources first, as discussed in paragraphs 11.33–.36. Because those quasi endowments are temporarily restricted gifts, rather than donor-restricted endowments, they are not subject to a time restriction until appropriated by the governing board. Thus, the resources are entirely available to support expenditures for the specified purpose even if the governing board does not appropriate them; and the net assets will be reclassified to unrestricted net assets as the purpose restrictions are met. The net assets of board-designated endowment funds are required to be disclosed per FASB ASC 958-205-50-1B.

Fund balances that are quasi endowments should be classified as net assets without donor restrictions if they were created by a designation of the NFP's governing board from resources in that net asset class. Fund balances that are quasi endowments should be classified as net assets with donor restrictions if they were created by a designation of the NFP's governing board from resources in that net asset class and the restrictions are not yet met. For example, if an NFP receives a large gift restricted for a specific purpose and the gift is far in excess of the NFP's current needs, the governing board may decide to invest the gift and use a spending rate to determine the amount it will annually spend for the restricted purpose. Over time, the restrictions on the quasi endowments are met because of the requirement to use restricted resources first, as discussed in paragraphs 11.33–.36. Because those quasi endowments were not created by contributions with perpetual restrictions, they are not subject to a time restriction until appropriated by the governing board as are the net assets of a donor-restricted endowment fund (see paragraph 4.72). Thus, the resources are entirely available to support expenditures for

---

[15] The amendments in FASB ASU No. 2016-14 are effective for annual financial statements issued for fiscal years beginning after December 15, 2017 (for example, years ending December 31, 2018, and years ending June 30, 2019), and for interim periods within fiscal years beginning after December 15, 2018. Application to interim financial statements is permitted but not required in the initial year of application. Early application of the amendments is permitted.

the specified purpose even if the governing board does not appropriate them; and the net assets will be reclassified to net assets without donor restrictions as the purpose restrictions are met. The net assets of board-designated endowment funds are required to be disclosed per the "Pending Content" in FASB ASC 958-205-50-1B and the "Pending Content" in FASB ASC 958-210-45-11.[16]

Annuity and Life-Income (Split-Interest) Funds

16.22 Annuity and life-income (or split-interest) funds may be used by NFPs to account for resources provided by donors under various kinds of agreements in which the NFP has a beneficial interest in the resources but is not the sole beneficiary. These agreements include charitable lead and remainder trusts, charitable gift annuities, pooled (life) income funds, and life interests in real estate. Split-interest agreements are discussed in chapter 6, "Split-Interest Agreements and Beneficial Interests in Trusts."

16.23 Fund balances of annuity and life-income funds represent an NFP's beneficial interest in the resources contributed by donors under split-interest agreements. Any portion of the fund balances representing amounts that will become part of perpetual endowment when the agreements terminate should be classified as permanently restricted net assets. Any portion of the fund balances representing amounts that will be available for restricted purposes or for unrestricted use by the NFP when the split-interest agreements terminate should be classified as temporarily restricted net assets. If the donor gives the NFP the immediate right to use the assets it receives without restriction, as discussed in paragraph 6.19, the fund balance should be classified as unrestricted net assets.

Fund balances of annuity and life-income funds represent an NFP's beneficial interest in the resources contributed by donors under split-interest agreements. Generally, the net assets subject to a split-interest agreement are subject to a time restriction until the death of the beneficiary (or other specified event) and may also be subject to a purpose restriction on the use of the resources provided to the NFP under the agreement, therefore, the fund balance should be classified as net assets with donor restrictions. If the donor gives the NFP the immediate right to use the assets it receives without restriction, as discussed in paragraph 6.19, the fund balance should be classified as net assets without donor restrictions.[17]

---

[16] The amendments in FASB ASU No. 2016-14 are effective for annual financial statements issued for fiscal years beginning after December 15, 2017 (for example, years ending December 31, 2018, and years ending June 30, 2019), and for interim periods within fiscal years beginning after December 15, 2018. Application to interim financial statements is permitted but not required in the initial year of application. Early application of the amendments is permitted.

[17] The amendments in FASB ASU No. 2016-14 are effective for annual financial statements issued for fiscal years beginning after December 15, 2017 (for example, years ending December 31, 2018, and years ending June 30, 2019), and for interim periods within fiscal years beginning after December 15, 2018. Application to interim financial statements is permitted but not required in the initial year of application. Early application of the amendments is permitted.

Agency (Or Custodian) Funds

16.24 Agency (or custodian) funds are used by NFPs to account for resources held by the NFP as an agent for resource providers until those resources are transferred to third-party recipients specified by the resource providers. The NFP has little or no discretion over the use of those resources. Accounting for agency transactions and distinguishing agency transactions from contributions are discussed in chapter 5, "Contributions Received and Agency Transactions." Because the assets and liabilities are always equal in agency funds, the fund balances of agency funds are always zero and no net assets are reported.

Summary

16.25 The following exhibit summarizes the net asset classes into which various kinds of fund balances will typically be classified.

Typical Classification of Fund Balances

	Net Asset Class		
Fund Type	*Permanently Restricted*	*Temporarily Restricted*	*Unrestricted*
Unrestricted Current (or Unrestricted Operating or General)	Not applicable	Fund balances with donor-imposed restrictions that expire with the passage of time (not usually present in unrestricted current funds).	Unrestricted fund balances, including those designated by governing bodies for specific purposes.
Restricted Current (or Restricted Operating or Specific Purpose)	Not applicable	Fund balances with donor-imposed restrictions that expire with the passage of time or that can be fulfilled or removed by actions of the not-for-profit entity (NFP).	Fund balances that are limited as to use by legal or contractual restrictions, rather than donor-imposed restrictions, including those designated by governing bodies for specific purposes.[1]

Typical Classification of Fund Balances—*continued*

	Net Asset Class		
Fund Type	*Permanently Restricted*	*Temporarily Restricted*	*Unrestricted*
Plant (or Land, Building, and Equipment)	Fund balances with donor-imposed restrictions that do not expire with the passage of time or cannot be fulfilled or removed by actions of the NFP.[2]	Fund balances with donor-imposed restrictions that expire with the passage of time or that can be fulfilled or removed by actions of the NFP.[3]	Fund balances that are limited as to use by legal or contractual restrictions, rather than donor-imposed restrictions, including those designated by governing bodies for specific purposes.[4]
Loan	Fund balances with donor-imposed restrictions that do not expire with the passage of time or cannot be fulfilled or removed by actions of the NFP.	Fund balances with donor-imposed restrictions that expire with the passage of time or that can be fulfilled or removed by actions of the NFP.	Fund balances that are limited as to use by legal or contractual restrictions, rather than donor-imposed restrictions, including those designated by governing bodies for specific purposes.
Endowment	Permanent endowment.[5]	Temporary (or term) endowment[6] or quasi endowment created from temporarily restricted resources for which the restrictions are not yet met.	Quasi endowment created from unrestricted resources.

(continued)

Typical Classification of Fund Balances—*continued*

	Net Asset Class		
Fund Type	*Permanently Restricted*	*Temporarily Restricted*	*Unrestricted*
Annuity and Life-Income (Split Interests)	Donor-restricted in perpetuity.	Amounts available for unrestricted or time-or-purpose restricted use when agreement terminates.	Fund balances for which the donor gives the NFP the immediate right to use the assets it receives without restriction, including those designated by governing bodies for specific purposes.
Agency (or Custodian)	Not applicable.	Not applicable.	Not applicable.

1 Any portion of the fund balances representing unearned revenue from exchange transactions should be classified as a liability.

2 This would include contributed assets such as land and capitalized collection items that must be held in perpetuity and other contributed assets when donors have stipulated that the proceeds from their ultimate sale or disposal must be reinvested in perpetuity.

3 Amounts representing assets contributed without donor-imposed restrictions about how long the land, building, or equipment must be used should be classified as unrestricted or temporarily restricted net assets, depending on the accounting policy adopted by the NFP, as discussed in paragraphs 16.13–.15.

4 Amounts representing assets contributed without donor-imposed restrictions about how long the land, building, or equipment must be used should be classified as unrestricted or temporarily restricted net assets, depending on the accounting policy adopted by the NFP, as discussed in paragraphs 16.13–.15.

5 Includes gains and losses on perpetual endowment when donor restrictions or law permanently preclude their use.

6 Includes gains on perpetual endowment if donor restrictions or law specify their use, if the gains have not been appropriated for expenditure, or both.

	Net Asset Class[18]	
Fund Type	*Net Assets with Donor Restrictions*	*Net Assets without Donor Restrictions*
Unrestricted Current (or Unrestricted Operating or General)	Fund balances with donor-imposed restrictions that expire with the passage of time (not usually present in unrestricted current funds).	Fund balances without donor-imposed restrictions on use, including fund balances designated by governing bodies for specific purposes.
Restricted Current (or Restricted Operating or Specific Purpose)	Fund balances with donor-imposed restrictions that expire with the passage of time or that can be fulfilled or removed by actions of the not-for-profit entity (NFP).	Fund balances that are limited as to use by legal or contractual restrictions, rather than donor-imposed restrictions, including those designated by governing bodies for specific purposes.[1]
Plant (or Land, Building, and Equipment)	Fund balances with donor-imposed restrictions.[2]	Fund balances that are limited as to use by legal or contractual restrictions, rather than donor-imposed restrictions, including those designated by governing bodies for specific purposes.[3]
Loan	Fund balances with donor-imposed restrictions, including those requiring the future principal and interest payments to used to make new loans (a revolving fund).	Fund balances that are limited as to use by legal or contractual restrictions, rather than donor-imposed restrictions, including those designated by governing bodies for specific purposes (such as matching funds).
Endowment	Perpetual and term endowment created by a donor restriction.[4] Quasi endowment created from donor-restricted resources for which the restrictions are not yet met.	Quasi endowment created from resources that are not subject to donor-imposed restrictions.

(*continued*)

[18] The amendments in FASB ASU No. 2016-14 are effective for annual financial statements issued for fiscal years beginning after December 15, 2017 (for example, years ending December 31, 2018, and years ending June 30, 2019), and for interim periods within fiscal years beginning after December 15, 2018. Application to interim financial statements is permitted but not required in the initial year of application. Early application of the amendments is permitted.

	Net Asset Class	
Fund Type	*Net Assets with Donor Restrictions*	*Net Assets without Donor Restrictions*
Annuity and Life-Income (Split Interests)	Fund balances subject to a time restriction until the death of the beneficiary (or other specified event) and/or subject to a purpose restriction on the use of the resources provided to the NFP under the agreement.	Fund balances for which the donor gives the NFP the immediate right to use the assets it receives without restriction, including those designated by governing bodies for specific purposes.
Agency (or Custodian)	Not applicable.	Not applicable.

[1] Any portion of the fund balances representing unearned revenue from exchange transactions should be classified as a liability.

[2] This would include fund balances related to (*a*) land and capitalized collection items that must be held in perpetuity, (*b*) contributed long-lived assets for which donors have stipulated that the proceeds from their ultimate sale or disposal must be used for restricted purposes, (*c*) contributed long-lived assets if the donor specified a purpose for which the property and equipment must be used and the asset has not yet been placed in service, and (*d*) contributed cash or other assets restricted for the purchase of long-lived assets if asset has not been acquired and placed in service.

[3] This would include amounts representing assets contributed with donor-imposed restrictions specifying how the donated or acquired land, building, or equipment must be used provided the asset has been placed in service as well as long-lived assets purchased with resources that were not subject to donor restrictions.

[4] Includes investment return on perpetual and term endowments when its use is limited by donor restrictions or a law that extends donor restrictions, and investment return on perpetual and term endowments that is available for general purposes but that has not been appropriated for expenditure.

Appendix A

The New Not-for-Profit Financial Reporting Model Standards: FASB ASU No. 2016-14

This appendix is nonauthoritative and is included for informational purposes only.

Overview

In August 2016, the Financial Accounting Standards Board (FASB) issued Accounting Standards Update (ASU) No. 2016-14, *Not-for-Profit Entities (Topic 958): Presentation of Financial Statements of Not-for-Profit Entities*. The ASU, which is the first phase of a two-phase project, makes significant changes in seven areas:

- Net asset classes
- Liquidity and availability of resources
- Classification and disclosure of underwater endowment funds
- Expense reporting
- Statement of cash flows
- Investment return
- Release of restrictions on capital assets.

The amendments in ASU No. 2016-14 are effective for annual financial statements issued for fiscal years beginning after December 15, 2017 (for example, years ending December 31, 2018 and years ending June 30, 2019), and for interim periods within fiscal years beginning after December 15, 2018. Application to interim financial statements is permitted but not required in the initial year of application. Early application of the amendments is permitted.

The amendments are to be applied on a retrospective basis in the year that they are first applied. However, if presenting comparative financial statements, a not-for-profit entity (NFP) has the option to omit the following information for any periods presented before the period of adoption:

1. Analysis of expenses by both natural classification and functional classification (the separate presentation of expenses by functional classification and expenses by natural classification is still required). NFPs that previously were required to present a statement of functional expenses do not have the option to omit this analysis; however, they may present the comparative period information in any of the formats permitted in ASU No. 2016-14, consistent with the presentation in the period of adoption.
2. Disclosures about liquidity and availability of resources.

In the period that the amendments are first applied, an NFP should disclose the nature of any reclassifications or restatements and their effects, if any, on changes in the net asset classes for each period presented.

Net Asset Classes

The three classes of net assets used in financial statements of not-for-profit organizations (unrestricted, temporarily restricted, and permanently restricted) will be replaced with two classes of net assets—net assets with donor restrictions and net assets without donor restrictions. Because the definition of donor-imposed restriction is essentially unchanged, the effect of the change is that temporarily restricted net assets and permanently restricted net assets are combined in the statement of financial position and the statement of activities to become a single class—net assets with donor restrictions. Unrestricted net assets are now referred to as net assets without donor restrictions. (Changes in classification of underwater endowment funds and in the release of restrictions on capital assets are discussed later in this appendix.)

An NFP will be required to present, on the face of the statement of financial position, net assets with donor restrictions and net assets without donor restrictions, as well as the currently required amount for total net assets. On the statement of activities, an NFP will be required to present the change in each of the two net asset classes as well as the currently required amount of the change in total net assets.

The current requirement to provide relevant information about the nature and amounts of donor restrictions on net assets (either on the face of the statement of financial position or in the notes) has been retained. Information about how the restrictions affect the use of resources is also required. Note B in the "Pending Content" in FASB ASC 958-205-55-21 provides the following example of such a disclosure:

> Net assets with donor restrictions are restricted for the following purposes or periods.

Subject to expenditure for specified purpose:	
Program A activities:	
Purchase of equipment	$ 3,060
Research	950
Educational seminars and publications	240
Program B activities:	
Disaster relief	745
Educational seminars and publications	280
Program C activities: general	210
Buildings and equipment	2,150
Annuity trust agreements for research	2,815
	10,450
Subject to the passage of time:	
For periods after June 30, 20X1	3,140

Subject to NFP spending policy and appropriation:	
Investment in perpetuity (including amounts above original gift amount of $122,337), which, once appropriated, is expendable to support:	
Program A activities	33,300
Program B activities	15,820
Program C activities	16,480
Any activities of the organization	109,100
	174,700
Subject to appropriation and expenditure when a specified event occurs:	
Endowment requiring income to be added to original gift until fund's value is $2,500	2,120
Paid-up life insurance policy that will provide proceeds upon death of insured for an endowment to support general activities	80
	2,200
Not subject to appropriation or expenditure:	
Land required to be used as a recreation area	3,000
Total net assets with donor restrictions	$193,490

In addition to information about net assets with donor restrictions, NFPs will also be required to disclose, as of the end of the reporting period, the amounts and purposes of governing board designations, appropriations, and similar actions that result in self-imposed limits on the use of resources that are free of donor-imposed restrictions. Note DD in the "Pending Content" in FASB ASC 958-205-55-21 provides the following example of such a disclosure:

> Not-for-Profit Entity A's governing board has designated, from net assets without donor restrictions of $92,600, net assets for the following purposes as of June 30, 20X1.

Quasi-endowment	$36,600
Liquidity reserve	1,300
Total	$37,900

Liquidity and Availability of Resources

Among the key objectives of FASB's NFP reporting project was the need to make it easier for readers of the financial statements to assess the organization's liquidity and to determine the availability of restricted resources to fund general expenditures. An organization will be required to disclose both qualitative and quantitative information about how it manages its liquid resources. The "Pending Content" in FASB ASC 958-210-50-1A requires an NFP to provide the following:

a. Qualitative information useful in assessing an entity's liquidity that communicates how the NFP manages its liquid resources available to meet cash needs for general expenditures within one year of the balance sheet date.

b. Quantitative information that communicates the availability of an NFP's financial assets at the balance sheet date to meet cash needs for general expenditures within one year of the balance sheet date. Availability of a financial asset may be affected by:

    i. Its nature

    ii. External limits imposed by donors, laws, and contracts with others

    iii. Internal limits imposed by governing board decisions

ASU No. 2016-14 doesn't provide standards as to the types of qualitative or quantitative information to include. However, there are three examples of notes that meet the requirements (Note G in FASB ASC 958-205-55-21 and Example 2 in FASB ASC 958-210-55). Combined (but not each individually), those examples include qualitative disclosures about:

- The organization's responsibility to maintain resources to meet donor restrictions, which may make those resources unavailable for general expenditures
- The organization's goals for maintaining financial assets
- The organization's policies for investing excess cash
- The organization's policies for spending from board-designated endowment funds
- Contractual agreements that make certain financial assets unavailable to fund general expenditures
- Lines of credit that would be drawn down if the organization did not have any liquid, available financial assets.

ASU No. 2016-14 does not define general expenditures. Because the determination of which expenditures are general expenditures affects the determination of whether a financial asset is available to meet cash needs for general expenditures, the additional qualitative information required by FASB ASC 958-210-50-1A(b) may need to include a description of how both general expenditures and availability of financial resources are determined by the NFP.

The "Pending Content" in FASB ASC 958-205-55-21 provides quantitative information in the form of a reconciliation, as of the financial statement date, of total financial assets to financial assets available to meet cash needs for general expenditures within one year. The reconciling items include amounts for financial assets that are not available for general expenditures, as shown in example Note G that follows:

> The following reflects Not-for-Profit Entity A's financial assets as of the balance sheet date, reduced by amounts not available for general use because of contractual or donor-imposed restrictions within one year of the balance sheet date. Amounts not available include amounts set aside for long-term investing in the quasi-endowment that could

be drawn upon if the governing board approves that action. However, amounts already appropriated from either the donor-restricted endowment or quasi-endowment for general expenditure within one year of the balance sheet date have not been subtracted as unavailable.

Financial assets, at year end	$234,410
Less those unavailable for general expenditures within one year, due to:	
Contractual or donor-imposed restrictions:	
Restricted by donor with time or purpose restrictions	(11,940)
Subject to appropriation and satisfaction of donor restrictions	(174,700)
Investments held in annuity trust	(4,500)
Board designations:	
Quasi-endowment fund, primarily for long-term investing	(36,600)
Amounts set aside for liquidity reserve	(1,300)
Financial assets available to meet cash needs for general expenditures within one year	$5,370

Not-for-Profit Entity A is substantially supported by restricted contributions. Because a donor's restriction requires resources to be used in a particular manner or in a future period, Not-for-Profit Entity A must maintain sufficient resources to meet those responsibilities to its donors. Thus, financial assets may not be available for general expenditure within one year. As part of Not-for-Profit Entity A's liquidity management, it has a policy to structure its financial assets to be available as its general expenditures, liabilities, and other obligations come due. In addition, Not-for-Profit Entity A invests cash in excess of daily requirements in short-term investments. Occasionally, the board designates a portion of any operating surplus to its liquidity reserve, which was $1,300 as of June 30, 20X1. There is a fund established by the governing board that may be drawn upon in the event of financial distress or an immediate liquidity need resulting from events outside the typical life cycle of converting financial assets to cash or settling financial liabilities. In the event of an unanticipated liquidity need, Not-for-Profit Entity A also could draw upon $10,000 of available lines of credit (as further discussed in Note XX) or its quasi-endowment fund.

The "Pending Content" in paragraphs 6–8 of FASB ASC 958-210-55 (example 2) provides fact sets and example disclosures for two additional cases. They provide quantitative information in the form of a list of financial assets that are available to meet cash needs for general expenditures.

Based on the fact set in FASB ASC 958-210-55-6, the following disclosure is illustrated:

NFP A has $395,000 of financial assets available within 1 year of the balance sheet date to meet cash needs for general expenditure consisting of cash of $75,000, contributions receivable of $20,000, and short-term investments of $300,000. None of the financial assets are subject to donor or other contractual restrictions that make them unavailable for general expenditure within one year of the balance sheet date. The contributions receivable are subject to implied time restrictions but are expected to be collected within one year. NFP A has a goal to maintain financial assets, which consist of cash and short-term investments, on hand to meet 60 days of normal operating expenses, which are, on average, approximately $275,000. NFP A has a policy to structure its financial assets to be available as its general expenditures, liabilities, and other obligations come due. In addition, as part of its liquidity management, NFP A invests cash in excess of daily requirements in various short-term investments including, certificate of deposits and short term treasury instruments. As more fully described in Note XX, NFP A also has committed lines of credit in the amount of $20,000, which it could draw upon in the event of an unanticipated liquidity need.

Based on the fact set FASB ASC 958-210-55-8, the following disclosure is illustrated to accompany a classified statement of financial position:

NFP A's financial assets available within one year of the balance sheet date for general expenditure are as follows:

Cash and cash equivalents	$4,575
Accounts and interest receivable	2,130
Contributions receivable	1,825
Short-term investments	1,400
Other investments appropriated for current use	10,804
	$20,734

NFP A's endowment funds consist of donor-restricted endowments and a quasi-endowment. Income from donor-restricted endowments is restricted for specific purposes and, therefore, is not available for general expenditure. As described in Note Y, the quasi-endowment has a spending rate of 5 percent. $1.65 million of appropriations from the quasi-endowment will be available within the next 12 months.

As part of NFP A's liquidity management, it has a policy to structure its financial assets to be available as its general expenditures, liabilities, and other obligations come due. In addition, NFP A invests cash in excess of daily requirements in short-term investments. To help manage unanticipated liquidity needs, NFP A has committed lines of credit in the amount of $20 million, which it could draw upon. Additionally, NFP A has a quasi-endowment of $33 million. Although NFP A does not intend to spend from its quasi-endowment other than amounts appropriated for general expenditure as part of its annual budget approval and appropriation process, amounts from its quasi-endowment could be made available if necessary. However, both the quasi-endowment and donor-restricted endowments contain investments with lock-up provisions that would reduce the total investments that could be made available (see Note X for disclosures about investments).

Classification and Disclosure of Underwater Endowment Funds

In conjunction with the changes in the net asset classes and new required disclosures about liquidity and availability of financial assets, there are new accounting and disclosure requirements for underwater endowment funds. ASU No. 2016-14 adds a definition of an underwater endowment fund to the FASB ASC Master Glossary as follows:

> A donor-restricted endowment fund for which the fair value of the fund at the reporting date is less than either the original gift amount or the amount required to be maintained by the donor or by law that extends donor restrictions.

Current standards require the deficit of a donor-restricted endowment fund to be included in unrestricted net assets. The "Pending Content" in FASB ASC 958-205-45-13H states that "If a donor-restricted endowment fund is an underwater endowment fund, the accumulated losses should be included together with that fund in net asset with donor restrictions." In other words, the endowment fund's balance is simply reduced. The fund balance of a donor-restricted endowment fund is entirely within net assets with donor restrictions, and the fund balance for a board-designated endowment fund is entirely within net assets without donor restrictions (unless the governing board designated resources that were purpose restricted by the donor to serve as an endowment).

In addition, the "Pending Content" in FASB ASC 958-205-50-2 requires that for each period for which a statement of financial position is presented, an NFP disclose each of the following, in the aggregate, for all underwater endowment funds:

a. The fair value of the underwater endowment funds

b. The original endowment gift amount or level required to be maintained by donor stipulations or by law that extends donor restrictions

c. The amount of the deficiencies of the underwater endowment funds ([a] less [b]).

To help readers of the financial statements understand the effects on availability of resources caused by an underwater condition, the pending content in FASB ASC 958-205-50-1B requires disclosures of the governing board's interpretation of laws affecting the ability to spend from underwater endowment funds, the organization's policies for spending from underwater endowment funds, and any actions taken during the period concerning appropriation from underwater endowment funds.

Analysis of Expenses by Function and Nature

ASU No. 2016-14 expands to all not-for-profit organizations the requirement to present an analysis of expenses by functional and natural classifications. That information, currently required only of voluntary health and welfare entities (paragraph 1.06), must be provided in one location—either on the face of the statement of activities, as a schedule in the notes to financial statements, or in a separate financial statement. The analysis must disaggregate the expense information by functional expense classifications, such as major classes of program services and supporting activities, and by natural expense classifications, such as salaries, rent, electricity, interest expense, supplies, depreciation, awards and grants to others, and professional fees. Expenses that are reported by other than their natural classification (such as salaries included in cost of goods sold or facility rental costs of special events reported as direct benefits to donors), must be reported by their natural classification in the analysis. Investment expenses that have been netted against investment return and items that are typically reported in other comprehensive income of for-profit entities (FASB ASC 220-10-45-10A) should not be included in the functional expense analysis. The "Pending Content" in FASB ASC 958-205-55-21 provides an example of the analysis in Note F.

In addition to the analysis, NFPs will be required to provide a description of the methods used to allocate costs among program and support functions. To make those allocations more comparable between NFPs, the "Pending Content" in paragraphs 171–175 of FASB ASC 958-720-55 provide examples of activities that constitute direct conduct or direct supervision of program activities (and thus are program expenses) rather than management and general expenses. There are examples for the costs related to the chief executive officer, the chief financial officer, the human resource department, and for grant accounting and reporting. The "Pending Content" in FASB ASC 958-720-55-176 provides an example of the required disclosure.

Statement of Cash Flows

The new standards continue to permit an organization to choose whether to provide a statement of cash flows using the direct or indirect method of reporting operating cash flows. However, to encourage greater use of the direct method, if an NFP chooses to present cash flows from operations using the direct method, the indirect reconciliation will no longer be required. There are no changes to the classification of operating, investing and financing cash flows.

Investment Return

ASU No. 2016-14 distinguishes between programmatic investing (the activity of making loans or other investments that are directed at carrying out a not-for-profit entity's purpose for existence) and total return investing (the activity of investing for the general production of income or appreciation of an asset). The new standards require that investment expenses related to total return investing be netted against investment return on the statement of activities and eliminate the requirement to disclose investment expenses that have been netted. That change was made to provide a more comparable measure of investment return across all not-for-profit organizations, regardless of whether the investment activities are managed internally or by outside investment managers, volunteers, or some combination. The new measure is also more comparable across organizations that invest in mutual funds, hedge funds, or other vehicles for which the management fees are embedded in the investment return of the vehicle. Because the disclosure of the netted expenses is eliminated, the difficulties and related costs in identifying embedded fees are eliminated, and the resultant inconsistencies in the reported amounts of investment expenses are avoided. Although no longer required to do so, an NFP may choose to continue to provide information about the netted investment expenses if it so desires. Netted investment expenses are limited to external investment expenses and direct internal investment expenses incurred during the period.

In addition, the ASU eliminates requirements for following disclosures about investment return. Although it may continue to do so, an NFP is no longer required to:

- Disclose investment income (for example, interest, dividends, rents) separately from the net appreciation or depreciation of investments
- Disclose the composition of investment return (investment income, net realized gains or losses on investments reported at other than fair value, and net gains or losses on investments reported at fair value)
- Provide a reconciliation of investment return to amounts reported in the statement of activities if investment return is separated into operating and nonoperating amounts.

Investment expenses that are netted against investment return are prohibited from inclusion in the analysis of expenses by functional and natural classifications.

Release of Restrictions on Capital Assets

ASU No. 2016-14 requires NFPs to use the placed-in-service approach to report expirations of restrictions on gifts of long-lived assets and cash or other assets to be used to acquire or construct long-lived assets (in the absence of specific donor restrictions stating otherwise). It eliminates the option of an NFP to adopt an accounting policy to imply a time restriction that expires over the useful life of the donated assets and recognize the release of the restriction ratably over the useful life of the asset.

In Conclusion

The AICPA encourages you to visit its website at aicpa.org and the Not-for-Profit Section at www.aicpa.org/interestareas/notforprofit.html to assist in understanding the new standards and in implementing them. Certain content on the AICPA's website is restricted to AICPA members and the content in the Not-for-Profit Section is restricted to section members.

Although the changes seem numerous, implementing the majority of them should not be onerous. FASB staff members are encouraging early adoption of the standard. They point out that most of the new requirements are currently available as options within existing standards and can be used without formally adopting ASU No. 2016-14 early. Any of the following changes can be voluntarily included in financial statements now because they are not inconsistent with the existing standards:

- Use of the term net assets without donor restrictions rather than unrestricted net assets
- Disclosure of board-designated net assets
- Increased detail in the disclosure of the restrictions on temporarily and permanently restricted net assets

- The qualitative liquidity and availability disclosures
- The quantitative liquidity and availability disclosure
- Presentation of an analysis of expenses by function and nature in one location
- Disclosure of cost allocation methods and bases used to allocate costs among functions
- Disclosure of the aggregate fair value and aggregate of original endowment gifts (or other level required by donor stipulation or by laws) for underwater endowment funds, in addition to the currently required aggregate deficit for underwater endowment funds
- Disclosure of policies for spending from underwater endowment funds.

The following changes would be inconsistent with current standards and should only be incorporated in financial statements when ASU No. 2016-14 is fully adopted:

- Combining the temporarily restricted and permanently restricted net asset classes into one net asset class
- Presenting a deficit in a donor-restricted endowment fund in a restricted net asset class rather than in unrestricted net assets
- Eliminating the disclosure of investment expenses that are netted against investment return
- Eliminating the three disclosures about investment return
- Eliminating the indirect method reconciliation when using the direct method on the statement of cash flows.

Appendix B

The New Revenue Recognition Standard: FASB ASC 606

This appendix is nonauthoritative and is included for informational purposes only.

Overview

On May 28, 2014, the International Accounting Standards Board (IASB) and FASB issued a joint accounting standard on revenue recognition to address a number of concerns regarding the complexity and lack of consistency surrounding the accounting for revenue transactions. Consistent with each board's policy, FASB issued Accounting Standards Update (ASU) No. 2014-09, *Revenue from Contracts with Customers (Topic 606)*, and the IASB issued International Financial Reporting Standard (IFRS) 15, *Revenue from Contracts with Customers*. FASB ASU No. 2014-09 will amend the FASB *Accounting Standards Codification*® (ASC) by creating a new Topic 606, *Revenue from Contracts with Customers*, and a new subtopic 340-40, *Other Assets and Deferred Costs—Contracts with Customers*. The guidance in FASB ASU No. 2014-09 provides what FASB describes as a framework for revenue recognition and supersedes or amends several of the revenue recognition requirements in FASB ASC 605, *Revenue Recognition*, as well as guidance within the 900 series of industry-specific topics.

As part of the boards' efforts to converge U.S. generally accepted accounting principles (GAAP) and IFRSs, the standard eliminates the transaction- and industry-specific revenue recognition guidance under current GAAP and replaces it with a principles-based approach for revenue recognition. The intent is to avoid inconsistencies of accounting treatment across different geographies and industries. In addition to improving comparability of revenue recognition practices, the new guidance provides more useful information to financial statement users through enhanced disclosure requirements. FASB and the IASB have essentially achieved convergence with these standards, with some minor differences related to the collectibility threshold, interim disclosure requirements, early application and effective date, impairment loss reversal, and nonpublic entity requirements.

The standard applies to any entity that either enters into contracts with customers to transfer goods or services or enters into contracts for the transfer of nonfinancial assets, unless those contracts are within the scope of other standards (for example, insurance or lease contracts).

Effective or Applicability Date

The guidance in ASU No. 2014-09 was originally effective for annual reporting periods of public entities beginning after December 15, 2016, including interim periods within that reporting period. Early application was not permitted for public entities, including not-for-profit entities (NFPs) that have issued, or are conduit bond obligors for, securities that are traded, listed, or quoted on an exchange or an over-the-counter market and for employee benefit plans that file or furnish financial statements to the SEC.

For nonpublic entities, the amendments in the new guidance were originally effective for annual reporting periods beginning after December 15, 2017, and interim periods within annual periods beginning after December 15, 2018.

On August 12, 2015, FASB issued ASU No. 2015-14, *Revenue from Contracts with Customers (Topic 606): Deferral of the Effective Date*, to allow entities additional time to implement systems, gather data, and resolve implementation questions. This update allows for public business entities, certain NFPs, and certain employee benefit plans to apply the new requirements to annual reporting periods beginning after December 15, 2017, including interim reporting periods within that reporting period. Earlier application is permitted only as of annual reporting periods beginning after December 15, 2016, including interim reporting periods within that reporting period.

All other entities will now apply the guidance in ASU No. 2014-09 to annual reporting periods beginning after December 15, 2018, and interim reporting periods within annual reporting periods beginning after December 15, 2019. Application is permitted earlier only as of an annual reporting period beginning after December 15, 2016, including interim reporting periods within that reporting period, or an annual reporting period beginning after December 15, 2016, and interim reporting periods within annual reporting periods beginning one year after the annual reporting period in which an entity first applies the guidance in ASU No. 2014-09.

Overview of the New Guidance

The core principle of the revised revenue recognition standard is that an entity should recognize revenue to depict the transfer of goods or services to customers in an amount that reflects the consideration to which the entity expects to be entitled in exchange for those good or services.

To apply the proposed revenue recognition standard, ASU No. 2014-09 states that an entity should follow these five steps:

1. Identify the contract(s) with a customer.
2. Identify the performance obligations in the contract.
3. Determine the transaction price.
4. Allocate the transaction price to the performance obligations in the contract.
5. Recognize revenue when (or as) the entity satisfies a performance obligation.

Under the new standard, revenue is recognized when a company satisfies a performance obligation by transferring a promised good or service to a customer (which is when the customer obtains control of that good or service). See the following discussion of the five steps involved when recognizing revenue under the new guidance.

Understanding the Five-Step Process

Step 1: Identify the Contract(s) With a Customer

ASU No. 2014-09 defines a *contract* as "an agreement between two or more parties that creates enforceable rights and obligations." The new standard affects contracts with a customer that meet the following criteria:

- Approval (in writing, orally, or in accordance with other customary business practices) and commitment of the parties
- Identification of the rights of the parties
- Identification of the payment terms
- Contract has commercial substance
- Probable that the entity will collect substantially all the consideration to which it will be entitled in exchange for the goods or services that will be transferred to the customer

A contract does not exist if each party to the contract has the unilateral enforceable right to terminate a wholly unperformed contract without compensating the other party (parties).

Step 2: Identify the Performance Obligations in the Contract

A *performance obligation* is a promise in a contract with a customer to transfer a good or service to the customer.

At contract inception, an entity should assess the goods or services promised in a contract with a customer and identify as a performance obligation (possibly multiple performance obligations) each promise to transfer to the customer either

- a good or service (or bundle of goods or services) that is distinct, or
- a series of distinct goods or services that are substantially the same and that have the same pattern of transfer to the customer.

A good or service that is not distinct should be combined with other promised goods or services until the entity identifies a bundle of goods or services that is distinct. In some cases, that would result in the entity accounting for all the goods or services promised in a contract as a single performance obligation.

Step 3: Determine the Transaction Price

The *transaction price* is the amount of consideration (fixed or variable) the entity expects to receive in exchange for transferring promised goods or services to a customer, excluding amounts collected on behalf of third parties. To determine the transaction price, an entity should consider the effects of

- variable consideration,
- constraining estimates of variable consideration,
- the existence of a significant financing component,
- noncash considerations, and
- consideration payable to the customer.

If the consideration promised in a contract includes a variable amount, then an entity should estimate the amount of consideration to which the entity will be entitled in exchange for transferring the promised goods or services to a customer. An entity would then include in the transaction price some or all of an amount of variable consideration only to the extent that it is probable that a significant reversal in the amount of cumulative revenue recognized will not occur when the uncertainty associated with the variable consideration is subsequently resolved.

An entity should consider the terms of the contract and its customary business practices to determine the transaction price.

Step 4: Allocate the Transaction Price to the Performance Obligations in the Contract

The transaction price is allocated to separate performance obligations in proportion to the standalone selling price of the promised goods or services. If a standalone selling price is not directly observable, then an entity should estimate it. Reallocation of the transaction price for changes in the standalone selling price is not permitted. When estimating the standalone selling price, entities can use various methods, including the adjusted market assessment approach, expected cost plus a margin approach, and residual approach (only if the selling price is highly variable and uncertain).

Sometimes, the transaction price includes a discount or a variable amount of consideration that relates entirely to one of the performance obligations in a contract. Guidance under the new standard specifies when an entity should allocate the discount or variable consideration to one (or some) performance obligation(s), rather than to all the performance obligations in the contract.

Step 5: Recognize Revenue When (or as) the Entity Satisfies a Performance Obligation

The amount of revenue recognized when transferring the promised good or service to a customer is equal to the amount allocated to the satisfied performance obligation, which may be satisfied at a point in time or over time. *Control of an asset* refers to the ability to direct the use of, and obtain substantially all the remaining benefits from, the asset. Control also includes the ability to prevent *other entities* from directing the use of, and obtaining the benefits from, an asset.

When performance obligations are satisfied over time, the entity should select an appropriate method for measuring its progress toward complete satisfaction of that performance obligation. The standard discusses methods of measuring progress, including input and output methods, and how to determine which method is appropriate.

Additional Guidance Under the New Standard

In addition to the five-step process for recognizing revenue, ASU No. 2014-09 also addresses the following areas:

- Accounting for incremental costs of obtaining a contract, as well as costs incurred to fulfill a contract
- Licenses
- Warranties

Lastly, the new guidance enhances disclosure requirements to include more information about specific revenue contracts entered into by the entity, including performance obligations and the transaction price.

Subsequent Developments

Subsequent to the issuance of ASU No. 2014-09, FASB issued updates to clarify guidance on performance obligations, licensing, principal versus agent considerations, and other narrow-scope improvements and practical expedients.

ASU No. 2016-08, *Revenue from Contracts with Customers (Topic 606): Principle versus Agent Considerations (Reporting Revenue Gross versus Net)*, was issued in March 2016 to clarify the guidance in FASB ASC 606 with respect to principal versus agent. There is little disagreement that an entity who is a principal recognizes revenue in the gross amount of consideration when a performance obligation is satisfied. An entity who is an agent (collecting revenue on behalf of the principal) recognizes revenue only to the extent of the commission or fee that the agent collects. This ASU hopes to eliminate the potential diversity in practice when determining whether an entity is a principal or an agent by clarifying the following:

- An entity determines whether it is a principal or an agent for each distinct good or service.
- An entity determines the nature of each specified good or service (including whether it is a right to a good or service)
- When an entity is a principal, it obtains control of
    - — a good or another asset from the other party that it then transfers to the customer;
    - — a right to a service that will be performed by another party, which gives the entity the ability to direct that party to provide the service to the customer on the entity's behalf; or
    - — a good or service from the other party that it combines with other goods or services to provide the specified good or service to the customer.
- Indicators in the assessment of control may be more or less relevant or persuasive, or both, to the control assessment, depending on the facts and circumstances.

Additional illustrative examples are also provided in ASU No. 2016-08 to further assist practitioners in applying this guidance. The effective date of this update is in line with the guidance in ASU No. 2014-09, as amended by ASU No. 2015-14.

ASU No. 2016-10, *Revenue from Contracts with Customers (Topic 606): Identifying Performance Obligations and Licensing*, was issued in April 2016 to reduce potential for diversity in practice at initial application of FASB ASC 606, as well as the cost and complexity of applying FASB ASC 606 at transition and on an ongoing basis. When identifying promised goods and services in a contract, this ASU states that entities

- are not required to assess whether promised goods or services are performance obligations if they are immaterial to the contract.

- can elect to account for shipping and handling activities as an activity to fulfill promises within the contract, rather than as an additional promised service.

When assessing whether promised goods or services are distinct, this ASU emphasizes the need to determine whether the nature of the promise is to transfer

- each of the goods or services, or
- a combined item (or items) to which the promised goods or services are inputs.

With regards to licensing, ASU No. 2016-10 clarifies whether revenue should be recognized at a point in time or over time, based on whether the license provides a right to use an entity's intellectual property or a right to access the entity's intellectual property. Specifically,

- if the intellectual property has significant standalone functionality, the license does not include supporting or maintaining that intellectual property during the license period. Therefore, the performance obligation would be considered satisfied at a point in time. Examples of this type of intellectual property include software, biological compounds or drug formulas, and media.
- licenses for symbolic intellectual property include supporting or maintaining that intellectual property during the license period and, therefore, are considered to be satisfied over time. Examples of symbolic intellectual property include brands, team or trade names, logos, and franchise rights.

Lastly, ASU No. 2016-10 provides clarification on implementation guidance on recognizing revenue for sales-based or usage-based royalty promised in exchange for a license of intellectual property. The effective date of this ASU is in line with the guidance in ASU No. 2014-09, as amended by ASU No. 2015-14.

FASB ASU No. 2016-12, *Revenue from Contracts with Customers (Topic 606): Narrow-Scope Improvements and Practical Expedients*, was issued in May 2016. Topics covered in this ASU include

- clarification on contract modifications. This amendment permits an entity to determine and allocate the transaction price on the basis of all satisfied and unsatisfied performance obligations in a modified contract as of the beginning of the earliest period presented in accordance with the guidance in FASB ASC 606. An entity would not be required to separately evaluate the effects of each contract modification. An entity that chooses to apply this practical expedient would apply the expedient consistently to similar types of contracts.
- how to assess the collectibility criterion. The amendment introduces new criteria to meet the collectibility requirement. An entity should assess the collectibility of the consideration promised in a contract for the goods or services that will be transferred to the customer, rather than assessing the collectibility of the consideration promised in the contract for all the promised goods or services.
- how to report sales taxes and similar taxes. This amendment states that an entity may make an accounting policy election to exclude from the measurement of the transaction price all taxes

assessed by a governmental authority that are both imposed on and concurrent with a specific revenue-producing transaction and collected by the entity from a customer (for example, sales, use, value added, and some excise taxes). Taxes assessed on an entity's total gross receipts or imposed during the inventory procurement process should be excluded from the scope of the election. An entity that makes this election should exclude from the transaction price all taxes in the scope of the election and should comply with the applicable accounting policy guidance, including disclosure requirements.

- when to measure noncash consideration. This amendment clarifies that the measurement date for noncash consideration is contract inception. If the fair value of the noncash consideration varies because of the form of the consideration and for reasons other than the form of the consideration, an entity should apply the guidance on variable consideration only to the variability resulting from reasons other than the form of the consideration.
- how to apply transition guidance. This amendment clarifies that a completed contract for purposes of transition is a contract for which all (or substantially all) the revenue was recognized under legacy GAAP before the date of initial application. Accounting for elements of a contract that do not affect revenue under legacy GAAP are irrelevant to the assessment of whether a contract is complete. In addition, the amendment permits an entity to apply the modified retrospective transition method either to all contracts or only to contracts that are not completed contracts.

The effective date of this ASU is in line with the guidance in ASU No. 2014-09, as amended by ASU No. 2015-14.

FASB also issued ASU No. 2016-20, *Technical Corrections and Improvements to Topic 606, Revenue from Contracts with Customers*, in December 2016. These amendments affect narrow aspects of guidance issued in ASU No. 2014-09, including but not limited to, guidance on

- impairment testing. When performing impairment testing, an entity should consider expected contract renewals and extensions. In addition, the assessment should include both the amount of consideration it already has received but has not yet recognized as revenue, and the amount it expects to receive in the future.
- additional scope exceptions. The term "insurance" is removed from the scope exceptions of Topic 606 to clarify that all contracts within the scope of Topic 944, *Financial Services – Insurance*, are excluded.
- provisions for losses on construction-type and production-type contracts. Such provisions should be determined at least at the contract level; however, an entity can make an accounting policy election to determine the provision for losses at the performance obligation level.
- disclosure of remaining performance obligations. Optional exemptions from the disclosure requirement are provided for remaining performance obligations when an entity is not required to estimate variable consideration to recognize revenue.

Consistent with the other ASUs, the effective date of ASU No. 2016-20 is in line with the guidance in ASU No. 2014-09, as amended by ASU No. 2015-14.

In February 2017, FASB issued ASU No. 2017-05, *Other Income—Gains and Losses from the Derecognition of Nonfinancial Assets (Subtopic 610-20): Clarifying the Scope of Asset Derecognition Guidance and Accounting for Partial Sales of Nonfinancial Assets*. The amendments in this ASU include, but are not limited to

- a definition of the term *in substance nonfinancial asset*, to clarify the scope of FASB ASC 610-20. An in substance nonfinancial asset is, in part, a financial asset promised to a counterparty in a contract if substantially all of the fair value of the assets (recognized and unrecognized) that are promised to the counterparty in the contract is concentrated in nonfinancial assets. An in substance nonfinancial asset also includes a financial asset that is held in an individual consolidated subsidiary within a contract if substantially all the fair value of the assets (recognized and unrecognized) that are promised to the counterparty in that subsidiary is concentrated in nonfinancial assets.
- a clarification that nonfinancial assets within the scope of FASB ASC 610-20 may include nonfinancial assets transferred within a legal entity to a counterparty. For example, a parent may transfer control of nonfinancial assets by transferring ownership interests in a consolidated subsidiary. A contract that includes the transfer of ownership interests in one or more consolidated subsidiaries is within the scope of Subtopic 610-20 if substantially all of the fair value of the assets that are promised to the counterparty in a contract is concentrated in nonfinancial assets.
- removal of the scope exception for transfers of equity method investment that were considered in substance nonfinancial assets. All transfers of equity method investments will be accounted for in accordance with FASB ASC 860, *Transfers and Servicing*.
- derecognition of each distinct nonfinancial asset or in substance nonfinancial asset promised to a counterparty. Each asset will be derecognized when a counterparty obtains control of it. The amendments also clarify that an entity should allocate consideration to each distinct asset by applying the guidance in FASB ASC 606 on allocating the transaction price to performance obligations.
- partial sales transactions. An entity will derecognize a distinct nonfinancial asset or distinct in substance nonfinancial asset in a partial sale transaction when it (1) does not have (or ceases to have) a controlling financial interest in the legal entity that holds the asset in accordance with FASB ASC 810, *Consolidation*, and (2) transfers control of the asset in accordance with FASB ASC 606. Once an entity transfers control of a distinct nonfinancial asset or distinct in substance nonfinancial asset, it is required to measure any noncontrolling interest it receives (or retains) at fair value. If an entity transfers ownership interests in a consolidated subsidiary and continues to have a controlling financial interest in that subsidiary, it does not derecognize the assets and liabilities of the subsidiary and accounts for the transaction as an equity transaction. Therefore, no gain or loss is recognized.

- contributions of nonfinancial assets to a joint venture or other noncontrolled investee. These contributions will be within the scope of FASB ASC 610-20, and an entity will recognize a full gain or loss on transfers of nonfinancial assets to equity method investees.

Consistent with the other ASUs, the effective date of ASU No. 2017-05 is in line with the guidance in ASU No. 2014-09, as amended by ASU No. 2015-14.

FASB also issued ASU No. 2017-13, *Revenue Recognition (Topic 605), Revenue from Contracts with Customers (Topic 606), Leases (Topic 840), and Leases (Topic 842): Amendments to SEC Paragraphs Pursuant to the Staff Announcement at the July 20, 2017 EITF Meeting and Rescission of Prior SEC Staff Announcements and Observer Comments*, in September 2017. The amendments in this ASU state that public entities that do not meet the definition of a public business entity except for a requirement to include or the inclusion of its financial statements or financial information in another entity's filing with the SEC may adopt the effective date for nonpublic entities.

Conclusion

Upon implementation of the new standard, consistency of revenue recognition principles across geography and industry will be enhanced, and financial statement users will be provided better insight through improved disclosure requirements. To provide CPAs with guidance during this time of transition, the AICPA's Financial Reporting Center (FRC) offers invaluable resources on the topic, including a roadmap to ensure that companies take the necessary steps to prepare themselves for the new standard. In addition, the FRC includes a list of conferences, webcasts, and other products to keep you informed on upcoming changes in revenue recognition. Refer to www.aicpa.org/interestareas/frc/accountingfinancialreporting/revenuerecognition/pages/revenuerecognition.aspx to stay updated on the latest information available on revenue recognition.

In addition, the AICPA continues to update the Revenue Recognition – Audit and Accounting Guide to include key accounting implementation issues across 16 industry task forces. Although the implementation issues have not all been finalized across the 16 task forces, this guide is currently available for purchase at https://www.aicpastore.com/accounting/revenue-recognition—audit-and-accounting-guide/prdovr~pc-012516/pc-012516.jsp, including updates to the guide as they become available.

Appendix C

The New Leases Standard: FASB ASC 842

This appendix is nonauthoritative and is included for informational purposes only.

Overview

Issuance and Objective

On February 25, 2016, FASB issued Accounting Standards Update (ASU) No. 2016-02, *Leases (Topic 842)*. The objective of the ASU is to increase transparency and comparability in financial reporting by requiring balance sheet recognition of leases and note disclosure of certain information about lease arrangements. This ASU codifies the new FASB ASC topic 842, *Leases*, and makes conforming amendments to other FASB ASC topics.

The new FASB ASC topic on leases consists of these subtopics:

a. Overall
b. Lessee
c. Lessor
d. Sale and leaseback transactions
e. Leveraged lease arrangements

Applicability and Effective Date

ASU No. 2016-02 is applicable to any entity that enters into a lease and is effective as follows:

	Fiscal Years Beginning After	*Interim Periods Within Fiscal Years Beginning After*
Public business entities, certain not-for-profit entities with conduit financing arrangements, and employee benefit plans	December 15, 2018	December 15, 2018
All other entities	December 15, 2019	December 15, 2020

FASB ASC 842 applies to all leases and subleases of property, plant, and equipment; it specifically does not apply to the following nondepreciable assets accounted for under other FASB ASC topics:

a. Leases of intangible assets
b. Leases to explore for or use nonregenerative resources such as minerals, oil, and natural gas
c. Leases of biological assets, such as timber
d. Leases of inventory
e. Leases of assets under construction

Main Provisions

Overall

Identifying a Lease

Key changes in the guidance are illustrated by comparing the definition of a lease in FASB ASC 840 (extant GAAP) and FASB ASC 842.

FASB ASC 840	*FASB ASC 842*
An agreement conveying the right to use property, plant, or equipment (land and/or depreciable assets) usually for a stated period of time.	A contract, or part of a contract, that conveys the right to control the use of identified property, plant, or equipment (an identified asset) for a period of time in exchange for consideration.

The identification of a lease under FASB ASC 842 should be based on the presence of key elements in the definition.

Separating Components of a Lease Contract

Under FASB ASC 842, a contract that contains a lease should be separated into lease and nonlease components. Separation should be based on the right to use; each underlying asset should be considered to be separate from other lease components when both of the following criteria are met:

a. The lessee can benefit from the right-of-use of the asset (either alone or with other readily available resources)

b. The right-of-use is neither highly dependent on or highly interrelated with other underlying assets in the contract

The consideration in the contract should be allocated to the separate lease and nonlease components in accordance with provisions of FASB ASC 842.

Lessees can make an accounting policy election to treat both lease and nonlease elements as a single lease component.

Lease Classification

When a lease meets any of the following specified criteria at commencement, the lease should be classified by the lessee and lessor as a finance lease and a sales-type lease, respectively. These criteria can be summarized as follows:

a. Transfers ownership to lessee

b. Purchase option reasonably certain to be exercised

c. Lease term for major portion of asset's remaining economic life

d. Present value of lease payments and residual value exceeds substantially all of the fair value of the underlying asset

e. Specialized nature of underlying asset results in no expectation of alternative use after the lease term

If none of the above criteria are met, the lease should be classified as follows:

Lessee—classify as an operating lease

Lessor—classify as an operating lease unless (1) the present value of the lease payments and any residual value guarantee that equals or exceeds substantially all of the fair value of the underlying asset and (2) it is probable that the lessor will collect the lease payments plus any residual value guarantee. If both of these summarized criteria from FASB ASC 842-10-25-3 are met, the lessor should classify the lease as a direct financing lease.

Lease Term and Measurement

The lease term is the noncancellable period of the lease together with all of the following:

a. Period covered by the option for the lessee to extend the lease if the option is reasonably certain to be exercised

b. Period covered by option for lessee to terminate the lease if reasonably certain not to be exercised

c. Period covered by option for lessor to extend or not terminate the lease if option is controlled by lessor.

Lease Payments

Lease payments relating to use of the underlying asset during the lease term include the following at the commencement date:

a. Fixed payments less incentives payable to lessee

b. Variable lease payments based on an index or other rate

c. Exercise price of an option to purchase the underlying asset if it is reasonably certain to be exercised

d. Payments for penalties for terminating a lease if the lease term reflects exercise of lessee option

e. Fees paid by the lessee to the owners of a special purpose entity for structuring the lease

f. For lessee only, amounts probable of being owed under residual value guarantees

Lease payments specifically exclude the following:

a. Certain other variable lease payments

b. Any guarantee by the lessee of the lessor's debt

c. Certain amounts allocated to nonlease components

Reassessment of the lease term and purchase options, and subsequent remeasurement by either the lessee or lessor are limited to certain specified circumstances.

Lessee

Recognition and Measurement

Commencement Date

At the commencement date of the lease, a lessee should recognize a right-of-use asset and a lease liability; for short term leases, an alternative accounting policy election is available.

The lease liability should be measured at the present value of the unpaid lease payments. The right-of-use asset should consist of the following: the amount of the initial lease liability; any lease payments made to lessor at or before the commencement date minus any incentives received; and initial direct costs.

A short term lease is defined by the FASB ASC master glossary as a lease that, at the commencement date has a lease term of 12 months or less and does not include an option to purchase the underlying asset that the lessee is reasonably certain to exercise. The accounting policy election for short term leases should be made by class of underlying asset. The election provides for recognition of the lease payments in profit or loss on a straight-line basis over the lease term and variable lease payments in the period in which the obligation for those payments is incurred.

After the Commencement Date

After the commencement date, the lessee should recognize in profit or loss (unless costs are included in the carrying amount of another asset) the following:

- Finance leases:
  - *a.* Amortization of the right-of-use asset and interest on the lease liability
  - *b.* Variable lease payments not included in the lease liability in the period obligation incurred
  - *c.* Any impairment
- Operating leases:
  - *a.* A single lease cost calculated such that the remaining cost is allocated on a straight line basis over the remaining lease term (unless another allocation is more representative of the benefit from use of the asset)
  - *b.* Variable lease payments not included in the lease liability in the period in which the obligation is incurred
  - *c.* Any impairment

Subsequent Measurement

FASB ASC 842-20-35 provides guidance for subsequent measurement.

Presentation and Disclosure

Key presentation matters include the following:

- Statement of financial position.
  - — Separate presentation of right-of-use assets and lease liabilities from finance leases and operating leases.
- Statement of comprehensive income.
  - — Finance leases—interest expense on the lease liability and amortization of right-of-use asset in a manner consistent with how the entity presents other interest expense and depreciation or amortization of similar assets.
  - — Operating leases—expense to be included in the lessee's income from continuing operations.

- Statement of cash flows.
  - Presentation within financing activities—the repayment of the principal portion of the lease liability arising from finance leases.
  - Presentation within operating activities—payments arising from operating leases; interest payments on the lease liability; variable lease payments and short term lease payments not included in lease liability.

Disclosure requirements include qualitative and quantitative information for leases, significant judgements, and amounts recognized in the financial statements, including certain specified information and amounts.

Lessor

Recognition and Measurement

FASB ASC 842 provides recognition guidance for sales-type leases, direct financing leases, and operating leases. The following table summarizes the guidance:

Sales-Type Leases	
At the Commencement Date	**After the Commencement Date**
Lessor should derecognize the underlying asset and recognize the following: *a.* Net investment in the lease (lease receivable and unguaranteed residual asset) *b.* Selling profit or loss arising from the lease *c.* Initial direct costs as an expense	Lessor should recognize all of the following: *a.* Interest income on the net investment in the lease *b.* Certain variable lease payments *c.* Impairment
Direct Financing Leases	
At the Commencement Date	**After the Commencement Date**
Lessor should derecognize the underlying asset and recognize the following: *a.* Net investment in the lease (lease receivable and unguaranteed residual asset reduced by selling profit) *b.* Selling loss arising from the lease, if applicable	Lessor should recognize all of the following: *a.* Interest income on the net investment in the lease *b.* Certain variable lease payments *c.* Impairment

(*continued*)

Operating Leases	
At the Commencement Date	**After the Commencement Date**
Lessor should defer initial direct costs.	Lessor should recognize all of the following: *a.* The lease payments as income in profit or loss over the lease term on a straight line basis (unless another method in more representative of the benefit received) *b.* Certain variable lease payments as income in profit or loss *c.* Initial direct costs as an expense over the lease term on the same basis as lease income

FASB ASC 842-30-35 provides guidance for subsequent measurement.

Presentation and Disclosure

Key presentation matters include the following:

For sales-type and direct financing leases:

- Statement of financial position
  - Separate presentation of lease assets (that is, aggregate of lessor's net investment in sales-type leases and direct financing leases) from other assets.
  - Classified as current or noncurrent based on same considerations as other assets.
- Statement of comprehensive income
  - Presentation of income from leases in the statement of comprehensive income or disclosure of income from leases in the notes with a reference to the corresponding line in the statement of comprehensive income.
  - Presentation of profit or loss recognized at commencement date in a manner appropriate to lessor's business model.
- Statement of cash flows
  - Presentation within operating activities—cash receipts from leases.

For operating leases:

- Statement of financial position
  - Presentation of an underlying asset subject to an operating leases in accordance with other FASB ASC topics.

- Statement of cash flows
  - Presentation within operating activities—cash receipts from leases.

Disclosure requirements include qualitative and quantitative information for leases, significant judgements, and amounts recognized in the financial statements, including certain specified information and amounts.

Sale and Leaseback Transactions

FASB ASC 842 provides guidance for both the transfer contract and the lease in a sale and leaseback transaction (a transaction in which a seller-lessee transfers an asset to a buyer-lessor and leases that asset back). Determination of whether the transfer is a sale should be based on provisions of FASB ASC 606, *Revenue from Contracts with Customers*. FASB ASC 842-40-25 provides measurement guidance for a transfer that is either determined to be a sale or determined not to be a sale.

FASB ASC 842-40 provides guidance for subsequent measurement, financial statement presentation, and disclosures.

Leveraged Lease Arrangements

The legacy accounting model for leveraged leases continues to apply to those leveraged leases that commenced before the effective date of FASB ASC 842. There is no separate accounting model for leveraged leases that commence after the effective date of FASB ASC 842.

Subsequent Developments

In January 2018, FASB issued ASU No. 2018-01, *Leases (Topic 842): Land Easement Practical Expedient for Transition to Topic 842*. This ASU permits an entity to elect an optional transition practical expedient to not evaluate under FASB ASC 842 existing or expired land easements not previously accounted for as leases under FASB ASC 840. The effective date of FASB ASU No. 2018-01 is in line with the guidance in ASU No. 2016-02.

Appendix D

FASB Accounting Standards Codification 958, Not-For-Profit Entities, *Topic Hierarchy*

This appendix is nonauthoritative and is included for informational purposes only.

The purpose of this appendix is to assist readers in their understanding of the structure of the FASB *Accounting Standards Codification* (ASC).

Within this guide, FASB ASC references follow the style articulated in FASB's notice to constituents, which can be found on the FASB ASC home page at http://asc.fasb.org/home. The basic reference format is FASB ASC 958-10-05-1, in which 958 is the topic (*Not-for-Profit-Entities*); 10 is the subtopic ("Overall"); 05 is the section ("Overview and Background"); and 1 is the paragraph.

The following table provides the list of subtopics and sections included within FASB ASC 958, *Not-for-Profit Entities*, as of March 1, 2013.

958	Not-for-Profit Entities		
	10	Overall	
		00	Status
		05	Overview and Background
		15	Scope and Scope Exceptions
		20	Glossary
		45	Other Presentation Matters
		60	Relationships
	20	Financially Interrelated Entities	
		00	Status
		05	Overview and Background
		15	Scope and Scope Exceptions
		20	Glossary
		25	Recognition
		35	Subsequent Measurement
		45	Other Presentation Matters
		50	Disclosure
		55	Implementation Guidance and Illustrations
		60	Relationships
		75	XBRL Elements
	30	Split-Interest Agreements	
		00	Status

	05	Overview and Background
	15	Scope and Scope Exceptions
	20	Glossary
	25	Recognition
	30	Initial Measurement
	35	Subsequent Measurement
	40	Derecognition
	45	Other Presentation Matters
	50	Disclosure
	55	Implementation Guidance and Illustrations
	75	XBRL Elements
205	Presentation of Financial Statements	
	00	Status
	05	Overview and Background
	10	Objectives
	15	Scope and Scope Exceptions
	20	Glossary
	45	Other Presentation Matters
	50	Disclosure
	55	Implementation Guidance and Illustrations
	60	Relationships
	65	Transition and Open Effective Date Information
	75	XBRL Elements
210	Balance Sheet	
	00	Status
	05	Overview and Background
	15	Scope and Scope Exceptions
	20	Glossary
	45	Other Presentation Matters
	50	Disclosure
	55	Implementation Guidance and Illustrations
	60	Relationships
220	Income Statement	
	00	Status
	05	Overview and Background

	15	Scope and Scope Exceptions
	20	Glossary
	45	Other Presentation Matters
	50	Disclosure
	55	Implementation Guidance and Illustrations
	75	XBRL Elements
230	Statement of Cash Flows	
	00	Status
	05	Overview and Background
	15	Scope and Scope Exceptions
	20	Glossary
	55	Implementation Guidance and Illustrations
	75	XBRL Elements
310	Receivables	
	00	Status
	05	Overview and Background
	15	Scope and Scope Exceptions
	20	Glossary
	25	Recognition
	30	Initial Measurement
	35	Subsequent Measurement
	45	Other Presentation Matters
	50	Disclosure
	55	Implementation Guidance and Illustrations
320	Investments—Debt and Equity Securities	
	00	Status
	05	Overview and Background
	15	Scope and Scope Exceptions
	20	Glossary
	25	Recognition
	30	Initial Measurement
	35	Subsequent Measurement
	45	Other Presentation Matters
	50	Disclosure
	55	Implementation Guidance and Illustrations

	60	Relationships
	75	XBRL Elements
321	Investments—Equity Securities ("Pending Content")	
	00	Status
	05	Overview and Background
	15	Scope and Scope Exceptions
	20	Glossary
	25	Recognition
	30	Initial Measurement
	35	Subsequent Measurement
	50	Disclosure
325	Investments—Other	
	00	Status
	05	Overview and Background
	15	Scope and Scope Exceptions
	20	Glossary
	25	Recognition
	30	Initial Measurement
	35	Subsequent Measurement
	45	Other Presentation Matters
	50	Disclosure
	60	Relationships
	75	XBRL Elements
360	Property, Plant, and Equipment	
	00	Status
	05	Overview and Background
	15	Scope and Scope Exceptions
	20	Glossary
	25	Recognition
	30	Initial Measurement
	35	Subsequent Measurement
	40	Derecognition
	45	Other Presentation Matters
	50	Disclosure
	55	Implementation Guidance and Illustrations

405	Liabilities	
	05	Overview and Background
	15	Scope and Scope Exceptions
	20	Glossary
	25	Recognition
	30	Initial Measurement
	35	Subsequent Measurement
	45	Other Presentation Matters
	50	Disclosure
	60	Relationships
450	Contingencies	
	00	Status
	05	Overview and Background
	15	Scope and Scope Exceptions
	20	Glossary
	25	Recognition
	50	Disclosure
470	Debt	
	00	Status
	05	Overview and Background
	15	Scope and Scope Exceptions
	25	Recognition
605	Revenue Recognition	
	00	Status
	05	Overview and Background
	15	Scope and Scope Exceptions
	20	Glossary
	25	Recognition
	30	Initial Measurement
	35	Subsequent Measurement
	45	Other Presentation Matters
	50	Disclosure
	55	Implementation Guidance and Illustrations
	75	XBRL Elements
715	Compensation—Retirement Benefits	

	00	Status
	05	Overview and Background
	15	Scope and Scope Exceptions
	20	Glossary
	25	Recognition
	35	Subsequent Measurement
	45	Other Presentation Matters
	50	Disclosure
	55	Implementation Guidance and Illustrations
	65	Transition and Open Effective Date Information
720	Other Expenses	
	00	Status
	05	Overview and Background
	15	Scope and Scope Exceptions
	20	Glossary
	25	Recognition
	30	Initial Measurement
	45	Other Presentation Matters
	50	Disclosure
	55	Implementation Guidance and Illustrations
	60	Relationships
	65	Transition and Open Effective Date Information
805	Business Combinations	
	00	Status
	05	Overview and Background
	10	Objectives
	15	Scope and Scope Exceptions
	20	Glossary
	25	Recognition
	30	Initial Measurement
	35	Subsequent Measurement
	45	Other Presentation Matters
	50	Disclosure
	55	Implementation Guidance and Illustrations
	65	Transition and Open Effective Date Information

	75	XBRL Elements
810	Consolidation	
	00	Status
	05	Overview and Background
	15	Scope and Scope Exceptions
	20	Glossary
	25	Recognition
	45	Other Presentation Matters
	50	Disclosure
	55	Implementation Guidance and Illustrations
	60	Relationships
	65	Transition and Open Effective Date Information
	75	XBRL Elements
815	Derivatives and Hedging	
	05	Overview and Background
	15	Scope and Scope Exceptions
	25	Recognition
	55	Implementation Guidance and Illustrations
840	Leases	
	05	Overview and Background
	15	Scope and Scope Exceptions
	20	Glossary
	55	Implementation Guidance and Illustrations

Appendix E

Information Sources

This appendix is nonauthoritative and is included for informational purposes only.

Further information on matters addressed in this guide is available through various publications and services listed in the table that follows. Many nongovernment and some government publications and services involve a charge or membership requirement.

Fax services allow users to follow voice cues and request that selected documents be sent by fax machine. Some fax services require the user to call from the handset of the fax machine, others allow the user to call from any phone. Most fax services offer an index document, which lists titles and other information describing available documents.

Electronic bulletin board services allow users to read, copy, and exchange information electronically. Most are available using a modem and standard communications software. Some bulletin board services are also available using one or more Internet protocols.

Recorded announcements allow users to listen to announcements about a variety of recent or scheduled actions or meetings.

All telephone numbers listed are voice lines, unless otherwise designated as fax (f) lines.

Information Sources

Organization	*General Information*	*Website*
American Institute of Certified Public Accountants	*Order Department* 220 Leigh Farm Road Durham, NC 27707 (888) 777.7077 *Audit and Accounting Technical Information Hotline* (877) 242.7212 Information about AICPA CPE programs is available by calling (888) 777.7077	www.aicpa.org
Financial Accounting Standards Board	*Order Department* P.O. Box 5116 Norwalk, CT 06856-5116 (800) 748.0659	www.fasb.org
National Association of College and University Business Officers	1110 Vermont Avenue NW Suite 800 Washington, D.C. 20005 (202) 861.2500 (800) 462.4916 (202) 861.2583 (f)	www.nacubo.org

(continued)

Information Sources—*continued*

Organization	*General Information*	*Website*
National Health Council	1730 M Street NW Suite 500 Washington, D.C. 20036 (202) 785.3910 (202) 785.5923 (f)	www.nationalhealthcouncil.org
U.S. Department of Education	Office of Inspector General U.S. Department of Education 400 Maryland Avenue SW Washington, D.C. 20202 (800) 872.5327	https://www.ed.gov/
U.S. Government Accountability Office	U.S. GAO 441 G Street NW Washington, D.C. 20548 (202) 512.3000 Publications (866) 801.7077	www.gao.gov
U.S. Office of Management and Budget	Office of Administration, Publications Office 725 17th Street NW Washington, D.C. 20503 (202) 395.3080 (202) 395.3888 (f)	www.whitehouse.gov/omb/ *Uniform Administrative Requirements, Cost Principles, and Audit Requirements for Federal Awards*, technical corrections, and other resources related to the Uniform Guidance are available at https://cfo.gov/cofar/.
Other		*The Rutgers Bulletin Board* at http://accounting.rutgers.edu/ includes various accounting related databases.

Appendix F

Overview of Statements on Quality Control Standards

This appendix is nonauthoritative and is included for informational purposes only.

This appendix is a partial reproduction of chapter 1 of the AICPA practice aid *Establishing and Maintaining a System of Quality Control for a CPA Firm's Accounting and Auditing Practice*, available at www.aicpa.org/interestareas/frc/pages/enhancingauditqualitypracticeaid.aspx.

This appendix highlights certain aspects of the quality control standards issued by the AICPA. If appropriate, readers should also refer to the quality control standards issued by the PCAOB, available at www.pcaobus.org/standards/qc/pages/default.aspx.

1.01 The objectives of a system of quality control are to provide a CPA firm with reasonable assurance[1] that the firm and its personnel comply with professional standards and applicable regulatory and legal requirements, and that the firm or engagement partners issue reports that are appropriate in the circumstances. QC section 10, *A Firm's System of Quality Control* (AICPA, *Professional Standards*), addresses a CPA firm's responsibilities for its system of quality control for its accounting and auditing practice. That section is to be read in conjunction with the AICPA Code of Professional Conduct and other relevant ethical requirements.

1.02 A system of quality control consists of policies designed to achieve the objectives of the system and the procedures necessary to implement and monitor compliance with those policies. The nature, extent, and formality of a firm's quality control policies and procedures will depend on various factors such as the firm's size; the number and operating characteristics of its offices; the degree of authority allowed to, and the knowledge and experience possessed by, firm personnel; and the nature and complexity of the firm's practice.

Communication of Quality Control Policies and Procedures

1.03 The firm should communicate its quality control policies and procedures to its personnel. Most firms will find it appropriate to communicate their policies and procedures in writing and distribute them, or make them available electronically, to all professional personnel. Effective communication includes the following:

- A description of quality control policies and procedures and the objectives they are designed to achieve

---

[1] The term *reasonable assurance*, which is defined as a high, but not absolute, level of assurance, is used because absolute assurance cannot be attained. Paragraph .53 of QC section 10, *A Firm's System of Quality Control* (AICPA, *Professional Standards*), states, "Any system of quality control has inherent limitations that can reduce its effectiveness."

- The message that each individual has a personal responsibility for quality
- A requirement for each individual to be familiar with and to comply with these policies and procedures

Effective communication also includes procedures for personnel to communicate their views or concerns on quality control matters to the firm's management.

Elements of a System of Quality Control

1.04 A firm must establish and maintain a system of quality control. The firm's system of quality control should include policies and procedures that address each of the following elements of quality control identified in paragraph .17 of QC section 10:

- Leadership responsibilities for quality within the firm (the "tone at the top")
- Relevant ethical requirements
- Acceptance and continuance of client relationships and specific engagements
- Human resources
- Engagement performance
- Monitoring

1.05 The elements of quality control are interrelated. For example, a firm continually assesses client relationships to comply with relevant ethical requirements, including independence, integrity, and objectivity, and policies and procedures related to the acceptance and continuance of client relationships and specific engagements. Similarly, the human resources element of quality control encompasses criteria related to professional development, hiring, advancement, and assignment of firm personnel to engagements, all of which affect policies and procedures related to engagement performance. In addition, policies and procedures related to the monitoring element of quality control enable a firm to evaluate whether its policies and procedures for each of the other five elements of quality control are suitably designed and effectively applied.

1.06 Policies and procedures established by the firm related to each element are designed to achieve reasonable assurance with respect to the purpose of that element. Deficiencies in policies and procedures for an element may result in not achieving reasonable assurance with respect to the purpose of that element; however, the system of quality control, as a whole, may still be effective in providing the firm with reasonable assurance that the firm and its personnel comply with professional standards and applicable regulatory and legal requirements and that the firm or engagement partners issue reports that are appropriate in the circumstances.

1.07 If a firm merges, acquires, sells, or otherwise changes a portion of its practice, the surviving firm evaluates and, as necessary, revises, implements, and maintains firm-wide quality control policies and procedures that are appropriate for the changed circumstances.

Leadership Responsibilities for Quality Within the Firm (the "Tone at the Top")

1.08 The purpose of the leadership responsibilities element of a system of quality control is to promote an internal culture based on the recognition that quality is essential in performing engagements. The firm should establish and maintain the following policies and procedures to achieve this purpose:

- Require the firm's leadership (managing partner, board of managing partners, CEO, or equivalent) to assume ultimate responsibility for the firm's system of quality control.
- Provide the firm with reasonable assurance that personnel assigned operational responsibility for the firm's quality control system have sufficient and appropriate experience and ability to identify and understand quality control issues and develop appropriate policies and procedures, as well as the necessary authority to implement those policies and procedures.

1.09 Establishing and maintaining the following policies and procedures assists firms in recognizing that the firm's business strategy is subject to the overarching requirement for the firm to achieve the objectives of the system of quality control in all the engagements that the firm performs:

- Assign management responsibilities so that commercial considerations do not override the quality of the work performed.
- Design policies and procedures addressing performance evaluation, compensation, and advancement (including incentive systems) with regard to personnel to demonstrate the firm's overarching commitment to the objectives of the system of quality control.
- Devote sufficient and appropriate resources for the development, communication, and support of its quality control policies and procedures.

Relevant Ethical Requirements

1.10 The purpose of the relevant ethical requirements element of a system of quality control is to provide the firm with reasonable assurance that the firm and its personnel comply with relevant ethical requirements when discharging professional responsibilities. Relevant ethical requirements include independence, integrity, and objectivity. Establishing and maintaining policies such as the following assist the firm in obtaining this assurance:

- Require that personnel adhere to relevant ethical requirements such as those in regulations, interpretations, and rules of the AICPA, state CPA societies, state boards of accountancy, state statutes, the U.S. Government Accountability Office, and any other applicable regulators.
- Establish procedures to communicate independence requirements to firm personnel and, where applicable, others subject to them.
- Establish procedures to identify and evaluate possible threats to independence and objectivity, including the familiarity threat that may be created by using the same senior personnel on an audit

or attest engagement over a long period of time, and to take appropriate action to eliminate those threats or reduce them to an acceptable level by applying safeguards.

- Require that the firm withdraw from the engagement if effective safeguards to reduce threats to independence to an acceptable level cannot be applied.
- Require written confirmation, at least annually, of compliance with the firm's policies and procedures on independence from all firm personnel required to be independent by relevant requirements.
- Establish procedures for confirming the independence of another firm or firm personnel in associated member firms who perform part of the engagement. This would apply to national firm personnel, foreign firm personnel, and foreign-associated firms.[2]
- Require the rotation of personnel for audit or attest engagements where regulatory or other authorities require such rotation after a specified period.

Acceptance and Continuance of Client Relationships and Specific Engagements

1.11 The purpose of the quality control element that addresses acceptance and continuance of client relationships and specific engagements is to establish criteria for deciding whether to accept or continue a client relationship and whether to perform a specific engagement for a client. A firm's client acceptance and continuance policies represent a key element in mitigating litigation and business risk. Accordingly, it is important that a firm be aware that the integrity and reputation of a client's management could reflect the reliability of the client's accounting records and financial representations and, therefore, affect the firm's reputation or involvement in litigation. A firm's policies and procedures related to the acceptance and continuance of client relationships and specific engagements should provide the firm with reasonable assurance that it will undertake or continue relationships and engagements only where it

- is competent to perform the engagement and has the capabilities, including the time and resources, to do so;
- can comply with legal and relevant ethical requirements;
- has considered the client's integrity and does not have information that would lead it to conclude that the client lacks integrity; and
- has reached an understanding with the client regarding the services to be performed.

1.12 This assurance should be obtained before accepting an engagement with a new client, when deciding whether to continue an existing engagement, and when considering acceptance of a new engagement with an existing client.

---

[2] A *foreign-associated firm* is a firm domiciled outside of the United States and its territories that is a member of, correspondent with, or similarly associated with an international firm or international association of firms.

Establishing and maintaining policies such as the following assist the firm in obtaining this assurance:

- Evaluate factors that have a bearing on management's integrity and consider the risk associated with providing professional services in particular circumstances.[3]
- Evaluate whether the engagement can be completed with professional competence; undertake only those engagements for which the firm has the capabilities, resources, and professional competence to complete; and evaluate, at the end of specific periods or upon occurrence of certain events, whether the relationship should be continued.
- Obtain an understanding, preferably in writing, with the client regarding the services to be performed.
- Establish procedures on continuing an engagement and the client relationship, including procedures for dealing with information that would have caused the firm to decline an engagement if the information had been available earlier.
- Require documentation of how issues relating to acceptance or continuance of client relationships and specific engagements were resolved.

Human Resources

1.13 The purpose of the human resources element of a system of quality control is to provide the firm with reasonable assurance that it has sufficient personnel with the capabilities, competence, and commitment to ethical principles necessary (*a*) to perform its engagements in accordance with professional standards and regulatory and legal requirements, and (*b*) to enable the firm to issue reports that are appropriate in the circumstances. Establishing and maintaining policies such as the following assist the firm in obtaining this assurance:

- Recruit and hire personnel of integrity who possess the characteristics that enable them to perform competently.
- Determine capabilities and competencies required for an engagement, especially for the engagement partner, based on the characteristics of the particular client, industry, and kind of service being performed. Specific competencies necessary for an engagement partner are discussed in paragraph .A27 of QC section 10.
- Determine the capabilities and competencies possessed by personnel.

---

[3] Such considerations would include the risk of providing professional services to significant clients or to other clients for which the practitioner's objectivity or the appearance of independence may be impaired. In broad terms, the significance of a client to a member or a firm refers to relationships that could diminish a practitioner's objectivity and independence in performing attest services. Examples of factors to consider in determining the significance of a client to an engagement partner, office, or practice unit include (*a*) the amount of time the partner, office, or practice unit devotes to the engagement, (*b*) the effect on the partner's stature within the firm as a result of his or her service to the client, (*c*) the manner in which the partner, office, or practice unit is compensated, or (*d*) the effect that losing the client would have on the partner, office, or practice unit.

- Assign the responsibility for each engagement to an engagement partner.
- Assign personnel based on the knowledge, skills, and abilities required in the circumstances and the nature and extent of supervision needed.
- Have personnel participate in general and industry-specific continuing professional education and professional development activities that enable them to accomplish assigned responsibilities and satisfy applicable continuing professional education requirements of the AICPA, state boards of accountancy, and other regulators.
- Select for advancement only those individuals who have the qualifications necessary to fulfill the responsibilities they will be called on to assume.

Engagement Performance

1.14 The purpose of the engagement performance element of quality control is to provide the firm with reasonable assurance (*a*) that engagements are consistently performed in accordance with applicable professional standards and regulatory and legal requirements, and (*b*) that the firm or the engagement partner issues reports that are appropriate in the circumstances. Policies and procedures for engagement performance should address all phases of the design and execution of the engagement, including engagement performance, supervision responsibilities, and review responsibilities. Policies and procedures also should require that consultation takes place when appropriate. In addition, a policy should establish criteria against which all engagements are to be evaluated to determine whether an engagement quality control review should be performed.

1.15 Establishing and maintaining policies such as the following assist the firm in obtaining the assurance required relating to the engagement performance element of quality control:

- Plan all engagements to meet professional, regulatory, and the firm's requirements.
- Perform work and issue reports and other communications that meet professional, regulatory, and the firm's requirements.
- Require that work performed by other team members be reviewed by qualified engagement team members, which may include the engagement partner, on a timely basis.
- Require the engagement team to complete the assembly of final engagement files on a timely basis.
- Establish procedures to maintain the confidentiality, safe custody, integrity, accessibility, and retrievability of engagement documentation.
- Require the retention of engagement documentation for a period of time sufficient to meet the needs of the firm, professional standards, laws, and regulations.

- Require that
  - — consultation take place when appropriate (for example, when dealing with complex, unusual, unfamiliar, difficult, or contentious issues);
  - — sufficient and appropriate resources be available to enable appropriate consultation to take place;
  - — all the relevant facts known to the engagement team be provided to those consulted;
  - — the nature, scope, and conclusions of such consultations be documented; and
  - — the conclusions resulting from such consultations be implemented.
- Require that
  - — differences of opinion be dealt with and resolved;
  - — conclusions reached are documented and implemented; and
  - — the report not be released until the matter is resolved.
- Require that
  - — all engagements be evaluated against the criteria for determining whether an engagement quality control review should be performed;
  - — an engagement quality control review be performed for all engagements that meet the criteria; and
  - — the review be completed before the report is released.
- Establish procedures addressing the nature, timing, extent, and documentation of the engagement quality control review.
- Establish criteria for the eligibility of engagement quality control reviewers.

Monitoring

1.16 The purpose of the monitoring element of a system of quality control is to provide the firm and its engagement partners with reasonable assurance that the policies and procedures related to the system of quality control are relevant, adequate, operating effectively, and complied with in practice. Monitoring involves an ongoing consideration and evaluation of the appropriateness of the design, the effectiveness of the operation of a firm's quality control system, and a firm's compliance with its quality control policies and procedures. The purpose of monitoring compliance with quality control policies and procedures is to provide an evaluation of the following:

- Adherence to professional standards and regulatory and legal requirements
- Whether the quality control system has been appropriately designed and effectively implemented

- Whether the firm's quality control policies and procedures have been operating effectively so that reports issued by the firm are appropriate in the circumstances

1.17 Establishing and maintaining policies such as the following assist the firm in obtaining the assurance required relating to the monitoring element of quality control:

- Assign responsibility for the monitoring process to a partner or partners or other persons with sufficient and appropriate experience and authority in the firm to assume that responsibility.
- Assign performance of the monitoring process to competent individuals.
- Require the performance of monitoring procedures that are sufficiently comprehensive to enable the firm to assess compliance with all applicable professional standards and the firm's quality control policies and procedures. Monitoring procedures consist of the following:
  - — Review of selected administrative and personnel records pertaining to the quality control elements.
  - — Review of engagement documentation, reports, and clients' financial statements.
  - — Summarization of the findings from the monitoring procedures, at least annually, and consideration of the systemic causes of findings that indicate that improvements are needed.
  - — Determination of any corrective actions to be taken or improvements to be made with respect to the specific engagements reviewed or the firm's quality control policies and procedures.
  - — Communication of the identified findings to appropriate firm management personnel.
  - — Consideration of findings by appropriate firm management personnel who should also determine that any actions necessary, including necessary modifications to the quality control system, are taken on a timely basis.
  - — Assessment of
    - the appropriateness of the firm's guidance materials and any practice aids;
    - new developments in professional standards and regulatory and legal requirements and how they are reflected in the firm's policies and procedures where appropriate;
    - compliance with policies and procedures on independence;
    - the effectiveness of continuing professional development, including training;

  - decisions related to acceptance and continuance of client relationships and specific engagements; and
  - firm personnel's understanding of the firm's quality control policies and procedures and implementation thereof.

- Communicate at least annually, to relevant engagement partners and other appropriate personnel, deficiencies noted as a result of the monitoring process and recommendations for appropriate remedial action.
- Communicate the results of the monitoring of its quality control system process to relevant firm personnel at least annually.
- Establish procedures designed to provide the firm with reasonable assurance that it deals appropriately with the following:
  - — Complaints and allegations that the work performed by the firm fails to comply with professional standards and regulatory and legal requirements.
  - — Allegations of noncompliance with the firm's system of quality control.
  - — Deficiencies in the design or operation of the firm's quality control policies and procedures, or noncompliance with the firm's system of quality control by an individual or individuals, as identified during the investigations into complaints and allegations.

  This includes establishing clearly defined channels for firm personnel to raise any concerns in a manner that enables them to come forward without fear of reprisal and documenting complaints and allegations and the responses to them.

- Require appropriate documentation to provide evidence of the operation of each element of its system of quality control. The form and content of documentation evidencing the operation of each of the elements of the system of quality control is a matter of judgment and depends on a number of factors, including the following, for example:
  - — The size of the firm and the number of offices.
  - — The nature and complexity of the firm's practice and organization.
- Require retention of documentation providing evidence of the operation of the system of quality control for a period of time sufficient to permit those performing monitoring procedures and peer review to evaluate the firm's compliance with its system of quality control, or for a longer period if required by law or regulation.

1.18 Some of the monitoring procedures discussed in the previous list may be accomplished through the performance of the following:

- Engagement quality control review

- Review of engagement documentation, reports, and clients' financial statements for selected engagements after the report release date
- Inspection[4] procedures

Documentation of Quality Control Policies and Procedures

1.19 The firm should document each element of its system of quality control. The extent of the documentation will depend on the size, structure, and nature of the firm's practice. Documentation may be as simple as a checklist of the firm's policies and procedures or as extensive as practice manuals.

---

[4] *Inspection* is a retrospective evaluation of the adequacy of the firm's quality control policies and procedures, its personnel's understanding of those policies and procedures, and the extent of the firm's compliance with them. Although monitoring procedures are meant to be ongoing, they may include inspection procedures performed at a fixed point in time. Monitoring is a broad concept; inspection is one specific type of monitoring procedure.

Appendix G

Schedule of Changes Made to the Text From the Previous Edition

This appendix is nonauthoritative and is included for informational purposes only.

As of March 1, 2018

Entries in the following table reflect current numbering, lettering (including that in appendix names), and character designations that resulted from the renumbering/reordering that occurred in the updating of this guide.

Reference	*Change*
Preface	Updated.
General	Editorial changes, including rephrasing, may have been made in this guide to improve readability where necessary.
General	Guide content included in gray-shaded areas and "Guidance Update" boxes within the chapters have been updated to appropriately reflect guidance not yet effective as of the date of the guide, primarily FASB Accounting Standards Update (ASU) No. 2016-14, *Not-for-Profit Entities (Topic 958): Presentation of Financial Statements of Not-for-Profit Entities*. See the preface of this guide for more explanation to this "dual guidance" treatment. Prior years' guidance update boxes are removed if the standards are now effective.
Paragraphs 2.122–.132	Revised to reflect issuance of Statement on Auditing Standards (SAS) No. 132, *The Auditor's Consideration of an Entity's Ability to Continue as a Going Concern* (AICPA, *Professional Standards*, AU-C sec. 570).
Paragraph 3.10	Revised for clarity.
Exhibit 3-1	Revised for clarity.
Exhibit 3-2	Revised to reflect issuance of FASB ASU No. 2015-02, *Consolidation (Topic 810): Amendments to the Consolidation Analysis*, and FASB ASU No. 2017-02, *Not-for-Profit Entities—Consolidation (Subtopic 958-810): Clarifying When a Not-for-Profit Entity That Is a General Partner or a Limited Partner Should Consolidate a For-Profit Limited Partnership or Similar Entity*.

(continued)

Reference	***Change***
Paragraphs 3.73, 3.81–.82, 3.84–.85, 3.88, and 3.90–.92	Revised to reflect issuance of FASB ASU No. 2015-02 and FASB ASU No. 2017-02.
Paragraphs 3.94 and 3.96	Added to reflect issuance of FASB ASU No. 2015-02 and FASB ASU No. 2017-02.
Former paragraph 3.96	Deleted.
Former paragraph 3.97	Deleted, see paragraph 3.96.
Paragraph 3.98	Revised to reflect issuance of FASB ASU No. 2015-02 and FASB ASU No. 2017-02.
Paragraph 3.104	Revised for clarity.
Paragraph 3.164	Revised to reflect the issuance of FASB ASU No. 2015-07, *Fair Value Measurement (Topic 820): Disclosures for Investments in Certain Entities That Calculate Net Asset Value per Share (or Its Equivalent) (a consensus of the FASB Emerging Issues Task Force)*.
Paragraph 3.174	Revised to reflect the issuance of FASB ASU No. 2014-15, *Presentation of Financial Statements—Going Concern (Subtopic 205-40): Disclosure of Uncertainties about an Entity's Ability to Continue as a Going Concern*.
Paragraph 3.189	Revised to reflect issuance of FASB ASU No. 2015-02 and FASB ASU No. 2017-02.
Paragraph 3.192	Revised for issuance of SAS No. 132.
Paragraph 3.193	Revised to reflect issuance of FASB ASU No. 2017-02.
Paragraph 3.194	Added to reflect the issuance of FASB ASU No. 2016-14.
Paragraph 4.06	Revised to reflect the issuance of FASB ASU 2017-02.
Exhibit 4-1	Revised to reflect issuance of FASB ASU No. 2015-02 and FASB ASU No. 2017-02.
Paragraphs 4.20–.21	Revised to reflect issuance of FASB ASU No. 2015-02 and FASB ASU No. 2017-02.
Paragraph 4.22	Revised to reflect issuance of FASB ASU No. 2015-02.
Paragraphs 4.23–.24 and 4.26	Revised to reflect issuance of FASB ASU No. 2015-02 and FASB ASU No. 2017-02.
Paragraph 4.27	Revised to reflect the issuance of FASB ASU No. 2017-02.

Reference	*Change*
Paragraph 4.28	Added to reflect the issuance of FASB ASU No. 2017-02.
Paragraph 4.43	Revised to reflect the issuance of FASB ASU No. 2015-07.
Paragraph 4.44	Revised to reflect the issuance of Technical Question and Answer (Q&A) section 2220.28, "Definition of *Readily Determinable Fair Value* and Its Interaction With the NAV Practical Expedient" (*Technical Questions and Answers*).
Paragraphs 4.66 and 4.81	Revised for clarity.
Paragraphs 4.97 and 4.101	Revised to reflect the issuance of FASB ASU No. 2015-07.
Paragraph 4.107	Revised for clarity.
Paragraph 4.118	Revised to reflect the issuance of Q&A section 2220.28; revised to reflect the issuance of FASB ASU No. 2015-07.
Paragraph 5.49	Revised to reflect the issuance of FASB ASU No. 2014-09, *Revenue from Contracts with Customers (Topic 606)*.
Paragraphs 5.52–.53, 5.56, 5.75, 5.105, 5.137, 5.165, 5.222, and 5.227	Revised for clarity.
Paragraph 5.242	Added a box before the paragraph saying that appendix B has not yet updated the Technical Questions and Answers for the amendments in FASB ASU No. 2016-14.
Paragraphs 6.46, 6.67–.69, 6.80, 6.86, and 6.91	Revised for clarity.
Paragraph 6.95	Added footnote 5 as a notice to readers that paragraph 54 has not been updated to reflect the issuance of FASB ASU No. 2016-14.
Paragraph 7.06	Revised to reflect the issuance of FASB ASU No. 2015-11, *Inventory (Topic 330): Simplifying the Measurement of Inventory*.
Paragraphs 7.19, 9.34, and 10.18	Revised for clarity.
Paragraph 10.19	Revised to reflect the issuance of Q&A section 7100, *Definition of a Public Business Entity* (*Technical Questions and Answers*).

(continued)

Reference	*Change*
Paragraph 10.24	Revised to reflect the issuance of Q&A section 7100.03, "Use of the Term 'Over-the-Counter Market' in the Definition of a Public Business Entity" (*Technical Questions and Answers*).
Paragraph 10.116	Revised to reflect the issuance of Q&A section 7100.05, "FINRA TRACE and MSRB EMMA Data and a Public Business Entity" (*Technical Questions and Answers*).
Paragraph 10.117	Revised to reflect the issuance of SAS No. 133, *Auditor Involvement with Exempt Offering Documents* (AICPA, *Professional Standards*, AU-C sec. 945); revised to correspond more completely with chapter 18 of the AICPA Audit and Accounting Guide *State and Local Governments* and chapter 7 of the Audit and Accounting Guide *Health Care Entities*.
Paragraph 10.117	Paragraphs B-3 and B-9 revised for clarity.
Paragraph 11.06	Revised for clarity.
Paragraph 11.20	Revised for the issuance of FASB ASU No. 2017-11, *Earnings Per Share (Topic 260); Distinguishing Liabilities from Equity (Topic 480); Derivatives and Hedging (Topic 815): (Part I) Accounting for Certain Financial Instruments with Down Round Features, (Part II) Replacement of the Indefinite Deferral for Mandatorily Redeemable Financial Instruments of Certain Nonpublic Entities and Certain Mandatorily Redeemable Noncontrolling Interests with a Scope Exception*.
Paragraph 11.21	Deleted.
Paragraph 11.21	Revised for the issuance of FASB ASU No. 2017-11.
Paragraph 11.63	Revised for clarity.
Paragraph 11.64	Added to reflect the issuance of FASB ASU No. 2016-14.
Paragraphs 12.03–.04, 12.06–.08, 12.12–.14	Revised to reflect the issuance of FASB ASU No. 2014-09.
Paragraph 12.25	Added to include includes excerpts from chapter 8, "Not-for-Profit Entities," of the AICPA Audit and Accounting Guide *Revenue Recognition*.
Paragraphs 13.15, 13.17–.18	Revised for the issuance of FASB ASU No. 2014-09.
Paragraphs 13.112 and 13.118	Revised for clarity.

Reference	*Change*
Paragraph 13.122	Footnote 25 added for clarity.
Paragraph 13.129	Revised for clarity.
Paragraph 14.11	Revised to reflect issuance of SAS No. 132.
Paragraphs 16.03 and 16.06	Revised for clarity.
Appendix B	Revised to reflect the issuance of FASB ASU No. 2017-05, *Other Income—Gains and Losses from the Derecognition of Nonfinancial Assets (Subtopic 610-20): Clarifying the Scope of Asset Derecognition Guidance and Accounting for Partial Sales of Nonfinancial Assets*, and FASB ASU No. 2017-13, *Revenue Recognition (Topic 605), Revenue from Contracts with Customers (Topic 606), Leases (Topic 840), and Leases (Topic 842): Amendments to SEC Paragraphs Pursuant to the Staff Announcement at the July 20, 2017 EITF Meeting and Rescission of Prior SEC Staff Announcements and Observer Comments (SEC Update)*.
Appendix C	Added.
Glossary	Revised to reflect the issuance of FASB ASU No. 2016-14.
Index of Pronouncements and Other Technical Guidance	Updated.
Subject Index	Updated.

Glossary

Gray shaded text in this chapter reflects guidance issued but not yet effective as of the date of this guide, March 1, 2018, but becoming effective on or prior to June 30, 2018, exclusive of any option to early adopt ahead of the mandatory effective date. Unless otherwise indicated, all unshaded text reflects guidance that was already effective as of the date of this guide.

The following terms can be found in the FASB *Accounting Standards Codification* (ASC) glossary:

acquiree. The business or businesses that the acquirer obtains control of in a business combination. This term also includes a nonprofit activity or business that a not-for-profit acquirer obtains control of in an acquisition by a not-for-profit entity (NFP).

acquirer. The entity that obtains control of the acquiree. However, in a business combination in which a variable interest entity is acquired, the primary beneficiary of that entity always is the acquirer.

acquisition by a not-for-profit entity. A transaction or other event in which a not-for-profit acquirer obtains control of one or more nonprofit activities or businesses and initially recognizes their assets and liabilities in the acquirer's financial statements. When applicable guidance in FASB ASC 805, *Business Combinations*, is applied by an NFP, the term *business combination* has the same meaning as this term has for an NFP. Likewise, a reference to business combinations in guidance that links to FASB ASC 805 has the same meaning as a reference to acquisitions by not-for-profit entities.

acquisition date. The date on which the acquirer obtains control of the acquiree.

activities. Activities are efforts to accomplish specific objectives. Some activities include producing and distributing materials. For example, if an NFP undertakes a mass mailing that includes a letter and a pamphlet, producing and distributing the letter and pamphlet are part of the activity. Other activities may include no materials, such as an annual dinner or a radio commercial.

affiliate. A party that, directly or indirectly through one or more intermediaries, controls, is controlled by, or is under common control with an entity.

agency transaction. A type of exchange transaction in which the reporting organization acts as an agent, trustee, or intermediary for another party that may be a donor or donee. See **agent**, **trustee**, and **intermediary**.

agent. An entity that acts for and on behalf of another. Although the term *agency* has a legal definition, the term is used broadly to encompass not only legal agency, but also the relationships described in FASB ASC 958, *Not-for-Profit Entities*. A recipient entity acts as an agent for and on behalf of a donor if it receives assets from the donor and agrees to use those assets on behalf of or transfer those assets, the return on investment of those assets, or both to a specified beneficiary. A recipient entity acts as an agent for and on behalf of a beneficiary if it agrees to solicit assets from potential donors specifically for the beneficiary's use and to distribute those assets to the beneficiary. A recipient entity also acts as an agent if a beneficiary can compel the recipient entity to make distributions on its behalf.

board-designated endowment fund. An endowment fund created by an NFP's governing board by designating a portion of its unrestricted net assets to be invested to provide income for a long but unspecified period (sometimes called funds functioning as endowment or quasi endowment funds). See **endowment fund**. See also **designated net assets**.

An endowment fund created by an NFP's governing board by designating a portion of its net assets without donor restrictions to be invested to provide income for a long but not necessarily specified period (sometimes called funds functioning as endowment or quasi-endowment funds). In rare circumstances, a board-designated endowment fund also can include a portion of net assets with donor restrictions. For example, if an NFP is unable to spend donor-restricted contributions in the near term, then the board sometimes considers the long-term investment of these funds. See **endowment fund**.[1]

board-designated net assets. Net assets without donor restrictions subject to self-imposed limits by action of the governing board. Board-designated net assets may be earmarked for future programs, investment, contingencies, purchase or construction of fixed assets, or other uses. Some governing boards may delegate designation decisions to internal management. Such designations are considered to be included in board-designated net assets.[2]

business. An integrated set of activities and assets that is capable of being conducted and managed for the purpose of providing a return in the form of dividends, lower costs, or other economic benefits directly to investors or other owners, members, or participants. Additional guidance on what a business consists of is presented in paragraphs 4–9 of FASB ASC 805-10-55.

business combination. A transaction or other event in which an acquirer obtains control of one or more businesses. Transactions sometimes referred to as *true mergers* or *mergers of equals* also are business combinations. See also **acquisition by a not-for-profit entity**.

charitable gift annuity. A transfer of assets to an NFP in connection with a split-interest agreement that is in part a contribution and in part an exchange transaction. The NFP accepts the contribution and is obligated to make periodic stipulated payments to the donor or a third-party beneficiary for a specified period of time, usually either a specified number of years or until the death of the donor or third-party beneficiary.

charitable lead annuity trust. A trust established in connection with a split-interest agreement, in which an NFP receives distributions of a fixed

---

[1] The amendments in FASB Accounting Standards Update (ASU) No. 2016-14, *Not-for-Profit Entities (Topic 958): Presentation of Financial Statements of Not-for-Profit Entities*, are effective for annual financial statements issued for fiscal years beginning after December 15, 2017 (for example, years ending December 31, 2018, and years ending June 30, 2019), and for interim periods within fiscal years beginning after December 15, 2018. Application to interim financial statements is permitted but not required in the initial year of application. Early application of the amendments is permitted.

[2] See footnote 1.

amount during the agreement's term. Upon termination of the trust, the remainder of the trust assets is paid to the donor or to third-party beneficiaries designated by the donor.

charitable lead trust. A trust established in connection with a split-interest agreement, in which the NFP receives distributions during the agreement's term. Upon termination of the trust, the remainder of the trust assets is paid to the donor or to third-party beneficiaries designated by the donor.

charitable lead unitrust. A trust established in connection with a split-interest agreement, in which an NFP receives distributions of a fixed percentage of the fair value of the trust's assets during the agreement's term. Upon termination of the trust, the remainder of the trust assets is paid to the donor or to third-party beneficiaries designated by the donor.

charitable remainder annuity trust. A trust established in connection with a split-interest agreement, in which the donor or a third-party beneficiary receives distributions of a fixed amount during the agreement's term. Upon termination of the trust, an NFP receives the assets remaining in the trust.

charitable remainder trust. A trust established in connection with a split-interest agreement, in which the donor or a third-party beneficiary receives specified distributions during the agreement's term. Upon termination of the trust, an NFP receives the assets remaining in the trust.

charitable remainder unitrust. A trust established in connection with a split-interest agreement, in which the donor or a third-party beneficiary receives distributions of a fixed percentage of the fair value of the trust's assets during the agreement's term. Upon termination of the trust, an NFP receives the assets remaining in the trust.

collections. Works of art, historical treasures, or similar assets that meet all of the following criteria: (*a*) they are held for public exhibition, education, or research in furtherance of public service rather than financial gain, (*b*) they are protected, kept unencumbered, cared for, and preserved, and (*c*) they are subject to an organizational policy that requires the proceeds of items that are sold to be used to acquire other items for collections. Collections generally are held by museums, botanical gardens, libraries, aquariums, arboretums, historic sites, planetariums, zoos, art galleries, nature, science, and technology centers, and similar educational, research, and public service organizations that have those divisions; however, the definition is not limited to those entities nor does it apply to all items held by those entities.

compensation or fees. Reciprocal transfers of cash or other assets in exchange for services performed.

conditional promise to give. A promise to give that depends on the occurrence of a specified future and uncertain event to bind the promisor.

contribution. An unconditional transfer of cash or other assets to an entity or a settlement or cancellation of its liabilities in a voluntary nonreciprocal transfer by another entity acting other than as an owner. Those characteristics distinguish contributions from exchange transactions, which are reciprocal transfers in which each party receives and sacrifices approximately equal value; from investments by owners and distributions to owners, which are nonreciprocal transfers between an entity and its owners; and from other nonreciprocal transfers, such as impositions of taxes or legal judgments, fines, and thefts, which are not voluntary transfers. In a contribution transaction, the value, if any, returned to the resource provider is incidental to potential public benefits. In an exchange transaction, the potential public benefits are secondary to the potential proprietary benefits to the resource provider. The term *contribution revenue* is used to apply to transactions that are part of the entity's ongoing major or central activities (revenues), or are peripheral or incidental to the entity (gains). See also **inherent contribution**.

control of a not-for-profit entity. The direct or indirect ability to determine the direction of management and policies through ownership, contract, or otherwise.

costs of joint activities. Costs incurred for a joint activity. Costs of joint activities may include joint costs and costs other than joint costs. Costs other than joint costs are costs that are identifiable with a particular function, such as fund-raising, program, management and general, and cost of sales. For example, some costs incurred for printing, paper, professional fees, and salaries to produce donor cards are not joint costs, although they may be incurred in connection with conducting joint activities.

designated net assets. Unrestricted net assets subject to self-imposed limits by action of the governing board. Designated net assets may be earmarked for future programs, investment, contingencies, purchase or construction of fixed assets, or other uses.

The term **designated net assets** will be replaced by **board-designated net assets** upon the effective date of FASB ASU No. 2016-14.[3]

donor-imposed condition. A donor stipulation that specifies a future and uncertain event whose occurrence or failure to occur gives the promisor a right of return of the assets it has transferred or releases the promisor from its obligation to transfer its assets.

donor-imposed restriction. A donor stipulation that specifies a use for the contributed asset that is more specific than broad limits resulting from the following: (*a*) the nature of the NFP, (*b*) the environment in which it operates, and (*c*) the purposes specified in its articles of incorporation or bylaws, or comparable documents for an unincorporated association. A donor-imposed restriction on an NFP's use of the asset contributed may be temporary or permanent. Some donor-imposed restrictions impose limits that are permanent, for example, stipulating that resources be invested in perpetuity (not used up). Others are temporary, for example, stipulating that resources may be used only after a specified date, for particular programs or services, or to acquire buildings and equipment.

A donor stipulation (donors include other types of contributors, including makers of certain grants) that specifies a use for a contributed asset that is more specific than broad limits resulting from the following: (*a*) the nature of the NFP, (*b*) the environment in which it operates, (*c*) the purposes specified in its articles of incorporation or bylaws or comparable documents for an unincorporated association. Some donors impose restrictions that are temporary in nature, for example, stipulating

[3] See footnote 1.

that resources be used after a specified date, for particular programs or services, or to acquire buildings or equipment. Other donors impose restrictions that are perpetual in nature, for example, stipulating that resources be maintained in perpetuity. Laws may extend those limits to investment returns from those resources and to other enhancements (diminishments) of those resources. Thus, those laws extend donor-imposed restrictions.[4]

donor-restricted endowment fund. An endowment fund that is created by a donor stipulation requiring investment of the gift in perpetuity or for a specified term. Some donors may require that a portion of income, gains, or both be added to the gift and invested subject to similar restrictions. The term does not include a board-designated endowment fund. See **endowment fund**.

An endowment fund that is created by a donor stipulation (donors include other types of contributors, including makers of certain grants) requiring investment of the gift in perpetuity or for a specified term. Some donors or laws may require that a portion of income, gains, or both be added to the gift and invested subject to similar restrictions. The term does not include a board-designated endowment fund. See **endowment fund**.[5]

donor-restricted support. Donor-restricted revenues or gains from contributions that increase net assets with donor restrictions (donors include other types of contributors, including makers of certain grants).[6]

economic interest. An NFP's interest in another entity that exists if any of the following criteria are met: (*a*) the other entity holds or utilizes significant resources that must be used for the unrestricted or restricted purposes of the NFP, either directly or indirectly by producing income or providing services, or (*b*) the NFP is responsible for the liabilities of the other entity.

An NFP's interest in another entity that exists if any of the following criteria are met: (*a*) the other entity holds or utilizes significant resources that must be used for the purposes of the NFP, either directly or indirectly by producing income or providing services, or (*b*) the NFP is responsible for the liabilities of the other entity.[7]

endowment fund. An established fund of cash, securities, or other assets to provide income for the maintenance of an NFP. The use of the assets of the fund may be permanently restricted, temporarily restricted, or unrestricted. Endowment funds generally are established by donor-restricted gifts and bequests to provide (*a*) a permanent endowment, which is to provide a permanent source of income, or (*b*) a term endowment, which is to provide income for a specified period.

---

[4] See footnote 1.
[5] See footnote 1.
[6] See footnote 1.
[7] See footnote 1.

An established fund of cash, securities, or other assets to provide income for the maintenance of an NFP. The use of the assets of the fund may be with or without donor-imposed restrictions. Endowment funds generally are established by donor-restricted gifts and bequests to provide a source of income in perpetuity or for a specified period. See **donor-restricted endowment fund**. Alternatively, an NFP's governing board may earmark a portion of its net assets as a **board-designated endowment fund**. See **funds functioning as endowment**.[8]

equity interests. Used broadly to mean ownership interests of investor-owned entities; owner, member, or participant interests of mutual entities; and owner or member interests in the net assets of NFPs.

financial asset. Cash, evidence of an ownership interest in an entity, or a contract that conveys to one entity a right to do either (*a*) receive cash or another financial instrument from a second entity or (*b*) exchange other financial instruments on potentially favorable terms with the second entity.

financial flexibility. The ability of an entity to take effective actions or alter amounts and timing of cash flows so it can respond to unexpected needs and opportunities.

financial liability. A contract that imposes on one entity an obligation to do either (*a*) deliver cash or another financial instrument to a second entity or (*b*) exchange other financial instruments on potentially unfavorable terms with the second entity.

financially interrelated entity. A recipient entity and a specified beneficiary are financially interrelated entities if the relationship between them has both of the following characteristics: (*a*) one of the entities has the ability to influence the operating and financial decisions of the other and (*b*) one of the entities has an ongoing economic interest in the net assets of the other.

functional classification. A method of grouping expenses according to the purpose for which the costs are incurred. The primary functional classifications are program services and supporting activities.

The term **functional classification** will be replaced with **functional expense classification** upon the effective date of FASB ASU No. 2016-14.[9]

functional expense classification. A method of grouping expenses according to the purpose for which the costs are incurred. The primary functional classifications of an NFP are program services and supporting activities.[10]

fund-raising activities. Activities undertaken to induce potential donors to contribute money, securities, services, materials, facilities, other assets, or time.

funds functioning as endowment. Unrestricted net assets designated by an entity's governing board, rather than restricted by a donor or other outside

[8] See footnote 1.
[9] See footnote 1.
[10] See footnote 1.

agency, to be invested to provide income for a long but unspecified period. A board-designated endowment, which results from an internal designation, is not donor-restricted and is classified as unrestricted net assets. The governing board has the right to decide at any time to expend the principal of such funds. (Sometimes referred to as quasi endowment funds.) See also **designated net assets**.

Net assets without donor restrictions (donors include other types of contributors, including makers of certain grants) designated by an entity's governing board to be invested to provide income for generally a long but not necessarily specified period. A board-designated endowment, which results from an internal designation, is generally not donor-restricted and is classified as net assets without donor restrictions. The governing board has the right to decide at any time to expend such funds. In rare circumstances, funds functioning as endowment also can include a portion of net assets with donor restrictions. For example, if an NFP is unable to spend donor-restricted contributions in the near term, the board sometimes considers the long-term investment of these funds. (Sometimes referred to as **quasi-endowment funds** or **board-designated endowment funds**.)[11]

goodwill. An asset representing the future economic benefits arising from other assets acquired in a business combination or an acquisition by an NFP that are not individually identified and separately recognized. For ease of reference, this term also includes the immediate charge recognized by NFPs in accordance with FASB ASC 958-805-25-29.

identifiable. An asset is identifiable if it meets either of the following criteria: (*a*) it is separable, that is, capable of being separated or divided from the entity and sold, transferred, licensed, rented, or exchanged, either individually or together with a related contract, identifiable asset, or liability, regardless of whether the entity intends to do so, or (*b*) it arises from contractual or other legal rights, regardless of whether those rights are transferable or separable from the entity or from other rights and obligations.

inherent contribution. A contribution that results if an entity voluntarily transfers assets (or net assets) or performs services for another entity in exchange for either no assets or for assets of substantially lower value and unstated rights or privileges of a commensurate value are not involved.

intangible assets. Assets (not including financial assets) that lack physical substance. (The term *intangible assets* is used to refer to intangible assets other than goodwill.)

intermediary. Although in general usage the term *intermediary* encompasses a broad range of situations in which an entity acts between two or more other parties, in this usage, it refers to situations in which a recipient entity acts as a facilitator for the transfer of assets between a potential donor and a potential beneficiary (donee) but is neither an agent or trustee nor a donee and donor.

---

[11] See footnote 1.

joint activity. An activity that is part of the fund-raising function and has elements of one or more other functions, such as programs, management and general, membership development, or any other functional category used by the entity.

joint costs. The costs of conducting joint activities that are not identifiable with a particular component of the activity. For example, the cost of postage for a letter that includes both fund-raising and program components is a joint cost. Joint costs may include the following costs: salaries, contract labor, consultants, professional fees, paper, printing, postage, event advertising, telephones, airtime, and facility rentals.

lead interest. The right to the benefits (cash flows or use) of assets during the term of a split-interest agreement, which generally starts upon the signing of the agreement and terminates at either of the following times: (*a*) after a specified number of years (period-certain) or (*b*) upon the occurrence of a certain event, commonly either the death of the donor or the death of the lead interest beneficiary (life-contingent).

legal entity. Any legal structure used to conduct activities or to hold assets. Some examples of such structures are corporations, partnerships, limited liability companies, grantor trusts, and other trusts.

management and general activities. Activities that are not identifiable with a single program, fund-raising activity, or membership-development activity but that are indispensable to the conduct of those activities and to an entity's existence.

Supporting activities that are not directly identifiable with one or more program, fundraising, or membership-development activities.[12]

medium. A means of mass communication, such as direct mail, direct response advertising, or television.

membership-development activities. Membership-development activities include soliciting for prospective members and membership dues, membership relations, and similar activities. However, if there are no significant benefits or duties connected with membership, the substance of membership-development activities may, in fact, be fund-raising.

merger date. The date on which the merger becomes effective.

merger of not-for-profit entities. A transaction or other event in which the governing bodies of two or more NFPs cede control of those entities to create a new NFP.

natural expense classification. A method of grouping expenses according to the kinds of economic benefits received in incurring those expenses. Examples of natural expense classifications include salaries and wages, employee benefits, supplies, rent, and utilities.

A method of grouping expenses according to the kinds of economic benefits received in incurring those expenses. Examples of natural expense

---

[12] See footnote 1.

classifications include salaries and wages, employee benefits, professional services, supplies, interest expense, rent, utilities, and depreciation.[13]

net assets. The excess or deficiency of assets over liabilities of an NFP, which is classified into three mutually exclusive classes according to the existence or absence of donor-imposed restrictions. See **unrestricted net assets, temporarily restricted net assets, and permanently restricted net assets**.

The excess or deficiency of assets over liabilities of an NFP, which is divided into two mutually exclusive classes according to the existence or absence of donor-imposed restrictions. See **net assets with donor restrictions** and **net assets without donor restrictions**.[14]

net assets with donor restrictions. The part of net assets of a not-for-profit entity that is subject to donor-imposed restrictions (donors include other types of contributors, including makers of certain grants).[15]

net assets without donor restrictions. The part of net assets of a not-for-profit entity that is not subject to donor-imposed restrictions (donors include other types of contributors, including makers of certain grants).[16]

net income unitrust. A trust established in connection with a split-interest agreement, in which the donor or a third-party beneficiary receives distributions during the agreement's term of the lesser of the net income earned by the trust or a fixed percentage of the fair value of the trust's assets, with or without recovery and distribution of the shortfall in a subsequent year. Upon termination of the trust, an NFP receives the assets remaining in the trust.

noncontrolling interest. The portion of equity (net assets) in a subsidiary not attributable, directly or indirectly, to a parent. A noncontrolling interest is sometimes called a *minority interest*.

nonfinancial asset. An asset that is not a financial asset. Nonfinancial assets include land, buildings, use of facilities or utilities, materials and supplies, intangible assets, or services.

nonprofit activity. An integrated set of activities and assets that is capable of being conducted and managed for the purpose of providing benefits, other than goods or services at a profit or profit equivalent, as a fulfillment of an entity's purpose or mission (for example, goods or services to beneficiaries, customers, or members). As with an NFP, a nonprofit activity possesses characteristics that distinguish it from a business or a for-profit business entity.

nonreciprocal transfer. A transaction in which an entity incurs a liability or transfers an asset to another entity (or receives an asset or cancellation of a liability) without directly receiving (or giving) value in exchange.

not-for-profit entity. An entity that possesses the following characteristics, in varying degrees, that distinguish it from a business entity: (*a*)

---

[13] See footnote 1.
[14] See footnote 1.
[15] See footnote 1.
[16] See footnote 1.

contributions of significant amounts of resources from resource providers who do not expect commensurate or proportionate pecuniary return, (*b*) operating purposes other than to provide goods or services at a profit, and (*c*) absence of ownership interests like those of business enterprises. Entities that clearly fall outside this definition include the following: (*a*) all investor-owned enterprises and (*b*) entities that provide dividends, lower costs, or other economic benefits directly and proportionately to their owners, members, or participants, such as mutual insurance companies, credit unions, farm and rural electric cooperatives, and employee benefit plans.

ongoing economic interest in the net assets of another. A residual right to another NFP's net assets that results from an ongoing relationship. The value of those rights increases or decreases as a result of the investment, fund-raising, operating, and other activities of the other entity.

owners. Used broadly to include holders of ownership interests (equity interests) of investor-owned entities, mutual entities, or NFPs. Owners include shareholders, partners, proprietors, or members or participants of mutual entities. Owners also include owner and member interests in the net assets of NFPs.

permanent restriction. A donor-imposed restriction that stipulates that resources be maintained permanently but permits the NFP to use up or expend part or all of the income (or other economic benefits) derived from the donated assets.

The preceding term will be deleted upon the effective date of FASB ASU No. 2016-14.[17]

permanently restricted net assets. The part of the net assets of an NFP resulting from the following: (*a*) contributions and other inflows of assets whose use by the NFP is limited by donor-imposed stipulations that neither expire by passage of time nor can be fulfilled or otherwise removed by actions of the NFP, (*b*) other asset enhancements and diminishments subject to the same kinds of stipulations, and (*c*) reclassifications from (or to) other classes of net assets as a consequence of donor-imposed stipulations.

The preceding term will be deleted upon the effective date of FASB ASU No. 2016-14.[18]

pooled income fund. A trust in which donors are assigned a specific number of units based on the proportion of the fair value of their contributions to the total fair value of the pooled income fund on the date of the donor's entry to the pooled fund. Until a donor's death, the donor (or the donor's designated beneficiary or beneficiaries) is paid the actual income (as defined under the arrangement) earned on the donor's assigned units. Upon the donor's death, the value of these assigned units reverts to the NFP.

program services. The activities that result in goods and services being distributed to beneficiaries, customers, or members that fulfill the purposes or mission for which the NFP exists. Those services are the major purpose for and the major output of the organization and often relate to several major programs.

---

[17] See footnote 1.
[18] See footnote 1.

programmatic investing. The activity of making loans or other investments that are directed at carrying out a not-for-profit entity's purpose for existence rather than investing in the general production of income or appreciation of an asset (for example, total return investing). An example of programmatic investing is a loan made to lower-income individuals to promote home ownership.[19]

promise to give. A written or oral agreement to contribute cash or other assets to another entity. A promise carries rights and obligations—the recipient of a promise to give has a right to expect that the promised assets will be transferred in the future, and the maker has a social and moral obligation, and generally a legal obligation, to make the promised transfer. A promise to give may be either conditional or unconditional.

quasi endowment funds. See **funds functioning as endowment**.

readily determinable fair value. An equity security has a readily determinable fair value if it meets any of the following conditions:

- *a.* The fair value of an equity security is readily determinable if sales prices or bid-and-asked quotations are currently available on a securities exchange registered with the U.S. Securities and Exchange Commission (SEC) or in the over-the-counter market, provided that those prices or quotations for the over-the-counter market are publicly reported by the National Association of Securities Dealers Automated Quotations systems or by OTC Markets Group Inc. Restricted stock meets that definition if the restriction terminates within one year.
- *b.* The fair value of an equity security traded only in a foreign market is readily determinable if that foreign market is of a breadth and scope comparable to one of the U.S. markets referred to above.
- *c.* The fair value of an equity security that is an investment in a mutual fund or in a structure similar to a mutual fund (that is, a limited partnership or a venture capital entity) is readily determinable if the fair value per share (unit) is determined and published and is the basis for current transactions.

reclassification. Simultaneous increase of one class of net assets and decrease of another, usually as a result of the release or lapsing of restrictions.

The term **reclassification** will be replaced with **reclassification of net assets** upon the effective date FASB ASU No. 2016-14.[20]

reclassification of net assets. Simultaneous increase of one class of net assets and decrease of another. A reclassification of net assets usually results from a donor-imposed restriction (donors include other types of contributors, including makers of certain grants) being satisfied or otherwise lapsing.[21]

remainder interest. The right to receive all or a portion of the assets of a split-interest agreement at the end of the agreement's term.

---

[19] See footnote 1.
[20] See footnote 1.
[21] See footnote 1.

restricted support. Donor-restricted revenues or gains from contributions that increase either temporarily restricted net assets or permanently restricted net assets. See also **unrestricted support**.

The term **restricted support** will be replaced with **donor-restricted support** upon the effective date of FASB ASU No. 2016-14.[22]

spending rate. The portion of total return on investments used for fiscal needs of the current period, usually used as a budgetary method of reporting returns of investments. It is usually measured in terms of an amount or a specified percentage of a moving average market value. Typically, the selection of a spending rate emphasizes the use of prudence and a systematic formula to determine the portion of cumulative investment return that can be used to support fiscal needs of the current period and the protection of endowment gifts from a loss of purchasing power as a consideration in determining the formula to be used.

split-interest agreement. An agreement in which a donor enters into a trust or other arrangement under which an NFP receives benefits that are shared with other beneficiaries. A typical split-interest agreement has the following two components: (*a*) a lead interest and (*b*) a remainder interest.

stipulation. A statement by a donor that creates a condition or restriction on the use of transferred resources.

supporting activities. All activities of an NFP other than program services. Generally, they include the following: (*a*) management and general activities, (*b*) fund-raising activities, and (*c*) membership development activities.

temporarily restricted net assets. The part of the net assets of an NFP resulting from the following: (*a*) contributions and other inflows of assets whose use by the NFP is limited by donor-imposed stipulations that either expire by the passage of time or can be fulfilled and removed by actions of the NFP pursuant to those stipulations, (*b*) other asset enhancements and diminishments subject to the same kinds of stipulations, and (*c*) reclassifications from or to other classes of net assets as a consequence of donor-imposed stipulations, their expiration by passage of time, or their fulfillment and removal by actions of the NFP pursuant to those stipulations.

The preceding term will be deleted upon the effective date of FASB ASU No. 2016-14.[23]

temporary restriction. A donor-imposed restriction that permits the donee to use up or expend the donated assets as specified and that is satisfied either by the passage of time or by actions of the donee.

The preceding term will be deleted upon the effective date of FASB ASU No. 2016-14.[24]

term endowment. An endowment fund established to provide income for a specified period. See **endowment fund**.

---

[22] See footnote 1.

[23] See footnote 1.

[24] See footnote 1.

total return. A measure of investment performance that focuses on the overall return on investments, including interest and dividend income as well as realized and unrealized gains and losses on investments. Frequently used in connection with a spending-rate formula to determine how much of that return will be used for fiscal needs of the current period.

trustee. An entity that has a duty to hold and manage assets for the benefit of a specified beneficiary in accordance with a charitable trust agreement. In some states, NFPs are organized under trust law rather than as corporations. Those NFPs are not trustees as defined because, under those statutes, they hold assets in trust for the community or some other broadly described group, rather than for a specific beneficiary.

unconditional promise to give. A promise to give that depends only on passage of time or demand by the promisee for performance.

underwater endowment fund. A donor-restricted endowment fund for which the fair value of the fund at the reporting date is less than either the original gift amount or the amount required to be maintained by the donor or by law that extends donor restrictions.[25]

unrestricted net assets. The part of net assets of an NFP that is neither permanently restricted nor temporarily restricted by donor-imposed stipulations. The only limits on the use of unrestricted net assets are the broad limits resulting from the following: (*a*) the nature of the NFP, (*b*) the environment in which the NFP operates, (*c*) the purposes specified in the NFP's articles of incorporation or bylaws, and (*d*) limits resulting from contractual agreements with suppliers, creditors, and others entered into by the NFP in the course of its business. Unrestricted net assets generally result from revenues from providing services, producing and delivering goods, receiving unrestricted contributions, and receiving dividends or interest from investing in income-producing assets, less expenses incurred in providing services, producing and delivering goods, raising contributions, and performing administrative functions.

The preceding term will be deleted upon the effective date of FASB ASU No. 2016-14.[26]

unrestricted support. Revenues or gains from contributions that are not restricted by donors. See also **restricted support**.

The preceding term will be deleted upon the effective date of FASB ASU No. 2016-14.[27]

variance power. The unilateral power to redirect the use of the transferred assets to another beneficiary. A donor explicitly grants variance power if the recipient entity's unilateral power to redirect the use of the assets is explicitly referred to in the instrument transferring the assets. Unilateral power means that the recipient entity can override the donor's instructions without approval from the donor, specified beneficiary, or any other interested party.

---

[25] See footnote 1.
[26] See footnote 1.
[27] See footnote 1.

voluntary health and welfare entities. An NFP that is formed for the purpose of performing voluntary services for various segments of society and that is tax exempt (organized for the benefit of the public), supported by the public, and operated on a not-for-profit basis. Most voluntary health and welfare entities concentrate their efforts and expend their resources in an attempt to solve health and welfare problems of our society and, in many cases, those of specific individuals. As a group, voluntary health and welfare entities include those NFPs that derive their revenue primarily from voluntary contributions from the general public to be used for general or specific purposes connected with health, welfare, or community services. For purposes of this definition, the general public excludes governmental entities when determining whether an NFP is a voluntary health and welfare entity.

The following is a list of additional terms that have been used in this guide:

assets held in trust. Resources held and administered, at the direction of the resource provider, by an outside trustee for the benefit of an NFP, frequently in connection with a split-interest agreement or permanent endowment.

> Resources held and administered, at the direction of the resource provider, by an outside trustee for the benefit of an NFP, frequently in connection with a split-interest agreement or perpetual endowment.[28]

corpus. The principal amount of a gift or trust. Usually refers to the portion of a split-interest gift or an endowment fund that must be maintained over a specified period or in perpetuity.

equity. See **net assets**.

help accomplish the not-for-profit entity's mission. Actions that help accomplish the NFP's mission are actions that either benefit the recipient (such as by improving the recipient's physical, mental, emotional, or spiritual health and well-being) or benefit society (by addressing societal problems).

life interest in real estate. Also referred to as a life estate, is the right of an individual to use or live in property during their lifetime. Upon the death of the life tenant, or their relinquishment of the right to use, the remainder interest owner receives the property without limitation. A charitable life estate provides for a charitable contribution deduction under U.S. tax law when a donor transfers ownership of a residence or farm to a qualified charitable organization and retains a life tenant interest in the property. Under such an arrangement, the charitable organization receives title and ownership of the property outright, subject to the life use rights.

life tenant. One who possesses a life-use right to property, frequently used in connection with a split-interest agreement.

net investment (equity) in land, buildings, and equipment. The total carrying value (after accumulated depreciation) of all property and equipment, less directly related liabilities. This amount is exclusive of real properties that are held for investment purposes.

---

[28] See footnote 1.

official statement. The common term used for the offering document or offering circular prepared in connection with a new issue of municipal securities. Although functionally equivalent to the prospectus used in connection with registered securities, an official statement for municipal securities is exempt from the prospectus requirements of the Securities Act of 1933.

program activities. See **program services.**

restricted net assets. Resources whose use is restricted by donors as contrasted with those over which the NFP has complete control and discretion. Restricted net assets may be permanently or temporarily restricted.

The preceding definition will be deleted upon the effective date of FASB ASU No. 2016-14.[29]

---

[29] See footnote 1.

Index of Pronouncements and Other Technical Guidance

A

Title	*Paragraphs*
402, *Audit Considerations Relating to an Entity Using a Service Organization*	2.57–.59
450, *Evaluation of Misstatements Identified During the Audit*	2.25, 2.112–.113
500, *Audit Evidence*	4.105, 4.108, 4.115, 5.227, 6.91–.92, 7.37, 7.42, 9.42, 10.112, 11.62, 12.21, 13.127, 15.73
501, *Audit Evidence—Specific Considerations for Selected Items*	2.121, 4.105, 7.37
505, *External Confirmations*	5.238, 12.23
530, *Audit Sampling*	2.30
540, *Auditing Accounting Estimates, Including Fair Value Accounting Estimates and Related Disclosures*	2.79, 5.226, 6.90, 7.37, 9.45
550, *Related Parties*	2.34–.35, 2.37
560, *Subsequent Events and Subsequently Discovered Facts*	10.114
570, *The Auditor's Consideration of an Entity's Ability to Continue as a Going Concern*	2.122–.132, 3.192, 14.11
580, *Written Representations*	2.133–.141, 4.108
600, *Special Considerations—Audits of Group Financial Statements*	2.14, 2.16, 2.18
620, *Using The Work of an Auditor's Specialist*	2.19–.24, 7.45
700, *Forming an Opinion and Reporting on Financial Statements*	1.12, 2.37, 2.114, 2.122, 2.132, 14.02–.05, 14.20
705, *Modifications to the Opinion in the Independent Auditor's Report*	2.37, 4.107, 6.93, 14.10
706, *Emphasis-of-Matter Paragraphs and Other-Matter Paragraphs in the Independent Auditor's Report*	1.12, 14.10
720, *Other Information in Documents Containing Audited Financial Statements*	10.117, 14.13
725, *Supplementary Information in Relation to the Financial Statements as a Whole*	
Interpretation No. 1, "Dating the Auditor's Report on Supplementary Information"	14.14

C

F

Title	*Paragraphs*
210, *Balance Sheet*	3.06, 3.10–.12, 3.21, 5.215, 6.45, 10.62, 12.15
220, *Income Statement—Reporting Comprehensive Income*	3.33, 3.38, 10.80
230, *Statement of Cash Flows*	3.47, 3.50
235, *Notes to Financial Statements*	5.15
250, *Accounting Changes and Error Correction*	1.15, 3.33–.34, 3.150, 3.174, 6.23, 13.112
275, *Risks and Uncertainties*	3.176, 3.184
280, *Segment Reporting*	3.02, 13.55
305, *Cash and Cash Equivalents*	4.83
310, *Receivables*	5.105, 5.201, 6.95, 8.08, 8.10, 8.34, 8.36, 8.39–.44, 8.47, 8.49–.52, 12.16–.17
320, *Investments—Debt and Equity Securities*	3.38, 4.38, 4.62, 4.88, 4.99, 8.60
323, *Investments—Equity Method and Joint Ventures*	3.62, 3.76–.78, 3.92, 3.94, 4.11, 4.13, 4.18–.19, 4.26–.27, 8.56
330, *Inventory*	7.02, 7.06
340, *Other Assets and Deferred Costs*	7.11, 13.18
350, *Intangibles—Goodwill and Other*	3.37, 7.14, 7.29–.35, 13.27
360, *Property, Plant and Equipment*	3.37, 7.22, 7.24, 7.33–.35, 9.20, 9.25, 9.27, 9.34–.35, 9.37, 9.49, 10.99
405, *Liabilities*	6.43–.44, 8.37, 10.14–.17, 10.26–.27, 10.33–.34, 10.36
410, *Asset Retirement and Environmental Obligations*	9.30–.32, 10.99
420, *Exit or Disposal Cost Obligations*	3.37, 10.99
450, *Contingencies*	3.175, 10.95, 10.101–.102, 10.108, 13.29
460, *Guarantees*	5.168–.169, 8.08, 8.26, 10.101

Title	*Paragraphs*
825, *Financial Instruments*	3.79–.80, 3.86–.88, 3.92–.95, 3.138, 3.147, 3.169–.171, 3.181, 3.184, 4.15, 4.18, 4.21–.25, 4.27, 4.37, 4.89–.90, 4.94, 4.96, 4.98, 5.128, 5.171, 5.180, 5.192, 5.199, 6.35, 6.38, 6.49, 6.86, 8.38, 8.59, 8.63, 10.02, 10.93, 12.15
830, *Foreign Currency Matters*	1.15
835, *Interest*	5.202–.203, 5.218, 8.10–.14, 8.16, 8.24, 8.30, 8.32, 9.14–.19, 9.37, 9.46, 10.81, 10.93, 13.77
840, *Leases*	9.08, 9.23, 9.37
845, *Nonmonetary Transactions*	3.138, 7.18, 12.09
850, *Related Party Disclosures*	2.34, 3.71, 3.182–.183, 5.18, 5.34, 8.51, 10.107, 13.68, 13.122
855, *Subsequent Events*	3.177–.179, 4.39, 5.102, 10.85, 11.08
860, *Transfers and Servicing*	3.138, 4.94, 10.37, 10.77, 10.81
920, *Entertainment—Broadcasters*	1.16, 12.06
926, *Entertainment—Films*	7.14
944, *Financial Services—Insurance*	3.102, 6.43
946, *Financial Services—Investment Companies*	4.43
954, *Health Care Entities*	3.09, 3.106, 3.119, 10.56, 11.27
958, *Not-for-Profit Entities*	1.14, 1.16, 3.55, 5.90, 13.123, 14.05–.06, 16.03, 16.05, Appendix C
10, *Overall*	1.15, 6.33
20, *Financially Interrelated Entities*	4.59, 5.29–.31, 5.36–.38, 10.98, 13.121, 13.123

Title	Paragraphs
30, *Split-Interest Arrangements*	6.01, 6.04, 6.07, 6.12–.16, 6.18–.20, 6.28–.34, 6.36, 6.40–.42, 6.48–.49, 6.92–.30
205, *Presentation of Financial Statements*	1.22–.23, 3.02–.05, 3.10, 3.27, 3.35, 3.40–.41, 3.55, 3.118, 3.173, 4.03, 4.38, 4.53, 4.68–.75, 4.77–.79, 4.97–.98, 5.217, 11.14, 11.26, 11.29–.30, 11.34, 11.36, 11.41–.43, 11.45, 11.47–.50, 11.54, 11.57, 11.60, 13.04, 13.64, 16.01, 16.07, 16.21
210, *Balance Sheet*	1.22, 3.02, 3.06–.16, 3.23–.27, 3.51, 3.53, 3.91–.92, 4.82, 6.46, 6.51, 6.87, 8.64, 9.37, 11.07, 11.09, 11.11, 11.52, 11.54, 16.04, 16.07, 16.09
220, *Income Statement—Reporting*	1.22, 3.02, 3.28–.33, 3.36–.37, 4.47, 5.21, 5.78, 5.147, 5.201, 9.33–.34, 11.28–.30, 11.53–.54, 11.63, 12.05, 12.10, 12.15, 13.03, 13.12, 13.38–.40, 13.47–.51
230, *Statement of Cash Flows*	3.02, 3.46, 3.52, 5.18, 7.21
310, *Receivables*	2.80, 5.197, 5.200, 5.203–.204, 5.206, 5.208–.209, 5.211–.212, 5.215–.216, 12.15
320, *Investments—Debt and Equity Securities*	3.80, 4.03, 4.11, 4.13, 4.17, 4.27, 4.45, 4.56–.57, 4.84–.90, 4.95, 4.97, 4.99, 6.07, 6.32, 6.35, 6.41, 8.38, 8.59, 8.66, 11.26, 11.52

Title	*Paragraphs*
325, *Investments—Other*	3.80–.81, 3.86, 3.97, 4.11, 4.13, 4.15–.16, 4.18, 4.20–.21, 4.23–.25, 4.38, 4.57, 4.90, 4.96, 4.116, 6.07, 6.13, 6.41, 6.86, 8.60, 8.68–.69
360, *Property, Plant, and Equipment*	7.17, 7.22–.23, 7.25–.27, 7.41, 7.44–.45, 9.03, 9.07, 9.10, 9.21–.22, 9.26, 9.29, 9.35, 9.37, 11.46
405, *Liabilities*	10.93, 10.95, 11.20
450, *Contingencies*	3.174, 10.102, 11.08
605, *Revenue Recognition*	2.79–.80, 3.176, 4.62, 4.99, 5.03, 5.09–.10, 5.14–.15, 5.19–.21, 5.24, 5.27, 5.30, 5.34, 5.37, 5.45, 5.47–.51, 5.59, 5.63, 5.65–.74, 5.76, 5.79, 5.83–.86, 5.91–.95, 5.97–.101, 5.105–.107, 5.114–.115, 5.117, 5.119–.121, 5.125–.127, 5.129–.130, 5.141, 5.145, 5.149–.150, 5.152–.153, 5.161–.162, 5.164–.165, 5.180–.181, 5.185, 5.188, 5.190–.191, 5.193–.194, 5.196, 5.206, 5.211, 5.213, 5.216, 5.238, 5.240, 6.04, 6.20, 6.24–.25, 6.27, 6.64–.65, 7.03–.05, 7.17, 7.24, 8.26, 8.28, 9.02, 9.04, 9.06, 9.10–.11, 9.36, 10.91, 10.97–.98, 11.03, 11.37, 11.45, 11.47, 11.52, 12.12, 13.13, 13.29, 13.34, 13.68–.70, 16.15

Title	*Paragraphs*
No. 2016-14, *Not-for-Profit Entities (Topic 958): Presentation of Financial Statements of Not-for-Profit Entities*	1.22, 2.28, 2.150, 3.03–.04, 3.64, 3.103–.105, 3.119, 3.134, 3.194, 4.03, 4.35, 4.37, 4.45–.53, 4.56, 4.65, 4.67–.79, 4.82, 4.84, 4.87–.89, 4.95–.98, 4.102, 4.117, 5.62, 5.78–.88, 5.95–.96, 5.98, 5.164, 5.173, 5.191, 5.203–.204, 5.213, 5.217, 5.222, 6.18–.19, 6.29–.31, 6.41–.42, 6.51, 6.57–.58, 6.60–.61, 6.64–.65, 6.69–.70, 6.72–.73, 6.76–.77, 6.81–.82, 6.85–.86, 6.96, 7.26, 7.28, 8.04, 8.65, 9.04–.05, 9.26, 9.29, 9.33, 9.36, 9.40, 9.42, 9.44, 9.47, 10.103, 11.64, 12.10, 12.21, 13.03–.04, 13.12, 13.22, 13.33, 13.38, 13.40–.41, 13.49, 13.66, 13.71, 16.07, 16.09, 16.11–.15, 16.17, 16.19–.21, 16.23, 16.25, glossary
FASB SFAC	
No. 4, *Objectives of Financial Reporting by Nonbusiness Organizations*	1.05
No. 5, *Recognition and Measurement in Financial Statements of Business Enterprises*	5.188, 12.07
No. 6, *Elements of Financial Statements*	3.173, 5.81, 11.60, 12.03, 13.02
FASB SFAS	
No. 76, *Extinguishment of Debt*	10.82
No. 116, *Accounting for Contributions Received and Contributions Made*	5.72, 5.189
No. 125, *Accounting for Transfers and Servicing of Financial Assets and Extinguishments of Liabilities*	10.82
Financial Reporting Alert *Not-for-Profit Entities: Accounting Issues and Risks*	1.26, 15.02

I

P

Q

Title	*Paragraphs*
6140.07, "Functional Category of Costs of Special Events"	13.45
6140.09, "Reporting Bad Debt Losses"	5.201, 12.15
6140.11, "Costs of Soliciting Contributed Services and Time That Do Not Meet the Recognition Criteria in FASB ASC 958"	13.67
6140.12, "Nondiscretionary Assistance Programs"	5.17
6140.13, "Note to Sections 6140.14–.18—Implementation of FASB ASC 958—Classification of a Beneficiary's Interest in the Net Assets of a Financially Interrelated Fund-Raising Foundation (in the Beneficiary's Financial Statements)"	5.242
6140.14, "Application of FASB ASC 958—Classification of a Beneficiary's Interest in the Net Assets of a Financially Interrelated Fund-Raising Foundation (The beneficiary can influence the operating and financial decisions of the foundation to such an extent that the beneficiary can determine the timing and amount of distributions from the foundation.)"	5.242
6140.15, "Application of FASB ASC 958—Classification of a Beneficiary's Interest in the Net Assets of a Financially Interrelated Fund-Raising Foundation (The beneficiary cannot influence the operating and financial decisions of the foundation to such an extent that the beneficiary can determine the timing and amount of distributions from the foundation.)"	5.242
6140.16, "Application of FASB ASC 958—Classification of a Beneficiary's Interest in the Net Assets of a Financially Interrelated Fund-Raising Foundation (More Than One Beneficiary—Some Contributions Are Designated)"	5.242
6140.17, "Application of FASB ASC 958—Classification of a Beneficiary's Interest in the Net Assets of a Financially Interrelated Fund-Raising Foundation (The beneficiary makes an expenditure that meets a purpose restriction on net assets held for its benefit by the recipient entity—The beneficiary can influence the operating and financial decisions of the recipient to such an extent that the beneficiary can determine the timing and amount of distributions from the recipient.)"	5.242

Title	Paragraphs
6140.18, "Application of FASB ASC 958—Classification of a Beneficiary's Interest in the Net Assets of a Financially Interrelated Fund-Raising Foundation (The beneficiary makes an expenditure that is consistent with a purpose restriction on net assets held for its benefit by the recipient entity—The beneficiary cannot influence the operating and financial decisions of the recipient to such an extent that the beneficiary can determine the timing and amount of distributions from the recipient.)"	5.242
6140.19, "Application of FASB ASC 958—Classification of Distributions From a Financially Interrelated Fund-Raising Foundation to a Health Care Beneficiary"	13.123
6140.20, "NPEs Reporting No Fund-Raising Expenses"	13.68–.69
6140.21, "Should an NPE Report Amounts Charged to the NPE by a Professional Fund-Raiser Gross, as Fund-Raising Expenses, or Net, as a Reduction of Contributions?"	5.21, 13.12
6140.22, "In Circumstances in Which the Reporting NPE Undertakes a Transaction in Which Another NPE Raises Contributions on Behalf of the Reporting NPE..."	5.21, 13.13
6140.23, "Changing Net Asset Classifications Reported in a Prior Year"	11.60
6140.24, "Contributions of Certain Nonfinancial Assets, Such as Fundraising Material, Informational Material, or Advertising, Including Media Time or Space for Public Service Announcements of Other Purposes"	5.153
6140.25, "Multiyear Unconditional Promises to Give—Measurement Objective and the Effect of Changes in Interest Rates"	5.202
6960.12, "Allocation of Overhead"	13.76
7100.01, "Use of the Term 'Security' in the Definition of a Public Business Entity"	10.19
7100.03, "Use of the Term 'Over-the-Counter Market' in the Definition of a Public Business Entity	10.19, 10.24
7100.04, Use of the Term 'Conduit Bond Obligor' in the Definition of a Public Business Entity	10.19

Title	*Paragraphs*
7100.05, "FINRA TRACE and MSRB EMMA Data and a Public Business Entity"	10.116
8200.07, "Considering a Substantive Audit Strategy"	2.100
8700.03, "Auditor's Responsibilities for Subsequent Events Relative to a Conduit Debt Obligor"	10.114
9160.27, "Providing Opinion on a Schedule of Expenditures of Federal Awards in Relation to an Entity's Financial Statements as a Whole When the Schedule of Expenditures of Federal Awards Is on a Different Basis of Accounting Than the Financial Statements"	14.29
QC section 10, *A Firm's System of Quality Control*	Appendix E

S

Title	*Paragraphs*
SOP 78-10, *Accounting Principles and Reporting Practices for Certain Nonprofit Organizations*	3.108

U

Title	*Paragraphs*
Title 2 U.S. Code of Federal Regulations Part 200, *Uniform Administrative Requirements, Cost Principles, and Audit Requirements for Federal Awards* (Uniform Guidance)	2.10.11, 2.29, 2.54.56, 13.73, 14.26.29

W

Title	*Paragraphs*
White paper, *Measurement of Fair Value for Certain Transactions of Not-for-Profit Entities*	3.140, 5.111, 5.183, 5.185, 5.241, 6.05, 6.17, 6.26, 6.52, 6.76, 6.95, 8.14

Subject Index

A

C

D

E

G

H

I

S